Environmental Law in Social Context

A Canadian Perspective

edited by

Allan Greenbaum
York University

Alex Wellington
Ryerson University

Ron Pushchak
Ryerson University

Captus Press

Environmental Law in Social Context: A Canadian Perspective

Captus Press Inc.
Mail: Units 14 & 15, 1600 Steeles Avenue West
         Concord, Ontario
         Canada   L4K 4M2
Telephone: (416) 736–5537
Fax: (416) 736–5793
Email: info@captus.com
Internet: http://www.captus.com

National Library of Canada Cataloguing in Publication

Environmental law in social context : a Canadian perspective : edited by Allan Greenbaum, Alex Wellington, Ron Pushchak.

Previous ed. published as v. 2 of Social conflict and environmental law : ethics, economics and equity / edited by Allan Greenbaum, Alex Wellington, Ellen Baar.

Includes bibliographical references.
ISBN 1–55322–046–3

1. Environmental law — Canada. 2. Environmental policy — Canada.
I. Greenbaum, Allan   II. Pushchak, Ronald   III. Wellington, Alex, 1958–

KE3619.E587 2002   344.71'046   C2002-904003-5

Canada ▐♦▌ *We acknowledge the financial support of the Government of Canada through the Book Publishing Industry Development Program (BPIDP) for our publishing activities.*

0 9 8 7 6 5 4 3 2 1
Printed in Canada

Table of Contents

Preface. vii

Acknowledgements. ix

Introduction: A "Law and Society" Approach to Environmental Law
Allan Greenbaum and Alex Wellington 2

One: Elements of the Legal System
Editors' Notes
Alex Wellington and Allan Greenbaum 24

A.   Concepts and Terms **38**
    (a)   The Canadian Legal System: Theories and principles
       Victor S. MacKinnon 38

B.   Common Law Actions **45**
    (a)   Common Law and Environmental Protection: Legal realities and
       judicial challenges
       William Charles and David VanderZwaag 45
    (b)   Civil Litigation — Negligence
       Elizabeth J. Swanson and Elaine L. Hughes 46
    (c)   Common Law and Environmental Protection: Legal realities and judicial
       challenges (Continued)
       William Charles and David VanderZwaag 48
    (d)   Civil Litigation — Remedies
       Elizabeth J. Swanson and Elaine L. Hughes 56

C.   Constitutional and Statutory Framework **59**
    (a)   The Institutional Contexts
       Melody Hessing and Michael Howlett 59

(b) Federalism, Environmental Protection, and Blame Avoidance
Kathryn Harrison 66

D. **Criminal Prohibitions** **76**

(a) Applying the Tests of Real Crime to Environmental Pollution
Law Reform Commission of Canada 76

E. **Regulation and Standards** **86**

(a) Controlling Corporate Misconduct through Regulatory Offences:
The Canadian experience
Kernaghan Webb 86

F. **The International Institutional Context** **91**

(a) The Institutional Contexts (Continued)
Melody Hessing and Michael Howlett 91

Two: **The Regulatory System: Standard Setting, Implementation, Monitoring
and Enforcement**
Editors' Notes
Allan Greenbaum and Alex Wellington 98

A. **The Political Context** **128**

(a) On Lawmaking
William J. Chambliss 128

(b) Environmental Assessment and Democracy
Stephen Hazell 134

(c) Environmental Protection and the Role of Government
Anita Krajnc 142

B. **Standard Setting** **150**

(a) A Model Procedure for Setting Environmental Standards ...
M.A.H. Franson, R.T. Franson, and A.R. Lucas 150

(b) Environmental Standards-Setting and the Law in Canada
Kernaghan Webb 155

(c) Setting Standards
Keith Hawkins 165

C. **Implementation and Instruments** **171**

(a) Instruments in Policy Implementation
Law Reform Commission of Canada 171

(b) The Case for Pollution Taxes
Nancy Olewiler 179

(c) Environmental Regulation: The economics of tradeable permits — a survey of
theory and practice
The Australian Bureau of Industry Economics 188

(d) Voluntary Initiatives and the Law: The practice and promise of voluntary
environmental initiatives depend heavily on a productive partnership with
legal instruments
Kernaghan Webb 197

D. **Monitoring and Enforcement** **203**

   (a) Environmental Regulation as a Bargaining Process: The Canadian approach
      Murray Rankin and Peter Z.R. Finkle 203

   (b) Persuasion, Penalties, and Prosecution: Administrative v. criminal sanctions
      Richard Brown and Murray Rankin 206

   (c) A Case for Strict Enforcement of Environmental Statutes
      John Z. Swaigen 212

   (d) The Impact of Prosecution of Corporations and Their Officers and Directors
      upon Regulatory Compliance by Corporations
      Dianne Saxe 217

   (e) Weak Environmental Law Enforcement in Canada: A well-kept secret
      David Donnelly and Leah Hagreen 223

   (f) Monitoring and Enforcement of Environmental Policy
      Mark A. Cohen 232

   (g) Taking Matters Into Their Own Hands: The role of citizens in Canadian
      pollution control enforcement
      Kernaghan Webb 242

   (h) Kingston Resident Wins Fisheries Act Prosecution of City
      Dawn Pier 254

Three: Assessing Environmental Change

Editors' Notes
Ron Pushchak, Alex Wellington and Allan Greenbaum 258

A. **Environmental Assessment** **287**

   (a) Assessing Environmental Impacts in Canada
      Thomas Meredith 287

   (b) The New *Canadian Environmental Assessment Act* — Bill C-78:
      A disappointing response to promised reform
      Michael I. Jeffery, Q.C. 294

   (c) "The Nasty Game": The failure of environmental assessment in Canada
      Andrew Nikiforuk 303

   (d) Reforms to the Environmental Assessment Program
      Environmental Assessment Advisory Committee 314

   (e) Environmental Impact Assessment and the Fallacy of Unfinished Business
      Kristin S. Shrader-Frechette 318

B. **Science and the Law: Facts and Values and Interpretation** **324**

   (a) The Conflict between Law and Science
      Hajo Versteeg 324

   (b) Science and the Tribunal: Dealing with scientific evidence in
      the adversarial arena
      Michael I. Jeffery, Q.C. 336

   (c) Science in the Courtroom: The value of an adversarial system
      Stuart L. Smith 342

   (d) Ethics, Science, and Environmental Regulation
      Donald A. Brown 346

   (e) Using Science in Environmental Policy: Can Canada do better?
      Ted Schrecker 357

C. Risk Assessment **368**

   (a) A Critical Review of Current Issues in Risk Assessment and Risk Management
      Steve E. Hrudey 368

   (b) Is a Scientific Assessment of Risk Possible? Value Assumptions in the Canadian
      Alachlor Controversy
      Conrad Brunk, Lawrence Haworth and Brenda Lee 376

   (c) Comparative Risk Assessment and the Naturalistic Fallacy
      Kristin S. Shrader-Frechette 383

   (d) Current Status and Implementation of the Precautionary Principle
      Joel Tickner and Nancy Myers 384

   (e) Our 'Stolen Future' and the Precautionary Principle
      Elizabeth M. Whelan 388

   (f) Debating the Precautionary Principle
      Nancy Myers 389

Four: Responses to Environmental Conflict

Editors' Notes
Allan Greenbaum, Alex Wellington and Ron Pushchak 394

A. Avenues for Citizen Participation **406**

   (a) Procedural Rights
      Elaine L. Hughes 406

   (b) Ontario's Environmental Bill of Rights Weakened, But Still Viable
      Averil Guiste 407

   (c) Conclusion: Continuing the process...
      Gerald Cormick, Norman Dale, Paul Emond, S. Glenn Sigurdson and Barry D. Stuart . . 408

B. Environmental Mediation **414**

   (a) Alternative Dispute Resolution and Environmental Conflict: The case for law
      reform
      Elizabeth J. Swanson 414

   (b) Environmental Mediation: From theory to practice
      Steven Shrybman 420

   (c) How Efficient Are Environmental Dispute Resolution Processes?
      Gail Bingham 426

   (d) The Politics of Environmental Mediation
      Douglas J. Amy 435

Appendices

Notes and References
Section One *Elements of the Legal System* 446
Section Two *The Regulatory System* 455
Section Three *Assessing Environmental Change* 472
Section Four *Responses to Environmental Conflict* 488

Glossary of Terms and Concepts 493

Preface

The forerunner to the present book is the two-volume *Social Conflict and Environmental Law* (Captus Press, 1995). That book was originally created to serve as the text for a full year, undergraduate, interdisciplinary social science course of the same name, developed by the editors, Allan Greenbaum, Alex Wellington and the late Ellen Baar. The course aspired to present a "law and society" perspective on the topic of environmental law and policy in Canada. No existing text or collection quite fit the bill, and we were challenged by this circumstance to assemble a collection of diverse materials, bridging disparate fields such as law, political science, economics, philosophy, sociology and environmental studies.

We initially divided up the terrain into two parts. The first (covered in Volume One of *Social Conflict and Environmental Law*) focused on critical social science approaches to, and ethical perspectives on, environmental conflict. It included case studies and thematic and topical approaches to contemporary environmental issues. The other part (Volume Two of the former book) surveyed the Canadian legal system, the regulatory framework governing environmental protection, environmental assessment and mediation. The second volume provided the template for the present book, which retains the same general structure: I. Elements of the Legal System; II. The Regulatory System; III. Assessing Environmental Change; IV. Responses to Environmental Conflict.

The present work was conceived when the publishers suggested that we update *Social Conflict and Environmental Law*. So much had changed in the meantime, however, in terms of the issues, the law, and the scholarly literature, that we found the "update" quickly turning into a major overhaul. It turned out, moreover, that the two volumes of the former book had found distinct markets. We therefore decided to succeed Volume Two of *Social Conflict and Environmental Law* with this stand alone title. We have endeavoured, nevertheless, to incorporate some of the material from the former Volume One as well.

The new book reflects the aforementioned changes in many ways. There is an abundance of new material, for one thing. We have included over two dozen entirely new pieces, and also commissioned several original articles specifically for this new book. Yet, we have still kept about twenty articles from the previous two volumes — a few from Volume One, and the remainder from Volume Two. The editors' notes and introductory essay have been revised considerably, in order to reflect the changes occurring to the law and policy, and in society, during the interim, and to connect, supplement and elaborate on the new materials. The glossary has been completely redone, and offers an extensive collection of terms and concepts to enhance and optimize the book's usefulness as a teaching tool.

Thematically, there are significant differences from the earlier volume. The discussion of the regulatory system has been expanded to include treatment of the drive towards deregulation, downsizing and downloading on the part of the federal and provincial governments. We have broadened the focus to include substantial coverage of the topic of risk assessment, in addition to environmental assessment. Both those topics are situated within the complex and crucial intersection of science and the law. We have also added a subsection on "avenues to citizen participation" to highlight the important role of non-state actors in environmental decision making. The present book, *Environmental Law in Social Context: Canadian Perspectives*, continues to provide a distinctive approach to social studies of environmental law and policy. The book aims to help the reader not only to learn something about the law as it actually is, at present, but also about how it got to be the way it is, as well as how it ought to be in the future, according to a diverse range of commentators and would-be reformers. This book will help students to appreciate that the law pertaining to the environment is not fixed and static, that it is not simply words on paper, but rather a set of social practices engaged in, and carried out by, many people performing distinct roles, including judges, lawyers, bureaucrats and politicians. These social practices both lead and follow, influencing and being influenced by other trends and patterns in contemporary life.

We suggest that taking a "law and society" approach to environmental law and policy in Canada means "taking it to the streets", in the sense that we address the following questions: How do environmental laws and policies actually work at the street level, i.e., what is the "law in action", not just in the books or on paper? What do those who are taking to the streets — protesting, marching, demonstrating — object to in the existing regime of environmental law and policy? What kinds of changes are citizens lobbying for or advocating, as they attempt to make their views known and aspire to fuller and more complete participation in the process?

Please feel free to contact the editors if you have any questions pertaining to the materials, or their potential uses as teaching materials.

Allan Greenbaum <eggplant@yorku.ca>

Alex Wellington <awelling@ryerson.ca>

Ron Pushchak: <pushchak@ryerson.ca>

Acknowledgements

The precursor of the present book was Volume Two of *Social Conflict and Environmental Law: Ethics, Economics and Equity* (North York: Captus Press, 1995), edited by Allan Greenbaum, Alex Wellington and Ellen Baar. Sadly, Professor Ellen Baar, of the Division of Social Science at York University, died before this newer incarnation of the work took shape. The current book has been so substantially revised that Ellen's work is no longer represented in it, yet her foundational contribution to the conceptual framework of the previous volume continues to shape the present book as well. It is fitting, therefore, that we dedicate this book to her memory. We are grateful to Ellen's husband, Carl Baar, for his encouragement in going ahead with the revision of the earlier volume. Allan and Alex are especially thankful to Ron Pushchak for agreeing to come on board, bringing to this project his enormous fund of knowledge and experience in the fields of environmental planning, assessment, and hazardous facility siting. We would all like to thank the authors of the commissioned pieces, written for this book: David Donnelly and Leah Hagreen, Anita Krajnc, and Kernaghan Webb.

Special thanks are due to Pauline Lai, at Captus Press, for instigating the revision of *Social Conflict and Environmental Law*, for her patience in waiting for the book to come to fruition, and for applying her exceptional organizational skills to keep us on track. Thanks to Lily Chu, also at Captus, for her diligence in helping to assemble the "manuscript" and in obtaining the necessary copyright permissions. Last, but certainly not least, thanks to all the instructors who have used the previous texts, and the many students and readers who have kept this book in print.

Introduction

A "Law and Society" Approach to Environmental Law

Allan Greenbaum and Alex Wellington ────────────────────────

LAW AND SOCIETY: DIVIDING UP THE TERRAIN

The first stage in the development of a "law and society" approach to an area of law is to address the question of what is meant by the term "law". This may seem unnecessary, for we all think we know what we are referring to when we think about the laws of a particular country, or the laws on a particular topic, or just what it is that lawyers work with on a daily basis. For instance, we can readily recognize and differentiate "Canadian" and "American", or "real estate law" and "intellectual property law". And yet, the task of providing a simple and comprehensive definition covering the whole set of social practices that fall under the rubric of "law" can be much more challenging than it first seems. It is especially hard to come up with a definition inclusive enough to cover legal systems that vary across a wide variety of cultures, nations, and localities, and that derive from distinct historical traditions. Such definitions are of crucial importance, nonetheless, in order to ground scholarship that extends not only to existing law, but also to prospective legal reform and comparative analysis.

To come up with a formal definition of "law", we have to abstract certain elements as essential and as common to a seemingly heterogeneous set of practices, institutions and norms. Numerous definitions and theories of law have been recommended by scholars from diverse disciplines, with distinct areas of expertise. Those efforts represent various points on a continuum that ranges from the perspectives of "insiders" or "participants" to the approaches adopted by "outsiders" — academics, and other observers of the system. Fitzgerald and Wright (2000: 1) distinguish between the "internal" and "external" approaches. "Internal" approaches comprise analytic jurisprudence and, at a stretch, philosophy of law. "External" accounts include a myriad disciplinary and interdisciplinary approaches to law in its social, political, economic and cultural context. We identify and characterize these latter approaches as social scientific ones.

Analytic jurisprudence rests initially upon what Donald Black (1976; 1989) calls the "participant's view" of the legal process — participant here referring to the practising lawyer or judge. This perspective originates in, and arises from, the internal logic of law, and focuses on the implications of various rules, doctrines, and principles, especially as they bear on the outcome of particular cases. It gathers together, under one umbrella, all the significant and relevant statutes and decisions, resulting in treatises that set out the "Law of Contracts", the "Law of Torts", "Property Law", or "Criminal Law", for instance. Lawyers (either as advocates or judges) are critically interested in the legal justification of particular outcomes — predicting them in advance and understanding them retrospectively. They need to be able to show that particular outcomes are or are not consistent with the relevant legal rules and principles. The emphasis here is on the "law on the books", what the law is like in its promulgated, expressed form; the law made manifest in authoritative pronouncements.

Lawyers as such seldom have occasion to ponder the definition of law. They operate, by and large, within a system of existing institutions and practices that can be taken for granted. The problem of defining law arises for them mainly when it is legally necessary to consider the line between law, on the one hand, and, on the other, extra-legal norms —

policy, fairness, community standards, and so on. Then, they do need to reflect on the extent to which the extra-legal norms may (or must) be taken into account in framing a legally justifiable outcome. Legal scholars will, by contrast, be provided with opportunity and motivation to engage in such enquiries on a regular basis. They will then be pursuing a common field of enquiry with other, non-legal academics — philosophers, political scientists and others.

Analytic jurisprudence can also encompass overtly philosophical variants, which seek to provide an abstract, conceptual understanding of law. These philosophical approaches aim at displaying the conceptual and linguistic structure of the concept of law, and effectively freeze the institution of law at some moment in time (Shiner, 1993: 205). The analytic jurisprudence perspective can then be expanded to include normative inquiry into the justification of principles, rules, or ways of decision making. In this sense, it represents a decidedly normative orientation, and is associated and affiliated with the wider fields of contemporary moral and political philosophy. This latter approach can be identified specifically as normative jurisprudence.

The social scientific study of law, instead, adopts the external "observer's view" (Black, 1976; 1989) of the legal system. These approaches begin with the institution of law as it "functions in the contemporary or historical world, or both, and presents accounts [predominantly descriptive or explanatory, but sometimes also normative] of that functioning" (Shiner, 1993: 205). Typically, but not always, a law and society approach is identified with a social scientific orientation. Such an approach is expected to do more than merely describe the law of a particular jurisdiction, concerning a particular issue or topic, or heading of law. Description of this sort is a necessary starting point for understanding an existing or historical legal regime, but it is not sufficient. We have provided the reader in Section One with an overview of the elements of the legal system as the necessary background material. The other sections of the book include pieces that represent the "something more" that constitutes a law and society approach. Taking such an approach requires giving, or at least attempting to give, an account of the social, political and economic contexts that gave rise to, and affect, the institutionalization and implementation of specific laws and policies, as well as of divergent proposed reforms. Much more is said below about the distinct strands of the social scientific study of law.

The two general approaches, or clusters, are complementary. Analytic jurisprudence can help to provide scholars with criteria for the "identification of the institution that the social study of law examines" (Shiner, 1993: 205). Normative jurisprudence can offer moral frameworks for assessing and criticizing the functioning of legal institutions in social context. In turn, the social scientific approaches to law offer a reality check, a balance and counter to the (at times) overly idealized accounts of law on the books.

The beginning of this Introduction will deal with those two different and general approaches to defining law: one that is philosophical, and the other that is rooted in social scientific method and theory. We then go on to discuss "the law in action", the nature of environmental conflict, and various perspectives on the relationship between law and environmental conflict. Last, we briefly survey the literature on the nature of national differences, and their influence on legal responses to environmental conflict.

Defining Law

Understanding Law, Philosophically

Concerns about the relationship between law and morality have been a central preoccupation of the philosophy of law. There are three main strands or schools of legal philosophy typically taught in courses on philosophy of law — natural law, legal positivism and legal realism. Increasingly, these are supplemented by coverage of critical legal studies and feminist jurisprudence. Here, we will briefly survey the three main traditions.

Versions of natural law theory have been proposed and promoted since ancient times, and there are contemporary variants still being debated to this day. The earliest systematic accounts of natural law theory were developed by theologians: for example, St. Augustine (writing in the early fifth century) and St. Thomas Aquinas (writing in the thirteenth century). Natural law theory claims that there is a necessary connection between law and morality, such that moral validity is, in effect, a necessary condition for legal validity. To understand why this is so for an adherent of natural law theory, it is necessary to appreciate some of the central features of their world view. Jeffrie Murphy and Jules Coleman (1990: 13) explain as follows: Nature has fixed a set of ends or purposes for human beings, according to the natural order of things. Moral duty consists in acting in accord with those purposes. The virtuous human life, moreover, entails living consistently with our natural purposes, or functions. Systems of social coercion may properly be called "legal" only if they are consistent with such purposes, or functions.

St. Thomas Aquinas put it thus: "Law is nothing else than an ordinance of reason for the common good, promulgated by him who has the care of the community... Human law has the nature of law in so far as it partakes of right reason... So far as it deviates from reason, it is called an unjust law and has the nature, not of law, but of violence... Such are acts of violence rather than laws because, as Augustine says, a law that is not just seems to be no law at all" (Murphy and Coleman, 1990: 15). The implication is that an unjust law (contrary to natural law) is not legally valid, and need not necessarily be obeyed, except perhaps for reasons of maintaining social order.

Natural law theory has elicited sustained and trenchant criticism from other legal philosophers, and provoked the development of legal positivism in opposition to it. The main line of criticism is summarized by Murphy and Coleman (1990: 14): natural law theory remains open to the "charge that it must be based either on the dogmatic acceptance of an implausible worldview, or on the subjective deliverances of the private conscience of each individual". Furthermore, the theory appears to conflate matters of definition — what counts as law *per se* — with matters of evaluation — what counts as "good" law. The term "law" becomes a "morally honorific title"; critics argue that intellectual clarity would be better served "by a more neutral analysis" (Murphy and Coleman, 1990: 18). The theory does go some way towards distinguishing law from mere force by ushering in the concept of obligation, and thus provides inspiration for theories that follow.

Legal positivism rests upon the notion of positive law as that which is set, or posited, or put into place by human authority (hence, *posit*ivism). John Austin, an early-nineteenth century British philosopher, worked out the initial construction of the theory in terms of a command theory of law, which rested upon empirical facts (habitual obedience, probability of sanction, etc.). Austin insisted that law must be defined without reference to morality, that "the existence of law is one thing, its merit or demerit is another".

According to Austin, a person who is habitually obeyed by the bulk of the population, and who does not him or herself habitually obey another, is sovereign. If that person expresses desires that something be done, or not be done, and then makes a credible threat to inflict harm on those who do not obey, the sovereign has commanded. Given his or her status as the sovereign — he or she who must be obeyed — the command is law (Murphy and Coleman, 1990: 23). For Austin, law is a coercive method of social control, which demands the attention and the compliance of those to whom it is directed, who are, in turn, under a duty to obey (Murphy and Coleman, 1990: 20). They are *obliged* to obey.

Subsequent legal philosophers have found numerous flaws in Austin's theory. Two main problems are identified by H.L.A. Hart: (i) Austin's theory does not provide for the continuity of the authority to make law possessed by a succession of different legislators; (ii) the theory cannot account for the persistence of laws long after their maker and those who rendered him/her habitual obedience have perished (Murphy and Coleman, 1990: 24). The sovereign ultimately has authority to make rules on the basis of other rules that are presupposed by the sovereign's authority in the first place. H.L.A. Hart's own theory is founded upon his critical insight about the nature of law as a system of rules that impose obligations.

Austin's great contribution to legal philosophy is said to be his insistence on the distinction between analytic and normative jurisprudence, and his articulation of two foundational ideas for positivism: (a) the sharp separation of law and morality; and (b) a pedigree test for legal validity. H.L.A. Hart preserved these features, and then went on to build his theory upon the distinction between primary and secondary rules. Primary rules are those "directed to all individuals in a social group telling them how they ought to act in certain circumstances" (Murphy and Coleman, 1990: 28). These rules are addressed to citizens, and concern their behaviour. Primary rules, moreover, "impose obligations or duties in the sense that they serve as standards of criticism or justification" (Murphy and Coleman, 1990: 29). Secondary rules specify ways in which "primary rules may be conclusively ascertained, introduced, eliminated, varied", and ways to determine conclusively when they had been violated (Murphy and Coleman, 1990: 30). Hart divided secondary rules into rules of recognition (i.e., criteria for distinguishing legal from moral, customary, or other kinds of rules), rules of change (e.g., procedures for enacting and amending laws) and rules of adjudication (e.g., rules of procedure, precedent and so on). Constitutional and administrative law consist mainly of secondary rules, while criminal law, tort law and so on consist mainly of primary rules.

Hart asserted that a theory of law had to respect the distinction between being *obliged* and being *obligated*. The former could consist in being forced to obey — such as when a gunman holds a gun to one's head and tells one to obey — whereas the latter means that one is under a duty to obey, and could be subjected to criticism for failure to fulfil that duty. Austin's theory of law as the command of the sovereign, Hart quipped, amounted to the "gunman writ large". It made adherence to law a matter of being obliged, but not necessarily obligated, to obey. Hart's own theory was intended to remedy that defect. Other problems that Hart's theory addressed included uncertainty about the rules, or conflict between the rules, and the static character of these primary rules (Murphy and Coleman, 1990: 29). Hart proposed the existence of secondary rules to solve these problems, as well as to provide for efficiency in dispute resolution.

Legal realism is the most recent of the legal philosophies, and it was developed in America by practising lawyers and judges during the early twentieth century (Justice Oliver Wendell Holmes, Jerome Frank, and Karl Llewellyn). It represents very much of a lawyer's perspective, reflecting a general scepticism about the value of any general and abstract theory of law. Legal realists developed a conception of law that was associated with empirical research on the behaviour of legal officials. Justice Holmes said that "the life of the law has not been logic", and he characterized the alternative as the "bad man view of the law" (Murphy and Coleman, 1990: 33). By that phrase he meant to refer to the perspective of the person facing the application of the legal rules by actual judges in actual courts, who is interested in the particular favourable outcome rather than in the formal justification of outcomes. That person would experience the law not as a system of rules waiting to be mechanically applied by judges, but instead as a more discretionary and creative exercise on the part of the judges. Rules allow judges considerable free play, and how they will actually decide a case will be more of a function of such factors as the judge's psychological temperament, social class, and values than of the application of rules *per se* (Murphy and Coleman, 1990: 33). As we note again below, the legal realists viewed legal theory as a matter of "prediction of what the courts will decide" (Murphy and Coleman, 1990: 33).

One major criticism of the legal realists has been that the theory cannot capture a crucial feature of legal decisions: "that certain considerations (for example, precedents) function not merely to explain a judge's decision but also rationally and publicly to justify that decision in terms of standards shared by (and thus definitive of) a particular legal community" (Murphy and Coleman, 1990; 34). Since then, legal philosopher Ronald Dworkin — while not a follower himself of legal realism — has developed a wide-ranging theory of law that places adjudication at its centre. In his many books and articles (including *Taking Rights Seriously, A Matter of Principle* and *Law's Empire*), he has provided a critique of

H.L.A. Hart's positivism, and proposed his own account of judge's reasoning in "hard cases" (ones for which the rules do not present a ready answer). That reasoning, he contends, is based on the application and weighting of various principles, meant to uphold the rights of the parties (Murphy and Coleman, 1990: 46). Thus, he calls his approach the "rights thesis", in contradistinction to Hart's "Model of Rules". Dworkin's approach to the articulation and elaboration of judicial reasoning makes moral and political philosophy a central and irreducible component of legal theory.

One can see from this cursory survey that the main focus for legal philosophers is "getting the theory right", aspiring to logical coherence and consistency and plausibility, criticizing and improving on earlier theories. They are typically not as concerned with developing empirical hypotheses, and testing them against the data of the real world. Now we turn to theories that are concerned with such matters.

Social Scientific Approaches to Law

Various legal scholars, anthropologists and sociologists have focused on different aspects of functions of Western and non-Western legal systems, and have arrived at very different accounts of law. We can identify two of the more influential tendencies by the phrases, "law as social control" and "law as conflict resolution", respectively.

A famous definition of law representing the "social control" type was offered by the sociologist Max Weber. Law, according to Weber (1946: 180),

> exists when there is a probability that an order will be upheld by a specific staff ... who will use physical or psychical compulsion with the intention of obtaining conformity with the order, or of inflicting sanctions for infringement of it.

For Weber, then, law is an activity of an organization (pre-eminently, though not exclusively, the state) in which compliance with rules or commands is enforced by personnel whose particular job it is to do so. Note that Weber's definition of law mentions neither courts nor litigants. Weber does not discount the dispute settlement role that legal institutions play in some societies (such as our own), but he chooses to call any rule enforcement bureaucracy a "legal system" whether or not it is available to parties (other than the state itself) for dispute resolution purposes. The Marxian and Durkheimian sociological traditions, though disagreeing on many points, have tended to concur with the Weberian tradition in defining law as a mechanism of social control (enforcing class domination or collective values, respectively).

Other social scientists, especially anthropologists, have defined law as an institution for conflict resolution (Nader, 1967). They regard the existence of courts, tribunals or other fora where disputes are heard and decisions (or agreements) rendered as the essential or defining features of legal systems, and some may regard the elements of compulsion or enforcement as incidental. Legal institutions are distinguished in this definition from other institutions by the distinctive task they perform — i.e., the settling of disputes. Such a definition may be called a "functional" definition in a very broad sense. (It may or may not also be "functionalist" in the more specific sense discussed below.) Other ways of defining law focus not on *what* law distinctively does, but on *how* law distinctively does it. Law, for example, might be seen as one way of resolving disputes; negotiation or unilateral force might be others. Law in this analysis might be defined as dispute resolution by an impartial third party, or in accordance with rules, and so on.

An instance of this kind of analysis can be found in the work of the political theorist John Dryzek. Dryzek (1987: 55f.) defines law in a functional sense as the institution concerned with conflict resolution, but he also identifies it (p. 64f.) as one of several "social choice mechanisms", that is, ways of deciding what gets done. Each social choice mechanism is defined in terms of its distinctive "co-ordination mode". In markets, things are decided by reference to price signals, in administrative systems by commands, in moral persuasion by promulgated values, in bargaining by negotiation, in armed conflict by force, and so on. In law, things are decided in terms of formal, general, consistent rules and rights. In comparing this definition with Weber's, we can see that Weber's definition of law overlaps at least two of Dryzek's categories, law and administration, neither of which is defined by Dryzek in terms of coercive enforcement. Indeed, like others in the conflict resolution camp, Dryzek has a tendency to identify law rather narrowly with the specific operations of tribunals that exercise (in Alexander Hamilton's words) "neither force nor will, but only judgement" (ibid.: 147). Dryzek's typology has some conceptual value, but his social choice mechanisms do not map onto actual social institutions. All these mechanisms interpenetrate one another in practice. Dryzek is not actually interested in identifying social choice mechanisms with concrete institutions, but in assessing the potential of each to contribute to "ecological rationality". Law, he concludes, can serve important co-ordination and negative feedback functions in helping society adapt to ecological constraints, but only insofar as these functions are expressible in terms of rights and rules. The potential of law is limited by the inherent rigidity of its distinctive co-ordination mode.

Debates about definitions of law inevitably touch on wider debates about the nature of law and society. Let us consider, for example, the views of the American anthropologist Paul Bohannon, one of the leading proponents of the conflict resolution definition of law. Bohannon (1965) defined legal institutions as specialized bodies to which disputes are transferred and settled in accordance with set rules. Bohannon thus agrees with Weber that legal rules are those which are enforced (or at least applied) by a distinct set of persons. Unlike Weber, however, Bohannon pictures legal institutions as processing disputes that arise external to the legal system. Bohannon's definition is primarily concerned with distinguishing "law" from "custom". Customs, for Bohannon, are rules or norms around which there is a high degree of social consensus. Substantive law consists of customs — social norms or rules — that have been explicitly restated and that are applied by legal institutions in accordance with specifically legal procedural rules. According to Bohannon, then, legal institutions are specialized institutions that settle conflicts arising in the wider society by reference to explicated versions of norms also originating from the wider society.

Some aspects of this definition might seem odd. True, in Western societies courts certainly do resolve disputes originating from outside the legal system, as when they hear civil law suits. It is also certainly true that both civil and criminal law incorporate many norms originally derived from custom, religion and morals. It seems a stretch, though, to regard much criminal law, for example, as being primarily about dispute resolution. Criminal *courts* do, of course, resolve disputes between the prosecution and the defence over the guilt of the accused, but such disputes arise *within* the operation of the legal system. In a broader or vaguer sense, one could argue that criminal law is about "resolving" conflict between criminals and victims or "society"; but then the sense of "conflict resolution" becomes so broad as to become coterminous with "social control". By the same token, it is hard to see tax law as being a restatement of custom, even if it incorporates various originally extra-legal norms and concepts such as "fairness" or "literal meaning". Bohannon's definition is most plausible if we identify "legal institution" narrowly with "court" or "tribunal". It is a less plausible definition of "law" in contexts where we speak of legislation as "law making" and policing as "law enforcement". One critic of the dispute resolution definition of law, anthropologist Stanley Diamond (1984), has pointed out that the earliest laws promulgated in the development of state legal systems concerned matters like taxation and conscription that directly served the consolidation and extension of state power and that had no basis in customary norms. Only later did state legal institutions come to serve as fora for the resolution of civil disputes.

What, then, would lead scholars such as Bohannon to define law the way they do? Legal anthropologists have often been interested in identifying legal institutions or practices in non-state societies. Bohannon is also interested in situations in which multiple "legal" systems coexist within state societies, not all of which may be backed by the coercive power of the state — an interest shared by the more recent "legal pluralist" scholars (e.g., Arthurs, 1984; Tie, 1999). Non-state societies lack a "sovereign" or central apparatus for producing rules, issuing orders and applying sanctions, but many possess institutions strongly analogous to courts. One might understandably be reluctant to adopt a definition of "law" according to which such societies would be considered lawless. Social control definitions such as Weber's arguably exhibit a state-centred bias, and/or take in many kinds of organized coercion that do not comport with our intuitive conception of "law". The definition from Weber quoted above would not, for example, distinguish between "the rule of law" and the most arbitrary acts of authority exercised by or through an enforcement apparatus. Proponents of the social control definition might not balk at the latter objection, though. They might argue that legitimacy and non-arbitrariness are always matters of degree, and do not go to the essence of law. In that respect, their views could be said to resemble Austin's version of legal positivism discussed above.

Conflict and Consensus

This debate over definitions is no mere lexicographical quibble. The positions are embedded in broader theoretical perspectives on law and society. Bohannon's analysis is typical of the functionalist perspective that dominated American social science in the 1960s, when the article we are discussing was published. This version of functionalism is associated with a "consensus theory" of law and society. For Bohannon, laws are derived from shared social norms recognized as binding by all. Conflict is not pervasive or structural; rather, conflicts are discrete clashes among specific parties. Conflicts, moreover, are dysfunctional aberrations that threaten the institutions in which they arise. All institutions, according to functionalism, have a specific function in society. The specific function of the legal system, Bohannon suggests, is to "disengage" conflict ("difficulties", "trouble") from other institutions and to resolve it according to legal rules "so that society can continue to function in an orderly manner".

Starting in the late 1960s, "consensus" theories of law and society came under increasing challenge from what were called "conflict" theories. According to conflict theories, law and the state exist in societies where some groups dominate and exploit others. Conflict is structurally inherent in such societies, and cannot be resolved by law. Rather, law serves ultimately to maintain the relations of domination. Diamond's critique of Bohannon is representative of this conflict perspective. For Bohannon, to define "law" in such a way as to classify non-state societies as "lawless" would be to imply (misleadingly) that such societies were exceptionally disorderly, chaotic and conflict-ridden. For Diamond, even more than Bohannon an admirer of non-state societies, such societies are orderly precisely because they are regulated by custom and reciprocity rather than by law (defined in terms of coercive social control).

In modern industrialized countries such as Canada, the issue of social control versus conflict resolution definitions of law (if not the broader debate between consensus and conflict theories) is a moot one, because social control and dispute resolution are inextricably linked in modern legal systems. Indeed, courts and tribunals — institutions that play a dispute resolution role within the rule-enforcement apparatus of the state — represent the intersection of the two definitions. Traditional legal scholarship has always focused on the rule-making activities of legislatures and the rule-making and rule-interpreting activities of courts. A law and society approach draws on the two broader definitions of law we have just discussed. The Weberian definition draws our attention to the activities (including rule-interpreting, and what in practice amounts to the rule-making, activities) of officials other than legislators and judges. Several studies relevant to this topic are found in Section Two of this book on the setting, implementation and enforcement of regulatory standards. On the other hand, the definition of law as conflict resolution draws our attention to institutions other than courts and practices other than trials that serve to settle disputes between parties. Section Four includes a number of readings on environmental mediation, one such mode of "alternative dispute resolution". Finally, a law and society approach embraces insights from political science and sociology that draw our attention to the way law may be used to serve purposes, such as symbolic ones, directly related neither to social control nor to dispute resolution. As several readings in this book suggest, governments may pass laws when it is politically expedient to be seen to be doing something about a matter of public concern, although the laws in question may go unenforced or be otherwise of little practical effect.

THE LAW IN ACTION

The foregoing points bring us to a consideration of the second topic that we have chosen to illustrate the distinctiveness of a law and society approach — the contrast between "the law on the books" and "the law in action". Many activities are legally forbidden (jaywalking, speeding, littering, etc.), but among laws that purport to forbid certain activities, some have far more social efficacy than others. Law enforcement officials are not automata blindly seeking to maximize the enforcement of law on the books. Rather, sociological studies find that officials use laws selectively to achieve specific ends related to the conceptions of social order (in the case of criminal or family law) or of environmental quality and economic efficiency (in the case of environmental law) that prevail in the officials' organizational culture. Police, for example, do not attempt systematically to apprehend everyone in simple possession of proscribed drugs, but will enforce drug possession laws against individuals singled out for some other reason. Littering is an example of environmental pollution, but bylaws against littering are seldom enforced. Industrial pollution, on the other hand, may attract significant legal sanctions, but enforcement of industrial pollution laws tends to vary with the political priorities of government, the relative clout of industry and environmentalists, and so on.

In other situations, laws that are not systematically enforced are brought into effect as tools not by officials but by private parties. We are not referring here to private law rights and remedies, but to public criminal and quasi-criminal laws. (The distinction between public and private law is discussed in the editors' notes to Section One, "The Elements of the Legal System".) Some such laws are complaint driven — that is, infractions are prosecuted by officials, but only in response to a complaint by a member of the public. Many municipal bylaws are enforced in this way. The complaints that trigger bylaw enforcement often arise from long-standing conflicts between neighbours that have little to do with the substance or objective of the bylaw. In other instances, officials have declined to enforce public law even after complaints have been made, leaving enforcement to private parties. Citizen enforcement of Canadian pollution laws is discussed in Kernaghan Webb's article, "Taking matters into their own hands", reproduced in Section Two, Part D of this book.

Traditional legal scholarship and analysis is preoccupied with "the law on the books" — constitutional provisions, statutes, regulations, and judicial decisions. It places less emphasis on "the law in action" or "the law on the streets" — what actually gets implemented, enforced and sanctioned, and how that affects people's lives (and, we might add from an ecological perspective, the lives of non-human beings and systems). Now, we have suggested that traditional legal scholarship and analysis is a product of the legal profession, and it is obvious that practising lawyers, as well as law reform advocates and analysts, have a strong pragmatic interest in the "law in action". At the same time, lawyers and judges play a particular role in the broader legal process; they specialize in the legal justification of sought or rendered judicial decisions. Many factors bear on why clients and their lawyers seek particular judicial decisions, and why judges decide what they do; but lawyers must try to justify the decisions they advocate, and judges the decisions they render, in terms of the law on the books. The law on the books will at least constrain the range of possible outcomes, even if it does not uniquely determine the outcome of any particular case.

Legal thought has long recognized that "law" is not reducible to a corpus of authoritative texts. The "Legal Realist" movement (introduced above) famously defined the law as the behaviour of courts, so that a statement of the law governing any to-be-decided case amounts to a prediction of what the court of final appeal will decide. An accurate prediction will be based not only on knowledge of the "law on the books", but also on knowledge of the attitudes and biases of the judges, the resources of the parties, and so on. The Legal realists introduced an empiricist, sociological dimension into the jurisprudential understanding of law, but retained the lawyer's traditional focus on courts and judges.

Law and society researchers have extended the Realists' insights in a several directions. As we have seen, the "law in action" is a product not only of the behaviour of judges but also the behaviour of many other categories of officials and functionaries, as well as the responses of the non-officials whose behaviour the law is intended to influence. (Economists and sociologists have devoted much attention over the years to the unintended — though often predictable — consequences of law. In particular, certain classical and neo-classical economists have long maintained — rightly or wrongly — that since market behaviour follows its own natural laws of supply and demand, attempted interventions such as minimum-wage laws, price controls, worker safety laws and so on are doomed to failure.) Law and society scholars have also sought to investigate empirically the behaviours that constitute the law in action, and to use the results of these empirical studies to build and test theories — generalizable, abstract models or interpretations of how the law works.

Donald Black, for example, undertakes what he calls "the sociology of the case" (1989: 4). He hypothesizes that the outcomes of legal cases are largely determined by the relative social location or status of the participants. He distinguishes between "adversary effects", "lawyer effects" and "third-party effects". As Black (1989: 13) puts it, "the social structure of a case is defined not only by who has a complaint against whom, but also by who supports whom and by who intervenes as a third party". Adversary effects are the effects of the relative status of the parties to a legal conflict. Black summarizes the main adversary effects as follows:

> [A] high status defendant accused of an offense against [an] equally high status victim is likely to be handled more severely than a low status defendant accused of an offense against an equally low status victim.... But when people offend a social superior or inferior, another pattern becomes evident. Those accused of offending someone above them in social status are likely to be handled more severely than those accused of offending someone below them. Those victimizing a social superior inhabit a legal space all their own, with a risk of severity vastly greater than anyone's (1989: 10).

Black also contends that the "relational distance" between parties also affects the behaviour of law. As he puts it (1989: 11), "[t]he closer people's relationships are, the less law enters into their affairs".

The second hypothesis that Black discusses concerns "lawyer effects". Lawyers differ in terms of their social status, as do the adversaries. The legal impact of the social status of the lawyer depends on the social status of the client. Black suggests that higher-status lawyers improve their clients' prospects more than lower-status lawyers. Furthermore, this effect benefits lower-status clients more than clients who already have the benefit of higher status (1989: 13). "Third-party effects" have to do with the effect of the difference in status between the judge or jury, on the one hand, and the litigants on the other. For example, Black suggests (1989: 15) that a judge who is much higher in status than the parties will be less lenient and more likely to "decide totally" for one side or the other, than will a judge whose social status is closer to that of the parties.

The status of clients, lawyers, and judges is not incorporated into the jurisprudential explanation of the outcomes of cases, for the social characteristics of the parties and advocates are not legally relevant (i.e., not mentioned in the applicable legal rules). Nevertheless, social scientists observe that these social characteristics seem to affect the outcomes of legal cases.

Consider, while reading this book, the extent to which the evidence presented in the materials reproduced here tends to support or contradict Black's hypotheses. Arguably, the behaviour of Canadian pollution regulation law, as described in these materials, conforms to what Black would predict on the basis of his "adversary effects". There is evidence to suggest that, considering the amounts of pollution discharged in each case, small businesses (presumably lower status) are more likely to face legal penalties than are big businesses. Pollution that primarily affects poor people or minorities is less likely to attract legal intervention than is pollution that primarily affects people with wealth and high social status (see, e.g., Lavelle and Coyle, 1993). Pollution-control officials are less likely to prosecute pollution offences than police officers are to prosecute other offences, in part because pollution control officers typically have closer working relationships with the offenders than police officers do. On the other hand, it might be less clear whether, for example, the differences between the behaviour of American environmental law and that of Britain and Canada can be explained in terms of Black's theory.

The relationship between "law on the books" and "law in action" is further complicated in the case of environmental law because, unlike criminal law, the application of environmental statutes to actual behaviour is often mediated by chains of policy statements, regulations, guidelines, approval conditions and so on. What is "the book", then? If each link in the policy implementation chain departs imperceptibly from the prior one, the law in action may fall well short of stated policy even if behaviour more or less conforms to documents that prescribe specific actions. Freudenburg and Gramling (1994a: 104f.; 1994b), who have studied this phenomenon in detail, call it "bureaucratic slippage".

TAKING A LAW AND SOCIETY APPROACH TO ENVIRONMENTAL ISSUES

Defining "Environment"

The definition of "environment" has important implications for environmental law (Kiss and Shelton, 1997: 5). *Webster's Dictionary* defines environment as the "circumstances, objects or conditions by which one is surrounded" and, more usefully for our purposes, as "the complex of physical, chemical, and biotic factors (as climate, soil and living things) that act upon an organism or an ecological community and ultimately determine its form and survival". As Kiss and Shelton (1997: 5) note, environmental law "springs from this understanding", especially the emphasis on ensuring the "continued viability of the planet and the sustainability of its myriad species".

Defining the environment is crucial for "determining the application of legal rules and the [existence of and] extent of liability when harm occurs" (Kiss and Shelton, 1997: 3). The "environment" is the subject of protection measures, and laws are developed to regulate human behaviour in order to prevent, ameliorate or remedy "environmental degradation". Environmental assessment and environmental auditing likewise rest upon notions of "the environment" to which they are to be applied. A very significant associated term is "pollution", commonly defined as "the introduction by [humans], directly or indirectly, of substances or energy into the environment resulting in deleterious effects of such a nature as to endanger human health, harm living resources and ecosystems, and impair or interfere with amenities and other legitimate uses of the environment" (Kiss and Shelton, 1997: 6). This definition would include noise, vibrations, heat and radiation.

Much of environmental law rests upon determining when human activity reaches such a level or is of such a nature as to harm or endanger people, property, non-human organisms (especially living resources), or ecosystems. Certain laws try to spell out what that would amount to; for instance, the *British Environmental Protection Act* defines "harm" as "injury to the health of living organisms or other interference with ecological systems of which they form a part", and also includes offence caused to human senses and harm to property within the definition of pollution (Kiss and Shelton, 1997: 6). Definitions of environment that broaden out to include "the aggregate of social and cultural conditions that influence the life of an individual or community" will also cover "urban problems such as traffic congestion, crime and noise within the field of environmental protection" (Kiss and Shelton, 1997: 4). The *Ontario Environmental Assessment Act* is an example of a statute employing such an expansive definition of environment.

Legal definitions of prohibited environmental harm typically build in reference to standards set as part of a regulatory process. Thus, "pollution" only counts as such if it could cause harm *and* if it exceeds the prescribed standards; such standards will typically reflect other concerns and values as well as environmental protection (such as economic efficiency or political expediency). This topic is discussed in the editors' notes and readings for Section Two, "The Regulatory System".

Environmental law has several features that are likely to lead to social conflict: the indeterminancy of the focus; dynamism of the environment; and the irreversibility of harm. The first, the difficulty of providing with any exact precision just what is or is or not covered by "environment", and just what does or does not cause serious and severe "environmental harm", is a constant source of debate and discussion. The environment, however it is defined, is a complex and interrelated system, and it is also dynamic and constantly evolving. There is, therefore, a need for integrated measures to address environmental problems, and also for flexibility and the ability to respond rapidly to new and often unanticipated circumstances. As Kiss and Shelton point out (1997: 9), "irreversibility of environmental harm is a third element that impacts upon decision making". Environmental harm can be permanent, as in the case of the extinction of species; it can also be effectively irreversible in cases where rehabilitation and repair are prohibitively expensive. For many people, this is a justification for measures that are preventative, that anticipate potential harm and curb or severely curtail it. The proper balance between prevention and "cleaning up messes" after the fact is just one of the many areas of controversy and contention within the field of environmental law.

The Nature of Environmental Conflict

Whether one takes the view that "conflict resolution" is part of the essence of law, or that law is a manifestation of pervasive structural conflict in society, it is evident that social conflict sets the stage for environmental law. The creation of environmental law is a response to conflict around environmental issues, and the implementation of environmental law is an occasion for still further conflict. Before addressing the relationship between law and environmental conflict, it is worth making a few very schematic comments about environmental conflict itself.

Values and interests. One way to categorize and theorize about environmental conflict is to focus on the nature of the parties' stakes. Some are drawn into environmental conflict through their pursuit or defence of their own material well-being. We will refer to such stakes as "interests". Others are struggling on behalf of the interests of human or non-human others, or for the sake of moral or political principle, or for a position or policy that symbolically validates the honour of a way of life in which they are invested or of the group to which they belong. We will, for short, call all such stakes "values". This analysis yields a three-way typology of conflict: interests versus interests, interests versus values, and values versus values. This typology is too simple, because there are different kinds of interests and values, and because real conflicts usually involve alliances among parties with different kinds of stakes.

The situation is also complicated by the close connections between interests and values. These terms can be given a broader meaning than we have given them here; in this broader sense, all interests are derived from values, and all values give rise to interests. But even in the narrower meanings we have assigned these terms here, interests and values can be closely linked. On the one hand, interests are often defended on the basis of value claims. For example, to say that I have a *right* to something (say, to breathe unpolluted air, or to develop my property) is to claim that my interest in doing so is protected by a legal or moral *principle* that imposes a correlative *duty* (if only one of non-interference) on others. On the other hand, people's values may affect the way they perceive, interpret, or prioritize their interests. Proponents of the cultural theory of risk selection argue that the kind of social order people value determines which threats to their material well-being they are most concerned about: for example, those who value social hierarchy worry about crime while egalitarians worry about toxic pollution (Douglas, 1992; Douglas and Wildavsky, 1982; Wildavsky and Dake, 1990).

Interests vary in strength. The most compelling interests are generally those related to immediate physical survival, or even of survival of a way of life. In many parts of the world, threats to survival interests posed by environmental degradation and scarcity are important factors contributing to armed conflicts that may not commonly be thought of as "environmental conflicts" (Homer-Dixon, 1999; Homer-Dixon and Blitt, 1998). Compellingly strong interests are also important factors in environmental conflicts commonly understood as such. Strong interests can normally be expected to trump other considerations in shaping parties' positions on contentious issues. This is a key point in understanding many conflicts of interests versus values. As David Schmidtz (2000) points out, it is a mistake to assume that such conflicts arise because the parties differ in their environmental values. Rather, it may be that for those on one side of the dispute, the environmental values in question have a high priority because they do not conflict with a compelling material interest, while for those on the other side, the values do so conflict and, therefore, have a lower priority. Immediate survival interests almost inevitably eclipse peoples' other concerns, including both values and long-term interests.

Symmetrical and asymmetrical conflicts of interests. Conflicts of interests versus interests take different forms. The simplest, conceptually, are those in which the parties are at odds just because they want the same thing. An example might be a dispute between upstream and downstream industrial water users in a situation where the upstream use so diminishes the quality or quantity of water in the river as to impair the downstream use. The parties want the same thing — water — for the sake of the same goal — making money. We might refer to such disputes as "symmetrical interest conflicts", or, following Schmidtz (2000: 398), as "conflicts in use". Other interest versus interest conflicts are asymmetrical in the sense that the parties have very different *kinds* of interests at stake.

One common kind of asymmetrical interest conflict occurs when an industrial use of the environment serving the economic material interests of one party detracts from another party's personal use of the environment, or clashes with that other party's material interest in health, safety, comfort or amenity. Many theorists have emphasized this form of environmental conflict. Gould, Schnaiberg and Weinberg (1996: 5, 13–18), for example, suggest that environmental conflicts "are fundamentally struggles over the different capacities of social groups to meet their needs by gaining access to natural resources", and that such struggles are generated by a structural conflict between the use values derived from environments by local residents and the exchange values derivable from them by business. In a similar vein, O'Connor (1998: 308) locates the essence of environmental conflict in the "struggle to defend or redefine conditions of *production* as conditions of *life*", while Murphy (1994: 172) points to the relation of "indirect exploitation" between privileged "environmental classes", who accumulate wealth in part by externalizing the costs of waste disposal, and unprivileged environmental classes who bear those costs. Unlike the situation characterized by symmetrical interest conflicts discussed above, the parties here make different kinds of use of the particular "resources" over which they struggle. For example, the polluting industrialist uses a river as a waste disposal medium in the interests of economic gain, while the local residents use it as a source of drinking water or a source of fish for food. Note that while the local residents and the industrialists in this example have opposing interests in respect of the river, they do not necessarily have diverging preferences or values, since the locals also like to make money, and the industrialists also like to drink clean water. The conflict arises insofar as the industrialists — not the locals — get the profits, and the locals — not the industrialists — get the pollution. As in the symmetrical situation, these conflicts arise ultimately not because people *want* different things, but because they *get* different things.

Another kind of asymmetrical conflict of interests involves a clash of incompatible use values. We may speak here of a "conflict of tastes". Golfers and birders disagree about whether a wood should be turned into a golf course. Neighbours disagree about whether a park should be kept neatly mown or encouraged to go wild. The issue here is not that the parties get different things; quite the contrary, they get the same thing, but differ in what they want. These conflicts may be about interests insofar as the preferences at stake are self-regarding ones rather than matters of principle, but they are in other respects like conflicts of values.

Conflicts of values. Conflicts of values or principles arise when the parties do not agree on what is valuable, good or morally right. Examples of this kind of conflict include the controversies over abortion, capital punishment, and euthanasia. An environmental example of a conflict of this kind might be a controversy over water pollution from a mine in a remote wilderness area. For the some, non-human nature has moral worth, and harm to non-human nature is wrong in itself. Others may disagree, and believe that only human beings have moral worth. Here, a conflict of value might arise over whether the law should penalize an instance of pollution that harms only organisms of no use to humans.

The distinction between conflicts of interests and conflicts of values is salient in the social study of law and conflict resolution because of the notion that different legal responses are appropriate to each. Aubert (1969) argued that conflicts of interests were most suited to mediation, which can provide for a positive sum arrangement that satisfies most of the interests of both sides. Conflicts of value, on the other hand, were most suited to adjudication, which provides for a zero-sum outcome. One party wins, and the other party loses. This is necessary in a case where there is a conflict of values because there is no compromise on matters of principle; rather, both sides want to be vindicated by law. This analysis has become the conventional wisdom in the literature of negotiation and alternative dispute resolution, as reflected in several of the readings in Section Four, Part B of this book.

Aubert, though, seems to be confusing two separate issues: whether the conflict is one of interests or one of values, and whether the conflict is by its nature a zero-sum conflict. A dispute over the ownership of a particular asset, or over who is entitled to a specific position (e.g., being president of a certain company), would represent a zero-sum conflict of interests. It is a symmetrical conflict of interests because each of the parties wants the same thing (i.e., the asset or the position). It is a zero-sum conflict because one party will lose to the extent that the other wins. Assuming the object of the conflict is highly valued by both parties, negotiations will likely reach an impasse, and the matter could be settled only by adjudication. Conversely, although many conflicts of values do not lend themselves to negotiated settlement (the abortion issue is a good example), a conflict of values need not be a zero-sum conflict if a way can be found simultaneously to accommodate the different values of the parties. A conflict between those who value the preservation of an endangered species and those who value the livelihood of a logging community might be resolved by finding a way of logging that does not adversely affect the species in question. Negotiation theorists (Fisher and Ury, 1991) urge parties to shift their attention away from their positions and to focus instead on the underlying interests that the positions are meant to advance. This advice is sometimes interpreted as: shift attention from values to interests. But values are no more to be automatically identified with positions than interests are; in cases of value conflict, the logic of the negotiation theory suggests we shift attention from positions to values.

There is, however, one important difference between conflicts of interest and values, and that concerns the role of payment or compensation as a means of dispute resolution. The dispute over the asset or the position could be resolved if one party offered the other an acceptable sum of money to drop their claim. With conflicts of value it is different. The species preservationists might be willing to compromise in the face of conflicting values, but they would not (if they were principled) be willing to drop the issue in return for a cash payment. Because they are not representing their own interests in the first place, they could not be compensated by money for the loss of the species. The species is not theirs to sell (see Sagoff 1982a,b).

There is another kind of dispute that Aubert does not mention. This is a dispute over facts. Disputes over facts play an important role in both conflicts of values and conflicts of interests. Conflicts where crucial facts are in dispute may not be amenable to mediation, regardless of the nature of the conflict. See the editors' notes and readings in Section Three for more discussion of the relationship between facts and values, and on the adjudication of fact disputes.

Diffuse versus concentrated interests. Conflicts of interests can be characterized according to whether the benefits or costs of the disputed activity are concentrated or diffuse. Again, let us consider some pollution-related examples. In the simplest case, an upstream industry saves money by dumping inadequately treated wastes in a river, and thereby imposes costs on a downstream industry that also uses water from the river. Here, both the costs and the benefits are concentrated. Now consider a case where the pollution is caused by one factory, but the pollution harms a large number of downstream users. In this case, the benefits are concentrated, but the costs are diffuse. The reverse may be true — a large number of parties may be involved in polluting the river, and this pollution affects relatively few. Here, the benefits of pollution are diffuse, but the costs are concentrated. Finally, for some kinds of pollution (for example, automobile exhaust) both the benefits of the polluting activity and the harm done by the pollution are fairly diffuse (though not evenly distributed) in the population.

Generally speaking, if the total levels of costs and benefits are comparable, more concentrated interests will tend to prevail over more diffuse interests. If the polluter saves $1,000 a year in waste treatment costs by dumping waste in the river, and the pollution does $10-worth of damage to each of 1,000 people, the harm done by the pollution far outweighs the benefit to the polluter. Nevertheless, the polluter has a major stake in continuing to pollute, and none of the victims is sufficiently harmed to make it worth their while to invest much effort in stopping the pollution. Conversely, a few well organized environmentalists may have relatively little difficulty forcing industry to invest in environmental protection measures if the relevant market is not highly competitive and the costs can easily be passed on as small price increases borne by large numbers of consumers. The situation would be very different if the industry in question were faced with stiff price competition from producers in jurisdictions where the environmental movement is weak and laws are lax. This is why globalization is (depending on the point of view one brings to this analysis) a bane to the environment or a boon to consumers.

Conflicts of all kinds can be classified according to the relative power of the parties. Conflicts between social "equals" can be distinguished from conflicts between parties with unequal access to resources. Almost always, in conflicts between parties with unequal resources, the more powerful party has the advantage. In legal conflicts, those with more resources can, for example, afford better lawyers and more expert witnesses. Interests that are both concentrated and powerful have a very great advantage in social conflict over interests that are both diffuse and powerless. This helps to explain why pollution impairing the general quality of life in low-income and minority communities is often the last to be controlled (see, e.g., Lavelle and Coyle, 1993; Bryant, 1995).

Formulations of the Relationship Between Law and Environmental Conflict

Law is sometimes described as a means of conflict resolution, dispute settlement, or grievance arbitration. We suggest that this view idealizes and oversimplifies the relationship between law and social conflict. Law interacts with social conflict in a complex set of ways. We have identified four different ways to formulate or characterize the relations between law and social conflict. These are: (1) articulation of conflict; (2) creation of conflict; (3) transformation of conflict; and (4) resolution or apparent resolution.

1. Law functions to articulate pre-existing social conflict. For instance, in a situation where an industry has been polluting the local environment for some time, a legal action (criminal prosecution or private lawsuit) may serve to articulate the conflict. The legal proceeding highlights and gives legal expression to the pre-existing conflict between the polluting industry and the surrounding town or settlement. This is a role that comports well with Bohannon's definition of law (see above), except that articulation does not always result in a socially "functional" resolution.

2. Indeed, law can create further social conflict. The creation of further social conflict occurs by a sort of "spiral" effect. A certain legal mechanism — for example, a zoning ordinance or bylaw — gives expression to, or articulates conflicts between, different citizens (e.g., landowners versus preservationists, or industrialists versus homeowners). The legal mechanism itself may then pit both sets of citizens (both landowners and preservationists, industrialists and homeowners) against the government in terms of application and enforcement. The legal mechanism provides the conditions for litigation over the ordinance or bylaw. The litigation could simply articulate the conflict between the litigating citizen parties (plaintiff and defendant), or it may produce new levels or locations of conflict if the litigation expands to include the government as a party. In the Rafferty Alameda and Oldman River dam cases, environmentalists sought to stop provincially sponsored developments by requesting federal environmental assessments of the projects. The conflict was thus expanded from one between environmentalists and developers to one including a jurisdictional dispute between the federal and provincial governments. Legal intervention both transformed the nature of the conflict and added new elements of conflict.

3. Law, as we see in the example discussed above, can transform social conflict. Sometimes substantive conflicts over land uses get transformed into disputes over procedure and jurisdiction, or disputes over the viability of scientific and technical evidence. Examples of this process include the environmental assessment cases like the Oldman River and the Rafferty Alameda (discussed in Section Three, Part A), or the Alachlor risk assessment (see the article by Brunk, Haworth and Lee in Section Three, Part C of this book, and the Section Three editors' notes). The original dispute concerns the attempt to have a dam or other development stopped, or to have a pesticide removed from the market. What happens, however, is that the focus of the dispute then shifts to technicalities concerning jurisdiction, procedure, or rules of evidence. Environmental cases involving complex scientific issues often turn into a dispute between expert scientific witnesses. Both sides bring in experts who disagree, and it then becomes a question of the credibility of the expert witnesses. Many parties to legal proceedings find themselves drawn to the use of legal procedural mechanisms to bring about desired substantive results.

   This last aspect of law as dispute transformation is an especially significant feature of the Canadian legal scene. Canadian environmental law (as compared with that of the United States) offers relatively little opportunity for litigation on substantive issues. Much environmental law everywhere is administrative law — it has less to do with what ought to be decided than with who has the authority to decide what. Until the *Charter of Rights and Freedoms* was added to the Canadian *Constitution* in 1982, Canadian constitutional jurisprudence was almost exclusively concerned with the division of powers between provincial and federal levels of government. The occasion for this jurisprudence was seldom an issue of inherent constitutional relevance, but rather litigation launched (usually by commercial interests, though sometimes by parties with civil liberties concerns) with the aim of striking down some inconvenient piece of legislation on the ground that it was enacted by the wrong level of government. As mentioned, the Rafferty Alameda and Oldman

River dam cases were largely of this character. More recently, the Supreme Court of Canada heard a case brought by the Spraytech and Chemlawn lawn care companies to quash a bylaw enacted by the town of Hudson, Quebec, banning "cosmetic" pesticide use. The Court upheld the bylaw, but despite a passing mention of the precautionary principle (see Section Three, Part C of this book) by one of the judges, the decision had next to nothing to do with the environmental merits of the bylaw. The legal issue was one of municipal administrative law: whether a municipal corporation has the jurisdiction to pass such an ordinance.

4. Finally, law can resolve social conflict in the sense of settling the dispute, or there can simply be a lack of resolution in the sense that the issue disappears legally. This may only look like a resolution, since the conflict that disappears from the legal realm will move to, or continue in, the political, social, or economic realm. Adjudication produces winners and losers; even if their case is settled in the legal sense (there are no more avenues of appeal), one or both parties may not feel satisfied with the outcome. Although the particular legal dispute is settled, the underlying conflict continues to simmer, and may either erupt in future litigation or give rise to attempts at mediation or negotiation.

While reading through the materials in this book, consider how the reliance upon a particular element or feature of the legal system — mediation or negotiated standards, for example — exemplifies one or more of these factors.

NATIONAL DIFFERENCES IN LEGAL CULTURE AND RESPONSES TO ENVIRONMENTAL CONFLICT

Legal responses to environmental conflicts can differ quite a bit even among similar societies: for example, among the advanced capitalist liberal democracies of Western Europe and North America. A "law and society" approach to environmental law must at least take account of, and ideally try to explain, such differences. Here we focus particularly on comparing Canada and the United States. Such comparison is crucial for understanding Canadian environmental law. On the one hand, the Canadian legal culture and political-institutional framework is very different from the American; on the other hand, Canadians' understandings of law and of environmental issues — which form the social context of environmental law — are largely shaped by the overshadowing American influence. The pressure to harmonize environmental law and policy between the two countries created by the Canada-U.S. and subsequent North American free trade agreements makes this topic all the more salient.

Recent comparative scholarship on Canadian and American approaches to environmental law and policy builds on a body of research and discussion from the 1980s comparing American and British approaches. Braithwaite (1987: 560) summarizes the thrust of David Vogel's influential 1986 comparison of American and British "styles of regulation" as follows:

> While American regulation is adversarial, litigious, and rule-bound, British regulation is mostly cooperative and consensual and grants great discretion to government officials. There is more conflict in American environmental regulation: the process is more open at multiple points to nonindustry interest groups, notably the environmental movement. Environmental decisions are mostly made by cross-cutting institutions of the state (the regulatory agency, Congress, the courts) that adjudicate gladiatorial battles between industry and various public interest groups. In Britain decisions are more likely to be made by a single institution of the state — the civil service — obtaining the consent of industry, and occasionally community groups, for a negotiated compromise.

The relationship between government and business is also, according to this research, more adversarial in the United States. The transparent and rule-bound structure of American regulation leads officials to adopt an inflexible "by the book" style of enforcement, which in turn confronts an "organized culture of resistance" (Bardach and Kagan, 1982). This contrasts markedly with the give-and-take relationship between British water officers and polluters described by Hawkins (1984), in which co-operation on the part of industry and "reasonableness" on the part of enforcement officials were the norm, and where the mere threat of prosecution was an infrequently invoked escalation.

What explains these differences? Vogel (1986: 240–45) sees the greater deference of British business executives to civil servants as being in part rooted in the different historical class systems of the two societies. In Britain the rising capitalist class had to accommodate itself to a state still dominated by an aristocratic upper class; the businessman aspired to be a gentleman. In the United States, capitalists formed the ruling class almost from the outset, and tended to look down on civil servants. This explanation does not, however, entirely account for the greater litigiousness of American society. Kagan (1988) emphasizes the different constitutions and institutional structures of the two countries. The United States is a country with a written constitution in which individual rights against the state are entrenched. More important, from Kagan's point of view, is the structure of the state. In the British and Canadian "Westminster" model of parliamentary government, the executive or administrative branch of the state — the ministries or departments and their agencies — answer to cabinet ministers who are members of the governing party in parliament (legislature) and who are appointed by the prime minister (premier), who is the leader of the governing party. (For more details, see the reading on the Canadian constitution in Section One, Part C.) Moreover, party discipline is maintained, so that on important matters members of the legislature must vote as directed by their party leader. This means that control over both the legislative and executive functions of government (i.e., both law making and law implementation and enforcement) are concentrated in the office of the prime minister. In the American model, by contrast, there is a separation of powers. The executive branch answers to a cabinet appointed by a separately elected president, and there is little party discipline — individual members of the legislature (Congress) decide for themselves how they will vote on the matters that come before them. Power is thus more diffuse in the American model.

How do these differences in government structure explain the different styles of environmental law? Kagan (1988) suggests the diffuse power structure in American government provides more avenues for sufficiently well organized and funded pressure groups, including environmental groups, to affect the contents of laws. It also means that those who write the laws do not control (and therefore do not entirely trust) those who implement and enforce them. This results in two distinctive features of American environmental law. First, there is a greater tendency to write specific rules, standards and procedures into legislation, rather than leaving these details to be filled in through regulations or by administrative discretion. Second, legislation may include provision for citizens to take officials to court on the grounds that they have not adequately or properly implemented the law. Inspired by the gains accomplished by the civil rights movement through litigation in the 1960s, American environmentalists since the 1970s eagerly embraced a litigious approach; this strategy achieved only modest results overall, however, as courts proved rather deferential to administrators and have also taken an increasingly restrictive line on who has legal standing to sue (Bogart, 2002: 238–41).

Canadian environmental law has more closely resembled the British "compliance" model than the American "sanctioning" approach. "The Canadian political process is less pluralist, less open, less adversarial and more informal than is the U.S. process" (VanNijnatten, 1999: 270). Canada resembles the United States, however, in being a federal state. Indeed, Canada is a more decentralized federation than is the United States; the federal level of government plays a more modest role than does its American counterpart. The implications of federalism for Canadian environmental law are discussed in the readings in Section One, Part C.

We will comment briefly on two of the main themes addressed by comparative research on Canadian and American environmental law. The first concerns what difference, if any, the different policy styles of the two countries make to substantive levels of environmental protection. The second has to do with whether, and in what respects, the two systems are converging.

Vogel thinks that the Americans might have something to learn from the British, whose less legalistic, less adversarial (and presumably less expensive) approach to regulation ended up providing similar levels of environmental protection (though he doubts that the British model could be transplanted). How does the Canadian version of the British model stack up against the American approach in terms of protecting the environment? When it comes to regulating hazards from toxic and radioactive substances, Harrison and Hoberg (1994) found that neither country has stricter controls overall; some toxics are more tightly restricted in Canada, and others in the United States (for more detail, see the editors' notes and readings in Section Three, Part C). Regarding the results of enforcement, Harrison (1995) found that a much higher proportion of American than Canadian pulp and paper mills were in compliance with water pollution regulations, suggesting that the "sanctioning" approach may more effective than a flexible "compliance" approach. Rabe's (1999) comparison of the effects of American versus Canadian federalism casts doubt on the hypothesis that a stronger federal role impedes creative policy innovation at the sub-national (provincial or state) level.

Are Canadian environmental law and policy becoming Americanized? Howlett (1994) compared rates of environmental litigation and avenues for judicial review of administrative action in the two countries and concluded that "there is no pattern of convergence in Canada-US environmental policy in terms of an increased legalization or judicialization of Canadian environmental processes or policy style". VanNijnatten (1999) discerns three periods in the recent history of American and Canadian environmental policy. During the first period, from the 1960s to the mid-1980s, American and Canadian policy-making diverged. Throughout the 1970s the United States expanded opportunities for public participation in environmental decision-making, and established a strong, relatively centralized regime of environmental law. During the second period, from the mid-1980s to the mid-1990s, a degree of convergence occurred, as Canada increased the role of the public through multistakeholder consultations, adopted American "alternative dispute resolution" methods (see Section Four of this book), and moved towards a stronger federal role through the 1988 *Canadian Environmental Protection Act* and 1992 *Canadian Environmental Assessment Act*. Perhaps the high water mark of this phase (oddly overlooked by VanNijnatten) was the 1994 enactment of the *Ontario Environmental Bill of Rights*. The late 1990s saw a renewed period of divergence. In Canada, public participation was undermined by cutbacks and privatization (see the reading by Krajnc in Section Two, Part A), moves toward voluntary initiatives (see the reading by Webb in Section Two, Part C), and an increased role of for closed-door intergovernmental (interprovincial, federal-provincial) negotiations in environmental policy-making. In the United States, meanwhile, efforts by the Republican-controlled Congress to roll back environmental laws were successfully resisted by the Clinton administration. VanNijnatten suggests that during the 1990s environmental deregulation proceeded more slowly in the United States than in Canada (though this pattern may change again under the Bush administration).

NOTE

For the first few paragraphs in this introduction, and in several other passages early on in this introductory essay, we borrow from earlier pieces of ours: "Defining Law" by Alex Wellington and Allan Greenbaum, and "Theories of Law and Society" by Allan Greenbaum and Alex Wellington. Both pieces appear in *Readings in Law and Society*, edited by Jane Banfield and Dorathy Moore, and published by Captus Press. The piece overall is a substantially revised, reworking of the introductory essay which appeared, under the same name, in the previous two volumes of Social Conflict and Environmental Law.

REFERENCES

Arthurs, Harry W. 1984. *Without the Law: Administrative Justice and Legal Pluralism in Nineteenth Century England*. Toronto: University of Toronto Press.

Aubert, Vilhelm. 1969. Law as a way of resolving conflicts: the case of a small industrialized society. In *Law in Culture and Society*, ed. Laura Nader. Chicago: Aldine.

Bardach, Eugene, and Robert A. Kagan. 1982. *Going by the Book: The Problem of Regulatory Unreasonableness*. Philadelphia: Temple University Press.

Black, Donald. 1989. *Sociological Justice*. New York: Oxford University Press.

———. 1976. *The Behavior of Law*. New York: Academic Press.

Bogart, William. 2002. *Consequences: The Impact of Law and Its Complexity*. Toronto: University of Toronto Press.

Bohannon, Paul. 1965. Differing realms of the law. *American Anthropologist* 67 (6 pt. 2): 33–42.

Braithwaite, John. 1987. "Review essay: Negotiation versus litigation: industry regulation in Great Britain and the United States." *American Bar Foundation Journal* 2–3 (Spring–Summer): 559–74.

Bryant, Bunyan (ed.). 1995. *Environmental Justice: Issues, Policies and Solutions*. Washington: Island Press .

Diamond, Stanley. 1984. "The rule of law versus the order of custom." *Social Research* 51 (Summer): 388–418.

Douglas, Mary. 1992. *Risk and Blame: Essays in Cultural Theory*. London: Routledge.

Douglas, Mary, and Aaron Wildavsky. 1982. *Risk and Culture: an Essay on the Selection of Technological and Environmental Dangers*. Berkeley, CA: University of California Press.

Dryzek, John S. 1987. *Rational Ecology: Environment and Political Ecology*. Oxford: Basil Blackwell.

Fisher, Roger, and William Ury. 1991. *Getting to Yes*, Second Edition. New York: Penguin.

Fitzgerald, Patrick, and Barry Wright. 2000. *Looking at Law: Canada's Legal System*, Fifth Edition. Toronto: Butterworth's.

Freudenburg, William R., and Robert Gramling. 1994a. *Oil in Troubled Waters: Perception, Politics, and the Battle over Offshore Oil Drilling*. Albany: State University of New York Press.

Freudenburg, William, and Robert Gramling. 1994b. "Bureaucratic slippage and failures of agency vigilance: the case of the Environmental Studies Program." *Social Problems* 41: 214–39.

Gould, K.A., A. Schnaiberg, and A. Weinberg. 1996. *Local Environmental Struggles: Citizen Activism in the Treadmill of Production*. Cambridge: Cambridge University Press.

Harrison, Katherine. 1995. "Is cooperation the answer? Canadian environmental enforcement in comparative context." *Journal of Policy Analysis and Management* 14: 221–44.

Harrison, Katherine, and George Hoberg. 1994. *Risk, Science and Politics: Regulating Toxic Substances in Canada and the US*. Montreal: McGill-Queens University Press.

Hawkins, Keith. 1984. *Environment and Enforcement: Regulation and the Social Definition of Pollution*. Oxford: Clarendon Press.

Homer-Dixon, Thomas. 1999. *Environment, Scarcity and Violence*. Princeton: Princeton University Press.

Homer-Dixon, Thomas, and Jessica Blitt (eds.), 1998. *Ecoviolence: Links Among Environment, Population and Security*. Lanham, MD: Rowman and Littlefield.

Honore, Tony. 1995. *About Law: An Introduction*. Oxford, UK: Clarendon Press.

Howlett, Michael. 1994. "The judicialization of Canadian environmental policy, 1980–1990: a test of the Canada-United States convergence thesis." *Canadian Journal of Political Science* 27: 99–125.

Kagan, Robert A. 1988. "What makes Uncle Sammy sue?" *Law and Society Review* 21: 717–39.

Kiss, Alexandre, and Dinah Shelton. 1997. *Manual of European Environmental Law*, Second Edition. Cambridge, UK: Grotius Publications/Cambridge University Press.

Lavelle, Marianne, and Marcia A. Coyle. 1993. "Unequal protection: the racial divide in environmental law." In *Toxic Struggles: The Theory and Practice of Environmental Justice*, ed. Richard Hofrichter. Philadelphia: New Society.

Murphy, Jeffrie G., and Jules L. Coleman. 1990. *Philosophy of Law: An Introduction to Jurisprudence*, Revised Edition. Boulder, CO: Westview Press.

Murphy, Raymond. 1994. *Rationality and Nature: A Sociological Inquiry into a Changing Relationship*. Boulder, CO.: Westview Press.

Nader, Laura. 1969. *Law in Culture and Society*. Chicago: Aldine.

O'Connor, J. 1998. *Natural Causes: Essays in Ecological Marxism*. New York: Guildford Press.

Rabe, Barry. 1999. "Federalism and entrepreneurship: explaining American and Canadian innovation in pollution prevention and regulatory integration." *Policy Studies Journal* 27: 307–27.

Sagoff, Mark. 1982a. "At the Shrine of Our Lady of Fatima, or, why political questions are not all economic." *Arizona Law Review* 23: 1283–98.

———. 1982b. "We have met the enemy and he is us: conflict and contradiction in environmental law." *Environmental Law* 12: 283–315.

Schmidtz, David. 2000. "Natural enemies: an anatomy of environmental conflict." *Environmental Ethics* 22: 397–408.

Schnaiberg, Allan, and Kenneth A. Gould. 1994. *Environment and Society: The Enduring Conflict.* New York: St. Martin's Press.

Shiner, Roger A. 1993. "Jurisprudence: Ideology of Analysis?" Review Essay. *Canadian Journal of Law and Society* 8, 2 (Fall/Autumn): 205–24.

Tie, Warwick. 1999. *Legal Pluralism: Toward a Multicultural Conception of Law.* Aldershot: Ashgate/Dartmouth Press.

VanNijnatten, Debra L. 1999. "Participation and environmental policy in Canada and the United States: trends over time." *Policy Studies Journal* 27: 267–87.

Vogel, David. 1986. *National Styles of Regulation: Environmental Policy in Great Britain and the United States.* Ithaca NY: Cornell University Press.

Weber, Max. 1946. "Class, status, party." In *From Max Weber*, ed. H.H. Gerth and C. Wright Mills. New York: Oxford University Press.

Wildavsky, Aaron, and Karl Dake. 1990. "Theories of risk perception: who fears what and why?" *Daedelus* 119, 4: 41–60.

One

Elements of the Legal System

Editors' Notes

Alex Wellington and Allan Greenbaum ─────────────────────────

It is most important to acknowledge right at the outset that there are many different ways of dividing up law. We use the term "elements" to signify that there are numerous discrete and identifiable components, aspects, or dimensions to any legal system; all of them will fall under the broad heading, or umbrella term, "law". Legal rules may be organized according to their source and to the kinds of cases or situations to which they apply. When organizing legal rules according to their source, it is customary to distinguish between those rules created by judges, legislatures and government officials. When organizing legal rules according to the kinds of case or situation to which they apply, it is customary to distinguish between public and private law. These conventional distinctions may not always hold up under close scrutiny; nevertheless, they provide a useful framework for our initial analysis in this book.

TYPES OF LAW

Here, we will survey the following distinctions between types of law: (i) civil law versus common law legal systems; (ii) common law versus equity; (iii) legislation versus judge-made law; (iv) federal versus provincial law; (v) substantive law and procedural law; (vi) public law versus private law and, more specifically, criminal law versus civil law; and (vii) international versus domestic/national law. All these elements are sources of law. Throughout the readings in the remainder of this book, it will often be helpful and useful, if not even necessary, to clarify which particular type of law an author is referring to at a given time and on a given point.

In these notes, we will also clarify the importance of crucial concepts and practices, such as precedent, judicial review and the rule of law.

I.   Civil Law and Common Law Systems

The terms "common law" and "civil law" have several different and distinct meanings. The context in which the term is used provides guidance on when and how a particular meaning is being relied upon. The most general characterization of these terms relates to two different systems of law, or "families of national legal systems" (Merryman, 1985: 1). The civil law system is contrasted with the common law system. A legal tradition, as John Henry Merryman explains, is a "set of deeply rooted, historically conditioned attitudes about the nature of law, about the role of law in the society and the polity, about the proper organization and operation of a legal system, and about the way law is or should be made, applied, studied, perfected and taught" (Merryman, 1985: 2).

Civil law, as a system, derives from Roman law, which was integrated and codified in the Justinian Code (*Codex Justinianeus* or *Corpus Juris Civilis*), published in A.D. 533 (the items themselves date back further, even to 450 B.C.). The civil law tradition continues today in many countries of continental Europe, as well as in some countries in South America. It is not easy to give a simple account of civil law, since it is really, as Merryman notes, a "composite of several distinct subtraditions" (Merryman, 1985: 6). The oldest, the Justinian Code, covered the law of persons, the family, inheritance, property, torts (discussed below), contracts and remedies; this material is sometimes referred to as "Roman civil law". During the nineteenth century, "the principal states of Western Europe adopted civil codes... of which the French Code Napoleon of 1804 is the archetype" (Merryman, 1985: 10). That code was in turn almost identical with the subject matter of portions of the

Justinian Code (the *Institutes*). France, Germany, Italy and Switzerland ultimately incorporated, or received the Roman civil law, into their national legal systems, although those systems are still differentiated to this day (especially the French, Germanic and Scandinavian traditions) (Kiss and Shelton, 1997). Quebec, as former colony of France, has a civil law system (one derived from the French Civil Code), while the rest of Canada inherited their legal system (i.e., common law) from Britain.

The common law tradition originated in England during the Norman Conquest, and thus began around A.D. 1066 (Merryman, 1985). "Historically, common law refers to the law common to the whole of England as distinct from customary local laws" (Fitzgerald and Wright, 2000: 22). The term "common law" is also used to distinguish the law that developed in "common law courts" from the law that emerged from the Chancery Courts, which is known as the law of equity. Equity is defined and discussed just below (in sub-section II). Canada's history as a colony of England led to the adoption and "formal reception" by Canada (except for in Quebec) of the common law of England.

II. Common Law and Equity

The common law includes rules derived from two bodies of law developed by what were originally two separate court systems in England (since combined). These two bodies of rules are, respectively, "common law" proper and "equity". The former was developed by the common law courts, and the latter was formulated and administered by the Court of Chancery. The term equity has an everyday meaning, and a specific or technical legal meaning. Equity in a general sense means justice or fairness. Specifically, it means "the discretionary power to do justice in particular cases where [the strict application of rules] would cause hardship" (*Canada Law Dictionary*). The rules of equity were developed to provide fair and sensible decisions where the application of the strict letter of the common law seemed manifestly unfair and arbitrary in the instant case. Thus, the principles of equity were intended to supplement the rules and procedures of common law. These rules subsequently came to be formalized themselves.

The *Judicature Act* of 1873 amalgamated the Common Law Courts and the Court of Chancery, and "provided for the fusion of law and equity, with the supremacy of equity in case of conflict" (*Osborn's Concise Law Dictionary*). Some rules and remedies are still referred to as "equitable doctrines" or "equitable relief". Examples of influential equitable principles include: "He who comes to equity must come with clean hands"; "He who seeks equity must do equity"; "Equity acts on the conscience"; "Equity will not suffer a wrong without a remedy"; "Equity aids the vigilant"; "Equity, like nature, does nothing in vain"; "Equitable remedies are discretionary" (*Osborn's Concise Law Dictionary*).

The first meaning of common law demarcates the legal systems of civil law countries or states from the legal systems of common law countries (former and current colonies of Britain). The second meaning of common law distinguishes it from equity. There is yet a third meaning of common law, which differentiates judge-made case law from statutory laws made by parliament or legislatures, and we now turn to that third meaning.

III. Judge-Made (Common) Law and Legislation

Within common law legal systems, common law itself can be distinguished from statute law on the basis of its source. In this sense, common law refers to judge-made law, and statute law refers to law made by the legislative branches of government. Statutes were initially "enacted to remedy defects in common law", but now it is the common law that "occupies the gaps left unaddressed by statutes" (Fitzgerald and Wright, 2000: 24). Outside of Quebec, there are some core aspects of private or civil law, such as torts, contracts and property, that remain under the governance of common law rules. However, legislation has gradually supplanted the common law in a great many areas of public and private law (contrasted and discussed below, in sub-section VI), including criminal law, commercial law, the family, the environment, and landlord-tenant law. Therefore, the most familiar source of law in the contemporary context is legislation. Below, in sub-section nine, we contrast the potential of common law with the regulatory system for environmental protection.

Precedent

Judge-made law rests upon the practice of precedent. Decided cases function as precedents for cases to be decided in the future. A case that has already been adjudicated thus furnishes an example, or sets out an authority for other cases that cover similar questions of law. Courts make concerted efforts to decide cases on the basis of the principles that have been established in previous cases. A precedent is a "rule of law" governing a particular type of case and that is referred to, and relied upon, by courts when they are dealing with similar cases (Gall, 1990: 274).

A few important terms need to be clarified: *ratio decidendi* is the "part of the case that is said to possess authority", the part of the decision that contains the "rule of law upon which the decision is founded"; *obiter dictum* is any statement of law made by a judge that is part of a case but that does not contain the particular rule of law upon which that case is decided. Then, *stare decisis* is a Latin phrase meaning "to stand by decided matters"; it is an abbreviation of *stare decisis et non quieta movere*: to stand by decisions and not to disturb settled matters (Gall, 1990: 274).

The doctrine of *stare decisis* means that the decision of a higher court acts as binding authority on a lower court within the same jurisdiction. The rulings of the Supreme Court of Canada are binding on all other courts in Canada, which includes the provincial Supreme or Superior Courts (Supreme, or Superior Court of Ontario, British Columbia, or Nova Scotia, etc.). Courts of co-ordinate jurisdiction — for example, Courts of Appeal of different provinces — are not bound to follow each other, even in applying the national constitution to a federal statute (thus, for example, the Court of Appeal for Alberta does not have to follow a decision of the Court of Appeal of New Brunswick) (Gall, 1990: 274).

The decision of a court of another jurisdiction (for instance, the Supreme Court of the United States) only acts as persuasive authority. The degree of persuasiveness depends upon various factors — the level of the court and the type of court, i.e., domestic jurisdiction (same country), common law jurisdiction, Commonwealth jurisdiction, etc. Future judges typically are bound by the *ratio decidendi* but not the *obiter dictum*; the doctrine of *stare decisis* is not applicable to obiter dictum (although it has persuasive force) (Gall, 1990: 274).

The purposes and advantages of *stare decisis* are certainty and predictability, continuity and stability, consistency and orderly development of legal rules. But there are disadvantages arising from *stare decisis*: these include rigidity and inflexibility in the law; the danger of illogical distinctions; and the vast magnitude and complexity of detail in the common law. The desirability of certainty must be balanced against the dictates of justice and fairness. The process of distinguishing provides a way for judges to avoid the binding or persuasive nature of precedent decisions. To distinguish a case, a judge can find that the precedent case has features that are absent in the instant case (the case at hand); or, alternatively, that the instant case has features absent in the precedent case: then the judge can deny the necessity of following the precedent case (Gall, 1990: 274).

Statutes and Regulations

In Canada and other liberal democracies, legislatures are assemblies of elected politicians. Legislation, as already noted, consists of statutes passed by Parliament (the federal legislature) and the provincial legislatures, which are often called legislative assemblies. The *Criminal Code* of Canada and the *Fisheries Act* are examples of federal statutes. The *Ontario Highway Traffic Act* and the *Ontario Environmental Assessment Act* are examples of provincial statutes. The *Constitution Act* is a special statute that governs the division of powers between different levels of government (and is discussed below, in sub-section four).

Some statutes, such as the *Criminal Code*, provide detailed rules that apply directly to members of the public. For example, the *Criminal Code* sets out the definition of first-degree murder. Anyone who commits an act falling under that definition is guilty of first-degree murder. Many statutes, including most of those that are important in environmental law, are not like that. The rules they include are mainly procedural, or provide for the devolving of powers to other institutions, agencies and bodies. These statutes, such as the *Pest Control Products Act*, may create government agencies (like the *Pest Management Regulatory Agency*) and stipulate the extent and nature of their powers. They may also provide for the government to pass regulations governing specific matters, such as the Pest Control Products Regulations. Statutes of this kind are called "enabling legislation", because their main function is to enable the government to do something, rather than to provide rules that directly govern the affairs of individuals and corporations.

The *Fisheries Act* is a familiar and important piece of enabling legislation that deals with the control of water pollution. Section 36(3) of the Act prohibits "the deposit of a deleterious substance of any type in water frequented by fish", but the prohibition does not apply if the pollution in question is authorized by a regulation made under Section 36(4) of the Act. This means that the specific rules that govern how much, and of what kind, of pollutants factories can emit into a lake or river are not found in the statute that was passed by Parliament. Instead, they are found in regulations issued "pursuant to" the statute. Parliament has, in effect, delegated the power to make legal rules on this particular matter to the "governor in council". Technically, the "governor in council" means the Cabinet — the Prime Minister or Premier, and the Ministers responsible for the various departments and ministries of the government. Members of Cabinet are usually members of the legislature who belong to the governing party. In reality, those dealing directly with regulations are the Minister and department staff of the relevant department or ministry. In this case, for example, staff of the Department of Fisheries and Oceans and/or the Department of the Environment normally oversee the regulations pertaining to water pollution. In other cases, legislation delegates rule-making power directly to agencies, such as the Environmental Assessment Board or the Canadian Radio-television and Telecommunications Commission (CRTC).

Practically speaking, regulations are legal rules created by unelected government officials, acting in accordance with legislation that empowers them to make such rules. The scope of the rule-making power of officials is confined by the terms of the enabling legislation. Nevertheless, the vast bulk of the legal rules governing every aspect of life — for example, the speed limit on your street, how much of air pollution-causing substances your car can emit, or how much Canadian content broadcasters must play — are created in this way.

The three sources of legal rules that are most prominent today — statutes, regulations and case law — correspond to the three main "branches" of government — the legislature, the executive (government officials), and the judiciary. Democratic countries distribute power to separate and independent institutions, and thereby effect a system of "checks and balances". The legislature has the power of making, altering and repealing the laws. The executive has the power of governing, administering and enforcing the laws. Then the judiciary has the power of adjudicating on disputes according to law, including adjudicating disputes about the exercise of executive and legislative powers. (Fitzgerald and Wright, 2000: 38) Moreover, the courts rule on, or pronounce upon, the proper division of powers between different levels of government.

IV. Federal and Provincial Law and the Constitution

There is a further factor that complicates law making in Canada, and that did not apply in Britain, a unitary state. Canada is a federal state, which means there is a division of powers between the federal and provincial governments. The United States and Australia are also federal states. Canadian jurisdictions became increasingly self-governing after the *Colonial Laws Validity Act* of 1865, and then especially so after the passing of the *British North America Act* in 1867. The *British North America Act* (now the *Constitution Act*) "established the Confederation, set up the institutions of federation and distributed legislative powers between the new Dominion government in Ottawa and the provinces" (Fitzgerald and Wright, 2000: 42). Section 91 and Section 92 of the *Constitution Act 1867* divvy up powers between the two levels of government, so that neither level can "encroach, or trench, as lawyers put it, on the law-making authority of the other" (Fitzgerald and Wright, 2000: 45). It is the role of the courts, through the exercise of judicial review, to ensure that laws are *intra vires* (within the powers), inside the valid jurisdiction of that level of government, and to determine whether and when a government is trying to act *ultra vires* (beyond the powers).

In 1982, the Canadian constitution was "patriated", when Britain passed the *Canada Act* (proclaimed by the Queen in Ottawa on April 17, 1982). This package included: "provisions that gave Canada full power to amend its constitution without reference to the British Parliament, and provided for constitutional entrenchment" of the *Charter of Rights and Freedoms* (Fitzgerald and Wright, 2000: 44). Thus, the new constitution contained a "formula setting out procedures for the future amendments" of the Constitution, attempted unsuccessfully in the Meech Lake and Charlottetown Accords (Fitzgerald and Wright, 2000: 44). The *Charter* was a more encompassing and constitutionally entrenched form of a Bill of Rights. Previously, Canada had inherited the Canadian *Bill of Rights* from England. Judges are now empowered to review a piece of legislation or government policy to ensure that it conforms to the *Charter*, and to either send it back for rewriting or to declare it invalid if it does not. The *Charter* has, it is said, "opened up the means for citizens to challenge the state"; it has also "extended the role of the courts in protecting individual rights and enhanced their role in Canadian public policy" (Fitzgerald and Wright, 2000: 47). That more extensive and expansive role has been the subject of considerable controversy (Mandel, 2002).

To summarize, in Canada there are the following checks on parliamentary supremacy: (1) the division of powers between the federal and provincial governments; (2) the need to follow a constitutional amending formula; (3) laws are subject to the *Charter*, and thus subject to judicial review to ensure conformity with the Charter (Fitzgerald and Wright, 2000: 41). The rule of law is ensured by the interaction and interpenetration of parliamentary supremacy and an independent judiciary, and by the presence of responsible government.

The Supreme Court

In 1875, the Supreme Court of Canada was established as "an appeal court of civil and criminal jurisdiction for the entire country. Until then appeals proceeded directly from provincial appeal courts to the Judicial Committee of the Privy Council in England" (Fitzgerald and Wright, 2000: 101). Nevertheless, the Privy Council continued to be the final court of appeal for some time. The Supreme Court became the final court of appeal in 1933 for criminal cases, and in 1949 for all other cases. The Supreme Court has discretion over whether to grant appellants leave to appeal, and may thus choose only the cases that involve matters of public importance (Fitzgerald and Wright, 2000: 101). The Supreme Court also hears reference cases directly; typically, these cases are constitutional ones, which concern the division of powers and authority between the federal and provincial governments.

V. Substantive Law and Procedural Law

This is an important distinction for practising lawyers, and for those who wish to avail themselves of legal tools and undertake legal actions. As Fitzgerald and Wright clarify, "substantive law tells us what our rights and duties are, while procedural law tells us how to enforce them" (Fitzgerald and Wright, 2000: 53). Criminal law sets out what offences exist, and criminal procedure then regulates the enforcement of that law, including the prosecution, trial and ultimate punishment (of the guilty) of those who commit (or are charged with) the offences. Civil procedure, on the other hand, regulates the methods of bringing a lawsuit, making claims, and enforcing legal rights, under the headings of civil law, which are elaborated upon in the next sub-section (six). The law of evidence, although related to the law of procedure, could yet be designated as a category of its own. Evidence law "consists of rules concerning witnesses, evidence and its admissibility, and burden of proof" (Fitzgerald and Wright, 2000: 88). As such, it "regulates the admission and weighing of the factual details of a case", and "helps to determine how a court will handle a dispute" (Fitzgerald and Wright, 2000: 88). For our purposes here, it is not necessary to delve into the intricacies and niceties of either civil or criminal procedure. We will return briefly to the topic of evidence in the editors' notes on "Science and the Law", Section Three, Part B of this volume.

VI. Public and Private Law

Fitzgerald and Wright provide the following definition of public law: "Public law, as its name suggests, regulates the institutions of the state, their relations with one another and their relations with the citizen" (Fitzgerald and Wright, 2000: 55). Public law, then, includes constitutional and administrative law, as well as criminal law. Constitutional law, as detailed above (in sub-section IV), "sets out the principles upon which society rests" and "lays down how the power of the state is divided" up between levels of government, officials, judges and others (Honore, 1995: 7). Administrative law "deals with the relations between officials and citizens", and sets out "the ways in which people can object to official decisions" (Honore, 1995: 7). In the case of criminal law, the "state prohibits activity in the public interest and deploys public institutions [and officials] to enforce the law and punish offenders" (Fitzgerald and Wright, 2000: 55). The state treats criminal "offences as its own concern even when the victims are individuals" (Honore, 1995: 7).

Private or civil law is said to be primarily concerned with the rights and duties of individuals towards one another, with relations between individuals, and with the "organized interests that serve private purposes" (Fitzgerald and Wright, 2000: 55). Examples include the duty to carry out a contract, or the duty to avoid injuring another person by your negligence (Honore, 1995: 7). The main headings of private law include torts, contract, property, the family, the environment, and labour law. The state, in the case of private law, "leaves it to the individual whose rights have been infringed to take action" (Honore, 1995: 8). The distinction — between public and private law — is often said to be quite arbitrary, since the activities covered by criminal law decisively affect the interests of individuals (i.e., the victims), and yet the activities of corporations (organizations serving private purposes) affect collective economic life, and impact upon the public good considerably (Fitzgerald and Wright, 2000: 55). Nevertheless, the division between private and public law has continued to have purchase in scholarly treatments and discussions. As mentioned above, private law includes many areas of law in which common law (i.e., judge-made law) continues to have contemporary influence and significance.

There is thus yet another meaning of civil law, as distinct from the meaning discussed above (in sub-section one). Earlier, civil law was contrasted with the common law as a type of legal system. We have just distinguished "private" or civil law from "public" law. We will now focus more specifically on the differences between civil law and criminal law.

Civil and Criminal Law

Civil law includes (but is not restricted to) laws having to do with relations between private citizens. Criminal law, instead, has to do with "public wrongs": that is, acts prejudicial to the community or disruptive of the "King's peace". Criminal law is often said to be based on fundamental values, and thus crimes are breaches of those norms. Criminal law in Canada is federal; it is based on the *Criminal Code of Canada*. Civil law is instead predominantly under the purview of the provinces. One crucial way in which these two types of law — civil and criminal — differ is that they each involve a different kind of procedure: civil procedure and criminal procedure, respectively. The other differences are set out just below.

The differences between civil and criminal law are outlined by Fitzgerald and Wright as follows: (1) criminal cases are ones in which the Crown (on behalf of the Queen, or *Regina*, in Canada) pursues an action (a prosecution) against the accused (thus criminal cases are titled, "*R.* versus the *accused*"); (2) criminal law begins with a summons or arrest; (3) criminal law involves the use of preliminary hearings; (4) the burden of proof in criminal cases is on the Crown, who must prove the guilt of the accused *beyond a reasonable doubt* (thus, the accused gets the benefit of the "presumption of innocence"); (5) finding of guilt is followed by punishment. With civil law, instead, the (1) proceedings take place between a plaintiff (who initiates legal action) and the defendant (who defends against that action); (2) cases begin with a statement of claim and continue with (3) written pleadings; (4) the plaintiff bears the burden of proof, and must show, on a *balance of probabilities* (just over 50% certainty, or persuasively probable) that the defendant should be found liable; and then (5) a finding of liability is followed by a remedy, usually (but not always) compensation for loss or harm (Fitzgerald and Wright, 2000: 77).

VII. National and International Law

National law (Canadian law, for instance) also needs to be distinguished from international law. International law, as Tony Honore explains, is "an extra system on top of the state systems" of law; it is "about the relations between independent states" (Honore, 1995: 3). Each state — being "a political unit with a territory" that is treated as independent by the international community — has its own system of law; international law aspires to govern relations between states (Honore, 1995: 2). International law is comprised of rules and general principles of general application — often instantiated in treaties — that deal with the conduct of nations and of international organizations (*Black's Law Dictionary*).

Environmental problems are increasingly understood to be global problems, requiring (at least in part) some global solutions. This has led to an increasing reliance upon "concerted action among nations to halt degradation" (Bogart, 2002: 242). Examples of the kinds of environmental matters that are covered by multilateral, international agreements, declarations, and treaties include the following: hazardous wastes and their disposal, nuclear risks, international watercourses, the marine environment and conservation of marine living resources. There are conventions that address liability for environmental damage, and ones that codify international environmental law (such as the convention on environmental impact assessment in a transboundary context) (Birnie and Boyle, 1995). As Jamie Benidickson (1997: 49) notes, "The United Nations Conference on the Human Environment (Stockholm, 1972), the report of the WCED [The World Commission on Environment and Development], Our Common Future (1987), and the UN Conference on Environment and Development at Rio de Janeiro (1992) have been landmarks in the development of principles of international environmental law".

Benidickson (1997: 50) describes the workings of international law in relation to Canadian environmental law as follows: "The process for incorporating international law into Canada's domestic legal regime varies as between customary and treaty law; the former is presumed to apply automatically in the absence of conflict with statute or judicial precedent, while treaty obligations are implemented only by means of legislative enactment". The responsibility for implementation of treaty obligations is divided between the federal and provincial governments, "depending on the subject matter in question" (ibid.).

International trade agreements such as those under the auspices of the World Trade Organization and the *General Agreement on Tariffs and Trade* (GATT) — all have important implications for domestic environmental protection, and are the source of continuing controversy to this day. There are critics of such trade arrangements who worry that they will "require the dilution of national standards", because those will be deemed impediments to the "free flow of goods" (Bogart, 2002: 242). The threat of "unfair trade practices", along with the demands for harmonization, have caused many environmentalists to worry that levels of environmental protection will be weakened in the wake of expansive trade negotiations and agreements. Shrybman (1990) and Henderson (1993) articulate the argument that harmonizing standards on a global basis could serve to undermine national efforts to establish effective and comprehensive environmental protection measures. They contend that international harmonization is associated with a loss of national control in setting regionally and nationally appropriate environmental standards. The underlying concern is that the framework of trade negotiations does not place environmental protection on a "sound legal footing" by recognizing it as an objective or goal on par with trade liberalization (Henderson, 1993). Shrybman and Henderson's pieces focused on the Canada-United States Trade Agreement (CUSTA), formerly known as the Free Trade Agreement (FTA), but their points apply to subsequent trade agreements as well. Critics of trade agreements are also troubled by what they view as insufficient efforts made by governments to facilitate public participation in the negotiation, implementation and interpretation of trade agreements. The topic of citizen participation is addressed in the editors' notes and readings for Section Four, Part A.

Particular episodes have exacerbated the fears of environmentalists. For instance, the overseers of the *General Agreement on Tariffs and Trade* "nullified US trade restrictions on tuna caught in a manner that also ensnared a substantial number of dolphins" in 1991 (Bogart, 2002: 246). The United States had wanted to exert its regulatory power over products produced elsewhere in the pursuit of conservation of marine mammals, but the GATT decision limited the power to do so. More recently, the World Trade Organization "judged that the USA was wrong in prohibiting shrimp imports from countries that fail to protect sea turtles from entrapment in the trawls of shrimping boats" (Bogart, 2002: 246).

On the other side are those who insist that "efforts to increase international trade are not inevitably a limit on the effectiveness of domestic law" (Bogart, 2002: 246). Furthermore, some defenders of trade agreements argue that they could ultimately buttress, or shore up, regulatory standards (ibid.: 243). Some free trade advocates and promoters do attack certain environmental regulations as "disguised trade barriers", but others point to a convergence of the goals of environmental protection and free trade. David Vogel (1995), for instance, emphasizes the parallel development of enhanced environmental and consumer regulatory requirements along with global and regional economic integration, and contends that trade liberalization can reinforce environmental protection regulation. The connection will hold, however, only under certain conditions; for instance, "when wealthy nations... stipulate more onerous standards, their trading partners are, generally forced to comply with them so as to retain their export markets" (Bogart, 2002: 242). Critics of Vogel's argument think it will not hold when one looks at the situation of less-developed countries (ibid.: 245).

Steven Globerman (1992) also argued that international trade liberalization could lead to improvement in environmental amenities rather than further deterioration. (The notion of "amenities" is subject to debate, however.) In addition, he relies upon social science research to examine two types of claimed connections between trade liberalization and environmental protection: industry relocation due to environmental protection measures and the harmonization of standards. He presents evidence that geographic and regional differences in environmental standards have a relatively small impact on the location decisions of firms (Globerman, 1992). He disputes the claim, then, that trade liberalization will create "pollution havens" — areas with lower environmental standards that will attract business away from areas with higher standards. Globerman concedes, however, that there is less direct empirical evidence available regarding the potential for environmental standards or their enforcement to be relaxed as a result of harmonization.

VIII. First Nations Peoples and the Law

It is important to emphasize that prior to colonization, the original inhabitants — the First Nations (the Indigenous, Aboriginal peoples) of North America — had well developed societies and their own systems of governance. However, the "British North American colonies resisted recognition of aboriginal rights", and the current constitutional status of the First Nations is extremely complex (Fitzgerald and Wright, 2000: 19). Provincial governments have jurisdiction over natural resources, but only the federal government has jurisdiction over native people. First Nations peoples, and their political organizations, are increasingly asserting their own inherent sovereignty against both levels of government. They argue that their rights to use and control their ancestral lands and resources are not subject to infringement or restriction by either level of government. The courts have become involved, in numerous cases dealing with the difficulties of interpreting centuries-old treaties in the current context and in light of the *Charter*.

There is a troubled historical legacy that has resulted in mistrust and a sense of betrayal on the behalf of Native people, and tensions with the larger, non-native society. As Patrick Fitzgerald and Barry Wright point out: "With Confederation and the creation of the Dominion of Canada in 1867, the federal government took on the Crown's responsibilities for native affairs and treaty obligations. Native people were registered under the *Indian Act* and regulated by paternalistic administrative measures of segregation and assimilation. Ottawa, and indeed most people of European background at the time, saw these measures as civilizing. Native people experienced them as devastating and destructive to their culture. They were regulated by a huge array of incomprehensible foreign rules that they had little or no hand in shaping. The courts continued to neglect treaty obligations until relatively recently" (Fitzgerald and Wright, 2000: 19). The Constitution was, in effect, largely silent on native rights until the passing of the *Charter* (in 1982), which contains several sections addressing the topic, expressly and explicitly. As Fitzgerald and Wright go on to say, before native contributions can be incorporated into Canadian law more formally, "our courts and legislatures must take formal steps to redress wrongs, settle land claims, and empower native communities" (ibid.: 20).

There have been some high profile court cases over the past few decades, ones in which the assertion of Aboriginal rights in relation to natural resources has conflicted with provincial jurisdiction. Examples include the case of the Cree and the James Bay Hydro-electric development in northern Quebec; mining exploration near Baker Lake in the Northwest Territories; logging on Meares Island in British Columbia; and disputes over oil and gas exploration near Lubicon Lake in Alberta (O'Reilly, 1988). In those cases, Native groups went to court to block resource developments that they claimed infringed their Aboriginal rights. The groups sought temporary court orders (called "interlocutory injunctions") to stop the development pending the ultimate outcomes of the court cases (which can take many years to work their way through the courts). An injunction prevents the continuation of an activity by the defendant that is claimed to infringe the rights of the plaintiff. The injunction requires that the activity cease until the legal issues concerning the claimed infringement of rights have been determined/resolved. A legal issue in deciding whether to grant such an injunction has to do with whether the feared/alleged infringement of rights would result in irreparable harm, such that it could not be sufficiently compensated for by money.

The Native groups argued that the developments in question threatened Native culture and "way of life", in ways that cash compensation could not properly repair or remedy. They insisted that an injunction was thus necessary. Some judges found in favour of the Natives, and did award temporary injunctions; others, however, found against the First Nations. Certain judges tended to doubt the existence of a distinct and intact Native culture that would be worth saving, and thought that the interests of Natives would best be served instead by assimilation into the dominant culture. Such ethnocentric decisions exemplify the problem of judicial bias that many commentators have lamented (O'Reilly, 1988).

One type of conflict arises from the impact of resource development by the non-Native society upon Native communities. Another type of conflict arises from Native resource extraction activities. First Nations people, in exercising their rights to harvest fish and wild-life, may come into conflict with other non-Native resource users and with resource management officials (Driben, 1987/1988; Wagner, 1991). In recent years, there have been ongoing disputes over the lobster fishery in Burnt Church, New Brunswick, and fishing around Cape Crocker, Ontario, and in various parts of British Columbia.

One very important legal case was that of Sparrow, a British Columbia Native person charged under the *Fisheries Act* with using an illegal net to fish. The Supreme Court of Canada passed judgement in the *Sparrow* case in 1990. Sparrow successfully argued that in exercising his Aboriginal right to fish he was not subject to governmental regulations (Usher, 1991). Since then, the Supreme Court has had to grapple with these issues again in the *Marshall* case. Marshall is a member of the Mi'kmaq First Nation, and he asserted Aboriginal rights to fish, hunt and trade into perpetuity, on the basis of a treaty, regardless of conservation regulations. The Supreme Court found in favour of Marshall, and then subsequently issued a "clarification" ruling, which attempted to reassert the right of governments to exercise control over natural resources for conservation purposes.

IX. Environmental Protection and the Law

Common Law/Private Law

Private lawsuits based on common law rules are still sometimes brought against polluters. The category of private law that is most relevant to environmental cases is that of torts. Many of the tort actions that have been used against polluters, such as private nuisance, trespass, and riparian rights, exist to protect rights in private property. The ownership of land is said to consist of a "bundle of rights". These rights are called "incidents of ownership". Landowners have the right to use and enjoy land without undue interference, and to have the quality and quantity of water flowing in streams across their land unimpaired by the actions of upstream users. The latter rights pertain to the cause of action labelled riparian rights, whereas the former relates to private nuisance. Landowners will have a potential "cause of action", and thus may sue, if their rights in land are affected by pollution or other kinds of environmental impairment.

Since these common law actions tend to protect rights in property, their effectiveness in combating many forms of pollution is very limited. However, because the common law has traditionally given the protection of property rights paramount importance, the remedies provided can, in specific instances, be very powerful. This has been particularly evident in Canada, where the courts have been reluctant to weaken the property rights of pollution victims for the sake of encouraging industrial activity (or at least, more reluctant to do so than the courts in the United States or Britain).

Despite the dim view taken of pollution by many common law judges, these common law actions have seldom had a significant impact on the overall quality of the environment. There are several reasons that have been put forth as explanation for this result. First, private litigation is expensive. Lawyers, expert witnesses and court costs must be paid. Those who are socio-economically disadvantaged tend to live in areas where rental and housing costs are cheaper, which are also areas most affected by pollution. The poor, however, are not typically in a position to make use of common law rights against pollution, even if they do own property. Furthermore, if a lawsuit is unsuccessful — the plaintiff is unable to persuade the court to find the defendant liable — the litigant may actually be required to pay some of the other side's costs. In the famous *Palmer* v. *NSFI* case (excerpted in this volume), those costs were substantial.

In tort cases, the litigant must find the wrongdoer; try to prove the case against the wrongdoer; and induce the wrongdoer to pay, if successful or, potentially, pay the wrongdoer's costs, if not. Litigation is thus extremely costly, stressful, and uncertain; some have even called it a "forensic lottery" (Fitzgerald and Wright, 2000: 66). Few people victimized by pollution will be willing to sue unless the degree of harm inflicted by the pollution is substantial enough to justify the risk and expense.

There is a second reason why the common law is not very effective in dealing with pollution. Pollution often involves conflict between concentrated and diffuse interests. Although a polluter may do a great deal of damage to property interests protected (in principle) by the common law, that damage may be diffused among a large number of victims. If so, then none of these victims may be, individually, so seriously affected as to make a lawsuit worthwhile. The third reason for the inefficacy of common law reflects the opposite situation, or circumstances. Sometimes the harms done by pollution are sufficiently concentrated and of such a kind that they would be readily recognized by common law, and thus a lawsuit seems appealing. However, the sources of that pollution may be diffuse. Tort law requires that a plaintiff prove that this particular defendant is responsible for precisely this harm. If there are several sources of pollution simultaneously affecting the property of the plaintiffs, it may, for obvious reasons, be impossible to isolate the damage done by each. In such a situation, the plaintiff's case will not be successful.

Finally, even if the plaintiff succeeds and obtains a court injunction forbidding the pollution, the economic consequences of the injunction may be deemed politically unacceptable to the legislature, and the injunction could be dissolved by statute. This has happened in several important Canadian cases, and the legislative over-ride may be seen as a consequence of the common law courts taking a strict view of the plaintiff's rights, and not taking into account the economic value of the defendant's activities. The legislatures are prone to take into consideration those economic concerns.

In their review of the literature (mainly United States), Dewees, Duff and Trebilcock (1996) evaluated the impact of environmental regulation and assessed the general efficacy of tort law. Tort law was assessed in terms of its ability to realize the three goals most commonly ascribed to it: deterrence, compensation and corrective justice (restoration of the victims to a pre-injury state by the morally culpable wrongdoers) (Bogart, 2002: 232). The findings for each of these goals are outlined just below. Dewees et al. examined cases involving "injuries to persons, and to property caused by the discharge of air and water pollution from fixed or mobile sources such as factory smoke stacks, sewers, and automobiles and by the discharge and disposal of solid and liquid wastes" (ibid.: 233). Their conclusions have been summarized by W.A. Bogart as follows (2002: 233): "Tort litigation has contributed only modestly to environmental protection, primarily in problems of soil contamination and severe local water pollution by isolated sources. Its limitations are inherent in the lack of clarity as to the source of many pollutants and the uncertainty of science regarding their effects".

Tort law is said to perform "poorly as a means of compensating victims of environmental harms" (Bogart, 2002: 235). Many individuals experience an increased risk, albeit often quite marginal, for certain diseases or conditions, as a result of exposure to a variety of environmental harms. Some of those people may go on to develop diseases as a result of that exposure, but few recover compensation (ibid.: 235). The few that do succeed in litigation will usually not "recover the full amount of their losses" (ibid.: 235). The great difficulty, in such cases, is establishing causation: "most victims cannot be distinguished from those of non-environmentally caused diseases or conditions" (ibid.: 235). As noted above, pollution damage can come from many sources, and it is exceptionally difficult to establish the source of any particular harm, and thus to present the required proof of cause-and-effect relationships (ibid.: 235). If only a small fraction of victims who suffer harm get compensated (even if only partially), then there is not the prospect of achieving corrective justice. Regulatory measures, it should be recognized, may also be somewhat ineffective with regard to compensation and corrective justice.

As for deterrence, tort law was effective only in certain kinds of situations, namely those in which "a large amount of pollution is discharged from an isolated source, resulting in harm in a substantial amount to individuals or their property" (Bogart, 2002: 233). It is surmised that lawsuits that involve contaminated land or water, specifically, are easier to win "because the costs of cleanup form a benchmark for measuring damages" (ibid.: 234). In some such cases, common law liability has been found. Empirical data has shown, by contrast, that overall decreases in pollution have been brought about by "government regulation at the local, state and federal levels"; these "reductions would not have occurred in the absence of regulation" (ibid.: 234). Traditional air emissions, for instance, have declined significantly in the United States since 1970, even while population has increased, and coal use has increased as well. Improvements in water quality have been more modest, but still recognizable.

Thus, although regulatory intervention itself has flaws, it was nevertheless determined to be "the better instrument for deterring pollution" in cases of factual uncertainty (Bogart, 2002: 233). The regulatory system, moreover, rather than the adjudicatory context, was thought to provide a preferable forum for debating evidence regarding the effects of pollutants. This topic — i.e., the comparison between adjudication and regulation for dealing with factual uncertainty — will be a focus of the editors' notes for Section Three, Part B ("Science and the Law"). Further discussion of the social and political context of regulation can be found in the editors' notes and readings for Section Two, "The Regulatory System".

Statute Law/Public Law

The impact and influence of enabling legislation and regulation over environmental matters is the subject matter of the next section of this book (Section Two). Here, we will just cover a point of clarification, concerning the difference between regulatory penalties, quasi-crimes and criminal prohibitions. Crimes, such as those set out in the *Criminal Code*, are considered to be the most serious legal infractions. They not only tend to carry the most severe maximum sentences, but they are also generally considered to carry a significant moral stigma. Regulatory offences (such as speeding) tend to involve less serious penalties and little, if any, moral stigma. Most pollution control laws in Canada create penalties that fall into the category of quasi-criminal. Examples include the *Fisheries Act* and the *Canadian Environmental Protection Act*.

In the case of true criminal liability, it is necessary that the accused be shown to have had both *mens rea* ("guilty mind") and *actus reus* ("guilty act"). If both are present, than the accused can be found guilty, unless there are exemptions or excuses that apply. Exemptions "take a defendant outside the ordinary operation of the criminal law": for instance, in cases of infancy or insanity (Fitzgerald and Wright, 2000: 59). Excuses "serve to negate culpability for a wrongful act"; they include duress, necessity and mistake of fact (Fitzgerald and Wright, 2000: 59). Outside of the *Criminal Code*, it is rare to find offences that require true criminal liability.

It may be helpful to think of a continuum with "true crimes" at one end, and administrative penalties at the other end. The fuzzy middle would be taken up by quasi-crimes, including strict and absolute liability offences. To begin with the simpler category, administrative penalties are doled out by administrative agencies or tribunals for breaches or infractions of a regulation. The agency or tribunal does not have to prosecute the violator (i.e., take the violator to court), but can simply impose the penalty. The agency or tribunal can make use of relatively informal procedures, and employ a civil standard of proof (see above, sub-section six). Administrative penalties are usually fines. An example of an administrative penalty is the penalty for late filing of an income tax return. Tax evasion is, instead, a criminal offence.

Quasi-crimes are a step up from administrative infractions that garner penalties, but they are not "true crimes". Quasi-crimes do require that an offender be convicted in a court of law, and resemble crimes in the standard of proof demanded. Thus, the formal and cumbersome criminal procedure must be followed in these cases. There are two distinct kinds of quasi-crimes, ones that rest upon absolute liability, and those that relate to strict liability. Absolute liability offences accord liability regardless of intention. The prosecution need only prove the *actus reus* of the offence, and conviction will follow automatically. Strict liability adds another element, the defence of due diligence. As with absolute liability, strict liability is also liability without intention; but after the *actus reus* has been established by the prosecution (beyond a reasonable doubt), the accused has the option of invoking a due diligence defence. That defence requires showing that the defendant took reasonable precautions to avoid the offence. The defence is established on a balance of probabilities (the civil standard of proof). It has been noted that courts "generally require strong evidence of a legislative intent to statutorily create strict liability offences" (*Canadian Law Dictionary*).

The readings included in this book may at times use the same terminology differently. An example is the use of the term "crime". In the reading excerpted (here, in Section One) from the Report of the Law Reform Commission, "Crimes Against the Environment", the Commission is referring to "true crimes", excluding quasi-criminal regulatory offences, when they discuss the possibility of including environmental offences in the *Criminal Code*. Yet, in the reading by Brown and Rankin (Section Two, "The Regulatory System"), which contrasts administrative and criminal sanctions, they are including quasi-criminal regulatory offences in the category of crimes.

The Law Reform Commission argue that some environmental transgressions are so serious and deserving of moral stigma — as violations of the fundamental values of society — that they ought to be included in the *Criminal Code*. Certain forms of pollution constitute a serious threat to human health and life, and infringe the fundamental value of the right to a healthy environment. Brown and Rankin take the opposite tack; they argue instead for greater use of administrative penalties in environmental law, ones that offer more flexibility. Some might say that the quasi-crime approach combines the worst aspects of both ends of the spectrum — or perhaps lacks the best of both — because it lacks both the gravity of true crimes and the flexible efficiency of administrative penalties.

The Readings

Victor MacKinnon provides a brief historical survey of the sources of law, which is supplemented by this editors' note. The common law is covered in the first portion of the section. William Charles and David VanderZwaag canvas the main kinds of legal cause of action available through the common law, in the two excerpts provided here. The two excerpts by Elizabeth Swanson and Elaine Hughes look at the topics of standard of care and remedies. The readings by Melody Hessing and Michael Howlett, and Kathryn Harrison both survey the constitutional framework in Canada, and discuss the social and political context of federal-provincial relations. Then, Kernaghan Webb surveys the regulatory system, and standard-setting, situating them in relation to other aspects of the Canadian legal system. The Law Reform Commission piece is summarized just above, and is followed by Melody Hessing and Michael Howlett's piece on international law.

REFERENCES

Benidickson, Jamie. 1997. *Environmental Law*. Concord, ON: Irwin Law.

Birnie, Patricia W., and Alan Boyle. 1995. *Basic Documents on International Law and the Environment*. Oxford, UK: Clarendon Press.

Bogart, W.A. 2002. *Consequences: The Impact of Law and Its Complexity*. Toronto: University of Toronto Press.

Dewees, D., A. Duff, and M. Trebilcock. 1996. *Exploring the Domain of Accident Law: Taking the Facts Seriously*. New York: Oxford University Press.

Driben, Paul. 1988. "Fishing in Uncharted Waters." *Alternatives* 15, 1 (December 1987/January 1988): 19–26.

Fitzgerald, Patrick, and Barry Wright. 2000. *Looking At Law: Canada's Legal System*, Fifth Edition. Toronto: Butterworths.

Gall, Gerald. 1990. *The Canadian Legal System*, Third Edition. Toronto: Carswell.

Globerman, Steven. 1992. "Trade Liberalization and the Environment." In *Assessing NAFTA: A Trinational Analysis*, ed. S. Globerman and Michael Walker. Vancouver, BC: The Fraser Institute.

Henderson, Laurie A. 1993. "Forging A Link: Two Approaches to Integrating Trade and Environment." *Alternatives* 20, 1 (November/December).

Honore, Tony. 1995. *About Law: An Introduction*. New York: Oxford University Press.

Kiss, Alexandre and Dinah Shelton. 1997. *Manual of European Environmental Law*, Second Edition. Cambridge, UK: Grotius Publications/Cambridge University Press.

Mandel, Michael. 2002. *The Canadian Charter of Rights and the Legalization of Politics in Canada*. Toronto: Wall and Thompson, 2002.

Merryman, John Henry. 1985. *The Civil Law Tradition: An Introduction to the Legal Systems of Western Europe and Latin America*, Second Edition. Stanford, CA: Stanford University Press.

O'Reilly, James. 1988. "The Courts and Community Values: Litigation Involving Native Peoples and Resource Development." *Alternatives* 15, 2 (April/May): 40–47.

Shrybman, Steven. 1990. "International Trade and the Environment: An Environmental Assessment of Present GATT Negotiations." *Alternatives*, 17, 2 (July/August): 20–28.

Usher, Peter J. 1991. "Some Implications of the *Sparrow* Judgement for Resource Conservation and Management." *Alternatives*, 18, 2: 20–21.

Vogel, David. 1995. *Trading Up: Consumer and Environmental Regulation in a Global Economy*. Cambridge, MA: Harvard University Press.

Wagner, Murray W. 1991. "Footsteps Along the Road: Indian Land Claims and Access To Natural Resources." *Alternatives*, 18, 2: 22–27.

Yogis, John. *Canadian Law Dictionary*, Third Edition. New York: Barron's Educational Series, Inc.

PART A
Concepts and Terms

(a) The Canadian Legal System: Theories and principles[†]

Victor S. MacKinnon ───────────────────────────────

Systems of Law

There are three principal systems of law which survive today: Islamic Law; Roman Law; and Anglo-American Common Law. (Although the Soviet Union and China contain a large proportion of the world's population, their legal systems are not sufficiently distinctive in substance or in procedural rules as to constitute completely separate "systems." Their main differentiation is as regards their being so completely within the continuous control of one particular political party.)

The common law originated in England, principally during the reign of Henry II (1154–1189). In earlier medieval England, law was localised, and tended to follow the old political boundaries such as those of the formerly separate Anglo-Saxon kingdoms such as Wessex and Mercia. The most durable result of Henry's reign was that the whole of English law was centralised and unified by the institution of a permanent court of professional judges. This sat mainly at Westminster but there were also itinerant judges who systematically visited the various counties of England and who eventually replaced the local courts presided over by the local nobility. The law thus became "common" in the sense of its being uniform. Even before the end of the twelfth century the judicial rolls contain many accounts of law-suits about very small pieces of land between persons of lowly rank. In the seventeenth-century struggles between King and Parliament the common law finally emerged as the bastion of defence against the arbitrary exercise of executive power by the Crown.

British settlers who colonised various areas around the world including those territories which eventually became Canada and the United States of America, took with them English common law. This became the foundation of the legal system in those colonies, almost all of which are now sovereign independent members of the international family of nations. The development of this system of law which has occurred outside England itself, particularly in the United States, is such as to justify adoption of the name "Anglo-American common law" to refer to it.

Sources of Law

At the earliest stages of social life, "justice" means not much more than a system of order imposed by someone with the authority to do so. In such a context "authority" can broadly be equated with "power." It is not until later in societal development that we take practical

---

† From *Public Administration: Canadian Materials*, 2d ed., ed. R. Hoffman, V. MacKinnon, J. Nicholson and J. Simeon (Toronto: Captus Press, 1993), pp. 168–77. Reproduced by permission of the author.

account of conflicts between positive law and justice, arising mainly out of abuses of authority. This problem of the relation between positive law and justice is of major, perhaps supreme importance, but this is not the place to discuss it. We are concerned here only with positive law, the law as we find it.

Accordingly we may confine ourselves to a consideration of law in its earliest forms as being based on custom, on usages and practices, on traditions. In various parts of the world, as for example on the African continent, we still find substantial portions of the legal system comprised of "customary law." Knowledge of the customs of the societal group is usually entrusted to some well-respected members of it, for example the tribal elders. This knowledge also usually entitles these elders to resolve disputes which may arise among other members of the tribal unit. Knowledge of the customs i.e., the "laws" is usually handed down from father to son, orally, and the resolution of a major dispute is, like the law itself, stored in memory, not written down.

The establishment of permanent courts, such as the common law courts of twelfth-century England referred to above, can be viewed as a formal institutionalization of the dispute-resolution process. The *source* of the law remains custom, usages, practices. The more these customs and usages, and the solutions to disputes about them, are recorded in writing however, the more these records become the source of the law, rather than the actual customs themselves. When this happens, we say that what started off as a custom or usage, has now "hardened" into law in the legal sense. It has become a "rule of common law." We preserve the connection with the original customs and practices by asserting that judges do not "make" the law, but simply "declare" what it is. They attach the necessary stamp to a particular customary practice, so that from here on we know for certain that customary practice is "law." (A famous American judge, Mr. Justice Cardozo, once described this as "the process by which forms of conduct are stamped in the judicial mint as law, and thereafter circulate freely as part of the coinage of the realm.")

Before leaving the topic, mention should be made of two other sources of common law — Roman Law and Canon Law. Canon Law is ecclesiastical or church law. For many centuries after the birth of Christ, the prevailing church in Western countries was the Roman Catholic church. The law of this church, the Canon Law, was based in large part on Roman Law, and, inasmuch as the church was, in this period, the principal source of the educational system, many of the royal judges were themselves clerics. These judges therefore were familiar with these other bodies of law on which they could draw to provide a problem-solving principle in situations where custom and usage gave them no answer.

In the early development of the common law, Roman Law concepts were therefore influential, but as the role of the clerics declined in later centuries, so also the influence of Roman Law diminished and the common law developed along its own separate and special path. The influence of canon law persisted the longest in the areas of the law of marriage, and succession to property, and as regards the regulation of the conduct of members of the clergy.

The other main source of law in the modern era is legislation, that is, the rules made by the organ of government known as the "legislature."

At the same time as it performs its function of making laws, the legislature also performs the function of being the vehicle through which are made known the views of the individual citizens in society as to how they should be governed. This is described as the "democratic" function, from the Greek words "demos" meaning "people" and "kratein" meaning "to rule" or "kratos" meaning "authority." It took thousands of years for the concept that the authority to rule a society should be derived from the people forming that society, to become fully developed. Consequently the decisions of the courts administering the common law were, for many centuries, the most important source of our law. In the last hundred and fifty years or so, however, the growing strength of the principles of democracy and the rapidly increasing complexity of modern societies have made legislation, produced by elected legislatures, far and away the pre-eminent source of new law.

Some Basic Legal Terminology

We have already introduced two important terms — *common law* and *legislation*. Common law is the law declared to be such by the courts and is therefore sometimes referred to as *judge-made* law. The judges perform this function in the disputes or cases which come before them for resolution, and therefore another term used in this regard is *case law*. Decided cases are frequently referred to as *precedents* for the case currently before the court. When the decisions (precedents) in a number of cases on related points of law are assembled together, we frequently find a more general principle or rule emerging, a *rule of common law*. This occurs, therefore, through a process of inductive reasoning, an inferring of general law from particular instances. This is in contrast to the deductive reasoning used when we apply a statute and draw an inference from the general to the particular.

Once a court has laid down a principle of law as applicable to a certain set of facts, it will adhere to that principle and apply it to all future cases where the factual situation is substantially the same, even although the parties involved are different. Courts of equivalent rank are not absolutely bound to follow each other's decisions, but usually do so. Lower courts are considered to be bound by the decisions of higher courts. All of this is described as the principle of *stare decisis*.

The term *statute* just employed above is one of a number of more or less interchangeable terms used to describe the end product of the work of a *legislature*. Legislature is a generic term (derived from the Latin word "lex" meaning "law") used to describe the modern organ of government which affords the general mass of citizens a degree of participation in the process of government. This occurs by virtue of the fact that in modern times the legislature in most of the countries of the world is elected by the citizens. The legislature therefore acquires two principal functions (a) that of *representing the interests of the people* and (b) making laws. As we have already noted, in modern times the laws made by the legislature have surpassed the laws declared by the courts in volume and in significance.

There are specific names for the legislature in various countries. In Canada the federal legislature is called Parliament, which copies British usage. (The word "Parliament" is derived from the French word "parler" meaning "to speak." The French legislature is thus called *le Parlement*.) The legislatures of the Provinces of Canada are most commonly called *Legislative Assembly*, the principal exception being Quebec, where it is called the *National Assembly* (l'Assemblee Nationale) for reasons of history and politics.

The legislature of the United States is called *Congress*. It is divided into houses or chambers called the *House of Representatives* and the *Senate*. The Parliament of Canada also has two chambers, the *House of Commons* and the *Sen-

ate*. The two chambers of the British Parliament are called the House of Commons and the *House of Lords*. Many legislatures have only one chamber however. This is the case with the Legislative Assembly of all ten Canadian Provinces, the national legislature of Israel (the *Knesset*) and the national legislature of Sweden (the *Riksdag*).

Another word used to describe what a legislature produces is *Act* — Act of Parliament, Act of the Legislative Assembly, Act of Congress, etc. Individual statutes will have names such as the Labour Relations Act, the Finance Act, and so on. More generally we can speak of *enacted law* or *enactment*, or alternatively, *statute law*, or *legislation*.

While a statute is still in process of being enacted, i.e., while it is still passing through the various procedures employed by the legislature concerned, and has not yet become a completed Act of that legislature, it is referred as a *Bill*.

It is also open to a legislature to group together the various common law rules which have been developed in this or that area of the law, and to re-enact them in a comprehensive form as legislation. The word commonly used to describe the result is *Code*. In Canada we can find both federal and Provincial examples of this e.g., the Canadian Criminal Code (federal) or the Quebec Civil Code. The latter is a Canadian adaptation of the older Napoleonic Code of France, which was a major restatement and revision of the numerous customary laws existing rather chaotically in France prior to the reign of the Emperor Napoleon Bonaparte. A codification need not necessarily bear the label of "code" e.g., the Sale of Goods Act enacted in 1893 by the British Parliament is a codification of the case law on this topic. All of the Provinces of Canada except Quebec have done the same thing in this area of the law.

The law can be classified in a variety of ways. A contrast is usually made between *civil law* and *criminal law*. Basically, civil law is everything which is not criminal. Criminal law deals with the commission of offences which have a typically criminal purpose and which lead to the imposition of some kind of punishment. (The definition of what is a "typically criminal purpose" can present the courts with difficulty from time to time.)

A specialised use of the term *civil law* may be noted here. In the Roman Empire the term *ius civile* denoted the general law which was applicable to, and available only to, Roman citizens. (Where non-citizens were involved in a dispute, the applicable law was the *ius gentium*, the "law of peoples" or the "law of nations." It is from this latter body of principles that portions of modern international law are derived.) In countries where the legal system is based on Roman law, the term *civil law* usually refers to *that* fact. Thus as regards, say, France, or Germany or the Canadian Province of Quebec we commonly say that these jurisdictions each have a civil law system, meaning that their law derives principally from the Roman law system, not the common law system.

Another contrast frequently made is that between *private law* and *public law*.

Private law sub-divides into a number of separately distinguishable topics. The law of *Contracts* regulates the manner in which binding agreements are made between or among individuals, and how these are enforced if necessary. The law of *Torts* deals with civil, as distinct from criminal, wrongs. (The word itself is simply the French word for "wrong.") Thus if I unintentionally, but negligently, knock you down with my automobile and injure you, the law requires me to make good to you this non-criminal wrong that I have done you. The most common form of reparation is by payment of a sum of money, called *damages*, by the negligent person to the injured person. The law recognises a substantial number and range of torts.

The law of *Marriage and Divorce* regulates this very personal set of relationships — how does one get married, what are the rights and duties of the partners during the subsistence of the marriage, and how does one terminate the legal status of being married. This is a branch of the broader topic of *Family Law*, under which the rights of the children of a marriage are also dealt with. *Property Law* deals with how you acquire legal rights to all kinds of property, both tangible (e.g., automobiles, land and buildings) and the intangible (shares in a company, rights under an insurance policy) and how those rights may be sold or otherwise transferred.

On your death your property will pass to somebody else and this is regulated by the law of *Wills and Succession*, dealing with the way in which you can personally control what is to happen to your property by drawing up a document called a will, or the general rules for identifying the persons who will succeed to your property in the event that you die without leaving any personal instructions in the form of a will. *Company (Corporation) Law* and the *Law of Partnerships* will deal with these particular ways of carrying on a business and *Bankruptcy Law* provides the rules for dealing with a situation where your business has failed.

Public Law involves the regulation of relationships between individual citizens and the state or its organs of government. It too can be sub-divided. *Constitutional Law* lays down the structure of the governmental system, specifying the organs of government and their powers. Frequently also, as is now the case in Canada since 1982, it will regulate the political and human rights of the individual citizen vis-à-vis the state. *Administrative Law* is the law regulating the dealings of the individual citizen with the bureaucracy i.e., the "public service" or "civil service," as distinct from the "politicians." *Criminal Law*, as defined earlier, deals with the commission of offences which have a typically criminal purpose and which lead to the imposition of some kind of punishment. It falls under the heading of public law because in modern societies the state has taken over the vindication of criminal violations of the rights of individual citizens. The majority of crimes are committed by individuals against individuals, but we no longer allow self-help in such situations. We do not allow the injured party to take revenge on the offending party. Instead, the state acts in the public interest, on behalf of us all, in seeking to punish the guilty. *International Law* is the most obviously "public" of these various areas. It regulates the dealings of countries (nations) with one another and with international organizations such as the United Nations.

In this regard we may also mention the *Law of Evidence* and the *Law of Procedure*. These are in a sense neutral topics, in that they are neither specifically private nor specifically public in their reach. Their adjunct nature leads to their being described on occasion as *Adjectival Law*. We may also note, however, that in certain circumstances they may become substantive in character, for example, where refusal to admit a particular piece of evidence, or a failure to observe minimum procedural standards might lead to the individual citizen thus affected making a claim that rights guaranteed by the constitution were being infringed.

Finally the term *jurisdiction* should be noted. In general terms this refers to the legal power possessed by a judge, or a court or other tribunal to inquire into a matter and to make a decision upon it. We can also note some more specific usages. *Original jurisdiction* is possessed by the tribunal where you are entitled to commence your case. If you are dissatisfied with the original decision, and if the law so permits, then you may appeal to a higher tribunal in an effort to get that decision altered. This second tribunal is said to have *appellate jurisdiction*. A court or tribunal will usually have limits on its *territorial jurisdiction*. The courts of the Province of Ontario have no jurisdictional power to decide cases which arise in Manitoba. The Supreme Court of Canada cannot decide cases which arise in Italy. Lastly, courts may have specialised powers as regards their *substantive jurisdiction*. For example, some courts may have power only in criminal cases, while similarly, other courts may have only civil jurisdiction. In the lower levels of courts we may find those which deal only with road traffic matters, or only with family law disputes. A rapidly developing modern phenomenon is the growth of administrative tribunals which deal, somewhat more informally than a regular common law court, with disputes arising in particular areas of administrative law, for example, a labour relations board or a municipal assessment appeals tribunal.

The Constitution and the Law

The constitution of a country is sometimes referred to as a "higher law." The extent to which this is true relates to the extent to which that constitution is enforceable in the courts or through some other institution.

For example, the former Soviet Union had quite a lengthy and complex written constitution, but no procedure existed whereby an individual citizen could compel the government to observe any provision of that document. Again, it is frequently said that Britain has an "unwritten" constitution. What this really means is that there is no one single document that can be pointed to as "the British constitution," although there exist several individual documents which are of constitutional significance in Britain. Again, apart from a few procedural rights, there is no procedure for individual citizens to achieve enforcement of constitutional principles. Indeed, one of the most cherished principles of the British constitution is the complete authority of the legislature or, as it is more usually expressed, "the sovereignty of Parliament." This refers to the inability of any

other institution of government in Britain to contradict what Parliament says, leading to the situation where, as is often said, "In Britain, the constitution is what Parliament says it is." (This position has been somewhat modified in recent years by Britain's membership of the European Common Market.)

The preamble to the Canadian Constitution expresses Canada's desire to have "a Constitution similar in principle to that of the United Kingdom." Consequently, in broad principle, this "sovereignty of Parliament" or "legislative supremacy" is a feature of the Canadian constitution also. However, this principle has to be modified in Canada to take account of the fact that Canada also has a "federal" system of government. This means that we have a duplication of the organs of government — legislature, executive and judiciary — i.e., not *one* set of each, as in a "unitary" state such as Britain, but *two* sets each. One set comprises the national, central or "federal" organs of government, situated in Ottawa, and the other set is divided into ten units, comprising the organs of government of each of the ten member units (called "Provinces") which together form the Canadian federal union. Governmental power is therefore *distributed* between the federal legislature and cabinet in Ottawa on the one hand and the ten legislatures and cabinets in each of the ten Provincial capitals (Toronto, Fredericton, Winnipeg, etc.) on the other hand. There is an analogous distribution as regards judicial power.

In Canada, therefore, we describe the federal organs and the provincial organs as "each being supreme within its own sphere." Putting them all together, we have the *totality* of Canadian governmental power, as viewed from the outside. Viewed from the inside, however, we see a provincial sphere and a federal sphere of power.

The written constitution of Canada makes a formal distribution of powers between those two spheres. (See Sections 91 and 92 of the Constitution particularly.) Consequently, if the federal government seeks to exercise powers which the constitution allocates to the sphere of power of the Provincial governments — or vice versa — then it is acting beyond its powers or, as we more usually say, using a Latin phrase, it is acting *ultra vires*. If a challenge is made in the courts, the courts have the power to declare the action to be of no force and effect, to be null and void, on the ground that the action is *ultra vires.* Conversely, after detailed scrutiny of the action involved, the courts may declare that the government concerned has acted *within* its sphere of power, that it has acted *intra vires.* The power of the courts to do this is referred to as the power of judicial review.

Until 1982, the ground of *ultra vires* was the only ground on which Canadian legislation, federal or Provincial, could be invalidated. In that year some major amendments were made to the Canadian constitution.

When the constitution was first enacted in 1867 it was entitled the British North America Act, but in 1982 it and all the amendments made to it between 1867 and 1982 were re-named the "Constitution Act, 1867, as amended." A new procedure for future amendments was added, but perhaps the most significant addition to the original constitution was 34 new sections collectively forming the Canadian Charter of Rights and Freedoms. (Note that what occurred in 1982 was the making of substantial additions and amendments to the 1867 constitution which, nonetheless survived intact in large measure. Canada did *not,* in 1982, receive a *new* constitution, although one occasionally still sees loose and wholly inaccurate statements to that effect.)

The Charter of Rights and Freedoms inserted into the constitution various principles such as freedom of speech and press, the right to vote, the right to enter and leave Canada, the right not to be arbitrarily detained or imprisoned, and so on and so forth.

This is not to say that such rights and freedoms did not exist in Canada prior to 1982. Most of them did in some form or other, but they were not formally incorporated into the text of the constitution. Rather, the same view was taken in Canada as still prevails in Britain today, that, as the noted English legal scholar A.V. Dicey expressed it, "most of these rights are consequences of the more general law or principle that no man can be punished except for direct breaches of law (i.e., crimes) proved in the way provided by law (i.e., before the courts of the realm)."

Section 52(1) of the 1982 Constitution Act declares that "The Constitution of Canada is the supreme law of Canada, and any law that is inconsistent with the provisions of the Constitution is, to the extent of the inconsistency, of no force or effect."

The result is that, since 1982, legislation which is *intra vires* as regards its falling within the sphere of power assigned by the constitution to the legislature which enacted it, may nevertheless be declared by the courts to be *unconstitutional* and therefore of no force or effect, on the ground that it conflicts with one of the rights or freedoms contained in the Charter of Rights and Freedoms. (It continues also to be possible to invalidate legislation on the ground that it is *ultra vires.*)

(For the sake of completeness, there must also be mentioned the Canadian Bill of Rights Act, 1960. Under this, the courts could declare legislation "inoperative" if it offended against certain principles enunciated in that Act. The Act applied to federal legislation only, and it did not form part of the constitution itself. Its precise role and status were therefore somewhat obscure. While it has not been repealed, it is more relevant for our purposes here to concentrate on the Charter of Rights and Freedoms.)

Administrative Law

It has already been indicated above that Administrative Law is that branch of public law which regulates the relationships between the individual and the state, while Constitutional Law deals with the rules, practices and institutions which *constitute* the state. Let us now explain the scope of administrative law a little further.

From a descriptive point of view, administrative law involves noting the various government institutions which the citizen may encounter. The most comprehensive of these is the 'Ministry' or 'Department', a division of the government, usually under the charge of a politician — or 'Minister' — who is a member of the political executive branch i.e., of the government for the time being. In conjunction with these Ministries or Departments we find a large array of other bodies with lesser powers and more narrowly specialized functions. These go under a wide variety of names, with no particular reason for the selection of one title rather than another. Thus we find an 'Agency' or 'Board' or 'Commission' or 'Tribunal' or 'Bureau' of this, that or the other, to mention only some of the more common names found.

From another descriptive point of view we might say that a study of administrative law involves a study of the actual rules, decisions and policies that administrators make. Those are a matter of content and substance, and many scholars prefer to refer to them as 'regulatory law' and to reserve the label 'administrative law' for the *procedures* for making policies. Professor Lief H. Carter has expressed it as that "Administrative law refers to the way the legal system, primarily the courts, translates the philosophy of the rule of law into controls on bureaucratic power." (Administrative Law and Politics, 1983, p. 35).

There are many ways in which administrative functions may be classified. Perhaps the simplest and certainly the broadest is to break them down into 'economic regulation' and 'benefit distribution'. The former would include such bodies as the federal Canadian Radio-television and Telecommunications Commission (CRTC), provincial egg marketing boards, professional organizations such as law societies or colleges of physicians, labour relations boards both federal and provincial, and so on. The latter would include a range of agencies administering various forms of health care and of income support and other social welfare benefits. Some bodies would straddle the two areas, such as agencies dealing with pollution control or wildlife protection.

Again as already mentioned, the courts are the principal agency through which controls over the administrative process are exercised. The courts have, on certain terms and conditions (which are themselves part of the substance of administrative law) the power of 'judicial review' over the propriety of administrative actings.

In the first place, they may examine the validity of the delegation, by the legislature to an administrative agency, of the power to act — the extent and nature of the grant and conditions under which it is granted; are these authorized by other principles of law, including the law of the constitution itself, or has there been an excessive or inappropriate delegation of power. Next the courts may inquire into what is called the 'rule-making process', if the particular agency has been given this quasi-legislative power — has the agency exercised this power to make rules of general application within the terms of the power delegated to it or has it exceeded them. Finally the courts may examine the propriety of the way in which the administrative agency has exercised what is called its 'adjudicative power', its power to make decisions involving individual citizens — has the agency observed the general rules which apply in this area.

Over a long period of time, sometimes stretching over centuries, the courts have developed a number of principles to which they require administrative bodies to conform when they act in ways which affect the rights of individual citizens. Many of these principles are comprehended within the concept of 'the principles of natural justice'. They have, for example, upheld the doctrine of *audi alteram partem* — that the individual must be given an opportunity to represent his or her side of the issue, whether this be done by means of a formal hearing or by some other process. Involved in these processes are the right to be represented by legal counsel (not always granted); to be given adequate advance notice of any proceedings and disclosure of what the state proposes [to] say on the matter; to cross-examine witnesses (again, not always granted); and the right to have one's representations considered by an un-biased adjudicator. Increasingly in recent years the courts have expanded the 'principles of natural justice' and developed a concept of 'fairness' as their yardstick for assessing administrative action. They have also expanded the range of persons and organizations which they will consider to have 'title' or 'standing' to bring actions.

The courts have also developed the principles upon which they will, or will not, overturn an administrative decision or acting because it is based upon an error of law, or an error of fact, or is based upon inadequate evidence, and upon which they will decline to intervene at all because they consider that the administrative side of government must be allowed a certain amount of latitude or discretion to act untrammelled.

Lastly, the courts will have to consider the remedy which they will provide to the aggrieved citizens if successful in his or her case before them. The court may 'quash' the administrative decision or acting which has been challenged. This may lead to the particular administrative decision or acting being repeated in revised form so as to take account of the court's criticism, or, quite frequently, to the decision or acting simply being abandoned. The court may issue an order to a public authority compelling it to take some action which it has failed to take, or forbidding it from taking some action which it ought not to take. Another alternative is for a court to issue an order declaratory of the rights of the parties, which can pave the way for a variety of other solutions to the problem at hand.

Common Law Actions

(a) Common Law and Environmental Protection: Legal realities and judicial challenges[†]

William Charles and David VanderZwaag ―――――――――――――――

INTRODUCTION

Private litigation is not an ideal route to secure environmental protection for numerous reasons. Private litigation, replying on the happenstance of a motivated and financially able plaintiff, cannot replace the need for long-term planning processes. The costs of litigation may be prohibitive because of attorney fees and the financial drain of securing witnesses. Private lawsuits tend to be reactive and adversarial with traditional legal requirements, such as the need for a property interest, often favouring defendants.

Nevertheless, private litigation may have a critical role to play in environmental protection. Litigation may be the only way to air legitimate grievances where governmental officials have refused to act or polluters have failed to listen. The profile of an environmental issue might be elevated through a lawsuit, and a court offers a decision-making forum less prone to political pressures.

Just how active judges should be in policy making will remain a controversial issue. A call for conservative approaches might be based on the notion that elected officials are the more proper vehicle for social policy decisions. However, common law doctrines carry inherent value judgments that are open to creative and jurisprudential evolutions based on changing societal perspectives.

Longstanding common law actions of negligence, nuisance, strict liability, riparian rights, and trespass to the person have been developed and used to protect individual rights to physical integrity and property. We have not, however, to this point, developed a legal theory that would give us a justiciable right to be free of the harmful effects of toxic substances. This, in spite of our growing awareness of the dangerous realities.

The English common law's focus on property rights as the basis for several of the actions relevant to environmental protection is illus-

―――――――――――――――――

† From *Environmental Law and Policy*, ed. Elaine L. Hughes, Alastair R. Lucas, and William A. Tilleman, 2d ed. (Toronto: Emond Montgomery Publications Limited, 1998), pp. 79–80. Reproduced by permission of the publisher.

trated by the comments of Lord Scarman who explained:

> For the environment a traditional lawyer reads property: English law reduces environmental problems to questions of property. Establish ownership or possession and the armoury of the English legal cupboard is yours of command. This is not to say that English law is, or has ever been, helpless in face of a threat to the environment. Trespass and nuisance have proved over the centuries potent causes of action enforceable by the effectual remedies of injunction and damages; and, on occasion, the law permits self-help as well, e.g. in the abatement of nuisance by going on one's neighbour's land and rooting it out. [L.A. Scarman, *English Law — The New Dimension* (London: Stevens & Sons, 1974), at 51.]

This chapter, in a two-part format, illustrates the potential power, but also key limitations, of common law to protect the environment. The following section highlights the basic legal requirements of negligence (including public authority liability), private nuisance, public nuisance, strict liability, riparian rights, trespass to the person, and trespass to land. The final section focuses on judicial challenges in toxic torts where plaintiffs are exposed to toxic agents (chemical, biological, or radiological).

OVERVIEW OF COMMON LAW DOCTRINES

Negligence

The most important tort action today, both in terms of the number of claims made and its theoretical importance, is the negligence cause of action. Unlike other torts, which protect specific interests from wrongful interference, the negligence action seems to have few limits. In a broad sense, negligence law deals with the compensation of losses caused by unintentional but unreasonable conduct that harmfully affects legally protected interests. Unreasonable conduct has been defined as "the omission to do something which a reasonable [person] guided by those considerations which a prudent, reasonable [person] would not do" (per Alderson B in *Blyth v. Birmingham Water Works Co.* (1856), 156 ER 1047, at 1049).

A negligence action, in which a defendant is held to the standard of care of a reasonable person, may be effectively used in the area of environmental litigation. To be successful, a plaintiff must establish, on the balance of probabilities, five key elements of the tort. These elements are legal duty, breach of the standard of care, cause in fact, proximate cause, and damage to the plaintiff.

(b)   Civil Litigation — Negligence[†]

Elizabeth J. Swanson and Elaine L. Hughes ――――――――――――――――

Standard of Care

The law of negligence imposes upon us a duty to avoid an unreasonable risk of harm to those who are likely to be affected by our actions. What constitutes an "unreasonable risk" depends, in part, on a balancing of the likelihood and severity of harm against the utility of the conduct and the costs of reducing or eliminating the risk.[283] Very generally, as the first two factors (likelihood and severity of harm) increase the more probable is a finding of negligence.[284]

The usual standard of care to meet is that of the "reasonable man", a fictional creature created by the courts to assist in the assessment of negligence. The relevant question is this: "given these factors (likelihood, severity, utility and cost) would a reasonable man in like circumstances have assumed this risk of harm?"

---

† From *The Price of Pollution: Environmental Litigation in Canada*, ed. Elizabeth J. Swanson and Elaine L. Hughes (Edmonton, Alta.: Environmental Law Centre (Alberta) Society, 1990), pp. 57–59. Reproduced by permission of the publisher. See Appendix for notes or references.

There are circumstances in which the standard of the "reasonable man" is replaced by other judicial measuring sticks. Defendants possessing special knowledge or expertise (doctors or lawyers, for example) are required to exercise the same degree of competence and skill which would be expected of their prudent colleagues.[285] In addition, legislation may impose a specific standard to be met by those acting pursuant to the legislation.[286] For a time it appeared that breach of a statute *per se* amounted to an actionable wrong for which an injured party could sue for compensation. This concept of a "tort" of statutory breach was laid to rest by the Supreme Court of Canada in *The Queen in Right of Canada* v. *Saskatchewan Wheat Pool*.[287] Instead, a breach of statute is to be treated as evidence of negligence. More particularly (but depending upon the nature and language of the legislation in question) departure from conduct prescribed by statute may indicate that, in the circumstances, the defendant failed to meet the standard of care required by law.[288]

Although this exact issue does not appear to have come before the courts as yet, failure to comply with terms of a license (to discharge effluents into water, for example) might be considered evidence of negligence, with the license provision being the standard of care to be met by its holder. Where a breach of the license results in loss or injury, arguably the injured party can rely upon that breach as proof of negligence.[289]

Customary or usual practices are particularly relevant to the "reasonableness" of business or industrial conduct, although compliance with those standards does not necessarily determine the question of negligence.

On occasion the courts seem to impose a higher standard of care upon those who engage in activities which are inherently dangerous or "risky." In *North York* v. *Kent Chemical Industries Inc.*, for example, the Ontario Supreme Court found the defendant chemical company liable for damage to municipal sewage lines resulting from the discharge of acidic wastes into the system. The basis for their liability was negligence, although it had been argued that those who deal in "inherently dangerous substances" should be held strictly liable for any resulting damage.[290] It is not clear from the decision in *North York* whether this argument was meant to establish the applicability of the rule in *Rylands* v. *Fletcher* or was advanced as a "new" basis for imposing liability.[291]

Although the language of Mr. Justice Krever suggests a new dimension to the setting of a standard of care, it is suggested here that the nature of the activity in question is part and parcel of the existing formula; that is, the more dangerous the activity, the more likely the risk of serious injury.

Actual Loss

Negligent conduct, however blameworthy, will not result in liability unless the plaintiff has suffered some actual loss or injury.[292] The proof of loss rests with the plaintiff who must establish on a balance of probabilities not only that he suffered injury but that the defendant's negligent conduct was the direct cause, or cause in fact, of the harm complained of.[293] The test for causation has sometimes been referred to as the "but for" test: but for the negligence of the defendant, would the plaintiff have suffered any harm? It is not necessary for the plaintiff to prove that the defendant's conduct was the only contributing factor. It is enough to show that the defendant contributed in a real and direct way to the injury.[294]

In some circumstances liability may be apportioned between defendants, each of whom are responsible, to some degree, for the plaintiff's loss. Quite commonly, multiple defendants are held "jointly and severally liable" for the damage. This means that the plaintiff may look to any of the defendants for full recovery of the damages awarded, regardless of the degree to which that particular defendant may have been found at fault. That party, in turn, may seek contribution from his fellow wrongdoers, each to the extent of their of liability.[295]

The loss alleged must be incurred directly by the plaintiff. This point was clearly made by the Exchequer Court of Canada in its 1961 decision in *Her Majesty the Queen* v. *Forest Protection Limited*.[296] In that case the Crown sued the defendant Forest Protection Limited for damages in excess of $5,000 alleging that the defendant had negligently caused the death of almost a million fish by allowing aerially sprayed insecticide to drift onto the waters of a state-owned hatchery. Although causation was at issue, the Court ultimately found the defendant responsible for the loss and awarded damages in the amount of $500, an amount significantly less than that sought by the plaintiff. The damages were awarded with respect to the cost of feeding the lost fish prior to their destruction, and for the inconvenience and disruption to the operation of the hatchery. No amount was awarded to compensate for the loss of fish themselves as:[297]

> The fish that were lost had no commercial value to the plaintiff: they were not for sale and there could be no loss or profit involved. The small fry serve to restock the streams and rivers, and the destruction of nearly one million of them could cause loss or inconvenience, not to the plaintiff, but to the public and only to those persons who years later might have caught them.

(c)   Common Law and Environmental Protection: Legal realities and judicial challenges (Continued)[†]

William Charles and David VanderZwaag ————————————

Public Authority Liability

A field of negligence law that is bound to take on increasing importance is the liability of public authorities. The ever-expanding role of government officials in regulatory activities may lead to future lawsuits over the adequacy of official conduct in preventing or controlling polluting activities. The doctrine of Crown immunity which, historically, has provided protection against civil liability, has in recent years, been significantly limited, courts have strained to develop an appropriate test for determining governmental civil liability. The Supreme Court of Canada's decision in *Just v. British Columbia*, [1982] 2 SCR 1228 is the seminal authority in Canada and is applied by the Ontario court in the environmental case that follows. In the *Gauvin* case, the plaintiffs suffered damages in the form of costs for replacing a negligently installed septic system, and the court found the Ontario Minister of Environment and the negligent contractor jointly and severally liable.

. . . .

Private Nuisance

A private nuisance is usually defined as an unreasonable interference with the use and enjoyment of land that is owned or occupied by another person. Liability may be imposed, even though the defendant did not intend and was not negligent in causing the interference. If the interference involves a form of physical damage to the land itself or personal injury to occupants, courts have been quick to conclude a finding of nuisance, given the substantial gravity of interference. Where the interference involves interference with the plaintiff's enjoyment of the property — for example, by loud noises or noxious odours — courts will weigh various factors in determining whether a nuisance exists. Key factors include duration of the interference, gravity, the neighbourhood (for example industrial/urban versus rural), utility of the defendant's activity, and whether the plaintiff has abnormal sensitivities.

. . . .

Public Nuisance

A public nuisance has been defined as an "action brought to protect the public interest in freedom from damages to health, safety, morality, comfort or convenience" (O.M. Reynolds, "Public Nuisance: A Crime in Tort Law" (1978), 31 *Oklahoma Law Review* 318). This civil action has its roots in the criminal law and more specifically in the common law offence of common nuisance. The civil action of public nuisance was developed in the 18th and 19th centuries and was intended to supplement the criminal offence. However, the modern tort of public nuisance

† From Elaine L. Hughes, Alastair R. Lucas, and William A. Tilleman, eds., *Environmental Law andd Policy* (Toronto: Emond Montgomery Publications Limited, 1998), pp. 83, 85, 93–95, 97–106. Reproduced by permission of the publisher.

does not require an unlawful act as its basic requirement and has grown from its function as an ancillary criminal remedy into an independent common law tort.

Originally designed to deal with obstructions of public highways, rights of way, or navigable waters, this tort has expanded to cover the pollution of beaches and shoreline properties, as well as noise-generating activities and street prostitution.

In order to determine whether a particular activity interferes unreasonably with the public interest, a court must balance, in a general manner, the defendant's right to engage in an activity, without undue restriction, against the public right to have its interests protected. Several factors may be considered by the court, such as the trouble or inconvenience caused by the activity, the ease or difficulty involved in taking steps to avoid the risk, the general practice of others, the utility of the activity, and the character of the neighbourhood. (L.N. Klar, *Tort Law*, 2d ed. (Scarborough, ON: Carswell, 1996), 527, citing *Chessie v. J.D. Irving Ltd.* (1982), 140 DLR (3d) 501 (NB CA). "The more harmful and less useful the activity, the more likely it is that it will be termed a (public) nuisance. Where the activity results not in material damage to public property but to questions of public's comfort and sensibilities, the balancing is more difficult."

In general, actions in public nuisance must be commenced by the attorney general on the theory that the rights of the public are vested in the Crown, and the attorney general, as an officer of the Crown, is the only person entitled to enforced those rights. The only exception to this rule occurs when the public right interference is such that some private right is interfered with at the same time. For example, where an obstruction is so placed on a highway that the owner of the premises abating upon the highway has his or her own private access to and from the property interfered with, that person can be considered to have suffered "special damage." Clearly, in cases where a public nuisance results in personal injury or damage to or interference with the plaintiff's property, the special damages requirement is met. However, where the plaintiff suffers loss of business profits (or economic loss), the issue is more difficult and the answer less clear as to whether this type of loss qualifies as "special damage." Courts have differed in their view of whether the plaintiff's loss must be particular or special in kind as compared with the public loss or harm or whether a greater degree of damage of the same kind is sufficient. In several cases, Canadian courts have taken a narrow view of special damages. The *Hickey* case that follows is one such case.

Hickey
v.
Electric Reduction Co. of Canada, Ltd.
(1970), 21 DLR (3d) 368 (Nfld. TD)

FURLONG CJ: ... For our present purposes then, I am assuming that the plaintiffs' assertion is true in substance, and that is, that the defendant discharged poisonous material into the waters of Placentia Bay, from its plant at Long Harbour, Placentia Bay, polluting the waters of the bay, poisoning fish "and rendering them of no commercial value."

So at the outset, we are put on inquiry to consider whether the facts disclose the creation of a tortious act, that is to say, the creation of a private nuisance, or the commission of a criminal act, which is to say, a public nuisance. The former is a civil wrong, actionable at the suit of an affected person.

The latter has been defined by Sir James Stephen in his *Digest of the Criminal Law*, 9th ed. (1950) (using the term "common nuisance"), in these words at p. 179:

> A common nuisance is an act not warranted by law or an omission to discharge a legal duty, which act or omission obstructs or causes inconvenience or damage to the public in the exercise of rights common to all His Majesty's subjects.

Salmond, *The Law of Torts*, 15th ed. (1969), expresses it more succinctly at p. 64:

> A public or common nuisance is a criminal offence. It is an act or omission which materially affects the reasonable comfort or convenience of life of a class of Her Majesty's subjects ...

and he adds:

> A public nuisance falls within the law of torts only in so far as it may in the particular case constitute some form of tort also. Thus the obstruction of a highway is a public nuisance; but if it causes any special and peculiar damage to an individual, it is also a tort actionable at his suit.

What has happened here? The defendants by the discharge of poisonous waste from its phosphorous plant at Long Harbour, Placentia Bay, destroyed the fish life of the adjacent waters, and the plaintiffs, as all other fishermen in the area suffered in their livelihood. I had said "all other fishermen," but the resulting pollution created a nuisance to all persons — "all Her Majesty's subjects" — to use Stephen's phrase. It was not a nuisance peculiar to the plaintiffs, nor confined to their use of the waters of Placentia Bay. It was a nuisance committed against the public....

Counsel for the plaintiffs, Mr. Robert Wells, argued that when a public nuisance has been created anyone who suffers special damage, that is direct damage has a right of action. I am unable to agree to this rather wide application of Salmond's view that a public nuisance may become a tortious act. I think the right view is that any person who suffers peculiar damage has a right of action, but where the damage is common to all persons of the same class, then a personal right of action is not maintainable. Mr. Wells suggests that the plaintiffs' right to outfit for the fishery and their right to fish is a particular right and this right having been interfered with they have a cause of action. This right which they enjoy is a right in common with all Her Majesty's subjects, an interference with which is the whole test of a public nuisance; a right which can only be vindicated by the appropriate means, which is an action by the Attorney-General, either with or without a relator, in the common interest of the public.

· · · ·

Strict Liability

An example of liability regardless of fault on the part of the defendant is found in cases where the defendant collects things on his or her land that are likely to do mischief if they escape. If they do escape, the defendant will be held strictly liable — that is, liable for the damages resulting from such an escape, even though the defendant may not have been careless or at fault in allowing the escape. This so-called rule has its origins in the case of *Rylands v. Fletcher* (1868), LR 3 HL 330, affirming *Fletcher v. Rylands* (1866), LR 1 Ex. 265. The essential elements of the tort created by the decision in this case can be listed as follows:

1. the defendant is in lawful occupation of property,
2. on which is stored a dangerous agent or thing constituting a non-natural of land,

3. escape of the agent or thing from the defendant's property, and
4. causing damage to the plaintiff.

The non-natural use requirement created by Lord Cairns has, traditionally and historically, been the factor most frequently considered by courts, but they have given it both a broad and a narrow meaning. Considered broadly, a non-natural use has been held to be any use that exposes the neighbourhood to special dangers. It has been suggested that some courts adopt a narrower view of "non-natural" by requiring that the use be not only hazardous but also unusual or special in the sense that it is not one originally conducted on land. See L.N. Klar, *Tort Law*, 2d ed., supra, at 456.

In *Cambridge Water Company v. Eastern Counties Leather*, [1994] 1 All ER 53 (HL), a case involving the pollution of a plaintiff's water supply by chemicals previously considered "safe" but later coming under government regulations, the House of Lords continued to embrace the traditional technical distinctions of non-natural use and escape from land but added the additional requirement of foreseeability of damage. There, the trial judge had found the storage of organochlorines in the vicinity of an industrial village to be a natural use of land. When the case reached the House of Lords, Lord Goff expressed the opinion (at 79) that the storage of substantial quantities of chemicals on industrial premises was to be regarded as an "almost classic case" of non-natural use. Lord Goff also rejected the American interpretation and application of *Rylands* that imposes strict liability in cases where damage is caused by "ultra-hazardous operations" (at 75). He did so on the basis that the law commission had expressed serious misgivings about the adoption of this test and that this decision should be made by Parliament. Lord Goff concluded (at 76) that because *Rylands v. Fletcher* was "essentially as an extension of the law of nuisance to cases of isolated escapes from land" and because foreseeability was already an element of nuisance, that the defendant could not be held liable for the unforeseeable damage from escaped chemicals.

Note that the strict liability rule of *Rylands v. Fletcher* requires some abnormal non-natural use of land that results in actual damage to the land, goods, or person of the plaintiff whereas nuisance merely requires a natural or usual but "unreasonable" use of land that can result in mere inconvenience to the occupier. G.H.L. Fridman, *The Law of Torts in Canada*, vol. 1 (Scarborough, ON: Carswell, 1989), 177–78.

. . . .

Riparian Rights

Riparian rights — rights held by the owner of land bordering a river, like, or stream — are often argued by plaintiffs in environment cases because of the potential for a high environmental standard to be imposed. The most important riparian rights, for environmental purposes, are those to natural quantity and natural quality of water flow.

The extent to which courts may dilute such strict rights is subject to some uncertainty. A "domestic use" or "ordinary use" exception is quite clear where a riparian owner may use water for domestic purposes such as drinking, stock watering, and washing, without incurring liability to a lower riparian. See G. LaForest, *Water Law in Canada — The Atlantic Provinces* (Ottawa: Dept. of Regional Economic Expansion, 1972), 224. Other secondary uses, such as waste disposal, have also been accepted and actions will lie only if the use is "unreasonable," a standard subject to case-by-case interpretation.

The case of *Gauthier v. Naneff*, [1971] 14 DLR (3d) 513 (Ont. HC), demonstrates a strict judicial approach toward environmental protection. There plaintiff riparian landowners sought an injunction against the holding of a speedboat regatta on Lake Ramsay in Sudbury and argued outboard motorboats would negatively effect the purity and potability of the water. The court, noting the need to interpret the word "unreasonable" in the light of present day knowledge of and concern for pollution problems, indicated every riparian proprietor has an entitlement to water quality without sensible alternation. The court refused to consider the economic arguments of the defendants, such as the goal of raising money for charities, and granted an injunction.

Other courts have been willing to consider social and economic interests, particularly at the stage of deciding whether to grant an injunction for riparian interferences. For example, in *Lockwood v. Brentwood Park Investments Ltd.* (1970), 10 DLR (3d) 143 (NS CA), the court, while willing to find a violation of riparian rights by the defendant apartment complex developers, who diverted brook waters with resultant loss of

amenities to the downstream plaintiff, refused to grant an injunction stopping further diversions. The court questioned whether the traditional strict approach to riparian rights developed in England should be applied in present urban situations with their population pressures.

Riparian rights have also been stated to extend to lands abutting the sea or other tidal waters. See LaForest, supra, at 200. For example, in *Corkum v. Nash* (1990), 71 DLR (4th) 390 (NS TD), affirmed (1991), 87 DLR (4th) 127 (CA), the court granted the owner of property abutting on the high-water mark of a salt water harbour an injunction requiring defendants to remove wharves on the shore which interfered with the owner's riparian right of access. It remains to be seen how far courts are willing to protect the natural quality of marine waters through the doctrine of riparian rights.

Trespass to the Person in the Form of Battery

The general tort of trespass to the person covers three more specific sub-torts called battery, assault, and false or wrongful imprisonment. The sub-tort of battery is the most relevant weapon to be used in the environmental context but even this tort has limited use because of the need to prove intention.

Battery is defined as the deliberate application of force to the person of another that results in harm to that person or offensive contact. The wrong that the law seeks to prevent by awarding damage compensation is the violation of a person's bodily integrity.

Although actual intention may be difficult to prove in environment cases, the doctrine of substantial certainty may assist a plaintiff. An act is intentional in law when the defendant can be said to desire the consequences that flow from the act or can be said to have been substantially certain that such consequences would occur.

The case of *Macdonald v. Sebastian* (1988), 81 NSR (2d) 189 (TD) demonstrates the applicability of battery in the environmental context. Three plaintiffs, a mother and her two children, were exposed to unacceptable levels of arsenic in the water supply of their leased premises owned by the defendant. Since the defendant, a medical doctor, had knowledge of the high arsenic levels and obvious damages to the health and safety of tenants, the court was willing to find a deliberate act of battery. Punitive damages in the amount of $7,000 per plaintiff were awarded in addition to $1,000 in general damages for each plaintiff.

Trespass to Land

Trespass to land involves an intended but unjustifiable interference with another person's possession of land. No physical damage to the property need occur. Interference with the legal right of possession is sufficient.

The tort consists of an act of direct physical entrance upon land in the possession of another or remaining upon such land after being told to leave or placing or projecting any object upon the land. In each case, the act must be done without lawful justification. The two key elements of the tort are intention and direct entry. The latter requirement particularly has caused problems for plaintiffs in cases involving the spraying of insecticides and other toxic chemicals where wind drift causes the chemicals to depart from their intended target and to be deposited upon the plaintiff's property (see L.N. Klar, *Tort Law*, 2d ed., supra, at 88). Similarly, oil jettisoned into the water by the defendant and carried into the plaintiff's foreshore was found not to constitute a trespass because the interference with the plaintiff's land was not the direct result of the defendant's act, *Southport Corp. v. Esso Petroleum Co.* (1954), 2 QB 182, reversed on other grounds (1955), 3 All ER 864 (HL). Such an approach clearly poses a problem for a plaintiff whose land has been affected by toxic chemicals that are dumped upon the defendant's land and are carried by percolating groundwater to the plaintiff's land. There would seem to be considerable weight to the argument that in these circumstances where the interference was "set in motion by the defendants assisted only by natural and inevitable forces" they ought to be treated as sufficiently direct to constitute a trespass (see L.N. Klar, *Tort Law*, 2d ed. supra, at 89).

What constitutes a physical entry upon land may be a legal issue. It is doubtful whether vibrations constitute physical entry and certain smells do not (*Phillips v. California Standard Co.* (1960), 31 WWR 331 (Alta. TD)). Some US courts grappling with the problem in the English tradition have insisted upon the entry of something tangible having appreciable mass and visible to the naked eye. This approach would not allow for the recognition of industrial dust or noxious fumes. (See W.P. Keeton et al., eds.,

Prosser and Keeton on Law of Torts, 5th ed. (St. Paul, MN: West Publishing, 1984), 71). However, other US court decisions have found a trespass to land in the entry of invisible gases and microscopic particles where they do harm or cause a substantial interference. See, for example, *Martin v. Reynolds Metals*, 342 P2d 790 (Or. 1959), where the court noted that by requiring a substantial interference, the doctrine of trespass to land would tend to merge with the doctrine of nuisance. See also *Bradley v. American Smelting and Refining*, 709 P2d 782 (Wash. 1985).

CHALLENGES AND JUDICIAL STRUGGLES IN TOXIC TORTS

Toxic torts, a term commonly used to describe civil lawsuits brought by plaintiffs to address exposure to toxic agents (chemical, biological, or radiological), tend to fall into three major categories, each with jurisprudential challenges. First, plaintiffs may try to prevent a threatened exposure to toxic agents, such as preventing the spraying of herbicides on a nearby property, by arguing a defendant's activity if allowed would be tortious (wrongful) and, therefore, an injunction should be imposed prohibiting or restricting the activity. Scientific uncertainties regarding toxic substances/agents often abound, with limited and sometimes conflicting studies making conclusions on genetic or biological effects difficult.

Various challenges are raised for the judiciary. Should traditional burden and standards of proof be followed with plaintiffs having to establish all the elements of causes of action, including causation, on a balance of probabilities? In light of the precautionary principle/approach evolving under international environmental law, where decision makers are urged to err on the side of caution in situations of scientific uncertainty, should the burden of proof be shifted to defendants? What type and level of risk should form the basis for judicial and injunctive action? What should be the role of courts in an age of specialized regulatory agencies? The case of *Palmer v. Nova Scotia Forest Industries*, infra, involving plaintiff actions trying to stop spraying of herbicides in Nova Scotia forests, highlights the prevention of threatened toxic exposure situation and introduces what is almost certainly to be a continuing controversial area of a Canadian common law doctrine.

A second category of cases involve plaintiffs suffering a present injury, such as a serious disease like cancer, where establishing a causal link to a defendant's tortious activity is often a central obstacle. Long latency periods for disease may make it difficult to point the legal finger at a particular defendant, especially where numerous defendants may have been involved in the manufacture and distribution of a particular toxic agent. Scientific uncertainties are usually prevalent with probabilistic evidence often central. Epidemiological studies of increase of disease among a given population usually does not rule out the possibility that a particular plaintiff's disease was caused by other than defendant's activity (for example, natural causes). Extrapolating the results of toxic tests on animal subjects to humans also carries uncertainties.

Again courts are faced with various jurisprudential challenges. Should the traditional common law "but for" test for establishing causation — that is, the plaintiff must establish on the balance of probabilities that but for the defendant's tortious activity, injury would not have occurred — be rejected? If so, what should replace the test? Various judicial innovations, such as the material contribution or material increase of risk/reverse onus tests have been suggested. The article by Bruce Pardy, infra, surveys a range of doctrinal approaches to causation, while the excerpt from the Supreme Court of Canada case of *Snell v. Farrell*, infra, shows an acceptance of a flexible, pragmatic approach to causation in line with the material contribution approach.

A third category of cases involves plaintiffs exposed to a toxic agent or agents but who have no "present injury" in the traditional sense of a manifest physical or personal injury. Various types of "damage" may nevertheless be claimed including recovery for an enhanced risk of future disease, money to monitor health and/or ecological impacts, compensation for the fear of getting cancer (or other serious disease), and a reduction in property value linked to public perceptions of risk/fear. Again, judicial challenges are raised such as the potential to open litigation floodgates unless some strict legal limits are imposed. Excerpts from the US cases of *Ayers v. Jackson Township*, *Potter v. Firestone Tire & Rubber*, and *Adkins v. Thomas Solvent Co.*, infra, demonstrate judicial struggles in this field of legal debate.

Prevention of Threatened Exposure to Toxic Agents

Palmer v. *Nova Scotia Forest Industries*
(1983), 2 DLR (4th) 397 (NS TD)

NUNN J: ... This is an application by the named plaintiffs in their individual capacities and as representatives of others for an injunction restraining the defendant, a company engaged in the forest industry in Nova Scotia, from spraying certain areas in the Province of Nova Scotia with phenoxy herbicides....

The subject of dioxins and chlorophenols has been widely disputed in many countries of the world both politically and before regulatory agencies. To my knowledge this is the first occasion where the dispute has reached the courts in Canada....

In the present case the allegation is that these offending chemicals, if they get to the plaintiffs' land, will interfere with the health of the plaintiffs thereby interfering with their enjoyment of their lands. Clearly such an interference, if proved, would fall within the essence of nuisance. As a serious risk of health, if proved, there is no doubt that such an interference would be substantial. In other words, the grounds for the cause of action in nuisance exist here provided that the plaintiffs prove the defendant will actually cause it, *i.e.*, that the chemicals will come to the plaintiffs' lands and that it will actually create a risk to their health. With this, I will deal later....

Again there is no doubt in my mind that, if it is proved that the defendant permits any of these substances on the plaintiffs' lands, it would constitute a trespass and be actionable....

The complete burden of proof, of course, rests upon the plaintiffs throughout for all issues asserted by them. If the spraying had actually occurred, they would have to prove by a preponderance of probabilities the essential elements of either or all of the alleged causes of action as I have set them out. However, the spraying has not occurred and this application is for a *quia timet* injunction. This can be translated as "which he fears." In other words, a plaintiff does not have to wait until actual damage occurs. Where such damage is apprehended, an application for a *quia timet* injunction is a appropriate avenue to obtain a remedy which will prevent the occurrence of the harm.

That remedy also, however, is not without its limitations.

In *Attorney-General v. Corporation of Manchester*, [1893] 2 Ch. 87, Chitty J States at p. 92:

> The principle which I think may be properly and safely extracted from the *quia timet* authorities is, that the plaintiff must show a strong case of probability that the apprehended mischief will, in fact, arise.

This passage was approved by Anglin J in the Supreme Court of Canada in *Matthew v. Guardian Ass'ce Co.* (1918), 45 DLR 32 at p. 42, ... and is still the proper principle to consider in an application of this kind....

The plaintiffs must, however, prove the essential elements of a regular injunction, namely, irreparable harm and that damages are not an adequate remedy as they are also essential elements of the *quia timet* injunction.

Finally, any injunction is a discretionary remedy and sufficient grounds must be established to warrant the exercise by the court of its discretion.

I am satisfied that a serious risk to health, if proved, would constitute irreparable harm and that damages would not be an adequate remedy. Further, recognizing the great width and elasticity of equitable principles, I would have no hesitation in deciding that such a situation would be one of the strongest which would warrant the exercise of the court's discretion to restrain the activity which would create the risk.

This matter thus reduces itself now to the single question. Have the plaintiffs offered sufficient proof that there is a serious risk of health and that such serious risk of health will occur if the spraying of the substances here is permitted to take place?...

Because of the nature of the issues in dispute, the witnesses produced and the testimony given, the enormous publicity attached to the trial and the public interest involved, the evidence went far beyond the particular substances involved and related to all the phenoxy herbicides and their derivatives. The whole trial took on the aura of a scientific inquiry as to whether the world should be exposed to dioxins. Scientists from all over North America, as well as from Sweden were called and testified. Scientific reports and studies from scientists the world over were filed as part of the evidence. In order to give both sides full opportunity to present their cases fully, it was necessary to grant this latitude although both parties were aware that the final decision would have to relate to the particular facts between the parties before the court.

As to the wider issues relating to the dioxin issue, it hardly seems necessary to state that a court of law is no forum for the determination of matters of science. Those are for science to determine, as facts, following the traditionally accepted methods of scientific inquiry. A substance neither does nor does not create a risk to health by court decree and it would be foolhardy for a court to enter such an inquiry. If science itself is not certain, a court cannot resolve the conflict and make the thing certain.

Essentially a court is engaged in the resolution of private disputes between parties and in the process follows certain time-honoured and well-established procedures and applies equally well-established principles of law, varying and altering them to adjust to an ever-changing society. Part of the process is the determination of facts and another part the application of the law to those facts, once determined, and designing the remedy. As to the occurrence of events, the court is concerned with "probability" and not with "possibility."....

As to Canada and the United Kingdom, both have registered 2,4-D and 2,4,5-T for forestry use with a maximum TCDD [dioxin] level of 0.1 parts per million. Registration for use in Canada for 2,4-D was in 1947 and 2,4,5-T in 1952. In both jurisdictions reviews are made periodically after reviews of the literature and independent study by highly trained and competent scientists. The evidence indicates this to be an ongoing process. In both countries registration for use is still in effect and neither jurisdiction has accepted that there are valid studies which could cause them to cancel the registration....

I do not mention regulatory agencies of other countries but there are some countries, notably Sweden, where 2,4,5-T is either restricted or prohibited. However, I have no evidence before me indicating that any such restriction or prohibition is the result of a scientific inquiry. All seem to be political decisions made for whatever reason. Even in the United States no such inquiry has been made and completed. Those decisions, therefore, are of no help to me....

To some extent this case takes on the nature of an appeal from the decision of the regulatory agency and any such approach through the courts ought to be discouraged in its infancy. Opponents to a particular chemical ought to direct their activities towards the regulatory agencies or, indeed, to government itself where broad areas of social policy are involved. It is not for the courts to become a regulatory agency of this type. It has neither the training nor the staff to perform this function. Suffice it to say that this decision will relate to, and be limited to, the dispute between these parties....

Having accepted Mr. Ross' testimony and accepting the evidence of Donald Freer and ex. D-70 that the defendant's supply of 2,4,5-T is formulated with a TCDD content of "non-detectable" at 0.01 parts per million, it is obvious that the amount of TCDD to be sprayed in Nova Scotia by the defendant is infinitesimally small.... It is, therefore, in the light of this concentration of TCDD that I must consider whether the plaintiffs have met the burden of proof....

A great deal of the evidence submitted related to animal studies where TCDD was reported to have caused various effects indicating it to be, among other things, foetotoxic, teratagenic, carcinogenic and to cause immunological deficiencies, enzymatic changes, liver problems and the like. Also it is alleged to bioaccumulate and be persistent both in soil and in tissue. I do not pretend to have included all of its effects, but those are the most major. I was asked to make findings of fact in all of these areas, but I decline to do so. Nothing would be added to the body of scientific fact by any such determination by this court. That TCDD has had all of these effects is undoubtedly true in the experiments described, but, in every case, the effect must be related to dose. In the animal studies the doses are extremely high and, in all cases, many, many thousands of times greater than any dose which could be received in Nova Scotia....

This brings me to the next suggestion by the plaintiffs which is that cancer, as a disease, has a long incubation period and the effects of dioxin cannot be known until time passes, approximately 40 years, so that it can be determined whether dioxin is indeed carcinogenic in humans. This again is not my function. I am to determine only if there is a probability of risk to health. To this point in time there is not sufficient acceptable evidence despite 35 years of use. One of the plaintiffs' witnesses, Dr. Daum, suggested that the only approach is to wait that period without permitting any further use. I cannot accept that. She is working from the premise

that any substance should be proved absolutely safe before use but, as commendable as that may be, it is not practical nor is it in conformity with currently accepted determinations for use of many substances. I doubt very much if any substance can be proved absolutely safe.

If all substances which are carcinogenic or otherwise toxic were removed from use, we would have no air to breathe or potable water and many common everyday products, necessary to our life, would be removed. The key to the use of all these is dosage. Where it can be determined that there is a safe dosage, according to acceptable scientific standards, then a substance can be used. Our regulatory agencies and scientists around the world are daily involved in this very area.

As well, virtually all chemicals are toxic, but hose in use generally are safe if used below the toxic levels, *i.e.*, if the dose received is below the safety levels. Scientists also determine a "no observable effect level." That is a level of intake of any particular substance where no effect is observed. It is, in most cases, far below the safe level, at least several orders of magnitude (each order being a multiple of 10) lower.

In these determinations effect on humans is assessed by extrapolation from animal studies. This is a well-known and widely accepted approach and some of the evidence here was based on this method.

I am satisfied that the overwhelming currently accepted view of responsible scientists is that there is little evidence that, for humans either 2,4-D or 2,4,5-T is mutagenic or carcinogenic and that TCDD is not an effective carcinogen, and further, that there are no-effect levels and safe levels for humans and wildlife for each of these substances....

Having reached this point it is appropriate to add that the evidence of risk assessments clearly indicates that any risk here in Nova Scotia, if, indeed, there is a risk at all, is infinitesimally small and many, many times less than one in a million which level, apparently, is regarded as a safe and acceptable risk by most of the world's regulatory agencies. Putting this in perspective, as indicated by Dr. Wilson in his evidence, the risk of cancer to a smoker is 1 in 800 and for a non-smoker continuously in the same room with smokers it is 1 in 100,000, while the risk to a person drinking two litres of water per day from a stream immediately after being sprayed (which will not happen with buffer zones) is 1 in 100,000 million or 100,000 times less than 1 in a million, which itself is regarded as a *de minimus* risk....

I am unable to accept that the plaintiffs have proved any strong probability or a sufficient degree of probability of risk to health to warrant the granting of the remedy sought, a *quia timet* injunction....

There is, accordingly, no nuisance, real or probable. As to trespass, none has been proved as probable to occur. Possibilities do not constitute proof. Similarly, there has been no basis established for the application of the rule in *Rylands v. Fletcher*, as neither the danger of the substance nor the likelihood of its escape to the plaintiffs' lands has been proved.

(d) Civil Litigation — Remedies[†]

Elizabeth J. Swanson and Elaine L. Hughes ——————————

NUISANCE

Remedies

There are three forms of relief usually granted in respect of a nuisance: injunctions, damages and abatement.[165] The first two are granted or awarded by the courts; abatement is an extra-judicial remedy employed by the affected individual as a form of "self-help."[166] The remedies are not necessarily exclusive; it is quite common in a nuisance action for the plaintiff to seek damages for past wrong doing and a prohibitory injunction to prevent future harm. In some circumstances damages may be awarded in lieu of an injunction if the court feels an injunction is not warranted.

Injunctions

It should be recalled that injunctions come in various shapes and sizes. A mandatory injunction requires some action to be taken; a prohibitory injunction forbids it. An injunction may be granted on an interim or interlocutory basis pending final resolution of the dispute at trial or may be permanent.[167] The courts have on occasion suspended the effect of an injunction to allow voluntary remediation by the defendant or have limited its operation to a certain time.[168]

Historically, an injunction was the only judicial remedy available for nuisance, and issued almost as of right once the plaintiff had proved

his claim.[169] Now, however, damages may be substituted in lieu of an injunction if (1) the injury to the plaintiff's legal rights is small; (2) and is one capable of being estimated in money; (3) and can be adequately compensated by a small money payment; and (4) the circumstances are such that it would be oppressive to the defendant to grant an injunction.[170] It is quite common in environmental litigation for the defendant to argue against an injunction on the basis that it would mean certain economic ruin (for the defendant, the entire community or both) or that the technology required to correct the nuisance does not yet exist. If the circumstances otherwise warrant the remedy, the courts have not generally received such arguments favourably.

In *Canada Paper Company v. Brown*,[171] for example, the Supreme Court Canada upheld a permanent injunction restraining the defendant pulp and paper mill from creating a nuisance through its operations. The nuisance consisted of odors and fumes which were so offensive that the plaintiff's neighbouring residence was, at times, rendered uninhabitable. The defendant argued that an injunction would have the effect of shutting down its business, which, in turn, would unquestionably result in economic ruin for the wider community. Mere personal inconvenience and discomfort (so the argument went) should not justify interference with indus-

† From *The Price of Pollution: Environmental Litigation in Canada*, ed. Elizabeth J. Swanson and Elaine L. Hughes (Edmonton, Alta.: the Environmental Law Centre (Alberta) Society, 1990), pp. 35–36, 52–53. Reproduced by permission of the publisher. See Appendix for notes or references.

try, particularly when damages might be awarded instead. These arguments were soundly rejected by the majority of the Supreme Court. Mr. Justice Idington was particularly outspoken. He said:[172]

> The invasion of rights incidental to the ownership of property, or the confiscation thereof, may suit the grasping tendencies of some and incidentally the needs or desires of the majority in any community benefiting thereby; yet such a basis or principle of action should be stoutly resisted by the courts ...
>
> And, I respectfully submit, that as long as we keep in view the essential merits of the remedy in the way of protecting the rights of property and preventing them from being invaded by mere autocratic assertions of what will be more conducive to the prosperity of the local community by disregarding such rights, we will not go far astray in taking as our guide the reasoning of any jurisprudence which recognizes the identical aim of protecting people in their rights of property when employing their remedy of perpetual injunction.

In the same case, Mr. Justice Duff was less certain of the irrelevance of the defendant's argument. He was "... far from accepting the contention" that the effects of an injunction upon the community at large should not be considered when granting an injunction.[173] Instead, he found the defendant's assertions of economic disaster to be unfounded. Cases decided both before and after *Canadian Paper Company* v. *Brown* indicate some judicial sympathy to the sentiments expressed by Mr. Justice Duff.[174] In *Huston* v. *Lloyd Refineries Ltd.*, a 1937 decision of the High Court of [Ontario], Mr. Justice Greene refused to grant an absolute injunction against the defendant refinery because to do so "would destroy an investment of half a million dollars where adequate relief might be granted by awarding damages."[175] On the basis of these decisions it would appear that economic hardship remains an argument available to a defendant to defeat a request for an injunction. However, the argument is likely to succeed only if the court is convinced that the hardship is real and substantial and damages will provide adequate compensation for the injured plaintiff.

. . . .

RIPARIAN RIGHTS

. . . .

Remedies

Infringement of riparian rights, like trespass is actionable *per se*; that is, the plaintiff is entitled to compensation or other relief without having to prove actual loss or injury.[263]

In the absence of actual harm or loss, the usual practice is to award nominal damages either as the only relief or together with an injunction. In 1912 for example, a riparian received one dollar in damages and an injunction to prevent pollution anticipated from the construction of drainage works.[264] If the plaintiff has actually incurred loss or suffered harm, however, damages may be substantial.[265]

Whether in anticipation of or in response to a violation of riparian rights, the courts do not seem reluctant to issue injunctions to restrain the offending behavior. As noted by Mr. Justice Kerwin for the Supreme Court of Canada in *McKie*: "The rights of riparian owners have always been zealously guarded by the Court"[266] and neither the economic hardship resulting to the defendant, nor the beneficial or charitable purpose of the offending conduct will prevent the granting of an injunction to which a plaintiff is otherwise entitled.[267]

In the case of *Gauthier* v. *Naneff*, for example, a riparian owner (with others) sought an injunction to prevent the holding of a speedboat regatta planned by a local rotary club to raise money for charitable purposes. The basis for concern was that the discharge of gas and motor oils from the boats in question would foul the waters of the lake upon which the regatta was to take place. Notwithstanding the [advanced] stage of preparations nor the money expended by the club in organizing the event, an injunction was issued together with these comments:[268]

> It is unfortunate that in the circumstances of this case, the rights of a riparian land proprietor come into conflict with the laudable objects of a charitable pursuit formulated and prosecuted with sincerity and dedication by the defendants Naneff and company on behalf of their club and endorsed and supported by the other defendants. Nonetheless, the most honourable of intentions alone at no time can justify the expropriation of common law rights of riparian owners.

It is this concern, that of depriving an individual of private rights without compensation, which argues against the substitution of damages for injunctions, particularly when the offending behaviour is of a continuing nature. Nonetheless the award of "once and for all" damages to a riparian might provide a solution of sorts to a court faced with pollution or water shortages resulting from licensed use. By providing compensation for prospective losses likely to result should the licensed behaviour continue, the courts might avoid the undesirable result of expropriation without interfering with rights of the defendant acquired under legislation.

Constitutional and Statutory Framework

(a) The Institutional Contexts[†]

Melody Hessing and Michael Howlett ——————————————

THE CANADIAN INSTITUTIONAL STRUCTURE

The analysis of Canadian resource and environmental policy-making, must take into account not only historical changes but the institutional order that establishes the basic political structure within which governments in Canada operate.[26] This order, broadly defined, is composed of two legal regimes. The first is the constitutional order in Canada itself. As will be discussed below, the fact that Canada is a democratic, parliamentary, and, above all, federal country has a significant impact on determining how governments act in response to any set of their own or public concerns. The basic constitutional order determines which government is responsible for which area of legislative activity and, within governments, which branch or level of government is able to make authoritative and binding decisions. The second regime is the set of international treaties, organizations, and rules that sovereign states have agreed should set the broad parameters within which domestic governments will operate. These *international regimes* exists in virtually every area of government activity and can have a significant impact by limiting or otherwise con-

straining the policy choices available to governments.[27] This is as true of the natural resource and environmental sector as it is of many other areas of state activity.[28]

THE CONSTITUTIONAL STRUCTURE OF CANADIAN GOVERNMENT

Canadian governments make public policy. However, it is the Canadian constitution that determines exactly which actors are entitled to make policies and decisions for the Canadian state. Like the international order, the constitutional structure of a country is an important component of the institutional context of policy-making.

The Canadian constitution creates a democratic parliamentary system similar to that found in Great Britain. This 'Westminster' model of parliamentary democracy has several characteristics that affect how policies are made.[29] The most significant characteristic relates to the strength of the executive in such systems. Unlike in many countries, notably the United States (where the powers of the executive are offset by powerful legislatures), in Canada the Westminster-style governments — the legislature and the

---

† Reproduced with permission of the publisher. From *Canadian Natural Resource and Environmental Policy: Political Economy and Public Policy* by Melody Hessing and Michael Howlett, pp. 52–62. © University of British Columbia Press, 1997. All rights reserved by the publisher. See Appendix for notes or references.

executive — are merged in a single body: Parliament. This fusion, all other things being equal, gives the executive much latitude in ensuring that its wishes become law.[30] In this regard, Canada has a strong form of executive government in which major decisions are made by political leaders and administrative officials and debated or publicized in legislative bodies.

Not all the aspects of Canada's parliamentary style of government are identical to those found in the United Kingdom. The most significant difference is that Canada has two distinct levels or orders of government, rather than one. While the United Kingdom is a 'unitary' or centralized state, Canada is a *federal* system. That is, it has two levels of government — the federal and the provincial — that are sovereign within their established jurisdictions.[31] This division of powers is significant for policy purposes because it determines which government will actually be entitled to make policy decisions in a particular area. Resource and environmental policy has been a significant locus of federal-provincial struggle, an arena in which power between levels of government may be contested. To a great extent, as is discussed below, the question of the division of powers regarding Canadian environmental policy flows from that relating to resources.[32]

The Division of Powers over Natural Resources and the Environment before 1982

Prior to 1982, the division of federal and provincial powers over natural resources and the environment was determined by colonial practices, the enactment of the British North America Act (1867), and subsequent judicial and parliamentary activities.[33]

The constitutional arrangements for the distribution of federal and provincial authority over natural resources at the time of Confederation established the framework within which policies aimed at environmental protection have since been created. At the time, the environment was not perceived as a coherent subject for the legislators' attention.[34]

At Confederation, the British North America (BNA) Act followed British colonial practice — itself with a history extending back to the Norman conquest — of according jurisdiction over natural resources to the level of government that controlled the territory in which they were located. Hence, Section 109 of the BNA Act awarded ownership of land and resources to the provincial governments, while Section 92(5) and 92(13) awarded provincial governments the exclusive right to legislate concerning the management and sale of public lands and resources and, more generally, 'property' within the province, including privately owned land and resources.[35]

The only significant exception to this rule concerned the fisheries, which, under Section 91(12), fell into exclusive federal jurisdiction. This exception, of course, befitted the nature of the ocean and anadromous fisheries, which transcended provincial boundaries and prevented the provinces from delimiting property relations. This was also in keeping with a second tenet of the BNA Act, which was to place interprovincial matters within federal jurisdiction — as occurred, for example, with interprovincial ferries and other forms of interprovincial transportation and communication. The fact that fisheries installations were private property and that some inland fisheries did not cross provincial boundaries, however, was not lost on the provinces, which quickly engaged the courts in upholding their rights in these areas. This resulted in the attenuation of the 'exclusive' federal power and the emergence of a complex jurisdictional situation in this area. At present, some activities (ocean fisheries) are exclusively federal, some are exclusively provincial (aquaculture), and some are joint (recreational fisheries).[36]

The terms of Confederation also gave the federal government the right to control resources on its lands. Although these lands were minor at the time of Confederation and restricted to Indian reserves, military installations, and the like, in 1869 they were greatly expanded by the purchase of Hudson's Bay Company lands by the federal government. British Columbia, Prince Edward Island, and Newfoundland entered Confederation on much the same terms as the original provinces of Nova Scotia, New Brunswick, Quebec, and Ontario and consequently owned and controlled their resources. However, this was not the case with the three provinces carved out of the federally owned Northwest Territories. Manitoba, Saskatchewan, and Alberta did not receive jurisdiction over their land and resources until this power was conveyed to them by the federal government in 1930.[37] The federal government still retains jurisdiction over the land and resources of the remaining Yukon and Northwest Territories, although it has begun to transfer some responsibilities in these areas to the two territorial governments in recent years. This pattern is likely to continue in 1999 when the new territory of Nunavut is carved out of the existing Northwest Territories.

In addition, the federal government, citing international treaty obligations in the area of nuclear materials, invoked its little-used 'declaratory power' (Section 92[10c]) in 1945 to assume full responsibility for the control of uranium production and the nuclear industry.[38] The federal government was also the beneficiary of a 1967 Supreme Court of Canada decision that awarded the offshore regions to it and not to the provinces. As part of the 'Canada Lands,' resources located offshore — such as oil and gas but also including some significant mineral deposits — are the sole responsibility of the federal government.[39]

Exclusive federal powers in the areas of trade and commerce and wide-ranging powers in the area of taxation have also limited provincial constitutional supremacy in many resource matters.[40] Control over the natural resource industry has often been debated as a question of the provincial right of ownership versus the federal right to regulate trade and commerce, a right contained in Section 91(2) of the Constitution Act (1867). This has been the case because of the high percentage of Canadian natural resources destined for interprovincial or international markets. These resources elude provincial property-based jurisdiction and enter into the federal domain as soon as they cross provincial boundaries.[41]

In the area of taxation, the provincial governments have also had to defer to the more extensive right under Section 109 to levy royalties on resources in their territories, these royalties relate only to the extraction stage of the process can be appropriated process. Revenues arising at later stages of the process can be appropriated by both levels of government. At this point, however, provincial governments were restricted under Section 92(2) to levying 'direct' taxes (that is, taxes paid directly to the government by the taxpayer), while the federal government's powers under Section 91(3) are unlimited.[42]

The result of this tangled constitutional situation prior to 1982 was for both levels of government to respect a slowly developed and court-regulated natural resource *modus vivendi* in which the hallmark of Canadian natural resource

decision-making was provincially led intergovernmental collaboration.[43] This occurred first in bilateral dealings with the federal government and, since World War II, in multilateral forums such as the Canadian Council of Resource and Environmental Ministers (CCREM) and the Canadian Council of Forest Ministers (CCFM).[44]

The Division of Powers over Natural Resources and the Environment after 1982

In 1982, a major round of constitutional negotiations climaxed in the patriation of the BNA Act and the creation of the Constitution Act. The only change to the division of powers between the federal and provincial governments invoked at the time affected natural resources. This was the establishment of Section 92a of the Constitution Act, 1982.

The six clauses of Section 92a address all the main issues of Canadian natural resource constitutional politics since Confederation: federal/provincial jurisdiction and ownership, control over extraprovincial trade and commerce, and the division of taxation authority. First, Section 92a(1) provides an exclusive provincial right to legislate in the areas of non-renewable natural resource exploration, development, conservation, and management, including the generation of electrical energy. Section 92a(5) defines natural resources as those described in the Sixth Schedule to the Act, while Section 92a(6) assures that the new language will not be interpreted in such a manner as to restrict preexisting provincial legislative rights. Second, Section 92a(2) provides for an extension of provincial legislative jurisdiction to include interprovincial exports, subject to the caveat that 'such laws may not authorize or provide for discrimination in prices or in supplies exported to another part of Canada.' Provincial legislative authority is further limited by the establishment of federal paramountcy in Section 92a(3).[45] Third, Section 92a(4) establishes a provincial right to tax non-renewable natural resources, and electrical energy and facilities, by any mode of taxation whether or not these goods are exported from the province, but subject to the caveat that 'such laws may not authorize or provide for taxation that differentiates between production exported to another part of Canada and production not exported from the province.'[46]

The provisions of Section 92a reaffirm previous provincial powers, allow provinces to levy indirect taxation on natural resource revenues, and provide provincial legislatures with control over interprovincial resource and energy exports, subject to several non-discriminatory caveats and federal paramountcy.[47] In terms of resource regulation, the caveats contained in Section 92a(2) provide that a province may discriminate between products destined for intraprovincial markets and those destined for interprovincial trade, but the caveats insist that each province treat all extraprovincial Canadian markets equally. In terms of resource taxation, the caveats contained in Section 92a(4) prohibit discrimination between intraprovincial and interprovincial exports.

The most significant difference between the two sections, however, concerns provincial control over international exports. Provincial regulatory control over natural resource trade is explicitly limited by Section 92a(2) to that concerning the 'export from the province to another part of Canada.' The regulation of international trade hence remains an area of exclusive federal jurisdiction. Provincial taxation requirements, however, are not limited to those affecting exports to domestic markets. Instead, Section 92a(4) refers more generally to 'whether or not such production is exported in whole or in part from the province.'

Thus, Section 92a represents, in the convoluted fashion typical of Canadian constitutional debate, a significant rearrangement of the pre-1982 federal-provincial *modus vivendi*. It not only reaffirms provincial control over many important aspects of natural resource management but also, subject to several caveats protecting the national interest, gives the provincial governments additional powers in the areas of interprovincial regulation and resource taxation, which had previously formed part of the established federal jurisdiction.[48]

Subsequent rounds of constitutional talks in Canada have, of course, failed to alter the constitutional status quo. While discussions have focused on the possibility of the increased devolution of responsibility for the environment to the provincial level, this has not occurred.[49] Some aspects of federal powers have been undermined by court decisions, especially the effort by the federal government to impose its authority on the provinces in the area of water pollution under the purview of the Fisheries

Act.[50] Other aspects of federal powers, however, including the ability to authorize environmental assessments in areas of provincial jurisdiction, have been strengthened.[51]

This situation has led to a patchwork response to environmental concerns by both levels of government in Canada.[52] Different aspects of environmental problems are dealt with by different levels of government in accordance with resource ownership and jurisdiction as initially laid out in 1867 and modified in 1982. While the federal government is able to deal with some problems that have a national scope, the most effective problem-solving is often accomplished through intergovernmental agreement rather than legislative dictates.[53]

Aboriginal Jurisdiction
Another significant element of the post-1982 Canadian constitutional situation relates to aboriginal right to, and jurisdiction over, lands and resources.[54] Although the claims and rights of First Nations in Canada date back to the initial contacts with European colonizers and subsequent seventeenth, eighteenth, and nineteenth century treaties and administrative arrangements,[55] they began to receive explicit constitutional status binding the actions of Canadian governments only after 1982.[56]

Paralleling developments in Alaska and elsewhere,[57] in the 1960s Native groups began to challenge the restricted interpretations of Native rights contained in Canadian jurisprudence. These groups engaged in numerous activities — such as demonstrations, court challenges, and media campaigns — aimed at changing the political and administrative status quo.[58] A persistent lobbying effort in the following decade contributed to an improved climate for, and visibility of, Native concerns. In the early 1970s, Canada's aboriginal organizations managed to secure a place at the constitutional negotiating table as the federal government grappled with an unrelated crisis provoked by threats of Quebec's secession.

Although they were eventually left out of the eleventh-hour bargaining that resulted in the 1982 Canada Act and amendments to the Canadian constitution, Natives did secure several provisions in the new document entrenching existing treaties. They also secured a promise that the next round of constitutional discussions would focus entirely on their aspirations, which had come to be recognized as instances of collective identity and rights similar to those of Quebec.[59] While the promised aboriginal round ended in failure in 1987, it did serve to place Native demands for self-government high on political, public, and constitutional agendas.[60]

While First Nations may have failed at the constitutional negotiating table, they did manage of effectively use the courts to expand their control over many areas of life, including lands and resources. Beginning with the *Calder* decision in 1973, legal challenges by aboriginal organizations began to produce results as the Supreme Court of Canada affirmed the continued existence of aboriginal title even in areas in which that title had often been considered extinguished.[61] At about the same time, other courts began to grant injunctions against various projects stated for construction on lands subject to claims disputes, notably in the case of the massive James Bay hydroelectric project in northwestern Quebec.[62]

These actions ultimately resulted in the establishment of a new land claims policy by the federal government and the successful negotiation of six claims covering most of northern Canada and Quebec between 1974 and 1995, as well as the beginnings of negotiations over additional claims covering British Columbia, Labrador, and the remaining areas of the Northwest Territories.[63] The successfully negotiated 'modern treaties' include two land claims in Quebec, three in the Northwest Territories, one in the Yukon, and a self-government arrangement in British Columbia.[64] Native claims, of course, have included not only these 'comprehensive claims' but also those covering Métis lands and smaller or 'specific claims' arising out of disputes over the implementation of existing treaties.[65]

By the late 1980s and early 1990s, court decisions clarifying the 1982 constitutional changes had come down in favour of a broad interpretation of aboriginal rights in many areas, especially rights to the fishery.[66] However, due to recurrent constitutional setbacks, the proposals made by First Nations for additional rights to self-government have not yet been successfully institutionalized. Discussions clarifying the nature of aboriginal self-government, rights, and title continue,[67] however, they have only resulted in some tentative steps toward implementation, and even these efforts came to a halt with the failure of the Canadian public to endorse the self-government provisions of the Charlottetown Accord on the Constitution in October 1992.[68]

The current situation concerning aboriginal land and resource jurisdiction is thus complex. In areas covered by treaties, First Nations control a variety of aspects of resource management, depending on the nature of the treaty involved. With treaties signed prior to the 1970s, Native peoples usually have complete control over land and resources on Indian reserves established by the federal government, although they are unable to alienate these lands except through an extremely cumbersome political-administrative process. Some bands, such as those located in parts of southern Alberta with substantial oil and gas reserves, do very well from the sale of resource rights — although, again, control over the expenditure of funds remains governed by complex arrangements between local bands and federal "Indian' administrators.

Most reserves, however, are small and contain few resources; in most cases having been established in the nineteenth century with the potential for future Native agricultural pursuits in mind. One of the few resources accessible to bands on many reserves is the fishery, and a protracted court battle is under way in this area. To date, it has provided Native bands with a greater role in catches and fishery management, subject to government conservation measures and the need to establish, on a case-by-case basis, the existence of an aboriginal right to a commercial — as opposed to a food — fishery.[69]

For treaties signed after 1970, the situation is very different. Many of these treaties cover vast areas of land (especially in the Yukon and Northwest Territories) and are extremely dense and complex. Following loosely the precedents set by Native land settlements in Alaska, these agreements contain provisions concerning educational, political, social, and cultural life, as well as those relating to the economy and environment of the area covered by the treaty.[70]

Although each agreement is unique, the general tendency has been for the First Nations involved in each land claim to receive a small area of land for which they have all surface and subsurface rights. They have also received larger areas over which they may exercise only various specified surface and subsurface rights. Because most of these agreements have covered areas in Canada's far north, forestry issues have not received a great deal of attention (although this situation is bound to change as agreements are signed in British Columbia), and the most attention has been paid to mineral, oil, and gas rights and, especially, to hunting and trapping rights. In Quebec, issues related to hydroelectric generation have also been key.[71]

For the most part, First Nations have traded control over minerals, oil, gas, and hydroelectricity for financial compensation, recognition of aboriginal title, and protection of hunting and trapping rights.[72] Nevertheless, the manner in which hunting and trapping rights intersect with provisions governing resource project approvals — especially entrenched treaty rights related to habitat and environmental protection — has given aboriginal groups a major voice in many resource policy areas. Thus, Native groups may not actually control a mineral resource, for example, but they may control access to the resource across lands dedicated to hunting and trapping.[73]

Thus, although aboriginal jurisdiction remains a dynamic, evolving entity, in certain areas of the country covered by modern treaties, aboriginal groups play a major role in resource development and environmental protection. Traditional aboriginal pursuits such as hunting, trapping, and fishing have been defined by the courts or old treaties as Native rights. In these areas, First Nations can also play a major role regardless of the part of the country in which these pursuits are undertaken. Both federal and provincial governments in recent years have begun to take aboriginal concerns much more seriously than in the past and in these areas aboriginal rights and title act as significant constraints on government actions.[74] As we will see in Chapter 7, however, the extent of Native participation in areas not explicitly covered by land claims or aboriginal rights remains very limited.

SIGNIFICANT FEDERAL AND PROVINCIAL ENVIRONMENTAL LEGISLATION

While most resource and environmental laws and regulations are implemented under provincial authority, there are several federal acts currently of particular significance to environmental protection. As we have seen, federal regulatory activity is constitutionally 'limited to international and interprovincial contamination, federal lands and developments and controlling the import, manufacture, use and ultimate disposal of toxic substances.'[75] Federal legislation most signification in dealing with environmental issues includes the Canadian Environmental Pro-

tection Act (CEPA), the Canadian Environmental Assessment Act (CEAA), the Fisheries Act, the Canada Shipping Act, and the Transportation of Dangerous Goods Act.

The CEAA, passed in 1992, provides for the planning, monitoring, and evaluation of projects that have an environmental impact. The CEPA was proclaimed in 1988, and it governs activities under federal jurisdiction such as international or cross-border air pollution (e.g., acid rain), the dumping of substances into oceans and navigable waterways, and the regulation of toxic substances. The Fisheries Act pertains to fish habitat and its harmful alternation or destruction. This statute has been especially relevant to concerns with pulp mill and other water pollution. Other federal statutes that are sometimes relevant to environmental matters are included in Figure 3.1.

The Department of the Environment (DOE) has been the federal agency primarily responsible for environmental matters. It has administered elements of a number of statutes, including those derived from federal powers over fisheries, such as the Fisheries Act and the Fish Inspection Act, both used extensively to control water pollution, as well as newer statutes such as the Canada Water Act, the Clean Air Act, and the Environmental Contaminants Act.[76] Other federal departments also administer statutes for environmental protection, primarily to regulate federally owned or administered lands or activities. The Department of Indian and Northern Affairs, for example, has administered the National Parks Act, while the Department of Transport has administered several statutes, including the Canada Shipping Act, the Railways Act, the Aeronautics Act, and the Navigable Waters Protection Act. The Department of Energy, Mines and Resources has been responsible for the independent Atomic Energy Control Board, which operates the Atomic Energy Control Act.[77]

While the establishment of Environment Canada anticipated its direct involvement in regulatory activity, the administration of regulatory standards set forth in federal legislation is, for the most part, in the constitutional domain of the provinces. Federal activity is geared to the establishment of policies and guidelines for provincial regulatory standards, the coordination of provincial activities, and scientific research.[78] Many different instruments are utilized to carry out these functions.

Various provincial and territorial statutes also deal with environmental protection, either

Figure 3.1 Significant federal environmental legislation

Name of act	Governs (if unspecified)
Canadian Environmental Protection Act	International air pollution Ocean and waterways Dumping Toxic substances
Canadian Environmental Assessment Act	
Fisheries Act	Protection of fish habitat
Canada Shipping Act	Shipping, fuel, ballast, cargo, pollution
Canada Water Act	
Transportation of Dangerous Goods Act	
Arctic Waters Pollution Prevention Act	
Navigable Waters Protection Act	
Migratory Birds Convention Act	
Atomic Energy Control Act	
Hazardous Products Act	
Pest Control Products Act	

Sources: Statistics Canada, *Human Activity and the Environment*, Catalogue 11-509E (Ottawa: Ministry of Industry, Science and Technology 1991), 34–5.

Figure 3.2 Significant provincial statutes governing environmental protection

Jurisdiction	Act
Newfoundland	Department of Environment Act
Nova Scotia	Environmental Protection Act Water Act Dangerous Goods Transportation Act Beverage Containers Act
Prince Edward Island	Environmental Protection Act
New Brunswick	Clean Environment Act
Quebec	Environment Quality Act
Ontario	Environment Protection Act Ontario Water Resources Act
Manitoba	Environment Act
Saskatchewan	Environmental Management and Protection Act
Alberta	Clean Air Act Clean Water Act Environmental Protection and Enhancement Act
British Columbia	Waste Management Act Environment Management Act Health Act Pesticide Control Act Litter Act
Yukon and Northwest Territories	Area Development Act, Northern Inland Waters Act

Source: Roger Cotton and Kelley M. MacKinnon, 'An Overview of Environmental Law in Canada,' in G. Thompson, M.L. McConnell, and L.B. Huestis, eds., *Environmental Law and Business in Canada* (Aurora, ON: Canada Law Book 1993), 8–11.

directly or indirectly. This legislation has primarily focused on 'the environmental effects incidental to manufacturing, natural resource and economic development projects, and contamination of land within the province.'[79] Differences in statutory provision for environmental protection are reflected in Figure 3.2, which identifies the most significant statutes in the provinces.

(b)   Federalism, Environmental Protection, and Blame Avoidance[†]

Kathryn Harrison ──────────────────────────────

The renewed salience of environmental issues in recent years has given rise to environmental policy initiatives by both the federal and provincial governments and, not coincidentally, to increased intergovernmental conflict. Federal-provincial disputes have emerged over the Québec government's James Bay hydro development, the Al-Pac pulp mill and the Oldman River Dam in Alberta, and the Rafferty-Alameda Dam in Saskatchewan, to name but a few. As a result, questions concerning to the appropriate balance of federal and provincial roles in environmental policy have assumed increasing prominence. This chapter examines how the current division of federal and provincial responsibilities for environmental protection evolved during the 1970s and 1980s, and speculates about future directions.

In light of recent conflicts concerning the environment, it is striking that there were remarkably few intergovernmental disputes over environmental matters until recently. As late as 1989, scholarly publications praised the cooperative atmosphere of federal-provincial relations in the environmental field (Dwivedi and Woodrow, 1989). The degree of intergovernmental cooperation with respects to environmental protection during the 1970s and early 1980s was particularly noteworthy in contrast to the often hostile climate of federal-provincial relations in other fields, including energy policy and constitutional reform, during the same period.

What happened in recent years to disrupt that climate of intergovernmental harmony? It is argued here that the low level of intergovernmental conflict from the early 1970s to the late 1980s reflected the fact that the federal government did not challenge provincial dominance in the environmental and natural resources field. Prior to the late 1980s, the federal government played a largely supportive role of conducting research, offering technical expertise, regulating

mobile source emissions, and gently encouraging the provinces to adopt consistent national standards (Thompson, 1980). In contrast, provincial governments assumed the role of front-line protectors of the environment — setting standards for environmental and effluent quality, issuing permits for individual sources, and enforcing both provincial and federal standards.

This chapter argues that the balance of federal and provincial roles and the tenor of federal-provincial relations in the environmental field have evolved in response to trends in public opinion concerning the environment. Federal (and provincial) jurisdictional assertiveness in recent years can be attributed to electoral incentives to claim credit from the public during a period of heightened attention to environmental issues. In contrast, previous federal deference can be seen as an effort to avoid blame from industries resistant to environmental regulation during a period of public inattentiveness. Provincial jurisdictional sensitivities are attributed to efforts to maintain control of natural resources and thus cater to those same interest groups.

EXPLAINING INTERGOVERNMENTAL CONFLICT AND COOPERATION

Two explanations for the historically weak federal role in the environmental field traditionally have been offered: constitutional constraints and provincial resistance. Many authors have suggested that the federal government has played a limited role because it is constrained by limited constitutional authority (Dwivedi, 1974: 180; Lundqvist, 1974: 135; Alhéritière, 1972: 571; Webb, 1983: 1–4). As discussed below, there is little disagreement that the provinces have strong claims to jurisdiction over the natural resources within their borders. In contrast, federal jurisdiction over the environment is both indirect and uncertain. The

[†] From François Rocher annd Miriam Smith, eds., *New Trends in Canadian Federalism* (Peterborough, ON: Broadview Press, 1995), pp. 414–17, 420–429, 431–432. Reproduced by permission of the publisher. See Appendix for notes or references.

problem with the constitutional constraint argument, however, is that uncertain authority has not always stopped the federal government before. Why would the federal government display such self-restraint with respect to the environment, when it did not do so with respect to health care, post-secondary education, or oil-pricing?

Legal scholars have been more inclined to argue that the federal government has taken a limited view of its own environmental powers (Saunders, 1988: 28–29; Percy, 1984: 86; Muldoon and Valiante, 1988: 26; Tingley, 1991: 132). For instance, Franson and Lucas have suggested that "the excuse of constitutional difficulties [has been] used as a smokescreen" by the federal government (Franson and Lucas, 1977: 25). Legal scholars generally attribute federal timidity to an unwillingness to confront the provinces, which tend to be highly protective of their jurisdiction over natural resources (Lucas, 1986: 39; Thompson, 1980: 22; Saunders, 1988: 21; Muldoon and Valiante, 1988, 27; Rabe, 1989: 262). Again, however, it is noteworthy that the federal government has not been so reluctant to provoke the provinces in other fields. For instance, when an opportunity arose to tax windfall profits from the oil industry in the late 1970s, the federal government did not hesitate to challenge provincial authority with respect to natural resources. One is left to wonder why provincial resistance in the environmental field was so successful during the same period.

These two explanations also fail to account for the disruption of cooperative federal-provincial relations in the environmental field that occurred in the late 1980s. Clearly, there was no change in the constitution to account for increasing federal jurisdictional assertiveness.[1] Nor is there evidence that the provinces let down their guard concerning natural resources. The one factor that has received too little attention to date in the literature on federalism and environmental policy is public opinion concerning the environment. While not denying the existence of either constitutional uncertainty or provincial resistance, this chapter argues that an explanation for federal and provincial roles in environmental protection is not complete without considering governments' electoral incentives to extend or defend their jurisdiction over the environment in the first place.

Two kinds of questions in public opinion polls offer insights concerning public attitudes toward the environment. First, the degree of public concern is indicated by close-ended questions, such as those asking respondents to rank the severity of environmental problems. Second, the salience of environmental issues is revealed by open-ended questions asking respondents to identify the "most important problem" facing the country today. Although the two measures have tended to move together over the last two decades, trends in the salience of environmental issues have been much more pronounced, suggesting that although there may be a high level of latent public concern for the environment, environmental issues are not always top of mind for most people.

Since the late 1960s, there have been two cycles of public attention to the environment. Environmental concerns rose to prominence for the first time in the late 1960s, coinciding with the first Earth Day (Parlour and Schatzow, 1978). However, public concern for the environment subsequently declined nationally from the early 1970s to the mid-1980s.[2] Thereafter, the trend began to reverse, concluding with a surge in environmental concern in the late 1980s and culminating in the second Earth Day (Bakvis and Nevitte, 1992). The prominence of environmental issues again subsided with the onset of a recession in the early 1990s.[3]

When environmental concerns are prominent on the public agenda, as was the case in the late 1960s and late 1980s, federal and provincial governments alike face strong incentives to claim credit from voters by responding to public demand with environmental issues is low, as was the case in the period between the first and second green waves, the diffuse benefits and concentrated costs associated with environmental protection present important obstacles to government action (Wilson, 1975; Weaver, 1986). Because each member of the general public who benefits from improvements in environmental quality has a relatively small stake in the outcome, people tend to be inattentive to governments' particular environmental policies. In contrast, industries that stand to bear the costs of environmental regulations remain not only attentive but adamantly resistant. Environmental regulation holds the promise of making more enemies than friends, and a government motivated to avoid electoral blame would be expected to take a more restrictive view of its jurisdiction. Thus, the absence of electoral incentives, rather than constitutional constraints or provincial opposition *per se*, may explain why the federal government did not pursue a large role in environmental protection throughout the 1970s and early 1980s (Harrison, 1993).

Why, then, have provincial governments been so eager to defend their environmental jurisdiction, even during periods of low salience? A crucial difference between the federal and provincial perspectives is that the provinces are the owners of Crown resources within their borders. Although both orders of government would be expected to respond preferentially to the concentrated interests of resource development industries rather than the diffuse interests of the beneficiaries of resource conservation during periods of public inattentiveness, in the province's case, their ability to do so is inextricably tied to their authority to control the terms of resource exploitation. Thus, the provinces would be expected to defend their jurisdiction over natural resources even during periods of low salience, though not so much to protect them as to manage their exploitation.

Since pollution was not a prominent issue in 1867, it is not surprising that responsibility for environmental protection was not explicitly allocated to either the federal or provincial legislatures by the BNA Act. In light of this omission, both federal and provincial authority with respect to environmental protection is derivative of other fields of jurisdiction explicitly mentioned in the constitution. Since almost every aspect of human endeavour has some environmental impact, "The powers that may be used to combat environmental degradation are liberally sprinkled through the heads of power given to each level of government" (Franson and Lucas, 1976: 251). The result is a substantial degree of overlap between federal and provincial powers.

Sources of Provincial Authority

Provincial governments have extensive authority to protect the environment in their capacity both as owners of public property and as legislators. With respect to the former, the constitution confers on the provinces ownership of public lands within their borders. As noted by Thompson and Eddy, that "ownership confers a form of jurisdiction over resources that is scarcely less far-reaching than legislative jurisdiction" (1973: 76). In particular, the provinces have extensive proprietary authority to conserve and protect their natural resources within their borders (Gibson, 1973).

The provinces also have important sources of legislative authority over natural resources, the most significant being that concerning "property and civil rights." The combination of proprietary powers and legislative jurisdiction over property and civil rights gives the provinces authority to legislate with respect to both publicly and privately owned resources within the province. However, an important limitation of provincial jurisdiction is that a province cannot control sources of environmental contaminants beyond its borders that affect the quality of the environment within the province (*Interprovincial Cooperatives*, 1975).

Sources of Federal Authority

The constitutional position of the federal government with respect to the environment is less clear. Like the provinces, the federal government has extensive authority with respect to its own property. Federal ownership is extensive offshore and in the northern territories, but much less significant within the provinces. As a result, federal proprietary powers cannot support comprehensive federal policies to protect the environment within provincial borders.

Indirect federal authority to protect the environment is associated with a number of specific subject areas, such as fisheries, navigation, and agriculture. Environmental jurisdiction associated with those powers is circumscribed, however, because federal actions taken under them must relate to the particular constitutional subject. In that respect, the federal power over fisheries is of greatest interest, since the fact that most water pollutants are harmful to fish gives the federal government considerable latitude to control water pollution using its fisheries power (Lucas, 1982).

Federal powers that have the potential to support a more comprehensive role in environmental protection include trade and commerce, criminal law, and "peace, order, and good government." Although the limits of each are unclear, the extent of federal authority concerning the environment under the residual power to make laws for the peace, order, and good government of Canada is particularly controversial. Most critics agree that some federal role is justified to address discrete interjurisdictional spillovers (LaForest, 1972). However, proponents of greater federal involvement argue that the environment is a subject that is inherently interjurisdictional and thus within federal jurisdiction (Gibson, 1969; Emond, 1972). Others oppose such expansive interpretations of federal powers by arguing that environmental protection is not a coherent subject in the constitutional sense, and that assignment of a matter so pervasive to one level of government or the order would have profound implications for the Canadian federal system (Landis, 1970; Tremblay, 1973; Beaudoin, 1977; Lederman, 1975).

Judicial Review

There are surprisingly few indications of how the courts will interpret federal powers concerning the environment. However, two recent decisions by the Supreme Court offer considerable support for federal jurisdiction over environmental matters.

In the 1988 *Crown Zellerbach* decision, a majority of the Court accepted marine pollution as a valid subject under "peace, order, and good government" with surprisingly little discussion and apparently few reservations (Saunders, 1988: 19). While the dissenting opinion argued that allocating matters of environment protection exclusively to the federal government "would effectively gut provincial legislative jurisdiction," the minority nonetheless clearly envisioned extensive federal jurisdiction with respect to the environment (*R. v. Crown Zellerbach*, 1988: 53). Following this decision, one prominent legal scholar observed that "Large chunks of the broad 'environment' subject now appear to be fair game for federal legislators" (Lucas, 1989: 183).

Perhaps the most significant constitutional case to date was the 1992 Supreme Court decision concerning the Oldman River Dam. In unanimously upholding the constitutionality of a federal environmental assessment regulation, the Court embraced a broad interpretation of federal authority concerning the environment. The decision was not, however, unanimous on questions of administrative law. While the Court maintained the traditional requirement that federal legislation must relate to a particular constitutional head of power, it nonetheless condoned federal reliance on narrow heads of power, such as navigation, as an indirect means to promote environmental protection (*Friends of the Oldman River Society*, 1992: 45). The Court also noted in passing that "In any event, [the federal regulation at issue] falls within the purely residuary

aspect of the Peace, Order and good Government' power" (*ibid.*: 49).

The federal government clearly faces two limitations concerning its jurisdiction over the environment. First, many federal powers with respect to the environment are indirect. A second and arguably more important constraint on federal powers is uncertainty. The courts might find comprehensive federal jurisdiction within the criminal law, trade and commerce, and peace, order, and good government powers, but the limits of federal authority remain unclear twenty years after the passage of the first generation of contemporary environmental statutes. The courts cannot be blamed for this persistent uncertainty; they have had few opportunities to clarify federal environmental jurisdiction. The persistent jurisdictional uncertainty reflects the fact that the federal government has taken a limited view of its own powers, and thus has not provoked many constitutional tests.

THE FIRST GREEN WAVE

Public consciousness of pollution problems in the Western Hemisphere grew throughout the 1960s, prompted by a series of high-profile events, including discovery of the impact of DDT on wildlife and oil spills of the coasts of England and Santa Barbara, California. By 1970, Canadians were confronted by environmental problems closer to home, when the tanker *Arrow* ran aground in Chedabucto Bay off Nova Scotia and when mercury contamination of waterways prompted extensive fishing bans. As public interest in pollution grew in the late 1960s, federal and provincial politicians also turned their attention to environmental protection.

This first green wave witnessed a dramatic change in federal politicians' attitudes toward their environmental jurisdiction. Prior to the late 1960s, federal cabinet ministers resisted occasional calls from the opposition for a federal response to pollution problems by arguing, for instance that, "the conservation of natural resources within the provinces is primarily a provincial responsibility" (House of Commons, 1953: 1941). However, in the face of public demand and opposition pressure in the late sixties and early seventies, they underwent a change of heart and passed nine environmental statutes, in addition to creating a Department of the Environment to administer them (Dwivedi, 1974). The Canada Water Act, passed in 1970, was the flagship of the package of federal environmental statutes introduced during the 28th Parliament. It was followed by, among others, the 1970 amendments to the Fisheries Act, which authorized uniform national effluent standards to control water pollution, and the Clean Air Act of 1971.

At the same time, provincial governments also were scrambling to satisfy public demands for pollution control. During this period, all ten provinces passed environmental protection statutes, with some preceding the federal initiatives (most notably, British Columbia and Ontario) and others trailing. Provincial reactions to the federal proposals also varied. Although there was quiet support for federal legislation among the smaller provinces, the four largest provinces — Ontario, Québec, British Columbia, and Alberta — openly resented what they depicted as unnecessary federal intrusion in provincial jurisdiction. As a result, federal-provincial relations concerning environmental protection during this period were characterized by tension and conflict (Dwivedi and Woodrow, 1989). Intergovernmental accommodation was facilitated, however, by the existence of an institutional forum for ministerial discussions, the Canadian Council of Resource Ministers, which was renamed the Canadian Council of Resource and Environment Ministers (CCREM) during this period.

THE FEDERAL RETREAT

When the economy took a turn for the worse in the early 1970s, the environment was soon displaced on the national agenda by bread and butter issues like inflation and unemployment. Federal and provincial governments thus confronted the formidable challenge of implementing their new environmental protection statutes in a less supportive political environment than that which gave rise to them.

The pace of legislative activity in the environmental field declined sharply after 1971. At the federal level, there was sufficient momentum in the early 1970s to carry through two additional statutes already under development: the Ocean Dumping Control Act and the Environmental Contaminants Act. Thereafter, although minor amendments were made to the Fisheries Act in 1977 and to the Clean Air Act in 1980, no new environmental legislation was passed until 1988.

It is not entirely surprising that legislative activity declined in the early 1970s, since the recently enacted statutes offered ample tools to combat pollution. The task at hand was to implement them. However, the promise of the first wave of federal environmental statutes was not fulfilled. The water quality provisions of the Canada Water Act, which had been hailed as the centrepiece of federal environmental protection efforts, simply were never implemented. The federal government made greater progress in implementing the Fisheries Act, but even there, national regulations were issued for only six industries under the Act, though twenty had originally been planned (Edgeworth, 1973: 5). In comparison, over fifty broad industrial categories were regulated during the same period under the U.S. Clean Water Act.

During this period, the balance of federal and provincial roles in environmental protection shifted back toward the provinces. By the mid-1970s a clear division of responsibilities emerged, with the federal government developing national guidelines but leaving their implementation and enforcement to the provinces (Giroux, 1987). The origins of this arrangement lay in long-standing agreements concerning the federal Fisheries Act, in which the federal government delegated administration of the Act to all but the Atlantic provinces (Parisien, 1972). That informal delegation of responsibility for enforcement was clarified and extended to other federal environmental statutes by a series of federal-provincial accords signed in the mid-seventies. All provinces but Québec, British Columbia, and Newfoundland signed bilateral accords with the federal government, which set out mutually agreed roles for the federal and provincial governments in the environmental field.[4] The federal government was to develop national discharge guidelines in consultation with the provinces, while the provinces were to "to establish and enforce requirements at least as stringent as the agreed national baseline requirements." In turn, the federal government agreed not to take action to enforce its own regulations unless the provinces failed to do the job.

In theory, delegation of responsibility for implementation of national standards to the provinces was conditional. In practice, however, despite a record of widespread and persistent non-compliance with federal standards, the federal government rarely intervened. Even in provinces where the accords expired or were never signed, provincial governments were given priority in enforcement (Huestis, 1985: 53; Webb, 1983: 5–187).

By 1979, the federal government further withdrew from the commitment to establish national standards, nominally assuming the mantle of advocate rather than regulator (Henley, 1985). Standard setting under the Fisheries Act ground to a halt.[5] By 1984, Environment Canada's annual report noted that federal "Regulatory powers are used sparingly as a last resort" (Environment Canada, 1984: 1).

While, like the federal government, most provinces faced little electoral pressure to aggressively pursue environmental protection during the 1970s and early 1980s, they did have incentives to defend their jurisdiction over natural resources. In light of federal deference in the environmental field, they had little to fear. It is thus not surprising that, as observed by Woodrow, "the early 1970s seemed to witness federal-provincial relations with regard to pollution control and environmental management turn its face from confrontation to co-existence" (1977: 480). The turf battles that accompanied the passage of the Canada Water Act subsided as the federal government assumed a welcome supporting role of providing research and technical expertise to the provinces and facilitating consensus on national standards.

In explaining the cooperative character of federal-provincial relations during this period, much has been made of the institutional form of CCREM, in which federal and provincial ministers participated as equals, with the chair rotating among them (Whittington, 1974; Jenkin, 120–24). However, in light of federal deference to provincial jurisdiction during this period, the absence of federal-provincial conflict can be seen more as a reflection of the fact that there was little to fight about than as a tribute to the mechanisms available to resolve intergovernmental conflicts. As Skogstad and Kopas (1992) have noted, federal and provincial governments were equality willing to turn a blind eye to widespread non-compliance with environmental standards.

The short-lived burst of federal government concern for the environment around 1970 did have lasting impacts. Federal leadership prompted many provinces to adopt comparable standards based on national guidelines (Franson, Lucas, and Lucas, 1982: 22) — though they did not necessarily enforce them. In addition, Environment Canada's regional officials occasionally succeeded in pressuring individual provinces to tighten permit conditions or prosecute persistent violations, and on rare occasions federal officials pursued unilateral enforcement action (Nemetz, 1986).

Ultimately, however, federal officials' impact on provincial standards was limited by the provinces' willingness to accept federal input. It was as if the federal government volunteered to conduct an orchestra, without any guarantee that the musicians would be playing the same tune. When the musicians were eager to play together, the conductor provided a valuable service. But when they were intent on playing solo, all the baton-waving in the world could not produce a symphony.

THE SECOND WAVE

In the second half of the 1980s, public fears concerning the environment were rekindled by reports of a seemingly endless series of ecological disasters, including Bhopal, Chernobyl, and the *Exxon Valdez*. In addition, the discovery of a hole in the stratospheric ozone layer and emerging evidence of global warming contributed to a growing recognition that environmental issues are global in scope. Within Canada, the 1980s brought discovery of a toxic "blob" in the St. Clair River, detection of dioxins in pulp mill effluents, and a PCB warehouse fire at Saint-Basile-le-Grand, among others.

Brown reports that Environment Canada's own public opinion polls revealed an important shift in Canadians' attitudes concerning the environment as early as 1984 (Brown, 1992: 31). However, it was not until the late 1980s that heightened public interest in the environment was reflected in a dramatic surge in salience of the environment in national opinion polls, only to be followed by an equally rapid decline with the onset of a recession in the early 1990s.

In many respects, the governmental response to the second green wave was a replay of the first. Brown and Siddiq (1991) report an average increase in provincial expenditures on environmental protection of 6.6 per cent per year between 1985 and 1989, more than three times the overall rate of growth in provincial expenditures. The federal government also was increasingly active concerning the environment. Reminiscent of the early seventies, the increased federal presence in the environmental field provoked federal-provincial tensions.

An important difference between the first and second green waves was the role played by environmentalists. The early seventies had witnessed the birth of dozens of local environmental associations, which were ill-prepared to participate in the first round of environmental policy-making (Woodrow, 1977: 124). By the late eighties many of those groups had matured to become professional organizations with respectable, if not extravagant, budgets.

With the possible exception of environmentalists in Ontario and Québec, many Canadian environmentalists distrusted the provinces more than the federal government, to the point of labelling them "the environmental ogres of our time" (Buttle, 1990: B4). Although far from satisfied with federal policies, they sought the reassurance of overlapping federal and provincial jurisdiction. Their ability to achieve that goal was reinforced by significant changes in the environmental policy-making process. In the late 1980s, federal consultation processes traditionally limited to federal and provincial governments and regulated industries were expanded to include environmental groups (Hoberg, 1993). Environmentalists thus were able to provide a voice for diffuse public concerns and, in so doing, to serve as a counterpoint to industry and provincial resistance to federal initiatives.

The Canadian Environmental Protection Act

When Tom McMillan was appointed Environment Minister in 1985 after the disastrous tenure of Suzanne Blais-Grenier, his first order of business was to repair both his own department's morale and the new Conservative government's reputation at a time of growing public concern for the environment. McMillan responded by asserting a stronger federal role in environmental protection in the form of new legislation that placed renewed emphasis on uniform national standards.

Like the Canada Water Act before it, the Canadian Environmental Protection Act (CEPA), proclaimed in June 1988, was offered as the centrepiece of a new federal environmental strategy (Lucas, 1989; Giroux, 1989; Tingley, 1991). In addition to consolidating several existing environmental laws, the new statute proposed to strengthen significantly the federal government's role in toxic substance control. CEPA rejected the supplementary federal role envisioned by earlier environmental statutes.

As with the Canada Water Act two decades earlier, provincial resistance was strongest from Ontario, Alberta, British Columbia, and especially Québec. In response to Québec's continuing concerns, a committee of federal and provincial officials proposed the concept of "equivalency," an arrangement in which federal regulations under CEPA could be revoked in a particular province if the federal government and that province agreed that the province's own regulations were equivalent to federal standards. The proposed federal legislation was amended accordingly after second reading to authorize equivalency agreements.

Ironically, provincial efforts to resist federal involvement in the environmental field resulted in a more intrusive statute. In introducing equivalency amendments in the face of opposition demands for an ever stronger federal role, the federal Minister included a number of statutory conditions on equivalency. Thus, although equivalency was envisioned by the provinces as a mechanism to limit federal involvement within their jurisdiction, as adopted, it has the potential to inject an element of hierarchy into the federal-provincial relationship, since any province seeking equivalency agreements must agree to be held accountable to federal conditions (Duncan, 1990: 55). Not surprisingly, many provinces are wary of the potential for federal oversight of provincial policies, and only one equivalency agreement was signed in the first six years following the passage of CEPA.

Lucas (1989: 184) has aptly characterized CEPA as a turning point in federal environmental policy. The late 1990s will reveal whether CEPA will sustain a stronger federal presence in environmental protection or succumb to the fate of the Canada Water Act. However, the early indications suggest a path closer to the latter. Although the federal government fulfilled its promise to evaluate forty-four categories of priority substances within five years of the publication of the Priority Substances List, as of July, 1994, it had issued control regulations for only one. A parliamentary review of the statute was scheduled for completion in 1994–95, and there are indications that Environment Canada will seek relaxation of the existing conditions on equivalency (Environment Canada, 1993, vii)....

. . . . .

Environmental Impact Assessment

Although the passage of CEPA had already disturbed the long-standing federal-provincial détente in environmental matters, the impact of a subsequent series of court decisions concerning environmental assessment was much more profound. In 1989, the Federal Court ruled that the federal government was required under the terms of its own Environmental Assessment and Review Process (EARP) guidelines to conduct an environmental review of two dams being constructed by the Saskatchewan government on the Rafferty and Alameda rivers. The decision was significant because it previously had been assumed that the federal government could exercise discretion in interpreting its own guidelines. However, the Court ruled that by using inflexible terms such as "shall" to describe ministerial responsibilities in a formal regulation, the federal government had, in effect, regulated itself and, short of revising the regulation, would thus have to abide by its own Guidelines Order.

The combined effect of the *Rafferty-Alameda* and subsequent *Oldman Dam* decisions was to force the federal government to acknowledge and exercise its considerable jurisdiction over the environment. Although a 1992 Supreme Court ruling in the Oldman Dam case subsequently restored some federal discretion to perform environment reviews, in the intervening three years the federal government was forced to operate under the assumption that it could be compelled to perform an environmental review of virtually any project that impinged on federal jurisdiction. As a result, although only thirty-three full environmental reviews were performed by the federal government in the fifteen year period from 1974 to 1989, there were twenty-four reviews in the first year alone after the Rafferty-Alameda decision (Ross, 1992: 323).

It warrants emphasis that the expansion of the federal role in environmental assessment following the Rafferty-Alameda and Oldman Dam decisions was not the result of a federal power grab. Rather, at the behest of environmental groups, the courts thrust jurisdiction upon a reluctant federal government. Indeed, Canadians were given a rare opportunity to see a federal Minister at a loss for words because he was granted more extensive power vis-à-vis the provinces than he had sought (Howard, 1990, A5). Moreover, the federal government time and again vigorously opposed environmentalists' legal arguments that it should apply its own law.

Both federal and provincial governments were frustrated in the aftermath of the EARP litigation. The federal government resented the loss of control of its agenda to environmental groups and the courts, while the provinces resented the uncertainty introduced by belated federal reviews of projects that they had already approved. However, the nature of the EARP decisions greatly limited the ability of the two levels of government to resolve their differences through compromise. In granting citizens enforceable claims to federal actions, the courts effectively empowered private litigants to drive a wedge between the federal and provincial governments.

The fact that these events occurred during a period of unprecedented public concern for the environment may explain the federal government's unwillingness to accede to provincial pressure to amend the EARP regulation. Instead, the federal government proceeded with legislation to replace the regulation altogether. The resulting Canadian Environmental Assessment Act (CEAA) received royal assent in June, 1992.

Led by the Alberta government, the provinces displayed unprecedented consensus in their opposition to the federal legislation. Their objectives were threefold. First, the provinces argued that federal involvement was unnecessary since they were already doing the job. Provincial bureaucrats and politicians alike complained of a federal "cherry-picking syndrome," arguing that the federal government sought involvement only in the few prominent cases that capture the public's attention.

Second, many provinces were highly defensive of their jurisdiction concerning natural resources. It was significant that the most prominent EARP disputes, including the Rafferty-Alameda and Oldman dams and the James Bay hydroelectric development, challenged the provinces' authority to develop their own Crown resources. As the Alberta Forestry Minister stated, "We fought hard for control of the resources in this province, and we're against the federal government coming into this process through the side door: (*Western Report*, 1989: 30).

Finally, as one provincial official put it, "The bottom line is not environmental protection here, but economic development" (confidential interview). The potential invasiveness of federal environmental jurisdiction was brought home by the efforts of environmental groups to use the EARP regulation to block dozens of major projects in virtually every province. The provinces' desire to control the pace and direction of economic development within their own jurisdictions spurred them to present a common front in opposition to federal proposals. In the end, although the federal government agreed to amendments to make consultation with the provinces mandatory under certain conditions, it denied all of their more substantive proposals, including ones for a form of equivalency in the environmental assessment field.

. . . .

WHITHER OF WITHER
THE FEDERAL ROLE?

Federal-provincial relations in the environmental field have been cooperative for the most part in the last two decades largely because the federal government has not provoked the provinces by testing the limits of its environmental jurisdiction. The extent of the federal government's hesitance concerning its constitutional jurisdiction has varied over time, however, in parallel with trends in public opinion.

For decades prior to the late 1960s, the federal government resisted sporadic calls for federal involvement in pollution control. However, when public interest in the environment surged in the late 1960s, the same politicians who had deflected calls for a stronger federal role only a few years earlier began to talk tough about the need for national standards. When public attention subsided in the early 1970s, politicians' enthusiasm for environmental protection also diminished. Between 1972 and 1985, when environmental issues virtually disappeared from public opinion polls, federal politicians gradually retreated from their earlier assertions of authority.

Finally, as the public rediscovered the environment in the late 1980s, so, too, did their elected representatives. Federal politicians again expressed confidence in the constitutional basis for a strong federal role in environmental policy and renewed their efforts to establish uniform national standards. This resurgence of the federal role was hastened by court decisions concerning the federal environmental assessment regulation, which effectively forced the federal government to acknowledge the breadth of its environmental jurisdiction and, more importantly, to exercise it.

Thus, while the federal government was advancing tentatively on its own in response to growing public demand in the late 1980s, environmental groups used the courts to give the federal government a powerful push.

The temptation to resist imposition of concentrated costs is ever-present in all democratic political systems. However, in the Canadian context, federalism provided a convenient means of escape from jurisdiction that presented politically difficult regulatory responsibilities. It is significant that the avenue through which the federal government retreated from implementation of its early environmental statutes during the 1970s and early 1980s was delegation to the provinces. Yet, rather than trying to pass the buck right back to the federal government, many provinces were highly motivated to defend their jurisdiction over natural resources because it is so closely related to their authority to pursue resource-driven economic development. Thus, as the salience of environmental issues rose and fell, the balance of federal and provincial roles in the environmental field shifted accordingly.

An implicit assumption in much of the literature on Canadian federalism is that both levels of government invariably seek to expand or at least to exploit fully their jurisdiction (see Norrie, Simeon, and Krasnick, 1984: 123; Cairns, 1988: 150–51).[6] But, in the environmental field, intergovernmental competition for jurisdiction over environmental protection has been the exception to the rule. The apparent hesitance of the federal government in environmental policy forces reconsideration of the common assumption that governments compete to extend their jurisdictional grasp. In light of potential political costs and benefits, federal and provincial politicians can be expected to perceive some fields of jurisdiction as worth fighting for and others worthy of surrender without a fight. Moreover, the possibility that governments can use the federal system to avoid responsibility for environmental protection cautions against the optimism of authors who have argued that two heads of power are better than one (Gibson, 1983; Nemetz, 1986; Thompson, 1980).

. . . .

Although public concern for the environment remains high, the prominence of environmental issues has subsided since the late 1980s. Many of the same conditions that prompted the federal retreat in the 1970s are replicated in the 1990s. The crucial difference this round could be the watchdog role of environmental groups. Environmentalists now routinely have a place at the table in government-sponsored consultations, and they will also retain considerable legal resources with respect to environmental assessment. But their effectiveness in preventing a federal (and provincial) retreat in the years to come ultimately will depend on their ability to mobilize support from a public increasingly preoccupied with other concerns.

PART D
Criminal Prohibitions

(a) Applying the Tests of Real Crime to Environmental Pollution[†]

Law Reform Commission of Canada ——————————————————————

This chapter is a particular instance of what *The Criminal Law in Canadian Society* identified as "... the need to examine some forms of conduct, not presently dealt with as criminal, with a view to assessing the advisability of treating them as criminal."[11] It should be noted at the outset that neither in *Our Criminal Law*, nor in *The Criminal Law in Canadian Society* were the similar tests of criminality proposed meant to be strict rules to be applied literally as the last word in every respect. They were meant rather to provide signposts or guidelines, and therefore were left somewhat general in formulation. Nevertheless, the five general tests or criteria of criminality to be applied here are of great and lasting value. We turn now to the first of these, the contravention of a fundamental value.

THE CONTRAVENTION OF A FUNDAMENTAL VALUE: A SAFE ENVIRONMENT

Just as the tests of criminality themselves are not written in stone, neither in every case is the boundary line between environmental pollution which should incur a response and sanction in the *Criminal Code* as most deserving of societal repudiation, and pollution which is more properly and effectively controlled by regulatory statutes and administrative sanctions. It has been rightly observed about the distinction between crimes and regulatory offences that:

> These boundaries will always be indistinct, and the definition of the boundary in respect to a specific issue, a particular form of conduct seen as posing a social problem, will always be subject to dispute and the application of the individual judgment of Canadians and, more particularly, Parliamentarians, whose collective decision it is to call an act a "crime" or not.[12]

An additional point should be made as well. Such decisions by legislators or proposals by law reformers should clearly not be a reflection only of the personal morality and preferences of some individuals, or merely responses to the political pressures and perceptions of the moment. Something more is required, namely a coherent philosophy of criminal law, one which gives a

---

† From Law Reform Commission of Canada, *Crimes Against the Environment — 'Protection' of Life*, Working Paper 44 (Ottawa: Law Reform Commission of Canada, 1985), pp. 7–16, 20–26, 28–29. Source: Department of Justice Canada. Reproduced with the permission of the Minister of Public Works and Government Services Canada, 2001 and Courtesy of the Department of Justice Canada. See Appendix for notes or references.

high priority to determining whether the conduct in question seriously contravenes what is widely acknowledged to be, and ethically defensible as, a fundamental value in our society. It is the view of this Commission that a fundamental and widely shared value is indeed seriously contravened by some environmental pollution, a value which we will refer to as the *right to a safe environment*.

To some extent, this right and value appears to be new and emerging, but in part because it is an extension of existing and very traditional rights and values already protected by criminal law, its presence and shape even now are largely discernible. Among the new strands of this fundamental value are, it may be argued, those such as *quality of life*, and *stewardship* of the natural environment. At the same time, traditional values as well have simply expanded and evolved to include the environment now as an area and interest of direct and primary concern. Among these values fundamental to the purposes and protections of criminal law are the *sanctity of life*, the *inviolability and integrity of persons*, and the *protection of human life and health*. It is increasingly understood that certain forms and degrees of environmental pollution can directly or indirectly, sooner or later, seriously harm or endanger human life and human health.

"Environmental Rights": The Options

An indispensable task in exploring and justifying our proposal to add environmental crimes to the *Criminal Code* is that of determining, with as much precision as possible, the particular value and interest legitimately within the scope of criminal law protection. There can, in other words, be a number of reasons why one might wish to make serious harm or danger to the environment a crime. But it does not follow that each reason has the same weight, or that each of the interests in mind equally merit the involvement of criminal law. The principle of restraint in the use of criminal law obliges us not to extend its already wide scope, except to include identifiable and deserving targets.

Expressed very broadly and in terms of environmental rights, there are potentially five related but different levels of "environmental rights" one might wish to enshrine in law, and corresponding activities one may wish the law to prohibit:

1. A right not to have one's life or health harmed or endangered as a result of environmental pollution, the health effects of which are known, predictable, serious and relatively immediate.

In effect this category can be thought of as an extension and application of the more general right and interest already the primary focus of the *Criminal Code* — that of physical integrity and security.

2. A right to a reasonable level of environmental quality, even when a specific pollutant or pollution source cannot now be identified with certainty as the cause of specific health damage or risk, on the grounds that sooner or later serious pollution of the environment will threaten human life and health as well.

Although the right in this case would be to environmental quality, the ultimate concern and basis, as in the first category, is human health. Unlike the first category, however, its scope would extend beyond just those instances of pollution with known, predictable and serious dangers to human life and health, to include all instances of serious environmental pollution. Proponents of this view would and do argue that, in the long run, to badly damage particular aspects of the natural environment, especially in an irreversible manner, may do serious harm to human health — if not to those now living, then to those in a future generation; in other words that, from an ecological perspective, there is no discontinuity between serious environmental harm and harm to the health of humans in general. Because of that risk, the law should directly prohibit all pollution which seriously harms or endangers environmental quality. This level and category of right does not assume or promote victimless crimes. Rather, it assumes that there will be specific and identifiable victims; it is simply that we do not yet know their identity or the particular form of their victimization.

3. A right to a reasonable level of environmental quality, but one which is violated by pollution instances which deprive people of the use and enjoyment of the environment, even when there are no health effects or dangers.

This right and category differs from the previous two in that the interest underlying the right is not the protection of human life or health, but a wide range of uses of the natural environment and natural resources which can be seriously interfered with by pollution ranging from noise to toxic contamination. These amenity considerations could range from a dirty (but not unhealthy) river, to the inability to exploit a particular natural resource for commercial purposes because of pollution damage. The fundamental question which must be faced in this regard is whether the scope of criminal law should be extended into the environmental arena to protect amenity rights alone, when there are no significant human health implications. Important rights can, of course, be infringed in both cases, and various branches of law other than criminal already are involved in protecting, for various purposes, the use and enjoyment of the environment; but the case for involving the criminal law would appear to be much stronger when claims to the use and enjoyment of the environment also involve direct or indirect health risks. In other words, the emission of very large quantities of highly carcinogenic or mutagenic compounds into city air would appear to constitute a much more serious and hence potentially criminal infringement of environmental rights than the emission of pollutants making a river objectionable to swim in, but not unhealthy.

4. A right of the environment to be protected from serious pollution for its own sake, even if pollution incidents should result in no direct or indirect risk or harm to human health or limitation upon the use and enjoyment of nature.

The previous three categories permit the focus upon, and protection of, the environment *itself*, although ultimately for the sake of human life, human health, and the use and enjoyment of the environment by humans. However, this last right would protect the environment *for its own sake*, quite apart from health or amenity considerations. From this perspective, it is the environment which should have various rights, not people who should have environmental rights. The implications of environmental pollution for humans would be quite incidental to this right. The extension of criminal law protection to encompass the first three rights could be considered *evolutionary* (although not necessarily justifi-

able in each case). However, for the criminal law, or law generally for that matter, to acknowledge this fourth category and right in the strict and literal sense would be truly *revolutionary*. It would be, in effect, to assign rights to nonhuman entities, and it has always been thought that only humans can have rights. Interesting and tempting though it may be to do so, efforts to argue that case have so far not been met with anything approaching general support, whether in philosophical or legal thinking. Some very real conceptual problems stand in the way of such efforts.[13] In our view, there are more than adequate grounds for more rigorous environmental protection right now, whether or not nonhuman entities are granted legal rights at some future date.

5. A right to have one's private property protected from damage by pollution caused by others.

It is doubtful in our view that this new environmental crime should include within its scope pollution which only damages or endangers the private property of others. The implications of some pollution for private property can be very serious; but when there are no serious dangers to human health or to the environment itself as well, what is at issue is not environmental rights, but (private) property rights. To include property considerations as a direct and exclusive object of this new crime against the environment would be to blunt its focus and diffuse its effect. It is in part at least to focus clearly on the environment itself as opposed to (private) property that this new environmental crime is being proposed. When only private property is harmed or endangered by pollution, the more direct and effective legal routes would seem to be the civil route or prosecutions for crimes against property.

A number of signs exist that there is a real and expanding concern for environmental protection: on the part of the general public; in the evolution of various legal concepts proposed to respond more adequately to environmental threats; and in the positions of environmentalists themselves. It would be too much to claim that there is yet a single and definable "environmental ethic" in place, or that its directions and implications are as yet clear or equally compelling to everyone or that all these concerns and proposals are equally persuasive. However, there is at least ample evidence that there is a widespread and growing commitment to a safe environment. Considering those signs briefly at this point will assist us in drawing some firmer conclusions about the five options just described, as regards the appropriateness or inappropriateness of criminal law.

Public Concerns and Pressures

If it ever was true that only the "lunatic fringe" was concerned about environmental protection, that is certainly not so in our times. For example, a 1978 national survey found that eighty-nine per cent of Canadians consider deterioration of the environment to be a major concern.[14] A 1982 survey of Edmonton residents indicated that seventy per cent of respondents favoured enforcement of air pollution standards, eighty-eight per cent supported the prosecution of pollution industries, and seventy per cent supported more rigorous enforcement of environmental statutes even if it led to higher prices.[15] More recently, another social policy research group reported that environmental health concerns are consistently in the top ten issues of concern to Canadians, and that most Canadians do not see environmental health and safety as a luxury to be traded for jobs or other values.[16]

Another indication of public concern is the strong desire for public participation in various aspects of environmental policy making. Particularly when the policy under consideration is perceived to have a *local* environmental and health impact, the interest and participation are at a very high level. The public is increasingly insistent that the opportunity to participate be provided when it presently is not. Among such occasions are, for example, hearings to select a waste disposal, treatment or storage site, or hearings to deal with the environmental impact of a proposed industry, or efforts of the public to obtain information about a potential environmental hazard.

There is, in some jurisdictions, an increasing resort to the prosecution of alleged polluters by various environmental agencies under the offence sections of their regulatory statutes. One of the reasons for this appears to be a pervasive pattern of noncompliance with administrative requirements by some regulated industries. But it has been argued that another related reason is the growing political profile of environmental issues, resulting in part from a greatly increased public awareness of actual or potential environmental abuses.

The Public Trust Doctrine, Environmental Quality and Bills of Environmental Rights

Another strand of an environmental ethic given increased attention in our times is the notion of "public trust" applied to environmental rights and duties. That notion is contributing to an evolution in our concept of private ownership. At present, most environmental protection legislation in Canada gives governments (through their environmental agencies) only a discretionary role *vis-à-vis* protection of the environment. That is, it *may* apply and enforce the legislation, but it *need not*. There are few obligations imposed on those who administer statutes.

However, the emerging public trust notion would impose duties to manage and use resources in *trust* for the public. It is already generally accepted that *governments* have public trust duties, in that land and resources owned by the government cannot be disposed of to private interests without taking into account the broad public interest. However, many argue that this notion should be applied to business as well, and to the land resources they own. While industries and developers would continue to be allowed the reasonable use of resources they own, their ownership and use would be qualified by their "public trustee" responsibilities.[17] Involved in this notion is in effect an evolution in our concept of ownership. The right to the private ownership and use of its land and resources by an industry would not be denied, but a new dimension would be added. That new dimension would be a responsibility to use it not only for private gain but also in the light of the common good. Consideration of the common good and the public heritage dimension of privately owned land and resources would rule out, for example, disposal of one's industrial wastes in ways likely to create public harm or risk.

This general notion of a dimension of common ownership is not in reality entirely new to law. It is only being rediscovered in our times. It was already expressed in the Institutes of Justinian:

> By natural law the following things belong to all men, namely: air, running water, the sea, and for this reason the shores of the sea.[18]

The concept of public trust — of the environment as a public heritage — is one of the foundations of efforts on many fronts in recent years to establish environmental Bills of Rights. Between 1976 and 1981 alone, a number of such Bills were proposed or introduced — in Alberta, Ontario, Saskatchewan and in the federal Parliament (by the then Minister of the Environment). As well, a proposal was made to the Parliamentary Joint Committee on the Constitution in 1980 to enshrine in the new Constitution a clause committing both levels of government to protecting the environment.[19] While none of these proposals have yet been successful in the strict legislative sense, their mere introduction and the not inconsiderable support for them are at least important signs of the priority many today give to environmental quality.

An example of an enactment which incorporated some of the major aspects of an environmental rights perspective was Michigan's 1970 *Environmental Protection Act*. It recognized the concept of public trust and placed a duty on the government agency, as well as businesses and developers which own natural resources, to protect them from pollution and degradation. It went a considerable distance towards providing citizens with a right to environmental quality — a right to a clean and healthy environment — by authorizing government agencies and others to "provide for actions for declaratory and equitable relief for protection of the air, water and other natural resources and the public trust therein."[20]

A related and equally central element in these Bills of Rights is that, in one form or another, they seek to shift at least some of the burden of proof from the plaintiff and Crown to the defendant and accused. Not only would a plaintiff, for example, not have to claim *personal* injury to have standing to bring an environmental action before a court, but if the activity complained of could be shown to endanger the environment, then the burden would shift to the alleged polluter to establish the safety of that activity.

From a "Homocentric" to an "Ecocentric" Ethic

A number of commentators have observed that the dominant environmental ethic both politically and intellectually until about the 1960s envisaged humans at the centre of the universe. Generally speaking that view made two assumptions as a result: that humans have dominion over all other forms of life and inanimate entities; and that we could and would make perpetually greater demands on the natural environment by way of production, consumption and waste.[21] To a large extent, that "mankind at the centre" perspective characterized as well the arguments and positions of those pushing for a safer and cleaner environment. What counted as the measure of defensible environmental policies was the value of the environment to us — the need to protect it because it is indispensable to the satisfaction of human needs and desires. That view also fueled the environmental legislation in the United States and Canada. Harm to the environment was to be avoided and controlled, implicitly because we humans would otherwise be affected in some manner; continuing and expanding resource consumption and production would be constrained, our enjoyment of nature curtailed, and our health put at risk.

However, more recently environmentalists and others have underlined what they see as some serious limitations of that homocentric or "mankind at the centre" perspective, and many have promoted instead an ecocentric or "environment at the centre" stance. They claim, for instance, that the older view was wrong to assume that we could have adequate environmental protection at no cost to our appetites, desires or life-styles — that we could continue and expand production, consumption and waste and at the same time have a safe and clean environment — that nature is definitely resilient and flexible. They now argue that there are always cost, some payable now, some later, that some resources are not renewable, and that there are thresholds and limits to what can be used and destroyed in the environment and each ecosystem. They maintain that there is a balance, harmony and interdependence in nature to be protected and respected for its own sake.

Some environmentalists also argue that, pushed to its logical conclusion, a policy of environmental protection based only on *human* goals and rights could progressively weaken claims for the protection of endangered aspects of the environment, the pollution or destruction of which would not constitute economic or aesthetic loss, or danger to human health. Some fear that as our capacity increases to supply by artificial means those human needs and desires now supplied by the natural environment, the checklist of those forms of life and inanimate entities in nature which we deem worthy of protecting would progressively shrink.

To some extent then, these and similar views constitute a shift away from a largely homocentric to an ecocentric ethic, one which in effect seeks the protection of the environment *for its own sake*, quite apart from its relevance to humans. There are, of course, many important and laudable insights provided by proponents of this more recent stage of environmental concerns. At the very least, they further demonstrate that the environment itself in the view of many ought to be a legally protectable interest; but, as already suggested above, there remain some serious conceptual and practical obstacles to the provision of legal protection to the natural environment *for its own sake*, apart from considerations of human benefits, wishes, uses and health risks. It would amount to granting rights to non-human entities. From a practical standpoint, it is inconceivable that natural resources could ever be totally insulated from economic and political considerations. Nor is it evident that we cannot provide adequate protection for the natural environment itself by continuing to permit a homocentric ethic to underlie our environmental regulations and laws, but one which now gives more scope to the *quality* of human life, and to our responsibility of *stewardship* or trusteeship over the natural environment.

Conclusions

In view of the preceding analyses about fundamental values and interests, we are now able to make the first of our conclusions. At this point, this first set of conclusions will encompass only the matter of the particular environmental values and interests to which the *Criminal Code* could and should legitimately extend. The five options in this regard were described above.... These conclusions will of course need supplementing and clarifying by the analyses, additional criteria and conclusion to follow in the remainder of this Working Paper. What we conclude at this point in the Paper is not meant to prejudge the question of whether pollution should be prohibited by the *Criminal Code*, either by the use of existing sections or by new ones formulated explicitly for that purpose. A final conclusion on that point can only be made after we weigh all the evidence to be considered in Chapters One and Two.

1. The scope of a *Criminal Code* offence against the environment should not extend to protecting the natural environment for its own sake, apart from human values, rights and interests.

2. However, a fundamental value is seriously contravened by some instances of environmental pollution, one which can be characterized as the right to a safe environment, or the right to a reasonable level of environmental quality.

3. This value may not as yet be fully emerged or universally acknowledged, but its existence and shape are already largely discernible. In protecting it, the *Criminal Code* would be essentially reflecting public perceptions and expanding values traditionally underlined in the *Code* — the sanctity of life, the integrity of persons, and the centrality of human life and health. At the same time, the Criminal Code would be playing an educative and advocacy role by clearly articulating environmental concerns and dangers not always perceived as such, and by incorporating newer concerns such as quality of life and stewardship of the natural environment.

4. More specifically, the scope of a Criminal Code pollution offence should extend to prohibiting environmental pollution which seriously damages or endangers the *quality of the environment*, and thereby seriously harms or endangers *human life or health*.

5. The pollution activities prohibited by a *Code* offence should include not only those which are presently known to constitute immediate and certain health harms or risks, but also those *likely* to cause serious harm to human health in the foreseeable future.

6. The scope of a *Criminal Code* pollution offence should not normally extend to prohibiting pollution which deprives others of the *use and enjoyment* of a natural resource but causes no serious present or likely harm or risks to human health. Only by express exception should an interest other than life or health fall within the scope of such an offence. Such an exception would be, for example, when a form of pollution would deprive an entire community of its livelihood.

7. Environmental pollution which destroys or damages *private property* without, as a result, causing or risking serious harm to

human life or health, should not fall within the scope of a *Code* offence against the environment, but should be the object of civil remedies or prosecuted as a crime against property.

. . . .

Latency, Accumulation and the Ecosystem Approach

In many cases, the pollution activities which are potentially the most harmful are those involving damage, destruction or injury which is not immediate and not harmful to identifiable aspects of the environment or identifiable human victims. Yet the damage can nevertheless be very grave. Two of the reasons why this can be so have to do with *latency* and *accumulation*. Latency is the delay between the release of, or exposure to, a hazard and the appearance of its injurious effects. Some of the most catastrophic effects can take the longest time to appear. An example is some carcinogens which can be latent for up to thirty years. The mutagenic effect of some hazardous chemicals may only show up several generations after the initial exposure. The process of accumulation means, in effect, that while an individual release of a pollutant may not in some cases be seriously or obviously harmful, many such acts, from one or many sources, may in the aggregate produce an accumulated threat to the environment, health and property, one going well beyond the threshold of what a particular species, resource, ecosystem or human body can tolerate without serious harm. A lake can finally lose the ability to cope with accumulated acid rain, and will die. Or a child exposed to lead over a long period of time can finally become seriously ill and even die because too much lead has accumulated in the body.

One explanation of the mechanics and implications of environmental damage and destruction is that provided by the ecosystem approach. That approach is not without its limitations when pushed to extremes, and it is not our intention to promote it or to justify legal prohibitions and reforms purely on the basis of one or another environmental school of thought. Nevertheless, some findings of ecologists are not disputed, and the general lines of the approach help to underline the potential seriousness of some environmental pollution.[23]

This relatively new approach is a synthesis of the insights and skills of a number of disciplines, especially biology, chemistry, geography and climatology. Whereas those and other fields study the threads of nature, the ecosystem approach studies its "whole cloth." Its proponents insist especially upon two points. They argue first of all that it is erroneous to speak of man *and* environment, or of man as *external* to the natural environment. Rather, humans are internal to, and partners with, the rest of nature. They argue, secondly, that serious harm done to one element in an ecosystem will invariably lead to the damage or even destruction of other elements in that and other ecosystems.

What ecologists mean by an "ecosystem" is any relatively homogeneous and delineated unit of nature in which nonliving substances and living organisms interact with an exchange of materials taking place between the nonliving and living parts. The term "ecosystem" is somewhat flexible and the boundaries between them somewhat arbitrary. Those boundaries are generally based upon what is most convenient for measuring the movement of energy and chemicals into and out of the system. Typical and important interrelated and overlapping ecosystems are: units of land along with the surrounding air and water, or lakes, or river basins, or forests, or climatic zones, or the earth itself or the biosphere (the outer sphere of the earth inhabited by living organisms and including lakes, oceans, soil and living organisms, including man). Within each ecosystem there is, they maintain, a delicate balance and interdependence between all the elements. Systems can cope with and adapt to some interferences, but not others. The overall long-range effect of some intrusions is not yet known with certainty or in detail. Ecologists argue that ecosystems are now known to be subject to very definable and immutable processes, which impose corresponding ecological constraints. They stress two organizational rules, namely, the first two of the three laws of thermodynamics. The first rule (that of conservation of matter and energy) is that matter and energy cannot be destroyed, only *transformed*. The second (the law of entropy) is that all energy transformations are *degradations*, whereby energy is transformed from more to less organized forms. In simpler terms, they explain those rules by the following principles and examples.

The first is that *everything in the environment or individual ecosystems is related*. If one breaks a link in the food-chain, for example, or introduces a substance not biodegradable, there are consequences for the entire ecosystem. Examples of the resulting serious and often irreversible harm are DDT and mercury. Since its massive use in the 1940s, the footsteps of DDT can be followed from wheat, to insects, to rodents, to larger animals and birds, and to man. In its wake it left whole species of animals more or less extinct or with serious reproductive problems. To illustrate the degree of interaction involved and the insignificance of time and distance, traces of DDT can now be found in the flesh of polar bears. The industrial discharge of *mercury* is another illustration. It has been followed from its discharge by pulp and paper industries into the air and water, to its transformation in the water into methyl-mercury by the water's micro-organisms, to its accumulation in the sediment of lakes or its absorption by the fish. Among its victims in the next stage, it is argued, have been the Indians of northern Ontario and Québec who eat those fish and are frequently inflicted with the horrors of what has come to be known as Minamata disease.

The second principle underlined by ecologists is that *unless neutralized, every contaminating substance remains harmful somewhere to something or someone* in the natural environment. Sooner or later we will pay, in some cases dearly, for discarding, for example, nonrecycled industrial toxins into rivers and dumps. Matter cannot be destroyed — only transformed. The atoms and molecules of matter are always preserved by ecosystems in some form. Moreover, if they are not or cannot be transformed, degraded, recycled or neutralized, it is an illusion to hope that that form will become a benign and harmless one.

Limitations of an Unqualified Ecosystem Approach

From the perspective of harm, however, there may be some difficulties and limitations of the ecosystem approach pushed to its extreme. It has been observed that some (by no means all) of its proponents are unjustifiably pessimistic and too rigorous. Some imply that each now stable and healthy ecosystem has inherent worth and must be preserved exactly as it is, that any harm or modification to it would be immoral, and that all human impacts upon, or changes to, an aspect of the environment are necessarily unnatural. However, that view has at least three limitations.

Viruses and Diseases: Good or Bad?

First of all, if every ecosystem, every species, is to be preserved and protected "as is" in its natural state, if human values, human judgment and human benefit are to be considered irrelevant, we would be forced to *tolerate many threats and diseases* generally perceived to be themselves harmful if not attacked and even wiped out if possible. An unqualified ecosystem approach pushed to its logical extreme might, for example, force a conclusion that the extinction of the smallpox virus was not a good thing, or that grasshoppers, mosquitoes, noxious weeds, various pests and disease organisms should not be combatted but protected, or that the building of human settlements was wrong because some ecosystems were necessarily harmed in the process. Few if any ecologists seem actually to intend those conclusions, but they do perhaps illustrate the sort of dilemmas implicit in attempts to determine and evaluate environmental harm, and the need to qualify the "deep ecology" stance in the light of some other considerations.

The Adaptive Capacity of the Environment

A second limitation of an extreme and rigorous ecosystem approach used to measure environmental harm, is that ecosystems are not only in many respects vulnerable, but also *adaptive and evolutionary*. Up to a point and in some respects, ecosystems can respond to and accommodate change. Some man-made alterations of an element of the environment can, in particular cases, trigger adaptive responses. Ecosystems are not in all respects fixed; there is a degree of rhythm and fluctuation. It becomes important in this regard to weigh impacts of polluting contaminants and activities as to whether they are degradable and noncumulative (for example, many pulp and paper wastes), nondegradable and cumulative (for example, mercury, lead, PCBs), reversible or irreversible, natural yet likely to cause damage to some environments in large concentrations (for example, sulphates, chlorides). There are undoubtedly good reasons for policy makers to give more attention to the "inherent worth" view of the natural environment, but this adaptive mechanism itself of ecosystems has an inherent worth and should be added to the calculations of harm. In some cases, the conclusion will be that a substance or activity goes well beyond the adaptive capacity of an ecosystem; in other cases it may not.

Tolerating Pollution for Legitimate Social Purposes: Balancing the Human Health Standard

There is yet a third and most important factor to be weighed in calculations of serious pollution harm, a factor more or less incompatible with an ecosystem approach which is strict and absolute. It is generally acknowledged in our political and economic system, and in our environmental policies and laws, that there are a number of legitimate social purposes which can justify, at least for a period of time, varying degrees of pollution, deterioration and risk — which permit downgrading the pollution harm and risk from serious and intolerable to less-than-serious and tolerable. It is not, of course, uncommon for the law to conclude that what would be reckless and unacceptable behaviour in some circumstances, can be justified if socially desirable for one reason or another. For example, a very risky medical operation can, in some circumstances, be acceptable and even desirable if it offers the only chance to save a life.

Primary among the goals and purposes implicitly or explicitly underlying environmental policies, regulations and statutes are economic ones. An environmental agency may judge, for example, that a particular existing industry should be allowed to exceed, at least for a specified time, the statutory emission standard for a particular contaminant, because there may be good reason to believe the expense of strict compliance will bankrupt the company and cause widespread unemployment. Similarly, it may be judged that the only way to secure the establishment of a new industry in an economically depressed area and to develop and market local resources is to permit it to do some widespread ecological damage, and/or, at least for a time, exceed by a considerable margin the statutory emission standards. It would, of course, be naive and unrealistic to assume that all such judgments are equally defensible, or that the economic viability and employment arguments of industry should be accepted uncritically by agencies. However, it would be equally naive and Utopian to expect that environmental decision making can ever be completely insulated from economic and political considerations.

It should be noted that the mere emission of a particular contaminating substance beyond the standard established in the relevant statute or regulations need not in itself always imply serious (or even minor) environmental and health harm. In the first place, the standard itself may be open to legitimate debate as to its accuracy and appropriateness. In some cases the standard may, by some criteria, be too strict, or based upon uncertain evidence. On the other hand, it may be felt by some to be not strict enough. Secondly, it is at least the intention of regulation and standard makers to build into the emission standards a certain margin of safety.

The "social utility" and other factors just indicated demonstrate that judgments before or after the event about the types and degrees of pollution which will be characterized and treated as serious and intolerable, as opposed to minor and tolerable within regulated limits, are not and cannot be strictly and exclusively "scientific" in nature. Determinations of harm and degree of harm are to a large degree value-judgments, rather than scientific calculations. More precisely, such judgments are based upon criteria which themselves imply or import value-judgments. Therefore, these judgments about the acceptability of harm and risk should not be made only by the scientist as scientist.[24]

There is, then, a major distinction to be made between pollution offences and the "paradigm" (criminal) offences of homicide, assault and theft, as regards seriousness. The latter are *always* considered seriously harmful to individuals and fundamental societal values, and therefore criminal (if the *mens rea* conditions are met), no matter what the degree of injury or loss. However, especially given the "social utility" factor, it is possible at present for pollution which by some criteria is endangering to the environment (and human health) to be characterized in the final analysis [as] not serious and even tolerable. To characterize the harm and danger as not serious need not, of course, mean that the conduct should be subject to no legal prohibitions and sanctions, only that the conduct in question would not fall within the scope of the *Criminal Code*.

That balancing of the environmental risks involved in permitting harmful pollution, with (for example) the economic implications of prohibiting it, is to at least some extent inescapable "before the event" in the formulation of environmental policies, standards and regulations. However, that same balancing is also [legitimate] "after the event," that is, in determining the seriousness of the alleged offence. At this stage, the social utility factor as a criterion of gravity can be one of the considerations in the choice among various compliance mechanisms authorized by the relevant statute, and in the decision about how rigorously to enforce the statute in this case, including whether or not to prosecute.

However, weighing the social utility of an alleged incidence of pollution to determine its seriousness is also inevitable if we go the further step being proposed in this Paper and characterize some of these activities as potentially *criminal in nature*. One of the criteria of pollution as a crime would be that it must be proved to be seriously harmful. That would be determined, at least in part, by whether conduct which is harmful or endangering by some scientific criteria, may in the final analysis be less than seriously harmful and endangering, or even justifiable and tolerable, in part because it promotes valid social goals. It has been suggested to us by one of those consulted that an alternate or more specific way of highlighting the social utility factor would be to make it a defence, or simply leave it to guide prosecutorial discretion. Both approaches appear to us essentially compatible with the analysis to this point. However, ... we feel the jury may have a unique and important role to play in the balancing of harm and social utility.

In any event, the life and health of others cannot be traded off for other apparent benefits, whether economic or other. We do not permit such a trade-off for other criminal offences involving serious harms or dangers to human life and bodily integrity. That being so, we may formulate the following by way of a general criterion: (1) the more certain is the evidence or likelihood of present or future harm and danger to human life and health, and the more serious the nature of that harm and danger, the less legitimate and persuasive should be other socially useful goals as justifications for the pollution or for reducing its classification from serious to minor, and the more compelling would be arguments for the criminal nature of that activity;

(2) the less likely are the serious present and future human health harms and dangers, and the more likely the interests affected are exclusively those of the use and enjoyment of the environment, the more relevant and legitimate is the weighing of other societal goals by way of mitigating its classification as potentially serious harm.

. . . .

CONCLUSIONS

1. The existing *Code* prohibitions examined do not directly and explicitly prohibit seriously harming or endangering the natural environment. They have as their direct objects quite different conduct and the direct interests in mind are those of property or life and bodily integrity.

2. In principle, one or another of those existing *Code* prohibitions could be revised to accommodate environmental pollution. But given the many considerations specific to crimes against the environment, such revisions would require "major surgery" and result in *Code* sections with too many very different goals. To change existing prohibitions to incorporate the many factors and priorities underlined in this Paper would blunt the present legitimate objects of those offences. At the same time it would make impossible a strong and sharply focused affirmation of the priority criminal law should give to the fundamental value at stake — a safe environment.

3. Environmental quality is a value so fundamental, unique and threatened, that very seriously to harm or endanger it merits express prohibition in a new and distinct offence we have labelled a "crime against the environment." To conclude thusly [*sic*] implies the addition of a third category, "offences against the environment," to the two major categories of offences in the present *Criminal Code*: "offences against persons," and "offences against property."

PART E
Regulation and Standards

(a) Controlling Corporate Misconduct through Regulatory Offences: The Canadian experience[†]

Kernaghan Webb ——————————————————

Regulatory offences[1] may lack the 'glamour' of crimes,[2] but they are the most effective penal option[3] available to address corporate misbehaviour in Canada.[4] An examination of recent legislative activity[5] and court cases[6] suggests that they will probably remain the preeminent penal tool used to control corporations. While use of criminal sanctions to counter environmental and workplace harm has become the darling of reformers,[7] legislators and enforcement agencies have no such fixation: certain characteristics of crimes render them of little use against corporations, particularly in environmental and workplace contexts.

An apt way of comparing the main features of crimes and regulatory offences is to use the metaphor of the differences between cannons and guns. With crimes — the legal equivalent of cannons — prosecutors have to prove subjective intent in order to obtain a conviction — someone 'knowingly' or deliberately engaged in a harmful act or was criminally wanton or reckless.[8] Satisfying the court that intent exists may be particularly difficult if the accused is a corporation, with a diffuse 'directing mind' and responsibilities divided among may individuals.[9] In regulatory offences (the guns), no proof of intent is required to obtain a conviction. With regulatory offences of strict liability, the corporate accused can escape liability by showing that it exercised due diligence or that there was a reasonable mistake of fact. The onus is thus on the corporation to explain its operations and justify its behaviour. With both crimes and regulatory offences, large financial penalties and imprisonment are available as sentencing options.[10]

No one denies that crimes carry a stigma that is anathema to any law-abiding citizen or corporation. But in most cases, the real question is whether the criminal approach is worthwhile, given the problems of proof associated with it, and in light of an alternative method that is both more appropriate and easier to enforce. Cannons make a lot of noise, but they are cumbersome and miss their target as often as they hit it. Guns are comparatively easy to use, and their lethal precision is well recognized. For good reason, then, outside the Criminal Code,[11] Canadian legislators and enforcement agencies pack guns, not cannons.

A number of debates and developments have occurred in Canada over the past two decades

---

† From Frank Pearce and Laureen Snider, eds., *Corporate Crime: Contemporary Debates* (Toronto: University of Toronto Press, 1995), pp. 339–46. See Appendix for notes or references. Reproduced by permission of University of Toronto Press, Incorporated.

bearing directly on the form, substance, and use of penal offences to control corporate misconduct. These events were shaped by unique features of the Canadian legal landscape, such as the Charter of Rights and Freedoms,[12] but many of the same issues have occurred or are likely to occur elsewhere.[13]

The focus in this chapter is on three controversial issues pertaining to penal offences. The first is the need for new crimes and for increased use of existing crimes to address corporate wrongdoing in such areas as environmental protection and workplace safety. I suggest that such efforts are misguided, given that regulatory offences are more appropriate and are now beginning to be used effectively. The second issue relates to prosecution by enforcement agencies. Analysis reveals that increased use of public compliance and enforcement policies, and of specialized enforcement units, is more effective. The third issue is legal justification for different standards of fault and burdens of proof for regulatory offences, when compared with criminal offences. Courts are developing a distinctive legal approach to regulatory offences, which is being held consistent with *Charter* standards of fundamental justice.

A Word on Terminology

Before proceeding any further, we must define the terms *criminal* and *regulatory* offences. The typology of offences used here is that developed by the Supreme Court of Canada in the landmark 1978 decision *R. v. City of Sault Ste. Marie.* Its three-tiered system divides offences into true crimes, strict liability, and absolute liability and has been essentially upheld in subsequent cases and proven workable. In my opinion, this system is not simply a semantic device resorted to by legally trained individuals to confuse non-lawyers. Rather, it makes important substantive and procedural distinctions that underlie the position taken here — that strict- and absolute-liability offences — the main regulatory offences in use — are both more appropriate and effective in addressing most types of corporate wrongdoing.

In the *Sault Ste. Marie* decision, Mr. Justice Dickson (as he then was) described criminal offences as those in which the prosecution must prove both the actus reus of the offence and the subjective intent — the mens rea — of the accused. The vast majority of criminal offences

are located in the *Criminal Code*, but there are also mens rea offences in other pieces of federal and provincial legislation, including those pertaining to environmental protection,[14] workplace safety,[15] and consumer protection.[16] Criminal offences, however, are extremely rare outside the Criminal Code and are seldom used.

Most offences contained in non-Criminal Code legislation involve either strict or absolution liability.[17] For this reason, I refer to both types as 'regulatory offences.' With both types, the prosecution need not prove the subjective intent of the accused. With absolute liability, it need prove only the actus reus of the offence, and a conviction will automatically result. With strict liability, after the prosecution has proven the actus reus, the accused is given the opportunity of establishing that due diligence was exercised or that there was a reasonable mistake of fact.

Strict liability offences are often referred to as negligence offences,[18] because of the type of fault element involved. The offence incorporates an *objective* standard of negligence through use of due diligence, so that the mere fact that the accused may have believed that his or her actions were careful or reasonable (a subjective standard) is not sufficient to avoid liability: what matters is whether the courts would consider that a reasonable person in the accused's position would have behaved in a similar manner.

In *Sault Ste. Marie*, the Supreme Court of Canada held that absolute-liability offences, because they impose penal liability without providing an accused an opportunity at least to demonstrate that he or she did everything reasonable, were contrary to the principles of penal justice.[19] More recently, in *Reference Re: S. 94(2) of the B.C. Motor Vehicles Act*, the Supreme Court stated that absolute-liability offences are contrary to the Charter's section 7, where deprivation of liberty such as imprisonment or probation is provided as a penalty. Such offences are comparatively rare in Canadian regulatory legislation.

In *R. v. Wholesale Travel*, a 1992 decision, the Supreme Court of Canada upheld strict-liability offences in regulatory legislation, including offences that may lead to imprisonment. Most regulatory offences in Canada are strict liability in nature.[20] Because such offences with imprisonment have been approved by the Supreme Court, and because of their heavy usage in regulatory legislation, they are the focus of analysis below

CRIMES VERSUS REGULATORY OFFENCES

In Canada, some quarters[21] have called for new crimes, or for more extensive use of existing crimes, to protect the environment or workplace safety. Legislators' reluctance so far to resort to the criminal approach seems to me eminently sensible.

There are three main arguments in favour of the use of crimes. First, the types of harm and suffering caused to humans and the greater environment are serious and deserving of serious denunciation. Second, there are occasions when this harm is inflicted deliberately or with criminal (subjective) negligence. Third, failure to use the criminal law to address this type of wrongdoing, often perpetrated by corporations, reflects an ideological bias in favour of certain powerful classes.

The position against expanded use of the criminal law in these contests can be summarized as follows. First, there are already numerous criminal offences well suited to deliberate or criminally negligent harm to individuals or property.[22] Second, it is agreed that there may be occasions when harm to workers or the environment is inflicted deliberately or in a criminally negligent manner. However, problems of proof make the criminal approach not as practical or as effective as enforcement through regulatory offences. Third, there are already a wide range of regulatory offences pertaining to environmental or workplace harm, with large penalties attached and the potential for imprisonment.[23] These offences clearly indicate societal disapproval and should be the main penal tool used to control misbehaviour in these contexts.

Fourth, it is considerably easier to enforce these regulatory offences, for both intentional or negligent misconduct, so this should be the preferred route. Fifth, the fact that these regulatory offences exist, and are easier to enforce, reflects societal recognition that regulated actors are in a different position than non-regulated actors — that the former are held to higher standards of conduct and are subject to more demanding legal treatment than the latter. Sixth, development of effective, publicly approved and disseminated compliance and enforcement policies[24] that set out in what circumstances prosecutions will take place should lead to more effective enforcement.

Regulatory offences hold corporations and natural persons to a higher standard than do crimes, for two reasons. First, not only intentional but also negligent behaviour is considered unacceptable.[25] Thus strict-liability offences hold corporations and natural persons to higher standards of care than crimes. Second, the onus is put on the regulated accused to demonstrate the reasonableness of its behaviour. This burden compels regulated persons to put in place preventive measures (e.g., safety or environmental audits[26]) if they wish to be able to establish due diligence to the satisfaction of courts. It is suggested that the largely abysmal enforcement record for criminal offences in addressing harm to workers or the environment,[27] in contrast to evidence of considerable success with regulatory offences,[28] is support for the regulatory-offence approach.

The push for more extensive use of criminality, while well-meaning and eloquently argued, appears to have been motivated more by reasons of doctrinal consistency than any real need. Thus, for example, the Law Reform Commission of Canada seems to have proposed new crimes against the environment and to address workplace harm as part of its suggested revision of the Criminal Code, not because of any pressing demand from the legal community or greater public or because of any deficiencies in the regulatory-offence approach.

Enforcement of Regulatory Offences

Legal and non-legal pressures have led government departments to develop more explicit, open, and effective approaches towards prosecutions of regulatory offences. The due-diligence defence allows accused to raise the issue of the acquiescence of governmental officials to a situation of non-compliance (i.e., 'officially induced non-compliance').[29] This has been one motivation for governments to develop compliance and enforcement policies that set out, for the public, the regulated sector, and inspectors, how and when regulatory offences and other sanctions will be used. The existence of a compliance and enforcement policy, when its terms are followed, decreases the likelihood of officially induced non-compliance and of its being successfully raised as part of a due-diligence defence.

Successful tort actions against government in recent years for negligent law enforcement[30] have led to greater realization in government that a systematic and predetermined approach to enforcement, as through use of compliance and enforcement policies, is desirable. Again, such policies, when strictly adhered to, tend to prevent tortious official-enforcement situations.

The possibility that inconsistent or uneven enforcement could be contrary to Charter principles of justice and equality[31] represents yet another stimulus for development of compliance and enforcement policies, since such policies, if the terms are followed, can lead to more equal enforcement and potentially be a defence to Charter challenges.

Enforcement by citizens or workers can be perceived by the public and government as indicative of governmental ineptitude.[32] Use of compliance and enforcement policies helps to bring citizens into the process earlier and may obviate the need for private enforcement. At a non-legal level, increasing public concern with environmental and health-and-safety matters, coupled with growing scepticism about the motivations and activities of government, has made the public more critical and vigilant. For all these reasons, governments seem to be realizing that the old, ad-hoc approach to prosecution is no longer acceptable.

Compliance and enforcement policies commit government to apply the law in a certain manner. They set out the powers, sanctions, constraints, and approaches of a department and the situations in which various sanctions will be used.[33] To be legitimate and effective, they are developed in consultation with regulatees, the public, other departments, and governments and are made available to the public. Where adhered to, such policies can become the basis for consistent, predictable, and fair implementation of policy. Growing numbers of government departments are developing these policies.[34]

Several environmental departments have set up special enforcement units, separate from the units that engage in day-to-day communications with regulatees.[35] These units have the expertise to bring successful prosecutions where such actions are necessary. They are not impeded by the tactical and practical constraints that might affect officials who regularly communicate with regulatees concerning compliance.

There are indications that limited but consistent use of regulatory-offence prosecutions can be effective against individuals, corporations, and corporate officials. In Ontario, for example, conviction rates for regulatory environmental offences have been high,[36] and empirical studies suggest that corporate officials take the threat of such prosecutions seriously.[37] Officials with the Ministry of Environment note a marked increase in cooperation from regulatees,[38] as well as improved abatement,[39] since the ministry began concerted enforcement of regulatory offences in 1985.[40] Private-sector representatives support this observation.[41]

The trend towards prosecuting corporate directors and officials as well as corporations represents the latest and most aggressive use of regulatory offences.[42] If such offences can survive Charter challenges,[43] as strategy of prosecuting corporate directors and officials will probably be a major additional impetus for corporations to develop effective environmental safeguards.[44]

By imposing a burden on the regulated accused to establish due diligence, the strict-liability offence requires regulated people to put proactive, preventive systems in place that tend to minimize the likelihood of offences arising.[45] Thus, for example, more environmental regulatees are hiring independent 'environmental auditors' to inspect their facilities and alert them to possible violations. If, despite hiring of such an auditor and following his or her advice, a violation does occur and is prosecuted, then the regulated accused can introduce the audits to support a claim of due diligence.[46]

In short, consistent enforcement of regulatory offences, when undertaken pursuant to compliance and enforcement policies, has proven an effective sanctioning tool to control environmental misconduct by corporations and individuals alike. There is no obvious reason why this approach could not be extended to other policy contexts, such as workplace health and safety and consumer protection, with similar positive results. Regular and concerted enforcement of regulatory offences can be an effective backdrop for administrative actions and can lead to regulatees' adopting proactive and preventive strategies.

. . . .

CONCLUSIONS

Regulatory offences have come into their own in Canada over the past twenty years. They have proliferated in statutes, been strengthened and elaborated on in amendments, and been judicially approved, and they are increasingly being enforced pursuant to coherent and explicit enforcement policies. Prosecution of regulatory offences represents a considerably more practical and effective method to imposing penal sanctions on corporations and other regulated actors than does criminal prosecution. Strict-liability offences, the main type of regulatory offence, impose responsibility for exercising due diligence on regulated actors and are easier to enforce, since the burden is on the accused to establish due diligence. The penalties for regulatory offences can range from million-dollar-a-day fines to imprisonment and probation.

It is both reasonable and fair to impose penal liability through regulatory offences, given the privileged position of regulatees in our society as persons who engage in potentially harmful activity, often for profit, and given the practical difficulties associated with requiring prosecutors to prove lack of diligence.

If courts build on the solid foundations for regulatory offences they have articulated in cases such as *Sault Ste. Marie, Reference Re: S. 94(2) of the B.C. Motor Vehicles Act, Thomson Newspapers, R. v. Wholesaler Travel*, and *R. v. Ellis-Don*, the ability of the state to control corporate misconduct will be on considerably more sound footing than if only a criminal approach were available.

The International Institutional Context

(a) The Institutional Contexts (Continued)[†]

Melody Hessing and Michael Howlett ⸻

INTERNATIONAL AGREEMENTS, CANADA'S RESOURCES, AND THE ENVIRONMENT

Governments operate within the context of the international system of states. While the activities of domestic governments affect the nature of the international system, events and actions in the international system can also have a major impact on the activities of domestic states.[80] Foreign military or environmental crises are good examples of the links between national and international actors, but the interaction continues on a day-to-day basis because of treaties, understandings, and commitments made by states to various international organizations.[81]

The nature of international agreements in the resource and environmental policy area is of significance, because they can restrict the choices of governments on policy issues.[82] Once again, these agreements tend to reflect the Canadian interest in resource exploitation rather than environmental protection per se, although this emphasis has been changing in recent years.

International Trade Agreements: From Empire to NAFTA

Great Britain's move toward free trade through the repeal of the Corn Laws in 1846, with its inadvertent effect of terminating the Canadian producers' preferred access to the British market, can be seen as the beginning of Canada's efforts to develop its own resource trade policy. The British action signified that Canada's interests were no longer a factor in the mother country's trade policies. Consequently, the five colonies forming British North America signed the Reciprocity Treaty with the United States in 1854, offering preferred access to each other's markets. The treaty was terminated in 1866 at the request of the American government. The reasons for its abrogation included Canada's huge trade surplus, pressures from US interests that were adversely affected by Canadian exports, and Britain's support for the South in the American Civil War, which caused much resentment in the eventually victorious North.[83]

The end of the treaty led Canadian policy-makers to search for alternative means of estab-

---

† Reproduced by permission of the publisher. From *Canadian Natural Resource and Environmental Policy: Political Economy and Public Policy* by Melody Hessing and Michael Howlett, pp. 62–69. © University of British Columbia Press, 1997. All rights reserved by the publisher. See Appendix for notes or references.

lishing access to a large market for Canadian producers, one of the results of which was Confederation in 1867. At the same time, the newly established Canadian government continued to pursue another reciprocity agreement with the United States, but to no avail. Frustrated with the American government's lack of interest in negotiating a trade deal, the Canadian government under Macdonald announced the National Policy in 1879, the cornerstone of which was a drastic increase in tariffs on imports.

One reason for this measure was to exert pressure on the American government to negotiate reciprocal reductions in tariffs. Another was to foster industrial development by protecting Canadian 'infant industries' from imports and by encouraging foreign manufacturers to establish plants in Canada in order to avoid tariffs. The second goal was largely accomplished, as many manufacturing plants, both Canadian and foreign (mostly American), were established toward the end of the century. However, the goal of negotiating reciprocity with the United States remained as elusive as ever. Nonetheless, the efforts continued, covertly by the Conservatives and overtly by the Liberals. The 1879 offer of preferential access to imports from Britain remained similarly unreciprocated by the British government.[84]

The goal of a free trade agreement with the United States was almost reached in 1911, when the Liberal government under Laurier announced that it had reached an agreement to reduce tariffs on a reciprocal basis on a range of natural products and some manufactured products. It was clearly designed to support western and eastern agricultural and primary producers, while only marginally reducing the protection afforded central Canadian manufacturers. But 1911 was an election year, and the Conservatives, in cohort with business and labour in the manufacturing sector and with staunchly anti-American British loyalists, mounted a bitter campaign that ended in a humiliating defeat for the Liberal Party. The lesson from the election was not lost on either main party, and neither dared raise the topic for several decades.[85]

The anti-American, pro-British sentiments that market the 1911 election were out of tune with the time, however, for the United States was rapidly emerging as the world's foremost military and economic power. Despite the rejection of the free trade deal, Canada's trade with the United States continued to expand, and increasingly large amounts of American capital poured into the country. Canada was on the march toward closer integration with the US economy, punctuated only by the Great Depression in the 1930s. In 1935, the two nations signed an agreement to lower their tariffs substantially; this was the first trade pact between the two neighbours since 1854. It was followed by further attempts to reduce tariffs, and in 1938 an agreement was reached between the United States, Great Britain, Australia, New Zealand, and South Africa to provide easy access for each other's goods. The process of multilateral reductions in trade barriers had begun, and it gained momentum after World War II.

The United States emerged from the war as clearly the dominate technological, economic, and military power in the world. It was in its interest to organize an open world trading order, and this goal was supported by Canada, which also emerged from the war as a beneficiary of increased world trade. The American efforts led to the negotiation and signing of the General Agreement on Tariffs and Trade (GATT) between twenty-three nations in 1947. This agreement, which has expanded considerably in both membership and scope since its inception, still forms the basis for trade between the non-Communist nations.[86]

The postwar international economic order has been characterized by *multilateralism*, a principle fully supported by Canada. Canadian leaders, aware of the nation's high degree of trade dependence, have recognized that a multilateral arrangement provides the best guarantee against protectionism and the economic and diplomatic powers of the larger nations. This guarantee explains the active Canadian participation in all the rounds of GATT negotiations and its support for other international institutions such as the World Trade Organization (WTO), created to succeed GATT following the Uruguay round of trade talks.

While Canada's commitment to multilateralism is beyond doubt, in practical terms the multilateral framework has worked mainly toward expanding Canadian trade with the United States.[87] The purpose of GATT/WTO is to promote a liberal international economic order based on the principle of comparative advantage. The organization establishes reciprocal rights and obligations among its members to reduce barriers to international trade, and it offers exporters opportunities to sell in the markets of member nations. But it also imposes an obligation not to erect barriers to imports, except under special circumstances provided for in the agreement. This obligation has been problematic for Canada, which, as we have seen, has wanted to reduce foreign barriers to its exports while maintaining its own barriers to imports of manufactured goods.[88]

Since the establishment of GATT, the value of world trade has increased more than six times. During this period, the growth in exports has been higher than the rate of economic growth in most developed and developing nations. While GATT cannot be credited with all the expansion in international trade, it certainly played a key role in facilitating the expansion.

GATT was critical in promoting international trade and increasing the economic prosperity of trade-dependent nations such as Canada, but by the 1980s there were justified fears about its future. For one thing, its membership had increased fourfold since its inception, making multilateral negotiations difficult because of the wider variety of interests that had to be accommodated. Moreover, there was no nation that could act as the United States did between the 1940s and the 1960s to prod negotiations and enforce discipline. In fact, a gigantic trade deficit had made protectionism politically popular in the United States even though it was the architect of GATT and the modern liberal trading order. The European Community's preoccupation with integration in Western Europe and its disregard for the interests of the nations outside the region also did not bode well for the future of GATT.

The fear that GATT might not be as effective in the future as it was in the past had led many countries to look for alternatives. After the Uruguay round, GATT was restructured, emerging as the WTO. But Canada had already shifted its focus toward solidifying and furthering its already relatively open trade relations with the United States. The Mulroney government, soon after its election in 1984, declared its intention to pursue free trade with the United States. The agreement was reached in October 1987 and came into effect on 1 January 1989.[89]

The Canada-US Free Trade Agreement (CAFTA) signified the *de facto* recognition of Canada's special trade relations with the United States, which had existed for almost a century, and reflected a sense of resignation among policymakers that it is not possible to utilize state actions to diversity Canada's trade relations

to any substantial degree from the pattern imposed by the international marketplace. In 1992, this agreement was extended to Mexico in the North American Free Trade Agreement (NAFTA).[90] Talks are under way to extend membership to Latin American nations in a new Free Trade of the Americas (AFTA) agreement, while other talks have centred on the creation of a new free trade area in the Pacific Rim under the aegis of the Asia-Pacific Economic Council (APEC).[91]

The free trade agreements have affected many areas of Canadian resource policy, although their effects on environmental policy-making have been less significant.[92] The provisions regarding the energy sector, in particular, have been some of the most far-reaching and contentious in Canada. Energy production is undoubtedly a vital sector in the Canadian economy: about 14 per cent of total Canadian investment is in this sector, which accounts for about 10 per cent of total Canadian exports.[93] The United States is the world's largest consumer and importer, as well as producer, of energy, and Canada is currently its largest foreign supplier. Many of the Trudeau government's measures to Canadianize the sector under the terms of the National Energy Program (NEP) were a major irritant to the United States, and it is doubtful whether the American government would have signed the FTA without an assurance that such measures would not be repeated.

The energy sector as defined in the agreements includes oil, natural gas, light petroleum gas, coal, uranium, and electricity. The FTAs eliminate almost all barriers to trade in these commodities. The agreements explicitly prohibit measures that make export prices higher than domestic prices, measures such as the export tax imposed under the NEP by the Trudeau government. Moreover, the agreements, while not prohibiting restrictions on the amount of energy exports to the United States in times of shortage, require that Canada permit American imports to purchase an amount no smaller than that used in the past thirty-six-month period. The US interest in insisting on this provision was to secure a guarantee that in times of shortage the Canadian government will introduce cuts that will affect consumers on both sides of the border equally. While this provision is in keeping with those implicit in GATT (Article 20) and with Canada's obligations under the International Energy Agreement pertaining to oil, the FTAs go further by explicitly specifying the proportion of supplies to be shared. Critics allege that, insofar as the Canadian government cannot reduce supplies to American consumers in times of shortage without hurting Canadian consumers as well, this is a serious erosion of Canada's sovereignty.

INTERNATIONAL ENVIRONMENTAL ORGANIZATIONS AND STRUCTURES

The GATT/WTO and CAFTA/NAFTA treaties are probably the most significant international commitments made by Canadian governments in the resource policy area.[94] While most of these treaties deal only indirectly with the environment, Canada does participate, with the United States and Mexico, in the (North American) Commission on Environmental Cooperation (CEC), an organization set up to mitigate the environmental aspects of North American free trade through the North American Agreement on Environmental Cooperation (NAAEC). Canada has specific exemptions from several practices of the NAAEC because of its federal structure, which exempts the provinces unless they choose to participate.[95]

Other international organizations and treaties have had a more direct impact on Canadian environmental policy-making.[96] Canada participates in all major international organizations with an environmental focus and has taken a lead role in the major international organization devoted to the environment, the United Nations Environmental Program (UNEP), which originated at a conference led by a Canadian and which has been head by Canadian.[97]

In addition, Canada belongs to the World Bank, which, along with the International Monetary Fund (IMF), plays a major role in financing industrial development in many countries, and is a member of organizations such as the Organization for Economic Cooperation and Development (OECD) and the G-7, which can affect the environment through their role in establishing international investment patterns and activities.[98] Canada is also a member of international organizations such as the World Meteorological Organization (WMO), the International Maritime Organization (IMO), the International Union for Conservation of Nature and Nature Resources (IUCN), and the World Health Organization (WHO), which also deal with environmental concerns in the course of their activities.[99]

Canada is a major participant in the international environmental regime and is a signatory to treaties such as the Rio Declaration on Bio-Diversity, the Montreal and Helsinki Protocols on Ozone Depletion, and the Agenda 21 proposals of environmental action into the next century.[100] Other major international agreements include the United Nations Economic Commission for Europe-sponsored Convention on Long Range Transboundary Air Pollution (LTRAP); protocols on sulphur emissions, nitrogen oxides, and volatile organic compounds; the United Nations Framework Convention on Climate Change; the UNESCO Convention for the Protection of the World Cultural and Natural Heritage; the UNESCO Convention on International Trade in Endangered Species of Wild Fauna and Flora; the Basel Convention on the Control of Transboundary Movements of Hazardous Wastes and Their Disposal; and the International Convention for the Prevention of Pollution of the Sea by Oil. Major bilateral agreements with the United States also cover areas such as air quality and acid rain, migratory birds and caribou, the Great Lakes, and waterfowl management.[101]

All of these treaties and agreements commit the governments of Canada to observing certain rules and principles of conduct. In its own way, each establishes minimum standards for national conduct and, with beneficial intent, limits the options open to governments in addressing domestic policy issues.[102]

CONCLUSION: INSTITUTIONAL CONSTRAINTS ON GOVERNMENT ACTION

Just as resource and environmental policy-making is affected by the socio-economic context in which it occurs, so it is affected by the broad institutional context of government. How a country fits into the international system of states, and the dynamics of this international system, influence both domestic and international policies. The ways in which the political institutions of a country are constructed, and the shifts in the powers of central and local governments relative to one another, are also significant components of the context of public policy-making. Furthermore, the powers of government(s) relative to those of the private sector must be considered, especially in an era when transnational corporations exert such extensive influence on domestic politics.

The aspect of Canada's position in the international system of states that is most significant for resource and environmental policy-making is the open nature of its resource-based economy. Canada is one of the most trade-dependent nations in the world, and its high degree of trade dependence, makes it very vulnerable to international pressures. The types of goods produced and the prices at which they are sold are determined by international market forces, which diminish Canada's capacity to control its political economy. As such, the international arena imposes an enduring constraint on Canada. The country has, as a result, negotiated a series of treaties and participated in the creation of a series of institutions designed to minimize uncertainty stemming from international conditions. Likewise, Canada has participated in a series of environmental treaties and arrangements, although they do not have the same singularity of purpose and the broad scope of trade arrangements.

On the domestic front, the most important aspect of Canada's institutional structure is its federal nature, which has resulted in the situation whereby more than a dozen senior governments make resource and environmental policy in this country. Environmental considerations per se were not dealt with in the British North America Act and remain the subject of divided authority and complex jurisdictional debate. Although the nature of Canadian federalism has changed over the years, the original divisions of powers set out in 1867 has largely been retained. Resources were originally divided between the provinces and the federal government on the basis of land ownership. As the federal land base has decreased over the years, so too has the federal government's ability to affect resource policy-making. The progressive decentralization of powers, the privatization of many previously public functions, and increasing funding constraints all exert pressures on government regulatory capacity. Conversely, areas of the country under the jurisdiction of aboriginal land claims have grown, as has the role of aboriginal organizations in land, resource, and environmental policy-making.

Two

The Regulatory System:
Standard Setting, Implementation,
Monitoring and Enforcement

Editors' Notes

Allan Greenbaum and Alex Wellington ————————————————————

The regulatory system — with its "tool kit" combining legislation, standard setting, licensing and certification — has become the most significant legal mechanism for dealing with pollution in contemporary society. As was discussed in the editors' notes to Section One, "The Elements of the Legal System", legislation has generally overtaken the common law in prominence and relevance, and that is particularly evident in the case of the environment. In those notes to the previous section, we outlined some of the reasons the common law is considered insufficient for dealing with modern day pollution and other environmental problems. Here, we will canvass some of the crucial reasons that environmentalists have had "high hopes", and their expectations disappointed, with regard to the workings of the regulatory system.

COMPONENTS OF THE REGULATORY SYSTEM

In this section, we address the whole environmental regulatory system. The system comprises several components, stages or levels — policy making, implementation, monitoring and enforcement. Each level represents the outcome of a social decision process. The first level, *policy making*, involves deciding on the objectives, goals, targets and measures of environmental regulation — how clean, how green an environment (and in what respects) will the law aim to bring about, given competing social demands. The political context of regulation, analyzed in the readings in Part A of this section, is particularly relevant to the policy-making level but has a pervasive effect on implementation and enforcement as well. We will have more to say about this topic below.

The next level, *implementation*, involves a choice of policy instruments — of carrots and sticks, and a multitude of decisions regarding the detailed rules and standards that will give shape and effect to those instruments. It also involves the staffing of a bureaucracy to design and operate the regulatory regime, and hence decisions about how much of resources will be assigned to the task. Implementation is typically carried out by means of regulations enacted under "enabling" legislation (discussed in the editors' notes to the previous section). One important aspect of implementation is the translation of the broad environmental quality goals developed in the policy making stage into precise, legally enforceable standards. Standard setting is discussed in the readings in Part B of this section. Different kinds of instruments are discussed in Part C. The reading in Part C by the Law Reform Commission of Canada sets out criteria for choosing among instruments, and discusses some of the more traditional pollution-control instruments: command-penalty mechanisms, financial incentives (subsidies) and persuasion. The other readings in Part C address what are sometimes advanced as more economically efficient and less cumbersome instruments: pollution taxes (Olewiler), tradable pollution credits (Australian Bureau of Industry Economics), and voluntary initiatives (Webb).

We speak of "implementation gaps" when governments fail to act upon stated public policy objectives. Gaps can occur at various stages of implementation. In some cases legislation is drafted and even introduced, but no statute is actually passed — as has been the situation with the continually delayed federal endangered species legislation. In other cases, a statute is passed but is not promulgated (brought into effect). In still other cases, enabling legislation comes into effect, but relatively little use is made of it by the government — few regulations are put in place, few parks created, for example.

Next (assuming policy has been implemented), decisions must be made about *monitoring*, both to detect non-compliance with the rules and to discover the effect of compliance and non-compliance on the environmental quality criteria with which the policy goals are concerned. These decisions include what to test (measure, inspect, observe, etc.), how to test, how much to test, who will test, and how much of resources will be devoted to monitoring. The last of these, of course, in large part determines how all those other issues will get resolved in practice. "Monitoring lapses" result when insufficient resources are assigned to compliance inspection and to monitoring environmental quality. Monitoring lapses may be caused by budgetary constraints or by a preference on the part of government to "see no evil and hear no evil" (a kind of deregulation through the back door).

Finally, in the event that non-compliance is detected (which presupposes that there has been implementation and adequate monitoring), decisions about *enforcement* must be made. For example, officials must decide (again, in light of the resource constraints they face) whether to prosecute, to impose administrative sanctions such as orders or penalties (if the applicable legislation so provides), or to exercise forbearance in return for promises of future compliance. If the violator is prosecuted, the court must then decide whether to convict or acquit. If it convicts, the court must choose, from a among the range of sentencing options provided by the relevant statute, a penalty of appropriate severity or leniency to impose on the guilty party. These enforcement and sentencing decisions are among the thorniest and highest profile ones in the whole regulatory process. The term "enforcement deficit" is sometimes used to describe the situation that results when little or nothing is done about non-compliance with environmental protection measures. Implementation gaps, monitoring lapses and enforcement deficits all contribute to the distance between the law in the statute books (or the policy in the election campaign platform) and the "law in action".

The components of the regulatory system comprise both conventional sorts of legal elements canvassed in Section One — statutes, regulations, courts, tribunals and so on — and partially extra-legal elements such as negotiation and voluntary initiatives. Negotiation as a mode of conflict resolution among stakeholders is addressed in Section Four, Part B; here we are concerned primarily with negotiation between regulators and those regulated. As discussed in the reading by Rankin and Finkle in Part D, negotiation has traditionally occurred at all stages of the regulatory process in Canada. Not only have the terms of regulations, licences, approvals and orders been subject to negotiation, but when these terms have been violated, the response on the part of authorities has often been to negotiate the terms of abatement or compliance measures rather than prosecuting or imposing mandatory abatement. The advantages to negotiation include greater flexibility and responsiveness, and the potential for effective consultation in decision making. There are, however, "those who view bargaining between regulators and industry as an abdication on the part of the former and an effort at manipulation on the part of the latter" (Benidickson, 1997: 239). We will have more to say about these issues in the discussions to follow of the political context of regulation and of enforcement issues.

Another increasingly important extra-legal element of the regulatory process is voluntary initiatives on the part of industry, which can be "implemented with or without government participation, assistance, and consent, and with or without the involvement of other interested parties", and which may be "adopted at the level of individual companies with comparatively localized objectives, or they may be developed in relation to the needs and capacity of an entire industry or sector with much broader implications" (Benidickson, 1997: 243–44). As Kernaghan Webb details in his article in Part D, voluntary initiatives, while not part of the law *per se*, come about within a context of existing and proposed regulation, and may have significant legal implications (such as helping define "reasonable" conduct for the purposes of assigning civil or quasi-criminal liability). However, as critics are quick to point out, the resort to voluntary initiatives may be seen both as a symptom of, and as contributing to, the "withering" and "shrinking" of the state's role in implementation, monitoring and enforcement (see the article by Krajnc in Part A).

FACTS AND VALUES: APPROACHES TO ANALYSIS

Concerning each of the aspects, components or levels in the regulatory process discussed above, we can ask two fundamentally different kinds of questions, which we may call "fact questions" and "value questions". Fact questions ask for descriptions, predictions or explanations. Descriptions are statements about the way things were or are; predictions are statements of how they will be; explanations are accounts of how they came (or will come) to be the way they are (or will be) — of causes and effects. Value or normative questions, on the other hand, concern matters of right and wrong, good and bad, just and unjust. They ask what goals we ought to seek and what means of attaining them are morally worthy. Answers to fact questions are justified on the basis of evidence and scientific reasoning; answers to normative questions are justified on the basis of value commitments and ethical reasoning, in addition to relevant facts. Value questions cannot be answered on the basis of facts alone (see "fact/value distinction" and "naturalistic fallacy" in the glossary). Facts and values come together in strategic questions: what, given the facts as we understand them, is the most effective way to realize or follow the values and norms we espouse?

People often find this distinction confusing because in ordinary conversation we often use the word "fact" to mean something definitely true, as opposed to "opinion". When we are contrasting matters of fact and matters of value, however, it is important to keep in mind that fact questions can be answered on the basis of theories, hypotheses, uncertain generalizations and, indeed, opinions — so long as they are opinions about matters of fact. Opinions about facts are beliefs concerning what is, was, or will be the case, as opposed to judgements about what ought to be the case. Of course, an answer based on well-founded evidence is more likely to be true than one based on mere opinion, but a false or uncertain statement of fact is still one of fact, not values.

The notes and readings to follow address both kinds of questions. Fact questions might include: How are environmental objectives set? What kinds of regulatory instruments are in use, and how did they come to be? Why do officials make the enforcement decisions they do? What are the effects on polluter behaviour and on the environment of different kinds of regulatory instruments, legal sanctions and enforcement practices? Value questions might include: How ought environmental objectives to be set? Should they take into account only human well being, or are non-human organisms and ecosystems also morally considerable? Should we make environmental decisions on the basis of the overall balance of costs (harms) and benefits, or should we also be concerned that the distribution of harms and benefits is fair? If the latter, what notion of fairness or justice should we appeal to? Should we make decisions about penalties and enforcement practices solely on the basis of predicted effects on polluter behaviour in light of our environmental quality objectives, or should we consider what people "deserve"? To what extent ought people to have a say — individually or collectively — in decisions that affect their environment?

Although these kinds of questions are distinguishable in principle, they are often very closely intertwined. It is a useful exercise to try to tease apart the issues of fact and the issues of value in the materials to follow.

THE POLITICAL CONTEXT

The readings in Part A of this section examine the political context of environmental law and law making from several angles. The reading by William Chambliss is from a seminal paper in the "law and society" literature on lawmaking. Chambliss's approach to the study of law differs in several respects from that of Donald Black (discussed in the introductory essay). Chambliss is primarily concerned with legislation, especially legislation that brings about major changes in the law. While Black emphasizes the social factors that affect the outcome of particular cases, Chambliss is interested in the social forces and processes that affect the creation and change of laws. Black is interested in explanations that will allow the observer to predict *how* legal institutions will behave, but he does not try to explain *why* the law behaves as it does. He tries to arrive at generalizations that are true across a wide range of times, places, and cultures. Chambliss, on the other hand, is interested in explaining why law behaves as it does, and especially why it changes when and how it does in the particular way that it does. Though his analysis is motivated and informed by particular (mainly egalitarian) values, he is, like Black, addressing "fact questions" — namely, those concerning the causes of legal change.

As discussed in the Introduction, social scientific accounts of law have traditionally divided between "consensus" and "conflict" theories. "Consensus" theories "view the law as merely the codification of mutually agreed upon norms for the smooth functioning of society" (Caputo et al., 1989: 2), while conflict theories see law and society as "arenas of struggle between social groups, and law is one means by which the powerful are able to oppress and exploit their subordinates" (Greenbaum and Wellington, 1993: 3). Conflict theorists do not deny that consensus plays a role in social life, but they do insist that "there is little consensus on ... important moral, political, and economic issues related to the exercise of power in society" (Caputo et al., 1989: 5).

Pluralist theories have been as influential as conflict and consensus theories. A pluralist conception of law is implicit in liberalism. Liberalism has been characterized as a political morality premised upon the commitment to state neutrality between competing conceptions of the good life. Treating citizens as equals, which is required for liberal political morality, means that laws and policies must respect the autonomy of individuals with respect to their public and private choices and actions. Ronald Dworkin is the best known proponent of this view (see Dworkin, 1978). Liberal democracy is premised upon the notion of rule of law, and committed to tolerance for diversity, and to accommodation of a plurality of interest groups. The "rule of law" refers to the settling of disputes by means of the application of impersonal legal rules and principles, rather than by the imposition of the arbitrary will of the powerful. The rule of law is an ideal particularly associated with liberal democracy.

Pluralism recognizes the "existence of conflict in society between competing interest groups"; yet, law functions to "keep disparate elements together" and to maintain order. (Caputo et al., 1989: 3) Pluralism differs from consensus theory in that it does not assume that a social consensus exists on substantive values. It does assume, however, that consensus exists about the political structures and institutions that mediate and resolve conflicts over specific issues. Pluralist theory tends to treat the law as being neutral in principle, i.e., not necessarily biased towards some interests and against others. The law is regarded as a referee, able to ensure that all sides in the struggle for power abide by the "rules of the game". For pluralists, the rules of the game are not themselves at stake in the struggle, as they are for conflict theorists. Conflict theorists suggest that such neutrality is unrealizable.

Conflict theories divide into "instrumental" and "structural" versions (Caputo et al., 1989: 7). The distinction between these two concepts has to do with the degree of autonomy accorded social institutions such as law. According to instrumental accounts of law, which represent a relatively pure form of conflict theory, the state is the instrument of the ruling class, and law in capitalist society originates in the needs of the capitalist elite. Chambliss finds few scholars still willing to defend such a stark view (but see Domhoff, 1996). Structuralism tries to take account of those features of law that make aspects of consensus and pluralist theories at least superficially plausible. For structural accounts, the state in capitalist societies is relatively autonomous, but ultimately supportive of capitalism. Law, in this view, reflects the needs of capitalism as a social formation rather than simply the will of those who happen to occupy the dominant class at a given moment; hence the importance of the rule of law. Structural conflict theories accept that the law may be applied impartially, and that this may sometimes go against the interests of powerful parties, but claim that this impartial system will nevertheless tend to favour the privileged and perpetuate inequality. For example, a system that gives equal protection to the property rights of the rich and the poor will tend to favour the rich, because they have more property to protect. This is true even if the law may defeat the attempt of a rich person to rob or defraud a poor one.

Chambliss argues for the need to go beyond the dichotomy between instrumentalism and structuralism. He advocates a "dialectical" approach to law, summed up as follows:

> People ... make choices, respond to realities, and struggle against oppression. Those at the top act as a class to perpetuate their privilege; those sprinkled below do likewise. The contrary interests generate conflicts, in response to which the government becomes complex, interactive and ever-changing. In a word, it is dialectical (Chambliss and Seidman, 1982: 316).

As Chambliss puts it, the dialectical approach "sees law creation as a process aimed at the resolution of contradictions, conflicts, and dilemmas which are inherent in the structure of a particular historical period" (1979: 152; reproduced in this volume). The legislation enacted to resolve certain social conflicts will itself lead to further contradictions and conflicts that will result in yet other legislative innovations. His theory attempts to acknowledge the complexity of social and legislative change.

Chambliss argues that pollution control laws highlight the conflicts between public interest representatives and those who own the industries. He points out that the failure to realize the fundamental contradiction between industrialization and the quality of the environment indicates a short-sighted position on the part of the owners of industry. Chambliss also emphasizes the contradictions within social classes. For example, at least some members of industry support some environmental pollution control measures. Chambliss mentions that big business might support regulation to impede competition from small business that will be more adversely affected by compliance with the regulation. Big business can more easily absorb the costs of compliance, assuming they do comply. As Rankin and Finkle (Part D of this section) mention, they often need not even comply. Small businesses will often (naively or powerlessly) comply with environmental regulation, while big businesses, which may pollute more, are able to negotiate compliance on their own terms with the government authorities — something about which a senior Department of Fisheries official complained in a leaked 1989 memo (VanderZwaag and Duncan, 1992: 15–16).

Generally speaking, investments in environmental protection (such as pollution-control equipment) do not, or are not perceived to, contribute to a firm's profit maximization. Since, especially in a competitive market and especially in the case of firms whose shares are publicly traded, profitability is a survival imperative for the firm or for its management, firms will tend to resist investing in environmental protection. Governments, meanwhile, are under pressure from environmentalists and their supporters in the public to force firms to make these investments. Corporations in polluting sectors will therefore have an incentive to resist environmental regulation. Resistance will be carried out at every stage of the regulatory process: law-makers will be lobbied to weaken legislation, to deregulate, or to cut funding for implementation, monitoring and enforcement; companies will use their bargaining clout (e.g., threats to close down) to extract forbearance from enforcement officials; finally, if prosecuted, companies will, of course, use their resources to defend themselves vigorously in the courts. Yet all of these forms of resistance are themselves costly and of uncertain benefit to the bottom line (Schnaiberg and Gould, 1994: 50–65). The particular balance of compliance and resistance costs to businesses, as well as the resources and political support available to environmentalists, will shape the specific outcome of the dialectic that Chambliss describes.

This is not to say that the behaviour of any of the parties involved is entirely a matter of simple, dispassionate economic (or ecological) rationality. Business routinely exaggerates the costs of proposed environmental protection policies, while environmental groups regularly play up the direst possible results of not adopting the policies they advocate. One might wonder why corporations have spent resources staunchly resisting (ostensibly on economic grounds) environmental rules that have proved to be either quite affordable (see, e.g., McHardie, 2000) or even economically beneficial to the firms involved (Porter and van der Linde, 1995). Schnaiberg and Gould (1994: 61) suggest that "firms resist regulat*ions* in order to protect themselves from regulat*ors* and their political supporters, who will coerce them to make other 'uneconomic' revisions of production in future circumstances".

The political economy of Canada, shaped by this country's distinctive history and geography, poses special obstacles to effective environmental regulation (Schrecker, 1990; MacDonald, 1991; Wellington et al., 1997). Canada has had a "staples economy", one largely driven by the export of raw materials (first fish and furs, then grain and lumber, then a range of forest products and minerals). Why does this matter? As we have mentioned, environmental regulation typically imposes costs, but costs are a problem for business mainly insofar as they cannot be passed on in the price of the product. This depends on whether the company is producing for a market with a high degree of price competition. The commodity export market is a competitive one, and producers are competing mainly on the basis of price, against foreign producers who may not be subject to the same kinds of regulations. At the same time, the dependence of resource producing hinterland regions on single industries, and the dependence of many towns on single companies, gives resource industries so vulnerable to the costs of regulation a powerful weapon to resist it: the "job blackmail" threat of disinvestment. This threat seldom need be made explicit:

> The nature of capitalist economies means that conflicts characterized by overt job blackmail are exceptional rather than routine. Since both governments and affected communities are aware of the economic consequences, overt threats of disinvestment are often unnecessary. Governments in all capitalist or mixed economies rely heavily on an ongoing flow of private investment to sustain the economic growth which both provides income and employment for their citizens and finances the provision of state services of various kinds. Thus, public policy must operate in a context of more or less continuous latent tension between the state's various other mandates, such as eliminating the damaging effects of economic activity on the environment, and the need to sustain the conditions for capital accumulation — that is, to maintain a favourable business climate. (Schrecker, 1990: 172)

This analysis is an instance of the structural conflict approach. Although capitalists as a class are not necessarily in a position to dictate details of public policy, and indeed may be strongly opposed to certain laws that are ultimately adopted, the dependence of the economy on maintaining investor confidence structurally constrains the outcome of policy conflicts in ways that systematically favour business interests.

Although the Canadian economy (at least in urban centres, where an increasing majority of Canadians live) is less dependent on staples exports than it was, other changes since the 1980s have exposed all sectors to pressure from foreign competition and capital flight. These changes have been an effect, as well as a contributing cause, of a shift to neoliberal policies favouring trade and investment liberalization, deregulation and privatization. The reading in this section by Anita Krajnc discusses this move to reduce the role of government in environmental affairs. Krajnc's article offers an explanatory analysis of some of the causes and effects of environmental deregulation, and also makes a normative case for the role of government.

Global restructuring (Cox, 1994) not only constrains the amount or degree of environmental regulation that states are willing or able to undertake, but also affects the nature and target of environmental regulation. Alan Hall (1998) points out that pesticide regulation in Ontario expanded during the 1990s to include a new attention to the use of pesticides by farmers (as opposed to stricter regulation of the products or the manufacturers). He explains this by reference not just to the clout of the manufacturing corporations, but to broader shifts in agricultural economics and policy away from maximizing yield toward "lean production" and minimizing costs. In an era of low agricultural commodity prices and global competition, encouraging farmers to cut pesticide use, Hall suggests, fits in with a more general strategy that encourages farmers to be more competitive and cost-efficient by economizing on inputs.

So far, we have focused on the relationship between politics and socio-economic structures. Another crucial aspect of the political context of regulation is the structure of government itself. We have already touched on some of the distinctive aspects of the Anglo-Canadian "Westminster" model of parliamentary government towards the end of the introductory essay, in the context of comparing it with the American model. One of the striking features of the Canadian system is the concentration of power over both the legislative (law making) and executive (law implementing and enforcing) functions of government in the Cabinet. The reading by Stephen Hazell explores, as he puts it, "the tensions between the conflicting imperatives of secretive Cabinet-centred government and the public demand for participatory democracy that occurred in the debates over environmental assessment reform". As such, the reading is directly relevant to the topics of environmental assessment and public participation taken up in Sections Three and Four of this book. In particular, the editors' notes and readings on environmental assessment in Part A of Section Three provide background that the reader might find helpful in understanding the specific policy context of Hazell's argument. We include Hazell here because his comments are relevant to all facets of environmental regulation.

Like Krajnc, Hazell engages in both explanatory and normative analysis. On the one hand, he seeks to *describe* certain institutional arrangements and decision-making practices characteristic of the Canadian government, and to *explain* how these tend to *cause* certain kinds of outcomes. On the other hand, he is offering a normative critique of these arrangements and practices that appeals to the *values*, *principles* and *ideals* such as participatory democracy and communicative rationality. His normative analysis draws on the work of political scientist John Dryzek, who is influenced in turn by the philosopher and social theorist Jurgen Habermas.

NORMATIVE ISSUES IN POLICY AND STANDARD-SETTING

Here we survey some of the normative theories used to justify and criticize particular environmental policies and standards. Such theories play a crucial role in making explicit the often unexplored value assumptions implicit in arguments about what the law ought to be concerning environmental protection. Facts cannot in themselves determine what ought to be done; attempts to derive normative judgements from statements of fact alone are said to commit the "naturalistic fallacy". The notes and readings in Section Three, Part B have more to say about this point. For example, the fact that a given level of some effluent increases the mortality of fish by a certain amount, or increases the risk of cancer in humans, does not in itself indicate that such a level should be prohibited. It only does so if coupled with specific norms concerning what kinds of harms ought to be illegal. Three general normative issues are salient in debates on environmental policy and law. The first has to do with the fair *distribution* of benefits and harms; this is emphasized in discussions of equity and social justice. The second has to do with the overall balance of aggregate benefit versus aggregate harm; this *efficiency* criterion has been especially emphasized by economists, and underlies cost-benefit analysis techniques. Both of these issues are familiar from debates about environmental protection and other areas of public policy. The third issue, whether and how harms and benefits to non-human beings should be taken into account, is distinctive of environmental (and animal welfare) policy questions.

The notion of equity is often opposed to the notion of economic efficiency, and debates over social policy often turn on tensions between these two overarching goals or ideals. For many areas of social policy, it comes to seem as if promotion or realization of one goal — such as efficiency — will come at the expense of the other. It is often charged, by those in favour of efficiency, that the pursuit of egalitarian policies will usher in economically inefficient outcomes. Yet the opposition between "utility" or "efficiency" and "equity" or "fairness" or "justice" is often not that simple. It is important to keep in mind that the notions of efficiency and fairness are rhetorical and ideological resources, at the disposal of actors in social conflicts, but it is not always evident how the same concept is linked across a range of distinctive situations. The meaning of equity, for instance, shifts depending on the context, which changes the dynamic of the opposition.

To make things even more complex, the various identifiable groups of actors or members of interest clusters are not unified, and they usually speak with many different voices, representing and reflecting a whole range of interests, values and concerns. There is not one "environmentalist" position, nor just one "industry" or "business" perspective; nor is there just one "union" position either. These cautionary words call for more subtle and nuanced analyses.

Equity and Social Justice

Considerations of equity and social justice provide a context for understanding social conflict about the environment. Many instances of social conflict or public policy debate over environmental issues feature claims about equity and social justice in conflict with appeals to economic efficiency. The common meaning of equity is "fairness and freedom from bias or favouritism" (*Webster's Dictionary*). Equity does not mean exactly the same thing as equality, but it is often linked to the idea of equality. The notion of equality is extremely complex, and subject to a multitude of interpretations, including equality of opportunity and equality of result (Turner, 1986). The former is often characterized in terms of "level playing fields", making sure that people start out on equal footing, in order to have a fair competition. Once the competition is over, however, people may end up in widely divergent positions, due to the inequities resulting from differential levels of acquired ability, innate talent, training, skills and so on. Equality of result instead refers to people ending up as fully equal, having roughly equal shares of social resources at any given time, however that equal distribution is brought about. Another interpretation of equality is the one embodied in law: "equality before and under the law".

A social justice perspective begins with an appreciation of the fundamental importance of the value of equality. If there are significant violations of equality interests, these amount to injustice, and should be remedied. This is particularly the case if the inequalities in question seem to be the result of bias or discrimination (whether deliberate, intentional prejudice or systemic). Note that because of the very different interpretations of "equality", debates rage over whether certain policies, such as affirmative action, are required to combat past injustice, or whether they are themselves instances of inequality, as reverse discrimination.

In the social science and social theory literature, the term equity is usually applied to concerns arising from discrimination on the basis of race, ethnicity, religion, gender, sexual orientation, class, age, (dis)ability, or other characteristics of identifiable groups. Thus, the term equity is used in the context of systemic discrimination on any such grounds. One other type of systemic inequality that has been explored in Canadian social science literature, at least in a preliminary way, is regional inequality. Resource development and management issues can be characterized as questions of control — who gets to control the use of the resource, who gets to benefit from its use, and who suffers the negative effects from its use. There is often a geographical dimension to environmental conflicts over resource use. These conflicts sometimes pit "urban" against "rural" dwellers, province (or territory) against province (or territory), region against region, and so on.

Another perspective on the notion of environmental equity is the concern with public participation in the formulation of environmental policy. For many "ordinary citizens" who are subjected to the effects of environmental decisions and policies, it is extremely important that there be sufficient avenues for public participation and citizen input, and that there be sufficient mechanisms to ensure government accountability to the general public. These topics are the focus of the editors' notes and readings for Section Four, Part A. It needs to be emphasized here that environmental issues are often characterized in ways that seem to exclude the general public, and that environmental policies are typically developed on the basis of scientific and technical expertise. It is thus a matter of fairness that the process of law and policy formation be designed to accommodate and welcome citizen participation.

There is, at times, a rather uneasy tension between the goals of social justice, and equity, and those of environmental protection, especially in terms of the preservation of natural areas. On occasion, the relationship between them has been cast in terms of opposition, exemplified by the simple formula, "social justice versus environmental protection"

(Paehlke and Rosenau, 1993). Groups committed to social justice and the eradication of racism, sexism and poverty have taken mainstream environmental organizations to task for not being sufficiently progressive; this has led to considerable debate and discussion within the leadership and membership of environmental organizations (Lavelle and Coyle, 1993). Yet, as Paehlke and Rosenau (1993; see also Paehlke, 1989) and many others have argued, there is actually much more basis for "common purpose" between social justice movements and environmental movements than is sometimes recognized. This is especially the case when environmental concerns are characterized in terms of concerns about long-term human health, and when the focus is on problems in the urban environments in which most North Americans reside.

In the context of environmental issues, the term equity normally covers the conventional meaning, and then is expanded to apply to issues of systemic inequality in the distribution of the benefits and burdens of environmental policies. The term "environmental racism" (Bullard, 1990; 1993; Westra and Wenz, 1995) has been used to signify the conjunction of discrimination and environmental impacts. Several collections of articles and book length treatments situate an environmental justice analysis in the context of toxic waste issues, specifically: Phil Brown and Edwin Mikkelsen, *No Safe Place: Toxic Waste, Leukemia, and Community Action*; Richard Hofrichter, editor, *Toxic Struggles: The Theory and Practice of Environmental Justice*; Michael R. Reich, *Toxic Politics: Responding to Chemical Disasters*; and Andrew Szasz, *Ecopopulism: Toxic Waste and the Movement for Environmental Justice*.

The general theme of environmental justice is that harmful environmental effects are experienced disproportionately by members of visible minorities or by (already) economically disadvantaged persons. The activities that generate these harmful environmental impacts are ones that generate economic and other benefits for, at least, some members of society — pollution and waste are by-products of industry, which produces goods for consumers. The less that companies spend on waste disposal and pollution control, or cleaning up the environment, the cheaper the goods can be for consumers to purchase. Environmental injustice covers situations in which the already disadvantaged get further disadvantaged, and the already advantaged are further advantaged.

Luke Cole (1992: 620) points out that "poor people bear the brunt of environmental dangers", and yet poor people "have the fewest resources to cope with these dangers, legally, medically or politically". Marianne Lavelle and Marcia Coyle (1993) provide an account of the findings of a *National Law Journal* investigation into the American federal government's pollution policies. The study looked particularly at the record of the Environmental Protection Agency's performance at Superfund toxic waste sites. That study, and other similar studies, have found that there are disproportionately high impacts of environmental pollution on minority communities (often called "communities of colour"). Areas or settlements in which the overwhelming majority of residents are people of colour, usually African-American and Latino-American, tend to be where toxic waste disposal sites are located. In Canada, there has been preliminary research suggesting that predominantly low-income and Aboriginal communities in Nova Scotia tend to be closest to the highest emitting polluters (Thompson, 2002).

Winona LaDuke (1993) has addressed the themes of pollution, sovereignty and control over natural resources in the context of the consequences of colonial occupation for native peoples. LaDuke recounts instances of environmental racism that are part of the colonial legacy, including nuclear-waste contamination and hydroelectric exploitation. Legal issues concerning First Nations people are briefly touched upon in sub-section eight of the editors' notes to Section One, "The Elements of the Legal System". In her work, LaDuke (1993) has elaborated on the relationship between indigenous values, which she describes as being in line with natural law (as distinct from positive law), and sustainable communities and economies. The struggles of native peoples over their homelands is often linked, strategically and conceptually, with those poor people, and with communities of colour who come together to "fight back" against environmental racism and unite in the demand for environmental justice.

Many commentators and activists recommend that government officials should factor race and poverty into the environmental policy and decision-making process. Marianne Lavelle and Marcia Coyle (1993) suggest that considering the disparate impact of environmental laws on poor people and communities of colour would be analogous to considering the negative impacts in terms of costs to industry, which is a long-standing practice. The U.S. Environmental Protection Agency did establish an Office of Environmental Equity, in acknowledgement of the need to design environmental legislation and policy to protect "special groups from the particular risks they face" (Paehlke and Rosenau, 1993: 683).

Recently, Richard Hofrichter (2000: 6) has insisted that much more is needed than is typically considered in conventional policy debates. There is, he asserts, need for a "major structural transformation to prevent increasing levels of toxicity, ill health and inequitable living conditions". Moreover, the "absence of a broader challenge to a system [i.e., contemporary capitalism] that generates ill health typically channels public attention to a limited legal and policy terrain on which to engage the issues" (ibid.). Hofrichter does not wish to endorse the focusing of energy and attention on that limited terrain. Instead, he advocates "organized action to combat ... the power arrangements that drive the capitalist social order", an order that is blamed for generating a toxic culture (ibid.: 1). This "toxic culture" consists of "exposure to an expanding array of toxic conditions in the air, water, and soil", presenting a long-term threat to public health. It also comprises the "social arrangements that encourage and excuse the deterioration of the environment and human health (ibid.: 1). Activists should, and do, he says, turn to community organizing, alternative media, art and other forms of cultural expression to counter the mainstream, toxic culture.

The kind of analysis, and rhetoric, pertaining to the ultimate "ineffectiveness of law" exemplified above leads William Bogart (2002: 220–21) to point to a "strange convergence of critics of the law on both the left and the right". Attacks on the inadequacy and futility of environmental laws by left-wing environmentalists, Bogart suggests, give succour to right-wing advocates of free markets and deregulation. The latter "argue that when even environmentalists pronounce the laws as not working there is no way that their costs can be justified. The solution is obvious: repeal most environmental regulation" (ibid.). This "solution" is, of course, quite the opposite of what the environmentalists seek. Nevertheless, according to Bogart, both ends of the ideological spectrum are guilty of a failure to appreciate the overall effectiveness and efficiency of the existing (admittedly imperfect) environmental law in North America. Then again, on any number of issues anti-capitalists and laissez-faire zealots share a scorn for the regulated capitalism of the welfare state.

A Few Important and Illustrative Cases

There are two very important cases that can help to illustrate the ways in which courts may apply the reasoning of an economic analysis or a social justice perspective. The first case of note is *Boomer v. Atlantic Cement Co.*, a case that went from a district court to the highest court (on appeal) in New York State during the 1970s. A group of residents led by the Boomer family, living near a cement plant outside Albany, New York, filed suit (in nuisance) against the company. They claimed that "dust and vibrations caused by the plant were damaging both their health and their property" and sought an injunction (DesJardins and McCall, 2000: 453). An injunction is a remedy available under common law, which requires a party to refrain from wrongdoing. At the time, there was no technology available that would allow the Atlantic Cement company to continue its operations without causing the dust and vibrations that the local residents wanted stopped.

The lower court did find in favour of the plaintiffs, but it did not, however, issue an injunction. The court instead "reasoned that the costs that would be involved in closing down the plant far outweighed the costs of the harms being done to the neighbours" (DesJardins and McCall, 2000: 453). The lower court ordered the company to pay the residents a lump sum for damages already suffered, and to pay them "ongoing monthly payments to compensate them for the harms that they would continue to suffer" (ibid.). The monthly payments were calculated on the basis of "fair market value for what they could receive if they were to rent their property" (ibid.). The court thus allowed the plant to continue operating, provided the company made compensation to the victims of the ensuing pollution. Upon appeal, the higher court agreed the neighbours had established the civil wrong of nuisance, but also refrained from issuing an injunction, as would be normal in such cases. The higher court likewise rationalized the refusal to issue an injunction on the basis of the disparity between the costs of the nuisance to the plaintiffs and the costs to the defendant of closing the plant. The higher court, however, decided that the Atlantic Cement company had to pay "permanent damages for the total present and future economic loss" to the property of the local residents (Ibid.).

A dissenting judge in the *Boomer* case argued that potential harm to health — which had been a crucial concern of the residents — should have been factored into the calculation of costs (DesJardins and McCall, 2000: 453). Furthermore, he emphasized that the harms to the general public were not being taken into account in the decision at all. The majority judgement in the case is often held to be a model of the use of economic analysis in the determination of a private dispute, an approach to common law adjudication that is endorsed very strongly by Richard Posner (1973).

A much more recent case is *South Camden Citizens in Action v. New Jersey Department of Environmental Protection*, decided by the U.S. District Court in New Jersey during 2001 <http://lawlibrary.rutgers.edu/fed/html/ca01-702-2.html>. This case also involved, interestingly, a cement plant proposed for Camden, New Jersey. The St. Lawrence Cement plant was approved by the New Jersey Department of Environmental Protection, after the company received all the appropriate permits and authorizations required. A group of residents in the Waterfront South area of Camden — with help from the Public Interest Law Center of Philadelphia and the Center on Race, Poverty and the Environment in San Francisco — filed a lawsuit alleging that the permits were in violation of civil rights law.

The cement plant was going to be located in an area the population of which has the following characteristics: (i) poor — the neighbourhood's residents earn a median household income which is less than one fourth of the state-wide median; (ii) mostly non-white — about 90% of the residents are from racial or ethnic minorities; (iii) already overburdened with locally unwanted land uses (LULUs) — there are already an incinerator, a sewage treatment plant, a power plant, a scrap metal yard and two Environmental Superfund sites in Waterfront South (Lazaroff; *New York Times*).

The litigants (residents) argued that although the permit granted had satisfied air pollution limits established by the Environmental Protection Agency (EPA), more was needed. The Department of Environmental Protection, they claimed, should have undertaken a broader review, "based on guidelines of the E.P.A. that call for incorporating the heavily industrialized neighborhood's racial and ethnic makeup, existing pollution sources and potential cumulative health effects from the plant" (*New York Times*). The litigants (residents) asked for a preliminary injunction, and one was granted by a district court judge. The judge ruled that the plaintiffs had "established a prima facie case of disparate impact discrimination based on race and national origin in violation of the E.P.A.'s regulations" (*New York Times*).

The judge ordered the plant to be closed while the Department completes a full review. The ruling has been appealed to a higher court by the St. Lawrence Cement Company. The company built the plant at a cost of US$50 million, and was promising to create 15 jobs for local residents, and several times that many "spinoff jobs" (Lazaroff; *New York Times*). The company claims that the non-operation of the plant will cost it US$200,000 a week (*NJBIA*). Some other residents of Camden have made a public appeal to politicians for "economic justice", concerned about the potential jobs at stake (*NJBIA*).

This case — being called the first significant "environmental justice" ruling from a court — could (if upheld on appeal) set a very significant precedent. It may ultimately require environmental regulators to consider cumulative impacts of polluting industries before issuing emissions permits (Lazaroff; *New York Times*). It serves meanwhile as an illustration of the potential impacts of applying an environmental justice perspective through adjudication.

The Economic Analysis Debates

The *National Law Journal* study (discussed above) showed that in the United States, pollution sources and hazardous facilities were more often located in minority communities, and that penalties for environmental damage done to minority communities tended to be lower than for damage in non-minority communities. The putative rationale for both siting decisions and compensation decisions is the same: "property values". Put simply, toxic wastes sites will be located where the land is cheapest, and those who are poor will tend to live in those areas where land is cheapest. Compensation for economically measured harm, in terms of declines in property values, will tend to be less when land is cheaper to begin with (all other things being equal). This all makes sense in terms of an economic analysis.

Some people — mainly economists — argue that an economic analysis is the most, or even the only, appropriate ethical perspective to apply to environmental problems. Cost-benefit analysis (discussed more fully below) is the method of application for economic analysis. The objective of economic analysis — which has both descriptive (empirical) and prescriptive (normative) components to it — is to identify and promote economically efficient, or optimal, outcomes in the allocation of scarce resources.

It is important to point out that the proponents of economic analysis would agree with proponents of a social justice or environmental justice perspective that environmental issues are inherently moral and political ones. They would disagree, nevertheless, about which fundamental value ought to be pursued, whether through social policy or individual activity. Social justice advocates, as explained above, base their perspective on the value of equality, whereas the economic analysis perspective is best understood in terms of the value of utility, understood in a highly specific way.

Economic analysis, as an ethical perspective, developed out of the branch of moral philosophy known as utilitarianism. The classic formulation of utilitarianism was developed by Jeremy Bentham and John Stuart Mill, who wrote during the early and mid-1800s (respectively) in England. The simple version of utilitarianism stipulates that one should choose whichever action would produce "the greatest good for the greatest number". Bentham and Mill claimed that it is morally required for us to try to bring about the state of affairs that produces the most net (positive) utility. Utility, for these classical utilitarians, was measured in terms of the presence of pleasure and happiness (positive utility), and the absence of pain, suffering or unhappiness (negative utility, or disutility). Utilitarianism is a consequentialist moral theory; it determines right and wrong, good and bad, on the basis of consequences (amounts of utility and disutility produced). It is also aggregative and maximizing.

An aggregate is a group of distinct things taken together. The utility and disutility of all concerned — everyone affected by a particular course of action or policy — is added up into a total, and it is the size of the total (the amount of utility) that is, in turn, to be maximized. Utilitarianism requires moral agents to be impartial — to weigh each unit of utility equally and evenly, without favouring their own utilities or those of anyone near and dear to them. It also requires moral agents to make decisions that "sum across persons", lumping together the impacts of decisions on distinct individual persons. Utilitarianism is committed to the maximization of net utility for society taken as a whole, and to attempting to predict what the likely effects of our actions will be, in terms of the generation of happiness and unhappiness.

Thus, the three main aspects of utilitarianism are the following: (i) welfarism — judging states of affairs by their capacity to generate utility or disutility; (ii) sum ranking; and (iii) consequentialism (Sen, 1979). Sum ranking refers to aggregating utility, as explained above. Economic analysis is also consequentialist and welfarist, and engages in aggregation of utilities (sum ranking). However, it makes use of a different interpretation of utility than that of the classical utilitarians. The ultimate goal is still to maximize net (positive) utility, but that is now understood in terms of economic efficiency, or preference satisfaction, or, on some accounts, wealth maximization, rather than psychological states of mind such as happiness or pleasure (and the absence of unhappiness or pain). Economic analysis entails a commitment to maximizing the realization of preference satisfaction and, ultimately, economic efficiency for society as a whole. Economic efficiency has a rather specialized meaning in economic theory. This concept is explained more fully below.

The adoption of an economic analysis, as a social policy perspective, rests upon a set of overlapping and interlocking assumptions that are set out below. Some of these are background assumptions, and some of them are building blocks for the theory itself. The critics of economic analysis tend to fall into two groups. One group accepts the basic assumptions of economic analysis, but recognizes the limitations and shortcomings of the theory — their criticisms are "internal" to the theory. The other group of critics reject most, if not all, of the basic assumptions of the theory, and counter with objections that are "external" to it. We will first set out the background assumptions, then the building blocks of the theory, and then survey the criticisms.

Background Assumptions

The background assumptions to economic analysis include the following: (a) preconditions for markets, (b) factors of production, (c) scarcity of resources, and (d) opportunity costs. The preconditions for markets include: (i) private property rights, (ii) enforceable contract law, (iii) information and (iv) competition. Property rights, exclusive and alienable, and enforcement of contract provisions enable those who produce to trade or sell the fruits of their labour for the fruits of others' labour. Perfect markets — the "ideal type" postulated by economists — require perfect information for consumers — full knowledge about the quality, availability, safety and efficacy, and the relative prices of all goods and services. Perfect markets also entail perfect competition, which means no monopolies (single seller or producer), no monopsonies (single buyer or purchaser), and no oligopolies (a few sellers dominating the market), or any other measures that would distort the market, or amount to restraint of trade. No one seller or buyer should be able to affect the price of any good or service by deciding whether or not to sell or buy.

Perfect markets would, by definition, not be vulnerable to problems of market failures, such as externalities, public goods or common property. Market failures usher in a distortion of incentive structures, resulting in too much or too little production or provision of the items in question. These market failures are discussed in more detail below. The real world, which has to deal with imperfect markets, nevertheless relies upon the preconditions of markets: private property rights, enforceable contracts, (imperfect) information for consumers, and (imperfect) competition. Factors of production are also relevant for the real world. The categories of "factors of production" include capital (which generates interest), labour-time (compensated for by wages and salaries), land (which generates rent), and then human resources, including creativity and entrepreneurship (Primeaux and Stieber, 1997: 182).

The Problem of Market Failures

Economists have given considerable attention to the problem of market failures. They have come up with several suggestions for understanding and dealing with such situations. Freeman (1986: 312) suggests that the existence, and the problem, of pollution can be explained in "terms of the incentives faced by firms and others whose activities generate waste products". He continues as follows: "Each unit of pollution discharged imposes costs or damages on other individuals. But typically, the dischargers are not required to compensate the losers for these costs. Thus, there is no economic incentive for the discharger to take those costs into account. This is the essence of the market failure argument" (ibid.).

Another way that the problem of environmental harm and the need for control measures is characterized is in terms of the "tragedy of the commons". This theory was first put forth by Garrett Hardin in a highly influential and widely reproduced piece with that title (1968). He describes the development of the tragedy in this way: "Picture a pasture open to all. It is to be expected that each herdsman will try to keep as many cattle as possible on the commons. Such an arrangement may work reasonably satisfactorily [for a time]. Finally, however, comes the day of reckoning, that is, the day when the inherent logic of the commons remorselessly generates tragedy" (ibid.: 1245). That depiction exemplifies the depletion of a resource, after the carrying capacity of the ecosystem has been reached and exceeded. The tragedy of the commons is also applied to the problem of pollution: the ability of the ecosystem to perform as a "sink" for human generated wastes is reached and exceeded, and the environment becomes a "cesspool", as Hardin puts it.

There are several ways to address these problems. One suggestion is to attempt to establish a "private market" in environmental services; by, in effect, creating property rights to units of clean air or clean water. Another way of describing this scenario is in terms of "privatizing the commons". Creating private property rights in environmental amenities would help markets to achieve an efficient allocation of environmental services (Freeman, 1986: 311). People have an incentive to protect what they can personally benefit from, and thus are motivated to take conservation measures. Economists do acknowledge, though, that the "air and waters surrounding us cannot readily be fenced, and so the tragedy of the commons as a cesspool must be prevented by different means" (ibid.). These other means consist of taxation or government regulation. As Freeman (1986: 311) explains, regulations, taxes and subsidies, on an economic approach, should "create incentives which replicate the incentives and outcomes that a perfectly functioning market would produce" (ibid.).

An Optimal Level of Pollution

The assumption concerning scarcity is that all physical materials are effectively scarce over the long run. There is some debate over whether they are inherently scarce, or only conditionally so. Some economists, such as Julian Simon, in *The Ultimate Resource*, contend that innovations of technology will always be able to produce acceptable substitutes, and thus there is no real scarcity. Other economists are much less sanguine, and insist that there will be actual scarcity of certain things, such as endangered species. Generally, it is assumed on most accounts that human needs are effectively unlimited. To meet human needs and satisfy human interests, to whatever extent, requires resources. Thus, it is of crucial importance that scarce resources are subjected to the optimal allocation in order to try to satisfy those presumably limitless human preferences.

Opportunity costs, at their most basic, are "foregone goods and services that could have been produced from a given set of resources that were used to produce other goods and services" (Primeaux and Stieber, 1997: 182). The notion of scarcity is linked to opportunity costs: if resources are used for purpose A, those very same resources cannot then be used for purpose B. William Baxter (1986 [1974]) uses the example of building a dam. Such a project would require: X hours of labour, Y tons of steel and concrete (material), Z amount of capital (to purchase tools, designs, plans, and technology). Those resources, if they are spent on building the dam, cannot be used to build something else, such as a school, a library, or a hospital. Specific resources, once allocated to use or purpose A, are no longer available for use or purpose B. There is thus an opportunity cost, which amounts to the value of alternatives that have to be foregone in order to achieve something.

Baxter suggests that better insight into environmental problems could be gained by the application of economic analysis. He claims that pollution, in particular, should be addressed as an economic problem — as an issue concerning the use of resources so as to maximize human satisfaction. Baxter argues that pollution control should be determined by the optimal level of pollution. The optimal level of pollution represents the optimal trade-off, the point at which further reducing pollution would require diversion of resources from activities society would prefer more than it would prefer reduced pollution. Baxter points out that environmental issues raise technical questions of how to achieve a given objective, but they also raise normative questions concerning what ought to be done. Baxter's treatment of pollution is part of his overall ethical framework, which includes: (a) a claim about the importance of the sphere of freedom; (b) the claim that waste is a bad thing; and (c) the claim that every individual should have "the incentive and the opportunity to improve his share of satisfactions" (Baxter, 1986: 215).

Economic Analysis and Standard-Setting

Freeman provides an interesting analysis of the relationship between environmental standards and economic efficiency, understood in terms of Pareto optimality (Pareto optimality is explained just below, under assumption one). It is worth quoting him at length (1986: 311–12):

> An environmental quality standard is a legally established minimum level of cleanliness or maximum level of pollution in some part of the environment, for example, an urban air shed or a specific portion of a river. A standard, once established, can be the basis for enforcement actions against a polluter whose discharges cause the standard to be violated. The principle of Pareto Optimality provides a basis for determining at what level an environmental quality standard should be set. In general, Pareto Optimality requires that each good be provided at the level for which the marginal willingness to pay for the good (the maximum amount that an individual would be willing to give up to get one more unit of the good) is just equal to the cost of providing one more unit of the good (its marginal cost).
>
> Consider for example an environment which is badly polluted because of existing industrial activity. Consider making successive one-unit improvements in some measure of environmental quality. For the first unit, individual's marginal willingness to pay for a small improvement are likely to be high. The cost of the first unit of clean-up is likely to be low. The difference between them is a net benefit. Further increases in cleanliness bring further net benefits as long as the marginal willingness to pay is greater than the marginal cost. But as the environment gets cleaner, the willingness to pay for additional units of cleanliness decreases, while the additional cost of further cleanliness rises. At that point where the marginal willingness to pay just equals the marginal cost ... is the point at which the environmental quality standard should be set.
>
> There are two points to make about this approach to standard setting. First, an environmental quality standard set by this rule will almost never call for complete elimination of pollution ... The second point is that the logic of benefit-cost analysis does not require that those who benefit pay for those benefits or that those who ultimately bear the cost of meeting a standard be compensated for those costs.

Freeman's account of the rationales of the environmental standard setting process has drawn upon the core building blocks of economic analysis: Pareto optimality, willingness to pay, potential compensation principle. It will now be fruitful to examine the particular assumptions that are building blocks to the theory of economic analysis, and then to explore the criticisms of those assumptions.

Theoretical Building Blocks of Economic Analysis

The assumptions of neoclassical economic analysis, which function as building blocks to the theory, are as follows: (1) commitment to economic efficiency; (2) utility understood in terms of preference satisfaction; (3) preference satisfaction is measured in terms of willingness to pay; (4) substitutability; (5) potential Pareto criterion; (6) measurability related to market pricing; (7) cost-benefit analysis deemed appropriate for situations involving the imposition of risk to health or life; (8) economic analysis as public policy.

1. Efficiency, in common usage, refers to the production of a desired effect with a minimum of effort, expense, or waste. Efficiency in economic theory refers to the extent that a particular allocation of resources maximizes overall value (measured in terms of preference satisfaction). If, for example, fuel is cheap, a form of transportation that is less efficient from an engineering point of view may be more efficient from an economic point of view.

   Jules Coleman (1988: 97) points out that "economists as well as proponents of economic analysis of law employ at least four efficiency-related notions". These four notions are: (i) productive efficiency, (ii) Pareto optimality, (iii) Pareto superiority and (iv) Kaldor-Hicks efficiency. These concepts "express standards for ranking or describing states of affairs".

Coleman's characterizations of the Pareto optimal and Pareto superior criteria are as follows:

> Resources are allocated in a Pareto-optimal fashion if and only if any further reallocation of them can enhance the welfare of one person only at the expense of another. An allocation of resources is Pareto superior to an alternative allocation if and only if no one is made worse off by the distribution and the welfare of at least one person is improved. These two conceptions of efficiency are analytically related in that a Pareto-optimal distribution has no distributions that are Pareto superior to it.... Pareto-optimal distributions are Pareto non-comparable; the Pareto-superior standard cannot be employed to choose among them. Another way of putting this last point is to say that the social choice between Pareto-optimal distributions must be made on nonefficiency grounds. (Coleman, 1988: 97)

As Coleman (1988: 97) explains, the relation to utility is as follows: "Pareto improvements increase total utility, although not all increases in total utility constitute Pareto improvements". Typically, however, "Pareto judgements are expressed in terms of individual preferences rather than in terms of total utility". Put another way, Pareto judgements, unlike utilitarian judgements, do not involve "sum ranking". The Pareto criterion demands "win-win" outcomes, and does not allow some people's losses to be balanced against others' gains.

Economists initially tried to develop the Pareto criterion as a tool for evaluating social policy. As long as you could improve the lot of one person, while making no one else any worse off, then you could claim to have made a Pareto improvement. An example of such a situation would be one in which there are some "unowned" resources, unclaimed resources that one person could take and make use of. Economic theory conjectures that in a perfect market, such a state will be reached through free exchange, via the working of the "invisible hand", since both parties to such exchanges are presumably better off, or the trade would not have occurred.

It is important to emphasize, as Coleman and others do, that what is Pareto optimal or Pareto superior will depend upon the initial distribution of entitlements. As Amartya Sen (1985: 10) has argued, "a situation can be Pareto optimal but nevertheless be highly objectionable, if the initial conditions are sufficiently egregious"; for example, "if the utility of the deprived cannot be raised without cutting into the utility of the rich, the situation can be Pareto optimal, but truly awful". The situation might be regarded as "awful" because, from an egalitarian point of view, it is one of distributive injustice. But it might also be regarded as awful from a utilitarian point of view if the total utility to be gained by improving the lot of the deprived would exceed the utility lost by the rich. In that case, the (classical) utilitarian would support measures to improve the lot of the poor even though such measures would contravene the Pareto criterion. Moreover, the pure Pareto criterion is of little practical use for evaluating social policy since, in the real world, virtually any policy will negatively affect *somebody*, if only slightly.

The shortcomings of the Pareto criterion have led economists to develop an alternative criterion for public policy, known as the Kaldor-Hicks, Potential Pareto, or Potential Compensation Principle, and it is discussed below (assumption five).

2. The appropriate measure of utility, so the theory holds, is the satisfaction of subjective wants or preferences. To the extent that a particular course of action would bring about the maximal satisfaction of preferences, that course of action is deemed to produce maximal net utility. These preferences tend to be of the kind normally satisfied by market transactions (see substitutability — assumption four below). The claim is that the basis of analysis should be the realization of *subjec-*

tive preferences, wants and desires, rather than *objective* standards of welfare or illfare — what will actually make people better off. With economic analysis, whatever people think they want, at the point of decision making — not even what would actually make them happy, after the fact — is what should be maximized. This account is said by its defenders to be respectful of the autonomy of individuals, since each person is assumed to be the best judge of what is in her or his own interests. Not all contemporary utilitarians favour this approach, but the adherents of economic analysis certainly do.

3. How, one might ask, can we tell what preferences people have, in order to assess whether, and how much, they have been satisfied? The answer the theory provides is the notion of "willingness to pay". The claim that the most appropriate and reliable way to measure preferences is by measuring "willingness to pay" is the third assumption. Asking someone how much she would be willing to pay to acquire something, or how much she would accept to give something up, is taken to be a reflection of that person's preferences in relation to that thing. The willingness to pay indicator presupposes substitutability (the fourth assumption).

4. Economists like to say that market behaviour consists of ranking options, assigning different weights to various potential "consumption bundles" (Freeman, 1986). The latter are simply the lumped together packages of economic goods and services, which people are asked to compare, and rate, in terms of which ones are more likely, or less likely, to satisfy their preferences. The notion of substitutability refers to the substitution of components of the consumption bundles. Consumers are asked to give higher rankings, or greater weight, to the consumption bundle that would most satisfy their preferences. It is then claimed that for any particular good or service, some other good or service could stand in for it, and effectively produce the same amount of utility.

    Furthermore, the substitution amounts should be calculable in monetary terms, which provides a conceptual linkage to the sixth assumption concerning measurability and market pricing (discussed below). If someone is willing to pay a certain amount (X) of money for something (Y), economists assume that the person is indifferent to the distinction between having Y and having some other thing, Z, for which she would also pay the same — X — amount. The amount of money that a person is willing to pay for something reflects the amount of expected preference satisfaction from having that thing. The same amount of satisfaction, it is assumed, could be obtained from spending that amount of money on something else.

5. As explained above, the Pareto Criterion "says to accept only those policies that benefit some people while harming no one" (Freeman, 1986: 221). As Myrick Freeman and others point out, this is a very stringent standard, and few policy proposals could actually meet it. There are few policies, as Freeman notes, "which do not impose some costs on some members of society. For example, a policy to curb pollution reduces the income of those who find it more profitable to pollute than to control their waste" (ibid.).

    The criterion that economists have developed for use in policy analysis, instead of the Pareto Criterion, is the Kaldor-Hicks, or Potential Pareto Principle. The framework for evaluating entails the tallying up of wins and losses, under any particular plan or policy, or course of action. Freeman (1986: 221) says of this other criterion: "[It] asks whether the aggregate gains to those made better off measured in money terms is greater than the money value of the losses to those made worse off. If the gains exceed the losses, the policy is accepted by this criterion... This criterion is justified on ethical grounds by observing that if the gains outweigh the losses, it would be possible for the gainers to compensate fully the losers ... and still themselves be better off with the policy. Thus if the compensation were actually paid, there would be no losers, only gainers" (ibid.).

This criterion is sometimes referred to as the "Potential Compensation Principle", and as Freeman points out, it is the "basis of the cost-benefit analysis of public policy" (1986: 221). The criterion effectively asks whether the winners under a policy win so much that they could potentially compensate the losers, and still win by achieving a net gain. As Herman Leonard and Richard Zeckhauser (1986) say, the assumption is that hypothetically, if compensation could be paid, all affected would agree to the decision/action/plan/policy promising the highest net benefits (after calculating expected benefits minus costs). There is a notion of hypothetical consent being invoked here.

6. One of the simplest and easiest ways to discover people's expression of preferences is to look at market pricing. When economists are faced with the problem of things for which there are no existing markets, they hypothesize that there are ways to infer their preferences through "shadow pricing", or imputed prices, for instance. Environmental amenities, such as peace and quiet, fresh air and clean water, are often considered to be non-market goods for which it is possible to calculate a value. One method might be looking at real estate prices of otherwise comparable properties, one with (access to) environmental amenities and one without. The difference between the prices should reflect consumers' willingness to pay extra for the amenities.

7. Proponents of economic analysis often join forces with those who propose the use of cost-benefit analysis in risk management. J. Fraiberg and Michael Trebilcock (1997) recommend that the political process be disciplined by "technocratic tools such as the use of science in risk assessment and cost-benefit analysis in risk management". They recognize, however, that the experts making such decisions must be accountable, and allow room for meaningful public participation. The criteria that they propose include these: (i) maximize expected values; (ii) avoid catastrophes; (iii) dismiss remote possibilities; and (iv) adopt equitable regulations (Fraiberg and Trebilcock, 1997).

Even in cases in which the activities in question threaten risk to health or life, proponents of economic analysis advocate its use. The field of workplace safety has been a prominent area for the application of cost-benefit analysis in the United States in recent history, as discussed by Steven Kelman (1986), Mark Sagoff (1981), and Ted Schrecker (1984). In 1981, an Executive Order of (then) President Ronald Reagan ushered in the requirement that administrative agencies and departments support any new major regulatory initiative with a cost-benefit analysis, in order to establish that the benefits of the regulation outweigh its costs, though the courts held that the agencies need not do so if this ran counter to the express goals of the enabling legislation (Sagoff, 1981).

Proponents typically support the application of cost-benefit analysis to risk on two main grounds. First, society can afford more safety overall if laws do not force businesses and consumers to waste economic resources on measures that are very expensive for the amount of risk they reduce. This is a cost-effectiveness argument, and is consistent even with accepting that safety should be the overriding social goal. See the editors' notes on risk analysis in Section Three. Second, safety is not the only goal that people value. People in their daily choices regularly trade off safety against other goods, such as convenience and pleasure, and policies are good insofar as they maximize the satisfaction of preferences rather than privileging some preferences (e.g., for safety) over others.

8. This leads us to the final premise, that public policy should be based on economic analysis. In part, as we have seen, this is based on the fundamental utilitarian norm of maximizing aggregate welfare. But the way welfare is understood and operationalized in this analysis also embodies certain particular kinds of liberty values. It is based on the notion discussed above that defining well-being in terms of people's willingness to pay respects individual autonomy because it does not substitute the preferences of policy-makers for those of the public. Advocates of this view often imply that those who would pursue policy goals other than economic efficiency or wealth maximization in the name of the public good are paternalistic elitists, inasmuch as wealth is, in economic theory, by definition, just whatever people think is in their own good, as revealed by their choices. This argument assumes that people's "true" preferences are those they reveal as consumers rather than as citizens (Sagoff, 1981), a point to which we will return when we take up the critique of economic analysis.

Critique of Economic Analysis

Each of the assumptions of economic analysis has been subjected to extensive and penetrating critical scrutiny. We will again go through each of the eight building blocks of neoclassical economic analysis set out above, this time outlining the *criticisms* that have been levelled at each, as well as some of the rejoinders offered by defenders of the approach.

1. The main line of criticism is that the concept of economic efficiency, being aggregative, pays no attention to the distribution of welfare (Schrecker, 1984). It has been a long-standing complaint against utilitarianism that it is "distribution insensitive" — by lumping together everyone's utilities and disutilities, it fails to take into account just who benefits and who suffers, and by how much. Likewise, economic analysis is unconcerned with matters of distributive justice: the fairness of allocating society's benefits and burdens. It does not require that there be an equitable distribution, or allocation, of society's resources (benefits), nor of its pollution or waste (disbenefits, or burdens).

    The response of many economists to this line of argument is to counter that inequalities should be addressed through taxation and redistributive measures of government policy rather than through distorting the market. Leonard and Zeckhauser (1986) argue that if distributional concerns are considered everywhere, they will end up not being treated adequately anywhere. Moreover, they point out that project-based redistributions will only go to the groups affected by the project, and that this will be less comprehensive than redistribution via taxation or direct expenditures of government.

2. It has already been pointed out above that preference satisfaction is a subjective standard; some critics prefer to endorse an account of human flourishing, which rests instead upon objective criteria or indicators of well-being.

3. The "willingness to pay" assumption has probably produced the most sustained and frequently encountered criticism of economic analysis. Environmentalists and others argue that willingness to pay should not be the only, or perhaps even the main, determinant for public policy. The simple problem with willingness to pay is that it is dependent upon "ability to pay". As Ted Schrecker (1984) has pointed out, "willingness to pay is irrelevant unless it is backed by ability to pay". Willingness to pay is intricately and irreducibly tied into the existing distribution of wealth in a society. Proponents of the economic analysis sometimes suggest that the market is the ultimate democracy, in which people "vote with their dollars" for what they prefer to have society provide. In this market democracy, however, those with more dol-

lars have more votes, and the preferences of the rich thus have greater proportional effect than those of the poor. Actual market prices ultimately reflect the preferences of those who have the resources at their disposal to give effect to their preferences.

Economists have acknowledged this criticism, and respond in several ways. One response is to point out that there are, overall, more poor people than rich people, so that, on balance, the aggregate preferences of poor people will add up to more than those of the rich (Leonard and Zeckhauser, 1986). This response does not address the problem of disproportionality, however; and thus an alternate response is to suggest that poor people's preferences could, in principle, be weighted more heavily than rich people's preferences. Leonard and Zeckhauser (1986) question how this could actually be done as a practical matter.

4. Assumption four, substitutability, has been challenged by those who claim that some things cannot be substituted for; that there are simply some things that are irreplaceable. Further, there are some things that are priceless, that should not be subjected to the pricing mechanism of the market. This raises the issues of measurability and non-market goods, dealt with below (criticism of assumption six).

5. The potential compensation principle is an easy target. The criterion is "silent on the question of whether compensation should be paid or not" (Freeman, 1986: 221), or whether consent would actually be granted. There is thus no requirement that the winners should actually pay the losers; it is only necessary that the winners could do so, and still benefit. There is thus no guarantee that the affected parties would actually agree to the decision or policy.

Economists defend the use of the potential compensation principle (or the Kaldor-Hicks principle) for carrying out cost-benefit analysis. They insist that it is simply not feasible to develop policy criteria that would ensure that everyone would actually win, or at least be compensated for losses, and thus ensure consent. Leonard and Zeckhauser (1986) argue that society already tends to compensate for large losses, where possible, or to avoid adopting policies or pursuing courses of action that would impose large losses where it is not possible to compensate. This, however, is a debatable assumption, and is not accepted by critics of cost-benefit analysis.

6. Critics charge that cost-benefit analysis is irredeemably quantitative, and that this will tend to create systematic bias towards consideration of certain aspects, or features; of situations, but will overlook others, namely ones that are inherently qualitative in nature. Some costs and benefits will thus be ignored, because they are much more difficult to measure than others. In response to the measurability and quantitative bias complaint, economists will admit this limitation of cost-benefit analysis. Leonard and Zeckhauser (1986) argue, though, that this is ethically neutral, unless it could be shown that the quantifiable considerations systematically push decisions in a particular direction, or skew the results. Some environmentalists do assert that there is a systematic bias in the application of cost-benefit analysis in favour of development, but there are counter-examples — cases in which a project disfavoured by environmentalists on ecological grounds is also rejected by economists on economic grounds. The rationales in favour of such projects would then tend to be overtly political.

There are several ways to deal with the qualitative, or not easily quantified, aspects: either leave them out altogether, or try to price them. Neither approach is really satisfactory to the critics. Critics of economic analysis have pointed out that some things cannot be substituted for, as noted just above. Such things should be deemed priceless, beyond price, outside the purview of the marketplace. Kelman

(1986) makes this point very eloquently: things such as love or friendship or kindness are cheapened, or devalued, by the very act of trying to put a dollar value on them. Thus, some have suggested that there needs to be a distinction drawn between "unpriced goods", which may be appropriate for market approximations of value, and those "unpriceable unpriced goods". In Kantian terms, there are certain human qualities or activities that derive their value from the human trait of "dignity" or "inherent worth", rather than having an instrumental value, which could potentially be measured in price (Kelman, 1986; Sagoff, 1981). For many people, rights to life, to workplace safety, or to environmental quality should be treated as "unpriceable unpriced goods".

Some economists will concede that some values will never fit, and should never be fit, within a cost-benefit analysis framework; that instead they should be treated as additional considerations or as binding constraints (Leonard and Zeckhauser, 1986). The debate over just which values should be treated this way, and to what extent, is the source of political dialogue, debate and deliberation.

7. Those who object to applying economic analysis to issues of risk often complain that doing so involves "putting a price tag on human life". In a sense this is so: in conducting a cost-benefit analysis of, say, a particular regulatory standard for air pollution, among the benefits quantified in dollars will be the lives saved (or aggregate years of life prolonged) if the standard is met, and these benefits will be weighed against the total cost to society of meeting the standard. There are two kinds of objections: that any dollar value assigned to life will be arbitrary, and that it is morally offensive to even contemplate pricing life in this way.

The first objection has considerable force, though one might reply that people regularly price their own lives and the lives of their loved ones when they buy life insurance. (The concern about willingness to pay reflecting ability to pay is relevant here.) More fundamentally, economists would argue, individuals tacitly price their own lives (in the sense of trading off safety against other goods) every time they spend money on anything other than increasing their safety or prolonging their lives. Individual lives may be priceless in the sense of having infinite moral worth, but it makes little sense to say that saving or prolonging one life is worth the infinite expenditure of resources (if only because that would cost the lives of others). Other criticisms of the economic analysis of risk are bound up with the critique of quantitative risk analysis generally, discussed in the notes and readings of Section Three, Part C.

8. A final very important criticism of the economic analysis is based directly on the notion of democracy. On the economic analysis, it seems as if there is no difference between private and public choice. This is mistaken, according to those who think (as do Mark Sagoff and Steven Kelman) that citizen values differ from consumer choices. Public political and social decision-making fora provide opportunities for people to express different values and assess options differently than do private economic transactions. Kelman (1986) and Sagoff (1981) argue that people do not have a fixed set of preferences that apply to both the public and private arena. Preferences expressed at the individual level about consumption may be quite at odds with the preferences expressed at the collective level. It would be arbitrary for economists to maintain that the preferences expressed in the marketplace are truer reflections of peoples' values than the choices expressed through the political process.

Jacobs (1994) thinks Sagoff's dichotomy of consumer and citizen preferences is too simplistic. Sagoff, like the economists, is advancing a normative argument under the guise of a conceptual analysis: economists think that consumer preferences ought to carry the day, and Sagoff thinks citizen preferences ought to; but neither looks at the complex ways people actually value the environment. Jacobs cites research that suggests that theories about valuation affect valuation behaviour (in experiments, economists are more likely to be free riders, because their theory tells them that's how people behave).

What Sagoff and Kelman want to emphasize is that it is important to distinguish between reliance upon economics as a tool, or a *means* to achieving the goals of public policy, and the reliance upon economics to determine the *ends* or goals of public policy. In the case of the former — economic analysis treated as a tool — the actual goals of public policy (such as the importance of environmental protection or workplace safety) are selected on other grounds. Economics then provides guidance on the most efficient ways to realize those goals. It is the latter use of economic analysis that is most contested — its use to actually select the goals of public policy. It is important also to carefully distinguish between the use of economic analysis to determine the overarching or underlying goals of environmental policy, and the use of economic instruments (discussed below) to implement those policies. We take up this distinction again in the discussion of economic instruments for policy implementation, below.

The Anthropocentrism Debate

The other debate concerns the moral justification of anthropocentrism, or the insistence that only human interests count morally and legally. Proponents of anthropocentrism insist that only human beings should have moral and legal standing. If a being has moral standing, the interests of that being must be taken into account in any decision, action, policy, or law that affects it. If a being has moral standing and a particular decision could harm the interests of that being, then the potential harm to that being must be a factor in the decision. The harm should be avoided or justified by reference to some other moral imperative. If a being has legal standing, then the interests of that being have legal import. When a being with legal standing suffers a legally significant wrong, the being has a claim that the legal system must acknowledge. That being can institute legal action.

Many argue that environmental issues should only be addressed in terms of human interests, that any resolution of an environmental conflict need only recognize the interests of human beings. Aldo Leopold's influential essay "The Land Ethic" argues against this assumption. Leopold (1966) advocates the adoption of a non-anthropocentric environmental ethic.

Aldo Leopold wrote "The Land Ethic" shortly before his death in 1948. He had started out in game management, and had written a classic text on conservation of game species. As Leopold learned more about the newly developing science of ecology, he came to reformulate his views about the appropriate relationship between humanity and nature. He said that ecology helped one to appreciate the interconnectedness of nature, and that it caused one to recognize that even the supposedly "dead" earth possessed a certain kind of life. On the basis of his understanding of ecology, he claimed that ecological knowledge gives us an intuitive respect for nature, and suggests "why we cannot destroy the earth with moral impunity". He claimed that there were moral implications to the findings of ecological science. That is, he attempted to develop a moral position based on scientific knowledge. Leopold has been one of the most influential figures in the development of an ecocentric environmental ethic.

Leopold describes an evolution of moral concern. He starts out his classic essay in this way:

> When God-like Odysseus returned from the wars in Troy, he hanged all on one rope a dozen slave-girls of his household whom he suspected of misbehaviour during his absence. This hanging involved no question of propriety. The girls were property. The disposal of property was then, as now, a matter of expedience, not of right and wrong. Concepts of right and wrong were not lacking from Odysseus' Greece: witness the fidelity of his wife through the long years before at last his black-prowed galleys ·clove the wine-dark seas for home. The ethical structure of that day covered wives, but had

not yet been extended to human chattels. During the three thousand years which have since elapsed, ethical criteria have been extended to many fields of conduct, with corresponding shrinkages in those judged by expediency only (1966: 237).

Leopold wants to advocate a further expansion of ethical criteria. He goes on to say:

There is as yet no ethic dealing with man's relation to land and to the animals and plants which grow upon it. Land, like Odysseus' slave girls, is still property. The land-relation is still strictly economic, entailing privileges but not obligations ... All ethics so far evolved rest upon a single premise: that the individual is a member of a community of interdependent parts ... The land ethic simply enlarges the boundaries of the community to include soils, waters, plants, and animals, or collectively: the land ... (1966: 238–39)

Leopold argued that people needed to develop an "ecological conscience", which would reflect a shift in moral thinking from a position that views nature as having only instrumental value to a position that views nature as having inherent worth. If nature has only instrumental value, any and all of non-human nature is important only if it serves to further human interests. It has value indirectly, only as a means to human ends. However, if nature is perceived to have inherent worth, value in and of itself, then moral claims can be made on behalf of nature or parts of nature. The interests of nature or parts of nature can count directly in moral decisions.

Leopold implicitly argued for a "holistic", ecocentric approach to ethics. He recommended the extension of moral standing to include land, plants, and animals, and he proposed that the land community (a whole rather than simply a collection of individuals) itself be granted moral standing. The focus of moral value was not just life-forms, as it would be for a biocentric approach to environmental ethics. He also included the soil, water and other abiotic elements of the ecosystem, or the "land". Humans, for Leopold, are "plain citizens" in the land community.

Leopold himself did not really explore the implications of his proposed land ethic for environmental law and policy, but Christopher Stone (1972), in a famous article, did just that. Stone recommends that society give legal rights to "natural objects" — forests, oceans, rivers, and so on. Stone describes the successive extension of rights to some new entity that was "unthinkable" prior to the extension. He argues that the extension of legal rights to "natural objects" is simply the next development in that historical progression, a point made by Leopold and explored at greater length by Roderick Nash (1989). He provides criteria for determining whether some thing is a holder of legal rights, and then discusses the application of the criteria to natural objects. Stone says that natural objects are analogous to inanimate objects, such as corporations, municipalities, nation states and so on. Since inanimate objects are legal "persons" in the sense that these objects are granted legal standing and legal rights, natural objects should likewise be granted legal standing and legal rights. Stone has attempted to operationalize the intuitions contained in Leopold's vision of the "land ethic".

William Baxter (1986: 215) — whose work is discussed above — argued explicitly for anthropocentrism. He urged that environmental policies ought to be people oriented. He said:

My criteria are oriented to people, not penguins. Damage to penguins, or sugar pines, or geological marvels is, without more, simply irrelevant. One must go further, by my criteria, and say: Penguins are important because people enjoy seeing them walk about rocks ... I have no interest in preserving penguins for their own sake.

He claimed that "every human being should be regarded as an end rather than as a means to be used for the betterment of another". He is recommending the adoption of a Kantian conception of respect for persons. Persons, for Kant, are "ends in themselves", and have intrinsic value or inherent worth. Only human beings should be so regarded, says Baxter. Baxter is thus asserting that only human beings have inherent worth, and that non-human nature can only be considered to have instrumental value.

He appeals to pragmatism to justify the exclusion of considerations other than human interests. He says:

> Insofar as we act collectively ... only humans can be afforded an opportunity to participate in the collective decisions. Penguins cannot vote now and are unlikely subjects for the franchise — pine trees more unlikely still (216).

Baxter contends that if polar bears or pine trees or penguins "are to count in our calculus of social organization", someone must figure out how much each one counts, how "these life-forms are to be permitted to express their preferences" (216). Baxter then goes on to question the workability of using human proxies to represent non-human interests.

Stone (1972) addresses these claims. He asserts that it is possible to determine what the interests of natural objects are, what their needs are in terms of health or well-being. He says: "I am sure I can judge with more certainty and meaningfulness whether and when my lawn wants (needs) water, than the Attorney General can judge whether and when the United States wants (needs) to take an appeal from an adverse judgement by a lower court". Stone's point is that the law already recognizes the needs of non-human, institutional entities and takes their interests into account. He thinks there is no good reason not to recognize the needs of non-human, natural objects and to take their interests into account. Further, he thinks it is not impossible to figure out economic equivalencies for the calculation of damages and compensation for natural objects.

Critics have pointed out fundamental difficulties with both Leopold's and Stone's proposals. Concerning the specifics of Stone's proposal, for example, critics like Baxter have challenged the claim that we can know with certainty what the interests of natural objects are. A related difficulty is the prospect of determining what is appropriate compensation, or what counts as suitable restoration. Critics have also pointed out the difficulty of determining who the appropriate guardians for natural objects should be. There would be a range of possible candidates for guardians who could claim to represent the interests of nature, but their recommendations would differ markedly.

This debate has continued up to the present among both lawyers and philosophers. Environmental lawyer P.S. Elder (1984) rejected Stone's proposal to extend rights to nature as both legally untenable and wholly superfluous to an adequate system of environmental law. In a similar vein, philosopher Bryan Norton (1991) has argued that it is unnecessary to invoke philosophically controversial biocentric and ecocentric ideas, since, he suggests, all environmentalists' policy goals can actually be justified on anthropocentric grounds. Discussions of alternative normative foundations for environmental law and policy are, in this view, a waste of time and distract environmentalists from the politically effective task of making the case for environmental protection in terms that most people can accept (i.e., human centred terms). Others are unpersuaded by these arguments. Lawyer Jerry DeMarco (1997) concedes that it is often imperative to make the legal case for protecting nature by whatever means are available, and these are often anthropocentric laws and legal doctrines. He worries, though, that this is a short-sighted strategy that ultimately serves to reinforce principles and attitudes that are inimical to his own nature centred values. Philosopher J. Baird Callicott (1995, 1999), a leading contemporary exponent of Leopold's land ethic, has responded sharply to Norton's position. Callicott argues that such "at-first-bizarre" ideas as intrinsic values in nature and ecocentric ethics, initially articulated and elaborated by environmental ethicists and other thinkers, are gradually coming to permeate public discourse on environmental issues and promise to exert a powerful influence on environmental politics, policy and law.

IMPLEMENTATION ISSUES: THE DEBATE OVER "ECONOMIC INSTRUMENTS"

In considering the role that "economic instruments" should play in the implementation of environmental policy, it is important to distinguish between the use of economic (or "market based") instruments to *implement* policy goals (however arrived at) and the use of market-oriented economic analysis to *set* environmental policy goals and standards, as discussed above. These two are often conflated, particularly by critics of market economic approaches in general. That they should be so conflated is understandable, since both are based on neoclassical economic theory and make use of notions of economic efficiency. It is necessary to grasp the difference between them, however, in order to understand why even some quite radical critics of mainstream economics and industrial capitalism can find at least qualified common ground with neoclassical economists in supporting pollution taxes or in preferring performance to prescriptive standards (e.g., Milani, 2000: 191–98).

Michael Jacobs (1994) distinguishes three approaches often conflated under the rubric of "market" approaches to environmental issues. The first is a true "free market" model (e.g., Anderson and Leal, 1991; Brubaker, 1995) that calls for the creation of real markets in environmental goods by the extension of property rights in the environment itself, not just marketable policy instruments. These property rights, like any other, would be protected through civil (and in some cases criminal) law remedies. In this model there is neither separation between the setting of environmental goals and their implementation nor, indeed, public environmental policy at all. Rather, to the extent that the ideal market conditions are met, a Pareto optimal level of environmental quality would be brought about automatically through the "invisible hand" of the market itself. This approach has attracted little support outside of libertarian circles. Apart from the normative objections to Pareto optimality as a criterion of environmental quality discussed above, there are formidable practical barriers to creating anything like an ideal market in environmental goods such as air. The drawbacks of using civil law actions such as nuisance to protect the environment have been discussed in the editors' notes to Section One and the readings in Section One, Part B.

The other two "market approaches" Jacobs (1994) calls the first and second stages of the "neoclassical project", respectively. The "first stage of the neoclassical project" in environmental economics involves policy and standard setting in which Kaldor-Hicks potential-Pareto optimal levels of environmental quality (given existing consumer preferences and wealth distribution) are determined via cost-benefit analysis. We have already discussed this use of economic analysis to determine the goals of environmental policy.

The "second stage of the neoclassical project" is concerned with developing economically efficient means of attaining policy goals (whether set via first stage neoclassical methods or otherwise). These means assume economically rational actors, and rely on what Jacobs prefers to call "financial incentive" or "price mechanism" instruments like green taxes and tradable permits (he thinks terms like "market mechanism instruments" invite confusion with the property rights approach). The readings in Part C of this section by Nancy Olewiler and the Bureau of Industry Economics reflect this "second stage". It is important to note that the use of these kinds of instruments does not entail a commitment to achieving (only) economically efficient levels of environmental quality, but are intended to offer an efficient (socially cost-effective) means of achieving pollution targets, however set, by creating financial incentives, for those polluters who can abate most cheaply, for them to do so. Critics commonly complain that pollution taxes and tradable pollution rights constitute a "licence to pollute". Supporters of these instruments reply that traditional command-penalty instruments, insofar as they do not prohibit pollution altogether (and few do), are also licences to pollute; but, unlike economic instruments, they are *free* licences. A law that makes it an offence for a factory to emit more than a ton of effluent a day is, in effect, a free licence to emit less than a ton of effluent, and provides no incentive to reduce emissions below that level. Having to pay to pollute "effectively *removes* rights that polluters enjoy under a regulatory system" (Jacobs, 1993: 160).

A related complaint against economic instruments is that taxes and fees, unlike penalties, do not morally stigmatize pollution. (This raises themes that also come up in the comparison of criminal versus quasi-criminal, regulatory versus administrative penalties addressed in Section One, Part E and Section Two, Part D.) Supporters reply that the purpose of pollution control law is to control pollution, not to punish polluters, and that if a less punitive approach is more effective in reducing pollution than a more punitive one, it is to be preferred (Hardin, 1998).

Economic instruments are not without their drawbacks, however. In the first place, even if these instruments are less costly to the economy as a whole than are command-penalty instruments, they may actually be more expensive for the state to administer, and depend even more on thorough monitoring and strict enforcement to be effective (Jacobs, 1993: 154–55). Nobody will pay to pollute if they think they can get away with polluting for free. Also, as Jacobs (1994) suggests, these mechanisms may be more effective on paper than in practice, since they are based on simplistic theories about the effects of incentives on behaviour. He argues that economic instruments assuming economic rationality don't always produce optimal outcomes because actors' rationality is bounded in various ways (e.g., "information lack, management costs, attitudes toward discount rates, and structural inertia"). Jacobs (1993: 156–59) points out several structural reasons energy taxes, as advocated by Olewiler, may fall short of their theoretical effectiveness. Consumers, for example, may not be able to afford to invest in energy conservation and efficiency measures, even if these would pay for themselves over the medium term. Landlords have no incentive to invest in insulation and higher efficiency furnaces and appliances if tenants are responsible for paying fuel and electricity bills. In such situations, Jacobs suggests, energy taxes would be less effective than regulations that would impose energy efficiency standards or would require utilities to finance consumers' conservation investments.

There are also normative concerns to do with fairness. For example, under a system of tradable air pollution rights, those firms able to reduce emissions more cheaply can sell their (now surplus) quotas to other firms who have more difficulty cutting pollution and therefore find it cheaper to buy pollution rights than to abate. Under such a system, the total amount of pollution allowed is no greater, and may be less, than if all firms were required to reduce their pollution by a fixed amount. Nevertheless, the air quality just down wind of the factory selling its pollution quota will be much better than that just down wind of the factory buying the quota. Arguably, people living near the two plants are not being treated equally. The factory buying the quota is likely to be an older plant, and those living nearby might justly complain that they have already breathed more than their fair share of bad air. Jacobs (1993: 173–75) argues that energy taxes, unless coupled with targeted rebates and subsidies, are likely to impact disproportionately on the poor, who spend a larger proportion of their income on fuel and who are less able to afford to insulate their homes or buy newer, more efficient appliances and vehicles. Olewiler responds to a number of efficiency, effectiveness and equity arguments against pollution and energy taxes, and comments on the circumstances in which taxes are or are not appropriate pollution control instruments.

FACT AND VALUE ISSUES IN ENFORCEMENT

Analytically, questions about enforcement fall into three categories. First, there are fact/explanatory questions concerning official behaviour. What kinds of sanctions or other responses to non-compliance do environmental enforcement officials make, under what circumstances, and what affects why they act as they do? Second, there are hybrid fact/value or strategic questions concerning the effectiveness of different enforcement practices in terms of advancing policy goals (be they environmental protection, economic efficiency, or something else). Answers to these questions often depend on the answers to fact questions about the effects of different enforcement strategies on polluter behaviour, as well as about the costs of the strategies themselves. Finally, there are deontological normative questions to do with the justice or procedural fairness of different approaches, irrespective of their effectiveness in accomplishing policy goals.

Canadian environmental law enforcement practice has tended to follow the British "compliance" approach rather than the American "sanctioning" approach. In his classic study of British water pollution law enforcement, Keith Hawkins (1984: 191–207) discovered a practice of using law (that is, prosecution or other formal sanctions) as a "last resort" in dealing with polluters. Formal sanctioning was generally reserved for cases of especially flagrant, malicious or defiant rule-breaking on the part of regulated companies. He found that enforcement officials had an ongoing relationship with regulated firms, and the officials believed that future violations and resulting environmental harm could be more effectively prevented by maintaining an open, co-operative relationship with company management, a relationship that would be breached by strict punitive enforcement. Managers generally reciprocated by being open and co-operative in turn, and by making good faith efforts to abate excessive emissions or prevent future spills. Hawkins argued that conflict theory explanations that focus on power relations could not account for both the forbearance on the part of officials and the deference to officials usually displayed by business managers. He turned instead to consensus theory, and explained the pattern in terms of social values. He suggested that there was no social consensus that non-compliance with environmental regulations was blameworthy in itself, so society would not support a policy of strict enforcement. There was, however, a social consensus that law ought to be respected; hence, "scofflaw" violators who made no effort to come into compliance — or, worse, who tried to deceive or defy officials — did deserve to be punished by the law.

Readings in Part D by Murray Rankin and Peter Finkle, John Swaigen and Dianne Saxe all make the case that Canada ought to move in the direction of the sanctioning approach. Their arguments are mainly based on considerations of effectiveness (that is, deterrence), but also appeal to normative considerations of justice and desert. Swaigen asserts that some pollution violations are morally blameworthy; interestingly, his criteria are much like those of the pollution officials studied by Hawkins. Saxe reports empirical research she conducted that suggests that Hawkins' officials are mistaken both in thinking that prosecution is usually ineffective and in thinking it fatal to the working relationship between officials and firms.

The arguments for strict enforcement are of particular significance in light of David Donnelly and Leah Hagreen's report on the pervasive pattern of under-enforcement of environmental law in Canada. While the reading by Donnelly and Hagreen is mainly descriptive and concerned with the particular situation in Canada, the reading by Mark Cohen, an economist, takes an analytic, explanatory approach. He reviews the literature (mainly from economics but also from the other social sciences) on the causes and effects of environmental law enforcement behaviour. He is interested in generalizing, in constructing abstract models that will help us to predict when and under what circumstances officials will enforce environmental regulations, and what effect on polluter behaviour different enforcement strategies will have. Both these readings are in Part D.

The rest of the articles in Part D address alternative modes of enforcement. Richard Brown and Murray Rankin argue for greater use of administrative penalties. Administrative remedies fall into two classes: orders and penalties. Orders come in various kinds, and are well established elements in the pollution abatement and law enforcement repertoire (see the entry on "orders" in the glossary). Orders and related instruments are sometimes called "mandatory abatement" measures, as distinct from the voluntary abatement measures informally worked out in negotiations between officials and polluters. There is thus a continuum of response to non-compliance: voluntary abatement, mandatory abatement, and prosecution (in ascending order of formality and coerciveness). Orders themselves need to be enforced, however, so they are not substitutes for penalties. Administrative penalties (sometimes called "administrative monetary penalties") are fines that can be imposed by officials or tribunals without the need for prosecution. Brown and Rankin argue that the lack of moral stigma attaching to administrative penalties is actually an advantage, since officials may be less reluctant to impose them. Environmental legislation in Canada has made relatively little use of administrative penalties. *Bill 82*, a 1998 piece of Ontario legislation, amended environmental statutes so as to enable the creation by regulation of administrative penalties, though this provision had not yet been implemented as of 2001 (Environmental Commissioner of Ontario, 2001: 77).

One final response that citizens can initiate when enforcement officials are reluctant to prosecute infractions is private prosecution. Private prosecutions are distinct from private law suits, since they are actions under public (criminal or regulatory) law rather than private (civil) law. In essence, a private party takes on the role normally occupied by the Crown attorney. The readings by Kernaghan Webb and Dawn Pier in Part D discuss this option.

REFERENCES

Anderson, Terry, and David Leal. 1991. *Free Market Environmentalism*. San Francisco: Westview Press.

Bannock, Graham, R.E. Baxter, and Ray Rees. 1978. *Penguin Dictionary of Economics*. New York: Penguin.

Baxter, William. 1974. *People or Penguins*. New York: Columbia University Press. Excerpt reprinted as "People or Penguins: The Case for Optimal Pollution". In *People, Penguins and Plastic Trees*, ed. D. VanDeVeer and C. Pierce. Belmont, CA: Wadsworth, 1986.

Benidickson, Jamie. 1997. *Environmental Law*. Concord, ON: Irwin Law.

Bogart, W.A. 2002. *Consequences: The Impact of Law and Its Complexity*. Toronto: University of Toronto Press.

Brubaker, Elizabeth. 1995. *Property Rights in Defense of Nature*. Toronto: Earthscan.

Bullard, Robert. 1990. *Dumping in Dixie: Race, Class, and Environmental Quality*. Boulder, CO: Westview Press.

Bullard, Robert (ed.). 1993. *Confronting Environmental Racism: Voices From the Grassroots*. Boston, MA: South End Press.

Callicott, J. Baird. 1995. "Environmental Philosophy *is* Environmental Activism: The Most Radical and Effective Kind." In *Environmental Activism*, ed. Don E. Marietta and Lester Embree. Lanham, MD: Rowman and Littlefield.

———. 1999. "Silencing Philosophers." *Environmental Values*, 8, 4: 499–516.

Caputo, Tullio, Mark Kennedy, Charles E. Reasons and Augustine Brannigan. 1989. *Law and Society: A Critical Perspective*. Toronto, ON: Harcourt, Brace and Jovanich.

Chambliss, William, and R. Seidman. 1982. *Law, Order and Power*. Second Edition. Boston, MA: Addison-Wesley.

Cole, Luke. 1992. "Empowerment as the Key to Environmental Protection: The Need for Environmental Poverty Law." *Ecology Law Quarterly* 19: 619–83.

Coleman, Jules. 1988. *Markets, Morals and the Law*. Cambridge, UK: Cambridge University Press.

Cox, Robert. 1994. "Global Restructuring: Making Sense of the Changing International Political Economy." In *Political Economy and the Changing International Order*, ed. R. Stubbs and G.R.D. Underhill. Toronto: McClelland & Stewart.

DeMarco, Jerry Valen. 1997. "The Long and Short of Environmental Defence." In *Canadian Issues in Environmental Ethics*, ed. Alex Wellington, Allan Greenbaum and Wesley Cragg. Peterborough, ON: Broadview Press.

DesJardins, Joseph R., and John J. McCall. 2000. "Decision Scenario B: *Boomer v. Atlantic Cement Co.*" In DesJardins and McCall, *Contemporary Issues in Business Ethics*, Fourth Edition. Belmont, CA: Wadsworth.

Domhoff, G. William. 1996. *State Autonomy or Class Dominance? Case Studies in Policy Making in America*. New York: Aldine de Gruyter.

Dworkin, Ronald. 1978. *Taking Rights Seriously*. Cambridge, MA: Harvard University Press.

Elder, P.S. 1984. "Legal Rights for Nature — The Wrong Answer to the Right(s) Question." *Osgoode Hall Law Journal* 22, 2: 285–95.

Environmental Commissioner of Ontario. 2001. *Having Regard: 2000–2001 Annual Report*. Toronto: Environmental Commissioner of Ontario.

Fraiberg, J., and M. Trebilcock. 1997. "Risk Regulation: Technocratic and Democratic Tools for Regulatory Reform." Unpublished Manuscript, Faculty of Law, University of Toronto. Cited by W.A. Bogart (2002).

Freeman, A. Myrick. 1986. "The Ethical Basis of the Economic View of the Environment." In *People, Penguins and Plastic Trees*, ed. D. VanDeVeer and C. Pierce. Belmont, CA: Wadsworth.

Greenbaum, Allan and Alex Wellington. 1993. "Theories of Law and Society". In *Readings in Law and Society*, ed. J. Banfield. Toronto: Captus Press.

Hall, Alan. 1998. "Pesticide Reforms and Globalization: Making the Farmer Responsible." *Canadian Journal of Law and Society* 13: 187–216.

Hardin, Garrett. 1968. "The Tragedy of the Commons." *Science*, 162: 1243–48.

Hardin, Russell. 1998. "Garbage In, Garbage Out." *Social Research* 65, 1: 9–30.

Hawkins, Keith. 1984. *Environment and Enforcement: Regulation and the Social Definition of Pollution*. Oxford: Clarendon Press.

Hofrichter, Richard. 2000. "Introduction: Critical Perspectives on Human Health and the Environment." In *Reclaiming the Environmental Debate: The Politics of Health in a Toxic Culture*, ed. Richard Hofrichter. Cambridge, MA: MIT Press.

Jacobs, Michael. 1994. "The Limits to Neoclassicism: Towards an Institutional Environmental Economics." In *Social Theory and the Global Environment*, ed. R. Redclift and T. Benton. London: Routledge.

———. 1993. *The Green Economy*. Vancouver: University of British Columbia Press.

Kelman, Steven. 1986. "Cost-Benefit Analysis: An Ethical Critique." In *People, Penguins and Plastic Trees*, ed. D. VanDeVeer and C. Pierce. Belmont, CA: Wadsworth. Originally published in *Regulation*, January/February 1981.

LaDuke, Winona. 1993. "A Society Based on Conquest Cannot Be Sustained: Native Peoples and the Environmental Crisis." In *Toxic Struggles: The Theory and Practice of Environmental Justice*, ed. R. Hofrichter. Philadelphia, PA: New Society Publishers.

Lavelle, Marianne, and Marcia A. Coyle. 1993. "Unequal Protection: The Racial Divide in Environmental Law." In *Toxic Struggles: The Theory and Practice of Environmental Justice*, ed. R. Hofrichter. Philadelphia, PA: New Society Publishers.

Lazaroff, Cat. 2001 "Environmental Injustice — Court Halts Operation of Cement Plant Dedicated By EPA Head Christie Whitman." *Environmental News Service* (24 April 2001), online: <http://ens.lycos.com/ens/apr2001L-04-24-06.html>

Leonard, Herman and Richard Zeckhauser. 1986. "Cost-Benefit Analysis Defended." In *People, Penguins and Plastic Trees*, ed. D. VanDeVeer and C. Pierce. Belmont, CA: Wadsworth. Originally published in the newsletter, *Report from the Center for Philosophy and Public Policy* 3, 3 (1983).

Leopold, Aldo. 1966. "The Land Ethic." In *A Sand County Almanac*. London, UK: Oxford University Press.

MacDonald, Doug. 1991. *The Politics of Pollution: Why Canadians are Failing their Environment*. Toronto: McClelland & Stewart.

McHardie, Daniel. 2000. "Rules have Pared Pulp Pollution." *Globe and Mail* (June 5, 2000): B9.

Milani, Brian. 2000. *Designing the Green Economy: The Postindustrial Alternative to Corporate Globalization*. Lanham, MD: Rowman and Littlefield.

Nash, Roderick. 1989. *The Rights of Nature: A History of Environmental Ethics*. Madison, WI: University of Wisconsin Press.

New Jersey Business and Industry Association Scrapbook. 2001. "Workers and Neighbors Rally To Oppose Court Shut Down of Camden Cement Plant" (June 4), online: <http://www.ngbia.org/jun401.htm>.

New York Times. 2001. "Federal Judge Halts Opening of Slag Plant" (April 21).

Norton, Bryan G. 1991. *Toward Unity Among Environmentalists*. New York, NY: Oxford University Press.

Paehlke, Robert. 1989. *Environmentalism and the Future of Progressive Politics*. New Haven, CT: Yale University Press.

Paehlke, Robert, and Pauline Vaillancourt Rosenau. 1993. "Environment/Equity: Tensions in North American Politics". *Policy Studies Journal* 21, 4: 672–96

Porter, Michael and Claas van der Linde. 1995. "Green *and* Competitive: Ending the Stalemate." *Harvard Business Review* (September–October): 120–34.

Posner, Richard. 1973. *The Economic Analysis of Law*. Cambridge, MA: Harvard University Press.

Primeaux, Patrick and John Stieber. 1997. "Economic Efficiency". In *Blackwell Encyclopedic Dictionary of Business Ethics*, ed. P. Werhane and E. Freeman. Malden, MA: Blackwell.

Sagoff, Mark. 1981. "At the Shrine of Our Lady of Fatima, or Why Political Questions Are Not All Economic." *Arizona Law Review* 23: 1283–98.

Schnaiberg, Allan, and Kenneth A. Gould. 1994. *Environment and Society: The Enduring Conflict*. New York: St. Martin's Press.

Schrecker, Ted. 1984. *The Political Economy of Environmental Hazards*. Ottawa: Law Reform Commission of Canada.

———. 1990. "Resisting Environmental Regulation: The Cryptic Pattern of Business-Government Relations." In *Managing Leviathan: Environmental Politics and the Administrative State*, ed. Robert Paehlke and Douglas Torgerson. Peterborough, ON: Broadview Press.

Sen, Amartya. 1985. "The Moral Standing of the Market." In *Ethics and Economics*, ed. E. Paul et. al. Oxford, UK: Basic Blackwell.

———. 1979. "Utilitarianism and Welfarism." *Journal of Philosophy* 76, 9: 463–89.

Stone, Christopher D. 1972. "Should Trees Have Standing: Toward Legal Rights for Natural Objects." *Southern California Law Review* 45: 450–501.

Thompson, Shirley. 2002. "Environmental Justice in a Toxic Economy: Community Struggles with Environmental Health Disorders in Canada." Unpublished paper presented at the Ninth Annual Conference of the Environmental Studies Association of Canada, Toronto, Ontario, 30 May 2002.

Turner, Bryan. 1986. *Equality*. London, UK: Ellis Horwood Ltd. and Tavistock Publications.

VanderZwaag, David, and Linda Duncan. 1992. "Canada and Environmental Protection: Confident Political Faces, Uncertain Legal Hands." In *Canadian Environmental Policy: Ecosystems, Politics and Process*, ed. Robert Boardman. Toronto: Oxford University Press.

Wellington, Alex, Allan Greenbaum and Wesley Cragg. 1997. "Themes in Canadian Applied Environmental Ethics." In *Canadian Issues in Environmental Ethics*, ed. Alex Wellington, Allan Greenbaum and Wesley Cragg. Peterborough, ON: Broadview Press.

Westra, Laura, and Peter Wenz. 1995. *Faces of Environmental Racism: Confronting Issues of Global Justice*. Lanham, MD: Rowman and Littlefield.

PART A
The Political Context

(a) On Lawmaking[†]

William J. Chambliss ——————————————————

There are literally thousands of laws enacted each year. In the United States with fifty state legislatures passing laws, thousands of municipal and county ordinances and the federal government, the sheer magnitude of law is overwhelming. In addition, there are court decisions at the state and federal level which often constitute the creation of new laws. Other nations, including most European countries and Scandinavia, where the law making function is more centralized, do not produce quite the magnitude of new law each year that the United States does, but it is nonetheless a very prolific enterprise, this business of making law.

It is not surprising, then, that attempts to generalize about the processes that lead to the creation of law should be wanting. Some laws are clearly passed for the specific interest of an individual; others emerge out of lobbying by groups representing substantial portions of the population; yet others, perhaps the majority, are no more than an expression of the views and interests of legislative committees.

Despite this, however, there remains the need for generalization to aid understanding. Fortunately, we are not hopelessly entangled in an endless number of laws for they are not all of equal significance. In fact, most bills and stat-

utes passed by legislators are concerned with tinkering with existing law. What we should be concerned with is not the mountain of *minutiae* produced as law but the critical events, the points at which laws are produced which provide a new approach to a problem, a basic revision of the existing relationships between state, polity, government and basic institutions; new innovation in the conception of legal contracts or the rights of children vis à vis parents; of women and work, and so forth. These laws are the ones that comprise the important turning points in the historical process and are therefore the ones about which we should be concerned to develop adequate sociological theory:

> Most cases, to be sure, are merely cumulative in their effect, moving in well-beaten paths, with some inevitable deviation but by and large within the lines laid down. Occasionally, however, comes a case of tremendous important [*sic*].[1]

These are the cases which "strike out in a new direction."

Explaining the Creation of Law
Social theories differ markedly on the relative weight they give to the ideological and the mate-

† From *British Journal of Law and Society* 6, 2 (1979): 149–53, 157–61, 164, 169–71. Reproduced by permission of Blackwell Publishers. See appendix for notes or references.

rial aspects of society. Theories which place greatest emphasis on ideology see the beliefs people have, their ideas of right and wrong, the things they value and their culture as the most important configuration of elements shaping the way people and their history behave. Theories which emphasize the importance of the social structure stress the way people organize the production and distribution of resources: food, shelter, clothing, money and power as the proper starting point for sociological analysis. There is a sense in which the entire history of western social thought can be seen as a struggle between exponents of these conflicting traditions.

In the zeal to defend one or the other theoretical paradigm it is not uncommon to find one side accusing advocates of the opposing position of having "completely ignored" or "relegated unimportant" those features of reality seen by the writer to be "salient." Those who attack ideological or normative theorists accuse them of neglecting entirely facets of social structure that are not part of the ideology of the times. Conversely those who argue against structural interpretations that de-emphasize the importance of culture or ideology like to characterize such theories as devoid of any emphasis upon ideology as a moving force. Attacks on Marxist theory are among the clearest examples of this erroneous [construction] of strawmen to strengthen one's own argument. Critics of Marxism invariably accuse this tradition of ignoring ideology and culture as forces shaping society. They also accuse Marxism of being "reductionist" and attributing everything to the force of economic determinism. No careful reader of Marx, Engels or those who have followed in that tradition could honestly make such an error. As Engels put this conflict between emphasizing social structure rather than ideology to a friend in a letter:

> ... because we deny an independent historical development to the various ideological spheres which play a part in history (we do not therefore) deny them any effect upon history.[2]

The point is given more concrete manifestation when it is observed that those nation-states that have based their political and economic organization on Marxist ideas have been among those most concerned to develop and foster an ideology among the people supportive of the state.

Critics of Weber and Durkheim often make the same oversimplification in the other direction, accusing them of emphasizing culture,

norms and ideology to the exclusion of social structure. The reduction of these complicated theories to such simple mistakes is as fallacious as is the characterization of Marxism as economic determinism.

This is not to say, however, that there is no significant difference in emphasis between sociological tradition [*sic*]. There are differences in emphasis which make for profound differences in the claims and explanations put forth. If one sees the most important force behind the development of the state in modern societies as resulting primarily from a tendency towards increasing rationalization and only secondarily from the demands and machinations of material conditions then a theory is suggested which is quite different from one that sees the state as developing primarily as a means of furthering the interests of those who control the means of production and only secondarily as being influenced by the ideology and norms extant at the time.

There was a time, not too long ago, when theories trying to answer the question of how laws are created followed directly from the two paradigmatic traditions discussed above. One theory suggested that the law represented "societal consensus." Durkheim, Sumner, and Hall (to mention the more obvious examples) saw the law as primarily a reflection of the "collective consciousness," the "norms and values" and the "customs" of a people. In opposition to this view was the "ruling class" model which argued that the law reflected the ideas and the interests of those who controlled the economic and power resources of the society, those who sat at the top of the political and economic institutions.

One is hard pressed to find examples of modern social scientists defending the pure forms of either of these models. Everyone, it seems, recognizes that there is some truth in both claims. Thus Richard Quinney invokes the idea that the law reflects extant ideology but integrates into this hypothesis the notion that extant ideology is largely a reflection of dominant class interests:

> As long as a capitalist ruling class exists, the prevailing ideology will be capitalistic. And as long as that ruling class uses the law to maintain its order, the legal ideology will be [capitalistic] as well.[3]

Lawrence Friedman has expressed a similarly eclectic view of the relationship between ideology and economic structure but his emphasis is on the role of consensually held values rather than economic structure: "What makes law, then, is not 'public opinion' in the abstract, but public opinion in the sense of *exerted social force*."[4] Friedman goes on to recognize that there are differentials of power which makes it more likely that some groups (and social classes) will be more successful in "exerting social force to create law" than will other groups. The "explanation" proffered is one of competing interest groups with different power bases as the moving force behind the creation of laws.

These two views of which the works of Quinney and Friedman are representative, characterize the current debate over law creation. They are logically derivative from earlier, less subtle characterizations of "ruling class" and "normative" theories of law. It is to the credit of the sociology of law as a scientific endeavour that the more sophisticated theoretical formulations take account of the empirical research and theoretical discussions which revealed the shortcomings of the more simplistic interpretations.

Several criticisms are nonetheless appropriate to the paradigms suggested by Quinney and Friedman. For one thing, neither is amenable to empirical test. As Friedman recognizes, if the test of whether or not one "interest group" has more power than another is that one is successful in its efforts to affect legislation while the other is not then the theory is a mere tautology which tells us that those groups whose interests are represented in the law are the groups who succeeded in having their interests represented in the law. On the other hand, the view that the law represents the ideology of capitalism so long as there is a capitalist ruling class begs the question of how this comes about. Is there an automatic response of all law or is there a process involved? Furthermore, this theory is also subject to the dangers of tautology. If we discover the passage of laws that are opposed by the "capitalist class" then does this contradict the theory? Perhaps it should but if we invoke the idea that "in the long run these laws turn out either to be unenforced or to represent the interests of the capitalist class" then we have once again suggested a paradigm which becomes true by (a) definition and (b) the invocation of auxiliary hypotheses.

There is a third theoretical paradigm which captures the best of these [alternatives] perspectives and is at the same time able to make sense of the extant empirical data on law creation. This is the dialectical paradigm which sees law creation as a process aimed at the resolution of contradictions, conflicts and dilemmas which are inherent in the structure of a particular historical period.

Contradictions and Resolutions

Every historical era has its own persistent dilemmas and conflicts. The most important dilemmas and conflicts extant in a particular time and place are those that derive from the economic and political structures of the times. Under feudalism a source of continuing conflict and irresolvable dilemmas was the attempt by feudal lords to expand their territory and provide protection for their serfs from attack by other feudal barons. These conflicts and dilemmas, in turn, were a direct result of the particular contradictions inherent in that economic form which we have come to call feudalism.

A contradiction is established in a particular historical period when the working out of the logic of the social structure and ideology must necessarily destroy some fundamental aspects of existing social relations.[5] This admittedly abstract depiction of what is meant by contradiction can best be comprehended by juxtaposing contradictions with other aspects of reality. Under capitalism, according to Marx, the basic contradiction is between capital and labour. This contradiction inheres in capitalism because if the workers and the capitalists both persistently and consistently pursue their own interests as defined by the logic of capitalism, then the relationship between workers and capitalists must eventually be destroyed. Without debating for the moment the validity of Marx's position we want only to illustrate the meaning of contradiction from this example. This contradiction of capitalism produces a wide range of dilemmas and conflicts. The attempt by workers to organize and demand higher wages, better working conditions, and tenure of employment, is a result of the basic contradiction. The attempt by owners to resist these demands by workers creates conflicts.[6] The dilemma for capital, the state and government is how to resolve the conflicts: how to maintain the capitalist system without fomenting a revolution. Note, however, that it is usually the conflicts which create the dilemma for the state. It is conflicts which the state and the government attempt to resolve, not the basic contradiction. Note also that this process is a dynamic one whereby the contradictions create conflicts and dilemmas which people try to resolve. In the resolution of particular conflicts and dilemmas, assuming that the basic contradictions are not resolved, we inevitably have the seeds for further conflicts. Often, resolutions of particular conflicts and dilemmas not only create further conflicts but spotlight as well other contradictions which were heretofore less salient.

. . . .

Pollution and Law

In recent years we have witnessed an explosion in the passage of public law relating to the environment and to consumer protection. For the most part processes by which these laws develop have not been the subject of systematic attention. One exception to this void, however, is the study of pollution laws conducted by Neil Gunningham. This area of legislation is particularly pertinent for our inquiry because it highlights the conflicts between public interest representatives (what Becker called "moral entrepreneurs") and those who own the industries which are largely responsible for the pollution.

Gunningham begins by pointing out the growth in recent years of concern over pollution. He singles out the publication of Rachel Carson's *Silent Spring* and the extent to which the media generally have brought the problem of pollution to public attention. But, he adds: "To explain the growth of environmental concern and the demand for legislation is not necessarily to explain the emergence of legislation. Only some legislative campaigns are successful, [others] fail."[16] The author goes on to point out that although public awareness about pollution problems increased in the years preceding passage of new laws there was certainly nothing approaching consensus:

> ... at one extreme are those who regard pollution as a minor problem and who deny that the environment is being threatened, while at the other, it is suggested that over-population, exploitation of natural resources and pollution will cause ecocatastrophe if present policies are not drastically amended.[17]

In his search for a plausible explanation for the emergence of pollution laws Gunningham also dismisses a simplistic "class conflict" explanation. He argues that the "working class" has not been particularly active or well organized in the campaign for anti-pollution laws. He acknowledges, however, that the most important groups opposing pollution control are "capitalists with strong economic interests in maintaining the status quo." Gunningham also notes that some government agencies (bureaucracies) develop a vested interest in opposing certain forms of environmental laws and come out strongly trying to influence legislation:

> In the pollution campaign, the clearest example of an agency engaged in status politics is the U.S. Department of Agriculture (U.S.D.A.) whose irresponsible attitude towards pesticides has been severely criticized. Why U.S.D.A. went overboard on new pesticides can be understood within an organization perspective. The department found its power and responsibilities diminishing in comparison with several other departments. Graham notes how the twentieth century has reached the farm, and the successful farmer-businessman, with his vast acreage, college degree and modern machinery was less dependent on the U.S.D.A. than the poorly educated struggling farmer with his scanty crop a decade or two earlier.[18]

Under these circumstances the U.S.D.A. was:

> ... in the tradition of all bureaucracies which feel their position threatened by shrinking responsibilities. The department's impulse to fabricate programmes which gave it the illusion of "business" has been especially apparent ... in the business of promoting pesticides, springing to arms at the first whisper of a pest.[19]

The position taken by the U.S.D.A. and the negative reflex action of capitalist owners to any pollution legislation was, however, shortsighted for it failed to realize a fundamental contradiction between industrialization and the quality of the environment. While short-term profits will be maximized by spewing forth industrial waste into rivers and oceans:

> It has become apparent with dramatic suddenness that, at the present more or less uncontrolled rate of industrial and urban development, the major rivers and lakes of the country will become incapable of supporting marine life and unsuitable for humans.[20]

In the long run it is apparent that the maximization of profits by ignoring environmental pollution will not be in the interests of capital.

Furthermore one of the most effective long-term profit maximization guarantees is the development of a monopoly. The law has often been used as a subtle means of increasing monopoly by creating law which gives an advantage to the largest firms in a particular industry. Thus the Meat Inspection laws in the United States were lobbied for and praised by large meat processing firms precisely because the added expense of meat inspection meant that the larger firms could more easily distribute the added expenses with a minimal loss of immediate profits; smaller firms would be forced out of business thus increasing monopoly for the larger companies.[21]

The same process is apparent vis à vis pollution legislation: In 1956 when the Clean Air Act was passed, industry was predominantly hostile to effective anti-pollution legislation inasmuch as this represented increased costs without any direct dividend....[22] However by 1968 another Clean Air Act was passed which met with little industrial opposition.[23] Gunningham explains this shift as occurring in part because of the change in the importance of management as contrasted with owner control over major corporations in the modern capitalist countries. More importantly, however, Gunningham observes:

> Thus, where a firm can afford to implement pollution controls and still make a sufficient profit to maintain expansion, research, etc., we may expect it to do so if it perceives it to be in its own long-term interests.[24]

Again we see the fit between our model and the reality of the legislative process culminating in the passage of law. The contradiction between exploiting the physical environment for maximum profit and destroying that environment to the eventual demise of the system (not to mention the people) creates conflicts between interest groups demanding change and owners attempting to maintain maximum profits and control. Ideology enters into the justification and protection of interests by arguing for the inherent morality of private ownership and private control of the profits derived therefrom. A resolution to the conflict emerges in the form of [legislation] that is in fact in the interests of the profit structure of the largest industrial firms and simultaneously placates the demands of those minority groups seeking state intervention in the industrial process. These laws, however, reveal other contradictions in the form of increased monopoly which itself will lead to further conflicts and dilemmas resulting in yet other legislative innovations.

It is important to note at this point that contradictions are not limited to those that exist between social classes. There are contradictions within particular classes as well. A recent study of the politics of public transportation in California by Alan Whitt is informative in this regard.[25] Whitt, focussing on the relative utility of what he calls the "pluralist, élitist and class-dialectical models," analyzes the forces behind five separate (but interrelated) referenda on public transportation which were voted on by the people of California. In California, as in many other states, voters are sometimes asked to approve or disapprove a particular piece of legislation. The five campaigns studied by Whitt were (1) the issue of whether or not to approve the construction of a mass transit system in San Francisco (BART); (2) Proposition A (1968) to establish rail and bus service public transportation in Los Angeles; (3) Proposition 18 which affected all of California and diverted revenues heretofore used for highway construction to public transportation; (4) Proposition 5 which was similar to 18; and (5) Proposition A which was a 1974 version of Proposition A above.

Each of the campaigns followed some typical patterns: groups mobilized to protect their own interests and support their values. They did not however mobilize in a vacuum. Some groups, city businessmen for example, favoured mass transit measures and would have supported them but were under pressure from the highway construction and oil industries to oppose them. What support was forthcoming was thus sometimes rather half-hearted. Opposition was often conspiratorially organized with contributions from various banks and industries being virtually "on demand": even to the point where each industry or financial institution contributed according to a predetermined percentage of the size of the market it controlled.

In some cases massive expenditures by large industry successfully defeated the referenda through advertising and political campaigns. But money was not always victorious. Furthermore, the "élite" or the "ruling class" was not only divided but it changed over time, opposing mass transit proposals at first but later coming to accept and support them (presumably because they discovered that it was not all that inimical to their economic interests). In short, Whitt's study forcefully reveals the shortcomings of both "pluralist" and "élitist" model — models in the tradition of "interest group" and "ruling class" models I have outlined above. Whitt's study also supports the explanatory power of a dialectical paradigm:

> It is this broader context which allows us to more fully appreciate the political events herein analyzed. Now we see more of the motivation behind such campaigns, the contradictions and conflicts manifested therein, and the reasons for the previously difficult-to-explain patter [*sic*] of political contributions. We can see these political events in the context of the contradictions which the dominant class must face: 1) the market economy *versus* the need for planning, 2) selling transportation as a private good *versus* the requirement for public services, 3) the competition among cities and among capitalists for growth-generating developments *versus* coherent structure and regularity in urban development, 4) the need to construct new urban transit systems *versus* the budget crisis and occasional mass resistance, 5) the desire for class hegemony *versus* the requirements of legitimacy and mass persuasion, and 6) the desire for class unity *versus* the divisive tendencies of intra-capitalist class differences and conflicts.... Rather than seeing (the political events in the five campaigns) as simply a clash of organized interest groups pursuing their own goals as the pluralist model would hold, or as the reflection of an élite working its will, we see that the situation is more complex than either of these models would lead us to believe. There is both competition and cohesion here, but that is not the real point. It is most important to understand that the capitalist class must respond to contradictions and crises in the economy, in the cities, and in the polity.[26]

Furthermore, and this point is essential, neither the "polity" nor the working class is impotent. The ruling class must respond somehow to forceful demands made by organized groups or risk losing not just the ideological legitimacy of the system but the ability to control their own destiny. In a word, the process is dialectical; it avoids "both the determinism of a completely materialist science, and the voluntarism of idealist philosophy."[27]

．．．．

The model I am suggesting for understanding the development of law differs from models which give law and society a life of their own which is independent of the decisions people make. A recent treatise on law by Donald Black attempts to construct a theoretical paradigm in which law moves, spreads, goes up and down, is higher and lower.[34] I shall not dwell on the absurdity of such conceptions here but the point is that in Black's model people are not resolving problems, settling disputes or struggling to survive. Social forces are moving automatically and inexorably towards some unknown (and probably unknowable) end. The model I am suggesting takes quite the opposite starting point: rather than law or society or even history determining the content of the law it is people in a particular historical context who are determining the content of the law. To paraphrase Marx, people make their own history but they do not make it out of whole cloth.

．．．．

While the re-interpretation of historical events according to a predetermined theoretical position is not unusual in science (see, for example, Hanson's superb analysis of physicists observing the same fact situation with different lenses,[50]) it is nevertheless incumbent on us to recognize what is left out of such an analysis. Furthermore, it is imperative that we understand the implications of the analysis as well. For if we see the law as shaped through struggle and conflict in relation to fundamental contradictions then the engine of social change becomes conflict, not harmony and equilibrium. The forces that are important to understand, then, are not the interstices of legal institutions (judges' reasoning, prosecutors' discretion) but the social forces of power, conflict, contradictions and dilemmas which create the "necessity" for legal institutions to respond, for law to change.

The more general point is that the creation of law reflects a dialectical process, a process through which people struggle and in so doing create the world in which they live. The history of law in capitalist countries indicates that in the long span of time the capitalists fare considerably better in the struggle for having their interests and views represented in the law than do the working classes; but the shape and content of the law is nonetheless a reflection of the struggle and not simply a mirror image of the short-run interests and ideologies of "the ruling class" or of "the people."

．．．．

Conclusion

In this paper, I have presented a model for explaining the larger social forces behind the creation of law. This model stresses the overriding importance of basic contradictions in the political economy as the starting point for a sociological understanding of law creation. It puts people squarely in the middle of these contradictions as the struggle to resolve the contradictions by fighting against existing law (laws supporting colonialism, wage discrimination, or racism for example) while others are creating new laws. In the process, ideological justifications develop, shift and change; these ideologies, in turn, become a force of their own influencing the development of legal institutions as it reflects the interplay between material conditions and ideology.

I have analyzed several laws in some detail by way of demonstrating both the utility of the theory and the kinds of data for which the theory is relevant.[52] I have looked particularly at laws pertaining to depressed areas in Britain, anti-pollution laws, and some of the laws relevant to labour and markets during capitalism's early and later stages of development. I have also indicated how the same general process characterizes law creation in socialist societies. That this process might be adumbrated in a truly classless society is a topic for another time.

(b) Environmental Assessment and Democracy[†]

Stephen Hazell

I think we will find that the more we talk about sustainable development, the more we will talk about democracy.

Ron Doering
(former executive director, National Round Table on Environment and Economy)

Secrecy in government has been a common theme in the story of reforming federal environmental assessment. Secrecy prompted the beginning of the public controversy when the Souris Basin Development Authority attempted to prevent federal scientists from assessing the environmental effects of the Rafferty-Alameda project. Secrecy was the downfall of Robert de Cotret in making a covert deal with Grant Devine to allow construction of the Rafferty-Alameda project to continue while a panel review was underway. The cone of silence damaged public confidence in the integrity of the federal government's regulation-making process under CEAA. In the end, these secrecies led to unwise single visions, unnecessary controversies, and public skepticism about government.

Yet, much of the process related to enacting the *Canadian Environmental Assessment Act*, as well as the substantive provisions of the law stand for democracy and openness in government

and against secrecy. The participatory democracy that occurred in the public and Parliamentary debates about Bill C-78 and Bill C-13 made for a better law with broader public support across Canada. As a key element in sustainable development, environmental assessment reform may be viewed as a vanguard for a democracy that is more participatory, and less secretive and Cabinet-centred.

This chapter explores the tensions between the conflicting imperatives of secretive Cabinet-centred government and the public demand for participatory democracy that occurred in the debates over environmental assessment reform. This process of reform illuminated two sources of tension that flowed from the Canadian system of governance, and particularly the parliamentary system.

The first source of tension is the high level of secrecy demanded by the decision-making process of the federal Cabinet. The second is the imbalance of power and authority between the government — specifically the federal Cabinet — on the one hand, and Parliament on the other. The two issues that relate to these two tensions are as follows:

† From Stephen Hazell, *Canada v. The Environment: Federal Environmental Assessment 1984–1998* (Toronto: Canadian Environmental Defence Fund, 1999), pp. 127–138. Reproduced by permission of Canadian Environmental Defence Fund.

- Must Cabinet decision making be so secretive?
- Must Parliament have such a marginal role in making environmental or other policies?

The balance of this chapter is a reflection on these issues linking environmental assessment to the practice of Canadian democracy, with suggestions for reform that would allow for a more participatory democracy in Canada.

First, a step back to review the theory underlying the current Cabinet-centred approach to the parliamentary system in Canada, often referred to as the Westminister model, and how this approach relates to participatory or discursive democracy.

According to Graham Wilson, the basic feature of the Westminister model is "the unity of the legislature and executive secured through a disciplined political party. The party that controls the legislature thereby controls the executive branch too; its control of both legislature and executive is conditional upon not losing that control of the legislature to another party or alliance of parties".[1] Related features of the Westminister model include:

- a government formed by the political party that can command a majority of members of the lower house of Parliament following an election;
- a career civil service largely free of political patronage appointees that constitutes the primary source of policy advice to ministers;
- a cabinet of ministers appointed by the prime minister that discusses policy issues in secret, and acts collectively in solidarity in providing policy direction; and
- a Parliament whose legislative agenda is controlled by the cabinet.

The rationale for confidentiality of Cabinet discussions and related documents is linked to the concept of Cabinet solidarity. If Cabinet ministers are to accept a single government position on any given matter, they must have full confidence that they may express their views candidly in meetings without fear that their personal views may be publicly revealed to differ from the Cabinet decision taken.

The dominant role of the bureaucracy in policy making is characterized by Van Loon and Whittington as follows:

> Policy formulation is the business of the bureaucracy, subject to the control of the cabinet.

> Parliament's role at this stage is very limited, because of the generally technical and complex nature of the problem of formulating policy alternatives. In terms of expertise and available time, the MP is ill-equipped to contribute much at this stage of policy making.[2]

Thus, a key advantage of the Westminister mode is that it allows governments to be decisive in policy making "unencumbered by the need to steer legislation through a separate, potentially recalcitrant legislature".[3] Another cited advantage is that it places limits on the political power of interest groups. In the case of the development of the regulations under CEAA, this was clearly not the case. Cabinet secrecy did severely limit the ability of public interest groups to affect the decisions that were made, since these groups depend upon an open exchange of information with government. But interest groups that do not rely on appeals to public opinion for their influence and that have close associations with ministers or the governing party, are not disadvantaged by Cabinet secrecy rules to nearly the same extent as environmentalists who, for example, do not receive dinner invitations to 24 Sussex Drive.

The clear disadvantage of the Westminister model is that it does not provide Parliament or concerned citizens with access to information about policy options being proposed for Cabinet consideration as these options are formulated within the bureaucracy, nor does it allow Parliament or concerned citizens to participate meaningfully in the development of those policy options. If the current popular disdain for governments and politicians is any guide, the Westminster model simply is not working.

Westminster-model governments, such as the current federal government, have difficulty solving what Frank Fischer calls "wicked" policy problems[4] precisely because of their heavy, sometimes exclusive, reliance on expert bureaucratic advice and decision making by a small group of Ministers. Wicked policy problems are problems such as drug addiction, the homeless, and the siting of incinerators that have "no solutions, only temporary and imperfect resolutions".[5] Wicked problems differ from traditional problems, such as building railroads or paving roads, in that they cannot be solved exclusively through technical means or instrumental rationalities. Fischer argues that collaborative or participatory approaches to policy analysis are viable if not essential to the solution of wicked policy problems. Environmental assessment is a leading example of the participatory approach.

John Dryzek has posed the argument that instrumental rationality "underlies or environmental predicament".[6] Instrumental rationality "invokes a Cartesian dichotomy between subject and object. The human mind is subject, all else — including the natural world, and other people — consists of objects, to be manipulated, therefore dominated, in the interests of the mind's desires".[7] Instrumental rationality is a manifestation of single vision.

Dryzek argues that rationality results from interaction with others. Communicative rationality, as he calls it, is a "property of intersubjective discourse" and is "rooted in the interaction of social life".[8] Thus, wicked policy problems — such as those presented in environmental assessments of development projects — should not and cannot be solved through some Cartesian calculus (instrumental rationality) but demand public input and debate (communicative rationality). In practical terms, this would mean that wicked policy problems cannot in principle be solved by Cabinet Ministers and their bureaucratic experts working in isolation. Participation by informed publics and stakeholders in the debates is essential, not just for reasons of political expedience, but to provide foundations of rationality to the policy development exercise.

As its best, environmental assessment can easily be considered as a form of communicative rationality. Paul Emond described the importance of public comment on information provided by experts as follows:

> Neither the environmental assessment nor the review are value-free scientific documents. They depend very much on someone's interpretation of the data. There may be more than one reasonable interpretation, yet this will never surface unless all interested persons have access to all relevant information upon which the environmental assessment and review are based.[9]

This discussion is not intended as a proof that decisions made by the federal Cabinet are inherently irrational. Rather it is intended to demonstrate just how far the Westminster model of parliamentary government is removed from even a modest form of participatory democracy.

As argued in Chapter 6, the extraordinary secrecy associated with the preparation of submissions to Cabinet damages the confidence of the public in government. The damage caused is particularly acute when an agency — FEARO in the case of the CEAA regulations — has made substantial efforts to consult with stakeholders and the public before beginning work on a Cabinet submission.

The issue of Cabinet secrecy relates closely to the second issue: Cabinet and bureaucratic dominance of the substance and process of legislation in Parliament. The extent to which Ministers of the Crown and senior bureaucrats control every step of the legislative process in Parliament is significant. This control goes far beyond merely setting the agenda for Parliament and controlling ultimate passage of legislation by the House of Commons and Senate. As described in Chapter 5, this control by the government, through the Privy Council Office and parliamentary secretaries, extends even into legislative committees of the House of Commons such that even seemingly minor amendments not approved by Cabinet in advance are not usually permitted to pass. Cabinet edicts are enforced by the parliamentary secretary working for the minister responsible for the legislation, as well as by the chair of the committee. These individuals are almost invariably members of Parliament representing the governing party. That the rules were relaxed and a measure of democracy permitted to occur for Bills C-78 and C-13 represents a partial exception to the rule. But even for these bills the highly complex structure of the legislation was never open for public debate, only the details were.

What is most egregious is that this Cabinet control over legislation being debated in Parliament is largely hidden from public view. Unlike Members of Parliament, the official from Privy Council Office is never identified to those present when a Parliamentary Committee is in session — and he/she should be because he/she is usually the most powerful person there. Is it surprising, then, that Parliamentarians are held in such disrepute given that they effectively have no vote except on those rare occasions when there is a minority Parliament, or a vote on a matter of conscience such as an abortion law?

Patrick Boyer, a member of Parliament from 1984 to 1993, has thought as deeply as any of his former colleagues about the role of Parliamentarians in democracy and the direct democracy of referendums.[10] He writes of his acute frustration with life as an MP:

> After seven years, I have serious doubts about whether the role of an MP in Canada today is of much consequence. The reasons for this are

many — and hard to admit. Hard because it means that for thirty-nine years I may have been on the wrong trajectory and that all those who have worked loyally to support me may have not a dream but an illusion. Hard because I believe that those of us in public life, no matter how desperate we feel or bleak the circumstances, have a duty to foster hope.[11]

Like many Canadians I have been smug about Canadian political ways compared to American practices. Yet after seven years of trying to function within the Canadian party and parliamentary system, that smugness has completely evaporated. The U.S. system is more transparent than ours meaning everyone can see and understand when, where and how public business is being transacted. Legislation introduced in Congress is not "government legislation" as it is here — and senators and congressmen go to work on it. There is more room for shifts and changes. Furthermore, there are many more entry points in the American legislature and governmental system.

In Canada, legislation, budgets, and other government programs are generally prepared in secret. The pre-consultation is mostly in secret. Bureaucrats behind closed doors fine-tune government measures, and in most cases by the time the measures are set and approved by the cabinet, virtually no change by a mere MP is possible. Despite my being an elected member of Parliament, I have virtually no scope in the legislative process to alter even a phrase in the wording of government legislation, and then the party line is imposed on voting in the Commons to make the measure law. We certainly lack a wide-open legislative process; we have one that is hardly open at all.[12]

Boyer's surprise at being excluded from law making may strike some political scientists as naivety. As a statement of fact, Boyer is correct. Parliament has a marginal role in drafting the laws of the nation. Only in some antique mythology was Parliament ever supreme. John Meisel concurs in this view that the appointed technocrats must dominate legislative policy making:

> Up until World War I, the Canadian parliament dealt with only a small number of issues, met seldom and required little specialist and technical knowledge to operate.... The expansion of government activities and the increasingly complicated nature of government decisions have reduced the capacity of elected officials to deal with many important public issues and necessitated the restructuring of many government institutions.... In short, an important shift has occurred in the focus of power of liberal democracies from elected politicians to appointed civil servants....[13]

Meisel argues that this encroachment by the bureaucratic state has led to a decline in the importance of political parties. Certainly, party solidarity has frayed more than ever in recent Parliaments. A former Liberal Cabinet minister, Warren Almand, voted against Paul Martin's 1995 budget, and another Liberal MP John Nunziata was ejected from the Liberal caucus when he voted against the 1996 budget. Nine Liberals voted offside on the gun control legislation, and the vote among Reform and New Democratic Party members was also split. Several Liberal backbenchers voted against the government's proposed hate crime amendments to the Criminal Code, and opposed changes to the human rights legislation which would confirm that discrimination on the basis of sexual orientation is illegal. However, governing party MPs like John Nunziata who do not vote the party line continue to be punished by the government to the point of excommunication. Opposition parties, such as the Reform Party, are disciplinarians as well. A further decline in the power of political parties, especially the power to strongarm Members of Parliament to vote the party line, would probably benefit Canadian democracy. With less party discipline, Members of Parliament would be able to represent the interests of their constituents and make up their own minds about proposed legislation that comes before the House of Commons.

However, in the present Canadian democracy, Cabinet ministers and senior officials govern in secret with little interference from parliamentarians, protected as they are by the cone of silence and the whip of the party system. As observed above, the Westminister model and its adherents among political scientists argue that the primary policy-related job of parliamentarians is to polish up legislation that Cabinet and the bureaucracy have drafted, if not developed, in secret.[14]

Several commentators have lamented the lack of a policy role for Members of Parliament. Michael Atkinson has argued that:

> It is surely not too much to ask that a government that listens so closely to the pronouncements of the provinces, interest groups, OPEC, and Washington also remain in touch with the country's elected representatives.
>
> It is essential, however, that these representatives have something to say that merits attention ... it will also be necessary to challenge the fundamental principles of the Westminster model with a view to guiding its evolution. If ordinary MPs remain in splendid isolation, entirely neutralized by strictures of party discipline that very few Canadians understand, Par-

liament will increasingly become an irrelevant and obscure institution.[15]

How can the Westminister model in Canada be challenged so as to guide its evolution toward a democracy that is participatory for both Parliamentarians and concerned citizens?

A series of steps could be taken to temper the application of the principles of Cabinet solidarity and confidentiality, without denying the importance of the concept that ministers must be able to speak freely and candidly in Cabinet without fear of their remarks being disclosed publicly. A first step would be to impose a requirement of Cabinet secrecy only for final versions of the ministerial recommendations, memoranda to Cabinet, and annexed documents such as draft regulations, that are submitted through the Privy Council Office. Such secrecy should not apply to draft Cabinet documents that are circulated within the bureaucracy. Ministers should at least have the option of sharing these draft documents with the public. If FEARO had had this option in the summer of 1993, the regulations would undoubtedly have been improved, public controversy avoided, and government credibility enhanced.

In essence, this is the same proposal as the Hon. Michael Wilson made in an article published in The Globe and Mail on May 22, 1995.[16] A former Minister of Finance in the Mulroney Progressive Conservative government, Wilson argued that the process of budget making needs to be opened up in a way that "engages all MPs and the public in a fundamental way".[17] He stated that the Minister of Finance should issue "a white paper with a fiscal plan with detailed revenue and expenditure components, which would meet a deficit target set by the government". In other words, a draft budget. The white paper would be released for broad public debate, with the resulting input incorporated into the final budget approved by Cabinet. The budget is often the most important decision that a Cabinet makes. If the process can be opened up for budget making, there is no reason why other Cabinet decision making cannot be more open.

Cabinet secrecy is important because it stands as the key obstacle, from a political and policy perspective, to entrenching in law a requirement that the environmental effects of any proposed policy or program be assessed before Cabinet approves it. As well, secrecy has hindered implementation of strategic environmental assessment under the Cabinet Directive,

because so little information about implementation is made public.

At present, proposals for policies and programs to be considered by Cabinet, other than regulations, are subject to the Cabinet Directive approve in June 1990.[18] The stated objective of the Cabinet Directive is to systematically integrate environmental considerations into the planning and decision-making process. The information derived from an environmental study of proposed policy or program initiatives is intended to support decision making in the same way that economic and other factors do.

The Cabinet Directive provides that a statement on environmental implications should be included in Memoranda to Cabinet, and where appropriate, other documents submitted to Ministers.[19] At present, these statements and documents are secret. Where anticipated environmental effects are likely to be significant, a more detailed account of the environmental assessment and the rationale for the conclusions and recommendations should be included in the documents supporting the proposal. These more detailed accounts are also secret.

The Cabinet Directive gives broad discretion to ministers as to whether or not a public statement relating to the environmental effects of the policy or program should be released. For key initiatives likely to have significant effects, the Cabinet Directive suggests that the public announcements contain a summary of these anticipated effects and their significance, and information on mitigation measures and follow-up programs, if any.[20] In the six years since de Cotret announced the Cabinet Directive, there have been but a few such public announcements, a notable example being the environmental review of the North American Free Trade Agreement.[21]

Systematically assessing the environmental effects of changes in government policies and programs could obviate the need to assess individual projects carried out pursuant to them. From an administrative perspective, it may take little sense to conduct environmental assessments of each fishing licence or allocation given to every fisher in Atlantic Canada. But obviously each of these licences and allocations have environmental effects that are cumulative. Therefore, it would seem sensible to assess carefully, and with public involvement, the environment effects of proposed cod fishery policies and programs, including environmental criteria relating to issuance of licences, before they are approved by Cabinet.

At present, the difficulty with the Cabinet Directive is that Ministers are not publicly accountable for failing to comply with it, or more generally for failing to assess environmental effects of proposed policies and programs. Cabinet secrecy has virtually guaranteed a failure to comply. As Minister of Environment, Sheila Copps conducted a crusade to ensure that her Cabinet colleagues examined environmental issues in their submissions to Cabinet. But the public did not know that these discussions were taking place, far less the substance and merit of these discussions.

The conclusion is that legislation is required to ensure that Cabinet considers the environmental effects of proposed policies and programs, just as legislation was required to ensure that departments assessed the environmental effects of their development projects.

Environmental groups no doubt would support such legislation. Industry might also be supportive if it meant fewer or less rigorous assessments of projects that had been through a strategic environmental assessment. The primary opponents of such legislation would likely be central agencies in the federal government, especially the Privy Council Office itself. The Privy Council Office would argue that legislating policy environmental assessment would trench on the traditional prerogatives of Ministers of the Crown to bring forward policy matters to Cabinet whenever and however they choose. Permitting public notice of such strategic environmental assessments (even worse, public involvement in same) would infringe on time-honoured principles of Cabinet solidarity and secrecy.

All of the arguments cannot be addressed here. However, it may be useful to point out that the Ontario Legislature has enacted a statute entitled the *Environmental Bill of Rights, 1993 (EBR)*, which achieves objectives similar to those of strategic environmental assessment, apparently without destroying the edifice of the Cabinet system in Ontario.

When the New Democratic Party took power in Ontario in 1990, an Environmental Bill of Rights Task Force was established to develop proposals for an EBR. The Task Force included two environmentalists, an environmental lawyer, and three representatives of industry, and was co-chaired by two senior civil servants. In its June 1992 report, the Task Force presented a

draft statute that was achieved by consensus.[22] This bill was enacted by the Ontario Legislature with only modest changes. The purposes of the EBR, which was proclaimed on February 15, 1994, are:

    (a) to protect, conserve and, where reasonable, restore the integrity of the environment by the means provided in this Act;
    (b) to provide sustainability of the environment by the means provided in this Act; and
    (c) to protect the right to a healthy environment by the means provided in this Act.[23]

These purposes set out the overall intent of the EBR and should not be construed as substantive rights to a healthy environment.

The EBR sets out minimum levels of public participation which must be met before the government of Ontario makes decisions on certain kinds of environmentally significant proposals for policies, programs, statutes and regulations, among other categories of proposals.

The EBR provides that where a Minister considers that a proposal for a policy or statute could, if implemented, have a significant effect on the environment and the Minister considers that the public should have an opportunity to comment on the proposal before implementation, the Minister is legally obliged to give notice of the proposal to the public, with several exceptions. Similar, but more restrictive, obligations apply to proposals for a regulation.

The means by which Ontario Ministers of the Crown provide notice of proposals is through the Environmental Registry which is established pursuant to the EBR. This is an electronic registry similar to the Public Registry System under CEAA. Over a 17-month period ending December 31, 1995, over 10,000 "hits" were logged on to the Ontario electronic registry.[24]

After giving notice of a proposal, Ministers are legally obliged to take every reasonable step to ensure that all comments relevant to the proposal that are received as part of the public participation process are considered when decisions about the proposal are made. Finally, Ministers are required to give notice that a proposal has been implemented as soon as reasonably possible after that implementation.

The EBR also provides for Statements of Environmental Values which fourteen Ontario Ministries are required to develop. These Statements explain how the purposes of the EBR are to be applied by Ministries when decisions that might significantly affect the environment are made and how consideration of the purpose of the Act should be integrated into decision making.

A Minister is required to take every reasonable step to ensure that the Ministry's Statement of Environmental Values is considered whenever internal decisions that might significantly affect the environment are made.

The EBR also provides for an independent Environmental Commissioner who reports to the Legislative Assembly. His/Her role is to oversee the implementation of, and compliance with, the EBR.

The EBR was weakened by the newly elected Progressive Conservative government in late 1995 when it issued regulations exempting the Ministry of Finance from the EBR's requirements and temporarily suspending, until September 1996, public notice requirements for any environmentally significant proposals linked to the government's cost-cutting initiatives. However, EBR, taken as a whole, represents a remarkable array of constraints on decision making by Ontario Ministers of the Crown, and indirectly, on the Ontario Cabinet. The Environmental Commissioner's annual reports indicate that in the several years since it was proclaimed, the EBR has, in practice, led to a much higher level of accountability for integrating environmental considerations in government decision making.

The rights of public participation in government decision making in the EBR may go beyond what is currently realistic politically at the federal level. In comparison to the EBR, rights of public participation under Bill C-83, the amendments to the *Auditor General Act*[25] (which establishes a Parliamentary commissioner not unlike the Environmental Commissioner) are extremely limited. The federal Commissioner of the Environment and Sustainable Development reports to the Auditor General of Canada, who in turn reports to Parliament.[26] The Auditor General is required to make a record of any written petition on an environmental matter received from a resident of Canada, and to forward that petition to the appropriate Minister. The federal Commissioner monitors the responses of Ministers to these petitions. This is the only legal requirement for public participation under the Act.

A different approach to increasing the accountability of Cabinet to the public would be simply to make the *Access to Information Act*

apply to Cabinet confidences. At present, this legislation does not apply to Cabinet memoranda, discussion papers, briefing papers, meeting agenda, minutes or draft legislation. Thus, the only legislation that is relevant is the *Official Secrets Act*[27], which is designed to prohibit and control access to sensitive government information. Under the *Official Secrets Act*, the unauthorized release to the public of Cabinet confidences that have been in existence for less than 20 years can result in criminal charges being brought against the individuals involved.

In his 1993–94 Annual Report, John Grace, the former Information Commissioner of Canada, wrote that:

> Perhaps no single provision brings the *Access to Information Act* into greater disrepute than section 69 which excludes Confidences of the Queen's Privy Council for Canada from the legislation's reach.[28]

Neither the Information Commissioner nor the courts have authority to examine documents even to determine if they are bone fide Cabinet Confidences.

The Information Commissioner recommended that Cabinet Confidences be subject to an exemption rather than an exclusion, and that appeals of decisions relating to release of information alleged to be subject to the exemption be sent to the Federal Court after review by the Information Commissioner. He also recommended that "analysis portions of Memoranda to Cabinet be released if a decision has been made public, the decision has been implemented, or five years have passed since the decision was made or considered."[29]

A second series of steps would be to empower Members of Parliament to have greater involvement in the development of legislation. The notion that Parliament should not have a substantial policy role in law making should be rejected, as should the notion that civil servants can master the difficulties of formulating policy alternatives better than parliamentarians. There is surely little evidence of the special cleverness that many political scientists believe that bureaucrats possess. Indeed, it seems to make more sense to have Parliamentarians debating the proper balance of public interests, and setting out the principles and policies of the statute, and to have the bureaucrats and lawyers doing the language polishing; not the other way around.

The Westminister model of Cabinet and bureaucratic dominance of legislative initiatives has been tempered in recent years by the use of Parliamentary committees to consider policy issues prior to the introduction of a bill into the House of Commons, as well as in conducting statutory reviews of existing legislation, such as the five-year review of the *Canadian Environmental Protection Act*. The growth in the use of public and stakeholder consultation processes, such as the CEAA Regulatory Advisory Committee, has also been a healthy trend. But as described earlier, such processes are still subject to Cabinet decision-making conducted wholly in secret. The point is that Cabinet and the bureaucracy continue to dominate the agenda and substance of legislative initiatives. Proposals for sustainable development put forward from within the bureaucracy may serve the public interest, but they more surely will serve the interests of more powerful bureaucrats. Only those legislative proposals that have been tested and transformed in the fire of genuine informed parliamentary debate are likely to transcend bureaucratic single vision.

A second point about bureaucratic single vision is that the civil service is now largely reactive and on the defensive, responding to ideas and proposals put to them by ministers, other politicians, public and special interest groups, or the media, rather than generating new ideas. Imaginings of what could be or what should be is largely outside the frame of reference within which the bureaucracy now works. It could hardly be otherwise in an era when public sentiment against government is so high, and government action to protect the environment or promote equity among Canadians is often seen as mere intervention in the free market. Ronald Reagan's 1980 election promise to get government off the backs of the people still resonates in Canada today. So innovation concerning sustainable development is unlikely to be led by the federal civil service. To achieve an ecological vision of sustainable development, requires the passion and common sense that individual citizens and their elected representatives at all levels bring to bear. The issue then is how to nurture democracy so that the visions of sustainable development held by communities and citizens can be realized.

Parliament is part of the answer. At present though, Members of Parliament have too few resources to do their law making while the bureaucracy may have too many. The 295 Members of Parliament and 104 Senators often employ but one legislative assistant each. They have access to a handful of researchers at the Library of Parliament and the research offices of their respective political parties. In contrast, policy analysts and their bosses and lawyers in the federal civil service number in the thousands. The imbalance in resources to consider and develop new legislation could not be more stark.

In an era of strong anti-government feeling that does not discriminate between elected and appointed officials, the following suggestion flies in the face of conventional wisdom: it just may be that Parliamentarians need more and better tools to do their job. However, it must be acknowledged that this would only constitute a partial solution. So long as individual Members of Parliament allow themselves to be cajoled and bullied by party whips into voting along party lines, collectively they will have little real political power.

As explained above, the role of Parliament as a democratic institution for policy making is limited. Short of reforming the relationship between the government and Parliament, other means must be developed to give the public access to information upon which rational options for sustainable development can be fashioned outside government. This convenient access to information is exactly what is provided in the public registry system under CEAA and the Ontario Environmental Bill of Rights.

In conclusion, requiring federal authorities to assess the environmental effects of proposed policies and programs (strategic environmental assessment), and then providing convenient public access to information about these environmental effects are the most important and immediately attainable, steps towards sustainable development that Parliament and the government could take. Not coincidentally, strategic environmental assessment and an enhanced Canadian democracy support ecovision by making single vision and Newton's sleep less possible. These steps are essential if the Government of Canada is truly serious about achieving sustainable development.

(c) Environmental Protection and the Role of Government[†]

Anita Krajnc ─────────────────────────────────

INTRODUCTION

Questions about the role of government in environmental protection are being raised more frequently in Canada these days. The 1990s drive for *less* government, environmental deregulation, downloading and privatization at the federal and provincial levels has left in its wake an unprecedented number of smog alerts, unregulated urban sprawl, a failure to reduce greenhouse gas emissions, accelerating habitat loss and a growing list of endangered species and water quality crises across the country.

In Ontario, for example, the Walkerton tragedy in May 2000 put the spotlight on the neo-conservative policies of the Harris government after seven people were killed and more than 2,000 fell severely ill from *E. coli* contamination of their drinking water from a nearby cattle farm. The Walkerton Public Inquiry was subsequently set up to examine the causes of the most fatal contaminated water crisis in the country's recent memory. The inquiry learned that since 1995, budget and staff levels at Ontario's environment ministry were cut by more than 40%, water-testing laboratories were privatized, and civil servants were fearful of introducing new environmental regulations in a numbing climate of "regulatory chill." Canada's national paper, *The Globe and Mail*, declared in an editorial entitled "Water and Big Government" that "Ontario's water problems likely mark the limit on the limitation of Big Government" (July 31, 2000, p. A12).

This article will make the case for "Big Government" — the idea that it is primarily the role of government to protect the environment — by drawing on comparisons between the public and private sectors' performance in such areas as stewardship, availability of resources for environmental protection, public accountability, access to information, public participation, and policy learning. Next, the article will explore a

host of old and new threats to the role of government, including domestic factors, such as fluctuations in public awareness and concern for the environment, the rise of neo-conservative ideology and attempts at devolution of environmental responsibilities to lower levels of government arising from Prime Minister Chrétien's national unity strategy and cost-cutting agenda. Then there are such international factors as the growing corporate globalization and the limits placed on state sovereignty by international and regional treaties and institutions like the North American Free Trade Agreement (NAFTA) and World Trade Organization (WTO). Finally, I will examine the growing pressures for rebuilding the state's role, and outline a preferred environmental vision of a strong and democratic state.

THE CASE FOR BIG GOVERNMENT

The maintenance of a strong state is advantageous for both process-oriented and substantive concerns. Process-oriented concerns include improved public access to information, public accountability, democratic citizen participation and state capacity to engage in coordination, planning, control, and policy learning. Substantive concerns involve the long-term stewardship of the environment and the special ability of governments to amass sufficient resources to address the growing number and severity of environmental challenges.

The Stewardship Function of Government
Markets and democratic governments have different purposes, and are consequently driven by distinct motivations. Businesses are driven primarily by the profit motive designed to accrue exclusive benefits for their members, and thus can be referred to as special interest groups (Schattschneider, 1960, p. 27). By contrast, government is the trustee of the public good: the

† An original article contributed by Anita Krajnc, Post-Doctoral Fellow, Globalism Project, Department of Political Science, University of Toronto. The author is grateful to the editors, Robert O. Matthews, and Jordan Berger and Timothy Hadwen of the Ontario Public Service Employees Union for their kind assistance.

role of democratic government is — together with its citizens — to identify and promote the public interest (Wamsley et al., 1987).

Herman Daly and John Cobb Jr. (1994: 44–61 and 138–158) argue that the free market is good at producing goods and services efficiently, but not at addressing social equity or environmental concerns. With respect to the environment, the first instance of market failure is the production of environmental externalities. That is, an industry on its own volition is likely to release harmful pollutants into the air, water or land, and impose these costs on society and the natural environment (a negative externality). A second problem relates to the possibility that unregulated business activity will surpass the proper scale of economic activities in relation to the limited capacity of the ecosystem to provide goods and services and absorb waste. Government intervention is required to correct these market failures. An activist state is necessary to ensure a just redistribution of goods and services, to internalize the costs of economic activities that harm the environment and to impose restraints on the scale of economic activities compatible with the carrying capacity of the ecosystem.

Resources

Related to the differences in purposes and motivations between states and markets is the question of the capacity of different actors to assemble and allocate resources for environmental protection and social equity. Although actors in civil society, such as environmental organizations, can and do implement environmental projects (Wapner, 1996), states are the only actors that have the coercive power and the ability to mobilize enough resources to deal with extant and emerging environmental challenges. Richard Falk (2001, p. 223), an international relations theorist, writes that: "Only the state, among existing political actors, has the potential capabilities to implement a degree of environmental regulation that will be needed to safeguard the health and well-being of peoples now alive on the planet and discharge responsibilities to future generations." Similarly, Gord Laxer (2001, p. 7) notes that "...the state is a more equal adversary of transnational capital than any other institution. The crucial battle is whether citizens will succeed in turning corporate-oriented states into citizen-oriented states."

The Brundtland Commission (WCED, 1987) has called for increased roles for the scientific community and non-governmental organizations (NGOs) in environmental decision-making processes, as was witnessed at the Earth Summit in Rio de Janeiro in 1992. Some of the problems with the drive for less government are the erosion of scientific capacity within ministries of the environment and the downloading of more and more environmental responsibilities to the non-profit sector. It is crucial that the NGO sector should only be supplementing, not supplanting, the role of government. Rather, as Elmer Schattschneider argues in his classic book, *Semi-Sovereign People* (1960), Big Business must be matched by Big Government in order to maintain an equilibrium between economic and political interests. The implications of Schattschneider's critique are that it is essential for governments to maintain their capacity to introduce, implement, and enforce environmental legislation and regulations in order to ensure the protection of public goods.

Public Accountability and Public Access to Information

Accountability refers to the obligation of subordinates to account to their superiors for the performance of services and to accept oversight and direction. Public accountability, also referred to as democratic accountability, is based on the principle that in a democracy, public officials (public servants and elected representatives) are seen as the people's representatives or trustees and are accountable to the public. Different instruments operate to achieve four different elements of accountability: reporting or informing, a duty of those accountable; information-seeking or investigation; oversight or verification; and a control or directing function. The latter three are performed by those in authority to whom accountability is owed (Mulgan, 1997b). No one instrument can ensure full public accountability.

There are important differences in the degrees of accountability in the public and private sectors. The range of instruments needed to ensure full public accountability, such as ministerial responsibility, parliamentary committees, ombudspersons, the auditor-general, administrative tribunals, Freedom of Information laws, public inquiries and media scrutiny, are much more limited in the case of the private sector than in the public sector. Some of these instruments involve oversight and control functions while others are information-seeking institutions that play a scrutinizing function and enhance opportunities for the public to participate in a democratic discussion of policy-making.

Ministerial responsibility is one of the most effective means of ensuring compliance from public service providers on behalf of the public. Contracting out functions to the private sector weakens the chain of responsibility that ties front-line bureaucrats to elected representatives. Public service accountability through the minister is achieved through immediate, day-to-day control in a chain of ministerial-departmental hierarchy. This day-to-day responsibility and accountability is surrendered with contracting out. Contracting out involves "a considerable diminution of public accountability because ministerial responsibility is one of the most effective means of enforcing compliance from public service providers on behalf of the public" (Mulgan, 1997b, p. 110).

Parliament, consisting of opposition parties, question period and parliamentary committees, among other institutions, provides the key difference between the public and private sectors, holding governments and ministers to higher standards of accountability than are commonly placed on corporations and their managers (ibid., p. 94). Mulgan (1997a, p. 35) believes that the main obstacle to improved accountability occurs at the reporting, investigating and assessing stages rather than at the control stage (i.e., ministerial responsibility), so that the priority should be on improving the scrutinizing function of parliament.

Another institution of parliament, the ombudsperson, loses jurisdiction to cover all contractors, leading to a further reduction in public accountability. Private contractors resist the general extension of the parliamentary ombudsperson's jurisdiction to their contracts, as this would add the costs of staff time needed to deal with investigations. "Accountability requirements are expensive and have the potential to undermine the efficiency gains from contracting out" (Mulgan 1997b, p. 113).

There is no equivalent to freedom of information legislation in relation to company policy. FOI rights are undermined as FOI law is partly or wholly excluded from functions transferred from government departments to arms-length, publicly owned special purpose agencies (e.g., Ontario Electricity Generation Corporation and Ontario Electrical Services Corporation); self-regulating, industry non-profit groups (e.g., Ontario Motor Vehicle Industry Council, Technical Standards and Safety Authority, Real Estate Council of Ontario, and Travel Industry Council of Ontario); and for-profit private contractors (e.g., Real/Data Ontario) (Roberts, 2000; Winfield et al., 2000).

There is generally much less media scrutiny as "private sector directors or managers do not open themselves to the same degree of media interrogation as politicians must accept, even on matters of clear public interest" (Mulgan, 2000, p. 94). Furthermore, companies do not face the same penalties for misleading the public on matters of general public concern. "Company directors are certainly subjected to significant legal liability if they mislead the investing public.... But there are no such obligations in relation to wider matters of public interest" (ibid.). While the interests of shareholders must be a top priority of company directors, this concern is not necessarily extended to other stakeholders. Yet the latter, including employees, customers, the local community or region and the natural environment, are affected by the activities of the company and should, in fairness, also be considered.

In sum, contracting out involves a trade-off between public accountability and efficiency, at best, and a loss in both public accountability and efficiency, at worst (Mulgan, 1997a). Privatization inevitably leads to less public access to information and less democratic control which, in turn, lowers the degree of public accountability. In fact, the very reduction of public accountability, and thus losses of democratic control and access to information, is seen by private contractor lobbies as one of the efficiency gains obtained in contracting out public services (Roberts, 2000; Mulgan, 1997a).

Public Participation

Making informed choices requires public input in a democratic process. Environmentalists consistently call for more democracy: increased transparency, more information and the public's right to know; more grassroots mobilization and full public participation in the decision-making process; and greater public accountability. Involving public input not only leads to more-informed decisions, but also produces more legitimate processes and outputs, and increases public trust.

Historically, progressive social movements have pressured governments to move issues from the private realm to the public arena. Elmer Schattschneider (1960, p. 7) argues that there is an enduring struggle between tendencies toward the privatization of conflict (particularly by powerful special interests in the business community) and the socialization of conflict (by weaker, diffuse interests such as public interest groups). The main way to promote the public interest is by expanding the scope of the conflict (i.e., involving a larger audience in the fight, to use Schattschneider's terminology), particularly through the invocation of universal ideas such as equality, justice, freedom of speech and association and the involvement of government.

Decisions about the future of public services should involve reasoned debate, involve citizens in that debate, and expand the opportunities for that involvement (Wamsley et al., 1987, p. 314). Unfortunately, public services are often privatized with little public input. For example, in Ontario, three out of four Ministry of Environment laboratories were privatized in 1996, and water testing was downloaded to municipalities with only eight weeks notice. Not only was the public not involved in these momentous decisions, but the Walkerton Inquiry learned that the government did not even undertake an evaluation of the impacts the move towards privatization might have on Ontario's drinking water quality.

Policy Learning

The long-term consequences of contracting out may be to diminish a state's capacity to engage in strategic management as the organization becomes more competitive, fragmented and "hollowed out". New Right ideologues and their academic counterparts in the New Public Management (NPM) school call for a "reinvention" of government so that its role is reduced to "steering" (making rules) rather than "rowing" (implementing policies). NPM theorists, dominated by economists, argue that conventional bureaucratic structures are slow and inefficient. They favour less government and the establishment of market-type, competitive arrangements between governments and the private sector. However, downsizing the public service may de-skill the public service and result in the loss of core competencies over the long term, thus diminishing the state's capacity to "steer". Stephen Cope (1995, p. 9) argues that contracting out "involves a gradual transfer of knowledge of service provision

from the client to the contractor, thus stifling policy learning. Competition between contractors and the consequent institutionalized fragmentation impede flows of information required for policy learning. The client may progressively lose its capacity to determine contract specifications, to control the contractor, and to select the 'best' contractor to run the contract." Ironically, a downsized public service may not possess sufficient knowledge to adequately supervise contracting out and, thus, may pose a threat to the goal of greater democratic control.

THREATS TO THE STATE

Canadian federal and provincial governments created ministries dedicated to the environment in the early 1970s and strengthened these ministries in the next twenty-five years in recognition of the necessity to develop an adequate state capacity to address the growing environmental crisis. The institutional capacity of governments is defined as the ability of governments to perform a series of functions in the environmental policy process: science and technology, monitoring, standard setting program development, program implementation and benchmark achievements (Victor, 2000). Thus environmentalists generally advocate greater government intervention in the areas of regulations, planning and programs of public expenditure.

In a sharp reversal, major decreases in public expenditures on environmental protection occurred in the mid 1990s at the federal level and in a number of provinces. The Chrétien government canceled the $3 billion Green Plan in 1995 and then launched two program reviews, cutting the Department of Environment's budget by about a third (from $737 million in 1995–96 to $503 million in 1997–98) and the staff by a quarter (1,400 of 5,700) across the country (Toner, 1997). The cuts were even more severe in Ontario, where the Harris government cut the Ministry of Environment budget by almost one-half and the staff by more than 40% from 2,430 in 1994 to 1,277 by the end of 1999 (OPSEU, 2001). By the beginning of the new millennium, the environment ministry's budget in real dollars (that is, taking into account inflation) was actually below the 1971 level — the year the ministry was created.

Part of this reduction can be explained by the historical rise and decline of environmental departments closely following the ebb and flow of green waves (Doern and Conway, 1994; Harrison, 1996). Green waves are periods of intense public awareness and concern about environmental issues that arise due to factors such as environmental crises, growing media coverage of environmental issues, and the work of scientists, environmental groups, and policy entrepreneurs. Governments tend to respond to heightened public concern by introducing new environmental legislation and programs. On the flip side, governments are often inactive or engage in minor retrenchment when the environment is no longer a top-of-mind issue for the public and gets bumped off the political agenda.

What is different now is a confluence of new forces that give the market and economic growth primacy above all else, and have led to an unprecedented retreat of the state on environmental matters. Ironically, this has occurred just when expectations were raised, following the 1992 Rio Summit, that governments around the world might redouble their efforts in what David Suzuki called the "turnaround decade," and move the planet towards ecological sustainability. Instead, the 1990s became a decade of unprecedented environmental retrenchment characterized by a reduction in the role of governments, decreased opportunities for democratic citizen input, and an expansion in the rights and power of corporations — the result of three domestic and international factors.

First, the rise of a neo-conservative ideology in provinces like Alberta (under Premier Ralph Klein), Ontario (Mike Harris) and, recently, in British Columbia (Gord Campbell) has reversed many of the institutional gains environmentalists had made in the previous three decades. The key principles of neo-conservatism are less government, a move away from government intervention towards an increased reliance on the market, and a redistribution of wealth from the lower to the upper classes (Brooke, 1999). In addition, neo-conservatives hold anti-environmental views similar to the extreme right-wing, anti-environmental "Wise Use" Movement in the U.S. Neo-conservatives are often antagonistic to environmentalism: they tend to show a fundamental lack of interest in environmental matters and a poor understanding of the concept of ecologically sustainable development; are hostile to the very notion of public goods and the implicit role for government in protecting these goods on behalf of society; and, in partnership with the Wise Use Movement, aim to further exploit and

commodify wildlife and the natural environment (Krajnc, 2000; Krajnc and Weis, 2000).

In addition to decreasing expenditures on environmental protection, neo-conservative governments have simultaneously undertaken a program of environmental deregulation, downloading and privatization. In Ontario, the Harris government set up a Red Tape Review Commission in December 1995, which was made a permanent body in May 2000, comprising nine Conservative MPPs, a secretariat attached to the Cabinet Committee on Regulations and an External Advisory Committee of business representatives. Its role is to review new and existing environmental, health and safety safeguards with a view to eliminating regulations that unnecessarily hinder business. Alberta also set up a Regulatory Reform Task Force in April 1995. In British Columbia, the neo-conservative Gordon Campbell government promised in its 2001 election campaign to reduce government regulations by a third through a new Minister of Deregulation — a bizarre *a priori* target for reduced regulation, avoiding even the pretence of a rational evaluation of what existing regulations are necessary (Goldberg, 2001). A similar deregulatory initiative at the federal level, the *Regulatory Efficiency Act*, was defeated by environmentalists in the mid 1990s.

Second, the federal government's role in environmental policy is threatened by its devolution or "dis-entanglement" strategy. In 1998, the federal government, all the provinces except Quebec, and both territories signed the new Canada Wide Accord on Environmental Harmonization and three sub-agreements on inspections, Canada-wide environmental standards, and environmental assessment. With this Accord, the federal government is devolving many of its environmental responsibilities to the Canadian Council of Ministers of the Environment (CCME) (an intergovernmental body) and the provinces. The first of a series of planned sub-agreements give the CCME a key role in setting national standards, and the provincial governments a larger role with respect to inspections and enforcement. For example, the environmental assessment sub-agreement makes way for "process substitution" in place of the current system of "process coordination," meaning that the responsibility for conducting environmental assessments in particular circumstances would be allocated to one order of government only, rather than involving two equal partners in managing coordinated responses, joint reviews, and joint panels; this would confine federal environmental assessments mainly to projects on federal lands (Kennett, 2000).

Federal transfer of power to the CCME and the provinces is bad news from an environmental point of view. The CCME is likely to drive environmental standards to the "lowest-common-denominator" with its consensus decision-making process in which each of the governments has a veto power, and to create pollution havens with its increased reliance on voluntary implementation measures. The provinces are generally less environmentally friendly than the federal government because resource industries tend to have more clout at the local level.

Observers link the harmonization initiatives to the federal government's national unity concerns, its cost-cutting agenda and business pressure (Winfield, 2001; Farford, 2000). In the aftermath of the October 1995 sovereignty referendum in Quebec, the harmonization initiative took on an added urgency for the Chrétien government, which was willing to sacrifice job training and the environment in order to prove its flexibility and to reduce irritants in federal-provincial relations. Environmentalists question the wisdom of the Chrétien government's approach to national unity: "Such a strategy puts the federal government in the position of declining relevancy to the day to day lives of Canadians, as it ceases to deliver services, and to be an effective guarantor of national standards in such areas as health care, social policy, and environmental protection" (Muldoon and Winfield, 1997, p. 7).

Third, increasing corporate globalization is threatening state sovereignty. International trade and investment agreements have given corporations new rights to sue governments for environmental regulations that lower their profits, and limit the range of tools available to governments and citizen campaigns to protect the environment (Marchak, 1998; Conca, 2000).

Recent international trade challenges and rulings on environmental policies highlight the way in which trade agreements are becoming "corporate rule" agreements (Johnston and Laxer, 2001). For example, a 1991 ruling by a General Agreement on Tariffs and Trade (GATT) panel found the U.S. prohibition on importing tuna caught by methods that killed dolphins at a higher rate than those used by U.S. fleets was inconsistent with GATT. This challenge, brought by Mexico before the NAFTA negotiations, galvanized U.S. public opinion about the environmental implications of trade regimes. The WTO, the successor to GATT, also views specific rules adopted to protect endangered species, such as those requiring that shrimp be caught in special nets that do not kill sea turtles, as non-tariff trade barriers.

The investment chapter of NAFTA, Chapter 11, increases corporate rights at the expense of government by giving corporations the right to sue governments for environmental regulations that hurt their profits. To date, ten out of the seventeen cases involving the investment chapter have involved environmental or natural resource issues, including management of hazardous waste, clean drinking water and gasoline additives (Mann, 2001). Corporate power is enhanced through the introduction of the notion of "regulatory takings," something the right-wing, U.S. property rights movement tried, and failed, to obtain at the national level. Canada and U.S. law recognizes the difference between expropriation of land and land use regulations. The property rights movement has unsuccessfully attempted to demand compensation for costs imposed on property owners as a result of land use regulations, such as the prohibition of development on environmentally sensitive shorelines (Weisbrot, 2001; Swenarchuk, 1998). Ironically, what the property rights movement failed to achieve at the national level, multinational corporations succeeded in obtaining in NAFTA's Chapter 11. In particular, the Ethyl Corporation of Virginia threatened to use the expropriation provisions of Chapter 11 to challenge Canada's ban of MMT, a gasoline additive that is an expected neuro-toxin and leads to an increase in air pollutant emissions (May, 1998). It filed a $250 million claim arguing that the regulatory ban was tantamount to an expropriation, but settled for $13 million in damages after the Canadian government (fearing it would lose the case) withdrew its 1997 import ban and apologized.

Furthermore, the WTO is limiting the use of various trade tools in new agreements and undermining existing international environmental regimes. Trade measures are an important tool for many environmental regimes, including the Convention on the International Trade in Endangered Species (CITES), which bans trade in endangered species; the Montreal Protocol, which uses trade measures to promote compliance with the regime; and the 1994 amendment to the Basel Convention, which bans north-south trade in hazardous waste. The use of such tools in new environmental agreements is now severely limited by trade treaties (Conca, 2000). Further, in the S. D. Myers case, the appointed NAFTA arbitration board made a ruling in November 2000 that appears to threaten existing environmental treaties that employ trade measures. S.D. Myers, an Ohio-based waste company, sued the Canadian government for US$50 million under NAFTA's Chapter 11 following Canada's nine-month-long ban on the export of PCB contaminated waste. The company launched a suit even though NAFTA specifically lists the Basel Convention as one of three international environmental treaties exempt from the general restriction of using trade measures to protect the environment. Canada is seeking a judicial review of the award through its own Federal Court.

Pressures to Rebuild the State

Pressures to return to an activist role for government are emerging from a variety of sources. Environmental crises play an important role here. Rod Rhodes notes that a return to bureaucracy often takes place following a catastrophe: "When catastrophe is coupled with limited central capability, there will be a strong imperative for a return to bureaucracy because governments will wish to strengthen their capacity to steer the system" (1994, p. 151). In addition, the public is increasingly aware of the fact that tax cuts are not cost-free, and that there are important environmental consequences arising from a drastic reduction in the size of government. In Ontario, the Walkerton Inquiry, the enormous media coverage of the tragedy and the campaigns of public interest groups have all increased this awareness.

In addition, the move away from regulation to voluntarism is clearly failing. For example, Canada's response to global climate change has been a voluntary approach calling on Canadian companies, governments and organizations to voluntarily take actions that limit or reduce their own emissions of greenhouse gases. The centrepiece of Canada's climate change policy has been the Voluntary Challenge and Registry (VCR) program, launched in 1995. This has clearly not worked, as Canada's greenhouse gas emissions are projected to increase by 19% from 1990 levels by 2010, rather than decrease by 6% as required by the Kyoto Protocol (Hornung, 1999).

Another green wave may be on its way, but one that links environmental protection to the need to defend the role of government and challenge corporate globalization. Traditionally, environmental organizations have focused their efforts on public education and lobbying governments and corporate actors. Now there is a recognition among environmentalists that they have an additional role: to defend the state. Previous strategies that focused on public pressure presumed that the state is competent, responsive and capable of acting. That assumption is being undermined.

The role of environmental groups has evolved rapidly. There is increasing participation of environmental organizations in trade matters and in WTO protests. In the 1980s, only a few environmental groups, such as the Canadian Environmental Law Association, were intimately involved in the movement to oppose Free Trade between the United States and Canada. By the early 1990s, the threat posed by international trade agreements was becoming more apparent to environmental groups, which were galvanized into fighting NAFTA (Ayres, 1998; Audley, 1997). More recently, 500 NGOs rallied against the proposed Multilateral Agreement on Investment (MAI), environmental groups were a major force in the collapse of the WTO's Millennium Round in Seattle at the end of 1999, and environmentalists helped organize protests at the April 2001 "Summit of the Americas" in Quebec City.

A sustained, broad-based coalition is a necessary condition for success. Important environmental and labour coalitions, such as the Mobilization on Development, Trade, Labour and the Environment, and Public Citizen's Trade Watch Campaign, were formed during the NAFTA negotiations. It is important to note that a number of more conservative environmental groups, like the National Wildlife Federation and the World Wildlife Fund in the U.S., which receive substantial corporate donations and have close ties with corporate elite, were initially supportive of the NAFTA agreement and helped promote it (Audley, 1997), though there is now a growing consensus that international trade agreements, particularly NAFTA's Chapter 11, have anti-environmental dimensions. Many of these environmental groups, along with more grassroots environmental groups such as Greenpeace, Public Citizen, Friends of the Earth, and the Sierra Club, have redoubled their efforts to oppose corporate-oriented trade agreements, and the latter have made important linkages with other progressive social movements. Also encouraging are the efforts of other actors in civil society, such as the American Society for Public Administration, which has mounted programs and campaigns to strengthen the image of the public service (Goodsell, 1994, p. 7).

VISIONS OF A STRONG AND DEMOCRATIC STATE

In 1987, the Brundtland Commission made a number of recommendations to strengthen environmental ministries and public input in its report, *Our Common Future*. They are even more relevant today. The Brundtland Commission identified six priority areas for institutional and legal change:

1. getting at the sources: It is essential to strengthen state capacity to monitor and evaluate sustainable development.
2. dealing with the effects: The Brundtland Commission recommended that governments should "strengthen the role and capacity of existing environmental protection and resource management agencies" (p. 319).
3. assessing global risks: The risks of new technologies are growing. "Governments, individually and collectively, have the principal responsibility to collect this information systematically and use it to assess risks, but to date only a few have developed a capacity to do so" (p. 324).
4. making informed choices: The Brundtland Commission notes that informing the public and securing its support will require the increased roles of the scientific community and NGOs.
5. providing the legal means: Instead of deregulating, governments should re-regulate on environmental matters. Writing in the late 1980s, the Brundtland Commission noted that there is an urgent need to "strengthen and extend the application of existing laws and international agreements in support of sustainable development." "National and international law has traditionally lagged behind events. Today, the accelerating pace and expanding scale of impacts on the environmental base of development is rapidly outdistancing legal regimes. Human laws must be reformulated to keep human activities in harmony with the unchanging and universal laws of nature" (p. 330).
6. investing in our future: It makes long-term economic sense to pursue environmentally sound policies. A healthy economy ultimately depends on a healthy environment.

Defenders of bureaucracy call for a reinvigorated state, noting that such policy options are available despite increasing economic globalization (Shields and Evans, 1998). However, the challenge is enormous. The role of government will need to be strengthened at the international level as well as at national and local levels. International environmental organizations and regimes are not well institutionalized at the regional and global levels, especially when compared to economic regimes. Richard Falk (2001, p. 224) notes that, at present, the United Nations Environment Program (UNEP) is mainly informational, and at most advisory, and "should not even be taken seriously as a participant in environmental governance.... the scale of its activity is so small relative to the scope of the environmental challenge, that it plays almost no role in serious global efforts relating to the environment.... It certainly makes as much, if not more, sense to create a capacity for global governance in the environmental sector as it does with respect to trade and development, but the ideological climate is not so inclined."

If left to the private sector, the environment will be ignored and the global environmental crisis will accelerate further, since the free market is not designed to deal with the degradation of the environment and the equitable redistribution of resources. The 1990s were supposed to be the "turnaround decade," moving the planet towards a more ecologically sustainable course. Instead, the rise of a neo-conservative agenda, corporate globalization and a misguided national unity strategy have led to the unprecedented retrenchment of environmental ministries and environmental laws. The environmental movement is now adding to its list of tasks the need to defend the state and its primary role in protecting the environment. Its success depends on the increasing realization among the public and policy-makers that a strong and democratic government is an essential component of any plans to stem and reverse the ecological crisis.

PART B
Standard Setting

(a) A Model Procedure for Setting Environmental Standards ...[†]

M.A.H. Franson, R.T. Franson, and A.R. Lucas ——————————

WHAT ARE STANDARDS?

One of the first barriers that must be overcome is terminological. Writers in different fields clearly mean different things when they write about standards, guidelines, and objectives. Some legal writers distinguish between guidelines and standards, for example, on the basis of their legal impact. For them, a standard is a legally enforceable specification of the amount of pollutant that may be discharged or present in the ambient medium. There is a tendency for the popular press to follow this distinction. In contrast, technical writers would not necessarily follow this distinction. For them, an objective might refer to the particular uses that are desired for the water or air. A standard would specify the amount of contaminant that could be discharged, but it might or might not be legally enforceable. The model we will outline in this report is intended to establish a consistent terminology for the purposes of this report.

DEFINITION OF TERMS

"Objective" denotes a goal or purpose toward which an environment control effort is directed. Examples of objectives are as follows: to preserve and enhance the salmon fishery in the waters; to prevent crop damage caused by air pollution; to protect the public health.

"Criteria" are compilations or digests of scientific data that are used to decide whether or not a certain quality of air or water is suitable for the chosen objectives. A simple example of a criterion that might be used to judge the suitability of water quality for a certain species of fish might be:

Concentration of Pollutant	Effect
A mg/L	No adverse effects noted
B mg/L	Lowest level at which sublethal effects noted
C mg/L	Lowest level at which mortalities noted
D mg/L	No survival

---

† Originally published in M.A.H. Franson, R.T. Franson, and A.R. Lucas, *Environmental Standards* (Edmonton: Environment Council of Alberta, 1982), pp. 23–47. Reproduced by permission of the authors.

"Standards" denotes a prescribed numerical value or set of values to which concentrations or amounts actually occurring in the ambient medium or the discharge to that medium may be compared, whether legally enforceable or not. Examples of standards are:

- Average concentration of Pollutant X in the air shall not exceed Y micrograms per cubic metre during any 24-hour period. (Ambient)
- Maximum daily discharge of Pollutant A from Point Source B shall not exceed Z kg. (Effluent)

HOW SHOULD STANDARDS BE SET?

The traditional, technically-based approach to setting standards is as follows:

1. Identification of uses of the ambient resource to be protected or *objectives* to be met.
2. Formulation of *criteria* through collection and/or generation of scientific information.
3. Formulation of *ambient quality standards* from the criteria.
4. Development of *effluent standards* for discharges into the environment that will produce a quality meeting the ambient standard.
5. Development of *monitoring and other information-gathering programs* that will refine the data inputs to the previous steps and provide feedback on whether the objects are being met.

Each of these components in the standards-setting process will be examined in the following sections.

IDENTIFICATION OF OBJECTIVES

The setting of objectives for pollution control and environmental preservation/restoration is the keystone of any rational standards-setting process.

Scope and Character of Objectives

Traditionally, selection of objectives has taken the form of identifying uses to be protected, implying human purpose. Surely this is an excellent starting point, and one still widely used in practice, but during the 1970's, with increased scientific and public awareness of ecological prin-

ciples, it came to be recognized that appropriate objectives might include more than just the very readily identifiable human uses such as water supply, water-based recreation, and fishing in the case of water, and respiration and damage-free agriculture in the case of air. A bold expression of the turning away from a purely anthropocentric approach to water quality objectives was the *US Federal Water Pollution Control Act of 1972* (PL92-500). In the words of Philip T. Cummings, who was Senate majority counsel for this bill, "One of the organizing principles of the 1972 act ... was that the policy of the government is to restore the integrity of the water. That is not dependent on some judgment about its use but about its original character. That is an ecological principle rather than the economic principle of beneficial use."

In practical terms, however, the objectives of the legislation were expressed in a way closely related to human uses. Section 101(a)(2) stated that "it is the national goal that wherever attainable, an interim goal of water quality which provides for the protection and propagation of fish, shellfish, and wildlife, and provides for recreation in and on the water be achieved by July 1, 1983." This is the so-called "fishable/swimmable" goal.

Objective-Setting Process

Decisions about objectives for air and water resource quality are fundamentally neither technical nor legal decisions. In a democratic society the objectives should express, as accurately as possible, the collective will and perceptions of all people likely to have some interest in the condition of the resource. While ultimately these expressions must be gathered, evaluated, and summarized by the regulatory authority, the opportunity for public input must be systematically provided for. This suggests that the formulation-of-objectives stage is one of the most important points in the standards-setting process for contact between the regulatory agency and the public....

QUALITY CRITERIA

Criteria [consist] of the supporting scientific data that enable us to answer questions such as, "Is this water safe to drink?" "Is the air safe to breathe?" "Can this lake support a healthy trout fishery?" Because of the extremely large number of elements and compounds now contained in our air and water resources and the many ways they affect potential uses of the resources, the answers to these questions can be very complex.

Information Needs

In contrast to the formulation of objectives, the formulation of criteria is strictly a scientific matter. It involves gathering of data on the effects of potential pollutants and combinations of pollutants on the uses in question, and in the absence of data, experimentation to generate such information. This is never a small task, and in the case of the more sensitive objectives, can be formidable indeed, for several reasons. First, the number of substances and other quality parameters that can affect sensitive objectives is very large. According to Loucks in the USSR over 400 harmful substances have been defined for drinking water, and over 60 for fish life. Janardan and Schaeffer state that an estimated 60,000 organic compounds are produced and used by various industries in the US. The number of substances is growing rapidly; many new chemicals are synthesized and thus added to our environment each year. Second, the effect of any substance in the air or water is rarely, if ever, expressible in black-and-white terms. That is, if a certain concentration of a substance clearly causes no harm at all, it is unlikely that a marginally higher concentration will clearly cause substantial harm. Rather, the effects of substances are usually more accurately represented by a continuum from states of nearly perfect safety (or perhaps even necessity in the case of certain trace elements), through states that may cause distress to certain sensitive individuals or species, to those causing more widespread and more severe harmful effects at increasing levels. Some pollutants appear to have a "threshold effect." Third, this approach does not take into account the possibility of synergistic and antagonistic effects among pollutants, that is, the possibility that one or several pollutants may either intensify or counteract the effects of one or several others.

. . . .

AMBIENT QUALITY STANDARDS

The third step is the formulation of ambient quality standards, that is, the prescription of the quality of water or air that is deemed necessary to protect the desired objectives, in the light of scientific knowledge supplied by the criteria and of socioeconomic factors affecting the control of pollution. Ambient standards may set upper limits on the mass or concentration of harmful substances, may set lower limits on the presence of desired substances such as dissolved oxygen, or may prescribe a range of desirable value (e.g., for pH). The values may be specified as averages over some given time period, extreme values never to be exceeded, or values that may be exceeded only for specified time periods.

The setting of ambient standards is not fundamentally a technical decision. Even if one assumes that the criteria provide a very complete technical background for decision, the standards set inevitably reflect value judgments. This is an important point, and one that has often been misunderstood.

Technical Evaluation

This phase of the standard setting will require specialized input not only from scientists but also from economists and experts in various industries. All this is not to say that the evaluation of benefits and costs should be limited to this input from the "experts" — it is well recognized that intangible and nonquantifiable benefits and costs will result from a water quality decision. These are recognized at a later state of the process.

The output of this technical evaluation stage will be a number of alternative water quality standards, with an evaluation of each in terms of how well it meets the proposed objectives, what risks it poses to the achievement of the objectives, and the benefits and costs that are likely to flow from the achievement of that standard. Each alternative standard will include recommended limits on the parameters relevant to the uses being protected. When these alternatives are being formulated, attention must be paid to two other practical problems.... First, does the standard, determined largely from laboratory study and the literature, make sense in the real world? For example, is it possible to conceive of a situation in which a body of water would be in regular violation of standards developed, on the basis of good technical data, to protect fish life, and yet be found to support a healthy fish population of the desired type? Second, is the proposed standard measurable by methods currently available for practical field use? A nonmeasurable standard not only cannot be enforced, but actually invites violation and disrespect of the entire regulatory process....

[T]he primary purpose of water quality standards is to maximize the level of protection of beneficial uses, and the second purpose is to minimize the cost of meeting the standards, and the job of the standards-setting body is to balance these conflicting objectives in a way that yields the greatest net social benefits. At this point in the process, the standards-setting agency has in hand (or should) the best information that the physical, biological, and social sciences can provide.

Political Choice Process

Information needs. If the regulatory agency has already done an effective job of securing public input into the setting of objectives, some information about public preferences may already be at hand. However, it may be appropriate to give members of the public and interest groups a further opportunity to consider and comment explicitly on proposed standards, to react to information generated in the technical evaluation, to bring forward new data that may not have been accessible to those performing the technical evaluation, to state preferences concerning hard or impossible-to-quantify matters such as aesthetic and spiritual values, and to give views on the acceptability of the risks inherent in the various proposed standards and willingness to pay for necessary measures....

Risk acceptability. The acceptability of a risk may depend not only on the character of the use that is at risk, but also on the attributes of the risk itself. ... Consider, for example, the case of a body of water supporting a fishery that is threatened by a waterborne discharge. Consideration of the economic importance of the fishery to the community will indicate a pressure toward a higher standard if the fishery is vital to the sustenance of a native community or if income from tourists who visit the area for fishing is an economic factor in the community, than if it is used only for recreational purposes by local people. Given, however, that *one* of these situations is the case, for example, that the fishery is vital to, and used only by, a native community, Jacobson's analysis [in his article that appeared in *Journal of the Air Pollution Control Association* 3 (1981)] predicts that more protection against risk will be demanded if, for example,

the type of damage predicted is rare, that is, alien to experience and therefore fear-inducing, rather than common, or if the pollution would come from an industrial plant owned by outsiders (innocent party at risk) rather than from the community's own waste collection system (polluter at risk)....

. . . .

Effluent Standards

The object of the next stage of the standards-setting process is to move from a statement of the desired condition of the air or water to standards defining limits on discharges to the resource that will permit the desired state to be attained. Ambient standards and effluent standards sometimes have been regarded as alternative approaches to regulation, but this view is incorrect. The approaches are supplementary and each is necessary; an ambient standard alone is unenforceable because it gives no indication of cause and effect nor any guidance to either regulatory body or the regulated about the necessary courses of action, and an effluent standard lacking a basis in an ambient quality goal has no reasonable foundation in reality....

Like the setting of ambient standards the setting of effluent standards requires both technical and nontechnical input.

Technical Considerations

Mathematical models. The science and art of constructing mathematical models to relate ambient quality to inputs of pollutants and to pollutant removal mechanisms inherent in the resource has made large advances over the last several decades. Before the widespread use of computers for such simulations, the possibilities for modelling were very limited and were restricted to cases involving only a few pollutants, sources of pollution inputs, and simple removal mechanisms. Present-day knowledge enables regulatory agencies to take account of more types of pollutants, a greater number of sources within an airshed or watershed, and more sophisticated behaviours of pollutants once they have entered the resource. The literature on the construction and use of mathematical models for investigations of air and water quality control is voluminous, and no attempt will be made here to review it. The regulatory agency will choose among the available approaches according to the complexity of the situation, and the ability of the model to produce results that approximate closely conditions in the "real world."

Many of the mathematical models used for pollution control have been intended to minimize an objective function, usually the cost of control measures, subject to a set of constraints, the most important of which is the desired quality of the pollution-receiving resource. Other constraints may include minimum treatment requirements, uniformity of treatment requirements, and prohibition of certain methods of treatment.

· · · ·

Coordination of control efforts in various media. [A] technical consideration, and one that is often overlooked and sometimes very difficult to perform because of the lack of administrative mechanisms for doing so, is the coordination of pollution control efforts to protect air, water, and land. Pollutants removed from a waste source must still be disposed of somewhere, somehow. Some methods of pollutant removal and disposal may amount to little more than intermedia transfers of problems. Consider, for example, an aqueous effluent treatment system that produces an effluent meeting standards for discharge to a receiving water as well as a sludge containing high concentrations of toxic chemicals. The sludge may be incinerated, with release of toxics to the air, or disposed of on land in such a way that the toxics may be leached out and returned to an aqueous environment. An effective means of accounting for such side-effects may be to rule out certain types of disposal options, such as sludge incineration, in constructing the mathematical models, when it appears that they may lead to substantial side effects.

Feasibility of effluent standard compliance. Like ambient standards, effluent standards generally should be set at levels that make the monitoring of compliance possible. However, in the case where serious reservations exist about the safety of extremely low or even non-detectable amounts of a substance, a very low or even "no-discharge" standard may be set and the cooperation of industry in the form of process change and of other government entities in restricting sale or use of the substance may be sought....

Nontechnical Considerations

Equity. The fundamental fairness of pollution control regulation is an important issue at this stage of the standards-setting process. As Lyon stated in 1965, "In any democratic country regulatory activity is attuned to the concept of equity. This concept is found in many other regulatory endeavours and is one that is always the approach most likely to gain general public acceptance. It is also a concept which very often is difficult to explain or justify in scientific terms."

Bargaining. A final non-technical consideration in the process of setting effluent standards is the bargaining process between the regulators and the regulated. While this is only one consideration at the final stage of the rational model of idealized standards-setting discussed in this section, it is, according to Thompson, actually the essence of the regulatory process in Canada. He states that "no matter how normative measures are expressed in a statute — whether as policy guidelines or as command prohibitions — the end result in the case of environmental regulation is a bargaining process."

The bargaining process also can act as an interface between the technology and economics of pollution control, which until this stage have been considered in isolation, and the economies of the country and the world. Because of the perceived need for confidentiality about financial matters, this may be the first opportunity given to the regulatory authority to consider the effects of proposed effluent standards and prospective expenditures on a particular discharger's competitive position within the Canadian economy, and, if standards for an entire industry are being set, to consider collectively that industry's position in the world market.

Finally, the bargaining process can vividly draw attention to the weak points of the scientific and economic information supporting the standards-setting process. Often, bargaining will take place precisely because such weak points exist and leave room for maneuvering.

Beyond the Effluent Quality Standard — Technology-Based Effluent Standards

Technology-based effluent and emission standards are defined by Freeman as "quantitative" limits placed on all dischargers, where quantities are determined by reference to the available technology defined in terms of what is "practical," "possible," or "achievable." These limits are designated without reference to any ambient standards, balance of benefits and costs, or other guiding principles.

The reasons for the adoption of the technology based approach are many are complex. One group of reasons centres around the practical difficulties of using a water-quality-based model of the regulatory process. Here are a few brief excerpts from the comments of some of the men who guided this approach into legislation: "One of the major problems with water quality standards was ... the fact that they were unenforceable." "The reason why water quality standards were not enforceable is that, at that time, and I think it is still true today, it was impossible to infer from stream characteristics, water quality, goals, standards.... By and large, water quality standards were measured in terms of four pollutants — biochemical oxygen demand, suspended solids, fecal coliform, and pH. There was a growing recognition in 1972 that they weren't sufficient." Freeman observes that technology-based standards are usually perceived as simplifying matters. A less kind observation might paraphrase the attitude as, "It's too hard to do it right, so let's not even try."

The other pressures leading to the adoption of technology-based standards were more political and related to the specific conditions in the US in 1972. Again, these same Congressional staffers: "... there were a number of things that were going on in the area of water pollution control that set the stage for another congressional look at the subject. Among these was the concern that abatement was not proceeding at the pace that anybody would consider acceptable under the *Water Quality Act* of 1965.... Another perception was more a function of the general political climate of that time. Earth Day ... brought about a general concern that the govern-

ment at all levels was not doing enough for environmental quality ..."

While some of the motivation came from the philosophical position that disposal of wastes is not a legitimate "use" for water resources, by far the greatest part seems to have come from the perceived need to adopt an uncomplicated approach that would produce results — fast.

How has it worked? Apparently, not too well. According to Freeman, the benefits claimed for this approach have been largely illusory. From the standpoint of how quickly water quality has improved, he says, this approach was not necessarily more successful than the water quality based approach because it has had its own problems in information gathering, procedural delays, and legal challenges. Language such as "best practical" and "reasonable cost" leaves a great deal to administrative discretion and leaves the door open to bargaining. Numerous issues have arisen: Should "exemplary" plants or a cross section of existing plants be used to determine "practicable" standards? Should guidelines give specific numerical values? Should in plant process changes be considered? So much for simplicity and quick results.

Another difficulty is that technology-based standards discourage innovation in treatment processes and encourage reliance on the prescribed technologies even when they seem unlikely to produce the desired quality of effluent. The latter is a particularly important point from the standpoint of enforcement, because a discharger that can demonstrate that in good faith it relied on the required technology is in a fairly safe position even should its effluent cause identifiable problems.

(b) Environmental Standards-Setting and the Law in Canada

Kernaghan Webb[†] ——————————————————————————————

Legislators, regulatory agencies, courts, industry associations, individual firms and non-

governmental organizations all use standards to distinguish acceptable from unacceptable types

† An original article contributed by Dr. Kernaghan Webb, Adjunct Research Professor to the Department of Law and School of Public Administration, Carleton University; Honorary Lecturer at the University of Dundee's Centre for Energy, Petroleum and Mineral Law and Policy; and Chief of Research for the Canadian Office of Consumer Affairs.

or levels of environmental conduct. Standards are essential "building blocks" of governmental and non-governmental environmental protection regimes, enshrined in licences and permits, regulations and codes, private tort law actions, offences and defences to liability. In their broadest sense, standards can be defined as pre-established measures of extent, quantity, quality, process or value that are to be applied in an objective, consistent manner. Thus, for example, the 1992 *Pulp and Paper Mill Effluent Chlorinated Dioxins and Furans Regulations* sets a standard requiring that all mills using chlorine bleaching processes achieve the maximum discharge limit in the final effluent of 15 parts per quadrillion (ppq) for dioxin and 50 ppq for furan, courts require that companies meet a reasonable care or due diligence standard as part of strict liability offences or private law tort actions of negligence, the Accelerated Reduction/Elimination of Toxics (ARET) program is a voluntary, non-regulatory initiative that has identified and set targets for the elimination of 117 toxic substances, and the World Wildlife Fund for Nature has spearheaded the development of sustainable forestry principles and standards through the Forest Stewardship Council.

But while the aforementioned definition of standards and the examples provided might give the impression that standard-setting is dry and uncontroversial, the reality is often quite different. In fact, as will become apparent from the discussion below, there are frequently bitter and protracted debates concerning what standards should apply in a particular circumstance. There are many questions associated with effective standards-setting: for example, who is the most appropriate body to develop standards? Through what process? How does one balance costs against benefits? What happens in situations of scientific uncertainty? What are the proper roles for legislators, courts, government departments, industry and environmental non-governmental organizations? How does one ensure that standards are both effective, credible and enforceable? In what ways does law constrain or facilitate standards-setting? These questions are explored in the following pages.

Who Should Develop Environmental Standards?

Because they are our elected representatives who sit in the primary democratic rule-making body in our society (e.g., Parliament and the provincial Legislative Assemblies), it would be easy to assume that legislators set most environmental standards in Canada, or at least oversee the process of setting environmental standards. But while statutes such as the *Canadian Environmental Protection Act, 1999* and the Ontario *Environmental Protection Act* do provide basic overarching environmental standards, legislators frequently delegate many environmental standards-setting responsibilities to others. Legislators delegate in apparent acknowledgement of their lack of expertise and, perhaps, in recognition that their time is better spent articulating broad policy frameworks rather than detailed regulatory prescriptions. Sometimes delegations take place in a direct manner (e.g., authorization for the Governor in Council to develop regulations), and in others the delegation is less obvious (e.g., where courts are by default left to ascertain what constitutes a "deleterious substance").[1] As standards-setting bodies, Parliament, Cabinet, government departments and regulatory agencies, the courts, industry associations, environmental non-governmental organizations, and others all have different features in terms of transparency, openness, accountability, expertise, formality, access to information and expense of process; and, as a result, the quality of standards developed by each type of body can vary significantly from one to the other. These points are discussed below.

Regulatory Standards-Setting

While Parliament and provincial legislatures establish overarching environmental protection frameworks in statutes, the detailed prescriptions and standards are typically embodied in subordinate statutory instruments such as regulations and permits. Generally, the authority to develop regulations is statutorily delegated by Parliament and provincial legislatures to the "Governor in Council," which is more commonly known as the Cabinet. Functionally, the Cabinet consists of the governing party's key Ministers. While the process of drafting regulations involves many checks and balances, it is important to understand at the outset that regulations are *not* the subject of scrutiny by the full Parliament or the provincial Legislative Assemblies. At the federal level, when the terms of proposed regulations are developed, the Special Committee of Council, consisting of ten ministers, reviews the proposed regulations and recommends that the Governor in Council make the regulations.

In practice, one Minister (and in turn, one Department) usually assumes the lead responsibility for ensuring that a regulation is passed. The process from initial review through to final publication is often long and tortuous. For example, in 1990, Environment Canada (working in close co-operation with the Minister of Fisheries and Oceans, who has nominal responsibility for the regulations) announced its intention to update and strengthen the 1977 *Metal Mining Liquid Effluent Regulations* (promulgated pursuant to the *Fisheries Act*).[2] In 1993, the Department established the "Assessment of the Aquatic Effects of Mining in Canada" (AQUAMIN) process to review the scientific data and develop recommendations for an improved regulation. The AQUAMIN process involved approximately 100 representatives from federal, provincial, and territorial governments, the mining industry, First Nations organizations, and environmental non-governmental organizations (ENGOs). Over the period 1993–1996, more than 700 reports related to over 95 Canadian mine sites were reviewed, and detailed case studies were conducted for 18 sites. The final report, issued in 1996, advanced more than 50 recommendations in three key areas: specific amendments to the existing regulations, the design of a national environmental effects monitoring program, and information gaps and research needs. The AQUAMIN process cost the federal government and the Mining Association of Canada $435,000 (split 78%–22%).[3]

A subsequent advisory process was established with the goal of completing revisions to the regulations by 2000. This phase involved another multi-stakeholder advisory group and several technical working groups to prepare recommendations for developing the new regulations. Prior to introduction of new or revised regulations, governments are required to undertake a regulatory impact assessment process, leading to publication of a Regulatory Impact Assessment Statement (RIAS), which is appended to the draft regulation circulated for public comment. The RIAS includes an economic analysis of the anticipated consequences of the proposed change in public policy, including its costs and benefits and alternatives considered, provides a summary of the consultation process and describes the compliance and enforcement strategy.

In July, 2001, the draft regulations and the RIAS were published in the *Canada Gazette* (the official newspaper for the federal government), and subject to a 60-day public comment period. At the time of their release as draft regulations, one area of controversy was whether the standards were currently achievable by all Canadian mines.[4] In this regard, the standards were based on what was determined through the AQUAMIN process to be the Best Available Technology Economically Achievable (BATEA). According to the RIAS, the requirements set in the standards are currently obtainable by the majority of Canadian mines and reflect similar provincial requirements: "BATEA does not imply that individual mine operators must have the final capacity to meet a proposed standard, but that technology must be affordable on a sectoral basis."[5] Thus, the BATEA approach can lead to adoption of a standard even if a particular mine does not currently have the capacity to meet it. While industry is reported in the RIAS as having supported the objective of producing effluents that are non-acutely lethal (i.e., the effluents will harm, but not kill an organism), it argued that it should not become a regulatory requirement until such time as BATEA was better demonstrated. On the other hand, ENGOs were on record as wanting regulations that were more "technology-forcing" (i.e., that stimulated companies to move beyond what they were now technologically capable of achieving).[6] In an apparent compromise designed to ensure the enforceability of the standard, and the acceptability of it to industry, the proposed regulation allows for authorized exemptions from the application of the standards for a period of up to two years. The requirement in the proposed regulation that there be ongoing environmental effects monitoring undertaken by each mine facility facilitates the ability of the federal government to upgrade the regulatory standards should information reveal new problems.

As part of the RIAS process, the federal government attempted to calculate the costs and benefits associated with the proposed regulations. Costs identified included those associated with upgrading and operating effluent treatment facilities ($224–$576 million over a 15-year period), costs of testing undertaken by mining companies ($3 million annually), environmental effects monitoring by mining companies (around $4 million annually) and costs to government of enforcement (about $2 million annually).[7] On the benefits side, identified elements included those associated with having uniform national standards with a level playing field (as opposed to the current patchwork), effects monitoring to determine effectiveness, reduced total suspended solids, reduced non-acutely lethal effluents, improved commercial, sport and aboriginal fisheries, increased value for properties located near affected watercourses, reduction in future costs of restoring polluted water courses, and a general improvement in quality of local ecosystems, among others. Illustrative of the difficulties of conducting cost-benefit analyses, the RIAS did not attempt to quantify these benefits, and indeed noted the problematic nature of such attempts.

The process of revision of the mine effluent regulations demonstrates the challenges associated with standards-setting through regulatory processes, including gathering the needed information, making an objective assessment, identifying costs and benefits, exploring options and devising appropriate protections, and ensuring that they are enforceable. When the new regulations are in place (projected date of operation: 2002), the process of development will have lasted 12 years and cost more than half a million dollars. The regulatory standards-setting process, through the use of concepts such as Best Available Technology Economically Achievable, authorized exemptions from the standards for up to two years, and ongoing environmental effects monitoring: attempts to ensure that the standards are both scientifically justifiable, but also practical and enforceable.

Federal-Provincial-Territorial Standard-Setting

Because legislative responsibilities for environmental protection in Canada are constitutionally split between the federal and provincial governments, there is considerable potential for conflict, duplication and lack of coordination regarding both standard-setting and enforcement activities. In recognition of this, in 1998 the Canadian Council of Ministers of the Environment (CCME), with the exception of Quebec, signed the *Canada-Wide Accord on Environmental Harmonization*, designed to lead to improved cooperation and better environmental protection across Canada.[8] Pursuant to the *Accord*, federal, provincial (except Quebec), and territorial governments agreed to a number of fundamental principles,

including the polluter pays principle, and the precautionary principle.[9] The *Accord* is based on, and respects, the pre-existing constitutional and legislative divisions of power. The *Accord* provides for sub-agreements to be developed, including one pertaining to environmental standards. The *Canada-Wide Environmental Standards Sub-agreement* was agreed to in 1998.

The aim of the *Standards Sub-agreement* is to encourage governments to work together on key issues requiring national standards. Canada-wide standards are to be based on "sound science and the evaluation of risk to human health and the environment," but are also to take into account socio-economic considerations.[10] The resulting Canada-wide standards are then available for use by governments as part of their regulatory initiatives. The *Sub-agreement* calls for the public to be given a meaningful opportunity to provide input into the selection of priorities, and development and implementation of standards.[11] However, because the Canada-wide standards are to be used by federal, provincial and territorial governments as part of their own regulations, there is a second, jurisdiction-specific opportunity for consultations, notice and comment.

An *Annex* to the *Accord* outlines principles for stakeholder involvement, as well as principles on how governments will be accountable for commitments made.[12] Generally, Canada-wide standards are to be developed using a risk-based approach, which ties together the scientific, technical, and socio-economic factors involved in developing and implementing the standards. A conceptual risk-based framework and a framework for the application of socio-economic analyses in setting environmental standards have been prepared. Pursuant to this process, Canada-wide standards have been established or are being finalized for ambient air quality for particulate matter and ground-level ozone, mercury emissions covering incineration and base metal smelting, and a national target to reduce benzine emissions and mercury for dental amalgam waste, and for dioxins and furans.[13] The Canada-wide standards for dioxins and furans are the only standards that address substances that are designated for "virtual elimination" under the *Canadian Environmental Protection Act* and the CCME Toxic Substances Management Policy. In January, 1999, a Development Committee composed of representatives from each jurisdiction was formed to develop the standards. A multi-stakeholder Core Advisory Group advised the Development Committee on stakeholder involvement in the development of the standard. Two national multi-stakeholder meetings were held. The Canada-wide standards for dioxins and furans for the incineration and coastal pulp and paper sectors were endorsed by the CCME in May 2001.[14]

A June, 2000 review of the Accord and sub-agreements undertaken for the CCME revealed that ENGOs and Aboriginal groups are in need of improved resources to enable them to participate on a more equitable basis with industry and other groups that have independent resources. According to the authors of the review, experience with the Canada-wide standards development process "demonstrated the complexity of the science, issues and analysis that must be considered in developing a standard."[15] In essence, the *Accord* and *Standards Sub-agreement* process are evidence of recognition by federal, provincial and territorial governments that, in order to have consistent, credible, and effective environmental standards across Canada, a framework for inter-governmental environmental standards-setting needed to be put in place that would ensure that a science-based, transparent and accessible process is used that has meaningful opportunities for all stakeholders to participate.

Standards-Setting in Permits and Licences

Although conducted at a considerably less visible level than that associated with regulations, governments also engage in standards-setting on an individuated basis when granting licences, permits, certificates of approvals and other site-specific approvals. Use of individuated permits is particularly prevalent in provincial resource management and pollution control activity, such as pursuant to the *Ontario Water Resources Act*[16] and the *Environmental Protection Act*.[17] From an environmental protection standpoint, a clear advantage of the individuated approval or permit approach is the enhanced ability to devise approvals that have standards specifically tailored to the particular features of the ecosystem and the resource extraction or industrial operation concerned. This advantage is particularly apparent when compared with regulations designed to operate on a sectoral basis — and that therefore lack the flexibility of setting separate standards in licences and permits. How-

ever, while, as we have seen, the process of setting standards through regulations can be quite transparent, with considerable opportunities for affected stakeholders to participate, the same may not be true for standards-setting in individuated permits. Typically, an official within a government ministry or department (e.g., the Director) will be charged with the responsibility of issuing licenses or permits.

In Ontario, since the introduction of the *Environmental Bill of Rights* in 1994, a publicly accessible environmental registry has been in place through which notice of all proposed permits and other instruments is disclosed, and, depending on the nature of the instrument, opportunities for comments are provided.[18] The Environmental Commissioner of Ontario has been charged with the responsibility of ensuring that registry, and the other provisions of the *Environmental Bill of Rights* are used in a proper fashion. Each year the Commissioner reports his or her findings to the Legislative Assembly.[19] The *Environmental Bill of Rights* also provides opportunities for review of existing instruments, and appeals of decisions made by the Ministry of Environment and other provincial ministries pertaining to the environment, including the right for citizens and companies to make appeals of decisions to grant permits.[20]

It is neither possible nor appropriate in an overview piece of this nature to describe the full range of opportunities and mechanisms available under the *Environmental Bill of Rights* and other provincial legislation, nor to explore their practical impact on standards setting. But it should be noted that local, affected citizens and groups have appealed decisions to grant permits to industry operations for, e.g., taking of water, arguing that the original decisions of the Director in the Ministry of Environment failed to obtain needed information in order to make a proper decision, failed to follow the Ministry of Environment's Statement of Environmental Values, or to apply appropriate principles such as the ecosystem or water basin approach.[21] In some cases, after hearing from all affected parties, the Environmental Appeal Tribunal has altered the terms of the permit, in apparent recognition that the standards initially developed by government officials were not adequate.[22] Thus, while more difficult, it has been possible for individual citizens to participate in individuated standards-setting activities such as those contained in permits, and to influence the standards set in those permits. However, this has largely been on a reactive basis, and thus represents the exception more than the rule.

Judicial Standard-Setting

By leaving key terms in legislation undefined or unclear, legislators can indirectly delegate environmental standard-setting to the courts. For example, pursuant to subsection 36(3) of the federal *Fisheries Act*, it is an offence for any person to deposit a deleterious substance in water frequented by fish, unless authorized pursuant to conditions set out in regulations. "Deleterious substance" is defined in the *Fisheries Act* as "any substance that, if added to any water, would degrade ... the quality of that water so that it is rendered ... deleterious to fish...." This is what is known as a circular definition, since it uses the word "defined" in the definition, thereby providing no real guidance as to its meaning. By providing a circular definition of "deleterious", Parliament has, in effect, delegated the decision concerning what constitutes a deleterious substance to the courts. Not too surprisingly, judges have not been overly pleased about taking on this responsibility, with one judge stating, "I must agree with the Provincial Court judge that a definition section that uses the word defined is awkward."[23]

There are several significant implications flowing from this type of statutory delegation of standard-setting to the courts. First, there is a decrease in transparency and accessibility of the decision-making process. Instead of Members of Parliament in the House of Commons or in Standing Committees deliberating on the issue of what constitutes water pollution (and potentially drawing on a wide range of industry, environmental organizations, government officials and scientists), the decision is typically made by single judges addressing specific fact situations, usually with only the assistance of the counsel for the prosecution and defence.[24] Second, from the standpoint of users of the law — industry, government officials, members of the general public and even judges — the offence provides very little certainty and guidance as to how the law is to be applied, leaving a large amount of discretion in the hands of those to enforce the law. How well equipped are courts to make decisions of this sort? Canadian judges, faced with decisions concerning what constitutes a significantly harmful substance, have stated, "...it hardly

seems necessary to state that a Court of law is no forum for the determination of matters of science."[25]

Stripped to its essence, the standard set by the *Fisheries Act* offence is basically one of "zero tolerance": that is, no substance, if found to be deleterious (as interpreted by the courts), can be deposited into water frequented by fish. With this offence, there is no balancing of environmental interests with economic interests or technological capability, as takes place in the regulation-making process: very simply, the protection of fish is the only interest to be taken into consideration. This, of course, is excellent from the standpoint of environmental protection, but raises serious questions in terms of practical implementation, compelling government officials to devise ways of structuring their enforcement discretion.[26] Moreover, the "zero tolerance" standard set in this offence conflicts with that established in other federal legislation. The *Pest Control Products Act*, for example, allows for some level of acceptable risk associated with the use of pesticides.[27] The federal Commissioner of the Environment and Sustainable Development has documented situations where the *Fisheries Act*'s zero tolerance approach embodied in s. 36(3) and the *Pest Control Products Act*'s "acceptable risk" approach have conflicted, with federal departments refusing to reconcile their differences, and provincial environmental departments and farmers (users of pesticides) left in the dark as to what standard is to be applied.[28]

There are other contexts in environmental law where courts play a key role in articulating standards. With both the strict liability regulatory offence, and private tort actions in negligence, accused firms can escape liability by establishing that they met a standard of "reasonable care" (also known as "due diligence"). It is important to recognize that with both the strict liability offence and the tort of negligence, the burden of proof for establishing due diligence rests not with the prosecutor or plaintiff, but rather with the accused. On the basis of the evidence put before them, and the persuasive abilities of opposing counsel, judges articulate what constitutes "due diligence." One of the most comprehensive discussions of the nature of the due diligence defence in recent years is provided by Justice Ormston in the case of *R.* v. *Bata Industries Ltd.*[29] According to Justice Ormston, to establish due diligence, courts are to examine whether the directors had established a pollution prevention system with adequate supervision and inspection, whether there is regular reporting back to the directors, what remedial and contingency plans for spills are in place, whether the company engages in ongoing audits, and whether there are training programs available. While court standards-setting activity allows for a case-by-case approach to decision-making, it also decreases certainty, since courts are not required to adopt the same standard as they would if it was established in regulations.

International Law and Environmental Standards-Setting

There are two aspects of international law of direct relevance to environmental standards-setting in Canada. The first is the ability of international legal conventions and treaties to establish standards and principles that are then applied domestically in Canada and elsewhere. The second is the ability of international legal agreements to constrain domestic standards-setting activities. Both of these aspects are briefly reviewed below.

It may be thought that standards-setting in international law is basically similar to that within domestic law-making institutions. In truth, it is considerably more difficult, primarily due to the fact that there is no binding rule-making body akin to Parliament or the provincial Legislative Assemblies. Instead, participation by nations in international treaty-making is ad hoc, and entirely consent-based. Thus, if a country does not wish to participate in the development of a treaty, or to ratify it, it does not have to, and if it does not wish to involve other parties in negotiation of the terms of treaties, such as environmental non-governmental organizations, it is under no obligation to do so. This has two significant implications from a standards-setting perspective. First, it can result in a tendency towards agreement of "lowest-common denominator" standards, in an effort to attract the consent of as many nations as possible. Second, it can result in very protracted negotiations and implementation processes that take place over years and even decades. For example, as early as 1974, scientists had identified chlorofluorocarbons (CFCs) as contributors to the thinning of the stratospheric ozone layer. But it took until 1987 for countries to agree to control measures as set out in the Montreal Protocol.[30] Nevertheless, in spite of these difficulties, an increasing number of international environmental conventions have been developed and ratified, and in turn have led to domestic legislation to implement the terms of the conventions.[31]

International environmental law can also be the source of general concepts such as sustainable development and the precautionary principle, which can find their way into, and be highly influential in, the domestic legal system. The precautionary principle may prove particularly important for environmental standards-setting activities, because it can act to stimulate and justify environmental action in the face of scientific uncertainty. The precautionary principle was articulated in the 1992 Rio Declaration on Environment and Development. Principle 15 stated that: "In order to protect the environment, the precautionary approach shall be widely applied by States according to their capability. Where there are threats of serious or irreversible damage, lack of full scientific certainty shall not be used as a reason for postponing cost-effective measures to prevent environmental degradation." Governments, judges, industry, ENGOs, and others are still struggling with exactly how to interpret and apply the principle, but in spite of this, it has already proven influential in Canada.[32]

In addition to inclusion of the precautionary principle in legislation such as the *Canadian Environmental Protection Act, 1999*, and in the *Canada-Wide Accord on Environmental Harmonization*, the Supreme Court of Canada has recently referred to it in support of its decision concerning the authority of a municipality to establish a by-law restricting use of pesticides.[33] Although it is too early to predict the precise impact of the precautionary principle on environmental standards-setting in Canada, its potential to assist in risk-based decision-making in the face of scientific uncertainty is great. In 2001, the federal government released a discussion paper setting out guidance on how to operationalize the principle.[34] Eleven principles are articulated, designed to respond to whether, and in what fashion, the federal government should act when faced with a situation where there is a potential for serious or irreversible harm, and where there is not full scientific certainty.[35]

The first six principles elaborate on the Canadian position with respect to precautionary decision making: for example, that it is legitimate for Canada to make precautionary decisions, and it is legitimate that decisions be based on Canadians' chosen level of protection; that while scientific uncertainty may exist, there still has to be some sound scientific basis for a decision; and that it is particularly important that there be increased transparency, accountability and public involvement. Five principles propose specific characteristics for precautionary measures: that they need to be reconsidered in light of evolving science and society's chosen level of protection; that they should be non-discriminatory and consistent as well as proportional to the level of protection being sought; that they should be cost-effective with the goal of generating an overall net benefit for society at least cost; and that, where more than one option meets these characteristics, they should be the least trade-restrictive option. The effect of the principles, if adopted, would be to create a framework for practical operationalization of the precautionary principle in environmental standards-setting.

At the same time as international law can establish environmental standards and articulate principles to be applied in domestic law, it can also constrain domestic standards-setting activity. This is most clearly evident in global trade agreements such as those of the World Trade Organization, and regional trade agreements such as the North American Free Trade Agreement (NAFTA). These agreements structure and restrict the ability of governments to put in place measures that impede trade unless the measures take an approved form and can be justified as compatible with certain identified legitimate public policy objectives (e.g., protection of health and safety and the environment). Where domestic legislation does not comply with trade agreements agreed to by the country in question, it can lead to legal actions, trade sanctions and compensation. In this way, international trade law can "discipline" domestic environmental standards-setting activity.

Two examples illustrate this point. In a challenge brought by the United States and others concerning European Union restrictions on imports of beef from cows that have been the subject of hormone injections, a WTO Dispute Panel and Appellate Body ruled that there was not adequate scientific evidence showing a serious identifiable health risk that would justify the EU import restrictions.[36] As a result, the European Union has been required to lift the restrictions, and/or provide some form of compensation.

A second case illustrating the ability of international law to constrain domestic environmental standards-setting concerns Chapter 11 of NAFTA, which pertains to investment. In April, 1997, the federal government banned the import and interprovincial transport (but not the use in Canada) of an additive in gasoline referred to as MMT. Because adequate data on the health risks of exposure to the elements in MMT was not available, the restrictions were established pursuant to a new Act, the *Manganese-Based Fuel Additives Act*,[37] and not the *Canadian Environmental Protection Act*.[38] The corporation that manufactures MMT, Ethyl, claimed that the ban on import was contrary to Chapter 11 of NAFTA, on the grounds that it constituted an illegal taking (i.e., an expropriation of the property of the investor that was not undertaken pursuant to acceptable grounds, such as to protect the health of Canadians, as justified by scientific evidence). In 1998, a settlement was reached between the Government of Canada and the Ethyl Corporation. As part of the settlement, the Government of Canada removed the measure that banned the product, issued a statement indicating that it had no evidence of harm to health caused by the product, and paid the company approximately $20 million.[39]

The two decisions show that domestic environmental standard setting that is not founded on a clear scientific basis will be vulnerable to challenge under international trade agreements.

Voluntary Approaches and Standards

We have seen that the process of regulatory standards-setting is onerous, expensive and lengthy, and must have a scientific basis to withstand legal challenges. This is, perhaps, nowhere more clearly demonstrated than with respect to the process of identifying and regulating toxic substances under the *Canadian Environmental Protection Act*. In his 1999 report, the federal Commissioner of the Environment and Sustainable Development concluded that:

> [t]he federal government has been slow to take action on some substances assessed and declared toxic under the *Canadian Environmental Protection Act*. The current programs are insufficient to ensure that risks will be adequately addressed in the future. Objectives for the protection of human health and the environment have not been specified, and agreed reductions in the release of toxic substances are not assured.[40]

Yet while regulatory processes are ponderous and, in some cases, insufficient, there are nevertheless some circumstances where preventative action is needed, and where industry may be prepared to act in the absence of the full scientific information needed to justify regulatory action. It was in this context that, in the early 1990s, Canadian industry, government and certain environmental groups came together[41] to draw up a list of 117 toxic substances, prioritize them, and begin a voluntary process to reduce their use. The substances were selected and agreed to on the basis of their persistence, bioaccumulative properties and toxicity.[42] A stakeholders committee, consisting of government and industry representatives, challenged participants to reduce releases of 30 high-priority toxic substances by 90 percent and the remaining 87 substances by 50 percent by the year 2000. This process, which eventually came to be known as the Accelerated Reduction/Elimination of Toxics (ARET) Challenge, has been credited with leading to reductions in usage far in excess of what could be established through the regulatory process.[43] Two commentators have stated:

> The federal government would not have been able to achieve the reductions realised under ARET by relying on the *Canadian Environmental Protection Act*, which regulates less than 10 per cent of ARET's 117 substances; it has neither the procedural tools to assess quickly the toxicity of so many substances, nor the necessary enforcement capacity to apply a purely regulatory approach.[44]

While the ARET program has quite rightly been criticized on many grounds that focus on implementation,[45] for present purposes its value is in demonstrating how non-regulatory programs may be able to employ a more rapid and informal standards-setting process that can act to stimulate action in advance of regulatory standards-setting initiatives.

Although generally it is government that initiates standards-setting activities, this is not always the case. There are increasing numbers of examples where industry associations and environmental non-governmental organizations (ENGOs) have taken the lead in developing standards. The Canadian Chemical Producers' Association (CCPA) has developed the Responsible Care program, which includes a statement of policy, guiding principles, and six codes of practice with 152 elements covering community awareness and emergency response, research and development, manufacturing, transportation, distribution, and hazardous waste management.[46] In developing and implementing the Responsible Care program, the CCPA has drawn on the input of a national advisory panel with ENGO and community representatives. In contrast to law-based standards setting, commentators have suggested that the CCPA program has stimulated the chemical industry to engage in pro-active changes in corporate culture, and has led to substantial reductions in emissions of many toxic chemicals.[47]

ENGOs have also taken the lead in voluntary standards-setting activities. Perhaps the best example of this is the Forest Stewardship Council (FSC), spearheaded by the World Wildlife Fund for Nature. Through a multi-stakeholder structure, the FSC has established principles and standards pertaining to sustainable forestry that have been adopted by forestry companies around the world. ENGO-initiated standards-setting provides non-governmental organizations with invaluable practical experience in working with a range of stakeholders, including industry.[48] Indeed, a strong argument can be made that ENGO-initiated standards-setting may have particular credibility in the eyes of consumers and, as a result, industry may be anxious to demonstrate their compliance with its terms in the hopes of gaining a competitive advantage.

Conclusions

In Canada, standards-setting is undertaken by a wide number of decision-making bodies, through a variety of processes. Parliament and provincial Legislative Assemblies generally set the overall environmental protection framework, but leave the detailed standards setting to subordinate bodies and the courts. As is evident from the metal mining liquid effluent regulation revision process, the regulatory standards-setting process can be very lengthy and thorough, involving extensive and expensive multi-stakeholder information gathering and consultation phases, numerous experts, cost-benefit analysis, and a review of options. The process is comparatively transparent, accountable and accessible, including publication in draft form with a Regulatory Impact Assessment Statement (RIAS) in the *Canada Gazette*. While the process of drafting regulations involves many checks and balances, it is important to recognize that regulations are not the subject of scrutiny by the full Parliament or the provincial Legislative Assemblies. As was demonstrated with the RIAS associated with the metal mining effluent regulations, while it is fairly easy to identify and quantify costs to industry and government associated with new regulatory measures, it is considerably more difficult to quantify benefits. In recognition of overlapping federal-provincial-territorial environmental responsibilities, the Canadian Ministers of Environment, with the exception of Quebec, have established an agreement and process for developing Canada-wide standards. The process is intended to reduce the potential for conflict, duplication, and lack of coordination in standards-setting, and has led to the development of several Canada-wide standards. While comparatively transparent and open, there have been criticisms that, in order to ensure effective environmental organization and aboriginal participation there is a need for greater resources.

In contrast to regulatory and inter-governmental standards-setting processes in Canada, the process of setting standards in permits is generally carried out within government bureaucracies, with only a notice of decisions made being made public, and is only rigorously reviewed by a range of parties on those rare occasions where appeals have taken place. Judicial standards-setting is also typically less comprehensive than regulatory standards-setting, is less open to full participation of all stakeholders, and lacks the access to information and expertise that is found using other techniques. In some cases, the courts could be described as engaging in standards-setting by default, in the sense that judges are compelled to set standards because legislators have left terms undefined or unclear. In some cases, such as with respect to the due diligence defence available for both strict liability offences and the tort of negligence, the onus of establishing compliance with the standard rests with the accused, not the prosecutor or plaintiff. The main advantages of judicial standards-setting are its ability to adjust over time, and its comparatively fast decision-making process; but this must be offset by the uncertainty caused for industry, governments, and the general public, who do not know from one case to another what standard will be applied.

Because of the consent-based nature of international environmental law, standards-setting at the international level is typically a very lengthy process, and can lead to "lowest-common-denominator" standards. Also, the participation of third parties (e.g., industry or environmental organizations) is more restricted than is normal for domestic regulatory approaches. Nevertheless, an increasing number of important domestic environmental obligations have their origin in international environmental treaties. International environmental law can also be the source of important principles that affect standards-setting, such as the precautionary principle. The precautionary principle stipulates that a lack of full scientific certainty should not be a barrier to development of cost-effective protections where there is a significant risk of harm. The Canadian government is in the process of establishing an operational framework for use of the precautionary approach, and has enshrined the precautionary principle in the *Canadian Environmental Protection Act, 1999*, and in the inter-governmental *Harmonization Accord*. International law — particularly trade law — can also constrain domestic environmental standards-setting activity. Recent WTO and NAFTA cases suggest that full documentation of the scientific basis for domestic health and environmental standards is essential to avoid successful challenges.

The review of regulatory standards-setting activities suggests that, while it is probably the most comprehensive and rigorous approach to standards development, it can also be very slow and expensive. Voluntary standards setting, on the other hand — be it instigated by government, industry, or ENGOs — can often be considerably quicker, even if it is less thorough. This can allow for quick, proactive measures that perhaps, can be followed by regulations at a later point. Industry and ENGO-led standards activity may be able to harness the energies of industry to demonstrate good environmental behaviour in a manner not normally associated with implementation of regulatory measures.

(c) Setting Standards[†]

Keith Hawkins ——————————————————————————————

Issues

The boundaries of regulatory deviance are drawn by administrative agencies: pollution, in other words, is an administrative creation. The broad legal mandate of the agencies about water pollution control is transformed into policy by senior officials and given practical expression in the setting of pollution standards.[1] Standards ("consents") are licences to discharge polluting matter. Pollution is, in effect, qualitatively controlled by the water authorities since standards are administratively negotiated. Not only, then, do the agencies possess power to enforce the law, they actually determine the reach of the law, for (in contrast with the police) they exercise a real legislative authority, enjoying broad discretion to define what makes "pollution." In this sense the water authorities create pollution, as Becker might say (1963:9), by making the rules whose infraction constitutes pollution. Definition and enforcement, a dual authority, are reciprocally related, a theme to be explored in this chapter.

For agency policy-makers the consent is an important tool expressing political and economic judgements about water quality. Its central purpose, as the head of one the agencies put it, is "to produce a river which is suitable for the uses which are needed downstream — providing a potable water supply, for fisheries, just amenity. We might even decide we just want an effluent channel.... The consents are geared to produce the quality water you want in the river for the use you want downstream." For the water authorities, in general, the practical significance of consents is that many rivers are now substantially comprised of effluent already discharged subject to consent. One of the southern authority's main potable supply rivers, for example, consists in dry weather of more than 50 per cent effluent; and another river flowing through a major city in the northern authority is over 90 per cent effluent.

Consents to pollute come in the form of emission or effluent standards which prescribe the temperature, amount, and kind of polluting matter which may be discharged from a particular source. Dischargers are, thus, permitted to pollute by the water authorities — but only (in theory) up to those levels set out in the discharger's consent document. A consent, however, is a movable threshold. Once fixed it may subsequently be reviewed and modified by the agency on consultation with the discharger. The pollution standards in a consent are defined locally by each water authority and are specific in application, with each consent negotiated on an *ad hoc* basis. Standards are expressed quantitatively and each one is formulated not to contemplate exceptional circumstances, instead addressing pollution without regard to mitigating features, such as accident. Simply by selecting those substances in impure water which are to be held potentially "polluting" (pollution parameters) and the point at which such contamination is to be regarded as "polluting" (pollution limits), together with temperature and volume restriction, the agency establishes theoretically enforceable boundaries,[2] exercising, in other words, power to control the *potential level* of pollution. And since the water authorities are enforcement agencies they also control, to a very great degree, what may seem to be some sort of *"real level"* of pollution which comes to light in amount and kind — those events or incidents which are detected and processed, becoming statistics of non-compliance or even, in some rare cases, of prosecutions in annual reports.

In setting standards the water authorities, like other regulatory agencies, are confronted by two crucial problems. First, pollution control means cost. Since the cost of control usually returns few, if any, financial benefits to the discharger and has to be met by increased prices, dischargers regard pollution control costs as a

---

† © Social Science Research Council 1984. Reproduced from *Environment and Enforcement: Regulation and the Social Definition of Pollution* by Keith Hawkins (Oxford: Clarendon Press, 1984), pp. 23–28, 32–36, by permission of Oxford University Press, U.K. See appendix for notes or references.

burden to be avoided wherever possible. There is no simple relationship between control and costs. To make a significant impact upon a bad discharge is not necessarily very expensive. But to make even a minor improvement to effluent which already consists of relatively good quality water may involve the discharger in very heavy expenditure indeed (see Kneese, 1973). The power to define and enforce consents is ultimately a power to put people out of business, to deter the introduction of new industry or to drive away going concerns.

The second, related, problem in standard setting is one of the distribution of costs. A tension between officials' perceptions of equity and efficacy is, for them, a familiar dilemma. The conflict is between an essentially moral stance which prizes consistency and uniformity in the application of standards (similar discharges should be similarly controlled in degree and kind) and a utilitarian approach concerned with effect on water quality, regardless (again, in theory, at least) of the means of the discharger or the demands fortuitously being placed unequally on similar dischargers (see generally Ackerman et al., 1974). "... [T]he load of polluting matter discharged should be controlled at all times to exactly the level that a river would accept without harming river uses or the environment" (unpubl. agency document). This is a recurrent dilemma in pollution control since efficacy insists that standards be tied to the setting of a discharge and settings vary enormously.

The weight to be given to the normally competing values of equity and efficacy is a persistent problem both in setting or reviewing standards and in enforcing them.[3] On one level, the dilemma is between standards of general and of individualized application. On another, the conflict is sometimes portrayed as between older, established ways of handling pollution control and newer, more "scientific" approaches in which environmental impact in its widest sense is the primary concern. The utilitarianism of the scientist tends to view the principle of equity with a certain disdain because of its potential inefficiency: "Equitability can be the biggest millstone," said a senior officer with a special interest in consents. "Often it goes against technical judgments. When it comes into play, some of the ultimate answers are not the best ones." In terms of formal policy, a shift in recent years has seen equity ostensibly yield place to efficacy. In practice this should mean that the design of con-

sents has been influenced less by conceptions about the similarity of discharges than by a scientific analysis of the impact a particular discharge may have on a particular watercourse and the polluting load that that watercourse can accept, according to agency plans for river quality.

Senior officials are firmly committed to the utilitarian view: "treating discharges alike in terms of ... the quality of the discharge, as distinct from the effect on the environment," said one, "is absolute nonsense." Yet senior staff and field men alike are aware of the fact that most dischargers are likely to be more sympathetic to an approach to standard setting and enforcement based on equity. Apart from the moral preference that like should be treated alike, dischargers' commercial instincts argue that no manufacturer or producer should be placed in a more favourable position than his competitors. The practical task, then, for a water authority setting or modifying a consent based on criteria relating to the particular watercourse becomes one of persuading a discharger disadvantaged by some criterion which makes sense in utilitarian —but not moral—terms of the force of the agency's position. In some cases this is apparently not as arduous a task as it may seem, simply because dischargers find it extremely difficult to portray themselves as "similar" to their rivals on more than a very few criteria.

An individualized approach based on a concept of efficacy can be sold to dischargers because it is "scientific." Equity can be played down:

> I don't know if it should be that important if everything we do is based on good sound scientific principles, because if people perhaps in the same industry are situated in different places in the estuary, y'know, if one was to point the finger at the other and say "But you allow him to discharge such and such and you only let us do this," then we should be able to turn round and say, "Ah yes, but you're discharging in a different place and the river quality in this different place needs different treatment." ... I think you can only treat them similarly if all other things are equal, if they're discharging into the same sort of watercourse in the same sort of position. Because obviously if you had one particular factory on the tideway and another producing an identical product and identical effluent in one of the tributaries, you couldn't treat them the same because they're patently different cases.

On this "scientific" view of standard setting, the design of consents to discharge polluted water is to be based on a dispassionate consideration of the amount and kind of pollution load any watercourse can bear. The capacity of a watercourse and the tolerable limits of polluting effluent are calculated according to a mathematical model, which ideally should be applied routinely and objectively to all dischargers regardless of their means, the costs of treatment, their prior efforts, or the demands made of their competitors.

Field men, however, are constantly reminded that industrialists and farmers work on a principle of equity: they can readily discover the standards which their competitors must observe and may complain if they are being handicapped. But the agencies prefer to avoid complaints wherever possible, and this encourages an administrative inclination for equity of treatment, even though "scientific" judgment may dictate otherwise. Negotiating about standards, especially when there is some disparity between apparently similar dischargers, though an infrequent event, can be one of the field man's trickiest tasks.

The picture of an agency which dispassionately administers scientifically-designed standards is blurred further by organizational practices. Later chapters will show that in pollution control work, standards are, by no means, treated as absolute proscriptions inexorably enforced. The agencies display a sometimes considerable flexibility, both in the standards set and in the enforcement policy adopted, in recognition of the technical difficulties and costs of complying, the potential for error, and the stigmatizing effect of strict legal enforcement. Furthermore, the processes giving rise to pollution sometimes produce erratic discharges in which effluents may become heavily polluting, and river water is also inherently variable in quality. The result is that a degree of leeway is normally granted to dischargers, and a certain amount of pollution allowed to occur with impunity. Such leeway is the means by which the enforcement agency adapts to uncertainty. "The present situation is that consent conditions are written as though they were absolute," a senior official said:

> The time it goes over — once in a lifetime — and you're a criminal. So the practice has been to regard them rather unofficially as having been satisfied if there is compliance on about ... three occasions out of four, or four out of five, or two out of three — practices are variable from one authority to another. We've adopted a three out of four.

Non-compliance with standards is thus organizationally sanctioned.[4] Though the consent may not be strictly enforced, however, it is significant as a benchmark for both dischargers and enforcement authorities. It remains the criterion of pollution, despite its irregular enforcement; as such it creates a zone of officially tolerated "pollution" which will vary as the standard and the setting of the discharge vary. And it remains the legally enforceable standard of pollution if customary enforcement practices are suspended.

In a substantial proportion of cases dischargers normally display little or no objection to the standards imposed by the agency, as a result of preparatory work in negotiations conducted by the field officer together with, in more important cases, his area supervisor. But where standards appear, to a discharger, to impose excessive demands, he may exercise a right of appeal to the Secretary of State. Although hardly ever employed, this right of appeal in effect confers bargaining power upon the discharger who seeks to counter administrative extravagance, since the agencies attempt to avoid appeal at almost all costs:

> It's certainly true that if people suggest they will go to the appeal procedure then we will do almost everything we can to avoid that, which means in some cases we're letting people get away with something that you wouldn't let others get away with, simply because they're being difficult — well, not being difficult, they would be just exercising their rights.

The desire to avoid appeal may partly be a reflection of the fact that standards have been selected by resort to the convention of established — but largely unexamined — practice which may be difficult to defend in a formal arena. Thus "you've got to be very sure of your ground, because you've got to get up, not in a court, but in an appeal situation, and give evidence." There is also a good organizational reason why agencies fear appeals: appeals introduce uncertainty (cf. Kaufman, 1960: 154–5) and threaten their control over the design of consents. An appeal may establish a formal precedent which an agency might find undesirable, since standard setting is then taken out of its hands by people regarded as possessed of less expertise and possibly differing interests. A principle informing negotiations about consents is to avoid the risk of creating a precedent on appeal injurious to the agency's interests, a principle of wide applicability, for to appeal and win — or even to appeal and lose — publicizes the possibility of remedy which itself is a threat to the agency's whip hand.[5] Appeal gives status and recognition to protest.

Ironically, recourse to precedent is a useful tactic for the field man to employ when negotiating about standards. Reference can be made to standards usually set by the agency "in cases of this kind," or attention drawn to practice in past cases. But the officer must maintain a certain flexibility and be able to deviate from usual practice where necessary, especially to avoid the risk that an administrative convention may be established which can subsequently be used by others with conflicting interests as a resource in their own negotiations. Obviously when the agency claims allegiance to an established precedent where its formal interests in pollution control or its organizational interests are served, it lends further support to the principle of equity. Indeed, the principle serves administrative interests well, for if standard conditions designed to be equitable as between apparently similar dischargers are routinely applied, the discharger who wishes to appeal against the standards imposed in his case is probably in a weak position if the agency is able to show the Minister that the standards were those typically in force. But in practical terms, the organizational imperative to avoid appeal means modifying demands in the course of negotiations if there is any suggestion that the agency might have to defend itself in a appeal: "we try to see," said a senior officer, "there are no grounds for reasonable objection."

.   .   .   .

Enforceability

Though the agencies do not regard standards as strict limits, their enforceability is important. From the field staff's point of view it is essential that the parameters in any consent should be clear and unambiguous. They should at least appear to be attainable, for standards which can be met, if at all, only after massive expenditure might tempt an unwilling discharger to question them by appeal. Unattainable standards, even though not appealed by a discharger, may still lead to practical problems of enforcement, since a continued reason which enforcement agents tolerate may suggest condonation by the agency of the continual breach of consent. Indeed in some cases in which there is a persistent failure to comply and no apparent harm to the watercourse, agency staff tend to assume that the

standards may be too tight, as a senior official suggested:

> somebody who's not complying with consent conditions and yet is not having much effect on the river, it probably means the consent condition is not right to start with.... This is I think one of the reasons that we can tolerate some non-compliance because some of the consent conditions are a bit too strict.

In areas of regulatory control like pollution, where the law regards conformity as essentially a matter of scientific measurement, deviance is conspicuous. While clear, uncomplicated standards are useful for an enforcement agent negotiating to secure compliance, economy in the design of standards is also important. To be parsimonious in the use of parameters assists in the display of deviance; in a prosecution it aids a portrayal of guilt, as an agency head explained:

> I always try and have as few conditions as possible in a consent.... In a court it would be so easy if I was on the other side to get up and say that in respect of eight of the conditions "We complied and we only contravened the suspended solids condition and we're very sorry it was 30,000 p.p.m. but you're not gonna cane us for that are you, Mr. Magistrate? We've got eight of them right." ... So the simpler the conditions the better, the fewer conditions the better.

Yet the use of few parameters, if they are well chosen, can still be an efficient means of pollution control. To have one or two strict parameters often means that other pollutants, which can remain unspecified in the consent document, are brought under control. Or parameters which provoke the discharger's concern can be framed leniently, control being assured by the insertion of a much stricter parameter of more general application.

The issue of enforceability was given a poignant twist following passage of the Control of Pollution Act 1974 which made an inroad into the virtual monopoly of pollution control enjoyed by the water authorities. The Act (much of which is not yet in force) requires publication of sample results and permits members of the public to bring legal action against a discharger who fails to comply with consent.[17] The agencies will have to have, available for public scrutiny, a register giving details of consents granted and results of effluent samples.[18] A source of particular vulnerability for the agencies is that in its reorganization of the water industry the 1973 Water Act gives them responsibility for the management of the great majority of sewage treatment works, which in many areas, are, themselves, significant — often principal — sources of pollution. The water authorities thus, not only set and enforce pollution standards, they are major polluters themselves. Yet the pollution control sections of the agencies are ultimately impotent to secure the compliance of their colleagues in sewage treatment, lacking recourse to the legal sanction (even if it were organizationally possible to prosecute fellow-workers). Many sewage treatment works have been consented in the ritual process to the usual 20 BOD and 30 suspended solids standards, which they have regularly failed to meet. While the agencies maintained almost total control over the enforcement of standards, a control which could be preserved in the absence of publicity, this posed no problem: "A lot of the standards were set by River Authorities; and the works weren't capable of achieving [them] anyway," a senior official said. "but the former River Authorities knew this and shut an eye to it."

After passage of the 1974 Act, however, the authorities had to contemplate the prospect that they themselves might be prosecuted for the polluting effluents from their sewage works. The new-found public accountability has produced a quite dramatic protective response from the agencies, illustrating the familiar point that a previously unreachable ideal may be achieved if reduced within the compass of the practically attainable. The agencies have simply embarked on a large-scale programme to revise consents, both of their sewage works, and of other discharges. Where a discharger would consistently do better than his existing consent, standards have sometimes been tightened. But where a discharger has regularly been outside consent, standards have been relaxed to accord with the existing performance in 95 per cent of samples taken. Thus, while standards were relaxed, this was accompanied by less tolerance of their breach, compliance being expected in 95 per cent, rather than 75 per cent, of samples: "exposing ourselves five per cent of the time," as a senior man put it, thinking of his agency's sewage works. The review was described by an agency director as

> an attempt to span out 95 per cent of the quality of effluent at present discharged from the [sewage] works, taking out the fliers and the obviously bad discharges .... This means in practice that one out of every twenty samples will

fail to comply with the standard and the Authority will be at risk from somebody, some member of the public, prosecuting.

This protective behaviour has occurred in reaction to the threat which publicity poses to the discretion with which the agencies would treat deviants — themselves and others. "We've learned in the last go it's the public accountability thing," said a senior official.

> The legal thing can go out the window. For the first time we've had to get our heads down and look at what we're doing.... We bend over backwards to do the thing [properly] ... but what happens in practice — do we mean it? And in many cases we realize we don't. We find a factory who's not met its standards eight times in a year, and what do we do about it? Nothing! ... So one reason [for reviewing consents] is it doesn't make any difference to the river system; another is that it means we're not prepared to follow the thing through on a legal basis.... It's going to be stupid when the booklet's published [giving details of sample results] — we'll get tons and tons of phone calls.... What we're now trying to do is say the river will stand a temperature of 30°C — if it'll stand it, don't let's bugger about. It takes some sort of public document for people to get you out of a rut.

Adaptive action by recasting the rules was necessary to preserve administrative control and avoid the public embarrassment of the authorities. Since financial, technical, and geographical constraints did not permit efforts to be made to bring their sewage works into compliance with the existing standards (even if time had been available), the only other means of demonstrably maintaining compliance was for the agencies to change the standards to fit the existing discharges.

For field staff, however, a review which led to the relaxation of a large number of consents appeared to be in direct contradiction to their efforts ostensibly to bring all dischargers into compliance — "trying to fiddle the books for when the Act comes into force" as a northern authority officer put it. For many, the task of policing relaxed consents was a source of considerable professional embarrassment following their attempts to secure compliance with the former, stricter standards. For the pragmatic field officer, the exercise was purely cosmetic, not an effort to overhaul consents to place more rational demands (in terms of what a river could accept by way of pollution) on the discharger. "To my way of thinking," said an officer of wide experience, "this is just paper — it's only figures on paper, this is — to prevent the general public being able to prosecute the authority if a sewage works has the odd bad sample."

Postscript

Pollution control standards are flexible markers of rule-breaking. How strict or lenient enforcement agents conceive them to be may well affect their enforcement behaviour. For example, working conceptions of cause may depend upon a judgment as to whether the standards breached were generally attainable at tolerable cost. If they were, a violation may prompt suspicions of deliberate wrong-doing in the interest of financial saving.

Until recently, pollution control standards were treated as guides rather than boundaries.

They were a species of organizational rhetoric (now menaced by public access to the monopoly of enforcement), embodying compromise between conflicting values and recognition of the vagaries of the environment to be controlled. Standards which cannot be attained by negotiation or legal enforcement may, at least, be achieved if made less demanding. The threat of the 1974 Act was the challenge posed to agency control over the enforcement of regulatory deviance by publicity and a strict liability law. By redrawing the individual boundaries of deviance the agencies have sought to retain control. Their response may be the occasion for added impetus to the ostensible shift from equity to efficacy as the guiding principle in the design of water pollution standards.

Implementation and Instruments

(a) Instruments in Policy Implementation[†]

Law Reform Commission of Canada

Government uses a wide variety of governing instruments to implement its policies, ranging from regulatory offence prosecutions to financial incentives, licences and persuasion.[34] This chapter outlines major categories of instruments, their characteristics, strengths and weaknesses. In order to facilitate comparisons, we put forward a number of evaluative criteria including speed of implementation, expense, degree of formality and intrusiveness. These criteria must be balanced against the general concern for fairness, responsiveness and effectiveness of administrative action.

We wish to stress the limitations of an instrumental approach. No matter how appealing descriptions of instruments may appear, "cataloguing" de-emphasizes the importance of *policy context* and *process*. ... Any description of the broad powers and capabilities associated with licences fails to acknowledge the importance of the policy context. The realities of policy implementation — perceived public support for a policy, government officials worried about their public image, insufficient manpower and

resources to carry out programs, and so on — are not considered in an instrumental approach....

CRITERIA FOR EVALUATION

A large number of factors can bear upon the design and implementation of instruments. Here is an admittedly incomplete list of questions[35] which policy planners should consider in the selection of a particular instrument.

1. How quickly can the instrument be implemented? An instrument which can be swiftly put in action brings home the policy message without delay. An instrument which can be implemented by administrators is more expeditious than one which requires the involvement of outside agencies (for example, the courts).
2. How expensive is it to use the instrument? Cost is a major concern of government: almost all institutions operate within a limited budget. Included here are costs of initial invocation, as well as follow-up expenses associated with inspection, moni-

† From Law Reform Commission of Canada, *Policy Implementation, Compliance and Administrative Law*, Working Paper 51 (Ottawa: Law Reform Commission of Canada, 1986), Chapter 3: 35–41, 45, 49–51, 54–56, 85. Source of information: Department of Justice Canada. Reproduced with the permission of Public Works and Government Services Canada, 2001 and Courtesy of the Department of Justice Canada. See appendix for notes or references.

toring, revision, and so on. A separate issue is the expense to the *administré*. Again, a distinction between initial start-up and maintenance costs can often be drawn. In recent years, the financial burden caused by regulations has become a concern to both government and the private sector.[36]

3. How formal are implementation activities? Closely related to questions about expense and speed are those pertaining to formality. Generally speaking, instruments involving formal processes and third parties (for example, public hearings) are both more expensive and more time-consuming. However, more formal instruments can have greater influence over *administrés* generally, since they are more public and enjoy a higher profile.

4. How intrusive is the instrument? Some instruments require a certain behaviour under threat of penalty or imprisonment; as such, they are clearly very intrusive. Others, while not compulsory or coercive, nevertheless entail divulging detailed information and maintaining close ongoing contact with the administrator. These, too, can be described as intrusive. Some *administrés* can be more concerned with intrusiveness and operational stringency than with threat of penalty (Rosenbaum, 1984). Serious questions remain about the permissible limits of intrusions such as administrative search. The guarantee of security "against unreasonable search and seizure" in section 8 of the Charter has brought such concerns to the forefront. However, intrusiveness is not *per se* undesirable; the intrusiveness of an instrument may be the very essence of its usefulness. Finally, certain activities necessary to effective administrative action are inherently intrusive: it is almost impossible to look for information without intruding.

5. Does invocation of the instrument change the nature of the relationship between the *administré* and the administrator? Does it inject a level of formality and adversariness into an otherwise harmonious relationship? This may, in certain circumstances, explain an administrator's reluctance to invoke an instrument. In other circumstances, the change in the nature of the relationship might help the *administré* to appreciate the seriousness of government policy objectives.

6. How certain is the outcome of the instrument invocation? Certainty in implementation can mean different things to different people. For the private sector, predictability in the use of an instrument is important. For the administrator, certainty entails confidence on his part that using the instrument will help implement the policy. If it is not clear that invocation will achieve policy objectives, there is little point in providing the instrument in the first place. From an implementation standpoint, it is important to distinguish between those instruments which generate heat and those which produce light: invocation of some mechanisms attracts much attention, but may not accomplish a great deal.

These are a few of the questions which policy planners might consider when selecting instruments for a particular regime. The answer to each question depends in large part on law-related issues. Thus, for example, a legal process can either speed up or slow down implementation of an instrument, increase or reduce costs, and so forth. This comes out clearly from reading this set of questions. However, in the final analysis, what may matter more is not what the legislator and policy planner think of a mechanism, but rather what the administrator thinks of it. If the administrator is intimidated by the complexity of implementation, or is reluctant to allow decision-making authority to shift to another agency (as certain mechanisms require), this may defeat the legislator's and policy planner's objectives.

Although we have addressed political and public administration issues, in earlier Papers,[37] such issues come into sharp focus in the context of discussions about policy implementation. Specifically, to implement its policies, government enacts legislation by which it delegates authority to its institutions to use legal instruments. A range of legal issues arise from delegation — matters of jurisdiction, procedure and controls. However, assuming that Parliament passes legislation within its constitutional authority, and assuming that private parties will benefit from appropriate procedural protections, then the government's principal concerns ought to be with achieving policy goals. With that in mind, we ask what kinds of institutions (departments, agencies, Crown corporations) can perform the kinds of activities necessary for implementation? What kinds of institutions and legal instruments ought to be combined to implement a given policy?

INSTRUMENTS

Command-Penalty Mechanisms: Regulatory Offence Prosecutions

Use of the regulatory offence instrument raises several fundamental legal issues. The Commission has taken positions on some of these issues. For example, in *Our Criminal Law* we suggested that regulatory offences should be required to meet a fourfold test: (1) "[I]s the act a potential source of harm to the community?" (2) "[A]re we satisfied that prohibition will not contravene our basic values regarding what the individual should be free to do?" (3) "[A]re we convinced that enforcing the regulatory prohibition will not do more harm than good?" and (4) "[A]re we sure that the regulatory prohibition will make a significant contribution in dealing with the problem?" We stated that those tests are lighter than the tests of criminality because "little stigma is involved in conviction for a regulatory offence; and prison should not be in general a permissible penalty for such offences" (Canada, LRCC, 1976a: 34).[38]

Within the general category, "regulatory offences," a number of further distinctions can be made: regulatory offences can be administratively or judicially imposed; they can pertain to social or economic activities; the offence can attach directly to the achieving of a policy or can supplement it (primary and secondary offences). While each of these subcategories carries with it significant consequences for implementation, by far the most important distinction is between administratively and judicially imposed offences. The vast majority of federal regulatory offences are judicially imposed; that is, an administrator or private citizen might *initiate* a prosecution, but the courts decide whether an offence has been committed and determine the sentence. And because courts are integrally involved, the adjudication process tends to be quite formal.

The Supreme Court of Canada has classified offences into three types: criminal, strict liability and absolute liability. A reading of the provisions creating regulatory offences may leave the impression that most are of the absolute liability type, requiring no proof of intention. In practice, the courts find many offences to be of the strict liability type, thus allowing the defence of due

diligence. In other cases, evidence of due diligence may mitigate the sentence. How deeply should courts look into the intentions of those accused of regulatory offences? Given that government policy is seldom expressly stated in moral terms, and that private parties are usually law abiding, an emphasis on the moral elements of a regulatory offence violation may be out of place (Eddy, 1981: 55).

Furthermore, there is no clear connection between culpability and policy implementation. Consequently, to the extent that punishment requires culpability, regulatory offences should not be the premier instrument for policy implementation. Yet, this appears to be the case, at least according to the statute book. By anyone's counting, federal statutes create an ominous number of regulatory offences: the Department of Justice counted more than 97,000 in 1983. The number of regulation-created offences is even more foreboding. And yet, comparatively few offences against those thousands of provisions have resulted in prosecutions. Moreover, little attempt has been made to accumulate and collect statistics on prosecutions commenced and on dispositional information about convictions, acquittals, imprisonment terms and fines. Such information could aid in an assessment of the usefulness of specific regulatory offence prohibitions for policy implementation.

The federal traffic offence regimes include "basket" clauses which illustrate some of the difficulties with regulatory offences. A basket clause provides that contravention of any provision of the particular Act or regulations made thereunder constitutes an offence. Such provisions reach a height of absurdity where the Minister responsible for the administration of a statute may be liable to prosecution under the statute's "basket" clause if he violates a reporting duty. In the administration of the several federal traffic offence regimes,[39] there is clearly need for a thorough consolidation and rationalization of offences and their administration.

Our main empirical research about policy implementation described experiences with the regulatory offence instrument in the areas of industrial water pollution control (Webb, 1983) and supervision of broadcast content (Clifford, 1983). In the former, the Administration did not prosecute mainly because it was expensive, slow and uncertain, and because financial incentives encouraging modernization may have been more appropriate. Third parties have, however, initiated some private prosecutions. These can disrupt implementation strategies but remain an important method for third-party participation. For their part, CRTC prosecutions for violation of the non-Canadian television programming regulations clearly bring out many of the difficulties in using regulatory offences: long trials, acquittals, cumbersome data collection processes and difficulties with definitions.

The creation of regulatory offences is sometimes a way for Parliament to establish or consolidate its jurisdiction to legislate in a given area. The problem with this approach is that probably "the criminal law power will not sustain a regulatory scheme which relies upon more sophisticated tools than a simple prohibition and penalty" (Hogg, 1977: 289). Consequently, it could be that Parliament can provide for better articulated implementation strategies only in those areas where it can claim jurisdiction under a heading other than criminal law.[40]

The presence of regulatory offences in a statutory scheme can greatly influence the Administration's activities and style. Even where few prosecutions are initiated, systems must be maintained to collect and analyse information about *administré* conduct. Administrators gather information so that they are able to identify "problem" *administrés* for closer monitoring. Ideally, this information is gathered in a manner that will make it admissible as evidence. On the other hand, even though reading the statutes may leave the impression that regulatory offences are in the foreground of policy implementation, much administrative activity is less confrontational. Much of it is conducted with the persistent possibility that prosecutions could be undertaken; none the less, given the many shortcomings of prosecutions (for example, delay, expense, effects on relations between the parties), regulatory offence prosecutions seem to be treated as a scarce resource[41] in practice, although the implicit threat of prosecutions may be omnipresent.

In the reform of federal regulatory offences, one might question the current institutional arrangements whereby provincial courts exercise jurisdiction over federal offences; whether this is done or not, reform, to be credible, must take into account the important differences that exist between crimes and other offences. Any reform should also begin by examining the purposes which regulatory offences are to serve. Among such purposes which may be relevant, in varying combinations, within a particular policy context, are punishment (with or without resort to imprisonment), disgorgement of income resulting from illegal activities, compensation, retribution, deterrence and revenue. Reassessing institutions would raise its own set of questions. Who should manage the system, prosecute charges, hear them at the trial level and on appeal? Would the division between the federal (criminal law) and provincial (administration of justice) jurisdictions require that "conjoint-provincial and federal action" (*McEvoy v. Attorney (N.B.)*, p. 722) be taken to create a discrete system of courts for federal (or federal and provincial) regulatory offences? Should agencies be allowed to create tribunals to adjudicate minor offences?[42] What procedures should govern? Can new systems serve the Administration's purposes better than the existing system? Should a new vocabulary be developed to distinguish non-criminal from criminal offences?

Some measures could also be taken to improve offence administration within existing institutional arrangements. The prosecutorial decision-making process could be more structured.... The Administration could establish controls allowing it to assess costs and perhaps better rationalize offence administration: this can begin by accumulating statistical information about prosecutions and their dispositions. Agencies could adjudicate or process minor offences on an experimental basis. Consolidation of similar kinds of offences, as in federal traffic offences, can visibly rationalize inconsistent practices. Attention can be directed to the issues associated with publicity, its timing and its effects on various kinds of parties in various circumstances. Finally, without the making of fundamental changes to the system, there still remains a need for addressing harm to third parties: in that sense, reform initiatives ought to include consideration of improved rights of private civil action[43] and clarification of rights in private prosecutions.[44] Consequently, it seems obvious that whether the approach taken is fundamental or within existing institutional arrangements, much can be done.

Command-Penalty Mechanisms: Licences

In public law, licences (including permits and permissions) convey authorization, and are issued for persons, things and activities for specified terms. Strictly speaking, a licence represents the authorization of the Administration (or the "licensing authority") to a person ("the licensee") for a specified term. The licensee is governed both by generally applicable legislated standards and by specific conditions included in his licence. Provided the licensee complies with legal requirements, he is free to pursue the relevant activity. Legally, the licensee has no right to licence renewal or to tenure in the licence, unless it is expressly so stated. At first glance, licensing appears to be an ideal instrument for accommodating the public's general concerns while at the same time addressing the peculiarities of individual *administrés*.

Licences are used to regulate occupations, trades and activities where the principal public concern is in the matter of eligibility standards. Licences also allocate use of public property, such as natural resources and the air waves. Administrative action associated with allocative licences commonly involves formal and elaborate procedural protections. The licensing authority has a number of available licensing sanctions, such as revocation, suspension, refusal to renew or short-term renewal. A variety of factors can influence the imposition of sanctions. Where private parties are significantly interested in the policy being implemented or in the performance of *administrés* (as in content regulation of broadcasting), public hearing of licence applications is the norm. Where the policy attracts little attention beyond the immediately affected licensee (for example, *Radio Act* licences, except for the use of vertical amplifiers which can threaten aviation safety), licensing sanctions may be imposed without a public hearing. In some cases, delayed suspension of licence could have grave public consequences: in such circumstances, administrators often have been given extraordinary powers to suspend permission without convening public hearings (for example, the aviation safety inspector's authority to suspend documents of entitlement).

Licensing has been recommended as an optimal instrument in policy areas "where the relevant pattern of activity can be defined with sufficient specificity" (Spigelman, 1977: 91). There ought to be "clearly identifiable activities capable of performance and review in accordance with particular standards" (Rice, 1968: 586). The success of licensing as a policy implementation instrument might therefore turn on the clarity [sic] of conduct prescriptions and the ease with

which a binary determination can be made about "correct" or "incorrect" behaviour. The certainty derived from such standards can greatly facilitate the task of the Administration. On the other hand, binary "yes-no" determinations about conduct may have little direct effect on policy implementation. In making public administration easier to perform and assess, the very basis for its existence, the implementation of policy, may be lost.

Individualized treatment of licensees is achieved mainly by the imposition of conditions and lesser prescriptions which address the particular circumstances of the individual licensee and the market in which he operates. These are supplemented by generally applicable licence conditions, statutes and regulations. Breach of a licence condition theoretically results in licence suspension or revocation. In some licensing schemes, compliance with regulations is made a condition of licensing, so that their breach can give rise to licensing action, prosecution for regulatory offence, or both.

A licensee acquires a kind of *de facto* tenure for the term of the licence even though its continuation is conditional on compliance. Where revocation or suspension for non-compliance with conditions is rare, tenure seems to extend beyond the term of the licence....

Ability and willingness to respond to licensee non-compliance by revoking or suspending licences depend substantially on the political support for the policy goals. None the less, we recognize the great variations, capacity for subtle treatment and flexibility of the licence for adjusting relations through licence conditions, and in those respects, we hold out licensing as a very important instrument for policy implementation.

Financial Incentives

In recent years, the federal government has increased its use of financial incentives to achieve policy objectives.... Government financial incentives can take a variety of forms and names, including "contributions," "grants," "subsidies," "low-interest" and "forgivable" loans, "loan guarantees" and "tax expenditures." Each type has distinctive implementation characteristics; indeed, within each incentive type there are many distinct examples.

Government financial incentives typically promote such policy objectives as creating or maintaining jobs, stimulating Canadian research and development, creating opportunities for Canadian suppliers, modernizing Canadian industrial machinery, and encouraging environmental protection. The fact that government financial incentives are used to encourage these broad types of goals at the same time as providing economic stimulus for specific private sector projects makes financial incentives, at one and the same time, multi-faceted and unwieldy instruments.

Although the federal government can regulate only those matters falling specifically within its legislative jurisdiction, commentators have suggested that it can nevertheless spend or lend its funds to any government, institution or individual it chooses for any purpose it chooses; moreover, it may attach to any grant or loan any conditions it chooses, including conditions it could not directly legislate (Hogg, 1977: 71). In short, the federal government may be able to influence the behaviour of the private sector through financial incentives (grants or loans) where it could not use command-penalty methods.

Regrettably, the state of legal research concerning incentives is still in its infancy in Canada....

. . . .

Definitions

For the purposes of discussion here, a grant is defined as "a conditional transfer payment made by government to a recipient ... for which the government will not receive any goods or services" (Fry, 1984:1). With loans, government focuses on recovering the money transferred at some later point, whereas with grants, government concentrates on levering a desired action from the recipient. With loan guarantees, government aims at recovering its money but pays out funds only if the recipient defaults on the loan. As well, government bears the costs of alternatives or other opportunities foregone in selecting another course of action (that is, opportunity cost) (see generally, Fry, 1984).

There are other, more subtle legal differences as well. For example, loan guarantees are payable directly out of the Consolidated Revenue Fund, and thus there is no need for annual appropriations; moreover, the authority for loan guarantees can be "buried" in a vote in an *Appropriation Act* where it is subject to minimal parliamentary scrutiny (von Finkenstein, 1984: 1–4).

Tax subsidies function as deductions from income or revenue; hence, they are most attractive to those who have income from which to offset the deduction. A "tax expenditure" is government revenue foregone rather than a positive act of appropriation of government funds (Webb, 1984: 7–9).

The above-outlined classification of financial incentives has some appeal. However, not everyone uses the same vocabulary,[47] and even federal personnel admit the distinctions sometimes blur in practice (Fry, 1984: 1).

. . . .

On a socio-economic level, because financial incentives involve very large expenditures of government money, some persons may find them more objectionable than command-penalty methods. This may be the case particularly where the incentives are intended to encourage behaviour which government is at the same time addressing through command-penalty instruments.

Effectiveness evaluations of financial incentives are often difficult: Would someone have installed pollution equipment, or explored for oil and gas in the North, or produced a Canadian television program even if the incentive scheme had not been in place? Perhaps what should be asked is not *would* the *administrés* have changed their behaviour without the existence of the incentive, but *when* would they have changed it?

Persuasion

Persuasion can be a principal instrument of policy implementation or an activity collateral to the operation of other instruments. For example, advertising may be conducted to "make perceived benefits greater than real benefits," and "to obscure the erosion of real benefits" (Trebilcock et al., 1981: 33). Persuasion can be used as an instrument in its own right, as has been the case in activities of the CHRC. It quite properly calls such activities "education" or "information sessions." For our purposes, all such activities are subsumed within the meaning of "persuasion."

To what extent can persuasion replace other policy-implementation instruments? Persuasion has great potential to influence private behaviour at less social and economic cost than other instruments (Adler and Pittle, 1984; Stanbury and Fulton, 1984). In policy implementation, persuasion is usually followed by more persuasion.

That may be accounted for in part by the characteristic absence of intermediate measures in Canadian public administration. There are as well several "attributes" of persuasion which commend themselves to administrators in the implementation of policy. Stanbury and Fulton (1984: 297) set out the nature of attributes such as informality and the somewhat "nebulous nature of [per]suasion [which] makes it more difficult for the 'targets' ... to challenge the constitutionality of the government's actions." Persuasion is highly reversible, flexible, targetable, potentially intense, useful to effect symbolic policies (that is, to show concern), immediately available, and may be popular when the marginal political cost of using other instruments is high (ibid.). However, the technical substitutability of persuasion may be rather limited (ibid.).

The Administration is commonly given authority to "supervise" (*Broadcasting Act*, s. 15) *administrés* which come under its authority: implicit in that power is the exercise of persuasion. In some instances, Administration is expressly given authority for persuasion.

> [The Commission] ... shall ... endeavour by persuasion, publicity or any other means that it considers appropriate to discourage and reduce discriminatory practices ... (*Canadian Human Rights Act s. 22(1)(g)*).

The persuasion instrument poses considerable challenges to the Administration: to be effective, persuasion, like propaganda, ought to encircle the whole person (Ellul, 1965) without reaching beyond the mandate of an administrative unit. Propaganda has been described in a way which conveys an indication of its scope:

> In the midst of increasing mechanization and technological organization, propaganda is simply the means used to prevent these things from being felt as too oppressive and to persuade man to submit with good grace (id.: xviii).

That view is consistent with Max Weber's opinion about why people comply with rules in the absence of force:

> [Weber] identified three types of legitimacy which lead people to submit to authority without constantly being forced to comply. These were traditional authority, charismatic authority and the legal-rational type based on the acceptance of generalized rules (Gerth and Mills, 1958: 78 ff.).

There are many historical examples about the ways in which traditional authority and charismatic authority have, through persuasion, led people to comply with policy (Thomson, 1977). As for the legal-rational acceptance of generalized rules, it is clear that education and other forms of persuasion are important for informing parties about the rules. While it is important to distinguish pure information from persuasion, the distinction is not always clear. Vocabulary can obscure their effects.

Persuasion is pervasive throughout most policy implementation; its substantive limits extend to the limits of the Administration's mandates. The limits and public acceptability of the persuasion instrument are more difficult to circumscribe. According to surveys, Canadians tend to frown upon partisan government advertising and to approve of persuasion campaigns directed at protecting society (for example, from drunk driving) or at improving the economy (for example, via tourism) (Goldfarb Consultants, 1982; Stanbury, Gorn and Weinberg, 1983). Deciding about acceptable limits for the use of the persuasion instrument poses major challenges for the reform of policy implementation.

In summary, the persuasion power of government has many manifestations. Education and persuasion may be side-effects or main thrusts of administrative activities. Publicity about noncompliance may have benign or intrusive effects on the *administré*. Persuasion can greatly improve the efficiency of implementation, and may in many instances be necessary for the effective invocation of command-penalty and incentive instruments. Persuasion, to be effective, requires a degree of organization and resource co-ordination which should arguably allow for due consideration of the probable effects of publicity on constituencies. So, notwithstanding the darker potential uses which can be made of persuasion, its importance for policy implementation is clear.

. . . .

SUMMARY

Parliament delegates to various institutions the authority to implement policy by means of activities associated with legal instruments. Important legal issues about institutions and instruments of government are critical to the implementation of policy.

Our focus for research to support this Paper was on administrative activities associated with particular legal instruments. This chapter has addressed mainly issues associated with such instruments. Thus, we have found that prosecutions for regulatory offences are commonly given too much prominence in policy design, legislation and implementation. Each particular instrument has some specific technical and operational strengths and weaknesses; the built-in weaknesses of legal instruments are too often ignored. For example, in licensing, administrators are able to develop standards specific to the individual *administré*; however, in some scenarios, the licensee acquires *de facto* tenure in the licence, because the licence is not revoked or suspended when non-compliance is detected. Furthermore, licensing often attracts procedural trappings which may unduly encumber policy implementation. In the administration of financial incentives such as grants, procedures are less formal; the rights of prospective applicants and third parties are unclear, as well as the legal characterization of grants. As for persuasion, legislation sometimes countenances such activities, but there are difficult questions about acceptable limits.

There are a number of other federal penalty-type instruments which are ripe for study and reform. Administrative imposition of fines for tax evasion deserves separate treatment. The revenue penalties are the most outstanding example of administratively imposed financial penalties. Another type, the "civil penalty," is more commonly used in the United States than in Canada (Diver, 1979). In Canada, some administrators would very much like to have available intermediate measures, such as civil penalties, to address minor instances of non-compliance. CATA may soon have such measures available, through amendment of the *Aeronautics Act*.

Ticketing is another instrument which shows promise. Already, the Department of Justice has explored ways of standardizing the numerous provisions in the area (*see note 39*). Questions remain, however, about the processing of ticketed offences: Should they continue to be treated as summary conviction offences? Should such matters be treated outside the criminal courts? What language, procedures and dispositions ought to be used? The expected implementation of a new ticketing plan by the Department of Transport, for *Transportation of Dangerous Goods Act* offences may eventually furnish needed empirical information in this regard.

. . . .

It would be out of place in this Paper to try to draw definitive conclusions about the relative value of different instruments in given contexts. Indeed, some may disagree even with the very broad statements we have made here. Our intention in this Working Paper is not to close the door on the area, but rather to raise issues in a way that will promote an optimal level of discussions.

. . . .

The relationships between instruments and institutions bring out difficult legal questions. Should the same institution administering command-penalty sanctions also be negotiating grants with *administrés*? The idea of co-ordination also highlights the interrelationship between institutions and their instruments. Co-ordination is important for several reasons. For example, institutions could agree about policy goals and use of instruments where legislation is silent or confusing. Numerous questions about co-ordination need discussion and analysis. To what degree should institutions share information about *administrés*? To what extent can or should institutions co-ordinate their use of instruments among a shared group of *administrés*? Given the variations of legal supervision of institutions, are they able to co-ordinate implementation effectively? Research of such legal issues about institutions would be useful for improving implementation.

Choice of institution can be as important to the effectiveness of implementation as is choice of instrument. The two decisions should be made together: the institution used to convey a particular policy should not be hastily considered as an afterthought to instrument choice. The two go hand in hand.

Generalizations about institutions and instruments are dangerous outside of specific policy contexts. That being said, however, one general observation does hold true: the practices of policy implementation are often quite different from the appearances of legal order. For example, bargaining between administrators and *administrés* pervades every part of the implementation process. Despite the many offence-creating provisions, few prosecutions are undertaken; departments which appear to be administering command-and-control instruments may give more attention to financial incentives. That conclusion underscores our fundamental observation that government policy cannot always be discerned from statutory descriptions of institutions and instruments; public policy is in the implementation activities of government administrators.

. . . .

CONCLUSION

In a letter to us in 1984, Professor J.W. Mohr succinctly stated a rationale for law reform work in the matter of compliance:

> "[C]ompliance" is one of those notions which is central to the relationship between law and human behaviour and yet is not locked into any specific legal form. And to the extent a law reform commission wants to re-form law, rather than adjusting and adapting it where this is necessary and possible, it must make use of notions which cut across the incredible constraints of given legal forms.

This comment expresses in a nutshell our reason for looking at policy implementation and compliance in the context of our work on administrative law. In their day-to-day work, lawyers are involved in many informal activities similar to what goes on in policy implementation. And yet, the substantive goal of policy implementation is sometimes overshadowed by formal legal processes and undue insistence on compliance with the letter of the law. Our legal culture characteristically prevents explicit recognition of less formal interactions among parties. Canadian

lawyers forge and wield instruments. They are trained mainly for the resolution of private disputes and for representing people accused of violating the law. This leads to an over-emphasis of formal responses to deviant conduct, to overjudicialization, to overreliance on adversarial processes and to over-use of sanctions in much of policy implementation. Undue focus on the instruments might not allow the freedom necessary to a full understanding of human behaviour and motivators. Better appreciation for the place of law in policy implementation is essential to reform in this area.

Law and legal instruments are useful for framing, facilitating and constraining activities of administrators and private parties. However, law has been too event-specific, centering on commands, strict compliance and penalties. To date, law has been unable to reflect the complexity of long-term relationships prevalent in policy implementation activities; as well, law does little to frame, constrain and facilitate government's use of persuasion and incentives. There is no need for this unsatisfactory state of affairs to continue any longer.

By making explicit some of the ways in which government policies are implemented, we hope that a synthesis may be forged between what lawyers and parties do in the implementation of policy. By linking law and implementation we have to bring together administrators, outside experts and the legal community to help resolve complex problems of governing in the 1980s and beyond.

(b)   The Case for Pollution Taxes[†]

Nancy Olewiler

Economists have long advocated taxation to deal with environmental problems. Taxes can correct the distortions in markets that arise because many of the goods and services provided by the

government are not priced. The disposal of waste products has been treated as a right freely available to all. The premise of an environmental tax or charge is quite simple. The tax establishes a

† From *Getting It Green: Case Studies in Canadian Environmental Regulation*, ed. Bruce Doern (Toronto: C.D. Howe Institute, 1990), pp. 188–208. © C.D. Howe Institute, reproduced with permission. See appendix for notes or references.

price for using the environment. The environment must then be treated as a scarce good by producers and consumers.

Taxation has many advantages apparent to economists, although their enthusiasm for taxes is not shared by decisionmakers in government and the private sector. Why? Opposition to taxation is often based on self-interest. Polluters are clearly worse off individually after the imposition of environmental taxes, although society as a whole may be much better off. The same cannot be said about command-and-control legislation. Taxes are generally unpopular with the public, which may view them as another revenue "grab" by governments. The impact of taxation on environmental quality is less certain than that of standards — if they are imposed and enforced. Physical standards establish targets for emissions or ambient environmental quality. These are easy to comprehend compared to the often complex features of taxes. The goal of reaching an efficient level of pollution that is generally positive is not welcomed by those who want major changes now. The argument that taxes are economically efficient does not convince the public that "something is being done" about pollution, nor does it elect politicians. It is not surprising that opposition to taxation has been both widespread and successful in Canada.

Why, then, rehash the debate about taxes versus other pollution policies? In today's political, economic, and environmental climate, we can no longer depend on the policies that have been used in the past. North America has now had over 20 years of experience with the extensive use of standards under command-and-control legislation. While there have been some improvements in environmental quality over this period, it would be difficult to argue that standards have been a rousing success. There are many serious problems that standards have not addressed. As well, Canadians have paid millions of dollars for pollution policies. Where does this money come from? It comes from taxpayers. Are we getting good value for our tax dollars? The simple answer is no. Command-and-control policies are expensive and must be financed out of general government revenue. In a time of crippling deficits, it is hard to be optimistic that the environment is going to be a major recipient of scarce government funds.

The object of this chapter is to make the case for the inclusion of pollution taxes and charges as one of the instruments in the arsenal for improving environmental quality. No single type of policy instrument is appropriate for all types of environmental problems. Canadian governments act as if command-and-control policies are the policy of first choice.[1] Taxation is rarely examined seriously. Marketable permits or tradable emissions rights have recently become a "fashionable" instrument to consider, but permits are not universally applicable to all environmental problems.

To make the case for taxes, this chapter first examines the benefits of taxation. The second part of the chapter considers some of the challenges to taxes and the responses to these criticisms. It concludes with a discussion of when taxes could be used.

TAXES: WHY NOW?

A series of arguments support the use of taxation to improve environmental quality. As mentioned above, the existing mix of policies being used in Canada has not worked as well or as quickly as many had hoped. It would not be prudent to ignore powerful instruments such as taxation.

Taxes Put a "Price" on Pollution

A tax or charge on the use of the environment as a waste depository forces people to treat pollution as another good. This allows the forces of supply and demand to lead to efficient use of the environment if the tax is set equal to the value of environmental damages resulting from production and consumption activities. Pricing the environment provides incentives for all who use it to change their behavior and to use it more conservatively. This is true for consumers of the goods and services generating pollution as well as for the producers of those goods. It is easy for those concerned about environmental quality to cast blame on the industries responsible for emissions. They forget that as consumers of the goods these industries produce, they too are responsible for deterioration of environmental quality. Under most circumstances, a tax on emissions, outputs, or the inputs in the production process will be passed along to consumers.[2] The tax makes the environmental cost of our activities apparent. A standard can camouflage the link between consumption activities and pollution. Standards may provide little or no incentive for consumers to alter the environmentally damaging activities. Taxes are thus in the spirit of the "environmental awareness" the pollsters say the public has. Taxes require all of us to pay for our use and abuse of the environment.

Taxes Minimize the Costs of Improving Environmental Quality

This argument involves the use of concepts familiar to economists, but often quite alien to others. Suppose an emissions tax is put on firms depositing a particular type of waste into the atmosphere or waterways. The tax rate is set per unit of the waste product emitted. Any firm facing this tax will have the choice of continuing to discharge just as much waste as it did before the tax, or to reduce its emissions. If the firm does not control any wastes, it will pay the government a tax bill consisting of the tax rate times the total emissions. If the firm reduces its emissions, it will incur costs for however much it abates, plus pay a tax bill on the uncontrolled emissions. The key point is that the firm decides how best to respond to the tax. If the costs of controlling emissions are lower than the tax per unit, the firm will stop discharging. If the costs of control exceed the tax, the firm will continue to pollute. Firms with the lowest costs of controlling emissions will abate the most.

The direct costs of controlling emissions — exclusive of costs of imposing and enforcing the policy — will be as low as they possibly can. Governments need not dictate to firms how to control their wastes, as is generally done in command-and-control legislation — in the form of requiring specific technologies for abatement be used. If society wants to minimize the costs of meeting some environmental target, the tax is the preferred instrument. It is hard for economists to imagine that people would want to pay more than is necessary to improve environmental quality.

Implications for Technological Change and Innovation

Taxes provide incentives to invest in technologies that control emissions at lower costs than existing techniques or that control more emissions at the same cost. This follows directly from the arguments made above. If a different production process can yield the same output with less pollution, a firm would lower its tax liability by adopting that process. Of course, the cost of the process must be weighed against the tax saving.

The process will be purchased if the present value of the tax saving incurred over the life of the technology is at least equal to the cost of the process.

This type of response means that there will be some uncertainty about when and if firms adopt new technologies. There may be an interval over which pollution does not decrease substantially as firms try to determine the cost-minimizing method of reducing their tax liabilities. But the private sector is very clever at finding ways to reduce taxes. It will not continue to pollute for long periods of time, especially if the tax rate is high enough to make the cost of "doing nothing" regarding wastes untenable.

Taxes should also spawn new industries trying to find these pollution-reducing technologies, for they will now have a market for their processes that did not exist before the imposition of the tax. These incentive effects are quite different from the impact of command-and-control policies with their requirements for specific technologies. Once the required technology is in place, there is no incentive to look for others that may be lower cost or more effective at reducing emissions. Pollution abatement is expensive and, once in place, firms will not be lobbying for alternative approaches to control emissions. For example, suppose an electrical generating station is required to install stack gas scrubbers to reduce emissions of sulfur dioxide. There will be no incentive for the utility to seek cheaper devices or less-polluting inputs — for example, low-sulphur instead of high-sulphur coal — unless the regulations change again.

The incentive to innovate and invest in new technologies also has implications for the competitiveness of industries. Competition in pollution-controlling technologies is encouraged by taxation of emissions. This may not be the case with command-and-control legislation. Take the example of the scrubbers above. Once a technology has been set by regulation,[3] there is little incentive to look for new ones. If the controlled industry contains few firms, there are likely to be few suppliers of the required technology simply because the market is small. It would be more difficult for a competitive pollution-control sector to develop under these circumstances.

Taxes Generate Revenue

A pollution tax or charge corrects the distortions that arise from the failure of markets to price the use of the environment as a waste depository. Unlike most other taxes levied by governments, pollution taxes do not create incentives for inefficiency; instead, they correct inefficiencies and improve social welfare. This is an important point that is easily overlooked when opposition to taxes is mounted by special-interest groups. Society as a whole can be better off with the introduction of a pollution tax.[4]

A key question arises: What should be done with the tax revenue obtained from pollution taxes? First, note that the amount of tax revenue collected depends on the tax rate and the ability of those taxed to reduce their emissions. If tax rates stay constant, governments can expect to collect more revenue in the short term when those taxed are more constrained in their response to the tax. Over time, revenue can be less than the taxes paid — as discussed above. Indeed, if taxes are doing their job to improve environmental quality, not a lot of revenue would be raised.

All this suggests that governments should not look to pollution taxes as a major revenue source. Some economists (and others) have been advocating environmental taxes to raise revenue and reduce government deficits.[5] Their argument is that the impact on the economy would be twofold. Revenue is raised in a distortion-reducing manner compared to other taxes, and environmental quality is enhanced. As already noted earlier, the revenue raised could be modest and falling over time. If these revenues were used for deficit reduction or in lieu of other taxes, governments would be very tempted to adjust the tax rates so as to maintain a constant (or increasing) flow to their coffers. The taxes would soon become tied to objectives other than efficient levels of pollution. Pollution tax rates should be tied to environmental quality, not other fiscal requirements.

What, then, could be done with the revenue raised? Two suggestions emerge, both of which are strong arguments to "sell" the use of taxes as policy for the environment. First, tax revenues could be used to improve environmental quality directly. Why not tie these taxes to specific types of expenditures on the environment? This makes the pollution tax a "benefit," or earmarked tax. Improvements in environmental quality come form three main sources: reductions in emissions — or the production and consumption of emissions-intensive goods — cleanups of the existing stock of contaminated ecosystems, and investment in new technologies that lessen the trade-offs between the environment and economic activities.

Standards, taxes, and marketable permits work on the first of these sources. How do we pay for the second? Some countries have started funds — for example, the Superfund in the United States — to clean up toxic sites. Part of the financing comes from levies on polluting industries, the rest from general revenues.[6] Canada should impose something similar. We have our own toxic sites and a long list of areas needing improvement. Taxes on polluters or pollution-intensive goods could be tied to these cleanups. That way, governments cannot divert these funds to other activities — for example, subsidizing megaprojects such as James Bay and Hibernia, which can lead to adverse environmental impacts. Benefit taxes would also be an important selling point to a public and a corporate sector suspicious of government motives. Politically, it would be difficult to oppose such taxes. Who wants to be on record as opposing the environment? As in the United States, the revenue raised from these taxes may be much too small to deal with major investment in improving the environment, but the revenue would help.

The revenue could also be used to augment private sector investment in environmental research and development (R&D). The case for government support comes if one feels that this sort of R&D would be undersupplied because of the difficulty of keeping technological information proprietary. The extent of the need for these funds is an empirical question that requires more investigation.

The second major way to use pollution tax revenues is for redistributive purposes. Governments could use the money to compensate those made worse off by the imposition of the tax. The need for compensation is likely to be short term. As tax revenues decline, so do losses incurred from the tax. It is well known that pollution taxes may be efficient but not equitable. Polluting firms with immobile capital would suffer capital losses with the imposition of an emission tax. Low-income consumers who cannot shift their consumption bundle in response to taxes on pollution-intensive commodities are other candidates for some compensation.

The key point is that if compensation is contemplated, it must not be tied to the amount of emissions or the consumption of the pollution-intensive good. It must be what economists call "lump sum." A payment can be made that offsets some of the profit or income loss, but the payment should not affect the relative price of pollution. Pollution taxes work by inducing people to substitute activities that pollute less for those that pollute more. Do I drive or walk to the park? The price of gasoline is certainly an important factor in this decision. A pollution tax on gasoline would induce a substitution of walking for driving. If the government then compensates people made worse off by the tax, it must do so in a way that is not dependent on the number of miles driven. Admittedly, it is very difficult to come up with compensation schemes, but not impossible.

Finally, the revenues can be used to "pay" for the cost of the government environmental bureaucracy. Regardless of the instrument used to improve environmental quality, there will be costs of administration. Only the pollution tax — and a marketable permit that is sold, not given away by the government — has the potential to help pay for these costs.

Administration Costs

Taxes should be no more difficult to administer than command-and-control regulations and, possibly, marketable permits schemes. Taxes could be cheaper to administer because they could make use of existing bureaucratic infrastructure and the tax system. For example, pollution taxes imposed at the retail level could be collected with provincial sales taxes (with provincial approval). Taxes on polluting inputs could be added to the goods and services tax (GST).[7] Taxes could be imposed faster than many command-and-control instruments because of the existing tax infrastructure and because governments have a lot of practice in setting tax rates and what to tax. The basic point is that taxes pose no additional administration costs compared with other policies. Some types of pollution taxes may be simpler to impose and collect than others. Implementation problems still exist — monitoring, compliance, and so on — but these problems apply to all pollution instruments.

Taxes and the Competitiveness of Canadian Industry

Pollution taxes can influence the structure of an industry. If the industry is perfectly competitive to begin with, the introduction of a pollution tax will not discourage competition. Taxation promotes competition, compared with standards that set tighter requirements for new firms than for existing firms and plants. As noted above, taxes can stimulate competition in the search for new pollution control technologies or less-polluting goods.

If an industry is noncompetitive, taxes can influence the number of firms in that industry. This is not unique to taxation, however. Command-and-control legislation, marketable permits, and every other pollution instrument can also influence competitiveness.

The problem is that, when one starts with a noncompetitive situation, there is distortion in addition to pollution. Generally, output levels are too low in noncompetitive industries, compared with outputs that would occur under perfect competition. A pollution tax typically will cut output even more. There is thus a tradeoff between the impact of the output reduction on environmental quality (a benefit to society) versus the impact of the reduction on noncompetitive profits (a loss to society).[8] It is possible to find tax rates (on the emissions/output) that do improve social welfare taking these tradeoffs into account. But small changes in the tax rates can lead to discrete jumps in the number of firms operating and, hence, can change market structure. The same could occur with standards or other instruments.[9] A key factor in the impact of taxation (or other instruments) is whether the tax is levied uniformly across the country and across different countries. This topic is examined below. I turn now to the challenges to taxes.

THE CASE AGAINST TAXATION

The focus in this section is on arguments opposing taxes specifically, not general arguments against pollution-control instruments.

Taxes Are Unfair

Taxes can create windfall losses for those who cannot at least partially shift the burden of these taxes to others. This is why firms vigorously oppose pollution taxes, which would make many of them worse off. In the short run, their profits would fall. What happens in the long run depends on their ability to substitute untaxed for taxed inputs and outputs. Taxes are different from standards or technology requirements of command-and-control policies.

They make polluting firms "pay" in two ways — first, for the costs of abating whatever emissions they do control; second, for the tax bill on uncontrolled emissions. Standards — yielding the same amount of emissions control — only impose the first type of payment. This may seem unfair. Any environmental policy can be seen as unfair compared to the status quo, where polluters get to use the environment for free. But this is not an argument that would receive much support anymore.

The fairness issue is thus seen as one where taxes are compared with other pollution-policy instruments. There are several rebuttals. First, the tax may only be "unfair" in the short term, compared with a standard. As noted above, a pollution tax continues to provide incentives to reduce the tax bill and to control more emissions, which a standard does not. If new abatement equipment is cheaper than the present value of the stream of tax liabilities, the firm will install it. There is no analogous incentive with standards.

Suppose the government wants higher environmental quality over time — a goal often established in command-and-control legislation. This requires increasingly tighter standards and often is accompanied by the use of specific technologies for control. Thus the government, not the firm, sets the timetable and determines the technologies. The record on governments' abilities to guess when new technologies will be implementable and how quickly to tighten standards has been abysmal in both Canada and the United States. Support for this statement comes from the record on air and water pollution after the imposition of the *Clean Air Act* and the *Clean Water Act* in the United States, and from the considerable body of ineffectual Canadian legislation. If the private sector really wants to be the best judge of how to control pollution, it should not be opposed to taxation. Taxation may save firms money in the long run.

The second rebuttal is that standards create their own sets of distortions that may be in the interests of certain firms but certainly not others. If standards are not uniform across all jurisdictions, if they differ for firms based on their location, vintage, or for some other reason, then what is beneficial to one firm, can be unfair to another.

If one really worries about fairness, then, as already noted, tax revenues can be used to compensate losers. It is more difficult to contemplate compensation under standards, for two reasons. First, the revenues for this must come from other (distortionary) taxes. Second, how does one compensate a potential entrant that is blocked by stricter standards imposed on it than on existing firms in the industry?

The arguments against taxation and in favor of standards may be self-serving for all involved. Why else might firms support standards rather than taxes? History suggests that they do so because they know that standards will not effectively constrain their polluting activities. Canadian and U.S. environmental policies are a legacy of unfulfilled promises. Elegant regulations exist on paper that have not been imposed in practice. Tough-sounding standards are approved, then regulators extend the deadlines for meeting these standards. It takes time to develop standards, especially if they are specific to regions and industries. Regulators recognize that some technological requirements cannot be implemented. Firms that "try" to reduce emissions cannot be charged Legal challenges to standards are common in the United States and even occur in Canada.[10] These actions can keep regulations tied up in court for years.

Command-and-control regulations thus can give the appearance that a lot is being done for the environment when, in fact, the progress is minimal. Regulations look forceful. The U.S. *Clean Water Act* — passed in 1972 and later amended — set up an ambitious timetable for controlling emissions to that country's waterways, the culmination of which was to have been a ban on all deleterious discharges to waterways by 1984. By the time, the United States' water was to be swimmable, fishable, and drinkable! Obviously, these targets were not met. Even the interim provisions of the act — to establish specific standards, BATs, and BPTs for each major polluting industry — met with delays and legal battles, and the U.S. federal government did not have the resources to determine these extensive standards.[11] The act received widespread support in Congress, and a cynical observer cannot help but wonder if support was strong because the politicians knew the provisions of the act would not be realized. Polluters are also more apt to support legislation they know will not be effective.

In Canada, much of the federal government's command-and-control legislation sounds as though Ottawa is taking charge, but again, very little has ever been implemented. The *Can-*

ada Water Act (1970) provided for the establishment of regional water-quality agencies, which might have been very useful forces in the control of emissions. Not one has been created. The act also was to have established federal water-quality standards. There are none. In Ontario, pollution regulations for a number of environmental problems have been dealt with by agreements between the provincial government and polluters. Under these agreements, as long as polluters were working toward compliance, they would be allowed to exceed the standards. Finally, in Canada — unlike in the United States — the federal government does not play the major role in setting and enforcing standards. It is beyond the scope of this chapter to examine the complex federal-provincial wrangling over regulatory powers that also characterizes and hamstrings Canadian environmental policy.[12] Simply put, Canada's political system is not well designed to provide for strong federal regulatory powers. National taxes stand a better chance of being implemented.

Taxes Have an Uncertain Impact on Environmental Quality

One cannot predict with certainty what proportion of a firm's effluent will be abated under an emissions tax, nor can one tell exactly how much substitution of environmentally friendly inputs and outputs for pollution-intensive goods will occur with consumption taxes. This means that any given pollution tax rate will not guarantee that a specific environmental target is met. Indeed, some tax critics fear that polluters will simply pay the tax and continue to pollute as much as they did before. There are three responses to this concern.

First, tax rates may have to be adjusted if the reduction in emissions falls short of the target. This means that there is the potential for more tax adjustments than could occur under a system of standards. The long discussion of fairness above suggests, however, that we are far from having ideal standards. If it is difficult to adjust taxes and if achieving a specific pollution target is necessary, then yes, taxes may be less desirable than other policies. Second, recall the incentives for technological change. Over time, emissions will be reduced to a greater extent with a tax than with a standard. But if one needs relatively quick reductions in emissions, a tax may not do the job. Finally, if firms are not

abating, the government must be collecting tax revenues. As discussed earlier, they could use these revenues to help improve environmental quality.

Fear of Changing Tax Regimes

The negative side of the previous argument for changing tax rates when emissions reduction is insufficient is that the tax regime introduces business and consumer uncertainty into the economy. If firms and consumers do not know what tax rate they will face, it is difficult for them to plan efficiently. There is also a danger that taxes may become part of another political agenda, thus severing the link between tax rates and emissions. These are all serious concerns, but they could be mitigated somewhat by requiring government to give parties some lead time before making any changes.

Taxes Drive Out Jobs and Businesses to Untaxed Jurisdictions

This argument can apply to any government policy that imposes costs on firms in a sector that are not borne by their counterparts in other jurisdictions. Pollution taxes are not unique in this respect. And while it is true that tax harmonization — or general pollution policy harmonization — would certainly be preferred to a situation where only one jurisdiction levies the tax, this does not mean that no policy is better than a unilateral policy. What society should be concerned about is social welfare, *inclusive* of the damages to the environment caused by domestic activities, not just the value of production and consumption. Plants, industries, and people may move in response to differential taxes, but social welfare can still increase after the imposition of the tax. There is also no guarantee that these shifts in economic activity will occur. If the tax is a small share of total costs of business, it may affect emissions but not location decisions. Other possibilities exist.

In a framework where two jurisdictions have different pollution taxes, conditions exist where social welfare is enhanced by a unilateral tax even with noncompetitive firms.[13] Under certain tax rates, economic activity can even increase. For example, a pollution tax imposed in Canada but not another country — say, the United Sates — can deter the entry of a foreign firm, while the Canadian firm does not shut down. It also opens an additional plant in the United States because of the lack of taxes there. Domestic employment does not decrease, and Canadian incomes are higher because there is less pollution and because there are larger returns to the owners of the Canadian firm. The tax policy becomes a barrier to entry, and while this inhibits competition domestically, it reduces emissions and increases welfare. Other results are also possible. The point is that the "drive out jobs" argument may simply be false in a framework of trading regions or countries.

Taxes can also create jobs and general income. As noted before, the search for cost-saving technologies for abatement may spur economic activity. Green products, recycling, and less waste creation can be good business. The pollution tax helps this process along by providing financial incentives.

Why taxes? Why not? There are no arguments against pollution taxes so compelling that taxes do not warrant serious consideration in the policy arena. Self-interest should be recognized as a motive for opposition. Taxes share many practical difficulties with other policies; these difficulties have been articulated by many and are not repeated here. The point is whether or not we want to see improvements in environmental quality. If the answer is yes, then taxes should be considered along with the other policies.

Governments can no longer afford to ignore the benefits of taxation for fear of alienating special-interest groups. In the current political environment, the federal government has an opportunity to consider pollution taxes seriously in its Green Plan. Tax may be a dirty word after the GST, but these taxes are different. They are benefit taxes, in the sense that people are being asked to pay for the costs they impose on the environment and the costs of cleaning up the mess. Standards have a poor track record. They take a long time to promulgate, are often very ineffective, and are expensive for the economy. Finally, other countries are rediscovering taxes. Pollution taxes are a major agenda item for European economic integration. The United States is talking — perhaps seriously this time — about pollution taxes on energy inputs. Canada could be a leader, not a follower, in this process. Even if Canada were to go it alone, the gains could outweigh the costs.

WHEN AND WHAT TO TAX

Pollution taxes are appropriate for specific environmental problems, but not for all. No single instrument is appropriate in every case. The list below is not exhaustive, but suggests the characteristics of the type of environmental problem conducive to taxation. I conclude with suggestions for some specific taxes.

Conditions Conducive to Taxation

First, marginal changes in the level of pollution will increase environmental quality. It is not necessary to have predictable explicit changes per unit time. There is no threshold level of emissions beyond which catastrophic damages to the environment occur. If these conditions are present, the uncertainty associated with the impact of a pollution tax on emissions will not be a major concern.

Second, the time of release of emissions and their precise location is not crucial to environmental quality. This suggests that a uniform tax could be used to improve environmental quality. If taxes must be tailored to specific locations and times of day, then they become very difficult to implement, just as with individual standards. If uniform taxes are used when the impact of emissions on environmental quality differs across regions, "hot spots" of severe environmental degradation can occur. This may still be preferable to individual taxes. If hot spots occur, taxes could be used in conjunction with other policies, such as standards.

Third, the tax is more effective and generates fewer windfall losses when supply-and-demand curves for pollution-intensive products are neither perfectly elastic nor inelastic. Taxes would also generate fewer losses if the sources of emissions are many and each produces similar amounts. That way, tax rates can be relatively low and still elicit reductions in emissions.

Fourth, efficient tax rates can be set more precisely if the government has good information about the nature of environmental damages on the margin. If damages per unit of pollution emitted are relatively constant, then tax rates can be set with less information about the polluters' costs of control.

Finally, taxes can be combined with standards and can act as penalties for noncompliance.

Possible Taxes

Given these characteristics, what are possible candidates for pollution taxation?

Fuel Taxes

The combustion of coal, petroleum products, and natural gas emit a variety of by-products that can adversely affect environmental quality. These include sulfur dioxide, unburned hydrocarbons, nitrogen oxides, and of course, carbon dioxide. As well, the components of combustion form photochemical smog and ozone. Some of the environmental problems arising from combustion are global (warming from carbon dioxide), others are local (ground level ozone). The relationship between combustion and emissions is well known by scientists, while the link between emissions and environmental impact is less certain. Would a tax work in this case?

I would argue for national pollution taxes on all fossil fuels, including uranium.[14] A uniform rate could be set for each fuel type, depending on the environmental characteristics of the emissions. There are large numbers of emitters of all the pollutants, each contributing a small amount. The tax would be easy to administer and to collect, and need not be confiscatory. While there would be some short-term rigidities, these would dissipate over time as consumers and producers respond to the price increase. The "energy crisis" of the 1970s is evidence of the elasticity of both supply and demand in energy alternatives and substitute products.

The tax need not be based on any single pollutant, thus avoiding the difficult determination of marginal costs of control versus damages for each user. The tax would increase environmental quality directly and even more so if the revenues were reinvested in the environment. This is not a carbon tax *per se*, but a broader-based tax on the consumption of fuels.[15] Other pollution-intensive inputs might be similar candidates for taxation — for example, pesticides, herbicides, and solvents.

Pollution Taxes on Commodities

The federal government already taxes one consumer good responsible for an environmental problem — automobile air conditioners that contain chlorofluorocarbons (CFCs). The motive for the tax was to raise revenue with an excise tax on a luxury good, but there is no reason why this tax and others could not be imposed on consumer goods responsible for environmental degradation. Some of these types of taxes already exist in certain provinces. British Columbia has additional taxes on tires and car batteries, and removes provincial sales tax on environmentally friendly goods such as bicycles and certain energy-saving home improvements. Again, we are talking about diffuse environmental benefits and damages. These are cases where taxes can work well. They change the relative prices of goods, and people respond by substituting away from these goods.

CONCLUSION

Taxes are a neglected instrument in the process of environmental policy. They have not been extensively used by governments. This chapter has examined the case for taxation and addressed some of the concerns of those who are opposed to taxes. Taxes are not a general solution, but could be used to reduce the output of pollution and to generate revenues that, in turn, could be used to improve environmental quality. I repeat the appeal for benefit taxation. If taxes are tied directly to the environment, the opposition to them should weaken and the scope for government mismanagement (and hidden agendas) should diminish. Command-and-control legislation has had limited success in improving environmental quality and has done so at costs that are higher than necessary. We can no longer afford to ignore pollution taxes.

(c) Environmental Regulation: The economics of tradeable permits — a survey of theory and practice[†]

The Australian Bureau of Industry Economics ———————————

INTRODUCTION

Introduction

One of the features of environmental problems is that costs are imposed on individuals in a manner over which they have no control. There exist no obvious mechanisms for them to avoid further costs or obtain compensation for costs already borne. The source of the problem is often argued to be market failure or missing markets, and this leads to a demand for some form of regulation, part of which may be to define, change or create property rights.

An essential part of the environmental debate therefore, is the investigation of the type of regulation that is most efficient for achieving environmental goals. By most efficient is meant not only that the goals will be achieved, but also they will be achieved at least cost. There are a variety of regulatory instruments available from government ownership to proscription (command and control) to taxes and subsidies, to licenses and permits. None is universally superior to the others. The suitability of an instrument will frequently depend on the environmental problem with which the regulator must deal.

Recently, it has become popular to talk about economic (or market-based or incentive-based) instruments as opposed to other sorts of instruments. The economic instruments that are most often referred to are those that result in the creation of an artificial market. These have become significant; for example, as at 20 July 1990, there were 124 pieces of legislation before the United States Congress that related to economic instruments for regulating the environment (EPA, 1990).

This paper aims to provide a brief comparison of artificial markets with other forms of pollution control, a discussion of theoretical and practical issues likely to be encountered when implementing artificial markets; and the experiences of existing programs both in Australia and overseas. The commodities traded in the artificial markets in pollutants are commonly referred to as tradable permits. The reason for this focus is that tradable permits have captured the imagination of many economists and regulators, and are represented as the most efficient mechanism for controlling certain environmental problems.

Before proceeding to an examination of regulatory mechanisms, the issue of sustainable development is discussed briefly. It is likely that within the context of the sustainable development debate, new or modified regulations will be demanded. Consequently, the issues discussed in this paper are an important input into the sustainable development debate.

Sustainable development

The principle of sustainability

The popular perception of environmental issues has been that they are separate from economic issues. However, the dichotomy between economics and the environment is misconceived (for example, as discussed by Pearce, Markandya and Barbier (1989). Economics is fundamentally about efficiently allocating scarce resources to maximise welfare. Resources such as clean air and water, tranquility and aesthetic beauty, while difficult to price (and therefore excluded from measures of GDP) are still important components of economic welfare.

Economic theory can contribute to the resolution of environmental conflicts because it encompasses tools to account for environmental problems. A loss in the quality of the environment will, *ceteris paribus*, reduce a properly measured index of GDP. The fact that such effects are excluded is not a conceptual failure in economics, but rather a shortcoming in national

---

[†] Excerpts from *Environmental Regulation: The Economics of Tradeable Permits — A Survey of Theory and Practice*. Research Report 42. (Canberra: Australian Government Publishing Service, 1992), pp. 1–3, 4–5, 8–11, 20–21, Glossary and Executive Summary. © Commonwealth of Australia, reproduced with permission.

accounting techniques (Repetto, 1990). The notion of economic growth which takes account of these externalities is encapsulated by the term sustainable development.

The World Commission on Environment and Development Report (the Brundtland Report, published in Australia as Our Common Future (1990)) describes sustainable development as "... a process of change in which the exploitation of resources, the direction of investments, the orientation of technological development, and institutional change are all in harmony and enhance both current and future potential to meet human needs and aspirations". It is pointed out that

> Ecological interactions do not respect the boundaries of individual ownership and political jurisdiction. Thus:
> - In a watershed, the ways in which a farmer up the slope uses land directly affect run-off on farms downstream.
> - The irrigation practices, pesticides, and fertilizers used on one farm affect the productivity of neighbouring ones, especially among small farms.
> - The efficiency of a factory boiler determines its rate of emission of soot and noxious chemicals and affects all who live and work around it.
> - The hot water discharged by a thermal power plant into a river or a local sea affects the catch of all who fish locally.
>
> (1990; pp. 90–1)

All of these interactions are immediately recognisable as manifestations of externality effects and can easily be fitted into the theoretical framework discussed in Chapter 2.

In the Australian context, sustainable development has been interpreted as requiring the achievement of six objectives as follows:

- improving material and non-material well-being;
- intergenerational equity;
- intragenerational equity;
- maintaining biodiversity and ecological systems;
- dealing cautiously with risk and uncertainty; and
- recognising the global dimension.

(ESD Working Groups, 1991; p. 1)

A desire to attempt to define the parameters for meeting these objectives led to the establishment of Ecologically Sustainable Development Working Groups covering all forms of Australian industry. These working groups reported in November 1991. The recommendations of the Groups are now being considered and the implications of ESD investigated. An issue that is raised several times in the recommendations is the possible effectiveness of tradable permits for

regulating some environmental problems, and thereby furthering the goals of sustainable development.

. . . .

REGULATION OF THE ENVIRONMENT

The Case for Regulatory Solutions

Common Access and Free Goods and Externalities

Analysis of environmental issues involves addressing many of the complexities of economics that arise when departures from the theory of perfectly competitive markets are investigated. The following discussion examines these complexities and illustrates their relevance to the environment debate. The analytical framework used in this paper is an economic one and, in accordance with that framework, the broad categorisation of *goods* is used for all of those things that have or could have a market value.

It has been argued that all of the problems associated with both *common access* and *free* goods can be dealt with as particular forms of externality (Baumol, 1977; Ng, 1979). However, for greater clarity of exposition the goods are first described explicitly. Most of the environmental problems that arise affect common access and free goods. In turn, costs are imposed on individuals through the degradation of these goods. That is, the pollution of the atmosphere is not *per se* a problem. It is the consequences of this pollution that are a cause for concern.

On occasions these may be dealt with by the provision of a publicly controlled good as, for example, when government resumes forest lands for a national park. This is also an example of government regulation involving ownership. A discussion of public goods is not included. Interested readers are referred to Ng (1979).

COMMON ACCESS GOODS

Common access goods are those goods of which anyone can take advantage. They are contrasted with free goods in that the taking of a common access good reduces the amount available for other individuals. Fishing grounds are a favourite example of a such a resource. Air and water are frequently viewed as free goods.

One of the earliest models of the outcomes from a common access fishery was proposed by Gordon (1954). The main conclusion of the model is that free access always leads to over-exploitation if there are diminishing returns. This has been called the *tragedy of the commons*. The tragedy is reinforced by the fact that if an individual refrains from using the property, this confers benefits on other individuals none of the value of which can be appropriated by the person who shows restraint.

FREE GOODS

In principle, it is possible to imagine a class of goods that are costless and non-rival in consumption. By non-rival is meant a good where the consumption by one individual apparently does not reduce the amount available to be consumed by other individuals. These are referred to as *free goods*. In effect, they are treated as goods that depart from the normal economic tenet of scarcity.

In practice, it is difficult to think of any examples of free goods and it is easy to see that clean air and water, the usual examples, are definitely not free goods. The apparent state of abundance is illusory, since atmospheric and surface pollution occasion real costs to people and indeed to economic activity (as when fishing grounds or farm lands are degraded.)

EXTERNALITIES

The types of goods considered above have an important attribute in common — there are difficulties with the nature and extent of the property rights. The theory of perfect competition assumes that property rights are well-defined and costlessly enforceable. It says nothing about how the rights come into existence or what should be the appropriate allocative mechanism for these rights. This is significant, because a feature of many environmental disputes is that the property right is vested in the state. And if a market mechanism is desired to promote more efficient management of the resource, the first step must be to devise a mechanism to allocate property rights in the resource. The importance of the nature and extent of property rights is nowhere more clearly demonstrated than by an examination of externalities.

An externality is the effect which arises when the actions of an individual incidentally impinge upon activities (and therefore well-being) of another. Because externalities tend to arise from either ill-defined property rights, high enforcement costs of existing rights, uncertainty as to property rights, or asymmetric or deficient information, these additional costs (or health costs) are external to the polluter. The offending individual only figures those costs directly attributable to the production process, but does not consider those additional (external) costs imposed on others as a consequence of production.

For example, if an individual plays their stereo system loudly this may result in both negative and positive externalities. One neighbour may derive utility (pleasure) from being able to hear the music whereas another may derive a disutility (displeasure). In respect of the former, this is a positive externality arising from the loud music and in respect of the latter it is a negative externality.

Property Rights

The property rights approach aims to provide incentives for individuals to conserve the environment by clarifying their rights to and responsibilities in common property, for example, water catchment rights. An economy in which every asset is owned would satisfy one precondition necessary to internalise all externalities. Based on this view, pollution of the oceans and atmosphere results from the fact that these assets are not owned. If ownership was vested in a private individual or organisation, then the resolution of the damage and clean-up charges would be undertaken through the enforcement of property rights. These would be determined through the market or legal system; for example, if a chemical firm pollutes a river, the river owner is legally entitled to and will receive compensation.

This simple Coasian model (Coase, 1960) suffers from a number of deficiencies. In practice, the major global environmental problems arise in circumstances where property rights are difficult, if not impossible to define. In addition where there are a number of parties involved, there may be significant free-rider incentives and transactions costs reducing the efficiency of the bargaining process. This method also assumes well functioning markets, yet in reality this is rarely the case. If there is monopolistic competition for example, the bargaining process can become more complex. Although monopolisation of a natural asset may reduce pollution, it would also lead to a less than optimal employment of the asset. The use of the asset may well be restricted to enable the monopolist to extract monopoly profits.

TRADABLE PERMITS

These are a variant of property rights albeit qualified. The idea of regulating the environment through emission quotas which are tradable was first proposed in the United States during the 1960's. The recent history of tradable permits can be traced to Ronald Coase's (1960) seminal article *The problem of social cost*, which identifies one cause of market failure as the absence of defined and enforced property rights, and to Dales (1968) and Montgomery (1972) for formalising the tradable rights literature. Even though the effects of permits are equivalent to charges and taxes, they are not technically an economic instrument. Tradable permits are an attempt to create a market by establishing and enforcing individual property rights. Thus they are a legal construct devised for the purpose of exploiting the putative efficiency of the market.

Ownership of permits allows firms to pollute up to a certain limit. If firms wish to expand production, then they must either purchase more permits, and/or invest in control technology. Firms which choose to emit less than their allowances may sell their surplus permits to other firms or use them to offset excess emissions in other parts of their own facilities. Essentially, permits operate as a pollution quota.

With permits, sources with low abatement costs have an incentive to control more emissions, and high cost controllers have an incentive to buy permits instead of undertaking expensive control measures. If a source's private marginal cost of pollution abatement (PMC) is less than the price of purchasing a single pollution permit, the preferred strategy would be to sell permits at the going price and invest in the cheaper control equipment. If the PMC is greater than the market price, the firm would prefer to purchase additional pollution permits.

If the market for permits is competitive (implying a large number of participants, perfect information and no transaction costs), then continued trades of permits forces their market price to equal the private marginal cost of pollution abatement. In other words, the following condition applies at equilibrium:

$$P = PMC$$

Permits have one advantage over other forms of regulation, that of lower private compliance costs. Because permit systems allow firms to decide the most appropriate method of keeping to the ambient standards, private compliance costs under permit systems can never be more expensive than under a direct regulatory regime that seeks to achieve the same emissions reduction. If firms vary widely in terms of marginal abatement costs, compliance costs will usually be lower.

Permits may also provide an incentive for firms to develop new technologies in a bid to keep operating costs down, and then to sell their excess credits for profit. Similarly entry into an existing industry (or location) may require technological development if existing permits cannot be purchased by the new firm.

One of the major problems associated with this system of control includes the possibility that the pollutants emitted may not form a common pool, but may in fact have different externalities and different concentrations in particular areas. This raises the need to determine a complex system of transfer prices or coefficients for permits between different locations.....

At present the primary application of these mechanisms has been in the United States in the area of air-borne lead pollution control. A major national program is being introduced in the US for sulphur oxides. ... Other possible areas of application, however, include water pollution, chlorofluorocarbon (CFC) reduction (this has already been done in Australia with quotas for CFCs established under the Ozone Protection Act 1989) and control of global warming through international trading in greenhouse gas permits.

Traditional regulatory Instruments

In most countries where there is some form of environmental regulation, governments have typically resorted to direct regulation instruments coupled with systems for monitoring and sanctioning non-compliance. According to the OECD (1989a) the approach of directly regulating human interaction with the environment mainly consists of imposing standards through legislation regarding emissions and discharges, product and process characteristics, and the like, through licensing and monitoring. The polluter's compliance is mandatory and sanctions for non-compliance usually exist. The tradition for applying this approach has its historical roots in the urban sewage and other public hygiene programs of the nineteenth century.

The most obvious advantage of the direct regulatory approach is the degree of control the authorities have over the behaviour of polluters, with a more or less certain outcome in terms of the effectiveness of the control on the environment. The advantages can be summarised as follows:

- Authorities are more familiar with the command and control approach.
- Market-based instruments are considered to be too indirect.
- Revenues and costs of market-based instruments are too uncertain.
- Charges may have negative distributional effects.
- The effect of charges on environmental quality are too uncertain.
- Direct regulation emphasises that tolerance of a polluting activity is a concession, whereas other mechanisms may lead to it being viewed as a right.
- The theoretical advantages of other methods are not evident in practice.
- The systems may become too complex.

Furthermore it is not only regulators who may prefer direct regulation. Firms could also desire direct regulation because:

- Charges might be additional to other compliance costs.
- They may believe that they have more influence on regulations through negotiations.
- Implementation of new regulations often takes a long time because of negotiations.

Another reason that regulations may be preferred by firms is that enforcement of the legislated standards is often discretionary, with authorities granting polluters exemptions from the standards in a confidential agreement — see for example, the Environment Protection Act 1973 (Tasmania). Most environmental assessment legislation includes the scope for these agreements. The confidential nature of this process means that the public are persistently misled as to the standards that are being applied. Market-based mechanisms are more transparent. With tradable permits for example, not only are the public interested in the enforcement of standards, so are the polluters themselves, which may even result in an alliance between two otherwise competing groups. At the National Airport Washington, America West airlines sought landing rights (noise pollution permits) in addition to those already issued. The community fearing in-

creasing noise pollution and existing operators concerned about a devaluation of their permits, opposed the move and the proposed legislation was defeated.[2,3]

Summary

There are many methods that can be used for regulating environmental problems. Deposit-refund schemes in spite of having the advantages of pollution tax and discouraging illegal dumping, are only effective for a group of recyclable pollutants. For most emissions/effluents, both standard pollution taxes and permits are likely to prove more efficient.

Biomass offsets have a superficial appeal, but suffer from their inability to attack the problem at its source. Whereas offset schemes may prove useful in restocking forests they are less effective in restoring lost ecosystems. In this case preventing irreversible environmental damage by reducing emissions might be a preferred option. Pollution taxes and permits are best suited to that role.

Direct regulation (or command-and-control), despite its acceptability by government, is cost-ineffective in reducing emissions when compared to both pollution taxes and permits. High costs of compliance lead to protracted delays in achieving ambient standards.

Pollution taxes and tradable permits are more efficient than command-and-control in that, once the tax is set or the permits are issued, firms are left to decide how best to comply with the pollution abatement requirements. With both, low cost controllers will control more than high cost controllers. The low cost controllers will control more than they would with command-and-control, whereas the high cost controllers will control less. The aggregate outcome is one of lower private compliance costs, and high rates of compliance.

What advantage do permits have over pollution taxes? Conceptually the two systems approach the same question from different directions. Permits fix the amount of emissions traded, thereby allowing prices to vary endogenously. Tax systems set prices, and allow emissions to vary endogenously. Government may feel safer with permits than with taxes because emission rates are exogenously determined. Also, there is no need to calculate elasticities with permits: instead an emissions ceiling is fixed. In short, government may feel that it is able to exercise greater control over firm behaviour with tradable permits.

But economic instruments will not be suitable for all situations. Where there are irreversibilities or threshold levels of pollutions such that damage costs increase exponentially above the threshold, direct regulation is likely to be more efficient because the costs of getting a tax rate wrong even in the short-run may be large. Taxes and tradable permits are unlikely to be acceptable for toxic pollutants. For example, if a toxic waste is being disposed of in such a way as to seriously endanger life, it is unlikely that individuals will be assuaged by assertions that the disposal is conducted pursuant to a permit. Here, direct regulation will be more acceptable.

There is a *prima facie* case in favour of tradable permits over other regulatory tools, whether economic or traditional measures. The remainder of this paper concerns itself with further examining issues likely to arise when implementing such a system.

GLOSSARY

The following is a glossary of terms used in the text. Note that most refer to United States legislation and experience.

Air-shed: A basin of air, usually marked by geographic features, in which ambient pollution is contained.

Air Quality Control Regions (*AQCRs*, also *Air Quality Control District*): An administrative region approximating an air-shed for purposes of environmental policy and control. AQCRs are often used to geographically define an ambient permit market.

(National) Ambient Air Quality Standard (NAAQS): Prevailing air quality levels set by the U.S. Federal EPA to protect human health. There are two forms: *Primary* standards are long-term averages (for example, $80ug/m^3$ *per annum* for sulphur dioxide in the United States) and *secondary* standards are short term averages (for example, $1,300ug/m^3$ *maximum 3-hour concentration*).

Ambient permit: Permit designed for use with non-uniform mixed assimilative pollutions. The permit is usually defined in terms of allowable levels of concentration of pollutions (for example, parts per million/year).

Attainment regions: Regions with air quality better than ambient standards. In the United States these areas are subject to Prevention of Significant Deterioration (PSD) policies.

Background concentration: Prevailing levels of ambient pollution, originating either from natural sources or from neighbouring air-sheds.

Banking policy: Part of the United States EPA Emissions Trading Program which allows firms to put aside permits for future use.

Best Available Control Technology (BACT): Control technology which new sources must install if entering attainment regions.

Biological Oxygen Demand (BOD): Amount of oxygen in water needed by biological effluents to decay.

Bubble Policy: Part of the United States EPA Emissions Trading Program which allows existing sources in non-attainment areas to purchase emission reduction credits.

Direct regulation (also Command-and-control): Any government legislative mandate which penalises individuals for failing to comply, but does not offer economic incentives nor redefines private property rights.

Emission reduction credit: The basic 'currency' of the U.S. bubbles, banking, offset and netting programs. Credits are equal to the difference between the allowable legal limit (as determined by the number of permits owned by a source) and the actual level of emissions of the source.

Emissions permit: Permit designed for use with uniform mixed assimilative pollutants. It is specified as a rate of emissions per period (for example, tonnes/year).

Episodic permits: Permits ranked in order of priority, in order to accommodate irregular changes to the environment.

Grandfathering: A free issue of permits to firms (or sources) incumbent to an industry.

Hot spots: Clusters of sources in an area, whose actual local emissions exceed the ambient air quality standards.

Lowest Achievable Emissions Rate (LAER): A requirement that all new or expanding sources in non-attainment areas must control their emissions to the lowest achievable emissions rate. The benchmark for such a rate is the lowest rate anywhere in the country, required by SIP, and often corresponds to adopting BACT.

Mobile sources: Includes motor vehicles and other forms of transport. Important contributors of NOx and CO. Mobile sources are difficult to monitor and enforce standards upon.

Netting: Allows firms or plants to expand operations and avoid new source review, provided that overall (or 'net') emissions are not significantly increased. Netting allows emission reduction credits earned elsewhere in the plant to offset the increased emissions expected from the expansion.

New source bias: The disadvantage faced by new or expanding sources which are required to purchase permits, when incumbent sources were granted initial permits free of charge.

Non-attainment regions: U.S. regions which do not confirm to national ambient air quality standards.

Non-point source: A source which is not readily identifiable, monitored and whose standards are not easily enforced. For example, fertiliser run-off from agricultural lands.

Nonuniformly mixed assimilative: Pollutants with disparate geographic effects, but which over time are assimilated into the environment. For example, sulphur dioxide.

Offset policy: Requires new and expanding sources in non-attainment areas to obtain permit credits from existing sources. By buying credits, new entrants in effect control (and in some cases improve) the ambient air quality levels. The offset policy provides for industrial growth by requiring that the proposed emission increases be offset by adequate emission reductions in the same airshed. The procedure of review and approval is called *new source review*.

Periodic permits: Permits which have their rates of emissions set according to precise patterns over time.

Point source: Readily identifiable and monitored sources. Usually appear in the form of chimney stacks, exhaust and drainage pipes.

Prevention of Significant Deterioration (PSD): Policies aimed at preventing the worsening of ambient levels in attainment regions. Such policies usually require the adoption of best-available-control-technology.

State Implementation Plan (SIP): Policies developed by state controlling authorities and approved by the U.S. Federal EPA. The SIP spells out, for each separate air quality control region, procedures and time-tables for meeting ambient standards.

Stationary sources: Non-mobile sources of pollution, for example chimney stacks and drain pipes.

Transfer coefficient (also Offset ratio, Transfer ratio): The number of emission reduction credits which must be bought before the purchaser is able to make use of one credit. It is often used as an incentive in the location of new sources, and to reduce emissions over time.

Uniformly mixed accumulative: Pollutant which is uniform in its geographic effects, but cannot be readily assimilated harmlessly in the environment. For example, most ozone depleting gases.

Uniformly mixed assimilative: Pollutant which is uniform in its geographic effects, and can be readily assimilated by the environment over time.

Water-basin: See Air-shed.

Waste end tax: A tax levied on emissions or effluents themselves, such as a carbon dioxide tax.

EXECUTIVE SUMMARY

- Various Ecologically Sustainable Development (ESD) Working Groups have identified tradable permits as a potentially effective means of regulating some environmental problems, and thereby furthering the goals of sustainable development.

- Tradable permits are private (transferable) property rights. Possession of a pollution permit allows an individual to emit up to a prescribed amount of pollution. Essentially, they act as pollution quotas.
  - Under such a policy, the value of the permits reflect their scarcity, allowing individuals to trade-off the cost of a permit against the cost of abatement technology.
  - Polluters with low pollution control costs will control more pollution and demand fewer permits. High control cost polluters will prefer to control less and demand more permits.
  - Theory suggests that in appropriate markets (sufficient participants to ensure active trading, but not so large such that monitoring and enforcement costs are prohibitive), tradable permits and pollution taxes are more economically efficient than other means in controlling and abating some forms of pollution. The private costs of complying with required reductions in emissions or effluents, are lower than under direct regulation.
  - Tradable permits may be preferred to pollution taxes whenever policymakers need to determine a specific aggregate level of emissions.

- In the 1970s, the U.S. Federal Environment Protection Agency (EPA) enacted a number of amendments to the Clean Air Act (CAA), and the Federal Clean Water Act. By 1975 it became clear that many of the goals set in 1970 and 1972 would not be achieved.
  - High compliance costs arising from the 1970 amendments discouraged compliance and in some instances encouraged legal action against the EPA. In a bid to improve compliance the EPA gradually introduced a number of market-based mechanisms which collectively became known as the Emissions Trading Program (ETP).

. . . .

which could lead to the same problems as mentioned above. Although this is possibly only correct in the short-run, it is likely that there is no long-run where some environmental problems are concerned, especially when environmental degradation is an irreversible process. In this case the issue is not one of high compliance costs which can be corrected, but of irreversible environmental degradation.

Pollution subsidies may be also analysed in Figure 2.3 above. A target rate of emissions is determined, and firms receive subsidies to be spent on control equipment. This expenditure would pivot each firm's marginal cost downwards by an amount equal to the subsidy. An optimum subsidy is one which achieves the desired emission reduction (both O and F are at Q*), and minimises the total subsidy payment. Like the optimum tax case, an optimum subsidy has each firm controlling an amount of emissions according to their marginal costs. The higher the PMC of abatement the greater the required subsidy.

Both the tax and subsidy systems are conceptually similar. The difference between the two is that one can imagine that a subsidised firm acts as if facing an optimum tax, but is reimbursed by the government for its control expenditure. Difficulties arise with subsidies however, over the truthful revelation of firm abatement costs as there is an incentive to mislead authorities in order to maximise the subsidy.

Examples of Taxes and Subsidies

Examples of the variants of the types of taxes discussed above are found in a number of European countries, especially in relation to water pollution charges. The OECD (1989b) lists a number of examples of pollution charges:

- *Effluent charges* are charges to be paid on discharges into the environment and are based on the quantity of discharged pollutants;
- *User charges* are payments for the costs of collective or public treatment of effluents. Tariffs are uniform or may differ according to the amount of effluent treated, and in some cases are only intended to cover the costs of services provided rather than reflect social costs;
- *Product charges* are charges upon the price of products which exhibit polluting properties in the manufacturing or consumption phase, or for which a disposal system has been organised. Product charges can be based on some product characteristic, or on the product itself.

- *Administrative charges* such as control and authorisation fees are payments for services undertaken by public authorities, e.g. registration of certain chemicals.
- *Tax differentiation* may lead to more favourable prices for "environmental friendly" products and vice versa.

Examples of subsidy arrangements presently being used in member OECD countries are:

- *Grants* are non-repayable forms of financial assistance that are provided if certain measures are taken by polluters to reduce their future levels of pollution.
- *Soft loans* are repayable funds provided to polluters at rates set below the market interest rate level, and require certain anti-pollution measures to be undertaken.
- *Tax allowances* directly influence the income or profits of a polluter by permitting accelerated depreciation or other forms of tax exemptions or rebates, on the understanding that anti-pollution policies have been initiated.

Taxes on Inputs

Imposing a tax on the output of an industry (assuming that a negative externality exists) as with a Pigouvian tax, is likely to be less efficient than taxing the prime source of the externality. Placing taxes on either offending inputs or discharges relative to a simple output tax is considered more desirable. These incentives can be used not only to reduce pollution, but also to conserve non-renewable resources. A resource tax on a particular input, for example, can both reduce the depletion rate of a mineral resource and stimulate investment in renewable and technological substitutes for that resource as they become relatively more economical. In addition, a tax on the main offending input may lead to research which eventually results in decreased use of the input (which can indirectly result in reduced levels of pollution).

An example is a tax on coal. By raising the price of coal, firms will find it in their interest either to switch from using the fuel or improve the efficiency of using it. Emissions of pollutants, SO_2 for example, will fall. What such a tax will not do, is encourage the development or adoption of SO_2 filters, or 'scrubbing' technologies, as there is no reward for reducing SO_2 emissions.

- The ETP evolved over a number of years from about 1975, and provides the only extensive working example of the successes and failure of tradable rights. Experience with the ETP formed the basis for the sulphur dioxide program of the 1990 amendments to the CAA.

- The ETP was one of mixed success. From its introduction until 1985 it is estimated that compliance costs (in accordance with the given ambient air and water quality standards) were at least $US900 million lower than they would have been under a system of direct regulation. Despite these large gains, it is widely believed that certain policy components of the ETP underperformed, and that cost savings could have been much greater if permit markets had been constructed differently. Some reasons for the ETP's mixed success include:
  - Prohibitive transaction costs, for the most part due to too many regulatory controls.
  - The nature of legislation made it cheaper for firms to adopt control technology, rather than investigate the possibilities of purchasing permits, since standards were set in accordance with existing and available technology.
  - Current ETP regulation requires that firms comply with prevailing standards at the conclusion of each trade. This leads to trading of blocks of permits rather than smaller more divisible units and combined with the fact that control technology is lumpy, means that the opportunity for firms to find suitable trading partners is significantly reduced.

- Title IV of the U.S. **1990 Clean Air Act Amendments** prescribes a nationwide emissions trading program for sulphur dioxide emissions. Its aims are ambitious, to reduce emissions by 10 million tonnes *per annum* by the year 2000.
  - Confidence in the earlier ETP encouraged policy-makers in adopting the "... largest experiment in history in the use of incentive-based environmental regulation ..." (Bohi and Burtraw, 1991, p. 1).
  - The program is not yet fully operational and it remains to be seen whether the theoretical advantages of a national permit trading scheme are realised in practice.

- A variety of other case studies of tradable rights and similar quota systems (in both environmental and non-environmental fields) demonstrate the wide applicability of tradable rights systems, and highlight why particular permit systems may succeed or fail. A salient feature of the failures is the poor information base that was used as a starting point in the permit design process.

- It is clear that there are several areas in Australia where the discharge of pollutants may be amenable to regulation through the use of emissions permits. However, it is also clear that the information base on which the decisions are to be made as to what is appropriate regulation for a particular region (and what is not) is deficient. Even when sufficient information is obtain such that a decision on appropriate regulation can be made, in respect of schemes where there are cross-border effects, such as greenhouse gases or river system pollution, an additional factor will be the requirement for the States and Commonwealth to reach agreement on the approach to be adopted.

- Although permits are a potentially useful tool in the protection of environmental standards, they are subject to a number of problems. Permits could work well in certain provided that the regime is designed carefully by the respective controlling authority, and that both the permit and product markets are competitive. Otherwise, alternative pollution control systems such as pollution taxes and direct regulation may be more appropriate.

(d) Voluntary Initiatives and the Law: The practice and promise of voluntary environmental initiatives depend heavily on a productive partnership with legal instruments[†]

Kernaghan Webb ————————————————————————————

In spite of their seemingly innocuous name, voluntary environmental initiatives[1] can have significant links to the legal system, and important legal implications for individuals, environmental groups, the private sector, and governments. Indeed, the connections between voluntary measures and the law are critical to understanding why such arrangements do or do not work.[2]

Such connections are numerous and varied. An important impetus for industry developing voluntary initiatives is often the perception that the initiatives will decrease the likelihood of new regulations being imposed. Adherence to the terms of voluntary programmes may diminish the likelihood of enforcement actions being initiated or successful, while non-compliance with provisions of a voluntary programme can assist courts in finding firms penally liable. Through regulatory prosecutions and private legal suits for breach of care (known in the law as the tort of negligence), the terms of voluntary programmes can in effect be judicially imposed on firms who are "free riding" on the positive image created by those who voluntarily comply with the programme. Failure to adhere to the terms of voluntary programmes can lead to legal actions in contract by participating parties (e.g., firms, industry associations, environmental groups, consumers). Members of a community may be able to draw on the existence of voluntary initiatives in tort actions to assist in establishing liability against individual firms. Participation by government in the development of voluntary programmes can further or impede regulatory objectives, but may also leave government open to legal actions. Voluntary initiatives may be pursued to overcome limitation of legal instruments such as jurisdictional constraints, may have trade law implications, and may run afoul of competition law requirements.

As even this brief listing suggests, those who choose to ignore or downplay the linkages between voluntary measures and laws may be underestimating the power of such non-regulatory instruments, perhaps to their own detriment.

. . . .

The Regulatory System and Voluntary Initiatives

Voluntary environmental initiatives are frequently adopted by industry for reasons which do not relate directly to the regulatory system. For example, firms may sign on to non-regulatory programmes in response to consumer demand, to demonstrate good corporate citizenship within a community, or to enhance the efficiency of a firm's operations. But in at least two ways, the regulatory system can be a stimulus for voluntary action. First, firms may develop and adhere to voluntary standards in an effort to decrease liability under existing regulations. Such voluntary initiatives can be viewed as supplements or reinforcements to the regulatory system. Second, voluntary programmes may be put in place by industry in an attempt to forestall new regulations being developed. In this respect, voluntary initiatives represent alternatives to the regulatory system.

Voluntary Initiatives as Supplements to the Regulatory System

The main type of offence include in federal and provincial environmental regulations is called the strict liability offence.[3] With this type of offence,

---

† From *Voluntary Initiatives and the New Politics of Corporate Greening* ed. Robert B. Gibson (Peterborough, ON: Broadview Press, 1999), pp. 32–50. Reproduced by permission.

once the Crown has proven the facts of the contravention beyond a reasonable doubt, the accused will be convicted unless he or she establishes on a balance of probabilities that every reasonable action was taken to avoid the commission of the offence. This is often referred to as the due diligence defence.

When courts consider the due diligence defence, a key issue to be ascertained is whether particular behaviour constitutes reasonable care in a particular circumstance. Courts may look to evidence of industry standards when considering due diligence defences. The existence of a voluntary code or standard — particularly one which concentrates on management systems and involves third party compliance verifications[4] — can be of considerable assistance to a court's determinations of reasonable care. In a recent Ontario case, the court held that non-compliance with a recognized industry standard constituted evidence of lack of due diligence on the part of the accused.[5] Both judges and legal commentators have suggested that compliance with environmental management standards such as ISO 14000 (which involves auditing by independent third parties) can reduce legal liability.[6]

Industry-developed standards can also play a role in regulatory sentencing. Recently, courts have required compliance with a voluntary programme as a term of sentence in a regulatory enforcement action. In *R. v. Prospec Chemicals*[7], following a finding of guilt for exceeding Alberta sulphur emissions limits contrary to Alberta environmental legislation, defence counsel proposed that Prospec be permitted to seek ISO 14000 certification as part of the court-ordered sentence. The judge agreed.... One commentator has suggested that programmes such as ISO 14000, which can involve independent certifications that a firm has successfully passed an environmental management system audit, may be of particular use in sentencing by "judges who may be lacking the experience and time to devise an appropriate organizational structure for environmental compliance."[8] In the United States, draft sentencing guidelines stipulate that adherence to the terms of environmental compliance programmes can considerably reduce the penalties imposed.[9]

. . . .

[F]irms considering developing non-regulatory programmes should be aware from the outset that their efforts could affect regulatory enforcement actions.[10] Firms that agree to adhere to the terms of a non-regulatory programme need to understand that the sanctions for non-compliance may extend beyond whatever penalties may be imposed by their industry association to include conviction under regulatory regimes.[11]

At the same time, a firm which does not participate in a voluntary programme may nevertheless have the standard imposed on it through a regulatory enforcement action. In this way, the management of firms who believe they can take a "free ride" on the positive industry image produced by others who adhere to a voluntary programme may have an unpleasant surprise awaiting them when their non-compliance with the terms of the programme subsequently plays a role in a court's determination of regulatory liability or as part of sentencing.

. . . .

For governments, the incentives to participate in non-regulatory initiatives and monitor their development and implementation are considerable. The fact that voluntary programmes can play a role in determining regulatory liability suggests that governments need to participate in the development of such programmes so that the standards produced are as rigorous as possible. Should government fail to provide such input, there is the risk that the standards produced will be considered reasonable by judges (who may lack the time or expertise to delve into the detail of individual voluntary agreements) even though they may be viewed as inadequate by government. Involvement by government in the development of voluntary programmes can also be seen as providing needed guidance to the private sector about what constitutes reasonable care or due diligence for the purposes of regulatory liability.

In light of cutbacks and continued budgetary pressures, governments may welcome non-regulatory approaches which decrease some of the enforcement burden on regulatory agencies. ... Moreover, self-identification by industry of who is complying voluntary programmes and who is not can assist government in targeting inspection and investigation efforts. In the interests of keeping a good public image, industry associations may even feel compelled to come forward with information concerning "bad actors" in their sector.[13]

. . . .

Environmental groups [ ] need to consider seriously the merits of participating in the development and implementation of voluntary programmes in light of the considerable impact such programmes can play in stimulating good conduct from industry, and in influencing judicial interpretations of regulatory liability and sentencing. Environmental group involvement can help to encourage adoption of more rigorous standards and stronger inducements for implementation. At the same time, environmental groups need to consider how direct involvement in industry programmes will be perceived by their members and the broader community.[21]

Increasingly, environmental organizations seem to be recognizing the benefits of establishing direct relations with industry through the vehicle of voluntary programmes. Mike McCloskey, chair of the American Sierra Club, is reported as saying,

> The time is right for corporations and environmentalists to deal directly with each other and not filter everything through government. The companies that sign the CERES Principles (a voluntary code concerning environmental responsibility) identify themselves as ones that organizations like mine should approach in our desire to forge a new relationship.[22]

For courts, the challenge will be to examine non-regulatory programmes critically — to look behind assertions that a particular voluntary code represents "the industry standard" and determine who was involved in its drafting and implementation, and how they were involved. Increasingly, there may be more than one non-regulatory programme in operation, necessitating that courts compare the relative merits of each.[23] In turn, counsel for the prosecution and defence will need to become much more familiar with the details of voluntary standards and the processes of development and implementation.

Voluntary Initiatives as Alternatives to Regulation

The preceding discussion focused on voluntary initiatives as supplements to the regulatory system. But in some cases, voluntary initiatives are specifically adopted in an attempt to avoid the development and imposition of new regulations. For industry, new regulations may be viewed as a threat,[24] since government-imposed obligations represent a potentially undesirable unknown: regulations could set an unnecessarily high standard (from an industry perspective), and compliance with them could be more cumbersome, expensive and time-consuming than adhering to self-imposed standards. The challenge for industry is to ascertain the real likelihood that government will act through development of new regulations if effective voluntary measures are not put in place, and to develop non-regulatory systems which will be seen by government (and others) as sufficiently rigorous in substance and implementation to make new regulations unnecessary.

Where government has a responsive, up-to-date regulatory system, and a track record of acting decisively through regulatory measures when new problems arise, there is arguably a credible threat stimulus to galvanize voluntary industry action. In this respect, a well-functioning regulatory presence can help to create the right environment for voluntary action. A second, more positive governmental stimulus for industry self-management is the perception in the private sector that sincere attempts to initiate and implement effective non-regulatory approaches will be positively received by government. If this second, positive stimulus is missing, then industry might well decide that seizing the initiative to develop voluntary approaches will not be worthwhile. In short, government must be prepared to act decisively through regulatory measures but be alert to the potential for voluntary programmes in the right set of circumstances.

. . . .

Contracts and Voluntary Initiatives

Voluntary initiatives are in essence consent-based regimes, in the sense that in the normal course of events parties agree of their own volition to abide by the terms of the initiative (in exchange for receiving certain benefits) and are not required to do so by legislation. The main legal instruments used to formalize consent-based agreements are contracts. Parties to a contract who fail to comply with contract terms can be liable for restitution, damages or specific performance requirements.[28] In all legal suits in contract, it is necessary to establish that the terms of the agreement are sufficiently precise to be actionable, that there was agreement between the parties about those terms, that consideration was exchanged, and that breach of contract occurred.[29]

Courts have held that, through contract-based actions, industry associations can discipline their members for failure to meet agreed-upon standards.[30] It is also possible for individual firms to require suppliers to meet non-regulatory measures as terms of contracts.[31] Firms which pay for the right to use a particular logo indicating that environmentally sound practices are being used, and agree to comply to the terms of the programme underlying that logo, can be the subject of legal actions in contract brought by the organization which developed that logo if the contract terms are breached.

On some issues, a contract-based voluntary programme may have as high or higher credibility in the marketplace than regulatory initiatives enforced by government agencies, so that products endorsed by respected groups may be considered by shoppers to be more [reliable] than those which meet government standards. Particularly in developing countries, the compliance verification systems which are part of contract-based programmes may be superior to those provided through domestic regulatory regimes.

. . . .

The Tort of Negligence and Voluntary Initiatives

... Individuals who are not contractual parties to a voluntary agreement are less fortunate. While they can also be harmed, they cannot initiate a legal suit in contract. However, they may be able to bring legal actions based on the tort of negligence if they can establish that they were owed a duty of care by the defendant, and that duty of care (as reflected in the voluntary agreement) was violated.[38]

... While non-regulatory standards such as those of the Canadian Standards Association are not conclusive on their own, courts have interpreted compliance with such standards as evidence of reasonable care.[40]

In negligence actions, courts can impose liability in tort on a firm, drawing on the existence of a non-regulatory programme as evidence of the standard of care owed, even if the firm never directly participated in the non-regulatory initiative.[41] This provides a strong incentive for participation. Individual firms that might otherwise be tempted to take a free ride on an industry initiative are thereby encouraged to adhere to its terms as a protection against tort liability.

Jurisdictional Constraints and Voluntary Initiatives

One of the reasons why governments may initiate, participate in, or sponsor voluntary measures is because of jurisdictional constraints which hamstring more conventional legal instruments. For example, within Canada, it may be possible for a coalition of stakeholders to devise and implement a voluntary instrument concerning protection of wildlife or reduction of emissions where a legislative instrument pertaining to the same topic might fail due to federal-provincial constitutional difficulties.[42]

At the international level, trade agreements such as the *General Agreement on Tariffs and Trade* (GATT) and the *North American Free Trade Agreement* (NAFTA) restrict the ability of governments to develop measures which could be interpreted as barriers to trade. A key requirement is that trade measures do not discriminate between home-produced goods and imports, or between imports from or exports to different trading partners. In addition, trade measures are not to discriminate between like products on the basis of method of production.

Many voluntary environmental initiatives such as those pertaining to sustainable forestry harvesting could be described as instruments which discriminate on the basis of method of production and may have the effect of decreasing trade from countries where uncertifiable methods of production are used. However, because these programmes are developed by non-governmental parties (e.g., industry and/or environmental groups), are driven by consumer demand, are voluntary and are not legislatively required, at first glance it is difficult to envisage how they could be considered "trade measures" under GATT.

Given that the effect of voluntary programmes such as those pertaining to sustainable forestry practices is not to prohibit production by certain methods, or to prohibit imports from a particular firm or country, but rather to provide information to consumers about how particular firms have produced their products (and those consumers who do not care about such matters are free to buy uncertified products), it might be more proper to characterize such initiatives as increasing consumer choice and information rather than restricting trade. If, however, compliance with these voluntary standards were to be required as a term of a regulation or licence, or in procurement contracts, and thus amount to a governmentally imposed restriction on imports, then it is more likely that GATT could be considered to apply.

The *Agreement on Technical Barriers to Trade* (TBT), which was passed to further the objectives of GATT, applies to both technical regulations and voluntary standards.[43] The TBT agreement imposes many requirements on "recognized bodies" concerning the content of standards, as well as the processes for developing them, with the intention of minimizing the creation of new barriers to trade.[44] "Recognized body" is not defined in the technical barriers agreement. The most obvious recognized bodies existing in virtually every country are those which are part of the national standards system. For example, in Canada, the Standards Council of Canada, which is a creature of statute[45] reporting to the Minister of Industry and which participates on behalf of Canada in deliberations of the International Organization for Standardization, is a clear example of a recognized body. The Standards Council of Canada is statutorily empowered to oversee the operations of standards bodies such as the Canadian Standards Association (CSA), which would appear to be another example of a recognized body. The ISO 14000 environmental management standards would be an excellent example of a voluntary standard developed by a recognized body.

Characterizing industry associations, coalitions of private sector firms, environmental groups and aboriginal representatives, or even individual firms which have developed their own voluntary codes, as recognized bodies for the purposes of the technical barriers agreement, would appear to represent to a considerable expansion in the coverage of the Technical Barriers to Trade and GATT agreements.[46] The World Trade Organization (WTO) has yet to make a definitive determination on this issue. However, even assuming such a determination were made, it is not at all clear that the technical barriers agreement applies to non-product related[47] processes and production method standards such as those pertaining to sustainable forestry practices.[48]

. . . .

Conclusions

Voluntary environmental initiatives may be developed by industry, environmental groups, standards organizations, and government for a wide number of reasons which do not relate in any direct manner to the legal system: consumer demand, increased efficiency, supplier demand, public image, and community pressure are but a few of the non-legal impulses underlying voluntary initiatives. By the same token, however, the legal system can play an important role in stimulating the development of voluntary initiatives, or reinforcing the effectiveness of such measures. Governments may encourage voluntary programmes or assist in their development as a way of minimizing enforcement costs and decreasing the pressure for new regulations. Industry might develop them in an attempt to meet reasonable care requirements in regulatory and tort law. Judges might draw on them in their determinations of due diligence and in devising appropriate sentencing structures. And industry associations, standards organizations, and environmental groups may rely on the contractual basis to such programmes to stimulate compliance.

. . . .

... An attempt to explicitly "build" a voluntary environmental programme on a legislative base is currently being undertaken by the European Union (EU) through the Eco-Management and Audit Scheme (EMAS).[58] The legal framework encourages industry to adopt explicit and comprehensive environmental management procedures, as verified and audited by independent third parties. In the future, EMAS may become a mandatory system in Europe, but for now it is not....

Whether the current, largely "hands off" Canadian approach to voluntary initiatives is sufficient, or a more ambitious and aggressive approach following the European example will be necessary in Canada and elsewhere, is difficult to say at this point. What is clear is that voluntary measures are playing an increasingly important role in environmental protection in Canada and in other jurisdictions, and that a clear-headed understanding of the legal implications of such initiatives is essential for all stakeholders.

Analysis suggests that in Canada the incentives to participate seriously in voluntary initiatives are closely but accidentally linked to a set of legal instruments or stimuli — the threat of regulations, prosecutions, and tort and contract liability. None of these legal instruments was specifically designed to promote voluntary initiatives and, more significantly, none of them is now being applied directly for this purpose. Perhaps an intelligently integrated and well focused strategy of credible regulatory threats, exemplary regulatory prosecutions, tort legal suits, and contract law actions might provide a powerful boost for voluntary initiatives. This type of "strategic" encouragement of voluntary initiatives might be more effective at stimulating effective voluntary action than either the current "hands off" approach or the more interventionist European statute-based approach. If successful, this approach could be supplemented through strategic and co-ordinated use of economic instruments and education-based campaigns.

Monitoring and Enforcement

(a) Environmental Regulation as a Bargaining Process: The Canadian approach[†]

Murray Rankin and Peter Z.R. Finkle ─────────────────────

NEGOTIATION AND BARGAINING

The negotiation and bargaining process has been the subject of several excellent case studies recently prepared for the Economic Council of Canada.[2] These case studies have unanimously concluded that environmental regulation in Canada reflects a process of negotiation and bargaining. The Austinian "command theory" of law which underscores our criminal law system and, arguably, our entire jurisprudence, is asserted to be insignificant in practice. Dr. Thompson concludes:

> [T]he reality is that the rules of environmental regulation are never clearly stated or certain, except in a purely symbolic sense. Instead the norms of conduct are the subject of negotiation and renegotiation between the regulator and the regulated right down to the moment of compliance or noncompliance. In this sense, rules stated in statutes or regulations are merely points of departure for negotiating modifications of behaviour; and "compliance" or "noncompliance" means "agreement" or "disagreement." Only if there is an ultimate disagreement is the enforcement procedure utilized, and even then its role may be but another step in a drawn out negotiation process, of little more significance than a variety of other weights such as tax concessions, that the regulator may bring to bear.[3]

Often statutory standards are expressed in terms of absolute prohibition of certain polluting conduct. The most important example of this regulatory approach is found in the water pollution provisions of the Fisheries Act.[4] Sometimes, environmentally destructive conduct is licensed. Most provinces, for example, have legislation like the Pollution Control Act of British Columbia.[5] Under this type of arrangement, discharge into a receiving medium is permitted — up to a stipulated maximum level. Pollution beyond this level is theoretically prohibited and the pertinent legislation contains offence provisions under which offenders are to be prosecuted.[6] Sometimes, rather than specific rules, general guidelines are spelled out. For example, the National Ambient Air Quality Objectives, which have been established for sulphur dioxide and nitrogen oxides, have been enacted by the federal government.[7] These guidelines are advisory only and acquire legal effect only when incorporated into provincial regulations.

---

† From Murray Rankin & Peter Z.R. Finkle, "The Enforcement of Environmental Law: Taking the Environment Seriously," in *Environmental Law in the 1980's: A New Beginning*, ed. A. Lucas (Calgary, AB: Canadian Institute of Resources Law, 1981), pp. 172–78. Repoduced by permission of Alastair R. Lucas. See appendix for notes or references.

> The significant point is that no matter how normative measures are expressed in a statute — whether as policy guidelines or as command prohibitions — the end result in the case of environmental regulation is a bargaining process.[8]

One must indeed acknowledge the need for negotiation, as there is so much uncertainty in environmental regulation with respect to causation, economic costs, and the social and ecological benefits resulting from an abatement or avoidance programme. Negotiation amongst interest groups who are far from equal in their financial or information resources is, however, a relatively meaningless exercise. From the lawyer's perspective, the lack of formalized arrangements which experience has shown does not equalize the contest between the weak and the strong is a serious, perhaps fatal, deficiency in the bargaining process. For example, in a recent study of the coastal forest industry and its conflict with the salmon fisheries,[9] the authors note the lack of such formalized arrangements, even though the impact of such resource negotiations upon the public is enormous.

This informality can play into the hands of the regulated interests. The industry in question has better information on compliance costs than the regulator. It often does its own monitoring of pollution levels, prompted by considerations of cost internalization. When the rules and the agenda for negotiation are not clear, the company can always emphasize the economic consequences of a particular course of action, which may be very difficult to evaluate for a scientifically-trained official, for instance, within the Ministry of Environment. In addition, the federal/provincial division of powers in Canada in many cases presents constitutional constraints upon a comprehensive regulatory programme.[10] Since no one government can effectively deal with an overall problem, a "divide and conquer" strategy is available to many industries.

One must carefully distinguish between "is" and "ought" in considering negotiation in environmental law. In an effort to recognize environmental regulation as a bargaining *process*, it is possible to move too quickly from a descriptive to a prescriptive analysis. While it is becoming clear that a bargaining process now extends from the time of the formulation of an environmental standard to the application and enforcement of the standard, it does not necessarily follow that reform consists merely of improving the entire bargaining process. That would be to say uncritically, that what is, ought to be. In our opinion, the bargaining process should be reformed and formalized in order to make it more equitable as between weak and strong interest groups, particularly in the period up to the creation of an enforceable regulation.

However, once a particular standard has been set, it must be enforced, with more or less the same diligence as the state enforces criminal laws, or contracts to which it is a party. Otherwise, the behaviour of industries which have certain negative impacts on the environment will remain effectively unchecked. Likewise, the legislation in the field of environmental law will remain cosmetic at best — "full of sound and fury and signifying nothing." Thomas Schelling in his seminal work, *The Strategy of Conflict*[11] has written:

> Enforceable promises cannot be taken for granted. Agreements must be in enforceable terms and involve enforceable types of behaviour. Enforcement depends on at least two things — some authority somewhere to punish or coerce and an ability to discern whether punishment or coercion is called for.[12]

Moreover, as Professor D. Dewees has shrewdly observed, environmental legislation may be deliberately framed to include "symbolic measures intended to generate enthusiasm and approval from environmental advocates."[13] Politicians can curry favour at elections by pointing to ostensibly tough environmental legislation which has been passed. However, the necessary implementing regulations may never be passed. Federal/provincial agreements may never be concluded, for a great variety of reasons. A programme may never be adequately funded or legal resources may not be provided so as to enforce the laws on the books.

If standards are drafted in open-ended terms, or as "objectives," they remain unenforceable. The conclusions of the Fraser River Task Force are illustrative. Formed in February 1980, the Task Force included many officers from the British Columbia Ministry of Environment charged with the investigation of all illegal sources of pollution in the lower Fraser River. Its Final Report was submitted to the Pearse Commission on Pacific Fisheries Policy.[14] The Task Force had a great deal of difficulty in enforcing permits issued under the Pollution Control Act[15] as they were written in "ambiguous or vague terms and lacking specific information." Often the permits used the term "at the direction of the Regional Manager" when referring to methods of operation or construction of works. The Task Force came to several revealing conclusions:

> for in some cases two or three years, no legal action had taken place by the Waste Management Branch. This resulted in almost tacit approval by the Branch and caused problems for the Task Force when it came time for the decision to lay charges because of the "due diligence" rule.... Another problem centred around the actual finding of violations of permits by Waste Management Branch staff and the reporting of same on compliance checks. The teams would constantly encounter major violations which were easily identifiable yet would observe no record of the noncompliances of a permit which caused a deadly toxic substance to enter the Fraser River.... It was felt by the Task Force that because of the general attitude of "non-enforcement" which had been fairly consistent throughout the Province, many of these faults could not be laid against any specific individual or Region. Training in enforcement techniques, court systems, writing of orders, etc. should be provided to the Waste Management Branch staff to help rectify this situation.[16]

On the other hand, if standards are set forth in clear and unambiguous terms but are unreasonably strict — or prohibit pollution altogether[17] — then there is an effective delegation of enormous discretionary power to the regulator in question. The message is clear that this "black letter" rule is not the "real rule" in practice. For example, if driving over 50 kilometres per hour is prohibited by the "written rule" yet police officers *in fact* only stop and ticket motorists who exceed 65 kilometres per hour, then the "real rule" is the latter speed limit. In the pollution context, it is the sophisticated, often large and powerful polluter who has greater information resources. Such a firm is not only more likely to be aware of the "real rules" of game, but can easily shape those rules by its power. Often the small, marginal operator may foolishly obey the more stringent "black letter" rule, to its detriment. Moreover, the administrator is quite likely to enforce the "black letter"

law against the weaker polluter. Ironically, therefore, we often punish the law abider and reward the recalcitrant.[18]

How is this "real rule" created? There is a negotiation and bargaining process which precedes its implementation. But since all the players *know* that it is the result of a bargain, there is a natural incentive on the polluter to "stonewall" — the disturbing situation with the International Nickel Company of Canada Ltd. and its compliance with the Ontario Environmental Protection Act[19] serves as a recent example.[20] Similarly, there is a temptation to seek an unreasonably low standard on the part of the polluter, just as the regulator reciprocates with an attempt to achieve an unreasonably high standard. The predictable outcome is a compromise somewhere between these extremes. However, this compromise may in no way reflect ecological necessities; instead, it may be a pure and rare coincidence if the resulting standard is "right" from an environmental point of view.

Yet this bargaining process does not terminate when the "real rule" has been articulated. Victor and Burrell in a case study for the Economic Council of Canada's Regulation Reference[21] describe how the effluent regulations under the Fisheries Act[22] for the pulp and paper industry were established — negotiated *in camera* between the industry and federal and provincial officials. For existing mills, the standards established by the regulations[23] were to be applied only according to compliance schedules negotiated with particular mills. These schedules were not promulgated as regulations. Noncompliance, it was observed, usually led to the renegotiation of the schedule. The same, continuous renegotiation at the enforcement stage is the sad history of the International Nickel Company of Canada Ltd. in Sudbury. In summary, therefore, we would encourage bargaining up to the point at which a standard is set. After the rule is promulgated and clarified, we would urge that it be made as enforceable as any agreement in law is enforceable. The bargaining mode must cease once the standard is established.

(b) Persuasion, Penalties, and Prosecution: Administrative v. criminal sanctions[†]

Richard Brown and Murray Rankin ───────────────

Regulators respond to most environmental and occupational health and safety violations by ordering offenders to obey the law. Sanctions are seldom invoked. This conciliatory mode of implementation is documented in several empirical studies of environmental[1] and health and safety regulation[2] in Canada. Similar observations have been made about enforcement of these types of regulatory schemes in Britain,[3] Australia,[4] and several other countries.[5] While the strong preference of regulatory officials for persuasion over punishment is common knowledge, little is known about what success they enjoy in persuading offenders to obey legal requirements or about the fate of those who are impervious to persuasion.

As regulatory agencies in both the environmental and occupational health and safety fields have an ongoing relationship with firms regulated, the best way to determine how many offenders are persuaded to comply is to plot their long-term compliance records. This is something few researchers have done.[6] In this study, we tracked the relationship between two agencies of the British Columbia (BC) government — the Workers' Compensation Board and the Waste Management Branch of the Ministry of Environment — and the firms being regulated by them over a period of approximately three years. We found that a substantial number of firms habitually violate environmental and occupational health and safety regulations, despite the efforts of regulators to persuade them to comply.

As well as asking how many offenders are persuaded to comply, we set out to determine whether those who prove resistant to persuasion are ultimately punished. We were particularly interested in learning whether the difference between the two agencies being studied in the type of sanction used has any effect on the number of offenders penalized and the size of the

resulting penalties. Prosecution is the sanction of last resort for the Waste Management Branch as for most regulatory agencies, where the Workers' Compensation Board imposes administrative monetary penalties without resort to the courts. Very few regulatory agencies in Canada have a similar power.[7] The relationship between the type of sanctioning mechanism employed and the stringency of enforcement is another topic that researchers have largely ignored.[8]

We found that the number of employers penalized by the Workers' Compensation Board for health and safety infractions far exceeds the number of firms prosecuted by the Waste Management Branch for environmental offences and that the administrative penalties imposed by the board are far larger on average than the fines assessed by the courts in pollution cases. Our research suggests that these differences are a function of the type of sanction employed by these two regulatory agencies.

· · · ·

Differences between Administrative and Criminal Penalties

The Workers' Compensation Board's use of administrative penalties sets it apart from almost all other regulatory agencies in Canada, for which prosecution is the ultimate sanction for a regulatory offence. Only one federal regulatory scheme provides for imposition of administrative penalties without resort to the courts. Under recent amendments to the Civil Aviation Act, the federal minister of transport may levy administrative penalties of up to $1,000 for certain aviation safety offences. If a penalty is not paid, the matter is referred to the Civil Aviation Tribunal for adjudication.[17] In the United States, a handful of regulatory agencies have similar enforcement

[†] From *Securing Compliance: Seven Case Studies*, ed. M.L. Friedland (Toronto: University of Toronto Press, 1990), pp. 325–26, 337–48. Reproduced with permission of University of Toronto Press, Incorporated. See appendix for notes or references.

powers, one of them being the Occupational Safety and Health Administration (OSHA).[18]

Much more common than these purely administrative penalties are schemes that combine administrative and judicial elements. These hybrid schemes allow enforcement officials to propose monetary penalties and perhaps to engage in settlement discussions. But if a penalty is contested, and a consensual solution is not reached, the matter is referred to court for adjudication. Hybrid sanctions enjoy widespread use in the United States.[19] A similar approach is now followed by several regulatory agencies which issue tickets for minor infractions.[20]

Does the choice between criminal and administrative penalties influence the number and magnitude of penalties? The Workers' Compensation Board takes penalty action much more often than the Waste Management Branch initiates prosecutions, and the penalties levied by the board are much larger on average than the fines imposed by the courts for environmental offences. While there is no doubt these differences are partly attributable to other factors, our research suggests that the stringency of enforcement is a function of the type of sanction.

In addition to using different sanctions, the Workers' Compensation Board and the Waste Management Branch differ on other fronts. The costs and benefits of pollution control measures are not necessarily the same as the costs and benefits of health and safety precautions. There are also differences in the composition and organization of the populations exposed to occupational hazards and environmental risks. These and other economic and political factors almost certainly influence the level of enforcement.

Yet such differences should not be exaggerated. Both agencies were operating in the same province during the same period. Almost all the enterprises regulated by the Waste Management Branch as permittees were also employers regulated by the Workers' Compensation Board, although employers in some industries were not permittees. In other words, these two agencies were subject to the same general economic and political forces, not only at the provincial level, but also at the industry level in many cases.

Key actors in these two agencies also help determine the level of enforcement. The Workers' Compensation Board's "get tougher" campaign and schedule of recommended penalties were introduced by a new general manager of the Occupational Health and Safety Division

shortly after he was appointed. At the Ministry of Environment, home to the Waste Management Branch, there was no tough enforcement rhetoric emanating from politicians or senior civil servants. Environmental prosecutions could be launched only with the approval of the "Triad Committee," consisting of the director of the Waste Management Branch, the chief conservation officer, and a civil lawyer from the Ministry of the Attorney General. Although the ostensible purpose of this committee was to ensure that adequate evidence is available before charges proceed, some in the branch saw it as an attempt to curtail prosecutions.

As the two regulatory agencies studied are buffeted by somewhat diverse economic and political winds and have different personalities at their helms, the level of enforcement would probably differ even if both used the same enforcement mechanism. However, if the same mechanism was used, our research strongly suggests that any disparity in enforcement would be much smaller than now exists, with one agency using administrative penalties and the other relying on the criminal process.

While most readers are probably familiar with the general nature of the criminal process, a brief description of the penalty process at the Workers' Compensation Board is probably in order. The process begins with a "show cause" letter sent by the director of field services to an employer. This letter describes the violation in question, sometimes reviews the employer's compliance history, and closes by stating that the board proposes to apply a penalty of a certain amount unless the employer shows cause why this should not be done. An oral hearing is held if an employer requests one, but such requests are rare. The final decision whether to levy a penalty is made by the director of field services. His or her decision may be appealed in writing to the commissioners of the board.

This administrative process is staffed entirely by regulatory officials. Regulators play a much smaller role in the criminal process. The only decision made solely by them is whether to recommend prosecution. Decisions about whether to lay charges or enter into plea bargains, and about what fines to seek, are made by prosecutors, with more or less consultation with regulatory officials. Lower-court judges or magistrates determine guilt or innocence and fix sentence.

We now explore differences in the way administrative and criminal enforcement mechanisms operate, differences that help to explain the tendency of a system of administrative penalties to produce more penalties. We then consider the relative size of penalties generated in the criminal and administrative process.

Information about prosecutions by the Waste Management Branch was acquired for the Vancouver Island and Northern regions. Interviews were conducted with a small group of technicians and section heads as well as both regional managers. In addition, regional conservation officers, the chief conservation officer, and regional crown counsel were interviewed. To learn about the Workers' Compensation Board we observed nine officers at work for two days each, held discussions with those officers, and conducted a mailed survey of all officers. All documents in the files for 230 penalty proceedings initiated in 1984 and 1985 were also read.

Risk v. Harm

Although some health and safety and environmental infractions are detected only after they have injured people or the life systems on which people depend, many violations are detected before any damage occurs. Available evidence suggests that the administrative process is more likely than the criminal justice system to punish offenders whose transgressions create a risk of harm that never materializes.

An injury or fatality is involved in only 20 per cent of the cases in which penalties are imposed by the Workers' Compensation Board for safety violations. In other words, the vast majority of penalties are for offences that cause no actual harm before being detected. The huge number of administrative penalties imposed by OSHA leaves no doubt that it follows the same practice.[21]

In contrast, officials of the Northern Region of the Waste Management Branch, who were more inclined to prosecute than were their counterparts elsewhere in the province, failed to persuade the Triad Committee to lay charges in the absence of obvious damage, such as fish kills or patent human health concerns. Branch officials also have complained that judges show little concern about permit violations that do not cause harm. One county court judge even held that actual environmental degradation is a necessary element of an offence under the Waste Management Act and that mere risk of substantial harm is not enough to constitute an offence. Although this ruling was subsequently overturned

on appeal, prosecutions continue to be a rare event in the absence of actual harm.[22]

In jurisdictions where health and safety offenders are punished under the criminal justice system, the pattern of enforcement is similar to that found in pollution cases in British Columbia.[23]

What explains this apparent distinction between the administrative and criminal process in the treatment of risk? One plausible explanation is that regulators view risk as more serious than do prosecutors and judges. Regulators who spend most of their time conducting inspections to detect hazards before anyone is hurt are likely to take risk seriously. Indeed, Workers' Compensation Board officers rated the risk of harm as more important than its actual occurrence in determining whether to recommend a penalty.[24] By contrast, a large part of the daily fare of judges and prosecutors, at least prosecutors who do not work for regulatory agencies, is crimes that result in property loss or personal injury. Offences that hurt no one may appear less blameworthy to them.

Another equally plausible explanation attributes the ways in which the criminal and administrative process respond to risk not to the legal actors involved but to the differing degrees of stigma associated with these two types of sanctions. According to this interpretation, legal actors of all stripes, including regulators, view the criminal process as more stigmatizing than the administrative process. They believe the stigma of prosecution is not warranted by offenders who cause no harm, except perhaps in egregious circumstances.

Stigma

A conviction in criminal court is probably viewed by regulatory officials as more stigmatizing than assessment of an administrative penalty. While the greater stigma association with criminal penalties enhances their deterrent effect on potential offenders,[25] this stigma may also deter regulators from initiating prosecutions.

Some data on the way people perceive criminal and administrative penalties is offered by a survey of taxpayers who were asked about the impact on their reputation of "being penalized for negligently under-reporting taxable income to Revenue Canada" and "being found guilty in court of tax evasion." While 45 per cent rated the effect of a guilty verdict on their reputation as either substantial or extreme, only 16 per cent felt the same way about a penalty.[26] In the absence of any evidence to the contrary, there is good reason to believe that both regulators in the environmental and health and safety arenas and those they regulate view criminal penalties as more serious than their administrative counterpart.

Legal actors may be reluctant to stigmatize most regulatory offenders with criminal penalties because their offences are perceived to be morally ambiguous. This ambiguity distinguishes regulatory offences from conventional crimes that violate a well-established moral code. As already noted, many infractions cause no actual damage, and the absence of any injury may make the offender appear less blameworthy.

There is another reason why many regulatory offenders may be seen as significantly different than conventional criminals. Crimes like burglary and assault are not only harmful to victims but contribute nothing to the welfare of society as a whole, whereas the economic activity subject to occupational health and safety regulations is neither all bad nor all good. Enterprises that turn out socially valuable products also entail some risk of harm to workers. Like anything else, safety comes at a price, and greater safety can be had only by diverting resources from the production of goods and services. There is no clear-cut answer as to what precautions should be legally required or as to how stringently legal requirements should be enforced.

Given this ambiguity, not just prosecutors and judges but even many regulators are hesitant to label offenders as criminals, except in egregious circumstances.[27] This reluctance is not attributable entirely to moral concerns about treating regulated firms fairly. Regulators have other, more pragmatic reasons for not prosecuting offenders who are believed not to deserve the stigma of conviction. Regulatory officials value good relations with regulated firms not just because conflict is stressful for all concerned but also because good relations facilitate education and persuasion. The stigma associated with the criminal process may be seen as an unnecessary irritant in many cases and, therefore, as a reason for not prosecuting.

Regulators who shy away from prosecution, because they view it as draconian, may be willing to use less stigmatizing administrative penalties. The attitudes of regulators toward administrative and criminal penalties merit empirical investigation.

Strict v. Absolute Liability

Liability for regulatory offences is virtually always strict in the criminal process, whereas liability in the administrative process may be either strict or absolute. Strict liability offers enterprises that contravene regulatory requirements a defence of due diligence, a defence not available in a regime of absolute liability.

In formal legal terms, liability for almost all environmental and health and safety offences is strict. While many statutes do not explicitly recognize the defence of due diligence, the courts have allowed it to be raised where the legislation is silent.[28] Statutory provisions precluding this defence are rare. The courts have invoked the Charter to strike down such provisions where they apply to offences punishable by imprisonment.[29]

Yet even if criminal liability were absolute according to legislation and precedent, there is reason to doubt that regulators would recommend prosecutions against companies that exercised due diligence. For example, the now defunct factory inspectorate in Britain treated fault as a prerequisite to prosecution, even though liability was absolute according to black-letter law.[30] The explanation for this practice may be that the stigma of prosecution is thought not to be warranted for firms that contravene regulatory requirements through no fault of their own.

While the terms *absolute liability* and *strict liability* are not part of the vocabulary used at the Workers' Compensation Board, the board's practice does recognize the distinction. While liability for most types of violations is strict, employers are often held absolutely liable for committing one of the violations on a "high risk" list adopted recently as part of the new enforcement campaign.

The board's long-standing policy states that an officer shall recommend a penalty for an offence that exposes workers to a serious hazard known to the employer. For other violations, officers are directed to consider recommending a penalty for a repeat violation "when satisfied that persuasive means have failed to gain a meaningful commitment to comply from the employer." By reserving punishment for cases in which an employer is aware of a serious hazard or fails to remedy deficiencies pointed out by an officer, the sanctioning guidelines implicitly declare that liability is not absolute and acknowledge a defence of due diligence.

Violations on the "high risk" list aside, this policy is followed in practice. The written reasons that officers give in support of penalty recommendations are replete with references to management representatives being aware of the instant violation (mean score 6.5 out of 7.0) as the single most important factor in their penalty decisions. Senior board officials follow a similar track in reviewing penalty recommendations.

Some officers follow a different approach for at least some of the violations that appear on the high-risk list. The policy manual directs officers to consider recommending a penalty whenever one of these violations is encountered but does not mandate that a penalty be recommended.[31] Some officers have responded to this guideline by recommending a penalty for the first occurrence of a high-risk violation without inquiring into what steps were taken to ensure compliance. Indeed, 51 per cent of the penalty recommendations submitted in the first six months of 1985 made no mention of the offender being cited on a previous occasion for the same offence. In most of these cases, the written reasons provided by the officer recommending a penalty do not refer to any factors that would suggest the employer had failed to exercise due diligence. Some employers respond to a show-cause letter proposing a penalty for a high-risk violation by arguing that they took reasonable precautions, but they typically find their objection dismissed out of hand. In short, many employers are held absolutely liable for these infractions.

While the board alternates between absolute and strict liability, OSHA unequivocally embraces absolute liability in the imposition of administrative penalties. The efforts made by an employer to comply with regulatory requirements are relevant only to the amount of the penalty assessed, with wilful and repeat violations attracting larger penalties than others.[32]

The defence of due diligence can be a major obstacle in regulatory enforcement. If an accused has been cited on several occasions for the same offence, the prosecution can easily rebut a defence of due diligence by introducing the record of previous infractions. The problem arises where there is no such record with which to meet this defence. Consider, for example, the questions that would arise in a case where an employee allowed a dangerous contaminant to enter the environment for the first or second time. Did the company have proper written procedures? Was the employee adequately trained

and supervised? Was the physical plant designed so as to reduce, to a reasonable level, the risk arising from inevitable human error? Was the equipment properly maintained?

If this sort of wide-ranging inquiry is conducted, the time and energy consumed are likely to deter regulators from resorting to the courts. The alternative to comprehensive investigation is short-cuts, which may produce erroneous conclusions about the exercise of due diligence. Both of these problems are exacerbated by the limited technical expertise of judges and prosecutors.

Administrative and Criminal Procedures

Cumbersome criminal procedures also deter prosecutions for regulatory offences. The conventional criminal process is very labour-intensive. Summonses are served by hand. Officials must appear in court merely to set trial dates. The number of court appearances often multiplies because adjournments are granted. Plea bargains are frequently struck at the court-house, with both inspector and prosecutor in attendance.

Whether a trial is held, a guilty plea entered, or a plea bargain struck, regulators often must educate inexpert prosecutors and judges about the technical aspects of a case so that they are sufficiently informed to make whatever decisions are required. Both Waste Management Branch officials and conservation officers who assist them in preparing cases for prosecution complain that many judges and lawyers lack the expertise required to grapple with the complex evidence in pollution cases. In an attempt to improve the qualifications of prosecutors, a unit that specializes in environmental cases was recently established within the Ministry of the Attorney General.

The show-cause process used by the Workers' Compensation Board avoids much of this work. Notice of proceedings is delivered by mail. On the rare occasion that a hearing is requested, dates are arranged through correspondence or over the telephone. The administrative equivalent of a guilty plea is submitted by letter. If an employer ignores a show-cause letter, the board confirms the proposed penalty and proceeds to collect it. Regulators who are specialists in health and safety do not need a crash course in technical matters.

The standard of proof is also higher in criminal than in administrative proceedings. The criminal standard, which requires proof beyond a reasonable doubt, is sometimes difficult to meet

— for example, in proving sub-lethal deleterious effects in environmental cases. Stringent procedures must be followed in the gathering, custody, transfer, analysis and production of evidence. The administrative process requires proof on a balance of probabilities, a standard much easier to attain.

Criminal proceedings consume time as well as resources. Six months or a year commonly pass between citation of a violation and disposition of a prosecution. The Workers' Compensation Board functions much more quickly. The time lapse from violation to conclusion of show-cause proceedings is rarely more than two or three months, although in the small proportion of cases that are appealed to the commissioners several more months pass before final disposition. Speed is important in regulatory enforcement, because the official who recommends a sanction and the accused firm are cast in the role of adversaries while enforcement proceedings are pending. A co-operative relationship is not likely to be restored until these proceedings run their course.

Although the high cost of the criminal process is a drain on the public purse, these costs are also a disincentive to enforcement. The use of criminal sanctions severely restricts the number of enforcement proceedings launched. Senior regulatory officials shun time-consuming prosecutions because they believe that the energy of field staff is better spent conducting inspections.[33] A dislike for court appearances that disrupt their routine work may lead field officers, the gate-keepers of the enforcement process, not to recommend prosecutions in the first place.[34] Delays arising from long court dockets are an additional disincentive prosecution.

Our conclusion that substituting administrative for criminal procedures facilitates enforcement is buttressed by research on the US Securities Exchange Commission.[35] For some types of offence, the commission may choose among criminal, civil, and administrative sanctions, but only criminal prosecution is available for other types of violations. The percentage of criminal prosecutions that are contested is higher than the percentage of administrative sanctions. A larger proportion of offenders are spared legal action when only cumbersome criminal proceedings are available.

The Size of Monetary Penalties

A comparison of the administrative penalties levied by the Workers' Compensation Board, with the fines assessed by the courts in pollution cases, suggests that board officials view regulatory offences as deserving larger monetary penalties than do legal actors in the criminal justice system. The board has set a minimum penalty of $1,500, an amount three times as large as the average pollution fine.

Penalties imposed by the board may be larger on average than criminal fines in pollution cases because the board imposes much harsher punishment on large companies than small ones. The board's new schedule of penalties, introduced in June 1986, ties the amount of a penalty to the size of the offender's payroll. The amount of a penalty varies also with the severity of the violation and the number of previous penalties. First penalties for non-serious violations range from $1,500 to $4,000, depending on a firm's payroll. First penalties for serious violations range from $3,500 to $15,000, again depending on payroll. A second sanction for a more serious violation within five years of the first, or a second sanction for a less serious violation within three years of the first, results in doubling of the penalty.

Like the Workers' Compensation Board, OSHA adjusts the amount of administrative penalties according to an employer's size. Employers with the largest work-forces receive penalties almost twice as large as those with the least employees.[36]

Unlike these administrative agencies, the courts have not adopted a well-defined sentencing policy to deal with differences in the size and wealth of convicted offenders.[37]

Conclusion

Both the Waste Management Branch and the Workers' Compensation Board rely heavily on persuasion to bring offenders into compliance with the law, but persuasion leaves a large compliance deficit. A substantial number of firms habitually violate regulatory requirements.

Regulators who can impose administrative penalties are much better equipped to tackle this compliance deficit than those who must resort to criminal prosecution. The administrative process responds to risk rather than to harm, does not unduly stigmatize offenders who are thought not to warrant moral opprobrium, applies a standard of absolute as opposed to strict liability in at least some cases, entails minimal operating costs, and imposes monetary penalties large enough to have a reasonable prospect of deterring offenders. Criminal prosecution, the most common sanction of last resort among Canadian regulatory agencies, scores poorly on all these counts.[38]

While offering several advantages over criminal prosecution in regulatory enforcement, administrative penalties are not a panacea. The stigma of criminal sanctions is perhaps the greatest strength of prosecution, as well as one of its greatest limitations. On the one hand, the stigma of conviction may lead legal actors to refrain from prosecuting employers who are thought not to warrant moral opprobrium. On the other hand, this stigma is almost certainly a potent deterrent.[39] More important, the symbolic condemnation of offenders through the criminal process may alter public attitudes about environmental and health and safety offences and thereby enhance compliance with regulatory requirements. These benefits of the criminal process are more likely to be realized if prosecutions are brought under the Criminal Code rather than for regulatory offences, as is the present practice.

These observations suggest that both administrative and criminal penalties should be included in the regulatory arsenal. An enforcement strategy that allows the more appropriate sanction to be chosen on a case-by-case basis offers the best of both worlds. Criminal prosecution is available for the worst offenders. Yet administrative penalties can be assessed against offending firms that would escape punishment entirely if prosecution were the only sanction available.

(c) A Case for Strict Enforcement of Environmental Statutes[†]

John Z. Swaigen

Environmental enforcement agencies throughout Canada rely on a variety of tools to enforce the statutes they administer. These tools include persuasion, formal voluntary compliance programs, terms and conditions attached to licences and permits, binding orders, injunctions, and prosecutions. The purpose of this paper is to argue for greater use of prosecution.

Prosecution is only one of many potential enforcement tools, and each tool has its place. Prosecution is not the appropriate response to all situations, but I do think prosecution is underutilized. This failure to prosecute in appropriate circumstances, in my opinion, leads to extensive delays in pollution abatement and erodes the credibility of law enforcement agencies. I intend to make a case for using prosecution more frequently and to deal with some of the criticisms of prosecution as an enforcement tool that enforcement agencies and writers have raised.

In four years as a lawyer with the Ontario Ministry of the Environment, I have participated in discussions leading to voluntary abatement; in the drafting of formal voluntary compliance programs; in drafting and discussing with companies, licences and permits and the terms and conditions to be attached to them, and in drafting formal Orders to be issued requiring installation of pollution control equipment, clean-up of spills, and other procedures. However, most of my time has been spent prosecuting polluters.

During this process, I have seen numerous examples of prosecution working as an inexpensive, fast way of accomplishing pollution abatement measures. I have seen cases where requests by the Ministry of the Environment have fallen upon deaf ears for years, but the steps requested were taken within a short time after laying charges.

Here are a few examples:

† From *Environmental Enforcement: Proceedings of the National Conference on the Enforcement of Environmental Law*, ed. Linda F. Duncan (Edmonton, AB.: Environmental Law Centre, 1985), pp. 2–7. © John Swaigen. Reproduced by permission of the author. See appendix for notes or references.

In response to requests from the Ministry of the Environment, a company kept promising to install a "baghouse" — a device for controlling emissions of particulate or dust into the air — but kept finding reasons to delay spending the money. Meanwhile, the iron oxides emitted into the air were eating away at the finish of neighbours' vehicles and generally creating a nuisance. Finally, charges were laid. Approximately two months later, the company pleaded guilty to two charges of contaminating the environment and was sentenced. During those two months, it had submitted to the Ministry of the Environment an application for a certificate of approval for a baghouse; the design had been approved by the Ministry and the certificate issued, the company had ordered and paid for a baghouse costing $60,000, and the foundation for this structure had been constructed.

A man was using his rural property as a garbage dump, creating a nuisance and a public health hazard. He ignored repeated requests to stop dumping material and remove the waste from the property. He was charged with operating an illegal waste disposal site and convicted. By the time of sentencing, he had removed all the waste, graded the land, and planted trees and grass.

A company had a punch press which caused vibrations which shook the foundations of neighbouring residences in an urban area. After being charged with installing this punch press without a certificate of approval and emitting a contaminant, since vibration is considered a pollutant in Ontario, the company's board of directors made a decision to relocate in a rural area far from any neighbours. By the trial date, the new plant was almost completely constructed.

A solvent recycling company responsible for obnoxious odours, was charged with emitting contaminants. Two months after the charges were laid, the company pleaded guilty and was fined $10,000. More important, however, after the charges were laid the company retained a consultant to conduct a thorough review of its maintenance and monitoring procedures.

A person who had illegally dumped hazardous waste on someone else's property, pleaded guilty and was fined. Prior to sentencing, he had made complete restitution to that person for all the clean-up costs incurred.

After being charged with offences, a major chemical company and a major paint company both made decisions to discontinue the manufacturing processes causing the problems for which they were being prosecuted. These decisions were made prior to conviction and sentencing.

A major chemical company was prosecuted under the *Occupational Health and Safety Act* for exposing workers to buried wastes which made them feel ill and also under the *Environmental Protection Act* for illegally burying wastes. After charges were laid the company agreed to register a notice on title that the property had been used for waste disposal to protect any future purchasers of the property. It provided the Ministry of the Environment with an extensive list of chemicals that had been buried on various parts of the property over several decades; and it retained a hydrogeological consultant to monitor both groundwater and surface water to ensure that there would be no escape of contaminants from the site.

These are only a few of many cases of companies installing pollution abatement equipment, making repairs, stepping up inspections, and changing operating practices as a result of prosecution. However, effectiveness in deterrence or pollution abatement is not the only argument for prosecution.

There is some conduct that deserves to be punished, and administrative remedies are no substitute for this punishment. When a company chooses to ignore the standards of conduct imposed by the legislature, it gains an unfair advantage over its competitors and unjustly enriches itself at the expense of those who obey the laws. As Paul Weiler writes:

> Punishment of offenders serves as reassurance to the law abiding.... It stands as visible evidence of the State's readiness to perform the guarantees it has made to protect those who will obey it.... Interdependent social life requires mutual adherence to laws which impose sacrifices on all of us in the pursuit of some (more or less) common good. The State makes an implicit bargain with those of its citizens who do make the sacrifices and obey the laws, that, in return, it will do something about the few who do not. In particular, it will deliberately impose a similar sacrifice on the latter. The object is not simply to deter these offenders, though it is that as well; it is also to preserve the morale of the law-abiding by showing them that their sacrifices have not been and will not be in vain.[1]

There are situations where prosecution may not be appropriate. When companies have difficult pollution problems that arise from the age of their plants, limitations in availability of pollution control technology, where immediate rectification is physically or financially impossible, where the problems were not readily foreseeable, prosecution may not be an appropriate first response. Moral suasion or administrative remedies may be more appropriate.

However, where companies are negligent, or violate standards deliberately, where they ignore repeated warnings or requests by authorities, where they know of problems but prefer to spend money on expansion of their business rather than pollution abatement, where they violate permits or orders which they have had an opportunity to shape before these permits or orders have been finalized, prosecution is often the appropriate response.

In my opinion, environmental law enforcement agencies should have guidelines which differentiate between different kinds of problems and the appropriate responses to them. These guidelines should be available to the regulated industries and to the general public. The guidelines should place limits on the length of time the agency will engage in discussions with companies before resorting to more coercive measures. The discussions with companies should be public. Government cannot expect the public or the media to believe that these discussions are leading to the most effective remedy or that enforcement is stringent unless they have access to discussions. These guidelines should set out when prosecution is an appropriate response. I would suggest that the *Sault Ste. Marie*[2] case has provided the answer: when a company has failed to set up and implement an adequate system for control of foreseeable pollution, in the absence of compelling reasons for not doing so, prosecution should be initiated.

I want to deal now with some of the arguments against prosecution put forward by writers and by law enforcement agencies. Traditionally, prosecution has been a last resort for a variety of reasons. In my experience, few of these reasons are valid.

One argument is that the command-penalty (command-control) model of law is not appropriate for pollution offences. Essentially, this boils down to a claim that there should be no prohibitions against pollution. Writers who say it is inappropriate to pass laws prohibiting pollution argue that controlling pollution involves difficult technological, economic, and social issues which require negotiation and compromise. They are more appropriately dealt with through administrative procedures. Some of these writers even suggest that the law should be changed to resemble the law of contracts, so that enforcement agencies and regulated industries could negotiate written binding contracts, and the agency would sue the polluter for breach of contract if it did not comply.

Some of these writers feel that it is wrong to pass laws prohibiting pollution because such prohibitions are unenforceable. Since it is impossible to prevent all pollution, the enforcement agencies ignore the prohibitions in their own legislation, and this "hypocrisy," as these writers perceive it, throws the law into disrepute. Therefore, they would solve this problem by deleting the prohibitions against polluting.

This argument is based on a misunderstanding of how the legislation actually works. None of the legislation in Canada places an absolute prohibition on pollution. The prohibitory sections are surrounded by other sections providing for regulation of pollution through licences, permits, voluntary compliance programs, Orders and financial incentives.

Moreover, all of the prohibitory sections are qualified by exemptions and restrictions. In some cases, the pollution is prohibited only when it has or is likely to have certain harmful effects. In other cases it is prohibited at levels which exceed numerical standards or when it is in a form which contravenes specific regulations. Moreover, the Supreme Court of Canada has added the caveat that these prohibitions do not apply to unforeseeable or uncontrollable pollution.

There is room for both the prohibitions and the other remedies. The prohibitions can be enforced through prosecution where they are violated through carelessness, greed, laziness, or a refusal to give priority to environmental matters.

For infractions that are less foreseeable or more difficult to control, other remedies are provided, and may be more appropriate. Indeed, there is room for "contracts," but as a supplement to other remedies, not a replacement. For example, many of the unenforceable "gentleman's agreements" between regulatory agencies and regulated companies might be replaced by formal contracts, whose breach is visited with financial penalties.

The next argument is that prosecution is too costly and time-consuming compared to informal agreements and administrative remedies. Where a problem can be solved quickly through good-will or moral suasion, there is no question that persuasion is less costly than prosecution, or other coercive methods of obtaining compliance. However, once it becomes necessary to invoke any kind of formal sanction, it is unlikely that prosecution is any more time-consuming or expensive than other tools available to enforcement agencies. An authority wishing to convince a recalcitrant industry to install pollution abatement equipment or to impose a binding order on such an industry, has to do the same groundwork to justify its demands in an administrative process as it must in preparation for prosecution.

Before an agency can impose its will on a resisting industry, it has a legal duty to act fairly. This requires the agency to give notice of its intention, supply reasons for its intended actions, and give the person an opportunity to reply. Most legislation also provides a person to whom administrative action is directed with one or more opportunities for appeal to senior administrators, Ministers, administrative tribunals, and courts.

The administrative process frequently involves the agency in extensive investigations, followed by numerous meetings and studies which may extend over many years. Any administrative action which is not based on solid evidence and fair procedure, is in danger of being rejected by the regulated industry and invalidated by the courts and tribunals.

In contrast, many prosecutions are completed within six months and few take more than a year to come to court.

The length of environmental trials is also cited as a reason for their high cost. While it is true that environmental trials often last two or three days and involve complicated expert testimony, and may last as long as several weeks on very rare occasions, it is important to realize that most cases do not involve a trial at all. In Ontario, during the period from January, 1981 to January, 1984, approximately two-thirds of the people charged with offences under the *Environmental Protection Act* and the *Ontario Water Resources Act* pleaded guilty. When good judgement is exercised in deciding to prosecute, most offenders will realize they are inescapably caught and will plead guilty. Most cases will be resolved without a trial.

The high degree of uncertainty of success in prosecutions is also cited as a reason for avoiding them. Critics claim that the need to prove the case beyond a reasonable doubt and the defence of reasonable care make it extremely difficult to prosecute successfully and make the outcome of a case problematic.

The statistics suggest otherwise. A study done by two university students last year found that the conviction rate of the Ontario Ministry of the Environment between 1975 and 1981 averaged 79 per cent. The Ministry itself keeps its records on a fiscal, rather than a calendar, year basis. These records show that in 1982–1983, the conviction rate was approximately 90 per cent. In 1983–1984, there were 40 convictions and two dismissals.

These statistics suggest to me that when investigation is carried out by experienced investigators, sound judgement is exercised in the decision whether to prosecute, and the trial is handled by experienced counsel, the outcome is highly predictable. Despite the heavy onus on the Crown, evidentiary difficulties, and defences available, a very high level of success will be attained.

Finally, critics argue that the low fines meted out by the courts are evidence of the ineffectuality of the prosecution process. Judging the success of a prosecution by looking at the size of a fine is like judging the quality of a wine by the size of the bottle. First, in a large percentage of cases, the mere laying of the charges results in substantial pollution abatement measures being taken before any sentence is rendered. In fact, the low sentences often reflect the court's recognition of large expenditures that have been made. Earlier, I gave a list of examples of abatement achieved through prosecution. In every one of those cases, the abatement action was taken *before* the Court handed down its sentence.

Secondly, although the fine may be low for the first conviction, companies know that they are vulnerable to higher fines for subsequent convictions. Both the firm and the agency know that having convicted once, the courts are likely to convict again and again if the same conduct continues. Once convicted, few firms are willing to gamble that the agency will turn a blind eye to future violations. They improve their performance after sentencing if they have not already done so before sentencing.

Environmental agencies are reluctant to prosecute for a different reason. They feel that prosecution will create an atmosphere of resentment and distrust and result in less cooperation from regulated industries.

I think the agencies are wrong for two reasons. First, law enforcement is not a popularity contest. The operative word is not "likeability," but respect. Even if prosecution did result in some friction between the regulators and the regulated, the regulators would still have a duty to prosecute flagrant offenders.

Secondly, in my experience, prosecution does not reduce co-operation, it increases it. Despite some short-term stress, discussions leading towards detailed compliance programs continue even while prosecution is pending.

Following prosecution, companies that had a tendency to ignore problems, hide information from the Ministry, or delay finding solutions are much quicker to report problems and consult with Ministry officials. Lines of communication between management and government officials improve after prosecution. Environmental problems are often symptomatic of other sloppy and unproductive practices within a corporation. Prosecution sometimes acts as a catalyst to create changes in management that are beneficial both to the company and to the environment. The new management is often more receptive to the enforcement agency's concerns than the old one.

I have spoken with many of the inspectors who have prosecuted companies over the years. They report that with few exceptions, the co-operation they receive has either been unaffected or has increased.

Moreover, I believe that successful prosecution improves the morale of enforcement agency staff. An inspector who knows that senior officials will back up his recommendations to prosecute and who knows he is part of a team that wins in court will feel better about his job and more confident in his dealings with industry.

Prosecution has benefits that are not available from any administrative remedy. One result of prosecution is that distant head offices tend to take notice. Canada is largely, as we all know, a branch plant economy. Administrators can negotiate with branch plants to little avail because the officials they are dealing with have limited power to authorize major expenditures. The decisions are made elsewhere. As long as the process remains one of polite discussion or

even the application of administrative remedies, the head office will resist providing the resources needed. Launch a prosecution, however, and the resources are suddenly forthcoming.

Secondly, no amount of persuasion or administrative action will bring to light the deliberate and surreptitious activities going on in certain industries the way a prosecution can. Witnesses subpoenaed to testify at trials and defendants seeking leniency from the courts have come forward with important information about unlawful activities in Ontario that probably never would have surfaced in any other context. Through such informers, the Ontario Ministry of the Environment has a much more comprehensive picture, for example, of the extent of illegal waste disposal today than it had in 1980 when the Minister of the day set up a Special Investigations Unit and stepped up prosecutions of offenders in the waste management industry. Any environmental agency that really wants to know the extent of pollution and particularly unscrupulous practices within its jurisdiction would be well advised to launch a vigorous prosecution program.

Thirdly, enforcement enhances credibility. An enforcement agency that will not prosecute may be generally effective in controlling pollution and be well-liked by the regulated industries, but it will have almost no credibility with victims, environmental groups, the general public and the press.

In conclusion, it is likely that in many cases, prosecution is just as cost-effective or even more so than prolonged negotiation or administrative remedies. However, the argument for prosecution does not depend on cost-effectiveness. It is important to uphold the law and to punish wrongdoers even if it isn't cost-effective. The most recent data from Statistics Canada indicate that it costs the public $63,000 a year to keep an offender in a maximum security prison. It would be cheaper to buy habitual criminals condominiums in Hawaii and pay them a salary to live there than to bring them to trial and incarcerate them. We spend this money not because it is cost-effective, but because it is the right thing to do.

Prosecuting flagrant environmental offenders is also the right thing to do. It is likely that every prosecution has a ripple effect throughout the industry and that a single prosecution has a much greater deterrent effect on other potential offenders than administrative remedies. However, even if prosecution had no deterrent effect, it would still be appropriate to punish those who choose by breaking the rules to give themselves an unfair advantage over the rest of the corporate community which chooses to play by the rules.

(d) The Impact of Prosecution of Corporations and Their Officers and Directors upon Regulatory Compliance by Corporations†

Dianne Saxe

Corporate directors and officers must resolve difficult conflicts between regulatory compliance and resource constraints. Is prosecution of corporations and their executives an effective tool to encourage greater regulatory compliance?

THE PROBLEM

Compliance with regulatory statutes in an important element of socially acceptable behaviour by corporations. How can such compliance be achieved? In particular, is prosecution of corporations important to promote regulatory compliance? Is personal prosecution of corporate officer and directors desirable?

Although much has been said about these questions, they have not been investigated empirically. This study examined the impact of prosecution on environmental protection by corporations.

It is difficult to study the impact of prosecution on corporate behaviour. Ideally, one would want to study comparable groups of corporations, operating under controlled conditions which were identical except for the extent of prosecution. One would then monitor their behaviour over time and measure differences in their regulatory compliance.

Unfortunately, such a study is impossible. There are no comparable groups of corporations operating under conditions which vary only in the use of prosecution. It is therefore necessary to approach the problem indirectly.

The first part of this article outlines the theoretical and factual background of prosecution in

the environmental field. The second part reports the results of a survey of corporate officers and directors concerning the effect of prosecution on environmental protection by their companies.

PROSECUTION AND THE THEORY OF REGULATORY COMPLIANCE

Why Is Regulatory Compliance by Corporations Important?

Compliance by corporations with regulatory statutes is increasingly essential to our society. As the Ontario Court of Appeal said in 1982:

> [P]ublic welfare...statute[s] are legion and cover all facets of life ranging from safety and consumer protection to ecological conservation. In our complex, interdependent modern society such regulatory statutes are accepted as essential in the public interest. They ensure standards of conduct, performance and reliability by various economic groups and make life tolerable for all.[1]

However, regulatory statutes cannot "ensure" anything unless they are complied with, and in particular, unless they are complied with by corporations. In the environmental field, for example, corporations are an essential focus of concern over regulatory compliance because:

(1) they are major sources of environmental degradation,[2] although by no means the sole sources,[3]
(2) larger corporations commit a disproportionate number of violations of law;[4]

† From *Journal of Environmental Law and Practice* 1 (1990): 90–95, 98–102, 104–109. Reproduced with permission of Diane Saxe, Saxe Law Office, Toronto.

(3) corporations handle the most dangerous types of pollutants (individuals rarely have the resources or the need to handle heavy metals, radioactive waste, or chemical residues);

(4) the environmental degradation which corporations cause is relatively concentrated and large in scale compared to the activities of individuals,[5] and so corporate activity is more likely to overwhelm natural equilibria;

(5) corporations have very extensive resources with which to reduce pollution, resources which they have accumulated in part by using up clear air, clear water and other public goods; and

(6) the localization and scale of corporate pollution typically make it easier to control than the equivalent amount of pollution from individuals.[6]

In other words, effective protection of the environment depends in large part upon the environmental behaviour of corporations.

Prosecution of Corporations and Regulatory Compliance

. . . .

Prosecution is certainly not a tool which can be used effectively to respond to all environmental problems. It costs far too much, takes too long, requires evidence which is often unavailable, and is frequently grossly out of proportion to the breach itself.[8] Even in the province with the most active prosecution policies, the number of prosecutions is necessarily very low compared to the flood of inspections, of known breaches, and of administrative measures.[9]

Some commentators have pointed out that prosecution and punishment are not always the best ways of changing deviant or undesirable behaviour. ...

. . . .

Ontario's environmental regulators focused primarily upon administrative tools from the early 1970s to the mid 1980s. They used disclosure requirements; permits, for example, to take water to discharge sewage; administrative orders; and environmental assessments. As late as 1984,

the province of Ontario conducted only 54 environmental prosecutions.

Unfortunately, environmental regulation which concentrated almost exclusively on negotiation and administrative remedies also proved to have limited effectiveness. A study for the Law Reform Commission of Canada described the regulatory process of the 1970s as somewhere between "cautious" and "captured" by industry.[11] This should not have been a surprise. Regardless of how one prefers to deal with the majority of regulatory breaches, there is an indisputable need for some enforcement:

> If the regulations were not enforced by the use of sanctions, they would come to be perceived not as regulatory requirements but merely as statements of aspiration.[12]

. . . .

Personal Prosecution Officers and Directors

. . . .

... In *R. v. United Keno Hill Mines*,[25] His Honour Judge Stuart of the Yukon Territorial Court emphasized that prosecution of those persons who shape corporate policy is the most effective method of deterring corporate violations. In his opinion, the possibility of personal prosecution ensures that those responsible for the direction of significant corporations have a strong personal incentive to demonstrate and to require environmentally acceptable behaviour.

The usual argument is that businessmen, professionals, and middle class people are extremely sensitive to the risk of personal prosecution, to the social stigma of a conviction, and to the financial impact of a personal fine. To them, even a remote prospect of imprisonment is a matter of the utmost seriousness. In contrast, prosecution and fining of a corporation leaves its upper echelon policy makers relatively unscathed. Corporation cannot be imprisoned. The fine is simply passed on, either to customers or to shareholders; it is never paid by the directors and officers themselves. If the corporation is a small one and the fine is substantial, the officers may simply dispose of the assets and abandon the corporate shell, leaving the fine unpaid.[26] Corporations may suffer some embarrassment from the adverse publicity of a conviction, but it does not have the same impact that it would upon an individual.

Unfortunately, there has been almost no empirical research to buttress these beliefs. This may be partly due to the fact that while corporate offences are common, prosecution of corporate directors and officers has not been.[27]

THE SURVEY

Hypothesis

The hypothesis of the survey was that prosecution of corporations would increase their regulatory compliance. Regulatory compliance was expected to be particularly likely if corporate directors and officers were liable to personal prosecution.

Method

The survey focused on environmental protection. A questionnaire was developed containing two parts. The first part requested factual information about the individual respondents and their corporation. These questions were the same for all respondents, and included questions about the present environmental behaviour of the corporation and its history (if any) of environmental prosecution. All respondents were asked about their response to three possible policies on the personal prosecution of executives.

The second part of each questionnaire was an experiment. The respondents were divided randomly into three groups, using a table of random numbers. The respondents in each group were asked to assume that regulators had adopted a specified policy on personal prosecution of corporate executives. One group was asked to assume that they could not be personally prosecuted for corporate pollution, the second to assume that they would rarely be personally prosecuted, and the third to assume that they would be prosecuted for any environmental offence for which the corporation were charged. Each assumption was repeated twice before the questions, and at the top of each page.

The respondents were then asked what they would do in five hypothetical situations which pitted environmentally protective behaviour against significant costs for the company. The respondents selected their response from a five-point scale ranging from definitely favouring the environment to definitely limiting costs.

The questionnaire was mailed to approximately one hundred major corporations carrying on business in Canada. ...

The questionnaires were addressed to chairmen of the board and to chief executive officers. ...

... 47 completed questionnaires (24 per cent) were returned, although one was received too late to be included in the results.

The respondents appeared to be representative of the original sample. 2 of the respondents were directors, 7 were officers, and 34 were both directors and officers of their corporations. They represented corporations carrying on business in all parts of Canada and in other countries. This included companies in the business of mining and milling, forestry, pulp and paper, petroleum, chemicals, general manufacturing, retailing, transportation and communications, utilities, and other industrial and commercial activities. 86 per cent of the companies had revenues exceeding $100,000,000 per year.

RESULTS

The survey indicated that prosecution has a strong, statistically significant impact upon the environmental behaviour of corporations, both in actual, past behaviour and in predictions of future behaviour. Corporations which had been prosecuted reported that they spent more on environmental protection than corporations which had not been prosecuted. Corporate executives indicated that, if they could be personally prosecuted for environmental offences, they would ensure that their corporations did more to avoid such offences.

The survey indicates that the most effective policy for regulators, with the fewest adverse side effects, would be one of holding corporate executives personally responsible for corporate environmental offences, but only if they could have prevented the commission of the offence and failed to do so.

The survey also indicated that large corporations now take a number of significant steps to avoid environmental offences.

Part 1: Actual Behaviour

Current Environmental Expenditures

50 per cent of the respondents reported that their corporations spend 1 per cent to 5 per cent of their annual budgets on environmental mat-

ters; 16.7 per cent spend more than that. One forestry and pulp and paper company, which wishes to be known for its environmental leadership, stated that the company spent $250,000, over 50 per cent of its gross revenues, on environmental matters.

95.3 per cent of the respondents reported that the resources devoted to environmental matters by the corporation had increased in the past five years. The average increase was 10 per cent to 50 per cent (46.5 per cent of the respondents); 18.6 per cent of the respondents reported increased of more than 100 per cent. The reasons given for these increases included: (1) increased public awareness and concern; (2) more stringent laws; (3) company commitment to manage its business in an environmentally responsible manner; (4) new scientific information about the danger of contaminants, such as dioxins; (5) improvements in available technology, both process technology and effluent control equipment; (6) switching production to more environmentally benign products; and (7) increased efforts to remove contaminants from effluents and waste streams, such as PCBs and asbestos.

Both the percentage of budget and its rate of increase were greater if the corporation had been prosecuted for an environmental offence. Of the 14 corporations who reported spending less than 1 per cent of their budget on environmental matters, 12 had never been prosecuted. In contrast, 21 of the 28 who spent more than 1 per cent had been prosecuted at least once.[28] Corporations which had been prosecuted also had greater rates of increase in resources devoted to environmental matters, although the difference was not statistically significant.[29]

. . . .

EFFECT OF GOVERNMENT POLICIES RE PERSONAL PROSECUTION

. . . .

All the respondents were asked to consider four possible government policies: (1) a policy of never prosecuting directors and officers personally; (2) a policy of prosecuting directors and officers who authorized pollution, whenever they prosecute the corporation;[34] (3) a policy of prosecuting all the directors and officers who could have prevented pollution but failed to do so, whenever they prosecute the corporation; and (4) a policy of prosecuting all the directors and officers whenever they prosecute the corporation.

They were asked to consider the impact of each of these policies upon three types of behaviour: (1) recommending or voting for greater environmental expenditures by the corporation; (2) resigning their position as director or officer; and (3) ceasing the company's operations or moving out of the jurisdiction.

A policy of never prosecuting directors and officers personally would have relatively little impact upon any of the behaviours.

A policy of prosecuting directors and officers, who authorized pollution, whenever the corporation is prosecuted, would be more effective in increasing environmental expenditures, with relatively few adverse side effects.

A policy of prosecuting all the directors and officers who could have prevented pollution, but had failed to do so, whenever the corporation was prosecuted, was the most effective in increasing environmental expenditures, without increasing the adverse side effects.

The fourth possible policy, one of prosecuting all directors and officers whenever the corporation is charged, would be less effective in

TABLE 1   Executives' Responses to Government Policies On Personal Prosecution

Policy	Vote for more environ. $	Resign	Cease Operations
Never prosecute directors/officers	12.5%	2.4%	2.5%
Prosecute directors/officers who authorize pollution	28.7%	14.6%	10.0%
Prosecute directors/officers who could have prevented pollution, but didn't	31.6%	12.2%	12.5%
Prosecute officers/directors whenever company charged	23.7%	34.1%	35.0%

increasing environmental expenditures, and would have substantial adverse side effects.

The advantages of the third policy, namely that of charging corporate executives only when they failed to prevent offences within their control, were highly significant.[35]

Part 2: The Experiment

The second part of the questionnaire, the experiment, also yielded significant and consistent results.[36] The majority of the respondents would take environmentally protective action regardless of the assumption made. Of the three groups, respondents who were asked to assume that they would always be prosecuted when an offence occurred were more likely to report that they would bring environmental problems to the attention of the board of directors and to take action to resolve them than were respondents who were asked to assume that they were immune from personal prosecution. However, it was the second group, those asked to assume that personal prosecution was possible but not inevitable, who were the most likely to report that they would bring environmental problems to the attention of the board of directors and to take action to resolve them.

The first hypothetical question asked respondents to

> Assume that new research shows that waste water from the corporation's main operation is reaching a nearby lake and may promote cancer among the 1,000 people who eat fish or drink water from the lake. No one outside the corporation yet knows this.
>
> It is illegal to impair the quality of water; it is also illegal to adversely affect the health of any person. Staff advise that the only equipment which can eliminate the increased cancer risk will reduce the company's profits by 50% for the next two years.
>
> In your company, would this information be put before the board of directors?
>
> Would you recommend or vote to install the equipment in view of its cost and the fact that the research is not conclusive?

95.2 per cent of the respondents would be likely to put this information before the board of directors; 64.3 per cent would be likely to install the equipments.

The second question asked respondents to

> Assume that an environmental audit shows that one of the company's profitable operations has a significant risk of serious spills of toxic materials, which are stored there in large quantities. Some minor spills have occurred there in the past, but no major spills. An uncontrolled spill could cause major, possibly irreversible, environmental damage to a nearby river, and could endanger human life in the town. If there is a spill, environmental regulations are likely to consider prosecution.
>
> Staff advise that the only way to control a major spill would have a capital cost equal to the annual profits of that operation. The company is considering moving the operation in two years' time. It is not possible to move it this year.

Respondents were asked what should be done "this year".

95.2 per cent of the respondents would be likely to put this information before the board of directors; 82.1 per cent would be likely to close the operation immediately (35.9 per cent) or install the spill control system (46.2 per cent).

The third question asked respondents to

> Assume that your company has a very large and valuable machine that was the state of the art when installed. It is ten years old and its remaining useful life is another 10 years. It has now been 75% depreciated. The machine generates substantial noise and vibration. The company has tried to reduce the noise by ordering the doors to be kept closed, but the employees keep opening the doors to get fresh air. The neighbours in this mixed industrial and residential area frequently complain that the noise and vibration deprive them of sleep, give them headaches, interfere with enjoyment of their property and cause their houses to settle. There are other noises in the area, but the neighbours say that your company's noise bothers them the most.
>
> A new machine has just become available, 50% more expensive than the original machine, that will do the same job with almost no noise or vibration. It is illegal to cause material discomfort to others or to damage their property.

70.7 per cent of the respondents would be likely to put this information before the board of directors; 61 per cent would be likely to install the equipment, considering, among other things,

TABLE 2   The Impact of Assumptions about Personal Prosecution on Environmentally Protective Actions

Assume:	Never prosecuted personally	Rarely prosecuted personally	Always prosecuted personally	F	Probability
Envir. Protection Score (out of 37)	27.87 (8)	33.08 (12)	30.87 (15)	4.559	.018

the cost of the new machine and the nature of area.

The fourth question asked respondents to

Assume that your company can reduce the likelihood of spills of all toxic materials by 50%. The spill reduction program would use funds originally earmarked for plant expansion, and so would delay the expansion by one year. The expansion is important if the company is to maintain its market share. It is not possible to proceed with both the spill reduction program and the expansion in the same year.

60 per cent of the respondents would be likely to recommend or vote to delay the plant expansion so that the spill reduction program could proceed immediately.

The fifth question asked respondents to

Assume that the corporation has had a long dispute with the government over air pollution from the plant. On bad days, the pollution causes vegetation damage, sore throats and watery eyes to nearby residents. Staff advise that they have reduced pollution as much as they readily can, but that further reductions cannot be accomplished without installing scrubbers.

The scrubbers are so expensive that they would increase the capital cost of the plant by 20%; the company has numerous other demands for the same funds for everything from wage increases to retooling. Government staff continue to press for further reductions in pollution.

Having considered the high cost of the scrubbers, 87.2 per cent of the respondents would be likely to recommend or vote to buy them.

The differences between the three experimental groups were not statistically significant when each question was considered separately,[37] but were highly significant when all questions

were considered together. An "Environmental Protection Score" out of 37 was calculated for each respondent.[38] Executives who assumed that they might be prosecuted had the highest scores.

CONCLUSIONS

This survey provides empirical evidence to support the decision of environmental regulators to give greater emphasis to prosecution, both of corporations and of their officers and directors. Corporations which have been prosecuted allocate significantly more of their resources to environmental protection than do corporations which have not been prosecuted. In addition, corporate attention to environmental matters, and corporate efforts to avoid pollution, would be greater if corporate executives faced the possibility of personal prosecution for pollution.

However, the second-rate showing of a policy of alwaysprosecuting executives underscores the importance of restricting personal liability to those with influence and control over the commission of environmental offences. As the Law Reform Commission of Canada said in *Criminal Responsibility for Group Action:*[39]

The simple imposition of criminal responsibility will not achieve regulatory aims where it does not reinforce realistic patterns of responsibility within the organizational structure of the corporation.

The survey may also provide empirical support for the social value of the due diligence defence. The higher environmental protection score of corporate executives who face only the possibility of prosecution, can most plausibly be interpreted as reflecting an assumption that those who do "the right thing" will not be chosen for prosecution. Only in this way do individual executives have the strongest inducement to prefer environmental protection over cost saving. As

Dickson J. (as he then was) said in *R. v. Sault Ste. Marie:*[40]

> If a person is already taking every reasonable precautionary measure, is he likely to take additional measures, knowing that however much care he takes, it will not serve as a defence in the event of breach? If he has exercised care and skill, will conviction have a deterrent effect upon him or others? Will the injustice of conviction lead to cynicism and disrespect for the law, on his part and on the part of others?

(e)   Weak Environmental Law Enforcement in Canada: A well-kept secret

David Donnelly and Leah Hagreen[†]

The Failure in Enforcement

Canada deserves a failing grade for enforcement of its environmental laws. From province to province, the number of inspections, prosecutions, convictions and amounts of fines collected has plummeted over the past decade. The federal government's performance in enforcing its environmental laws has declined even more precipitously. In virtually every jurisdiction, governments have robbed their environment departments, depriving them of the resources required to adequately enforce their laws. Poor enforcement is a clear compromise of environmental protection, even though governments admit that prompt and certain enforcement of environmental laws serves as a general deterrent to others who might be tempted to break environmental laws and regulations (Compliance Guideline, 1995). This paper is an initial foray, an overview and assessment of the fourteen Canadian jurisdictions that have the major responsibility for enforcing environmental laws.

Enforcement History

Enforcement of environmental standards can be traced to the epidemics of water-borne diseases that swept North America and Europe in the nineteenth century. In 1832, a cholera epidemic wiped out one-seventh of the population of Montreal, and 20,000 people throughout Canada. In response, the first boards of health were established along with public health legislation authorizing the cleaning up of fetid urban living conditions (Bilson, 1984).

Starting in 1884, discharge of polluting materials into watercourses, water supplies, sewage works and private septic systems was governed by the first *Public Health Act* (Estrin and Swaigen, 1979). Starting at the turn of the twentieth century, landowners abutting waterways began asserting their common law rights to the use and enjoyment of waterfronts. These actions were infrequent, and protected private property for the most part, with the protection of public resources happening merely as a collateral benefit.

In Ontario, two successful common law actions by riparian landowners downstream from municipally operated sewage treatment plants (*Stephens* v. *Richmond Hill*, 1955; and *Burgess* v. *Woodstock*, 1955) prompted the government of Premier Leslie Frost to create the *Water Resources Commission Act* (Estrin and Swaigen, 1993: 530). This Act, and those that followed in other provinces, were accompanied by rules to limit discharges, first into water, and then into air and soil. All provinces now have some form of environmental protection legislation that governs undertakings such as sewage and septic

† An original article contributed by David Donnelly and Leah Hagreen. David Donnelly is the Legal Director for Environmental Defence Canada. He has appeared before the Ontario Municipal Board regarding the Oak Ridges Moraine and the O'Connor Inquiry into Ontario's tainted water supply. Leah Hagreen is a consultant with Lourie & Love for Environmental Defence Canada on environmental enforcement issues. Ms. Hagreen works with Pollution Probe on mercury policy, and with the Clean Air Foundation, developing and implementing public engagement programs to improve air quality in Canada.

systems and waste disposal sites, and each uses enforcement instruments such as "control orders", "stop orders", "remedial orders" and "preventative orders" to protect the environment from illegal discharges (AEPA, 1995: ss. 7, 8, 17 and 18). Enshrined in each statute is the requirement that industrial facilities must obtain a Certificate of Approval: in effect, a licence to pollute. If a certificate's limits are exceeded, EPA statutes also state it is the right of government and the public to prosecute the offenders.

The Importance of Enforcement

Prosecutions are the foundation of most environmental compliance and enforcement programs across Canada. A prosecution is generally defined as an action undertaken by the government (the Crown), in which one or more charges are laid against one or more defendants. Charges sometimes lead to court cases that can result in fines or imprisonment[1] being imposed upon the offender.

Detecting and prosecuting pollution offences committed by governments, industries and individuals is a complicated process that relies on two types of programs: those that examine the actions of governments and companies to determine whether they are in "compliance" with environmental laws, and those that ensure "enforcement" when laws are broken. Consultation, routine and spot inspections, data collection and monitoring are some of the tools of compliance monitoring; but enforcement programs rely on investigations, warnings, orders and, ultimately, prosecutions to compel compliance.[2]

Enforcement is an essential partner to compliance; it ensures that polluting an environment is a serious offence. The failure to prosecute has the effect of excusing unlawful behaviour, and it has the added effect of diminishing any urgency for industries to stop polluting (Swaigen, 1985). The benefit to society of proper enforcement cannot be overstated. A vigorous prosecution policy can have a significant, positive influence on corporate behaviour. Anyone who has sat in a boardroom, listening to a corporate crisis management meeting that involved possible litigation and negative media coverage, accepts this premise as common sense.

According to Mr. Justin Dubin, in his report on aviation safety:

> Enforcement should play an important role in accident prevention programs. It is presently not

doing so, and that is why the aviation community does not take enforcement seriously, and that is one of the reasons why the Canadian aviation safety record is not as good as it should be (Saxe, 1990a).

There is strong reason to believe this effect is no less substantial for environmental compliance (Saxe, 1990a). Hence, the importance of monitoring and improving Canada's enforcement record. Given this importance, Canadians have a right to expect effective and vigorous enforcement of their environmental laws.

Despite this importance, many provinces in Atlantic Canada and the prairies do not rely on enforcement; instead they use alternative means of achieving compliance, including educating and persuading polluters, and using formal programs to gain voluntary compliance, among others. The question that has yet to be resolved is whether a voluntary approach is more effective in winning real compliance than an aggressive enforcement program.

Assessing Enforcement

Even in provinces where enforcement is done, knowing whether environmental laws are fully and fairly enforced is difficult because there are few performance measures of aggressive enforcement. For too long, the enforcement of environmental laws has occurred almost as if by happenstance, depending upon the political administration of the day. This piecemeal approach to enforcement is unjustifiable, knowing that prosecutions naturally have a deterrent effect even if they are unsuccessful. This deterrence can increase the likelihood of cooperation by an offender, especially since compliance programs are often negotiated while a prosecution is pending (Swaigen, 1985).

Undermining the deterrence effect of prosecutions is the current trend to promote and adopt voluntary compliance agreements in administrative programs.[3] These agreements are advertised as a constructive, less costly and more effective alternative to the traditional "command and control" means of limiting pollution. And yet, the primary strength of these agreements — flexibility and lack of certainty — is also their chief weakness.

Peter Krahn, federal Head of the Inspections Division for the Pacific and Yukon Region, has documented a number of failings with the voluntary monitoring and compliance programs he supervises. The industrial sectors that relied solely upon self-monitoring or voluntary compliance had a compliance rating of 60%, versus a 94% average compliance rating for those industries that were subject to federal regulations combined with a consistent inspection program (North American Working Group, 2001). It is no wonder industries lobby government for less regulation and enforcement, and at the same time press for greater use of voluntary measures.

Finally, dramatic cuts to the enforcement budgets in many provinces have underscored the need to produce conclusive evidence that stricter enforcement leads to overall improvements in environmental quality.[4] The first step in proving this common sense proposition is the development of indicators of effective environmental enforcement, which is fitfully underway (Castrilli, 1999; Swanson, 1999).

The Benefits of Enforcement

While the evidence so far has been piecemeal, concentrated inspection efforts (leading to prosecutions) have been shown to result in a high level of compliance, thereby reducing emissions and improving overall environmental quality. For example, in the 1980s, British Columbia's pulp and paper industry had been discharging acutely lethal effluents into freshwater and marine environments that supported valuable stocks of salmon, other fish and shellfish. Persistent dumping of chemicals culminated in the dramatic closure of 1,200 square km of crab and shellfish harvesting areas in 1988 and 1989.[5]

A series of initiatives were undertaken to reduce the amount of effluent being discharged. An intensive inspection and investigation program was undertaken, targeting six mills in the Greater Vancouver region. The benefits of the program were immediately felt; "discharges of acutely lethal effluent immediately fell off — and continued to do so in essentially three waves of reductions, under the pressure of continuing inspections, as successive mills implemented physical and operational changes — until a level of nearly zero effluent discharges was achieved in 1998 (a 94% reduction from 1991 levels)" (North American Working Group, 2001: 3-34).

The Consequences of Poor Enforcement

The number of inspections conducted and enforcement actions taken is not the only mea-

sure of success. The inspections also have to be adequate and comprehensive. Many jurisdictions have developed checklists to track the requirements of a permit and a facility being reviewed for compliance. In Quebec, the Ministry of Environment has established procedures that specify everything from dress code, hours of inspection and how to deal with uncooperative owners (North American Working Group, 2001: 3-25).

Failure to conduct adequate inspection, testing and enforcement programs can lead to tragic consequences, as witnessed in Walkerton, Ontario. In the summer of 2000, the municipal water supply was contaminated by surface waters that had entered the municipality's well after heavy summer rains. The contamination was known by the operator of the municipality's water treatment equipment, and by the laboratory that tested the town's water samples. The results were not reported to the Medical Officer of Health; seven people in Walkerton died, and 2,000 became ill from drinking water contaminated with a lethal strain of *E. coli*.

In 1990, the Government of Ontario had initiated the Sewage and Water Inspection Program (SWIP) to ensure the province's high priority water treatment plants were inspected. Between 1990 and 1994, municipal waterworks were inspected on a bi-annual basis. Following 1994, government resources were cut, priorities changed and the inspection cycle was reduced to once every four years. By 1998, inspections were optional. In his final submissions to the Walkerton Inquiry, counsel for Environmental Defence Canada concluded:

> More detailed scrutiny of the Walkerton waterworks in 1998 would likely have resulted in the issuance of an order [a "control order", the normal precursor to prosecution]. This in turn may have helped prevent the events that occurred. The incompetence of the management was extensive and not subtle enough to escape detection under a system of more rigorous review and inspection (Solokov, 2001: 22).

Priorities can change quickly. After the tragedy at Walkerton, all 600 Ontario municipal water treatment plants were inspected in 2000 and 2001. MOE officials confirm that after the Walkerton tragedy occurred, inspections will now be conducted on an annual basis. In addition, a SWAT team of 140 inspectors and investigators has been deployed with a mandate to conduct 1,000 inspections each year, and to vigorously prosecute offenders.[6]

In the absence of a tragedy like Walkerton, it is difficult for decision-makers to prioritize the "right" issues for enforcement. Often, they have to choose between competing scientific opinions and interest groups. While most of Canada is rapidly deploying strict water quality standards and inspection programs, other priorities are being neglected. For example, the Ontario Medical Association estimates that in 2000, approximately 1,900 premature deaths occurred in Ontario as a result of air pollution. Poor air quality resulted in another 9,800 hospital admissions, 13,000 emergency room visits and 47 million minor illness days attributable to air pollutants caused by humans. These numbers are expected to increase substantially by the year 2015.[7]

The majority of these illnesses are attributable to the concentration of small particles in the air, such as PM_{10}[2] (Particulate Matter with a particle size of 10 microns), with ozone accounting for about half the hospital admissions and emergency room visits. These health damages equate to a total of about $600 million in costs to the health-care system and another $560 million in direct losses to employers and employees. This represents over $1 billion in direct costs to the people of Ontario. If one uses conservative estimates of the value of pain and suffering, and loss of life, these add a staggering $5 billion and $4 billion respectively to the total. This gives a total annual economic loss of $10 billion in 2000, rising to $12 billion by 2015. Despite this warning, little monitoring and enforcement is being done to detect and prevent ground level ozone emissions.

Prosecution of Offences — The Nuts and Bolts

Canada's *Constitution* divides responsibility for environmental protection between the federal government (for example, fisheries) and the provincial governments (wildlife). These governments are also responsible for different types of environmental enforcement. Generally, the federal government is responsible for enforcing laws pertaining to fisheries, migratory birds, national protected areas such as national parks, manufacture, trade and transport of toxic and hazardous materials and ozone-depleting substances. Provincial governments are responsible for the management of natural resources, including forests, wildlife, and authorization and verification of all activities likely to have an impact on the environment,

such as emissions and hazardous wastes[8] (North American Working Group, 2001). It is this last responsibility that has ensured that provincial governments have historically conducted most of the environmental prosecutions in Canada.

An environmental prosecution inevitably starts with an offence, such as an emission of pollutants that exceeds a permitted level or that causes harm to the environment. Prosecutions may not be initiated for some types of contaminants, even at very high concentrations (for example, CO_2), whereas the discharge of very low levels of acutely toxic substances may trigger a prosecution. Even though a wide range of chemicals and toxic substances are regulated, there are still some types of emissions that are almost never prosecuted, even though they may be harmful, such as mercury.

A discharge of a harmful substance into the environment can take many forms. Offences that can be prosecuted range from direct discharge of a toxic substance in a watercourse, to a spill of a toxic material from the back of a truck. Generally, offences against the environment occur from what are commonly called point sources, such as a smokestack or effluent lagoon. By and large, pollution events from point sources are well known and are relatively easily inspected. In contrast, polluted run-off from paved surfaces or farms, for example, is far less easy to detect and is rarely prosecuted.

Inspections: The Starting Point

Inspections are usually the starting point for an enforcement action and are considered the primary component of any compliance program. Inspectors, or members of the public, may be thought of as the cop on the beat, first on the scene of an offence against the environment. In most cases, investigators are the sleuths that put together a case by painstakingly gathering evidence to prove that an offence has occurred. In some cases, this requires the investigator to prove that the accused intended for the offence to occur, and that the emission caused actual harm to the environment.

In general, inspections are on-site searches of facilities to ensure compliance with the law. Most often, this involves a review of the operation, maintenance, waste disposal and emissions of the subject facility. Almost all inspections will involve a data-gathering exercise to ensure compliance with the terms of the Certificate of

Approval — the licence to pollute. It is becoming common for authorities to require industries to conduct self-monitoring and to regularly report this information: for example, in monitoring pulp and paper effluents. Although this form of "honour" system can lead to abuse, there are serious consequences for failing to provide accurate information that are potentially more serious than being convicted for polluting. Providing government with a false or misleading report is now punishable by $1,000,000 and/or up to six months imprisonment [CEPA s. 114].

Who Is Inspected?

The first step in establishing an inspection program is determining what facilities are at a high priority for review. Prosecution agencies such as Environment Canada create an annual Inspection Plan that establishes a priority list of facilities for inspection based on the degree of threat posed to the environment and human health, the age of the regulation (newer regulations receive greater attention), current levels of compliance and the past level of inspection.

It is obvious that this list is subjective, leaving room for decision-makers to exercise discretion. Typically this discretion has resulted in different priorities in different areas. For example, federal inspectors in the Ontario region have tended to place greater emphasis on enforcement of industrial pollution regulations under the *Canadian Environmental Protection Act*, whereas inspectors in the Pacific and Yukon regions have set a high priority on enforcement of the *Fisheries Act* (North American Working Group, 2001: 3-21).

Determining who gets inspected is done in different ways across Canada, but is normally done by assessing environmental risk factors (ERF). ERF can include any number of factors, but normally they include (1) the risk that the substance or activity presents to the environment or to human health; and (2) the compliance record of the individual or company (Environment Canada, 1988). Once the ERF for types of activities has been established, regulators can develop guidelines or rules for the frequency of inspecting different types of facilities. For example, guidelines in British Columbia set objectives requiring that every site be physically inspected at least once every three calendar years, that low risk sites be inspected every three to six months, high risk sites be inspected bi-monthly;

and sites deemed to be in non-compliance be inspected every month [B.C. Ministry of the Environment, 1994: 5]. As impressive as this appears, it has been noted that in British Columbia, the number of inspections is declining, while self-monitoring and reporting are becoming more common (Castrilli, 1999).

Finally, the indicators used to conduct an inspection are critical to the success of any inspection program. In Ontario until 1995, water-sampling tests conducted by the MOE covered microbial parameters including *E. coli*. However, Drinking Water Surveillance Program documents confirm that at the beginning of 1996, the testing of microbial parameters was discontinued. This weakened water quality and trend-monitoring efforts, and it also undermined public safety and health.

In the same year, the provincial government transferred the responsibility for municipal water testing to private laboratories. Prior to handing over the duty to private labs, public labs were required to alert local Ministry officers when problems were detected. Labs would in turn warn public health officials, who could issue boil-water advisories. No such rule was in place for the private labs, which created a gap in the regulations for alerting the public to unsafe drinking water. This gap prevented the timely notification by authorities of the contamination of Walkerton's water supply.

Measuring Inspection Performance

The easiest criterion for evaluating the effectiveness of a given inspection program is the number of inspections. It stands to reason that the greater the number of inspections, the wider the regulatory net is cast. As will be discussed below, the depth and thoroughness of inspections is another key measure of effectiveness (quality rather than quantity); but by and large, provinces that conduct a larger number of inspections have a more effective enforcement program.

Given the importance of inspections in relation to enforcement, it is shocking to observe the low numbers of inspections conducted each year across Canada. More alarming is the refusal of nearly half of Canada's provinces to compile and release the number of inspections conducted.

Table 1 is the result of a review of Canada's provinces.

In Ontario, the number of inspections has decreased 34% since 1996. This decrease has

TABLE 1 Inspections Reported Across Canada

Government	# Inspections	Years*	Avg. # Inspections 1995–2000	Avg. # Inspections 1990–1994
Federal	3,305	1999/00	1,902	1,986
British Columbia	1,604	1998/99	1,744	3,498
Alberta	NA	NA	NA	NA
Saskatchewan	NA	NA	NA	NA
Manitoba	4,770	1999/00	5,105	6,051
Ontario	4,400	1999/2000	4,400	NA
Quebec	9,53	2000	10,584	NA
New Brunswick	NA	NA	NA	NA
Nova Scotia	NA	NA	NA	NA
Prince Edward Island	NA	NA	NA	NA
Newfoundland and Labrador	NA	NA	NA	NA
Northwest Territories	177	1999	114	113
Nunavut	53	1999/00	53	NA
Yukon	59	2000	47	NA

* The most recent years available

occurred despite the fact that over 20,000 pollution occurrences were reported to the Ontario Ministry of the Environment in one year, as noted by the Ontario Provincial Auditor. In addition, there are approximately 220,000 Certificates of Approval in Ontario, and almost 8,000 new certificates issued each year. The Auditor has estimated it costs $80,000 in salaries to monitor just one mining operation (Office of the Provincial Auditor, 2000: 116).

The federal government has dramatically increased its inspections after being condemned by the Standing Legislative Committee on Sustainable Development for not enforcing the Acts for which it is responsible (Caccia, 1998). In 1998/99, the federal government conducted 1,555 inspections, fewer than half the number conducted in 1999/2002. The rate of inspections has fallen dramatically in British Columbia, given that the province conducted over 4,000 inspections in 1995/96. Nova Scotia's inspection effort is reflected in the fact that it employs a single inspector.

It should be noted that the public plays an important but limited role in detecting and reporting suspected violations. For a number of reasons, regulators are ambivalent about the role the public plays in enforcement. For example, each year, over 20,000 pollution occurrences are reported to the Ontario Ministry of Environment, some of which constitute significant violations. If inspectors chase each complaint, however, there would not be sufficient staff resources to conduct programmed or spot checks of known, repeat offenders and polluters. When these reports are not investigated, members of the public become justifiably upset, believing that government is ignoring their legitimate concerns.

Investigations: Gathering the Evidence

Once a report of a suspected violation has been prepared, it is forwarded to an Investigations and Enforcement Branch (IEB) office. A supervisor must then determine whether an investigation is warranted. Investigations are done to determine whether reasonable and probable grounds exist for laying charges. In some provinces, inspectors are given the same powers and responsibilities as investigators, such as the powers of search and seizure. If enough evidence of an offence is collected, a written recommendation to prosecute is forwarded to the Legal Services Branch of a Ministry or a local prosecutor.

Number of Investigations

Regarding enforcement generally, many provinces do not report the number of investigations in a given year. Table 2 is the result of a review of Canada's provinces.

By far the most radical swings in enforcement effort occur when investigations are done.

TABLE 2 Enforcement Effort Across Canada — Investigations

Government	# Investigations	Years*	Avg. # Investigations 1995–2000	Avg. # Investigations 1990–1994
Federal Government	64	1999/00	56	139
British Columbia	NA	NA	NA	NA
Alberta	NA	NA	NA	NA
Saskatchewan	NA	NA	NA	NA
Manitoba	603†	1999/00	NA	NA
Ontario	1,159	1999	1,054	1,532
Quebec	1,018	1998‡	NA	NA
New Brunswick	NA	n/a	NA	NA
Nova Scotia	NA	NA	NA	NA
Prince Edward Island	n/a	NA	NA	NA
North West Territories	78	2000	78	NA
Nunavut	5	2000	5	NA
Yukon	NA	NA	NA	NA

* The most recent years available

† Manitoba does not list formal investigations, but publishes "Complaints responded to".

‡ This reporting was a one-time report to the North American Commission on Environmental Cooperation Annual Report.

For example, the federal government performed just eight investigations in 1995/96.

It is interesting to note that the number of charges laid in a province in a given year roughly reflects the number of investigations undertaken. In Ontario since 1991, there were a greater number of charges laid than inspections undertaken in five of those years. This statistic is similar in other provinces that reported the number of investigations. This outcome indicates that when serious complaints are investigated, there is a very high probability that an offence has occurred. This begs the question why more investigations are not undertaken, and also why investigations are the least reported statistic among the measures of enforcement effort.

Prosecution: The Best Measure of Enforcement

The best measure of enforcement success is the number of prosecutions: charges laid, parties charged, convictions and amounts of fines levied for environmental offences. The final enforcement effort lies in prosecuting, obtaining fines and convictions. It is not clear, however, that Canadian prosecutions have fundamentally reflected the number of serious environmental offences, nor is it clear that the effort to obtain prosecutions has been even across Canada.

Comparing Jurisdictions: A Choppy Sea of Enforcement Information

All across Canada, governments are pursuing different enforcement agendas. Enforcement across the country is conducted in such an uneven and piecemeal fashion that our national enforcement can only be described as dysfunctional. Alberta lurched from 7 to 51 convictions in the period 1999/00 to 2000/01, a swing that defies explanation. In Ontario, the total number of prosecutions has ridden a rollercoaster ride, from 315 in 1992 to a low of 143 in 1996, ascending again to 368 in 1999. Some provinces, including Nova Scotia, Newfoundland and Labrador, P.E.I. and New Brunswick, do not seem to be prosecuting — except in the most extreme cases. Enforcement levels are so uneven across Canada that conservative estimates indicate an Ontario rate of convictions at least 35 times higher than the federal government (Caccia, 1998). In 1992, Saskatchewan actually did not record a single conviction in an entire year, while other provinces have collected less than $10,000 in fines for all environmental offences.

The amount of the average fine is an important indicator of the seriousness of offences prosecuted and the deterrent effect of such prosecutions. In Alberta several years ago, the government obtained a conviction against Bovar Inc.

TABLE 3   Enforcement Effort Across Canada — Convictions, Prosecutions, Charges and Fines

Government	Convictions	Prosecutions	Charges	Fines	Year*
Federal	10	NA	NA	97,000	2000/01
British Columbia	NA	60	298	223,666	1999/00
Alberta	51	NA	54	539,692†	2000/01
Saskatchewan	14	NA	28	2,755	2000
Manitoba	175	NA	187	57,048	1999/00
Ontario	288‡	NA	805	1,500,000	1999
Quebec	113	NA	NA	241,700	2000
New Brunswick	19	23	27	35,233	NA
Nova Scotia	8	9	9	9,895	2000
Prince Edward Island	NA	NA	30	NA	2000/01
Newfoundland and Labrador	NA	NA	NA	NA	NA
Northwest Territories	0	0	NA	NA	1999/00
Nunavut	0	0	0	0	1999/00
Yukon	2	NA	NA	200	2000

* The most recent years available
† Alberta obtained judgments for $212,075 in 1999/00.
‡ Reported as "Parties Convicted".

for release of toxic substances that carried a $625,000 fine. By way of contrast, its neighbour, Manitoba, wins average fines of less than $400. Overall, Ontario courts have imposed fines greater than those of the rest of the country combined (including the federal government). There is no rational way to explain these discrepancies. It is a clear sign that jurisdictions treat violations of their environmental statutes differently. While a permissive or cooperative approach to dealing with minor violations is expected locally, the decision by some provinces to excuse serious pollution offences undermines the efforts of others competing for scarce investment dollars. Lax enforcement can make some provinces appear to be "pollution havens" to investors.

Adding to the lack of understanding about enforcement is that many provinces simply do not report the number of investigations, prosecutions or convictions in a given year. Table 3 is the result of a review of Canada's provinces.

Evaluating Canada's Enforcement Program

It is a commonly held belief that the enforcement of Canada's environmental laws is inadequate. According to Diane Saxe, former prosecutor for the Ontario Ministry of the Environment, "Even in provinces with the most

active prosecution policies, the number of prosecutions is very low compared to the volume of inspections of known breaches, and administrative measures such as control orders or formal warnings" (Saxe, 1990b).

Despite the importance of enforcement to environmental protection, and the over-riding right of the public to know the effectiveness of environmental enforcement, the most surprising finding of this research is the unwillingness of some governments to provide basic enforcement information. Most do not publish or post on the internet their annual compliance or enforcement reports. Some jurisdictions do not even attempt to compile them. Only Manitoba can claim to have a comprehensive, coherent and accessible environmental enforcement information registry. Governments must not only stop hiding this information from their citizens, they also need to have the information compiled in a form that can be used by government officials to assess the effectiveness of its own regulations.

Resources Are Critical

Prosecutions do not happen without adequate funding. Resources are needed to carry out inspections, to lay charges, prepare cases and prosecute them in court. However, across Canada, budgets for environmental departments have been slashed over the past five years: Environment Canada was reduced by 30%; Quebec by 64.9%; Newfoundland by 60%; New Brunswick by 50%; Alberta by 37%; Ontario by 43%; and the cuts have continued (Gallon, 1998). Enforcement staff and resources such as laboratories, cameras and vehicles are the essential components of an effective enforcement capacity. Staff levels that used to be marginal are now dangerously thin. Budget cuts have left a legacy of reduced staff, unfilled positions and patchwork monitoring and compliance programs. Prosecutors rely on inspectors to compile their briefs and verify that regulations have been complied with. The federal government employs just eight inspectors for the entire Quebec region. This lack of staff forces the department to arbitrarily limit its mandate. According to one federal staff member: "In the Quebec Region, we enforce 32 acts and regulations. Over the next year, 10 of these 32 acts and regulations will be a high priority, some will be medium to low priority, and 16 will not be enforced at all" (Gonthier, 1998). For several years, New Brunswick has employed only one investigator for the entire province.

How vast is the gap between current enforcement capacity and the resources needed to have environmental laws enforced? In 1998, the House of Commons Standing Committee on Environment and Sustainable Development ("the Committee"), Chaired by Mr. Charles Caccia, MP, found the federal enforcement program to be "woefully understaffed". Why? There are 60 enforcement personnel enforcing federal laws in Canada, complemented by 22 support staff at the national Office of Enforcement. An internal study prepared by Environment Canada conservatively estimated that over 300 full-time staff would be needed for effective enforcement (Caccia, 1998). Anecdotal evidence in the study suggested that the provinces are continuing to further cut their enforcement capacity.

Alternative Penalties and Sentencing

While some governments are making efforts to correct historically poor enforcement performance, some are seeking alternatives to vigorous enforcement programs. Enforcement officials in government frequently complain that there are insufficient resources to launch a significant number of prosecutions because of their cost and time needed to take them through the courts. Additionally, administrators would prefer that in certain circumstances, courts could impose penal-

ties that benefited the environment, as opposed to the traditional payment of a fine into Consolidated General Revenue.

Federal administrators have testified that the imposition of an Administrative Monetary Penalty (AMP) would improve enforcement performance (House of Commons, 1995). The Ontario Ministry of the Environment is considering an Administrative Monetary Penalty (AMP), a U.S.-inspired enforcement tool somewhat comparable to a parking ticket that results in a large number of small fines. The benefits of administrative penalties for governments lacking resources are clear, and include:

- Consume fewer resources and less time;
- Allow for enforcement on a wider scale;
- Lead to quicker resolutions;
- A smaller procedural burden; and
- Preserve resources for bigger cases.

For example, Ontario's Investigations and Enforcement Branch currently receives 20,000 Occurrence Reports annually, which result in the discovery of 6,000 suspected violations. Due to limited enforcement resources, these violations result in only 1,200 investigations and approximately 350 prosecutions. An AMP could be used to target the large number of violations that are never investigated or prosecuted.

The cost of an AMP program is significantly less than prosecuting all those who break environmental laws. Jurisdictions using AMPs typically report that over 90% of AMPs are paid without appeal.[9] However, critics fear that AMPs would be used primarily as a substitute for a strong enforcement program, and could only work if the deterrent of successful prosecution remained. The public also expects that pollution offences would be treated similarly to other serious crimes; that is, the punishment would fit the crime.

The Role of the Public

Often, a form of conflict of interest can occur as provincial governments compete against one another for economic development projects, and offer reduced environmental enforcement of their regulations as an inducement. In the United States, citizen lawsuit provisions in statutes permit citizens to fill the enforcement void, during periods of administrative reluctance to prosecute environmental offences. In 1983 (during the Reagan Administration), citizen suits actually outnumbered Environmental Protection Agency actions under the *Clean Water Act* (Miller, 1994). By and large, Canadians who launch private prosecutions can typically expect the Attorney General's intervention in the case and a stay of proceedings (Kostuch, 1995). Recently, provincial governments have been introducing rights for citizens to request investigations of suspected offences; however, citizen actions have not yet affected prosecution results appreciably.[10]

In absence of a meaningful citizen's right to sue, Canada may be in violation of its commitment to the North American Agreement on Environmental Cooperation (NAAEC). When Canada signed the side-agreement to the North American Free Trade Agreement, it pledged to protect its environment. More important, Article 22 of NAAEC can be used to punish a country found to be persistently failing to effectively enforce its environmental laws. Citizens have begun applying to the North American Commission for Environmental Cooperation to censure Canada for not prosecuting environmental offenders.

Conclusion

It is the conclusion of this study that Canada does not currently effectively enforce its laws, even though polls consistently show that Canadians want their governments to do more to protect the environment (Duffy, 1998). First, it is clear that governments are not reporting what efforts are being made to monitor compliance with law, and what is being done to punish offenders. Second, a review of the enforcement records reveals a shockingly low number of investigations being initiated, charges being laid, prosecutions undertaken, convictions being obtained and fines being imposed. There can be only one explanation for such a low level of enforcement: governments have unilaterally decided that political and economic priorities rank ahead of environmental protection. Finally, future enforcement policies should not be set without full disclosure, by government and industry, of data on environmental violations and prosecutions to inform public decision-making. Otherwise, one must ask who is keeping whose secrets.

(f) Monitoring and Enforcement of Environmental Policy[†]

Mark A. Cohen —————————————————————————————

Economic Theories of Firm Behavior

Any study of optimal government monitoring and enforcement policy should start first with a more basic understanding of firm behavior. After all, there would be no need to study enforcement if all firms complied with the law. Since not all firms do comply with the law, it is interesting to start with a more fundamental question — why do firms comply at all? An obvious economic reason for compliance is that firms respond to both positive and negative incentives. If expected penalties are sufficiently high, the threat of being punished for noncompliance should be an adequate reason. However, as Russell, Harrington

and Vaughn (1986) and Harrington (1988) note, government monitoring activities are often quite limited. Moreover, even if discovered to be in noncompliance, fines are low. For example, the median administrative fine imposed by the U.S. EPA in 1995 was $4,000, while the average fine was $10,181 and the maximum fine was $125,000 (Lear, 1998). Moreover, fewer than 200 firms were fined in 1995. Despite these facts, most sources in the U.S. are thought to be in compliance a large fraction of the time. For example, Magat and Viscusi (1990) report an average level of compliance of 75% in the U.S. pulp and paper industry between 1982 and 1985.

† From *International Yearbook of Environmental and Resource Economics* 3 (1999): 44–106. Online: http://www.worldbank.org/nipr/work_paper/cohen/ (last accessed: 01-08-29). Reproduced with permission of Edward Elgar Publishing Ltd..

To explain the phenomenon of high compliance in the absence of strict enforcement, Harrington (1988), Harford and Harrington (1991), and Harford (1991) adapted existing models of income tax enforcement.[7] These models have been referred to as "state-dependent" enforcement, since government policy depends on the firm's previous compliance status. The basic idea is that firms are assigned to groups based upon their known compliance history. Ignoring firms that are never monitored, a simple two-group scheme would involve firms found to be in compliance at their last inspection (group 1) and those found to be out of compliance at their last inspection (group 2). Firms placed into group 2 would be subject to some combination of a higher monitoring probability, tougher regulatory standards, or higher fines than would firms in group 1. It has been shown that this type scheme allows the regulatory agency to increase the fraction of firms in compliance for a given level of monitoring or expected penalties. Extra incentives for compliance are created by the threat of being faced with a tougher regulatory regime (i.e., being forced into group 2) if found to be out of compliance. Harrington (1988) calls this added incentive "enforcement leverage." Such a scheme tends to make the level of compliance appear high relative to the fines actually imposed and the average fine threatened.[8] ...

Although it is possible firms comply with environmental laws because of the threat of being placed on the enforcement agency's target list, this is unlikely to be the sole reason for compliance. Downing and Kimball (1982) documented the low penalties for noncompliance and the relatively high compliance rates in the U.S. First, they note that firms receive cost subsidies in the form of tax breaks and special financing. Although a cost subsidy does not provide an incentive for compliance the way a penalty does, it will affect the cost-benefit calculus a firm must undergo when determining the expected cost of compliance in the presence of noncompliance penalties. Second, they argue that industry might want stringent regulation as an entry barrier to new firms. Although this is plausible, it is not clear how this explains compliance (as opposed to regulation). Third, they note that risk aversion might help explain compliance. The fact that subsequent violations are dealt with more harshly provides an impetus for a risk averse decision maker to comply now instead of risking future monitoring. Finally, Downing and Kimball (1982)

raise the possibility that managers care about their corporate image, a hypothesis that they claim is supported by survey evidence....

There are other reasons why firms might comply with environmental standards. It is possible, for example, that firms do not realize how low the expected penalty is for violating the law. Hammit and Reuter (1988), for example, cite survey evidence that small quantity generators of hazardous waste significantly overestimate the chance the government will monitor them. Alternatively, it is possible that the expected penalty for noncompliance is not as low as it appears on the surface. For example, there is growing evidence that the relative law administratively imposed fines noted by previous authors are not the only penalties imposed on firms that fail to comply with environment laws. ... [F]irms that violate the law might be sanctioned by market forces.

It is also possible, for example, that managers who make the decisions about compliance simply believe that compliance is the right thing to do. In other words, social norms might operate to yield significant compliance rates — even without the threat of penalties. ... It is also possible that the marketplace rewards firms that comply with environmental regulations if a segment of consumers are more likely to buy their products (Arora and Gangopadhyay, 1995).[9]

. . . .

Finally, an interesting question to ponder is whether noncompliance may be partly explained by ignorance, not willful behavior. Brehm and Hamilton (1996) consider this possibility in the case of new rules requiring certain emitters of toxic chemicals to report their emissions to the U.S. EPA. They develop a model in which violations may occur due to ignorance or evasion. For example, "ignorance" was operationalized by measuring the extent to which a facility had other environmental permits or requirements. It is assumed that firms with other environmental permits were more likely to know about the new reporting requirement. Alternatively, if a firm that failed to report its TRI emissions had a previous violation under other environmental laws, that would suggest evasive activity. Brehm and Hamilton (1996) found considerable support for an "ignorance" explanation for noncompliance, although there was also evidence of evasive activity. Their paper highlights the importance of considering the information set of firms subject to regulations.

. . . .

Positive Theories of Government Behavior

. . . .

The environmental compliance literature includes a variety of assumptions about enforcement agency behavior. Some of these theories of behavior are based on the general propositions of the political economy or public choice literature, others are based on more detailed interactions between the Congress and the regulatory agency. In this section, I explore several theories of enforcement behavior: (1) net political support maximization, (2) bureaucratic behavior theory, (3) the law enforcement goal of maximizing compliance, (4) maximizing the benefits of compliance without regard to compliance costs, and (5) a median voter model with asymmetric information about enforcement effort and compliance costs.

. . . .

Economic Theory of Regulation/ Net Political Support Maximization

The economic theory of regulation posits that agencies wish to maximize net political support (Peltzman, 1976).[14] That is, the agency wants to maximize the difference between the number of supporters and the number of detractors of its enforcement policy. One way to do this is to impose the least amount of regulatory burden on private interests that are concentrated and well organized. Deily and Gray (1991) model the regulatory agency in this manner. They note that if a firm finds compliance too costly and will otherwise shut down, it is a likely candidate to pressure the agency and to generate political opposition. In particular, that firm's employees and other local citizens who will be hurt from a plant-closing are likely to be vocal opponents of any such stringent regulatory enforcement activity. Thus, they hypothesize that the government will fail to enforce as stringently when the cost of compliance is very high or when the plant is in danger of closing. They also expect to find less enforcement when the plant is a significant employer in the area.[15]

Bureaucratic Behavior Theory

Bureaucratic behavior theory (Niskanen, 1975) is based on the notion that government personnel derive benefits (through higher salaries, perks, and stature) when they have larger budgets. Asymmetry of information between the bureaucratic agency and Congress results in an agency that is driven more by budget maximization than social welfare maximization.

Lee (1983) examines the problem of collecting an emissions fee when the enforcement authority acts as a budget maximizing agency. Not surprisingly, he finds that the agency will spend an excessive amount of resources monitoring for violations. Although the Lee (1983) paper is intuitively appealing and is a nice application of bureaucratic behavior theory, it does not appear to help explain how pollution control laws are enforced in the U.S. As we have shown, an optimal penalty will involve are relatively low level of monitoring, and the empirical evidence suggests that minimal monitoring actually occurs.[16]

. . . .

Maximizing Compliance with the Law

The enforcement arm of a regulatory agency often has more in common with police or other law enforcement agencies in government than with the regulatory agency itself. In the U.S., EPA enforcement officials work closely with the Department of Justice and some EPA officers even have criminal arrest powers and carry guns. Thus, an alternative view of enforcement is that it is a pure law enforcement function designed to achieve the highest possible level of compliance. In contrast to "maximizing social welfare," which would require the agency to balance the cost of compliance against the benefits of compliance, "maximizing compliance" ignores costs altogether. Keeler (1995) adopts this somewhat apolitical view of the enforcement agency, and assumes a limited enforcement budget that must compete with other agency functions. As long as the agency does not fully account for the cost of compliance in its decision process, Keeler's model thus predicts an excessive amount of enforcement relative to the socially desired level and relative to the other functions of the agency (e.g., writing new regulations, research, etc.). Garvie and Keeler (1994) also assume the enforcement agency's goal is to achieve the highest level of compliance given their enforcement budget. Thus, the agency must take into account the fact that if it tries to impose a very steep penalty, it will incur additional enforcement costs as firms attempt to evade, challenge enforcement actions in court, etc. In such a setting, Garvie and Keeler's model predicts relatively low penalties and more frequent contact with enforcement officials and less formal negotiations when the regulated industry has a lot of political power or when there is a high probability of judicial leniency due to unclear regulatory standards. On the other hand, we expect low monitoring/probability of detection and high penalties when the activity is judged to be especially damaging and the regulator can be certain of legal and public support for prosecution. Examples of the latter are midnight dumping of hazardous wastes. To my knowledge, there have been no empirical tests of these testable implications.

Maximizing Environmental Benefits of Enforcement

If we allow the goals of the regulatory agency and its enforcement arm to be somewhat more closely aligned, it might be reasonable to assume that the enforcement goal is to maximize the environmental benefits of compliance. This is different from maximizing compliance, which would involve focusing on a 'easy' enforcement targets even if they yield little environmental benefits. Maximizing environmental benefits would focus the enforcement agency on those facilities that have the highest environmental payoff per dollar of enforcement effort. It is also different from maximizing the *net* benefits of compliance, which would explicitly consider the firm's compliance cost.

. . . .

Median Voter Model

Casual observation suggests there is often an asymmetry between the law and its application. Although stringent environmental regulations might be on the books, one cannot necessarily assume that compliance and enforcement will take place. Selden and Terrones (1993) formalize this notion by adopting a median voter model where the legislature and voters have asymmetric information about the costs of pollution control and enforcement zeal. The voters demand and are "given" very stringent environmental legislation since they are less readily able

to see the cost of these rules. However, the voters are also less able to observe the extent to which the government is enforcing its environmental standards. Thus, we expect more stringent regulations than might be socially optimal, and we expect less than stringent enforcement to compensate. Note that if this model is realistic, one should be cautious about allowing private citizen suits ... to enforce when the government does not. In this context, citizen suits would only cause over deterrence.

The Role of Federalism and Multi-level Enforcement Agencies

An interesting question that has only seldom been discussed in the literature is the extent to which enforcement and compliance differs with the level of government in a federal system. Should monitoring and enforcement be delegated to a state or local jurisdiction, or remain with the Federal enforcement agency? The scarcity of literature on this topic reflects both the difficulty in obtaining sound data that would allow for such a study, and the lack of definitive theoretical models of federalism that yield strong predictions of enforcement behavior. Thus, the little empirical literature devoted to this topic tends to be focused on policy implementation issues.

. . . .

EMPIRICAL ANALYSIS OF ENVIRONMENTAL ENFORCEMENT

Until recently, there have been surprisingly few empirical studies of environmental enforcement. Diver (1980) suggests that the reason is that enforcement is so difficult to study. Agencies are reluctant to reveal their enforcement policies and many decisions are made at relatively low levels within the agency and without formal proceedings. Data on compliance and enforcement are often impossible to obtain. Until recently, the U.S. EPA did not have comprehensive compliance data available themselves, let alone make it available to researchers. Thus, the few studies that have been published focused either on oil spills (where the Coast Guard maintains a comprehensive data set), or on specific industries such as the pulp and paper industry, where EPA funded and/or assisted researchers in their data collection efforts. Outside the U.S., data appear to be even scarcer....

. . . .

Government Monitoring and Enforcement of Environmental Regulation

Empirical studies of enforcement generally ask two questions: (1) How does the regulatory agency enforces its regulations? and (2) Does more enforcement lead to an increase in compliance or improvement in the environment? Although the first question is primarily descriptive, it provides insight into whether the enforcement authority targets its efforts and whether it acts as if it is interested in an efficient enforcement scheme. The second question often leads to policy implications such as whether monitoring or penalties should be increased or decreased.

Although empirical studies have demonstrated the effectiveness of government activities such as inspections and monitoring, one must take care in drawing strong policy implications from these studies. Each empirical study is necessarily limited by the scope of the data and choices made by regulatory authorities. Further, few studies have attempted to characterize the social costs and benefits of government monitoring or enforcement activities. Thus, a finding that increased monitoring leads to increased compliance, for example, does not tell us if the marginal cost of increased monitoring is outweighed by the benefits of increased compliance. It also does not tell us if there are other less costly methods of monitoring and enforcement or more productive methods that could be employed for the same level of government expenditures. A few studies have attempted to answer these latter questions and are highlighted below.

. . . .

Manufacturing Industry Emissions in the U.S. and Canada

. . . .

... Magat and Viscui (1990) document the fact that higher levels of enforcement activity result in lower levels of pollution.[38] They are able to document a "specific" deterrent effect with a one quarter lag.[39] However, Magat and Viscusi (1990) are less sanguine about whether current enforcement policy passes a cost-benefit test. Although they show that the estimated value of benefits exceed the cost of inspections,

it is not clear that they exceed the cost of regulatory compliance.

Liu (1995) replicates the Magat and Viscusi (1990) study with updated data and more complete information on monitoring activity. Unlike Magat and Viscusi, Liu finds that increased monitoring does *not* reduce the number of known violations. However, Liu explains this result by noting that during the more recent time period, EPA undertook two types of inspections — discretionary and routine. Routine inspections designed to detect reporting violations are likely to increase the number of know violations. On the other hand, discretionary inspections are targeted towards firms known to be out of compliance and those with previous violations. Discretionary inspections are expected to deter both false reporting and noncompliance. The combination of these two inspection mechanisms thus has an indeterminate effect on the number of observed violations. Liu's empirical analysis confirms this hypothesis about the differential impact of inspections, thus helping to explain the observation of no "deterrent" effect at the aggregate level. This is an important lesson for future researchers to keep in mind when conducting an empirical analysis of enforcement and deterrence.

Monitoring of pollution at pulp and paper mills has also been studied in Canada (Laplante and Rilstone, 1996).... Consistent with previous studies using actual inspection rates, Laplante and Rilstone find that the treat of inspections (or "expected inspection rate") also induces compliance. They also find that inspections are effective at including more frequent self-reporting.

Nadeau (1997) conducted another study of EPA enforcement effectiveness, but extended the analysis to include the length of time of violation. Thus, Nadeau explicitly models the fact that firms are usually out of compliance for more than one day at a time. He also studies the U.S. pulp and paper industry, and finds that a 10% increase in monitoring activity leads to a 0.6 to 4.2% reduction in violation time. A 10% increase in enforcement (e.g. fines) is more effective, resulting in a 4.0–4.7% reduction in violation time.

Having established that monitoring and enforcement deters regulatory violations, Helland (1998) turns to a different question — whether or not government monitoring and enforcement policies are consistent with the 'targeting' approach described by Harrington (1988) and others. In other words, do firms that have been found to be in violation of the law have a significantly higher probability of being inspected in subsequent periods? The answer, according to Helland (1998), is a qualified yes. Firms found to be out of compliance are more likely to be inspected in subsequent periods. These firms are also more likely to self-report a violent, consistent with the view that they are trying to regain credibility with the government so that they are taken off the 'target' list. However, Helland also finds that other "political" factors help explain inspections, including the per-capita level of pollution, the affluence of the community, and the probability that a plant will close if it is forced to comply.

Moving from the pulp and paper industry to the steel industry, Deily and Gray (1991) examine the government's enforcement policy during the years 1977–1986....

. . . .

Consistent with theory, they find that plants with a higher probability of closing have lower inspection rates. A lower inspection rate is also prevalent when a plant's workers are a large fraction of the local labor market. However, they are unable to explain the contrary finding that plants in high unemployment areas are found to have a higher risk of inspections.

A subsequent paper by Gray and Deily (1996) examines steel industry behavior and government inspections in a simultaneous model. They not only ask the question of whether increased monitoring and enforcement leads to increased compliance, but they also ask if increased compliance by firms yields reduced levels of government activity....

... Consistent with most of the other published empirical papers, Gray and Deily (1996) find that increased monitoring and enforcement leads to higher compliance in subsequent periods. They also find that firms who were found to be in compliance in prior periods were less likely to be inspected in subsequent periods. Plants that had higher emissions had higher inspection rates — even controlling for compliance in prior periods. At the firm level, larger companies had lower enforcement rates, which they note is consistent with "regulatory sensitivity to firms' political power". One interesting finding is that there appears to be a pattern of compliance or noncompliance across plants owned by the same firm, and multi-plant firms are more likely to be in compliance than single-plant firms.

This suggests that corporate policies on environmental compliance might be important, and that enforcement authorities might target plants whose owners have been known to be out of compliance elsewhere. Note that financial status of the firm did not affect compliance, which rules out a purely financial explanation for the last result.

A similar study of enforcement in the pulp and paper industry in Canada confirms some — but not all — of the findings by Deily and Gray (1991) and Gray and Deily (1996). Dion, Lanoie and Laplante (1998) employ a virtually identical model of government monitoring and find similar results that past compliance history explains enforcement activity. They also have a measure of environment damages and find that monitoring is concentrated where damages are largest. Unlike Deily and Gray (1991), they find that a plant with a larger share of local employment is *more likely* to be inspected. They posit that the difference between the two studies lies in their measurement of government enforcement. Deily and Gray (1991) measure government activity as the number of actions taken — including inspections, remedial orders and penalties. In contrast, Dion, Lanoie and Laplante (1998) measure only inspections. Thus, it is possible that enforcement agencies are more likely to inspect more visible plants, but if found to be in noncompliance, they are less likely to impose remedial actions or punitive sanctions. Contrary to Deily and Gray, they also find that areas with higher unemployment are likely to have *lower* enforcement levels. This is certainly an area that could benefit from further empirical research.

. . . .

Finally, Harrison (1995) is one of the few cross national studies of enforcement. She compares the different approaches to enforcement policy existing in the U.S. and Canada, once again focusing on the pulp and paper industry. Harrison characterizes the strategy in Canada to be "cooperative" relative to the more stringent approach adopted in the U.S. Canadian enforcement officials are more willing to negotiate and revise compliance programs instead of forcing compliance or imposing a sanction. Empirically, Harrison finds that Canadian pulp and paper mills are not in compliance as much as in the U.S. Moreover, she shows that U.S. enforcement is more even handed across plants — suggesting that Canadian officials are more likely to give in to plants that face higher control costs.

Illegal Disposal of Wastes in the U.S. and Canada

Illegal disposal of wastes presents a somewhat more complicated problem than normally encountered in the study of enforcement policies. Unlike most areas of environmental regulation, this inherently involves a new policy parameter — the cost of *legal* disposal. Not only does the government decide how to "price" noncompliance (through a monetary penalty) and how much effort to expend on monitoring, but now the government also needs to price "compliance" by setting the price of legal disposal.[41] As Sullivan (1987) shows, if the price of legal disposal is too high, the government actually encourages illegal disposal. Conversely, one way to encourage legal disposal is to subsidize it. Thus, the government has a third policy option available when determining optimal enforcement against illegal disposal — subsidizing legal disposal....

Sullivan (1987) provides an initial estimate of the optimal subsidy and enforcement budget for hazardous waste disposal and determines the conditions under which a subsidy is preferable to increased enforcement and vice versa. Similar analyses are conducted by Fullerton and Kinneman (1995) in the context of household garbage, and Sigman (1998) for used oil disposal. All of these studies highlight the tradeoff between raising the cost of legal disposal and the amount of illegal disposal that is observed. For example, Sigman (1998) estimates that a ban on used oil disposal (requiring instead that used oil be recycled or reused) will result in 34% of the waste previously disposed legally being illegally dumped. Since illegal dumping is likely to be worse than the previous method of legal disposal, one cannot say a priori whether a ban on used oil disposal is socially beneficial. This is an excellent example of how enforcement concerns can make an otherwise socially desirable policy change counter productive.

Finally, returning to a model of bureaucratic behavior, Hamilton (1996) examines EPA data on administrative fines imposed on hazardous waste violators and finds that political pressures affect the magnitude of sanctions imposed. Fines are higher in regions where key Congressional Committee members reside and where there are higher levels of environmental group membership. Hamilton also finds that fines are significantly higher when EPA does not resort to the use of a "formal" rule and instead negotiates an informal settlement. He suggests that this is partly due to the fact that regulators are more likely to have strong environmental preferences and thus impose higher sanctions when they are not constrained by the regulatory process.

Government Enforcement Outside the U.S. and Canada

Most of the empirical work on environmental enforcement has focused on the U.S. and Canada. One exception is the U.K., where sociologists and political scientists have studied regulatory enforcement for quite some time. Fenn and Veljanovski (1988) employ an economic approach to study enforcement in the U.K. They model government enforcement authorities as having discretion over whether or not to prosecute offenders who have violated the law. In that case, bargaining, selective enforcement and negotiated agreements without penalties become important enforcement tools. However, only credible threats of punishment and credible promises of compliance will make an informal system like this work. If firms know that they are always able to negotiate a compliance agreement without further penalty, they will take a 'wait and see' approach to compliance. Fenn and Veljanovski (1988) argue that in reality there is uncertainty about the enforcement agency's strategy. Although they might agree to a negotiated settlement involving no penalties, there is no guarantee they will do so. In a repeated game, they find that if the cost of compliance is less than the social harm, it is possible to find a cooperative solution involving negotiated compliance. Employing data from health and safety inspections at factories in the U.K., they find evidence in support of their model. For example, inspectors are more likely to negotiate when compliance costs are very high and there are significant employment concerns.

. . . .

Criminal Enforcement of Environmental Laws in the U.S.

Virtually every environmental law in the U.S. includes criminal provisions (Cohen, 1992). Some of these criminal provisions are designed to ensure truthful self-reporting..., while others apply to the polluting activity itself. Economic theory does not generally distinguish between criminal law and civil or administrative law. A penalty is a penalty regardless of who imposes it. All of the goals of punishment — except incapacitation (holding an offender in prison so they cannot commit a new offense) — can be realized with either a criminal or civil sanction. Yet, criminal laws have different legal procedures, standards of proof, and enforcement personnel. In general, it is thought that imposing a criminal sanction is more costly to the government than imposing a similar sanction through the administrative process.[42] Most economists have thus argued that criminal sanctions should be reserved for cases in which the optimal penalty is too high to be collected (Cohen, 1992: 1061–2). In that case, one might mandate a period of incarceration for the individual violator. An alternative view of criminal sanctions is that they help educate or shape preferences of the public who are potential violators (Dau-Schmidt, 1990). Given these competing theories, there is a need for future empirical research on the distinction between civil and criminal enforcement.

While the U.S. EPA has a civil penalty policy that systematically assesses penalties, there is no comparable policy for environmental crimes. Judges are free to assess any monetary sanction as long as it is not greater than the statutory maximum.[43] Cohen (1992) examines criminal sanctions imposed on companies that have violated U.S. environmental laws and compares the penalty structure implied by these sanctions to that which we would expect under an optimal penalty. One of the difficulties with this type of analysis is the lack of comprehensive data on harm. In the absence of such data, Cohen (1992) used monetary harm — any known restitution or payments for direct losses suffered by victims plus cleanup costs. Both criminal fines and total monetary sanctions are found to increase with this measure of harm. Sanctions are also higher for hazardous waste violations. However, Cohen (1992: 1090, Table 6) finds that sanctions are higher for larger firms and are higher when individuals are convicted along with their firms. These findings appear to be inconsistent with optimal penalty theory. There is no economic reason to increase fines for larger firms — only for larger harms. However, since large firms are less likely to have individuals convicted for the same offense, the larger penal-

ties might simply reflect the inability to trade-off individual for corporate sanctions. That is, judges might be increasing the monetary penalty to companies when there is no individual to sanction. This is a plausible explanation, since in a restricted sample of small, privately held firms convicted of environmental crimes, monetary fines are found to be negatively related to the likelihood of an individual going to jail (Cohen, 1992: 1095, Table 8).

Private Enforcement of Environment Law

Although enforcement is ultimately the government's responsibility, the government does not necessarily initiate all enforcement activity. In some instances, private parties are given the right to initiate enforcement actions through the administrative agencies or the courts. There are several reasons why governments might adopt this dual enforcement approach. Private citizens who are directly affected by pollution might be better situated to detect environmental violations in their neighborhoods and can be a good judge of whether or not they are concerned enough about this pollution to take some action. It is also possible that private enforcement is less costly as private enforcers are not subject to the inefficiencies of government bureaucracies. Finally, the government enforcement agency might simply lack the funds to adequately enforce, and instead would have to rely upon private enforcement agents to fill in the gaps.

Despite these apparent benefits, private enforcement might also serve the less noble goal of enhancing private interests at the expense of public interests. As Landes and Posner (1975) show, private enforcement might lead to too much enforcement, i.e., over deterrence. This is especially a concern if private enforcement is allowed as an adjunct to public enforcement and the public agency does not take private enforcement into account when setting their enforcement policy. For example, ... it may be optimal for the government to set a high fine and low probability of detection. Assuming that such an enforcement policy is set optimally, allowing private enforcement would yield a higher expected penalty than is optimal. This might lead to too much enforcement and overdeterrence — a situation whereby the firm spends more than is socially optimal to prevent pollution. As Tietenberg (1996) shows, if the regulatory standard is too stringent (but not enforced), private enforcement can lead to excessive regulations. Polinsky (1980) argues just the opposite, however, if the optimal enforcement scheme involves high monitoring costs. In that case, relying on private enforcement might lead to under deterrence. Thus, if the government is to allow private enforcement, it should take into account the level of enforcement expected from private parties in determining the correct penalty level to impose.

Cohen and Rubin (1985) propose an alternative approach to private enforcement, whereby EPA turns all of its monitoring and enforcement activities over to private parties. The payment the private enforcer receives is based on the net social benefit of enforcement. In theory, their proposal would overcome both of these objections. However, even in an era of privatization, the practical and political difficulties of implementing this proposal appear to be insurmountable.

. . . .

Information and Market Forces as Enforcement Tools

Information that a firm has been sanctioned for violating environmental laws (fines, cleanup costs, damage compensation, etc.) may be of interest to shareholders or lenders of that firm. To the extent that the monetary sanction reduces the expected value of the firm, this will affect the share price and/or bond rating of the firm. It may also give lenders pause about risking more capital on that particular firm. In addition to the direct monetary sanctions and cleanup costs associated with the enforcement action, the firm may incur additional costs in the future. For example, if being convicted of an environmental crime automatically causes a firm to be barred from doing business with the government (as it oftentimes does in the U.S. — even though this is a temporary suspension), then investors may take this additional information into account. Similarly, if the government enforcement agency follows the suggestion of Harrington (1988) and others..., and implements a targeted enforcement strategy, the threat of future sanctions may now be higher. It is also possible that this environment law violation will result in the loss of goodwill to employees or customers, thus reducing the long run profitability of the firm. Some socially conscious investors might even shun the firm's stock, thereby depressing its value. Finally,

it is possible that investors will update their assessment of the quality of management in the firm and take this environmental law violation as a signal that the firm is not as well managed as they thought.

The role of non-regulatory enforcement tools such as the impact of information disclosure on firm behavior is an important emerging topic in the economics of enforcement. One impetus for this growing interest appears to be the experience in the U.S. with the "toxic release inventory" (TRI) information disclosure requirements. Firms emitting more than a certain amount of chemicals in to the air, water or land are required to report the type and amount of emissions to the EPA — even for emissions that are legal. Hamilton (1995) estimates that the first such disclosure had a significant effect on the market value of publicly traded firms — a negative abnormal return of -0.3 for the average firm. However, the distribution of abnormal returns varied considerably, with some firms receiving stock price reductions of several percentage points, and others actually receiving positive abnormal returns. Hamilton's analysis does not provide a means of determining the underlying reason for the stock price decline. We do not know, for example, whether these stock price effects reflect investor expectations of future targeted enforcement scrutiny of high emitters (which has been hinted at by EPA). Another potential explanation for the stock price decline is the expectation that public pressure would cause firms to voluntarily reduce emissions. It is also possible that investors simply take this information as a signal of an inefficient production process and/or bad management. Regardless of the reason, we know that firms have dramatically reduced their TRI emissions following the initial disclosure. Konar and Cohen (1997) compared the firm-specific reductions to the abnormal returns estimated by Hamilton (1995), and find that the firms with the largest negative abnormal returns upon the initial announcement of TRI emissions are the firms that reduced their emissions the most.

It is important to keep in mind that information disclosure under the TRI program is about legal emissions. Mandatory disclosure programs such as TRI are best thought of as substitutes for regulatory programs that attempt to use community or other external pressures to encourage firms to reduce emissions voluntarily. In contrast, information disclosure about law violations is best thought of as another form of penalty in addition to any direct government imposed monetary fine. Thus, to the extent that information disclosure about *legal* emissions had an effect on firm valuation and subsequent *legal* emissions, we would expect similar if not greater effects for information disclosure about *illegal* emissions....

. . . .

Several recent experiments with information disclosure as an enforcement tool have yielded promising results. Most of these efforts are being promoted by the "New Ideas in Pollution Regulation" (NIPR) program of the World Bank, and are reported on at their internet site, http://www.worldbank.org/nipr. Although some of these experiments are designed to fill a void where no regulations are in place, others have explicitly used the power of information disclosure as a method of pressuring firms to comply with government regulations. This is particularly useful in countries where government enforcement resources are limited....

SUMMARY AND FUTURE RESEARCH NEEDS

It has long been recognized that enforcement is an important element of regulatory policy design. Yet, the economics literature on environmental enforcement is highly fragmented and not easily accessible. I had two main goals in writing this article: (1) to bring this diverse literature together in a format that provides researchers and policy makers with a laundry list of enforcement issues to consider when evaluating environmental policy, and (2) to provide researchers with new and interesting topics for further study.

Over the past 25 years, we have learned a lot about the effect of monitoring and enforcement on firm behavior. We know that increased monitoring and inspections can increase compliance. We also know that enforcement does not occur in a vacuum and that understanding the motivations and incentives of both polluters and enforcement agencies should be an important component of any study of enforcement. However, there is a lot yet to be learned.

We probably know the least about the most important and fundamental topic in enforcement — why firms comply with the law. Two promising areas of research on this topic appear to be developing: (1) incorporating social norms, community pressure and firm reputation into the analysis, and (2) opening up the "black box" of the firm and incorporating incentives within the organization. These are both complex topics that require an understanding of a diverse set of literatures — including topics such as corporate governance, principal-agency theory and economic models of social norms. This is also an area where economists can learn from other disciplines and from other empirical studies outside economics. Although recent attempts to empirically estimate the factors that cause firms to voluntarily reduce emissions have been promising, they have often been unable to substantiate the theoretical models that others have proposed. Further empirical and theoretical work in this area could be beneficial.

Another significant gap in our knowledge relates to the interaction of the various institutions that affect compliance behavior. Are citizen suits a substitute or a complement to government enforcement? What role do firm reputation and market forces play in the enforcement equation? Does organizational structure affect a firm's propensity to comply? If so, how should this be taken into account in designing appropriate enforcement policies? Is "information" really an enforcement tool that government agencies can use at a very low cost? If so, what are the social costs and benefits of providing information to the public in an effort to affect firm behavior? How can a diverse set of institutional actors with their own agendas (e.g., EPA, Sentencing Commission, courts, private enforcement activities, market forces) coordinate so that the outcome at least approximates optimality? These are just a few of the questions that arise when we look beyond the simple question of designing an optimal penalty when there are only two actors — a polluter and enforcement agency. Opening up the model to account for real world complexities make our task much more difficult — but also much more interesting.

(g)   Taking Matters Into Their Own Hands: The role of citizens in Canadian pollution control enforcement[†]

Kernaghan Webb —————————————————————————

> The history of the last 20 years in North America affords a number of instances of why citizens and taxpayers distrust government or are highly skeptical of government actions and promises.[1]

> Historically, our law has not found favour with the idea that members of the general public should be entitled to invoke the aid of the courts whenever they perceive a wrongful invasion of public as opposed to private rights.... The spectre of the "busybody" or "meddlesome interloper" has loomed large....[2]

INTRODUCTION

When citizens initiate or conduct pollution offence prosecutions,[3] two diametrically opposed (and simplistic) reactions are commonly expressed. Either it is concluded that government officials have been co-opted by industry, thus necessitating citizen action; or, alternatively, private prosecutors are characterized as being on some type of personal vendetta against industry and/or government — they are "gadflies" or busybodies, meddling where they have no business to interfere.

As the case descriptions of citizen-initiated prosecutions included in this article reveal, the truth normally lies somewhere between these two extremes: in two of the three citizen initiated actions described,[4] government officials actually assisted citizens with their prosecutions. This hardly fits the stereotypical behaviour of an industry co-opted bureaucracy. In all three cases, courts found the polluters guilty. Assertions that citizens are meddling are difficult to maintain when the courts vindicate their concerns.

In effect, analysis of these cases suggests that private prosecutions are but a symptom of a larger problem — determining how much enforcement is necessary and the proper role for citizens in that enforcement. To address this larger problem it is necessary to focus on why citizen actions have provoked such strong and divergent reactions. Once the causes of the tensions created by private prosecutions are revealed, it may be possible to alleviate them.

The position taken here is that private prosecutions straddle an extremely important cleft which exists in our society. It is the cleft between promise and performance. The promises exist on a number of levels, embodied in expectations that elected officials represent the views of and are accountable to the public, that citizens can meaningfully participate in decisions which affect them, and that what is said in legislation is what will actually occur. To initiate a private prosecution is to put these promises to the test, and to demand that they are kept or that satisfactory explanations are provided for why they are not. The strong emotions expressed when citizens launch prosecutions of pollution offices are indications of the gap between promise and performance.

Perhaps not surprisingly given their educational and practical experience, the natural predilection of many legally trained persons confronted with problems having legal dimensions is to launch into the debate at the level of legislation and caselaw and emerge triumphantly sometime later with the sought-after "technical" legal solution. But, by approaching problems in this manner, there is a real likelihood that the solution arrived at will have missed the mark: for example, it may be based on tacit assumptions about the governing process which cannot withstand critical examination, or it may fail to fully take into account the broader context in which the problem originally arose.

Thus, determining the role that the citizen can and should play in pollution control enforcement necessitates a more fundamental examination of the extent and practical implications of participatory democracy, the historical evolution and development of regulatory processes, and the efficacy and weaknesses of current governmental efforts to protect the environment. This

---

† From *McGill Law Journal* 36 (1991): 772–74, 776–78, 781–82, 784–86, 801–17. Reproduced by permission of the author and the publisher. See appendix for notes or references.

article explores legal aspects of these three issues in an attempt to arrive at solutions which can simultaneously reduce the acrimony which surrounds private prosecutions, enhance the ability of the citizen to participate in enforcement, and improve the effectiveness of government pollution control efforts.

. . . .

DEMOCRACY, PUBLIC PARTICIPATION AND PRIVATE PROSECUTIONS: CONCEPTS AND MECHANICS

The Basic Concepts
The question of the relation between public participation and democracy is a vexing one which has occupied the attention of political theorists for centuries. It underlies any understanding of the role and function of citizen prosecutions, and so a brief discussion of the meanings and linkages between the concepts of democracy, public participation and the ability to engage in private prosecutions will be provided here prior to examining how these ideas have been synthesized in the Canadian governmental system.

The concepts of democracy and public participation overlap to a significant extent, yet the two notions are not identical. The word democracy is derived from the Greek roots *demos*, meaning the "people," and *kratos* meaning "authority."[6] In some ancient Greek city-states, democracy was literally government by the many, with all citizens regularly and directly participating in both the making and implementing of laws.[7]

While today such "direct democracy" systems are rare, some commentators have advocated a return to the small scale populist approach, in the interests of bringing a mass-consumption world economy back under control.[8] Direct democracies assume an active, capable, civic-minded populace, which has the time, resources and inclination to involve itself in both making and carrying out the laws. For most intents and purposes, the direct democratic approach can be described as idealist.

In today's mass population, complex societies the most common form of democracy is known as "representative democracy." Instead of rule by the people as a whole, representatives are elected to make laws and govern on the basis of competitive elections in the interest of the citizenry. In theory, then, the decisions of the representatives derive their authority from popular elections. Actions of those who govern are controlled through elections and a host of other monitoring techniques.

It should be immediately apparent that any system which elevates some individuals to act on behalf of others is susceptible to abuses of power and will inevitably create questions in the minds of some as to who is being represented on any particular decision, and the adequacy of that representation. In effect, this division of responsibilities is an inherent source of tension in society, and the issue of "trust" in the governors by the governed is an on-going concern. The existence of elections, question periods in legislatures, the courts, ombudspersons, etc., perform the function of "checks and balances" and "controls" on the behaviour of the governors. It is probably apparent that Canada operates under a form of representative democracy.

The expression "public participation" is here taken to mean those processes whereby individuals and groups can influence government decisions which affect or matter to them.[9] The term "influence" is also in need of definition. As one commentator has put it, "[t]o be in a position to influence a decision is not the same thing as to be in a position to ... determine the outcome or to ... make that decision."[10] Thus, the notions of influence and public participation do not necessarily imply control. Rather, they denote a clearly articulated and recognized input into the process.

Ideally, the decision-making process should provide an opportunity for the citizen's individual input, and not simply an interchangeable and generic (perhaps symbolic) gesture. While spontaneous and unstructured forms of public participation are important, the emphasis here is on institutionalized forms of public participation through legally and administratively sanctioned processes.[11]

While both direct and representative democratic systems are inherently linked to the concept of public participation, there are certain forms of public participation particularly associated with each. In the ancient Athenian model of direct democracy, popular assemblies were a key mode of public participation which allowed all citizens to involve themselves directly in the processes of governing. A major difficulty with such a system might be determining ways of achieving consensus in a fully participatory polity.

In representative democracies the elemental forms of public participation are indirect (for example, elections, question period in Parliament), and so the need for supplemental forms of public participation at the procedural and administrative level to ensure effective representation is increased. The further one strays from the direct democracy model, the more one needs to incorporate every possible form of public participation to compensate for the inadequacies of indirect, representative democracy. Dussault and Borgeat refer to the work of French legal commentator Isaac for the proposition that procedural administrative democracy is becoming an essential tenet in the welfare state, for it

> allows a more elaborate degree of democratization ... by situating the democratic process within the procedure for carrying out the decisions themselves, and no longer in the context of designating even local representatives.[12]

Cairns, in a recent article focusing on the symbolic and practical implications of Canada promulgating the *Charter*,[13] notes that

> [s]tate purposes now require so much popular support and participation if they are to succeed that we have no alternative but to move in the direction of a more participant citizenry, which shares on a day to day basis in the task of governing itself.[14]

In short, as a general rule, all institutionalized forms of public participation should be encouraged in representative democracies. And given that private prosecutions are a method of influencing government decisions, this form of public participation should be encouraged in the interest of ensuring effective representativeness of government.

. . . .

Private Prosecutions and the Machinery of Government

The decision to initiate a prosecution is a very serious one in our society, for it directly brings into question the character of the accused, and could result in deprivations of liberty or other interests. Damage to the character of the accused and enormous legal defence expenses may be incurred even though eventually the accused could be acquitted of all charges.[25] Reflecting the seriousness with which society treats such accusations, the rights of the accused in the pre-arrest (for example, investigation), arrest and trial stages

are preserved in the *Criminal Code*[26] and the *Charter*.[27]

In addition, in an apparent effort to ensure that only technically and substantively sound charges are proceeded with, responsibility for investigation of offences and initiation of prosecutions within government is usually divided among several Ministers. In theory these Ministers are politically accountable to Parliament or the legislatures and the electorate. Whether or not she is aware of it or desires it, the private prosecutor is a part of this process.

The question then becomes, where do citizen legal actions to enforce public wrongs fit, when there are officials who have been elected on the basis of popular consensus, and have been designated the responsibility of carrying out the functions of protecting the environment and supervising the justice system, on behalf of the public? To answer this it is necessary to examine the governmental prosecution decision process and its weaknesses. Once there is recognition of the inherent limitations in this process, the role for private prosecutions becomes clearer.

The prosecution process can be broken into three separate functions: detections, investigations and where warranted, prosecutions. In government, the prosecution functions are divided among several actors, and are subject to certain checks and balances. A major problem, from the perspective of the concerned citizen, is the visibility of this process: if it is difficult to observe what is happening, then there is greater potential for suspicion to arise. The recent British Columbia *Discretion to Prosecute Inquiry*,[28] established because of perceived wrongdoing concerning certain enforcement decisions in that province, is a perfect example of the dangers of government proceeding in a non-visible way. The Inquiry revealed that with respect to a government decision not to prosecute a certain public official, a credible, thorough investigation considering the merits of prosecutorial action had taken place and that there was no political or other improper influence or interference at any stage.[29] But this had not been made clear to all members of the public. As a result, one of them engaged in a private prosecution.[30]

With respect to environmental enforcement, responsibility for the process leading to prosecutions is divided primarily between the Minister of Environment and the Attorney General. Officials under the Minister of Environment are in the logical position to detect offences, and conduct investigations concerning them, relying primarily on information obtained through inspections, monitoring reports, and communications with regulatees and members of the public. This may lead to recommendations for prosecutions to the Attorney General, or to other enforcement actions, or to no action whatsoever. As will be discussed in greater detail later in the article, the need for the Minister to develop a publicly vetted and disseminated implementation policy which explains the Minister's approach to implementation and the criteria upon which responses are made, is clear. The need for publication of non-compliant regulatees is also readily apparent.[31]

. . . .

The Attorney General has the authority to intervene in any private prosecution to either conduct or stay it.[42] The authority of the Attorney General to supervise private prosecutions and ensure that improper actions do not proceed seems to be a sensible check on the private prosecutorial power, given that, at least theoretically, political accountability exists for this decision, and some private prosecutions may be ill-conceived. When the Attorney General *does* intervene and/or stay a private prosecution, the question of whether the public interest is being appropriately represented becomes an issue. The ability of Parliament and the courts to hold the Attorney General accountable for such decisions has increasingly been the subject of question in recent years.[43] The political accountability of Ministers of the Crown to the House of Commons, in the form of being called upon to answer questions and being censured in the case of wrongdoing, is limited in practice by party solidarity and the "after-the-fact" nature of any questioning which does take place.[44]

There is also a limited possibility of judicial accountability with respect to the Attorney General's decision to initiate and continue prosecutions and to intervene in the actions of private citizens. The most recent cases suggest that courts would not interfere with an Attorney General's decision to stay a proceeding absent proof of flagrant impropriety[45] or demonstration to the satisfaction of the court that the Attorney General acted with bias or had abused the law.[46] The introduction of the *Charter* may open further avenues for review and control of prosecutorial discretion, particularly in relation to the notions of fundamental justice[47] and equality.[48] Since *Operation Dismantle* v. *R.*[49] it has been clear that all executive powers are subject to scrutiny under the *Charter*: however, to date, the *Charter* has not been invoked successfully to overturn a decision of the Attorney General to stay a prosecution.[50]

The need for publicly vetted and disseminated criteria upon which decisions to stay or intervene are made is, again, readily apparent. Some jurisdictions, such as Alberta and British Columbia, have express policies that private prosecutions will not be allowed to proceed: the actions will either be conducted by the Attorney General or stayed.[51] Given the possible impact such a policy can have on the actions of citizens, a strong argument can be made that such policies should be publicly vetted and disseminated, and that the criteria upon which such decisions are made should be included. A general policy of providing reasons upon request for a decision to stay would appear to be a sensible additional check on the Attorney General's stay power, bearing in mind the limitations of political and judicial accountability at the present time.

It can be seen, then, that as the elected official appointed the task of supervising the prosecution, the Attorney General is the *primary* although *not* the exclusive guardian of the public interest. To some degree, her actions are accountable to Parliament and to the courts. However, in the absence of private prosecutions, it may be more difficult to hold the Attorney General accountable for decisions *not* to undertake prosecutions, than for decisions to prosecute.

In effect, a decision by the Attorney General not to prosecute can be all but invisible to Parliament, the public, and the courts. Private prosecutions force this decision process to the surface: either the Attorney General allows the private action to go ahead (raising the issue of why the Attorney General did not bring the action herself), intervenes and conducts the prosecution (raising the same issue), or stays the proceeding (which provokes questions as to why an enforcement action should not take place).

In light of these difficulties and the potential for conflict of interest, the importance of private prosecutions seems self-evident. It can be seen that emphasis on the function of private prosecutions as a check on government enforcement action or inaction bespeaks of its negative, constraining, and reactive characteristics as a means of participation — that is, in keeping with the philosophy underlying the representative theory of democracy, its purpose is to control the elected officials and the administrators responsible to them.

In a more positive light,[52] private prosecutions offer the opportunity for direct citizen involvement in the criminal justice process. One commentator remarks as follows:

> [A] criminal justice system that makes provision for private prosecution of criminal and quasi-criminal offences has advantages over one that does not.... In any system of law, particularly one dealing with crimes and quasi-crimes, it is of fundamental importance to positively involve the citizen. Giving him the opportunity of presenting his case before a court, even where a public official has declined to take up the matter, is one way of ensuring such participation.[53]

Thus, private prosecutions can be viewed as a useful supplement to government action, and not merely a check on government efforts. As will be seen, historically, this was the primary function of citizen enforcement.

. . . .

Summary Observations

This brief examination of the public participation provisions in environmental protection legislation suggests that there has been a significant evolution in approaches to citizen involvement in the past thirty years. The initial pollution control legislation was silent as to the role of the public, but the problems produced by letting the government and private sectors work without citizen participation soon became apparent. The next step was administrative recognition (in enlightened jurisdictions) of the role of the public through notice and comment procedures.

Finally, statutory integration of public participation in pollution control is now taking place in some leading jurisdictions. If the experience with other progressive legislation such as freedom of information and human rights statutes is any indication, once one Canadian jurisdiction has "taken the plunge" by establishing new, more rigorous standards, other jurisdictions will likely follow suit. The Manitoba *Environment Act* and the federal *C.E.P.A.* have taken the lead by formally recognizing the important role played by citizens in the pollution control process. Draft legislation for Alberta seems to follow this lead.[145] Unless there prove to be problems with this approach, it seems inevitable that the other provinces will soon adopt similar provisions in their own legislation.

The situation facing a private prosecutor in 1991 is not, however, a promising one. Administration of pollution control regimes is still largely an on-going technical liaison between government and regulatees, enveloped in informal intra- and inter-governmental agreements. There are few publicly disseminated compliance and enforcement policies, and information concerning the non-compliance of regulatees is not easily available. Thus, the citizen is still outside the "inner circle" of decision-making, and still has solid grounds for suspicion and distrust of government actions.

THREE CASE STUDIES: THE POLLUTION CONTROL APPROACH IN PRACTICE

Discussion to this point suggests that governments are beginning to appreciate the need for citizen involvement in environmental decision-making. In some enlightened jurisdictions there seems to be recognition that the legitimacy of government decisions is enhanced, and the likelihood of these decisions being challenged is reduced, when there is early and meaningful citizen participation. Usually, it is only when government fails to accommodate the concerns of the public in the early stages that private prosecutions occur. As the following three case studies demonstrate, private prosecutions are initiated out of fear, lack of understanding and frustration, in addition to genuine concern about the environment. Private prosecutions are the cry of the disenfranchised.

The three prosecutions included here all involve proceedings under the *Fisheries Act*,[146] and took place during the first half of the 1980s. The *Fisheries Act* has become the private prosecutor's vehicle of choice for a variety of reasons.[147] First, the Act is national in scope, so that its provisions are applicable in every region. Second, at the present time, it can be used in spite of existing provincial legislation,[148] and in spite of compliance with provincial standards.[149] Indeed, as we shall see, it can even be used when *federal officials* are satisfied with provincial actions.[150] Third, penalties for breach of the *Fisheries Act* pollution provisions are significant — higher than in some provincial legislation.[151] Fourth, the *Fisheries Act* is binding on both the federal and provincial Crown, thus permitting actions against both levels of government. Finally, regulations passed pursuant to the Act entitle those who initiate or conduct prosecutions to one half of any penalty imposed.[152]

These three actions have been chosen for their variety: the proceedings take place in three different provincial jurisdictions, concern both spill and continuous pollution incidents and demonstrate both citizen-conducted and citizen-initiated litigation. All three illustrate the range of obstacles which face citizens wishing to initiate actions against perceived industrial emission polluters and the range of governmental reactions to such proceedings.

R. ex rel. Howe v. Cyanamid Inc.[153]

Over the period of 1976 through 1980, Michael Dickman, an associate professor of biology at Brock University, with the assistance of some of his students, monitored the effluent deposited into the Welland River by Cyanamid Canada of Niagara Falls, Ontario. The Cyanamid plant manufactures chemical fertilizers. The results of Dickman's monitoring efforts indicated that Cyanamid was discharging substances which were highly toxic to fish into the Welland River. Dickman learned that Cyanamid was the subject of a Control Order issued under the provincial *Environmental Protection Act*.[154] The terms of the Control Order permitted Cyanamid to discharge air and water pollution until 1984, as long as specified improvements and additions to the plant's pollution control equipment were introduced at various dates in the interim.

In 1979, Dickman contacted officials of the provincial Ministry of Environment (M.O.E.) and expressed his concerns with respect to the toxic discharge. In a letter to the Director of Legal Services of the M.O.E. dated February 27, 1979, Dickman concludes: "I feel that I lack the legal experience to pursue this much further and I'm seeking your advice re a vehicle for pursuance."

In reply to this letter, the Director of Legal Services of the M.O.E. pointed out that Cyanamid was in compliance with the terms of the Control Order, and that, by what was then ss. 102(2) of the *E.P.A.*, compliance with a Control Order renders an operation virtually immune from prosecution under that Act. The Director also noted that prosecution of Cyanamid by the M.O.E. under another statute, be it provincial (for example, the *Ontario Water Resources Act*[155]) or federal (for example, the *Fisheries Act*), in the

absence of some new development or indication of bad faith on the part of Cyanamid, would detrimentally affect the credibility of the M.O.E. However, in closing, the Director added "[i]t may be that these considerations would not be serious obstacles to yourself or some private prosecutor taking action under the Fisheries Act."[156]

In 1980, Dickman, in conjunction with a local environmental group, Operation Clean, and the Canadian Environmental Law Association (C.E.L.A.), began preparations in earnest for a *Fisheries Act* prosecution. Officials from the Ontario Ministries of Environment and Natural Resources were contacted. They confirmed that the Ontario position had not changed from that expressed in the 1979 letter to Dickman from the Director of Legal Services of the M.O.E.[157]

The federal Departments of Environment (D.O.E.) and Fisheries and Oceans were also contacted. Officials from the D.O.E. provided the Dickman group with technical advice on how to successfully prosecute under s. 33(2) of the *Fisheries Act*. However, the D.O.E. itself declined to conduct the actual prosecution against Cyanamid. The Honourable John Roberts, speaking for the D.O.E. replied:

> I understand that the Cyanamid Company (Welland Plant) has so far been in compliance with the water pollution control requirements outlined in the Ontario Ministry of the Environment Control Order. While I recognize the current problem with fish toxicity at the Cyanamid plant, the Control Order does specify future requirements for the complete installation of control measures to achieve the Ministry's objectives for fish toxicity and other parameters. Therefore, in this particular instance, we accept the Ministry of the Environment Control Order issued under provincial legislation as being a satisfactory means of achieving our objectives. My officials and I do not believe that there is anything to be gained through unilateral legal action against the company or further bioassay tests by the Department.[158]

Finally, on March 23, 1991, Margherita Howe, head of Operation Clean, laid an information against Cyanamid, alleging that the company discharged substances deleterious to fish into Welland River contrary to the terms of the *Fisheries Act* ss. 33(2) (as it then was). The case was closely followed by the press from the time of the laying of the information through to the court's verdict.[159]

At trial, Wallace J., noted that "[t]he charge is a private complaint, Federal Justice and/or

Fisheries authorities having declined an invitation to prosecute."[160]

Wallace J. observed that the only fish in the canal are catfish, "a scavenger fish not prized by sport fishermen."[161] He also noted that the Welland river system empties into the Ontario Hydro generating plants and turbines, so that "[a]ny fish finding their way into the hydro canal system are doomed."[162]

Dickman conducted the toxicity tests for the prosecution and provided expert testimony regarding the effluent at trial. The prosecutor's cause was also furthered by the testimony of an Ontario M.O.E. toxicity scientist. Wallace J. noted that tests using rainbow trout placed in the effluent revealed that "[w]ithin 51 seconds all fish placed in the aquariums containing effluent were dead. All of the fish in the aquariums containing Welland River water lived for many hours."[163]

In his summary of the facts of the case, Wallace J. made the following observations which foreshadowed his eventual decision:

> The effluent in issue was being deposited into the Welland River under the watchful eyes of Ontario environmental authorities. These authorities ... had spent more than a year in attendance daily at the Cyanamid factory studying the Cyanamid production processes and preparing an engineering emission study with respect to both air pollution and water pollution. These authorities had complete cooperation and assistance from Cyanamid executives at all times.
>
> The efforts of the Ontario environmental authorities culminated with their issuing ... a Control Order, directing and ordering Cyanamid to install certain pollution control equipment by certain dates set out in the Control Order. Certain of the equipment was to be installed during the first year of the order, certain of it to be installed in the second year of the Order and so on until the year 1984, by which time all equipment would be in place.
>
> The Ontario authorities therefore, set up a schedule of priorities concerning pollution control. They gave higher priority to air pollution control than to water pollution control, presumably on the basis that air pollution affecting thousands of citizens was of higher priority than water pollution affecting a handful of catfish.
>
> The cost to Cyanamid by the conclusion of the program in 1984 will be about 20 million dollars. Nine million dollars has been spent by Cyanamid up to the end of 1980. ... All equipment has been installed on time and Cyanamid is not in default under the pollution Control Order.
>
> At all times the Ontario pollution control and authorities [sic] have monitored the progress of Cyanamid. At all times the cooperation of Cyanamid with these authorities has been exemplary.

> Some difficulty has been encountered with respect to the installation of equipment ... There was a delay to permit the necessary technology to be developed. Then some processes considered were found unsuitable because they would not function in cold weather. ...
>
> Because of the provision of ... the *Environmental Protection Act*, ... and because Cyanamid Canada Inc. is not in default under the provisions of the Control Order ... Cyanamid ... cannot be prosecuted under the provisions of the said ... *Act*.[164]

Counsel for Cyanamid raised three defences: first, that the prosecution had failed to prove the *actus reus* of the offence beyond a reasonable doubt; second that the *Fisheries Act* pollution offence applies only to commercial waters; and third, that the company had exercised due diligence.[165] With respect to the *actus reus* contention, although there were some weaknesses in the evidence of the prosecution,[166] the court held that there was proof beyond a reasonable doubt.[167] On the basis of several cases and dictionary definitions. Wallace J. held that the *Fisheries Act* pollution offence applied to the protection of the entire natural resource of the fishery, not merely commercial fisheries as maintained by the counsel of the defence.[168]

Wallace J. then considered the defence of due diligence. The defence had a district engineer with the Ontario Ministry of Environment testify that the company was complying with the provincial Control Order and that the control program would cost Cyanamid about $20 million when completed in 1984. Nevertheless, Wallace J. rejected the defence in the following manner:

> It appears to this Court to be obvious that the due diligence to be established must be referable to the specific offence before the court. The test is whether Cyanamid did all that a reasonable corporation would have done in the circumstances and took all reasonable steps to avoid the outflow of ammonia effluent from its factory into the Welland River *on March 23rd, 1981*.
>
> The evidence discloses and I find that Cyanamid has done all that a reasonable corporation would have done in the circumstances and has taken all reasonable steps to avoid the outflow of ammonia effluent from its factory into the Welland River *as of the year 1984* when all processes required by the Control Order of February 10th, 1978, have been installed and are operational.
>
> I find, however, that due diligence to prevent an offence in 1984 is not an answer to an offence to have occurred on March 23rd, 1981 (emphasis added).[169]

Wallace J. found Cyanamid guilty as charged. He added the following comment:

> I appreciate the fact that it would have created a tremendous financial burden upon the accused corporation to have closed and sealed the pipe on or before March 23rd, 1981, and it may have required that the Cyanamid factory be shut down and that many jobs be lost. These factors, however, do not relate to the issue of guilt or innocence with respect to the charge before this Court. They are mitigating factors which will be weighed by the Court in the imposition of sentence.[170]

He then considered sentencing, and began by enumerating eleven "mitigating circumstances which are to the benefit of Cyanamid."[171] These included the poor quality of fish in the Welland River, the fact that there was no evidence of a fish kill in the Welland River because of the Cyanamid effluent and no evidence of deterioration of the water because of the ammonia effluent, the compliance of Cyanamid with the Ontario Control Order, the approval of Ontario officials of Cyanamid's activities, the excellent co-operation with Ontario officials, the substantial financial commitment of Cyanamid to abatement, and the fact that shutting off the pipe would cause a loss of jobs and severe financial consequences to Cyanamid.[172]

Wallace J. concluded by saying "I trust that the penalty that I am about to impose will reflect where I consider this case rests on any scale of severity," he then levied a penalty of one dollar with one month to pay.[173] Subsequently, Cyanamid installed a $23 million ammonia waste treatment plant.[174]

R. v. *Crown Zellerbach Properties Ltd.*[175]

From March 1977 through January 1980, Crown Zellerbach Properties Ltd. of British Columbia and its associates (Crown Zellerbach) were engaged in a landfill operation on a site which had two creeks flowing through it. The creeks eventually emptied into the Fraser River. On February 11, 1977, Crown Zellerbach applied for what was then called a pollution discharge permit from what was then known as the British Columbia Pollution Control Board (P.C.B.). The P.C.B. referred the application to federal D.O.E. officials for comment, as was the agreed upon practice, and on October 17, 1977 the P.C.B. permit was granted. The interactions between P.C.B. and D.O.E. officials with respect to the landfill operations from 1977 to 1980 indicate

continuous friction between the two authorities, with the D.O.E. desirous of stricter terms and stricter enforcement by P.C.B. (the lead agency).

While it is quite evident that the D.O.E. was not satisfied with the enforcement efforts of the P.C.B., there is no available information suggesting that the D.O.E. intended to prosecute on its own. In 1980, a federal official privately assisted a citizen, David Aldcroft, with the gathering of samples for a prosecution. Aldcroft was a member of the environmental group the Fraser River Coalition. He laid an information against Crown Zellerbach, alleging breach of s. 33(2) of the *Fisheries Act* (as it then was).

As in the Cyanamid situation, the local media took a strong interest in the action: Aldcroft told a reporter that he laid the charges "to shame the federal government into acting."[176] In fact, agents of the federal Department of Justice actually conducted the prosecution. At trial, Groberman J. took full cognizance of the P.C.B.-D.O.E. referral system, and noted that D.O.E. concerns were not being fully met by the P.C.B. enforcement actions.[177]

Expert testimony from D.O.E. personnel played an integral role in the eventual findings of the Court. Crown Zellerbach raised a defence of due diligence, claiming that it was conforming with the terms of a provincial discharge permit, which had itself received federal input. Groberman J. rejected the due diligence defence:

> Vendev [an associate of Crown Zellerbach] did respond to problems raised by the Pollution Control Branch but did not carry out a sufficient site inspection which, in my opinion, is a serious flaw in the system.
>
> I am also mindful of the differing opinions expressed between the Provincial Pollution Control Branch and the Federal Environmental Protection Services. However, they both agreed, "No leachates."[178]

Two of the four corporate members of the Crown Zellerbach landfill operation were found guilty as charged, and fined a total of $28,000. Pursuant to the *Fisheries Act Forfeitures Regulations*, Aldcroft received one half of this penalty ($14,000). At the conclusion of the trial, Aldcroft announced his intention to "sink the money into further prosecutions against polluting industry, individuals or municipalities."[179]

The problems with Crown Zellerbach did not end with the private prosecutions. In 1981, the federal Department of Fisheries and Oceans brought several more charges against the company.[180] The Provincial Court held that Crown Zellerbach had acted with due diligence by co-operating with authorities, setting up a regular inspection process, and attempting to contain the leachate.[181] The Court held that there were no leachate solutions available prior to the spring of 1982, at which time the company installed power aeration units costing $250,000 which solved the problem.[182]

R. v. Suncor Inc.[183]

In 1964, the Great Canadian Oil Sands Company (G.C.O.S.) began construction of a plant for the extraction and commercial recovery of oil from the Athabasca tar sands. Located at Tar Island, some thirty five miles north of Fort McMurray in northern Alberta, the facility commenced operation in 1967, the first of its kind. Later, G.C.O.S. amalgamated with Sun Oil to form Suncor.[184]

As part of plant operations leading to the extraction of oil, the facility uses large volumes of water from the Athabasca river, and eventually, through a wastewater system, liquid effluent is deposited back into the river. The plant itself is massive, occupying 7500 acres, designed to produce 58,000 barrels of oil a day. It employed over 1700 persons at the time of the prosecutions under study here.[185] The wastewater pond alone is 45 acres.[186] Because oil sands themselves are unique, in turn, the methods and technology used to extract oil have been distinctive, and defy comparison with traditional extraction and refinery techniques. One judge who viewed the plant facilities said the following:

> After completing this [tour of the plant] I could not help but be struck by the magnitude and complexity of this facility which consists of a mining operation and extraction plant, a refinery and a power generator and steam generator plant, and one becomes totally aware of the tremendous amount of materials that are required to be handled under high temperature and high pressures in all kinds of weather conditions and it was thereafter much easier to conceptualize the difficulties faced by Suncor in pioneering these methods and in applying this new technology to oil sands extraction.[187]

The only other major oil sands recovery operation, Syncrude, came on stream in the 1970s, years after the original G.C.O.S. facility had been constructed, and uses what is known as a "closed water system" which apparently avoids many of the effluent problems associated with the G.C.O.S./Suncor facility.[188] While the federal government has developed regulations under the *Fisheries Act* for the discharge of effluent from conventional refineries,[189] none have been forthcoming for oil sands recovery plants.[190]

The Fort McKay Indian Band is located downstream from the Suncor plant,[191] as is a fish plant.[192] Lake Athabasca, also downstream, supports commercial fishing.[193] The Chief of the Fort McKay Indians, Dorothy Mary McDonald, is reported to have said, "Our problems began in 1976 when Suncor opened. We've had to stop using river water that we have used for generations. Our babies especially started getting sick."[194] In 1978, permission was granted by the Alberta government for a major expansion of the plant, scheduled for completion in 1981. While there have been many water pollution problems at the G.C.O.S./Suncor plant since its inception,[195] the focus of discussion here will be on the period beginning immediately prior to the laying of charges in February and March, 1982.

Although both federal and provincial governments have jurisdiction (and legislation) to control water pollution, in Alberta and across the country, it is provincial officials who play the lead role.[196] During the time period under consideration here, the main regulatory tool pertaining to Suncor's wastewater effluent was the provincial *Clean Water Act*,[197] and more specifically, a licence to operate issued pursuant to that legislation. The Alberta Ministry of Environment had (and continues to have) the lead responsibility with the respect to pollution matters, although, as well shall see, provincial Ministry of Public Lands and Wildlife officials in the Fish and Wildlife division and Energy Resources Conservation Board officials in the Ministry of Energy also participate in environment-related decisions. Provincial Fish and Wildlife officials have been appointed fisheries officers under the federal *Fisheries Act*.[198]

Expansion of the plant was authorized in 1978 by a *Clean Water Act* licence, which was subsequently amended in November, 1980 to include further reporting requirements.[199] For the whole of 1981, Suncor experienced many serious operational problems which the plant associated with the completion of the expansion in the year.[200] Records submitted by Suncor pursuant to its licence of operation indicate that in all but one month in 1981, oil and grease emissions were above permitted levels.[201] According to one report, Alberta Environment officials were aware of problems with the release of water contaminants since June 1981, but apparently had not required any specific studies or followup action by Suncor at that time.[202]

In November 1981, Alberta Environment officials met with Suncor representatives and requested that the company investigate certain matters and report back to the department.[203] In December, 1981 and again in January, 1982, the plant was hit by a series of fires and explosions, which caused significant damage and forced shutdowns of some processes.[204] It was evident following a major fire on the wastewater pond on January 21, 1981, that a large amount of oil had escaped from the plant into the water pond.[205] Suncor attempted to clean up this oil using vacuum trucks for several weeks after the fire.[206]

One report indicates that a meeting took place between Suncor and Alberta Environment on January 26, 1982, but that prior to that time "the company showed no concern for the safety of downstream users of the Athabasca River."[207] As a result of that meeting, Suncor was ordered to warn the Fort McKay Indian Band.[208] Nevertheless, as we shall see, the Fort McKay Indian Band was not notified until late February.

While records kept by Suncor indicated substantial increases in effluent starting on February 9,[209] company employees showed no "particular concern."[210] An external habitat biologist flying over the site between February 12 and 15 observed "orange substances" on the ice beside the Suncor plant, and on February 15 notified a Fish and Wildlife officer who attended the site on February 16, and contacted the water quality manager from Suncor. The two men observed excessive oil in the wastewater pond and a sheen of oil in the river.[211] On February 17 and March 9, samples were taken by the Fish and Wildlife officer.[212]

On February 18, an official from the Energy Resources Conservation Board inspected the site and suggested remedial measures to Suncor or contract employees of Suncor.[213] Members of the Fort McKay Indian Band were not informed of the situation until February 24.[214] On February 25, Alberta Environment officials issued a Water Quality Control Order with respect to Suncor's problems.[215] On February 26, Chief McDonald laid five separate informations, alleging breaches of s. 33(2) of the *Fisheries Act* between February 21 and 25, 1982.[216] Chief McDonald testified that band members began complaining of mouth sores, diarrhea and headaches while drinking

melted river ice during January and February.[217] Following this, the Alberta Attorney General's office laid an additional fifteen charges under the *Fisheries Act* and two others under the *Clean Water Act*.[218]

The first actions to reach the court were with respect to the *Clean Water Act*, for exceeding licence effluent limits for the period February 20 through 24, 1982, and failing to report the incident to Alberta Environment on or about February 21, 1982. With respect to the charge of exceeding the licence limits, Suncor raised a due diligence defence, maintaining that the fires and explosion of December 1981 and January 1982 were disasters not caused by their negligence, that the disasters occurred during the worst winter in twenty-five years, and that they had acted reasonably in the circumstances.[219] Because there was no suggestion by the Crown that the disasters were caused by negligence (i.e., the due diligence defence was not challenged by the Crown), the Court accepted the due diligence defence.[220] The company was, however, found guilty of failing to report, and a fine of $500.00 was levied.[221]

The lack of challenge to the due diligence defence, and failure on the part of the Attorney General to appeal the verdict was to haunt the Crown in subsequent proceedings. The next set of informations to be decided upon by the Court were those *Fisheries Act* charges initiated by Chief McDonald. The Attorney General of Alberta assumed responsibility for conducting the case. Shortly after proceedings began, the original Crown prosecutor became "emotionally and mentally prostrated and was unable to continue with the Trial."[222] A long delay followed (the defence unsuccessfully made an application for relief on the grounds of s. 11(b) of the *Charter*), after which the Court dismissed four out of five charges on grounds of issue estoppel. The Court ruled that since the *Fisheries Act* deleterious deposit and *Clean Water Act* licence contravention charges overlapped for all but one day, and since the Court had already found that due diligence had been exercised with respect to the *Clean Water Act* contraventions, it would lead to inconsistent verdicts for the court to find Suncor guilty under the *Fisheries Act* for those overlapping days.[223]

However, as there was no overlap between the *Clean Water Act* verdicts and the February 25 *Fisheries Act* charge, the Court proceeded to consider this charge. After considering extremely technical arguments concerning (1) the inaccuracy of measuring techniques used by the accused Suncor in its effluent reports which were relied upon by the Crown in its case (it was held that the inaccuracies were not significant[224]); (2) whether the emissions were deleterious (the oil and grease concentrations were held to be "capable of giving rise to sublethal effects in fish" and therefore deleterious[225]); and (3) a due diligence defence (hiring of an inexperienced official to clean up oil spills, failure on the part of the company to properly react to inspector's warnings[226]), Suncor was found guilty. In sentencing, the Court made several strong criticisms concerning the response of government to Suncor's situation. First, that "the people responsible for producing regulations for Plants have not seen fit to produce regulations for Plants of this nature and it's a factor I take into account."[227] Second, the Court took into account the fact that Suncor had been exceeding permitted limits on numerous occasions and that

> this seems to have taken place without causing any excitement in the authorities who were supposed to look after this and, you know, if the watchdogs aren't going to get worried, it is a little difficult to see why the company should get excessively worried in those circumstances.[228]

A fine of $8,000 was imposed.[229] Proceedings had begun on October 21, 1982, but, because of problems with the prosecutor and the "complicated and technical nature of the proceedings,"[230] the verdict was not delivered until June 3, 1983.

On October 17, 1983, the Provincial Court commenced hearings concerning two other alleged deposits of substances deleterious to fish contrary to s. 33(2) of the *Fisheries Act*, occurring February 17, 1982 (i.e., *before* the other already decided upon charges) and March 9, 1982. The information had been laid by officials from the Ministry of Fish and Wildlife, not private citizens; however, they were initiated after charges had been brought by the Fort McKay Indian Band concerning the same situation. As with the previous proceedings, the trial was extremely lengthy and convoluted. There were some 49 witnesses called, many of whom were expert. The trial lasted 76 court days, with final supplementary written argument from the Crown being submitted on March 26, 1985, and the decision being rendered May 25, 1985. The court waded through evidence and arguments concerning the legal definition of "deleterious of fish," the actual

deleteriousness of the deposits, the correct testing procedures and constitutional arguments.[231] Eventually, Suncor was found guilty on both counts and a total fine of $30,000 was levied.

Total prosecution costs for the February and March, 1982 incidents at Suncor have been estimated to be several million dollars.[232] In March, 1982, the wastewater system was altered and upgraded with considerable success.[233] The real impact of the Suncor trials, however, appears to have been on the Alberta Ministry of Environment. Following the trials, in 1987, Alberta Environment established a Review Panel on Environmental Law Enforcement which reported in January, 1988. Among other things, the Panel recommended promulgation of a government approved, publicly reviewed, enforcement policy outlining detailed criteria for enforcement responses, and the creation of an environmental enforcement unit. The Review Panel also recommended changes in the legislation which would improve administrative and court powers to respond to pollution incidents, and place new responsibilities on polluters.[234]

In 1988, the Pollution Control Division was reorganized, with two branches, one responsible for investigating complaints and responding to emergencies (the Investigation Branch), the other responsible for reviewing draft licences and making decisions on correct compliance responses (the Compliance Branch).[235] Negotiation no longer takes place at the enforcement state regarding, for example, the type of enforcement or whether there should be an enforcement response.[236] In 1990, new draft legislation was announced which followed many of the Review Panel's recommendations,[237] and a formal enforcement policy is currently being drafted;[238] in the meantime, officials maintain that they are following the general approach contained in the Action Plan.[239] Several private prosecutions have been attempted since the Suncor incident, but have been stayed or are still under consideration at the time of writing.[240]

Analysis

It would be impossible to assert that these three case studies of private prosecutions are in some way typical or indicative of the range of outcomes and issues which arise when citizens take matters into their own hands. Nevertheless, they do illustrate many of the problems which face private prosecutors: the attitudes of courts in such cases, the technical nature of many pollution incidents, and the extent of inter- and intra-governmental, as well as government regulatee, interactions. For this reason, these cases provide a factual backdrop for the analysis which will follow.

A first and self-evident observation that emerges from the case studies is that private prosecutions can be successful. Obviously, however, "success" is a relative term. There are a host of possible criteria for determination of a successful prosecution. These include convictions, penalties and the effect on the reputation of the private prosecutor. Measured in terms of convictions, all three prosecutions were a success. If some modicum of penalty were to be imported into the equation, arguably the *Cyanamid* case was a failure. Those who maintain that citizen prosecutors are mere "busybodies" and meddlers might point to *Cyanamid* and the thinly veiled irritation of Wallace J. for support of their position. On the other hand, the Cyanamid company *did* install a major ammonia recycling plant after the prosecution.

In fact, in all three cases, significant pollution abatement actions took place following the prosecutions. While one cannot state with certainty that the abatement action itself, or the speed of that action, was due to the prosecutions, the alternative theory available — that clean up was merely a coincidence — seems considerably less plausible.

All three actions forcefully illustrate the inadequacies of informal and *ad hoc* inter-governmental agreements. These agreements are strung like tripwires across the hazy enforcement landscape, ready to fell the unwary. Their status is unclear: the public may or may not be aware of them, governments may or may not follow them, and judges may or may not choose to recognize them. An alternative system is necessary....

Equally problematic are the on-going relationships between government and regulatees. As can be seen from all three of the case studies, the fact that regular communication between government and regulatees takes place as technical solutions are worked out appears to be a necessary evil. But there is a heavy price to pay for this necessity. There is the increased likelihood that on-going relationships will compromise government's ability to make decisions to prosecute when the time is right. To a certain extent, the dangers of on-going government-

regulatee relationships can be avoided: each of the milestones toward an abatement solution can be formally set out in a licence or Control Order (as in the *Cyanamid* case, at the Ontario M.O.E. level, but formal federal approval of the Ontario actions was missing), special enforcement squads can be created, separate from the negotiators.[241] ... Private prosecutions can act as an important check on relations becoming too cosy. The difficulty is, how can an outsider to the process determine when a prosecution is appropriate? The technical and non-public nature of these relations raise suspicions and present major obstacles to private prosecutions.[243]

Evident in all three of the case studies were the tremendous informational, technical and financial resources necessary to secure convictions for pollution offence violations. The fact that in all three cases the accused raised due diligence defences is indicative of a particularly difficult obstacle facing the private prosecutor. In all three cases, the actions of government officials seemed to be on trial as much as those of the accused. Usually, only government officials will be in a position to refute arguments by the accused that government acquiesced with company plans. Yet if government does not intervene and conduct the prosecution, there is the possibility that the due diligence defence will succeed, thus potentially estopping other actions.[244]

The impression left by all three of the case studies is that the citizen has been left "out in the cold" — outside of the pollution control process. But the private prosecutions succeeded in pointing a very powerful spotlight on the actions of government, and in many cases found them wanting: they exposed unstructured enforcement discretion as well as loose and informal arrangements between government agencies. Taken together, it is no wonder that citizens have become suspicious and have engaged in such actions. Some might contend that the situation has changed since these prosecutions took place. This is undoubtedly true. As we have seen, new legislation has been put into place in some jurisdictions, and is contemplated in others. Enforcement units have been established in many provinces.[245] Approaches toward enforcement have changed in some jurisdictions. But ... [u]ntil ... reforms are made, private prosecutions are likely to continue to be viewed by government and industry as a problem, rather than a useful adjunct to government enforcement.

(h) Kingston Resident Wins Fisheries Act Prosecution of City[†]

Dawn Pier ─────────────────────────────────────

Janet Fletcher is one of the few private citizens in Canada to prosecute a government successfully for an environmental offence.

In December 1998, Justice of the Peace Jack Bell of the Ontario Court found the City of Kingston guilty on seven out of eight counts of violating the federal *Fisheries Act*. In February, Justice Bell sentenced the city to pay a fine totalling $150,000 and ordered that the city develop a remediation plan within one year.

Under the unusual "fine-sharing" provisions of the federal fisheries law, Fletcher was awarded one half of the fines resulting from the four charges she initiated. Justice Bell explained that it was the Court's hope that this would "reinforce the intent of the [*Fisheries Act*] legislators to encourage public participation in the protection of community interests."

Fletcher's charges relate to the Belle Island Park dump site, located on the western shores of the Great Cataraqui River in Kingston, Ontario. The city operated a dump at the site between 1952 and 1974. Anecdotal evidence suggests that everything from industrial and laboratory waste to household garbage were disposed of in the dump. The site was later converted into a public golf course and a children's recreational day camp.

Evidence of the dump's effects on the adjacent river has been visible during several winters when the ice nearby is stained brown by iron-rich leachate coming out of the north end of the dump. Local residents, concerned about the brown staining, contacted the municipality and local Ministry of the Environment and Energy (MOEE) officials on several occasions. Nothing was done to address their concerns.

In 1991, Fletcher obtained evidence that the Belle Island site was a potential source of contamination to the Great Cataraqui River. While investigating the effects of a different dump on the river, she and six other local citizens found information in MOEE documents obtained through access-to-information requests indicating the dump was leaking contaminants.

A 1992 MOEE inventory of all Ontario dump sites placed the Belle Island dump in the category of greatest concern for environmental impact. The local MOEE abatement office tried to persuade the city that something had to be done about the site, but no charges were laid.

Stella Couban, of the MOEE legal services branch, explains that "the Investigations and Enforcement Branch [IEB] were at the mercy of huge cutbacks under the Harris government. The only IEB officer in the local office, David Kerr, was laid off during this period. They just didn't have the resources to follow-up on this issue."

In 1996, Fletcher's interest in the dump was renewed when she was approached by a concerned citizen aware of her activism. Together with Sierra Legal [Defence] Fund lawyers Doug Chapman and Mark Mattson, Fletcher collected samples of leachate that was "oozing" out of the dump in December of that year.

Analysis and testing of the samples by Beak International Laboratories indicated that they contained a toxic mixture of benzene, chlorobenzene, undisclosed heavy metals and ammonia. Standardized toxicity tests demonstrated that rainbow trout exposed to the leachate quickly died.

In March 1997, Fletcher brought charges under Section 36(6) of the *Fisheries Act* that on four days between December 5 and 17, 1996, the City of Kingston unlawfully permitted the deposit of a deleterious substance into the Great Cataraqui River, which is frequented by fish, and therefore committed an offence contrary to Section 40(2) of the act.

In a unique twist, three months after Fletcher laid her charges, the MOEE laid a set of similar charges against the city and its environmental engineer Mirka Januszkiewicz. It

─────────────────────────────

† Reproduced with permission from "Citizen Case," *Alternatives Journal: Environmental thought, policy and action* 25, 3 (1999): 10. Annual Subscriptions $25.00 (plus GST) from Alternatives Journal, Faculty of Environmental Studies, University of Waterloo, Ontario N2L 3G1 <alternat@fes.uwaterloo.ca>.

was later agreed that the eight charges laid by Fletcher and the MOEE would be heard concurrently by the court. The court upheld all four of Fletcher's charges and three out of four of the ministry's charges.

The Fletcher *vs.* City of Kingston pollution case has brought a number of environmental law enforcement issues to public attention. On the day Kingston was sentenced in the Belle Island case, *The Globe and Mail* featured an article exposing a new MOEE policy that directed ministry investigations officers not to pursue specific types of complaint. Examples of offences that the inspectors were told to ignore include raw sewage discharges to rivers by pleasure craft, many pesticide infractions, and littering.

Fletcher says she does not relish her role as environmental watchdog, and feels that she should not have to be doing the job of government enforcers. She maintains that her activism is necessary only because "legislation has been abandoned" by federal and provincial government ministers responsible for environment law enforcement.

Even in the Belle Island Park dump case, Fletcher's job is not done. The City of Kingston is now appealing Justice Bell's decision.

Three

Assessing Environmental Change

Editors' Notes

ENVIRONMENTAL ASSESSMENT

Ron Pushchak ————————————————————————————

The term Environmental Assessment (EA) refers to two things: first, it is an administrative process intended to determine, avoid and mitigate the environmental impacts of new projects. As David Estrin and John Swaigen (1993: 188) put it: "[a]n environmental impact assessment is a planning process designed to identify and assess the effects that a program, plan, project, or other undertaking might have on the natural and human environment". Second, an EA is a document that records the process of assessing the predicted environmental impacts or facts of a new project. It is a public record that shows the scope of the environmental investigations, the prediction of impacts and the value judgments made about whether the impacts are acceptable. It is open to review by all who are affected by the decision and, in many jurisdictions, it is subject to a hearing by a board or panel that determines whether the EA is adequate in assessing environmental impacts.

The environmental assessment process has become the modern focal point for conflicts about ecosystem facts and values because it provides a single opportunity to reject a project if it is expected to cause unacceptable environmental impacts. Because the EA represents a "one time only" chance to reject an action that will harm the environment, it has become a critical locus of environmental disputes for opponents and proponents alike. Further, the EA reveals how much a society values its environmental resources by the number of economically beneficial projects it rejects on the basis that the impacts on the natural environment are expected to be too damaging. The EA process is used to determine whether undertakings should proceed and, if so, what steps should be taken to reduce or mitigate the negative impacts. The environmental assessment process, as Estrin and Swaigen note, is intended to shift the emphasis away "from the technological emphasis on pollution control approvals ... to a wider concern for the social, economic, cultural, and environmental implications of development" (Estrin and Swaigen, 1993: 190). Michael Jeffery (in this volume) describes the development of the environmental impact assessment process as "a radical departure from existing regulatory models in environmental policy". It has changed the "focus from regulation and control to planning and prevention"; it is anticipatory rather than merely reactive.

Environmental Assessment Origins

The process of environmental assessment was first created in the United States in the *National Environmental Policy Act* (NEPA) of 1969. It arose as a response to the public outcry against many large public and private projects that caused significant environmental losses, and that could not be stopped because no environmental approval was required. Those who participated in the environmental movement leading up to NEPA argued that once a project was built, its impacts thereafter could not be avoided. The government was pressed by the public to provide an environmental approval process for new projects, and NEPA was the result. NEPA also established the first environmental assessment process by requiring that every agency of the federal government prepare an environmental impact statement (EIS) on all policies they propose or actions they take that will significantly affect the environment. Beginning with NEPA, federal agencies had to evaluate the environmental consequences of their activities before they could carry them out. Since NEPA, the EIS process has been adopted to some degree in many jurisdictions, including Canada and the provinces.

Canadian Environmental Assessment Origins

The first (and, some would suggest, still the strongest) piece of environmental assessment legislation in Canada was the Ontario *Environmental Assessment Act*, passed in 1975. However, until the recent enactment of the *Canadian Environmental Assessment Act* (CEAA) in 1992, there was no formal federal environmental assessment legislation in Canada. Instead, federal environmental assessment was carried out under a Guidelines Order put in place through a series of Cabinet directives from 1972 to 1977. At the time, the view of government was that the order was discretionary, and departments could apply it or not as they wished.

Although the guidelines were reinforced in 1984 as the Environmental Assessment and Review Process (EARP) guidelines, there was no federal law that clearly required an EA until 1992. In reality, the EARP guidelines did not give the Minister the statutory authority to force an agency to do an EA. Because it was not a legislated, formal requirement, the process depended on the co-operation of departments and agencies in assessing environmental impacts. This continued until 1979, when the *Government Reorganization Act* provided a statutory basis for a federal EA process by giving the federal environment minister the power to establish environmental assessment guidelines for federal departments and agencies. The minister could establish guidelines, but still could not compel a federal department or agency to assess the environmental impacts of their projects (see Steven Hazell's discussion in Section Two of this volume). Court rulings, such as the Rafferty-Alameda and Oldman River dam cases discussed below, made clear that what the government believed was a non-binding guideline was, in fact, a legal requirement for federal projects with significant environmental impacts. These court decisions paved the way for passage of the federal act in 1992.

Provincial Environmental Assessment

Thomas Meredith outlines the legal basis for EA, and he notes that the purposes of EA in Canada and the provinces were to both avert environmental disasters at the local scale and to educate decision-makers in adapting to new environmental pressures. He notes that the legal and institutional framework for EA varies somewhat from one jurisdiction to another. The following description is based mainly on the Ontario legislation, but the process is broadly similar in other provinces. The environmental assessment process typically involves the submission to a government agency of an assessment document prepared by the proponent of the undertaking. This document is both a scientific report on the predicted environmental impacts of the proposed project, and a policy decision on whether the project's impacts on the environment are acceptable. The document is reviewed by government(s) and other interested parties, including members of the general public. If the issue is controversial, a hearing may be held before a special tribunal, such as the Ontario Environmental Assessment Board. In such a hearing, evidence is presented and witnesses can be cross-examined.

In Ontario, an EA is done for each "undertaking". Undertakings are new proposed projects; examples include proposals to construct a dam, to site a landfill or to build a new highway. In Ontario, undertakings include physical projects (enterprises or activities) by government, but they also include proposals, plans or programs by provincial government agencies, public bodies or municipalities. While the current Ontario process does not generally include private commercial or business projects, the Minister of the Environment can designate commercial or business projects as undertakings for the purpose of conducting an environmental assessment.

In Ontario, environmental assessment applies not only to discrete projects, but to categories of frequent, similar projects, each one thought to be too small to warrant an assessment of its own. Such an assessment of a category of undertakings is called a "Class EA". For example, it is not necessary to undertake an EA every time a road is built across a stream; stream-crossing practices and standards were assessed once and for all in a Class

EA. Because the implications of a Class EA decision can be far-reaching, the fact and value issues raised can be extremely complex. For example, the longest and most contentious hearing ever conducted by the Ontario Environmental Assessment Board thus far concerned the Class EA for forestry practices in northern Ontario. In other jurisdictions, rather than exclude a class of projects, lists of projects are often identified for exclusion. In most EA systems, there is some attempt to exempt from EA those projects assumed to have little or no effect.

In approving an environmental assessment, two decisions must be made. First, is the document acceptable; that is, is it scientifically adequate, and does it consider all the alternatives? Second, is the proposed undertaking acceptable? Knowing what changes will happen to the environment because of the project, should it go ahead and, if so, what conditions should be imposed on it? The first decision is clearly a policy issue, the second reveals how the environment is valued.

From the point of view of proponents, the EA process may be frustrating and onerous because of the large and indefinite range of issues that must be taken into account and because clear standards for assessment are lacking. Environmental assessment legislation typically defines "environment" very broadly, and provides little guidance on what kinds of impacts must be examined or what kinds of issues must be addressed. Nor does it typically provide an indication of the level of scientific rigour with which environmental impacts must be predicted, or how the acceptability of those impacts will be judged. If the assessment document is found wanting because some issues of concern to other government agencies or members of the public have been neglected, or because the scientific quality of some aspect of the report is poor, further studies may be ordered. The proponent is thus liable to incur unpredictable costs and delays. Even if the assessment document is accepted, the predicted environmental impacts may be judged by the EA agency or tribunal to be unacceptable, so that the project may be rejected or approved subject to unanticipated terms and conditions.

Because of these risks, experienced proponents try to involve interested parties much earlier in the assessment process than the legislation may require. They make an effort to discover what aspects of the proposed undertaking are likely to be controversial, so as to focus the range of issues to be considered. This procedure is often referred to as "scoping", because it sets out what components of the environment will be assessed and for which impacts. In Ontario, the recent 1997 changes to the EA legislation have made scoping an official part of the EA process. The act requires proponents to draft a "Terms of Reference" document that identifies the scope of the assessment at the beginning of the EA, and mediation can be imposed by the government to resolve conflicts about the scope of the study before the EA begins.

Where the potential for conflict over the proposed undertaking is large, stakeholders may attempt to achieve consensus by means of mediation. Environmental mediation is discussed further in this volume (see Section Four). Environmental mediation uses negotiation to try to arrive at a proposal that is minimally acceptable to all parties. In the Ontario EA process, parts of it are subject to mediation to assist negotiations among parties to the conflict. Mediation can occur at the beginning in accepting the terms of reference (ToR) for the EA, and at the end concerning the decision whether to approve or reject the EA. The minister may appoint the EA Board as mediator to assist the negotiation (see mediation and arbitration). At the federal level, the 1992 *Canadian Environmental Assessment Act* specifically provides for mediation in lieu of, or in addition to, a hearing before a tribunal panel.

In this volume, the Ontario legislation is examined in an excerpt from the report of the Environmental Assessment Advisory Committee. Environmental assessment in Ontario has been criticized for the following: "the government's failure to apply the Act to the private sector, its exemption of many significant public undertakings, the lack of requirements for information sharing and public involvement, and the failure to provide intervenor funding at the planning stages of assessment" (Estrin and Swaigen, 1993: 188). The Environmental Assessment Advisory Committee was formed to address the issue of reforms to the Ontario

Environmental Assessment Act. The excerpt from the report of the EAAC in this section elaborates on the context of decision making and the factors considered in the reform process.

Federal Environmental Assessment

Under the *Canadian Environmental Assessment Act*, all projects are screened for potential environmental impacts that might require a full investigation. Where it is determined by the screening process that significant environmental effects might occur, the project is referred to an EA panel. The panel is appointed by the Minister of the Environment, in consultation with the federal agency (responsible authority) that has proposed the project. The panel is intended to be free of conflicts of interest and to have knowledge or experience relevant to the anticipated environmental effects of the project. The panel holds hearings and hears evidence about the EA. However, the minister has the power to set the terms of reference for the panel, and set the scope of the hearings for the project.

The EA panel has the authority to conduct public hearings on an environmental assessment that is contested. The hearings are to be public, and the panel acts as a quasi-judicial body with some of the procedures found in a court of law. The panel acts as a judge: it can summon witnesses and compel them to testify, it hears evidence, and can compel the presentation of documents, and allows cross-examination of witnesses. It judges the adequacy of the EA and makes recommendations to the minister about acceptance or rejection.

In his review of the federal process in this volume, Andrew Nikiforuk points out the weaknesses of federal Environmental Assessment, its lack of coherence and limitations in following democratic process that make it a bureaucratic exercise rather than a means of protecting the environment from substantial ecological losses. He draws attention to the many opportunities for government interference in the EA process and the failures of a number of EAs to reject projects that would cause significant environmental impacts. Nikiforuk concludes that: "Environmental Assessment has become a cynical, irrational and highly discretionary federal policy in Canada. What should be a coherent and democratic filter to ensure that ecological and economic follies do not ruin Canada's natural riches has become a bureaucratic exercise that is neither cost-effective nor conservation-minded" (Nikiforuk, 1997: i).

Environmental Assessment Effectiveness

Kristin Shrader-Frechette points out that environmental assessments tend to focus on technical and scientific issues of fact and, accordingly, they seldom seriously address alternatives to the undertaking at the level of broad policy goals. Arguably, however, this is a problem inherent in the EA approach, where proponents are required to assess whether the environmental impacts of their own projects are acceptable. In most cases, proponents have little reason to seriously consider alternatives to their own preferred projects. Also, the proponent is often in no position to implement policy alternatives even if they were to be considered. For example, in assessing the impacts of a highway, the Ministry of Transportation may confine its attention to details of routing and impact mitigation, rather than addressing social alternatives, such as whether the need for the highway could be eliminated by more compact urban form and higher energy prices. These latter factors are, however, far beyond the control and jurisdiction of the proponent.

Questions about the effectiveness of EA have been raised because proponents who originally objected to having EA imposed on their projects have now institutionalized EA. Where proponents once resisted EA because it delayed projects, raised costs and hindered development initiatives, they now include EA in their development plans, served by a large consulting industry where the expense of an EA and its legal and scientific experts is simply part of the "cost of doing business". Furthermore, if proponents are successful in the

EA, the approval tends to make other opportunities for opposing a new project more costly for the opponents and less likely to be successful.

Furthermore, at neither the federal nor provincial level are all activities subject to environmental assessment. Except for some waste management facilities, private sector projects on private land — whatever their scale and potential environmental impacts — are not generally subject to assessment under the Ontario legislation. As both Jeffery and the EAAC point out, both federal and provincial assessment processes have tended to regard only discrete physical projects such as highways, dams and fossil fuel extraction facilities as "undertakings". Government policies, for example, have not regularly been subject to environmental assessment, although Ontario Hydro, the provincial utility, found its plans to expand its energy production facilities were subjected to an EA and were turned down because the need for additional power could not be justified.

The article by Michael Jeffery reproduced here discusses the origins and some of the shortcomings of the new federal legislation. Jeffery undertakes a sustained analysis of the significant features and serious shortcomings of the previous system — based on the Environmental Assessment Review Process (EARP) guidelines. He finds the two main weaknesses of the former system to be: (1) that it is based on the principle of self-assessment, and (2) that there was a lack of authority for review panels. These panels effectively had an advisory function only.

Jeffery also evaluates the proposed reforms contained in the CEAA, and finds the proposed act disappointing "primarily because it fails to address many of the more insidious deficiencies inherent in the existing" process. The proposed act, as Jeffery puts it, "does not remove conflict of interest concerns, both real and perceived, associated with the underlying principle of self-assessment". The responsible authority, which tends to be the proponent of a project, continues to have the ultimate decision making power. This problem highlights the difficulty of public confidence in a process that does not seem to embody due process or that lacks fairness and justice. Further, it is not clear whether the public is entitled to participate in the environmental assessment process in any meaningful way.

Jurisdictional Conflicts

The highest-profile legal issues surrounding environmental assessment in Canada have had to do with conflicts between federal and provincial jurisdictions. Since environmental assessment legislation exists at both the federal and provincial levels, it is necessary to determine under which jurisdiction an undertaking falls. If an undertaking falls under provincial jurisdiction, it is subject to provincial assessment; if it falls under federal jurisdiction, it is subject to federal assessment. Most private undertakings will fall under provincial jurisdiction. Some projects impinge on both federal and provincial jurisdiction. Even projects where the proponent is a provincial government or Crown corporation may involve overlapping jurisdictions, if the project may "have impacts on matters within federal jurisdiction, such as fisheries, navigable waters, or nuclear power" (Estrin and Swaigen, 1993: 191). Jurisdictional disputes featured prominently in the Rafferty-Alameda and Oldman River dam cases.

The Rafferty-Alameda and Oldman River sagas serve to illustrate a pattern of relationships between provincial governments, the federal government, and environmental advocates that can be observed in the context of pollution as well as environmental assessment (see Harrison, 1995, and the Webb article "Taking Matters into Their Own Hands" in Section Two; see also chapter 4 in Steven Hazell's *Canada v. the Environment*, which reviews the secrecy and political interest brought to bear in the Rafferty-Alameda case). Provincial governments jealously guard their jurisdiction over natural resources, but may be reluctant to exercise that jurisdiction in ways that environmentalists would like. The federal government seeks a positive record on environmental protection, but also attempts to avoid the blame for measures that might impose economic costs. As a result, it is often happy to defer to the provinces on matters of environmental jurisdiction, and to shift to the provinces the responsibility for implementing federal environmental laws and policies. Environmentalists, dissatisfied with provincial governments' administrative decisions, have attempted to use the courts to force the application of federal law. Private prosecutions for pollution infractions under the *Fisheries Act* are instances of such citizen invocation of federal jurisdiction, as are the Rafferty-Alameda and Oldman River suits.

The difference between the *Fisheries Act* prosecutions and the EA dam cases is that the former are instances of quasi-criminal law, whereas the latter are instances of administrative law. In administrative litigation, the courts may be asked to force government agencies to act in accordance with their legal mandates. In the dam cases, the courts ruled that the federal EA guidelines orders legally required the federal government to conduct assessments on projects falling within federal jurisdiction. The federal cabinet had originally created guidelines orders rather than legislating an environmental assessment process, mainly because it did not want to be legally bound and did not want to invite U.S.-style administrative litigation. Ironically, the courts interpreted the guidelines as being legally binding, and the dam cases ended up being the closest Canadian equivalent to American environmental administrative litigation. Because the federal government's strategy backfired, it had little to lose by moving to a statutory framework for environmental assessment (Doern and Conway, 1994).

The legal and political wrangling concerning these two water resource management projects are detailed in the article by Jeffery in this section, and the article by Charles and VanderZwaag in this volume. In the Oldman River case, "the Supreme Court of Canada confirmed that projects will often require assessment under both federal and provincial EA processes". The new *Canadian Environmental Assessment Act* "contains several provisions to permit its application to projects that appear to be primarily local", such as ones "where the project relies on any federal funding, or where it requires any federal licence or approval". Consequently, Ontario's 1997 revisions to the EA Act provided for the "harmonization" of federal and provincial requirements so that if a federal EA was done, an Ontario environmental assessment would not be required.

The promise of environmental assessment at the outset was "revolutionary" because it suggested to proponents and the public alike that projects causing significant and unacceptable environmental impacts could be prevented (Lang, 1979). It was also revolutionary because in an EA, decisions about the acceptability of a project's impacts would not be made by its proponents, but through a public process that predicted impacts objectively and documented them openly. It was also a sea change in public decision-making, because it promised, in the last resort, that proponents or governments would not make the crucial decision, and that an impartial panel or board would, rather, assess the impacts fairly. Despite the widespread adoption of EA as a decision method in more than 100 countries and by many international organizations, the papers in this section indicate some of the distance that still lies between the facts of environmental damage caused by new projects and the values society uses in protecting the environment.

SCIENCE AND THE LAW

Alex Wellington

The Interdependence of Science and (Environmental) Law

Both science and law are, in effect, institutionalized fact-finding processes, with the crucial difference that in law there are added elements that go above and beyond simply finding out the facts. To the extent that they share ground as fact-finding institutions, they embody and instantiate certain epistemic goals: (i) descriptive accuracy; (ii) identification, characterization and reduction of uncertainty; and (iii) provision of a transparent evidentiary basis (Walker, 2001: 358). There are similar institutional constraints that bear on the processes of scientific research and on legal decision-making, such as the pressure of administrative efficiency, the need to ensure fairness to the parties (or to research subjects and consumers of end products of research), and to merit and maintain public confidence (ibid.). Stephen Breyer (1998) points out that science and law are interdependent. On the one hand, "[t]he practice of science depends on sound law" to set the parameters within which research is carried out (Breyer, 1998: 537). Actions of government officials, legislatures and courts "profoundly affect not only the resources and opportunities of the scientific community but also the conduct of its affairs" (Kennedy and Merrill, 2000: 49). On the other hand, "the law itself increasingly requires access to sound science" (Breyer, 1998: 537). As Kennedy and Merrill (2000: 49) say, "decision makers in all three branches of government increasingly rely on, and to decide wisely must understand, the disciplines and products of science". Society depends for its well-being on both "scientifically complex technology" and the legal regulation of its use and application (Breyer, 1998: 537).

A host of issues of contemporary concern involve the law-science interface: the reliability of polygraph lie detector tests or DNA "fingerprinting" quality control; the validity of expert predictions of defendants' future dangerousness; the reasonableness of an administrative agency's conclusions about the safety of a drug, or about the risks attending nuclear waste disposal, or the leakage potential of a toxic waste dump, or the threat to wildlife associated with the building of a dam (Breyer, 1998: 537). Many of those issues pertain to environmental matters. Environmental law, as is alluded to in the "definition" of environment presented in the "Introductory Essay", is interdisciplinary and complex, dealing with evolving ecological processes and systems. Environmental law, as Kiss and Shelton (1997: 9) explain, "uses science to predict and regulate the consequences of human behaviour on natural phenomena". Thus, a proper understanding of environmental law requires a firm grounding in, and respectful consideration of, scientific knowledge (Kiss and Shelton, 1997: 9).

It will be helpful to provide a nutshell summary of the basic characteristics and rationales of the scientific method. As Ayala and Black (1993: 234) explain, empirical science is distinguished from other forms of knowledge by the principle of empirical testing. Any scientific explanation, i.e., one that "tries to explain why events take place and organize that knowledge systematically", must be subject to testing (ibid.). Therefore, a scientific explanation is always vulnerable to being proven false. The hallmark of science, then, is testable predictions and the "possibility of rejection based on observation or experiment" (ibid.). Furthermore, such testing must be repeatable, and it must be undertaken in a careful and fruitful manner. Science is inherently a "cumulative endeavour in which each scientist must build on the work of others", and thus the "scientific community places great emphasis on weeding out false ideas" (Ayala and Black, 1993: 238). To minimize the potential for error and bias, and "to facilitate reliance on previous work when conducting new research, science has developed a number of institutional review mechanisms", as Ayala and Black (ibid.) note. Foremost among those is the system of "peer review".

Ayala and Black (1993: 238) provide this account of its rationale and importance:

> Peer review represents both an effort to police scientific claims and an attempt to assure their widest possible dissemination. The pressure on scientists to publish derives not only from narrow concerns about recognition and career advancement, but also from the desire of all scientists to learn of new developments that may guide their work. Because submitting a paper for peer review is the best way to establish priority for a new discovery or idea, the process serves to get new information out fast as well as to control its quality... Any claim that would significantly add to or change a body of scientific knowledge must be regarded quite sceptically if it has not been subjected to some form of peer scrutiny, preferably by submission to a reputable journal.

Sociologists of science have themselves expressed scepticism about the ability of "novel" or "unorthodox" findings or theories to find their way past the "peer review" process, which is far from perfect, in their estimation. "Policing the boundaries" of disciplines or fields of enquiry has, at times, as much to do with issues of professional prestige and status, power and control, and competition in the access to limited sources of funding, or other factors than simple quality control. In the field of "environmental science", for instance, there are hotly contested struggles over what counts as the "real science" relating to climate change, genetically modified organisms, and so on. It is important to note that judges, in their determination of what counts as valid and thus credible, and even admissible, evidence in court proceedings, have relied upon the social practice of peer review (as discussed below).

A proper understanding of environmental law also entails an appreciation of the special role played by scientific expertise in legal proceedings. Such expertise is needed, as Kiss and Shelton emphasize (1997: 9), "not only to advise on the current state of knowledge, but to predict and assess risks in areas of scientific uncertainty". The court relies upon experts to present scientific evidence, but often the legal experts (judges and juries alike) who are charged with interpreting and assessing that evidence lack sufficient "scientific literacy" to enable them to be good consumers (Malone, 2000: 83). The problems caused by pervasive scientific uncertainty and the difficulties of evaluating expert testimony are the focus of many of the readings in this section. How court and, specifically judges, deal with that expertise in the trial setting is dealt with below.

While recognizing the commonalities and connections between science and law, it is nevertheless crucial to see their differences clearly, and also to keep in mind the fact-value distinction. In addition, the differences between law and both facts and values will be a theme of these notes.

Facts, Values and Interpretation

Facts and values have already been contrasted, and elaborated on, in the context of regulatory policy-making and standard-setting, in the editors' notes to Section Two, "The Regulatory System". There, we emphasized the role of economics in relation to the fact-value distinction. Here, we want to revisit the topic, and emphasize the role of science in relation to the fact-value distinction. Then we will broaden the analysis in order to incorporate an emphasis on "interpretation". First, we will focus on the relevance of the distinction between facts and values for regulation, and environmental assessment or risk assessment.

Questions of fact are questions about the nature of the case. They concern descriptions of the world, accounts of states of affairs. Whether exposure to a certain chemical increases the risk of cancer is a question of (scientific) fact, although there may be very little actually known about the specific causal mechanisms by which it does so. How much an exposed individual's risk of cancer goes up is a question of fact, and the increased risk is usually presented in probabilistic terms. The evidence for that increased risk may come from toxicological sources — experiments on animal models and extrapolation to humans, or from epidemiological data, concerning the incidence of disease in given populations. How much it would cost to ban the chemical, or to protect people from exposure to it, for instance at the worksite, is also a question of (economic) fact.

Questions of value are questions of good and bad, right and wrong, fair or unfair, just or unjust. Values pertain to judgments of importance, and prescriptions about what ought or ought not to be done. Whether reducing the risk of cancer by a given amount is judged to be worth the cost of restricting the carcinogenic chemical is a question of value. Whether the government should ban a particular chemical in order to prevent harm to health due to exposure is a question of policy. Thus, the policy issue of how the chemical in question should be regulated, and whether or not it should be approved or allowed, is a matter of both fact and value.

In setting out to analyze policy issues, it is important to keep the following in mind. Issues of fact and issues of value, as we emphasize in the notes to Section Two, need to be carefully distinguished. The failure to clearly distinguish fact claims and value claims in an analysis can lead to the failure to appreciate that both play a role in policy formation. It is a mistake in logic to claim to derive evaluative or prescriptive conclusions from purely factual premises — what is known as the "naturalistic fallacy", or "Hume's is-ought dichotomy" (after David Hume, a philosopher who identified it).

Kristin Shrader-Frechette, whose article is reproduced in Part A of this section, diagnoses this kind of mistake in environmental assessment. The problem arises from treating policy questions or policy judgments as if they were purely scientific or technical questions — that is, as if they were purely questions of fact. Shrader-Frechette and Donald Brown, whose article is reproduced in Part B of this section, point out that discussing, or treating, policy judgments as solely scientific does not actually mean that values are not operating. It just means that the value assumptions implicit in the discussion are taken for granted, and therefore go unchallenged. Those value assumptions cannot be properly justified, if at all, unless they are made express and explicit. Brunk, Haworth and Lee's piece in Part C of this section provides a sophisticated analysis of the role of value assumptions in risk assessment. In it, they report that different scientists, on the basis of honest and competent analyses of the same raw data, came up with vastly different estimates of the cancer risk posed by the herbicide Alachlor. The differences reflected the different values and biases of the scientists. Those who favoured the use of agricultural chemicals tended to arrive at low estimates of risk, while those who valued caution where toxic health risks are concerned arrived at high estimates.

As both Brown and Shrader-Frechette argue, focusing on technical (seemingly factual) issues to the exclusion of value issues often has the effect of biasing the analysis in favour of "business as usual". Nevertheless, one often finds that parties on both (or all) sides of an environmental controversy argue as if the issues in dispute could be settled entirely by appeals to fact claims. Those who want to see a chemical banned, for example, may emphasize the fact that the chemical increases the risk of cancer, while those who oppose the ban may emphasize the fact that the risk is small, or they may highlight the fact that the economic cost of banning the chemical is substantial. However, the weight and significance of these different claims depends upon value assumptions that may not be explicitly addressed. In this case, the argument for banning the chemical may rely on the unstated value assumption that any increase in the risk of cancer is unacceptable, regardless of the benefits that may be obtained from the product. The argument against banning the chemical, on the other hand, may rely on the unstated value assumption that small risks are morally insignificant — especially by comparison with much larger risks that people voluntarily assume — or that all policy questions should be decided on the basis of economic efficiency (the application of economic analysis, covered in the notes to Section Two).

Donald Brown points out that even decisions about what to study, and how much to spend on studies, are ultimately questions of value. Values, or ethical perspectives, will determine what weight or emphasis facts are given, and what role particular facts will play in justifying a certain course of action or policy. Different parties to social conflicts tend to emphasize different facts, as illustrated just above, and it is thus crucial to identify which facts are relied upon by which parties when analyzing the conflict. As Donald Brown makes clear, however, it can be just as problematic to attempt to treat fact and value issues as completely separate. That can lead to a failure to appreciate the subtle, complex, and influential connections between fact claims and value claims in the formation of policy.

Brown's article provides a comprehensive account of various factors and influences on environmental policy-making that distort the process. These factors include: the presumed separation of facts and values (detailed just above); the translation of all value questions into economic language (the over-reaching application of economic analysis); the pressure to make decisions through cost-benefit analysis; the pressure for limiting government regulatory activity; the tendency for technical analysis to be incomplete; and the distortions caused by narrow focus on risk assessment. Brown also provides recommendations to improve public policy procedures, and to increase the involvement of concerned citizens.

Patrick Malone (2000: 84) has this to say about the potential of science to influence law: "the power of science to make good public policy lies more in the rigor of its method than in the 'facts' it discovers, which are always subject to revision. The power of science to make bad policy lies in the failure to scrutinize critically the unspoken values implicit in many scientific 'truths'". Donald Brown and Mark Sagoff (1985) caution policy-makers to carefully distinguish between the reliance upon science to determine the means to achieve goals that are chosen on some other grounds, and the reliance upon science to determine goals, or ends. The former — using science to select optimal means of achieving goals — is necessary, and even desirable; but the latter, they contend, is not. Science, like economics (see editors' notes to Section Two), is thus appropriate for determining the means (to realize ends), but not for determining the ends, or goals, or policy objectives. Law-makers should refrain from "hiding their value judgments behind ostensibly objective science" (Malone, 2000: 84), and should engage in political discussion, debate and deliberation over values. In addition to the political points being made here is a prudential one: that science is, in effect, "always up for grabs", subject to revision as new data comes in. Mark Sagoff (1985) details several situations where the understanding of the ecology changed, and the revised account no longer directly supported the policy claims that had rested upon it. The need to base policy — at least in part — on value claims, while seemingly a "tougher sell", will ultimately, be inescapable.

Legal Interpretation

We now need to bring in the crucial notion of legal interpretation. It is evident that interpretation plays a central role in law. Indeed, as Ruth Sullivan (1997: 1) points out: "It is impossible to do anything in law without interpreting the words of others and anticipating how others will interpret (or misinterpret) one's own words". The need for the act of interpretation is pervasive throughout the various elements of the legal system, discussed in the editors' notes to Section One — legislation, judgments, rules of court and statements of claim. The law is, as Sullivan puts it, "extracted from these texts through interpretation" (ibid.). Judicial interpretation decides whether a particular act of government, legislation or policy, is or is not *ultra vires*, or outside the bounds of its constitutionally authorized jurisdiction, and whether it does or does not conform to the requirements of the *Charter of Rights and Freedoms*. Judicial interpretation also determines whether an administrative agency has acted "reasonably", within the terms of its jurisdiction (*intra vires*), through the mechanism of judicial review.

It is worth saying a bit about how the process of legal interpretation is normally carried out. Initial impressions of the meaning of legal texts are arrived at through the same application of "ordinary linguistic intuition" and "common sense", as other acts of interpretation make use of (Sullivan, 1997: 2). However, that is just the beginning; those initial impressions must be "informed by legal values and principles", which are themselves introduced and developed through the use of specific "rules" of statutory interpretation (ibid.). Such rules consist of "principles, policies, presumptions, doctrines, maxims and directives" and they perform several functions. Those rules: (i) tell interpreters what to take into account when dealing with legislative texts; (ii) supply the vocabulary for analyzing and explaining the texts; and (iii) shape the arguments that interpreters use to defend their preferred interpretations, and — if they are judges — to justify their decisions (*ibid.*). A text in statutory interpretation will cover the various approaches to interpretation: contextual analysis, purposive analysis, consequential analysis, and the "plausible meaning rule". In addition, there are situations in which courts will introduce policy analysis into statutory interpretation, and circumstances under which they will rely upon so-called extrinsic aids to interpretation (typically, the legislative history).

What legal decision-makers are doing is discerning or discovering the "facts of the case", and then applying the relevant law — statutes, common law precedents and legal principles — to those facts. There is, in effect, a division of labour in cases involving both a judge and a jury, which is much more common in the United States than in Canada. Juries perform the fact-finding function (deciding on guilt or innocence, liability or absence of the same). Juries apply the law as it has been explained to them by the judge. Juries, as Fitzgerald and Wright (2000: 112–13) explain, "are a 'lay presence' in the administration of law", and they are meant to be broadly representative of the community. It is worth saying a bit more about the relative prominence and significance of juries. In commonwealth countries, "[t]he right to trial by a jury of one's peers has long been regarded as an important constitutional liberty" (Fitzgerald and Wright, 2000: 113). Yet, in Canada today, "less than ten percent of criminal trials" involve juries, and "juries in civil cases are even more rare than in criminal proceedings" (ibid.). In the United States, however, the right to jury trial is constitutionally mandated by the Seventh Amendment. Even then, the common law and the codified Federal Rules of Evidence give "judges the authority to limit the admissibility of evidence if it will cause confusion or unfair prejudice" (Ayala and Black, 1993: 230). This power to exclude testimony, and its implications, are discussed below, in the discussion of "The American Experience".

What, then, is the role of the adjudicator? The adjudicator (judge or jury) selects, from among the various witnesses and pieces of testimony offered up as evidence, the most credible. In certain situations, as just mentioned, the judge decides for the jury which particular experts and which types of evidence will be presented to them. The adjudicator thus determines which account of the facts will be the legally validated one, and applies the law to that account. The distinction between fact and law is thus of crucial importance. It is also critical to distinguish the concept of "law" from the notion of "value", generally, although this is much more difficult to do.

We can remind the reader that the Legal Realists — discussed in the Introductory Essay, "A Law and Society Approach to Environmental Law" — insisted that law was simply a prediction of what the courts (i.e., judges) will decide. The judges have their "values", beliefs and attitudes arising from their education and training, class position and family background, life experiences, and so on, and those values lead judges to decide the way they do. Some commentators emphasize the more elite background of judges, as compared, for instance, to the "regular folk" who serve as members of juries (Jasanoff, 2001). This picture, however, is too simplistic (as we pointed out in the Introductory Essay). It seems to conflate several distinctive aspects of judicial decision-making, and overlooks crucial dimensions of legal reasoning.

When a judge is making a ruling, whether it involves statutory interpretation or interpretation of precedent, the judge is applying the applicable law as he or she understands it. Judges may find themselves having to apply rules that are valid laws yet are not in concordance with their personal substantive values or with the values of the wider society. These rules are not any the less law for being unpopular, although they may end up being targets for legal reform campaigns, and understandably so. The rules of equity were developed by judges who felt that the strict application of common law rules could lead to injustice or unfairness. Those maxims of equity include value claims, of a sort: "equity aids the vigilant"; "he who comes to equity must come with clean hands", "equity looks to the intent rather the form", "delay defeats equity" (*Osborn's Law Dictionary*). Some of these are more substantive in orientation, and some sound more procedurally based. The principles reflect and represent different values than the ones the judges interpreted to be at work in the common law rules they hoped to supplement, or even supplant.

Different parts of the law may be related to different values or policy goals. For instance, the goal of general or compensatory damages is to ensure compensation of the victim. Punitive or exemplary damages, on the other hand, are intended to achieve the goals of deterrence, and other non-utilitarian goals of punishment, such as retribution (a deontological approach) or public denunciation of the defendant's conduct. The goal of rehabilitation is another value that is not served by either of these types of remedies, and can provide a critical perspective, and potential inspiration, for future reform.

Once the judge has decided, then the law on that topic — as a matter of social fact — is what the judge has said it is, unless and until a higher court overrules or overturns that initial decision. The subsequent ruling by an appeal court may replace a different interpretation of the law for that earlier one, and the law then becomes that subsequent interpretation. The appeal court judges rely upon their understanding of the "correct" law, the "right" interpretation, in order to substitute their judgment for that of the lower court judge. From the judge's perspective, which is a participant's view, there is "law" to which they are endeavouring to be true. From the legal scholar's perspective, or the viewpoint of any observer, the law may simply seem to be "what the courts in fact decide"; but that can only ever be merely part of the story, never the whole story.

There are, then, distinctively different values at play at any given time, including ones that are embodied or manifest in the law, and ones that provide a critical perspective on that law. The subtle nuances of the connections between law and morality, particularly in "hard cases", where judges can and often must exercise their discretion, or in situations involving constitutional interpretation, with its foundation in political morality, are the focus of much of the work of contemporary philosophers of law.

Process values, rather than substantive values, are also relevant to an understanding of the judge's perceived duty, and for assessing the merits or demerits of a legal system as a whole. Stephen Breyer, a judge of the United States Supreme Court, elaborates on the unique and distinctive role of judicial decision-makers. Their role differs from that of scientists and other fact-finders or truth-seekers, and from that of politicians and policy-makers. Judges are generalists, he says, who deal with wide ranging and highly variable kinds of cases. Their main focus is on the parties before them and the instant case. Their primary objective is usually process related, i.e., "seeing that a decision is reached fairly and in a timely way" (Breyer, 1998: 537). Judges are committed, moreover, to the "transparency of the adversary process" (Jasanoff, 2001: 34). They are also committed to the underlying rationales of the adversary system — with its techniques of discovery and cross-examination, which we touch on briefly below.

There are "legal" values that apply at the level of a legal system. It is argued that any legal system needs to satisfy "procedural" moral demands of justice or fairness. These demands relate to impartial enforcement of rules that apply prospectively (not retroactively) and that are publicly promulgated, and so on. Lon Fuller calls these demands the "internal morality of law", or the "morality that makes law possible" (Murphy and Coleman, 1990: 39). A legal system that rested upon vague or ambiguous rules, ones that changed constantly on a case-by-case basis, or were applied "after the fact", or enforced arbitrarily, would not be considered an adequate legal system, even if admitted to be one. These norms are formal or procedural, however, and do not speak to the content of the specific rules that constitute the law.

Science in the Courtroom

Rules of Evidence and "Scientific" Findings

In the editors' notes to Section One, "The Elements of the Legal System", we pointed out that rules of procedure (civil and criminal) need to be distinguished from the rules or law of evidence, although they do intersect. The distinction between them was noticed initially by legal philosopher (and proponent of utilitarianism) Jeremy Bentham, and explicitly emphasized by the famous legal scholar Wigmore (Shapiro, 1983: 182). The latter — rules governing the admissibility of evidence, and especially expert testimony, have been a particular concern of scholars writing on environmental issues.

Toxic Torts: Hajo Versteeg's piece reproduced here focuses on the specific problems of evidence in toxic tort cases, a very important area of environmental law. Toxic tort cases, as William Charles and David VanderZwaag (this volume, Section One, Part B) explain, are "civil lawsuits brought by plaintiffs to address exposure to toxic agents (chemical, biological, or radiological)". "Toxic tort", it should be said, is not itself a legal category: the specific legal cause of action could be negligence, nuisance, trespass, riparian rights, strict liability (tort), etc., depending on the particular facts of the case. Some commentators (Berger, 2000: 57) call toxic tort cases a "subspecies of product liability litigation", but the category can be broader than that. Generally, a toxic tort case is one in which the harm to the victims' health or property is due to exposure to toxic substances.

Charles and VanderZwaag (this volume) differentiate between three distinct categories of toxic tort cases. One of these — the "no present injury" kind — involves plaintiffs who have been exposed to toxic agents and are at risk, but who have not yet manifested signs of injury, personal or physical (to land). The plaintiffs will still try to claim for recovery, based on several factors: (a) the expenses of monitoring their health or ecological impact to land, (b) compensation for the fear of developing a serious disease, and/or (c) decline in property value due to the "stigma" effect, the negative public perception attending the risk. Another kind of case involves exposed plaintiffs who do suffer a present injury, but have difficulty establishing a causal link to a particular defendant's tortious activity. The complicating factors include the long latency periods of certain conditions, during which time numerous potential defendants were involved with the manufacture, distribution and use of a toxic agent.

There is a third kind of toxic tort case identified by Charles and VanderZwaag. In these cases, involving "preemptive legal action", the plaintiffs pursue litigation to prevent a threatened exposure to toxic agents. The remedy would consist of an injunction prohibiting or restricting the activity in question. A case of this third sort is the much discussed *Palmer v. Nova Scotia Forest Industries*, a brief excerpt of which is included in the readings for Section One, Part B (see the second of the pieces by William Charles and David VanderZwaag). The plaintiffs were trying to stop the spraying of phenoxy herbicides (specifically a 2,4,5-T and 2,4D blend) used to control woody vegetation in forestry. The particular herbicide had dioxin-contaminants, which were generated as a by-product of the production process. Evidence from both toxicology and epidemiology had provided cause for concern about dioxin, as Versteeg (this volume) notes. The toxicology tests had demonstrated that dioxin produced "cancer, mutation and birth defects in laboratory animals". Epidemiological studies indicated that human beings "exposed to dioxin have a statistically significant increased incidence of cancer and birth defects". Dioxin-contaminated herbicides were also the focus of the Agent Orange litigation in the United States (Schuck, 1987). The company, Stora Kopparbergs, had obtained permits from the appropriate regulatory authorities for the use of the herbicide in spraying. The plaintiffs asked the court to grant an injunction to prevent the spraying, on the basis that they would be exposed to a higher risk of injury if it were allowed. They based their case mainly on nuisance and trespass to land, although they also alleged other causes of action.

The judge in the *Palmer* case (Justice Nunn) denied an injunction to the plaintiffs, and in so doing dismissed the significance of evidence of harm from high-dose animal exposure to the substance in question (TCDD — dioxin). Bruce Wildsmith (1986) notes that shortly after the Nova Scotia court decision in the *Palmer* case, the Dow Chemical company — the major supplier of 2,4,5-T products — announced that it would no longer market products containing 2,4,5-T. Ultimately, the U.S. Environmental Protection Agency totally banned the use of that product for any purpose in the United States (Charles and VanderZwaag, this volume). The case became the focus of a 1984 National Film Board of Canada documentary, *Herbicides Trials* (directed by Neal Livingston). The case is mentioned again (several times) briefly below.

Versteeg's discussion of toxic tort cases begins with an account of the policy rationales underlying legal burdens and the onus of proof. Pardy (1989) likewise focuses on the evidentiary problems and standard of proof issues in his treatment of the topic. In the editors' notes to Section One, we drew a sharp contrast between criminal and civil law, in terms of burden of proof and other characteristics. Versteeg emphasizes the different burdens of proof, but he also highlights the common foundation, historically, for the presumption of innocence in criminal law, and the development of burden and onus allocations in civil proceedings.

Versteeg's account emphasizes the general goals of tort law, which have been mentioned or discussed elsewhere in this volume. Those goals are to compensate victims, deter socially unacceptable conduct, and to provide for fairness and justice (Versteeg, this volume). There are good policy reasons, Versteeg writes, for requiring plaintiffs to establish the cause-effect nexus in tort cases, and having to prove that a particular activity caused that plaintiff's particular injury. In the bulk of tort cases, the "wrongful conduct of the defendant and the resulting damage to the plaintiff are contemporaneous and obvious", Versteeg says (this volume). Yet, ensuring that justice is done may not be so easy in certain kinds of tort cases that depart from this norm.

Tort law generally "assesses civil liability for injury or death", and thus it "often requires difficult determinations about the degree of risk of death or injury" represented by human activity (Breyer, 1998: 537). In toxic tort situations, the activities that pose the risk, that threaten death or illness, involve the use of chemical substances and a highly uncertain causal relationship. Toxic tort cases are typically ones in which the plaintiffs bringing the action allege that their injuries or disease (such as cancer or a birth defect) were caused by exposure to the defendant's product, or activity (such as spraying or waste disposal and storage). Some of the most common, yet the most vexing, testimony that courts have to deal with is of the form of an assertion such as that exposure to X causes disease or condition Y.

Given the current state of scientific knowledge, what can be determined, at best, is that exposure to a certain substance can increase the risk or likelihood of someone so exposed suffering an injury or subsequently developing an illness. Yet those same conditions can occur in people who are not so exposed and, thus, the etiology (cause or origin) is multiple and variable. Bruce Pardy (1989: 277–78) uses the distinction between "signature disease" and "non-signature disease" to describe the problem. Diseases lack signatures, Pardy explains, when the cause cannot be "discerned by looking at the injury itself" (ibid.). Cancer has been classified as a "non-signature" disease, and it is often the focus of toxic tort cases. The plaintiff, for a start, "must demonstrate a higher disease rate in the population exposed to the defendant's substance than occurs in its absence" (ibid.). The statistical relationship being claimed needs to be close enough to establish a causal link. In the tort context, the plaintiff must establish that the product, or activity in question, is more likely than not (over fifty percent chance) to have caused her injuries or illness. The common law test for causation has been called the "but for" test. As Charles and VanderZwaag (this volume) articulate, the plaintiff "must establish on the balance of probabilities that *but for* the defendant's tortious activity, injury would not have occurred". That is often extremely difficult to do.

There is a lot at stake in toxic court cases, whichever way the decision goes. Stephen Breyer explains why that is (1998: 537): If compensation is wrongly denied to the plaintiff, then it "can deprive not only the plaintiff of warranted compensation but can discourage other similarly situated individuals from even trying to obtain compensation and can encourage the continued use of a dangerous substance. On the other hand, a decision wrongly granting compensation, although of immediate benefit to the plaintiff, through the strong financial disincentives that accompany a finding of tort liability, can improperly force abandonment of the substance".

Toxic tort cases can be very expensive for all parties to litigate, because they are usually "class action lawsuits", and because they often involve "punitive damages". These legal measures are a reflection of the influence of American law upon Canadian law. Class actions were first devised in the United States, and they have since been legislatively authorized in the three largest Canadian provinces (Bowal, 2002: 11). Punitive damages were also first imposed in the United States in civil cases, and the Supreme Court of Canada has recently expanded the "availability of large punitive damages awards" (ibid.). Toxic tort cases typically require extensive expert testimony, and confront courts with decisions about what kinds of testimony decisions should be based on, or even should be allowed into the courtroom.

Commentators have drawn a contrast between the proof of risk, in risk assessment, and proof of causation in tort cases. With risk assessment, there is often a risk-benefit or cost-benefit analysis being done. In such situations, an administrative agency "may decide to bar a substance or a product if the potential benefits are outweighed by the possibility of risks that are largely unquantifiable because of presently unknown contingencies" (Berger, 2000: 62). Moreover, when the research is inconclusive from a scientific perspective, that is seen to be a call for more research. Regulations and standards can be modified once the further research is available. However, in a court of law, causation is understood in different terms: was it more likely than not that the substance (or activity) caused the alleged harm (to the plaintiff)? In civil litigation, the specific case, for reasons of process values, needs to be decided definitively and as speedily as possible. As Margaret Berger explains (2000: 63), a court's "rejection of the plaintiff's expert proof means that the plaintiff will lose regardless of what future research might show, for the law has virtually no mechanism for deferring the resolution of disputes until additional scientific information is gathered".

To repeat a point made just above, the causal mechanisms of many diseases are not yet well understood. The kind of evidence that is available pertaining to causation is evidence that is used to assess risk. That evidence is described and categorized by Hajo Versteeg. Typically, it involves the use of "high-dose animal studies" that have to be extrapolated in two ways. The data have to be extrapolated from the animal species used to humans, and there has to be an extrapolation from the high doses given to animals to the normally much lower exposure experienced by the plaintiffs (Berger, 2000: 62). Some have argued, for these reasons, that "high dose animal studies have no scientific value outside the context of risk assessment and should be irrelevant to prove causation" (ibid.). As Versteeg points out, the value of such evidence was an issue in the *Palmer* case. The judge found the toxicology evidence to be of little "probative value" in light of the actual low possible exposure that the plaintiffs in the case would experience.

Justice Nunn (the judge in the *Palmer* case) indicated that there might be "safe doses" of substances such as dioxin, and that there could be "no observable effects levels" (NOELs). Ted Schrecker (1986: 4) has elaborated on the policy implications of such a claim:

> [W]e usually do not know (and indeed may well never know) whether NOELs emerging from experiments conducted with a specific substance represent a genuine absence of effect or merely reflect a failure to detect effects which might still be highly important when extrapolated to a large exposed human population. The use of safety/uncertainty factors takes this consideration into account. However, ... their use assumes the existence of biological thresholds. In the absence of this assumption, the choice of an uncertainty factor represents a normative decision about acceptable risk.

The judge in the *Palmer* case also relied upon the fact that governmental regulatory agencies had approved the activity in question (spraying of a herbicide), and insisted that the role of courts was not to "second guess" the government on broad areas of social policy. Versteeg discusses other cases — both Canadian and American — in which courts have tried to exercise discretion in response to the problems of indeterminate defendants and probabilistic evidence. When courts do try to fashion remedies, by relying upon "legal" constructions of proof rather than strictly scientific standards of proof, they have attracted criticism in some circles. Here again, we can see that there are crucially important policy issues underlying the question of whether and how to fashion flexible remedies, or apply legal rather than scientific notions of proof, in the face of "pragmatically irreducible uncertainty" (Jasanoff, 2001: 33). For instance, how much should the cost of what we do not know fall on technology's unintended and unsuspecting victims, as Sheila Jasanoff (ibid.) asks?

The Adversary System

How, then, should the law deal with issues of scientific uncertainty? In the Anglo-American legal tradition, evidence is brought before the court through the adversarial process. The judge plays a relatively passive role in this process; the presentation of evidence is controlled by the parties. Each side presents, through expert witnesses, evidence favourable to its own side. Each side also has the opportunity to cross-examine the other side's witnesses. The system is meant to be "equal to the task of sifting good evidence from bad" (Jasanoff, 2001: 28) through the techniques of discovery and cross-examination. The disparity of the parties' interests — which leads to the dispute between them — is itself part of the guarantee of the "integrity of fact-finding" (ibid.). Jasanoff (2001: 28) explains why this is: "The courtroom would simply function as the forum in which the adversaries, each motivated by the desire to win, would vigorously represent their own claims and as diligently contest their opponents'. From this spirited exchange the facts would emerge — or as much of them as needed to resolve disputes fairly". Liberalized discovery rules are, then, a way to level the playing field, and ensure the efficacy of the system. Supposedly, neither side could enjoy an unfair advantage in the "competition". It is another issue altogether whether the parties enjoy unfair advantages in terms of their disparate access to social resources — resources needed to pay lawyers, to pay experts, and to pay court costs or the opponent's costs (in case of loss). The litigants in the *Palmer* case (mentioned above) found the exorbitant expense of pursuing their case (and losing, and having costs awarded against them) prevented them from mounting an appeal.

The usefulness of this adversarial system where scientific controversy is concerned is itself a highly contentious issue. Some scientists and scholars have argued that scientific data is "routinely abused, mishandled or ignored in the interest of governance" (Malone, 2000: 84). David Faigan's book, *Legal Alchemy*, collects numerous anecdotes to back up those charges. The problem, according to one school of thought, "stems from the inability of lay juries to distinguish between valid scientific claims and 'junk science'" (Jasanoff, 2001: 27). (See http://www.junkscience.com/for more on junk science.) Junk science, a term with high rhetorical impact in public policy debates, refers to "expert assertions that would not pass muster with genuine scientists, but that seem nevertheless to carry weight when admitted as testimony before untutored fact-finders" (ibid.). Judges are, of course, also potentially vulnerable to being swayed by junk science, but the problem is seen to be more acute and pernicious in the case of juries.

Critics of the adversarial nature of the legal system have argued that cross-examination, rather than ameliorating, actually "exacerbates the problem by indiscriminately attacking experts' credibility, whether or not their testimony is technically meritorious" (Jasanoff, 2001: 27) The problem is two-fold: either unworthy scientific claims are accepted improperly, or else valid claims are rejected on frivolous grounds (due to personal characteristics of the witness that are not actually germane) (ibid.). The philosopher John Locke, writing during the 1600s, set out six criteria for evaluating testimony: "the number of witnesses, their integrity, their skill at presenting the evidence, their purpose, the internal consistency of the evidence and its agreement with the circumstances and lastly, the presence or absence of contrary testimony" (Shapiro, 1983: 183). To this day, there are continual debates over which factors should govern the evaluation of witnesses' credibility and to what extent, i.e., how to weight and balance competing factors. Some people still worry that the style or form or mode of presentation has too much sway over juries, to the detriment of the substance of the testimony. These kinds of concerns have led some commentators to call for the development of "science courts" (see concluding sub-section below).

There are plenty of arguments on the other side of the debate, nevertheless. Liora Salter (1988: 175) has argued that because scientists have their biases, the adversarial system with its cross-examination of witnesses is necessary for the full disclosure of information. "It is not likely that the expert witnesses would have falsified their data to suit the interests of those who hired them", she writes, "but circumstances decreed that they were also unlikely to speculate broadly ... about potentially contradictory findings" unless forced to do so under cross-examination (ibid.).

Stuart Smith, in his article reproduced here, concurs with Salter in supporting the adversarial system. He maintains that the logic of the adversarial system is very much akin to the logic of science itself. He is, however, more optimistic than Salter about the separability of scientific and value issues. Smith recommends that judges and tribunals must be very clear about: the actual scientific work being cited, the method by which conclusions are being drawn from the work, and the policy or value-laden issues that determine the final decisions.

Both Stuart Smith and Michael Jeffery ultimately defend the adversarial process as a means of truth finding, and they are both sceptical that the alternatives — science court and mediation — would work any better. Michael Jeffery, who wrote the article included in this book while serving as chair of the Ontario Environmental Assessment Board, is less enthusiastic about the adversarial system as it operates in courts of law, but maintains that it works well in administrative tribunals such as environmental assessment boards.

The American Experience

The U.S. Supreme Court Rulings

The rationale for including a discussion of American jurisprudence in this context is that Canada is quite "open to looking at international law and the domestic law of other common law countries to answer its current legal questions" (Bowal, 2002: 10). It is much more open that way than are American courts, who do not generally cite either international law or the domestic law of other countries (ibid.). Canadian legal scholar Peter Bowal selects that characteristic as one of the ten central differences between the Canadian and American legal system (in a piece written while he was working at the United States Supreme Court).

The United States Supreme Court has had occasion several times during the past decade to address the criteria for admission of scientific and other technical advice. It is worth presenting a brief summary of the issues and the rulings in one of these. The first, and most significant, of the cases is *Daubert v. Merrell Dow* from 1993. (The others are *General Electric Co. v. Joiner*, in 1997, and *Kumbo Tire Co. v. Carmichael*, in 1999.) Shulman (1994: 15) describes the background to the *Daubert* case as follows:

> [It] concerned an alleged link between birth defects and Bendectin, an antinausea drug for pregnant women. In the case, William and Joyce Daubert of San Diego, Calif., sued Merrell Dow Pharmaceuticals — the makers of Bendectin — when their son Jason was born with malformed limbs after Joyce Daubert took the drug during the first trimester of pregnancy.
>
> The science of the case was at issue because some in vitro and animal studies suggest that the drug does cause birth defects, and the pharmacological studies reveal similarities between the structure of Bendectin and other substances known to cause birth defects in humans. In fact, based on results such as these, Merrell Dow soon found itself facing thousands of lawsuits like the one brought by the Dauberts. In response, the company removed Bendectin from the market in 1983 after more than 10 million women had used the drug for two decades.
>
> But most of the lawsuits against Merrell Dow faltered because the courts generally demand direct evidence of injury to humans in such cases. And none of the more than 30 published studies involving over 130,000 patients have been able to establish a statistically significant link between Bendectin and birth defects in human infants.

During the *Daubert* proceedings, the California court, and a federal appeals court, both refused to admit the testimony of several key witnesses for the plaintiffs. The reason for refusal was that the research had not been published in a peer-reviewed journal. The courts were applying the common law "Frye" rule, articulated in a 1923 case, *Frye v. United States*, on expert testimony. That rule, as Sheila Jasanoff explains (1998: 80), was based on the evidence having gained "general acceptance in the particular field in which it belongs". The basic legal test for the "acceptability of novel scientific and technical evidence" rested on showing that the evidence was relevant and reliable, but also that it had "near unanimous support from experts in the appropriate fields" (ibid.). The rejection of the plaintiff's expert and the applicability of the "Frye" test in modern day society were the basis of the appeal to the U.S. Supreme Court.

The *Daubert v. Merrell Dow* case marked the first time that the high court "directly considered what standard should govern the use of science in the courtroom" (Ayala and Black, 1993: 230). It also "focused the spotlight of public attention on the judiciary's failure to develop clear and consistent guidelines for evaluating scientific evidence" (ibid.). The case attracted significant attention from the research community in particular; at least twenty *amicus* briefs (advice offered by "friends of the court") were filed (Shulman, 1994:

16). (The Canadian term used for *amicus* briefs is "intervenor" submissions.) The groups included the National Academy of Sciences, the American Medical Association, and the American Association for the Advancement of Science (ibid*.)*.

The judgment in the *Daubert* case concluded that "congressionally enacted Federal Rules of Evidence", and not the earlier common law rule, should govern the admissibility of evidence in federal litigation (Jasanoff, 2001: 29). Under those rules, "judges were authorized to keep out of court any expert testimony that was not both reliable and relevant", and the court went on to offer "four sample criteria for determining admissibility" (ibid*.)*. Those criteria are as follows: (i) "was the science in question testable and had it been tested"; (ii) "was it peer reviewed"; (iii) "did it have a known or potential error rate"; (iv) "was it generally accepted within the relevant scientific community?" (ibid*.)*. Although the fourth criterion seems to recapitulate the "Frye" rule, it was now characterized as just one factor to consider, and no longer determinative.

The case, it has been said, has "ushered in a new era of judicial scrutiny of science by declaring that judges must act as 'gatekeepers' to ensure that juries hear evidence only from expert witnesses offering 'valid' science" (Malone, 2000: 84). The sociological significance of the ruling has been emphasized by Sheila Jasanoff. The ruling was seen as a "victory for science", because it encouraged federal judges to "think like scientists" (Jasanoff, 2001: 29). What it also may have done was "left judges considerable latitude to decide, in practice, how scientists think" (ibid*.)*. The response on the part of at least some judges was to view the change in jurisprudence as an opportunity for alliances between adjudicators and working scientists. Stephen Breyer (2000) details the kinds of initiatives that have followed in the wake of *Daubert*.

Access to Research Data — the Shelby Amendment

It was a contested piece of environmental regulation that led to a much debated amendment to the U.S. *Freedom of Information Act* (FOIA), known as the "Shelby Amendment". It was passed in 1999 as an amendment to a federal appropriations bill. This amendment guarantees public access under the *FOIA* to all data that is produced by federally funded research scientists. The amendment was initially drafted very broadly, although it was meant to "apply only to nonprofit universities, teaching hospitals, and research centers, and not to federally funded research undertaken by for-profit companies" (Anderson, 2000: 71). The U.S. Office of Management and Budget has since issued guidelines reaffirming privacy and trade secret protections, and narrowing the application of the amendment. It is now supposed to be limited to providing access to research data used by government in developing legally binding actions of administrative agencies (ibid*.)*.

The particular case that led to the introduction of the "Shelby Amendment" involved particulate standards. As Anderson (2000: 71) explains, "business interests were denied access to confidential medical data" that had been compiled by a team of Harvard-based researchers, "whose studies prompted the Environmental Protection Agency (EPA) to tighten up costly air pollution standards". The Harvard-based researchers were concerned to protect the privacy of medical records of research subjects, whereas the business interests — led by the Chamber of Commerce — wanted to review all the data in order to challenge the validity of the data and/or its interpretation. The politician, Richard Shelby (R-Ala.), took up their cause and brought in the amendment. Following the U.S. Office of Management and Budget's attempt to constrain the application of the amendment, the Chamber of Commerce has continued to pursue legal action in order to get access to the disputed data.

As Anderson (2000: 71) notes, "industry stakeholders enthusiastically supported the amendment as a means of challenging scientific studies that underpin costly regulations, tort suits, and higher health risk estimates". Here we can see the interpenetration and cross-fertilization of economic rationales and scientific challenges. On the other side of the fence, many members of the scientific community were worried that the amendment could mean "increased paperwork... unwarranted access to personal information on research subjects, and even deliberate use of the amendment to harass researchers" (ibid.). Donald Kennedy and Robert Merrill (2000: 50) sum up the importance of the amendment as follows: "It can be said to recognize a new right of citizens to contest the scientific premises of governmental rules, but it may also burden and impede federally funded investigators and increase the cost of research". The amendment provides a tool for citizens to obtain detailed information about the data on which policy decisions are based, whatever their motivation. It could thus provide an adjunct "avenue to citizen participation" (see the editors' notes for Section Four, Part A).

Frederick Anderson (2000: 75) points out, however, that there are other ways to address the particulate standards controversy and others like it. In areas of general controversy, the U.S. National Research Council can be called upon by Congress to provide "broad, state-of-the-science consensus reports" (ibid.). Such reports can, and do, provide validation for policy-making. More might be needed in cases of highly specific controversy. Anderson endorses the potential of having an independent body undertake a reanalysis of critical scientific studies. Such a reanalysis was done, for the data in question, by the Health Effects Institute in Massachusetts, to see whether it "supported the researchers' conclusions on morbidity and mortality caused by air pollution" (ibid.). The advantages of this approach are fourfold. First, with an independent body, it avoids the potential for stakeholder bias during interpretation of results. Second, the time and expense involved would, one hopes, rule out frivolous or vexatious challenges. This approach should only be justified in cases of controversial research underpinning costly regulations. Third, "strict replication of results using the full data set (held confidential where warranted) rests on the very foundation of the scientific method: reproducible results" (ibid.). Fourth, the original researchers can have some involvement, in terms of participating in a "non-adversarial exchange of views", and defending their conclusions in the final report (ibid.). This promotes efficiency and fairness.

Should There Be Science Courts?

Hajo Versteeg (in this volume) discusses the once-popular idea of "science courts" — specialized courts or panels to be made up of distinguished experts. Advocates on opposing sides of a technical issue would present evidence and arguments to the panel, who would then "resolve the scientific issues". The courts and administrative agencies could then rely upon these factual conclusions, and apply the relevant law or policy to them. A variation on the theme would "allow litigants to argue their cases before a panel of judges with recognized scientific credentials". Science courts have been considered in both Canadian and American circles. But, as Versteeg notes, the idea has "generally fallen into disfavour".

The fundamental problem of "pragmatically irreducible uncertainty" (Jasanoff's term) would not disappear with the development of science courts. Those courts would continue to face the same difficulties, as Versteeg emphasizes, "in determining the cause-effect nexus faced by traditional courts". Science courts will not solve the major epistemological, ethical or political problems in toxic tort cases, nor the problems raised by a whole new area of concern, hormonally active agents in the environment. As Schrecker (2001: 56) notes, there are increasing concerns that certain chemicals can "mimic natural hormones, inhibit the action of hormones, or alter the normal regulatory function of the immune, nervous and endocrine systems". There are suspected effects of these chemicals, which include abnormal sexual development, reduced male fertility, alteration in pituitary and thyroid gland functions, and immune suppression (Colborn, 1997). These substances — found in pesticides and industrial chemicals — may be damaging the health of wildlife and of human beings.

Science courts, even if adopted, may not have wide appeal. U.S. judges already had the authority, under the federal Rules of Evidence, to "appoint independent experts" to advise them. Some judges had availed themselves of the opportunity, but it was not a common practice. There are many outstanding questions that attend the use of independent experts, as Stephen Breyer (1998: 538) has written. He asks: "Will use of an independent expert, in effect, substitute that expert's judgment for that of the court? Will it inappropriately deprive the parties of control over the presentation of the case? Will it improperly intrude on the proper function of the jury?" "Will the search for the expert create inordinate delay or significantly increase costs?" Furthermore, there are unresolved issues of finding truly "neutral" experts.

Beyond and above the particular questions of interpretation, adjudication and admissibility of evidence covered here, there are broader issues. As Sheila Jasanoff (2001: 35) has argued, "the deeper question for society is how to remedy harms if the facts cannot be definitively established, inside or outside the legal process". Ted Schrecker (this volume) comments that the regulation of toxic chemicals presents very different challenges than dealing with more familiar forms of pollution or resource depletion issues common to environmental law. Scientific uncertainty, and its policy implications, are an inescapable feature of modern life, as is the interdependence of science and law. Courts have been forced to deal with the problems raised by toxic tort cases. Governments may attempt to excuse failure to legislate or to regulate by pointing to scientific uncertainty, just as they use market conditions for "blame avoidance" (Kathryn Harrison's term), as Ted Schrecker (this volume) observes. But ultimately, they will be forced — by public pressure, if nothing else — to grapple with, and act on, the challenges.

RISK ASSESSMENT AND THE PRECAUTIONARY PRINCIPLE

Allan Greenbaum ⎯⎯⎯⎯⎯⎯⎯⎯⎯⎯⎯⎯⎯⎯⎯⎯⎯⎯⎯⎯⎯⎯⎯⎯

One of the more contentious issues currently surrounding environmental regulation concerns the role of quantitative (probabilistic) risk assessment. In simplest terms (we'll complicate things a little bit shortly), risk assessment is a set of procedures for estimating the probability that an individual potentially exposed to a particular hazard will be harmed in a particular way as a result, and for deciding whether that probability is high enough to justify taking (possibly expensive) steps to eliminate or mitigate the hazard. Proponents of projects, activities or technologies that are subject to environmental or health regulations typically argue that such regulations ought to be justified on the basis of risk assessment. Advocates argue that risk assessment provides an objective, scientific basis for consistent, rational and efficient risk regulation. Critics of risk assessment, who are also often opponents of controversial projects or technologies, maintain that it is a scientifically dubious and politically problematic exercise that is used to legitimate the imposition of unnecessary risks on an unwilling public and the environment (Shrader-Frechette 1991, 1993; O'Brien 2000).

Risk assessment is used in a variety of regulatory contexts, including project approval, product approval and standard setting. In a *project approval* process, such as the licensing of a nuclear power plant or the environmental assessment of a dam, it addresses the riskiness of a particular project (including both the risk of a catastrophic accident, such as a dam failure or reactor core meltdown, and the risks posed by ordinary operation, such as low level radiation release). Pharmaceuticals, pesticides and various kinds of consumer goods are subject to *product approval* processes. For example, all pesticides produced, sold or used in Canada must be registered under the federal *Pest Control Products Act*, and in order to be registered the active ingredients must be found to pose no more than an "acceptable" risk to human health and the environment. Risk assessment is a key stage in the process of determining whether a pesticide meets this approval criterion (Standing Committee on Environment and Sustainable Development 2000). Finally, risk assessment may play a role in *standard setting*: for example, in helping regulators decide the maximum allowable concentration of a particular hazardous substance in the air or water.

One of the readings in this section, by Brunk, Haworth and Lee, analyzes a risk assessment conducted as part of a product approval, an assessment of the agricultural herbicide Alachlor under the *Pest Control Products Act*. Before discussing risk assessment itself in more detail, it is helpful to say something about the legal and institutional context in which risk assessment occurs. We will use the Alachlor case as an illustration, and our account is based on the study by Harrison and Hoberg (1994). Alachlor, produced by Monsanto, was a much used agricultural chemical in the 1970s. It was originally licensed on the basis of test data supplied on behalf of Monsanto by IBT Laboratories. In the 1980s, it came to light that IBT had falsified data, and the test results were declared invalid. Health and Welfare Canada conducted a new risk assessment based on fresh data that suggested that Alachlor could cause cancer, and it recommended that Agriculture Canada deny Alachlor a licence. Monsanto appealed the ban, and the Alachlor Review Board (ARB), an appellate tribunal, was appointed. The ARB found that the ban should be overturned, but the Minister of Agriculture continued to refuse to license the product. In 1988, Monsanto brought an action in the Federal Court of Appeal, arguing that it was beyond the discretion of the Minister to withhold the licence in the face of the ARB's decision that a licence should be granted. The Court found against Monsanto, and the ban stood.

This saga illustrates some noteworthy points about the context in which risk assessment occurs. First, as with environmental assessment generally, the data on which the assessment is based is generated by or on behalf of the proponent, who has a stake in the approval of the product or undertaking under review. Even if this does not result in outright fraud (as in the IBT affair), and even if allegations of continued rampant distortion and suppression of data by the chemical industry (e.g., Fagin and Lavelle, 1999) are exaggerated, this arrangement is a source of systemic (if subtle) bias in the science of risk assessment. Second, risk assessment is embedded in an adversarial process. The adversaries directly involved were not "business versus environmentalists" or "business versus government"; the conflict was as much within the state as between the state and the corporation, as Agriculture Canada staff sided with Monsanto while Health and Welfare staff argued for banning the product. Among stakeholders who were not parties to the formal proceedings, those with values or interests opposed to Monsanto's included manufacturers of competing products, as well as environmentalists and health advocates. Last, note that at various stages this case involved many of the forms of official decision-making or dispute resolution that characterize "environmental law" in the broad ("law and society") sense: first there was a bureaucratic (administrative) decision, then adjudication by an administrative tribunal, then an act of political discretion and, finally, a judicial decision.

It is also revealing to compare the Canadian process with the parallel process going on in the United States. As is typically the case, the American approval process is more formal, rule-bound, transparent, open to public participation and adversarial, while the Canadian process is more closed and informal, with a greater role for bureaucratic and political discretion. In Canada, non-party stakeholders such as environmental groups were informally consulted at the "front end" of the process. In the United States, environmental and public health groups had a right to participate as parties in the formal process, and also had greater opportunity to seek judicial review of the administrative process if they were unsatisfied with the outcome ("back-end participation"). American environmental health advocates did not, however, exercise their participation rights in the Alachlor case, as they had other priorities at the time. In the end, Alachlor was banned in Canada but merely subject to minor restrictions in the United States. Although in this case the Canadian process had a less permissive, more risk-averse outcome than the American process, Harrison and Hoberg (1994) found that the reverse is often true; and that, on balance, neither regime is clearly stricter than the other. There are some other significant differences between the Canadian and American pesticide approval risk assessment processes, but before we can address them, we have to discuss risk assessment itself in more detail.

The excerpt by Hrudey sets out the elements of risk assessment. Risk assessment presumes to rest on a model of technically rational analysis. It comprises two conceptually distinct (but practically and, indeed, theoretically inextricable) components or stages. The first is scientific, and involves identifying hazards and calculating the probability that a potentially exposed individual will experience a particular adverse outcome (e.g., death, cancer, or property destruction) due to a particular hazard (e.g., an environmental pollutant, workplace hazard, or type of accident). The second is normative (evaluative) and strategic in nature; it involves deciding what ought to be done given the information produced in the first stage. Not all authorities use the same system of terminology to label these stages, which may give rise to some confusion. Hrudey follows the American convention established by the U.S. National Research Council (1983; see Powell, 2000: 134–37), according to which the first ("scientific") stage is called "risk assessment", and all of the second stage is called "risk management"; the overall process comprising both is sometimes called "risk analysis". The British convention (see Royal Society Study Group, 1992: 2–5) uses the term "risk management" in a broad sense to name the overall process (corresponding to the American "risk analysis"), but also uses "risk management" in a narrower sense to refer to the decision-making and implementation phases of the second stage. The first stage is called by the Royal Society "risk estimation", and those aspects of the second to do with determining acceptable levels of risk, "risk evaluation". Risk estimation and evaluation together comprise "risk assessment", according to the Royal Society nomenclature. The over-arching notion of separating the empirical and normative stages and addressing each in turn is sometimes called "sequential assessment of risk" (Harrison and Hoberg, 1994).

Quantitative risk assessment derives ultimately from actuarial science: it provides the sort of information that an insurer would require in order to make rational decisions concerning premiums. Risk from an actuarial point of view is a function of the size of a claim multiplied by the probability of a claim of that size. A relatively infrequent but costly type of accident would represent to the insurer the same level of risk as another kind of mishap that is ten times as frequent but that on average causes only one-tenth as much damage in each instance. Other considerations — such as whether the hazard in question is voluntary or involuntary, familiar or strange, public or private — are not relevant to the actuary, though they may be to the people exposed to the hazard.

The actuarial approach to risk is not controversial in the insurance context, but it is controversial in the regulatory context. In making public decisions about risky technologies or facilities, risk assessment is used not to determine how much it would cost to insure against unavoidable or voluntarily assumed risks, but rather to determine what risks imposed by the activities and undertakings of others are socially acceptable. As toxic hazard activist Lois Gibbs (1994: 329) put it, from the point of view of affected communities risk assessments are about "the risks that somebody else has chosen for you to take". The controversial aspects of environmental regulatory issues are further compounded by the fact that much greater scientific uncertainty surrounds risks typically addressed by environmental regulators (e.g., the ecological and health effects of a new pesticide) than those typically addressed by insurers (e.g., the frequency of house fires or car crashes). The normative and epistemological dimensions of risk controversies interact in complex ways, as our readings illustrate.

In order to clarify these issues, it is helpful to return to the idealized two stage model of risk assessment discussed above. Recall that the first stage addresses the empirical question of risk estimation: How big a risk does this hazard pose? The second addresses the ultimately normative (i.e., moral, ethical, political) question of risk evaluation: Is this risk acceptable? The first stage is itself made up of various components. The risk is analyzed into its component parts. (This is why some people prefer to reserve the term "risk analysis" to name this stage; unfortunately, as we have seen, usage is not consistent.) For example, if we are interested in estimating the cancer risk of a suspected carcinogen, we need to calculate the added frequency of cancer induced by various doses of the chemical (the "dose-response curve"). This is done on the basis of toxicological studies (usually animal tests), in some cases supplemented by epidemiological data from exposed human populations. We also need to establish the dose to which people will be exposed if the chemical is used. This calculation requires many complex studies of how the chemical behaves in the environment — how it is transported through various media (air, water, soil), the rate at which it breaks down or bioaccumulates — the extent to which it is absorbed by the human body, and so on. All of these calculations are fraught with scientific uncertainty, but none refers overtly to moral values. If it should turn out that the estimated exposure lies well below the threshold of harm (in this case, carcinogenicity) established by toxicology, then we can say that the risk is effectively zero, and so the explicitly normative questions of risk evaluation are moot.

How sharply and explicitly the two stages of risk analysis are distinguished depends in part on how the law authorizing the assessment is written and interpreted. To see how this is so, let us return briefly to Harrison and Hoberg's (1994) comparison of Canadian and American Alachlor assessments. The Canadian pesticide law required that the products must both have some benefit and pose no "unacceptable risk" in order to be approved, but did not require that the risks be weighed against the benefits. The vague "acceptable risk" standard was interpreted in the Alachlor case to mean that the product must not cause cancer under a "reasonable worst-case scenario". This implied a threshold approach to risk: the product either causes cancer (under "reasonable" circumstances) or it doesn't. This is apparently a question of fact and, as we shall see, the implicit value issues were played out around the interpretation of "reasonable". Risk estimation called for a yes/no answer, with no separate risk evaluation needed. The American pesticide law, by contrast, required the regulatory agency to weigh the risks against the benefits of product approval. This approach encouraged a dose-response interpretation of risk at the estimation stage: the fact issue at that stage was not, "Is there risk?", but, "How much risk?". It also called for a distinct risk evaluation stage in which the economic and value issues were explicitly addressed.

Although in theory the first stage of sequential assessment is empirical rather than normative, we can see that — especially in the Canadian process but, to some extent, in any — value-based decisions enter crucially into the first stage as well. Consider first the choice of which negative outcomes to assess. Gibbs (1994) complains that risk assessors, when analyzing toxic substance hazards, tend to focus too exclusively on cancer and fail to assess other health risks that these chemicals might pose. More generally, as Kristin Shrader-Frechette points out in the article reproduced in this section, when quantitative risk assessment is used to compare and rank risks from various hazards (a practice we will discuss shortly), death is usually the only negative outcome considered. True, there is a high level of consensus that premature death is bad; but, as she puts it, "death is not the only important 'end point' whose probability rational people might want to evaluate". Science can, in principle, tell us to what extent substance X contributes to outcome Y, but it cannot tell us that Y is itself a negative or bad outcome. To proceed as if it could is to commit the "naturalistic fallacy" (see "naturalistic fallacy" and "fact/value distinction" in the glossary). Risk assessment cannot get started, therefore, without a prior value judgement about what we are interested in avoiding.

Value judgements also enter into risk estimation partly because of high levels of scientific uncertainty that surround many of the variables that need to be plugged into the calculation. Hrudey's article in this section, and Versteeg's article in the previous one, touch on many of the normative issues to which uncertainty gives rise. Brunk, Haworth and Lee, in this section, draw a useful distinction between two kinds of value issues that enter into risk estimation. The first, which they call "conditionally normative issues", arises under the condition of uncertainty; they "come into play only where there is not enough information available to decide the issue on the basis of the scientific data alone. They could be settled without normative judgements if more or better information were available". The questions often take the form: In the absence of certain information, how conservative should our assumptions be? To what extent should we err on the side of caution? If, for example, different experiments yield different toxicity thresholds, do we use the average or the lowest number in our risk estimation?

Much can ride on the resolution of these conditionally normative scientific issues, and so they give rise to heated debate. It is standard practice in risk estimation to introduce at various points in the analysis conservative assumptions, such as an arbitrary factor-of-ten safety margin. For example, the toxicity threshold of a chemical will be assumed to be one-tenth what experimental results suggest it is. Including these safety margins at several points in the analysis results in "cascading conservative assumptions" that, according to some industry advocates, may result in analyses that significantly over-estimate risk and hence support excessively restrictive and economically burdensome regulatory decisions. Environmentalists, on the other hand, contend that these margins of safety are inadequate to correct for other sources of risk under-estimation in standard models (which, for example, do not calculate the special risks faced by vulnerable populations, such as children). When complex undertakings such as nuclear facilities are assessed, it is necessary to estimate risks arising from a great many contingencies about which no scientific data are available. Where data are lacking, "guesstimates" based on expert judgement must be inserted in the computations. Studies comparing expert judgments with subsequently obtained data reveal that expert judgement (like lay judgement) is systematically biased; in particular, experts tend to under-estimate risks of technologies with which they are familiar, and to over-estimate the accuracy of their own estimates (Freudenburg 1988; Shrader-Frechette 1991: 128f, 189f).

So far we have been considering aspects of risk estimation that in the real world are subject to value judgements but that could, in principle, be made on purely empirical grounds. Brunk, Haworth and Lee, in their article reproduced here, point out that risk estimation (never mind risk evaluation) also raises inherently normative issues. These are irreducibly value-laden risk management questions that are built right into the process of risk estimation. One cannot calculate a probability of harm without making certain assumptions concerning matters that are not, even in principle, empirically decidable. We have already considered one such inherently normative issue: What "harms" are we going to calculate the probability of? Another has to do with what assumptions to make about "human error". In the risk assessment of the herbicide Alachlor examined by Brunk, Haworth and Lee, it turned out to make an important difference whether the exposure calculation assumed that farmers use the product as directed and wear the recommended protective gear when spraying. The issue is not whether as a matter of fact users will follow directions when applying Alachlor, but whether as a matter of policy "safe enough to allow" means "safe enough when used as directed", or, "safe enough to use somewhat carelessly". Those on the side of industry in this dispute might maintain that it is unfair and economically perverse to ban as unsafe a product that would be found to be safe if used as directed; environmentalists and health advocates might reply that it is reckless and unrealistic to allow as safe a product that can cause cancer if used as many people are actually likely to use it.

We turn now to the overtly normative stage of risk evaluation. Risk evaluation asks the question, "How safe is safe enough?" Shrader-Frechette, in the article reproduced in this section, takes issue with one approach to addressing this question within the context of quantitative risk assessment: namely, "comparative risk assessment". Advocates of comparative risk analysis suggest that hazards that impose similar levels of quantitative (probabilistic, actuarial) risk be treated the same from a normative perspective. This perspective has several policy implications. At the level of broad regulatory agenda setting, it implies a "worst things first" approach, focusing attention on hazards that pose the greatest quantitative risk (see Finkel and Golding, 1994). At the level of risk evaluation of particular hazards, it implies that technological risks subject to regulation (such as pesticides, pollutants, food additives or nuclear energy facilities) should be deemed acceptable if they are smaller than natural "background" risks and risks from activities that people accept as a matter of course in their daily lives. Alvin Weinberg (1985), for example, whose views Shrader-Frechette cites, has argued against regulating "*de minimis*" risks, such as synthetic chemicals in the environment which have less effect than naturally occurring carcinogens.

These proposals are intensely controversial. Risk comparisons based on quantitative risk assessment are often very much at odds with public perceptions and environmentalist priorities (Covello, 1991). Indeed, quantitative risk comparisons play a central role in anti-environmentalist polemics that portray the concerned public as ignorant or irrational dupes of misleading environmentalist propaganda. Environmentalists, in turn, often dismiss comparative risk analysis results as dishonest and self-interested exercises in corporate public relations.

An extensive body of research (reviewed in Royal Society, 1992: ch. 5) exists on the nature and sources of the divergence between public risk perception and "objective" results of comparative risk analysis. In part, this is due (as risk analysis proponents might surmise) to misperception by the lay public of fatality frequencies. People tend to overestimate the frequency of deaths due to rare causes and underestimate the frequency of deaths due to common or familiar causes. In part, however, it is also due to the fact that risk as informally understood, unlike risk as defined in most quantitative comparative studies, is not entirely a matter of probability of death. People tend to be more concerned about risks perceived as involuntary, inequitable, uncontrollable and potentially catastrophic. Shrader-Frechette argues that these concerns are entirely rational. In any case, Freudenburg (1993) contends, there is no sociological evidence that those who are more concerned about these putatively small technological risks are less rational or well informed about the risks than those who are less concerned; rather, the degree of concern is inversely related to the level of trust in institutions and organizations that create and manage these risks. This finding is consistent with the cultural theory view that individuals and organizations emphasize risks on the basis of commitments to kinds of social orders (Douglas and Wildavsky, 1982; Douglas, 1992). The conflict is not between the scientific rationality of experts versus the intuitive perception of laypeople; rather, each side rests on intuitive perceptions shaped by particular discourses, and each develops bodies of expert knowledge and practices of scientific rationality consistent with those intuitions (Nelkin, 1992; Tesh, 2000). This is not to claim that objective scientific knowledge about risk is impossible in principle, only that we have good social scientific reason to believe that it is hard to establish in practice.

The normative basis of comparative risk analysis is not merely the notion that rational consistency requires treating (quantitatively) like risks alike. Proponents of comparative risk analysis also appeal to efficiency. Like proponents of economic analysis, they point out that reducing risk generally involves some (and often great) costs, and that resources are finite. Resources lavished on reducing minute risks could be better spent reducing greater risks. For example, it has been estimated that money spent on controlling radioactive waste could save a hundred times as many lives if spent on improved highway safety features (see Covello, 1991: 105). Comparative risk analysis allows society as a whole to save more lives per dollar spent on safety. Note that this is a utilitarian argument: it focuses on aggregate harm averted, not on issues of distribution of harm, compensation, voluntariness and so on, which Shrader-Frechette raises. Critics of risk assessment who take an environmental justice perspective emphasize these latter concerns. They point out that, for example, hazardous facilities are frequently sited in poor and minority communities, disproportionately burdening those already disadvantaged on the basis of class and race with a cumulation of individually "acceptable" risks, without consent or compensation. Defenders of comparative risk analysis, on the other hand, question whether those who reject the aggregative approach are actually interested in reducing risk at all, and accuse them of treating environmental protection as "merely an expedient vehicle for the achievement of other political objectives" — objectives hostile to business, technology and free enterprise (Belzer in Finkel and Golding, 1994: 168). As Brunk, Haworth and Lee found in the Alachlor case, the debates about risk comparison reveal that assessments of risk are shaped by the relative priority that actors assign to values such as social equality, efficiency, economic liberty, democracy, ecological integrity and so on.

Mary O'Brien, a leading critic of risk assessment, has proposed that quantitative risk assessment be replaced by an "alternatives assessment" approach modeled on the original ideal of environmental assessment (O'Brien, 2000). Instead of trying to decide whether the risks posed by a particular substance or undertaking do or do not meet some standard of "acceptable risk" (derived from comparison with fatality rates for relatively uncontroversial risks), the substance or undertaking would be assessed in comparison with a broad range of alternative means of attaining the same purpose. The decision would not be made on narrow technical criteria (as is the case with risk assessment), but through a democratic process informed by a holistic appraisal of all the options. For example, instead of deciding whether to approve a specific agricultural pesticide by determining whether it posed accept-able risks (compared with commonly accepted risks in general, or with pesticides in gen-eral), the advantages and disadvantages (including potential risks) of the pesticide would be weighed against the advantages and disadvantages of other chemicals, of integrated pest management techniques, organic agriculture and so on. One difficulty with this approach is that, as mentioned in our notes to the section of this book on environmental assessment, under current social arrangements neither the proponent (e.g., the pesticide manufacturer) nor the regulatory agency has a mandate or interest in implementing broadly conceived alternatives to the assessed undertaking. This approach implies a much greater role for collective decision-making, whereas risk assessment of individual products or projects fits within the regulatory structures adapted to a capitalist economy and liberal institutional order.

One of the commonest complaints about the risk assessment approach is that under it, chemicals and other potentially hazardous technologies are "innocent until proven guilty" — that the onus is on those interested in or responsible for health and environmental protec-tion to prove risk, not on industry to prove safety. As explained in the piece by Versteeg in this volume, this observation is certainly true in the context of "toxic tort" litigation. In the context of regulatory regimes in which certain kinds of products (e.g., pesticides) or under-takings must "pass" a risk assessment, it is more accurate to say that, whatever one might think about the *standard* of proof required, the *burden* of proof (or of "persuasion") is on those who propose to generate the hazard. Nevertheless, even in the case of the regula-tory system, there is some justice to the complaint. Risk assessment is an expensive pro-cess, and can only be applied to risks the basic mechanisms of which are fairly well understood. This means that only a small proportion of the synthetic chemicals in use have been subject to risk assessment. It also means that those chemicals that have been assessed have been assessed only for a fairly narrow range of risks (e.g., causing cancer), and only for their effects in isolation, not as they might interact with countless other sub-stances in the environment. It is therefore fair to say that in respect of unassessed technol-ogies and unassessed risks related to assessed technologies, the technologies do enjoy the "benefit of the doubt".

These concerns have led groups of scientists, activists and regulators to call for the adoption of a "precautionary principle" that would guide all stages of policy formation and regulation. One of many formulations of the principle, the Wingspread Conference definition, states: "When an activity raises threats of harm to human health or the environment, pre-cautionary measures should be taken even if some cause and effect relationships are not fully established scientifically" (http://www.sehn.org/wing.html). The precautionary principle, like risk assessment, has given rise to a great deal of controversy. Some versions of the principle appear to rule out any activities about which there is scientific uncertainty, others are more compatible with conventional risk assessment and cost-benefit analysis approaches (Foster et al., 2000). Despite the controversies, versions of the precautionary principle have been incorporated into the policies and laws of an increasing number of national and international jurisdictions (including, for example, the 1992 Treaty of the Euro-pean Union). The use of the precautionary principle in policy and law is surveyed in the article by Tickner and Myers reproduced in this section. (For a more extended treatment see Raffensperger and Tickner, 1999.) The reading by Whelan presents criticisms of the precautionary principle from a pro-industry point of view. It is taken from Whelan's response to the book, *Our Stolen Future* (Colborn et al., 1996). That book brought to public attention the theory that certain pollutants either mimic or disrupt the action of various hormones, and that exposure to even the most minute doses of these pollutants during key stages of development could have far reaching impacts on the health of organisms so exposed. The book called for vigorous action to eliminate suspected hormone disrupting pollutants on the basis of the precautionary principle: although the mechanisms and extent of hormone disruption are still poorly understood scientifically, the theory has some scientific basis and the harm it predicts is potentially very great. Whelan contends that the precautionary principle would hold economic and technological progress hostage to far-fetched and speculative scares. Myers, in the article entitled "Debating the Precautionary Principle", states and rebuts many of the commonest criticisms raised against the principle.

The debate over the precautionary principle recapitulates many of the themes in the debates over quantitative and comparative risk assessment. Strictly speaking, the issue is not the same, because in the former issues the normative concerned "how safe is safe enough", and how to proceed in the face of bounded scientific uncertainty about how safe something is; in the case of the precautionary principle, the debate is about how to proceed in cases where we don't even know what we don't know. Still, many of the arguments against taking expensive measures against putatively small risks are also made against taking expensive measures to avert a putatively remote chance that a big risk exists. Those who favour comparative risk assessment over the precautionary principle argue that risk-producing technological activities tend, on balance, to make the population safer and healthier, either directly or indirectly via the generation of wealth; implementing the precautionary principle, they fear, could actually result in greater risk overall (and thus, paradoxically, fall afoul of the precautionary principle) (Cross, 1996; Morris, 2000). Both sides of the debate implicitly assume a precautionary stance, and warn of the potentially catastrophic consequences of interfering with our fragile life-support system. For one side, the interference is technological and the life-support system is the environment; for the other, the interference is regulatory and the life-support system is the economy (Tesh, 2000).

REFERENCES

Anderson, Frederick R. 2000. "Science Advocacy and Scientific Due Process." *Issues in Science and Technology* 16, 4 (Summer): 71–76.

Ayala, Francisco J., and Bert Black. 1993. "Science and the Courts." *American Scientist* 81 (May–June): 230–39.

Berger, Margaret. 2000. "Expert Testimony: The Supreme Court's Rules." *Issues in Science and Technology* 16, 4 (Summer): 57–63.

Bowal, Peter. 2002. "Ten Differences." *Law Now* (June/July): 9–11.

Breyer, Stephen. 2000. "Science in the Courtroom." *Issues in Science and Technology* 16, 4 (Summer): 52–56.

———. 1998. "The Interdependence of Science and Law." *Science* 280 (24 April): 537–38.

Colborn, Theo, Dianne Dumanoski, and John Peterson Myers. 1997. *Our Stolen Future: Are We Threatening Our Fertility, Intelligence, and Survival? — A Scientific Detective Story*. New York: Plume Publishing Co./Penguin.

Covello, Vincent T. 1991. "Risk Comparisons and Risk Communication: Issues and Problems in Comparing Health and Environmental Risk." In *Communicating Risks to the Public*, ed. R.E. Kasperson and P.J.M. Stallen. Dordrecht: Kluwer Academic Publishers.

Cross, Frank B. 1996. "Paradoxical Perils of the Precautionary Principle." *Washington and Lee Law Review* 53: 851–925.

Doern, G. Bruce, and Ted Reed. 2000. "Canada's Changing Science-Based Policy and Regulatory Regime: Issues and Framework.." In *Risky Business: Canada's Changing Science-Based Policy and Regulatory Regime*, ed. G. Bruce Doern and Ted Reed. Toronto: University of Toronto Press.

Doern, Bruce, and Thomas Conway. 1994. *The Greening of Canada: Federal Institutions and Decisions*, Chapter 9. Toronto: University of Toronto Press.

Douglas, Mary. 1992. *Risk and Blame: Essays in Cultural Theory*. London: Routledge.

Douglas, Mary, and Aaron Wildavsky. 1982. *Risk and Culture: an Essay on the Selection of Technological and Environmental Dangers*. Berkeley, CA: University of California Press.

Estrin, David, and John Swaigen. 1993. *Environment on Trial. A Guide to Ontario Environmental Law and Policy.* Toronto: Emond Montgomery Publications Limited.

Fagin, Dan, Marianne Lavelle, and the Center for Public Integrity. 1999. *Toxic Deception: How the Chemical Industry Manipulates Science, Bends the Law and Endangers Your Health.* Monroe, ME: Common Courage Press.

Finkel, Adam M., and Dominic Golding (eds.). 1994. *Worst Things First? The Debate over Risk-Based National Environmental Priorities.* Washington, DC: Resources for the Future.

Fitzgerald, Patrick, and Barry Wright. 2000. *Looking at Law: Canada's Legal System*, Fifth Edition. Markham, ON: Butterworths.

Flynn, James, Paul Slovic, and Howard Kunreuther (eds.). 2001. *Risk, Media and Stigma: Understanding Public Challenges to Modern Science and Technology.* London, UK: Earthscan Publications Ltd.

Foster, Kenneth, Paolo Veccia, and Michael Repacholi. 2000. "Science and the Precautionary Principle." *Science* 288 (12 May): 979–80.

Freudenburg, William R. 1993. "Risk and Recreancy: Weber, the Division of Labour, and the Rationality of Risk Perceptions." *Social Forces* 71: 90–32.

———. 1988. "Perceived Risk, Real Risk: Social Science and the Art of Probabilistic Risk Assessment." *Science* 242: 44–49.

Gibbs, Lois. 1994. "Risk Assessments from a Community Perspective." *Environmental Impact Assessment Review* 14: 327–35.

Harrison, Kathryn. 1995. "Federalism, Environmental Protection, and Blame Avoidance." In *New Trends in Canadian Federalism*, ed. Francois Rocher and Miriam Smith. Peterborough, ON: Broadview Press.

Harrison, Kathyrn, and George Hoberg. 1994. *Risk, Science and Politics: Regulating Toxic Substances in Canada and the US.* Montreal: McGill-Queens University Press.

Hazell, Stephen. 1999. *Canada v. the Environment: Federal Environmental Assessment 1984–1998.* Toronto: Canadian Environmental Defence Fund.

Jasanoff, Sheila. 2001. "Judicial Fictions: The Supreme Court's Quest for Good Science," *Society* 38, 4 (May/June): 27–36.

———. 1989. "Science on the Witness Stand". *Issues in Science and Technology* 6, 1 (Fall): 80–87.

Kennedy, Donald, and Robert A. Merrill. 2000. "Science and the Law". *Issues in Science and Technology* 16, 4 (Summer): 49–51.

Kiss, Alexandre, and Dinah Shelton. 1997. *Manual of European Environmental Law*, Second Edition. Cambridge, UK: Grotius Publications/Cambridge University Press.

Lang, Reg. 1979. Environmental Impact Assessment: Reform or Rhetoric. In *Ecology Versus Politics in Canada*, ed. William Leiss. Toronto: University of Toronto Press.

Malone, Patrick. 2000. "Science and the Law: Review of *Legal Alchemy: The Use and Misuse of Science in the Law.*" *Issues in Science and Technology* 16, 4 (Summer): 83–85.

Morris, Julian (ed.). 2000. *Rethinking Risk and the Precautionary Principle.* London: Butterworth Heinemann.

Murphy, Jeffrie G., and Jules L. Coleman. 1990. *Philosophy of Law: An Introduction to Jurisprudence*, Revised Edition. Boulder, CO: Westview Press.

Nelkin, Dorothy. 1992. *Controversy.* London: Sage.

Nikiforuk, Andrew. 1997. *The Nasty Game: the Failure of Environmental Assessment in Canada.* Toronto: Walter and Duncan Gordon Foundation

O'Brien, Mary. 2000. *Making Better Environmental Decisions: An Alternative to Risk Assessment.* Cambridge, MA: MIT Press.

Pardy, Bruce. 1989. "Risk, Cause, and Toxic Torts: A Theory for Standard of Proof." *Advocates' Quarterly* 10: 277.

Powell, Douglas. 2000. "Risk-Based Regulatory Responses in Global Food Trade: A Case Study of Guatemalan Raspberry Imports into the United States and Canada 1996–1998." In *Risky Business: Canada's Changing Science-Based Policy and Regulatory Regime*, ed. G. Bruce Doern and Ted Reed. Toronto: University of Toronto Press.

Raffensperger, Carolyn, and Joel Tickner (eds.). 1999. *Protecting Public Health and the Environment: Implementing the Precautionary Principle.* Washington DC: Island Press.

Royal Society Study Group. 1992. *Risk: Analysis, Perception and Management.* London: The Royal Society.

Sagoff, Mark. 1985. "Fact and Value in Ecological Science". Environmental Ethics, 7, 2 (Summer): 99–116.

Salter, Liora. 1988. *Mandated Science: Science and Scientists in the Making of Science*. Dordrecht, Netherlands: Kluwer Academic Publishers.

Schrecker, Ted. 2001. "Using Science in Environmental Policy: Can Canada Do Better?" [excerpts included in this volume]. In *Governing the Environment: Persistent Challenges, Uncertain Innovations*, ed. E. Parsons. Toronto: University of Toronto Press.

———. 1986. *The Pitfalls of Standards*. Hamilton, ON: Canadian Centre for Occupational Health and Safety.

Schuck, Peter H. 1987. *Agent Orange on Trial: Mass Toxic Disasters in the Courts*. Cambridge, MA: Belknap Press/Harvard University Press.

Shapiro, Barbara. 1983. *Probability and Certainty in Seventeenth Century England: A Study of the Relationships Between Natural Science, Religion, History, Law, and Literature*. Princeton, NJ: Princeton University Press.

Shrader-Frechette, Kristin S. 1993. *Burying Uncertainty: Risk and the Case Against Geological Disposal of Nuclear Waste*. Berkeley, CA: University of California Press.

———. 1991. *Risk and Rationality: Philosophical Foundations for Populist Reforms*. Berkeley, CA: University of California Press.

Shulman, Seth. 1994. "Doing Science Justice in the Courtroom." *Technology Review* (April): 15–17.

Standing Committee on Environment and Sustainable Development. 2000 *Pesticides: Making the Right Choice for the Protection of Health and the Environment*. Ottawa: Parliament of Canada.

Sullivan, Ruth. 1997. *Statutory Interpretation*. Concord, ON: Irwin Law.

Tesh, Sylvia Noble. 2000. *Uncertain Hazards: Environmental Activism and Scientific Proof*. Ithaca, NY: Cornell University Press.

U.S. National Research Council. 1983. *Risk Assessment in the Federal Government: Managing the Process*. Washington: National Academy Press.

Walker, Vern. 2001. "Defining and Identifying Stigma." In *Risk, Media and Stigma: Understanding Public Challenges to Modern Science and Technology*, pp. 353–60, ed. J. Flynn et. al. London, UK: Earthscan Publications Ltd.

Weinberg, Alvin. 1985. "Science and its Limits: The Regulator's Dilemma." *Issues in Science and Technology* 2, 1: 59–72.

Wildsmith, Bruce H. 1986. "Of Herbicides and Humankind: Palmer's Common Law Lessons." *Osgoode Hall Law Journal*, 24: 161–86.

PART A
Environmental Assessment

(a) Assessing Environmental Impacts in Canada[†]

Thomas Meredith ─────────────────────────────────

WHAT IS ENVIRONMENTAL ASSESSMENT?

. . . .

Environmental impact is approaching its twenty-fifth anniversary. In the quarter century since it was conceived, public understanding of what it can and should achieve has evolved markedly. The transition reflects several important developments. The first is the recognition of environmental vulnerability. From the eccentric environmentalism of the 1960s to the World Summit in 1992, humanity has come to accept that environmental protection is a global imperative (UNCED 1993). The second is that project proponents are now much less likely to see formal impact assessment as needless harassment. It is seen as part of the cost of doing business, but as with all forms of regulation, they expect to have clear, fair, and consistent guidelines (FEARO 1993). The third is the fact that those involved in the technical aspects of impact assessment are often beyond our scientific competence.... The fourth reflects the fact that formal impact assessment takes place within an institutional or regulatory setting....

. . . .

Forethought and Foresight

Impact assessment is no more than a process by which common-sense concerns about community futures are incorporated into decisions — public or private — that will affect the future. It originated as *environmental* impact assessment (EIA) and was soon twinned by *social* impact assessment (SIA) (see Lang and Armour 1981 for an overview), but as the cultural context of environment and the environmental context of culture became more evident, the term 'impact assessment' (IA) was widely adopted.

IA has been described as a tool for 'minimum regret planning' (Beanlands and Duinker 1983). It presents decision makers with information about possible unplanned consequences of planned change. Thus, it need consist of only two things: the commitment to forethought and some ability to foresee. Advances in the latter arise through science and the willingness to explore traditional ecological knowledge. Advances in the former originate in public opinion but, since IA can be 'whatever you make of it' (Livingston 1981), it requires institutional support. The policies, regulations, and legislation

─────────────────────────────────

† From Bruce Mitchell, ed., *Resource and Environmental Management in Canada: Addressing Conflict and Uncertainty*, 2d ed. (Toronto: Oxtford University Press, 1995), pp. 360–72, 375–79. Figures omitted. See Appendix for notes or references. Reproduced by permission of the author.

that underlie impact assessment are the topics of the next section.

ORIGIN AND PURPOSE

IA was to have been the flagship of the environmental movement. In its twenty-five-year history, it has won some victories, but has also faced many failures (see Rosenberg et al. 1981; Sadler 1994; Smith 1993; Westman 1985; Whitney and Maclaren 1985b for good overviews). There is still uncertainty as to how well the process can be expected to work. The history of impact assessment begins with public concern, but its operational significance begins with the law.

The Legal Basis

Origins in the United States

The US National Environmental Policy Act (NEPA 1969) is generally recognized as the pioneer of formalized impact assessment. It was the crystallization of widespread public concern for environmental quality. The purposes of NEPA are to 'encourage productive and enjoyable harmony between man [sic] and his environment; to ... prevent damage to the environment; [and] to enrich understanding of the ecological systems and natural resources important to the Nation.' The act also specifies something about how the objectives are to be achieved. Three central requisites for impact assessment studies are outlined: that studies be interdisciplinary, including natural and social sciences and environmental design arts; that unquantifiable externalities be considered; and that there be a formal written statement available to the public. These requirements give impact assessment a very special character.

The specific objectives of the process are outlined by the Council on Environmental Quality (CEQ 1973):

1. Each generation is to serve as a trustee for future generations.
2. A safe, healthful, productive, and aesthetically and culturally pleasing environment is to be assured.
3. A wide range of safe and compatible uses should be permitted.
4. Aspects of heritage and range of options for the future should be protected.
5. A balance between population and resource potential is to be sought.

6. Use of renewable and recyclable resources is to be encouraged.

It is obvious from these objectives that interpretation of and response to the guidelines could be both highly discretionary and imponderably complex because it requires a balance of social, economic, and scientific objectives.

Canadian Federal Policy and the Canadian Environmental Assessment Act

The origin of federal environmental assessment was a task force established in 1970 to study impact assessment policy and procedure. It established guidelines for impact assessment within federal jurisdiction. The Cabinet Committee on Science, Culture and Information agreed on 18 December 1973 on the need for a formal assessment process (FEARO 1978) and two days later established the Federal Environmental Assessment and Review Process (EARP) and the Review Office (FEARO) (see Couch 1994 for a chronology of events).

The EARP was intended to differ from the NEPA process in several ways, most notably in having no legislated basis so that it would not be enforceable through the courts. Reviews would be cooperative, constructive processes of negotiation and deliberation based on points of environmental substance rather than costly adversarial ones pivoting on legal technicalities (FEARO 1987). But there was public concern about accountability under EARP, concern that self-regulation had meant that EARP was 'carried out inconsistently and in some cases ... [was] ... not being implemented' (FEARO 1988).

There were calls for revisions to the EARP process that were highlighted in events involving two western Canadian water development projects, the Rafferty-Alameda Dam in Saskatchewan and the Oldman River Dam in Alberta. Both projects were initiated without formal environmental assessment and both involved federal jurisdiction (under the Navigable Waters Act). A court challenge stopped work on partially completed projects and, after expensive and acrimonious debates, the Supreme Court of Canada determined that the EARP did have the force of law wherever there was a federal 'affirmative regulatory duty', no matter how small. This was never the government's intent and federal departments have neither the resources nor skills for such universal assessments.

Somewhat ironically, the revision process that began with the goal of making a diffuse procedure more consistent and rigorous became an exercise in limiting power. After public consultation, the Conservative government passed the Canadian Environmental Assessment Act (CEAA) on 23 June 1992 (Government of Canada 1992), but never proclaimed it. Elections followed and the Conservatives vanished. The Liberal 'Red Book' campaign platform made a strong commitment to environmental protection, noting that 'preventive environmental care ... is a wise public investment' (Liberal Party of Canada 1993:63). Impact assessment is clearly preventive care, and the Liberals have pledged to proclaim the act but to make it 'greener' and more independent of government (Regulatory Advisory Committee 1994).

The major change from EARP is that the act is restricted to 'projects', which are defined as physical work (such as construction or decommissioning) or physical activity (such as military training exercises). This is a contentious restriction because it means that policy decisions that could have marked environmental effects (e.g., setting fishing quotas) or programs (e.g., subsidizing fishing wages) do not need to be assessed. Critics felt the Conservative government was deliberately narrowing the scope to minimize the effect of the act. Professionals at FEARO, who would be responsible for applying the act, support the restriction on pragmatic grounds — it makes their task manageable. They point out that very few jurisdictions in the world require program and policy assessment and that adopting it might give a competitive disadvantage to Canadians (Department of the Environment 1993). While the Liberal government is committed to program and policy evaluation, this could be achieved through their 'Commissioner of the Environment' (Standing Committee on Environment and Sustainable Development 1994) rather than through a process that would necessarily delay further the proclamation of the new act.

In 1994, the act created the Canadian Environmental Assessment Agency (also CEAA) to replace FEARO. It will oversee impact assessments triggered in four instances: where the federal government (or an agent) is the proponent, or where federal lands, funding, or jurisdiction is involved (e.g. navigable waters).... There are four major objectives (FEARO 1993): (1) ensure that environmental affects receive careful consideration before action is taken; (2) promote sus-

tainable development, a healthy environment, and a healthy economy; (3) ensure that projects do not have adverse environmental effects outside areas of jurisdiction in which they are carried out; and (4) ensure the opportunity of public participation.

The act makes some important innovations, for example, with respect to mediation (Para. 29), cooperation with provinces (Paras. 46 and 54), and access to information (Para. 55).....

. . . .

Despite the apparent limitations of the EARP process, many of Canada's most important impact studies have been done under federal auspices. Examples include proposals for Boundary Bay airport near Vancouver, oil exploration off the West Coast, oil drilling in the Beaufort Sea, oil shipping through Lancaster Sound, gas transhipment along the Alaska Highway, uranium refineries at several locations, new port facilities near Montreal, gas exploration on Sable Island, NATO fighter plane training over Labrador, and service facilities for Hybernia oil in St. John's, Newfoundland. The final reports provide good practical insight into the nature of impact assessment and are very useful study documents. They are available from FEARO/CEAA offices.

Provincial Regulations and the Quebec Example

The provincial regulations vary from province to province (reviewed in Couch 1985; Emond 1978; Franson and Lucas 1978; Lucas 1981; Malvern et al. 1992; Thompson 1980), but invariably some form of environmental assessment is required. Industry groups on the Regulatory Advisory Committee feared that a single project could trigger 'cascading', a tangled series of independent impact assessments for different levels of governments and different ministries.

To eliminate duplication of effort and streamline impact assessment, the Canadian Council of Ministers of the Environment (CCME) is attempting to develop 'single-window' guidelines for impact assessment that give proponents a clear, *a priori* statement of regulations that they will have to satisfy. Alberta has made a commitment to open an office to provide such a service. The discussions with Quebec are, predictably, the most complex. But there are ongoing, mutual efforts to establish 'equivalency' so that any federal processes will at least await, and perhaps be made superfluous by, the resolution of the provincial assessments.

Quebec is a particularly interesting case to consider because, more than any other province, it is concerned about clarifying (or changing) jurisdictional issues and because of the enormous public visibility of the massive James Bay development projects. The act that empowers and regulates impact assessment in Quebec was adopted after the early work at James Bay. The Environmental Quality Act (1978) identifies categories of projects requiring impact assessment and specifies the material to be covered within impact reports. It is, in fact, a very progressive act. The most fundamental protection associated with the act derives from Article 19.1, which states that 'every person has a right to a healthy environment and to its protection, and to the protection of living species inhabiting it to the extent provided for by this act ...' This protection arises from (and accountability is achieved through) Article 22, which says that 'no one may ... carry on activity ... if it seems likely that this will result in ... a change in the quality of the environment, unless he obtains from the Deputy Minister a certificate of authorization.'

Within the private sector, all activities are permitted provided that they conform with local land-use regulations and do not breach environmental quality regulations. Major zoning changes of the kind required for complete new sitings of industry may require impact assessment, and activities that involve the government or their corporations, or which require law changes or licensing, can be submitted to the process. The effectiveness of the process can be limited by the fact that recommendations arising from the impact assessment procedure are for the minister's advice only (as is the case in all Canadian jurisdictions).

Bill 61 (1992) is an act to amend the Environmental Quality Act of 1978. Most of it deals with impact assessment. Three major objectives are addressed by the bill, the first of which is to ensure that 'consideration be given to any environmental questions involved in policies or programs of the Government' or its agents (Government of Quebec 1992). Note that programs and policies are included here. The second is to ensure public consultation or formal public hearings. The third is to provide intervenor funding for 'encouraging individuals, groups or municipal-

ities to take part in public hearings'. The act has a number of very significant provisions: the possibility of treating several projects with a common objective as a single project (Section 31.8), the right to prescribe measures for monitoring project (Section 31.8), the right to prescribe measures for monitoring project effects (Section 31.9.9), and to require that proponents produce 'attestations of conformity' at various predetermined stages of the project development process. Perhaps of most political significance is the right to make the provisions of this act applicable to any project subject to environmental legislation under another jurisdiction (Section 31.9.16). In other words, this act automatically applies to anything that would be subject to federal assessment. While this may be an attempt to co-opt authority or assert sovereignty, it does make more feasible the goal of 'single-window' assessments under harmonized procedures.

Quebec is still anxious to expand hydro production in northern Quebec despite recent international controversies regarding the development and cancellation of major export contracts, but the day of developments unconstrained by social and environmental impacts may be over. The government has been persistent in its effort to get northern Natives to endorse further development and has constructed impact assessment procedures that should ensure more effective studies.

THE REQUISITES FOR IMPACT ASSESSMENT

With the legal mandate to conduct impact assessment, it becomes necessary to define the terms and objectives of any particular study. The information requirements are considered below, as are the mechanisms for making the study manageable and effective.

Spheres of Knowledge

The Proposed Activity

Before the nature of probable impacts can be predicted, it is necessary to know what the proposed activity encompasses. Depending on the type of project, there may be significant impacts associated with the planning or the exploration stage, the construction or implementation stage, the period of normal use and operation, and perhaps with a decommissioning or 'winding down' phase, and a postuse period. This is particularly important where toxic or hazardous wastes may contaminate sites for indefinite periods. In the case of nuclear waste material, it is unclear how the essentially external costs of keeping waste can be incorporated into planning decisions.

There may also be secondary or derived effects. Consider, for example, the opening of a 'destination area' ski resort at Panorama, British Columbia. Direct impacts are only related to slope clearance, but derived impacts come from road improvements, hotel development, sewage outfall, traffic congestion, increased pressure on local services (including hospitals), and further development of residential and service facilities in the area. In other situations, secondary impacts may be more difficult to predict, such as the mercury contamination of reservoirs in James Bay. Determining derived impacts may require detailed knowledge of complex industrial processes, waste management principles, and natural ecological responses.

The Development Environment

An impact may be defined as a change in the state of the environment. Because of the weblike interdependencies of ecosystem's components, a shift in one component will frequently result in compensatory adjustments in other parts of the system. In order to predict impacts, it is necessary (but not sufficient) to know what the components of the development environment are. Understanding ecological principles permits prediction of change: 'guestimation' based on concepts such as succession or biological magnification or numeric prediction based on models such as those for pollution diffusion or the responses of lakes to nutrient enrichment.

．　．　．　．

The Canadian North continues to present many unique challenges. The need for basic inventories may seem greater there than in the more fully researched South, but it should be noted that northern residents are often much more fully aware of their environment than people in industrial settings. Folk knowledge, ethnoscience, and conventional wisdom can often be valuable in conducting species inventories, doing ecological mapping, or describing behaviour or activities such as migration routes or staging times. Inuit hunters know where, when, and how to hunt. That information can often give ecologists all they need to know.

Screening for Significance

Determining what to study — an exercise commonly known as 'scoping' — can be based on an assessment of the following:

1. The possibility of occurrence: If a result appears to be extremely unlikely, it will warrant less concern than if the same result appears to be extremely likely. However, the probability must be assessed with reference to the gravity of the consequences.

2. The magnitude of the change: If an event will result in a large change, be it positive or negative, it may warrant consideration even if the possibility of that result is low. Conversely, if the change is trivial, even a highly probable event may be ignored. Cumulative and synergistic changes need special attention and the perception of those experiencing the change must be considered.

   The interaction of the probability and magnitude of factors is demonstrated by comparing the relatively low probability of failures in nuclear systems with 'triple redundant' safety systems with the virtual certainty of noise disturbance from a highway, but magnitude may make the former unacceptable and the latter acceptable.

3. The perception of change: Value judgement is an essential part of the impact assessment process, not only at the stage of evaluating the impact predictions but also at the stage of selecting the impacts to be studied. Evaluators must therefore either be representative of or responsive to the constituency on whose behalf the impact assessment is being made. Hence, the importance of public hearings in IA.

   This concern is particularly important in Canada where many resource and land-use issues involve Native rights. It has always been difficult for developers to understand, for example, the value placed on traditional lifestyles by northern Natives. The case of the NATO training flights over Native hunting grounds highlights the conflict. It is difficult if not possible for anyone not of that culture to understand what the value of the hunting experience might be or how low-level, high-speed flights might alter it.

4. The timing of the occurrence. If an event is likely to take place at some time in the distant future, its impact on decision making will usually be different from something that is imminent. For a result that has a measurable cash value, a process called 'discounting' may be used to compensate for time differences. For example, something that yields a value of $100 but only after a delay of, say, seven years would be considered as being equal in value to something that has an immediate benefit worth about $10 (if interest rates of roughly 10 per cent are assumed). This has the effect of diminishing the importance of future events, whether good or bad. The net effect of discounting is that benefits tend to be brought forward and costs tend to be delayed. 'Short-term gain, long-term pain' makes economic sense, although it puts an unfair ethical burden on the generations that will miss the benefits but be left to settle the costs.

Thus, on the basis of probability, magnitude, significance, and imminence, the vast array of potential elements to study must be reduced to a manageable few. Still, before studies are conducted, it must be clear that there are rational means of interpreting results. This means comparing alternatives.

Identifying Alternatives

... [I]mpact assessment implies comparison. The comparison is often between a future as influenced by the development project and a static present, but, of course, such a comparison is meaningless. The only useful comparison is among possible futures, none of which will be identical with the present.

When impact assessment is undertaken in response to an application for a specific project, the onus is on the proponent to establish that the total social costs will not be unacceptable. This situation ... normally results in comparison of with-project and without-project futures. This is a situation that arises when a single site is available for an optional project — for example, when determining whether a dam site should be developed or not. This is by far the most common context for practical impact assessment.

In other cases, impact assessment is undertaken to minimize the costs of what is necessary, for example, building a road or constructing a sewage treatment plant. Here, the essence of the project remains the same, but the environment varies; that is, several possible sites are considered. The study may be duplicated for all likely sites and the range of problems and the magnitude of the task multiplies accordingly.... The task is to locate the site at which the ratio of costs to benefits will be most favourable.

In situations where the motivation for impact studies derives from a regional or national development initiative, the situation is complicated in a different way. The site remains constant, but the possible futures are made to vary, that is, for a specific site a number of different development alternatives are considered.... This is the situation that community or regional planners encounter as they try to consider a range of alternative development strategies (Meredith 1992).

In Canada, any one of these situations may arise. Impact assessments undertaken in the first situation may be seen as being defensive or reactive. In the second, assuming the motivating need is perceived by local people, it is neutral (a necessary concomitant of meeting community needs). But in the third it may be seen as a positive program of considered planning leading to proposals based on environmental capability.

.   .   .   .

LINKING WITH DECISION MAKERS

The specific functions of impact assessment are to reduce the frequency of unexpected change, reduce unexpected and undesirable consequences of planned or inevitable change, and permit mitigation planning (or compensation) for unavoidable negative changes. The collection, interpretation, and presentation of salient data are critical, but represent only the first steps. The information has to enter the decision-making process somehow. Just how that occurs depends on how facts or probabilities are evaluated and then on how they influence change.

Evaluating Results

'Good' and 'bad' are not words that are found frequently in impact assessment literature, although the words 'cost' and 'benefit' pervade it. Benefit-cost analysis compares net benefits with net costs to produce an overall evaluation of the ultimate impact of an action or event. It is a process fraught with difficulties because of the breadth of its scope: it presumes an ability to compare elements measured or valued in different units (see Westman 1985 for discussion).

One application of benefit-cost analysis to decision making in resource planning is the inclusion of externalities. Externalities are costs that can be imposed — directly or indirectly — on third parties or on the community at large. If a pulp mill causes a decline in commercial fishing, that loss is an externality. Justice suggests that those profiting from the mill should compensate fishers for their loss.

Impact assessment can help to reveal externalities, but the situation is complicated by two factors: (1) many costs may not be quantifiable or commensurable (that is, capable of being converted to easily compared units such as dollar value), and (2) evaluations must consider *total* community welfare, not merely the self-interest of single actors.

. . . .

The Boundaries of Evaluation

Because technology varies among regions (or among cultures in different regions) and because the needs of one community may differ from the needs of another community, what is seen as the optimal use of a given resource will depend on the cultural context of the resource system.

Within a culturally homogeneous area, a common focus of controversy is what has been dubbed the NIMBY syndrome (Not In My Backyard): a culture group collectively accepts the need for a project — say a landfill site, an airport, or a nuclear power plant — but no one wants it near them (see Pushchak and Burton 1983). In such cases the decision may be simply one of numbers; that is, one of finding a site that affects the fewest people.

In situations where developments are undertaken in one area for the benefit of communities in another, as is the case for most northern development in Canada, the situation is more complex. It may be that if only the residents of the North are considered when evaluating the efficiency of the resource systems, the most efficient system is one that emphasizes the preservation of nature and sustainable exploitation of local renewable resources.

If a broader constituency is included, the relative importance of local renewable resources

will be greatly reduced and the relative value of the non-renewable industrial resources will be increased. The Berger Commission on the MacKenzie Valley Pipeline proposal exposed these conflicts in what has become a landmark study (Berger 1978). The title of Berger's report, *Norther Frontier, Northern Homeland*, captures the essence of the 'boundary of evaluation' question. What makes sense at the frontier may not make sense within the homeland, and when these are the same location, only viewed from different perspectives, there is a potential for conflict. How this is resolved depends on where decision-making authority resides.

Locus of Control

Another study that broached the issue is that of oil exploration proposals for Lancaster Sound in the Canadian Arctic. A statement from the Government of Canada quoted in the report (Dirschl 1982) notes that 'the needs of people in the North are more important than resource development'. Also quoted is a statement from the minister of Indian and Northern Affairs (then John C. Munro) noting the objective of 'greater political, social and economic self-sufficiency' for norther people. However, the frame of reference for the study was the Canadian public interest, and 'the Canadian public' was given the 'opportunity to consider potential and future uses for the Lancaster Sound Region'.

It is evident that while the involvement of northern residents in planning is seen as a desirable objective, the power for allowing northern input and the discretion for accepting or rejecting it lies in the South. ...

Likewise, the situation for Cree and Inuit in Quebec is characterized by the introduction to the James Bay and Northern Quebec Agreement: 'a comprehensive settlement that would establish ... Quebec's national policy'. It is certainly far from self-evident that Quebec's 'national' priorities will always also be in the best interest of local communities....

IMPROVING THE EFFECTIVENESS OF IMPACT ASSESSMENT

The role that impact assessment plays in decision making is, ideally, one in which externalities are identified, evaluated, and incorporated into the decision-making process. Without this connection, even scientifically excellent impact assessment will not necessarily lead to responsive decisions — decisions that are rational within the local context.

If impact assessment has no input into the decision-making process, its only value is to allow prospective victims of negative change to prepare for the change. If its inclusion in decision making is discretionary and beyond the control of those initiating the study, then its prime value will derive not primarily from its accuracy or precision but from its rhetorical value. How well impact assessment can work depends on what it is intended to do, so those involved in the process must be clear on the context.

In a short statement of priorities for enhancing impact assessment, the Canadian Environmental Assessment Review Council (1988) suggests that 'Three concerns remain central...: first, the accuracy of predicting; second, the degree to which mitigatory and compensatory measures actually reduce impacts...; and third, the efficiency and fairness with which the assessment process itself accommodates the needs, concerns and values of all the interested parties.' Improving the basic science — whether it is natural or social science — is a matter for the professionals in the various fields (see Beanlands and Duinker 1983 for statement of problem, and Hart et al. 1984, and Maclaren and Whitney 1985 for discussions). Improving mitigation and compensation programs requires improvements in follow-up studies of programs that have been implemented (see Munro et al. 1986 for discussions).

The most problematic is the third because needs, concerns, and values are so difficult to manage in a quantitative, reductionist way. There is evergrowing interest in the study of measures of quality of life (Miles 1985). Until interested parties can identify and articulate which aspects of their socioecosystem are essential to preserving or enhancing their own quality of life, impact assessment will risk overlooking critical determinants.

There is an allegory of a man who lost his wallet in a dark street and decided to look for it in the next street where the light was better. It is relevant here. Impact assessment is part of a cultural adaptation to new environmental pressures. Planning and development, the precursors of most impact assessments, are ostensibly undertaken to improve human well-being. Impact assessment attempts to ensure that those goals are achieved, but invariably we rely on indicators that are easy to measure and understand, often forsaking what is most important only because it is so nebulous.

(b) The New *Canadian Environmental Assessment Act* — Bill C-78: A disappointing response to promised reform[†]

Michael I. Jeffery, Q.C. ————————————————————————

BACKGROUND

Environmental impact assessment (E.I.A.) first appeared in Canada at the federal level in the early 1970s.[1] It represented this country's response to an earlier initiative of the Nixon administration in the United States, which culminated in the enactment of the *National Environmental Policy Act*[2] in 1969.

In terms of both methodology and purpose, E.I.A. marked a radical departure from existing regulatory models in environmental policy, changing the focus from regulation and control to planning and prevention. The regulatory model invariably contains a general prohibition against the discharge of pollutants into the natural environment, with permissible levels or concentrations set out in accompanying regulations. In contrast, E.I.A. is anticipatory in nature, involving the evaluation of alternatives to the proposed undertaking, and alternative methods

† This article was originally published in the *McGill Law Journal* 36 (1991): 1070–1088. Reproduced by permission of the author and the publisher. See appendix for notes or references.

of carrying it out, prior to the start of any construction. This approach is viewed as the principal means of ensuring an environmentally acceptable solution in matters of development. In essence, E.I.A. may be characterized as preventative rather than reactive. Unlike the regulatory approach, which emphasizes adherence to predetermined standards, E.I.A. is primarily used as a planning tool to provide the regulatory authority with an objective basis upon which to grant or deny project approval.

The underlying philosophy of E.I.A. is illustrated by the wording of s. 102 of *N.E.P.A.*, which states as a matter of policy that all federal government agencies must

> utilize a systematic interdisciplinary approach which will ensure the integrated use of the natural and social sciences and the environmental design arts in planning and in decision making which may have an impact on man's environment.[3]

It is not uncommon for courts in the United States to refer to the inherent objectives of environmental legislation in the context of specific decisions. For example, in the case of *Boston (City) v. Volpe*,[4] Coffin J. stated that

> the purpose of the statute [*N.E.P.A.*] was to "build into the agency decision process" environmental considerations, "as early as possible," taking into account "the overall, cumulative impact of the action proposed (and of further actions contemplated)" and "environmental consequences not fully evaluated at the outset of the project or program."[5]

Although the scope of the American legislation is extremely broad, it is nevertheless considered by many to be fundamentally flawed because it fails to provide an independent regulatory/enforcement mechanism or process. This lack of a separate administrative structure has meant that the task of enforcing statutory norms has gradually fallen to the courts.[6]

Until recently, reliance upon the courts in the United States for the necessary supervision with respect to environmental impact legislation stood in sharp contrast to the Canadian perception of the proper role of the judiciary in the process. In light of the more activist role of the U.S. Supreme Court, particularly with respect to social policy issues, it is not surprising that the American people and their governments remain more willing to have environmental assessment legislation and policy interpreted and enforced

through judicial intervention. In Canada, the opposite is certainly the case, for notwithstanding the increased role of the judiciary following the enactment of the *Canadian Charter of Rights and Freedoms*[7] in 1982, any supervisory function similar to that exercised by U.S. courts would most certainly be perceived as an unwarranted intrusion into the administrative and regulatory realm of government.[8]

THE LEGAL FRAMEWORK FOR THE FEDERAL ENVIRONMENTAL ASSESSMENT PROCESS

For reasons which are still not fully understood, the government which first introduced comprehensive environmental assessment at the federal level chose to do so by means of a Cabinet directive in the form of a Guidelines Order, rather than by way of legislative enactment. The "self-assessment" nature of the Guidelines Order clearly indicates that the government wished to retain as much flexibility as possible with respect to the environmental assessment of federal undertakings. In fact, right up until the Federal Court decisions in the *Rafferty Alameda*[9] cases, the government resisted any suggestion that the application of the E.A.R.P. was mandatory with respect to projects or proposals falling within the scope of the Guidelines.

By adopting guidelines as opposed to enacting specific E.I.A. legislation, the government quite reasonably assumed that the E.A.R.P. provisions were just that: guidelines to be followed when and if the governmental authority responsible for their application, in its unfettered discretion, thought it appropriate to do so. Supporters of this interpretation could also point to the wording of the supporting legislation which provided the basis in law for the Guidelines, and attested to the discretionary nature of the power of the Minister of the Environment to promulgate guidelines in the first place. Section 6 of the *Department of the Environment Act*[10] states:

> 6. For the purpose of carrying out his duties and functions related to environmental quality, the Minister of the Environment *may*, by order, with the approval of the Governor in Council, establish guidelines for use by departments, boards and agencies of the Government of Canada and, where appropriate, by corporations named in Schedule D to the *Financial Administration Act* and regulatory bodies in the exercise of their powers and the carrying out of their duties and functions [emphasis added].

At the time the Guidelines Order was made, there appeared to have been no statutory obligation compelling the Minister to establish guidelines at all, for s. 6 uses the word "may," not "shall," in outlining the Minister's powers.

In hindsight it is reasonable to conclude that, until recently, both the government and indeed many others were oblivious to the possibility that the courts might find the E.A.R.P. Guidelines Order to be "not a mere description of policy or programme" but instead a Regulation which "may create rights and be enforceable by way of mandamus."[11]

The far-reaching decisions of the Federal Court in the *Rafferty Alameda* cases[12] generated shockwaves within the federal bureaucracy which are still being felt today. The result in these cases accelerated the pace of and gave a sense of urgency to reform already underway.

Before reviewing the circumstances giving rise to the Federal Court decisions in the *Rafferty Alameda* and *Oldman River*[13] cases, and their impact upon the proposed new *Canadian Environmental Assessment Act*, it will be useful to outline briefly the relevant provisions of the Guidelines Order.

The Guidelines Order

2. In these Guidelines,

"Environmental Impact Statement" means a documented assessment of the environmental consequences of any proposal expected to have significant environmental consequences that is prepared or procured by the proponent in accordance with guidelines established by a Panel;

"department" means ...
(a) any department, board or agency of the Government of Canada, and
(b) any corporation listed in schedule D to the *Financial Administration Act* and any regulatory body;

"initiating department" means any department that is, on behalf of the Government of Canada, the decision making authority for a proposal;

"Minister" means the Minister of the Environment:

...

"proponent" means the organization or the initiating department intending to undertake a proposal;

"proposal" includes any initiative, undertaking or activity for which the Government of Canada has a decision making responsibility.

3. The Process shall be a self assessment process under which the initiating department shall,

as early in the planning process as possible and before irrevocable decisions are taken, ensure that the environmental implications of all proposals for which it is the decision making authority are fully considered and where the implications are significant, refer the proposal to the Minister for public review by a Panel.

4.(1) An initiating department shall include in its consideration of a proposal pursuant to section 3
(a) the potential environmental effects of the proposal and the social effects directly related to those environmental effects, including any effects that are external to Canadian territory; and
(b) the concerns of the public regarding the proposal and its potential environmental effects.

(2) Subject to the approval of the Minister and the Minister of the initiating department, consideration of a proposal may include such matters as the general socio-economic effects of the proposal and the technology assessment of and need for the proposal.

5.(1) Where a proposal is subject to environmental regulation, independently of the Process, duplication in terms of public reviews is to be avoided.

(2) For the purpose of avoiding the duplication referred to in subsection (1), the initiating department shall use a public review under the Process as a planning tool at the earliest stages of development of the proposal rather than as a regulatory mechanism and make the results of the public review available for use in any regulatory deliberations respecting the proposal.

6. These Guidelines shall apply to any proposal
(a) that is to be undertaken directly by an initiating department;
(b) that may have an environmental effect on an area of federal responsibility;
(c) for which the Government of Canada makes a financial commitment; or
(d) that is located on lands including the offshore that are administered by the Government of Canada.[14]

THE RAFFERTY ALAMEDA CASES

What have become known as the *Rafferty Alameda* cases in fact represent a number of interrelated proceedings before the Federal Court of Canada involving both the trial and appellate divisions. In view of the limited scope of this commentary, only the initial decision of Cullen J. of the Trial Division will be discussed in detail.[15] It is primarily this decision which gave rise to the controversy which followed regarding the binding nature of the Guidelines.

The Facts

In order to alleviate fluctuating flood and drought conditions in the Souris River basin in southern Saskatchewan, the provincial government indicated its intention to construct two dams, the Rafferty dam, to be located on the Souris River near the town of Estevan, and the Alameda dam on Moose Mountain Creek, which flows into the Souris near Alameda, Saskatchewan.

The Souris River is an international waterway, flowing from Saskatchewan. The project was to be undertaken by the Government of Saskatchewan through the Souris Basin Development Authority (S.B.D.A.) as agent for another Crown corporation, the Saskatchewan Water Corporation.

The S.B.D.A. prepared a provincial environmental impact statement which was publicly released and, after a review by a Board of Inquiry, the Saskatchewan Minister of the Environment and Public Safety granted the authority to proceed subject to certain conditions. On June 17, 1988 the federal Minister of the Environment (the Minister), determined that the review of the provincial environmental impact statement by Environment Canada, together with the conditions to be attached to the Saskatchewan licence, were sufficient to protect the interests of the Federal Government. He issued a licence for dam construction to the Saskatchewan Water Corporation pursuant to the *International River Improvements Act*.[16]

The Canadian Wildlife Federation (C.W.F.) had on several occasions requested that the Minister conduct an assessment and review under the E.A.R.P. Guidelines Order before approving the licence application. The E.I.A. prepared in Saskatchewan did not contain an assessment and review of the environmental impact of the project in North Dakota or in Manitoba, nor was one prepared in Manitoba with respect to the environmental impact there. The federal Minister nevertheless did not heed the request of C.W.F. for a more comprehensive review. In its subsequent application to the Court, C.W.F. sought: (i) an order for *certiorari*, quashing and setting aside the licence issued by the Minister under the *International River Improvements Act*; and (ii) an order for *mandamus* requiring the Minister to comply with the E.A.R.P. Guidelines Order, to subject the proposed project to an initial environmental screening to assess potentially adverse environmental effects. According to the Guidelines, wherever a proposal may cause significant adverse environmental effects, it must be referred to the Minister for public review by an Environmental Assessment Panel.

The Decisions

The Court held that the Guidelines Order was an enactment or Regulation as defined in s. 2 of the *Interpretation Act*,[17] and as such could create rights enforceable by way of *mandamus*.[18] In considering whether the Minister was required to comply with the provisions of the Guidelines Order, the Court found that the project was a "proposal" that would "have an environmental impact upon a number of areas of federal responsibility, namely, international relations [by virtue of], the *International Boundary Waters Treaty Act*,[19] ... migratory birds (by virtue of the *Migratory Birds Convention Act*),[20] ... interprovincial affairs and fisheries."[21] In addition, the project would have an environmental effect on "4,000 acres of land 'owned' or at the very least held in trust and administered, by the Federal Government."[22]

Compliance with the E.A.R.P. Guidelines Order was held to be a condition precedent to the granting of a licence by the Minister under the *International River Improvements Act*. The Minister's failure to comply with the Guidelines constituted an excess of his jurisdiction entitling the applicant to an order of *certiorari* quashing the licence.

The Court further held that despite the apparently discretionary language of the Guidelines, the Minister had breached a duty by not complying with the provisions of the Guidelines Order. The applicant was therefore also entitled to an order of *mandamus* compelling the Minister to carry out an appropriate environmental assessment, as required by the Guidelines.

The Federal Court of Appeal upheld the decision of Cullen J.[23] Following these proceedings, the Minister ordered that a draft Initial Environmental Evaluation (IEE) be prepared, to be followed by a public consultation process prior to the preparation of the final IEE in August 1989. Without appointing a public review panel under the provisions of the Guidelines Order, the Minister granted a second licence for the projects on August 31, 1989. His decision was based on advice from his officials that any significant adverse environmental effects could be almost entirely mitigated. The Minister's decision triggered a further round of litigation, with two more applications for *certiorari* and *mandamus* being launched. Once again the Trial Division found the decision of the Minister not to appoint a panel review unlawful, and issued an order of *mandamus* requiring the Minister to comply with the provisions of the E.A.R.P. Guidelines Order by appointing a panel to review the project. The Court also ordered *certiorari* to quash the second licence unless a panel was appointed within a specified time.[24]

This decision was appealed on the grounds that the order of *certiorari* should have quashed the second licence absolutely as long as a review panel had not been appointed and its report had not been considered by the Minister prior to the issuance of the licence. The Saskatchewan Water Corporation cross-appealed.

The Federal Court of Appeal, in a decision issued December 21, 1990, once again upheld the decision of the trial judge and dismissed both the appeal and cross appeal.[25] The Court confirmed that "a panel review must take place unless potentially adverse environmental effects that may be caused by the proposal are found to be insignificant."[26]

Construction of the Rafferty dam had continued virtually unabated even as court proceedings were being undertaken from 1989 to 1990. The dam was virtually completed by October 1990 when the panel appointed by the Minister in compliance with the Court's order resigned in protest at the continuing construction.

The federal government applied to the Saskatchewan Court of Queen's Bench in November 1990, for an injunction to stop Saskatchewan from proceeding with construction until public hearings were completed. The Court rejected federal arguments that continuing construction of the project could cause irreparable harm to the environment, and refused to issue a stop work order. Chief Justice Donald MacPherson referred to the federal E.A.R.P. as "badly flawed," and severely criticised the federal government for its procedural and legislative handling of the entire matter.[27]

At the same time, an application for an injunction to halt construction of the project pending completion of the review was brought by two local ranchers concerned over the potential loss of grazing land for their cattle in the vicinity of the proposed Alameda reservoir. The application for injunction was rejected by the Federal Court Trial Division, but in his reasons,

Muldoon J. affirmed the Minister's obligation to appoint a new panel.[28] The Court would not intervene to halt construction as long as panel hearings were taking place, but failure to appoint a new panel could lead to the issuance of an injunction to stop the project from proceeding further. In the words of the Court, "no panel — no licence — no construction."[29] Three days before Muldoon J. rendered his decision on February 8, 1991, the Minister had advised the Court that a new panel would be appointed.

In addition, the Saskatchewan Water Corporation and the Souris Basin Development Corporation recently launched two suits in the Saskatchewan courts claiming damages against the federal government in excess of $600 million.

THE OLDMAN RIVER CASE[30]

Only a few months after the initial decision in *Rafferty Alameda*, the Federal Court was again asked to compel Ministers of the federal government to comply with the E.A.R.P. Guidelines Order.

The *Oldman River* case involved a proposal to construct a dam on the Oldman River in Southern Alberta to ensure a secure supply of water within the South Saskatchewan River Basin. The decision to proceed with construction was reached after several years of planning by the Alberta government, which included numerous studies and reviews by various provincial committees, with input in some cases from federal officials.

In 1986 the Alberta Department of the Environment applied for and subsequently obtained approval from the federal Minister of Transport for the dam site and plan pursuant to s. 5 of the *Navigable Waters Protection Act*.[31] No initial environmental assessment or screening was undertaken, and the application was not referred to the Minister of the Environment for review. Although the Southern Alberta Environmental Group had requested that the Minister of Fisheries and Oceans comply with the Guidelines Order, the Minister replied that environmental issues were being addressed by the Province, and refused to intervene.

The Friends of the Oldman River Society then requested that the Minister of the Environment subject the project to review under the Guidelines Order. Once again the request was refused by the Minister, who believed that any potential environmental problems were being adequately mitigated by those responsible for the project, rendering a separate federal assessment unnecessary. The Minister also cited long-standing administrative arrangements with the province, governing the management of joint concerns such as environmental assessment and fisheries.

Many of the issues first raised in *Rafferty Alameda* were reconsidered by the Trial Division in *Oldman River*. In the *Oldman* case, however, Associate Chief Justice Jerome remained unconvinced of the applicability of the Guidelines Order in the circumstances and dismissed the application.[32]

The Federal Court of Appeal allowed the appeal, and granted an order of *certiorari* quashing the approval of the licence by the Minister of Transport under the *Navigable Waters Protection Act*. In addition, orders of *mandamus* were issued directing both the Ministers of Transport and of Fisheries and Oceans to comply with the E.A.R.P. Guidelines Order.[33] The reasoning of the Court of Appeal in *Oldman River* was similar to that of the same court in *Rafferty Alameda*;[34] however, some points of distinction should be noted. The Court specifically rejected the notion that the Guidelines Order does not apply to cases where specialized statutory provisions require consideration of criteria not directly related to environmental concerns. In reaffirming the position taken by the Court in *Rafferty Alameda*, Stone J. stated:

> By virtue of s. 6 of the *Department of the Environment Act*, any guidelines established are to be used "by departments ... in the exercise of their powers and the carrying out of their duties and functions" in furtherance of those duties and functions of the Minister of the Environment (Canada) himself which are "related to environmental quality" ... the Guidelines Order was intended to bind the Minister in the performance of his duties and functions. It created a duty which is superadded to the exercise of any other statutory power residing in him. The source of the Minister's jurisdiction and responsibility to address environmental questions in areas of federal responsibility springs not from the statutory law but from the Guidelines Order itself. The Minister had a positive obligation to comply with it.[35]

The Court found that the word "proposal," as it is used in the Guidelines Order,[36] goes beyond its ordinary meaning, which would signify something in the nature of an application. A Minister might become aware of the existence of an "initiative, undertaking or activity, in some other way than having received an application for approval of a proposal that may have an environmental effect on an area of federal responsibility for which he was the decision making authority."[37]

In this case the Minister of Fisheries and Oceans was required by statute to intervene to protect fisheries resources. As this was an area of federal responsibility under the *Fisheries Act*,[38] the Minister became the decision making authority with respect to determining what action would be taken. Having notice of the "proposal," he became obliged to comply with the Guidelines Order.[39]

The effect of *Rafferty Alameda* and *Oldman River* on the federal environmental assessment process has been profound. The cases reinforced the desire of the federal Minister of the Environment to ensure swift passage of the new *Canadian Environmental Assessment Act*. The following section will briefly examine the proposed legislative scheme, as well as some of the underlying factors which led to its introduction.

THE CANADIAN ENVIRONMENTAL ASSESSMENT ACT

At least two years prior to the initial decision in *Rafferty Alameda*, the federal government initiated a series of studies and public consultation sessions aimed at reforming the E.A.R.P. process at both the structural and procedural levels. The process had long been criticised on a number of fronts, and the government at last appeared to be responding to an increasingly vocal minority calling for substantive reform.

The criticism most often levelled at the existing federal process is that it is based upon a principle of self-assessment. The process is triggered only when an initiating department with decision making responsibility determines that the potential impact of a proposal warrants referring the matter to the Minister of the Environment for public review. It must be remembered that in many cases the initiating department is also the proponent proposing to undertake its own project. It is only in recent years that the federal *Access to Information Act*[40] has helped the public obtain information concerning both the proposal and, more importantly, the decision of the initiating department with respect to the initial screening or assessment, thus providing a potential check on the dangers inherent in self-assessment.

A second perceived weakness concerned the lack of authority of the review panel, which under the Guidelines Order performs an advisory function only. Decision making powers were reserved for the Minister of the Environment and the Minister of the initiating department, significantly increasing the potential for politicizing the process.

Critics have also pointed to the absence of a quasi-judicial forum in which to rigorously examine a proposal using adversarial techniques for testing the truth of conflicting evidence.[41] This lack of an independent structure raises significant concerns where the process lacks a statutory foundation, and is therefore less insulated from the possibility of political interference. It is true that a quasi-judicial process might also be subject to political pressures. Even the decisions of a formally independent, quasi-judicial tribunal may often be varied by the government by way of appeal or petition to a Minister or Cabinet.[42] Nevertheless, the credibility of quasi-judicial decision making processes is maintained by the fact that the public hearing or review is conducted in an atmosphere that is generally perceived by those taking part to be fair, just, and devoid of political interference. This was not the case with E.A.R.P. hearings under the procedures outlined in the Guidelines Order.

In January 1987 the Federal Environmental Assessment Review Office (F.E.A.R.O.) announced the establishment of a study group to be chaired by the Honourable Allison M. Walsh, Q.C., a retired justice of the Federal Court. The study group was to review the existing procedures followed by F.E.A.R.O. in conducting public reviews, and to determine whether a more structured adversarial hearing format was required.

The study group released its report in January of 1988,[43] and concluded that the informal hearing procedures then in place should be continued. The report recommended that panels be given subpoena powers, but not the power to swear in participants. The report also recommended, however, that principles of procedural fairness guide the hearing process to a greater extent. Panels should be composed of panelists who were independent of both the government and the proponent, unbiased with respect to the particular project under review, and yet possess special expertise in the matters at issue.

In September 1987, the federal Minister of the Environment released a Green Paper[44] calling for the reform of the E.A.R.P. after a period of extensive discussion and consultation. The Green Paper canvassed a variety of options for improving the initial assessment phase, and alluded to the possibility of some form of environmental assessment legislation in lieu of guidelines issued under the authority of an Order in Council. The discussion paper also suggested improvements to the public review phase, and attempted to address the contentious issue of self-assessment. In addition, it suggested that measures be developed to prevent duplication of environmental hearings by more than one regulatory agency with respect to a particular proposal.

Although the *Rafferty Alameda* and *Oldman River* decisions did not in themselves provide the impetus for reform, they did provide the basis for pushing the government's reform package to the top of its political agenda. With the courts having decided that the E.A.R.P. Guidelines Order was enforceable as a regulation to be applied with respect to areas of federal responsibility, there seemed little point in delaying introduction of the long-awaited legislation. The new *Canadian Environmental Assessment Act* was tabled in the House of Commons on June 18, 1990.

In introducing the new Bill, the then Minister of the Environment, the Honourable Robert de Cotret, stated:

> I want to emphasize that the new Act will go much further than the original Guidelines. In fact, this legislation and Reform Package will result in an environmental assessment process which is more powerful in its impact on decision making than any other environmental assessment in the world.[45]

Not surprisingly, the Minister's enthusiastic endorsement of the proposed *C.E.A.A.* is not shared by all, particularly since many of the perceived areas of deficiency remain. The principal elements of the proposed legislative scheme are described in the following paragraphs.

Provisions of the New Canadian Environmental Assessment Act

Federal authorities subject to the Act include federal Ministers, agencies, departments and Crown corporations.[46] An initial screening and report concerning possible environmental effects are to be carried out with respect to proposed projects where: the federal authority is the proponent; the authority provides financial assistance; the project is to be carried out on federal lands; or in circumstances where a federal permit, licence or approval is required.[47]

The Act provides for the development by Cabinet of exclusionary and mandatory study lists for different types of projects. The exclusionary list will list projects which have been determined by Cabinet to have negligible environmental effects, which should be excluded for reasons of national security or which entail minimal federal involvement. Mandatory study lists will include all projects deemed by Cabinet to have significant adverse environmental effects.[48]

The Federal Environmental Assessment Review Office is to be replaced by a new agency — the Canadian Environmental Assessment Agency. Although separate from Environment Canada, the Minister of the Environment will continue to be responsible for the agency, which will perform essentially the same advisory, as opposed to decision-making, role as that of its predecessor.[49]

Unless exempted by virtue of being located on the exclusionary list, the responsible authority, after completing a screening report, may proceed with the project if in its opinion:

> (i) the project is not likely to cause significant adverse environmental effects, or
> (ii) any such effects can be mitigated.[50]

Where the project is to be found on the mandatory study list, the responsible authority must conduct a mandatory study and submit a mandatory study report to the Agency, or refer the project to the Minister who will arrange for mediation or review by a panel.[51]

Where in the opinion of the responsible authority the project is likely to cause significant adverse environmental effects that may not be mitigable, or where public concern warrants it, the project must be referred to the Minister for mediation or review by a panel. The responsible authority may not in these circumstances proceed with the project while the environmental assessment is being conducted.[52]

The new legislation gives the Minister of the Environment the sole discretion to determine the need for panel review, and provides him with the option of referring the project to mediation. In addition, where the Minister is of the opinion that the project is likely to cause significant environmental effects that may not be mitigable,

or that public concern warrants it, he may after consulting the responsible authority refer the project to mediation or a review panel.[53] The responsible authority retains the ultimate decision making power with respect to the project following the submission of the report by the mediator or review panel.[54]

Environmental assessments are to take into account the environmental effects of a project, including cumulative environmental impacts, comments concerning those effects received from the public and mitigation measures that are technically and economically feasible. Every mandatory study, mediation or panel review must also include a consideration of the purpose of the project, and of alternative means of carrying it out that are technically and economically feasible, as well as the environmental effects of any such alternative means. In addition, studies must examine the need for, and the requirements of any follow-up program, as well as the capacity for short and long-term regeneration of renewable resources.[55]

A public registry is to be established for panel reports, supporting documents, and other information relative to the assessment, other than restricted information protected by the *Access to Information Act*.[56]

The Act also provides for the establishment of joint review panels in circumstances where jurisdiction with respect to a project is jointly shared with a province, foreign government or international organization of states.[57]

The extent to which the proposed legislation represents an improvement over the existing federal process has been the subject of considerable debate during past months. The following section will canvass some of the strengths and weaknesses identified to date with respect to the proposed legislation.

STRENGTHS AND WEAKNESSES OF THE NEW *C.E.A.A.*

The proposed *C.E.A.A.* is disappointing in several respects primarily because it fails to address many of the more insidious deficiencies inherent in the existing environmental assessment process.

As presently drafted, the Act does not remove conflict of interest concerns, both real and perceived, associated with the underlying principle of self-assessment. The ultimate decision making power continues to rest with the responsible authority, which is often the proponent of the project itself. The credibility of the government's efforts to improve the existing environmental assessment process would be enhanced if the ultimate decision making power with respect to the environmental assessment of projects were given to an independent tribunal or, failing this, to the Minister of the Environment.[58] The intense debate in Cabinet leading up to the introduction of the new *C.E.A.A.* in the House of Commons indicates that other Ministers were reluctant to allow the Minister of the Environment or an independent tribunal to place environmental constraints upon projects or policy initiatives considered to be within their own specific areas of jurisdiction. This "turf battle" has once again left the federal process open to serious and justifiable criticism.[59]

The same protectionist sentiment is all the more evident in concerns voiced by many provincial officials, who worry about federal encroachment upon specific areas of provincial jurisdiction, such as the ownership and control of provincial natural resources.[60] The Act has attempted to overcome some of these objections by including provisions for joint review panels in areas where jurisdiction overlaps with that of provinces or foreign states. Nevertheless, the federal Minister of the Environment retains the power to appoint the chairperson, or a cochairperson, and one or more members of the panel. The federal Minister also retains the power to require that the public be given an opportunity to participate in the assessment by the panel, and may fix or approve its terms of reference.

Although the Act provides for mediation in prescribed circumstances, it does not appear to contemplate mediation in the event of a disagreement between a province and the federal government. Further, the Act does not oblige the responsible federal authority to accept the findings or recommendations set out in the report of a joint review panel. Section 38 of the Act stipulates only that upon completion of the assessment, the report of the panel must be submitted to the Minister and be published. The responsible federal authority appears to retain the decision making power with respect to the project, even in cases where it has been subject to a joint panel review.

These elements of federal control over matters in which provinces have a clear interest, such as natural resources, will undoubtedly contribute to a further polarization of the constitutional debate now raging across the country. This danger is evident in the continuing controversy over *Rafferty Alameda*, as the province of Saskatchewan continues to assert its right to make its own decisions free of federal encroachment through the environmental assessment process. The thrust of the recent decisions of the Federal Court will do little to quell the mistrust on the part of the provinces with respect to what some perceive as an unwarranted incursion into provincial affairs.[61]

In addition, many of the most important aspects of the process have not yet been spelled out in the Act, but remain to be addressed in future regulations. Essential elements such as which projects or classes of projects will be included on the mandatory study or exclusionary lists; the setting of procedures and relevant time periods relating to the environmental assessment process; and provisions concerning the conduct of assessments by review panels, all remain to be prescribed by regulations.[62] Although provision for public participation is contained in the proposed legislation, no participant funding program has been included, and might well succumb to political and/or budgetary pressures.[63] In addition, while subpoena powers have been given to review panels to compel witnesses to attend and give evidence, no mention is made of the right to counsel or the right to cross-examine witnesses.[64] The extent to which the public is entitled to participate in the process in any meaningful way is thus left ambiguous.[65]

Of particular concern is the apparently more restrictive scope of the *C.E.A.A.* Its application is limited to "projects" which, in turn, are defined in terms of physical works or physical activities.[66] In contrast, under the existing Guidelines Order the E.A.R.P. applies to a "proposal," which is defined to include "any initiative, undertaking or activity for which the Government of Canada has a decision making responsibility."[67] It is therefore doubtful that the legislation in its present form would support the assessment of government policy initiatives, if those initiatives did not include in their implementation phase a physical work or physical activity. Many potentially important government policies impacting upon millions of Canadians will not be subject to assessment under the proposed Act.

The exclusion of policy review from the provisions of the *C.E.A.A.* is more difficult to understand in light of the announcement by the

Minister of the Environment of March 19, 1991 that the Environment Committee of the House of Commons will review all major government policies.[68] By confining policy review to the political arena, the government has once again stepped back from allowing the affected public to examine the environmental effects of government policy in a non-partisan arena, as would more likely be the case if review took place under a legislative scheme.

On the positive side, the proposed legislation contains provisions for the design and implementation of follow-up monitoring programs not available under the Guidelines.[69] The new legislation also provides for mediation as an option to panel reviews in cases where the potential for reaching consensus appears promising;[70] and specifically provides for the assessment of transborder environmental effects.[71]

CONCLUSION

Overall, the environmental assessment process envisaged by the new *C.E.A.A.* remains susceptible to political pressure and interference. The federal government has squandered a prime opportunity to remedy a number of the systemic deficiencies present in the existing E.A.R.P. process.

The situation of *Rafferty Alameda* illustrates the danger of not specifically providing in the legislation that construction must stop while assessment is ongoing, if the process of environ-

mental review is to be credible and achieve its purpose. Madam Justice Reed of the Federal Court (Trial Division) in the case of *Naskapi-Montagnais Innu Association* v. *Minister of National Defence*[72] found that there was no mandatory obligation in the Guidelines that a project be halted until a panel review was completed and its report submitted.

Under the existing Guidelines initiating departments and Ministers are able to ignore whatever recommendations a Panel might make. They, of course, do so at their peril insofar as public opinion is concerned. Under the scheme of the Guidelines it is the watchful eye of public opinion which is to operate as the leverage to ensure that environmentally responsible decisions are taken.[73]

As the *Rafferty Alameda* and *Oldman River* decisions amply illustrate, the task of ensuring that the government follows its own Guidelines fell to the courts when it continued to ignore the watchful eye of public opinion.

Instead of capitalizing upon the opportunity to implement a federal environmental assessment process capable of meeting the expectations of an increasingly sceptical public, the government has provided draft legislation that will neither silence its critics, nor avoid the protracted litigation of the recent past.

Indeed, for many, the watchful eye of public opinion may not be sufficient to ensure environmentally sound and responsible decision making by the federal government.

(c) "The Nasty Game": The failure of environmental assessment in Canada[†]

Andrew Nikiforuk ———————————————————————

What's an EA?

Environmental assessment is a big term for a simple idea. A proper impact audit makes sure that all the big effects of a project, program or

policy, are well known to the public at the early stages of planning. Given a jumble of conflicting numbers and eloquent words, an EA asks a fairly unique question: "And then what?" After

† An independent public report commissioned by the Walter & Duncan Gordon Foundation, Toronto, Ontario, in September 1996. Released January 1997. Excerpts from pp. 2–22, 24–25. Figure omitted.

weighing the impacts and costs to creatures, plants and human communities, an EA gives a public agency or public representatives all the evidence they need to make an informed decision: a go or no-go....

As a democratic planning tool, an effective EA presents citizens with economic alternatives to the project. It also estimates costs and benefits. By its nature, an EA is both an evolving science and a predictive art. It, too, is a profoundly conservative practice that should serve as a filter against folly. Many businesses call it a "look before you leap" policy....

To identify, predict and assess the consequences of industrial activity on the land, an EA must respect three basic principles.

It must be done before the project has been approved or designed.

It must be focus on significant effects or the big issues.

It must do so as even-handedly as possible.

. . . .

Both environmentalists and the business community now agree that Canada's assessment process routinely violates all three principles. Dams have been built while under review and no-go recommendations such as the gigantic bridge to Prince Edward Island have been overturned by politicians intent on buying regional votes.[6] Big issues such as cumulative effects are either not understood or blatantly ignored.

Although the principles of EA are simple, its evolving practice is complicated and value-laden. Predicting the impacts of a particular pulp mill on the boreal forest might look like a basic engineering exercise but it's never that straightforward. The infant science of understanding ecosystems invariably comes with incomplete and inadequate information and many unknowns. As a result EA more closely resembles the dilemmas of good parenting or weather forecasting: once the known facts are established (the science), the final conclusions are based on wisdom, experience and a moral code that respects, for want for a better word, Province or Creation.

. . . .

Effective EA, for example, would recognize that certain regions of the country, such as the Fraser River basin, are now overloaded by industrial activity, and can house no more development without irreparable harm. Good EA, then,

can only be effective by imposing limits and discipline on an economy. Fred Roots of Environment Canada recently wrote that a well-tailored EA program forces a nation to ask an important question: "How much do we really want to change our practices and institutions today in order to reduce costs and environmental degradation tomorrow?"[7]

. . . .

Canada's very first EA, the Mackenzie Valley Pipeline, still stands as a singular model of excellence. Established by the Privy Council in 1974, it focused on the social, economic and environmental effects of the Arctic Gas Pipeline or what the company boasted would be "the greatest construction project, in terms of capital expenditure, that private enterprise has ever taken anywhere."[8]

Headed by Justice Thomas Berger, the public inquiry reviewed what scientists, economists and native elders had to say about bringing more than $8 billion worth of progress to the Arctic, namely 1,100 miles of pipeline, 6,000 construction workers and 600 water crossings. Berger looked at alternatives such as diversifying the native economy and all the potential effects, good and bad, for caribou as well as the Inuit, the Dene and the Métis. After three years and $5 million, Berger found the environmental losses irreparable, the social impact devastating and the economic benefits limited. He prohibited development in northern Yukon and recommended a 10-year postponement of industrial activity in the Mackenzie Valley until land claims had been settled. It was Canada's first "no-go" and it was written in plain English.

Industry, of course, never built a pipeline and thereby saved tens of billions of dollars. As Berger recommended, national parks and ecological reserves have since been established; a few land claims have even been settled. Berger achieved these national savings by respecting the basics of EA: he looked at all the big issues early and in a balanced manner. The Canadian government, which owns or manages 41 per cent of the nation's land mass, has yet to establish a coherent process that duplicates the spirit or integrity of Berger's public review.

HISTORICAL TERMS OF REFERENCE

In 1973, just before Berger began his great pipeline narrative, the Canadian government established its first "environmental assessment and review process." ...

. . . .

... William Rees, an ecologist at the University of British Columbia, performed the first and only complete audit on federal environmental assessments in 1987.[10] ... Rees found that of 18 government departments only one, Transport Canada, had a screening process and kept reliable records. Then, as now, the government wasn't really committed to the principle of EA at all. "Ottawa likes to look at politics, technology and feasibility," says Robert Gibson, an environmental professor at the University of Waterloo. "They still don't want an environmental agency to have more power or to upset the way they decide things."

As a result, little got reviewed. And politics solely determined what projects made it to a public panel. Due to the popularity of the Berger inquiry and the influence the Canadian Arctic Resource Committee (a public interest group representing northern concerns) most of the projects that got "EARPed" [Federal Environmental Assessment and Review Process] were largely northern or rural. These included an exploratory drilling well in Lancaster Sound, oil and gas developments in the Beaufort Sea and uranium mines in northern Saskatchewan. Meanwhile significant developments such as funding for the Westray Mine, the reduction of the Atlantic cod fleet and the construction of the Mirabel Airport, a fiscal disaster of white elephant proportions, conveniently escaped scrutiny.

In the beginning public review panels often consisted of government employees as opposed to citizens with particular expertise. At the hearings on oil projects for South Davis Strait, the oil companies had much higher standards of environmental safety than the bureaucrats. During the Lancaster Sound review, citizens had to threaten legal action in order to open hearings for public questioning. And cabinet ministers continued to undermine the whole process by bluntly informing panels that a "no-go" decision was unacceptable. During the lengthy and controversial hearings studying low-level military flights over Labrador and eastern Quebec, the Minister of the Environment even lectured the panel that they couldn't rule against more flying[11] and so on. For these and other reasons, the Innu still call the process "a nasty game."

In spite of these failings, the panel reviews established some milestones in EA. They secured the right and reinforced the significance of public participation. (At the Alberta Pacific Environmental Impact Assessment review in 1989, public comment on a giant pulp mill led to scientific studies on gender-bending chemicals, now one of the hottest fields in environmental science.[12]) Panels such as the Westcoast Offshore Hydrocarbon Exploration Review in 1986 proved the need "for government reviews of broad industrial activities within large geographic regions." And some panels actually stopped a lot of bad energy projects. (To this day many oil executives exclaim that, "If the government didn't force us to do EAs, we would have to invent to ourselves."[13])

For a while "no-go" was part of the EA vocabulary. The Lancaster Sound panel recommended a "no-go" because it didn't think the government should spend or exploit natural capital for which no inventory existed. Uranium mines and plants got no-gos. And many other projects were delays or postponed because of unacceptable risks or poor impact statements. As a consequence nearly a half dozen developments never got built.

In 1984, the government introduced very clear guidelines for conducting public screenings and public reviews. Although Ottawa said the guidelines "shall apply" to all government projects and programs, political discretion ruled the day. Most departments still considered EARP a nuisance or "an ineffectual paperwork ritual." The majority of government screenings simply flashed a green light and public reviews took place with the frequency of solar eclipses.

The public, however, took the guidelines more seriously than Ottawa did and launched approximately 70 court cases towards the end of the 1980s.[14] Most of these cases simply asked the government to abide by its own "shall apply" guidelines. Even inshore cod fishermen asked for an environmental audit of licencing policies, a request that might have lessened Canada's greatest economic disaster of this century. But most of the challenges failed — with three important exceptions.

In northern Quebec, the Cree launched a series of aggressive court actions in 1991 to force federal and Quebec officials to honour the law and begin an EA of the multi-billion-dollar Great Whale Hydroelectric Project. Faced with a public audit and strong U.S. opposition, Hydro

Quebec then canceled the scheme. Numerous court decisions also forced panel reviews of two politically motivated dams with clearly bad economic and ecological impacts on the prairies: Alberta's Oldman Dam and Saskatchewan's Rafferty-Alameda Dams. In a complete mockery of EA, both reviews occurred after construction was well advanced. But theses embarrassing court decisions, which interpreted the guidelines as an enforceable order, warned Ottawa that it had a legal obligation to properly assess projects, whether it wanted to or not.

The other rulings, however, show that Canada's justice system has a much more myopic understanding of EA than the public. Although Canadians need the courts to take a tough-minded approach to conservation in public interest, [Rod] Northey's exhaustive review of CEAA reveals that public panel reviews and the courts have chosen different paths.

Panels have tended to occupy the high ground by emphasizing the need for EAs of policies, programs and megaprojects. The courts, however, have applied EA only to physical developments. While panels have called for early assessment, the courts have favoured getting reviewed projects built. Although panels have sought regional studies of impacts, the courts have focused on narrow projects-by-project definitions. Last, but not least, the panels have repeatedly described the need for independent and objective decisions. The courts, however, have championed self-assessment and politics as usual. The current law reflects the narrowness of these judicial interpretations.[15]

The court decisions effectively weakened an ad hoc program. "Ever since the courts got involved, the big picture need for EA has been obscured," says Northey. "We've had narrower application, less objectivity and little long-term planning."

By the 1990s, both industry and the environmental movement realized that EA had become a political fiasco. The provinces, which considered the process "a Trojan horse" of federal intervention, flaunted the and pursued their own resource extraction projects anyway. And when Ottawa didn't like what the panels recommended, the federal government simply set up alternative panels that quickly rubber-stamped federally funded make-work projects such as the fixed link with Prince Edward Island. With political discretion defining the game, the integrity of the process evaporated. When the Innu of Lab-

rador and Quebec, the people most affected by low-level buzzing of military aircraft, boycotted the public hearings studying impacts of the flights, federal EAs lost even more credibility. To this day, many prominent scientists and citizens refuse to participate in public panel reviews. In the last six years most panels have ended with litigation, controversy or dissatisfied parties all around.

Six years ago Environment Minister Robert de Cotret finally promised "an assessment process which was more powerful in its impact on decision making than any other environmental assessment legislation in the world."[16] Few citizens or business leaders held their breath.

THE LAW

The Canadian Environment Assessment Act fills more than 50 pages and came into force in 1995 after five years of dithering and debate. The government calls it "a tool for decision makers," and claims that the act sets up an open and balanced process to gauge environmental effects. Yet lawyers, business leaders and citizens unanimously agree that it is one of the most complicated pieces of legislation they have ever read.

Ecologist William Rees of the University of British Columbia correctly notes that "the law is a book and impenetrable unless you are a lawyer." Adds Northey, a lawyer: "If anyone can read CEAA in one sitting, then they should have their head examined. ... Clearly, it wasn't written for anyone who wants to do an environmental assessment." Ian Scott of the Canadian Association of Petroleum Producers observes: "If you want public input then why does the government make it so complicated that the public can't get into it?"[17]

To assist government employees in deciphering the law, a training manual comes in a thick binder. It includes six different sections including a copy of the law, regulations, a user's guide and a citizen's guide — a total of 491 pages. The old EARP review guidelines consisted of six pages and no training manual.

The preamble of the act commits Canada to using EA as a tool to conserve and enhance environmental quality and to ensure "that economic development is compatible with the high value Canadians place on environmental quality."

Contrast these ambiguous words with the mission statement of the Nunavut Impact Review Board: "to use traditional Inuit knowledge and recognized scientific methods in an ecosystem analysis to assess and monitor on a site-specific and regional basis the environmental, cultural and socio-economic impacts of proposals. ... and to determine whether proposals should proceed to develop, and if so, under what conditions." In other words the tundra, rivers and coast of the Nunavut Settlement Area come first.

CEAA defines its purposes as threefold: to guarantee that environmental effects are duly considered by federal departments or "responsible authorities;" that significant adverse effect don't affect communities outside of the project area; and that the public has a say. Period. According to the act, just about any agency or government can be a responsible authority except a province. There is no clear mention of ever making a go or no-go decision. Worse still is the exclusion list. Crown corporations and harbour commissions, for example, don't have to follow the rules. To find out who or what is included and excluded, one has to wade through four regulations.

The act is narrow in scope. It confines assessments to projects or "physical activities." The old EARP guidelines applied to all kinds of undertakings and even permitted regional planning and reviews of big industrial developments. CEAA doesn't really allow for such flexibility. Policies and programs whose impacts could be more ruinous than any one project are excluded from the act.

An EA only happens when the government does not of [these] things: when it proposes a project, funds a project or allows one to take place on federal land. A number of federal laws such as the Fisheries Act or Navigable Waters Act can also trigger an assessment.

An assessment ... always begins with a screening or simple evaluation of significance. The screening may, in turn, lead to comprehensive review (most mining projects fall into this category), a public panel review or mediation.

. . . .

The new act ... refers to projects "not likely to cause significant effects," "likely to cause significant adverse environmental effects that cannot be justified in the circumstances," "uncertainty about likely effects" and public concern about a project. ...

While the old EARP guidelines clearly considered the "general socio-economic effects of the proposal," the new act doesn't. The only time the act mentions social or economic effects is when "any change that the project may cause in the environment" affects people. "CEAA doesn't look at the full socio-economic picture. How is that compatible with sustainable development?" asks Northey. Although the law includes a provision for looking at "cumulative effects" in public reviews, the term is never defined.

When it comes to final decisions, ministerial discretion is king. The act is full of "mays" instead of "shalls." Public reviews may recommend a "no" but the cabinet can always say "say." Like the old EARP guidelines, panel decisions are not binding.

The principle of self-assessment, which defined EARP, also dominates the spirit of CEAA. This means that the government agencies proposing projects are responsible for assessing the impacts as well as the quality of any follow-up program. As a consequence the law allows the self-interest of government bureaucracies to constantly supersede the public interest. Moreover, the act imposes no penalties for those who fail to uphold the law or uphold it badly.

. . . .

BHP: THE LAW IN ACTION

No event better illustrates the crisis of EA than the great diamond rush in the central Arctic. Ever since geologist Charles Fipke found the precious gem in kimberlite pipes under Arctic lakes in 1990, a small army of companies has staked claims throughout the Great Slave Geological Province in the Northwest Territories, an area larger than Italy.

The region's first diamond mine is grand in scale and impact. Owned largely by BHP, one of the world's biggest mining firms, the mine's mega-economics promise to transform the NWT into a "diamond republic" just as surely as Inco's $5-billion mine in Voisey's Bay will turn Labrador into a "nickel republic."

Provided the diamond cartel remains stable (a subject never addressed during the review), the mine could increase Canada's GDP by $6.2 billion over its predicted 25-year life span. With revenues of half a billion a year, the mine will also become the largest purchaser of goods and services in the North, as well as its largest industrial employer, with an annual payroll of $32 million.

Pulling diamonds out of the Arctic doesn't involve chemicals but it does take a lot of earth moving. The company estimates that the mine will create 40 million tonnes of "waste rock" a year. Because the diamond-bearing kimberlite pipes are located underwater, BHP proposes to "dewater" 15 lakes or fill them with tailings. Another 43 streams will lose their lives. Moreover, the $750-million development sits smack in the middle of one of the world's last great wildernesses, Canada's barren grounds. What was once a home only to the Bathurst caribou herd, grizzly bears and wolves has now become the industrial economy's self-professed "corridor of hope."

After viewing videos in 1995 supplied by BHP, the Department of Indian Affairs and Northern Development (DIAND) finally became a diamond believer. It belatedly recommended an impact study and public review under the old EARP guidelines but "in the spirit of CEAA." The government first approached David Schindler of the University of Alberta, one of the world's top aquatic scientists, to serve on the panel. "Their terms of reference focused on one little spot and everyone knows there is going to be more than one mine," says Schindler. "I told them unless you do a regional assessment, I won't consider it." The government never phoned Schindler back.

DIAND, the so-called responsible authority, eventually appointed a four-person panel. Not one member had any expertise in ecological science. Nor did the panel hire any technical experts during the 18-month-long hearings to help wade through BHP's eight-volume, 37-kilogram impact statement. While the company paid $14 million for this environmental analysis, the government provided only $250,000 for the public to challenge or review it. BHP submitted its impact report just four months after Ottawa decided what significant things should be examined.

Throughout the hearings the government acted as much as a proponent of the development as BHP. From the beginning, DIAND declared that the mine was good and that its environmental effects could easily be managed. This had a dramatic impact on the hearings. "In doing so they ruled out any dissenting voices from government," notes Robbie Keith, the former chair of the Canadian Arctic Resources Committee (CARC). "What government scientist is going to stand up and say, 'I have some reser-

vations,' when Ottawa takes a side like that?" Most international courts of law would have recognized the behaviour of the Canadian government as "conflict of interest."

As a consequence federal scientists and bureaucrats set new lows for public accountability at the hearings. Human Resources, the people responsible for job training, never appeared. Heritage Canada and Environment Canada never spoke about wilderness protection. And so on. ...

In the end the review panel gave the mine "a go." It concluded that "environmental effects of the project are largely predictable and mitigable." It did so even though the panel and the government admitted that the Great Slave Geological Province, like Lancaster Sound in 1979, remained an ecological mystery.[20] Nobody really asked how scientists could safely predict significant effects in a region with little baseline ecological data. The cumulative effects of other developments, including an existing gold mine, a proposed second diamond mine, an infant road network, and the dramatic borings and earth moving of further diamond exploration were ignored. ...

A recent CARC newsletter aptly summed up what many environmentalists thought of the EA game: "We conclude that the environmental assessment of the BHP diamond mine was fundamentally flawed; the process was neither rigorous, comprehensive, nor fair. This, we believe, is why the recommendations of the four-person panel are weak and insipid. Once more, environmental assessment itself is at issue."[21]

From BHP's perspective the process was equally bizarre and unjust. When the company learned a public review was imminent, it approached the federal assessment office in Vancouver and asked for a model panel report. It got none. "We wanted to know what was going to be involved and didn't get any answers," says Karen Azinger, BHP's manager of external affairs. "Maybe we asked the wrong questions." Yet other private-sector proponents have been similarly frustrated for 25 years.

Company research revealed that more than 50 projects had been EARPed and that reviews had taken anywhere from eight months to 10 years. It also discovered that the only mining projects ever to be reviewed were a group of five Saskatchewan uranium properties. "It's still not clear to me what projects have to go through a review and why we had to go through what we did," says Azinger.

When the government set its terms of reference, it delivered a big surprise to BHP: "full and equal consideration of traditional knowledge." "We asked DIAND what this meant and the government was pretty unhelpful," says Azinger. "Not a single federal department had any regulations or guidelines for traditional knowledge. Not a single department has yet incorporated it." Even CEAA doesn't have a pamphlet on what it means. Yet BHP was asked to do what the government is not doing. Both the panel and BHP later admitted that traditional knowledge, a people's memory of the land, was not truly considered.

. . . .

But the most damning event came at the end of the process, when the panel tabled its report. DIAND Minister Ron Irwin accepted "the go" but then imposed more conditions on the company. He gave BHP just 60 days to conclude Impact Benefit Agreements (IBA) with aboriginal communities as well as to negotiate a final environmental agreement for an independent monitoring agency. "We jumped 10 feet, then they raised the bar and piled this stuff on us," says Azinger. "The minister had no legal right to comment on these things. It was precedent setting." These important issues, which a reasonable EA process should have addressed and spelled out, once again reflected the weaknesses of Canada's irrational system.

. . . .

BHP: RATIONAL ALTERNATIVES

A responsible government would not have put so many carts before so many horses. For starters, it would have begun a study of the land and its wildlife in the diamond zone as early as 1992 during the rush. This would have provided the science and traditional histories needed to shape an effective assessment. This work, which Ottawa still considers a separate issue, has not yet begun.

Good government would have settled the land claims before embarking on a panel review or set up a regional planning board in the interim. An honest and focused bureaucracy then would have provided BHP with clear criteria and standards to ensure the company spent money on science that mattered as opposed to science

that covers all the political bases. It would have recognized the need for a regional or generic industrial activity review as opposed to a single project review. Last but not least, as a proponent of the project, DIAND would have ensured the independence and objectivity of the review by turning it over to another agency.

(A prudent government would also have recognized that Impact Benefit Agreements, private deals between companies and communities that often involve monetary compensation for the loss of clean air or hunting grounds, have the potential to undermine the entire EA process. "Here we have these private agreements" notes Robbie Keith, "but EA is a public process designed to protect the public interest. Somehow or other we've got to sort this thing out.")

Given the government's negligence and sloppiness, it's not surprising that the EA ended up being used for things it was never intended for: a debate about land claims, as opposed to a debate about the effects of diamond mines in the North. And nobody knows whether the second diamond mine will be submitted to the same tortuous, costly and frameless exercise. As one government official noted: "In the end a lot of cheques were cut and everyone got a deal. But it's not clear an environmental assessment was ever done."

To appreciate the poor standards set by the BHP review, just consider the terms of reference recently set for a $5-billion nickel mine in Labrador. The proponent, the Voisey's Bay Nickel Company (VBNC), a subsidiary of Inco Limited, might well ask why the government demands that it pass an altogether different environmental test by establishing "need," "purpose," "alternatives to the undertaking" and "effects on biodiversity" when BHP was never asked such questions.[22] And BHP might well inquire why Inco is not being asked to incorporate "full and fair consideration of traditional knowledge." Inconsistency, it seems, is the only consistent hallmark of federal assessments.

SIGNIFICANT ISSUES

Alternatives
Unlike Canadian law, the U.S. National Environmental Policy Act recognizes that EA should encourage full and open discussion of economic alternatives, "which would avoid or minimize

adverse impacts or enhance the quality of the human environment."[23]

... "The heart of any impact statement is a thorough discussion of alternatives so that objective decision makers can pick the most environmentally acceptable development," says William Tilleman, a lawyer and chairman of Alberta's Environmental Review Board. "But this issue is unanimously ignored at the federal level in Canada."

When public outcry forced Ottawa to assess northern pulp mills in Alberta, the forests were excluded from any impact statement. This meant citizens could not ask if tourism and smaller wood projects would achieve more employment and revenue with less cost. And it's unlikely that the current review of an open-pit coal mine in the Rockies by Cardinal River Coals will ask if the region's natural capital could better be spent on the creation of another national or provincial park. ...

Several years ago, a New Brunswick Crown corporation proposed a $45-million coastal highway along the Bay of Fundy.[24] The object was to make a wild and beautiful place just another roadside attraction. A comprehensive impact statement looked at all kinds of things except an alternative development. The agency argued that the government had set aside money for a highway and that was that.

The public didn't agree. When the EA came to public review, several groups pointed out that "rubber-tire tourism" was not only dying but made poor use of the region's natural capital. A coalition of citizens, including New Brunswick's Economic Development and Tourism Department, argued for more jobs and less damage — a $10-million eco-tourism project with only a small highway upgrade. In this case a half-million-dollar EA led to a scaled-down project that saved 35 million tax dollars and actually protected the coast. Unfortunately this is the exception, not the rule, in EA.

Non-compliance

The recent sale of CANDU reactors to China, one of the world's least democratic and least environmentally sensitive nations, illustrates the degree to which the Canadian government selectively applies the law. According to CEAA, whenever the government provides "financial assistance to the proponent" whether in or "outside of Canada," an assessment for adverse

effects must be done. The multi-billion-dollar loan to China to buy old nuclear technology long subsidized by Canadian taxpayers clearly falls in this category. But the government has exempted this bad sale from public scrutiny.

Ottawa argues that the true lender is the Export Development Corporation, a Crown agency. The government says no EA is required because the law doesn't apply to Crown corporation with no EA commitments. This cynical interpretation of the law and cynical use of taxpayers' money means that as long as any federal department gets friendly Crown corporations to do its bidding, the project will go unexamined.

. . . .

Canada's reluctance to enforce the law is also the subject of a complaint before NAFTA's Commission for Environmental Cooperation. Under NAFTA, the citizens of Mexico, Canada or the United States can file cases of bad environmental work. Both the governments of Mexico and Canada have charges pending against them.

In Canada's case, the complaint concerns pure and simple law breaking. Consider, for example, Sunpine Forest Product's attempt to build a 41-kilometre-long road with 22 river or stream crossings in the eastern slopes of the Rocky Mountains.[26] Because this project will affect prime trout habitat, an EA should have been triggered under the Fisheries Act. The Department of Fisheries and Oceans (DFO) initially refused to uphold the law and refused to screen the project. When finally pressured to do so, it failed to identify the correct species of fish (cutthroat trout) or even to acknowledge provincial assessments which found the project unnecessary. Existing roads, said provincial authorities, would serve the company's needs just fine.

But Sunpine is just part of much larger problem of non-compliance....

. . . .

Since the beginning of CEAA, the government claims to have screened more than 6,000 projects, performed 10 comprehensive studies and started four panel reviews: Sunshine Ski Development (Alberta), Express Pipeline (Alberta), Voisey's Bay Project (Labrador) and Cheviot Coal Mine Project (Alberta). These numbers indicate that either the government has become an environmental saint or that it's just as reluctant to launch an assessment in the 1990s as it was in the 1980s. The Mining Association of Canada and most environmentalists suspect the latter.[27] So, too, does William Ross, an environmental profess at the University of Calgary who has served on five different public review panels: "The expectation was that a great number of public reviews would be done under CEAA, when in fact we have headed in the other decision. Why is that? Are we building fewer projects? I don't think so." Ross suspects that decisions are simply being made in the interests of developers and government agencies to avoid reviews and thereby cut costs.[28]

Focus

Without clear criteria, fair standards or a powerful focus, EA has degenerated into a paper game. Cardinal River Coals, a firm proposing a $250-million open-pit coal mine outside of Jasper National Park, has already amassed 12 volumes of data for its impact statement for a panel review scheduled for next year. BHP produced a "small coffin" of documents that came in eight volumes. "I am not sure who it is serving," says Charlie Ferguson, Inco's vice-president of environmental affairs. Adds CEAA expert Rodney Northey: "Without a focus you get a mass of data with no highs or lows. You just have one big, thick grey mass."

Because each of these companies had to prepare impact studies for different "responsible authorities," there is no continuity. And in the absence of clarity and focus, proponents try to make up the difference with snowdrifts of paper that contain more data than assessment. "In our case," says Ferguson, "we'll be supplying one of these big, fat, intimidating documents to an agency (DFO) that would rather we didn't and they should admit that." By making every government department responsible for doing EAs, Ottawa has effectively enshrined a lot of irresponsibility — something industry knows all too well.

Forests of paper also hide bad science. In BHP's impact opus, one study claimed to identify all the aquatic organisms to genus when in fact it only named them to a family or order. "In another ecosystem their level of taxonomic distinction would have failed to show the difference between humans and chimpanzees," explains David Schindler of the University of Alberta.[29]

"It's a totally inadequate job and makes it difficult to go back and assess losses in biodiversity."

．　．　．　．

This proliferation of bad science is also aggravated by the fact that proponents are free to hire their own EA consultants to do an impact statement....

One study on the Beaufort Sea oil and gas development[31] found proponents consistently underplayed bad effects while inflating project benefits. Proponents took an original consultant's work and reworked it to sound even more benign, with the consequence that 86 per cent of the changes favoured a "go." In the impact statements prepared by Cardinal River Coals, consultants refer to the mine's "significant" potential to wipe out grizzly bears in the area. Yet the company's summary refers to these matters as insignificant. Most consultants will alienate the environment before they alienate their clients with damning conclusions that could foreclose on future business opportunities. The current system pretends such serious and untenable conflicts of interest do not exist.

Jurisdiction

In Canada the federal government and each of the provinces now have their own EA policies, some strong and some weak. But given the nation's constitutional battles and the Quebec crisis, the focus is never on best practice but who should do (or avoid) an EA and when. Alberta and Quebec, provinces that behave like quasi-national states, have been the most adamant about being above federal law. To complicate matters, the northern land claim settlements, Nunavut and Inuvialuit, actually have much more comprehensive policies than Ottawa and want nothing to do with CEAA.[32]

But that's just the beginning of the EA maze. When various agencies and boards such as the National Energy Board or Alberta's Energy and Utilities Board are added to the picture, Canada actually has as many as 200 "major EA regimes."[33] Notes William Ross of the University of Calgary: "I have yet to see any research that explains why Canada needs all these different EAs.... It just leads to confusion on behalf of all participants."

It also leads to overlap, duplication and the latest development, a myriad of joint federal/

provincial hearings. As a result there is a great deal of talk about "harmonization," which often means letting everyone do what they want, doing EA twice or doing it once with two discretionary sets of rules. Mining companies report as many as 60 bureaucrats showing up at one "harmonized" review in British Columbia led by a young fisheries biologist who knew nothing about mining or EA. Other companies report finishing one provincial process only to find they had just triggered a federal review with additional costs and no apparent benefits to the public.[34]

. . . .

... Ottawa ... didn't want to stop Alberta from building a $500-million dam on the Oldman River or prevent Grant Devine's Tories from erecting two dams on the Souris River. Aboriginal concerns, the fisheries and international treaties spoke of clear federal responsibilities. But it look extensive court action to force Ottawa to accept its responsibilities and only then half-heartedly.

Such willingness to blithely ignore or contract out federal obligations has created big problems of "political legitimacy and legal validity" as well as many shoddy EAs. It has also undermined the public interest.

As Robert Page, dean of environmental design at the University of Calgary explains, federal/provincial wrangling about EA is really an adolescent dispute in a house with no adults. "The provinces are arguing vigorously for control of EA because they own the natural resources and believe the environment should be an aspect of resource planning. The feds no longer have the money or the will to enforce national standards in the environment. The provinces want the jurisdiction in order to exploit resources as opposed to enforcing standards. For them it's really a matter of excluding the feds from properly enforcing environmental regulations." The vague agreements pouring out of meetings attended by provincial environment ministers merely underscore this point, as do the highly inconsistent terms for joint federal/provincial reviews. The provinces almost invariably use discretion as liberally as Ottawa in order to get forestry plans and other developments exempted.

. . . .

Uncertainty

To corporations, a federal assessment still represents a swamp of legal and fiscal uncertainties. In the absence of clear standards, companies don't know what or even how much assessment to do. They often can't figure out when the law will be triggered or what the requirements will be or who the responsible authority is.

This lack of clarity, in turn, results in big expenses as companies scramble to cover all conceivable bases. It also explains why BHP spent $14 million on its impact statement and why Inco has already spent $20 million on its EA for Voisey's Bay. Most of these sums were spent before any responsible authority identified what might be significant. "After 10 or 15 years of doing assessments on mines or dams the costs should come down," argues Husain Sadar at Ottawa's Impact Assessment Centre. "But that hasn't happened." Scientists have amassed an incredible volume of research on the downstream effects of dams in the last 30 years, yet none of this science has ever been used to fashion a comprehensive template for any proposed dam in Canada. Instead, the government prefers to reinvent the wheel with every project, inflate costs and exercise its political discretion.[39] The alarming and increasing expenditures beg another simple question: What government could say no to a proponent after asking so much and providing so little to the process?

Monitoring

EA is a unique exercise about making predictions. And forecasting can be a dangerous task if no one tries to find out how accurate the forecasts were, what really happened and if any mitigation worked. "If you spend $10 million on an EA, isn't it worth following up?" asks Husain Sadar, director of Ottawa's Impact Assessment Centre. "Yet Canada has continually failed to do that."

Whenever projects have been monitored, surprising and unforeseen effects have often appeared. For example, an EA of a mine developed by Charlie Ferguson at Inco Limited predicted an acid problem with mine tailings. "We were wrong," says Ferguson. "The waste rock created an alkaline problem. We just sampled the wrong thing."

The South Indian Lake reservoir in northern Manitoba (all part of the Churchill River diversion scheme) missed many significant effects and killed a local, self-sufficient economy. By raising water levels and increasing the muddiness of the water, the project changed the colour of whitefish, an important commercial fishery for aboriginals. Whitefish that aren't white don't sell well. As annual incomes of $35,000a year [plummeted] among fishermen, alcohol abuse rose. So, too, did other social problems. Yet no one had predicted this horrible chain of effects.[41] Most of Manitoba's hydroelectric projects have not been monitored.

This lack of accountability is well known both to business leaders and scientists. Without any follow-up, bad science is not exposed, ineffective mitigation methods are not abandoned, politicians or technicians are not held accountable for their bad work and the land continues to be ruined by unforeseen effects. "There is just no learning curve in our system," says David Schindler of the University of Alberta.

. . . .

CONCLUSION: THE CUMULATIVE EFFECTS OF BAD WORK

Nearly 800 years ago, the inhabitants of Easter Island drove their economy to ruin by destroying the island's forests, soils, fisheries and sources of fresh water. As a consequence, a population of 10,000 people collapsed and free market cannibalism prevailed. By the time Europeans arrived on the scene, no one remembered how the famous stone monuments had been erected.

Had Easter Island employed Canada's EA program, only individual projects of tree cutting or dolphin netting would have been reviewed. No big studies of forestry programs or policies would have occurred and significant issues would have been kept hidden. The motto of "more jobs, less damage" wouldn't have been heard on the island.

The chief and his retinue of "responsible authorities" would have exercised discretion as opposed to doing the right thing. They would have set inconsistent and narrow terms of reference for reviews. They would have replaced any Polynesian panel recommending a "no-go" with a more agreeable group. Proponents of big tree-cutting schemes would have spent large amounts of labour and capital on isolated impact statements without ever knowing their effect on conservation or future developments. And so on. With "the tyranny of small decisions" prevailing, Easter Island would have spent all its natural capital before recognizing there was nothing left in the island's natural resource base except human flesh. Yet at international conferences it could have boasted, "We're OK. We do EAs."

Just about everyone involved in federal EA knows it is largely a political opera. It provides little or no guidance for business yet demands they participate in an inconsistent and unpredictable process with no standards and no cost controls. And it creates the illusion of environmental responsibility, when in fact no one is defending the public interest or the environment. When all government departments are responsible authorities, it seems all are equally irresponsible. "Ottawa just doesn't want to do things that subvert the old ways of how they like to work," concludes Robert Gibson of the University of Waterloo.

Both business and citizens' groups generally agree that the law has to be set up to allow a fair process that leads to an explicit "go" or "no-go" decision. "Until that happens," argues Alastair Lucas, "we are going to spend money in ways that any good auditor general would have trouble with. And the public will remain suspicious about the whole process."

Canada is further from that goal now than it was a decade ago.

(d)   Reforms to the Environmental Assessment Program[†]

Environmental Assessment Advisory Committee ————————————————

INTRODUCTION TO PART 1

History of EA

Ontario's Environmental Assessment Act (EA Act) was, when it was proclaimed in 1975, and still is, considered to be a fundamental and progressive piece of legislation needed to ensure that the environment is fully considered in decision making. The Act requires the proponent of a proposed project, plan, or program (called an undertaking) to evaluate the environmental effects of the undertaking and its alternatives in order to ensure that the proposed undertaking provides "for the protection, conservation and wise management in Ontario of the environment." Today more than ever, the public routinely expects the decisions will be made with full consideration of the environment, and that they will be consulted about actions that may affect them.

Over the past 15 years, the EA Act has been an important instrument for environmental protection — for helping to change the "business as usual" attitude toward the environment by improving the way decisions are made. But experience with environmental assessments in Ontario has also led to considerable criticism of the EA program, including both the requirements of the Environmental Assessment Act and its administration. Proponents have complained about the length of time it takes to receive approval under the Act and the lack of direction on how to comply with its requirements. Public concerns have focused on the limited application of the Act and on barriers to effective public involvement in the process.

Review of EA Act by Ministry and Referral to EAAC

Because of such concerns, the Ministry of the Environment launched a major review of Ontario's EA program in April 1988. This resulted in a Discussion Paper, "Toward Improving the Environmental Assessment Program In Ontario." In December 1990, the Minister of the Environment released the Paper for public review and in her covering letter ... highlighted the need to consider the EA program in terms of its effectiveness, fairness and efficiency. She asked the Environmental Assessment Advisory Committee (EAAC) to undertake the public consultation and provide its advice on the recommendations contained in the Paper and on several matters raised in her covering letter. The Committee was established in 1983 and is comprised of three independent persons appointed by the Minister.

Over 170 groups and individuals made submissions to the Committee. Although the Committee was to report to the Minister by the end of May, we requested more time to address these submissions carefully and to consult further about concerns raised by submitters. The Minister agreed with the Committee's proposal to report in stages, and asked us to give an initial report by mid-October. This is the first of two parts of the Committee's Report to the Minister.

THE ENVIRONMENTAL ASSESSMENT ACT

EA Approval Process

The Environmental Assessment Act, as currently interpreted, requires the proponent to follow a planning process which addresses potential environmental impacts of alternative ways of addressing a problem or opportunity, and to choose and design the preferred alternative (the proposed undertaking) on the basis of these impacts. Under the Act, the environment is defined very broadly to include the social, economic, and built, as well as natural, environments. The proponent must prepare and submit a document, called an environmental assessment (EA), which describes the purpose of and rationale for the undertaking, potential environmental

[†] Report No. 47 to the Minister of Environment, 1992, pp. 1–3, 6–13. © Queen's Printer for Ontario, 1992. Reproduced with permission.

effects of the undertaking and the alternatives, ways of mitigating adverse impacts, and an evaluation of the advantages and disadvantages of the undertaking and the alternatives. There is then a formal, government review of the EA, after which the public may comment on both the EA and the government's review, and request a hearing by the Environmental Assessment Board. Before the proponent may be given any other government approvals for the undertaking and proceed with it, the EA must be accepted and the undertaking must be approved. The Minister makes the decisions on acceptance of the EA and approval of the undertaking unless these matters are referred to the Board. The Act also sets out a number of detailed requirements for the process, including requirements for public notices.

Application

The Act requires this process for all public sector undertakings, which include "enterprises or activities or proposals, plans, or programs in respect of enterprises or activities" by the provincial government, municipalities and other public bodies such as Ontario Hydro and conservation authorities. The Minister of the Environment may, with the approval of Cabinet, exempt a public undertaking from the requirements of the Act.

In contrast to public sector undertakings, the private sector is not subject to the Act unless the Minister, with the approval of Cabinet, designates the undertaking by regulation. Except in the area of waste disposal facilities, only a few private sector undertakings have been made subject to the Act.

· · · ·

CONCERNS AND ISSUES RAISED

Submissions to EAAC

In the many [ ] thoughtful submissions received by the Committee, concerns were raised about both the legislation and how the Act is implemented and administered. Although there is support for the purpose of and need for the EA Act, submitters expressed a range of views about the Act. Some consider it to be sound legislation which is being poorly administered; others see the Act as being fundamentally flawed and in great need of review. There were a number of recurring, interrelated themes in the submissions,

which relate to the need to make the EA program more effective, fair and efficient, as discussed below.

The Lack of Government Commitment

Government Commitment

Throughout the submissions there was an overwhelming consensus that one of the major problems with the EA process has been the weakness of government commitment to effective and efficient implementation of the Act. This was evident, for example, in complaints about difficulties in getting clear and timely comments from government reviewers, about the junior status and inexperienced staff of the EA Branch, and about the continued resistance of some government agencies to the breadth and openness of decision making required under the Act. The Regional Chairmen of Ontario, for example, submitted that there is a "need for better educated, better trained and more experienced EA Reviewers." The Federation of Ontario Naturalists stated that "at the present there is a lack of any comment by the agencies who have every reason to be concerned about the effect of the undertakings on their responsibilities" and that "this lack of comment demonstrates an unwillingness to get involved in the process."

Resources and Commitment

To some extent these concerns point to a failure to allocate sufficient resources to the environmental assessment program — a failure that reflects a lack of appreciation for the economic as well as environmental costs of delays and other inefficiencies in the EA process. But submitters also stressed the apparent lack of political and bureaucratic commitment which has tolerated avoidance of assessment and review obligations, has encouraged efforts to restrict application of the Act and narrow the scope of required considerations, and has left environmental administration as a minor function of a line Ministry. Some submitters suggested that these problems could be reduced by reaffirming and clarifying EA obligations and by establishing a more senior and independent body for administering the process. But the consensus seems to be that a package of policy, structural and resource improvements are needed to demonstrate and implement a substantially increased government commitment to EA. The Canadian Environmental Law Association (CELA), for example, submitted, "If this government is serious, as we think it should be, about increasing certainty, efficiency, fairness and effectiveness in the EA Program, both the preparation and the administration of a reformed EA Program will require significant political, financial and human resource commitments to accomplish these goals."

The Length of Process

Another major theme through the submissions centred around the excessive length of the process. The extended time required for government reviews and hearings, in particular, was seen to result in inefficiency and increased expense. Firm time limits for the process were sought by most submitters.

The Need for Greater Direction and Certainty

The EA process was generally seen to be too uncertain in that many participants do not know what is expected of them. Proponents stated that they received little guidance on how to focus their studies and therefore feel that they must "study everything." They also are unclear on the role of the public and how they should respond to public concerns. They want better information, clearer advice and policy direction on what alternatives need to be considered, what kinds of environmental studies to conduct, the environmental priorities of government and the concerns of the numerous government agencies, and how to consult effectively with the public. The public needs to have a more clearly defined role which includes the right to timely information and information on how they will be consulted, especially in the early planning stages.

The Emphasis on Process Rather than Results

Many submitters also expressed the view that there is too much emphasis on how to "get through" the EA process rather than on better environmental planning and decision making. The Association of Municipalities of Ontario submitted that "the process has become an end unto itself, to the detriment of achieving environmental protection goals." The result of this focus was seen to be a process that necessitates lawyers and consultants, and intimidates the public from getting directly involved.

The Need for Early and Effective Public Involvement

There was also general support for the public being involved and consulted from the beginning of the process. The Regional Chairmen submitted that "there should be a requirement that there be public consultation from the beginning." It was a common view, however, that the complexity of the process does not facilitate public involvement. The Metro Toronto Remedial Action Plan Advisory Committee, for example, submitted that "the application of EA leaves many concerned citizens puzzled, frustrated, and, at times, cynical" and "the EA system seems to be geared for full time agency people, consultants and lawyers."

The need to provide funds to the public to assist in their participation in the process was also widely recognized. However, there was a range of opinions about when and how such funding should be provided and who should pay for it. The EA Board, for example, submitted that "a mandatory program for the distribution of funding to participants should be available at the earliest stages of the EA and prior to any scoping hearing...." The AMO submitted that "If the Province wishes to establish a system of intervener funding, it should provide the financial resources...."

Limited Application of the Act

Need for Fundamental Change

Submitters also raised concerns that to "simply fine tune the EA Act" will not address the fundamental need to improve environmental decision making on matters to which the Act does not currently apply, and that there is a need either to broaden the application of the Act or to address environmental concerns properly through other legislation. These fundamental questions were raised in a number of different ways as submitters responded to the Task Force recommendations concerning public sector exemptions, private sector designations and class EAs. Approvals of private land development projects were given as examples of cases where the EA Act does not apply and the Planning Act does not require an adequate degree of environmental analysis.

Application of EA

Some submitters stated that the Act is not being applied to the right set of activities—

while EAs are carried out on relatively small, individual public sector projects, there is no assessment and public input on more environmentally significant decisions, for example, on government programs and plans and certain types of private sector projects, many of which involve cumulative impacts.

Concerns were raised about the artificial distinction between public and private sector undertakings when there may be no difference in their environmental significance. Submitters stated that there has been no government commitment to applying the Act to environmentally significant private sector projects, with the exception of waste disposal facilities, as evidenced by the fact that virtually all designation requests have been denied. There was a range of opinions, however, on the best way of addressing this problem (e.g., by individual designation decisions or by designating similar types of private projects at the same time), and about whether and how the requirements of the Act should be adjusted to accommodate special needs of the private sector. Concerns were also raised about the adequacy of the criteria and procedures proposed by the Task Force for making both designation and exemption decisions.

Finally, submitters generally supported the use of class EAs in order to apply the Act efficiently to a number of similar projects with relatively minor effects, and agreed that there is a need to provide clear legal authority for them. However, they complained about the Ministry's poor handling of bump-up requests. There was a range of opinions on what class EAs should apply to, and on what requirements and procedures are needed to ensure that class EAs are effective.

THE COMMITTEE'S VIEW

Concerns and Criticisms

The concerns and criticisms raised about the EA program are both significant and valid. Taken together, it is apparent that the program presents significant practical problems for proponents and other participants, and that the EA Act has not fully met the needs of the environment nor the expectations of the public. Unfortunately, because of these real and perceived problems, the EA program has gained a reputation that has been a major reason, in our view, for the lack of government will to apply the Act more widely, and ironically for the lack of suffi-

cient resources for efficient administration of the process.

Strengths of EA Act

Despite these problems, the EA program has significantly improved environmental decision making. It has helped to broaden the way we now approach environmental problems such as waste management, and the public has come to expect such changes as a matter of course. The principles embodied in the EA Act — consideration of alternatives and their environmental impacts, the broad definition of the environment, proper documentation, public and government consultation and review, and where warranted consideration by an independent tribunal — are sound. In today's world, it is no longer acceptable that decisions affecting the environment may be made without first critically and publicly considering alternatives and the full range of effects on the environment. Toronto's Ataratiri housing project, which was exempted from the Act, is an example of an undertaking that could have benefitted from an environmental assessment prior to the government making the costly decision to build housing on the contaminated lands.

It is largely due to a lack of understanding of the principles embodied in the Act, its poor administration and the natural aversion of proponents to open up their decision making to public scrutiny that the EA program has not nearly achieved its potential. However, before the environmental assessment process can win wider acceptance, it must, as stated by the Minister, become more effective, fair and efficient.

Historical Perspective

The EA program, as we know it today, is largely the result of decisions made over the past 15 years by the provincial agencies acting as both proponents of undertakings and as administrators of the Act. During our public consultation and other Committee reviews over the past six years, the Committee has heard over and over how the EA Act is being poorly administered. This includes poor and inconsistent advice and direction from the EA Branch, the long and uncertain time it takes for completion of government reviews which are often of limited value, inappropriate bureaucratic and political involvement in the process, the consistent denial of designation and bump-up requests, and the length and cost of EA Board hearings.

If the EA Act had been strongly supported and administered properly, it would likely not be in such disrepute today. Significant improvements can be made immediately through administrative changes and a fundamental change in commitment to the EA program by the government and senior civil servants. Such changes are absolutely necessary for the program to work, regardless of changes to the Act itself. The Task Force made a number of recommendations for administrative changes which would move in the right direction. But in the Committee's view these would not be nearly enough to correct current weaknesses of the process and its implementation.

Amendments to EA Act

Amendments to the EA Act will also be needed to address some significant problems, particularly if the needed changes in administration and commitment are not made. The Task Force made recommendations for such legislative changes. It was evident from the submissions that both proponents and the public see the need to build requirements into the Act that will help to address their concerns.

We therefore begin our review with recommendations for legislative changes to the EA approval process. Subsequent sections deal with matters needed to support the process and its implementation, including: policies, regulations and guidelines; participant funding; the EA Board; and the administration of the process. We end with a brief discussion of other important matters including class EAs, the application of the Act and its relation to the Planning Act, which are to be addressed in Part 2 of our report to the Minister.

(e) Environmental Impact Assessment and the Fallacy of Unfinished Business[†]

Kristin S. Shrader-Frechette ————————————————————

Nearly all current attempts at environmental impact analysis and technology assessment fall victim to an ethical and methodological assumption that Keniston termed "the fallacy of unfinished business." Related to one version of the naturalistic fallacy, this assumption is that technological and environmental problems have only technical, but not social, ethical, or political solutions. After using several impact analyses to illustrate the policy consequences of the fallacy of unfinished business, I suggest how it might be overcome. Next I present three standard arguments, repeatedly used in technology and environmental impact assessments, by those who subscribe to this "fallacy." I briefly examine the logical, consequentialist, and historical reasons for rejecting all three arguments in favor of this assumption. If my suggestions are correct, then environmental impact analysis is not only a matter of discovering how to finish our technological business, but also a question of learning how to recognize the ethical and epistemological dimensions of our assessment tasks.

Introduction

It is a truism that the wise person is not necessarily known by the answers he gives, but by the way he formulates the questions. Perhaps this is because even the best of us often cannot resolve a problem when it has been formulated in terms of the wrong questions.

For the last several decades, at least, we have intently formulated our environmental problems in terms of technological questions about purely technological solutions to them. We have asked, for example, whether we ought to store radioactive waste in salt mines, or in deep-drilled wells, in solidified ceramic form or as a liquid inside double-walled steel tanks.[1] Not surprisingly, we have been getting technologi-

† From *Environmental Ethics* 4, 1 (Spring 1982): 37–47. Reproduced by permission of the author and the publisher. See appendix for notes or references.

cal answers, ones which respond to the questions asked, but which fail to resolve the more difficult problems which generated the original inquiry. In the case of the environmental hazard posed by radioactive wastes, the really intractable problem is not the technical one of what storage technique to adopt, but the ethical and social ones, such as what risk we can impose on future generations and how we ought to determine the acceptability of a given risk. We have not answered questions such as these in part because we have been asking, not wrong questions, but incomplete ones, questions that are epistemologically loaded, questions that presuppose a definition of a given problem for which only an answer in terms of the technological status quo counts as a solution.

Suboptimization and the Status Quo

In a recent EPA (Environmental Protection Agency) assessment on which I worked, this was exactly what happened. The question we gave ourselves was simple: ought we to develop coal or nuclear fission in the nine-state Ohio River basin area, in order to meet electricity demand between now and the year 2000?[2] Our "allowable" technological answers to this question were not very satisfying, owing both to the well-known problems besetting nuclear utilities since 1974 and to the atmospheric and geographical characteristics (air inversions and cascading effects) unique to the Ohio River valley. Precisely because our formulation of this technological question admitted only of a technological answer, in terms either of coal or nuclear fission, our EPA assessment ignored alternative ethical, social and political solutions to the problem. As members of the assessment team, we did not consider that, as the authors of the recent Harvard Business School study pointed out, up to the first ten-million barrels per day of oil equivalent, conservation, and some low-technology forms of solar power are all cheaper than any conventional energy source, including coal and nuclear power.[3] Quite typically, we were willing to look at all the *technological options* that might render coal or nuclear power most cost effective, but we were not willing to examine all the ethical, social, and political parameters, e.g., prices incentives, regulations, public preferences, and values, that could make conservation or on-site solar more cost effective than conventional energy sources. For this reason, our technological

question gave us a purely technological and, to that extent, incomplete and unsatisfying answer.

The same sorts of unsatisfying answers appear in nearly all environmental impact analyses and technology assessments, and it can be shown that their incompleteness stems from a common methodological assumption. In a recent OTA (Office of Technology Assessment) study of automobile technology, for example, the authors calculated existent and predicted rates of pollution caused by automobiles and analyzed the effectiveness of various pollution control devices. Because they investigated largely *technological solutions* (e.g., better pollution-control equipment) to the environmental problems caused by automobile technology, they failed to consider adequately the role of social-political solutions, such as regulatory incentives for mass transit. By their own admission, the price paid for failure to assess alternative social and political solutions will be that, by the year 2000, approximately half of all persons in the U.S. will be regularly exposed to dangerous levels of toxic chemicals from automobile emissions.[4]

As the EPA energy study and the OTA auto assessment illustrate, even though assessment teams working under U.S. government contract are specifically directed to examine alternative means of solving impact problems and attaining given goals,[5] many environmental impact analyses and technology assessments fail to evaluate nontechnological or non-status-quo options. This situation seems to present a classic case of what Boulding called *suboptimization*. He defined suboptimization as finding the best ways to do things which might better be left undone.[6] In assessing automobile technology, apparently the OTA authors fell victim to suboptimization. Apparently they studied the auto's impacts and found the best way to continue to use something, conventionally designed automobiles for private travel, even though this mode of transport may not itself be a truly optimal alternative. Likewise, in [assessing] energy technology, apparently policy makers found the best and the cheapest way to do something, import fifty percent of this country's oil, even though such an extensive import policy should not have been followed at all. The policy weakened the dollar, discouraged conservation, and threatened political security.[7] If these examples about "suboptimal" technology and environmental impact assessments are representative, and I think they are, then they lead one to question the methodological and ethical assumptions undergirding many assessment results. (1) Do evaluators merely find the technically optimal solution to a problem which is prematurely and perhaps erroneously defined purely as technical? Or (2) do they also generate a number of possible ethical, social, and political solutions whose complexity requires more than merely technical analyses? A comprehensive review of recent environmental impact and technology assessments suggests to me that most studies fit the paradigm of (1) and not (2).[8] Because of the way most impact questions are formulated, it is rarely the case that key ethical, social, or political parameters are either recognized or analyzed, particularly if solution scenarios in which they might appear are built on atypical presuppositions, such as that more technology is not necessarily better technology,[9] or that need for a technology or commodity is not accurately defined by demand for it.[10]

The Fallacy of Unfinished Business and the Naturalistic Fallacy

What does all this mean? It means, I think, that assessors of environmental and technological impacts have too often fallen victim to a certain epistemological naivete, to what Keniston calls "the fallacy of unfinished business."[11] This is the error of assuming that more of the status quo, and more technology (whether contraceptives [for] India or broad-spectrum pesticides for Malaya [now part of Malaysia]), is all that is needed to cure our technological, environmental, and social malaise. It comes down to the belief that "real" answers are technical, or scientific, but assuredly not ethical or social. In the light of the facts, for example, that India's population is a consequence, not of the dearth of contraceptives, but of the desire for parents to have survivors to care for them in old age, and that pest infestation in Malaya has worsened in the face of chemically induced pest immunity, it is clear that providing more of the status-quo technology is not necessarily the answer to all environmental problems. Why, then, do persons subscribe to the fallacy of unfinished business?

This fallacy appears to have the same philosophical roots as one version of the famous naturalistic fallacy. A variant of the latter error occurs, according to Moore, whenever one attempts to give scientific reasons, alone, as a justification for ethical beliefs.[12] (If one argued, for example, that taking a certain environmen-

tal risk were moral, solely because it had a low probability of causing catastrophe, then one would commit this error. The problem here would be the assumption that purely scientific property, i.e, a low probability, constitutes a sufficient condition for judging a risk as morally acceptable.[13]) As Moore pointed out, empirical, inductive, or statistical considerations represent only a part of what must be addressed in making ethical judgements.[14]

Insofar as they subscribe to the fallacy of unfinished business, a number of assessors appear to assume that empirical, statistical, or technical considerations are sufficient for making judgements about environmental and technological impacts. Admittedly, most assessors would not claim to be making *ethical* judgements by means of the *technical* considerations. Although most impact studies do avoid overtly normative statements, however, they nevertheless fall into implicit normative assumptions by virtue of what they are willing to count as relevant to the problem at hand. For example, consider the EPA ORBES assessment on which I worked. I am sure that my co-workers, who were directed to find the best way of meeting energy demand in the basin, would not claim to be making any ethical judgements about what ought to be done. Yet, by virtue of their own decision that coal and nuclear fission were the only viable options to be assessed, they did make an implicit evaluative judgment about whether society ought to consider alternatives such as on-site solar or nuclear fusion.[15] In this sense, assessors' subscribing to the fallacy of unfinished business does seem to have reduced their (implicitly ethical) impact studies to purely scientific considerations, and this reduction represents perhaps the least controversial variant of the naturalistic fallacy.

I say "least controversial variant" because the naturalistic fallacy in some of its forms has been subject to great dispute.[16] It seems largely indisputable, however, that if one reduced environmental and technological policy studies to purely scientific analyses, then a number of obviously undesirable consequences could be shown to follow. Perhaps most importantly, policy makers would have to equate the criteria for the moral acceptability of an action, e.g., using broad-spectrum pesticides, with the criteria for assessing the purely scientific or technical impacts of that action, e.g., increasing crop yield. By definition, considerations such as (1) whether a given action is accepted voluntarily or involuntarily, (2) whether the costs and benefits of the action are distributed equitably, and (3) whether the action is "worth it" would be excluded from consideration. Hence the attempt to reduce policy considerations to purely scientific analyses obviously ignores a number of relevant, and perhaps central, parameters.

One of the most important questions about environmental impacts is not whether to choose polluting technology *A* or polluting technology *B* as a *means* to attain some end, *C*, but whether to choose *C* or some other *end*. But, if assessments deal with purely technological questions, then of course they deal solely with choosing *means* to an assumed (usually status-quo) end, rather than with also evaluating alternative ends.

One desirable result of avoiding the fallacy of unfinished business is thus likely to be that once ethical, social, and political solutions to given problems are considered, then the ends of policy actions, and not just the means to them, will be assessed. In other words, environmental impact and technology assessments would likely stop investigating merely the impacts of various technical means to some presupposed end (e.g., generating more electricity), and instead would begin evaluating the impacts of alternative ends (e.g., generating more/less/the same amounts of electricity) as well. Only when impact analyses make the consequences of the broadest scope of public choices apparent, can those choices be rationally evaluated.

One Solution: Broadening the Scope of Assessments

Practically speaking, avoiding the ethical and methodological assumption known as the fallacy of unfinished business and learning to assess ends as well as means might be accomplished by broadening the scope of one of the criteria expressly used for technology assessment and environmental impact analysis in the U.S. In the third of its eleven criteria, the OTA enjoins assessors to determine the costs and benefits of "various policy options regarding a given technology."[17] If this criterion could be interpreted, such that the concept of "policy options" were understood in the widest possible sense, then environmental impact analysis and technology assessment methodology might move a long way in the right direction.

"Various policy options" could be defined so as to include alternatives that might be viable within different ethical, legislative, fiscal, regulatory, social or political frameworks. With this new understanding of the options, policy makers would have before them alternatives which differed in ends as well as in means. They would have various ethical alternatives, some of which challenged, and others of which supported, existing assumptions about, for example, the necessity of growth, the environmental price of progress, and the value of particular pollution controls.

By redefining what we mean by "policy option," and broadening it to include nontechnological solutions, we could expand the range of choices open to a policy maker confronted with the given problem. One such range of choices was exhibited recently by Ben-David, Schulze, and Kneese, who illustrated how different social, ethical, and political assumptions could be used to generate alternative environmental/technological policies, each of which could be said to be cost-effective depending on the assumptions used. They concluded, for example, that on the basis of their respective value judgments, the Nietzschean, Benthamite, and Golden Rule ethics indicate that strict standards for automobile emissions are not cost-effective, but that they are cost-effective when considered in the light of Rawlsian ethics.[18]

Such a proliferation of policy alternatives is likely to increase both the freedom and the power of those who make public decisions. Freedom is, after all, not only a function of the number of different alternatives that one has, but also a function of the number of distinct and different options he has. This is why using various ethical, social, and political assumptions to weight the costs and benefits being assessed, as Kneese et al. have done, clearly expands the range of public choices in environmental and technological decision making.

Broadening the Scope of Assessments: Objections and Responses

To these proposals for expanding the concept of "policy options," the experienced assessor of environmental impacts has several clear responses. (1) Such an expansion would require every impact analysis team to spend much more time and much more money examining policy alternatives having only a small probability of ever coming to be. (2) There would be no way to obtain "hard data" on new, untested, or alternative technologies or policy options. And

(3) predicting impacts on the basis of alternative ethical, social, or political, e.g., institutional and governmental, frameworks, is risky and problematic, and would provide only a questionable basis for policy making.

While each of these objections raises a central and important point, a number of considerations suggest that they are not as devastating, to the notion of expanding the concept of "policy option," as might appear. Objection (1) is a particularly compelling one because it focuses on the practical impossibility of indefinitely expanding the list of policy alternatives. Although it is true that all possible alternatives could never be assessed, practically speaking, the force of this objection could be mitigated by two considerations. First, if a study only considers highly probable alternatives under the technological status quo, then the assessment itself wrongly encourages a self-fulfilling prophecy and implicitly sanctions the status quo, regardless of how praiseworthy or blameworthy it may be. Only by consideration of less probable, more complex, but perhaps more desirable, policy options, is it likely either that those desirable options will become reality, or that the circularity of many assessments will be avoided. Secondly, although a study realistically cannot assess all possible policy options, an achievable goal might be simply to evaluate, not necessarily a greater number of policy options, but a greater variety of alternatives.

On the last assessment team of which I was a member, for example, the project members considered possible energy scenarios for the year 2000 of only four kinds: 100 percent nuclear, 100 percent coal, 80 percent nuclear/20 percent coal, and 20 percent nuclear/80 percent coal, based on BOM (Bureau of Mines) statistics regarding energy demand.[19] Obviously our team could have narrowed the number of alternatives considered by eliminating some of these scenarios as unrealistic for the year 2000 (e.g., the 100 percent nuclear option). At the same time, they could have provided an evaluation of more *kinds* of options, e.g., one with twenty percent on-site solar, or one with twenty percent cogeneration. They could also have helped to present a varied policy list by assessing some options based on Ford Foundation energy demand statistics, rather than BOM data, which are much higher. In other words, increasing the variety of policy options does not necessarily entail increasing the overall number of options assessed.

Objection (2) also has force because it rightly points out that there is little hard data on new, untested, or alternative technologies and policies. This is the obvious problem with anything new. If one refrained from analyzing new policies or technologies because there was little hard data to assess, however, then more data would never be generated. Thus, new policies and technologies would never be studied, and environmental policy, environmental goods, and technology all would stagnate. When carried to its logical consequences, objection (2) clearly leads to false and undesirable consequences.

It is also not apparent that there is in fact as little data on new options as is often alleged. In this regard, U.S. assessment teams have much to learn from their colleagues abroad. Canadians, for example, have done outstanding work on social and political alternatives (legal, regulatory) for avoiding the negative impacts of rail accidents and railroad technology. Their studies have enabled them to cut their rail accidents per train mile traveled to half that of the U.S.[20] The varied policy alternatives represented in their technology assessments and environmental impact analyses have much to teach U.S. teams. Likewise China, which feeds its own people (and exports rice as well) has much to tell us about the policy option of nonchemical pest control, a low technology alternative not widely practiced in this country and inadequately considered by U.S. assessment teams.[21] The Swedes, too, have had much success in cutting automobile pollution and traffic accidents by means of regulatory incentives for mass transit.[22] To my knowledge, their experiences have not been used to assess U.S. policy options in the same area. In fact, the latest U.S. auto assessment is recalcitrantly pro auto and pro status quo.[23] Finally, we have much to learn from the English, who appear to have done a commendable job of pricing the social costs (externalities) of some environmental impacts.[24] Because of this economic assessment technique, they have provided an alternative policy option for responding to the problems posed by numerous technological developments. U.S. teams, on the other hand, are only beginning to assess such pricing mechanisms as possible solutions for holding down social costs.

Although the cultural, economic, social, and political differences among the U.S. and countries such as Canada, China, Sweden, and England, are great, there might be some profitable data (admittedly assumption-laden and context-dependent) which could help U.S. assessment teams broaden the list and types of policy options they typically consider. More probably, the widened scope of assessment methodology sometimes used in other countries could very likely be modified for use in the U.S.

Objection (3) focuses on the well-known difficulty that any forecasting is tricky business, but predicting consequences of policy options under alternative (perhaps nonexistent) regulatory, price, political, ethical, or social frameworks is doubly problematic because both the future and the effects of an untried framework are unknown. While this objection focuses on unarguably correct points, its wholesale acceptance could lead to devastating consequences, for it ultimately leads to the conservative position of sanctioning only the status quo, and only allegedly known and understood policy options. This position, however, is both questionable and inconsistent with current practice. The impacts of many conventional technological policies are not fully known and understood prior to the policy's being adopted. Consider, for example, the extent to which the effects of a nuclear (fission) core melt are understood.[25] It is also false that policies are considered and adopted only after their long-term consequences have been or can be spelled out. Current U.S. policy allows the annual generation of exponentially increasing amounts of nuclear wastes, for example, and yet we have as yet to discover whether it can be safely stored in perpetuity.[26] U.S. society is likewise now using nonrenewable natural resources at an exponential rate, while we have yet to determine what the effects of such actions will be. Clearly the claim, "but I don't know the environmental impacts of the future effects of the technology," has not stopped numerous policies from being implemented. Hence, the unknowability of the consequences of alternative-technology scenarios does

not appear, in itself, to be *a priori* grounds for failing to include an analysis of them in assessments.

Perhaps the controlling reason why this is the case is that the ability of a given scenario to yield good predictions is less important than the value the society or the assessors place on realization of the scenario in question. Assessment scenarios involving solar energy, for example, are often seen as incapable of yielding hard predictive data because the technology has not been used as extensively as others. Yet, as a recent government study indicated, the impacts of solar technology are far easier to predict than those of conventional energy sources, since the latter are complicated by the possibility of cartels and other international political-legal maneuvers.[27] Many assessors, nevertheless, resolutely pursue predictions based on conventional energy sources, but describe solar predictions as too difficult to assess. What just might be going on here is an implicit value judgement about the relative merits of conventional versus nonconventional energy sources. Perhaps this judgement has far more to do with accepting the fallacy of unfinished business than with looking for hard data.

Conclusions

If these brief outlines of possible responses to objections are partially correct, and if there are no compelling methodological reasons against expanding the concept of "policy options," then such an expansion (via OTA assessment criteria) may well provide a basis for avoiding "the fallacy of unfinished business." Perhaps then we will move closer to assessing environmental assets and liabilities in a way that is less an *apologia* for the status quo and more a challenge for real ethical and technological analysis.

PART B
Science and the Law

(a)   The Conflict between Law and Science[†]

Hajo Versteeg ─────────────────────────────────

In 1982 a small group of Cape Breton landowners sought a *quia timet* injunction to prevent the spraying of a dioxin-contaminated herbicide near their homes by a Swedish-owned multinational forest company.[1] They were concerned that the dioxin would irreparably damage their health and their natural environment. Following an exhaustive review of the voluminous evidence presented by both the plaintiffs and the defendant, the trial judge concluded:[2]

> This matter thus reduces itself now to the single question. Have the plaintiffs offered sufficient proof that there is a serious risk of health and that such serious risk of health will occur if the spraying of the substances here is permitted to take place?

By confining the legal issue to burden and onus rules, the Nova Scotia Court merely echoed a long-standing precedent for resolving legal disputes.

This paper argues that litigants attempting to use traditional common law doctrines to minimize the potential adverse impact of environmental risk activities, such as spraying pesticides, invariably lose. Part II of this paper explains the inherent limitations in the law and the science of environmental risk activities which promote this result. Part III explores the desirability of extending tort doctrines to allow recovery in "environmental risk" lawsuits. Part IV briefly canvasses various mechanisms for moderating onus and burden rules in appropriate circumstances. Where appropriate, the Noval Scotia Herbicide Trial will be used for illustrative purposes.

I.   PROOF OF CAUSE/EFFECT RELATIONSHIPS: LAW VS SCIENCE

A. Legal Burdens and the Onus of Proof

Historically, the procedural backbone for resolving legal conflict in our society has focused on the rules dealing with proof of harm and burden of proof.[3] Generally, the injured party has the onus of presenting to the factfinder enough information to prove the alleged injury, and to prove that the injury was in fact caused by the wrongful conduct of the injuring party. Criminal law affords an excellent example of these rules. A person is presumed innocent until the State can prove the guilt of that person beyond a reasonable doubt. If the accused person is

† From Raymond Cote, Dawn Russell and David VanderZwaag, eds., *Law and the Enforcement: Problems of Risk and Uncertainty* (Montreal: Canadian Institute for the Administration of Justice, 1993), pp. 209, 211–34. Reproduced by permission of Canadian Institute for the Administration of Justice, Faculté de droit, Université de Montreal <http://www.ciaj-icaj.ca>.

not demonstrably proven guilty of the particular charges brought by the State, the case has not been made out. The accused must be set free, without restrictions. Thus, traditional dispute resolution principles irrebutably presume that the inability to establish enough information to prove guilt means conclusive evidence of innocence. In the result, an accused person who is *in fact* guilty of a crime will be declared innocent whenever the State cannot establish enough information to prove that the accused caused the illegal activity. Society consciously promotes this result because high priority is accorded to the principles of individual liberty and freedom from coercion by the State. These principles are exemplified in the maxim: "Better that 100 guilty people be declared innocent than one innocent person be declared guilty."[4]

Civil lawsuits adopt similar notions of proof of harm and burden of proof. In a typical tort action, the party alleging injury must prove, on a balance of probabilities, three elements: injury in fact, unacceptable conduct by a particular defendant and a causal nexus between the injury and the unacceptable conduct of the defendant.[5]

The allocation of the burden of proof to the party alleging harm (the State of a plaintiff) normally represents an efficient and fair mechanism for regulating legal proceedings. The field of tort law is illustrate.[6] Tort liability concerns itself with distributing losses which are inevitable by-products of organized society. Practically all human activities involve some risk of interference with the rights of others. But tort law does not attempt to shift the loss in every case where one person's conduct adversely impacts upon the interest of another. Rather, tort liability compensates a party who has been injured, by compelling the wrongdoer to pay for the damage that has been done to that injured party where the harm to the individual is greater than he ought reasonably be expected to bear in the circumstances. The function of tort law is to determine how best to allocate these losses, in the interest of the public good.[7]

Procedural rules placed the onus and burden of proof upon the party alleging injury generally help to uphold these principles. A legal regime which allows a person to initiate a lawsuit without presenting appropriate information to justify a change to the status quo would be inefficient.[8] Such a system would promote the unreasonable use of judicial processes because there would be minimal costs attached to the plaintiff's initia-

tion of a lawsuit. The plaintiff would have little incentive to proceed with prudence. In addition, it would be difficult and costly to the judicial process, and to defendants, to assess the merits of the case. Defendants would be forced to speculate about the case of the plaintiff and produce volumes of evidence, much of which would be of doubtful relevance.

In addition to arguments of efficiency, considerations of fairness dictate that plaintiffs should not be able to restrain the conduct of a defendant simply by instituting a lawsuit. As one commentator observed:[9]

> [T]he plaintiff's starting point on the road to a tort recovery is to be able to pick the defendant out of the crowd; that is, to demonstrate factually that *there is a reason why this particular person is the defendant*. (emphasis added)

The concept of fairness is most evident in criminal law. The presumption of innocence is the cornerstone of criminal law in most civilized societies.[10] Our society is opposed in principle to allowing the State to interfere with the freedoms and liberties of an individual without first showing good cause as to why that interference is justifiable. This is particularly so where the complex and sophisticated fact finding capability of the State gives a powerful advantage over an individual accused.

The following illustration highlights a reason for the development of burden and onus allocations. In many civil proceedings which may be characterized as "environmental" cases, a non-consumer of a resource is inevitably the injured party, while the consumer of a resource is inevitably the injuring party.[11] For example, an individual living downstream from a pulp and paper mill may use the shared river for drinking purposes. The non-consumptive drinking use will never restrict the use of the water to carry off effluent. However, the mill's use of the water as a sewer (the consumptive use) will inevitably interfere with the use for drinking purposes. A legal system which allocates the burden of proof upon the non-consumptive user, *ex hypothesi* allows the consumptive activity to continue unabated until such times as a lawsuit is initiated. Further, the non-consumptive user must prove, on a balance of probabilities, injury and causation-in-fact by the resource consumer. In cases of doubt about any material component of the lawsuit, the consumptive user will prevail.[12] Thus, the common law has traditionally encouraged economically productive activity by casting the onus and the burden of proof on the non-consumer. This preference reflected society's approval of industrial expansion, frontier settlement and economic growth over the conservation of natural resources. This was based in large part upon an understandable, but drastic misconception that natural resources were inexhaustible.

A final argument supports the historical allocation of burden and onus rules.[13] In the vast majority of legal disputes, the wrongful conduct of the defendant and the resulting damage to the plaintiff are [contemporaneous] and obvious. Indeed, identification of the injury has rarely been a problem. Most lawsuits have dealt with accidental injuries, wherein a relatively sudden cause gives rise to an immediate and visible effect (injury) to person or property. In most tort cases the person alleging injury can point to identifiable harm over and above that which is associated with the everyday risks of life. In the result, the injured party can immediately gather all of the relevant information needed to prove the harm and to prove that the harm was caused by the wrongdoer. This information can then be preserved and presented to the decision maker charged with resolving the dispute. In most disputes, the decision maker would have available *all* of the relevant information needed to make an equitable decision. The decision maker could fairly conclude upon the *available* information that the plaintiff had proven the case or had not proven the case. Thus, the contemporaneous nature of the cause-effect nexus is well suited to allocating burden and onus rules upon a plaintiff.

B. Characterizing Environmental Risk Activities

Environmentalism in its modern form was born during the 1960s in the writing of Rachel Carson, René Dubos and Barry Commoner.[14] During this time there was general agreement over the nature of environmental insults and the methodologies needed to resolve them.[15] This was so because the data needed to assess and resolve problems such as air pollution and the eutrophication of water systems was readily available and understandable. By the mid-1970s, observers of environmental disruption became more sophisticated. They began to realize that a special category of serious environmental insults had dimensions that were not amenable to sim-

ple solutions. Society was being confronted with newly recognized, poorly understood and amazingly complex environmental *risk* problems.

The term "environmental risk" describes an activity which has apparent benefits, but which has concomitant *potential* adverse consequences, the underlying probabilities of which are *uncertain* and knowable, if at all, at some future time.[16] This is so because the scientific information needed to assess the potential of a toxic substance to cause harm, and the extent of harm, is either equivocal, or simply not available. Examples of environmental risks include the risk of groundwater contamination near hazardous waste disposal facilities, the risk of leakage from toxic chemicals storage sites and the risk of using pesticides which may adversely affect human health or damage the receiving ecosystem.

The fact that the information necessary to define the boundaries of a risk activity is uncertain or unavailable is *fundamental* to understanding the conflict between law and science. Therefore, the next subsection will describe a series of legal paradigms which highlight the reasons *why* scientific information concerning risk activities is usually uncertain or unavailable, and its consequent impact in a courtroom setting.[17]

C. Environmental Risk Problems in Court

When attempting to establish causation, a litigant exposed to a toxic chemical may realistically encounter one of two scenarios. Either one will defeat the case if traditional procedural rules are adopted. In the first scenario, the injury of the plaintiff is obvious (cancer, birth defect, etc.), but the plaintiff cannot establish that it was more likely than not that a particular wrongdoer in fact caused the injury in question. In the second scenario, the defendant is obvious, but the plaintiff cannot establish that it is more likely than not that he has, or will develop, a particular injury. The reasons for, and the legal consequences of each paradigm are discussed below.

Indeterminate Defendants

ONE OF A NUMBER OF WRONGDOERS
In *Cook* v. *Lewis*,[18] the plaintiff suffered injury caused by one of two hunters, both of whom fired negligently in his direction. Unfortunately, the plaintiff could not prove which one of the two hunters in fact caused his injury. To assist the faultless victim, the Court shifted the

burden onto each hunter to prove that he was not responsible for the plaintiff's injury. The consequence of this ruling is that liability was imposed on someone who did not cause the harm. The Court reasoned that it was impossible for the plaintiff to establish who caused the injury. As between an innocent victim and negligent defendants it would be fairer that the burden be placed upon each defendant to exculpate himself, even if he had not in fact caused the harm. As stated by Fleming, the "law prefers a 50% chance of doing justice to the certainty of doing injustice."[19]

The doctrine developed in *Cook* v. *Lewis* was extended in the California Supreme Court, in *Sindell* v. *Abbott Laboratories*.[20] The plaintiff, a cancer victim, was able to establish that her injury resulted from the ingestion of diethylstilbestrol (DES) administered to her mother during pregnancy. However, she was not able to produce any evidence to point to the particular manufacturer(s) from whom her mother purchased the drug. She therefore sued the nine major manufacturers of the drug, arguing that each should bear the burden of proving that it had not produced the drugs her mother had ingested. The Court upheld her suit as an extension of the *Cook* v. *Lewis* principle.[21] When many of the manufacturers were unable to absolve themselves, the court held each liable in proportion to its share of the DES market. The court stated:

> [i]n our contemporary complex industrialized society, advances in science and technology create fungible goods which may harm consumers and which cannot be traced to any specific producer. The response of the courts can either be to adhere rigidly to prior doctrine, denying recovery to those injured by such products, or to fashion remedies to meet these changing needs. [...] [W]e acknowledge that some adaptation of the rules of causation and liability may be appropriate in these recurring circumstances.[22]

These cases indicate a willingness by the courts to expand causation principles to assist worthy plaintiffs who are unable, *through no fault of their own*, to identify the cause(s) in fact of their injuries.[23]

WRONGDOER MAY NOT HAVE CAUSED INJURY

Exposure to toxic chemicals has the potential to cause a broad range of physical harm, including cancer, genetic mutations, central nervous system disorders, fetal and birth injuries, lung disease, and sterility.[24] A tremendous difficulty that must be confronted by toxic tort litigants is the fact that virtually all of these adverse health impacts are also caused by "natural" events.[25] Science does not understand the etiology (the established pathways explaining how and why an exposure produces an effect) of many diseases.[26] Thus, it is often impossible to distinguish between a disease induced by toxic chemicals and the normal background incidence of the same disease.

The inability to distinguish between natural causes of a disease (which would not be recoverable in a tort action) and human causes of a disease, reflects the inability of the natural sciences to establish cause-effect relationships with any degree of certainty.

Two types of evidence are used to identify toxic substances that may pose unacceptable health hazards: (1) epidemiologic evidence derives from studies of exposed human population, and (2) toxicological evidence derived from acute, short-term and long-term experiments on animals.[27]

Epidemiological Proof of Probability

Epidemiology is the study of the distribution of disease and the search for causes of the observed distribution in human populations.[28] The two main types of investigations used to develop evidence of a particular chemical hazard are "cohort studies" and "case-control studies".

Cohort studies involve the comparison of the rates of a particular disease in two groups that were differentially exposed to a substance. Ideally the two groups are identical in demographic makeup (age, sex, race, living and working environment, etc.) except that one group was totally unexposed to the chemical in question and the other was significantly exposed to the chemical.

Case-control studies involve a comparison of people who already exhibit a given disease with a group that is identical demographically, except that they do not exhibit the disease. The purpose of the study is to ascertain if the two groups differ in exposure to the chemical under investigation. Case-control studies are usually retrospective. Researchers take a group that has contracted the disease, and collect data back in time to compare characteristics of that group with those of the control group. The investigator then searches for distinguishing factors that might have caused the disease. Cohort studies can be either retrospective or prospective. In a prospective study, a sample population exposed to a toxic suspect chemical is followed forward in time. The incidence of disease is recorded and then compared with the disease rate of the control group. In a retrospective study, the researcher examines the historical record of a group of people exposed to the suspect chemical over a definite time period to establish their disease rate. That rate is then compared with the disease rate for a similar group not exposed to the chemical.

A number of practical and theoretical limitations severely restrict the value of epidemiological studies in a courtroom.[29] Retrospective studies require accurate and well-documented data. Information concerning the past and present whereabouts of individuals, exposed or diseased, lengths of exposure, and exposure rates is critical. Effective studies often need to go back in time for 10 to 20 years. In many cases, records have not been kept, data about past events is sketchy or unavailable and members of the exposed population are difficult to track. In addition, it is often impossible to segregate and measure the effect of a suspect chemical because of unknown exposures to other toxic substances. Retrospective studies are susceptible to bias because both the researcher and the subject are usually aware of the hypothesized causal connection between exposure and disease.

Prospective cohort studies have additional problems. Since many diseases of concern have lengthy latency periods, all cohort studies require large numbers of subjects and a long follow-up period. There are ethical problems involved in exposing subjects to suspect chemicals in prospective studies. In addition, the criteria and methodology may change over time as new information becomes available. Subjects may tire of the study and respond sporadically or not at all.

All epidemiological studies are extremely expensive and time consuming. In addition, the selection of control groups must be done with extreme care to ensure as much similarity as possible between the groups being studied.

Independent of practical limitations, a number of serious theoretical problems restrict the usefulness of these studies in a courtroom. The mathematical models used to quantify the risk of harm associated with exposure to particular substances are highly complex and fraught with uncertainty. There is no single correct protocol for analyzing the results of a particular epidemiological study. Different models, which are considered equally legitimate within the scientific community, may give rise to radically different conclusions.[30]

Even if an association between a chemical and a disease is found, it must always be understood that epidemiology, by definition, is a study of populations, not individuals.[31] Epidemiology may assist in answering the question: "Could the substance have caused this disease?" It offers much less guidance when attempting to answer the question: "Did this particular substance cause the particular disease complained of by this particular plaintiff?" At best, epidemiology can only give statistical, probabilistic estimates of injury and causation.

The following example (which will be used throughout this paper) is illustrative.[32] Suppose that a spill exposes a group of 100 workers (hereafter, the workers) to a chemical suspected of being a carcinogen. [Epidemiologists] would assemble another group of 100 workers with similar demographic characteristics (age, sex, race, etc.) who were not exposed to the spill. The two groups would be observed in a prospective cohort study to determine the number of persons in each group that developed particular diseases. Assume that ten years after the spill, the investigators find the following results:

Prospective Cohort Study:
Development of Liver Cancer Among 100 Exposed
and 100 Unexposed Workers

Group	Total	Liver Cancer	No Liver Cancer
Exposed	100	15	85
Unexposed	100	10	90
Total	200	25	175

The risk of contracting liver cancer after ten years for the unexposed group is 10/100 or .10. This figure is extremely important; it establishes that the chemical in question cannot be the only cause of liver cancer since the disease occurs in the *unexposed* group as well. The exposed group has a risk of contracting liver cancer of 15/100 or .15. Thus, the increased risk of contracting liver cancer as a result of the exposure to the chemical is .15 minus .10, or .05 (5/100). Stated another way, it could be said that of the 15 liver cancers in the exposed group, 10 were caused by natural factors and 5 were caused by the exposure to the chemical. Therefore one individual in the exposed group can only show a 33% probability (5/15) that his particular injury was caused by the toxic chemical.

In a lawsuit against the chemical company, a victim could use the epidemiology study (assuming it could withstand procedural and theoretical scrutiny) to show that the defendant caused an increased incidence of liver cancer among a *group* of workers. However, the individual must prove, on a balance of probabilities, that his injury was in fact caused by the defendant's conduct. Two tests are commonly used to establish causation-in-fact.[33] Under the "but-for" test, the plaintiff must establish that but-for the defendant's conduct the injury would not have occurred. The "material and contributing factor" test requires that the plaintiff shows that the conduct of the defendant contributed materially to his injury. Our worker cannot satisfy either test because there is a 66% chance that the liver cancer was caused by an agency acting totally independent of the defendant. When the independent or the concerted conduct of two or more [*tortfeasors*] harm a plaintiff, caselaw such as *Cook* v. *Lewis* and *Abbott* v. *Sindell Laboratories* will assist the plaintiff in recovering for proven injury. But when one of two alternative causes does not involve unacceptable conduct (i.e., where the cause may be natural), the court has usually insisted that the plaintiff prove causation on a balance of probabilities.[34]

However, two cases lend support to modifying this traditional approach declared that a defendant who negligently "intermixes" human causation *with natural causation* so as to destroy the plaintiff's "power of proof" would bear the burden of disproof on the issue of causation.[35] This statement was *obiter dicta*, however, as it was established that the injury was caused by one of two negligent human agents.

In *McGhee* v. *National Coal Board*,[36] the plaintiff contracted dermatitis while working in the defendant's brick works. The defendant conceded that it had breached its duty of care to the plaintiff by not installing showers. However, the plaintiff had not proven that failure to provide the showers had caused the harm. The medical evidence established that other factors may have caused the dermatitis.

The majority of the court acknowledged that the medical evidence made it impossible for the plaintiff to prove that the defendant's negligence had caused his harm. Nevertheless, the court held the defendant liable. Lord Wilberforce stated:[37]

> [T]he question remains whether a pursuer must necessarily fail if, after he has shown a breach of duty, involving an increase of risk of disease, he cannot positively prove that this increase of risk caused or materially contributed to the disease while his employers cannot positively prove the contrary [...] In my opinion, there are further considerations of importance. First, it is a sound principle that where a person has, by breach of duty of care, created a risk, and injury occurs within the area of that risk, the loss should be borne by him unless he shows that it had some other causse. Secondly, [...] why should a man who is able to show that his employer should have taken certain precautions, because without them there is a risk, or an added risk, of injury or disease, and who in fact sustains exactly that injury or disease, have to assume the burden of proving more: namely, that it was the addition to the risk, caused by the breach of duty, which caused or materially contributed to the injury? In many cases of which the present is typical, this is impossible to prove, just because honest medical opinion cannot segregate the causes of an illness between compound causes. And if one asks which of the parties, the workman or the employers, should suffer from this inherent evidential difficulty, the answer as a matter of policy or justice should be that it is the creator of the risk who, ex hypothesi, must be taken to have foreseen the possibility of damage, who should bear its consequences.

Toxicological Studies

As outlined above, epidemiological studies have a number of inherent limitations. In addition, the studies are most effective *after* a population has been exposed to a suspect chemical. Therefore, scientists have begun to rely on animal studies as an aid to predicting the potential of a chemical to cause unacceptable harm, prior to exposure.[38]

The effects of a particular chemical on an individual are dependent upon a number of complex, interrelated factors. The single most important factor that determines the effect of a chemical is the amount taken up by a living system (the dose). It is also important to consider how often the exposure occurs (the frequency). Other factors that influence the toxic effect of a chemical on humans include sex, age, state of health, nutrition, individual sensitivity and the presence of other chemicals. Different species of animals may respond to exposure to a chemical differently. Different species of animals may respond to exposure to a chemical differently. Toxicity is also dependent upon the route of exposure. The three principle routes are the gastrointestinal track (oral), the skin (dermal) and the lungs (inhalation). The effect of a chemical itself may be immediate or delayed, and may occur in the exposed individual or in subsequent offspring.

Three types of tests are used to evaluate the toxicity of a particular chemical.[39] Acute toxicity tests are designed to determine the amount of chemical that will cause death in 50% of a given number of test animals (the lethal dose — commonly written "LD$_{50}$").

Sub-chronic tests involve repeated administration of the chemical for up to 90 days. Two species of animals are used (usually rats and dogs) with three dose levels given to each of the two species. At the end of the test, all animals are subjected to complete postmortems, including microscopic examinations of all organ systems.

Chronic tests are those in which a low dose of the chemical is administered for a substantial portion of the lifetime of the test animal. Several species of animals could be used but mice, rats and hamsters are preferred. Their natural lifespans are short, they are easy to breed and handle in large numbers, they are relatively inexpensive and easy to care for. As well, scientists have a relatively good understanding of the biological mechanisms of these animals. This allows for a good assessment of background disease rates, susceptibility to specific diseases at specific organ sites, longevity, and response to husbandry systems. Established scientific protocol recommends that thorough chronic testing of the disease potential of a chemical must include two species of rodents, both sexes of each, adequate controls, a sufficient number of animals to allow for the detection of a potential effect, three dose ranges (including one level likely to yield maximum expression of disease potential), detailed pathological examination throughout the duration of the studies, observation extending to most of the lifetime of the animals, and statistical evaluation of the results.[40]

In addition to acute, sub-chronic and chronic tests, special tests aimed at analyzing effects on reproduction, the immune system, skin, eyes and behaviour may be required.

Despite the extremely useful information that toxicology can generate to assist in estimating potential health risks, there are serious problems in using animal studies to demonstrate a causal link between harm and exposure to a particular substance.[41]

The complexity and inexactitude of the experimental procedures listed above, including the amount and form of the test chemical, the routes of exposure, the selection of the test animals, the difficulty in assessing the results of postmortem examinations, the establishment of the protocols for the tests and the expense involved, all mitigate against the use of the final results to prove causal relationships. The predictive value to humans of adverse health responses in animal tests (the mouse-to-man extrapolation) is not universally accepted. In addition, the need to feed test animals much larger doses of a substance than humans could possibly consume has often been criticized.[42] Controversy also surrounds the selection of the mathematical models used to extrapolate the results from high dose to low dose levels in animals. Further extrapolation from animals to human beings compounds the uncertainty.[43] For example, the American National Academy of Sciences estimated that the expected number of bladder cancers resulting from the consumption of saccharin over a lifetime of exposure ranged between less than one to 1,144,000 cases, depending upon the particular extrapolation assumptions that were made.[44]

SUMMARY

The disciplines of toxicology and epidemiology are characterized by substantial uncertainties due to limitations in scientific understanding, data, models, and methodologies.[45] Contributing to the uncertainty are major difficulties in understanding the etiology of many human diseases, in determining expected levels of human exposure to specific chemicals, in estimating synergistic and antagonistic effects (interactions between two or more toxic chemicals), in estimating the length and effect of latency periods, and in understanding effects on sensitive populations such as children, pregnant women, the elderly and people with pre-existing sensitivities to diseases. The results of most tests are reduced to statistical, probabilistic statements, often with wide margins of error.

Given these limitations, litigants, through no fault of their own, encounter an insurmountable hurdle when forced to prove causation in fact using toxicological or epidemiological test results. As outlined in the next section, these scientific limitations also restrict a plaintiff's ability to establish injury in fact in certain situations.

Indeterminate Plaintiffs

In *Reserve Mining Co.* v. *EPA*,[46] the plaintiff claimed that the continued dumping of mine tailings into the atmosphere and into Lake Superior, the source of the drinking water for the city of Duluth, would increase the incidence of various forms of cancer among the exposed [population]. Some of the tailings contained amosite asbestos fibers. The EPA brought an action to stop the discharge under the injunction provisions of the *Federal Water Pollution Control Act. This Act requires that a pollution source be "presenting an imminent and substantial endangerment to the health of persons."*[47] The plaintiff argued as follows:[48]

(a) Animal studies had demonstrated that asbestos fibers were carcinogenic;
(b) Human exposure to asbestos fibers at occupational levels has been scientifically established to increase the incidence of cancer;
(c) The tailings contained asbestos fibers, and taconite fibers that are substantially similar to, or identical to asbestos fibers;
(d) Therefore Reserve Mining's discharges into air and water represented a potential human health hazard; and
(e) Therefore the plaintiff was injured because he was exposed to a higher risk, beyond normal background levels, of developing cancer.

In *Palmer* v. *Stora Kopparbergs* the plaintiffs presented the following argument in an attempt to obtain a permanent injunction to prevent the future spraying of a dioxin-contaminated herbicide near their homes:[49]

(a) Dioxin has been demonstrated to produce cancer, mutation and birth defects in laboratory animals (toxicology tests);
(b) Epidemiology studies indicate that humans exposed to dioxin have a statistically significant increased incidence of cancer and birth defects;
(c) The herbicide to be applied by the defendants would drift onto the person and property of plaintiffs, and would contaminate water system used by plaintiffs;
(d) Therefore, Stora Kopperberg's spraying activities represented a potential health hazard to plaintiffs;

(e) Therefore, the plaintiffs would be injured if spraying was allowed because they would be exposed to a higher risk of injury.

In essence, the position of the plaintiffs in *Reserve Mining* and *Palmer* was identical. In each case, the plaintiff could establish that the conduct of a particular defendant subjected the plaintiff to an uncertain risk of future injury. But they could not establish on a balance of probabilities that they would in fact develop the disease(s) of concern. Nevertheless, the decision of each court was radically different.

In *Reserve Mining*, the Court made the following determination:

> [A]lthough Reserve's discharges represent a possible medical danger, they have not in this case been proven to amount to a health hazard. The discharges may or may not result in detrimental health effects, but, for the present, that is simply unknown. [...] The medical and scientific conclusions here in dispute clearly lie on the frontiers of scientific knowledge. [...] In assessing probabilities in this case, it cannot be forecast that the rates of cancer will increase from drinking Lake Superior water or breathing Silver Bay air. The best that can be said is that the existence of this asbestos contaminate in air and water gives rise to a reasonable medical concern for the public health. The public's exposure to asbestos fibers in air and water creates some health risk. [...] The existence of this risk to the public justifies an injunction decree requiring abatement of the health hazard on reasonable terms as a precautionary and preventative measure to protect the public health.[50]

The Court then concluded:

> In fashioning relief in a case such as this involving a possibility of future harm, a court should strike a proper balance between the benefits conferred and the hazards created by Reserve's facility [...] A court is not powerless to act in these circumstances. But an immediate injunction cannot be justified in striking a balance between unpredictable health effects and the clearly predictable social and economic consequences that would follow the plant closing. [...] The [lower] court abused its discretion by immediately closing this major industrial plant. In this case, the risk of harm to the public is potential, not imminent or certain, and Reserve says it earnestly seeks a practical way to abate the pollution. A remedy should be fashioned which will serve the ultimate public weal by insuring clean air, clean water, and continued jobs in an industry vital to the nation's welfare.[51]

The Court granted a permanent injunction, but stayed the execution of the injunction. The Court was clearly impressed with the undertaking by Reserve to spend $245 million to abate its discharges into air and water by developing environmentally acceptable on-land disposal facilities.

In *Palmer* the Court made the following observations:

> The complete burden of proof, of course, rests upon the plaintiffs throughout for all issues asserted by them. If the spraying had actually occurred, they would have to prove by a preponderance of probabilities the essential elements of either or all of the alleged causes of action as I have set them out. However, the spraying has not occurred and this application is for a quia timet injunction [...] That remedy also, however, is not without its limitations [...]. The plaintiffs must [...] prove the essential elements of a regular injunction, namely irreparable harm and that damages are not an adequate remedy [...].[52]

Justice Nunn then questioned whether the plaintiffs have offered sufficient proof that there is a serious risk of harm to the health of the plaintiffs.[53] He then continued:

> A great deal of the evidence submitted related to animal studies where TCDD was reported to have caused various effects indicating it to be, among other things, fetotoxic, teratogenic, carcinogenic and to cause immunological deficiencies, enzymatic changes, liver problems and the like. Also it is alleged to bioaccumulate and be persistent both in soil and in tissue [...] That TCDD has had all of these effects is undoubtedly true in the experiments described, but, in every case, the effect must be related to dose. In the animal studies the doses are extremely high and, in all cases, many, many thousands of times greater than any dose which could be received in Nova Scotia [...] The human [epidemiological] information comes from a number of studies made in various countries of the world [...] I am satisfied that in all these cases the exposure was massive, either through accident or industrial exposure or the Vietnam War. [...] [I] am satisfied that, on the whole of the evidence, where risk to health is claimed in any study, the circumstance has been one of massive exposure and such are not of significant probative value in light of the actual low possible exposure here.[54]

In the end, the Court refused to issue the injunction, holding that the Cape Breton landowners had not proven their case in accordance with long-standing legal principles.[55]

D. Summary of Section I

Potential litigants contemplating common law action involving an environmental risk activity

may be assisted by the courts when they cannot establish which of a number of wrongdoers caused a visible injury. However, where the malfeasance of the defendant may or may not have caused an obvious injury, or where the plaintiff cannot establish an injury or the potential for injury is on a balance of probabilities, the plaintiff will have a very difficult time convincing the court of the merits of the case. Section II of this paper will determine whether this state of affairs accords with the goals of tort law.

II. THE GOALS OF TORT LAW

In part I above, it was argued that procedural rules placing the onus and burden of proof upon the party alleging injury were developed to help promote the tort goals of compensation, deterrence, economic efficiency and fairness. As stated by Lord Reid in *McGhee* v. *National Coal Board*:

> the legal concept of causation is not based on logic or philosophy. It is based on the practical way in which the ordinary man's mind works in the everyday affairs of life.[56]

A number of tort scholars have argued convincingly that causation is not simply a blind mechanical formula to be insensitively applied by the courts.[57] Indeed, these writers state that courts will modify causation rules when equity or public policy considerations warrant such relaxation. *Cook* v. *Lewis*, *McGhee* v. *National Coal Board*, *Reserve Mining Co.* v. *EPA* and *Sindell* v. *Abbott Laboratories* are all expressions of the court's insistence on an overriding policy of social justice. Ernest Weinrib, in a fascinating article entitled "A Step Forward in Factual Causation" makes the following observation in analyzing the *Cook* and *McGhee* cases:

> The allocation of the burden of proof is not always to be the plaintiff's, but it must be subservient to compelling requirements of justice. And the primarily evidential nature of cause in fact should not render it impervious to the considerations of policy, purpose and value.[58]

Weinrib continues:

> the very existence of the cause in fact inquiry is the expression of certain more abstract considerations of fairness. At stake is a balance between the innocent victim's claim to be compensated and the freedom of the defendant to be as wicked as he likes as long as no injurious consequences flow from that wickedness. The weighing of these competing interests is [...] not

a value-free process [...] we must always be prepared to test the cause in fact process against
the underlying policies and purposes that it embodies, and to adjust the ordinary method of
dealing with cause in fact if it fails adequately
to reflect our more basic notions of fairness.[59]

Does the status quo, which denies a remedy
to a toxic tort litigant, then promote the principles of tort law? The answer is "no". As outlined above, a primary function of tort law is to
compensate victims. If each of the 15 workers
who had contracted liver cancer were permitted
to recover fully for their damages, 10 would
receive a windfall because it was more likely
than not that the defendant did *not* injure them.
However, denying recovery to all of the 15 individuals denies compensation to the five plaintiffs
who were in fact injured by the defendant.[60]

A second goal of tort law is to deter socially
unacceptable conduct. Obviously, increasing the
incidence of cancer from 10 to 15 cases in a
group of 100 workers is socially unacceptable.
Granting a remedy to an individual worker in
those circumstances would force the defendant to
conduct his business in a more benign fashion.

Perhaps the most important reason for re-
evaluating tort law principles involves the notions
of fairness and justice. The rules governing onus
and burden of proof were developed to protect
individual rights and liberties. Therefore, traditional dispute resolution mechanisms presume
that lack of proof of guilt (harm) means probable proof of innocence (safety).[61] Society accepts
the potential for error when resolving traditional
disputes (better that 100 guilty be freed than one
innocent be convicted) because high priority is
placed upon individual liberty. But when managing toxic chemicals, the primary concern for society must be with *public* health, not individual
liberty or corporate growth.[62] When assessing
environmental risk problems, it would be absurd
to adopt the proposition that it is better than
100 harmful chemicals be declared safe than one
safe chemical be declared harmful.[63] When dealing with environmental risks, the inability to
prove injury must *not* be viewed as presumptive
proof of safety. The evidence that is equivocal or
unavailable today may prove at some future date
to have caused harm. And, in accordance with
the characteristics of an environmental risk activity, the harm, if it does materialize, will be serious and irreparable. Thus, policy considerations
dictate that, in appropriate circumstances, a toxic
tort litigant should not be precluded from a rem-

edy because, through no fault of his or her own,
he or she cannot meet standards which were
established to foster social policy goals different
from the goals that are sought to be preserved
in toxic tort litigation. Section III of this paper
will examine some mechanisms to affect appropriate changes to common law doctrine to allow
recovery in toxic tort litigation.

III. SUGGESTED MECHANISMS FOR REFORM

A number of writers have suggested various
approaches to overcome some of the inequities
resulting from the insistence on using traditional
burden and onus rules in toxic tort litigation.
These remedies include, but are not restricted to,
the establishment of no-fault insurance schemes,[64]
legislating a statutory cause of action for persons
injured by toxic chemical exposure,[65] establishing
governmental compensation boards,[66] and adopting risk/benefit analysis to regulate specific chemicals.[67] Many of these approaches are innovative
and must be carefully examined to assess their
merits, including the cost-effectiveness of implementation. No doubt the ultimate solution will
incorporate a number of different approaches.
Other papers in these proceedings deal primarily
with the role of civil courts in adapting traditional common law approaches to standing, class
action, damages and costs in toxic tort litigation.
Therefore, this section will highlights some of the
approaches that may be used to modify existing
causation rules to assist deserving litigants. The
ability to utilize any of these approaches will
depend to a significant extent upon the particular
facts of the case in front of the court.

A. Lower Plaintiff's Burden

Some writers have suggested that the courts
could lower the burden of proof to allow recovery where the plaintiff establishes that causation is "possible", or "conceivable", rather than
"probable".[68] An interesting expression of this
approach involves the replacement of the preponderance of evidence rule with proportional
liability.

Proportional Liability

Proportional liability overcomes the difficulties associated with causal indeterminacy (plaintiff cannot establish on a balance of probabilities
injury in fact, or injury caused by wrongdoing of

a particular defendant) by holding the defendant liable in proportion to the probability that the defendant caused the injury.[69] In the liver cancer example, if 15 workers develop the disease and epidemiological studies causally link the defendant to 5 of those cancers, the principle of proportional liability would allow the court to conclude that there was 1 33% chance (5/15) that the injury of each of the 15 victims was caused by the defendant. Proportional compensation would therefore allow each of the 15 plaintiffs to recover 33% of their damage claim. Proportional liability clearly undercompensates the five victims whose injuries were caused by the defendant, and provides a windfall for the 10 workers whose cancer was not caused by the defendant.[70] Nevertheless, to paraphrase Fleming, the law should prefer a 33% chance of doing justice, to 100% certainty of doing injustice.[71] The tort goal of deterring socially unacceptable conduct is also addressed by the concept of proportional liability.[72] The defendant could no longer expect to misuse toxic substances and remain exempt from tort liability. The remedy claimed by the 15 workers, each recovering 33% of their damages would, in the aggregate, equal the actual damage inflicted by the defendant. The threat of being made responsible for actual losses should deter the defendant from activities which give rise to liability.

Risk/Benefit Analysis

In *Reserve Mining* the Court modified the traditional standards for obtaining an injunction where it was clear that the citizens of Duluth were subjected to an uncertain, but serious and irreparable risk of harm to their health. Using a risk/benefit analysis, the Court made a number of threshold findings to the effect that the scientific information needed to quantify the potential harm was unavailable through no fault of the plaintiff.[73] The Court then balanced the benefits to the community of the defendant's mine, against the seriousness of potential injury. The remedy, an injunction with a stay of execution pending defendant undertakings to eliminate the discharges, clearly accommodated the tort goals of fairness and deterrence.

B. Shift Burden of Proof onto Defendant

Several writers recommend that the burden of disproving causation be placed upon the defendant.[74] Once a plaintiff had presented a threshold case, showing, for example, that the injury or the cause of the injury is indeterminate, that epidemiological studies can permit reasonable probabilistic calculations of the increased incidence of disease, or disease potential, and that the plaintiff is within the risk zone (that is, the plaintiff was significantly exposed to the activity in question) the burden would shift to the defendant to disprove causation as to individual victims.

While the arguments supporting a shift in the burden of proof seem compelling at first glance, there are two reasons why extreme caution should be exercised before a Court adopts this approach. First, the limitations inherent in epidemiological studies which, at best, produce probabilistic estimates of causal relationships can often work to the advantage of a defendant.[75] A worker may be able to demonstrate an increase over background levels, of five cancers, resulting in a 33% chance that his liver cancer was caused by the defendant. However, shifting the burden would allow the defendant to establish a 67% chance that he did not cause the plaintiff's injury!

Secondly, independent of probabilistic evidence (epidemiological and toxicology studies) a defendant might well be able to establish in certain cases that it is more likely than not that its activities are reasonable. For example, in the Nova Scotia Herbicide Trial, the Court made the following observations:[76]

> most countries, including Canada, have regulatory agencies, whose function it is to regulate and control the use of new chemical compounds before they are exposed to the environment. [...] In [Canada] reviews are made periodically after reviews of the literature and independent study by highly trained and competent scientists. In [Canada] registration for use is still in effect. [...] The provincial Department of Environment [...] has not restricted the use of these herbicides. [...] To some extent this case takes on the nature of an appeal from the decision of the regulatory agency and any such approach through the Courts ought to be discouraged in its infancy. Opponents to a particular chemical ought to direct their activities towards the regulatory agencies, or, indeed, to government itself where broad areas of social policy are involved. It is not for the Courts to become a regulatory agency of this type. It has neither the training nor the staff to perform this function.

Thus, in circumstances where the concern for safety amounts to an uncertain risk of future harm, it may well be easy for a defendant to dispel a shifted burden, simply by showing that governmental regulatory agencies have approved the activity in question.

C. Science Courts

It has been suggested that a specialized court be created to minimize the difficulties associated with the law-science interface.[77] One proposal would allow scientific advocates on opposing sides of a technical issue to present evidence and argument to a panel of distinguished scientists. The panel would resolve the scientific issues. The Court would then utilize these factual conclusions, supply the relevant legal or policy judgments, and make a final decision. Another variation would allow litigants to argue their cases before a panel of judges with recognized scientific credentials.

The concept of the science court has generally fallen into disfavour.[7] Judges have historically shown great adeptness at understanding the essentials of complex litigations. In this regard, toxic tort litigation is not unique. In any event, the problem faced by litigants is not that the science of environmental risk is complex but that the data needed to establish the case is equivocal or unavailable. Thus, the science court would be faced with exactly the same difficulty in determining the cause-effect nexus faced by traditional law courts.

D. Summary

Social policy considerations dictate that, in appropriate circumstances, courts may wish to modify traditional burden and onus rules to accommodate deserving toxic tort litigants. To be effective, variations from the norm and the justification for such variations, must be clearly articulated. Part V concludes with some suggestions that may assist lawyers and judges in accommodating the broader social goals reflected in toxic tort litigation.

CONCLUSION

As separate disciplines, law and science each exert tremendous influence over the world as we understand it today.[79] But the synergistic benefits of law and science acting in concert are much greater than the impact of each discipline acting independent of the other, or even worse, antagonistic to the other. If a goal of science is to seek physical truth, the goal of law is to seek justice — that is, truth tempered by mercy. In a very practical sense, when one discipline act independent of the other, each is incomplete.

To a significant extent, the conflict between law and science is the result of misunderstanding and ignorance of one discipline by the practitioners of the other.[80] Lawyers' lack of understanding of science, its role in society and methodologies is pervasive, and unacceptable. Scientists' ignorance of law, its role in society and its methodologies is equally pervasive and is also unacceptable. A pivotal first step in coming to terms with the conflict must be for each profession to begin to understand the strengths and limitations of the other. Professional associations must sponsor conferences with workshops and plenary sessions which specifically address the law/science interface. University [curricula] must encourage cross-disciplined education, at both the undergraduate and professional levels. The editorial boards of professional journals must solicit quality articles from various professional disciplines. Perhaps most importantly, lawyers must appreciate that they have a clear obligation to carefully assess the potential for winning toxic tort litigation, but only *after* they fully comprehend the implications of the science issues involved. In appropriate circumstances, lawyers *must* look at alternatives to litigation, including negotiation and mediation processes to resolve environmental disputes.[81] It is hoped that if some of these steps are taken, lawyers and judges will develop a better appreciation of the parameters of science. Armed with these new insights, they will undoubtedly be better able to accommodate the social goals which are at the very heart of tort law.

[POSTSCRIPT]

The reader is cautioned that both caselaw and academic writing on this topic have evolved since these articles were written by Professor John G. Fleming: "Probabilistic Causation in Tort Law" (1989) 68 Can. Bar Rev. 661; and "Probabilistic Causation in Tort Law: A Postscript" (1991) 70 Can. Bar Rev. 136.

(b) Science and the Tribunal: Dealing with scientific evidence in the adversarial arena[†]

Michael I. Jeffery, Q.C. ————————————————

Although regulation by the state, whether through legislation or otherwise, is hardly a new phenomenon, the rapid growth of a highly technologically-oriented society, in recent years, has served to focus attention on the mechanisms employed by governments in the exercise of their regulatory powers.

Since the early 1970's, decision making in the regulatory/approval context has increasingly encompassed public hearing processes before independent quasi-judicial administrative tribunals, which are obliged to observe the rules of natural justice and conduct hearings in a manner which ensures procedural fairness to all parties.

The purpose of this paper is to consider the appropriateness of dealing with scientific or technical evidence in the adversarial arena provided by an administrative tribunal. To provide a basis for evaluating effectiveness of the adversarial system, this paper will describe how scientific and technical evidence is presently dealt with by courts and tribunals, using the Environmental Assessment Board of Ontario as a role model for discussion purposes. In addition, an attempt will be made to address some alternative approaches which have been suggested as more appropriate, given the nature of scientific evidence.

The issues surrounding scientific evidence and the adversarial process are addressed here from a legal perspective, but recognizing that scientists and lawyers seldom approach this problem area in an other than partisan manner, every attempt is made to present the other side fairly.

Science and the Law — Defining the Problem

It is essential first to appreciate and understand the inherent differences and interaction between law and science. Science has been defined as

a branch of study in which facts are observed and clarified and, usually, quantitative laws are formulated and verified; it involves the application of mathematical reasoning and data analysis to natural phenomena[1]

whereas the concept of a legal system or process encompasses

a body of principles or set of rules recognized and applied by the state in the administration of justice.[2]

Both law and science are rooted in the facts of the particular issues in question, but many problems which face society today contain a broad spectrum of "value laden," or what has been often termed "quality-of-life" concerns over which there is little widespread agreement among various elements of society. It is especially difficult to apply firm rules to issues raised by evolving technologies that cannot be tested in the manner normally undertaken by the scientific community.

Many of the matters that routinely come before tribunals or courts for disposition are assessed not only upon information of a scientific or technical nature, but also, to some degree upon societal or community values which must be considered by the decision maker. This is particularly the case where environmental assessment methodology is used, and is evident from a review of environmental assessment legislation.[3] If, for example, the matter before the tribunal concerns the approval of an application for the establishment of a landfill site, the evidence must include a detailed hydrogeological site assessment. The site-specific portion of the assessment will be based upon a plethora of information derived from drilling logs, soil analysis, contour mapping, etc., most of which will depend upon

---

[†] Reproduced with permission from *Alternatives Journal: Environmental thought, policy and action* 15, 2 (Apr./May 1988): 24, 26–29. Annual subscriptions $25.00 (plus GST) from Alternatives Journal, Faculty of Environmental Studies, University of Waterloo, Waterloo, Ontario N2L 3G1 <alternat@fes.uwaterloo.ca>. See appendix for notes or references.

the subjective interpretation on the part of the individual presenting the information.

In addition, where a hearing is mandated, those in opposition will normally spend considerable time and effort attempting to convince the decision makers that there are more environmentally-suitable alternatives to landfilling, such as recycling, incineration or source separation, which will provide a more acceptable solution to society's waste disposal problems in a manner consistent with prevailing social values and preferences. It is not enough, therefore, to appreciate the nature of scientific or technical evidence in the absence of a clear understanding of the particular type of judicial or quasi-judicial process under which this evidence will be presented and tested.

There are, of course, many fundamental differences between courts and tribunals which to a large extent affect the nature of the adversarial proceedings, including the way in which evidence is both presented and received. It is obvious to anyone who has testified in a courtroom that the proceedings are extremely structured, formal and designed to follow a precise path scripted by the result of centuries of judicial and legislative refinement. All of the judicial trappings are present, from the sometimes intimidating solemnity of the courtroom itself, to the robed judge, gowned lawyers and other court officials.

Hearings before administrative tribunals are designed to be less intimidating and more accessible in the sense that they are less formal in terms of both structure and physical setting. The administrative hearing process, although also adversarial in nature, does not usually demand rigid adherence to roles and procedures known only to judges and lawyers.

Notwithstanding these very real differences, however, the principal function of both courts and quasi-judicial tribunals remains essentially the same: to render unbiased decisions based upon the evidence presented in accordance with the statutory or other framework relative to the case or application at hand. It is important to appreciate this similarity of purpose for, although the rules concerning the admissibility of evidence may differ rather significantly between courts and tribunals, both utilize virtually the same standards in assessing the evidentiary values attributed to such evidence.[4]

To what extent, then, can scientific information in the adversarial arena be relied upon, and to what extent does this type of information affect or influence the decision makers' choices? In order to arrive at any tentative conclusions it is necessary to appreciate the nature of the evidentiary tests applicable to expert opinion evidence.

Balance of Probabilities vs. Beyond a Reasonable Doubt

Most of us are familiar with the standard of proof articulated by the courts in relation to their criminal and civil jurisdictions.

In a civil case (or an application before a statutory tribunal), the degree of probability required to discharge the burden of proof is characterized as being "on a balance of probabilities." Lord Denning, in the case of *Miller v. Minister of Pensions*[5] in commenting upon the civil onus stated the following:

> It must carry a reasonable degree of probability but not so high as is required in a criminal case. If the evidence is such that the tribunal can say we think it more probable than not, the burden is discharged, but if the probabilities are equal it is not.[6]

The criminal burden of proof is that "beyond a reasonable doubt." While this is a much higher burden than the civil onus, it does not generally include the notion of 100 percent probability, for that degree of probability could virtually never be attained.

If at the low end of the scale the civil burden of proof could be as little as 51 percent, that is "more probable than not" how high is "beyond a reasonable doubt" in terms of degree of probability? It is readily apparent that these questions cannot be answered adequately in the absence of the totality of the circumstances surrounding the particular issues of fact.[7] It is interesting, however, to note that although the evidence before a tribunal charged with granting a planning or environmental approval, is subject to the lower civil burden of proof, the scientific community is generally in agreement that the standard scientific criterion for causality is based on a 95 percent confidence level in an animal or human study.[8] One could argue with some justification that the scientific standard of proof is much more akin to the criminal standard of proof, and that it is this latter standard that should be applied.

While I am not in a position to defend or attack the efficacy of the scientific community's adherence to a higher standard of probability, I am prepared to offer some practical reasons why such a standard does not form the basis of decision making at the tribunal level, at least in the context of environmental hearings. It is, I think axiomatic that the nature of the burden of proof required in certain types of proceedings is the result of inherent policy or societal objectives. For example, the societal justification for the criminal burden of proof, being that of "beyond a reasonable doubt," is to ensure within reasonable, attainable limits, that in the interests of justice an innocent person is not wrongly convicted.

In Western democracies, it is simply more important from a societal value perspective that the liberty of the individual is preserved at all costs unless the criminal burden of proof has been fully discharged. Thus, although this will mean that the accused will be exonerated if the facts are only proved on a balance of probabilities, the more stringent test is judged by society to be both desirable and necessary to protect the liberty of the individual and, one could argue collectively, the state.

Scientists by and large support a high standard of probability presumably in the interests of advancing theories and conclusions based upon empirical facts which are as close to representing the "truth" as is possible to attain at any particular point in time.

Although the purely scientific quest for knowledge is sometimes acknowledged as evolutionary in nature, it is not always grounded upon what one would call "hard" objective facts, as compared with the "soft" subjective opinions of humanists and politicians. Often the interpretation of scientific data is indeed subject to the personal biases and preferences of the individual involved, and these vagaries are compounded when the areas of investigation concern questions which are, in themselves, probabilistic in nature.

In contrast to the goals of both science in the pursuit of scientific knowledge and society in the interests of justice, the decision maker in the environmental context is faced with the immediate task of deciding whether to approve or reject a specific proposal. In doing so he or she must come to terms with the technological state of the art as presented by expert witnesses, while at the same time evaluating the social and economic considerations which frequently reflect conflicting community and societal concerns. Often the question is not whether the proposal is the "best possible" solution to a particular problem,

but rather whether it is "environmentally acceptable" or "suitable," taking into account the much broader range of criteria which must be fully canvassed and considered.

If one were to ask experts who routinely appear before tribunals whether or not "A" would cause "B" beyond a reasonable doubt, few would be prepared to answer affirmatively on this basis. If project approvals demanded such certainty, virtually no application would be approved. In practice, the level of confidence demanded depends on the context. Usually it is at least to some extent dependent upon the gravity of the consequences flowing from the evidence, for as the consequences of reaching the wrong conclusion increase, so also would the necessary degree of probability within the general range established by the case law.

Most decisions made in the context of environmental legislation are directed toward the protection and/or preservation of the environment, and are arrived at in terms of how the particular proposal will affect both the natural environment and that created by humans. What may be good for the economy, for example, may be detrimental to the natural environment, and rejection or approval will depend upon the decision makers' view of both the hard and soft evidence presented at the hearing.

Notwithstanding the difficulties facing tribunals in balancing a number of conflicting goals and interests, the fact remains that decisions must be made at a particular point in time in an attempt to solve or at least alleviate pressing environmental problems. More often than not the luxury of obtaining all of the facts or information of a technical nature simply does not exist and, even where there is a relatively adequate data base, the scientific community is by no means in agreement on either the raw data or the conclusions derived therefrom.[9]

Adversarial Processes

Victory vs. Truth

Some have argued that it is impossible to assess scientific and technical information properly in the context of an adversarial process. It is worth considering why this argument is made and whether alternative methods might handle this type of information better.

In the typical hearing format, scientific and technical information is presented by experts giving oral testimony and submitting in evidence written reports to a panel of (in most cases) non expert decision makers. The information presented must be in a manner that is not only comprehensible to the lay-person, but also sufficiently detailed and supported by scientific methodology to withstand firstly, an assault by opposing legal counsel (assisted by similarly qualified experts) in the course of often arduous cross examination and secondly, the impact of contradictory evidence that will undoubtedly be adduced by the experts testifying on behalf of those parties in opposition.

In this often unfamiliar setting, the ability of scientists to pursue the quest for truth effectively is frequently curtailed by limitations imposed by the judicial or quasi-judicial process.

Judge Marvin Frankel observed some years ago, in commenting upon the incompatibility of scientific truth-seeking and the adversarial process:

> Others searching after facts — in history, geography, medicine, whatever — do not evaluate our adversary system ... We know that many of the rules and devices of adversary litigation as we conduct it are not geared for, but are aptly suited to defeat, the development of the truth. To put that thought more exactly, the truth and victory are mutually incompatible for some considerable percentage of attorneys trying cases at any given time.[10]

Courtroom experience has led scientists as well as judges to question use of the adversarial process. As Dr. Stuart L. Smith, former head of the Science Council of Canada, observes in his article [also included in this volume], some scientists have been moved to "conclude that the adversarial method is anti-scientific, forcing simplistic answers where the truth is complex, jumping to conclusions before facts are assembled ..." But Dr. Smith himself comes to a conclusion which contrasts sharply with that of Judge Frankel and other critics:

> My own somewhat unusual set of careers leads me to believe that the experience of scientists in the courtroom can be beneficial to both domains (science and law). No doubt I am out of step with today's fashion, but I prefer more adversarial process in the regulatory system, not less.[11]

Although Judge Frankel's view may have some merit in the context of civil litigation, I believe it is entirely inappropriate to apply his observations to environmental regulatory/ approval proceedings. The inherent differences between courts and tribunals preclude a useful comparison of the adversarial nature of what are essentially two distinct processes with very different decisional implications.

In the Public Interest — Tribunals vs. Courts

Quasi-judicial administrative tribunals which function as regulatory/ approval authorities address issues involving the public interest. In environmental decision making there are no winners or losers in the traditional sense other than the environment and the whole public dependent on it. The parties in regulatory/approval matters being the proponents and those in opposition, are players on a larger stage where the environment and its protection are the central issue. The fate of the parties to the proceedings assumes a secondary role.

Courts in the civil context resolve disputes between specific parties and adjudicate on what is described as a "lis" (controversy or dispute between the parties). Little, if any, account is taken of the public interest, and if one party or the other fails to provide the court with the appropriate evidence, the court simply finds against that party. In contrast, many tribunals have a statutory duty to consider the public interest in the global sense and this often includes "different" publics, all of which may or may not be represented at the hearing.[12]

Environmental decision making involves findings of fact and determination of policy. It therefore requires some type of forum wherein information of a scientific nature, as well as other information of a non-scientific nature, can be communicated, tested and assimilated by both the public and the decision maker. This transfer of information must also be capable of reflecting the societal or communal values which, along with the hard data, will form the basis of the ultimate decision. In providing such a forum administrative tribunals in environmental cases rely heavily on the use of lawyers and adversarial legal procedures. Although it is true that most lawyers are not scientists and cannot participate in the development and understanding of scientific information in the technical sense, they are capable of organizing vast quantities of data and arranging for its presentation in a manner consistent with requirements of a particular statute or regulation.

Certain aspects of peer review are incorporated into the adversarial process through the review by other qualified experts of written reports, and the examination by counsel of witnesses both in chief and in cross-examination. In addition, it can be argued that the adversarial process forces scientists, to the extent that it is possible, to articulate this information in simple terms, for to fail to do so is to run the risk that it will be misinterpreted and provide the basis for an adverse ruling. The tribunal in this context often takes a much more active role than a court in terms of ensuring that it sufficiently understands the evidence, and frequently poses questions to witnesses directly.

In cases where the tribunal is having difficulty in comprehending the evidence or where it perceives that a particular area is not being appropriately addressed, expert witnesses are sometimes retained by the Board itself to, in effect, fill a void in the evidence.[13] The overriding interest of the tribunal, in the regulatory/approval type of proceeding, is not based upon the adversarial relationship between the proponent and those in opposition, but rather upon the necessity of ensuring that the "best" information is before the tribunal to enable it to arrive at a proper decision. It is for these reasons that hearings of this type, although in general adversarial in nature, are nevertheless subjected to procedural modifications to allow boards to deal effectively and efficiently with the matters before them.

There is, more importantly, an inherent element of fairness that should be considered as well, and this relates to the fact that the public, who will inevitably in some way be affected by the decisions, should be entitled at least, to have the opportunity to understand the rationale underlying a particular decision affecting their interests and, if in disagreement therewith, the opportunity to challenge the evidence prior to the decision being rendered.

Increased public participation in the decision-making process is a phenomenon witnessed by many jurisdictions in the past few years, and intervenor funding has served to assist the public in its capacity to deal more effectively with evidence of a scientific and technical nature.[14]

Attempts have been made by some tribunals, notably the Environmental Assessment Board of Ontario, as well as the Joint Boards appointed pursuant to the *Consolidated Hearings Act* to introduce procedural reforms into the hearing process to assist the understanding by both the Board and the public of the scientific and technical information presented during the course of the hearing.

These include a requirement that expert witnesses must exchange detailed witness statements and copies of their technical reports with other parties prior to the hearing, in order to allow review by other similarly qualified experts. Parties may also, with leave of the Board, file interrogatories to which written replies are given, and this procedure is often used to deal with non-controversial evidence of a technical nature.

One of the most important innovations in recent years has been the use of witness panels wherein several expert witnesses form a panel to present all of the evidence dealing with a particular area at one time. In this way the witness most qualified to deal with a specific part of the subject matter under discussion does so, and the evidence is covered and tested in cross-examination in a way which permits better comprehension rather than being presented in a disjointed manner, which is often the case where witnesses are examined individually.

An analysis of the advantages or disadvantages of dealing with scientific or technical evidence in the adversarial arena must therefore take into account the very basic difference of approach (both philosophical and legal) of courts and administrative tribunals, for to ignore these differences is tantamount to comparing apples and oranges.

Suggested Alternative Approaches

Although it is beyond the scope of this paper to outline in any comprehensive way alternative methods of dealing with scientific evidence, those opposed to the adversarial approach have put forward some alternatives which are of interest and worth mentioning.

The first alternative is that of a specialized or "science court," i.e, a court or tribunal comprised of scientists or persons with specific technical expertise in the subject matter of the particular application.[15] Many criticisms have been levelled at this suggested approach with the principle one being directed at the increased tendency for personal biases to become an inhibiting factor in the decision-making process.

The science court option is also problematic because scientific or specialized technical expertise may not necessarily reflect the societal value judgments which must be made when dealing with the social, economic and cultural issues relevant to environmental assessment legislation. The subject matter of each application before the tribunal or court will likely require substantially different areas of expertise, procedural consistency and policy continuity may be sacrificed in order to ensure for the decision makers, a high degree of scientific or technical understanding of the evidence put forward by the parties. Those who have had practical experience with the environmental regulatory/approval process will realize the difficulties encountered in trying to effectively separate factual and policy issues, and it is likely that the integrity of an environmental legal system designed to reflect public interest concerns will suffer if social policy issues are not dealt with in a consistent manner on a case-by-case basis.[16]

Others have suggested the use of environmental mediation as a possible alternative form of dispute resolution. Proponents of this process argue that the removal of contentious issues out of the public adversarial arena will facilitate the opportunity for settlement. In order to be effective, however, most if not all of the principal parties must agree to mediation for, unlike decision making by courts or tribunals where imposed solutions are ultimately rendered, mediation very much remains a consensual process.

In this writer's view, environmental mediation should only be used where appropriate in support of the existing quasi-judicial decision-making process and not as a substitute for it. In mediation the well-defined procedural safeguards inherent in an adjudicative process are largely absent and statutory requirements must nevertheless be observed. In addition, the ability of parties to deal with scientific evidence in the course of mediation in any different fashion than is the case in the adversarial arena is by no means assured.

In many jurisdictions including Ontario, public inquiries have been used to address specific problems with some success. For example, three members of the Environmental Assessment Board were appointed to a Commission under the provision of Ontario's *Public Inquiries Act*[17] and directed to hold public hearings and report on the Ministry of the Environment's proposed regulatory control of mobile PCB destruction facilities in the province.

Much of the evidence presented was of a scientific and technical nature and experts from many jurisdictions addressed a variety of issues in a procedural format which allowed extensive questioning by the Commission as well as by counsel for other interested parties. In addition, the Commission retained its own counsel to assist it throughout the course of the hearing. It may be that greater use of the public inquiry with extensive investigative powers may prove to be more useful in dealing with scientific evidence in certain cases. The public inquiry by its very nature, however, does not usually provide for the decision-making function required by regulatory/ approval legislation, and the absence of certain procedural requirements may not satisfy the rules of natural justice which are often applicable.

Concluding Comments

The adversarial regulatory/approval system has for the most part proved to be effective, efficient and fair in terms of providing a means to communicate and assess both scientific and non-scientific evidence in a manner which specifically meets the requirements of an increasingly informed public no longer content to remain outside the decision-making process.

Unfortunately, solutions to environmental problems cannot always be addressed through a process of peer review or other forms of dispute resolution such as environmental mediation. In many instances an imposed solution by a regulatory authority is the only practical means of effecting any solution or remedial action at all. To date, the case for doing away with the adversarial system has yet to be made.

(c) Science in the Courtroom:
The value of an adversarial system[†]

Stuart L. Smith

While an occasional brilliant flash of scientific insight can render the incomprehensible fully understandable, it is fair to say that, most of the time, new knowledge takes what used to seem simple and makes it far more complicated. We are less likely nowadays to throw fists at one another and more likely to throw complex molecules. The courts have changed accordingly and science is an every day participant.

Scientists appear in court or in front of legal tribunals generally in two situations. The first is a regulatory setting where their expertise is sought, usually in order to help prevent harm. The second is in regard to litigation where, often, some harm has allegedly occurred and efforts are made to assign responsibility. In the regulatory situation, there is an analysis of the risks and/or the benefits, the acceptability of the balance between them and the determination of how the balance might be affected by various actions. In litigation, there is often an analysis of the harm, the determination of the relative importance of various causes and whether steps might have been taken to avoid the damage. There is the assignment of responsibility wherever indicated.

In each case, be it risk/benefit ratio or analysis of causes, scientific understanding of cause and effect is a vital part of the process. Short of global annihilation, nothing will turn back the advance of knowledge and therefore, nothing will prevent the increase in these disputes. Scientists and lawyers are going to be spending more time with each other, like it or not.

To me this represents an exciting challenge and an opportunity for both the scientific and legal community. These contacts ought to help scientists to sharpen their logic and lawyers to broaden their understanding of causal mechanisms. Yet I am amazed at how much negative material is written on this relationship.

I have heard it said that there are unbridgeable gulfs between scientists and lawyers in that they have different concepts of truth. The scientists seek to understand the underlying laws of the universe while courts, only slightly ahead of politicians, seek sufficient argumentation to legitimize some action. I don't think they are really so different. "Scientific proof" is directly analogous to a basis for conviction in a criminal trial (beyond reasonable doubt), yet scientists are constantly dealing with "probabilities," just as a civil trial must do; the territory is familiar on both sides.

Some scientists are offended by the treatment they receive in court and conclude that the adversarial method is anti-scientific, forcing simplistic answers when the truth is complex, jumping to conclusions before facts are assembled. Some lawyers, for their part, despair when so-called experts contradict each other with equal certainty and when scientific witnesses seem inclined to favour the views of their employer or patron. My own somewhat unusual set of careers leads me to believe that the experience of scientists in the courtroom can be beneficial to both domains (science and law). No doubt I am out of step with today's fashion, but I prefer more adversarial process in the regulatory system, not less![1]

Benefits of the Adversarial System

An adversarial system is, after all, simply one type of formalized debate. Cross examination was characterized by Wigmore in 1923 as "the greatest legal engine ever invented for the discovery of truth."[2] Perhaps scientists would prefer to apply that description to the controlled experiment and even to the scientific method itself. But there is no contradiction here. The logical system underlying both the cross examination

---

[†] Reproduced, with permission of Dr. Stuart Smith, from *Alternatives Journal: Environmental thought, policy and action* 15, 2 (Apr./May 1988): 18, 20–22. Annual subscriptions $25.00 (plus GST) from Alternatives Journal, Faculty of Environmental Studies, University of Waterloo, Waterloo, Ontario N2L 3G1 <alternat@fes.uwaterloo.ca>. See appendix for notes or references.

method and the scientific method is identical. Scientific debate, including the use of "devil's advocate positions," is essential in order to make sure that the scientific method is being properly applied. Debate is beneficial, whether in the courtroom or the laboratory, and no scientist should complain of it.

Consider the main alternative to adversarial proceedings when it comes to regulatory decisions. That alternative is for such decisions to be made in discussion between a regulatory authority and a given industry. Standards are set and are often said to be based on the best science available and/or the "best available technology"; they are intended to be in the public interest. But it is well known that scientists have their biases or have limits to their knowledge. Unless the regulators are particularly good at cross-examination, analysis and argument, then even with the best of intentions they may fail to reveal these biases or limits.

The regulators themselves cannot possibly know everything that may be happening in a given field of science or technology and, to complicate matters further, they will be influenced by the economic situation of the country, the political situation of the government, and the need for continued co-operation with the industry. Regulators are in no position to scour the world looking for witnesses who might report recent examples of "best available science or technology," examples of which the industry itself may not be fully aware. Nor are they likely to delve deeply into every detail of the laboratory work that is said to indicate possible risk.

It is only people whose personal interests are directly affected and who are permitted a role in adversarial proceedings who will do those things. Regulators, despite themselves, are often captured by politics, by their regulated industry or even by their own biases, however innocently this may happen. In my experience, both the public and the industries are better served by an adversarial process.

Consider for the moment the celebrated case of urea formaldehyde foam insulation (UFFI). Both in Canada and the United States, a series of regulatory decisions led to chaos and misfortune.[3] But if we focus on one issue, namely that of the possible health hazard, the clearest, most thorough and most logical treatment of the issue is, in my view, that by Chief Judge Clark in the United States Court of Appeals, Fifth Circuit.[4]

In a painstaking, complex, thorough trial, Chief Judge Clark familiarized himself with all the scientific issues in dispute and rendered a verdict. Whereas the Consumer Products Safety Commission issued a ban on UFFI, based on indications that it was hazardous to health, the judge reviewed both the users' complaints and the original scientific papers, and concluded that a basis for the ban did not exist. In fact, he removed the ban. While some may disagree with his verdict, I believe that he did a better scientific analysis than some of the scientists did; his verdict should be required reading for scientists who involve themselves in the regulatory process.

A major concern in the adversarial system is its cost. The well-known case of herbicide spraying in Nova Scotia,[5] also one which involved an attempt at the logical analysis of many competing views from various scientists, placed an enormous burden of costs on persons who were unable to bear them. There needs to be a fund to which people who have a reasonable case can apply so as to finance the proper presentation of such a case, a kind of legal insurance for people who can't otherwise afford expert witnesses or who could be wiped out by having to pay all the costs of such a trial.

This issue of costs is crucial. Many of those who defend a mediated, behind closed doors, regulatory approach do so because it is cheaper than an adversarial system. That may be the case, but I believe that the decisions emanating from the closed door approach are more difficult for people to accept and are simply not as good as those the adversarial system would produce. Since lack of public acceptance often leads to prolonged political controversy, whereas "legal" decisions are often "the final word," even the cost difference may not be that great in the long run.

Dealing with Values and Uncertainties

Some scientists decry the pressure on courts to make decisions in the absence of sufficient evidence. Since our political and legal systems both are based on the need for decisions on the "best available evidence" and cannot come to a standstill while awaiting certainty, this criticism must be regarded as true but irrelevant.

Where all observers agree is that the basic difficulty in scientific disputes in the courtroom is the problem of separating issues of "fact" from issues of "policy." It is my view that much confusion would be avoided if we would further subdivide the area of "fact" into two sub-areas, namely the actual scientific work upon which conclusions are to be based, and the exact methods of inference used in order to draw conclusions from the work. In other words, the judge or tribunal must be absolutely clear about

- the actual scientific work being cited,
- the method by which conclusions are being drawn from that work, and
- the policy or value-laden issues that determine the final decision.

In most instances, the real questions are those of value judgements.[6] Is the certainty of unemployment in a given community, should a plant be closed down, more or less important than the possibility of serious illness from pollution? Is the benefit to the country's economy of certain mining operations more important than possible harm that might come to a traditional fishery used by native peoples? Is the probable benefit of genetic manipulation to remove inherited disease more important than the possible eventual misuse of genetic manipulation to produce a "superhuman?" Here is where the law must be at its wisest.

Even if the underlying facts, probabilities, inference mechanisms, and so on are understood, the decisions are still exceedingly difficult. Yet there is no other place for such decisions to be made. Judge H.T. Markey has commented:

> Science is mechanical, technical, value free and non-humanistic. Science pronounces the law as supplied by nature ... Law is dialectical, idealistic, non-technical, value-laden and humanistic. Law, in the non-scientific sense, seeks to free society from the rule of science. Law is the only tool that society has to tame and channel science and technology.[7]

The main job of the law is to deal with the subject of values in these disputes. Unfortunately, the law is also often called upon to deal with both the validity of the underlying science and the acceptability of the method of inference by which conclusions are drawn.

To return to the UFFI case I mentioned earlier, the judge had to go into details of each experiment in order to determine its validity as a basis for a ban on the substance. For example, rats were exposed to formaldehyde and many developed a form of cancer. That seemed simple enough. But it was revealed (in the adversarial proceeding) that the "average exposure" that the rats had might not have been an accurate reflection of what really happened; many of the rats had occasional exposures to vastly higher concentrations of the substance.

Since an occasional huge exposure might be toxic in itself, the meaning of an "average" exposure is open to serious question. Only an adversarial proceeding would be likely to bring out that kind of feature in a scientific experiment.

Moving to the issues of inference and drawing from the same example, it turns out that there is a frequently used mathematical model for determining how a particular dose/illness relationship in rats might imply a numerically expressed risk in humans. Only a thorough analysis of the model, however, would reveal that there are underlying assumptions which would limit its application to cases involving certain types of chemicals, used under certain conditions or on certain species. Such a model might provide, in given circumstances, no real basis for quantitatively stating a human risk.

It seems to me that scientists can make a real contribution to legal proceedings by confining themselves to clarifying issues about the actual underlying scientific work under discussion and by making clear the method of inference for drawing further conclusions. Scientists should avoid testifying on questions of values. Scientists are human and have values, but when they speak of values in the courtroom they are going beyond their areas of expertise.

Legal professionals must understand the distinction between the underlying science, the method of inference and the value decisions to be made; they should clearly separate these components in the process and avoid drawing scientists in to areas where they don't belong and where they often feel abused.

In order to achieve that kind of clarity, lawyers and judges need to understand the methods of science to some extent. They need some exposure, in their training or at continuing education conferences, to the scientific method and to issues of expert testimony. They must understand that laboratory experiments are almost never, as lawyers say, "right on the point" with regard to the case under consideration. The questions that scientists ask are being asked in another context and for another reason completely. To understand scientific bias, it is important to characterize knowledge along the lines of Randall Albury in Australia who asked two questions:[8]

- from what practice, by what means, and for what purpose was this knowledge developed? and
- within what practice, by what means, and for what purpose is this knowledge used as a tool?

When the answer to the first question is the laboratory and to the second, the courtroom, it would be rare indeed to have the work fit the problem exactly. Even worse, the court must evaluate evidence about which there may be disagreement among scientists. Lawyers cannot be expert in every area but should at least understand the nature of scientific disagreement in general.

Alternatives to the Adversarial Process

Are there alternatives to the courtroom and/or the adversarial process? There is much to be said for a particular alternative to the trial, namely the use of a specialized tribunal. In my view, that is the best solution of all since it retains the adversarial system but increases the likelihood of familiarity with the issues. The main problem with it is the selection of members of the tribunal so as to avoid the existence or the appearance of bias of a political or ideological nature. Since such tribunals do not enjoy the status or permanence of our courts, the issue of bias is an important one. Nonetheless, I believe that the system works extremely well.

The main alternative to the adversarial system is that of negotiated or reasoned regulations which take place in a department or agency of government. I have already indicated some deficiencies in this system. Another problem with it is the question of notice. People want to contribute evidence, even if they cannot cross-examine witnesses, but such interested parties need to know when a department or agency is taking up a certain issue that could affect them. For instance, not too long ago, there was a dispute concerning the dumping of tailings in an area which was of possible importance to a group of native persons but the notice of such impending discussions occurred in media that were rarely consulted by the native community.[9]

Many bureaucracies across Canada are now making their regulatory procedures more open and are trying hard to involve various public interest groups. Despite those welcome improvements, however, I still believe that, short of

actual cross-examination and public participation, there will be flaws in the system.

Some have suggested an alternative called the Science Court. The idea came from Kantrowitz[10] in 1967 and was advanced by an United States task force in 1976.[11] The system would work by having a special body to adjudicate only technologically complex issues after a "submitting agency" has separated fact from social policy. The court would be run by disinterested scientists from an adjacent field of science, assisted by legal counsel. Other judges would be scientists chosen by opposing parties from a list of qualified persons. Then quasi-legal procedures would take place to test each side's version of the facts. The report from the court would separate agreed facts from those which were challenged and would give the court's finding on the latter. It would also make recommendations for further research where no answer was possible.

I feel this is not a good idea. Scientists have their own personal biases and they do not have the tradition of judges in learning how to put them aside. Also, it would be difficult to identify exactly which cases to send to Science Court since, even in seemingly straightforward criminal cases, there can be complicated scientific testimony. Furthermore, it strikes me as cumbersome to have a three-stage process in which, first there is argument about separating the facts from the policy issues, then the facts are decided by the Science Court, and then the value-laden decisions are made somewhere else. I therefore reject the Science Court concept.

There are two methods by which the adversarial system could be improved. To some extent these are already used by tribunals in Canada and I recommend more general adoption.

- It is a good idea to have court-appointed experts, agreed upon by the parties and still subject to cross examination, in addition to those experts chosen by either side. An objective finding is much more likely to emerge from that situation.
- Perhaps the most important thing that a judge can do in preparing for a complex science-related trial is to have a pre-trial meeting with counsel from both sides and with scientific experts. At such a meeting the judge can be assured that both he or she and the competing lawyers have a thorough understanding of the basic issues involved. Pre-trial meetings are commonplace in Canada but might per-

haps be more effectively used to educate the judges and to sort out scientific and technological complexities in some cases.

In summary, there is an underlying logical unity between science and law. Both disciplines can be sharpened by proper debate and by exposure one to the other. With suggested modifications, an adversarial approach, preferably in flexible, specialized, public tribunals, but also in the courtroom, is still the best forum for serving the interests of society.

(d)   Ethics, Science, and Environmental Regulation[†]

Donald A. Brown ——————————————————————————————

Because complex environmental problems are relegated to scientific experts, the ethical questions that are embedded in these problems are often hidden or distorted in scientific and administrative methodology and communication. The administrative process requires that facts and values be separated. Those values that cannot simply be ignored are usually translated into technical economic language and settled in terms of economic costs and benefits. Calls for regulatory reform — i.e., to reduce or eliminate environmental regulation — create additional pressures on analysts that encourage them to focus on quantitative questions at the expense of qualitative ones. Distortion can also result from the use of standard risk assessment procedures and from the improper placement of burden of proof on government agencies. The greatest problem, nevertheless, is the narrow scientific training of technical experts which frequently leaves them unprepared to deal with the ethical and value issues in environmental public policy.

the attainment of consensus on political issues.[1] Communication about environmental problems and issues is particularly susceptible to the distortion that follows from the uncritical use of the language of science because of the technical complexity of most environmental problems and the accompanying need to relegate all complex environmental problems to "technical experts." In this article I explore some of the more frequent ways in which the translation of environmental problems into the language and methods of science all too often distorts the value questions inherent in environmental problems. By exposing the many ways in which questions of value are lost or distorted in technical discourse about environmental problems, I hope to help restore value questions to their appropriate central status in environmental policy making.

Introduction
Are important ethical and values questions distorted through the relegation of environmental problems to the language systems of technical "experts?" Does our growing faith in science often lead to confusion about important environmental issues? Many authors have written extensively about the impoverishment of human communication through the use of technology-laden language and the development of value-neutral sciences to analyze human value problems. Jurgen Habermas, for instance, has asserted that science and technology are sources of systematically distorted communication that prevents

The Regulatory Setting
We all know that the new age of science, computers, space missions, biotechnology, star wars weapons and other goodies of post-industrial society creates potential for new man-made environmental and social disasters. The dangers posed by hazardous chemicals, endangered and vanishing species of flora and fauna, the potential depletion of the ozone layer, the ever increasing contamination of domestic water supplies, problems relating to nuclear power, and the most recent concern over the gradual heating of the global weather patterns caused by the "greenhouse effect" are examples of pressing ecological

† From *Environmental Ethics* 9, 4 (Winter 1987): 331–49. Reproduced by permission of Donald A. Brown, Director Pennsylvania Consortium for Interdisciplinary Environmental Policy; and the publisher. See appendix for notes or references.

problems thrust upon society for the first time during the second half of the twentieth century. These problems are characterized by levels of complexity and uncertainty never before experienced by any society. Because faith in science is at an all time high, we tend not to blame the engineer or scientist for these problems. Instead, we believe that science will tell us which problems should be of concern and what steps should be taken to protect us.

In the United States the usual response to these complex problems has been to create complex laws that empower administrative agencies staffed largely by engineers, scientists, lawyers, and, with greater frequency, economists, to "regulate" these problems. Although many of the goals of public policy are set out in the authorizing legislation, very often much of the public policy is determined by administrative rule making.[2] For example, some environmental laws require the government to promulgate rules to balance health benefits against costs, such as the Toxic Substances Control Act,[3] while others appear to allow for considerations of health only, e.g., section 109(b)(1) of the Clean Air Act.[4] Even though environmental administrators are in this way constrained by the authorizing legislation in promulgating environmental rules, all the major environmental statutes give government agencies much discretion in formulating the final rules, for example, by allowing agencies to decide which pollutants shall be regulated or by allowing administrators to identify what levels of pollution are acceptable. For instance, under the Clean Air Act national ambient air standards are set at a level which "in the judgment of the administrator ... [allows] an adequate margin of safety" and a hazardous air pollutant is designated by "the judgment of the administrator."[5]

According to the model for an administrative agency accepted by most lawyers, administrators, and political scientists, the administrative expert breaks down all environmental problems into an "objective" technical problem and a "subjective" policy component. In developing policy the administrator looks at the guidance contained in the legislation and then applies the "objective" technical facts to the decision rule found in the policy-defining legislation. In this way, agency technicians apply science derived "facts" to politically derived rules. The model envisioned in this conventional view of administrative decision making assumes that the technical problems under consideration can be dealt with in technical, ana-

lytical terms and that the values of the administrator and the value problems embedded in the environmental controversy can be eliminated from the administrative process. Does the relegation of these "fact-value" questions to "technical" experts systematically distort the important values and ethical questions that are necessarily embedded in the environmental questions under consideration? I believe that the answer is clear.

Definition of Terms — Ethics and Science Distinguished

For purposes of definition, by ethics I mean the domain of inquiry that attempts to answer the question "What is good?" Ethical statements are propositions of the form that such and such is good or bad, right or wrong, obligatory or nonobligatory. Ethics should be distinguished from the social sciences, such as sociology and psychology, which attempt to determine why individuals or groups make statements about what is good, right, or obligatory. Furthermore, ethics is concerned with "prescriptive" statements, which attempt to transcend relative cultural and individual positions. Science, as used in this essay, is the discipline that attempts to make "descriptive" statements about the nature of reality through analysis of facts and experience. Science and its derivative technologies attempt to describe objectively, through an empirical methodology, facts and relationships between facts, and the laws of nature that govern the universe.

It is generally accepted that science cannot deduce prescriptive statements from facts.[6] That is, one cannot deduce "ought" from "is" without supplying a new minor premise. One cannot introduce an evaluative term, such as "optimal solution," into the conclusion of an argument if the prior premises of that argument are entirely nonevaluative (e.g., dose-response statistics). Although a description of certain facts may suggest an ethical position, one cannot through a description of the facts alone deduce an ethical conclusion. An ethical system such as utilitarianism may provide the minor premise needed for ethical reasoning. For instance, if one concludes that option "A" will create the greatest happiness, by applying the utilitarian maxim that one should choose the option that creates the greatest happiness, one can conclude that option "A" is the optimal solution. From a proposition that such and such a problem creates a particular risk, one cannot, however, deduce whether that risk is acceptable without first deciding on certain criteria for acceptability. Therefore, on this largely traditional view of the logic of ethics, science cannot answer ethical questions all by itself.

This is not to say, however, that science is irrelevant to ethics. Ethics is concerned with the ends that should be chosen by people. Science is extremely important in most environmental ethical discussions because, once a particular goal is chosen, science can evaluate various means that are available to achieve the goal. Science can also analyze which ends are feasible. If a society determines that it is good to build a nuclear power plant, for instance, science can analyze what structures or what types of institutions most effectively and safely achieve the type of power plant desired by the community. Science can also help determine what environmental impacts the community should expect from the power plant. On this view, however, science cannot fully determine whether the power plant should be built, precisely because no amount of descriptive analysis can logically certify a prescriptive course of action. Science is thus obviously fundamental to the description of the environmental problems discussed in this essay and is particularly useful in identifying, for example, the health risks that certain projects pose. Those who are interested in a full discussion of values positions in environmental policy making, therefore, are not anti-scientific. In fact, sound scientific analysis is essential in any attempt to fully define most of the environmental ethical questions considered here.

If we agree that the question of whether society should use nuclear power is essentially an ethical question, while admitting that science is extremely important in analyzing the facts, and thereby giving content to the ethical question, it must be admitted that there is no generally accepted consensus in the philosophical community about which ethical system to apply to any given problem. Several major philosophical systems attempt to define good, including utilitarianism, Kantian ethics, natural rights, and Rawlsian contract theory, just to name a few. Some philosophers assert that ethical assertions should be treated as nothing more than the emotive preferences of the person making the assertion on the grounds that they are entirely subjective and relative to the person making the value judgment. Additionally, it is sometimes difficult to determine which facts should be considered and what weight should be given to these

facts in any ethical calculus. Because most of the dominant Western philosophical systems make human interests the measure of value, human interests, some critics argue, are the only interests considered in Western ethical systems, with the result that such concerns as the rights of animals are not appropriately included in traditional ethical debate. In the last ten years, as concern about environmental problems has increased, environmental philosophers have attempted to create new ethical approaches to these complex environmental problems. Because there are so many approaches, showing that there are ethical questions that have not been adequately considered in public policy formulation is far easier than finding ethical solutions to these questions.

The Separation of Facts and Values in the Administrative Process

One of the most common ways in which value issues are hidden in environmental public policy making develops out of the expectation that the technical analysts can isolate the "facts" under dispute and employ these "facts" in accordance with the "value" formula given in the enabling legislation. The separation of "fact" and "value" issues, however, is often difficult, if not impossible. Philosophers who have been concerned about how people understand facts, a topic studied within a branch of philosophy called hermeneutics, have come to realize that what one sees is usually a product of cultural tradition; there are no acts of pure perception that are not dependent on prior value choices. In this context, the decision about which "facts" to focus on in the analytical stage of research cannot avoid value questions. For example, should the environmental impact analysis of a dam consider protection of the habitats of deer and elk or should it consider potential destruction of the habitats of skunk or coyote? The decision of what to study is frequently a question of value, not of fact.

Second, the decision about what resources will be used in performing the analyses of the facts is ultimately a value decision for which there is usually no objective standard. In a recent book entitled *Making Bureaucracies Think*, Serge Taylor reports that the determination of what methods and resources the Army Corps of Engineers will employ to predict the environmental impacts of a project often results from a negotiated settlement between the environmental analyst and the project manager, and frequently depends upon such nonscientific criteria as the amount of budget money that is available to perform the analysis.[7]

Many of the "facts" that the analyst attempts to collect for use in policy calculations are not susceptible to purely objective analysis. For instance, it is impossible to determine the visual impact of a water diversion project upstream from a dam, for there are simply no "objective" criteria for beauty or ugliness. Separating "facts" from values is also often impossible because the gathering of the facts must rest on hard-to-test or even presently untestable assumptions about the way the world works. The facts at issue in environmental disputes are very often nothing more than guesses based on high-level speculation. Likewise, how facts are arrayed by technical experts are often not policy neutral. A report by the Center for Philosophy and Public Policy entitled *Faith in Science* concludes that

> ... simply knowing some action will result in the deaths of some people who would not have otherwise died does not tell us whether the act is murder, killing, allowing some people to die, or even saving lives.... No matter how "neutral" the scientific work is, there may be no neutral description of it that can be incorporated into policy discussions. The psychological literature on decision making shows that people's preferences are often determined by the way a choice is described to them and can change under different descriptions that appear to be equivalent.[8]

Analysis of environmental "facts" usually requires prior value decisions about level of detail, burden-of-proof, and quality of data. Thus, a value choice is implicit in almost every choice the technical analyst makes. But for reasons discussed later, these value choices are rarely identified in the technical analysis or in the public policy debate.

The Translation of All Value Questions into Economic Language

Another way in which values questions are distorted in the technical process into which they are relegated is through the translation of value questions to economic language. When technical experts recognize that particular value questions have to be considered in environmental decision making, the values are usually discussed in terms of economic considerations, in terms of costs and benefits and efficient markets. Although economics, as social science, is a valid attempt to

describe and predict what will happen within a society if it chooses certain economic behaviors, many economists do not hesitate to make prescriptive statements about economic behavior. Many economists, for example, assert that the option that makes the most efficient use of resources ought to be the preferred option. Once an economist makes an "ought" statement, however, he or she is tacitly assuming some ethical position. When such recommendations are made, economists are choosing one ethical approach over others, and that approach is most often some form of utilitarianism. The underlying assumption of utilitarianism is that an option should be chosen that creates the greatest happiness for the greatest number of people. Since an efficient market maximizes happiness by satisfying the greatest number of individual preferences, the economist usually asserts that the option which maximizes the efficiency of the market place is the "optimal" solution. This is a utilitarian formulation of the good.[9] It is a different formulation than other ethical formulations, and to the extent that the value assumption is not identified and remains hidden, the ethical basis for the final decision is never exposed, and other viable approaches are completely ignored.

The utilitarian approach raises additional ethical problems that cannot easily be answered from within a utilitarian system.[10] A utilitarian, for instance, must decide which alternatives will be entertained in the utilitarian calculus, which consequences of a given action will be considered, whose assessments of harms and benefits will be allowed, and what time scale will be used in assessing those consequences. The utilitarian framework, therefore, often rests upon imprecise judgments independent of, and prior to, the utility calculus itself.

Utilitarian methodology, moreover, cannot easily accommodate the rights individuals may have either to be protected from certain pollutants or to be spared from death-threatening situations. Most contemporary philosophers hold that utilitarian approaches must be supplemented by other ethical approaches, such as a Kantian approach, which stress such concepts as rights, justice, and due process as fundamental. The Kantian would resist many developmental strategies that may be justifiable on utilitarian grounds. More importantly, the utilitarian approach often assumes that various questions can be reduced to a quantifiable amount. Quantification of environmental or health benefits, however, is often difficult and sometimes impossible. For instance, what is the value of human life? Even if the problem of quantification can be solved, utilitarianism is still incapable of answering how benefits or costs should be distributed among potential losers and winners.[11] As a result, most commentators agree that a utilitarian analysis must be supplemented by concepts of distributive justice. Nevertheless, almost all value discussions one encounters in the environmental public policy debate are limited to some variant of the utilitarian approach. Although more sophisticated utilitarian approaches are capable of dealing with some of the problems mentioned above, all too frequently the value analyses one actually finds in the environmental public policy debates are over-simplified utilitarian calculations that more sophisticated utilitarians would likely reject.

The Pressure to Make Decisions Through Analysis of Costs and Benefits

One manifestation of the propensity to discuss all value questions in economic terms is the recent ascendency of cost-benefit analysis as the paradigmatic decision-making tool. Although most academic observers agree that cost-benefit analysis as a descriptive tool may initially be helpful to decision makers, provided that the ethical limitations of this approach are understood, most philosophers agree that mandatory cost-benefit analysis should not be used as a prescriptive decision-making tool. It is ironic that despite the fact that much has been written in the philosophical community of late about the weakness of cost-benefit analysis as a prescriptive decision-making tool, because of inherent difficulties in dealing with certain values questions and in quantifying benefits, governments with increasing frequency are being required to perform mandatory cost-benefit analysis. For instance the federal government is required to perform mandatory cost-benefit analysis as a decision tool by Executive Order 12291, issued by Ronald Reagan in 1981,[12] and many states now require mandatory cost-benefit analysis by law or executive order.

The value approach encountered in mandatory cost-benefit analysis often involves the assumption that values are nothing more than subjective preferences that can be determined in market situations. This position, however, ignores

the view of many philosophers, namely, that values are not only subjective preferences, but also have an objective content — that is, that value claims are not just felt; that they are capable of being judged to be sound or unsound. Seen in this way, value claims are more than individual preferences. Pricing mechanisms measuring preferences measure only the intensity of wants; they cannot evaluate which beliefs are morally superior. For instance, the right of an individual to be protected from PCBs in his or her water supply may be greater than the utility of such protection recognized by the market place. Such cases show that ethical questions are not reducible to questions of economics understood as efficient markets. Nevertheless, all one usually hears during the public policy debate on environmental issues is oversimplified versions of the utilitarian economic approach.

The Pressure for Regulatory Reform

Another cause of value distortion is pressure for reform to limit governmental regulatory activity. Most state governments and the federal government have been acutely aware of the pressure for strong regulatory reform that has existed since the middle of the 1970s. It has been so strong in the last five years that no administrator can long survive without giving considerable attention to reform issues. As a result, the rule-making activities of almost all government agencies now include elaborate public participation procedures, "sunset" provisions which require that all programs be reviewed on a periodic basis, various legislative oversight provisions, and mandatory cost-benefit analysis procedures.

The net effect of all of these reforms has been the creation of a climate in which it is almost impossible for an environmental administrator to adopt a regulation without first establishing a strong political consensus that the regulation is "necessary." Lobbyists for regulated industries, nevertheless, continue to call for regulatory reform as an important political priority on the grounds that environmental agencies axiomatically always adopt regulations that are unnecessary and that go far beyond the intent of the authorizing legislation. As a result, there has been significant and continuing effort on the part of government to "reform" environmental rule making. Although some of this reform is valid, much of it is not. According to Webster's dictionary, *reform* means "to amend or improve by change or removal of faults or abuses." The most recent pressure to reform environmental regulation, nonetheless, has been directed at establishing a considerably restricted meaning for the word. Those who have been pushing most vigorously for environmental regulatory reform usually assert that rational decision making should rely on such procedures as mandatory cost-benefit analysis and that rule making should be prohibited unless government agencies can clearly demonstrate that a particular activity creates a serious environmental problem with a high degree of scientific certainty. "Regulatory reform," therefore, is often a euphemism for mandatory cost-benefit analysis and strict quantitative risk assessment approaches.

Regulatory reform so constituted is a force aimed at preventing government agencies from making decisions when those decisions cannot be quantitatively justified in accordance with a very specific methodology. Whenever such regulatory reform is adopted, the government expert is then under considerable pressure to quantify and balance all issues on a single scale. As a result of this pressure, administrators are forced to reduce all aspects of each problem to some common measure in terms of which "objective" comparisons can be made. According to some common versions of this approach, all of the "fuzzy" values, such as rights, are either reduced to "hard data" or ignored, and the objectified values are measured in terms of prices as determined in market situations. When values cannot be ignored or quantified as prices, they are then translated into matters of human personal preference. The transformation of these values into personal preference, in turn, serves to discredit policy choices based on general principles believed to hold universally, such as theories of distributive justice.

In most cases, regulatory reform as it has most recently [been] formulated obscures rather than clarifies the kinds of ethical concerns and issues discussed in this essay. Although regulatory reform in its broadest sense, as the "improving" and "removing of abuses," should be a goal of all concerned citizens, current pressure for regulatory reform may actually create significant abuses by forcing administrative officials to balance things which should not be compared on the same scale, to quantify values arbitrarily which are inherently unquantifiable, and to use a decision methodology which distorts interests and values concerns.

The Tendency of Technical Analysis to be Incomplete

Value distortions also appear in environmental public policy making when incomplete technical analyses are performed. One of the primary causes of incomplete technical analyses is the tendency of analysts to examine environmental problems exclusively in terms of their own disciplines. To illustrate this common phenomenon, let us consider the following twist in the ancient story of the blindmen and the elephant. Four specially trained blindmen are asked to examine an elephant and describe what it is after touching it. The first blindman, who is specially trained to examine legs, determines that the elephant is cylindrical in shape and has a body of considerable mass. The second blindman who is specially trained to examine surface texture, asserts that elephants are large masses of wrinkled soft material. The third blindman who is specially trained to find tails, examines the tail of the elephant and asserts that the major characteristic of an elephant is a long flexible structure having the thickness of a two-inch rope. The fourth blindman who is specially trained to be sensitive to smell, asserts that the distinguishing characteristic of an elephant is its unique mixture of organic, peanut, and haylike fragrances.

The regulation of the nuclear power industry in this country provides a dramatic example of the tendency of the technical community to concentrate on those aspects of a problem that are best understood by the persons responsible for the analysis. Almost all of the debate on nuclear energy has been centered on the risk of accidents that can cause a release of radiation. However, accident-induced radiation releases are not the only reason why many are concerned about the wisdom of nuclear power. Some are very concerned about the relationship between nuclear power plant development and the resultant loss of ability to control the spread of nuclear weapons. Some commentators have ranked the policy importance of nuclear power risks in the following (decreasing) order: proliferation, theft, sabotage, accidents, routine emissions.[13] Nuclear engineering data is only very useful at the lower end of the policy importance continuum. However, since the nuclear power debate is usually conducted by a technical community trained to think about how to build a nuclear power plant, and thereby to minimize the risk of accidents, the debate concerning nuclear power has largely ignored the nuclear proliferation issue. This sort of tunnel vision may yet prove to be the most serious folly of all.

The technical community often focuses on those aspects of a problem it knows something about while ignoring others. It is true, of course, that no one person can fully be an expert on all of the many issues and factual questions that are of concern. What the public usually sees, however, is a debate about a narrow range of the technical issues with the participants in the debate acting as though they understand and are dealing with all issues that should be of concern to the public. In this way, the public policy debate is often a language game in which the jargon of the specialty of the analysts sets the allowable limits of where to start and stop the investigation. Value conflicts which should be resolved politically are then hidden in what look like rational and objective calculations.

K.S. Shrader-Frechette has discussed still another variant of incomplete analysis, what she calls the fallacy of unfinished business.[14] This fallacy arises out of the assumption that technical and environmental problems have only technical, but not social, ethical, or political solutions. The fallacy of unfinished business is the practice of formulating questions about environmental issues in such a way that the answers necessarily include technical solutions for the problems identified. An example given by the author focuses on whether "to store radioactive waste in salt mines, or in deep drilled wells, in solidified ceramic form or as a liquid inside double-walled steel tanks."[15] Although the question posed in this way requires a technical solution,

> the really intractable problem is not the technical one of what storage technique to adopt, but the ethical and social one, such as what risk we can impose on future generations and how we ought to determine the acceptability of a given risk. We have not answered questions such as these in part because we have been asking, not wrong questions but incomplete ones, questions that are epistemologically loaded, questions that presuppose a definition of a given problem for which only an answer in terms of the technological status quo counts as a solution.[16]

As another example, Shrader-Frechette asks whether we ought "to develop coal or nuclear fission in the United States Ohio River basin area, in order to meet the electric power demand between now and the year 2000?"[17] She points out that precisely because the formulation of this technological question allows only

for a technical answer in terms either of coal or nuclear fission, the EPA assessment of this question ignores alternative ethical, social, and political solutions to problems such as the conservation of energy.

The propensity to ask the incomplete question is built into the way that we develop new technology and solve technological problems. When a technology goes wrong, someone schooled in that technology is brought in to fix or analyze that technology. Likewise, when a technology is under consideration for future use, someone knowledgeable about that technology is often asked to assess that technology. The result is public policy that does not consider other potentially appropriate options. Once again the ethical questions posed by the public policy issue are confused by the process of relegating the problem to a narrow technical elite.

Finally, there is the problem of time pressure. The technical expert within a government agency is usually under pressure to make a technical assessment of alternatives in a timely fashion and to ignore any arbitrariness in so doing. This pressure tends to force the technical expert to analyze only what is genuinely predictable and calculable. Since a known technology is usually taken to be more predictable than alternatives that depend upon social or moral considerations, the technical expert usually focuses his or her attention on those alternatives that are most easily calculable and predictable, namely alternative technologies.

Distortions Caused by Narrow Focus on Risk Assessment

Value questions can also be distorted in risk assessment studies. It is often asserted in environmental public policy debates that a comparison of the risks associated with the technology in question with the risks posed by other activities is of central importance to responsible environmental decision making. Quantitative risk assessment is a statistical process that uses data from laboratory tests, epidemiological studies, or material failure rates to predict the probability of health costs that result from the use of various chemicals or technologies. Many technical experts act as if a weighing of risks is all that is necessary to give direction to public policy questions. It is often stated, for example, that nuclear power is an acceptable energy option because the risks involved with it compare favorably to risks created by the mining and burning of coal. The basic argument presumably is that because more people will die from mining and burning coal than will die from exposure to an operational nuclear power plant, nuclear power is the acceptable energy option. Although on the surface such straightforward reliance on quantitative risk assessment seems reasonable, the approach, nevertheless, frequently ignores many ethical problems that need to be taken into consideration in the policy debate.[18] These problems include the following:

Problems of Scientific Uncertainty

Risk assessment involves so much scientific uncertainty that comparison of risks may often be no better than intuitive speculation. In some cases, for instance, risk assessment depends on the evaluation of epidemiological data about rates of exposure in laboratory animal experiments. There are many reasons why uncertainties arise: (a) epidemiological data relating to dose rates to human disease does not exist for most problems; (b) there are significant problems in extrapolating from animals to humans; (c) effects of exposure may take years or generations to materialize; (d) human experimentation is excluded on ethical grounds; and finally (e) experiments must often assume an average dose rate, thereby providing little or no information about very high dose rates. Because of these kinds of uncertainties, quantitative risk assessment cannot be relied upon to support the fine distinctions required for accurate public policy decision making.

Questions Concerning the Distribution of Harm

If a particular hazard is not equally distributed among subgroups in a population, certain ethical questions arise. For instance, migrant farm workers may be exposed to pesticides when picking oranges in concentrations thousands of times higher than those of city dwellers whose rate is determined solely by eating an occasional breakfast orange. Considerations of due process or other rights theories may require that the migrant worker be protected from a pesticide in addition to the average consumer of oranges.

The Need to Distinguish Accepted Risks from Those That Are Not Accepted

When a hazard is not well understood by the public that will bear the risks, questions arise

about due process and the protection of individual rights. A risk that is voluntarily accepted is different in kind from a risk that is involuntarily forced upon someone.[19] For instance, someone may accept the risk associated with his or her decision to smoke cigarettes alone, but resent the additional risks imposed by others who smoke in the same room. Free and informed consent to risks from toxic substances in the environment is not a realistic goal, since most exposure is indirect, involuntary, and difficult to observe.

The Need to Consider the Type of Harm That Will Be Created by the Risk

Risks that are grave and dangerous are different in kind from risks that involve less dire consequences. If certain activities create a risk of death, even though that risk may be small, that risk may be more objectionable than a risk of sickness, even though the risk associated with the sickness has a higher probability. The risk of a nuclear power plant accident, for example, although perhaps small, may be more objectionable than the risk to the public of an explosion at a fossil fuel plant.

The Need to Distinguish Background Facts from Ethical Questions

Questions of risk often confuse the normal with the moral. We often hear comparisons of a new risk with background conditions. Although we have no choice but to accept the background conditions, the new risks may, nevertheless, be objectionable. If one person in 100,000 dies because of background radiation from the atmosphere, it does not necessarily follow that it is ethically appropriate to choose deliberately to expose people to low levels of radiation that are likely to produce a rate of death from increased exposure equal to or less than one death in 100,000.

The Need to Describe Criteria for Acceptability of Risks

The term *acceptable risks* includes a normative dimension that is not usually defended in public policy debate. For example, risks to a small proportion of a human population are often asserted to be "acceptable." When large numbers of humans are involved, however, there can be a considerable number of statistical casualties. If the government accepts that one in 100,000 people will get cancer from a particular activity, it is willing to permit 2,500 cancer deaths in the United States. Despite the low risk statistically, few people would consider so many deaths to be a clearly "acceptable" risk. Nevertheless, small numerical risks may encourage policy makers to believe that they can responsibly proceed with an activity in some cases when it is not actually warranted. For instance, the Rasmussen Report, the report relied upon by the Nuclear Regulatory Commission before the accident at Three Mile Island, predicted that the probability of a meltdown was one in 17,000. Although this seemed to suggest a reasonable risk associated with nuclear power plant failure, when one added this risk to the risks of all other power plants that were expected to be in existence by the time the report was published, the risk increased to one meltdown every five years.[20]

Distortions Caused by Improper Placement of Burden of Proof

Another way in which value questions get distorted in public debate is through the improper placement of burden of proof. Because of the complexity of many public health and environmental issues and because of the economic consequences to those who are regulated when government action is taken, many of the laws that authorize government regulation put the burden of proof of showing risk or injury on the government agencies responsible for the rule making. Since the incredible complexities involved make it almost impossible for the party with the burden of proof to sustain that burden, government has been scandalously slow in regulating such substances as pesticides.[21] In such cases, there are so many technical difficulties with mathematical models, dose-response assumptions, and the statistical analysis that problems can nearly always be quickly identified by those who want to assert that the burden of proof has not been met. Precisely because of the inherent complexities of these issues, guesswork at almost all stages of problem analysis is necessary, with potential for mistakes in either direction.

If the benefit of the doubt does not go to the public, then those interested in restraining government can, with little effort, regularly succeed in preventing government regulation. Scientists inside and outside the agency are very skilled in exposing technical weaknesses in an adversary's position, particularly when that adversary is viewed to have the burden of proof.

Moreover, greater weight and authority is given to those insiders and outsiders that are viewed to have the greater technical resources, frequently a decisive advantage to those who can muster more resources than the government. As a result, government is often troubled about what to do when its knowledge is viewed to be inadequate but it is under pressure to take action. In such situations, however, the value questions that are created by inadequate information are very rarely identified as such. Instead, the public debate focuses on the "technical" aspects of the issue under consideration.

At various times the burden of proof shifts back and forth between government and regulated industry. For instance, although a permit applicant may be viewed to have the burden of showing that a new plant will not create a water pollution problem from a point source discharge, the permit reviewer may assume a presumption of innocence about the "non-point" pollution discharges to the stream. As Serge Taylor points out in *Making Bureaucracies Think*, burden of proof questions are often level of detail questions. In many permit review situations, when government is faced with the question of whether it has enough information at the proper level of detail to make an informed decision, it decides not to require additional information on the grounds that it is too costly.

The very posing of environmental questions in terms of empirical science often has the effect of enhancing the expectation that the agency technical analysts will be able to determine the environmental impacts of various projects with available methodologies. When public expectation is created in this way, the government may assume a burden of proof that it cannot meet, especially if the theoretical basis for predicting outcomes is not available. For instance, when a government agency accepts the responsibility for deciding whether a low-level waste dump will have adverse environmental impacts, the government may be assuming a burden of proof for which existing technology cannot provide answers with an acceptable level of scientific certainty. Because most environmental impact analysis is discussed in "science-like" terminology, notwithstanding the fact that the scientific predictive basis is sometimes so weak that prediction is not much better than untutored intuitive speculation, there is, nevertheless, nearly always a strong, but unfounded, belief in the credibility of the analysis that shifts burden of proof to the analyst.

Since scientists in environmental agencies are usually not in a position to suspend judgment until all of the proof is in, nor to wait out the long latency periods that may be necessary to determine whether the project will create the expected outcomes, the "science-like" jargon of the analysis is misleading. Environmental impact analysis should be distinguished from other areas of science in which the scientist can selectively focus on problems that can be settled by verifiable scientific procedures.

Because of the scientific uncertainty in environmental problems, technical experts within government have often refused to act out of fear that they will enrage a legislator who will then have them fired if it is discovered that they have imposed unsupportable costs upon a constituent. This reluctance is also consistent with most scientific training. The scientist is trained to be very conservative in asserting cause and effect relationships. No traditionally trained scientist will act quickly if there is reason to suspect uncertainty about the cause of an environmental problem. If a position, once taken, is later discredited by subsequent scientific research, the technical person who suggested the cause and effect relationship may suffer significant peer sanctions for being associated with a faulty scientific hypothesis.

Value Distortions Caused by
the Technical Training of the Analyst

Another cause of value distortion in environmental analysis is the narrow scientific training of most scientists. Scientists are taught to value scientific truths above other truths because, ideally, scientific truths are usually never accepted until they have been publicly tested. In contrast, since the "truth" of ethical positions cannot be empirically verified in the same way, and is therefore less "objective" than scientific truth, many scientifically trained people express open hostility to ethical discourse and value judgments. Ethical questions are often called "soft" or "fuzzy" in contrast with scientific questions and solutions that are supposed to be "hard." As a result, quantitative criteria tend to crowd out qualitative criteria. Because quantitative disputes can be resolved on technical grounds and value disputes cannot, disagreements tend to get settled on analytical technical grounds.

Some technically trained administrators go so far as to equate rationality with science and irrationality or raw emotion with ethics on the grounds that value questions cannot be decided scientifically. Those who do not go quite this far, nevertheless, often act as if ethical questions are less significant or less relevant than the "hard" scientific facts. Engineers often express open hostility and frustration with having to analyze the value questions that are raised in environmental impact analysis. On one occasion, for example, an environmental engineer who was given the task of analyzing the aesthetic impact of a substantial reduction in water flow on the Great Falls of the Passaic River in New Jersey in a proposed water diversion project asserted that aesthetic values were "Mickey Mouse" and that environmental groups that were raising aesthetic issues were being "irrational."

Because of the primacy given to scientific truths by technically trained persons, issues that can be dealt with on quantitative terms are more sympathetically considered than issues that involve more difficult qualitative or ethical concerns. Most environmental administrators, for instance, will deal more quickly, seriously, and sympathetically with an issue requiring the setting of standards for bacteria to prevent *living* people from getting a water-borne disease than they will with issues involving our duty to future generations to preserve wilderness areas or save species from extinction.

Scientists are trained to report impersonal data from which all subjective elements have been removed, to reduce all issues to a scale that can be quantitatively manipulated, to think of nature as lifeless substance with measurable analytic parameters, and to transform social questions into technical questions. When a problem has been reduced to quantitative terms, to the language of science and mathematics, technically trained people almost invariably critique the mathematical model exclusively on a scientific-mathematical basis, omitting any critique of the transformation of the qualitative values into quantitative terms. For example, although there was much discussion within the New Jersey Department of Environmental Protection during the 1970s about the science of modeling a river in order to predict pollution loads and set water-quality based effluent limitations, there was almost no discussion during that time about the ethical assumptions of the model, even though the model included provisions for distributing available stream capacity among various industrial and domestic users and for reserving the river's pollution-absorbing capacity for future use.

In distributing loads among users and reserving stream capacity for future use the engineers had to make value judgments and to translate those value judgments into quantitative factors that could be incorporated into the model. Although these factors had far-reaching consequences, never to my knowledge did any of the technical staff challenge the value assumptions that were used in determining them. This situation was startling, I believe, given the fact that at one point the model permitted all domestic sewage treatment plants in New Jersey to use as much of a stream's assimilative capacity as they needed provided that they employed a minimum secondary treatment, while industrial users, on the other hand, were required to accept whatever effluent limitations were necessary to meet stream standards after ten percent of New Jersey's stream capacity was reserved for *all* future uses. In the end, the public policy considerations that had the most important long-term consequences were based upon the value premises of a few engineers that were never disclosed, discussed, or critiqued by any of the technical experts inside or outside the agency.

Recommendations

Although it is admittedly important that we continue our attempts to enhance our analytical power to make mathematical estimates of risks, costs, and outcomes, it is even more important that we at long last develop the technical skill to deal with the ethical and value dimensions of our environmental problems. To this end, I recommend the following measures, which, if they are to be successful, require not only improvements in public policy procedures within government, but also the active support and involvement of concerned citizens.

First, environmental decision makers must come to understand value questions. At a minimum, concerned citizens must demand that environmental decision makers are capable of distinguishing issues of fact from ethical issues. In addition, it is vitally important to make sure that ethical questions and various ethical positions are adequately considered in environmental decision-making processes. To this end, persons concerned about environmental ethical issues should vigorously include themselves in debates about public policy and refuse to accept a narrow utilitarian calculus as the sole basis for a rational choice.

Second, ethical positions must be disclosed. As government inevitably increases its ability to calculate costs and benefits, reform of environmental rule making must insure that value assumptions are disclosed as part of the decision-making process. For example, if a given chemical is not going to be regulated because a human life has been assigned a value of $75,000, then surely that fact must be disclosed. Similarly, in risk assessments the value assumptions included in any risk comparison should be disclosed as well as the timetables used to calculate the consequences of any activity and any alternatives to that activity. Better access to information is a precondition of public decisions on regulatory standards.

Third, solutions to environmental problems must consider social alternatives. Everyone should strive to see that public policy questions are as open as possible to social as well as technical solutions. Environmental administrators should not adopt a technical solution until they have fully examined, identified, and rejected all possible social solutions.

Fourth, economic analyses must expose their value assumptions. Interested parties should critique all cost-benefit analyses in order to identify the basic ethical assumptions and presumptions. Citizens should resist any law that requires that all environmental decisions be made strictly in accordance with a cost-benefit calculation.

Finally, environmental decisions must be viewed primarily as ethical choices. It is important in an age of increasing scientific complexity that interested parties attempt to understand the value positions and ethical issues that lie underneath scientifically derived policy choices. Experts and concerned citizens must realize that crucial policy choices concerning environmental pollution, nuclear power, and toxic chemicals are value judgments, matters of morality, social and political judgments. In a democracy these judgments should not be made by "experts," but rather by the people and their elected representatives. As long as the value component of environmental decision making is relegated to technical experts who are not experts in ethics and value studies, and indeed are reluctant by training and disposition to deal with value issues at all, environmental policy that is critically flawed by value distortions will continue to be the rule, not the exception.

(e) Using Science in Environmental Policy: Can Canada do better?[†]

Ted Schrecker ──────────────────────────────

INTRODUCTION: LEARNING FROM THE HEADLINES

In the summer of 1997, Canadians were offered an unusually candid examination of how our government uses science in making environmental policy. Three respected scientists, one of whom had only recently left the Department of Fisheries and Oceans (DFO), published a stinging article in which they argued that 'bureaucratic influence' had seriously compromised the scientific basis for fisheries management.[1] To support this claim, they cited the history of overly optimistic stock assessments that contributed to the eventual collapse of the north Atlantic cod fishery in 1992, and the questionable scientific basis for DFO's position on the minimum water flows from Alcan's hydroelectric facilities on British Columbia's Nechako River that were consistent with the protection of salmon habitat.

By the time the article appeared, it was clear that grotesque mistakes had been made in the management of the cod fishery, leading to its collapse and the subsequent closure of the fishery by DFO.[2] The article described a process in which the raw data for fisheries stock assessments originated with DFO scientists in their roles as members of various subcommittees of the Canadian Atlantic Fisheries Scientific Advisory Committee (CAFSAC). Subcommittee reports, in turn, 'constituted the primary source of information for the CAFSAC Steering Committee,' but 'were not available to the public. Following its vetting of these reports, the Steering Committee prepared Advisory Documents which formed the primary source of scientific information for the Atlantic Groundfish Advisory Committee (AGAC), the committee of industry and government (federal and provincial) representatives that provided recommendations to the senior managers and planners within the management structure of the DFO.'[3] I suggest

later in the chapter that the channels of power and influence that led to the perpetuation of fisheries mismanagement can only be understood with reference to the broader political economy of fisheries management in Atlantic Canada.

By 1997, much of the history of the BC case had been well documented, because a newly elected BC government had directed the BC Utilities Commission (BCUC) in 1993 to conduct an environmental review of Alcan's current operations and of proposals to expand Alcan's hydroelectric facilities (the Kemano completion proposals). Before that review, the federal government had gone to extraordinary lengths to avoid a publicly visible examination of the environmental impacts of Alcan's operations. Its strategy included convening an ad hoc working group under the chairmanship of David Strangway, then president of the University of British Columbia, with instructions to take the flow rates that Alcan considered essential to its expansion plans and work around them. The four days of closed meetings held by the working group did not include the DFO scientists who had previously been most directly involved in assessing the environmental impacts of the proposed smelter expansion.[4] At the end of the BCUC's lengthy hearings, an environmentalist coalition (the Rivers Defence Coalition, or RDC) was moved to ask, 'How is it possible that new information arose in the Strangway Working Group negotiations in four days that satisfied the DFO members that the salmon would be protected under the Alcan flows when the best scientists in the DFO had insisted it was impossible for the better part of a decade?'[5] This seems like a reasonable question. It is also a question of the kind that outsiders to the process of decision-making in Canadian environmental policy do not usually get to ask, and indeed in this case did not get to ask until well after the fact. As if

---

† From E. Parson, ed., *Governing the Environment: Persistent Challenges, Uncertain Innovations* (Toronto: University of Toronto Press, 2001), pp. 31–72. Reproduced with the permission of the publisher.

to underscore this point, the federal government subsequently exempted the Kemano completion by Cabinet order from the application of the federal Environmental Assessment and Review Process Guidelines Order as it then existed. The legality of the exemption was challenged in the courts, but ultimately upheld.

Nothing about the fisheries science example is unique. Canadian studies have consistently identified a pattern of environmental policy-making that is secretive and opaque, organized around negotiations that involve only a limited number of parties and are insulated from public scrutiny.[6] ...

ELEMENTS OF CONTEXT: MARKET ECONOMY AND ORGANIZATIONAL STRUCTURE

Understanding the place of science in environmental policy requires reference both to the characteristics of industrialized market economies and to the organizational setting within which scientists work. Under each of these headings, many elements are common across national cultures and political institutions, but some are distinctive to the Canadian context.

Environmental policy in any market economy must be analysed with reference to the distinctive power of business,[14] and specifically to investors' 'power to define reality' by way of their investment or disinvestment choices.[15] Most environmental policy initiatives directly or indirectly imply some erosion of property rights, at least in situations where those rights are exercised for income-generating purposes. The qualifier is important because the history of Canadian environmental law provides a number of examples in which property rights (for example, riparian rights) established under common law were circumscribed by legislation in order to improve the prospects for industrial enterprise.[16] In any market economy, and especially given today's hypermobility of capital both within and among national jurisdictions, academic cant about the compatibility between environment and development ('jobs') is supremely irrelevant. The primary of investors' property rights gives them a unique ability to involve third parties in contests about the appropriate balance among the competing values of economic return and environmental protection: to practise 'job blackmail.'[17] Advocates for environmental conservation nor-

mally lack comparable resources, and both industry and government routinely oppose legislative changes that would create judicially enforceable environmental rights. Such rights would give litigants outside government the ability to involve third parties, with or without their agreement,[18] just as investors have always been able to do by way of the simple threat to close the mine or locate the new plant elsewhere. Even though environmental rights could never realistically compete for primacy with property rights over the long term, they might decisively alter the terms of specific conflicts.

Who are the environmentalists? The term is convenient, but also problematic from the perspective of political economy. At the personal level, they may be people who can take for granted a level of material security that much of the rest of the population cannot. Whether experiences of affluence are individual or shared, they may help to account for the spread of what Ronald Inglehart has called post-materialist values.[19] On the other hand, commitments to environmental conservation, however intense they are, may or may not motivate the politically effective segments of the public[20] to make investments of time, money, and other political resources comparable to those that may be mobilized with respect to such issues as local property values, cable rates, or the taxation of investment income. Another way of stating this point is that support for environmental conservation is often a mile wide, but only a few inches deep. The distinction is normally well understood by political elites; thus, polls like the one that found that '94% of Canadians from coast to coast would support a federal endangered species act'[21] are likely to be taken with a grain of salt, and addressed by way of responses that are largely symbolic.

Canada's economic mix introduces a further dimension to the analysis because Canada, although highly urbanized,[22] remains heavily reliant on non-urban resource industries and the export revenues they generate. This dependence is clear at the national level[23] and even more dramatic at the regional level. 'Natural resources, including agricultural products, make up 79 percent of Atlantic Canada's merchandise exports, 80 percent of Alberta's, 74 percent of Saskatchewan's, and 77 percent of B.C.'s.'[24] The one-industry town, usually reliant on a resource industry, remains a fundamental feature of the Canadian social and political landscape. It is only a slight exaggeration to say that if resource-based industries (including agriculture) were to disappear, there would be little economic rationale for the continued human habitation of large sections of Canada outside the Quebec-Windsor corridor beyond the levels sufficient to sustain subsistence production and an overwhelmingly export-oriented tourism and entertainment industry.

These facts of economic and political life can lead governments to permit (or require) the public to absorb extraordinarily high costs associated with environmental damage in situations where the economic future of a community dependent on a particular resource industry is at stake.[25] Kathryn Harrison has persuasively identified 'blame avoidance' as a central issue in environmental policy with reference to the relations among levels of government.[26] Blame avoidance is also relevant in other senses, and would be even if Canada were a unitary state. To paraphrase Tip O'Neil, all politics is regional politics. The incentives for short-termism in resource management, which is another way of describing the socialization of environmental costs, are immense. Few governments will risk policies that would have the effect of shutting down a town, or an industry, in the interests of environmental conservation. This is true *even if* the result of failure to do so is, as in the case of the Atlantic fishery, the eventual destruction of the resource base itself.[27] It is preferable, from a political point of view, for governments to permit continued exploitation until a moratorium is decided on by the fish,[28] or by the trees and the international trading regime.[29] The dynamic here is the same one encountered in policy toward industries that are declining for other reasons: they are allowed to struggle on, often with substantial public subsidy (including environmental subsidy in the form of unregulated and uncompensated environmental damage) until their demise can credibly be ascribed to market conditions in a way that minimizes the attribution of responsibility to governments.[30]

Prescriptions for improving the use of science in environmental policy must be cognizant of these elements of political economy. They must also incorporate an awareness of the organizational context within which scientists work, and within which scientific information is used by governments. Perhaps the most significant element of this context is hierarchy: few outsiders understand the intensely hierarchical structure of Canadian departments of government. Backbench Members of Parliament routinely misidentify the locus of decision-making authority by referring to mid-level managers in departments like Environment Canada or Health Canada as 'regulators.' Such individuals normally do not make binding decisions on their own, either in Canada or elsewhere, about the content or the implementation of regulations. Furthermore, their career paths may depend on the extent to which their findings and recommendations, as transmitted up the departmental or agency food chain, are viewed as congruent with or troublesome for the government's objectives — including concern with matters that are unmentioned in the relevant enabling legislation, such as regional economic development and trade policy, but are very much part of the policy context.

Hutchings and his colleagues may therefore have erred in emphasizing the 'bureaucratic' influence on science. Most people who work as scientists in government, and for that matter outside it, are also bureaucrats in the Weberian sense. They work in a context of fairly clear reporting relationships, in terms of both superiors and subordinates, and their work is structured in a way that would make them relatively easy to replace without extensive disruption of the organization's functioning. The reference to bureaucracy is highly relevant, however, with respect to the process by which scientific findings are communicated to senior management, ministers, and ultimately those outside government. In a delightful article on how resource-management agencies produce environmental-impact statements that support the objectives of their leaders, David Bella points out that routes of information transmission, and the process of converting scientific findings into policy advice and recommendations, are critically important for understanding how and why 'systemic distortion arises through the behaviors of ordinary people doing what is commonly expected of them within organizational systems.'[31] The nature of information flow, and the hierarchical and lateral division of labour within the organization, make it almost impossible to assign individual responsibility for such distortions. In Bella's hypothetical, the occupants of four roles — a high-level manager, a mid-level manager, a professional technologist, and a 'troublemaker' — have explanations that show each did his or her job as defined with reference to the organization's internal structure.

Bella's analysis suggests the value of understanding the role of scientists in government by way of the complementary concepts of filters and reinforcements. Philosopher of science Jon Elster notes the importance for social science of filter explanations, which involve choices made by a particular actor with a stake in the results. 'Military financed research may be analyzed by a filter-explanation. If academic personnel apply for military funds in order to be able to conduct the research that they would have done in any case ... the Department of Defence may serve as a filter that selects some applications and rejects others. The resulting composition of research will be beneficial to the military interests, while wholly unintended by the individual scientists, who can argue truthfully that no one has told him what to do.'[32] Filters may operate in another way as well. Staying with the example of academic scientists for the moment, one can argue that if attracting substantial research funding from external sources is a significant determinant of promotion and tenure decisions within the academic world, then the composition of academic departments will shift over time to emphasize specialties and normative orientations that are compatible with the priorities of external sponsors.

The operation of filters depends, however, on the availability of a highly receptive audience for the selective provision of reinforcements. Competition for income, promotion, and security within any organization demands the ability to learn fast, and security within any organization demands the ability to learn fast, and the successful adapt with striking facility to the moving target represented by changing objectives and changing requirements for success within the institution.... [I]ndividual self-interest, which must always be a central element of social-scientific explanation, leads those who work within an organization to alter their behavior in response to organizational priorities as they are reflected in the filtering process. Often, scientists and people working at the science/policy interface within government are not cynical or careerist; indeed, some have gone to extraordinary lengths to demonstrate their commitment both to sound science and to environmental conservation. The organizational context does, however, determine the price of that commitment, which can be very high.[34]

Some such limits on what scientists and other professionals in government can say or do are generic, while others are specific to Canada's political institutions. The latter include the extraordinary concentration of power in the hands of the political executive (Cabinet) and, within Cabinet, in the hands of the prime minister or premier and his entourage.[35] 'It is hardly possible to overemphasize the fact that the Canadian prime minister has no outer limits defining his political authority within the government.'[36] An organizational point of particular significance is that deputy ministers (the senior civil servants within any given department) normally control the flow of information, advice, and recommendations to ministers. They also have substantial political responsibilities, which are reflected in the fact that they are chosen not by the minister whom they serve but rather by the prime minister or premier.[37] '[B]oth Prime Ministers Mulroney and Chrétien reminded' deputy ministers 'from time to time ... that deputy ministers work for the prime minister.'[38] They would in any event not have risen so far in the bureaucratic ranks without demonstrating a substantial ability to adapt to the changing political agenda as defined from above: what the Privy Council Office calls 'being corporate.'[39]

. . . .

The organizational factors that give Canadian political executives a remarkable degree of control over the environmental policy and implementation agenda[42] are magnified by full line forcing. The term refers to the ability of political candidates or parties to define electoral competition in terms of a choice among a limited number of 'full lines' of policies, and it is central to understanding policy outcomes in all parliamentary systems because of the strength of party discipline. Students to whom this process is explained by analogy to a town with three or four supermarkets, each of which offers only one basket of groceries, are thereafter notably more sceptical about the rhetoric of democracy. They begin to understand the importance for political analysis of asking who has, and who does not have, the resources needed to convince the supermarket manager, or regional purchasing agent, to change the contents of the market basket.

The U.S. congressional system, by contrast, offers at least the potential for multiple reporting channels. Although the heads of executive-branch agencies like the United States Environmental Protection Agency (EPA) are appointed by the president, subject to congressional confirmation, the potential exists for congressional oversight with respect not only to annual appropriations, but also to the fit between agency policies and the stated goals of the legislation under which agencies operate. Such oversight can be initiated independently of the executive branch, and sometimes even in direct opposition to it. Neither executive-branch agencies like EPA nor legislative-branch agencies like the Congressional Budget Office or the now-deceased Office of Technology Assessment (OTA) are shielded from the demands of political expediency. This became particularly clear at EPA during the first Reagan administration;[43] the elimination of OTA by the Republican congressional majority shortly after the 1994 elections is another case in point. However, the complicated institutional connections among weak party discipline, the separation of powers, the fixed interval between elections, and the accessibility of judicial review of many regulatory decisions probably make it easier for U.S. agencies with environmental responsibilities to cultivate clienteles outside government than for their Canadian department counterparts. This fact is important because departments or agencies whose statutory mandates emphasize environmental conservation or protection of public health lack an obvious clientele, apart from an amorphous and geographically diffuse 'public.' By contrast, departments of agriculture, industry, or natural resources (to give but a few examples) define their roles with reference to the economic prospects of specific client industries and, at least by implication, of the regions that rely on those industries for jobs and tax revenue.[44]

SCIENCE AND UNCERTAINTY: NEITHER SCIENCE NOR POLICY IS 'VALUE-FREE'

One set of problems at the interface of science and policy involves situations in which scientists working for government agencies, or interacting with them in other capacities (for examples, as contractors or grant recipients) are directed to lie, to reinterpret findings in ways that support a policy position that has already been decided upon, or not to disclose findings that might be politically inconvenient. Such situations represent relatively straightforward confrontations between truth and power, to use Wildavsky's famous categories. The preceding discussion of filters and reinforcements suggests that a more common situation is likely to be the one in which scientists, especially those with administrative responsibilities, understand the context well enough to anticipate the reactions a particular set of findings will elicit, and to create the spin that corresponds to organizational priorities or promises to expand their own career horizons. As noted, the institutional characteristics of Canadian environmental policy make it very difficult even to identify the frequency with which each kind of situation occurs, much less to study individual cases in adequate detail.

A separate area of study, which raises a distinct set of substantive questions, involves the conceptually complicated set of problems associated with uncertainty and ambiguity in scientific findings. The most familiar examples of such uncertainty arise in the field of toxic-substances control. At first glance such questions as 'Will a particular chemical cause cancer or birth defects in human beings when they are exposed to it in the environment?' appear straightforward. However, even a strictly provisional answer to this question means resolving conflicts associated with pathways of exposure and uptake; dose-response relations; and the appropriate basis, if any, for extrapolating from toxicological findings in non-human species.[45] Although perhaps less familiar, the uncertainties in some other areas of science are if anything even more pervasive. For example: what is the minimum contiguous area of undisturbed habitat necessary to prevent the extinction of a particular wildlife population? Based on that conclusion, will a contemplated program of habitat protection prevent the extinction of a species like the Florida panther, the Sonora tiger salamander, or the northern spotted owl?[46]

These questions are deliberately stated in a naive and oversimplified manner in order to highlight the contrast between the view of science as an enterprise capable of delivering 'just the facts, ma'am ... and the multiple levels of inference and methodological choice that normally characterize the scientific research on which environmental policy depends. One of the most fundamental methodological choices involves the appropriate standard of proof. In 1978, Talbot Page[47] identified the regulation of toxic chemicals as exemplifying a class of 'environmental risks' that present challenges different from those associated with 'the more familiar pollution and resource depletion problems.' Central to Page's analysis, which has now been incorporated into numerous studies of regulatory policy, was the distinction between false positives and false negatives, or Type I and Type II errors. The scientific enterprise, very much like an idealized version of the criminal-justice system, is organized around minimizing the occurrence of false positives — that is, incorrect rejections of the null hypothesis. (The null hypothesis is that a particular chemical does not cause the harmful effect of concern in human beings who are exposed to it in the natural environment, or that the defendant did not commit the crime with which she is charged.) Indeed the process of scientific peer review often consists primarily of identifying all the possible methodological shortcomings of a study that might cause its authors incorrectly to have rejected the null hypothesis. One often-used illustration is the demand for statistical significance at the 95 per cent confidence level — corresponding to only one chance in 20 that the observed effect occurred by chance — before positive findings are considered sufficiently robust for publication.

Good reasons exist for conducting scientific research in this way, but many problems can arise when results of scientific research are used as a basis for public policy without an adequate understanding of uncertainty. For instance, the costs of acting on false negatives and false positives may be highly 'asymmetrical,' in Page's words. The consequences of adopting as the basis for public policy the same standards of proof that would be used by scientists may be catastrophic — for example, if discharges of an environmental contaminant that subsequently turns out to cause birth defects are permitted because the evidence of harm is unclear or equivocal. When the stakes are high enough, it is surprisingly easy to make the evidence appear unclear or equivocal, as economist Thomas Crocker suggests in his reference to a 'cigarette company standard of proof,' invoking the tobacco industry's long-standing claim that 'the etiology of cigarette smoking and lung cancer has not been "scientifically demonstrated."' Like the tobacco industry, generators of environmental impacts will clearly 'wish to minimize the probability of the policymaker treating as true some hypothesized environmental impact source that really is not true,' even when the evidence of harm is overwhelming.[48]

The choice to study a particular set of hypothetical cause-effect relations further before acting is unexceptionable in the laboratory context, where the stakes are limited to delays in publishing the next article or submitting the next grant application. The same may not be true in the policy context, where such choices may imply accepting a particular set of potential consequences on behalf of a large number of third parties.[49] Consequently 'a risk/benefit assessment,' which may be implicit or even intuitive, 'is part of every public policy action which is based upon the interpretation of the results of a scientific investigation.'[50] In the words of a former EPA official:

> The regulator's every action — or inaction — represents a decision of some kind. For example, postponing action on some chemical until there is better information is a decision; taking precautionary action in the meantime is a decision; delaying action for the time being because of limited resources or other priorities is a decision.
>
> There is no way to escape this difficulty. A regulator may say that he is postponing a decision, but this is just another way of saying that he has decided to postpone action. Whichever way he goes, he runs the risk of making the wrong decision in the midst of pervasive uncertainty. The law of average says that he will not be right every time. Therein lies the inevitability of being wrong.[51]

The task of those who make and implement environmental policy is best described in terms of integrating: the best available scientific evidence; the costs of obtaining additional evidence, recognizing that sometimes such evidence is simply impossible to obtain; and the potential consequences, which may themselves be highly uncertain, of being wrong in different kinds of ways.[52]

Science, qua science, simply cannot answer questions about the appropriate standard of proof in such contexts. The choices must be based on considerations of policy, or values, or ethics. Scientists have no special competence when it comes to making such choices. The choice of a threshold of statistical significance, for instance, is 'an issue of pure policy'; in other words, there is no reason a priori to demand a 95 per cent confidence level for policy purposes rather than 90 per cent, or 80 per cent, or even 51 per cent.[53] The appropriate basis for the choice involves the anticipated consequences, keeping in mind again the warning that one cannot always be right.

It may help here to return to the example of the legal system. In criminal cases, at least in theory, every element of an offence must normally be proved beyond a reasonable doubt before the defendant is found guilty. The underlying presumption is that allowing a few guilty defendants to go free is less objectionable than convicting innocent ones.[54] In civil cases, a defendant may be found liable for damages on the balance of probabilities, which is a considerably less demanding standard. This state of affairs reflects the belief, whether or not it is an accurate belief, that undeserved loss in a lawsuit is a less objectionable outcome than undeserved conviction on criminal charges, and therefore need not be guarded against with the same determination.

Meaningful questions that are relevant to environmental policy can seldom be resolved in the simple, dichotomous fashion that might be inferred from the preceding discussion. It is therefore particularly important for scientists and non-scientists alike the recognize and communicate the importance of what Shrader-Frechette and McCoy have called methodological value judgments.[55] Such judgments are in no way unscientific, and the phrase does not imply a criticism of scientists who make them. Indeed, 'scientists make methodological rule, rather than another. For example, whenever one uses a particular research design because of available computer software, one is making a methodological value judgment that the research design is adequate.... Even collecting data requires use of methodological value judgments because one must make evaluative assumptions about what data to collect and what to ignore, how to interpret the data, and how to avoid erroneous interpretations. For example, one must always simplify any scientific problem, in order to make it tractable.'[56] There is no hard and fast line between such methodological value judgments and what McGarity has called 'science policy' decisions in situations of incomplete or ambiguous evidence. The best one can do is to indicate that choices of the former kind usually occur, chronologically and institutionally, before scientific researchers present results or findings: for example, when study designs are being selected, standards of proof defined, or study populations chosen.

... The use of the theory of island biogeography as the basis for estimating the minimum appropriate size of nature reserves, according to Shrader-Frechette and McCoy, exemplifies the need for multiple methodological value judgments. With respect to the health effects of toxic substances, methodological value judgments are incorporated in choices about (for example) the

appropriate basis for extrapolating from high to low exposures, and the relative weight accorded to various forms of evidence from non-human species and to human evidence from epidemiological studies.[57] A common methodological value judgment in environmental-impact statements, especially when they are prepared by or for project proponents, involves identifying and quantifying the impacts of the development in question in isolation. Like the hypothetical studies of metal illness referred to above, each study that results may be a masterpiece, yet even taken together they will provide a fatally incomplete account of the project's effects on the environment. An alternative approach would instead consider those impacts in combination with those of other undertakings that are proceeding simultaneously, or that are actually required by the project.[58] Thus, value judgments are integral not only to the evaluation of scientific evidence for purposes of public policy, but also to the research enterprise itself.

Analysts of environmental policy therefore need to concentrate attention not only on 'better science,' but also on defining the appropriate values for environmental policy. We can draw important lessons from a real-world example: Cancer researcher Beverley Paigen was actively critical of governments' slow response to the health concerns of Love Canal area residents, who discovered in the late 1970s they were living on top of a disused chemical waste dump. She describes a conversation she had

> with a Health Department epidemiologist concerning the data on adverse pregnancy outcomes at Love Canal. We both agreed that we should take the conservative approach only to find that in every case we disagreed over what the conservative approach was. To him 'conservative' meant that we must be very cautious about concluding that Love Canal was an *unsafe* place to live. The evidence had to be compelling because substantial financial resources were needed to correct the problem. To me 'conservative' meant that we must be very cautious about concluding that Love canal was a *safe* place to live. The evidence had to be compelling because the public health consequences of an error were considerable. And so we disagreed on specific detail after specific detail.
>
> This is not a scientific issue, nor can it be resolved by scientific methods. The issue is ethical, for it is a value judgement to decide whether to make errors on the side of protecting human health or on the side of conserving state resources.[59]

In ecosystem management more broadly, the kinds and sources of scientific uncertainty are somewhat different,[60] but competing ideas of conservatism could be identified with respect, for example, to decisions about the maximum permissible harvest of a variety of renewable resources.

Cases like the one described by Paigen account for the growing appeal of the precautionary principle. The principle was apparently first articulated in the context of regulating toxic pollution of the North Sea, and with specific reference to the possible consequences of failing to take regulatory action in the absence of conclusive scientific evidence.[61] It has since been articulated in numerous other forms, some of which make explicit reference to 'the scientist's need for 95% certainty.'[62] A lukewarm version was also incorporated into *Agenda 21*, the document that emerged from the United Nations Conference on Environment and Development (the Earth Summit).[63] More expansive, even extravagant notions of the precautionary principle involve both standards of proof and the burden of proof. In one version, 'the precautionary principle ... presumes that any regulatory procedure should begin with a presumption against the discharge of wastes unless the proponent can adequately demonstrate that harm is not likely to occur.'[64] (But what should constitute an adequate demonstration that harm is not likely to occur? This formulation simply ignores the values embodied in the choice of a standard of proof.) Another author wonders: 'What if the burden of proof was [sic] on the other side? If chemical manufacturers or developers had to 'prove' with 95% certainty that a particular substance or activity did not cause an adverse effect on the environment....'[65]

The short answer is that any jurisdiction that imposed such a test on all pollutant discharges or industrial activities, unless it were imposed in a strictly rhetorical way — like the provisions on human rights in the old Soviet constitution — would rapidly cease to have an industrial economy. Such an economic cataclysm would have its own, highly destructive, consequences for public health. On a less apocalyptic scale, Leiss points out that applying such a test only to new technologies, chemical compounds, or industrial undertakings is likely actually to be counterproductive by slowing the replacement of old processes and products by new, more technologically sophisticated (and less environmentally destructive) ones.[66] So the precautionary principle must

itself be treated with caution when it incorporates reference to the burden of proof, as well as the standard of proof. The principle is, indeed, best described as (a) a commitment to acknowledging that values judgments are unavoidable when choosing a standard of proof for purposes of environmental management, and (b) an explicit rejection of unreflective 'conservatism' oriented toward minimizing false positives in the manner of laboratory science, without regard to the potential consequences.

EVALUATING THE USE OF SCIENCE IN ENVIRONMENTAL POLICY

In some respects, then, concern about the infusion of political (or, more broadly, non-scientific) considerations into environmental management is misplaced. Such considerations will *always* be involved, in the sense that governments must resolve tensions or conflicts among competing values and the scientific enterprise itself is not value-free. Some explicitly normative framework is needed to evaluate the way science is used in environmental policy. Such a framework is needed for another reason, as well. When governments make decisions about acceptable levels of harm, to their subjects and arguably to the natural environment as well, even rudimentary democratic principles dictate the importance of process and informed consent. 'An acceptable decision process reflects a political philosophy, that is, the principles that govern the interaction between different groups.'[67]

. . . .

The preceding considerations suggest the value of assessing the use of scientific evidence in environmental policy with reference to criteria that have to do with fairness and the nature of political obligation, but that are exogenous to any particular set of political institutions. Such an approach is exemplified by Elisabeth Paté's thoughtful and much-neglected effort to set out eight principles for the acceptability of risk-related decision processes:

- A sound legal basis with clear understanding of individual and societal rights, burden of proof, and treatment of economic effects.
- An information system (risks, costs, benefits, redistribution, etc.) with appropriate expression of uncertainties and assumptions.

- A communication system such that this information can circulate among concerned individuals and organizations and be fully understood.
- A good criterion for selection of experts and a mechanism of aggregation of experts' opinions that reflects the characteristics of the problem.
- A public review process in which the information used can be examined and criticized by intervenors, industry, etc.
- A clear but flexible set of decision criteria that reflect public preferences given the nature of the hazard, the state of information, and the economic implication of the considered regulations.
- An appropriate conflict-resolution mechanism (mediation, arbitration, etc.)
- A feedback mechanism gathered and used in an appropriate and predictable way to measure the regulatory effects a posteriori, including those that had escaped initial policy analysis.[72]

These criteria stand in dramatic contrast not only to the inference that risks are acceptable because formal mechanisms of accountability exists, but also to much of the contemporary literature on risk communication and risk management. I have drawn on Paté's work in order to identify three core institutional prerequisites for the responsible use of scientific evidence in Canadian environmental policy.

First, sound firewalls[73] must be constructed between the scientific inquiry that provides inputs for public policy and the process of evaluating those inputs. Scientific researchers working in or for government must be unrestricted in their ability to publicize their findings, without having to take into account considerations of political advantage or expediency. This is clearly what Hutchings and colleagues had in mind when they recommended that 'the science and stock assessments conducted for government be provided by a publicly funded, but politically independent, institution (somewhat analogous to the Canadian judiciary)' one perhaps modelled on the Fisheries Research Board of Canada, which was absorbed into DFO in 1979.[74] It also appears to be what Leiss has in mind in suggesting the potential usefulness of independent, issue-specific expert panels under the auspices of the Royal Society of Canada.[75] The depth of the chasm between this ideal and recent practice is

evident from DFO's own media-relations guidelines (as of 1997), described by DFO authors as 'similar to those of other government departments': 'Public servants should be prepared to openly provide *factual information* to the public and the media within their areas of responsibility *that describes or explains programs or policies that have been announced or implemented by this government....* Public servants should not go beyond this discussion of factual information.'[76] A more thoroughly Orwellian notion of what constitutes factual information, on full disclosure, is hard to imagine.[77]

Second, because of the pervasiveness of scientific uncertainty and because waiting for that uncertainty to be resolved itself represents a significant policy decision, the relevant decision-makers must articulate the principles on which they resolve scientific uncertainty in situations where the evidence is incomplete or inconclusive. These principles must include explicit reference to the values that guide the choice of a standard of proof. On this point the precautionary principle is genuinely significant, even though it does not represent a decision rule but rather a guide to choosing among competing decision rules. Principles for resolving scientific uncertainty must also include what Vern Walker has called 'a default rule for making a finding when the weight of evidence is in "equipoise" — that is, when it appears ... that the evidence for a proposition seems equal in weight to the evidence for its negation.'[78] In practice, such situations are relatively infrequent. Decision-makers often think such a situation exists when it does not, because of conceptual confusion about such issues as the distinction between failure to find an effect and a finding of 'no effect.'[79] However, unless decision-makers are required to articulate such a 'tie-breaking rule,'[80] they are unlikely to come to grips with such conceptual issues, since there are few rewards for doing so.

Third, and perhaps most importantly, the evidentiary basis for all environmental policy and management decisions must be publicly disclosed in enough detail to enable outsiders to identify each step in the decision-making process. This disclosure should include an identification of *all* the evidence, whether generated within government or outside it, that has been considered, and should contain enough detail to enable the outsider to identify methodological value judgments that have been incorporated in what might otherwise be opaque scientific 'findings.' This point is especially important with respect to un-published studies, and to assessments of scientific evidence that have been conducted within government.[81] Ideally, academic researchers whose work is used for purposes of governmental decision-making would further be required to disclose the sources and amounts of all their grant and contract support; in practice, this requirement is probably impossible to implement, since no scientific journal requires a comparable level of disclosure. The general principle here is that a comprehensive, publicly accessible record should document the evidence for governments' environmental policy and management decisions — including, crucially, the decision not to begin new policy initiatives or to change existing operational routines.

This third criterion is essential to ensuring the implementation of the first two. Without requirements for such extensive disclosure, governments with the best intentions in the world will find that existing patterns of accommodation, bargaining, and blackmail quickly reassert themselves. For better or for worse, openness or transparency with respect to the evidentiary basis for decisions need not entail transparency with respect to the decision-making process itself. 'The basic premise is simply increased transparency in the scientific advice used. Plainly decision makers may well still not act on such advice, but openness would assure that they could no longer claim to have done so, and their incorporation of other considerations would be more explicit.'[82]

Various actors may have a stake in confusing the conceptual issues I have identified, and consequently in opposing the disclosure that might aid in their clarification. For example, the federally appointed task force that surveyed the socio-economic wreckage created by the collapse of the cod fishery belatedly pointed out that evidence of overcapacity and overcapitalization in the fishing and fish-processing industries had been ignored for more than a decade.[83] This oversight may be attributable to federal efforts to 'restructure' the industry that actually intensified the economic pressure to catch more fish.[84] Under the circumstances, it was hardly to be expected that ensuring the long-term viability of the resource base would be a priority. Control over scientific information can also be used to forestall the development of potentially intractable conflicts between economic activity and environmental conservation.[85] Especially in Canada,

governments play a crucial role in financing scientific research, and they may simply decline to support a particular line of inquiry that promises to be politically troublesome, unless they can exert strict control over both the research design and the dissemination of findings. As Leiss and Chociolko point out, in such situations, 'Quite simply, *it is preferable not know.*'[86]

For this reason among others, further research is needed into the conditions under which government departments or agencies are most likely to conduct or support, and to disseminate, research on environmental quality that is likely to generate demands for substantive policy responses. One hypothesis is that departments without a clearly defined commercial clientele, like environment departments, are more likely to do so than are departments, such as agriculture or health, that have environmental policy and regulatory responsibilities but also well-defined relations with industrial client groups.

Firms or industries that view environmental conservation initiatives as an economic threat are likely to contend that all policy and regulatory decisions should be 'purely science-based,' or to use some similar phrase. They invoke the cognitive authority of science (who, after all, can be against science?) for strategic purposes, in order to avoid discussing concepts like standards of proof in the terms that are appropriate. Governments may pursue the same course of action in order to defend decisions that have been reached primarily on grounds unrelated to either science or the environment, such as trade-policy implications or the avoidance of major economic disruptions.[87] Thus, the idea of science-based environmental policy is superficially attractive, yet ultimately pernicious....

... [Needed] is a framework for making environmental policy decisions that is sensitive to the kinds of questions that can be answered by science, and the kinds that cannot — in other words, that incorporates the requisites identified in section 4 of this chapter.

Little evidence suggests that Canadian public policy at the national level is moving in this direction. The federal departments most directly responsible for protecting public health and the environment, Health Canada's Health Protection Branch (HPB) and Environment Canada, have suffered major cuts in their research budgets and complements of scientific personnel over the past few years. Whether or not the result was intended, the cuts have probably compromised both basic research and the ability to evaluate scientific research done by others.[112] Meanwhile three internal government initiatives have addressed the uses of science in policy: the Council of Science and Technology Advisors (CSTA), which reports to the Cabinet Committee on Economic Union and 'is composed of representatives of external advisory boards which report to Ministers of federal science-based departments and agencies';[113] the Committee of Science Assistant Deputy Ministers (ADMs); and the so-called 5NR group, which involves the five departments with natural-resource management responsibilities: Agriculture and Agri-Food, Environment, Fisheries and Oceans, Health, and Natural Resources.[114] However, few substantive statutory or organizational changes relevant to the use of scientific evidence in environmental policy have been implemented.

PART C
Risk Assessment

(a) A Critical Review of Current Issues in Risk Assessment and Risk Management[†]

Steve E. Hrudey ————————————————————————————

1. INTRODUCTION

Risk assessment and risk management are both activities which presume we already understand what we are attempting to assess or manage. Often this rudimentary requirement is not satisfied because various participants to these activities have failed to seek or to reach any consensus on what they mean by risk. To avoid replicating this flaw, I will adopt and expand the concept of Kaplan and Garrick (1981). They proposed risk to be the answer to three questions:

* what can go wrong?
* how likely is it?
* what are the consequences?

Kaplan and Garrick proposed that these answers can be represented as a set of triplets which correspond to:

* a set of hazardous scenarios
* a set of probability distributions for those scenarios occurring
* a set of consequences for the hazardous scenarios.

To complete this concept we should add:

* a time frame over which the risk will be considered and
* a perspective of reality.

The time frame is necessary to establish the scope of the risk being considered which the perspective of reality is necessary to reflect those inevitable judgments which [underlay] any characterization of risk. This conception leads to some unavoidable conclusions about risk.

1. Risk cannot be objective represented by a single number. The multidimensional character of risk can only be distilled into a single number by assigning implicit or explicit weighting factors to various numerical components and by adopting some algorithm to combine them. Any such decisions must involve judgment and therefore cannot be cloaked in the authority of strict objectivity.
2. Given the foregoing, risks cannot be ranked on strictly objective grounds. A strictly objective ranking scheme would be based upon numerical sorting from largest to

---

† "Eco-Research Chair: Environmental Risk Management." Working Paper. ERC 96–8, University of Alberta. An updated and modified version of this working paper was subsequently published as Hrudey, E.E. (1977) "Current needs in environmental risk management" *Environmental Reviews* 5: 121–29. Reproduced with permission of the author.

smallest, a task which can only be achieved unambiguously, by reducing risk to a single number.

3. Risk is not "real". Hazards, which are essential components of a risk, can be real. Likewise, the consequences can be real, as can the time frame. However, the essential probability component is always a prediction or expectation. While it may be based upon substantial relevant experience (e.g. extensive pipeline failure statistics), the composite notion of risk for any real circumstance always involves inference and judgment such that risk probability predictions are inevitably statements of belief (elaborated in section 5.1). When all the foregoing components of risk are combined, risk cannot be considered to be "real". We can and should focus on the reliability of the evidentiary basis for risk predictions. Most of us are likely inclined to place more reliance on a prediction based upon extensive, relevant experience than on any individual's intuition or "gut" reaction.

With these foundations specified:

> **risk assessment** should represent a rigorous, adaptive and interactive process of evaluating the nature and, to the maximum extent possible, the quantitative character of risks.
>
> **risk management** should represent an interactive design, planning, negotiation and/or regulation process aimed at reducing identified risks to levels which can be tolerated by potentially affected parties or by society overall.

The models for these processes which have dominated U.S. practices in health and environmental risk assessment, and consequently the risk literature, are largely derived from the "red book" proposals of the National Academy of Sciences (1983). This report stressed the importance of separating the practice of risk assessment from risk management to avoid having the political considerations involved in risk management interfere with the goal of having risk assessment make the best use of scientific knowledge to characterize the risks. An unfortunate byproduct of that separation has been a failure to recognize the inevitable interactions between risk management and risk assessment and the value of pursuing tiered and/or iterative processes. Some

redress on their linkage has been proposed by the National Research Council (1994). Likewise, an alternative model which explicitly offers the advantages of a staged approach has been proposed in the draft Canadian standard for risk management (Canadian Standards Association 1996).

2. INPUTS TO RISK ASSESSMENT AND RISK MANAGEMENT

This review is primarily focused on health and environmental risks, rather the entire spectrum of risks such as business, engineering process or financial risks, in search of comprehensive yet coherent treatment.

2.1. Model Issues

Models will be discussed in their broadest sense with some brief, specific applications. A model is simply a means for organizing information to express our conception of reality. In this sense, environmental and health risk assessment is predicted on a model involving a chain of causation whereby a receptor is exposed to an agent via one or more environmental media giving rise to a dose of the agent which may cause an adverse effect (Figure 1). This model must be recognized as an enormous oversimplification which does not realistically represent the web of causal and contributory risk factors we believe to be associated with any disease process. The disciplines of epidemiology and/or toxicology provide the primary methodologies for gathering evidence in support of this model.

This model incorporates several concepts and principles which govern the performance of health risk assessment. These include:

- health risks can only be studied quantitatively by studying populations rather than individuals (humans in epidemiology and animals in toxicology).
- individual health risk is an abstract quantity which must be inferred from evidence of population health risk.
- epidemiological studies can demonstrate association (correlation) of an effect with exposure to an agent, but cannot solely prove causation.
- there is a hierarchy of epidemiological study designs such that analytical studies (case con-

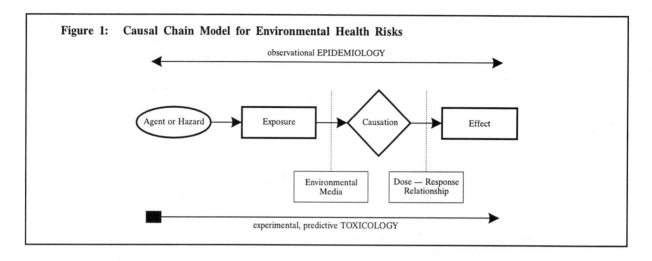

Figure 1: Causal Chain Model for Environmental Health Risks

trol or cohort studies) are needed to provide any substantial support for causal inference. Experimental designs (e.g. clinical trials), the strongest study designs for developing causal inference, are not available for environmental epidemiology because of practical and ethical limitations.

• toxicology is both an art and a science. The science goes with the observational and experimental activities while the art goes with the interpretation and predictive (risk assessment) activities.

• the dose makes the poison because all substances are toxic in sufficient dose.

• as the quantity of exposure to an agent increases within its harmful range, either or both the probability and/or the severity of adverse effects will increase, thereby forming the basis for the dose response relationship.

• humans are animals so that much can be learned from the study of toxic effects occurring in animals exposed to an agent, but anatomical and physiological similarities and differences must be recognized and reconciled.

• adverse effects of agents will not be universal in character, rather they will be specific to one or more mechanisms of action giving rise to various specific adverse effects.

• adverse effects will occur via molecular level chemical reactions and/or physical processes. They are classified as adverse because of their outcome with respect to the function of the affected host, but most of these chemical reactions are not otherwise uniquely or universally distinguishable from normal life processes.

• the consequences of exposure to any agent depend upon the toxicokinetics (absorption, distribution, metabolism and excretion) and the toxicodynamics (mechanisms of action at the target site) of the agent.

• there is a hierarchy of weight of evidence for identifying the potential hazard to humans associated with any agent which rises from theoretical predictions based on chemical structure as being least compelling, up to replicated, reliable epidemiological evidence, supported by plausible and specific biological mechanisms, as being most compelling.

• knowledge of the exposure (the dose) of an agent and the dose-response relationship of an agent is essential to provide the basis for any quantitative prediction of the likelihood of adverse health effects.

Elaboration of each of these premises is beyond the scope of this review. However, the underlying theme of causal inference and supporting scientific knowledge deserves some consideration. Causal inference underlines the entire activity of risk assessment. The tenuous nature of causal inference must be acknowledged because the evidentiary basis is entirely empirical. Consequently, the fallibility of our knowledge is subject to the fallibility of our finite observations (Rothman 1988: 6). Yet, humans have a compulsion to explain events according to a cause and we are extremely reluctant to accept events as occurring by random chance alone (Paulos 1995: 85).

We have adapted a variety of processes to improve our confidence in causal inference, including: seeking consensus, appealing to authority, performing replication and relying on inductive logic. However, none of these can overcome the limitations of our empirical approach. As Rothman notes: *"empirical science does not provide irrefutable statements about nature* (Rothman 1988: 9)." Although Susser (1988: 195) provides a convincing defense of inductive logic as an effective tool for advancing our knowledge of nature, we are left with an inescapable discrepancy between an ideal of the scientific search for the truth about nature and the reality of how our scientific knowledge develops. Science is the product of the efforts of scientists who are subject to all the individual failings of humans. Likewise, scientific institutions are subject to the organizational and sociological flaws of other human institutions so the realization of science as an idealized search for the truth is not attainable. Yet, these limitations are not grounds for accepting all theories, scientific or otherwise, as equally useful. Experience has shown us remarkable human progress through the use of our imperfect Science and we can usually distinguish theories which have negligible merit.

We need to be able to recognize the limitations of our scientific institutions and relate them realistically to decision-making approaches in society. In this regard, the advice of Paulos (1995: 25) for judging the reliability of social forecasts may be useful for judging risk assessments. He regards social forecasts as likely to be more reliable:

- if predictions are short term rather than long term,
- if they deal with simple rather than complex phenomena,
- if they deal with pairs of closely associated variables rather than many subtle interactions,
- if they are expressed as broad anticipations rather than precise assertions, and
- if they are not coloured by the forecaster's intentions.

A realistic perspective on the limitations of the scientific method is necessary to hold a nature perspective of the predictions generated by risk assessment, thereby leading to their wise use in risk management.

. . . .

Generally, more attention is directed to data issues than to model issues, perhaps because the former is easier to address with the skills we hold. Yet, incorrect models are more likely than incorrect data to cause major errors in risk assessment and risk management.

2.2 Data Issues

Data needs will be considered in relation to our ability to efficiently evaluate agents for the likelihood that they pose unacceptable risks to human health or the environment. In this regard the sequence of questions proposed by NRC (National Research Council 1994: 145) is helpful:

- Is the agent emitted to the environment?
- Is the agent stable enough to be transported from its source to a population?

These first two questions lead to a decision point. If there is no emission of the agent or if the agent is too unstable to survive to a point of population exposure (provided it is not transformed into some other harmful agent), the evaluation may be completed without further assessment. If there is emission and the agent survives to cause exposure, then we must ask:

- who is exposed, to how much and for how long?
- what is the relationship between exposure (dose) and response (effect) for humans or other ecological receptors?

Data is needed to characterize emissions, transport and fate, exposure and toxicity.

These needs commonly encounter common problems of:

- inadequate background exposure data
- inadequate guidance for monitoring and analytical methods which are both agent and media specific
- inadequate databases for collection, storage and efficient retrieval of relevant data.

General procedures for evaluating data were suggested by the National Research Council (1994: 255) as:

- develop data quality guidelines that require all data submitted to meet minimal quality levels relative to their intended use before being applied in risk assessment

- conduct critical review of data-gathering and data-management systems to insure that quality and quantity of data are sufficient for regulatory requirements
- document procedures used to develop data, including why particular analysis or measurement methods were chosen and their limitations (sources of systematic error, precision, accuracy, detection and quantitation limits)
- characterize and document data, including why particular analysis or measurement methods were chosen and their limitations (sources or systematic error, precision, accuracy, detection and quantitation limits)
- account for uncertainty and variability in collection of data

2.3 Uncertainty Issues

Uncertainty has received increasing attention in risk assessment and risk management in the past five years. This is a major improvement because previous reliance on point estimates of risk seriously misrepresented the reliability of risk estimates and the confidence we should place in them.

Another improvement has been a recognition of the need to distinguish uncertainty arising from variability (heterogeneity) from true uncertainty (lack of knowledge). These concepts are easily confused because both can be represented by probability distributions. However, these two concepts must be distinguished because they arise from different sources and they reflect different requirements for analysis and management.

Variability for any parameter means that there are truly values for that parameter (i.e. individual age or body mass in an exposed population). Additional study or research can only characterize variability better, but it cannot reduce variability.

True uncertainty, in contrast, is most easily recognized for a parameter which, in principle, has a single value, but that true value is not known (the population of Canada on this specific day in 1996, or the median age of all Canadians on this specific day in 1996). We can also be uncertain about each of the individual values in a variable distribution of values. True uncertainty can also exist about models and relationships, such as elements of the cause-effect chain model (Figure 1).

Variability applies to all the stages of data collection and modeling. Emissions will vary in amount and character over time and space. Transport and fate will vary as a function of environmental variables (wind speed, ambient temperature, solar radiation). Exposures will vary according to differences in activity over time and space and in response to physiological and behavioural variations (breathing rate, metabolic rates, food and water consumption). Dose-response behaviour will vary as a function of susceptibility among individuals, with an individual over time and as a result of differing individual characteristics (age, sex, body mass, nutritional and health status). ...

. . . .

True uncertainty deals with how confident we can be in our state of knowledge and what we should do with our knowledge. This consists of (Finkel 1990):

- parameter uncertainty (measurement errors, random errors and systematic errors)
- model uncertainty (surrogate variables, excluded variables, abnormal conditions, incorrect model form)
- decision-rule uncertainty (risk measures, summary statistics, definition of acceptability, utility functions, aggregation of utility for social welfare, tradeoffs).

Both risk assessment and risk management demand characterization of both variability and true uncertainty. Ignoring uncertainty means operating with blind faith, whereas confronting uncertainty means confronting reality.

In summary, we need to know the full scope of what we know and how sure we are about what we know. Confronting uncertainty can seem to be a discouraging exercise. But, just as there are clear limits to our knowledge, there are also limits to our lack of knowledge (Hoffman 1996). For illustration, there are three absolute certainties we should recognize with regard to health risk:

- everyone has a lifetime probability of death = 1
- there is a finite and non-trivial probability of the earth having another catastrophic collision with a celestial body capable of making our planet uninhabitable for humans
- zero risk does not, nor has it ever existed.

Explicit consideration of uncertainty, within the bounds of our knowledge, should protect risk assessors and managers from the charge which has been leveled at some regulatory risk assessors (Hattis and Kennedy 1986: 71): "*They're never right, but they're always sure*".

3. GOALS FOR RISK ASSESSMENT

. . . .

Risk assessment should provide sufficient understanding of the dimensions and character of risk to help us recognize the nature of the tradeoffs which must be made to manage risks in the face of uncertainty. This recognition is necessary to keep us from making decisions which our limited technical knowledge can reliably show us to be wrong. Put more directly, risk assessment of disinfection of drinking water with chlorine suggests that we should seek prudent means for reducing the formation of disinfection by-products while avoiding any compromise to be pathogen disinfection efficiency. But, risk assessment should not encourage anyone to abandon or impair chlorination of drinking water to avoid a predicted, but unverifiable cancer risk and simultaneously accept the inevitability of infectious disease transmission. Consequently, the decision by Peruvian environmental regulators to reduce chlorination of well waters over concerns with cancer risk, thereby contributing to a cholera outbreak of 300,000 cases with over 3500 deaths, provides a stark example of risk assessment failing to meet our minimum goal (Anderson 1991).

Risk assessment must be recognized as an aid to informed risk decision-making in risk management. However, risk assessment cannot make the decision. It may not even make clear what is the "best" decision, because the definition of "best" is unavoidably dependent on value-based preferences. As noted in section 2, most of the critical judgments required to characterize environmental risks require some imposition of science-policy to compensate for unattainable scientific knowledge (e.g. low dose extrapolation for evaluating health effects from environmental level exposures). In recognition of this reality the National Academy of Sciences review of U.S. Environmental Protection Agency risk assessment protocols (NRC 1994) noted: "*The principle of separation of risk assessment from risk management*

has led to systematic downplaying of the science-policy judgments embedded in risk assessment. Risk assessment is accordingly sometimes mistakenly perceived as a search for 'truth' independent of management concerns."

Even to the extent that risk assessment can approximate scientific "truth", knowing what to do with the "truth" can be as, or more difficult than knowing what is the "truth" (Finkel 1990). Consequently, more detailed and accurate risk assessment will not make risk management any easier, because difficult choices and tradeoffs will still have to be made. However, we should expect that better risk assessment should make the evidentiary basis for risk management decisions more reliable, thereby creating to the possibility of "better" risk management.

4. GOALS FOR RISK MANAGEMENT

Goals for risk management have been articulated for some time, yet our progress towards achieving more effective risk management has been slow. Morgan (1981) proposed five goals for improving risk management which remain valid today:

* improve how risk management systems characterize and deal with uncertainty
* broaden the focus of risk management systems so they do not miss the big picture or the inevitable risk tradeoffs
* avoid undue emphasis on immediate global solutions rather than allowing alternative and incremental approaches
* avoid the drive to assign blame which inevitably creates an adversarial process, rather than a flexible and adaptive risk management process
* improve the promotion of consensus and collaboration among stakeholders.

Risk management must be developed with a full understanding of the character and uncertainty of risk estimates. This understanding must be used to make informed judgments which weigh benefits of various risk management options so we will avoid making dumb decisions. In this regard, Hattis and Kennedy (1986: 71) quoted Ashford's pragmatic goal for risk management as being: "*to bound the set of not clearly incorrect answers.*"

Risk management also requires recognition of risk tradeoffs (Graham and Wiener 1995).

Figure 2: A global ranking for managing carcinogenic risk

Exposure (levels and/or numbers of people)

		HIGH	LOW
Potency	HIGH	BAD: develop actions	POSSIBLE CONCERN: identify problems
	LOW	POSSIBLE CONCERN: identify problems	LIKELY OK: watch for new evidence

Experience suggests that human nature is inclined to prefer, at least by default, unknown risks which will arise when risk management causes some activity to be abandoned or modified. As long as risk management only focuses on the reduction in risk achieved by modifying those activities being regulated, the true nature of the risk tradeoffs which may be involved will not be weighed. Clearly, if risk management seeks to reduce risks overall, rather than merely transferring them, risk tradeoffs must be fully explored. Likewise, we need to be sure that risk management is at least capable of sorting out the big issues before we get lost in the infinite detail of specific issues. So, for example, carcinogen risk management needs to recognize both the scale and the interactions of the carcinogenic potency (which ranges over 100,000,000 fold) with human exposure (which likely spans at least as wide a numerical range) to guide risk management (Figure 2).

An incremental and iterative process for risk management is both realistic and preferable. The premise that one should proceed linearly from a risk assessment through risk management to provide the ideal and ultimate solution is rarely attained nor even desirable. An incremental and iterative process has been effectively captured in the proposed CSA risk management standard (Canadian Standards Association 1996).

The problems with seeking to assign blame in adversarial risk management versus promoting consensus and collaborative solutions have been addressed by Leiss and Chociolko (1994). They demonstrate through the analysis of several case studies that stakeholders in a risk controversy generally seek to have some other party take responsibility for assuming the consequences of a risk. If risk management can be recognized by all stakeholders as a fundamentally political process demanding tradeoffs, then parties can avoid taking absolute positions of "right" and "wrong" based on claims of having scientific truth on their side. Having to negotiate the "truth" is not a viable prospect; negotiating policy choices may be. A multi-stakeholder process must acknowledge the inevitable uncertainties which create the need for science-policy choices. Only with a pragmatic approach can stakeholders develop a mature understanding of the issues and proceed with negotiating acceptable tradeoffs.

. . . .

5. GOALS FOR RISK COMMUNICATION

Risk communication has received enormous attention in the literature, as well as in practice over the past decade. Most attention has been directed towards risk communication with the public, based upon the mistaken belief that public misunderstandings about risks cause most risk controversies. The quality of communication among different disciplines involved in risk assessment and between risk assessors and risk managers has received much less attention. However, if confusion is rampant between risk assessors and risk managers, effective risk communication with the public will be unattainable.

5.1 Communication Among Risk Assessors and with Risk Managers

Carcinogens have dominated the environmental agenda since the 1960s and are only now being challenged by other issues like reproductive toxicology (e.g. "environmental estrogens") for top billing. Given the attention received and the billions of dollars devoted to biomedical research on cancer, the public should be forgiven for expecting the scientific community to have reached a consensus on cancer risk issues. Yet, when surveyed for agreement with the statement: *"There is no safe level of exposure to a cancer-causing agent"*, almost one in five toxicologists either agreed or strongly agreed that there was no safe level of exposure to a carcinogen (Kraus et al. 1992: 217). When subcategorized according to employer, only 5% of industry toxicologists believed in the absence of safety for carcinogens compared with 20% for government toxicologists and 34% for academic toxicologists. Given these disparities, is it any wonder that a majority of the public believe there can be no safe level of exposure to a carcinogen? Logically, if no level can be considered safe, then all of our environmental criteria for carcinogens must be unsafe. This paradox prompted Hrudey and Krewski (1995) to provide an explanation of quantitative cancer risk estimation for environmental scientists to demonstrate how they can reach their own informed conclusions, thereby avoiding contributing to public confusion.

A more recent polling of Canadian toxicologists for their agreement with the statement: *"Experts are able to make accurate estimates of health risks from chemicals in the environment"* found that 43% agreed or strongly agreed but 53% disagreed or strongly disagreed (Slovic et al. 1995). Clearly, the public has justification for being cynical about environmental risk assessment. Such confusion amplifies risk communication problems as in the recent mad cow disease crisis. Douglas Hurd (1996) observed that when the media is pressing politicians for absolute answers: *"The minister turns to the scientist. 'Well, Minister,' he says, 'it is not very simple, the risk is very small, we cannot exactly quantify it, more research is needed.' The minister is asked at once to convert the uncertainties of scientific life into the certainties of public reassurance. Since a minister is not an alchemist, he finds this difficult, even impossible."*

· · · ·

Finally, risk assessors need to explore the logic and language they use in communicating

their findings to risk managers. Problems such as failing to distinguish statistical inference from causal inference, statistical significance from practical significance and association from causation (e.g. referring to evidence of an association from an epidemiological study as showing a "rink" between exposure and outcome) are often encountered (Jardine and Hrudey 1996).

5.2 Communication of Risk Professionals with the Public

Because risk management invariably involves elements of human behaviour, risk communication with the public must be recognized as an essential element of risk management, rather than a simple public relations exercise to be undertaken once risk management decisions have already been made. Despite much rhetoric embracing the need for better risk communication, there remains a prevalent perspective that risk communication need only educate the public about the expert risk assessments so that the public's risk perceptions can be replaced with the expert's risk assessment. Rather than this top-down perspective, there must be a meaningful two way interchange between those proposing to manage the risks and those potentially affected by the risks. This exchange must involve the risk managers learning what the affected public already knows or believes about the risks and what insights the public may be able to offer about options for managing the risk and making the necessary and inevitable tradeoffs. Risk managers will not be able to achieve this dialogue if they do not fully appreciate the practical limitations of risk assessment predictions.

Ultimately, risk communication must develop a mature understanding of what we know about risks and what we can realistically expect to manage. We cannot hold our scientific knowledge to be so objective as to be beyond question without simultaneously raising unreasonable expectations for what risk assessment and risk management can and should achieve. As Douglas Hurd (1996) stated: *"Tolerable human existence depends upon the balancing of risks not their abolition.... The aim of political and business leaders, of educators in every profession, should be to reinforce our sense of balance, not to hold up the empty prospect of a risk-free world."*

(b)   Is a Scientific Assessment of Risk Possible? Value Assumptions in the Canadian Alachlor Controversy[†]

Conrad Brunk, Lawrence Haworth and Brenda Lee ——————————

INTRODUCTION

Increasingly our society relies upon government regulatory agencies to protect its people, its institutions and its environment from the negative impacts of new technologies. These agencies are saddled with the task of deciding among strongly conflicting viewpoints represented by a wide range of interest groups and "value communities" within the society. When regulatory decisions are made some interests and values are protected while others are curtailed.

Because the actions of government regulatory agencies profoundly affect the liberties and opportunities of individuals and corporations, the basic norms of justice require that these actions be based upon a clearly articulated rationale, not seriously biased in favour of the values of one interest group against the values of others. That is to say, within the liberal, democratic tradition the rationale by which the government intervenes in the lives of its citizens requires either a social consensus or neutrality vis-à-vis the competing values and interests affected by it.

The idea that this regulatory process might be conducted according to the terms of an objective and socially neutral "science" is a tantalizing prospect. If science is objective and value-free it can arbitrate between competing views about social policy options by demonstrating which ones impose the greatest costs or risks upon the society and which ones generate the greatest compensating benefits; and it can do so by appealing to empirically demonstrable data and scientific principles universally accepted across a pluralistic society. Hence, the emergence of "regulatory" or "mandated" science — the enlistment of science in the aid of government regulation.[2]

An increasingly significant aspect of this regulatory function of governments involves the attempt to protect consumers and the general public from products and activities that pose unacceptably high levels of risk. The private sector also must increasingly accommodate its activities to the requirements and standards imposed by the public regulatory sector. Both government and industry, therefore, have need of reliable risk assessments to undergird their regulatory or management decisions. Consequently, there has developed a strong market for rigorous and reliable risk assessment and risk management methodologies to aid in these decisions.

In its classical expressions risk assessment is said to have two stages. The first is the stage of risk estimation,[3] at which what is thought to be a purely factual determination of the level of risk, free of social and other value judgments, is made. It is simply a measure of the magnitude of the harm involved if a hazard occurs, multiplied by the probability of its occurrence — factors thought to be empirically discernible and measurable. Hence the popular references to "quantitative" or "scientific" risk assessment.[4] Risk, as the product of the two factors, is thus thought to be an objectively determinable fact resident in the world.

Only after an objective estimation of the level of risk has been completed is one qualified to move on to the second stage — that of risk evaluation. This second stage, unlike the first, is generally recognized to be normative: it is the stage at which a determination is made concerning the *acceptability* of the risk levels identified at the first. Since the second stage involves appeal to a norm or standard of acceptability (a "safety" standard), it requires an explicit invo-

---

[†] From *Dialogue* 30 (1991): 235–45. Reproduced by permission of the author and the Canadian Philosophical Association, University of Ottawa. See appendix for notes or references.

cation of values. Still, whatever norm of acceptability is appealed to, the resulting safety judgment is deemed by the classical view to be inherently flawed unless it is based on a scientifically reliable estimate of risk at the first stage. This is how risk assessment is supposed to function ideally. In this paper we summarize research we carried out to examine in detail a regulatory implementation of scientific risk assessment that invoked this classical model. It involved an appeal to a panel of scientific experts of a decision by the Canadian government to cancel the registration of an agricultural herbicide called Alachlor. Our aim was threefold. We wanted, first, to identify the actual assumptions made by the scientists to bridge the information gaps and other uncertainties with which they were confronted. Secondly, we wanted to identify the values implicit in these assumptions. And thirdly, we wanted to examine more closely the ideal of risk analysis itself as an objective, value-free science. Our research has convinced us that the conclusions generated by risk assessment are necessarily based upon important normative assumptions.[5] These are necessary, not only in order to bridge the gaps created by the nature of regulatory science, an aspect that has been observed by others, but also, surprisingly, in the very conduct of risk assessment itself.

An important finding was that many of these normative assumptions were unavoidable: the normative nature of the risk assessment was such that had the assessors managed to remain true to the classical model by maintaining a stance of pure objectivity, they could not have produced an assessment at all. This is to say, it was a condition of completing the assessment that normative assumptions be made. Unless the assessors invoke values, they cannot do their job.

A second important finding concerned the effect of divergent normative assumptions on the risk assessment, compared with the effect on the risk assessment of differing views concerning the purely empirical aspects of the case. So influential were the normative assumptions that it is fair to say that the real debate concerning the risks of Alachlor was normative, not empirical and scientific.[6] This feature of the debate was hidden from view because on the surface most of the issues on which the assessors were divided were empirical. But, as we show below, the differing positions taken on many of the ostensibly empirical issues were traceable to the different normative assumptions made by the assessors.

THE CASE OF ALACHLOR AND THE COMPETING ASSESSMENTS OF RISK

Alachlor is a chemical herbicide manufactured by Monsanto Corporation to inhibit weed growth in corn and soy bean fields. In 1985, Agriculture Canada cancelled the registration of the herbicide for sale in Canada. It was guided by a risk assessment provided by the Health Protection Branch of Health and Welfare Canada, which had concluded that Alachlor presented a serious risk of cancer to farmers. Monsanto appealed the cancellation decision, and a scientific Review Board was appointed to consider the appeal. After public hearings, in which it considered expert studies and testimony submitted by more than 50 parties, the Board concluded that the government had overestimated the risks of Alachlor and recommended that Alachlor's registration be reinstated.[7]

The Alachlor risk assessment focussed upon the risk of cancer which the chemical poses to those who apply this herbicide to fields planted in corn and soy beans. The assessment was based upon two basic estimates: the first of the quantity of Alachlor sufficient to induce cancer in humans; the second of the levels of exposure likely to be experienced by those who come into contact with Alachlor. The evidence suggested that 2.5 mg/kg/day was sufficient to induce tumours in rats. Since there was little or no direct evidence concerning the effects of the chemical in humans, 2.5 mg/kg/day was simply accepted as the best estimate of a potentially carcinogenic dose, and attention thus focussed on the question of likely human exposures. Actual exposure, of course, varies from individual to individual, depending on such variables as how careful the applicators are, the sort of protective clothing they wear, the amount of Alachlor they apply, the number of applications per year and the number of years they are employed applying Alachlor. As well, the exposure estimates will vary depending on which of various procedures for measuring exposure is adopted, and on whether it is decided to "amortize" exposure, and if so at what rate.[8]

Both the government and the manufacturer dealt with the exposure question by developing "reasonable worst-case exposure scenarios." The scenario of the Health Protection Branch (HPB) suggested a possible exposure to applicators of 2.7 mg/kg/day of Alachlor, slightly more than the minimum dose sufficient to induce a tumour in rats. At the other extreme, one of Monsanto's exposure estimates was nearly seven orders of magnitude less than this. The Review Board itself settled on a range between these extremes, concluding that in the reasonably expected worst case, Alachlor exposure would fall somewhere between .001 and .0001 mg/kg/day. The gap between this and the lowest dose to induce a tumour in rats, 2.5 mg/kg/day, the Board considered a reasonably wide enough margin of safety to pronounce Alachlor "safe."

What explains the wide range of exposure estimates — from .0000009 to 2.7 mg/kg/day? On the face of it, the issue is entirely empirical. The scientists working for Monsanto appear to have reached one view concerning the facts of the case; the scientists working for HPB, a very different one — with the Review Board scientists in the middle. This is the conclusion suggested by the classical model of risk assessment. In actuality, however, the discrepancy in exposure estimates did not result from differences concerning the facts of the case. Instead, it resulted from differing value assumptions.

We identified three levels of generality in the value assumptions that entered into the widely divergent exposure estimates. The first and least analytic level involved the way the risk assessors themselves priorized the basic values that were at stake in the decision concerning Alachlor — what we call their basic "framework of value." The second involved the role of inherently and conditionally normative issues in the assessment. The third level involved the influence of assessors' values upon their adoption of different argumentative strategies. It is primarily the second and third types of value influence that demonstrate most dramatically the unavoidable value-ladenness of risk assessments.

Priorized Values

At the most general level, the differing estimates largely resulted from the assessors having priorized different values. Monsanto and, to a lesser degree, the Review Board were especially sensitive to the economic benefits associated with

use of Alachlor and to Monsanto's freedom to market its product. By contrast, HPB was, understandably, especially sensitive to the human health implications of Alachlor use, and rather less concerned with the economic factors.

Looking behind, for example, the Review Board's emphasis on the economic benefits associated with use of Alachlor, which were spelled out in terms of the price and yield effects of discontinuing the marketing of Alachlor, it is possible to see three interlinked, normative assumptions at work. These are, first, an instrumental view of rationality, second, a pro-technology stance, and third, a liberal view of the political order.

These three normative assumptions formed a distinctive value framework that coloured many aspects of the Board's assessment of Alachlor's risks as well as its views concerning the substantive issue of whether Alachlor's registration should be cancelled. Commitment to the idea of instrumental rationality — that is, the definition of reason as the efficient adaptation of means to the achievement of non-rational ends — was especially clear in the Board's acceptance of the risk-benefit standard of risk acceptability as a virtually self-evident truth. Its pro-technology stance was most evident in its failure to consider the option of cancelling both Alachlor and Metolachlor (its main competing product), an option which would have opened discussion on the reduction in general of farm dependence on chemical pesticides. In the Board's view there were just two serious alternatives: the registration for use in Canada of both herbicides, or the registration of Metolachlor and cancellation of Alachlor (the government's own decision). The Board's liberalism was straightforwardly expressed in its concern for the freedom of Monsanto to market its product and in the weight it attached to its estimate of the price and yield effects of cancelling Alachlor's registration.

The government, on the other hand, seemed to be motivated by a somewhat different orientation to these value issues, being less open to a risk-benefit standard of acceptable risk and far less sympathetic to the traditional liberal concern for market fairness. Its position on the question of technology itself was less evident. The environmental groups represented at the hearings, however, were clearly operating from a more sceptical stance towards technological solutions and a different conception of rationality and market justice from that of the Review Board.

FIGURE 1 Alachlor Exposure Estimates

Mg/kg of body wt/day

2.7	HPB patch test, 100% absorption, no protective clothing, no amortization
2.5	*Lowest dose at which a tumour was observed in rat studies*
0.68	HPB patch test, 25% absorption, no protective clothing, no amortization
0.26	Biomonitoring, no protective clothing, no amortization
0.21	HPB patch test, 100% absorption, protective clothing, no amortization
0.063	HPB patch test, 100% absorption, no protective clothing, full amortization
0.05	HPB patch test, 25% absorption, protective clothing, no amortization
0.02	Biomonitoring, protective clothing, no amortization
0.0078	Biomonitoring, no protective clothing, no amortization
0.0056	HPB patch test, 100% absorption, protective clothing, full amortization, 1 day exposure/year
0.0047	Biomonitoring, commercial applicators, protective clothing, 15 days exposure/year
0.0042	HPB patch test, 100% absorption, no protective clothing, full amortization, 1 day exposure/year
0.001	*Upper limit of worst-case exposure scenario*
0.0006	Biomonitoring, protective clothing, no amortization
0.00038	HPB patch test, 100% absorption, protective clothing, full amortization, 1 day exposure/year
0.0001	*Lower limit of worse-case exposure scenario*
0.000014	Biomonitoring, commercial applicators, protective clothing, full amortization, 15 days exposure/year
0.000031	Biomonitoring, protective clothing, full amortization, 1 day exposure/year
0.000016	Biomonitoring, commercial applicators, protective clothing, full amortization, 1 day exposure/year
0.0000009	Biomonitoring, protective clothing, full amortization, 1 day exposure/year

Conditionally and Inherently Normative Issues

These large normative assumptions, or the "value framework" of the assessors, impacted on the risk assessment of Alachlor by influencing the way the assessors resolved two different kinds of normative questions embedded in the issue. We have identified these as "conditionally" and "inherently" normative. A closer look at the divergent exposure estimates alluded to in the preceding section will clarify the nature of these two different normative assumptions in the Alachlor risk assessment (see Figure 1).

Note that the divergent estimates, from 2.7 to .0000009 mg/kg/day, do not represent different measurements of actual exposure. Instead, for the most part, these estimates are based on the same raw data and result from subjecting those data to different assumptions. Prominent among these assumptions are the following: do applicators wear protective clothing? To how many acres do they apply the herbicide during a growing season? Over how many years do they apply the herbicide? Should the applicators' exposures be amortized over their entire lifetimes? If so, at what rate? That is, given a particular measurement of exposure, answering these questions in different ways yields widely divergent calculations of exposure.

If one assumes, as did the government, for example, that the applicator wears no protective clothing, that exposure is not amortized, that a patch test is the best method for measuring exposure, that 100% of the Alachlor deposited on the skin is absorbed, and that the applicator applies Alachlor 15 days per year, at a rate of 100 acres per day, over a 40 year period, the calculated exposure estimate of 2.7 mg/kg/day results. By contrast, if one assumes, as did Monsanto in one of its scenarios, that the applicator wears full protective clothing, that exposure is fully amortized, that biomonitoring is the chosen method for measuring exposure, and that the applicator applies Alachlor one day per year at the same rate of 100 acres per day over the same 40 year period, the calculated exposure falls to as low as .0000009 mg/kg/day.

The various exposure calculations, based on various sets of assumptions of the sorts identified in the preceding paragraph, are compiled in Figure 1. But even with this data in hand, no decision concerning the risks of Alachlor to applicators can be made until the exposure calculations are interpreted by deriving a "reasonable worst-case exposure scenario." That is, some of the calculated exposures may seem (from the point of view of safety) overly optimistic, some overly pessimistic. Thus, it may seem unreasonably pessimistic to assume a dermal absorption rate of 100% (given the evidence from the animal studies); and it may seem unreasonably optimistic to expect the applicator both to apply Alachlor only one day per year and to be wearing full protective clothing.

As the discussion below establishes, the assumptions employed to calculate exposure, as well as the assumptions that underlie decisions made in deriving an exposure scenario, are either inherently or conditionally normative. This is what leads us to conclude that the "risk" of Alachlor is not an objective fact but a value judgment.

Conditionally Normative Issues

The priorized values of risk assessors are able to influence a risk assessment owing to two nearly universal circumstances in risk assessments. First, the assessment must be carried out in the face of massive uncertainties. Second, despite the uncertainties the assessors must actually reach a conclusion concerning the product's risks. In these circumstances, the definite conclusion the assessors are required to reach must be based on something other than "the facts of the case." Their only recourse, short of tossing a coin, is to decide the issue by having in view the values they primarily want to protect. We designate issues decided in this way as *conditionally normative,* since they come into play only in the condition where there is not enough information available to decide the issue on the basis of the scientific data alone. They could be settled without normative judgments if more (or better) information were available.

As noted above, at work in the assessment of Alachlor's risks were two competing priorized values, economic benefits and human health. A result of the Review Board's sensitivity to the former was that in contexts of scientific uncertainty, where the facts did not speak sufficiently loudly to validate a definite view, it took positions that protected the economic benefits Alachlor was thought to promise, at the possible cost of the human health benefits associated with banning Alachlor. HPB, on the other hand, preferred to protect health over economic benefits.

For example, the question whether to amortize exposure over the entire lifespan of the applicators, and if so at what rate, presented an especially sensitive, conditionally normative issue. There was insufficient factual basis for deciding, but the issue could not be avoided: in calculating exposure one either will or will not amortize, and one cannot amortize without choosing a rate of amortization. Amortization minimizes exposure estimates; not amortizing maximizes them. Monsanto and the Review Board, sensitive to the projected economic benefits of Alachlor, amortized; HPB, conceiving itself as the guardian of health, did not.

In calling decisions of the sort referred to above "conditionally *normative,*" we are referring to the fact that in view of the uncertainties, one's decision will disclose values one wishes to protect. Remove those values from the deliberations and there is no basis for choosing between HPB's and the Review Board's widely divergent scenarios. This is one reason for insisting that risk assessment in a context of uncertainty has no alternative but to invoke value assumptions.

Inherently Normative Issues

The risk assessors' attempts to calculate Alachlor exposure were complicated by the fact that exposure conditions vary. Some applicators wear protective clothing, some do not. Some work but one day a year, some work many more. And so on. For these reasons, the assessors had to make a number of assumptions in order to calculate Alachlor exposure. These may be thought of as "normalizing" assumptions. The most decisive was that concerning protective clothing. Should one assume, for purposes of an exposure estimate, that protective gloves will be worn? If so, gloves of what quality and effectiveness? This is a mundane example of the sort of inherently normative issue assessors of Alachlor's risks confronted. If it were assumed that applicators would be wearing high-quality protective gloves, the resulting exposure estimate would be at least an order of magnitude lower than it would be under the assumption that no gloves would be worn. The lower of the two Alachlor exposure estimates might support a verdict of safe; the higher, a verdict of unsafe. Not surprisingly, Monsanto's exposure calculations were based on the assumption that gloves of good quality would be worn; HPB's were based on the assumption that they would not be.

Why call a normalizing assumption inherently normative? The reason is that the basis for any such assumption is necessarily normative, regardless of the reliability and completeness of the data. That is to say, the issue itself is normative, and cannot, therefore, be settled by any amount of empirical data. For example, the basis for Monsanto's and the Review Board's decision to assume that applicators would wear full protective clothing (despite the fact that most applicators do not) was that it would be unfair to Monsanto to include in the exposure estimate exposure that resulted from applicators' not taking due care. In other words, the increased risk in such a case should be attributed to the behaviour of the applicator, not to Monsanto's product itself (the "should be" here clearly identifies the normativeness of the judgment). By contrast, HPB's decision to include within the range of exposure risks the case in which applicators would not wear the recommended protective clothing was founded in its mandate, health protection. Thus, concern for fairness led to one set of assumptions; concern for health to another. The issues of fairness and of what due regard for farmers' well-being required were not fabricated by the assessors but were intrinsic elements of the decision problem they confronted. That is, they did not arbitrarily decide to conceive the protective clothing question as a normative one. It was itself normative. What the assessors did not grasp was the significance of their approach to the issue. Although they dealt with it properly, as normative and not empirical, they continued to think of their investigation into Alachlor's risks in the conventional way, as a value-free enterprise.

In addition to the protective clothing issue, other inherently normative issues arose: in estimating the danger of Alachlor contaminating well water, should the assessor include in the calculation seepage into poorly constructed wells? What attitude should be taken toward exposure that results from the clothing worn by applicators not having been laundered after use? Should account be taken of exposure that results from careless practices in mixing the solution? Should it be assumed that the solution will be incorporated into the soil at the time of planting, rather than sprayed on after germination? To how many acres a year shall applicators be assumed to apply Alachlor?

These were all issues that needed to be resolved in order to develop a "reasonable worst-case exposure scenario"; that is, in order to answer the question central to the risk assessment: what is the highest level of exposure to the hazards of Alachlor it is "reasonable" to expect? Any position concerning the reasonable worst-case exposure scenario was inherently normative. Monsanto's interpretation of the "worst case" roughly coincided with HPB's interpretation of the "best case," with the Review Board's falling somewhere in between. A genuine issue was thus posed. But what divided the parties was not differing views concerning the factual aspects of the case. Rather, HPB's more conservative interpretation of the "worst case" reflected the higher priority it attached to human health. By contrast, Monsanto's and the Review Board's less conservative interpretation of the "worst case" reflected a relatively higher concern for economic benefits, and the principles of individual responsibility and non-interference in the marketplace. In this way, one can see that the very idea of a reasonable worst-case exposure scenario is inherently normative.

It might be argued that there is no need to construe any of the decisions in an exposure estimate as inherently normative, and since there are advantages to keeping risk assessments scientifically pure, it is a mistake to do so. Thus, the argument would go, the protective clothing issue is simply the empirical one of determining what sort of clothing applicators actually do wear. In particular, do they wear adequate gloves or not? The exposure estimate should be based on the answer to this question.

The difficulty in this attempt to retain scientific purity is that practice is not uniform. Some wear very adequate protective clothing, some wear protective clothing of middling adequacy, and some are exceptionally careless in this regard. The same variation in practice is met with respect to the other exposure conditions. Some applicators apply ten times more Alachlor per year than others. So the question is *not* that of determining the level of exposure under a certain condition, but rather that of determining *which* exposure condition we should take as representing the risk of Alachlor to applicators. It is a matter of first *defining* the "reasonable worst, medium and best case," and then deciding among them, all of which requires normative choices.

Argumentative Strategies

A major way in which assessors' values influenced assessments of Alachlor's risks was through their adoption of argumentative strategies. These strategies formed procedural responses to the following questions: who has the burden of proof? How much scientific rigour is required? Shall the assessor be risk-aversive or risk-taking? In assessing Alachlor's risks, the assessor had no alternative but to take a stand on each of these issues. Are we to assume that Alachlor is safe unless it is proved to be unsafe? Or that it is unsafe unless proved safe? When assessing evidence that bears on Alachlor's risks shall we apply the same high standard as is applied when practising "laboratory science?" Or is a more relaxed "weight of evidence" standard satisfactory? When gaps in the data or conflicting data make a decision difficult, but there are risks associated with how the decision is made, shall we be cautious, risk-aversive? Or shall we be risk-takers, since caution may jeopardize benefits that can only be gained by taking a chance?

In the Alachlor debate, HPB was risk-aversive, applied a rigorous standard in assessing Monsanto's evidence concerning Alachlor's safety, and held that the burden of proof fell on Monsanto to establish Alachlor's safety, in the absence of which it must be regarded as unsafe. Monsanto and the Review Board opposed these argumentative strategies by holding that at the outset Alachlor should be regarded as safe and that the onus fell on the government to prove otherwise, that HPB's claims regarding Alachlor's carcinogenicity should be evaluated by applying a rigorous scientific standard, and that HPB had been excessively cautious or risk-aversive in, for example, estimating exposure levels.

It is obvious that these argumentative strategies form natural clusters. To lay the burden of proof on the government, to expect it to satisfy a rigorous standard of scientific credibility, and to adopt a risk-taking stance when assessing evidence concerning Alachlor's risks — these moves influence the debate in the same way. They create, as it were, a current in the argument, so that arguing the view that Alachlor poses high risk becomes rather like swimming upstream, and arguing the opposite position becomes more like swimming downstream.

On one hand, some assumption about burden of proof, some assumption regarding scientific rigour, and some assumption concerning risk-taking must be made. On the other hand, these assumptions cannot be supported by reference to the factual aspects of the risk assessment; rather, they control interpretation of those facts. The assumptions are value-laden because invoking them expresses values held by the assessor, or at least it requires the assessor to take a position in a normative debate. For example, if human health is the value the assessor has uppermost in mind, this will and should find expression in the assumption that Monsanto bears a burden of proof to establish Alachlor's safety. If economic benefits or economic freedom are deemed to be the values that most need protection, then the regulator should be required to prove that Alachlor represents a high risk to human health.

CONCLUSION

A risk debate is not primarily a debate between those who accept the verdict of scientific risk assessment and those who do not. It is not a conflict between those who understand the "objective" risks and those who are guided by an irrational, "subjective" perception of those risks. Neither is it primarily a debate within science itself. Rather, it is primarily a political debate — a debate among different value frameworks, different ways of thinking about moral values, different conceptions of society, and different attitudes toward technology and towards risk-taking itself.

If this is true, it raises serious questions about how these debates ought to be resolved, and whether their resolution should be put more or less exclusively in the hands of risk assessment experts and other scientists. To make such individuals the sole arbiters is in effect to allow one value framework within the social conflict represented in the debates to settle the issue in its favour. However, in this way, what is essentially a value-laden political decision becomes disguised as politically and morally neutral. There is no question that science and risk assessment experts have important contributions to make. The outstanding question is how to broaden the forum within which decisions concerning technological risks are made, so that other members of the larger community might have a voice as well.

(c)   Comparative Risk Assessment and the Naturalistic Fallacy[†]

Kristin S. Shrader-Frechette ———————————————————

Have we humans become risk-averse wimps? Many scientists think so. Nuclear physicist Alvin Weinberg, for example, claims that contemporary laypeople are often victims of 'environmental hypochondria', similar to the hysteria that drove 15th- and 16th-century witch hunts. Weinberg notes that witch hunts subsided only after the Inquisitor of Spain convened a group of savants who proclaimed there was no proof that 'witches' caused misfortunes. He concludes that environmental hypochondria likewise will disappear only after contemporary risk assessors dismiss most of the health problems allegedly caused by environmental threats such as pollution[1].

Arguing along similar lines, numerous scientists have claimed that if members of the public understood the extremely low probabilities associated with environmentally induced health hazards, they would not fear threats from sources such as pesticides, chlorinated drinking water and global warming. They reason that — because laypeople are much more likely to die in a traffic accident than in a nuclear core melt — they are irrational and inconsistent if they accept automobile travel but oppose commercial atomic energy. Fully rational people, they maintain, do not fear small risks while they dismiss much larger ones. Instead, they say that people who evaluate risks consistently and rationally do so on the basis of their respective probabilities of death. Rational people rank risks according to their likelihood of fatality, say many risk assessors, and they exhibit risk aversion that is proportional to the respective probabilities (see, for example, Ref. 2). In other words, a number of experts claim that rational and consistent risk behavior is based on comparative risk assessment.

Comparative risk assessment (CRA) is a set of quantitative techniques that scientists and engineers use to evaluate various environmental threats, from owning handguns or occupying a home without a smoke alarm, to eating meats treated with nitrates or living near a chemical plant. CRA ranks risks, highest to lowest, on the basis of their average annual probability of inducing (human) fatality. The rationale for such ranking, and for CRA-based public policymaking, is that it encourages more rational and consistent risk decisions; it helps prevent lawmakers from implementing 'irrational' policies of regulating supposed small risks while ignoring larger ones; it assists in reducing overall risk; it forces society to set environmental priorities according to science rather than politics; it saves industry from excessive spending to reduce very small risks; and it enables governments to use risk-abatement expenditures wisely and efficiently. Jumping on the bandwagon, a variety of industrial, scientific and governmental groups have endorsed CRA-based policymaking. There are at least three different 'risk' bills, for example, before the 1994–1995 US Congress, and all of them mandate both performing CRA as part of quantitative risk assessment and setting standards and regulations on the basis of CRA.

Despite the merits of rational policymaking regarding environmental risk. CRA probably raises more questions than it addresses. One problem is that CRA is easier said than done. For the approximately 50,000 human-made environmental contaminants, such as benzene and vinyl chloride, no more than a handful have gone through epidemiological testing. The newness of such hazards, and the expense of testing, mean that there are reliable frequency records for only a few risks. In the absence of empirical data, experts routinely use subjective probabilities in their risk assessments. On the few occasions when assessors have been able to check their risk predictions, they typically err by four to six orders of magnitude.[3]

Another difficulty with CRA ranking is that death is not the only important 'end point' whose probability rational people might want to evaluate. Other end points and/or effects include

† Reproduced from *TREE — Trends in Research in Ecology and Evolution* 10, 1 (January 1995): 50, with permission of from Elsevier Science and the author.

a variety of health, ecological and welfare risks — from eggshell thinning, mutagenic injury and loss of ecosystem functions — to inequities in risk distribution, lack of citizen consent to certain threats, and inadequate compensation (or denial of due process rights to recover damages) after exposure to hazards. Indeed, rational and consistent people arguably might prefer to take a voluntarily chosen risk (like driving an automobile) rather than an involuntarily imposed one (like living near a nuclear power plant), even though the probability of dying in a traffic accident is greater. In other words, rational people might ask not only 'how safe is safe enough?' but 'how safe is voluntary enough?', 'how safe is equitable enough?', 'how safe is fair enough?', 'how safe is compensated enough?'[4].

In its simplistic 'body-count' approach to environmental hazards, CRA ignores important questions, such as who calculates the relevant risk probabilities, who bears the risks, who benefits from the risks, whether the risk is avoidable, how the risk figures are averaged, who would pay for risk reduction, and who has the right to give or withhold consent to the risk. If one assumes a multi-attribute view of risk and denies that probability of fatality is the only relevant variable for comparing environmental risks, then one could just as well rank societal threats in terms of the respective threats they pose to the gene pool, to future generations, to political autonomy, to justice, or to some other value. All these considerations suggest that, like beauty, risk may be — in part — in the eye of the beholder.

By assuming that a wide variety of social and environmental values can be reduced merely to probability of fatality, proponents of CRA err in assuming that quantitative information — even when it is uncertain — trumps qualitative factors. This bureaucratic enthusiasm for number crunching in CRA illustrates Gresham's Law: monetary drives out nonmonetary information, and quantitative drives out nonquantitative information[4]. Assessors who follow Gresham's Law err in reducing questions of ethics (is this risk acceptable?) to questions of science (what is the probability of this risk?). British moral philosopher G.E. Moore warned, earlier in this century, that anyone who attempts to reduce an ethical question to a scientific one commits 'the naturalistic fallacy'[5]. Obviously we cannot learn how things ought to be, ethically, by looking only at how they are, scientifically. And if not, then although science and CRA are essential tools for risk comparisons, they are not the only tools. Indeed, they err in telling us that we ought to accept preventable environmental risks just because we cannot eliminate all risks.

(d) Current Status and Implementation of the Precautionary Principle[†]

Joel Tickner and Nancy Myers

Discussion of the role of the precautionary principle in environmental health policy has intensified..., especially in the European Union and in the international arena but also in the United States and Canada. Much of this debate has been fueled by trade controversies over beef and milk containing growth hormones and over genetically modified foods. The precautionary principle dominated discussions at the recent Biosafety Protocol meeting in Montreal and was at the core of the final protocol. At [the] World Trade Organization Ministerial meeting in Seattle, controversy swirled around the precautionary principle. The principle has been a central element in recent discussions of international food safety standards (Codex Alimentarius).

† From <http://www.sehn.org/ppcurrentstatus.html> (excerpts) (last accessed: 02-06-05). Reprdouced by permission of the publisher.

The Maastricht Treaty forming the European Union stated that Community environmental policy should be based on the precautionary principle and that environmental damage should be prevented at source. The European Commission has been debating the principle for several years and produced a Communication in February 2000 that solidifies the principle in European environmental policy and seeks to define its use.

Each EU member state accepts precaution as a general principle of environmental policy. ... Several other countries including Hungary and Brazil have adopted precaution as a guiding principle.

The United States has not adopted precaution as an explicit basis for environmental policy, even though this country has ratified the Rio Declaration on Environment and Development, which obliges nations to exercise the precautionary principle. Nonetheless, precaution has been articulated in some U.S. environmental laws and early court interpretations, as well as by the U.S. President's Council on Sustainable Development, in a 1996 statement of guiding principles for sustainable development. There has been little government or public debate about the precautionary principle in the United States, although this is changing. As the principle comes to the fore on the international arena and as environmental activists and academics embrace the principle with growing enthusiasm, U.S. officials are forced to come to terms with the principle and its meaning.

So far, U.S. official responses have been mostly negative. They come not from agencies with direct responsibility for environmental and health matters but from the U.S. Department of State, the U.S. Trade Representative, and the U.S. Department of Commerce, the latter two representing mainly economic and industrial interests. The bodies most competent to speak on matters of health and the environment — the Environmental Protection Agency, the Occupational Safety and Health Administration, and the Department of Health and Human Services — have been mostly silent.

That is partly because the World Trade Organization and other international economic institutions, such as the World Bank and the International Monetary Fund, are taking an increasingly important role in defining environmental policy throughout the world. By narrowly defining the basis for environmental decision-making (in terms of quantitative risk assessment),

WTO rules serve to limit the breadth of international discussions on the precautionary principle and the ability of countries to take precautionary measures. WTO rules require that countries who institute environmental or health protection measures that might inhibit trade can only do so on the basis of a quantitative risk assessment and so long as the action (or standard) is consistent with international standards set by agencies such as Codex Alimentarius. Any stricter standard is at risk of being challenged by another country as a trade barrier. Any weaker standard, however, cannot be challenged as environmental dumping. While countries can take emergency measures to protect health or the environment, these are only "temporary" until further scientific information can be gathered.

. . . .

The international trade regime is designed for economic liberalization and not for environmental protection or sustainable development. The priority given to the WTO and other trade harmonization schemes like Codex Alimentarius has contributed to certain weaknesses in the recent European Commission Communication on the Precautionary Principle. The statement also reflects the trend toward reductionism in environmental science and a lack of understanding of the complex nature of environmental threats:

- The Communication describes precaution as a risk management tool — only a part of a risk analysis framework rather than the overall guide to its implementation. According to this argument, precautionary action should only be taken after experts prepare an "objective" quantitative risk assessment.
- Precaution is discussed in the context of risk containment, not in terms of preventing risks and harm. This assumes that risks are inevitable and must be accepted by society — only the degree of acceptable risk is in question. The importance of assessing alternatives to potentially harmful activities is completely missing from the Communication.
- Precaution is seen as a temporary measure pending further scientific information. This is based on the assumption that science can eventually provide answers.

On the positive side, the Communication acknowledges the need to incorporate qualitative scientific evidence (not just quantitative evidence) and consider multiple disciplines and sources of information. While it calls for cost-benefit analysis, it notes that such quantitative analyses cannot always be undertaken. More important, it says that protection of health and the environment should come before economic concerns.

What is missing from such highly qualified, economics-based statements on precaution is the spirit of the original German framers of the Vorsorgeprinzip and the most thoughtful subsequent interpretations of the precautionary principle. The precautionary approach calls not only for foresight, but for "forecaring," to translate the German term directly. The principle embodies the idea of careful planning to avoid risks in the first place, rather than trying to determine how much risk is acceptable. The German framers of the principle believed that implementing the principle would not impose great economic hardship but would instead stimulate innovation and create jobs in the growing field of environmental technologies. Aggressive planning was viewed as central to sustainable development goals.

At the core of each subsequent statement of precaution is the idea that action should be taken to prevent harm to the environment and human health, even if scientific evidence is inconclusive. This essential component of the principle has been integrated into international environmental treaties, beginning with the Montreal Protocol and the Second International Convention on Protection of the North Sea in 1987. Since then, the principle has gained status as a customary principle of international environmental law. It has been built into virtually every international environmental treaty and declaration, including the 1992 Rio Declaration on Environment and Development, the 1990 and 1992 Global Climate Change Conferences, the 1992 Convention on Protection of the Environment of the Northeast Atlantic, and most recently the February 2000 Biosafety Protocol of the Cartagena Convention. The 1990 Bergen Ministerial Conference on Sustainable Development linked the concept of precaution to sustainable development.

The differences among these statements have to do mainly with how the principle should be carried out. The Rio Declaration calls for "cost-effective" measures to prevent degradation. The 1991 Bamako Convention calls for the implementation of clean production measures to prevent harm to the African environment. The 1998 Wingspread Conference on the Precautionary Principle summarized four components of the precautionary principle that should guide its implementation:

- action to prevent harm despite uncertainty,
- shifting the burden of proof to proponents of a potentially harmful activity,
- examination of a full range of alternatives to potentially harmful activities, including no action, and
- democratic decision making to ensure inclusion of those affected.

Elements of these four components have appeared in some statements of the principle and in some national implementation efforts. For example, in Sweden precaution is linked to the substitution principle, the ecocycle society principle, the sustainability principle, and the polluter pays principle. Unfortunately, however, most of the debate around precaution has focused on its interpretation and role in environmental policy rather than on tools and processes to guide precautionary action.

Precaution will be implemented in different ways in different countries. In the United States, implementing such an overarching principle will be especially challenging because industry holds great power over decision-making; because decision-makers rely on science to quantify environmental threats (to protect themselves in the courts); and because of the inflexible and often prescriptive nature of the U.S. environmental regulatory system. Innovation in U.S. environmental policy has been largely missing in recent years, due in part to increasing conservatism in national politics. As a result, the precautionary principle is likely to be debated and implemented on a local and state level, where there are more opportunities for innovative public policy. Legislation and policy implementing the principle at the local level can then influence national policy.

Implementating the precautionary principle is likely to be easier in Europe, where there is more flexibility in law and policy. There is more freedom to make political decisions in the face of scientific uncertainty, without having to quantify effects; less judicial review of decisions; and less influence by economic interests. The precautionary principle is more likely to be implemented on a national and international level in Europe.

Differences in the way the United States and European countries might implement precaution are illustrated in the controversy over phthalates in PVC children's toys. The Danish government banned phthalates in toys designed for children under three without calculating risks quantitatively.

Instead, they based the decision on qualitative considerations:

- exposure was occurring;
- phthalates are toxic to laboratory animals;
- children may be uniquely susceptible to toxic substances;
- alternatives were readily available.

By contrast, the U.S. government prepared a quantitative risk assessment of the impacts of phthalate exposure to children and found that the risk was very low. Nevertheless, officials called for a voluntary removal of phthalates based on residual uncertainties. And several major toy companies quickly complied, touting their decision, which was no doubt based on market pressures and the threat of litigation, as a voluntary move to protect the safety of children.

What structures and changes will be required to implement the precautionary principle? The first change should be the questions asked by decision-makers. Instead of asking, "What level of risk is safe or acceptable?" they must ask, "What alternatives exist to a potentially harmful activity?" and "Can harm be prevented?" These questions will shift the focus from analysis to careful planning.

Second, implementing precaution requires changes in science. The precautionary principle calls for more rigorous and honest science, drawing evidence from multiple disciplines and constituencies and being clear about uncertainties (including what is known, not known, and can be known).

Science must better anticipate harm and identify solutions. This requires qualitative methods in decision-making, that is, the exercising of good judgment. For example, a weight-of-evidence approach examines the cumulative sum of information, including common sense and experience. We must develop decision-making approaches that go beyond examining risk and causality to consider the magnitude of potential harm, reversibility, temporal and spatial scales,

vulnerable populations, need, and availability of alternatives.

Various components of a policy structure to implement the precautionary principle should be applied in all countries and all situations. Precautionary action need not always mean banning a potentially hazardous activity. There must be ways to say "yes" — with caution. Such tools and structures would shift the responsibility to those who create risks to examine and choose the most environmentally friendly options. Some of these components are:

- General duties to take preventive, precautionary action in the face of uncertainty. This would put in place a responsibility for government and businesses to act in a precautionary way if there is evidence that an activity (or substance) might pose a risk to health or the environment, even if there is no specific regulation of that activity. Such general duties can be accomplished through constitutional rights to a clean and healthy environment as well.
- Goal-setting for environmental and public health protection. Aggressive environmental health goals provide a stimulus for innovation and an acknowledgment of potential risks, even without proof of causality. For example, the Swedish government has proposed phasing out persistent and bioaccumulative substances in products by the year 2007 because they have characteristics that are not compatible with sustainability.
- Focusing on preventing harm by identifying safer and cleaner ways to provide specific services. Clean production is a well-known set of techniques to implement the precautionary principle. Clean production, which attempts to reduce the materials and toxics used in services and products, has been demonstrated not only to produce benefits to the environment but also to increase economic competitiveness and innovation. Other prevention-oriented methods include: pre-market testing; environmental impact assessments and audits; limitations pending further testing; labeling; and health-based exposure limits.
- Monitoring to continuously measure potential adverse effects of both current and alternative activities. Decisions made under a precautionary framework must be followed by continuous monitoring to ensure that they can be updated as new information becomes available. The goal should be to continuously

improve environmental conditions, anticipate potential impacts before they occur (obey warning signals), and take action to prevent harm based on this information.

- Economic incentives to promote precaution. Polluters should be responsible for paying the full costs associated with the health and environmental damage they create. Environmental bonds, for example, provide an incentive to prevent harm in the face of uncertainty.

- Democratic decision-making structures. Because decisions regarding health and the environment are "public" decisions, those who might be affected must have a say in the decision-making process. Structures such as lay person juries, citizen advisory committees, local negotiation, and science shops can ensure that citizens have both the knowledge and access necessary to influence complex decisions.

(e)   Our 'Stolen Future' and the Precautionary Principle†

Elizabeth M. Whelan

I don't buy into the Precautionary Principle, for several reasons. First, it always assumes worst-case scenarios. Second, it distracts consumers and policy makers alike from the known and proven threats to human health. And third, it assumes no health detriment from the proposed regulations and restrictions. By that I mean that the Precautionary Principle overlooks the possibility that real public health risks can be associated with eliminating minuscule, hypothetical risks. As an ancient philosopher said, "It is a serious disease to worry over what has not occurred."

We seem to be a nation fixated on hypothetical risks. My former colleague, the late Aaron Wildavsky, noted that the Precautionary Principle plays well to the crowd, by placing the environmental advocate on the side of the citizenry — "I care about your health, and I propose an intervention that will protect you." And it allows environmentalists to portray those disagreeing with them as indifferent or even hostile to the public health and perhaps motivated by a desire to profit from whatever product or process is held to be risky.

But in reality, the Precautionary Principle itself can be hazardous to our health. It's well known that the health of citizens is consistently correlated with their countries' standard of living. Dismantling our industrially-based high standard

of living ... [will] lead to poorer, not better, overall health.

In talking about hypothetical risks, we get into the distinction between what people perceive as risks and what has scientifically been established as risky. As a corollary to the Precautionary Principle, consumer activists now insist that if the public perceives something as risky, that perception should carry the day regardless whether there truly is a risk or not. In essence, these people argue that science should take a back seat to fear — whether that fear is justified or not — when it comes to setting policy.

An op-ed piece published several years ago exemplifies this cockeyed approach to assessing risks. It was written by Dr. Edward Groth III, director of technical policy and public service at Consumers Union, and Professor Peter Sandman of Rutgers University, and discusses Alar, the growth-regulating chemical for apples that was withdrawn from the market in 1989 because of the public outcry over its alleged carcinogenicity. Groth and Sandman conclude that the outrage over Alar was completely [justified] while acknowledging that the scientific evidence failed to show whether Alar was dangerous or not....

So why was the outrage justified? The authors offer several reasons:

---

† From <http://www.acsh.org/publications/priorities/0803/future.html> (excerpts) (last accessed: 02-06-05). Reproduced with permission of Dr. Elizabeth Whelan, Priorities Magazine and the American Council on Science and Health, 1995 Broadway NY 10023..

- "It's not fair." Only the apple growers were benefitting from Alar; and children, who "consume comparatively huge amounts of apples and apple products," will bear "much higher theoretical risks from Alar than adults do."
- "It's involuntary," and therefore "consumers reasonably may ask, 'who gave them the right to put my child at risk?'"
- "Someone's responsible" for Alar. Even if naturally occurring pesticides "pose cancer risks thousands of times greater than the hazards of synthetic pesticides and other agricultural chemicals," Nature is "not making a business decision to sell or spray Alar."
- It's unnecessary," and therefore, "if consumers don't want Alar in apples and apple products, it needn't be there."

Where is the science here? There is none, but only a reliance on fear and a hostile stance towards business.

Groth and Sandman believe that the perception of harm is more important than evidence of actual harm in determining public policy. I strongly disagree. We're not doing children nor the rest of society any favors by "dissing" science in this way. Faced with a multitude of risks, both hypothetical and real, and with limited resources for dealing with them, we must rely on science when deciding which risks truly merit our attention.

(f)   Debating the Precautionary Principle[†]

Nancy Myers

The precautionary principle has taken center stage in a number of recent international discussions on trade, the environment, and human health. As a result, it has stirred criticism as well as interest. In these discussions and in a growing number of media reports on the principle, certain criticisms and qualifications, enumerated below, have been repeated with some frequency.

The Science and Environmental Health Network offers the following responses to stimulate the thinking of others on these statements and on the precautionary principle. ...

"The precautionary principle is vague and has conflicting definitions."
The precautionary principle is worded differently each time it is articulated. This is not uncommon in international customary law. Although some statements of the principle are more detailed than others, there are no major conflicts among them. At the core of each statement is the idea

that action should be taken to prevent harm to the environment and human health, even if scientific evidence is inconclusive.

For example, the 1998 Wingspread Statement on the Precautionary Principle summarizes the principle this way: "When an activity raises threats of harm to human health or the environment, precautionary measures should be taken even if some cause and effect relationships are not fully established scientifically." (The Wingspread Conference on the Precautionary Principle was convened by the Science and Environmental Health Network.)

The February 2, 2000 European Commission Communication on the Precautionary Principle notes: "The precautionary principle applies where scientific evidence is insufficient, inconclusive or uncertain and preliminary scientific evaluation indicates that that there are reasonable grounds for concern that the potentially dangerous effects on the environment, human, animal or plant health may be inconsistent with the high level of protection chosen by the EU."

---

† From <www.sehn.org/ppdebate.html> (excerpts) (last accessed: 02-06-05). Reproduced by permission of Science and Environmental Health Network.

The January 29, 2000 Cartagena Protocol on Biosafety says: "Lack of scientific certainty due to insufficient relevant scientific information ... shall not prevent the Party of import, in order to avoid or minimize such potential adverse effects, from taking a decision, as appropriate, with regard to the import of the living modified organism in question."

. . . .

As the principle has been elaborated recently, it nearly always implies three additional ideas, beyond "harm" and "scientific uncertainty":

• the notion of seeking alternatives to harmful technologies;
• the idea of shifting to proponents of a technology the responsibility for demonstrating its safety; and
• the goal of transparency and democracy in making decisions about technologies.

Taken together, these concepts provide what we believe is a sound overarching approach to assessing and making decisions on products and technologies and other human activities that may impact health or the environment. That is how "precaution" operates at the broadest level. On this level it is something like the common-sense attitude we take in conducting our own lives and making decisions: We consider whether we need or want something, try to learn as much as we can about risks and benefits, consider alternatives, choose the best and (most likely) safest route, and hold responsible those who provide the services we choose. And when something we value is threatened, we tend to err on the side of caution.

But the precautionary principle, especially as articulated in international treaties and agreements, is also a specific justification for action in cases of likely harm and scientific uncertainty.

"If precaution applies to everything, precaution would stop all technology in its tracks."

This criticism confuses the broad, common-sense precautionary approach to decision-making with specific precautionary action. It is wrong on two counts. In the first place, precautionary action does not always mean calling a halt or implementing a ban. It can also mean imposing a

moratorium while further research is conducted, calling for monitoring of technologies and products already in use, adopting safer alternatives, and so forth. In the second place, a broad precautionary approach will encourage the development of better technologies. Using this approach, society will say "yes" so some technologies while it says "no" to others. Making uncertainty explicit, considering alternatives, and increasing transparency and the responsibility of proponents and manufacturers to demonstrate safety should lead to cleaner products and production methods.

"Precaution calls for zero risk, which is impossible to achieve."

Any debate over the possibility of "zero risk" is pointless. Our real goal must be to impose far less risk and harm on the environment and on human health than we have in the past. We must harness human ingenuity to reduce the harmful effects of our activities.

The precautionary principle is based on the assumption that people have the right to know as much as possible about risks they are taking on, in exchange for what benefits, and to make choices accordingly. With food and other products, such choices are often played out in the marketplace. A major factor in the controversy over genetically engineered food is the consumer understanding that benefits of these products (which accrue more to producers than to consumers) do not outweigh the risk of harm to themselves or the environment.

. . . .

A key to making those choices is transparency — about what products contain, and about the testing and monitoring of those ingredients. Another is support, by government and industry, for the exploration of — and rigorous research on — alternatives.

Sometimes it makes sense to eliminate even questionable risks if it is easy to do so. For example, most airlines forbid passengers to use electronic devices during takeoff and landing, even though studies have not confirmed that they pose a danger.

In other cases the risk will be small but the consequences severe. An example of this kind of precautionary action is the U.S. "zero-tolerance" standard for Listeria monocytogenes in ready-to-eat foods. Listeria infections are rare, but they are extremely dangerous. (See Edward Groth III, "Science, Precaution, and Food Safety: How Can We Do Better?" Consumers Union of the U.S., Inc., February 2000.)

Market and voluntary action is not enough, especially on issues that go beyond individual and corporate choice. It is the responsibility of communities, governments, and international bodies to make far-reaching decisions that greatly reduce the risks we now impose on the Earth and all its inhabitants.

"We don't need the precautionary principle: we have risk assessment."

Risk assessment is the prevalent tool used to make decisions about technologies and products. Its proponents argue that because conservative assumptions are built into these assessments, they are sufficiently precautionary.

Too often, however, risk assessment has been used to delay precautionary action: decision-makers wait to get enough information and then attempt to "manage" rather than prevent risks. Risk assessment is not necessarily inconsistent with the precautionary principle, but because it omits certain basic requirements of the decision-making process, the current type of risk assessment is only helpful at a narrow stage of the process, when the product or technology and alternatives have been well developed and tested and a great deal of information has already been gathered about them. Standard risk assessment, in other words, is only useful in conditions of relatively high certainty, and generally only to help evaluate alternatives to damaging technologies.

Under the precautionary principle, uncertainty is also given due weight. The nature of the uncertainties about a technology can suggest such things as whether short-term testing can provide adequate answers; and if not, whether longer-term testing and monitoring can do so; and whether the benefits of the technology warrant that investment. The precautionary principle calls for the examination of a wider range of harms — including social and economic ones — than traditional risk analysis provides. It points to the need to examine not only single, linear risks but also complex interactions among multiple factors, and the broadest possible range of harmful effects.

This broad, probing consideration of harm — including the identification of uncertainty —

should begin as early as possible in the conception of a technology and should continue through its release and use. That is, a precautionary approach should begin before the regulatory phase of decision-making and should be built into the research agenda.

What is not consistent with the precautionary principle is the misleading certainty often implied by quantitative risk assessments — that precise numbers can be assigned to the possibility of harm, that these numbers are usually a sufficient basis for deciding whether the substance or technology is "safe," and that lack of numbers means there is no reason to take action. The assumptions behind risk assessments — what "risks" are evaluated and how comparisons are made — are easily manipulated by those with a stake in their outcome.

"The precautionary principle is a tool of risk assessment."

This statement implies that the precautionary principle only applies to risk management, rather than a comprehensive approach to preventing harm. It implies that uncertainty will eventually be resolved through more research or trial and error. Related to the above arguments, this one assumes a narrow definition (and use) of the precautionary principle — a stop or holding action when scientific evidence is uncertain. We argue that this is only one aspect of the precautionary principle, and that, on the contrary, risk assessment as it is currently practiced may be a useful — but narrow — tool of a broader approach to precautionary decision-making.

"Precaution itself is risky: it will prevent us from adopting technologies that are actually safer."

This consideration is built into the precautionary principle. Current and prospective alternatives to harmful technologies (such as genetic modification to reduce pesticide use) must be scrutinized as carefully as the technologies they replace. It does not make sense to replace one set of harms with another.

"The precautionary principle is anti-science."

On the contrary, the precautionary principle calls for more and better science, especially investigations of complex interactions over longer periods of time. The assertion that the principle is "anti-science" is based on any or all of the following faulty assumptions:

- Those who advocate precaution urge action on the basis of vague fears, regardless of whether there is scientific evidence to support their fears. Most statements of the precautionary principle say it applies when there is reason to believe serious or irreversible harm may occur. Those reasons are based on scientific evidence of various kinds: studies, observations, precedents, experience, professional judgment, and so forth. They are based on what we know about how processes work and might be affected by a technology. However, precautionary decisions also take into account what we know we do not know. The more we know, scientifically, the greater will be our ability to prevent disasters based on ignorance. But we must be much more cautious than we have been in the past about moving forward in ignorance.
- Taking action in advance of full scientific proof undermines science. Scientific standards of proof are high in experimental science or for accepting or refuting a hypothesis, and well they should be. Waiting to take action before a substance or technology is proven harmful, or even until plausible cause-and-effect relationships can be established, may mean allowing irreversible harm to occur — deaths, extinctions, poisoning, and the like. Humans and the environment become the unwitting testing grounds for these technologies. Precaution says this is no longer acceptable. Moreover, science should serve society, not vice versa. Any decision to take action — before or after scientific proof — is a decision of society, not science.
- Quantitative risk assessment is more scientific than other kinds of evaluation.

. . . .

"The precautionary principle is a cover for trade protectionism."

The precautionary principle was created to protect public health and the environment, not to restrict valid trade. North American, Argentinian, and other representatives in trade talks have leveled this accusation against the European Union in response to EU action on beef containing growth hormones and on genetically modified foods and crops. Recent EU statements on the precautionary principle have emphasized that the principle should be applied fairly and without discrimination.

However, the real issue is not protectionism but whether a nation has the sovereign right to impose standards that exceed the standards of international regimes. The recent European Commission statement on the precautionary principle and Cartagena Biosafety Protocol both assert that right.

"Precautionary actions must be proportionate, cost-effective, and temporary (subjected to further research)."

These qualifications (along with "fairness") have been included in recent statements, no doubt partly to make the precautionary principle more palatable to U.S. officials. While it is difficult to argue against any of them, they could dilute the effectiveness of the principle. For example:

Action should indeed be generally proportionate to the severity of a threat and standards of protection. But (as noted above) sometimes the availability of alternatives or the ease of taking action makes decisive action appropriate even if the threat is not severe or imminent.

"Cost-effectiveness" and "cost-benefit analysis" have been used in the past to stop regulatory action. Cost considerations, like risk assessments, are easily manipulated: whose costs and whose benefits are considered? The European Commission precautionary principle statement makes the useful assertion that "protection of health takes precedence over economic considerations." If "cost-effectiveness" is defined in this way, then of course precautionary decisions are cost-effective, directing us to the least costly choices.

All decisions about technology, positive and negative, should be temporary — that is, open to review and revision based on new knowledge and experience. A precautionary approach has many feedback loops. As uncertainty is reduced, we may say "yes" to some things to which we previously said "no, " and vice versa. This implies that all stakeholders should have access to relevant information. But sometimes the judicious decision will be to turn away from technologies that pose too many uncertainties and offer too few benefits. It will not always make sense to invest limited government resources into continuing research into those technologies.

Four

Responses to
Environmental Conflict

Editors' Notes

Allan Greenbaum, Alex Wellington and Ron Pushchak ————————————

AVENUES FOR CITIZEN PARTICIPATION

The rise of public participation in environmental decision-making is rooted in several political trends in the last half of the twentieth century. First, there has been a decline in the willingness of people to defer to authority on environmental decisions. People have increasingly felt that decisions, particularly local ones affecting the quality of the air and water or potentially affecting their health, should not be made without their consent, and they have made that feeling known by successfully opposing a number of environmentally hazardous projects (Laird, 1989; Nevitte, 1996).

Second, there has been since the 1960s an increasing demand for participatory democracy in general and specifically for the democratization of environmental decision-making. Participatory democracy is contrasted with representative democracy (Macpherson, 1977). In representative democracy, citizen participation in the political process is generally confined to voting for representatives in periodic elections (and, for those with time or money to spare, volunteering in or donating to the campaign of a favoured candidate or party). Given that the Canadian political system is based on a model of representative democracy, many would argue that the electoral process remains a most crucial avenue of citizen participation, if only because most of the other avenues discussed here can be thwarted or closed altogether if a government antagonistic to them is elected.

Environmental issues, however, seldom dominate election campaigns, and even less often do they dominate the agendas of governments between elections. Environmental concerns, and especially the interests of communities threatened by the negative effects of projects and pollution, will often take a back seat to the imperatives of economic growth and the influence of powerful economic interests. Environmentalists argued that the environment could only be protected if the decision-making process was opened up to the involvement of people and points of view previously shut out of the closed and often secretive networks of politicians, bureaucrats and business executives that dominated the decision-making process (see Stephen Hazell's piece in Section Two, Part A of this book).

"Citizen participation" thus became a rallying cry of the environmental movement, and in this respect the movement has had a measure of success. Public participation has become something of an entitlement in Canada, and is expected by stakeholders in all environmental decisions. It is now required by many environmental laws, including federal and most provincial environmental assessment laws, as well as planning procedures for urban development, forestry, parks and so on. A major public role in decisions has meant that public concerns cannot be easily dismissed and require a response. On the other hand, public participation does not in itself guarantee better or more acceptable environmental decisions.

In order to understand the successes and limitations of citizen participation, we need first to clarify what this term refers to. "Citizen participation" is a broad rubric that covers a range of avenues. First, participation can occur at various *levels* of decision-making, from high-level policy agenda setting to particular decisions about law enforcement in individual cases. Second, there are various *kinds* of participation, such as consultation, consensus-seeking, intervention and litigation.

In consultation, concerned members of the public are invited to provide input into the decision-making process. The consultation process may be relatively structured (for example, hearings, multi-stakeholder conferences or formal calls for briefs) or less so (for example, open houses or informal outreach by officials to interested constituencies). In either case, the hallmark of consultation is that decision-makers are not bound to follow the advice they receive. Indeed, they could not be so bound, since those who are consulted seldom speak with one mind on the issues at stake. Consultation is often undertaken by public officials seeking feedback on proposed plans and policies. It is also undertaken by private proponents of projects that will become subject to public review or that have the potential to attract protest or political opposition. In such cases, corporations may use the information they receive to modify aspects of their proposals so as to allay the most serious or most easily accommodated public concerns, and also to be able to anticipate the attacks they will face concerning those aspects they are not prepared to change.

Consultation has been and remains the most prevalent mode of public participation built into the mechanisms of Canadian environmental decision-making. Landmark consultations include the Mackenzie Valley Pipeline Inquiry in the 1970s (Berger, 1977), which resulted in a decision to shelve a proposed natural gas pipeline through the Canadian north, and the British Columbia Commission on Resources and Environment (CORE) in the 1990s. Established by special provincial legislation in 1992 and abolished in 1996, CORE involved consensus as well as consultation; its mandate "encompassed the development and monitoring of regional land-use planning, community-based participatory processes concerning land-use, resources and environmental management, and a related dispute-resolution system" (Benidickson, 1997: 243). Although consultations are typically intended not to be adversarial affairs, whenever the subject matter is controversial the nature of the consultation process will tend to encourage adversarial, strategic behaviour on the part of participants, as each stakeholder group vies for an outcome favourable to itself or consistent with its values (Wondolleck, 1988). This tendency has encouraged an interest in consensus processes.

The reading in this section by Cormick et al. provides an introduction to the elements, advantages and challenges of consensus processes. Consensus processes differ from consultation in that the output is agreed to by all parties. In consultation, the decision-maker listens to all concerned, and then decides what to do; in a consensus process, representatives of all interested groups and constituencies deliberate together until they arrive at a resolution acceptable to all. Needless to say, consensus processes require a much greater investment of time and effort by all concerned. Since the achievement of consensus is never certain, some default position or fallback method of decision making must be available. Consensus processes are discussed in detail in the sections below on alternative dispute resolution (ADR) and environmental mediation. ADR methods may be seen as ways of settling disputes between parties, but they can also be understood as ways of making decisions on matters of public policy, implementation and planning. There is thus much overlap between the concepts of ADR, especially when applied to issues of public decision-making, and that of "deliberative democracy" (Pellizzoni, 1999; 2001). According to Pellow (1999), many environmental activists, even those operating from an oppositional "environmental justice" frame of reference, have come to embrace participation in consensus based decision processes, in part because they are thought to embody progressive values of democracy, sustainability, co-operation and accountability, and in part because changes in the larger political and economic scene have undercut the effectiveness of traditional confrontational strategies.

Intervention and litigation as avenues for citizen participation refer to the participation of citizens and citizen groups in proceedings involving courts or administrative tribunals. In litigation, the citizens in question are initiators of the legal proceedings, and are full parties to it. Citizens can also seek to participate in legal proceedings as intervenors. Intervenors are not parties to the legal case, but are persons or organizations with an interest in the outcome who are granted permission by the court to submit arguments and evidence. Two recent cases before the Supreme Court of Canada illustrate this role. In the first case (*114957 Canada Ltee [Spraytech] et al. v. Hudson [Town]* 2001 SCC 40), a group of lawn care companies sought to have the Court strike down a municipal bylaw restricting the use of pesticides; environmentalists intervened in support of upholding the bylaw. In the other case (decision pending at the time of writing), Harvard University brought an action to force Canada's patent office to grant a patent on a genetically engineered mouse developed by the university, and environmentalists (among others) intervened to oppose allowing patents on animals. [Supreme Court decisions can be found on-line at <http://www.lexum.umontreal.ca/csc-scc/en/pub/>.]

The term "intervenor" is also used to describe parties other than the proponent who participate in environmental assessment hearings and other administrative hearings concerned with approving projects or plans. Avenues for citizen participation in environmental assessment, then, include consultation at the early "scoping" stage of the process (see the discussion of environmental assessment in the editors' notes to Section Three, Part A) and intervention at the formal hearing stage. The term is appropriate because such administrative hearings, while not quite as formal, resemble trials in many respects. Expert witnesses are cross-examined at length by opposing lawyers. Citizen intervenors have contributed to better environmental decision-making on many occasions by exposing the shortcomings of faulty or incomplete proponent assessments. Effective intervention is expensive, however. Intervenors must pay for scientific studies, expert witnesses, and lawyers. Mindful of the value of citizen intervention, and aiming to "level the playing field" between what are often small, "grassroots" public interest groups and proponents, some environmental assessment regimes have instituted "intervenor funding" programs. Under these programs, intervenors who meet certain criteria have some of their expenses covered out of the public purse.

Starting with the Mackenzie Valley Pipeline Inquiry in the 1970s, provincial and federal governments have made intervenor funding available, if only on an *ad hoc* basis (Macdonald, 1991: 176–78). In 1988 the Ontario government established a provisional program to fund intervenors before the Environmental Assessment and Ontario Energy Boards, but allowed this program to lapse in 1996. The Ontario government still provides indirect funding for some citizen environmental litigation through the Canadian Environmental Law Association (CELA) in its capacity as a legal aid clinic. CELA (and the Canadian Institute for Environmental Law and Policy, or CIELAP) is also a donor supported non-governmental organization that engages in litigation, intervention, research, public education and law-reform advocacy. Environmental Defence Canada and the Sierra Legal Defence Fund are other donor supported non-governmental organizations that act as funders of last resort for major environmental legal fights.

In previous sections of this book we have addressed citizen litigation in the forms of civil lawsuits and private criminal or quasi-criminal prosecutions. Another avenue for citizens to affect environmental decision-making through the courts is administrative litigation — lawsuits in which courts are asked to review the actions of public agencies. In the United States there is much greater opportunity for this kind of litigation than in Canada (see the last section of the Introductory Essay). American law often gives concerned citizens and groups standing to sue government officials for failing to give effect to the substance of environment legislation, while Canadian law generally grants officials greater discretion on substantive issues, and courts will review administrative decisions only around issues of procedure and jurisdiction. The power of public (and private) interest groups to tie up American government decisions in the courts is another factor that has spurred interest in consensus models and ADR in the United States.

The quest for an "environmental bill of rights" in Canada was initially motivated by a desire to open up more avenues to public interest litigation by relaxing restrictive rules of legal standing. The effect of these rules was to make civil and administrative litigation available only to parties protecting their own special pecuniary interests. The 1970 *Michigan Environmental Protection Act* provided a model for Canadians seeking to reform Canada's standing and environmental laws. This quest to establish citizens' procedural rights to litigate on behalf of environmental quality is sketched in the reading by Elaine Hughes in this section.

Interestingly, Ontario's 1993 *Environmental Bill of Rights* (EBR), the most ambitious of these reforms to be enacted, ended up taking on a rather different, and arguably a distinctively "Canadian", shape. The EBR does relax common law standing rules for public nuisance litigation to some degree, and creates a tort of environmental law-breaking. This provision has been used to sue operators of waste disposal sites and, most recently, to sue the Canadian mining giant INCO for the toxic metal contamination of the town of Port Colborne by its refinery there (Environmental Commissioner of Ontario 2001: 150). The EBR's main thrust, however, is not to facilitate litigation, but to allow the public to have input into, and oversight of, the regulatory process. It requires that environmentally significant government proposals (including policies, legislation, regulations, standards, approvals and other instruments) be posted on an Internet registry. It gives Ontario residents rights to comment on these proposals and, in some cases, to appeal government decisions to a tribunal. It also gives residents the right to request that the government investigate suspected violations of environmental rules, and even to request that these rules be revised in light of the government's own "Statements of Environmental Values". The Ontario EBR, then, provides for citizen input at all of the *levels* of the regulatory process discussed at the outset of this note, from policy setting to specific instruments, and makes use of the full range of *kinds* of participation, from consultation to litigation.

The Ontario EBR is discussed in the reading by Averil Guiste in this section. The reading by Stephen Hazell on environmental assessment and democracy (in Section Two, Part A) also discussed the Ontario EBR at length. Hazell argues that the greatest merit of the EBR is that it provides transparency to aspects of environmental decision-making that in Canada have traditionally been shrouded in secrecy. More information on the EBR and its use can be obtained from the website of the Environmental Commissioner of Ontario: <http://www.eco.on.ca>.

The extent to which the avenues to citizen participation discussed here have improved environmental decision-making is a topic of lively debate. Two decades ago, conservationist John Livingston (1981: 33) denounced environmental assessment as a "fraud, a hoax and a con" because it allowed development to proceed as usual with a veneer of environmental scrutiny. What is clearer is the effect the proliferation of these avenues has had on the environmental movement and, specifically, on environmental non-governmental organizations (ENGOs). The opportunity, and hence the imperative, to participate in environmental decision-making has created employment for a legion of advocates, researchers, administrators, fundraisers and lawyers, all occupied almost entirely with participation in consultations, hearings and so on. Participation absorbs a corresponding proportion of the volunteer energies available to organizations without the resources to hire staff. Are the environmental benefits of "citizen participation" (as presently institutionalized) worth the costs, not just to government and business, but to the citizen participants themselves?

Alternative to or complementary with these institutional avenues of participation are other forms of public involvement in which citizen actors retain the initiative. One particularly interesting instance of a citizen initiated law reform effort was the Tin Wis Coalition in British Columbia, an alliance of environmentalists, community activists, First Nations and labour unions in the forestry and fishery industries, which developed and advocated model forest practices legislation based on ideas of ecological stewardship and local value-added processing of wood products (Tester, 1992; Pinkerton, 1993). Another approach, less broadly based but effective, was the campaign organized by Greenpeace in Europe to boycott B.C. forest products not certified as having been produced in an ecologically sound way by the Forest Stewardship Council, an international, independent, non-profit, non-governmental organization founded in 1993 (the website of the FSC's Canadian office can be accessed at <http://www.fsccanada.org>, and that of the head office in Mexico at <http://www.fscoax.org).

ALTERNATIVE DISPUTE RESOLUTION

Alternative dispute resolution, as a movement, and as a set of social practices, is part of a reform agenda to provide more "flexibility, informality, particularity and privacy" to disputing parties (Menkel-Meadow, 1997: 418).[1] The moniker "ADR" is applied to negotiation, mediation and arbitration, as well as the less familiar practices of mini trials, summary trials, and early neutral evaluation. The "alternatives" to litigation share some common elements, such as relaxation of procedural formality, non-application of substantive legal rules, and an emphasis on compromise to produce a resolution (Bush, 1989: 254, note 1). Alternative dispute resolution processes were intended to be more creative, contextual and responsive to the needs and interests of the disputing parties than what traditional, adversarial, formal justice systems typically provide.

The word "alternative" refers to something other than adjudication by state courts, i.e., to informal as opposed to formal justice systems. Adjudication specifies decision making by a third body whose "authority to decide is derived from the holding of an office", namely a judge, who provides a binding decision (Woodman, 1993: 137). Decisions reached by judges can "normally be enforced by official coercion"; they are backed up by the powers of the state (Woodman, 1993: 137). Included under the umbrella term "alternative" is a range of approaches and processes. The most like adjudication is arbitration, in which binding decisions are made by a person or body other than a court. Arbitration is quasi-judicial in nature, and "may be invoked at the instance of one party pursuant to some legislative regime or prior agreement of the parties" (Shrybman, 1984). Arbitration provisions are "common in union collective bargaining agreements", for instance (*Black's Law Dictionary*, 1991: 70). "The authority of the third party decision maker is typically derived from an over-arching agreement between the parties" (*Black's Law Dictionary*, 1991: 70). The process is usually less formal than adjudication, and it involves expedited fact finding. An arbitration decision is "binding only on the parties and in the instant case and carries no precedential effect" (Bush, 1987: 46). Arbitration is "intended to avoid the formalities, the delay, the expense and vexation of ordinary litigation" (*Black's Law Dictionary*, 1991: 70).

The other alternatives are mediation and negotiation.[2] Mediation is a relatively informal approach to dispute resolution that rests upon the intervention of a third party neutral who works to help parties reach a mutually agreeable outcome, whether or not a settlement is reached. The crucial aspects of mediation are that it is a voluntary process, a consensual process and a non-binding process. The mediator has "no authority to impose a settlement", and hence no coercive power (Cormick, 1982: 16). The "dispute is settled when the parties themselves reach what they consider to be a workable solution" (Cormick, 1982: 16). Otherwise, the dispute remains unresolved, and the parties may turn to other avenues, such as litigation or negotiation.

Negotiation may be defined as "any process directed towards an agreed resolution in which no third party plays a significant part" (Woodman, 1993: 138). Negotiation can be either facilitated or unfacilitated; that is, the parties can be assisted by third parties, or they can negotiate amongst themselves without any assistance. Negotiation comprises deliberative discussion, and communication with a view to reaching a settlement or agreement. In the context of contracts, it involves the process of submission and consideration of offers until an acceptable offer is made and then accepted. Negotiation ultimately is more generic than either mediation or arbitration; it "pervades life inside and outside of organizations" (Lax and Sebenius, 1986: 365). Yet, it is not completely unstructured; there needs to be "mutual awareness and explicit acceptance" of the recognized "rules of the game for negotiation". David Lax and James Sebenius identify the following as features of negotiation situations: "interdependence, some perceived conflict, opportunistic potential, the possibility of explicit or tacit agreement on joint action" (Lax and Sebenius, 1986: 365).

The term "dispute" is often used interchangeably with "conflict". A more specific definition of dispute is as follows: "the species of conflict which has developed to the point where there is a public assertion of the mutually inconsistent claims and the fact of the incompatibility" (Woodman, 1993: 136). This particular definition of dispute has the merits of focusing on the expression of conflicts in such a way as to call up a response, whether from the systems of formal justice or those of informal justice. It has the advantage of distinguishing disputes from generic conflicts, many of which remain unexpressed and are part of background social conditions. The term "resolution", as many have noted, is somewhat misleading insofar as it seems to suggest that conflicts actually are terminated or relieved. Some scholars, such as Frank Sander, use the term "dispute processing" instead. It may be safer to say the end result is a redefinition or a transformation of the conflict through the application of processes or modes of addressing the dispute. As Gordon Woodman put it, "a resolution is best viewed as an event which terminates a particular stage in the dispute by changing the normative relationship between the parties to a greater or lesser degree, but which does not necessarily terminate the dispute" (Woodman, 1993: 136). Successful resolutions are possible, of course, to the extent that the parties themselves are "fully aware of the alternatives" and "come to a mutually satisfactory agreement" (Sander, 1995: 329).

Alternative dispute resolution and, in particular, mediation, it is said, can provide a more complex form of "satisfaction", one in which the needs and interests of the parties determine the final outcome. It is not only that some disputants would be able to actually resolve their disputes were they to avail themselves of ADR, but also that even those who might fail to reach agreement if they tried ... would still benefit from the attempt, and may be less likely to be disaffected or disappointed from the adjudicative or other outcome to their dispute, having tried the other way.

There have been vocal critics of ADR from its earliest days, and one line of criticism has focused on the way that ADR constrains or limits conflict resolution, making it a "private matter" between the parties. One of the earliest articulations of a "justice" critique of ADR was penned by Owen Fiss in the mid-1980s (Fiss, 1984). The critique has since been updated by David Luban and others. The problem, as Fiss characterized it, was that dispute settlement trivialized the "remedial dimensions" of a lawsuit, and compromised the "moral fabric" of society by replacing "public", "authoritative" decision-making with "private" resolution (Fiss, 1984: 1073). David Luban, likewise, relies upon a "public-life conception of legitimacy" to offer criteria for choosing among settlements, in order to reject the "wrong" ones (Luban, 1995: 2662). Luban suggests that the title of Fiss' article, "Against Settlement", should be revised to read, "Against the Wrong Settlements". The wrong settlements are specifically ones that are shrouded in secrecy, ones where one or other of the parties insists upon confidentiality clauses. Such clauses prevent the public from obtaining the factual information that was unearthed or brought to light during the discovery process, or simply through the negotiation proceedings. Toxic tort cases, for instance, involve information about defective products or by-products of production that pose serious threats to public health and safety. Yet, it is in just such cases that the companies involved have insisted on tying their payments to plaintiffs up with confidentiality and non-disclosure provisions. These secret settlements are the ones to be resisted, Luban argues, rather than settlements generally. They pose a particularly pernicious threat to public good.

Other lines of criticism or areas of concern can be found in the literature on alternative dispute resolution. In the readings included in this volume, Douglas Amy emphasizes the problems in environmental mediation that arise from unequal bargaining power of the parties (discussed below). There are continuing debates about what the over-riding or underlying objectives or purposes of mediation should be. Should mediation, as a set of social practices, be aimed at achieving "peace" and social harmony, or should it instead be aimed at pursuing "social justice" and radical social change? The latter reflects a concern with the fate of society generally, and the welfare or illfare of identifiable social groups, rather than simply the disputing parties *qua* individuals.

The "peace and harmony" approach to mediation is often aligned, at least in the eyes of its critics, with enhancement of the social order. They charge that, since the approach is not affiliated with radical critiques of the existing social order, it is instead part and parcel of the problem. Many of the proponents of the "peace and harmony" conception of mediation, however, do see themselves as concerned with social change, but characterize the desiderata in terms of transformation of individuals, for example, rather than structural social change. That, for the adherents of the "social justice" approach, is simply not sufficient. Social justice includes, and even requires ameliorating and remedying discrimination, poverty, abuse and other social ills visited upon individuals as members of identifiable social groups. What is crucial, for the social justice mediator, is to avoid "pathologizing" social conflict, as the "peace and harmony" advocates are wont to do. Instead, social conflict must be recognized to be not only unavoidable, but necessary as a way to fight against oppression and injustice (whether one is fighting back as a victim, or as an advocate on behalf of victims).

To summarize, "alternative forms of dispute resolution have become increasingly popular" in situations where the "parties are in a continuing relationship, where fault is difficult to allocate, and compromise is the most equitable solution" (Fitzgerald and Wright, 2000: 95). They have also become increasingly attractive to governments concerned with court backlogs and looking for ways to cut administrative costs; some jurisdictions have begun to experiment with introducing court-annexed mediation programs. Negotiation is pervasive during all legal cases, since "most disputes are in fact settled before they get to court (Fitzgerald and Wright, 2000: 95). Environmental negotiation, or negotiation about environmental matters in particular, occurs throughout the processes of licensing and prosecutorial confrontations (Benidickson, 1997: 239). That topic is discussed in the editors' notes to Section Two, "The Regulatory System".

Other situations in which negotiation about environmental matters has been prominent or influential include what is known in the United States as "negotiated rule making" (Benidickson, 1997: 239). This occurred, for example, during the development of regulations under the *Canadian Environmental Assessment Act*. During that process, "[r]epresentatives of several federal departments, provincial governments, and various industry associations, public-interest organizations, and Aboriginal groups deliberated extensively" (Benidickson, 1997: 239). That process illustrates the kinds of developments surveyed just above in "Avenues to Citizen Participation". Environmental Assessment is discussed in detail in the editors' notes to Section Three, Part A. Next, we focus specifically on the importance of mediation for environmental matters.

ENVIRONMENTAL MEDIATION

An alternative framework for resolving environmental disputes has been a long sought-after solution to a widening range of prolonged and sometimes bitter conflicts that dot the environmental landscape. Conflicts that have arisen over the threatened loss of forest ecosystems, proposals to site hazardous waste facilities, waste incinerators, power plants, radioactive waste facilities, highways and dams have drawn the attention of many in law and public policy who wish for a better, less confrontational way of resolving environmental disputes. There has been a great deal of dissatisfaction with traditional legislated and legal processes that are adversarial and often result in large costs for all stakeholders, and that frequently fail to resolve disputes. The need for an alternative solution to environmental conflicts has been particularly great where the courts have not been able to resolve disputes in a timely manner or where legislated solutions have not been able to quell the intense public opposition arising with each new proposal. As a result, environmental mediation is frequently put forward as an alternative to litigation.

When self-interest prevails, litigation will usually be relied upon; however, where mediation can be accepted as an alternative, it can reduce the chance that a decision will be imposed on an affected population by the courts (Emond, 1991). In theory, both proponents and those who oppose their projects stand to benefit when their interests can be reasonably satisfied by having a project implemented through negotiation rather than a legal conflict. A growing recognition of the interdependence of stakeholders' interests provides the incentive needed for decision making by consensus. But, in the absence of that recognition, consensus decision-making is not likely to lead to an agreement on what constitutes an environmentally acceptable action.

Environmental mediation assumes that it is possible to make major decisions by reaching consensus among a number of competing interests. Early attempts at negotiating environmental conflicts recognized that it is the very nature of consensus that leads to negotiated settlements (B.C. Round Table on the Environment and the Economy, n.d.). The Round Table report outlined the place of consensus in a legal or policy decision process. The fact that consensus requires compromise is also at the core of negotiated agreements. The role of compromise was also examined in the context of a number of environmental conflicts in British Columbia that were addressed through alternative dispute resolution methods. In the end, the Round Table concluded that, among other features, a negotiated outcome is possible where the key stakeholders have a clear incentive to seek a decision by consensus, and where the participants support the process rules used to reach the consensus.

The growing use of mediation to resolve environmental conflicts has been supported by several advances in alternative methods of dispute resolution found in recent research and practice on methods of negotiating disputes. Some of the early examples included the development of principled conflict resolution methods at the Harvard Project on Negotiation in the 1980s that have been applied to environmental conflicts with considerable success (Fisher and Ury, 1981; Susskind and Cruikshank, 1987). Advances in Alternative Dispute Resolution methods (ADR) and a growing record of successes at resolving environmental disputes using ADR approaches have prompted governments and agencies involved in environmental conflicts to try these methods, including negotiating impact agreements with stakeholders directly, and compensating affected people to offset the losses of environmental projects (Bingham, 1984). The most popular ADR method has been environmental mediation, the process of submitting an environmental dispute to an informal negotiation process assisted by a mediator who is an impartial third party.

Rounthwaite has described environmental mediation as a voluntary process for resolving environmental disputes that requires the intervention of a neutral mediator (Rounthwaite, 1998: 516). He noted that it is a process where the procedures to be followed in the negotiation are agreed to by the participants themselves, and where the mediator assists the participants by bringing to bear a knowledge of mediation methods and experience in mediating a resolution to conflict. To be successful, an environmental mediation process must do several things. It must identify and include all of the relevant stakeholders involved in the conflict. The absence of an important constituent group might undo an agreement, if one is reached. Further, there must be a willingness on the part of the stakeholders to negotiate in good faith, because the stability of an agreement depends on the trust created among the parties. In addition, the mediator selected should have knowledge of the mediation process and experience in guiding the parties to a settlement (Rounthwaite, 1998: 518).

Environmental mediation is the most prominent of the major methods of ADR in Canada that have received attention in environmental decision-making (others include arbitration and negotiated agreements). Rounthwaite noted that the *Canadian Environmental Assessment Act* is one prominent example of an attempt to implement environmental mediation by legislation in the environmental assessment of federal projects. He suggested that instituting shared decision methods like environmental mediation is part of a transformative approach to making environmental decisions by balancing the unequal power that exists among the stakeholders in a conflict (Rounthwaite, 1998: 519).

An early example of institutionalized mediation was the *British Columbia CORE Act* (*Commissioner On Resources and Environment Act*, 1992). It required the B.C. commissioner to develop and facilitate a dispute resolution system to resolve land use, related resource and environmental conflicts. At the time, the argument for institutionalizing environmental mediation and other ADR methods voiced by the Commissioner was that: "[T]he traditional approach to land and resource allocation, based primarily on the responsibility of statutory decision-makers, is no longer accepted in British Columbia as necessarily the best way to make decisions" (Rounthwaite, 1998: 542). The expectation was that institutionalizing environmental mediation could produce a shared and more accepted decision-making process.

Swanson, in this volume, reviews the growing trend in the use of ADR methods in resolving environmental conflicts and the use of ADR legislation in Canada, and she also examines the question whether ADR methods should be institutionalized in legislation or whether they should remain outside the legal system as alternatives to traditional decision-making methods. She explains that alternative dispute resolution methods originally arose outside the law, and were last resorts when traditional methods failed. Moreover, it was frequently the threat of litigation and its potential losses that brought disputing parties together to negotiate their conflict outside the legal process. Swanson notes the use of institutionalized environmental mediation and other ADR methods in federal legislation, including the *Canadian Environmental Assessment Act*, and in provincial laws in Nova Scotia, Manitoba and Ontario (Swanson, 1995: 274).

In this volume, Swanson poses the arguments for and against institutionalizing environmental mediation. Institutionalized environmental mediation would provide clear mechanisms for the enforcement of any agreements reached by the parties in a conflict. It would also help make ADR procedures more consistent, and make the process of negotiation fairer for many public participants who lack experience and resources to successfully negotiate disputes. On the other hand, requiring environmental mediation by law may reduce the threat of litigation and the willingness of proponents to reduce environmental impacts. They know mediation will provide some measure of what they desire in an environmental decision, and that the entire project will not face rejection. On balance, Swanson favours law reforms that would build environmental mediation and ADR methods into legislation.

Steven Shrybman's paper outlines the types of environmental disputes mediation can be applied to, and the circumstances that are conducive to successful mediation that allow a skilled mediator to start a negotiation process that might otherwise not occur. For mediation to be successful, he notes that it must be a voluntary process where stakeholders cannot be compelled to participate in the negotiation process. Similarly, the agreement reached must be a consensual one where the participants are satisfied that it meets their collective needs, because the mediator does not have the authority to make the agreement binding. In every successful mediation, the outcome must be willingly accepted by the stakeholders. Shrybman notes that throughout the process, the role of the mediator is to persuade the parties to reach consensus, not to coerce them to do so, and he reviews the obstacles to successful mediation. While examining the positive outcomes that can result from mediation, he raises the important question of whether all environmental disputes are amenable to a negotiated solution. Further, he notes that many groups have identified the lack of a legal framework for ADR as a significant impediment to its successful use in resolving environmental disputes.

Further in this section, Bingham argues that environmental mediation is a step forward because it addresses issues that are important to the implementation of a project much more directly than litigation does. Typically, a mediated agreement focuses on how a project will be carried out and how its impacts might be reduced. As well, she contends that there is greater potential for both parties to benefit from the decision than there is when litigation is employed. The ratio of benefits to costs for each party may improve, since a court or tribunal does not define how and why costs and benefits should be distributed. Bingham believes that the outcomes of mediation may be more satisfactory to the parties than the outcomes of litigation. After all, litigation creates a zero-sum game. It creates winners and losers; not all parties benefit from the decision. She also suggests that environmental mediation seeks to reduce the cost and delay associated with litigation. In her article, Bingham uses American data to test the hypothesis that environmental mediation is more efficient, speedier and less costly than litigation. She concludes that the incentive to use environmental mediation will depend on the desire of the parties for greater satisfaction with the outcomes, not on the desire to curb costs and reduce delay.

Douglas Amy's examination of the politics of environmental mediation in this volume frames the debate about what issues should and should not be negotiated in the mediation process, and raises the question of whether some environmental resources are non-negotiable, where any compromise would be considered a significant and unacceptable impact on natural resources. He observes that, while it is often less costly and time consuming to resolve environmental disputes through mediation rather than litigation, non-negotiable environmental interests are at risk in a mediation, and that the promise of a settlement may "seduce" those representing environmental interests into making significant concessions in air and water quality, public health or ecosystems protection. Amy suggests that environmentalists in many negotiating situations are not able to evenly match the power that development interests bring to the bargaining table. He argues that there is a substantial problem of unequal bargaining power in most environmental conflicts, and points out three ways in which the imbalance in power "undermine(s) the assumed neutrality of the mediation process" (Amy, 1983: 7).

First, he suggests that significant economic and political power tends to provide development interests with greater access to the mediation process, particularly access to those who have the power to influence the mediation. Second, superior resources can, as in other environmental legal proceedings and hearings, endow proponents with greater technical expertise; and third, the lesser power of environmental participants tends to undermine their freedom to voluntarily reject a mediated agreement. In some cases, environmental negotiators are aware that the threat of legal action faces them if a settlement is not reached, and that the proponent's greater financial resources are available to pursue a court action.

Amy refers to such actions as "biased games with impartial referees", and notes that the fair resolution of games with such inherent biases lies in the hands of the mediator. If mediators were responsible, conscientious and politically aware, they would be able to recognize the biases in a negotiation, and could avoid promoting unfair compromises in a context of unequal power. He raises the question of the mediator's role in non-negotiable environmental issues where a compromise could mean significant environmental losses, even if conceded by environmental interests. He notes that it is an extremely difficult task for any mediator to distinguish between biased and unbiased negotiations, and between negotiable and non-negotiable environmental issues.

Recent developments in the use of conflict resolution to resolve public policy disputes include multi-stakeholder committees, round tables on the environment and the economy, and coalitions for co-management. These developments represent additional consensus-seeking responses to environmental conflicts by governments and citizens. They also reflect efforts on the part of governments to ostensibly provide more opportunities for citizen participation in response to agitation, lobbying and persistent requests for citizen involvement in environmental decisions. These initiatives concerning public participation reflect movement away from a reliance on the authority of the state toward a sharing of responsibility for environmental decisions between governments and stakeholders.

Currently, mediation is being legislated in a growing number of environmental laws. As Swanson notes, mediation is included in the *Canadian Environmental Assessment Act* and some provincial acts. In Ontario, the 1997 revisions to the *Environmental Assessment Act* provide for mediation where there is a dispute about the terms of reference for an environmental assessment study, before those terms are approved. Also, the Minister of the Environment determines who the parties are in a mediation process, and can appoint persons to act as mediators. The minister can also appoint the Environmental Assessment Board, a body that normally conducts an environmental assessment hearing, to itself act as a mediator in a dispute about the assessment.

The question raised in this section is whether the use of mediation is reasonable in all cases. Swanson argued that if mediation were institutionalized, as it has been in Ontario, the legal requirement would provide a clear mechanism for enforcing agreements. However, making mediation a requirement assumes that all participants have the power and resources to negotiate without being coerced to concede significant environmental losses (the imbalance of power in the mediation process raises the theme of justice that is a recurring theme throughout this book). As Emond observed, environmental mediation is a process that ideally involves those who are believed to have the clout required to veto implementation of a negotiated settlement (Emond, 1991). Those who are assumed to lack economic or political clout can be excluded from the negotiation process; their interests need not be considered in constructing a "solution". The costs they will bear, as a result of the siting or disposal practices adopted, need not be addressed when negotiating a settlement. The process does not take into account the consequences of the negotiated settlement for those not at the table.

Shrybman also notes the potential for mediation to have a pro-development bias that can lead to substantial concessions, including allowing proponents to avoid the environmental assessment process. He raises the central question, whether environmental mediation is a boon or a hindrance to environmentalists. It is conceivable that the environment can be compromised through biased mediation or negotiated away by those who have a personal or group interest in a negotiated outcome. Amy echoes this concern by suggesting that environmentalists who get involved in the (mediation) process tend to get co-opted, and are not successful in protecting environmental resources.

In the end, the environmental mediation process was not designed to promote the interests of the environment or of future generations. Instead, it is structured to meet the interests of the stakeholders involved in the negotiation, and the public interest is not necessarily reflected in a mediated settlement. Governments have seized on the opportunity to control conflicts and reduce delays in environmental proceedings by imposing mediation. Imposed mediation, in a sociological perspective, serves to structure and control social conflicts from within. Where mediation was previously voluntary and implied that those opposed to the project could veto the undertaking if consensus was not reached, imposed mediation mandates a settlement. While mediation was originally a method to resolve environmental conflicts outside the institutional context, it is now becoming an institutionalized way of internalizing the debate over natural resources, one that produces more predictable outcomes that do not impede major projects when environmental and development interests conflict.

NOTES

1. The next six paragraphs borrow heavily from the following pieces of one of the authors: Alex Wellington, "Taking Codes of Ethics Seriously: Alternative Dispute Resolution and Reconstitutive Liberalism", *The Canadian Journal of Law and Jurisprudence*, Volume 12, Number 2, July 1999; and Alex Wellington, "Professional Ethics for Mediators: Tensions Between Justice and Accountability," forthcoming in *Communication, Conflict, and Reconciliation*, edited by Cheryl Hughes and James Wong (*Social Philosophy Today* Book Series, Volume 17, 2003).

2. The legal literature often contains discussion of the following processes that are adjunct to litigation: ministerial, summary jury trial, and early neutral evaluation. See Frank E.A. Sander, "The Varieties of Dispute Processing" (1976) 70 *Federal Rules Decisions* 111; and Frank E.A. Sander and Stephen B. Goldberg, "Fitting the Forum to the Fuss: A User-Friendly Guide to Selecting an ADR Procedure" (January 1994) *Negotiation Journal* 49–68.

REFERENCES

Amy, Douglas. 1983. "The Politics of Environmental Mediation." *Ecology Law Quarterly* 11, 1: 1–19.

Benidickson, Jamie. 1997. *Environmental Law*. Concord, ON: Irwin Law Publishers.

Berger, Thomas. 1977. *Northern Frontier, Northern Homeland: The Report of the Mackenzie Valley Pipeline Inquiry*. Ottawa: Ministry of Supply and Services.

Bingham, Gail. 1984. *Resolving Environmental Disputes: A Decade of Experience*. Washington: The Conservation Foundation.

Black's Law Dictionary, Sixth Abridged Edition. St. Paul, MN: West Publishing, 1991.

British Columbia Round Table on the Environment and the Economy. n.d. *Concepts and Definitions*, Victoria, B.C. Round Table on the Environment and the Economy.

Bush, Robert Baruch. 1989. "Efficiency and Protection or Empowerment and Recognition?: The Mediator's Role and Ethical Standards in Mediation." *Florida Law Review* 41: 253–86.

———. 1987. "Using Process Observation to Teach Alternative Dispute Resolution: Alternatives to Simulation." *Journal of Legal Education* 37: 46–57.

Cormick, Gerald. 1982. "The Myth, The Reality and The Future of Environmental Mediation." *Environment*, 24: 14–39.

Emond, Paul. 1991. "The Greening of Environmental Law." *McGill Law Journal* 36: 743–69.

Environmental Commissioner of Ontario. 2001. *Having Regard: 2000–2001 Annual Report*. Toronto: Environmental Commissioner of Ontario.

Fisher, Roger, and Ury, William. 1981. *Getting to Yes: Negotiating Without Giving In*. New York: Houghton Mifflin.

Fiss, Owen. 1984. "Against Settlement." *Yale Law Journal* 93: 1073–90.

Fitzgerald, Patrick, and Barry Wright. 2000. *Looking at Law: Canada's Legal System*, Fifth Edition. Markham, ON: Butterworths.

Laird, Frank. 1989. "The Decline of Deference: The Political Context of Risk Communication." *Risk Analysis* 9, 4: 543–50.

Lax, David A., and James K. Sebenius. 1986. "Three Ethical Issues in Negotiation." *Negotiation Journal* 363–69.

Livingston, John A. 1981. *The Fallacy of Wildlife Conservation*. Toronto: McClelland & Stewart.

Luban, David. 1995. "Settlements and the Erosion of the Public Realm." *Georgetown Law Journal* 83: 2619–62.

Macdonald, Doug. 1991. *The Politics of Pollution*. Toronto: McClelland & Stewart.

Macpherson, Crawford Braugh. 1977. *The Life and Times of Liberal Democracy*. Oxford, UK: Oxford University Press.

Marentette, Roger F.X. 1992. "A Review of the Alternative Dispute Resolution System in Ontario and Canada." *Municipal World* (September): 8–9.

Menkel-Meadow, Carrie. 1997. "Ethics in Alternative Dispute Resolution: New Issues, No Answers From the Adversary Conception of Lawyers Responsibilities." *South Texas Law Review* 38: 418.

Nevitte, Neil. 1996. *The Decline of Deference: Canadian Value Change in Cross-National Perspective*. Peterborough, ON: Broadview.

Pellizzoni, Luigi. 2001. "The Myth of the Best Argument." *British Journal of Sociology* 52: 56–86.

———. 1999. "Reflexive Modernization and Beyond: Knowledge and Value in the Politics of Environment and Technology." *Theory, Culture and Society* 16, 4: 99–125.

Pellow, David N. 1999. "Emerging Environmental Movement Tactics: Mobilizing Consensus, Demobilizing Conflict." *Sociological Forum* 14: 659–83.

Pinkerton, Evelyn. 1993. "Co-management Efforts as Social Movements: The Tin Wis Coalition and the Drive for Forest Practices Legislation in British Columbia." *Alternatives* 19, 3: 33–38.

Rounthwaite, Ian. 1998. "Alternative Dispute Resolution in Environmental Law: Uses, Limitations, and Potentials." In *Environmental law and Policy*, Second Edition, ed. E. Hughes, A. Lucas and W. Tilleman. Toronto: Emond Montgomery Publishers.

Sander, Frank. 1995. "The Obsession With Settlement Rates." *Negotiation Journal* (October): 329–32.

Shrybman, Steven. 1984. *Environmental Mediation: From Theory to Practice*. Toronto: Canadian Environmental Law Association. [Excerpts published in this volume.]

Susskind, Lawrence, and Jeffrey Cruikshank. 1987. *Breaking the Impasse: Consensual Approaches to Resolving Public Disputes*. New York, Basic Books.

Swanson, Elizabeth. 1995. "Alternative Dispute Resolution and Environmental Conflict: the Case for Law Reform." *Alberta Law Review* 34, 1: 267–78.

Tester, Frank. 1992. "Environmentalism and the Evolution of Citizen Participation in Canada." *Alternatives* 19, 1: 41–43.

Wondolleck, Julia. 1988. *Public Lands Conflict and Resolution: Managing National Forest Disputes*. New York: Plenum Press.

Woodman, Gordon. 1993. "The Alternative Law of Alternative Dispute Resolution." In *Readings in Law and Society*, ed. J. Banfield. Toronto: Captus Press.

PART A
Avenues for Citizen Participation

(a) Procedural Rights[†]

Elaine L. Hughes ————————————————————————————

Numerous attempts to obtain an "environmental bill of rights" have been made in Canada since the early 1970s. These have arisen primarily at the provincial level, in the form of proposed legislation that, in the words of Doug MacDonald, *The Politics of Pollution* (Toronto: McClelland & Stewart, 1991), 144:

> if enacted, would grant the public a right to a healthy environment and introduce a series of reforms to increase the powers of private citizens to protect themselves, and their environment, from the effects of pollution and to initiate private prosecutions of pollution offenses in cases where government had refused to act. It would also provide increased access to information on pollution and rights to participate in standard-setting and other processes.

In "Details of a Canadian Environmental Bill of Rights," in D. Estrin and J. Swaigen, eds., *Environmental on Trial* (Toronto: CELRF, 1974), it was also suggested that an environmental bill of rights should require better environmental impact assessments, provisions addressing litigation costs, legislative limits on the exercise of administrative discretion, creation of an environmental ombudsman, and reverse onus provisions.

These proposals, in other words, have been primarily procedural in nature. Typically, the

basic idea has been to try to address a number of the existing deficiencies in the present law. For example, one of the earliest proposals was made in Alberta in 1979: Bill 222, The Environmental Bill of Rights, 1st sess., 19th leg. Alta. including standing to bring private prosecutions, a statutory cause of action for pollution if it significantly decreased environmental quality, some provisions altering the burden of proof in civil actions, better access to information, and some provisions dealing with remedies. Other proposals were made periodically, including those in Ontario in 1979, 1980, 1987 and 1989, and Saskatchewan in 1982; each proposal continued to emphasize the improvement of procedural rights, including costs, intervenor funding, and judicial review of administrative decisions, although some also included a few "substantive" provisions.

However, each time such bills were introduced, they either died on the order paper or were blocked by the majority government of the day. In fact, the only rights legislation successfully enacted in the 1970s and 1980s was section 19.1 of Quebec's Environment Quality Act, RSQ, c. Q-2, which, in 1978, gave every natural person "a right to a healthy environment and to its protection ... to the extent provided for by this act and the regulations." However, this section cre-

---

[†] From E.L. Hughes, A.R. Lucas and W.A. Tilleman, eds., *Environmental Law and Policy*, 2nd edition (Toronto: Emond Montgomery Publications Ltd., 1998), pp. 405–406. Reproduced by permission of the publisher.

ated little more than a statutory tort, protecting residents only from violations of the legislative requirements.

Finally, in 1990, the first "true" Canadian environmental rights legislation was enacted with the passage of the Northwest Territories' Environmental Rights Act, SNWT 1990, c. 28. The next year the Yukon Territory enacted more comprehensive environmental legislation that also included a set of environmental rights.

(b) Ontario's Environmental Bill of Rights Weakened, But Still Viable[†]

Averil Guiste ————————————————————————————

The new Ontario government has scaled back the province's ground-breaking Environmental Bill of Rights (EBR), but the province's environmental commissioner says the law remains a useful tool for government accountability.

Ontario Regulation 482/95, announced in late 1995, removes the Ministry of Finance from the list of ministries that must comply with the law. It also temporarily suspends public notice requirements for environmentally significant proposals linked to government cost cutting.

The environmental commissioner, Eva Ligeti, says the changes weaken the EBR and constrain her role, but should not be perceived as the death knell for the two-year-old law. She believes that the public can still use the law to demand government accountability and that the law's purpose remains essential.

"While the current climate of fiscal restraint may suggest otherwise, environmental protection and sustainability are achievable and essential," says Ligeti. "They're necessary to retain what we currently enjoy, for future environmental quality, and economic development and competitiveness."

The EBR requires each ministry to establish a Statement of Environmental Values outlining how the ministry will integrate the EBR into its work. The law also sets up an Environmental Registry, a computer bulletin board of information about proposed environmental policies, laws, regulations and instruments, or changes to existing ones.

The ministries to which the EBR applies must post this information on the registry and give the public a minimum of 30 days to comment. As well, the ministries are required to consider public comments when making their decisions.

"Because it is free and accessible at more than 300 libraries and community information centres across Ontario or from a home or office by modem, the registry opens up the government decision-making process to the public in ways never before seen in Ontario, or Canada, for that matter," Ligeti says. "Essentially, the Environmental Bill of Rights seeks to protect, conserve and restore the natural environment. Regulation 482/95 decreases opportunities to participate in these processes."

The government also failed to post Regulation 482/95 itself on the registry, a move which, Ligeti says, violated both the spirit and the intent of the EBR.

The Ministry of Environment and Energy, which developed the regulation, and the Ministry of Finance, which won exemption from EBR requirements, contend that the exemption is appropriate because most of the Finance Ministry's activities were already covered by the budgetary, financial and administrative exemptions in the EBR.

But Ligeti says the Ministry of Finance was one of the most crucial of the prescribed ministries because it decides how much money is spent and how. "The Ministry of Finance was in-

———————————————————————————

† From *Alternatives Journal* 22, 3 (July/August 1996): 9. Reproduced with permission of the Environmental Commissioner of Ontario.

cluded among the prescribed ministries because it has and will continue to play a vital role in this province's move toward sustainability," she says. "In fact, it's now recognized that the budget is one of the most important statements of environmental policy a government can make."

(c) Conclusion: Continuing the process...[†]

Gerald Cormick, Norman Dale, Paul Emond, S. Glenn Sigurdson and Barry D. Stuart ⎯⎯⎯⎯⎯⎯⎯⎯⎯⎯⎯⎯⎯⎯⎯⎯⎯⎯⎯⎯

The "pros" of consensus

Sustainability is largely about enjoying the fruits of the earth today in such a way that these benefits will be available tomorrow and far beyond into the future. If we did not cherish concern for unborn generations and for the countless other species inhabiting this world, many of today's decisions would be simpler. We would pay little attention to the more distant and subtle consequences of current development projects, enjoying like Aesop's proverbial grasshopper whatever gratifies for the moment. Some believe that, with little exaggeration, this is how modern industrialized and agrarian societies have been making decisions, at least until recently. Many people now recognize that making decisions based on what appears to be immediately "best" and technically feasible is to disregard consequences for other people, other species, and the future.

The importance attached to these concerns varies among the many groups who use or care about the environment. As well, despite several decades of increasingly sophisticated impact assessment, the consequences of development remain difficult to predict accurately. Amid diverse viewpoints and values and unimaginable ecological complexities, it is virtually certain that serious disagreements will abound.

The dangerous result is stalemate and inaction in the face of uncertainty and value conflict. In consequence, the environment is exposed to continuing threats whose extent cannot be agreed upon, while important economic opportunities are hamstrung by doubts and discord. Commonly, "pro-development" and "pro-environment" forces are each powerful enough to frustrate one another's plans, yet both find the status quo unacceptance. The high social and ecological costs of such impasses make it essential to find ways to break stalemates, to move forward in the face of uncertainty. Consensus processes can meet this need. What specifically do they offer in the quest for a sustainable future?

Meaningful involvement as equals in decisions that affect our lives

Involvement in decision making is meaningful because it is based on a clearly identified commitment and sense of purpose among all parties [ ]; because it is open to all significant interests [ ] who are participating because they want to [ ]; and because the process is designed by participants [ ] and can be adapted as circumstances require [ ].

One of the key and liberating assumptions of consensus is that everyone counts. That is true by definition. If any participant is unwilling to go along with a decision there is no consensus. This means that the views and values of each count equally. And [ ] the commitment to equality goes further. It says that parties must participate on an equal footing, having equal access to the resources needed to negotiate effectively. Otherwise the outcome is little more than coercion disguised as consultation.

† From Gerald Cormick, Norman Dale, Paul Emond, S. Glenn Sigurdson and Barry D. Stuart, *Building Consensus for a Sustainable Future: Putting Principles into Practice* (Ottawa, ON: National Round Table on the Enviroment and the Economy, 1996), pp. 104–113. Reproduced by permission of National Round Table on the Environment and the Economy.

A chance to negotiate and reach agreement on what we know — and don't

Debates and disputes about sustainability are inherently complex. They involve issues about how nature works; how benefits are to be counted; how impacts may cascade through environments near and far and in space and time; what the significance of environmental change may be and to whom; and how, if at all, negative impacts can be mitigated or compensated for fairly. This complexity is often what has enabled parties to hold vastly different views on what the "facts" really are. Through consensus processes, these adversaries have an opportunity to debate and reach agreement on what is known and not known; they can often negotiate a focused strategy for collecting data that can shed light on the issues; and they may fashion adaptive ways of coping with uncertainties that cannot be resolved.

In essence, although consensus processes involve people whose backgrounds may range from casual lay observers to well-known experts on the environment (and economy), such processes recreate one fundamental precondition of good science — direct and open discussion of the facts involving anyone who has an interest.

A shift from confrontation to accommodation

Most other forums for decision making rely in one way or another on adjudication. This is seen most obviously in the courts but also prevails when administrators make regulatory rulings. The typical "best" approach for stakeholders is to state their case in the most extreme terms in the hope of convincing a decision maker. Consensus instead requires parties to look for common ground in spite of their differences. The very nature of consensus implies that a decision can be reached only when all parties are satisfied. All-or-nothing decisions are not an option. Under this pressure, parties can bring to the table what no judge or administrator ever has: intimate knowledge of what they themselves most need and value.

An opportunity to (re)build relationships based on trust, respect, and understanding

Sound management of the environment cannot be achieved through one-time deals or decisions. It is a continuous challenge requiring diverse groups to work together despite differing views and values. It rests on relationships, ones that are constructive and ongoing. Again, consensus has a distinct advantage over other means of decision making in this regard. During a consensus process, emphasis is placed on developing a more empathic understanding of other parties [ ], because without this empathy, there may be no way to devise solutions that meet everyone's basic needs without offending their basic values. The satisfaction of having co-invented a mutually acceptable solution relationship, as does the contact usually entailed in successful implementation and monitoring [ ]. After a consensus process, parties often find that a simple telephone call can resolve difficulties that previously would have led to open confrontation.

A focus on "do-able" action rather than high-sounding advice

Consensus processes break with long-standing traditions of advisory consultations and planning. Over the years, Canadians have become progressively more frustrated as elaborate and expensive consultations and inquires are conducted, impressive reports are produced, and then nothing seems to happen. Or, something does happen but not what the inquiry recommended.

Consensus processes are not like this. They are deliberately directed at devising "do-able" actions and clearly identifying how agreements are to be fulfilled [ ]. The flexibility of consensus processes [ ] allows parties to fine-tune solutions as needed to implement them. By including everyone who has a stake in making the agreement work, especially those who will be needed for implementation [ ], practical and detailed plans can be spelled out.

Renewing and validating accountability

Consensus decisions are very different from those made in legislatures, bureaucracies, or judiciaries in terms of accountability to people most affected. Politicians must deal with an enormous array of issues, often trading one off against another in legislative bargaining. The bureaucracy is required to be accountable first and foremost to cabinet ministers and only through them to broad publics made of many competing interests. Judges and quasi-judicial panels are quite the opposite, obliged to maintain independence not only from the polity but also from many of the specifics and peculiarities in each case. Their accountability is chiefly to broad legal principles and precedents.

In contrast, negotiators of public policy issues have the paramount goal of protecting and advancing the case-specific interests of those who sent them to the table [ ]. They must, of course, do this with an eye to what will work for other parties. But, otherwise, constituency interests alone dictate their actions and their acceptance of particular solutions and outcomes. This makes accountability far more focused, direct, and uninhibited than is the case for decision makers in conventional dispute resolution settings.

Recapping the cross-cutting themes

. . . .

Role of the mediator

... Groups of stakeholders can sometimes reach consensus on their own. But as the complexity of disputes and the numbers of parties involved increase, it becomes harder for agreement to happen without someone whose principal and exclusive interest is seeing a fair and effective process take place. [There are] many distinct functions that a mediator can perform — conducting initial informal discussions to determine whether a process is wanted and possible [ ] working with initial disputants to identify other key stakeholders whose inclusion is important [ ]; providing general experience with procedural ground rules and ensuring that the parties do not neglect the necessity and opportunity of self-design [ ]; working with the parties to assist them in being effective participants in the process, and thus increasing the likelihood that the process will be effective [ ]. Mediators are in a unique position to act as sounding boards for ideas to be advanced in full group sessions. By attending to the details of meeting logistics and ensuring that progress is recorded, a mediator can help to head off relatively simple problems that might otherwise lead to process breakdown. In essence, by looking out for the details and defending one and only one interest — the integrity of the process — a mediator frees the negotiators to advance their interests in a more determined and effective manner.

The difficult but essential role for government

The emergence of consensus processes is taking place within an established and complicated system of government involvement and responsibilities. Almost every issue of sustainability is surrounded by myriad regulations and policies. Final say over sustainability controversies rests (and will continue to rest) with elected representatives, and often with the public servants who report to them. On the surface this creates an awkward situation in terms of direct government agency involvement in consensus processes. Government officials may want to stay out of such processes, claiming they need to maintain final and exclusive authority to "rule" freely on an issue. This position is sometimes supported by non-governmental organizations who argue that regulatory agencies have no business "bargaining away" their legal mandates.

[We adopt] a different perspective. Without the direct participation of key government agencies, most consensus processes will lack critical information and expertise. Moreover, successful implementation of the resulting agreement will be in question. Without these resources and incentives, other parties' motivation to participate will dwindle. The move toward consensus building has been strongly supported by Canadian governments at all levels because it is a chance for stakeholders to reach agreement on the most difficult public issues of our time. Government representatives, in coming to the table, are not there to compromise what is legally required of them. Instead, they have an unparalleled opportunity to educate others on the nature and rationale of regulatory policy and, also, to exercise such flexibility as their mandates may already provide.[14]

Making it happen

Accepting that consensus processes offer important advantages over the more formal and adversarial way of making environmental decisions, what has to happen to increase their use and effectiveness? Despite widespread interest in consensual negotiations, their use remains exceptional rather than the rule.

First, there is a need to dispel some of the misconceptions that surround the "theory" and practice of consensus building.

> *"You can't negotiate when values differ, which is usually the case in environment and development controversies."*

It is frequently asserted that negotiations can only take place over details and when the parties have basic shared understandings and values. No one, it is said, is going to bargain away the things they most cherish and value. So, for example, when a new transportation corridor means increased traffic and hazards to human safety, someone will inevitably say: "We can't negotiate our children's lives."

The response is to ask whether people prefer decisions on such matters to be made entirely outside their control, by judges or bureaucrats. Consensus processes give stakeholders a chance to convey critical values and to explore, with adversaries, ways of protecting these while still accomplishing what these others seek. No one is expected to give up what they most value. In fact, the consensus rule guarantees that no decision will be forthcoming as long as one or more parties feels that their most basic needs and interests are unmet.

Ironically, it is often the case that people with widely differing values are well placed to craft agreements that respect each other's interests precisely because of their differences. One party may care about the fate of a rare species; another may want to build a subdivision. They do not need to sped energy squabbling over why they care about or want these things. Instead, through candid discussion, they can look at options in terms of how well they meet both sets of values. To leave a final decision on such matters to a judge or regulator is to risk one party losing everything or missing an innovative solution that only the parties, by virtue of their intimate knowledge of what they value, could have found.

"Parties have differing 'power' and you don't negotiate under those conditions."

Negotiations are unlikely to work if one party has the power to get what it wants unilaterally. Whether this is the case must be assessed prior to undertaking a consensus process. [It is essential] that every party has a purpose best served through negotiations rather than another avenue.

Consensus processes can actually help to redress some of the inequality in resources that makes one party significantly weaker than others. [Also,] the decision by seemingly more powerful interests to negotiate with others marks a recognition of reciprocal influence and even empowers the weaker group.

"Consensus processes just go on and on and on ... they're an opportunity to stall."

Group decisions attract a lot of bad press, especially when consensus is the rule. Typical comments include: "We should just vote and let the majority rule" or "The buck should stop at one and only one point." These views are based on frustration with ineffective consensus decision making. The source of the problem is often ignorance of the preparations needed for constructive collaborative decision making. Simply sitting a group of adversaries down together without due care and planning will usually lead to disillusionment and sweeping generalizations about the ineffectiveness of all consensus processes.

Consensus does take time — although compared with, say, a full adjudication of an issue including appeals, it may not be all that long. But if parties follow the guiding principles, especially when they take the time to establish their own ground rules [ ], they can accomplish much more than a one-time agreement. Their investment of time and energy pays off in a better working relationship, increasing the odds of successful implementation and of constructive problem solving when the same parties face one another over other issues. ...

"Consensus is compromise and that means solutions are inferior — nothing but the lowest common denominator."

Consensus is commonly confused with compromise and "least bad" solutions. The Old Testament story in which Solomon proposes resolving a custody dispute by cutting a child in half is sometimes used to illustrate the shortcomings of compromise. But the message of the original story was quite different: Solomon had used a ploy to surface the true feelings and interests of the disputants in a manner analogous to those used occasionally by modern mediators. In fact, in consensus decisions over environmental issues, the resolution is almost never just a matter of "splitting the difference." Usually, many interwoven issues are involved and the challenge is to find creative ways to make everyone better off. As give-and-take options are considered, the parties frequently come to understand each other's interests well enough to devise a settlement from which all can gain.

"Consensus robs parties of their right to be heard by the courts and/or their elected officials; relatedly, consensus usurps or relieves accountable public officials of their legally required responsibilities."

Only the most extreme advocate of consensus would argue that the approach should replace all existing institutions and procedures of environmental decision making. In the last several decades important advances have occurred to improve the effectiveness of conventional forums such as courts, legislatures, and administrative agencies in dealing with sustainability issues. In particular, notable reforms have occurred making these institutions more open to public participation and more sensitive to complex environmental data. Consensus processes can further these ends and complement longer-established approaches. If conducted according to [ ] guiding principles, particularly [the principle] that parties participate voluntarily — consensus building is always subject to parties changing their minds and pursuing alternative ways of protecting and advancing their basic interests.

"Consensus presumes trust but there is virtually none when there's been a long and bitter struggle."

The confusion here is with conditions at the outset of negotiations versus those at the end. At the beginning of a process, no one would sensibly presume to trust parties with conflicting presume to trust parties with conflicting interests, especially when a controversy has been protracted and adversarial. At that point, no one is asked to make concessions or even commitments based on trust.

In the initial phase parties should focus on exploring the pros and cons of negotiations without prejudice to their interests or any obligation to continue to meet. Only when considerable effort has been made to talk about whether to talk and to draft process ground rules, should the parties decide whether to proceed. The process will help engender trust in an incremental manner. The pleasant surprise of finding some common ground with old adversaries and seeing them keep their commitments helps immeasurably. By the time that an agreement is reached, some of its elements may well be based on each party's word. Inevitably, however, settlements provide more formal, even legal, means to ensure compliance. To varying degrees, depending on the case, trust develops through consensus processes: it is never simply assumed.

"Sure consensus is worthwhile, but we're already doing it."

Two different, almost opposite responses are commonly encountered when suggestions are made to tackle environmental conflicts with a consensus-based approach. One is: "It won't work here." The reasons given are usually a variation of the misunderstandings already discussed. The other response is something to the effect of: "We're already using consensus — we held a public hearing just last week." The final misconception with which supporters of consensus must often deal is confusion with other forms of public participation that, on closer examination, do not have the core features of consensual negotiations. Broad consultative approaches are not the same as consensus. In consensus processes stakeholders talk directly to each other, not to an authoritative judge or regulator; the purpose is not for each interest individually to stick with its solution but to devise and commit to a single resolution reflecting all interests. Those who want to see consensus used more broadly must take care to make these distinctions when alternative approaches are considered.

.   .   .   .

A significant increase in the use of consensus for Canadian sustainability issues will require broader and more systematic commitment than can arise ad hoc through individual advocacy. Already, governments across the country are establishing laws, regulations, and institutions to open doors — and minds — to consensual negotiations. The recent federal Environmental Assessment Act enables government to use mediation as an alternative to full assessment panels, provided that parties are willing. In British Columbia the Commission on Resources and Environment (CORE) has made significant use of multiparty negotiations among stakeholders to develop broad regional land use plans. The National Round Table on the Environment and the Economy has facilitated several major process of policy dialogue, again centred on the involvement of spokespersons from all key interest groups. In Quebec, in 1993, the formal terms of reference for the Bureau d'audiences publiques sur l'environnement (BAPE) were expanded to recognize the agency's mediating role, a function it had carried out informally for a number of years when convening public hearings on environmental matters. In Nova Scotia, a law has been enacted naming "alternative dispute resolution" as a possibility for a wide range of environmental decisions. Also in Nova Scotia, a bill for municipal amalgamation is in preparation that includes a very specific requirement for multistakeholder processes in solid waste management for the Halifax region. These are critically important steps in ensuring that the opportunity is there, if parties are willing to use consensus building and respect its results.

Canadians have only begun to tap the huge stores of creativity, everyday common sense, and basic good will needed to build a sustainable future. Across the country recognition is growing that not despite but because of our diversity of cultures and perspectives, common ground can be found to accomplish this. Canadian — whether loggers from British Columbia, fishers in the Maritimes, corporate executives in Calgary, Montreal, or Toronto, First Nations in the many homelands, environmentalists working in tiny community groups or internationally known organizations, government officials and politicians at all levels, or millions of others with no clear affiliations — all share important commitments to

- fairness and the goal of protecting the interests and freedoms of all, even those with whom one disagrees,
- an environment that supports Canadians' core values, ranging from economic well-being to spiritual needs, and
- Canadian children, their children, and generations beyond.

These common commitments provide an excellent footing for finding solutions to sustainability issues that are much more than mere compromises, but rather allow everyone to gain. To harmonize the collective action of these diverse publics, consensus will be needed on a multitude of local, regional, and national issues and policies. Groups and individuals require the skill to get along with one another and an understanding of the core principles underlying sound and stable consensus. ...

PART B
Environmental Mediation

(a) Alternative Dispute Resolution and Environmental Conflict: The case for law reform[†]

Elizabeth J. Swanson ───────────────────────────────

INTRODUCTION

Given the diversity of values, interests and players involved, it is not surprising that conflict is a characteristic part of environmental decision making. Although traditional legal and political processes have succeeded in settling many disputes in the environmental arena, there is a trend towards the use of alternative dispute resolution ("ADR") techniques. By and large this has been an informal development; the result of governmental or private initiative rather than carefully structured law or policy. In some ways, the very informality and flexibility of *ad hoc* arrangements may enhance the success of ADR. However, in my view, the significance of such processes for the law and legal rights or interests calls for selective institutionalization through legislative reform.[1]

This article critically examines the case for law reform, describes the state of ADR-related legislation in effect or proposed in Canada and makes recommendations for further law reform required to promote the effective and fair use of ADR to resolve environmental conflicts. Before turning to these topics, some words about terminology.

Coming to Terms with ADR

The recent growth of the ADR industry, with its attendant scribes and scholars, has resulted in a virtual explosion of jargon. *Consensus, consensus building, mediation, negotiation, principled negotiation, and regulatory negotiation* are just a sample of terms encountered in the literature. Yet, as Gail Bingham notes:

Although several attempts have been made to develop a conceptual framework that clearly distinguishes different environmental dispute resolution processes, no generally acceptable framework has yet been devised. As a result, individuals and organizations involved in this field use different terms for similar approaches and similar terms for different approaches.[2]

"Traditional" v. "Alternative" Dispute Resolution Techniques

To begin with, a distinction is made between *traditional* and *alternative* dispute resolution processes: *traditional* processes include negotiation, arbitration, litigation, decision making, law and policy making, consultation and lobbying while *alternative* processes encompass consensus building and negotiation, with or without the assistance of a neutral third party or *mediator*. This

† From Alberta Law Review 34, 1 (1995): 268–278. Reproduced by permission of the author.

distinction is admittedly somewhat arbitrary and the two categories do overlap. The basis for the distinction is as follows: dispute resolution processes which have been so commonly employed that they are recognized as established techniques by law, policy or political and legal theory are classified as *traditional* processes; those of more recent practice and of different theoretical origins are classified as *alternative* processes. Using these criteria, arbitration, quite often thought of as a form of ADR, is considered to be a traditional process because (a) it has a long history of use, particularly in relation to labour disputes; (b) it typically has a legislative basis; and (c) resolution results from third party and adjudication rather than from direct negotiation between the disputants. A further distinction is made between various ADR methods on the basis of the intended outcome and the involvement of a neutral third party (mediator), and then only to the extent that such distinction is useful within the context of this article.

"Consensus Building"

Consensus building is a problem solving approach which emphasizes the common interest of the participants in jointly defining and solving problems. The primary outcome of consensus building need not be decision-making nor the development of recommendations. Instead, the objective might be the improvement of communications and relationships between groups that are normally opposed to one another, or to improve the quality and legitimacy of decision making by one or more of the participants.[3]

Consensus building differs from consultation in that it seeks to encourage agreement or foster understanding between participants, while consultation merely affords an opportunity for parties to express their individual positions in an attempt to influence or inform a decision maker.

"Negotiation"

Negotiation refers to a process of bargaining between parties adverse in interest in order to make a decision or provide recommendations based upon their consensus. Unlike consensus building, negotiation is directed towards decision-making. The parties to a negotiation either have the authority (power) to make the decision themselves or are confident that their consensus-based recommendations will influence decision-making by another.

"Mediation"

As used here, "mediation" simply to the use of a neutral third party to support consensus building or negotiation. Mediation is thus treated as a way of proceeding, rather than as a unique process, making it possible to speak of "mediated consensus building" or "mediated negotiation."

"Institutionalization"

The phrase, "institutionalization of ADR" means bring the practice of ADR within existing judicial and legislative systems by providing a legal mandate and establishing formal rules and standards.

"Environmental Dispute"

In the context of this article, an environmental dispute refers to disagreements between parties which are about or are directly relevant to the natural environment. The same meaning applies to the phrase "environmental conflict." The word "dispute" is used in its broader sense of conflict or controversy and not as a legal term of art.[4] Types or categories of environmental disputes include: (1) party-to-party disputes; (2) disputes about the issuance of permits or licences; (3) disputes about preliminary or "in principle" approvals; (4) disputes about the content of law and policy: and (5) disputes regarding compliance and enforcement. Each of these will be discussed briefly in the next section.

Types of Environmental Disputes

Identification of kinds or types of environmental disputes is, to some extent, an arbitrary exercise premised on the hypotheses that: (a) environmental disputes are distinguishable from other sorts of conflict; and (b) it is possible to meaningfully distinguish between disputes within that smaller universe. Still, such distinction is attempted here in order to provide a framework for discussion and analysis.

As defined above, a dispute becomes "environmental" when it is about or directly relates to the natural environment. The basis for this first distinction is thus the subject matter or content of the controversy. Subsequent distinctions are based upon the legal activity which gives rise to, or is the context for, an environmental dispute.[5]

"Party-to-party disputes" is a phrase used to describe conflict between private individuals; what legal theory terms a dispute *inter pares*.

Generally speaking, disputes of this sort involve a conflict of interest as opposed to a conflict of values.[6] This is also true of conflict arising in the context of enforcement action taken or licenses issued by government though disputes in such circumstances likely involve both private and public interests.

While the legal authority to enact legislation and develop policy remains vested in governments, various forms of consultation have become an expected part of the legislative and policy making process. Disputes that typically arise in this context tend to result from a conflict of values as opposed to a conflict of interests. Positions are advanced by various parties, each of whom hopes to influence the ultimate decision maker and "win the day."

TOWARDS RESOLUTION: ADR, ENVIRONMENTAL CONFLICT AND THE LAW

What does the law have to do with ADR? Very little, according to some people who consider them to be two solitudes and hope to keep it that way.[7] Others acknowledge the interaction, but have very different views about the nature of the relationship. Timothy Sullivan, for example, believes that:

> As long as litigation offers an acceptable, trouble-alternative to negotiation, then opposition groups and government agencies will seldom accept the heavy and often burdensome costs of training negotiators and undertaking the internal bargaining that successful negotiations require.[8]

while Gerald Cormick says:

> Actual or threatened litigation is often a necessary prerequisite to the willingness of a party proposing some action to negotiate; it is the source of power and influence that brings the parties to the table and to mediation....
>
> While the parties to a conflict may at some point choose to negotiate in lieu of initiating or continuing court action, mediation cannot reasonably be expected to supplant or negate the need for litigation until such time as protesting constituencies are provided with some other basis for their power and influence.[9]

In a recent study, the Environmental Law Centre reviewed the use of both traditional and alternative methods of dispute resolution and concluded that:

- the two approaches do interact in that the use of one may have implications for the other;
- this interaction can be either positive or negative; and
- while the law applies to and may be used to address many of the concerns surrounding the use of ADR, considerable uncertainty about important issues exists and needs to be addressed, if ADR is to be encouraged.[10]

The "important issues" referred to above include: (a) confidentiality and privilege; (b) mediator liability; (c) preservation of pre-existing legal rights; (d) subsequent right of legal action and standards for judicial review; (e) minimum qualification criteria or standards for mediators; and (f) participant rights, such as the right to funding and the right to information. While new reform is certainly one way to provide certainty and clarification, is it the *best* way?

The Case for (and against) Institutionalization through Law Reform

The case for the institutionalization of ADR, particularly through legislative reform, is neatly summed up by Vanderburgh and Hope:

> Advocates of institutionalized environmental mediation believe that institutionalization makes the process of mediation more predictable, provides a clear mechanism for enforcing the agreement and protects the parties that elect to use it, thereby encouraging its use. Institutionalization should also contribute to more successful mediation, measured not only by the numbers of agreements reached but by an increase in community participation in those agreements.[11]

Another commentator, Merton Berstein, also supports legislative reform, primarily because he is reluctant to let developments in the common law catch up with the practice of ADR. Though it may be nothing more than wishful thinking on his part, Berstein also believes that legislation providing for the enforcement of mediated agreements, in particular:

> would force the legal community to recognize the validity of the mediation process. Imposing a statutory process on mediation activities might overcome the general reluctance of lawyers to use any new approach which contains unfamiliar procedures and doctrines. Furthermore, the enactment of a statute adds a certain dignity and respectability to the use of mediation by lawyers.[12]

Opponents of institutionalization are no less interested in finding answers than their reform-minded colleagues but either believe that: (a) the law as it now exists provides acceptable solutions; (b) ADR processes are so intricate and engage so many issues that creating workable legislation would be next to impossible; (c) solutions will be developed through the common law, as needed; (d) institutionalization will destroy the utility of ADR processes by limiting flexibility and creativity in favour of certainty and predictability; or (e) ADR requires further time to develop on its own before any concerted effort is made to codify or formalize it.[13]

In his report, "Environmental Mediation: From Theory To Practice,"[14] Steven Shrybman summarizes the results of a survey of government officials, members of environmental non-governmental organizations (ENGOs) and industry representatives. All three groups identified the lack of a legal framework as a significant impediment to the successful use of ADR to resolve environmental disputes. Notwithstanding these results, Shrybman expresses the view that:

> Clearly the institutionalization of mediation as a readily available option must await a much greater awareness of, and positive experience with, this process.[15]

That statement was made more than ten years ago. Given the significant increase in both the use of ADR processes and public participation in environmental decision and rule making, it is argued here that the time Shrybman spoke of has come and law reform is a current, not a future, need.

Firstly, the use of ADR is proceeding, often in an *ad hoc* manner. Formalizing procedure through the enactment of legislation would, at a minimum, ensure consistency between ADR processes and might, in addition, be used to provide some level of fairness to participants.[16] Secondly, confidence in and support for ADR processes is adversely affected by uncertainty about significant issues; confidentiality, for example. This uncertainty needs to be addressed, and to the extent reasonably possible, eliminated. Finally, there is a need to provide remedies for those who are adversely affected by or dissatisfied with the results of an ADR process. Although opinion is divided as to the adequacy of existing law to provide such remedies legislative reform, in my review, is preferable to creative adjudication.

I do agree, however, with the caution that the task of merging certainty and fairness with flexibility and creativity (the hallmarks of ADR) is bound to be a difficult one.

That challenge has already been taken up is some jurisdictions, both here in Canada and in the United States, with the enactment of legislation providing for the use of ADR.

One the Road to Reform: Legislative Developments to Date

Legislative Models for Types

A review of existing ADR legislation in Canada and the United States suggests that there are two types, or models, to choose from: (1) legislation dealing only with ADR, applicable across legislative subject matter ("ADR specific"); and (2) legislation providing for the use of ADR processes in the context of a particular subject matter ("ADR inclusive").

Legislation dealing exclusive with ADR can be found in the United States at both the federal and state level.[17] Two enactments will be described here by way of example: the federal *Administrative Dispute Resolution Act*[18] and the *Dispute Resolution Act* of Colorado.[19]

The *Administrative Dispute Resolution Act* ("ADRA") authorizes the use of ADR processes by federal agencies to deal with conflict arising in the context of an administrative program. An administrative program is defined to include: "a Federal function which involves protection of the public interest and the determination of rights, privileges, and obligations of private persons through rule making, adjudication, licensing, or investigation...."[20] As provide by the ADRA, ADR is a voluntary process intended to supplement other resolution techniques and may not be used in certain circumstances.[21]

Colorado's *Dispute Resolution Act* takes a slightly different approach by establishing an office of dispute resolution under the administration of a director. The director must ensure that dispute resolution services are available through each of the various judicial districts. Anyone involved in a dispute may access mediation services, before or after filing a suit, and upon payment of a fee.[22]

The recently proclaimed *Canadian Environmental Assessment Act* ("CEAA")[23] illustrates the second type of legislative enactment: the incorporation of ADR provisions in a statute dealing with a discrete subject matter; in CEAA's case, environmental assessment.

The CEAA requires all federal authorities to undertake an environmental assessment of projects to which the CEAA applies. If the anticipated adverse environmental impacts of a project are significant (and unjustifiable) or unknown, or if public concerns so warrant, the project must be referred to the Minister of the Environment for a referral to a mediator or a review panel.[24]

Sections 29–32 authorize and provide details about mediation under the CEAA, including these:

- all or part of an environmental assessment can be referred to a mediator;
- a project may not be referred to a mediator unless interested parties have been identified and are willing to participate;[25]
- a mediation may be terminated at any time by the Minister of the Environment if the Minister or the mediator determines that it is unlikely to result in a result acceptable to all the participants;
- the selection of a mediator is left to the Minister of the Environment in consultation with the responsible federal authority and all parties who are willing to participate in the mediation;
- additional parties may be added to a mediation at any time, with the permission of the mediator; and
- upon the conclusion of a mediation, the mediator must submit a report to the Minister of the Environment and to the responsible federal authority.

An Overview of Legislative Developments in Canada

The CEAA, as described above, is currently the only piece of federal environmental legislation that specifically provides for the use of ADR. It should be noted that, in addition to authorizing and establishing a process for mediation in the context of environmental assessment, the CEAA addresses the issues of confidentiality and mediator qualifications. With respect to the latter, s.32(2) provides:

> No evidence of or relating to a statement made by a mediator or a participant to the mediation during the course of and for the purposes of the mediation is admissible without the consent of the mediator or participant, in any proceed-ing before a review panel, court, tribunal, body or person with jurisdiction to compel the production of evidence.

And, pursuant to s. 30(1)(a)(i), only persons with mediation experience or knowledge and who are unbiased and free from any conflict of interest may be appointed as mediators under the CEAA.

At the provincial level a number of statutes recently proclaimed or at the proposal (discussion) stage authorize the use of ADR. Of these, Nova Scotia's new *Environmental Act*[26] is the most comprehensive. Details are set out in s. 14 of the *Act*:

> **14**(1) For the purpose of resolving a dispute, the Minister may refer a matter to a form of alternate dispute resolution, including but not limited to, conciliation, negotiation or arbitration.
>
> (2) Where the Minister decides to use a form of alternate dispute resolution ... the Minister, in consultation with the affected parties and using criteria prescribed or adopted by the Department, shall determine which form of dispute resolution is most appropriate.
>
> (3) Any form of alternate dispute resolution used shall strive to achieve consensus to resolve procedural and substantive issues throughout the process.
>
> (4) Where a form of alternate dispute resolution is being used ... and where an independent party or neutral third party has been chosen to facilitate, mediate or arbitrate, at the conclusion of the process that person shall file a report ... whether or not the dispute was resolved.
>
> (5) Without limiting the generality [of the foregoing] ... a form of alternate dispute resolution may be used
>
> (a) in the case of a dispute over a certificate of qualification or certificate of variance;
> (b) in case of a dispute over an approval
> (c) in case of a dispute ... respecting responsibility for rehabilitation of a contaminated site; or
> (d) generally, for conflict resolution.

Legislative references to mediation, in particular, can also be found in the respective environmental protection statutes of Ontario, Manitoba, Yukon and the Northwest Territories.

Section of Manitoba's *Environment Act*[27] establishes the Clean Environment Commission which may, upon the request of the Environment Minister, "act as a mediator between two or more parties to an environmental dispute...."[28] In the Northwest Territories and Yukon, each Minister of the Environment is authorized to appoint a mediator to (respectively) resolve disputes or settle complaints.[29] Ontario's *Environmental Bill of Rights* provides for the use of mediation to resolve differences of opinion or issues with respect to proposed legislation.[30]

An environmental dispute mediation process is part of legislation proposed for British Columbia. Still at the discussion stage, the *British Columbia Environmental Protection Act* authorizes the Minister of the Environment to arrange for the mediation of environmental disputes.[31]

CONCLUSIONS AND RECOMMENDATIONS

The lack of a legislative basis for alternative dispute resolution has hampered, but not prevented, the use of ADR processes to address environmental conflict. While the informality and flexibility of *ad hoc* processes may be consistent with ADR theory and may, in some ways, enhance its success, there is a current and pressing need for law reform.

Formalizing ADR procedure through the enactment of legislation would, at a minimum, encourage consistency between ADR processes and could be used to provide some level of fairness to participants. In addition, the lack of certainty about significant issues, such as confidentiality of information and implementation of results, directly affects confidence in and support for the use of ADR. Finally, there is a need to provide remedies for those who are adversely affected by or dissatisfied with the results of an ADR process. All of these can be best achieved, in my opinion, through deliberate and thoughtful law reform.

We have already begun that process in Canada through the enactment of environmental legislation authorizing the use of ADR. The *Canadian Environmental Assessment Act* is one example of ADR-inclusive legislation; Nova Scotia's *Environment Act* is another.

Much more remains to be done. In particular, I recommend:

1. Negotiated rulemaking. If the desire of the federal or provincial governments is to provide for public participation in environmental law-making through structured negotiations, legislation should be enacted to: (a) authorize the practice; (b) provide for the implementation of the results; and (c) establish minimum procedural standards. A model to consider is the U.S. federal *Negotiated Rulemaking Act of 1990.*[32]

2. Dispute resolution. The use of ADR to resolve environmental (and other) conflict should be institutionalized through the enactment of both ADR-specific and ADR-inclusive legislation. ADR-specific legislation should deal with issues of common concern such as: (a) confidentiality and privilege; (b) mediator liability; (c) preservation of pre-existing legal rights; (d) subsequent right of legal action and standards for judicial review; (e) minimum qualification criteria or standards for mediators; and (f) participant rights; for example, the right to funding and the right to information. Other matters, such as authorization, participant selection and implementation, for example, should be addressed in their subjective context. The *Canadian Environmental Assessment Act* is an example of ADR-inclusive legislation and could be used as a model.

Finally, regardless of the specific intent or purpose of an alternative dispute resolution process, participation must remain voluntary and must not come at the expense of legal rights or recourse to traditional processes, like litigation. To do otherwise may deprive us of the full benefit of ADR and the full protection of the law.

(b) Environmental Mediation: From theory to practice†

Steven Shrybman ————————————————————

FIRST PRINCIPLES

Environmental Mediation: A Definition

The most often cited definition of mediation has been advanced by Gerald Cormick, one of the leading practitioners and theoreticians in this field:

> Mediation is a voluntary process in which those involved in a dispute jointly explore and reconcile their differences. The mediator has no authority to impose a settlement. His or her strength lies in the ability to assist the parties in resolving their own differences. The mediated dispute is settled when the parties themselves reach what they consider to be a workable solution.[1]

Although mediation might also be defined more simply as negotiation assisted by a neutral third party, Cormick's expanded definition highlights the key elements of this particular dispute resolution process:

1. **The Process is Voluntary:** No party is compelled to participate. The mediator has no coercive, as opposed to persuasive, power. Participation is without prejudice to any other remedy that might be available to any party.
2. **The Process is Consensual:** The issues and objectives of the process are defined by the participants. Agreement is reached upon consensus — there is no majority rule.
3. **The Process is Non-Binding:** The mediator has no authority to impose a settlement.

Given the fact that inter-party negotiation is the essential dynamic of environmental mediation, why then the interest in mediation as opposed to negotiation? Why not concentrate on ways in which to simply encourage the negotiation of environmental disputes? In part, one might respond that mediation may simply be regarded as a technique for encouraging those embroiled in an environmental dispute to consider and pursue face-to-face negotiation as opposed to more adversarial forms of dispute resolution....

. . . .

Apart from negotiation, it is also important to distinguish mediation from other related dispute resolution processes. When compared with two closely related approaches, these difficulties might briefly be described as follows:

1. **Arbitration:** Arbitration accords to a neutral third party the authority and responsibility to fashion and impose a settlement. Another distinction arises when the arbitration process may be invoked at the instance of one party pursuant to some legislative regime or prior agreement among the parties.
2. **Conciliation:** Conciliation differs from mediation in two respects. The first is that the intervening third party need not be neutral with respect to the matters in dispute. The second difference arises by reason of the fact that the third party need not have been invited to intervene by all of the parties to the dispute.

Not quite as easy to draw, however, is the line distinguishing mediation from "facilitation," "policy dialogue," "conflict anticipation" and other conflict management devices that do conform to the criteria engendered by the above-noted definition of mediation.

By whatever name, these intervention options may be very broadly characterized as dispute management processes that seek to resolve conflict before stalemate or impasse occurs.[4] The

---

† From *Environmental Protection Service*, 1983/84: 8–9, 11–12, 15–19, 36–38, 100, 102–12. (Quebec: The Canadian Environmental Law Association. Reprinted by permission of Environment Canada). Source of Information: Environment Canada. Reproduced with the permission of the Minister of Public Works and Government Services Canada, 2002. See appendix for notes or references. [Notes have been re-numbered in this reproduction.]

considerable discussion and debate that has taken place with respect to the differentiating characteristics of these dispute management processes has failed to yield any definitive characterization and indeed several practitioners have suggested that the efforts have proven largely to be little more than a waste of time. In the alternative, they propose functional categories that would be based upon the objectives of the process rather than the particular methods used.[5]

. . . .

National or International Policy

These major disputes invoke the interest and jurisdiction of the broadest constituencies and often transcend international boundaries. Policies pertaining to oil and natural gas exploration, natural resource use in coastal or international waters, and transboundary and long-range transport of toxic air pollutants provide generic examples here. Although the issues may be manageable from a technical perspective, the number of interested parties militates against resolving these disputes in any but the most encompassing political forum available. Even then, national boundaries may inhibit the opportunity of capturing, from a jurisdictional point of view, the ambit of interested parties, and the absence of an effective international forum for resolving these disputes has frequently kept the possibility of settlement out of reach.

Specific examples would include Acid Rain, Great Lakes Water Quality, Winter Navigation on the St. Lawrence River, the Garrison Water Diversion Project, and the recently settled High Ross Dam-Skajit [sic] River dispute.[9]

National Policy — Limited Constituency

Although many of the disputes within this category engender interests that are relatively unconfined geographically — both the locus of regulatory authority and the relatively limited number of affected interests [distinguish] them as being generally of a regulatory rule-making or a standard setting character. Regulation of certain toxic substances (Phenoxy herbicides, for example), disposal of radioactive wastes, specific performance standards with respect to lead content of fuel, and drinking water standards provide examples of such issues. There have been some successful efforts in the United States to address these issues using a consensual dispute resolution process designed to narrow or focus the subject of dispute.

. . . .

Provincial or Regional Policy Matters

Two types of disputes are encompassed under this heading. The first are disputes that pertain to activities or undertakings that are confined geographically but involve various government agencies, levels of government, and broadly based industrial and environmental interest groups. Hydro-electric development in northern Manitoba and northern Quebec provide good examples of this type of dispute. Although both projects might be considered examples of facility siting disputes (see below), the scope and dimension of environmental impact entails a very substantial resource allocation component. Such disputes are usually very difficult to resolve because of the number of affected constituencies and the very diverse nature of their respective interests. Typically, the costs and benefits associated with such activities will be borne or enjoyed by very different constituencies. As is illustrated by the Northern Flood Agreement, however, resolution of these disputes is possible when innovative approaches are developed for rationalizing those costs and benefits.[11] Other examples here would include oil and natural gas exploration in the Beaufort Sea and forest management issues.

The second category of dispute that may be seen as falling within this subheading is of a regulatory or standard setting nature and does not usually involve significant extra-provincial considerations. Ontario's initiative to establish a comprehensive policy with respect to waste management provides a good example, as do various provincial initiatives for developing licensing and emission guidelines and procedures for the disposal of PCBs. The multiplicity of parties involved is clearly an impediment to pursuing a comprehensive consensual resolution process. The existence of some shared and broadly accepted common interest, however, suggests that some opportunity for negotiation may exist. Thus while the waste disposal industry, government and environmentalists may disagree vehemently about the manner for disposing of hazardous wastes — all would agree that some disposal system and management program is necessary.

Site Specific Issues with
Secondary Impacts

Nuclear generation stations or centralized facilities for disposing of hazardous substances provide prototypical examples of this next category. The nature of the facilities themselves [involves] matters of provincial policy that are of considerable interest beyond the confines of the affected community. Because of the size and nature of the facility, impacts upon the local community may be very significant and entail socio-economic, planning and natural environment components. To this, however, must be added another level of environmental concern that might be considered generic in nature. Do nuclear reactors represent a viable option for providing our energy service needs? Do the user fees associated with hazardous waste disposal facilities ensure that most wastes will arrive at the facility — or operate as a disincentive to recycling? The specific interests of those opposed to any such project, as between the local community opponents and the more broadly based environmental groups, are often very difficult to accommodate. The Victoria Hospital EFW and Darlington Nuclear Generation Station case studies provide illustrations of this type of dispute and indicate that significant potential may exist for mediated resolution of many, if not all, of the matters at issue.

Site Specific Issues

These types of disputes have been those most amenable to mediated resolution.[12] The parties are easily identified and some sense of common objectives may be shared by them. An example would be a dispute concerning municipal waste disposal. Furthermore, this type of dispute occurs often and manifests similar characteristics.

One caveat, however, might be added. No matter how confined geographically, the ambit of environmental impact is often broader than was anticipated. Thus what one might have considered to be a very local problem, e.g., Love Canal, acquires a national character because of the severity of impact (the potential carcinogenic impact upon area residents) and an international dimension when toxic substances are found leaching their way toward Lake Ontario.

· · · · ·

Are the Issues Amenable to Compromise/Negotiated Resolution?

Whatever the costs and disharmony associated with protracted battles in judicial, administrative or public forums, it is clear that certain issues do not lend themselves to negotiated resolution. A commonly sited [sic] illustration here is the principled opposition expressed by certain environmental groups to nuclear reactors, a position that leaves no room for compromise. Although this particular example provides one of the clearest illustrations of a non-negotiable environmental issue, it is not infrequently the case that there is little and often no shared or common interest among antagonists to environmental disputes.

Whether the particular issue is the construction of high-voltage transmission lines to serve distant markets, or the regulation of pesticides, it is not uncommon to find the costs and benefits of such initiatives borne or enjoyed by entirely distinct "communities." Unlike the labour management analogue where both parties share a commitment to a common endeavour (the prosperity of the company), opponents to a wide variety of environmentally significant undertakings have virtually no interest in seeing the project proceed. Absent this common ground, delay represents victory. Local and public interest groups might stall development sufficiently to render it uneconomic. Alternatively, industry may stall regulatory initiatives to avoid the installation of costly pollution equipment. More often than not, however, opportunities for throwing roadblocks in the path of such undertakings are limited, and eventually exhausted: the inevitability of the endeavour is recognized. At this juncture, or in anticipation of it, the opposition may realize the wisdom of negotiating measures that will soften adverse impacts. Thus, notwithstanding the antithetical nature of the interests involved, compromise will often be recognized as a necessary, albeit unpalatable, fact of life.

On the other hand, certain issues would be regarded as non-negotiable as, for example, test case litigation brought to establish a precedent or settle some matter pertaining to due process. Other disputes will also have to be resolved in public forums, judicial or otherwise, in order to gain the high visibility necessary for general public acceptance. This is true with respect to issues that are sufficiently controversial to warrant considerable caution to avoid even the appearance of a backroom deal.[13]

In contrast with those factors that may easily disqualify any potential candidate, there are other dispute characteristics that indicate that mediation may be particularly well suited as a dispute resolution mechanism. Described as the hallmarks of mediability, they are:

1. The existence of some common ground between opposing parties, and;
2. The existence of feasible mitigative measures to alleviate problematic environmental impact.[14]

One illustration of the former often arises with respect to the siting by municipalities of local or regional waste disposal facilities. The interested parties commonly share the objective of disposing of waste in a cost effective manner that minimizes impact upon the community. In seeking to identify this common ground, one should recognize, however, that the existence of any mutual interest is often obscured by the confrontational positions taken for public relations reasons or for tactical advantage. Assessing the availability of feasible mitigative measures will also require some familiarity with the facts of the dispute, and those resources of the project proponent available to undertake any such mitigative action. Most often agreement on the appropriateness and feasibility of mitigative measures will be the single most important factor in determining the success of environmental mediation. The existence of available and adequate mitigation options would then militate in favour of mediation. Perhaps the most encouraging indicia of mediability will exist where the dispute is similar in character and dimension to disputes that have been successfully mediated elsewhere.

Finally on this subject, one point of clarification should be added. While mediation might not resolve all of the issues at hand in any given dispute, it may well accomplish more limited objectives. Thus, mediation may offer significant opportunities for scoping or narrowing the issues, resolving procedural problems, and facilitating information and data access and exchange.[15] Were these to be the only contributions that mediation would make on the Canadian scene (and experience to date already belies such limited expectations), it would still make a significant contribution if the relatively expensive and formal processes, carried out by tribunals such as those under FEARO or the Environmental Assessment Board were narrowed by resolving even a smaller proportion of the issues on their respective agendas.

. . . .

OVERCOMING THE OBSTACLES

Obstacles to Mediation

As with any new process or procedure, a variety of obstacles will present themselves to slow the process of implementation. Some of the impediments that are identified there are systemic and endemic to the regulatory process and/or the dynamics of the relationship among the various interests involved in that process. It is of course premature to suggest that, in aid of facilitating the implementation of environmental mediation, new and significant policy initiatives be taken to overcome these obstacles. Rather the object of this exercise is to optimize efforts to examine the utility and viability of this new approach to resolving environmental disputes. Practical efforts to assess the utility of the mediation process will benefit greatly if those involved foresee and appreciate some of the difficulties that may be encountered. Finally, awareness of potential impediments will serve as a further check upon the process of assessing the mediability of the particular dispute.

During phase 1 of this project, a summary survey was conducted of members of the various constituencies involved in the environmental regulatory process. A brief questionnaire was mailed to a sample of government officials, public and private industry executives and representatives of environmental non-governmental organizations (ENGOs).[16] Among the questions asked, was the following:

- "Are there barriers to using mediation? What kind? (e.g., attitudinal, administrative, legal, political, etc.) Would you rank any such barriers in order of importance?"

. . . .

ENGO's: Approximately half the respondents were able to identify potential barriers, these include:

- existing environmental legislation does not contemplate a process of negotiation between proponents, government, and impacted community

- the political objectives of government might undermine efforts to promote such tripartite resolutions
- the relative powerlessness of the ENGO and rate payer sector creates no incentive for either government or industry to deal with this constituency
- attitudinal — level of debate on the issue is relatively uninformed
- several respondents identify the lack of resources available to the ENGO network
- the ambivalence of government or industry to see their relatively significant power usurped.

Conceptually these obstacles may be differentiated into three categories:

- those barriers that will inhibit recourse to environmental mediation even where there is some indication that it might make a valuable contribution;
- those problems that may be encountered during the course of mediation, and;
- difficulties that will impede efforts at implementation or enforcement of any agreement that may be arrived at.

. . . .

Impediments to Using Environmental Mediation

The perspective offered of this issue by regulatory officials, project proponents and environmentalists, predictably varies. There are however some problems that are identified by all three constituencies. The first concerns the absence of administrative or legal regimes that might countenance or sanction the use of this approach to dispute resolution. Clearly the institutionalization of mediation as a readily available option must await a much greater awareness of, and positive experience with, this process. These developments will in turn depend upon an ongoing effort to educate and inform the prospective participants. A considerable degree of such activity is underway in Canada, and it is also interesting to note that significant public policy support for the process has already been expressed by senior public officials.[17]

Should the process prove its usefulness, a number of more concrete initiatives will be required to provide the financial and logistical support that implementing the process will require. Funding mechanisms will have to be cre-

ated, government officials will need a mandate to sanction the use of mediation in appropriate situations, and regulatory processes will require modification to accommodate mediation.

In addition to these practical obstacles however, a number of other impediments exist that may be regarded as essentially attitudinal in nature. Government officials may be want to relinquish their considerable discretion and ability to achieve objectives unilaterally, and may perceive mediation as a potential threat to their substantial power base. Public and private industry executives may be reluctant to recognize as legitimate, the interests of local citizens and environmental groups. Finally, ratepayer and interest groups may be reluctant to participate in any process that does not directly address their most pressing problem — access to sufficient resources to allow an effective opportunity to negotiate in the first place.[18]

Apart from those barriers that were identified by questionnaire respondents, practitioners have encountered additional disincentives to the use of mediation in this context. The first concerns the risks associated with even suggesting recourse to mediation: your opponent may consider such an overture to be a sign of weakness; your allies (already skeptical about the process) will begin to question your commitment to the group objectives.[19] Another obstacle arises when the parties become locked into their public postures with respect to the issues. Not only do the parties tend to take their own positions too literally, but [they] do the same for the other side's "propaganda" as well.[20]

To each of the above noted impediments one might offer a reassuring and pithy solution. An offer to negotiate can be taken as an indication that one is confident in one's position, reluctance to include opponents in an effective manner can yield to a dawning realization that it is far easier in the long run to proceed with an undertaking when it enjoys general support, than when it is the subject of wide scale opposition. More appropriately however, it is important here to recognize that overcoming some of these obstacles will simply be a function of garnering practical experience with environmental mediation. Some barriers may not materialize, others may prove very resilient. ...

. . . .

Environmental Mediation — A Boon or a Hindrance to Environmentalists

We have seen that those with the ability to unilaterally achieve their objectives, will predictably be reluctant to contemplate an exercise that implies compromise. This reticence may however, be shared by those who have only a nominal ability to influence the specific course of any environmentally contentious endeavour. In this regard, environmental groups have perceived the mediation process as just another public involvement scheme designed to do little more than co-opt the energies of project opponents.[22] To advocate negotiation and compromise without addressing in some concrete way, the disparity of resources and inequality of power between the bargainers is simply to distract environmentalists from pursuing a more effective means for putting forward their cause. Pursuant to this paradigm, participation without power equals co-optation.[23]

Critics also describe the mediation process as having an inherent pro-development bias.[24] Pursuant to this analysis, environmental mediation may operate not only to engender but as well to perpetuate an inherent imbalance of power that inevitably favours project proponents and government agencies. This would occur in a variety of ways. To begin with, only those with power to block or subvert project development are included in the mediation process. In this manner, environmental mediation may provide the practical mechanism for excluding a potentially problematic constituency from the bargaining process. This would isolate the relatively powerless local citizens or ratepayer group from its natural ally, a national or more broadly based environmental group.

The divide and conquer scenario that is sketched here does appear to represent a real threat to open and comprehensive participation in the decision-making process. The community impact [agreements] negotiated by Ontario Hydro with the Towns of Newcastle and Atikokan have often been assailed as little more than an effort designed to avoid adequate environmental assessment and public scrutiny of these two large energy projects. The criticism is particularly hard to counter when, as with the case of Darlington, substantial sums of money changed hands and where the impact agreement appears to have been the precondition for dispensing with a public environmental assessment process.

Should the concerns of the host community be "satisfied" in this fashion, it would be very difficult for a broadly based environmental group to intervene and insist upon rigorous and full environmental assessment. Without the support and active interest of local residents, the resources would simply not be available to sustain an effective campaign. On occasion regarded by project proponents as officious intermeddlers [sic], environmentalists would now also run the risk of alienating the local community should they challenge or retard the progress of a project that now offers very tangible benefits to that host community.

From the perspective of the local interest group, the resources of environmental groups often offer the most accessible and inexpensive source of expertise that is a necessary precondition of meaningful bargaining. Should the local group embark upon bilateral (as opposed to multi-lateral) negotiations, it may well cut itself off from that assistance. This would further tilt the bargaining process in favour of pro-development interests by denying to local opponents, even those scarce resources now available to them.

Critics have also described the negotiation process as defining environmental issues in a manner that tends to impute a pro-development bias. Thus the focus of the mediation process can easily become one of removing obstacles to development rather than questioning the rationale for the development proposal in the first place or, alternatively, examining the philosophical and moral issues that underlie opposition.[25] If "responsible development" is to be the compromise between competing environmental and development interests — it is easy to see then how "responsible development" (of nuclear power plants for example) can be regarded essentially as victories for pro-development interests. Critics argue that not all issues of right and wrong are capable of being translated into different but equally-valid interests.

Another criticism that has been made of the process relates to the congenial atmosphere that may be created during negotiations as offering a subtle opportunity for developers to seduce relatively unsophisticated environmentalists.[26] Thus the ability of the process to convert an atmosphere of confrontation to one of some civility may, in certain situations, disarm environmentalists who have sufficiently little political and economic power to render them virtually defenceless without the drama necessary to prompt media and public interest.

Clearly a number of these criticisms are well-founded. The relative powerlessness of environmental and local citizens groups certainly will work to their disadvantage whatever the forum of debate, however. One must be careful then not to confuse with mediation, the problems that are already endemic to this arena. The lack of legislative or legal recourse available to environmentalists tends to deny legitimization to their concerns and objectives. Most Canadian environmental organizations have in the alternative developed strategies that tend to maximize media coverage and politicize debate. Not uncommonly, among the objectives of such campaigns is the establishment of a formal public hearing process. Should mediation then operate to remove this public and often heated debate to the confines of the bargaining table, without first allowing for the development of the more formal structures, it might well operate to subvert environmental interests and leave the opposition with no recourse whatsoever should the mediation exercise fail. Indeed, without recourse to a more formal administrative or judicial remedy, environmental groups might be well advised to regard mediation as being little more than an effort to divert their attention from activities that may create very real problems for development.

On the other hand, problems associated with lack of sophistication on the part of interest groups are probably overstated as several corporate executives who have faced the articulate wrath of "unsophisticated" citizen groups spokespersons can well attest.

As for the possibility that mediation may somehow exacerbate the problems that already exist by reason of the inequality of power between proponents and environmentalists, one further comment might be made. Environmentalists are keenly aware of their relative disadvantage in this regard and have repeatedly shown little interest in negotiation without access to the resources necessary to make that process meaningful. Undoubtedly, one of the first demands that will be put forward during any mediation exercise will be for resources sufficient to enable opponents to acquire sufficient expertise to digest the proponent's technical information and reports, and to develop, where appropriate — an affirmative case in the alternative. The process might well then offer opportunities that do not now exist for addressing this problem.

With little practical experience, it is difficult to determine whether the concerns expressed here will prove to be well-founded. For environmentalists to focus too much attention upon the potential liabilities of the process however, may be to overlook the considerable advantages that mediation may offer. Indeed, proponent willingness to bargain in good faith may do more to legitimize the concerns of interest and environmental groups than do the formal public hearing processes that have to date remained little more than symbolic exercises. Should all concerned be alerted however, to the potential shortcomings of this innovative approach for resolving environmental disputes, the more likely it will be that environmental mediation will live up to its very significant promise.

(c) How Efficient Are Environmental Dispute Resolution Processes?†

Gail Bingham

Perhaps the single most common assertion made about environmental dispute resolution processes

— indeed, about alternative dispute resolution processes in general — is that they are cheaper

---

† From *Resolving Environmental Disputes: A Decade of Experience* (Washington, DC.: The Conservation Foundation, 1986), pp. 127–33, 135–41, 144–47. Reproduced with permission of RESOLVE, 1255 — 23rd St. NW, Washington, D.C. 200036. See appendix for notes or references.

and faster than litigation. No systematic attempt to test this claim by comparing litigation on environmental matters with environmental dispute resolution alternatives has ever been made, however, perhaps because very little evidence exists about how long it takes either to litigate or to mediate environmental disputes. Further, there are several conceptual problems in making comparisons between environmental dispute resolution alternatives and litigation. Through simple repetition, however, the notion seems to have become an accepted fact.

The very frequency with which claims are made that mediation is cheaper and faster than litigation is an indicator that people are interested in finding more efficient ways to resolve conflicts. Much has been written about problems in the American legal system and about potential reform measures. Legal scholars addressed judicial reform issues at least as early as the turn of the 20th century,[1] although concerns about resolving disputes in the courts go back to colonial times.[2] ...

. . . .

Although this chapter focuses on questions of time and costs, it also is important to remember that from the perspective of those involved in environmental disputes efficiency is not enough. In looking for dispute resolution processes that will take less time and cost less money, the parties to disputes also are looking for processes that are more effective in producing satisfactory outcomes. Therefore, from the perspective of the parties in a dispute, the most important question is not so much whether mediation, in general, takes less time than litigation, in general. Rather, the parties' concern is a balancing one — how to achieve the best results most efficiently in each specific case.

Evaluating how individual cases might have been more efficiently mediated or litigated requires a level of detail that lies beyond the scope of this study, however. Even a general comparison between mediation and litigation is difficult, because of the lack of parallel data between cases that were litigated and cases that were mediated. Despite these limitations, this chapter does discuss the factors that would have to be taken into account if such a comparison were performed. Some statistics that are available about both litigation and mediation are presented, although it must be remembered that the data are not comparable in any way. The assumption that litigation of environmental issues is a problem is reviewed, as is the idea that some parties use delay as a strategy in their efforts to produce a satisfactory outcome to a dispute.

Comparing Mediation With Litigation

Most individuals and organizations involved in environmental disputes can cite at least one dispute in which the parties became so locked in a legal stalemate that there seemed to be no way out. Such stories have helped build the case for the weakness in relying solely on litigation for settling disputes, but they also may have oversimplified the general public image both of litigation and of dispute resolution alternatives. A lawsuit that goes to trial may take a very long time, but few lawsuits go to trial. Some mediated environmental disputes may be resolved quickly, but voluntary dispute resolution processes are not necessarily fast if the issues are complex. In addition, although mediators generally charge less than attorneys, one is not necessarily a substitute for the other, and attorneys' and mediators' fees are not the only costs associated with resolving disputes. The costs of preparing for negotiation, for example, may be as high as or higher than the parallel costs of preparing for some kinds of litigation, particularly for public interest groups in cases requiring analysis of scientific information.

One example that is often cited as evidence that expensive, lengthy legal disputes can be better solved through mediation is a dispute that began in 1963 over a proposed pump-storage power station at Storm King Mountain in the Hudson River Highlands in New York.[4] During the course of the 17 years of litigation that ensued, three environmental groups, four public agencies, and five utility companies became involved at an estimated combined cost to the parties of over $6 million in legal fees and other court costs.[5] In April 1979, Russell Train, now chairman of the board of World Wildlife Fund and The Conservation Foundation and former administrator of the U.S. Environmental Protection Agency, was invited to step in as mediator, and, in December 1980, the parties formally signed an out-of-court settlement. The combined costs of the mediator's time and expenses, and the fees of the attorneys and technical people involved in the negotiations, must have been only a tiny fraction of the cost of the previous litigation — and an even smaller fraction of the total cost of the projects involved.

Such a simple comparison, however, although striking, can be misleading. Unlike the Storm King case, most civil disputes, including environmental disputes, never go to trial. In addition, in cases where all parties view the stakes as high, they are often not willing to negotiate until litigation has proved unable to settle the dispute in their favour. As a result, it is difficult to decide which costs to count in comparing litigation and environmental dispute resolution alternatives.

It may be unrealistic to begin counting the costs of mediation at the time that the parties agreed to negotiate, if the previous period of contention, litigation, or clarification of relative power contributed to the parties' willingness to negotiate a settlement. In the Storm King case, for example, the parties probably would not have agreed to mediation instead of litigation if the former had been available in the early 1960s. At the beginning of the dispute, the economic, environmental, and legal interests of all the parties did not give those parties sufficient incentives to compromise.

Filing a lawsuit also may be the only way that some of the parties to a dispute can get the others to talk to them. In almost 25 percent of the cases in this study, mediation was used to settle environmental disputes that were being litigated. In perhaps another 20 percent of the cases studied, there was the threat of a lawsuit. In a few cases, mediation actually occurred after a lawsuit had settled issues that were not easily negotiable.

A simple comparison of costs also leaves out perhaps the most important consideration in analyzing the worth of the settlement of a dispute — the nature and quality of the outcome itself. A more efficient process may not be more desirable if it leads to significantly poorer decisions in the view of one or all of the parties. The outcomes of litigation and environmental dispute resolution alternatives theoretically are very different. At the end of a trial, there is usually a winner and a loser. A clear win or loss may be the most desirable outcome in cases where what is at stake is a matter of principle or of law, because compromise may be neither possible nor desirable. In such cases, the publicity of even a hopeless fight might be better than an agreement that offers little or no real gain. Under other circumstances, however, neither the winner

nor the loser really benefits. Sometimes, the decisions in lawsuits are made on procedural grounds. Such an outcome could produce an improved procedure, or perhaps an improved environmental assessment, but no substantial change in the proposed project, plan, or policy. By contrast, in a voluntary dispute resolution process, the parties are much more likely to deal with the substantive issues in dispute.

The goal of negotiation or consensus-building processes is an agreement among all of the parties at interest. Because everyone supposedly agrees voluntarily, it is assumed that everyone wins something — or, at least, that all parties feel that the outcome is better than it might have been without an agreement. In measuring the relative costs of litigation and environmental dispute resolution alternatives, therefore, one may be measuring the costs of two very different kinds of results. Choosing a winner and a loser in a lawsuit also may preclude the search for new alternatives that achieve important joint gains for all parties, if they are successful at engaging in creative problem-solving during the negotiations.

The final major conceptual problem in asking whether environmental dispute resolution processes are really cheaper and faster than litigation is the difficulty of finding comparable samples of cases. Many variables significantly affect the complexity and, therefore, the duration and cost of environmental disputes, independent of the dispute resolution process used. As was noted in chapter 1, some disputes involve particularly thorny scientific and technical issues; others do not. Different statutes apply to different disputes. The cases may or may not have precedential value. The number and types of parties differ.

For example, a dispute over the siting of a new hazardous waste facility differs significantly from a dispute over whether an existing industrial facility is out of compliance with its water quality control permit. Multiple parties are involved in the former; usually two — the owner of the facility and the regulatory agency — are involved in the latter. The technical resources available to the parties are relatively even in the latter but unequal in the former. A local community may benefit from the status quo in the former, but the company probably benefits from the status quo in the latter. Despite these differences, however, these disputes may have more in common with each other than with disputes over plans for timber harvest, oil and gas exploration, or mining on public lands.

Significant variation can exist even within a category of disputes. For instance, it makes a big difference to the complexity of resolving a dispute over forest management plans whether logging operations are proposed in a potential wilderness area or in an area where logging previously has taken place.

The comparison of litigation and voluntary environmental dispute resolution alternatives can be further hampered by a misconception that lawsuits and voluntary approaches are mutually exclusive options. Most lawsuits never go to trial. In fact, it is commonly estimated that over 90 percent of all civil cases are resolved out of court through some form of voluntary settlement negotiations.[6] In addition, mediated dispute resolution processes can begin with a lawsuit or the threat of a lawsuit. Such overlap can easily blur a comparison of the duration and cost of litigation and environmental dispute resolution alternatives.

Moreover, the comparability of litigation and voluntary alternatives can be further confused because, in some disputes, either litigation or a voluntary approach simply is not a relevant alternative. In some cases, in which parties are attempting to set legal precedents, informal negotiations may not be appropriate. Sometimes, a dispute must be settled first in an administrative process by a public agency responsible for planning, permitting, or regulatory decisions. Litigation may not be an option in such cases until after several levels of administrative appeals are completed. In other cases, where a dispute is over a controversial solution to a difficult environmental problem, the most likely alternative, although not the most desirable one from all points of view, to a voluntary dispute resolution process may be no action at all.

Thus, finding comparable cases with which to assess the efficiency of environmental dispute resolution alternatives and litigation presents a considerable challenge. One would like to find a sufficient number of similar cases, some of which were mediated and some of which were litigated. A large enough sample should nullify the effects of case variability, and it might even be possible to find correlations between certain factors and the processes by which disputes were resolved — for example, whether cases were litigated and went all the way to trial, whether lawsuits were resolved through negotiated settlements, whether

mediation occurred, and whether mediation was used before or after lawsuits were filed.

Unfortunately, too few cases have been mediated in any one issue area to conduct such a comparison at this time. This should be possible sometime in the future, however.

Is Litigation Really a Problem?

The search for more efficient dispute resolution alternatives to litigation presumes that problems exist with litigation. If there are problems, what are they? Is there too much litigation of environmental issues? Does it take too long and cost too much? Is the problem really one of inefficiency, or is it that litigation often may not be the most *effective* way to solve a problem?

. . . .

Concerns about the overload on the judicial system are widespread, and statistics show that the overall burden on federal courts is increasing. The Administrative Office of the United States Courts reports that in the 12-month period ending June 30, 1983, 241,842 civil cases were filed in U.S. District Courts[8] and 29,630 appeals were filed in U.S. Courts of Appeals.[9] These totals constitute 74.3[10] and 56.6 percent[11] increases, respectively, over the same period five years previous.

Available figures, although limited, do not indicate that the number of environmental lawsuits has grown in a similar fashion, however.... Rather, the Council on Environmental Quality's *Annual Reports* show that the volume of litigation under NEPA involving federal agencies actually declined slightly between 1974 and 1982 — from 189 NEPA cases filed in 1974 to 157 filed in 1982.[13] In addition, the Judicial Conference of the United States, which keeps statistics about the federal courts, reports that between 1978 and 1983, the number of suits filed in U.S. District Courts under any environmental statute dropped from 519 in the 12-month period ending June 30, 1978 to 465 for the same period in 1982 and 1983.[14]

. . . .

Opinions differ over whether decreases in the number of environmental lawsuits filed is a positive or negative trend. Litigation has been the principal way for those interested in protecting the quality of the environment to make gains, and that often continues to be the case. Thus, a decrease in litigation could be seen as a retreat from the vigorous pursuit of environmental objectives. Unless comparable achievements in protecting human health and the environment can be demonstrated to result from alternatives to litigation, environmental advocates will understandably remain skeptical about what the use of those alternatives really signifies.

If indications are that the number of environmental lawsuits is not increasing, is the problem with litigation instead that these lawsuits take too long to settle? Many think so. Among other factors, it is argued that environmental disputes often involve uncertainty, which can increase pretrial preparation time as well as time spent in court. A search of the literature, however, turned up no published information about how long it takes to litigate any kind of environmental dispute. Instead, many questions were raised about whether the question can be answered at all. Too much uncertainty exists over where one would start the clock. Environmental disputes generally involve considerable administrative action prior to the filing of a lawsuit. In addition, questions remain about whether it is possible to ascertain how representative any particular sample of cases might be, who keeps what kinds of data, whether those data are in comparable forms, and whether the complete duration of a case can be accurately measured, if the case has been appealed from one court to another.

Information on how long it takes to litigate general civil litigation is available, but, previously, such information has not been published for environmental disputes. For this report, the Judicial Conference of the United States conducted a special computer search of its data to determine the duration of environmental disputes filed in U.S. District Courts (figure 16).[17] These data assume that litigation began at the time of filing. They are limited to those kinds of environmental disputes that are brought to a U.S. District Court and, therefore, may not be representative of the broad range of environmental disputes.[18] Also, the data do not take into account whether the case had been heard previously in another administrative or judicial forum or, for those few cases that went to trial, whether the case was appealed further. These figures, therefore, should only be considered general indicators.

The information on the median number of months that it takes to dispense with a dispute in federal court indicates that cases are concluded relatively expeditiously and usually without going to trial. The range in the length of time it takes to conclude cases is great, however. On the average, the median duration of civil suits in U.S. District Courts terminated in the 12-month period ending June 30, 1983, was 7 months. The median time from filing to disposition of lawsuits involving environmental matters during this same period was 10 months. Only 5.8 percent of the civil litigation and 7.7 percent of the environmental litigation included in this sample went to trial, however. The remainder were terminated without court action or were terminated before or during pretrial proceedings. The median number of months from filing to disposition for cases that went to trial was 19 months for all civil disputes and 23 months for environmental disputes.

More interesting than the median duration of these lawsuits, however, is the range among the cases. Ten percent of all civil litigation in this sample took more than 28 months from the time of filing to disposition regardless of when and how the case was terminated, while 10 percent of the environmental litigation took more than 42 months. For those cases that went to trial, 10 percent of the civil suits took longer than 45 months to be decided, and 10 percent of the environmental suits took more than a whopping 67 months — or over five and one-half years. It is likely, therefore, that it is the *threat* of protracted litigation that is most significant in creating the incentives to find alternative ways to resolve disputes.

The Strategy of Delay

The length of time it takes to resolve a particular dispute through the legal system depends on the complexity of the dispute, how much is at stake, whether one of the parties is using the system to hold up the process, whether the case goes to trial, and whether the decision is appealed. Because some courts have larger backlogs than others, similar cases filed in different courts also may take more or less time to decide.

The use of the legal system to stop a project through delay has been blamed for many of the ills of environmental disputes. The implication seems to be that the motives behind these

	All civil cases[1]	Environmental matters[2]
FIGURE 16 Time Interval from Filing to Disposition of Civil Cases in U.S. District Courts, by Nature of Suit and Method of Disposition during the 12-Month Period Ending June 30, 1983		
Total cases		
Number of cases	184,427	416
Time interval		
Bottom 10%	< 1 month	< 0 months
Median	7 months	10 months
Top 10%	> 28 months	> 42 months
Cases involving no court action		
Number of cases	93,661	116
Time interval		
Bottom 10%	< 1 month	< 0 months
Median	4 months	3 months
Top 10%	> 18 months	> 32 months
Cases involving court action — disposed before pretrial		
Number of cases	54,057	204
Time interval		
Bottom 10%	< 2 months	< 0 months
Median	7 months	12 months
Top 10%	> 24 months	> 42 months
Cases involving court action — disposed during or after pretrial		
Number of cases	26,052	52
Time interval		
Bottom 10%	< 6 months	< 5 months
Median	16 months	22 months
Top 10%	> 38 months	> 47 months
Cases involving court action — disposed through trial		
Number of cases	10,657	32
Time interval		
Bottom 10%	< 6 months	< 7 months
Median	19 months	23 months
Top 10%	> 45 months	> 67 months

[1] All civil cases filed in U.S. District Courts other than land condemnation, prisoner petitions, and deportation reviews.
[2] Includes, among others, cases filed under the National Environmental Policy Act, Clean Air Act, Federal Water Pollution Control Act, and Federal [Insecticide], Fungicide, and Rodenticide Act.

actions are cynical and, therefore, somehow suspect. A closer look at the strategy of delay, however, indicates that the picture is neither so simple nor so bleak as is often assumed. The reasons why parties use litigation to delay a decision vary, and no one type of party is uniquely "to blame." The effectiveness of voluntary dispute resolution processes to speed up the process, therefore, depends on a clearer understanding of what underlies the strategy of delay.

Although disputes are often escalated by accusations that one party or another is using lit-

igation as a strategy to delay a decision, the reasons why parties attempt to block a decision are more important for creating a successful dispute resolution process than who the parties are. Sometimes, a party to an environmental dispute may benefit from the continuation of the status quo. Citizens' and environmental groups benefit, for example, when they delay a proposed project that is expected to discharge pollutants into the air or water, generate additional traffic, or threaten natural resources and wildlife habitat, unless the problems that could cause negative impact on human health or the environment are solved. Delay is not always to the advantage of citizen and environmental groups, however, when they look to public agencies to solve problems such as the cleanup of abandoned toxic waste dumps or the reduction of pollutants in the environment. Delay also can work to the advantage of the party subject to regulation when stricter regulatory policies are being proposed or when enforcement actions are taken by a regulated agency. In such cases, change is likely to be expensive. The longer a decision is delayed, the longer a regulated company can postpone paying those costs.

Obviously, delay can be an end in itself if a party — whether it be a citizens' group, an environmental organization, or a company — thinks that, if it waits long enough, the opposition will walk away. Environmental dispute resolution processes do not, by themselves, offer a magic solution to the use of litigation for delay. The incentives to cause delays also must be changed, or the parties either will not agree to participate or will use the mediation process as one more way to delay the eventual decision.

Usually, however, delay is only a means that parties in disputes use to satisfy their underlying needs and objectives. Occasionally, when a company faced with large expenditures for new pollution control equipment goes to court to block an agency's requirement, it can be satisfied if the agency can find ways to take the company's costs into account.[19] For example, allowing longer compliance deadlines may give the company a chance to achieve greater pollution reductions through plant retooling; "averaging" approaches such as the "bubble" concept, if properly used, can give companies the flexibility to reduce emissions further than required and at less cost.[20]

Similarly, active environmental litigators are concerned about accomplishing environmental goals and often would prefer to negotiate mitigation measures in project proposals or other changes in agency actions to protect the environment. They often file lawsuits or threaten to file lawsuits principally to persuade their opposition to sit down with them and negotiate. In one example, environmentalists who sued to stop construction of a proposed dam were most interested, not in totally preventing the dam, but rather in preserving habitat areas for water-dependent species. When proponents of the dam

agreed to protect minimum in-stream flows, the environmentalists withdrew their lawsuit.[21]

One of the commonly cited strategies used by environmentalists to delay a proposed project has been to challenge the project on the grounds that an environmental impact statement (EIS) required under NEPA should have been prepared or that an existing EIS was inadequate. These suits, however, also illustrate the real dynamics behind the strategy of delay, described above. For the most part, environmental activists care more about the project and how to mitigate or compensate for environmental impacts than they do about EIS documents. It is not that they do not care about the value of environmental impact assessments in bringing out information that will be useful in sound project planning decisions but rather that they care most about the actual decisions that are reached. NEPA lawsuits can increase the incentives for project planners and public decision makers to respond to environmental concerns.

Realistically, however, not all issues are susceptible to compromise, either because matters of principle or of law may be at stake or because the parties are unable to invent new options that give each other more palatable choices and they remain opposed to an activity under any circumstances. In these cases, voluntary dispute resolution processes are not likely to be more efficient or more effective than litigation.

How Long Do Environmental Dispute Resolution Alternatives Take?

To describe the time it takes to resolve environmental disputes through some form of negotiation or consensus building, one must first select beginning- and end-points. Because the scope of this study is limited to mediated processes, the date that someone first contracted a mediator serves here as the beginning point from which to measure the length of a mediation process. Some may prefer to measure environmental dispute resolution processes from the date of the first meeting; others may propose another point. There is sufficient variability in these processes that exceptions will be found to any choice.[22] However, because so much of a mediator's assistance is in helping the parties agree on the nature, ground rules, and agenda of the process, the point at which a mediator begins to provide this assistance seems the most logical beginning.

The end of the dispute resolution process is considered here to be the date of the last meeting or the date that an agreement was signed or ratified, whichever was later. There are times that the formalities of an agreement are worked out after the last meeting but that the agreement is signed without another meeting. At other times, as has been noted, environmental dispute resolution processes are relatively informal, with agreements not put into writing.

The results of this study indicate that, at least in site-specific cases, the duration of voluntary dispute resolution processes varies considerably.* Of the 78 cases for which information is available on the length of time the case took to resolve, the parties took from a single meeting to over two years to negotiate a resolution of issues in dispute.... The variation can be explained easily by, among other factors, the variation in the complexity of issues, number of parties, and polarization among those parties. The median length of time these cases took to conclude was five to six months, whether agreements were reached or not. Over one third of the cases in which agreements were reached took less than four months to resolve; half the cases took less than half a year; and three quarters took less than a year. An encouraging note is that parties took significantly less time to conclude cases in which they failed to agree, indicating that, in calculating the risks of failure when considering a mediation option, parties need not be overly concerned about wasting their time. There appears to be no significant difference in duration among cases with different objectives.

Too little information is available on the duration of policy dialogues to draw reliable conclusion. A first impression, however, is that policy dialogues generally can be separated into two categories: those that took one or two meetings, one to three days long, with a few months of planning time before the meetings and a few months after for drafting a report; and those that involved a series of regular meetings over a period of nine months to two years.

How Much Do Alternative Dispute Resolution Alternatives Cost?

Advocates of environmental dispute resolution alternatives also frequently assert that these processes are cheaper than litigation. At first glance, this seems reasonable. Cost is, in large part, a function of time, and mediators on the average charge less for their time than do attorneys. As was noted earlier, there are many more factors to the comparative costs of litigation and voluntary alternatives than the relative cost of hiring mediators rather than attorneys or even the amount of time it takes to resolve cases.

It is important at the outset to consider who pays what costs. Taxpayers support the costs of the judicial system. To the extent that court reforms or alternatives to litigation reduce the burden on the courts, taxpayers benefit. If mediation services are adjuncts to the judicial system or are paid for by public agencies, the benefits are equal to the difference between costs of providing mediators and of supporting judges. The cost savings to the parties depend on (a) the extent to which the mediation reduces the use of attorneys, (b) whether or not the parties pay the mediator's fees, and (c) the difference between the expenses required for preparation for litigation or negotiation.

Mediators aren't always a substitute for attorneys. In some cases, parties may represent themselves directly in the negotiation process, thus avoiding legal costs. In other cases, parties in a mediation process may want the assistance of their attorneys during the negotiations and in reviewing any mediated agreement to ensure that its terms are in their interests, that the agreement itself is legal, and that it is adequately enforceable. The amount of time attorneys have spent participating in environmental dispute resolution cases has varied considerably, and it is not uncommon for the attorneys to represent their clients at the negotiating table. In such cases, the cost of the mediator generally does not offset the attorneys' fees.

Cases also vary considerably with respect to who pays the mediator. The first environmental mediation organizations were primarily financed by philanthropic foundations that paid their mediators' salaries, with corporate donations, government contracts, and in-kind support from citizens' groups and public interest organizations providing most of the remaining funding. In a few cases, fees were charged to the parties to a dispute resolution attempt, but, for the most part, the mediators' services were free of charge to the parties. This made sense at the time, because environmental dispute resolution alternatives were new, and, even without charging a fee for mediation services, it was difficult to convince all the parties to a dispute to attempt a voluntary resolution of the issues. Mediation ser-

> **FIGURE 18** Cost Estimates for Mediator's Time and Expenses
> (selected site-specific cases only)
>
> | | One mediator | Two mediators |
> | --- | --- | --- |
> | Agreement | 9 | 9 |
> | Average costs | $7,700 | $23,000 |
> | Average duration (in months) | 3.8 | 8.8 |
> | Average number of parties | 5.3 | 8.0 |

vices are available free of charge to the parties less frequently now than they used to be. In some cases, the parties must find ways to pay the mediator's fee; in many cases, however, the parties who pay are government agencies. Such arrangements are analogous to the support of the judicial system in that the dispute resolution process is paid for by the taxpayer.

Only a little information is available about how much it costs to employ environmental mediators. Average fees for the mediators' personal services in 1984 ranged from $250 per day to perhaps $700 per day, plus expenses. Under the earlier circumstances in which foundations supported most environmental mediation services, mediators often did not keep records about their time and expenses on individual cases. A few, however, were able to provide some figures on the costs per case for this report. Information about the cost of the mediator's time and expenses was available for 18 site-specific cases. In 9 of them, one mediator was involved; in the other 9, two mediators were involved (figure 18). The average cost for the cases with one mediator was $7,700. Half of those cases had costs below $5,000, and half had costs above $10,000. The range was from $1,000, for two cases involving two parties and one mediation session, to $26,000, for a case involving 10 parties over a 10 month-period. The average cost for the cases in which two mediators were involved was $23,000, with the range between $15,000, for a case involving six parties over a six-month period (including two and one-half months of intensive work), and $40,000, for a case involving 12 parties over a five-month period. Another case that cost about $30,000 involved 16 parties over a 12-month period. These figures, however, tend to come from organizations that still receive considerable grant support for general expenses. In addition, these figures, some of which are several years old, have not been adjusted for inflation.

Policy dialogues are estimated generally to cost somewhat more than site-specific disputes. Estimates range from $40,000 to over $100,000 per dispute, depending on the complexity and duration of the case.[23] A few particularly large cases have cost several hundred thousand dollars.

Environmental dispute resolution processes for both site-specific cases and policy dialogues tend to have substantial "indirect" costs for the parties, as well. The exact costs depend, of course, on a dispute's specific characteristics. In general, however, negotiation and other consensus-building processes usually require more direct — and therefore time-consuming — participation by the parties themselves than may be required in litigation. The costs of participation by company executives, engineers, planners, citizens, environmentalists, and their technical experts may be considerable. Miscellaneous overhead costs can also be large. Citizens' and environmental groups can be hit especially hard, and some have found that the costs of these approaches to them may exceed the costs of litigation.

Even assuming that the advantages of voluntary resolution of the issues outweigh the disadvantages, however, citizens' and environmental groups may still have a problem with lack of resources to participate. This can make it more difficult for these groups to choose negotiation. Not only may the investment in a lawsuit, if successful, set precedents for other similar cases; but, in addition, some kinds of legal action may be cheaper and faster for public interest groups than negotiation would be. For example, although the full process of preparing for and going to trial may be very expensive, procedural motions, injunctions, or other legal action short of a trial may be sufficient to cause expensive delays for project proponents without large expenditures by the public interest groups concerned about the project's potential impacts. In contrast, precisely because of its advertised benefits, negotiation can demand significantly more time and expense for environmental groups.

The advantage of negotiation over litigation for environmental groups often is that the substantive issues can be addressed more directly. It is one thing, however, to argue in court that the responsible party has not provided sufficient information about the environmental impacts of a project. If one is successful, the expense for further studies is carried by the project proponent. It is another thing entirely in a negotiation to obtain sufficient evidence to persuade others at the table that adverse environmental impacts will occur and that alternative courses of action are justified. If environmental groups propose alternatives, they also may need resources for adequate scientific and technical studies to support the feasibility of the proposed alternatives.

(d)   The Politics of Environmental Mediation[†]

Douglas J. Amy ——————————————————————————————

INTRODUCTION

Put most simply, environmental mediation is a process in which representatives of environmental groups, business groups, and government agencies sit down together with a neutral mediator to negotiate a binding resolution to a particular environmental dispute.[1] Since its beginning in the mid-seventies, environmental mediation has been the subject of serious political disagreement.[2] Proponents argue that environmental mediation is often less costly and less time consuming than litigation.[3] In addition, they claim mediated agreements are impartial and just.[4] It is assumed that the agreements are mutually beneficial to the parties. In part, this assumption is based on the fact that mediation, as opposed to arbitration, is seen as a purely voluntary process in which the mediator has no power to impose a settlement.[5] The voluntary nature of the process is thought to ensure that no party is forced into accepting a disadvantageous agreement.

Despite this reassuring view of mediation and despite a growing list of successful mediation efforts,[6] suspicion about mediation continues to exist among environmentalists. One environmental organizer recently complained that mediation "strikes me as being pro-establishment. I think that environmentalists who get involved in the process tend to be co-opted."[7] David

Brower has also criticized cooperative strategies such as environmental mediation. "Polite conservationists," says Brower, "leave no marks except the scars on the landscape that could have been prevented."[8] These kinds of intuitive suspicions have been fueled by several stories in environmental publications that have claimed that "industry clearly likes the idea" of mediation and that some mediation efforts and mediation institutes have been heavily funded by corporate foundations and by corporations with poor environmental records, including Dow Chemical, U.S. Steel, and Union Carbide.[9]

How reasonable are these suspicions? Are environmentalists indulging in guilt by association, or is the mediation process actually biased toward the interests of developers? Are mediated agreements always mutually beneficial? Are they always in the public interest? Are they always purely voluntary? These are important questions for those concerned with environmental policy. The answers bear on the issues of how fair and impartial mediation actually is and whether or not environmental groups should embrace this alternative to litigation. Despite their importance, very little effort has been made to examine these politically charged questions in a careful and systematic way. Legal scholars have done some work on the politics of mediation as it is practiced in neighbourhood justice centers,[10] but relatively few studies have been done of the politics of environmental mediation. Most of the scholarly work on environmental mediation has focused on mediation techniques or descriptions of particular cases;[11] little has been written specifically about the possibility of political bias in this process.[12] This article will begin to fill this gap and to help those involved in environmental policymaking and environmental disputes to evaluate and use mediation as a tool in dispute resolution.

There is little question that there are *potential* political biases against environmentalists in mediation. In particular, the possibility of co-optation is ever-present in mediation, as it is in all forms of citizen participation.[13] This essay will categorize and describe the various forms of bias and co-optation that can be present in mediation. The three forms that will be examined are: (1) the possibility that the congenial atmosphere created by mediators serves to disarm and co-opt environmentalists; (2) the possibility that superior political and economic resources create imbalances of power that allow pro-development interests to extract unfair concessions from environmentalists at the bargaining table; and (3) the possibility that the mediation process itself tends to redefine environmental issues in a way that favors pro-development interests. In addition, this essay will consider how proponents of environmental mediation attempt to rebut these charges of bias. Finally, this essay will conclude with some thoughts about how environmentalists should approach mediation.

MEDIATION AS SEDUCTION

The Charge
One of the most common charges leveled at environmental mediation is that the subtle conciliation techniques often used in mediation can "seduce" environmentalists into compromising their ideals and granting overly generous concessions to their opponents.[14] It is pointed out, for instance, that mediators bring conflicting parties together in informal settings, often over lunch or dinner, and encourage them to get to know and eventually like one another.[15] Opponents suggest that in this congenial atmosphere, environmentalists can lose their fighting edge and end up making too many concessions to their new found "friends." As James Benson of the Institute for Ecological Studies explains it:

> All of a sudden you are hobnobbing with industry leaders you used to think of as enemies, and now you are sitting down having dinner and drinks with them.... Environmentalists are not really very feisty people, and when they get around a bunch of high power corporate types they don't want to be unreasonable. They don't want to get into arguments. They want things to be peaceful and gentlemanly.... [They] get carried away, and really may lose sight of what it is they may be trading off. They may be trading off something in the negotiations that others may be unwilling to trade off.[16]

The focus here is not on the possibility that this problem is due to some personal bias against environmentalists on the part of the individual mediator; rather, the focus is on sources of co-optation that are built into the mediation process itself and that are at work irrespective of who the individual mediators are. There are good reasons to believe several inherent aspects of mediation encourage the kind of seduction to which Benson alludes. For example, most mediators would acknowledge that "[o]ne of the prime goals of negotiation/mediation is to promote an atmosphere of cooperation, reasonableness and understanding...."[17] Moreover, even proponents of mediation, such as Gail Bingham of the Conservation Foundation, admit that during prolonged negotiations "people tend to get to know each other and to like each other. There gets to be a personal bond — it's a natural human response."[18] Some mediators also use conciliation and facilitation techniques to diffuse hostility and minimize personal animosities. They encourage participants to move beyond the initial preconceptions and negative stereotypes they may have of each other.[19] Some environmentalists may be uneasy with this "touchy-feely" approach to negotiations, believing that they may become psychologically disarmed as they are encouraged to get to know and trust their opponents. In the eyes of the environmentalists, conciliation too easily becomes pacification.

The Defense
Proponents of mediation argue, however, that such appearances can be deceiving. According to proponents, conciliation efforts are attempts to clear away the emotional and psychological obstacles that often get in the way of rational negotiations, rather than attempts at seduction.

As negotiators from the Rocky Mountain Center on the Environment[20] have pointed out, opponents in mediation attempts often bring to the bargaining table a whole history of antagonistic relationships, misperceptions, and miscommunications that must be dealt with if serious and straightforward negotiations over the substantive issues are to take place.[21] Thus, in the eyes of mediators, conciliation techniques are an attempt to overcome the barriers that stand in the way of effective negotiations, not an attempt at seduction.

Should we rely simply on the assurances of mediators in this matter? After all, it would seem to be clearly in their self-interest to engage in seduction if it will increase the chances of reaching an agreement. Mediators point out, however, that in practice, attempts at seduction could easily backfire and actually interfere with the final dispute resolution.[22] For example, even if an environmental representative made unusually large concessions at the bargaining table, those concessions could easily be repudiated later by the organization he or she represents. As Gerald Cormick, executive director of the Institute for Environmental Mediation in Seattle, has argued, mediators must be careful not to construct an atmosphere that is too congenial. He points out that there is a danger that the participants:

> will begin to like and trust and understand each other to the point that they forget that their constituents have not had the benefit of the same intensive and cooperative interaction. Solutions that are not politically viable may gain credence in the rarefied atmosphere of cooperative negotiations, but be repudiated as a "sell-out" by constituents.[23]

Seducible Environmentalists

Most mediators could cite cases in which environmentalists made greater concessions than seem warranted by the situation: the key question in such cases is to pinpoint where the responsibility for making such overly generous concessions lies. Some mediators insist that the responsibility should lie with the participants, not with the mediators:

> Environmental organizers are wary of mediation because in mediation the grassroots type will be in a room with a bunch of corporate executives, and they will wind up saying, "Oh my God, the executives are only people. They put their pants on one leg at a time. They are nice guys. They buy me lunch. Gee, golf may not be such a bad game after all." And so all of these environmentalists who were full of good character and

right thinking are suddenly going to get perverted, because the mediator is going to seduce them by putting them together with the big shots. But that attitude is so naive, it's so flimsy, it's so indicative of never having done mediation. I can't change your character. If you have the courage of your convictions, you have it before you get there and I'm not going to take it away from you. If you are subject to being seduced, you are going to be seduced. But there is nothing I do that changes your character.[24]

This is probably mediators' strongest line of defense against the charge that environmental mediation seduces the unsophisticated participant. Even if one acknowledges that the tendency toward seduction is inherent in the conciliatory aspects of mediation, it is difficult to deny that a large part of the responsibility for any concessions must ultimately lie with the negotiators themselves. If environmentalists cannot have dinner with their opponents and engage in calm discussion without capitulating, it hardly seems fair to blame mediators or mediation. More likely these concessions indicate a weakness in the negotiating ability of environmentalists.[25]

This conclusion need not be a discouraging one for environmentalists. On the contrary, an understanding of the problem brings with it the promise that it can be at least partially overcome. If part of the problem lies in the naive attitude of environmental negotiators, then one can expect this problem to be ameliorated as environmentalists gain more experience at mediation and learn to be tougher negotiators. Thus, while the possibility of seduction will remain ever-present in environmental mediation, the problem may not be as intractable as some environmentalists suggest. There are, however, other forms of co-optation or political bias in mediation that may prove much more troublesome for environmentalists.

THE PROBLEM OF POWER

A second source of political bias in environmental mediation is the typical imbalance of power between environmental and pro-development groups. Pro-development groups, whether they are private concerns or public agencies, usually have a better established financial/political power base and greater access to economic and political resources than do environmental groups, especially local ones.[26] This situation has led one environmentalist to conclude that "mediation is not an even match between environmentalists and industrialists."[27]

Imbalances in power tend to favor developmental interests and thus undermine the assumed neutrality of the mediation process in three different ways: First, these imbalances can affect who is allowed to participate in mediation efforts; Second, superior resources can give pro-development groups the advantage of superior technical analysis; and Third, environmentalists' lack of power can make their participation less than voluntary.

Unequal Access to Mediation

Power may be a passport into the mediation process. Mediators are often faced with the task of choosing which groups will participate in the mediation effort, and in order to maximize the chance of agreement, some mediators prefer to limit participation to as small a number as possible. Often, the main criterion in choosing the participants is whether a group has enough power to block or subvert any final agreement. According to one mediator:

> One of the reasons that mediation works is that it is usually limited to people that have some impact on the situation.... I don't ask people who don't have clout to participate in the mediation. This is not public participation, this is cloutful people's participation. That's a real important difference.... I don't have anything to do with people without power because they can't affect what I'm doing. It's a pragmatic test.[28]

Although limiting participation on this ground is perfectly understandable from a mediator's point of view, some obvious political problems flow from that approach. A wide variety of interests are usually directly affected by an environmental dispute,[29] but not all have sufficient political and economic resources to insist that they be included in any mediation attempt. Local citizens and environmental groups especially have difficulty in amassing the resources that would allow them to wage the prolonged legal and political battles necessary to establish themselves as "cloutful people." The result is that these types of groups tend to be left out of the bargaining process, and this can skew the results of any settlement. In environmental mediation, as in pluralist political theory, the assumption of neutrality and fairness in the decisionmaking process rests largely on the presupposition that all interests have free and equal access to the process.[30] The fulfillment of this

requirement is in jeopardy when power serves as the passport to participation in mediation efforts.[31]

One example of how the choice of participants can affect the substance of negotiated agreements is found in the dispute over the White Flint Mall in Maryland.[32] Developers of the mall actively sought negotiations with the residents living in the area of the proposed site, presumably in the belief that the opposition of this group could do them the most damage. The final negotiated agreement reflected only the concerns of the two groups involved: the developers received neighborhood approval of their mall, and the residents received guarantees that the mall would be designed not to disrupt their neighborhood[33] and that the developers would buy their houses at pre-mall[34] prices if their property values decreased because of the mall. Although these two groups were satisfied with the agreement, the question remains whether building this modified mall met the interests of all the citizens in the area, especially those concerned with the detrimental effects of shopping centers on struggling downtown areas. While in this example the participants were essentially chosen by the developer rather than a mediator, the point is the same: mediated agreements can hardly be thought of as fair, just, or in the public interest when some interested groups are excluded from the negotiations.

Proponents of environmental mediation are not oblivious to the imbalances in power between disputants. Their primary focus, however, is often on how this problem threatens the expansion of mediation opportunities. As Gerald Cormick has pointed out, mediation "requires some relative balance of power between the parties."[35] In other words, disputing parties are unlikely to submit to mediation until it is clear to them that the other group has enough power to delay or block their own goals.[36] Thus, proponents of mediation worry that if environmentalists are too weak, they will not be able to force developers to the bargaining table. This likelihood has led to the argument that "[f]or mediation to become more broadly applied it will be necessary to develop sources of influence for protesting [environmental] constituencies."[37]

Another troublesome aspect of the imbalances of power is that instead of avoiding mediation or seeking to exclude other groups from the process, powerful interests may actively embrace mediation as a way of co-opting their weaker opponents.[38] Indeed, established groups might easily *prefer* mediation over more formal approaches like litigation because mediation can be considerably less costly in terms of both time and money.[39] For powerful groups, mediation may be the most efficient means to their ends, especially if they are able to translate their political and economic superiority into advantages at the bargaining table. Distribution of power may determine not only who participates, but also who has the upper hand in the negotiations themselves. Among the several types of advantages that more powerful groups can enjoy in the mediation process, the most obvious is greater access to expertise.

The Advantages of Expertise

Because most environmental disputes involve complex legal, economic, and scientific issues, effective negotiating usually requires access to experts in those areas. At a minimum, one needs professional advice on how to analyze various policy outcomes and help with devising plausible alternatives. As one might expect, scholars have found that groups with better access to information and expertise enjoy a substantial advantage over their opponents.[40] In practice, this means that the advantage goes to pro-development interests because they typically possess the economic resources necessary to purchase expertise. Of course, imbalances in expertise do not exist in every case. Large national environmental groups have been developing in-house experts to narrow this deficit, but even so, they remain outnumbered and outspent in most bargaining situations. The situation is often much worse for local environmental groups that have even smaller financial resources. Thus, there is probably much truth to the environmentalists' complaint that "environmentalists who get involved in mediation are certainly outmanned and perhaps even intimidated. It is clearly a mismatch when it comes to being able to counter the industries' side when they have a wealth of information, computer models, and analysts."[41] In politics, information is power, and this is true even in such "informal" political processes as environmental mediation.

The Illusion of Voluntariness

Imbalances in power can further undermine the equality and impartiality of negotiations by affecting whether or not the final agreement of all parties is purely voluntary. The question of voluntariness is crucial. Advocates often defend the fairness and neutrality of mediated agreements on the grounds that the process is purely a voluntary one, and that no parties are forced to accept unfavorable agreements.[42] Research has shown, however, that power and coercion can enter into mediation processes in subtle ways. For example, in her study of the mediation done in neighborhood justice centers, Christine Harrington found that subtle threats of outside sanctions often make mediation less than voluntary.[43] She points out that local prosecutors sometimes "persuade" people to participate in mediation by dangling over their heads the threat of formal prosecution.[44] Similar kinds of outside forces may introduce coercion into environmental mediation as well. Environmental groups that lack substantial sources of formal power may be forced into mediation because the other available options are even more undesirable. For instance, a local environmental group that cannot sustain a prolonged court battle and that has little influence on a city council might easily conclude that it has little choice but to mediate. It will thus enter into negotiations from a position of weakness. In contrast, a pro-development group may enter into negotiations from a position of strength, confident that if negotiations fail, it can always turn to more formal political avenues to pursue its case. In such situations, developers will be inclined to offer only token concessions to environmental groups. Because environmentalists are bargaining from a position of weakness, they will be inclined to accept what amounts to only a slight modification of an undesirable project, reasoning that even a few concessions are better than nothing. Indeed, James Benson argues that this is the actual result of many mediation efforts: "Basically, what industry is doing is giving crumbs to its opponents and walking off with pretty much what it wanted in the first place."[45]

The illusion of voluntariness that surrounds mediation not only obscures subtle forms of coercion, but also grants an air of reasonableness and legitimacy to mediated agreements. James Crowfoot made this point in his study of whether negotiations can be an effective tool for citizens' organizations:

> In terms of the elite's interests, negotiation/mediation is a very good tool if you have controlling power. It can be quite useful in a situation of conflict in which there is a need to provide a sense of participation to other interest groups....

Participation [of citizens' groups] in such processes can also make elite goals and perspectives seem to be fair and reasonable.[46]

This air of legitimacy and reasonableness may be difficult for developers to come by otherwise. When they are forced to use their financial and political clout to gain victories before legislative bodies or courts, developers risk being seen as the "heavies" in the public's view. If developers can achieve virtually the same goals through mediation, however, they have also achieved a public relations coup. Their (slightly modified) project now has the voluntary seal of approval from environmentalists. The advantage of such an approach was shown in the case of the White Flint Mall.[47] After the developers granted some design concessions to local residents, the residents actually testified on the developers' behalf before the zoning board.[48]

An Uncommonly Clear Example

It is very difficult, of course, to establish that developmental interests enter mediation with the intention of co-opting environmentalists in the ways described above. Few would readily admit that that was their purpose. Fortunately, there is a little-known government study that reveals in an uncommonly clear way the co-optive intentions that can lie behind mediation offers.[49] This report was intended to familiarize federal officials who must deal with environmental issues and groups with the various advantages of mediation:

> [I]t is the thesis of this paper that Federal decisionmaking and, specifically, public sector planning and regulation often can be improved by early involvement of all key interest groups likely to attempt to block a Federal action. Using conflict management tools such as conciliation, facilitation, and mediation — which build consensus among constituents with a stake in proposed Federal action — officials can in certain circumstances reduce unnecessary court delays, avoid regulatory standoffs and move opponents to mutually acceptable settlements. Environmental conflict will be less disruptive to agency decisionmaking if officials learn to use conflict management tools....[50]

While this passage contains such appealing phrases as "mutually acceptable settlements," it is clear that the overriding purpose of mediation efforts from the perspective of the authors is to "manage" conflict. They seem primarily concerned with avoiding or dampening conflicts that could "block" or "disrupt" the efficient imple-

mentation of agency policy. Later in the report, Clark and Emrich go into greater detail as to how an agency can give the illusion of negotiating with opposition groups while maintaining its authority to make the basic policy decisions:

> [Some agencies] fear a loss of agency authority in the context of a group negotiating process....
>
> [But] a properly managed mediation process *guarantees* retention of agency authority; it does not challenge or weaken it. At the very outset, the mediator requires the agency to outline its specific constraints — regulatory, political, economic — under which it must operate and within which any final agreements must fall.[51]

Thus, by using the notion of "constraints," an agency is able to set the parameters of what will be negotiable and what will not, and in that way retain the essential power in the situation. In practice, this means that although the agency may be willing to grant concessions on details, the basic policy decisions remain non-negotiable. This tactic is used by private developmental concerns as well. The issue of mall development again illustrates how this tactic can be applied in a specific conflict. As one environmental lawyer has complained, shopping center developers often seem eager to negotiate, but rarely over the basic question of whether the mall should be built at all:

> I was involved in a case in which a company wanted to build a massive regional shopping center in a suburban county. It would have effectively destroyed what had been accomplished downtown — a classic case....
>
> Of course we continually wanted to negotiate. But the developers wanted to negotiate things like how to make it pretty and how many parks they would give ... I refused to negotiate until they agreed to negotiate on the basic land use question. The truth is, we were telling them [that] our bottom line was no regional shopping center ... but we had to go to court because they were unwilling to put that issue on the table.[52]

Powerful public and private organizations using mediation to give the illusion of significant and widespread participation, while retaining essential policymaking power, is classic textbook co-optation: participation without power.[53] Thus, the most basic problem of co-optation in mediation may not be the problem of naive environmentalists being seduced by congenial mediators, but rather the illusion of meaningful participation in a process where other parties actually possess the decisive power.

Biased Games With Impartial Referees

Power imbalances obviously can compromise the impartiality of environmental mediation; the question is whether mediators and mediation should be held responsible for the problem. Proponents of mediation argue that power imbalances already exist in the outside world and are not created by mediation or mediators. In this sense, then, environmental mediation actually remains politically neutral. Just as a finely made mirror neutrally reflects what is presented to it by the outside world, mediation impartially reflects the imbalances of power in society itself. We do not blame a mirror for what we look like, and neither should we hold mediation responsible for what it reflects.

There is much truth to this argument; mediation obviously is not responsible for the maldistribution of political and economic power in our society. That fact does not mean, however, that mediation cannot be held responsible for its built-in tendency to institutionalize and perpetuate that maldistribution. Environmental mediation may actually work to legitimize imbalances in power by conferring an air of fairness to inequitable or co-optive agreements, and in this sense, mediation and mediators may be culpable. It is as if the mediator were a referee who comes upon an informal game of soccer that is being played on a slanted field and where one of the teams has more and bigger players. If the referee neutrally accepts the game as it is and merely attempts to ensure that the players act in a fair and sportsmanlike manner, the game remains a biased one. Although the referee may congratulate himself on his impartiality in enforcing the rules of "fair play," he inadvertently institutionalizes an inherently inequitable game and confers upon it a sense of legality and legitimacy that it did not possess before. It is this kind of contribution for which mediators can be held responsible.

DEFINITIONAL BIAS

A third potential form of political bias in environmental mediation is what might be called "definitional bias." In mediation, environmental issues tend to be defined in ways that implicitly favor pro-development interests. An effort is usually made not to cast issues in moral terms; rather, disputes are seen as taking place between groups with equally valid demands.[54] For media-

tors, this amoral perspective on environmental conflict reflects in part their desire to remain neutral, but it performs another valuable function as well by laying a conceptual groundwork favorable to compromise. If disputes were seen in moral terms, where one party is right and the other is wrong, the attractiveness of compromise would be minimized. Compromise with those who are wrong would itself been seen as immoral. If one views environmental conflicts as clashes of different but equally valid *interests*, however, then compromise becomes the logical solution to the problem. From this perspective, "splitting the difference" is the fair and just solution to the conflict because each party gets some of what it wants.[55]

On one hand, this view of environmental conflict as a clash between competing interests simply represents the mediators' commitment to neutrality and reasonable compromise. On the other hand, defining environmental conflict in terms of equally valid competing interests may work to the advantage of pro-development interests. In practice, it promotes the adoption of compromises that may actually come much closer to fulfilling the goals of developers than the goals of environmentalists. The logical compromise between the developers and environmentalists is usually some form of what is called "responsible development."[56] It is quite possible to see this approach as a reasonable integration of environmental and developmental interests. It is also possible, however, to see "responsible development" as satisfying developers more than environmentalists. This is particularly true if one believes that many pressing environmental issues do not involve choices between responsible and irresponsible development, but rather, choices between development and non-development.[57] Many environmentalists would undoubtedly argue that the responsible development of nuclear plants or the responsible development of oil drilling in national parks are "compromises" that are essentially victories for pro-development interests.

Some promoters of mediation will admit that responsible development is not a strictly neutral goal. This developmental bias poses little problem for them, however, because they believe that development is a natural part of social progress, and that mediation can ensure that this progress proceeds smoothly. According to Mernitz, "environmental mediation helps opposing parties to see the need for compromise as a means of furthering society's progress. Extensive delays, although sometimes valuable for selected interests, usually cause social, economic, emotional, and ecological traumas that are undesirable."[58]

Many environmentalists, of course, would question Mernitz's equation of continuous development with the good life. Many environmental writers have argued that the pursuit of the good life now requires limits to development.[59] They argue that continuous economic growth and development, even in their "responsible" forms, only drain valuable non-renewable resources and threaten to stress our ecosystem to the breaking point.[60] From this perspective, environmental disputes do not simply involve conflicts of interest, but involve basic structural choices between two different ways of life, one based on ever-increasing development and maximization of GNP, the other based on limits to growth and ecological viability.[61] When viewed this way, responsible development does not represent a reasonable compromise, but a destructive capitulation to the forces of growth. Understanding that what is at stake in many environmental controversies is a choice between two incompatible paths makes many environmentalists suspicious of mediation. One environmental lawyer thinks environmentalists "give away the whole ballgame" by agreeing to negotiate:

> My point is based on my involvement in certain environmental issues, that there are some cases where the chance to negotiate equals giving up what you're fighting for. There *are* some absolutes in the world and I think lawyers are just going to have to flat-out fight to preserve them. I disagree that there are always going to be negotiations. There *are* going to be some ultimate decisions, but it should be clearly recognized that there are times when you just can't negotiate, because there are some things in the world that are non-negotiable.[62]

Implicit in this statement is the idea that environmental mediation can obscure the fact that some environmental disputes involve fundamental moral and philosophical differences. Richard Abel, in his study of the political functions of neighborhood mediation and arbitration centers, makes a similar point.[63] He argues that these informal processes tend to obscure the systemic nature of many societal conflicts by defining disputes as individual grievances.[64] Mediators and arbitrators tend not to see disputes as basic clashes between classes or races, but rather as isolated problems involving individual landlords and tenants or particular merchants and customers. Consequently, according to Abel, the larger societal issues tend to drop from sight as mediators focus on the specific incidents and the particular personalities of the individuals.[65] A similar process of conflict redefinition occurs in environmental mediation; mediators would prefer to see disputes as conflicts of interests among local groups rather than as symptoms of larger structural and value choices facing society.

This approach not only tends to suppress the more fundamental environmental issues at stake, but also tends to shift the blame for the conflict away from pro-development groups. As Abel points out, mediators prefer not to see disputes as one-sided, or in the case of environmental issues, as caused by the forces of development threatening the environment.[66] When the blame rests on one party, compromise is hardly the just solution. The tendency on the part of mediators, therefore, is to see the conflict as caused by both parties' unreasonable demands and unwillingness to compromise. This assumption of mutual fault, which may be accurate in some cases, but certainly not all, serves to suppress the possibility that environmentalists are the wronged party and deserve vindication. This, in turn, morally disarms environmental groups. It puts pressure on them to be "reasonable," give up some of their "extremist" demands, and compromise on a "responsible" plan for development.

Avoiding the Problem

Although proponents of mediation are not unaware of this potential problem, they see it as one that can be avoided relatively easily. Politically sophisticated mediators recognize that some environmental issues are nonnegotiable and advise mediators to avoid trying to promote compromises on them.[67] For instance, Gerald Cormick cautions mediators not to attempt to mediate controversies over nuclear power plants. Recognizing that many environmentalists are philosophically opposed to nuclear power *per se*, he points out that "[t]here is no possible area of accommodation and no scope for good-faith negotiation and mediation."[68]

While it might seem that avoiding disputes where compromise is not appropriate would eliminate much of the problem of definitional bias, there are several reasons why this solution may not be workable. First of all, not all mediators are necessarily as responsible and conscientious as Cormick. Some have been known to distort the nature of disputes and to attempt to convince environmentalists to accept compromises on non-negotiable issues. Dr. Irving Goldaber of the Center for the Practice of Conflict Management, for example, sees no problem with trying to mediate disputes over nuclear energy.[69] He has held seminars for utility company executives to teach them his "win/win" approach to conflicts over nuclear energy, a process of negotiation in which both sides allegedly win. In one such seminar, a simulated negotiation resulted in "utility executives" and "environmentalists" finally agreeing to (1) co-sponsor public hearings on general nuclear issues; (2) form a joint consumer advisory committee; and (3) allow a peaceful demonstration outside the secured area of the plant.[70] One participant reported that Goldaber, quite happy with this agreement, declared, "You see? There *is* a win/win solution, ladies and gentlemen, even in your situation, which at times seems so hopeless."[71] When asked if he really believed that people in the anti-nuclear movement would believe they had "won" if the plant remained under construction, Goldaber responded that "[t]hey've made some concessions, of course; but look what they're going away with."[72] Undoubtedly some mediators would view Goldaber's efforts in the nuclear area as a disservice to their profession. But the fact remains that others say compromise is possible "in nearly every conflict situation."[73]

Another difficulty with the suggestion that mediators should simply avoid involvement in nonnegotiable issues is that it is often very difficult to distinguish between those conflicts that are negotiable and those that are not. Conflicts often involve a mixture of negotiable and nonnegotiable issues. In such cases, there is a natural temptation to try to suppress the more basic and controversial dimensions of the conflict and focus attention instead on the more negotiable — and peripheral — issues. The complex environmental disputes that arise over proposals to open up new uranium mines and mills are good examples. Issues range from local concern over disruption of the water table and the danger of radiation to local residents to the larger societal issues concerning the relationship of the mine to nuclear energy and nuclear weapons programs. While one could imagine arriving at mutually acceptable solutions to many of the local problems, the larger issues are more intractable. This is not simply a hypothetical situation; this narrowing of the issues has occurred in several controversies over uranium mines.[74] In one such case, the lawyer representing the environmental groups was quite eager to mediate the dispute but was frustrated in his efforts by a few environmentalists who refused to let go of some of the larger issues involved. He wrote:

> The mining company has talked to us about the possibility of mediating this dispute. They would match their experts on reclamation, hydrology, wildlife and outdoor recreation against ours at a negotiation table. And we would try to reason to a result. I like that idea, and *some* of my clients like it, also. Not all. The ones that don't like it are, by and large, "anti-nuclear" folks. Their main concern is not how good the reclamation or how restricted the hydrologic system will be. They simply don't want any contribution to the nuclear fuel cycle being made by our public land managers.[75]

The passage leaves the impression that those concerned with the larger nuclear issues are being unreasonable, and that if only those larger issues could be set aside, then negotiations could go ahead much more efficiently and the dispute could be resolved.[76]

While one can be sympathetic with the mediators' desire to keep discussion at a reasonable level, one can also see how this approach tends to downplay issues that are of greatest importance to some environmentalists. This tendency is not necessarily the result of any personal political bias on the part of individual mediators, but rather a function of the inherent limitations of the mediation process. Mediation sheds light only on certain types of disputes. It works best in disputes that are primarily local and that do not involve basic value conflicts or structural choices. There is a tendency for mediators to try to fit all disputes into this mold. If the only tool one has is a hammer, everything becomes a nail.

CONCLUSION

A number of potential sources of political bias and co-optation are inherent in environmental mediation. But how should an understanding of the political pitfalls of mediation affect whether environmentalists choose this alternative to litigation? There is no simple answer. As a rule, it would benefit environmentalists to have a healthy suspicion of mediation, especially when the offer to mediate comes from their opponents. It also should be kept in mind, however, that mediation can sometimes benefit environmentalists,[77] and the potential benefits will increase as environmentalists become more aware of the political traps built into this process and more adept at avoiding them. At times it may even be useful for environmentalists to actually embrace co-optation. If, for example, one is faced with a good possibility of losing entirely, it may be prudent to accept a mediated compromise even if one gains only token concessions. Something may be better than nothing. On the other hand, one might want to avoid this kind of mediation because of the air of legitimacy it might give undesirable developments. In short, the decision to enter into mediation is complex and difficult. It is an option that should not be entered into naively or precipitously, but neither should it be eliminated automatically because of its inherent political biases.[78]

Finally, it is helpful to keep in mind that the problems of mediation are in many ways simply reflections of the larger political problems faced by environmentalists in our society. In mediation there may be political biases toward those with the most power and ideological biases toward development, but these are most properly seen as functions of the fact that we live in a society in which power is inequitably distributed and in which the economic system has a structural bias toward continuous growth and development. Understanding the political problems of environmental mediation in this way suggests that environmentalists should not waste time avoiding or condemning mediation. Instead, they should turn to the more difficult task of changing the larger political landscape. This task involves building greater sources of formal political power and promoting greater societal appreciation of the importance of environmental values and the costs of continuous development. In the end, that will be the most effective way to overcome the political biases of environmental mediation.

Appendices

Notes and References
Glossary of Terms and Concepts

One
Elements of the Legal System

A. Concepts and Terms

(b) "Civil Litigation"
Elizabeth J. Swanson and Elaine L. Hughes

283. See generally Linden, *supra*, note 270 at 7–17.

284. A "mathematical" approach to the balancing of factors has been suggested by various authorities, including Linden. His "formula" involves a comparison between the products of (P)robability × (L)oss against (O)bject × (C)ost. Where (P × L) is greater than (O × C) liability should follow. *Supra*, note 270 at 8.

285. This, of course, refers to conduct within their area of expertise.

286. See, for example, *North York* v. *Kent Chemical Industries Inc.* (1985), 33 C.C.L.T. 184 (Ont. S.C.).

287. (1983), 143 D.L.R. (3d) 9.

288. *Ibid.* At p. 25 of his decision Mr. Justice Dickson (as he then was) concluded as follows:
    1. Civil consequences of breach of statute should be subsumed in the law of negligence.
    2. The notion of a nominate tort of statutory breach giving a right to recovery should be rejected, as should the view that unexcused breach constitutes negligence *per se* giving rise to absolute liability.
    3. Proof of statutory breach, causative of damage, may be evidence of negligence.
    4. The statutory formulation of the duty may afford a specific, and useful, standard of reasonable conduct....

    This Canadian approach towards breach of statute differs from that of England (where the nominate tort of breach of statute still exists) and of the United States (where an "unexcused" breach is treated as *prima facie* evidence of negligence with the resulting burden shifting to the defendant to rebut the presumption of negligence). *Supra*, note 270.

289. Linden, *supra*, note 12 at 86.

290. *Supra*, note 286.

291. Mr. Justice Krever found it unnecessary to go beyond the law of negligence. He said: I have rejected, as unhelpful in the circumstances of this case, the argument that the defendant's use of inherently dangerous substances exposed it to liability for the harm that resulted from their discharge into the plaintiff's sewer: The fact, however, that the defendant used corrosive chemicals which it knew would, if not sufficiently neutralized, cause damage to the sewer is not irrelevant. The simple point is that the greater the potential for harm the higher the standard of care that must be taken. The degree of care that is reasonably expected of a risk taken must be proportionate to the risk created or commiserate with the magnitude of the risk.... *Supra*, note 286 at 202.

292. Linden, *supra*, note 12 at 86.

293. Linden, *supra*, note 12 at 89–92. See also *Priestly-Wright* v. *Alberta* (1986), 74 A.R. 77 (Alta. C.A.).

294. Linden, *supra*, note 12 at 90–92.

295. The basis for joint and several liability is statutory. In Alberta, for example, see the provisions of the *Contributory Negligence Act*, R.S.A. 1980, c. C-23.

296. [1961] Ex. C.R. 263.

297. *Ibid* at 273.

(d) "Civil Litigation" (Continued)
Elizabeth J. Swanson and Elaine L. Hughes

165. See generally John G. Fleming, *The Law of Torts*, 7th ed. (Sydney: Law Book, 1987) at 411–416.

166. *Ibid.*

167. An interim injunction is usually granted on a pre-trial application to preserve the status quo or prevent further loss or damage before the whole action is heard by the courts. Factors taken into account in granting an interim injunction are different than those determining the availability of a permanent injunction. See text, *supra*, at 9–11.

168. ... the effect of an injunction was suspended for a specified time to allow the defendant to correct deficiencies in its air pollution control system.

169. See McLaren, *supra*, note 97.

170. *Shelfer* v. *London Electric Co.*, [1985] 1 Ch. 287; *Canada Paper Company* v. *Brown*, *supra*, note 110 (per Duff, J.). The burden of proving these "special circumstances" warranting the substitution of damages where injunctive relief has been requested rests with the defendant. *McKinnon Industries Ltd.* v. *Walker*, *supra*, note 119 at 581.

171. *Supra*, note 110.

172. *Supra*, note 110 at 248, 250.

173. *Supra*, note 110 at 252.

174. See in particular the decisions of Middleton J. of the Ontario High Court in *Chadwick* v. *Toronto* (1914), 32 D.L.R. 111 and *Black* v. *Canadian Copper Co.*, [1917] O.W.N. 243.

175. [1937] O.W.N. 53 at 56. See also *Rombough* v. *Crestbrook Timber Ltd.* (1966), 55 W.W.R. 577 (B.C.C.A.).

...

263. *Crowther* v. *Town of Cobourg*, *supra*, note 199; *John Young and Company* v. *The Bankier Distillery Company*, *supra*, note 194; *McKie* v. *The K.V.P. Co.*, *supra*, note 192; *Stephens* v. *Village of Richmond Hill*, *supra*, note 199.

264. *Crowther* v. *The Town of Cobourg*, *supra*, note 194.

265. See for example, *McKie* v. *The K.V.P. Co.*, *supra*, note 192 and *Steadman* v. *Erickson Gold Mining Corp.*, *supra*, note 208.

266. *Supra*, note 192 at 101.

267. See for example, *Mckie* v. *The K.V.P. Co.*, *supra*, note 192; *Groat* v. *The City of Edmonton*, *supra*, note 241; *Gauthier* v. *Naneff*, *supra*, note 194.

268. *Supra*, note 194 at 519.

C. Constitutional and Statutory Framework

(a) "The Institutional Contexts"
Melody Hessing and Michael Howlett

26. Michael Atkinson, ed., *Governing Canada* (Toronto: Harcourt Brace 1994); James G. March and Johan Olsen, *Rediscovering Institutions: The Organizational Basis of Politics* (New York: Free Press 1989).

27. Stephen D. Krasner, ed., *International Regimes* (Ithaca, NY: Cornell University Press 1983); Volker Rittberger and Peter Mayer, eds., *Regime Theory and International Relations* (Oxford: Clarendon Press 1993).

28. Peter M. Haas, Robert O. Keohane, and Marc A. Levy, eds., *Institutions for the Earth: Sources of Effective International Environmental Protection* (Boston: MIT Press 1993).

29. John Stewart, *The Canadian House of Commons* (Montreal and Kingston: McGill-Queen's University Press 1977).

30. R. Kent Weaver and Bert A. Rockman, 'Assessing the Effects of Institutions,' in R.K. Weaver and B.A. Rockman, eds., *Do Institutions Matter? Government Capabilities in the United States and Abroad* (Washington, D.C.: Brookings Institute 1993), 1–41.

31. Kenneth Wheare, *Federal Government* (Oxford: Oxford University Press 1964).

32. Bruce Mitchell, 'The Provincial Domain in Environmental Management and Resource Development,' in O. Dwivedi, ed., *Resources and the Environment: Policy Perspectives for Canada* (Toronto: McClelland and Stewart 1980), 49–76; Peter N. Nemetz, 'Federal Environmental Regulation in Canada,' *Natural Resources Journal 26* (1986): 551–608.

33. Canada, Department of Justice, *A Consolidation of the Constitution Acts 1867 to 1982* (Ottawa: Supply and Services 1983).

34. Roger Cotton and Kelley M. MacKinnon, 'An Overview of Environmental Law in Canada,' in G. Thompson, M.L. McConnell, and L.B. Huestis, eds., *Environmental Law and Business in Canada* (Aurora, ON: Canada Law Books 1993), 1–30.

35. Gerard V. La Forest, *Natural Resources and Public Property under the Canadian Constitution* (Toronto: University of Toronto Press 1969), 3–47, 164–95.

36. A. Scott and A. Neher, eds., *The Public Regulation of Commercial Fisheries in Canada* (Ottawa: Supply and Services 1981).

37. This was also true of a small portion of British Columbia originally transferred to the federal government for railway construction purposes in the terms of Confederation of that province in 1871; see Chester Martin, *'Dominion Lands' Policy* (Toronto: Macmillan 1938).

38. Ronald M. Burns, *Conflict and Its Resolution in the Administration of Mineral Resources in Canada* (Kingston: Queen's University Centre for Resource Studies 1976).

39. Cf. W.R. Lederman, 'The Offshore Reference,' in William R. Lederman, *The Courts and the Canadian Constitution: A Selection of Essays* (Toronto: McClelland and Stewart 1964).

40. Dale Gibson, 'Constitutional Jurisdiction over Environmental Management in Canada,' *University of Toronto Law Journal 23* (1973): 54–87.

41. S.I. Bushnell, 'Constitutional Law — Proprietary Rights and the Control of Natural Resources,' *Canadian Bar Review* (1980): 157–69.

42. Gerard V. La Forest, *The Allocation of Taxing Power under the Canadian Constitution* (Toronto: Canadian Tax Foundation 1981).

43. Michael Howlett, 'Forest Policy in Canada: Resource Constraints and Political Interests in the Canadian Forest Sector,' doctoral dissertation, Queen's University, 1988; A.R. Thompson and H.R. Eddy, 'Jurisdictional Problems in Natural Resource Management in Canada,' in W.D. Bennett et al., ed., *Essays on Aspects of Resource Policy* (Ottawa: Science Council of Canada 1973), 67–96.

44. See Michael Whittington, *CCREM: An Experiment in Interjurisdictional Co-Ordination* (Ottawa: Science Council of Canada 1978).

45. On the doctrine of paramountcy in Canadian constitutional interpretation, see Eric Colvin, 'Legal Theory and the Paramountcy Rule,' *McGill Law Journal 25.1* (1979–80): 82–98; and W.R. Lederman, 'The Concurrent Operation of Federal and Provincial Laws in Canada,' *McGill Law Journal 9.3* (1962–3): 185–99.

46. J. Peter Meekison, Roy J. Romanow, William D. Moull, *Origins and Meaning of Section 92A: The 1982 Constitutional Amendment on Resources* (Montreal: Institute for Research on Public Policy 1985).

47. Marsha A. Chandler, 'Constitutional Change and Public Policy: The Impact of the Resource Amendment (Section 92A),' *Canadian Journal of Political Science 19.1* (1986): 103–26.

48. On the negotiations and conditions that led to the enactment of Section 92A, see Michael Howlett, 'The Politics of Constitutional Change in a Federal System: Institutional Arrangements and Political Interests in the Negotiation of Section 92A of the Canadian Constitution Act (1982),' *Publius: The Journal of Federalism 21.1* (1991): 121–42.

49. K. Swinton, *Competing Constitutional Visions: The Meech Lake Accord* (Toronto: Carswell 1988); K. McRoberts and P. Monahan, eds., *The Charlottetown Accord, the Referendum and the Future of Canada* (Toronto: University of Toronto Press 1993).

50. Peter N. Nemetz, 'The Fisheries Act and Federal-Provincial Environmental Regulation: Duplication or Complementarity?' *Canadian Public Administration 29* (1986): 401–24. See also Alastair R. Lucas, 'Natural Resources and the Environment: A Jurisdictional (Edmonton: Environmental Law Centre 1987). These attacks continue: see Paul Waldie, 'Strike Down Green Law, IPSCO Asks: Steelmakers Want Supreme Court to Rule CEPA Unconstitutional,' *Globe and Mail* (2 April 1996): B8; and Steven A. Kennett, 'Nova Pipeline Jurisdiction: Federal or Provincial?' *Resources 54* (1996): 1–6.

51. This was the case with the acknowledgment of federal powers under the 'Peace, Order and Good Government' clause of the Constitution by the Supreme Court of Canada in the *Crown Zellerbach* case; see *R. v. Crown Zellerbach, National Report 84* (1988): 1–68; and J.B. Hanebury, 'Environmental Impact Assessment in the Canadian Federal System,' *McGill Law Journal 36* (1991): 962–1005.

52. For a partial list of Canadian environmental statutes in areas including land, water, air, hazardous wastes, noise, solid wastes, energy, wildlife, fish, and forests, as well as general laws relating to environmental pro-

tection, see Statistics Canada, *Human Activity and the Environment* (Ottawa: Ministry of Industry, Science and Technology 1991), 34–6.

53. Murray Rankin, 'Environmental Regulation and the Changing Canadian Constitutional Landscape,' in Thompson, McConnell, and Huestis, eds., 31–51; David VanderZwaag and Linda Duncan, 'Canada and Environmental Protection: Confident Political Faces, Uncertain Legal Hands,' in R. Boardman, ed., *Canadian Environmental Policy: Ecosystems, Politics and Process* (Toronto: Oxford University Press 1992), 3–23.

54. On aboriginal rights and title, see Peter Cumming and N.H. Mickenberg, eds., *Native Rights in Canada* (Toronto: General Publishing 1972); P.J. Usher, F.J. Tough, and R.M. Galois, 'Reclaiming the Land: Aboriginal Title, Treaty Rights and Land Claims in Canada,' *Applied Geography 12* (1992): 109–32; and D. Raunet, *Without Surrender, Without Consent: A History of the Nishga Land Claims* (Vancouver: Douglas and McIntyre 1984).

55. On the history of the treaties, see L. Upton, 'The Origins of Canadian Indian Policy,' *Journal of Canadian Studies 8* (1973): 51–61; E. Titley, *A Narrow Vision: Duncan Campbell Scott and the Administration of Indian Affairs in Canada* (Vancouver: University of British Columbia Press 1986); W.E. Daugherty and D. Madill, *Indian Government under Indian Act Legislation, 1868–1951* (Ottawa: Indian Affairs and Northern Development 1980); and E. Patterson, 'A Decade of Change: Origins of the Nishga and Tsimshian Land Protests in the 1880s,' *Journal of Canadian Studies 18* (1983): 40–54.

56. On the 1982 changes, see B. Slattery, 'The Constitutional Guarantee of Aboriginal and Treaty Rights,' *Queen's Law Journal 8* (1983): 232–73. On the earlier constitutional status of Native rights, see N. Bankes, 'Indian Resource Rights and Constitutional Enactments in Western Canada, 1871–1930,' in L. Knafla, ed., *Law and Justice in a New Land: Essays in Western Canadian Legal History* (Toronto: Carswell 1986), 129–64.

57. A.M. Ervin, 'Contrasts between the Resolution of Native Land Claims in the United States and Canada Based on Observations of the Alaska Native Land Claims Movement,' *Canadian Journal of Native Studies 1* (1981): 123–40.

58. J.A. Long, 'Political Revitalization in Canadian Native Indian Society,' *Canadian Journal of Political Science 23* (1990): 751–74; P. Tennant, *Aboriginal Peoples and Politics: The Indian Land Question in British Columbia 1849–1989* (Vancouver: UBC Press 1990).

59. B. Slattery, 'The Hidden Constitution: Aboriginal Rights in Canada,' *American Journal of Comparative Law 32* (1984): 361–92; B.H. Wildsmith, *Aboriginal People and Section 25 of the Canadian Charter of Rights and Freedoms* (Saskatoon: University of Saskatchewan Native Law Centre 1988).

60. K.L. Brock, 'The Politics of Aboriginal Self-Government: A Canadian Paradox,' *Canadian Public Administration 34* (1991): 272–86; D.E. Sanders, 'An Uncertain Path: The Aboriginal Constitutional Conferences,' in J.M. Weiler and R.M. Elliot, eds., *Litigating the Values of Nation* (Toronto: Carswell 1986), 63–77; D.E. Sanders, 'The Indian Lobby,' in R. Simeon and K. Banting, eds., *And No One Cheered: Federalism, Democracy and the Constitution Act* (Toronto: Methuen 1983), 301–32.

61. K. Lysyk, 'The Indian Title Question in Canada: An Appraisal in the Light of Calder,' *Canadian Bar Review 51* (1973): 450–80; W.H. McConnell, 'The Calder Case in Historical Perspective,' *Saskatchewan Law Review 38* (1974): 88–122; D. Sanders, 'The Nishga Case,' *BC Studies 19* (1988): 3–20.

62. T. Morantz, 'Aboriginal Land Claims in Quebec,' in K. Coates, ed., *Aboriginal Land Claims in Canada* (Toronto: Copp Clark Pitman 1992), 101–30; J. O'Reilly, 'The Courts and Community Values: Litigation Involving Native Peoples and Resource Development,' *Alternatives 15* (1988): 40–48.

63. On their negotiation, see T. Berger, 'Native History, Native Claims and Self-Determination,' *BC Studies 57* (1983): 10–23; F. Cassidy, ed., *Reaching Just Settlements: Land Claims in British Columbia* (Vancouver: Oolichan Books/Institute for Research on Public Policy 1991); H.A. Feit, 'Negotiation Recognition of Aboriginal Rights: History, Strategies and Reactions to the James Bay and Northern Quebec Agreement,' *Canadian Journal of Anthropology 1* (1980): 159–70.

64. Canada, *Northeastern Quebec Agreement* (Ottawa: Information Canada 1978); Canada, *Sechelt Indian Band Self-Government Act* (Ottawa: Queen's Printer 1986); Canada, *The Western Arctic Claim: The Inuvialuit Final Agreement* (Ottawa: Indian and Northern Affairs Canada 1984); Canada, *Comprehensive Land Claim Umbrella Final Agreement between the Government of Canada, the Council for Yukon Indians and the Government of the Yukon* (Ottawa: Indian and Northern Affairs Canada 1990); Canada, *Gwich'in Comprehensive Land Claim Agreement* (Ottawa: Indian and Northern Affairs Canada 1992); Canada, *Agreement in Principle for the Nunavut Settlement Area* (Ottawa: Indian and Northern Affairs Canada 1992); Quebec, *The James Bay and Northern Quebec Agreement....* (Québec: Editeur Officiel du Québec 1976).

65. Coates, ed., *Aboriginal Land Claims*.

66. D. Sanders, 'The Supreme Court of Canada and the "Legal and Political Struggle" over Indigenous Rights,' *Canadian Ethnic Studies 22* (1990): 122–9; M. Asch and P. Macklem, 'Aboriginal Rights and Canadian Sovereignty: An Essay on *R.V. Sparrow,*' *Alberta Law Review 29* (1991): 498–517. See also F. Cassidy, ed., *Aboriginal Title in British Columbia: Delgamuukw v. the Queen* (Vancouver: Oolichan Books/Institute for research on Public Policy 1992).

67. M. M'Gonigle, 'Developing Sustainability: A Native/Environmentalist Prescription for Third-Level Government,' *BC Studies 84* (1989): 65–99; M. Boldt and J.A. Long, 'Native Indian Self-Government: Instrument of Autonomy or Assimilation?' in J.A. Long and M. Boldt, eds., *Governments in conflict* (Toronto: University of Toronto Press 1988), 38–56; P. Macklem, 'First Nations Self-Government and the Borders of the Canadian Legal Imagination,' *McGill Law Journal 36.2* (1991): 382–486.

68. Mary Ellen Turpel, 'The Charlottetown Discord and Aboriginal Peoples' Struggle for Fundamental Political Change,' in K. McRoberts and P. Monahan, eds., *The Charlottetown Accord, the Referendum, and the Future of Canada* (Toronto: University of Toronto Press 1993), 117–51.

69. See P. Usher, 'Some Implications of the Sparrow Judgement for Resource Conservation and Management,' *Alternatives 18* (1991): 20–2. See also *R.V. Van der Peet,* SCC File No. 23803 (22 August 1996).

70. K. Lysyk, 'Approaches to Settlement of Indian Title Claims: The Alaska Model,' *UBC Law Review 8* (1973): 321–42; C. Hunt, 'Approaches to Native Land Settlements and Implications for Northern Land Use and Resource Management Policies,' in R.F. Keith and J.B. Wright, eds., *Northern Transitions* (Ottawa: Canadian Arctic Resources Committee 1978), 5–41.

71. M.W. Wagner, 'Footsteps along the Road: Indian Land Claims and Access to Natural Resources,' *Alternative 18* (1991): 22–8. On water rights in general, also a major issue on the Prairies, see Claudia Notzke, *Aboriginal Peoples and Natural Resources in Canada* (Toronto: Centre for Aboriginal Management, Education and Training 1994).

72. Notzke, *Aboriginal Peoples*.

73. J. Keeping, *The Inuvialuit Final Agreement* (Calgary: Canadian Institute of Resources Law 1989); L. MacLachlan, 'The Gwich'in Final Agreement,' *Resources 36* (1991): 6–11; E.J. Peters, *Existing Aboriginal Self-Government Arrangements in Canada: An Overview* (Kingston: Queen's University Institute of Intergovernmental Relations 1987).

74. Co-management of resources between aboriginal and non-aboriginal governments appears to be the order of the day. See Evelyn Pinkerton, ed., *Cooperative Management of Local Fisheries: New Directions for Improved Management and Community Development* (Vancouver: University of British Columbia Press 1989). More generally, see F. Cassidy and N. Dale, *After Native Claims? The Implications of Comprehensive Claims Settlements for Natural Resources in British Columbia* (Montreal: Institute for Research on Public Policy 1988).

75. Andrew Roman and Kelly Hooey, 'The Regulatory Framework,' in Thompson, McConnell, and Huestis, eds., 53–70.

76. G.B. Doern and Thomas Conway, *The Greening of Canada: Federal Institutions and Decisions* (Toronto: University of Toronto Press 1994).

77. All of these agencies have gone through a number of organizational and name changes over the years. For a survey up to the mid-1970s, see J.E. Hodgetts, *The Canadian Public Service: A Physiology of Government 1867–1970* (Toronto: University of Toronto Press 1973).

78. D. Macdonald, *The Politics of Pollution* (Toronto: McClelland and Stewart 1991), 143.

79. Roman and Hooey, 'Regulatory Framework,' 53–70.

(b) "Federalism, Environmental Protection, and Blame Avoidance"
Kathryn Harrison

1. It is true that the Supreme Court decisions in the *Crown Zellerbach* and *Oldman River* cases during this period clarified the extent of federal authority within the existing constitution. However, well before the first of these decisions, the federal government had already disrupted intergovernmental harmony by introducing the Canadian Environmental Protection Act.

2. Unfortunately, Gallup did not report responses to the "most important problem" question between 1969 and 1972, when other indicators, such as trends in Canadian media coverage and in public opinion in the U.S., suggest the salience of environmental issues peaked. In 1972, pollution was cited as the most important problem by 5 per cent of respondents. Thereafter, the frac-

tion of respondents citing pollution declined to the point where it was not even mentioned by Gallup in conjunction with this question between 1976 and 1987. (See, for instance, "Concern with Pollution Drops Among Canadians," *Gallup Report*, February 26, 1975.) Although a relatively high degree of residual concern was revealed by close-ended questions asking respondents how serious they perceive environmental problems to be, even there, the percentage responding "very serious" declined steadily from 63 per cent in 1970 to a low of 51 per cent in 1985 (*Gallup Report*, May 28, 1990.)

3. The fraction of respondents identifying the environment as the "most important problem" facing the country peaked in July, 1989, at 16.5 per cent, when the environment was the top-ranked problem, and thereafter declined to 2 per cent by late 1991. (See *Gallup Report*, October 3, 1991).

4. The Canada–New Brunswick Accord for the Protectio and Enhancement of Environmental Quality is reprinted in Standing Committee on Fisheries and Forestry, *Minutes and Proceedings of Evidence*, June 8, 1977, 29A: 51.

5. A revision of the pulp and paper regulations, which was ready for review by the Privy Council Office, and a proposed regulation for the textile industry, which was even further advanced, were abandoned when the advocacy approach was introduced in 1979.

6. An important exception is Young, Faucher, and Blais (1984).

References

Alhéritière, Dominique (1972). "Les problèmes constitutionnel de la lutte contre la pollution de l'espace atmosphèrique au Canada," *La Revue du Barreau Canadien,* 50: 561–79.

Beaudoin, Gerald A. (1977). "La protection de l'environnement et ses implications en droit constitutionnel," *McGill Law Journal,* 23: 207–24.

Bouchard, Lucien (1989). *Notes for an address at the Symposium 'Le Saint-Laurent, un fleuve a reconquérir*, November 3.

Brown, M. Paul (1992). "Organizational Design as Policy Instrument: Environment Canada in the Canadian Bureaucracy," in Robert Boardman, ed., *Canadian Environmental Policy: Ecosystems, Politics, and Process*. Toronto: Oxford University Press.

Brown, M. Paul, and Fazley Siddiq (1991). "The Dimensions of Provincial Environmental Protection Spending," paper presented at the annual meeting of the Canadian Political Science Association, Kingston.

Buttle, Jeff (1990). "Cutback in environmental role feared," *Vancouver Sun*, May 10: B4.

Cairns, Alan (1988). "The Governments and Societies of Canadian Federalism," in Cairns, *Constitution, Government and Society in Canada: Selected Essays by Alan C. Cairns*, edited by Douglas E. Williams. Toronto: McClelland & Stewart.

Canada (1990). *Canada's Green Plan*.

Canadian Council of Ministers of the Environment (1990). Statement of Interjurisdictional Cooperation on Environmental Matters.

Carlisle, Tamsin (1990), "Mixed Reactions in Alberta over Green Plan," *Financial Post*, December 28: 12.

Duncan, Linda F. (1990). "Trends in Enforcement: Is Environment Canada Serious about Enforcing its Laws?" in Donna Tingley, ed., *Into the Future: Environmental*

Law and Policy for the 1990s. Edmonton: Environmental Law Centre (Alberta) Society.

Dwivedi, O.P. (1974). "The Canadian Government Response to Environmental Concerns," in Dwivedi, ed., *Protecting the Environment: Issues and Choices – Canadian Perspectives.* Vancouver: Copp Clark.

Dwivedi, O.P., and R. Brian Woodrow (1989). "Environmental Policy – Making and Administration in a Federal State: The Impact of Overlapping Jurisdiction in Canada," in William M. Chandler and Christian W. Zollner, eds., *Challenges to Federalism: Policy-making in Canada and the Federal Republic of Germany.* Kingston: Institute of Intergovernmental Relations.

Edgeworth, Les (1973). "Canada's Approach to Environmental Pollution Control for the Pulp and Paper Industry," paper presented by F.G. Hurtubise to the 15th EUCEPA Conference, Rome, May 7–12.

Emond, Paul (1972). "The Case for a Greater Federal Role in the Environmental Protection Field: An Examination of the Pollution Problem and the Constitution," *Osgoode Hall Law Journal,* 10: 647–80.

Environment Canada (1984). *Annual Report,* 1983–84.

Environment Canada (1993). Environment Canada Regulatory Review. Environmental Protection Program: A Discussion Document.

Franson, M.A.H., R.T. Franson, and A.R. Lucas (1982). *Environmental Standards: A Comparative Study of Canadian Standards, Standard Setting Processes and Enforcement.* Edmonton: Environment Council of Alberta.

Franson, Robert T., and Alastair R. Lucas (1976). *Canadian Environmental Law.* Vancouver: Butterworths.

Franson, Robert T., and Alastair Lucas (1977). "Legal Control of Hazardous Products in Canada," in Science Council of Canada, *Canadian Law and the Control of Exposure to Hazards.* Ottawa: Science Council of Canada.

Friends of the Oldman River Society and The Queen in right of Alberta et al. (1992) DLR, 88: 1–60.

Gibson, Dale (1969). "The Constitutional Context of Canadian Water Planning," *Alberta Law Review,* 7: 71–92.

Gibson, Dale (1973). "Constitutional Jurisdiction over Environmental Management in Canada," *University of Toronto Law Journal,* 23: 54–87.

Gibson, Dale (1983). "Environmental Protection and Enhancement under a New Canadian Constitution," in Stanley M. Beck and Ivan Bernier, eds., *Canada and the New Constitution.* Montreal: Institute for Research on Public Policy.

Giroux, Lorne (1987). "Delegation of Administration," in Donna Tingley, ed., *Environmental Protection and the Canadian Constitution.* Edmonton: Environmental Law Centre (Alberta) Society.

Giroux, Lorne (1989). "Les nouvelles technologies et le régime de la protection de l'environnement au Canada: la nouvelle loi canadienne sur la protection de l'environnement," *Les Cahiers de Droit,* 30: 747–76.

Harrison, Kathryn (1993). *Passing the Buck: Federalism and Canadian Environmental Policy,* Ph.D. dissertation, University of British Columbia.

Henley, Doreen C. (1985). "The Advocacy Approach," in Linda F. Duncan, ed., *Environmental Enforcement: Proceedings of the National Conference on the Enforcement of Environmental Law.* Edmonton: Environment Law Centre (Alberta) Society.

Hoberg, George (1993). "Environmental Policy: Alternative Styles," in Michael Atkinson, ed., *Governing Canada:*

Institutions and Public Policy. Toronto: Harcourt Brace Jovanovich.

Hoberg, George, and Kathryn Harrison (1994). "It's Not Easy Being Green: The Politics of Canada's Green Plan," *Canadian Public Policy,* 20: 119–37.

House of Commons (1953). *Debates.* January 30: 1491.

Howard, Ross (1990). "Oldman dam ruling stuns federal officials – Bouchard non-committal, calls decisions 'interesting,'" Globe and Mail, March 15: A5.

Huestis, Lynne B. (1985). "Pilot Study Report, S. 33 Fisheries Act," Department of Justice, Federal Statutes Compliances Project. December.

Interprovincial Cooperatives Ltd. et al. v. The Queen in Right of Manitoba (1975). DLR 53: 321–59.

Jenkin, Michael (1983). *The Challenge of Diversity: Industrial Policy in the Canadian Federation.* Ottawa: Science Council of Canada.

LaForest, Gerard V. (1972). "Interprovincial Rivers," *Canadian Bar Review,* 50: 39–49.

Landis, Henry (1970). "Legal Controls of Pollution in the Great Lakes Basin," *Canadian Bar Review,* 48: 66–157.

Lederman, W.R. (1975). "Unity and Diversity in Canadian Federalism: Ideals and Methods of Modernization," *Canadian Bar Review,* 53: 597–620.

Lucas, Alastair R. (1982). "Constitutional Law – Federal Fisheries Power – Provincial Resource Management and Property and Civil Rights Powers – *Fowler v. The Queen and Northwest Falling Contractors Ltd. v. The Queen,*" *University of British Columbia Law Review,* 16: 145–154.

Lucas, Alastair R. (1986). "Harmonization of Federal and Provincial Environmental Policies: The Changing Legal and Policy Framework," in, J. Owen Saunders, *Managing Natural Resources in a Federal State.* Toronto: Carswell.

Lucas, Alastair R. (1989). "The New Environmental Law," in R. Watts and D. Brown, eds., *Canada: The State of the Federation, 1989.* Kingston: Institute of Intergovernmental Relations.

Lundqvist, L.J. (1974). "Do Political Structures Matter in Environmental Politics? The Case of Air Pollution Control in Canada, Sweden, and the United States," *Canadian Public Administration,* 17: 112–42.

Muldoon, Paul, and Marcia Valiante (1988). *Toxic Water Pollution in Canada.* Calgary: Canadian Institute of Resources Law.

Nemetz, Peter (1986). "The Fisheries Act and Federal-Provincial Environmental Regulation: Duplication or Complementarity?" *Canadian Public Administration,* 29: 401–24.

Norrie, Kenneth, Richard Simeon, and Mark Krasnick, (1986). *Federalism and Economic Union in Canada.* Toronto: University of Toronto Press.

Parisien, Richard W. (1972). *The Fisheries Act: Origins of Federal Delegation of Administrative Jurisdiction to the Provinces.* Ottawa: Environment Canada.

Parlour, J.W., and Schatzow (1978). "The Mass Media and Public Concern for Environmental Problems in Canada," *International Journal of Environmental Studies,* 13: 9–17.

Percy, D.R. (1984). "Federal/Provincial Jurisdictional Issues," in Harriet Rueggeberg and A.R. Thompson, eds., *Water Law and Policy Issues in Canada.* Vancouver: Westwater Research Centre.

R. v. Crown Zellerbach Canada Ltd. (1988) 84 NR I.

Rabe, Barry G. (1989). "Cross-Media Environmental Regulatory Integration: The Case of Canada," *American Review of Canadian Studies,* 19: 261–73.

Ross, Monique (1992). "An Evaluation of Joint Environmental Impact Assessments," in Monique Ross and J. Owen Saunders, eds., *Growing Demands on a Shrinking Heritage: Managing Resource-Use Conflicts*. Calgary: Canadian Institute of Resources Law.

Saunders, J. Owen (1988). *Interjurisdictional Issues in Canadian Water Management*. Calgary: Canadian Institute of Resources Law.

Skogstad, Grace, and Paul Kopas (1992). "Environmental Policy in a Federal System: Ottawa and the Provinces," in Robert Boardman, ed., *Canadian Environmental Policy: Ecosystems, Politics, and Process*. Toronto: Oxford University Press.

Smiley, Donald V. (1979). "An Outsider's Observations of Federal-Provincial Relations Among Consenting Adults," in Richard Simeon, ed., *Confrontation and Collaboration – Intergovernmental Relations in Canada Today*. Toronto: Institute of Public Administration of Canada.

Thompson, Andrew R. (1980). *Environmental Regulation in Canada: An Assessment of the Regulatory Process*. Vancouver: Westwater Research Centre.

Thompson, Andrew R. and H.R. Eddy (1973). "Jurisdictional Problems in Natural Resource Management," in W.D. Bennett *et al., Essays on Aspects of Resource Policy*. Ottawa: Science Council of Canada.

Tingley, Donna (1991). "Conflict and Cooperation on the Environment," in Douglas Brown, ed., *Canada: The State of the Federation, 1991*. Kingston: Institute of Intergovernmental Relations.

Toner, Glen (1994). "The Green Plan: From Great Expectations to Eco-Backtracking ... to Revitalization?" in Susan D. Phillips, ed., *How Ottawa Spends 1994–95: Making Change*. Ottawa: Carleton University Press.

Tremblay, André (1973). "La priorité des compétences provinciales dans la lutte contre la pollution des eaux," in Phillippe Crabbé and Irene M. Spry, eds., *Natural Resources Development in Canada*. Ottawa: University of Ottawa Press.

Weaver, R. Kent (1986). "The Politics of Blame Avoidance," *Journal of Public Policy*, 6: 371–98.

Webb, Kernaghan R. (1983). "Industrial Water Pollution Control and the EPS," unpublished background study prepared for the Law Reform Commission of Canada.

Western Report (1989). "Fjordbotten: No means No," December 25: 30.

Whittington, Michael (1974). "Environmental Policy," in G. Bruce Doern and V. Seymour Wilson, *Issues in Canadian Public Policy*. Toronto: Macmillan.

Wilson, James Q. (1975). "The Politics of Regulation," in James McKie, ed., *Social Responsibility and the Business Predicament*. Washington: Brookings Institution.

Woodrow, R.B. (1977). "The Development and Implementation of Federal Pollution Control Policy Programs in Canada, 1966–1974," Ph.D. thesis, University of Toronto.

Young, R.A. Philippe Faucher, and André Blais (1984). "The Concept of Province-Building: A Critique," *Canadian Journal of Political Science*, 17: 783–818.

D. Criminal Prohibitions

(a) "Applying the Tests of Real Crime to Environmental Pollution"
Law Reform Commission of Canada

11. *Supra*, note 4, p. 43.
12. *Ibid.*

13. See generally on this approach, C.D. Stone, "Should Trees Have Standing? — Toward Legal Rights for Natural Objects" (1972), 45 *Southern California Law Review* 450; L.H. Tribe, "Ways Not to Think about Plastic Trees: New Foundations for Environmental Law" (1974), 83 *Yale Law Journal* 1315; D.P. Emond, "Co-operation in Nature: A New Foundation for Environmental Law" (1984), 22 *Osgoode Hall Law Journal* 323.

14. The study was done for Environment Canada by the Centre de recherche d'opinion publique (CROP).

15. See "Environmental Issues in Alberta: The Opinions of Edmonton Residents," *RMD Report*, 82/17.

16. See "Canada Considers Legislation to Protect Quality of Water," *The Globe and Mail*, February 7, 1984. A 1985 poll of Canadian attitudes to the acid rain problem reported that seventy-five per cent of Canadians feel that their governments are doing little or nothing to solve the problem. The same newspaper article reported that a 1985 Harris Poll in the United States found that awareness of acid rain pollution has "soared to 94 percent from 30 in the past five years and a majority of the population wants to see polluters pay for the clean-up." See "Acid-Rain Awareness up to 94%, U.S. Poll Shows," *The Globe and Mail*, May 13, 1985, p. 11.

17. One of the strongest and earliest proponents of the relevance of this doctrine to environmental protection was Joseph Sax. See his *Defending the Environment: A Strategy for Citizen Action* (New York: Alfred A. Knopf, 1971). See also Constance D. Hunt, "The Public Trust Doctrine in Canada," in John Swaigen, ed., *Environmental Rights in Canada* (Toronto: Butterworths, 1981), pp. 151–94. A related approach encouraged by many argues for a new substantive right to environmental quality which could be enforced by government or any member of the public against business, or any member of the public against the government. See John Swaigen and Richard Woods, "A Substantive Right to Environmental Quality," in *Environmental Rights in Canada, supra*, pp. 195–241.

18. Institutes of Justinian, Book II, Title I, para. 1., in *The Civil Law*, a translation by S.P. Scott (Cincinnati: The Central Trust Company, 1931), vol. 2, p. 33.

19. In Alberta, the Leader of the Opposition introduced a private member's Bill in the Alberta Legislative Assembly in 1978 and again in 1979. The Bill was entitled "The Environmental Bill of Rights" (Bill 222, 19th Legislature, 1st Session), but it was blocked by the government without debate. A more comprehensive private member's Bill was that introduced by the Leader of the Opposition in the Ontario legislature in 1979. Entitled "The Ontario Environmental Rights Act" (Bill 185, 1979, 31st Legislature, 3rd Session), it was briefly debated but also defeated. In 1980, the Ontario New Democratic Party introduced its own Bill entitled "The Environmental Magna Carta Act" (Bill 91, 31st Legislature, 4th Session). It died on the Order Paper without debate. In 1978, the federal government introduced a Bill to amend the Constitution of Canada (Bill C-60, "An Act to Amend the Constitution of Canada," 30th Parliament, 3rd Session, tabled June 20, 1978). The 1980 proposal to the Parliamentary Joint Committee on the Constitution (by Aird and Love) would have committed the federal and provincial governments to "advancing the management and use of Canada's natural resources to meet the needs of soci-

ety in perpetuity." See Aird and Love, "Enshrine Resources in a New Constitution," *The Globe and Mail*, July 25, 1980, p. 7. See also G. Mains, "Some Environmental Aspects of a New Canadian Constitution" (1980), 9 *Alternatives* 14.

The Canadian Environmental Law Association (CELA) also made a brief to the same Joint Committee arguing among other things for a commitment from the government to the preservation of environmental quality across Canada. The Canadian Environmental Law Research Foundation (CELRF) also proposed an "Environmental Bill of Rights" in David Estrin and John Swaigen, eds., *Environment on Trial*, rev. ed. (Toronto: CELA and CELRF, 1978), pp. 458–81, in which it maintained at page 458 that "[l]ike freedom of speech, freedom of religion, and other basic civil rights, *environmental quality should be recognized by law as an inalienable right*, for without an environment capable of supporting the human race, all other rights are useless."

20. *Environmental Protection Act* (Michigan), Public Law 127 of 1970.

21. See, for example, N. Morse and D.A. Chant, *An Environmental Ethic: Its Formulation and Implications* (Ottawa: Canadian Environmental Advisory Council, 1975); R. Cahn, *Footprints on the Planet: A Search for an Environmental Ethic* (New York: Universe Books, 1978).

...

23. For details on the meaning and significance of the ecosystems approach, see: E.P. Odum, *Fundamentals of Ecology*, 3rd ed. (London: Saunders, 1971); H.T. Odum, *Environment, Power and Society* (New York: Wiley, 1971); B. Commoner, *L'encerclement* (Paris: Le Seuil, 1972); P. Lebreton, *Les chemins de l'écologie* (Paris: Éditions Denoël, 1978); A. Schnaiberg, *The Environment* (Oxford: Oxford U. Press, 1980).

24. See T. Page, "A Framework for Unreasonable Risk in the Toxic Substance Control Act (TSCA)" in W. Nicholson, ed., *Management of Assessed Risk for Carcinogens* (1981), 363 *Annals of the New York Academy of Sciences*, New York.

E.   Regulation and Standards

(a) "Controlling Corporate Misconduct through Regulatory Offences"
Kernaghan Webb

1. Also referred to by Canadian courts as 'public welfare' offences....

2. The reader may quite justifiably wonder what is 'glamorous' about crimes. The best way to explain this is by referring to a debate over regulatory offences versus crimes in which the author was involved, where I noted: 'I must admit, though, I'm at a psychological disadvantage, in trying to persuade you of the strengths of regulatory offences. The trouble is, when compared with the word "crimes," the phrase "regulatory offences" strikes fear in the hearts of no one. Imagine the blasé response of the literary world if Dostoyevsky had entitled his book Regulatory Offences and Compliance, instead of Crime and Punishment.' (Webb 1990, 59).

3. The word 'penal' is used here to denote sanctions with a deterrent and punitive element, including fines, pro-bation, and imprisonment. Both regulatory and criminal offences are penal in nature.

4. I am not suggesting that the penal approach is the only or necessarily the preferable method to control corporate misbehaviour. Other techniques include control orders, licensing arrangements, and warnings. For a discussion of the range of options used to control pollution, see Webb (1988, chaps. 1–3). I believe that administrative techniques such as those described above will be more successfully invoked where backed by effective penal sanctions, enforced pursuant to a public compliance and enforcement policy.

5. As evidenced by the offence provisions of the Canadian Environmental Protection Act, 1988, RSC 1985, 4th Supp., c. 16, the Manitoba Environment Act, SM 1987–88, c. 26; 1988 amendments to the Ontario Environmental Protection Act RSO 1980, c. 141, and Ontario Water Resources Act RSO 1980, c. 361.

6. See, especially, *R. v. Wholesale Travel Group Inc.* [1991] 67 CCC (3d) 193, *R. v. Ellis-Don* [1992] 7 OR (3d) 320; *Reference Re: S. 94(2) of the B.C. Motor Vehicles Act* [1985] 48 CR (3d) 289.

7. See Glasbeek (1984); Keyserlingk (1984); Schrecker and Tremblay (1986).

8. Dickson, J., in *Sault Ste. Marie*, 362, states: 'Where the offence is criminal, the Crown must establish a mental element, namely, that the accused who committed the prohibited act did so intentionally or recklessly, with knowledge of the facts constituting the offence, or with wilful blindness toward them.'

9. See *R. v. Canadian Dredge and Dock Co. Ltd.* (1985) 19 DLR (3d) 161.

10. On penalties available for regulatory offences, see below under the heading 'Crimes versus Regulatory Offences.'

11. RSC 1985, c. C-46.

12. Part I of the Constitution Act, 1982, being Schedule B of the Canada Act 1982 (U.K.), 1982, c. 11.

13. See U.S. court articulation of non-mens rea regulatory offence in *U.S. Dotterweich* 320 U.S. 277 (1943); discussion of regulatory offences in New Zealand in November (1990, 236–9).

14. S. 115 of the Canadian Environmental Protection Act.

15. S. 148(5) of the Canada Labour Code, RSC 1985, c. L-2.

16. S. 14 of the Consumer Packaging and Labelling Act, RSC 1985, c. C-38.

17. There are an estimated 97,000 regulatory offences created by federal statutes alone: see Clifford and Webb (1986, 38).

18. See Dickson, J., in *Sault Ste. Marie* 370.

19. Per Dickson, J., in *Sault Ste. Marie* 363.

20. See comment to this effect re environmental offences in Hughes and Swanson (1990, 159). My own research suggests that legislation on workplace safety and consumer protection also uses primarily the strict-liability offence. This is in keeping with the Supreme Court of Canada's guidance in *Sault Ste. Marie* that public-welfare offences should be presumed to be in the strict-liability category unless there are express legislative indications to the contrary.

21. See Glasbeek (1984); Keyserlingk (1984); Schrecker and Tremblay (1986).

22. See discussion of these in Webb (1988), chap. 4).

23. Under s. 113 of the Canadian Environmental Protection Act, RSC, 1985, 4th Supp., c. 16, every person who manufactures or imports a substance in contra-

vention of the act is guilty of an offence and liable, on summary conviction, to a fine not exceeding $300,000 and/or up to six months' imprisonment, or, on indictment, up to $1 million dollars and/or imprisonment for up to three years. In Ontario, corporations that pollute contrary to provisions of the Ontario Environmental Protection Act, RSO 1980, c. 141, as amended, s. 146a(1), are liable on conviction to fines of up to $100,000 for repeat-offences, while individual repeat offenders can be imprisoned for up to one year (s. 146a). Polluters in Manitoba can be fined up to $200,000 per day for repeat offences and to one year or both, pursuant to section 33 of the Manitoba Environment Act, SM 1987, c. 26.

24. Compliance and enforcement policies are defined and discussed in greater detail below.

25. Dickson, J., in *Sault Ste. Marie*, 363, makes the point as follows: 'Where the offence is criminal, the Crown must establish a mental element, namely, that the accused who committed the prohibited act did so intentionally or recklessly, with knowledge of the facts constituting the offence, or with wilful blindness toward them. Mere negligence is excluded from the concept of the mental element required for conviction. Within the context of a criminal prosecution a person who fails to make such inquires as a reasonable and prudent person would make, or who fails to know facts he should have known, is innocent in the eyes of the law.'

26. Environmental audits are discussed in greater detail below under the heading 'Enforcement of Regulatory Offences.'

27. As described in Schrecker (1984).

28. As discussed in greater detail below, 'Enforcement of Regulatory Offences.'

29. See *R. v. United Ceramics Ltd.* (1979) 52 CCC (2d) 19.

30. See *Just v. The Queen* [1989] SCR 1228; *City of Vernon v. Manolakos* [1989] SCR 1259; *Tock v. St. John's Metropolitan Area Bd.* [1989] 2 SCR 1181.

31. See discussion of this in Finkle and Cameron (1989, 34).

32. See discussion of the effect of private prosecutions on government enforcement action in Webb (1991, 770).

33. See Environment Canada (1988). This policy is discussed in some depth in Webb (1991, 819–24).

34. At the federal level, the Department of Fisheries and Oceans, in conjunction with the Department of Environment, is developing a compliance-and-enforcement policy for the pollution provisions of the Fisheries Act; the federal Department of Labour has a compliance-and-enforcement policy for the Canada Labour Code; the Department of Consumer and Corporate Affairs is developing such policies for some of its consumer-protection legislation.

35. Ontario, Quebec, and British Columbia have established such units.

36. In 1991, fines against polluters in Ontario totalled a record $2,575,145 on 485 convictions. In conversation of the author (November 1992) with David Kerr, regional supervisor, Investigations and Enforcement Branch, Southeastern Region, Ministry of Environment, he indicated that there is 85–90 per cent success rate for prosecutions (convictions and guilty pleas). There was also a shift in 1991 towards creative sentencing, either as an alternative or in addition to jail terms or fines. Companies have been stripped of profits, required to set up trust funds, and/or establish environmental scholarships. As well, directors and managers are increasingly being directly prosecuted and held liable for environmental offences. During the period 1985–91, the number of prosecutions increased 400 per cent; see Ontario Ministry of Environment (1992a). And see Ontario Ministry of Environment (1991).

37. See Saxe (1990, 91).

38. For example, in a November 1992 telephone conversation with the author, Mr Rob Dunn, district manager, Ottawa District, noted that 'prior to 1985, regulatees used to say "get off my back" when we came around. Now, they're reporting spills on time, and are much more forthcoming with information. On the other hand, when we do investigations, nowadays they have their lawyers present.'

39. Because of constantly changing economic, political, and regulatory conditions, officials were not able to supply me with statistical evidence to back up this assertion, but it is the considered opinion of all officials contacted that abatement practices of the private sector have improved since the 1985 enforcement campaign began.

40. Per my discussions with David Kerr. In 1985, the Ontario Ministry of Environment created its Investigations and Enforcement Branch. From fiscal year 1985–6 through to 1991, convictions increased from 100 per year to over 250 per year.

41. Conversations with Tony Pingue, vice president, Regulatory and Environmental Affairs, Philip Environmental Inc., November 1992.

42. Ontario Ministry of Environment (1992b, 2): 'In 1986 provisions were enacted by the Ontario Legislature in the Environmental Protection Act that made all directors or officers of a corporation personally accountable for offences committed against the environment. As a result of these provisions, more and more environmental prosecutions are resulting in the conviction of individuals as well as companies, and senior staff are being held personally responsible for their company's actions. Prosecutors are thinking not only in terms of fines, but also in jail terms – which can't passed on to someone else.' For a recent example of a successful conviction of corporate directors, see *R. v. Bata Industries Ltd.* [1992] 9 OR (3d) 329.

43. For discussion of defence bar concerns with such prosecutions, and the interpretation of Ontario director offences, see 'The Bata Case – the Inside Story: New Rules for Officers' and Directors' Liability' in Fasken Martineau, *Environmental Law Bulletin*) (August 1991), 1.

44. Of course, it may have additional effects, such as reorganization of corporate structures and resignations from boards of directors.

45. Iaccobucci, J., in *R. v. Wholesale Travel*, 235, talks of strict-liability offences as providing an 'effective inducement for those engaged in regulated activity to comply strictly with the regulatory scheme including adopting proper procedures and record-keeping.'

46. For further discussion of environmental audits, their strengths, and their weaknesses, see Edwards (1991, 1).

F. The International Institutional Context

(a) "The Institutional Contexts"
Melody Hessing and Michael Howlett

80. Gabriel A. Almond, 'The International-National Connection,' *British Journal of Political Science* 19.2 (1989):

237–59; Peter Gourevitch, 'The Second Image Reversed: The International Sources of Domestic Politics,' *International Organization 32* (1978): 881–912.

81. See Robert O. Keohane and Helen V. Milner, eds., *Internationalization and Domestic Politics* (Cambridge, UK: Cambridge University Press 1996); Miles Kahler, *International Institutions and the Political Economy of Integration* (Washington, DC: Brookings Institute 1995); and Martin List and Volker Rittberger, 'International Environmental Management,' in A. Hurrell and B. Kingsbury, eds., *The International Politics of the Environment: Actors, Interests and Institutions* (Oxford: Clarendon Press 1992), 85–109.

82. Oran Young, *International Environmental Regimes* (Ithaca, NY: Cornell University Press 1989); Oran Young, 'The Politics of International Regime Formation: Managing Natural Resources and the Environment,' *International Organization 43.3* (1989): 349–76.

83. W.T. Easterbrook and Hugh G.J. Aitken, *Canadian Economic History* (Toronto: Gage 1980).

84. M. Howlett and M. Ramesh, *The Political Economy of Canada: An Introduction* (Toronto: McClelland and Stewart 1992).

85. J.L. Granatstein, 'Free Trade between Canada and the United Stats: The Issue That Will Not No Away,' in D. Stairs and G. Winham, eds., *The Politics of Canada's Economic Relationship with the United States* (Toronto: University of Toronto Press 1985), 1–51.

86. GATT, *Basic Instruments and Selected Documents* (Geneva: GATT 1969).

87. In 1947, GATT was signed by twenty-three nations, including Canada, at the American initiative. Since then, the number of nations acceding to it expanded to eighty-nine, with another thirty maintaining de facto application of its rules. The original provisions of the agreement have remained essentially intact, even though many rules have been modified to strengthen, extend, or clarify these provisions through the adoption of a number of supplementary codes and agreements over the years. See Robert O. Keohane, 'Multilateralism: An Agenda for Research,' *International Journal 45* (1990): 731–64.

88. Howlett and Ramesh, *Political Economy*.

89. Canada, Department of Finance, *The Canada-U.S. Free Trade Agreement: An Economic Assessment* (Ottawa: Supply and Service 1988).

90. Steven Globerman, ed., *Continental Accord: North American Economic Integration* (Vancouver: Fraser Institute 1991).

91. Rod Dobell and Michael Neufeld, eds., *Beyond NAFTA: The Western Hemisphere Interface* (Lantzville, BC: Oolichan Books 1993).

92. Robert J. Gale, 'NAFTA and Its Implications for Resource and Environmental Management,' in B. Mitchell, ed., *Resource and Environmental Management in Canada: Addressing Conflict and Uncertainty* (Toronto: Oxford University Press 1995), 99–129.

93. Economic Council of Canada, *Venturing Forth: An Assessment of the Canada-U.S. Trade Agreement* (Ottawa: Economic Council of Canada 1988), 11–12.

94. See S. Shrybman, 'International Trade and the Environment: An Environmental Assessment of Present GATT Negotiations,' *Alternatives 17* (1990): 20–9; John Whalley, 'Regional Trade Arrangements in North America: CUSTA and NAFTA,' in J. de Melo and A. Panagariya, eds., *New Dimensions in Regional Integration* (Cambridge, UK: Cambridge University Press 1993), 352–89; and J. Kirton and S. Richardson, eds., *Trade, Environment, and Competitiveness: Sustaining Canada's Prosperity* (Ottawa: National Round Table on Environment and Economy 1992).

95. See especially Pierre Marc Johnson and André Beaulieu, *The Environment and NAFTA: Understanding and Implementing the New Continental Law* (Washington, DC: Island Press 1996); also Annette Baker Fox, 'Environment and Trade: The NAFTA Case,' *Political Science Quarterly 110.1* (1995): 49–68; C. Thomas and G.A. Tereposky, 'The NAFTA and the Side Agreement on Environmental Co-Operation,' *Journal of World Trade 27.6* (1993): 5–34.

96. Peter S. Thacher, 'The Role of the United Nations,' in A. Hurrell and B. Kingsbury, eds., *The International Politics of the Environment* (Oxford: Clarendon Press 1992), 183–211; Hayward R. Alker and Peter M. Haas, 'The Rise of Global Ecopolitics,' in N. Choucri, ed., *Global Accord: Environmental Challenges and International Responses* (Boston: MIT Press 1993), 205–54.

97. Tony Brenton, *The Greening of Machiavelli: The Evolution of International Environmental Politics* (London: Royal Institute of International Affairs 1994); Peter Bartelmus, *Environment, Growth and Development: The Concepts and Strategies of Sustainability* (London: Routledge 1994). Some major international environmental organizations are based in Canada. Montreal, for example, is home to the NAFTA Environmental Commission on Environmental Cooperation, as well as to the permanent secretariat to the UN Convention on Biological Diversity.

98. Kenneth Piddington, 'The Role of the World Bank,' in Hurrell and Kingsbury, eds., 212–27.

99. Statistics Canada, *Human Activity*.

100. Richard Benedick, *Ozone Diplomacy* (Cambridge, MA: Harvard University Press 1991); Michael Grubb, *The Earth Summit Agreements: A Guide and Assessment* (London: RIIA/Earthscan 1993).

101. Linda C. Reif, 'International Environmental Law,' in Thompson, McConnell, and Huestis, eds., 71–103.

102. For alternative perspectives on the effectiveness of these standards, see Daniel C. Esty, *Greening the GATT: Trade, Environment and the Future* (Washington, DC: Institute of International Economics 1994); and C. Fred Runge, *Freer Trade, Protected Environment: Balancing Trade Liberalization and Environmental Institutions* (Washington, DC: Council on Foreign Relations 1994).

103. The constitutional constraint on policymakers, however, is two-edged: that is, because the Constitution does not clearly demarcate jurisdictional boundaries in this area of social and economic life, some duplication and overlap in services, regulation, and monitoring are inevitable. While those concerned with efficient administration and accountable expenditures may decry this situation, there are some advantages, from an environmental perspective, to restricting the freedom of individual jurisdictions to do as they wish with their resources and environments. That is, as Peter Nemetz has pointed out, duplication in oversight ensures that no jurisdiction is able to 'opt out' of environmental protection and simply 'high grade' or stripmine its resources. Nemetz, 'Fisheries Act.'

Two
The Regulatory System

A. The Political Context

(a) "On Lawmaking"
William J. Chambliss

1. J. Hall, *Theft Law and Society* (Revised Edition, 1952). 3–4.
2. Letter from Engels to F. Mehring, 14 July 1893 in K. Marx and F. Engels, *Selected Works In One Volume* (1968) 701.
3. R. Quinney, *Critique of Legal Order: Crime Control in Capitalist Society* (1974) 138.
4. L. Friedman, *Law and Society: An Introduction* (1977) 99.
5. E. Mandel, *The Contradictions of Capitalism* (1970) 132–181.
6. For two excellent recent articles on dialectical methodology see (a) Appelbaum, "Marx's Theory of the Falling Rate of Profit" (1978), *Am. Sociological Rev.* 43 67–81; (b) Appelbaum, "Marxist Method: Structural Constraints and Social Praxis" (1978) 13 *The American Sociologist* 73–81.

...

16. N. Gunningham, *Pollution, Social Interest and the Law* (1974) 35. See also F. Graham, Jr., *Since Silent Spring* (1970) 225.
17. *Ibid.*, p. 35.
18. *Ibid.*, p. 40.
19. *Id.*
20. *Ibid.*, p. 46.
21. G. Kolko, *The Triumph of Conservation* (1963).
22. *Op. cit.*, p. 42.
23. *Id.*
24. *Ibid.*, p. 46.
25. Whitt, "Toward a Class-Dialectical Model of Political Power: An Empirical Assessment of Three Competing Models of Political Power" (1979) *Am. Sociological Rev.* 81–99.
26. *Ibid.*, pp. 38–99.
27. Appelbaum, *op. cit.*, p.78.

...

34. D. Black, *The Behaviour of Law* (1977).

...

50. N.R. Hansen, *Patterns of Discovery* (1958).

...

52. Because of the tendency in the sociology of law to concentrate on criminal law, I have intentionally focused primarily on civil law. The theoretical findings and trends, however, are applicable to criminal law as well.

(b) "Environmental Assessment and Democracy"
Stephen Hazell

1. Graham Wilson, "The Westminster Model in Comparative Perspective" in *Developing Democracy* pp. 189–201.
2. For example, see Richard Van Loon and Michael Whittington, *The Canadian Political System: Environment, Structure and Process* (4th ed.) (Toronto: McGraw-Hill Ryerson Ltd. 1978). p. 393.
3. ibid note 1 p. 195.
4. Frank Fischer, "Citizen participation and democratization of policy expertise: From theoretical inquiry to practical cases" *Policy Sciences Vol. 26* (1993) pp. 165–187.
5. Ibid p. 172.
6. John Dryzek, "Green Reason: Communicative Ethics for the Biosphere" *Environmental Ethics* Vol. 12, p. 196.
7. Ibid.
8. John Dryzek, *Discursive Democracy: Politics, Policy, and Political Science* (Cambridge Press, 1990) p. 14.
9. D. P. Emond, *Environmental Assessment Law in Canada* (Toronto: McClelland & Stewart, 1978) p. 98.
10. Patrick Boyer, *The People's Mandate: Referendums and a More Democratic Canada* (Toronto: Dundurn Press Limited 1992).
11. Ibid p. 226.
12. Ibid p. 224.
13. John Meisel, "The Decline of the Party" in *The Political Party System in Canada* (6th ed.) ed. Hugh Thorburn (Scarborough, Ontario: Prentice-Hall Canada Ltd., 1991), pp. 179–180.
14. Ibid note 2, p. 393.
15. Michael M. Atkinson, "Parliamentary Government in Canada" in *Canadian Politics in the 1990s (Third Edition)* Michael Whittington and Glen Williams (ed.) (Scarborough: Nelson Canada, 1990) p. 355.
16. Michael Wilson, "Wanted: a more open, useful way to deliver Canada's budget". *The Globe and Mail.* (May 22, 1995), p. A17.
17. Ibid.
18. Federal Environmental Assessment Review Office, *The Environmental Assessment Process for Policy and Program Proposals* (Hull, Quebec: FEARO, February, 1993).
19. Ibid p. 6.
20. Ibid p. 7.
21. As noted in Chapter 5, other strategic environmental assessments have been conducted by federal departments, but such strategic have not been publicly released in the form set out in the Cabinet Directive.
22. Task Force on the Ontario Environmental Bill of Rights, *Report of the Task Force on the Ontario Environmental Bill of Rights July 1992* (Toronto: Queen's Printer for Ontario, 1992).
23. *Environmental Bill of Rights*, 1993. S.O. 1993, c. 28.
24. Environmental Commissioner of Ontario, *Opening the Doors to Better Environmental Decision Making: Annual Report 1994–95* (Toronto: Environmental Commissioner of Ontario, 1996), p. 26.
25. S.C. 1995, c. 43.
26. Ibid s. 15(1).
27. R.S.C. 1985, c. 0–5, as amended.

28. John Grace, Information Commissioner of Canada., *Annual Report Information Commissioner 1993–94* (Ottawa: Minister of Supply and Services Canada, 1994).
29. Ibid p. 34.

(c) "Environmental Protection and the Role of Government"
Anita Krajnc

Audley, John. *Green Politics and Global Trade: NAFTA and the Future of Environmental Politics.* Washington, D.C.: Georgetown University Press, 1997.

Ayres, Jeffrey. *Defying Conventional Wisdom: Political Movements and Popular Contention against North American Free Trade.* Toronto: University of Toronto Press, 1998.

Bellone, Carl J. and George Frederick Goerl. "Reconciling Public Entrepreneurship and Democracy." *Public Administration Review.* March/April 1992, 52(2): 130–134.

Conca, Ken. "The WTO and the Undermining of Global Environmental Governance." *Review of International Political Economy.* Autumn 2000. 3(2): 484–494.

Cope, Stephen. "Contracting and Globalization: Implications for Governance, Policy Learning and Strategic Management" (Paper presented to the Twenty-Third International Congress of Administrative Sciences, Riyadh, July 1995).

Daly, Herman and John B. Cobb, Jr., *For the Common Good: Redirecting the Economy Toward Community, the Environment, and a Sustainable Future,* 2d ed. Boston: Beacon Press, 1994.

Doern, G. Bruce and Thomas Conway. *The Greening of Canada: Federal Institutions and Decisions.* Toronto: University of Toronto Press, 1994.

Fafard, Patrick C. and Kathryn Harrison (eds.), *Managing Environmental Union: Intergovernmental Relations and Environmental Policy in Canada.* Montreal: McGill-Queen's University Press, 2000.

Fafard, Patrick C. "Groups, Governments and the Environment: Some Evidence from the Harmonization Initiative" in Patrick C. Fafard and Kathryn Harrison (eds.), *Managing Environmental Union: Intergovernmental Relations and Environmental Policy in Canada,* pp. 81–101. Montreal: McGill-Queen's University Press, 2000.

Falk, Richard. "Humane Governance and the Environment: Overcoming Neo-Liberalism" in Brendan Gleeson and Nicholas Low (eds.), *Governing for the Environment: Global Problems, Ethics and Democracy,* pp. 221–236. New York: Palgrave, 2001.

Goldberg, Kim. "Corporate Elite Rules BC." *Canadian Dimension.* July/August 2001. 35(4): 3.

Goodsell, Charles T. *The Case for Bureaucracy,* 3d edition. Chatham, N.J.: Chatham House, 1994.

Hall, Michael and Paul Reed. "Shifting the Burden: How Much Can Government Download to the non-profit sector?" *Canadian Public Administration.* Spring 1998. 41(1): 1–20.

Harrison, Kathryn. *Passing the Buck: Federalism and Canadian Environmental Policy.* Vancouver: UBC Press, 1996.

Hornung, Robert. "VCR does not work" in Robert Gibson, ed., *Voluntary initiatives: the new politics of corporate greening* (Peterborough: Broadview Press, 1999).

Johnston, Josée and Gordon Laxer. "Solidarity in the Age of Globalisation: Lessons from the anti-MAI and Zapatista Struggles." Unpublished paper, July 2001.

Kennett, Steven A. "Meeting the Intergovernmental Challenge of Environmental Assessment" in Patrick C. Fafard and Kathryn Harrison (eds.), *Managing Environmental Union: Intergovernmental Relations and Environmental Policy in Canada,* pp. 105–32. Montreal: McGill-Queen's University Press, 2000.

Krajnc, Anita. "Whither Ontario's Environment? Neoconservatism and the Decline of the Environment Ministry." *Canadian Public Policy.* March 2000. 26(1): 111–127.

Krajnc, Anita and Tony Weis. "The new politics of bloodsport in Ontario." *Canadian Dimension.* September/October 2000. 34(5): 42–45.

Laxer, Gordan. "The Movement That Dare Not Speak Its Name: The Return of Left Nationalism/Internationalism." *Alternatives.* 26 (2001): 1–32.

Mann, Howard. *Private Rights, Public Problems: A Guide to NAFTA's Controversial Chapter on Investor Rights.* Winnipeg: International Institute for Sustainable Development and World Wildlife Fund US, 2001.

Marchak, Patricia. "Environment and Resource Protection: Does NAFTA Make a Difference?" *Environment and Development.* June 1998. 11(2): 133–154.

May, Elizabeth. "Fighting the MAI" in Andrew Jackson and Matthew Sanger (eds), *Dismantling Democracy: The Multilateral Agreement on Investment (MAI) and Its Impact,* pp. 32–47. Ottawa and Toronto: The Canadian Centre for Policy Alternatives and James Lorimer, 1998.

Muldoon, Paul and Mark S. Winfield. *Brief to the House of Commons Standing Committee on Environment and Sustainable Development Regarding the CCME Environmental "Harmonization" Initiative* (CIELAP Brief 97/4, October 21, 1997).

Mulgan, Richard. "Comparing Accountability in the Public and Private Sectors." *Australian Journal of Public Administration.* March 2000. 59(1): 87–97.

———. "Contracting Out and Accountability." *Australian Journal of Public Administration.* December 1997a. 56(4): 106–116.

———. "The Processes of Public Accountability." *Australian Journal of Public Administration.* March 1997b. 56(1): 25–36.

Ontario Public Service Employees Union. *Renewing the Ministry of Environment* (A submission to the Walkerton Inquiry, May 2001).

Rhodes, Rod A.W. "The Hollowing Out of the State: The Changing Nature of the Public Service in Britain." *The Political Quarterly.* April 1994. 65(2): 138–151.

Roberts, Alasdair S. "Less Government, More Secrecy: Reinvention and the Weakening of Freedom of Information Law." *Public Administration Review.* Vol. 60, No. 4, July/August 2000. pp. 308–320.

Schattschneider, Elmer. *The Semi-Sovereign People: A Realist's View of Democracy in America.* New York: Holt, Rinehart and Winston, 1960.

Shields, John and B. Mitchell Evans. *Shrinking the State: Globalization and Public Administration "Reform".* Halifax: Fernwood Publishing, 1998.

Swenarchuk, Michelle. "The MAI and the Environment" in Andrew Jackson and Matthew Sanger (eds), *Dismantling Democracy: The Multilateral Agreement on Investment (MAI) and Its Impact,* pp. 120–137. Ottawa and Toronto: The Canadian Centre for Policy Alternatives and James Lorimer, 1998.

Toner, Glen. "Environment Canada's Continuing Roller Coaster Ride," in Gene Swimmer (ed.), *How Ottawa*

Spends 1996–97: Life Under the Knife, pp. 99–132. Ottawa: Carleton University Press, 1997.

Victor, Peter. Personal communication, Dean, Faculty of Environmental Studies, York University, Toronto, Ontario, July 24, 2000.

Wamsley, G.L., Charles T. Goodsell, John A. Rohr, Camilla M. Stivers, Orion F. White, and James F. Wolf. "The Public Administration and the Governance Process: Refocusing the American Dialogue" in R. C. Chandler (ed.,), *A Centennial History of the American Administrative State*, pp. 291–317. London: Collier-Macmillan, 1987.

Wapner, Paul. *Environmental Activism and World Civic Politics*. Albany: State University of New York Press, 1996.

Weisbrot, Mark. "Tricks of Trade: The only thing 'free' about it is the free ride it gives giant corporations." *Sierra*, pp. 64–70 and 84–85. September/October 2001.

Winfield, Mark. "Environmental Policy and Federalism" in Grace Skogstad and Herman Bakvis (eds), *Canadian Federalism: Performance, Effectiveness and Legitimacy*. Don Mills, Ont.: Oxford University Press, 2002.

Winfield, Mark S. with Shelly Kaufman and David Whorely, *The 'New Public Management' Comes to Ontario: A Study of Ontario's Technical Standards and Safety Authority and the impacts of putting public safety in private hands*. Toronto: Canadian Institute for Environmental Law and Policy, 2000.

World Commission on Environment and Development (Brundtland Commission). *Our Common Future*. Oxford: Oxford University Press, 1987.

B. Standard Setting

(a) "Environmental Standards-Setting and the Law in Canada"
Kernaghan Webb

1. These types of standards-setting are explored in more detail below.
2. The following information is derived from the Regulatory Impact Assessment Statement which accompanied the proposed revised Metal Mining Liquid Effluent Regulations, published in the Canada Gazette Part I, July 28, 2001, pp. 2613–60, and downloadable at: <http://canada.gc.ca/gazette/part1/pdf/g1-13530.pdf>.
3. Per Commissioner of the Environment and Sustainable Development, *Report of the Commissioner of the Environment and Sustainable Development to the House of Commons 2000*, Chapter 6, esp. para. 6.100–6.112.
4. All the following information is derived from the RIAS that accompanied the draft regulation, *ibid.*
5. *Ibid.*
6. The RIAS also reports that ENGOs wanted the metals identified in the regulation to be subject to lower effluent limits, and that more metals be subject to the regulation. In addition, they proposed that there be a regulatory requirement for effluent to be non-acutely lethal to *Daphnia magna* (water fleas) as well as rainbow trout (under the proposed regulation, both species are used for monitoring only of acute lethality). Acute lethality means that the effluent kills the test organism.
7. *Ibid.*
8. The Accord was signed in January, 1998, and is downloadable at: <www.ccme.ca>

9. The polluter pays principle holds that those who generate pollution and waste should bear the cost of prevention, containment, cleanup or abatement. The precautionary principle holds that, where there are threats of serious or irreversible environmental damage, lack of full scientific certainty shall not be used as a reason for postponing cost-effective measures to prevent environmental degradation. Both of these principles are defined in the Accord. The precautionary principle is discussed in greater detail below.
10. The Standards Sub-agreement is downloadable from <www.ccme.ca>. The following information is from *Guide to the Canada-Wide Accord on Environmental Harmonization*, at <www.ccme.ca/3e_priorities/3ea_harmonization/3ea1_accord/3ea1a.html>.
11. The following from "What is a Canada-Wide Standard?" at <www.ccme.ca/3e_priorities/3ea_harmonization/3ea2_cws/3ea2b.html>.
12. Downloadable at <www.ccme.ca>.
13. Per "Canada-Wide Standards for Dioxins and Furans," September 2001, downloadable from <www.ccme.ca>.
14. *Ibid.*
15. Per CCME, "Two-Year Review of Canada-Wide Accord on Environmental Harmonization," (June, 2000), downloadable at <www.ccme.ca>.
16. E.g., section 34 of the *Ontario Water Resources Act*, pertaining to taking of water permits.
17. E.g., section 27 of the *Environmental Protection Act*, pertaining to approvals to operate a waste disposal site.
18. The Registry is accessible at: <http://www.eco.on.ca/english/registry/what_on1.htm>.
19. See, e.g., ECO Annual Reports, downloadable at: <http://www.eco.on.ca/english/publicat/index.htm>.
20. For discussion of the appeal process, see <http://www.eco.on.ca/english/publicat/guide/appinstr.htm>.
21. For example, recently citizens have successfully appealed the terms of a permit granted to OMYA pursuant to s. 34 of the *Ontario Water Resources Act* on these grounds. The decision is available at: <http://204.40.253.254/envregistry/013314ei.htm>
22. See OMYA decision, *ibid.*
23. *R.* v. *MacMillan Bloedel (Alberni) Ltd.* (1979) 2 Fisheries Pollution Reports 182 at pp. 184–185 (B.C.C.A.).
24. It does, however, de-politicize the decision-making process, in the sense that judges are not as vulnerable to lobbying activities, or "playing to the gallery", as are Members of Parliament in their law-making function.
25. Per Nunn J., in *Palmer* v. *Nova Scotia Forest Industries* (1983) 2 DLR (4th) 397 (N.S.T.D.).
26. On this point, see discussion in K. Webb, *Pollution Control in Canada: The Regulatory Approach in the 1980s* (Ottawa: Law Reform Commission, 1986).
27. The following discussion is derived from: Report of the Commissioner of the Environment and Sustainable Development, *Understanding the Risks From Toxic Substances: Cracks in the Foundation of the Federal House* (1999), pp. 3-16–3-17.
28. Report of the Commissioner of the Environment and Sustainable Development, *Understanding the Risks From Toxic Substances: Cracks in the Foundation of the Federal House* (1999), pp. 3-16–3-17.
29. (1992) 9 OR 329 (Ont. Prov. Ct.).
30. Per Commissioner of the Environment and Sustainable Development, Report of the Commissioner of the Environment and Sustainable Development — 1998, *Global Challenges*, Chapter 2, paragraph 2.44.

31. For example, the 1909 Treaty between the United States and Great Britain Relating to Boundary Waters, the 1916 Convention concerning Migratory Birds, the 1973 Convention on International Trade in Endangered Species of Wild Fauna and Flora (CITES), the 1985 Vienna Convention on the Protection of the Ozone Layer, the 1987 Montreal Protocol on Substances That Deplete the Ozone Layer, the 1989 Basel Convention on the Control of Transboundary Movements of Hazardous Wastes and Their Disposal, the 1992 United Nations Framework Convention on Climate Change, the 1997 Kyoto Protocol on Climate Change. See chart of Canada's Involvement in International Environmental Agreements and Instruments, in Report of the Commissioner of Environment and Sustainable Development — 1998, *ibid.*, Exhibit 2.8.

32. See discussion of the Government of Canada discussion paper concerning the precautionary principle below.

33. *114957 Canada Ltée (Spraytech, Société d'arrosage)* v. *Hudson (Town)*, 2001 SCC 40.

34. Government of Canada, A Canadian Perspective on the Precautionary Approach/Principle (September, 2001), downloadable at: <www.dfait-maeci.gc.ca/tna-nac/precaution-e.asp>.

35. The following is taken directly from a one-page summary of *A Canadian Perspective on the Precautionary Approach/Principle, op cit.*

36. See discussion in P. Holmes, "The WTO Beef Hormones Case: A Risky Decision?" (March–April, 2000) 10 *Consumer Policy Review* 61–70.

37. SC 1997, c. 11.

38. Regulation of substances pursuant to the *Canadian Environmental Protection Act* requires that there be an environmental or health risk basis for decision-making.

39. See <www.appletonlaw.com>.

40. Report of the Commissioner of the Environment and Sustainable Development — 1999, *Managing the Risks of Toxic Substances* at p. 4-5.

41. The environmental organizations later left. See D. VanNijnatten, "The Day the NGOs Walked Out," in R. Gibson, ed., *Voluntary Initiatives: The New Politics of Corporate Greening* (Peterborough: Broadview Press, 1999) at pp. 101–110.

42. The following information from *Managing the Risks of Toxic Substances, op cit.*, especially para. 4.91.

43. *Ibid.*, per para. 4.91

44. F. Bregha and J. Moffet, "From Challenge to Agreement? Background Paper on the Future of ARET," (Ottawa: Resource Futures International, December 8, 1997), p. 2.

45. Particularly in terms of problems of measurability, verifiability, accountability: see *Managing the Risks of Toxic Substances, op cit.*, at para. 4.98 and 4.99.

46. See e.g., discussion in J. Moffet and F. Bregha, "Responsible Care," in R. Gibson, ed., *op cit.*, at pp. 69–85.

47. *Ibid.*

48. See e.g,. discussion in M. von Mirbach, "Demanding Good Wood," in R. Gibson, *op cit.*, at pp. 211–225.

(c) "Setting Standards"
Keith Hawkins

1. See further Ackerman et al., 1974; Davies, 1970; Richardson et al., forthcoming.

2. It follows from this that the law may be irrelevant as a means of control or sanctioning unless the standard actually addresses 'pollution' specifically. What is visibly 'polluting' to a layman may legally be clean water. In one case, for example, a major water supply and fisheries river was contaminated by the escape of a large amount of chemical dye which ironically was normally used to trace the source of pollutions. As a result the water in the river for several miles turned conspicuously red. The chemical could not be treated, but simply passed through sewage works without effect. The dye did not affect the suspended solids, biochemical oxygen demand (see n. 10 below), or any of the other parameters laid down in the company's consent. The water authority in this case was theoretically powerless: there was no standard at the work where the pollution originated which addressed the colour of its effluent, therefore no pollution.

3. Consistent demands made of dischargers in the standards set, apart from expressing a deeply-held value of justice, also assist in efficient enforcement, Kagan (1978:81) argues, since rules which are uniformly and consistently enforced are more likely to meet with voluntary compliance.

4. An unpublished agency document reported that 'only about 50 per cent of samples of existing discharges conform with currently applicable quality conditions. ...' Subsequent chapters discuss the reasons for such official tolerance.

5. There is a parallel here in the reluctance of regulatory agencies to pursue prosecutions where defendants are likely to contest the charge strenuously: see, e.g. Cranston, 1979: 125.

...

17. Previously, an individual could only prosecute with the leave of the Attorney-General.

18. Control of Pollution Act 1974, s. 41.

References

Ackerman, Bruce A., Susan Rose Ackerman, James W. Sawyer jun., and Dale W. Henderson (1974) *The uncertain search for environmental quality* (New York: Free Press).

Becker, Howard S. (1963) *Outsiders. Studies in the sociology of deviance* (New York: Free Press).

Cranston, Ross (1979) *Regulating business. Law and consumer agencies* (London: Macmillan).

Davies, J. Clarence (1970) *The politics of pollution* (Indianapolis: Bobbs-Merill).

Enthoven, Alain C. and A. Myrick Freeman III (eds.) (1973) *Pollution, resources, and the environment* (New York: Norton).

Kagan, Robert A. (1978) Regulatory justice: implementing a wage-price freeze (New York: Russell Sage).

Kaufmann, Herbert (1960) The forest ranger. A study in administrative, behavior (Baltimore: Johns Hopkins University Press).

Kneese, Allen V. (1973) 'Economics and the quality of the environment: some empirical experiences' in Enthoven and Freeman (1973): 72–87.

Richardson, Geneva with A.I. Ogus and Pal Burrows (forthcoming) *Policing pollution: a study of regulation and enforcement* (Oxford: Clarendon Press).

Royal Commission on Sewage Disposal (1912) *Eighth Report: Standards and tests for sewage and sewage effluents discharging into rivers and streams* Cd. 6464.

C. Implementation and Instruments

(a) "Instruments in Policy Implementation"
Law Reform Commission of Canada

34. The use of the regulatory offence prosecution instrument is pervasive in federal legislation: we encountered examples of practice in several fields. As for licences, our main examples have been taken from research on the CRTC's broadcasting licence administration (Clifford, 1983). Various incentive instruments were exposed in our research of the EPS (Webb, 1983) and the CFDC (Lillico, 1985); our treatment of incentives is also supported by our "contract model" Paper (Barton et al., 1984). The persuasion instrument is used by every institution which we have studied, but our best example to date is derived from a study of the CHRC (Laberge, 1983).

35. See also the "attributes" of various instruments, described in Stanbury and Fulton (1984: 319–22).

36. See for example: Canada, House of Commons ... (1980); Canada, Economics Council (1981a); Canada, LRCC (1980 and 1985); Canada, Royal Commission ... (1979); Canadian Chamber of Commerce (1981).

37. In Reports 14 (Canada, LRCC, 1980a); 17 (Canada, LRCC, 1982); 18 (Canada, LRCC, 1982a); 26 (Canada, LRCC, 1985); in Working Paper 25 (Canada, LRCC, 1980); also in the following Study Papers by Hunter and Kelly (1976); Doern (1976); Carrière and Silverstone (1976); Issalys and Watkins (1977); Lucas and Bell (1977); Janisch (1978); Issalys (1979); Slayton (1979); Johnston (1980); Kelleher (1980); Slayton and Quinn (1981).

38. As to the relation of this issue to *mens rea* and regulatory offences, see *R*. v. *City of Sault Ste. Marie*, and *Ref. re Section 94(2) of the Motor Vehicle Act (B.C.)*. The Department of Justice has followed up our recommendation on imprisonment. See Canada, Department of Justice (1982). See also the work of the Federal Statutes Compliance Project of the Department of Justice. Initially a part of the *Criminal Code* Review, this project moved into other areas of public law.

39. *Airport Traffic Regulations; Government Property Traffic Act and Regulations; National Parks Highway Traffic Regulations; Indian Reserve Traffic Regulations; Band Council Reserve Traffic By-Laws; National Capital Act Traffic and Property Regulations; National Harbours Board Act and Regulations; Government Harbours and Piers Act and Regulations; The Harbour Commissions Act and Regulations; The Hamilton Harbour Commissioners' Act and By-Laws; The Toronto Harbour Commissioners' Act, 1911, and By-Laws; An Act respecting the National Battlefields at Quebec and By-Laws; St. Lawrence Seaway Authority Act and Regulations*.

40. The test for valid federal criminal legislation was set out by Rand J. In *Ref. re Validity of Section 5(a) of the Dairy Industry Act*, p. 50: "Is the prohibition then enacted with a view to a public purpose which can support it as being in relation to criminal law? public peace, order, security, health, morality: these are ordinary though not exclusive ends served by that law, ..." Canadian jurisprudence has also developed tests for assessing the validity of a regulatory provision. In *MacDonald* v. *Vapour Canada Ltd.*, for example, Laskin C.J. at p. 25 held that paragraph 7(*e*) of the *Trade Marks Act*, was "not a regulation, nor is it concerned

with trade as a whole nor with general trade and commerce. [...] One looks in vain for any regulatory scheme ... Its enforcement is left to the chance of private redress without public monitoring by the continuing oversight of a regulatory agency...." In the matter of fisheries jurisdiction, the courts continue to make fine distinctions about the *vires* of regulatory provisions in the *Fisheries Act*; see, for example *Attorney-General of Canada* v. *Aluminum Co. of Canada Ltd.*, where Berger J. upheld the Minister's order to discharge more water to ease salmon migration, because the court will recognize the Minister's authority to make such orders in the public interest, under subsection 20(10) of the *Fisheries Act* if he acts on evidence, not arbitrarily and not upon extraneous considerations unrelated to fisheries protection. See, however, *R*. v. *MacMillan Bloedel Limited*, where the court held that a subspecies of cutthroat trout was outside federal jurisdiction. See also *City National Leasing Ltd.* v. *General Motors of Canada Ltd.*, wherein the Ontario High Court held section 31.1 of the *Combines Investigation Act* invalid. That section purported to create a civil cause of action; Rosenberg J. at p. 662 held that "[i]t is clear that s.31.1 is not part of the complex scheme set up by the Act. [...] It cannot be justified as a *necessary* part of an administrative scheme set up by the Act. The only possible justification for s.31.1 is as legislation 'necessarily incidental' or 'truly ancillary' to other provisions in the Act or the regulation of trade and commerce."

41. "Precisely because the legitimate occasions for social intervention will continue to multiply as society becomes more complex, congested, and technologically sophisticated, the collective-coercion component of intervention should be treated as a scarce resource. Since some coercion is implicit in all social intervention, intervention should be reserved for times when it promises large benefits. And when we do intervene we ought to maximize the use of techniques that modify the structure of private incentives rather than those that rely on the command-and-control approach of centralized bureaucracies. ... [O]ur political system almost always chooses the command-and-control response and seldom tries the other alternatives, regardless of whether that mode of response fits the problem" [Schultze, 1977: 7, 13].

42. There is a plan to do so in the Department of Transport's regulation of aviation safety. Recent revisions to the *Aeronautics Act* enable a new Civil Aviation Tribunal to adjudicate on such matters.

43. Note, however, that the validity of a civil cause of action created by federal statute will probably depend on whether it is "necessarily incidental" or "truly ancillary" to other provisions in the same statute or to regulation under a head of federal constitutional authority. See, for example, *City National Leasing Ltd.* v. *General Motors of Canada Ltd.* See also *MacDonald* v. *Vapour Canada Ltd.*

44. Legal and social histories of private prosecutions are clearly beyond the scope of this Paper, but it is suggested that an analysis of actual private prosecutions can reveal the extent to which they aid policy implementation. A preliminary analysis of this kind was made by Webb (1983: 284–322).

...

47. See, for example, the Ontario description in Cass (1984).

References

Adler, R.S. and R.D. Pittle (1984) "Cajolery or Command: Are Education Campaigns an Adequate Substitute for Regulation?" 1 *Yale J. on Regulation* 159.

Barton, B.J., R.T. Franson and A.R. Thompson (1983) *A Contract Model for Pollution Control* (Unpublished LRCC Paper). See also B.J. Barton, R.T. Franson and A.R. Thompson (1984) *A Contract Model for Pollution Control*. Vancouver: Westwater Research Centre.

Brown, K.M. (1984) "The Elusive Carrot: Tax Incentives for R & D" (Jan.–Feb.) 8 *Regulation* 33.

Canada, Law Reform Commission (1976a) *Our Criminal Law* [Report 3]. Ottawa: Supply and Services.

Canada, Law Reform Commission (1980) *Independent Administrative Agencies* [Working Paper 25]. Ottawa: Supply and Services.

Canada, Law Reform Commission (1980a) *Judicial Review and the Federal Court* [Report 14]. Ottawa: Supply and Services.

Canada, Law Reform Commission (1982) *Contempt of Court* [Report 17]. Ottawa: Supply and Services.

Canada, Law Reform Commission (1982a) *Obtaining Reasons before Applying for Judicial Scrutiny: Immigration Appeal Board* [Report 18]. Ottawa: Supply and Services.

Canada, Law Reform Commission (1985) *Independent Administrative Agencies* [Report 26]. Ottawa: LRCC.

Canada, Royal Commission on Financial Management and Accountability (1979) Allen T. Lambert, Chairman. *Final Report*. Ottawa: Supply and Services.

Canadian Chamber of Commerce (1981) *Regulatory Cost of Compliance Methodologies*. Toronto, September 1981.

Canadian Human Rights Commission (1984) *Annual Report, 1983*. Ottawa: Supply and Services.

Carrière, P. and S. Silverstone (1976) *The Parole Process: A Study of the National Parole Board* (LRCC Study Paper). Ottawa: Supply and Services.

Cass, B.E. (1984) "Grants Subject to Repayment — The Ontario Experience" in *Seminar on Government Contribution and Loan Guarantees* (unpublished). Toronto: Ontario Ministry of Industry and Trade.

Clifford, J.C. (1983) *Content Regulation in Private FM Radio and Television Broadcasting: A Background Study about CRTC Sanctions and Compliance Strategy* (unpublished LRCC Paper).

Diver, C.S. (1979) *The Assessment and Litigation of Civil Money Penalties by Federal Administrative Agencies*, Final Report to the Administrative Conference of the United States. Washington, May 1979.

Diver, C.S. (1980) "A Theory of Regulatory Enforcement" 28 *Public Policy* 257.

Doern, G.B. (ed.) (1978) *The Regulatory Process in Canada*. Toronto: MacMillan.

Dunning, C. (1982) *Compliance and Administrative Law: Costs of Compliance* (unpublished LRCC Paper).

Eddy, H. (1981) *Sanctions, Compliance Policy and Administrative Law* (unpublished LRCC Paper).

Ellul, J. (1965) *Propaganda*. New York: Alfred A. Knopf.

Fry, E. (1984) "Contribution Agreements: The DRIE Experience" in *Seminar on Contribution Agreements and Loan Guarantees*. Legal Services — DRIE. Ottawa, 26 June 1984.

Gerth, H.H. and C.W. Mills (1958) *From Max Weber: Essays in Sociology*. New York: Oxford University Press.

Goldfarb Consultants (1982) *Public Reaction to Government Advertising: Executive Summary* (Paper presented to the First Canadian Symposium on Government Advertising). Montréal, 19 November 1982.

Hogg, P.W. (1977) *Constitutional Law of Canada*. Toronto: Carswell.

Hunter, I.A. and I.F. Kelly (1976) *The Immigration Appeal Board* (LRCC Study Paper). Ottawa: Supply and Services.

Issalys, P. (1979) *The Pension Appeals Board: A Study of Administrative Procedure in Social Security Matters* (LRCC Study Paper). Ottawa: Supply and Services.

Issalys, P. and G. Watkins (1977) *Unemployment Insurance Benefits: A Study of Administrative Procedure in the Unemployment Insurance Commission* (LRCC Study Paper). Ottawa: Supply and Services.

Janisch, H.N. (1978) *The Regulatory Process of Canadian Transport Commission* (LRCC Study Paper). Ottawa: Supply and Services.

Johnson, J.P. (1982) *Canadian Industrial Incentives Legislation: Government Financial Assistance Programs in Canada*. Toronto: Price Waterhouse.

Kelleher, S. (1980) *Canada Labour Relations Board* (LRCC Study Paper). Ottawa: Supply and Services.

Laberge, T. (1983) *Le conformisme et les droits de la personne au Canada* (unpublished LRCC Paper).

Lillico, D. (1985) *The Canadian Film Development Corporation: A Report on Financial Incentives As Mechanisms for Achieving Compliance with Agency Objectives* (unpublished LRCC Paper).

Lucas, A.R. and T. Bell (1977) *The National Energy Board: Policy, Procedure and Practice* (LRCC Study Paper). Ottawa: Supply and Services.

Rice, D.A. (1968) "Remedies, Enforcement Procedures and the Duality of Consumer Transaction Problems" 48 *Boston University L. Rev.* 559.

Rosenbaum, N. (1981) "Statutory Structure and Policy Implementation: The Case of Wetlands Regulation" in D.A. Mazmanian and P.A. Sabatier (eds.), *Effective Policy Implementation*. Lexington, Mass.: Lexington Books.

Schultze, C.L. (1977) *The Public Use of Private Interest*. Washington: The Brookings Institution.

Slayton, P. (1979) *The Anti-dumping Tribunal* (LRCC Study Paper). Ottawa: Supply and Services.

Slayton, P. and J.J. Quinn (1981) *The Tariff Board* (LRCC Study Paper). Ottawa: Supply and Services.

Spigelman, J.J. (1977) *Sanctions, Remedies and Law Reform* (unpublished Australia Law Reform Commission Paper).

Stanbury, W.T. and J. Fulton (1984) "Suasion As a Governing Instrument" in A.M. Maslove (ed.), *How Ottawa Spends 1984: The New Agenda*. Toronto: Methuen.

Stanbury, W.T., G.J. Gorn and C.B. Weinberg (1983) "Federal Advertising Expenditures" in G. Bruce Doern (ed.), *How Ottawa Spends 1983: The Liberals, the Opposition & Federal Priorities*. Toronto: Lorimer.

Thomson, O. (1977) *Mass Persuasion in History: An Historical Analysis of the Development of Propaganda Techniques*. Edinburgh: Paul Harris Publishing.

Trebilcock, M.J. et al. (1981) *The Choice of Governing Instruments: Some Applications* (Technical Report No. 12). Toronto: Economic Council of Canada.

von Finkenstein, K. (1984) "Loan Guarantees: The Crown's Side" in *Seminar on Contribution Agreements and Loan Guarantees*. Ottawa: Legal Services.

Webb, K.R. (1983) *Industrial Water Pollution Control and the Environmental Protection Service* (unpublished LRCC Paper).

Webb, K.R. (1984) *The Petroleum Incentive Program — An Alternative to Tax-Based Subsidies* (Paper submitted to

Professor J.P. Lacasse, University of Ottawa, Masters of Law Course on Taxation of Resource Industry).

(b) "The Case for Pollution Taxes"
Nancy Olewiler

1. Evidence of this is seen in the federal government's "Green Paper." Taxation is not mentioned. In Ontario, the Municipal/Industrial Strategy for Abatement (MISA) program apparently did not even consider the role of market incentives to deal with major sources of pollution.

2. If the tax is levied on output of goods and services, it will be shifted forward — at least partially — to consumers as long as the producers are not facing a perfectly elastic demand curve for their product — as long as the price of the good produced is not exogenously given or fixed by markets that are unaffected by the tax. If the tax is levied on pollution-generating inputs into the production (or consumption) of goods and services, the tax will be borne by producers and ... consumers as long as demand for that input is not perfectly inelastic — that is, unresponsive to changes in that input's price. It will also be felt by the owners of the inputs as long as they are not supplied perfectly elastically — at only one price unaffected by any taxes. Individuals will change their consumption habits in response to any of these taxes — including those levied at the retail level — as long as their demand for the good or service is not perfectly inelastic. While it is beyond the scope of this paper to examine in detail all the possible inputs and outputs that could be taxed, I would be surprised if many were supplied or demanded under conditions that led to no response in their use.

3. These technological requirements often have been in the form of "best practicable" or "best available" technologies (BPTs and BATs). The way many command-and-control policies have worked is to examine the industry's ability to control emissions — generally in consultation with the industry. The initial decision regarding technology determines the best one currently available — the BAT. Firms are required to install the BAT within some time frame. Meanwhile, the regulators and industry look for alternative technologies that are better and/or cheaper at controlling emissions, but still feasible — the BPT. A schedule for switching from BATs to BPTs is announced. Once these technologies are set, there is no incentive to seek others unless, of course, the emissions are still deemed to be too high. Then, regulations must be rewritten, an expensive and time-consuming process.

4. Obviously, certain groups could be worse off. This topic will be addressed below.

5. See, for example, D. Terkla, "The Efficiency Value of Effluent Tax Revenue," *Journal of Environmental Economics and Management* 11 (1984): 107–123; W. Oates, "Taxing Pollution: An Idea Whose Time Has Come?" *Resources* 91 (Spring 1988); and G.B. Doern, ed., *The Environmental Imperative: Market Approaches to the Greening of Canada*, Policy Study 9 (Toronto: C.D. Howe Institute, 1990).

6. Thus far, the levies under the Superfund legislation have been a small percentage of the total cost of cleanup.

7. The federal government ignored an opportunity to incorporate environmental taxes with the GST.

8. For a recent analysis of noncompetitive industries and pollution taxes, see J. Markusen, E. Morey, and N. Olewiler, "Environmental Policy When Market Structure and Plant Locations are Endogenous" (Department of Economics, Simon Fraser University, Burnaby, B.C., 1990, Mimeographed).

9. There is an extensive literature on marketable permits and industrial structure. Permits clearly work best when an industry is competitive. See, for example, R. Hahn and R. Noll, *Designing a Market for Tradable Emissions Permits*, Working Paper 398 (Pasadena: California Institute of Technology, 1981); R. Hahn, "Economic Prescriptions for Environmental Problems: How the Patient Followed the Doctor's Orders," *Journal of Economic Perspectives* 3 (1989); 95–114; and the other chapters in this volume. Industrial structure is a complicating factor for any instrument.

10. The company responsible for the "tire fire" in Hagersville, Ontario in 1990 had been fighting Ontario orders to divide the tire piles. The legal system protects polluters while these challenges are being adjudicated.

11. Ontario's MISA contains provisions very similar to those of the U.S. *Clean Water Act*. One fears that MISA may be similarly costly and of limited success. Market incentives play no role in this policy.

12. Pollution taxes levied by the federal government could cause some difficulty with provincial Crown corporations, notably utilities. Currently, these Crown corporations do not pay federal taxes. Standards do not share this problem.

13. See Markusen, Morey, and Olewiler, "Environmental Policy When Market Structure and Plant Locations are Endogenous."

14. For other discussions of fuel taxes, see Dewees, *Evaluation of Policies for Regulating Environmental Pollution*, Regulation Reference Working Paper 4 (Ottawa: Economic Council of Canada, 1980); and W. Oates, "Markets for Pollution Control," *Challenge*, May–June 1984, pp. 4–17.

15. The United States is currently considering a tax somewhat similar to this.

(c) "Environmental Regulation:
The Economics of Tradeable Permits —
A Survey of Theory and Practice"
The Australian Bureau of Industry Economics

2. Interview with Mr W Roberts, Legislative Director, Environmental Defense Fund, Washington D.C., 4 June 1991.

(d) "Voluntary Initiatives and the Law"
Kernaghan Webb

1. As used here, a voluntary initiative is a set of non-legislatively required commitments or obligations agreed to by one or more entities, designed to influence or control behaviour, to be applied in a consistent manner or reach a consistent outcome by all parties....

2. The issue of whether or not voluntary initiatives "work" is a separate topic in its own right. ... Voluntary initiatives succeed or fail for a variety of reasons, which may or may not be attributable to their legal dimensions. Nevertheless, the legal implications of volun-

tary initiatives can contribute to their effectiveness of their failure.

3. For example, s. 36(3) of the *Fisheries Act*, Revised Statutes of Canada 1985, c. F-14, as amended; or s. 16(1) of the *Ontario Water Resources Act*, Revised Statutes of Ontario 1990, c. O.40, as amended. For further information about regulatory offences, see K. Webb, "Regulatory Offences, the Mental Element and the *Charter*. Rough Road Ahead," *Ottawa Law Review 21* (1989), pp. 419ff.

4. For example, the ISO 14000 environmental management standards or the Canadian Chemical Producers' Association's Responsible Care initiative. For discussion of ISO standards see ... International Organization for Standardization, *Environmental Management Systems: Specifications with Guidance for Use* (ISO/DIS 14001, June 1995). ...

5. *R. v. Domtar* [1993] Ontario Judgments, No. 3415 (Ontario Court — General Division).

6. See, for example, comments to this effect by an American judge and a New Zealand lawyer in "Reducing legal liability with an ISO 14001 EMS," *Standards New Zealand Environmental Newsletter 1:1* (February 1996), p. 1. See also J. Melnitzer, "Fix environmental snags before seeking ISO 14000 certification," *Law Times*, June 16–22, 1997, pp. 14–15.

7. *R. v. Prospec Chemicals Ltd.* [1996] Alberta Judgment, No. 174, Alberta Provincial Court, January 25, 1996.

8. Environmental lawyer Diane Saxe, reported in Melnitzer, "Fix environmental snags," (n. 6). See also the discussion below on the needs for critical judicial scrutiny of voluntary standards.

9. See E. Orts, "Reflexive Environmental Law," *Northwestern University Law Review 89* (1995), pp. 1281–1283. The environmental compliance programmes must involve a commitment of resources and a "management process" that is reasonably calculated "to achieve and maintain compliance with environmental requirements" (Orts, p. 1282). The draft sentencing guidelines, which will be binding on federal courts, stipulate that firms which have put in place "environmental compliance programmes" can have their penalties reduced by up to 65 per cent (Orts, p. 1282).

10. Brian Wastle, vice-president, Canadian Chemical Producers' Association, has indicated that in the initial phase of development of the Responsible Care voluntary programme, legal counsel had noted the potential liability flowing from adoption of the Responsible Care principles. Personal communication, September 1996.

11. In this vein, some commentators have suggested that companies seeking certification to a voluntary standard should address any known issues of non-compliance with environmental law first, since the disclosure obligations associated with voluntary programmes can render the company vulnerable to regulatory enforcement actions. See Saxe in Melnitzer, "Fix environmental snags," (n. 6).

...

13. *J. Rees*, in *Hostages of Each Other: The Transformation of Nuclear Safety Since Three Mile Island* (Chicago: Chicago University Press, 1994), talks of an industry concerned about its image as a whole, and therefore motivated to identify non-complying parties who could bring the reputation of the sector into disrepute.

...

21. For insights on the perspective of environmental non-governmental organizations concerning voluntary stan-

dards development, see, e.g., T. Burrell, *CSA Environmental Standards Writing: Barriers to Environmental Non-Governmental Organizations Involvement* (Toronto: CIELAP, 1997). ...

22. J. Andy Smith, III, "The CERES Principles: A Voluntary Code for Corporate Environmental Responsibility," *Yale Journal of International Law 18* (1993), p. 309.

23. [In a 1995 New Zealand court case, *Department of Labour* v. *Waste Management NZ Ltd.* [1995] Court Registry Number 40040511262 (District Court, Auckland), the court rejected application of an American standard.]

24. In some instances, regulations may be welcomed by existing industry players because the regulations may create trade barriers that decrease competition from foreign companies, create a level playing field among existing firms, or provide comparative certainty about a standard and the roles of parties vis-à-vis enforcement.

...

28. See generally, Webb and Morrison, "Legal Aspects" (n. 19).

29. For scholarly explorations of the essential elements of contracts, see, for example, G. Fridman, *The Law of Contract in Canada* (Scarborough: Thomson, 1994).

30. See, e.g., *Ripley v. Investment Dealers Association (Business Conduct Committee)* [1991] 108 Nova Scotia Reports (2d) 38 (NS Court of Appeal). The court held that the Association's disciplinary (which generally apply only to government programmes).

31. See, e.g., K. Webb, G. Rhone, and J. Stroud, "The Gap's Code of Conduct for Treatment of Overseas Workers," in [D. Cohen and K. Webb, eds. *Exploring Voluntary Codes and the Marketplace* (Ottawa: Industry Canada, forthcoming).

...

38. For discussion of environmental negligence cases, see E. Swanson and E. Hughes, *The Price of Pollution: Environmental Litigation in Canada* (Edmonton: Environmental Law Centre: 1990), pp. 53–61.

...

40. See, e.g., *Visp Construction v. Scepter Manufacturing Co.* [1991] Ontario Judgments, No. 356 (Ont. Court of Justice — General Division).

41. See, for example, *Reed v. McDermid St. Lawrence Ltd.* (1991) 52 British Columbia Law Reports (2d) 265 (BC Court of Appeal).

42. This is not to suggest that a voluntary initiative would accomplish what a cohesive and coordinated federal-provincial legislative regime could accomplish, but rather that a voluntary initiatives may be more feasible, and in some respects (e.g., in that it specifically involves industry and environmental groups as partners) more successful.

43. Pursuant to Annex of the tbt Agreement, "Standard" is defined as a "document approved by a recognized body, that provides, for common and repeated use, rules, guidelines or characteristics for products or related processes and production methods, with which compliance is not mandatory...."

44. See especially Annex 3 of the tbt Agreement, which sets out a "Code of Good Practice for the Preparation, Adoption, and Application of Standards."

45. See the *Standards Council of Canada Act*, Revised Statutes of Canada 1985, c. S-16, as amended.

46. The Canadian delegation at a recent meeting of the WTO Trade and Environment Committee has sought to have all eco-labelling programmes brought under the WTO umbrella. See WTO Trade and Environment Bulletin No. 11 (9 August 1996), at http:/www.wto.org/ environ/teoII.htm.

47. A non-product related process is a process which does not affect the final outcome (e.g., the look, feel, use, and operation) of a product. Thus, for example, by simply looking at the final wood product of a sustainable forest harvest and one that was made using wood from a clear cut forest.

48. As noted above, the definition of "standard" focuses on a document that provides rules for "products or related processes and production methods...." The question is, what constitutes a rule for product or related production methods? This has yet to be the subject of a definitive statement by the WTO.

...

58. As discussed in Orts, "Reflexive Environmental Law," (n. 9).

D. Monitoring and Enforcement

(a) "Environmental Regulation as a Bargaining Process: The Canadian Approach"
Murray Rankin and Peter Z.R. Finkle

2. The research publications culminated in the final report of the Regulation Reference of the Economic Council of Canada entitled, *Reforming Regulation*, Ottawa, Supply and Services, 1981; chapter 8 deals with "The Regulation of Environmental Pollution." An "overview essay" drawing together the research produced in six case studies and four theme papers commissioned to deal with the environmental regulation component of the Regulation Reference was published as: Thompson, Andrew R., *Environmental Regulation in Canada: an assessment of the regulatory process*, Vancouver, Westwater Research Centre, The University of British Columbia, 1981.

3. Thompson, *id.*, at 33.

4. R.S.C. 1970, c.F-14, as am. See, in particular, s. 33(2).

5. Pollution Control Act, R.S.B.C. 1979, c.332.

6. See, for example, *id.*, s. 25.

7. Under the Clean Air Act, S.C. 1970–71–72, c.47.

8. Thompson, *supra*, note 2 at 34.

9. Dorcey, Anthony H.J., McPhee, M.W., and Sydneysmith, S., *Salmon Protection and the B.C. Coastal Forest Industry: environmental regulation as a bargaining process*, Vancouver, Westwater Research Centre, The University of British Columbia, 1981.

10. For example, the regulation of the disposal of hazardous wastes is hampered by disputes between not only the federal and provincial governments but also between municipalities and regional districts, all of which have overlapping jurisdictions in this field.

11. Schelling, T.C., *The Strategy of Conflict*, New York, 1963.

12. *Id.*, at 131.

13. Dewees, Donald N., *Evaluation of Policies for Regulating Environmental Pollution*, Vancouver, Westwater Research Centre, The University of British Columbia, 1981 at 18.

14. The Final Report of the Fraser River Task Force (July 30, 1980) presented by A. Ackerman, B. Clapp et al.

15. R.S.B.C. 1979, c.332.

16. *Supra*, note 14 at 13 to 15.

17. *E.g.*, Fisheries Act, R.S.C. 1970, c.F-14, s.33(2) as am.

18. See, generally, S. Wexler, "Discretion: The Unacknowledged Side of Law" (1975), 25 *U. of T. L.J.* 120.

19. R.S.O. 1980, c.141.

20. See, especially, Felske, Brian E., *Sulphur Dioxide Regulation and the Canadian Non-Ferrous Metals Industry*, Ottawa, Economic Council of Canada, 1981, especially chapter five.

21. Victor and Burrell, *Environmental Protection Regulation, Water Pollution, and the Pulp and Paper Industry*, a study prepared for the Economic Council of Canada, Regulation Reference, by Victor and Burrell, Economic Consultants, Toronto, 1981.

22. R.S.C. 1970, c.F-14, as am.

23. Pulp and Paper Effluent Regulations, C.R.C. 1978, c.830.

(b) "Persuasion, Penalties, and Prosecution: Administrative v. Criminal Sanctions"
Richard Brown and Murray Rankin

1. P. Nemetz, "The Fisheries Act and Federal-Provincial Environmental Regulation: Duplication or Complementarity?" (1986) 29 *Canadian Public Administration* 401; B. Barton, R. Franson, and A. Thompson, *A Contract Model for Pollution Control* (Vancouver: University of British Columbia, Westwater Research Centre, 1984); A. Thompson, *Environmental Regulation in Canada, An Assessment of the Regulatory Process* (Vancouver: University of British Columbia, Westwater Research Centre, 1980); *Report of the Royal Commission on the Economic Union and Development Prospects for Canada* (Macdonald Report), vol. II (Ottawa: Supply and Services Canada, 1985), chapter 13.

2. G. Reschenthaler, *Occupational Health and Safety in Canada* (Montreal: Institute for Research on Public Policy, 1979); Macdonald Report, chapter 17.

3. K. Hawkins, *Environment and Enforcement* (Oxford: Clarendon Press, 1984); W. Carson, 'White Collar Crime and the Enforcement of Factory Legislation' (1970) to *British Journal of Criminology* 383; W. Carson, *The Other Price of Britain's Oil* (Oxford: Martin Robertson, 1982); D. Vogel, *National Styles of Regulation* (Ithaca: Cornell University Press, 1986).

4. P. Grabosky and J. Braithwaite, *Of Manners Gentle: Enforcement Strategies of Australian Business Regulatory Agencies* (Melbourne: Oxford University Press, 1986); J. Braithwaite and P. Grabosky, *Occupational Health and Safety Commission* (Canberra: Australian Institute of Criminology, 1985).

5. F. Morgenstern, *Deterrence and Compensation: Legal Liability in Occupational Health and Safety* (Geneva: International Labour Office, 1982); P. Downing and K. Hanf, *International Comparisons in Implementing Pollution Control Laws* (Boston: Kluwer-Nijhoff, 1983). The most obvious exception to this general trend in regulatory enforcement is the US Occupational Health and Safety Administration. See E. Bardach and R. Kagan, *Going by the Book: The Problem of Regulatory Unreasonableness* (Philadelphia: Temple University Press, 1982).

6. One exception is Carson, 'White Collar Crime.'

7. See, e.g., the Civil Aviation Act, discussed below.

8. S. Shapiro, "The Road Not Taken: The Elusive Path to Criminal Prosecution for White-Collar Offenders' (1985) 19 *Law and Society Review* 179.

...

17. Similar sorts of penalties are found in taxation and social welfare legislation. Revenue Canada assesses administrative penalties for income tax evasion. The Canada Employment and Immigration Commission also levies such penalties for fraudulent unemployment insurance claims.

18. C. Diver, 'The Assessment and Mitigation of Civil Money Penalties by Federal Administrative Agencies' (1979) 79 *Columbia Law Review* 1435.

19. Diver, in ibid., found 141 federal statutory provisions empowering a federal department or independent agency to assess a monetary penalty.

20. After the period under study, the Waste Management Branch was given authority to implement a ticketing scheme. The Construction Safety Branch of the Ontario Ministry of Labour tickets workers for not wearing personal protective equipment. In Quebec, the Commission de la Santé et de la Sécurité du Travail issues a notice of violation for almost all infractions. An employer or employee who receives such a notice can avoid appearing in court by paying the minimum fine.

21. In 1986–7, OSHA levied 529 penalties for wilful violations, 1,800 for failure to abate violations, 3,505 for repeat violations, and 36,982 for serious violations. Although additional penalties were imposed for violations that do not fit any of these categories, the number is not reported in OSHA's annual summary of inspection data.

22. *R. v. Finlay Forest Industries Ltd.* (1987), 1 WCB (2d) 226 (BCCA).

23. Fifty-one per cent of the prosecutions initiated by the Ontario Industrial Health and Safety Branch in fiscal year 1985–6 were for infractions that caused a fatality or critical injury, as were 55 per cent in fiscal 1987–8. Between 1983–4 and 1986–7, there were sixteen prosecutions in Saskatchewan, all but one in response to an injury or fatality. In Newfoundland, five out of nine prosecutions from 1983 to 1986 involved harm to an employee. The experience abroad is much the same. A study of dealings between British regulators and two hundred firms revealed ten prosecutions, each and every one precipitated by an injury or fatality: Carson, 'White Collar Crime.' Senior Australian regulators rated the occurrence of harm as the most important factor in deciding whether to prosecute an offender: Braithwaite and Grabosky, *Of Manners Gentle.*

24. On a seven-point scale, officers gave the probability of harm a mean score of 6.0 and the severity of possible harm a mean score of 5.8, whereas the actual occurrence of serious harm received a mean score of 5.5.

25. See note 39, below.

26. This survey was conducted as part of the study in this volume by Brooks and Doob. The answers may have been coloured by a suggestion in the question that the offence being penalized by Revenue Canada (negligently under-reporting) is less serious than the one considered by the court (tax evasion).

27. Hawkins, *Environment and Enforcement.*

28. *R. v. Sault Ste Marie* [1978] 2 SCR 1299.

29. See *R. v. Cancoil Thermal Corp.* (1986), 52 CR (3d) 188 (Ont. CA).

30. W. Carson, 'Some Sociological Aspects of Strict Liability and the Enforcement of Factory Legislation' (1970) 33 *Modern Law Review* 396. In accordance with then prevailing usage, Carson uses the term *strict liability* to refer to what is here defined as absolute liability.

31. The eleven hazards on the current 'high risk' list are as follows:
    (1) unsloped and unshored excavations;
    (2) working within ten feet of a power line;
    (3) failure to lockout machinery for service or repair;
    (4) failure to remove snag trees;
    (5) domino falling (using one tree to push over another);
    (6) leaving cut trees up;
    (7) failing to control the fall of a tree;
    (8) working within two tree lengths of falling operations;
    (9) failure to wear seat belts where the possibility of roll-over exists;
    (10) permitting worker exposure to health hazards which are immediately dangerous to life or health; and,
    (11) inadequately protecting workers from health hazards with a high risk of chronic effect.

32. US Department of Labor, Occupational Safety and Health Administration (OSHA), *Field Operations Manual* (Rockville, Md: Government Institutes, 1987).

33. T. Ison, 'The Uses and Limits of Sanctions in Industrial Health and Safety' (1975–6) 2 *Workers' Compensation Reporter* 203. However, Hawkins, *Environment and Enforcement,* argues that cost is not an impediment to prosecutions for environmental offences in Britain.

34. Hawkins, *Environment and Enforcement.*

35. Shapiro, 'The Road Not Taken' 179.

36. OSHA, *Manual.* The penalties assessed by OSHA for wilful violations are much larger on average than those levied by the Workers' Compensation Board, while OSHA's penalties for other offences are much smaller on average. In 1986–7, the average penalty for 529 wilful violations was $23,978 and for 36,982 serious violations $230.

37. While Swaigen and Bunt contend that the courts do levy larger fines against large companies than small ones for environmental offences, they provide little data to support this assertion: J. Swaigen and G. Bunt, *Sentencing in Environmental Cases* (Ottawa: Law Reform Commission of Canada, 1985) 25–8.

38. Hybrid schemes fall in the middle ground between administrative penalties and criminal prosecutions. These schemes might appear at first blush to offer all of the advantages of the administrative process for uncontested cases. Yet the decision not to contest a penalty is made in the shadow of the courts which retain exclusive authority to impose a sanction.

39. Two studies of enforcement of environmental regulations in Britain concluded that the adverse publicity generated by prosecutions was an effective deterrent: Hawkins, *Environmental and Enforcement*; and Y. Brittan, *The Impact of Water Pollution Control Legislation: A Case Study of Fifty Dischargers* (Oxford: Centre for Socio-Legal Studies, 1984). See also B. Fisse and J. Braithwaite, *The Impact of Publicity on Corporate Offenders* (Albany: State University of New York Press, 1983). For a general discussion of the role that

stigma plays in deterrence see C.R. Tittle, *Sanctions and Social Deviance: The Question of Deterrence* (New York: Praeger, 1980).

(c) "A Case for Strict Enforcement of Environmental Statutes"
John Z. Swaigen

1. Weiler, Paul: "The Reform of Punishment," in *Studies on Sentencing*, Law Reform Commission of Canada, Ottawa, 1974.
2. *R v City of Sault Ste. Marie* 1976, 13 O.R. (2d) 113; *R v City of Sault Ste. Marie* 1978, 2 S.C.R. 1299.

(d) "The Impact of Prosecution of Corporation and Their Officers and Directors upon Regulatory Compliance by Corporations"
Dianne Saxe

1. *R. v. Cotton Felts Ltd.* (1982), C.C.C. (3d) 287, C.E.S.H.G. 95, 056 (Ont. C.A.).
2. Pulp and paper processing, iron and steel smelting and refining, cement and ready-mix concrete manufacturing, lime production, the auto industry and petroleum refining account for a high proportion of existing pollution; the same industries make important contributions to the gross products; Economics Council of Canada, Reforming Regulation, p. 84.
3. Much environmental degradation occurs as a result of the activities of individuals: e.g., burning fossil fuels to power their cars and heat their homes; pouring harsh chemicals such as toilet cleaner and solvents into the sewers; and creating mountains of garbage. Municipalities manage waste disposal and sewage treatment, some well but others very poorly. Other government activities can also be significant sources of environmental degradation, e.g., road construction, harbour dredging and dumping, and national defence.
4. Clinard and Yeager, Corporate Crime (1980), at p. 299.
5. Corporations have had at least 7 spills of toxic gas larger and more toxic than Bhopal; and 20 oil spills larger than that of the Exxon Valdez: Corporate Crime Reporter, April 3, 1989, p. 17 and May 8, 1989, p. 3.
6. E.g., it is likely to be easier and cheaper to control emissions from a single large factory stack than from 50,000 individual cars.

8. For discussions of the weaknesses of prosecution as a tool of regulatory compliance, see Grad, *ibid.*, and Barton, Franson and Thompson, A Contract Model for Pollution Control (1984).
9. In Ontario, there are approximately 300 prosecutions per year compared to nearly 50,000 inspections and thousands of permits, licences and certificates of approval; see Saxe, Inspections and Searches in the Environmental Context (1989), Appendix 1.

11. Law Reform Commission of Canada, Political Economy of Environmental Hazards (1984), Protection of Life Series Study Paper.
12. *Re Industrial Hygiene*, Decision No. 167 (1975), 2 W.C.R. 234 at 252.

25. (1980), 10 C.E.L.R. 43 (R.T. Terr. Ct.).
26. E.g., *Re Eagle Disposal Systems Ltd. and Min. of Env.* (1984), 47 O.R. (2d) 332, 12 D.L.R. (4th) 639, 13 C.C.C. (3d) 351, dismissing appeal from 44 O.R. (2d) 518, 5 D.L.R. (4th) 70, 9 C.C.C. (3d) 500, 13 C.E.L.R. 13 (C.A.).
27. Clinard and Yeager studied 582 of the largest American corporations engaged in manufacturing wholesale, retail and service industries. In the two years of 1975 and 1976, over 66 per cent were charged with federal offences; state and local offences were not studied. The average firm that was charged at all was charged more than four times. Of the 1,553 cases, only 56 corporate officers and directors were convicted; 91 per cent of those were for anti-trust violations; *supra*, note 4, at pp. 113, 279.

    Marilyn Matthews studied the regulatory offences enforced by only four federal offences, thus excluding anti-trust, employee health and safety, tax and many other offences, and again excluding all state and local offences. Even on this very limited base, she found that 196 of the 355 most profitable U.S. manufacturing companies committed offences between 1973 and 1980. 67 per cent were repeat offenders; "Corporate Crimes: External vs. Internal Regulation" University of California, Ph. D. thesis, 1984.

34. Some respondents objected to this question, saying, for example, that "No responsible director would authorize pollution". The question was asked because in a number of environmental cases, this is exactly what the directors did: e.g., *R. v. Jetco Mfg.* (1986), 1 C.E.L.R. (N.S.) 79, reversed 1 C.E.L.R. (N.S.) 243, 57 O.R. (2d) 776, 31 C.C.C. (3d) 171, 18 O.A.C. 313; *R. v. B.E.S.T. Plating Shoppe* (1986), 1 C.E.L.R. (N.S.) 85, reversed in part 1 C.E.L.R. (N.S.) 145, 59 O.R. (2d) 145, 19 C.O.C. (2d) 174, 32 C.C.C. (3d) 417, 21 O.A.C. 62; as well as the *J.B. Carroll Elec. Ltd.* and *Kemtron Inc.* cases.
35. Respondents indicated their response to each policy on a five-point scale: "yes", "probably", "possibly", "unlikely", or "no". Those responding "yes" or "probably" were aggregated as summarized in Table 1.

    Matched pair t-tests of the five-point scales were calculated. On the question of environmental expenditures, condition 1 was significantly different from condition 2 ($t=2.71$, $df=85$, $p=.010$) and from condition 3 ($t=2.95$, $df=37$, $p=.005$). Condition 4 was significantly different from condition 3 ($t=-2.32$, $df=37$, $p=.26$).

    On the question of resignation, condition 1 was significantly different from condition 2 ($t=2.75$, $df=40$, $p=.009$), from condition 3 ($t=3.45$, $df=30$, $p=.001$), and from condition 4 ($t=5.60$, $df=40$, $p=.001$). Condition 4 was also significantly different from condition 2 ($t=3.83$, $df=40$, $p<.001$), and condition 3 ($t=3.67$, $df=40$, $p<.001$).

    On the question of ceasing to operate in the jurisdiction, condition 1 was significantly different from condition 2 ($t=3.67$, $df=39$, $p=.001$), from condition 3 ($t=3.98$, $df=39$, $p<.001$), and from condition 4 ($t=5.80$, $df=39$, $p<.001$). Condition 4 was also significantly different from condition 2 ($t=3.79$, $df=39$, $p=.001$), and condition 3 ($t=-3.56$, $df=39$, $p=.001$).
36. Although several respondents stated that the hypotheticals did not contain enough details on which to found decisions.

37. Except for the question as to whether to advise the board of the availability of the new, less noisy machine: p<.038.
38. Respondents indicated their response to seven of the eight questions on the same five-point scale, from "yes" to "no", referred to in footnote 8. These were coded as 1 to 5; in each case, a higher number indicated more environmentally protective actions. The eighth question was answered by choosing one of three alternative actions. For scoring purposes, the two environmentally protective alternatives were recoded as 2, and continuing to operate the plant notwithstanding its environmental risk was recoded as 1. An analysis of variance was then performed of the aggregate scores (the Environment Protection Score) by the assumption which each respondent had been asked to make.
39. Working paper 16 (1976), at p. 16.
40. [1978] 2 S.C.R. 1299, 3 C.R. (3d) 30, 85 D.L.R. (3d) 161, 40 C.C.C. (2d) 353, 7 C.E.L.R. 53, 21 N.R. 295 [Ont.]

(e) "Weak Environmental Law Enforcement in Canada: A well-kept secret" David Donnelly and Leah Hagreen

1. "Petawawa man gets jail sentence for illegal dumping of waste" press release <www.ene.gov.on.ca/envision/news/0004.thm>, September 27, 2000 — 60 days in jail for illegally dumping solid and liquid waste in Renfrew County, Ontario.
2. Other means of preventing pollution include persuasion, formal voluntary compliance programs, terms and conditions attached to licenses and permits, binding orders, injunctions, administrative penalties and other means.
3. For example, ISO 14000 corporate environmental management programs are often taken as evidence of a company's intention to comply with environmental laws.
4. "Enforcement agencies need to develop the measurement tools and methodologies to link enforcement efforts to environmental improvement, in order to explain better the role enforcement plays in achieving broader environmental and public welfare objectives." Commission for Environmental Cooperation, *Special Report on Enforcement Activities* (Montreal: Commission for Environmental Cooperation, 2000), p. 30.
5. Commissioner Ligeti stated, "In recent years, Ontario has joined a global trend toward relying on voluntary approaches to environmental protection rather than on government regulation. However, our review of these approaches during 1997 shows that voluntary agreements in Ontario are usually negotiated without any involvement of the public or environmental groups." In Environmental Commissioner of Ontario, *Annual Report 1997: Open Doors — Ontario's Environmental Bill of Rights* (April 1998), p. 8.
6. CEDF Enforcement Paper, "In 1993–94, 75% of municipal water treatment plants in Ontario were inspected compared to just 29% in 1999–2000" [*The Toronto Star*, December 22, 2001]. From our interviews with MOE officials, we found that for two to three years prior to the Walkerton tragedy, inspection of water treatment plants were conducted approximately once every three to four years. Implementation of the recommendations was limited or non-existent, as were

follow-up and monitoring efforts. All plants were inspected in the year 2000/2001 and MOE officials confirm that inspections will now be conducted on an annual basis.
7. Ontario Medical Association, "The Illness Costs of Air Pollution in Ontario," (Toronto: OMA, 2000).
8. North American Working Group on Enforcement and Compliance Cooperation, "Special Report on Enforcement Activities" (Commission for Environmental Cooperation, June 2001), 3-11.
9. J. Flagel, "Administrative Monetary Penalties (AMPs): The Next Logical Step in Environmental Regulatory Law" Legal Emissions" (Toronto: Ministry of the Environment, 1998), p. 9.
10. S. 184 AEPEA and s. 74 EBR.

References

Ontario Ministry of the Environment. 1995. Compliance Guideline, Guideline F-2, Revised, June 16.

Alberta Environmental Protection, Pollution Control Division. *Business Plan 1995–96 to 1997–98* (Edmonton: Alberta Environmental Protection).

Bilson, G. 1984. "Cholera and Public Heath in Canada." *Canadian Journal of Public Health*, 75(5): 352–55.

British Columbia Ministry of the Environment, Lands and Parks. 1994. "Procedure for Rating Compliance of Permits and Regulated Sites Using the Waste System" (Draft).

Burgess v. *Woodstock* (1955), 4 DLR 615 (Ont. H.C.J.)

Caccia, C. 1998. Canadian Environmental Law Association, *Brief to the Standing Committee on Environment and Sustainable Development re: Enforcing Canada's Pollution Laws* (3 February 1998).

Duffy, A. 2000. "Clean air, water outrank lifestyle, health care: poll," *The Ottawa Citizen* (19 June) A1.

Estrin, D. and J. Swaigen. 1979. *Environment on Trial: A Handbook of Ontario Environmental Law*, p. 41. Toronto: Canadian Environmental Law Research Foundation.

Estrin, D. and J. Swaigen, 1993. *Environment on Trial: A Handbook of Ontario Environmental Law*, 2d ed., p. 530. Toronto: Canadian Institute for Environmental Law and Policy.

Environment Canada, 1988. *Canadian Environmental Protection Act*: Enforcement and Compliance Policy 5.

Flagel, J. 1998. "Administrative Monetary Penalties (AMPs): The Next Logical Step in Environmental Regulatory Law" *Legal Emissions*. Toronto: Ministry of the Environment.

Gallon, G. 1998. "Black Day for the Environment" *The Montreal Gazette* (31 January).

Gonthier, C. 1998. "Testimony," in *Enforcing Canada's Pollution Laws: The Public Interest Must Come First! Third Report*. Standing Committee on Environment and Sustainability (May), p. 9.

Hall, J. 1998. "Canadians want laws to be meaner and greener 30-country poll finds majority favours tougher protection for the environment," *The Toronto Star* (5 June) A2.

House of Commons Standing Committee on Environment and Sustainable Development. 1995. *It's About Our Health! Towards Pollution Prevention: CEPA Revisited*, pp. 247–49. Ottawa: Public Works, Canadian Communications Group..

Kostuch v. *Alberta (Attorney General)* (1995), A.J. No. 866.

Miller, J. 1994. "Citizen Suits: Part III" in *Environmental Law Review* 19, 10407 at 10424–25.

North American Commission for Environmental Cooperation, 2000. *Special Report on Enforcement Activities* (Montreal: Commission for Environment Cooperation), p. 30.

Office of the Provincial Auditor of Ontario. 2000. *Special Report: Accountability and Value for Money*, p. 116. Ontario: Queen's Printer.

Saxe, D. 1990a. "The Impact of Prosecutions of Corporations and Their Officers and Directors upon Regulatory Compliance by Corporations" *Journal of Environmental Law and Practice*, 1(1): 91.

Saxe, D. 1990b. *Environmental Offences: Corporate Responsibility and Executive Liability*, pp. 27–28. Toronto: Canada Law Book.

Sokolov, L. 2001. "Submissions of the Safe Drinking Water Coalition on Parts 1A and 1B of the Walkerton Inquiry" (Toronto: Canadian Environmental Defence Fund).

Stephens v. *Richmond Hill* (1955), 4 DLR 572 (Ont. H.C.J.).

Swaigen, J.Z. 1985. "A Case for Strict Enforcement of Environmental Statutes" in L. Duncan ed., *Environmental Enforcement* (Edmonton: Environmental Law Centre).

(f) "Monitoring and Enforcement of Environmental Policy"
Mark A. Cohen

6. Despite this widely held belief, several U.S. General Accounting Office reports (1979, 1990) suggest that these official estimates may be too high. For example, one study in 1979 found that only 200 out of 921 sources thought to be in compliance actually were. A more recent study in 1990 suggested that EPA's estimate of 86% compliance by major air pollution sources was too optimistic. Nevertheless, the 'stylized fact' that the vast majority of firms are in compliance persists.

7. Livernois and McKenna (1997) offer a somewhat different reason for compliance based on the fact that the enforcement authority offers a significant incentive for self-reporting violations....

8. Notwithstanding the above discussion, there is no necessary connection between the level of fines actually observed and the level of compliance. For example, Harford (1987b) provides a model in which high compliance rates result from high monitoring rates and no fines being imposed.

9. Although Arora and Gangopadhyay (1995) model firms that do better than regulatory standards, there is little difference between their model and one in which firms either comply or violate the law. They model "environmental leaders" as being of some value to a segment of consumers. In a world with only firms that comply or violate the laws, the complying firm could be thought of as an environmental leader. Thus, except for the threat of government-imposed sanctions, the underlying theories of why a firm might comply with regulations and why it might overcomply are virtually indistinguishable.

...

14. Magat, Krupnick and Harrington (1986) operationalize a model of net political support maximization in the context of EPA and the stringency of environmental regulations. However, they do not consider enforcement issues.

15. See Section 4.1.2 for a discussion of Deily and Gray's empirical results.

16. Harford (1985) makes this same point and corrects some errors in the Lee (1983) formulation. However, the basic result that budget maximization leads to excessive monitoring still holds.

...

38. Magat and Viscusi (1990) estimate current pollution levels as a function of last period's inspection rate. One reason for ignoring current period inspections is that they are endogenous. Indeed, one would expect and hope that enforcement authorities determine their enforcement priorities based on prior experience with each company, current market conditions that might affect compliance, etc.

39. A "specific" deterrent effect is one that applies to a specific person or firm that has been reprimanded for a past activity and subsequently refrains from that activity. Because of the difference in data availability, Cohen (1987) does not test for a specific deterrent effect, but instead finds a "general" deterrent effect — whereby the monitoring activities of the Coast Guard have an effect on the aggregate volume levels of oil spills.

...

41. In many ways, this is analogous to setting the regulatory standard itself. By requiring a more costly pollution control standard, the government raises the marginal value of noncompliance and hence affects enforcement....

42. However, this may not always be true. In the U.S., for example, charging a corporation with a crime makes it easier for the government to obtain documents that might provide evidence against corporate officials who were involved in the criminal activity.

43. In 1991, the U.S. Sentencing Commission issued mandatory guidelines for judges to follow in the case of organizations convicted of federal crimes. However, it did not include environmental crimes in the penalty provisions of these guidelines. Thus, judges are still free to impose any monetary penalty they see fit (up to the statutory maximum).

Bibliography

Arora, S. and S. Gangopadhyay. (1995). "Toward a Theoretical Model of Voluntary Overcompliance." *Journal of Economic Behavior and Organization* 28, 289–309.

Brehm, J. and J.T. Hamilton. (1996). "Noncompliance in Environmental Reporting: Are Violators Ignorant, or Evasive, of the Law?" *American Journal of Political Science*. 40(2), 444–77.

Cohen, M.A. (1992) "Environmental Crime and Punishment: Legal/Economic Theory and Empirical Evidence on Enforcement of Federal Environmental Statutes" *Journal of Criminal Law & Criminology* 82(4), 1054–1108.

Cohen, M.A., and P.H. Rubin. (Fall 1985). "Private Enforcement of Public Policy." *Yale Journal on Regulation* 3, 167–93.

Dau-Schmidt, K.G. (1990) "An Economic Analysis of the Criminal Law as a Preference-Shaping Policy" *Duke Law Journal* 1.

Deily, M.E. and W.B. Gray. (1991). "Enforcement of Pollution Regulation in a Declining Industry." *Journal of Environmental Economics and Management* 21(2), 260–274.

Dion, C., P. Lanoie, and B. Laplante. (1988). "Monitoring of Pollution Regulation: Do Local Conditions Matter?" *Journal of Regulatory Economics* (forthcoming).

Diver, C.S. (Summer 1980). "A Theory of Regulatory Enforcement." *Public Policy* 28(3), 257–299.

Downing, P. and J. Kimball. (1982). "Enforcing Pollution Control Laws in the United States", *Policy Studies Journal* 11, no. 1.

Fenn, P., and C.G. Veljanovski. (December 1988). "A Positive Economic Theory of Regulatory Enforcement." *The Economic Journal* 98, 1055–1070.

Fullerton, D. and T.C. Kinnaman (1995) "Garbage, Recycling, and Illicit Burning or Dumping" *Journal of Environmental Economics and Management* 29, 78–91.

Garvie, D. and A. Keeler. (1994). "Incomplete Enforcement with Endogenous Regulatory Choice." *Journal of Public Economics* 55, 141–162.

Gray, W.B. and M.E. Deily (1996). "Compliance and Enforcement: Air Pollution Regulation in the U.S. Steel Industry." *Journal of Environmental Economics and Management* 31(1): 96–111.

Hamilton, J.T. (1996). "Going by the (Informal) Book: The EPA's Use of Informal Rules in Enforcing Hazardous Waste Laws." In G.D. Libecap (ed.) *Advances in the Study of Entrepreneurship, Innovation, and Economic Growth.* 7, 109–155.

Hamilton J.T. (1995). "Pollution as News: Media and Stock Market Reactions to the Toxics Release Inventory Data." *Journal of Environmental Economics and Management.* 28, 98–113.

Hammitt, J.K. and P. Reuter. (1988). *Measuring and Deterring Illegal Disposal of Hazardous Waste: A Preliminary Assessment.* Santa Monica, CA: RAND.

Harford, J.D. (1991). "Measurement Error and State-Dependent Pollution Control Enforcement." *Journal of Environmental Economics and Management* 21, 67–81.

Harford, J.D. and W. Harrington. (1991). "A Reconsideration of Enforcement Leverage when Penalties are Restricted." *Journal of Public Economics* 45(3), 391–95.

Harrington, W. (1988). "Enforcement Leverage When Penalties Are Restricted." *Journal of Public Economics* 37, 29–53.

Harrison, K. (1995). "Is Cooperation the Answer? Canadian Environment in Comparative Context" *Journal of Policy Analysis and Management* 14(2), 221–244.

Helland, E. (1998). "The Enforcement of Pollution Control Laws: Inspections, Violations, and Self-Reporting." *The Review of Economics and Statistics* 141–53.

Keeler, A.G. (1995). "Regulatory Objectives and Enforcement Behavior." *Environmental and Resource Economics* 6, 73–85.

Konar, S. and M.A. Cohen. (1997). "Information as Regulation: The Effect of Community Right to Know Laws on Toxic Emission." *Journal of Environmental Economics and Management* 32, 109–124.

Landes, W.M. and R.A. Posner. (1975). "The Private Enforcement of Law." *Journal of Legal Studies* 4, 1–46.

Laplante, B. and P. Rilstone (1996). "Environmental Inspections and Emissions of the Pulp and Paper Industry in Quebec." *Journal of Environmental Economics and Management* 31(1).

Lear, K.K. (1998). "An Empirical Examination of EPA Administrative Penalties," Working Paper, Kelley School of Business, Indiana University (March).

Lee, D.R. (1983). "Monitoring and Budget Maximization in the Control of Pollution." *Economic Inquiry* 21, 565–575.

Liu, P.C. (1995). "Regulator Inspection and Violation Deterrence Under Clean Water Act Regulation of Pulp and Paper Mill Water Pollution." Ph.D. Dissertation, Standard University (August).

Magat, W. and W.K. Viscusi. (1990). "Effectiveness of the EPA's Regulatory Enforcement: The Case of Industrial Effluent Standards." *Journal of Law and Economics* 33, 331–360.

Nadeau, L.W. (1997). "EPA Effectiveness at Reducing the Duration of Plant-Level Noncompliance" *Journal of Environmental Economics and Management* 34, 54–78.

Peltzman, S. (1976). "Toward a More General Theory of Regulation" *Journal of Law and Economics* 19(2), 211–240.

Russell, C.S., W. Harrington, and W.J. Vaughn. (1986). "Enforcing Pollution Control Laws." *Resources for the Future.*

Selden, T.M. and M.E. Terrones. (1993). "Environmental Legislation and Enforcement: A Voting Model Under Asymmetric Information." *Journal of Environmental Economics and Management* 24(3), 212–228.

Sigman, H. (1998). "Midnight Dumping: Public Policies and Illegal Disposal of Used Oil." *RAND Journal of Economics.* 29(1) 157–178.

Sullivan, A.M. (1987). "Policy Options for Toxics Disposal: Laissez-Faire, Subsidization, and Enforcement." *Journal of Environmental Economics and Management* 14, 58–71.

(g) "Taking Matters Into Their Own Hands: The role of citizens in Canadian pollution control enforcement" Kernaghan Webb

1. *Waste Not Wanted Inc.* v. *R.* (1987) 1 F.C. 239, 2 C.E.L.R. (N.S.) 24 at 57, Collier, J. (T.D.). Note that the decision concerned an action in nuisance, whereas the focus of this article is on citizen enforcement of regulatory pollution control laws.
2. P.L. Bryden, "Public Interest Intervention in the Courts" (1987) 66 Can. Bar Rev. 490 at 492. Note that Bryden's article and comments are not directed specifically towards citizen enforcement of regulatory laws.
3. The subject matter of this article is citizen prosecution of regulatory offences. Regulatory offences, for the purposes of this article, are penal offences adjudicated upon the ordinary courts which normally do not require proof of subjective intent to obtain a conviction and are usually part of administrative regimes which control rather than prohibit a particular activity. This definition is based primarily on the analysis of Dickson J. (as he then was) in *R.* v. *City of Sault Ste. Marie* (1977), [1978] 2 S.C.R. 1299, 40 C.C.C. (2d) 353 at 373–75 [hereinafter *Sault Ste. Marie* cited to C.C.C.].

   The two most prevalent regulatory offence types are those of "strict" and "absolute" liability. A strict liability offence was defined by Dickson J. in *Sault Ste. Marie* as one where an accused will be convicted upon proof of the *actus reus*, unless the accused establishes on a balance of probabilities that due diligence or reasonable care was exercised, or that a reasonable mistake of fact occurred. Absolute liability offences were defined as those where the accused will be convicted upon proof of the *actus reus* (*supra* at 373–74). According to E. Swanson & E. Hughes, *The Price of Pollution: Environmental Litigation in Canada* (Edmonton: Environmental Law Centre, 1990) at 159, "the vast majority of environmental offences are ones of strict liability." Recently, the likelihood of certain absolute and strict liability offences withstanding s.7 and s.11 *Canadian Charter of Rights and Freedoms*, Part I of the *Constitution Act, 1982*, being Schedule B of the *Canada Act 1982* (U.K.), 1982, c.11 [hereinafter *Charter*], challenges has been questioned: see *e.g.*, K. Webb, "Regulatory Offences, the Mental Element and the *Charter*: Rough Road Ahead" (1989) 21 Ottawa L. Rev. 419 [hereinafter "Regulatory Offences"].

4. In *R. ex rel. Howe* v. *Cyanamid Inc.* (1981), 3 F.P.R. 151 [hereinafter *Cyanamid*], government officials alerted a concerned citizen to the possibility of private prosecution actions, and provided technical assistance and witnesses in the subsequent trial. In *R.* v. *Crown Zellerbach Properties Ltd.* (1981), 3 F.P.R. 84 (B.C. Prov. Ct), aff'd (1983) 3 F.P.R. 107 (B.C. Co.Ct) [hereinafter *Crown Zellerbach*] a government official actually "set up" the citizen prosecution, and then subsequently the Crown conducted the trial. See below for further details. As to the representativeness of these cases, see below at 801 & 815–17.

...

6. Discussion of basic concepts of democracy derived primarily from R. Jackson, D. Jackson & N. Baxter-Moore, *Politics in Canada: Culture, Institutions, Behaviour and Public Policy* (Scarborough: Prentice-Hall, 1986) at 24–25.
7. *Ibid.* at 24.
8. See, *e.g.*, E.F. Schumacher, *Small is Beautiful: A Study of Economics as if People Really Mattered* (London: Abacus, 1974), especially c.5.
9. For a similar definition, see R. Parenteau, *Public Participation in Environmental Decision-Making* (Ottawa: Supply and Services Canada, 1988) at 6. Parenteau also notes that participation may serve the political function of obtaining public support for decisions.
10. C. Pateman, *Participation and Democratic Theory* (New York: Cambridge University Press, 1970) at 69.
11. The phrase "legal and administrative processes" is intended to encompass both constitutionally and legislatively sanctioned techniques, such as elections, public hearings, private prosecutions, judicial review, and administrative activities, such as the practice of consultation prior to the passage of new policies or regulations, and complaints procedures relating to enforcement.
12. G. Isaac, *La procédure administrative non contentieuse* (Paris: Librarie générale de droit et de jurisprudence, 1968) at 240, para. 231, trans. in R. Dussault & L. Borgeat, *Administrative Law: A Treatise*, 2d ed. (trans. M. Rankin) (Toronto: Carswell, 1985), vol. 1 at 278 n. 247.
13. *Supra*, note 3.
14. A.C. Cairns, "The Canadian Constitutional Experiment" (1984) 9 Dalhousie L.J. 87 at 87.

...

25. The situation with respect to Nurse Nelles in Toronto is perhaps the best example of the damage which can take place to an accused who is eventually found to have been wrongly accused of a crime. In fact, the Nelles affair lead to an action for malicious prosecution against the Crown. See *Nelles* v. *Ontario*, [1989] 2 S.C.R. 170, 60 D.L.R. (4th) 609 [hereinafter *Nelles*], which set out the parameters for a successful prosecution. I am indebted to Mr. Glenn Gilmour of the Law Reform Commission of Canada for his assistance con-

cerning the *Nelles* case and *Criminal Code*, R.S.C. 1985, c.C-46 [hereinafter *Criminal Code*] provisions.
26. More specifically, regarding protection of potential accuseds at the pre-arrest (investigation) stage see, *e.g.*, *Criminal Code*, part VI concerning invasion of privacy by the use of wiretaps. See also procedures circumscribing the issuance of search warrants, especially ss 487 and 487.1. Concerning the limits of powers to arrest, the circumstances in which releases from custody can take place and the judicial obligation to release on bail, see ss 495–499, 515, 520 & 522. With respect to protections at trial see, *e.g.*, ss 603 and 605.
27. Ss 7–15. Regarding recent applications of s.7 and s.11 to regulatory offences see "Regulatory Offences," *supra*, note 3.

...

31. On this point, see recent initiative of the B.C. Ministry of Environment, described *infra*, note 290 and accompanying text.

...

42. *Criminal Code*, s.579(1). See, *Re Dowson and R.* (1980), 57 CCC (2d) 140, 19 C.R. (3d) 384 (Ont. H.C.), aff'd (1981), 24 C.R. (3d) 139, 62 C.C.C. (2d) 286, rev'd [1983] 2 S.C.R. 144, 35 C.R. (3d) 289; *R.* v. *Hauser*, [1979] 1 S.C.R. 984, 98 D.L.R. (3d) 193; *Controlling Criminal Prosecutions*, *ibid.* at 18 & 65.
43. See *Controlling Criminal Prosecutions*, *ibid.* at 11–15.
44. *Ibid.* at 11–12.

...

51. With respect to Alberta, see I. Cartwright, "Practice Note — A Private Prosecution in Alberta — A Painful Process" (1990) 1 J. Env. L. & Practice 110 at 110. For British Columbia, see Owen, *supra*, note 28 at 90–91.
52. *I.e.*, in the sense that private prosecutions are not merely constraints on improper government action.
53. Burns, *supra*, note 5 at 296. See an almost identical sentiment expressed in *Private Prosecutions*, *supra*, note 5 at 3.
54. To put it another way, assuming both private prosecutors and Crown prosecutors are competent, dedicated to their task, and in possession of the evidence needed to prove guilt, the technical constraints of the trial proof of guilt process require the prosecutor to closely follow certain steps. These include: proof of the *actus reus*, proof that the accused committed the *actus reus*, and, in the case of a strict liability offence where the defence of due diligence is in dispute, proof that the accused did not exercise reasonable care. These constraints do not provide prosecutors with the type of latitude which would facilitate the communication to the judge of a distinctive citizen, as opposed to Crown, perspective.

...

146. Now R.S.C. 1985, c.F-14 [hereinafter *Fisheries Act*].
147. In addition to the private prosecutions set out in the case descriptions below, the following other *Fisheries Act* prosecutions initiated by citizens have been reported: *R.* v. *Panarctic Oils Ltd.* (1983), 3 F.P.R. 429, 12 C.E.L.R. 78 (Terr. Ct); *R.* v. *Greater Vancouver Regional District and Greater Vancouver Sewage and Drainage District* (1981), 3 F.P.R. 134 (B.C. Prov. Ct); *F.C. Bellas* v. *A.G. British Columbia* (sub nom. *Re: Riley Creek*) (1980), 3 F.P.R. 58 (B.C. Prov. Ct). In 1986, a private prosecution with respect to Eldorado Mining Ltd. at Baker Lake Saskatchewan was stayed. In 1988, a private prosecution in relation to a permit

to construct under the Alberta *Clean Water Act*, R.S.A. 1980, c.C-13 [hereinafter *Clean Water Act*] was stayed. In that same year, a *Fisheries Act* private prosecution in relation to the Old Man Dam was stayed and another concerning the same Dam project was stayed in early 1990. Another action with respect to the same Dam activity is currently active. Information concerning these actions obtained from Mr. John MacLatchy, federal Department of Environment, and Ms. Jillian Flett, Alberta Ministry of the Environment.

148. This is particularly significant for those jurisdictions where consent of the Attorney General is required before private prosecutions can be entered; see, *e.g.*, New Brunswick *Clean Environment Act*, R.S.N.B. 1973, s.33.2, and Newfoundland *Department of Environment Act*, S.N. 1981, s.49 (consent of Minister required).

149. See, *e.g.*, *Cyanamid* case description below at 803.

150. Discussion of this characteristic of the current federal-provincial approach to emissions control follows the case studies below.

151. For example, penalties under the *Fisheries Act*, s.40(2) for first offences are fines not to exceed $50,000, whereas the comparable penalty under the Alberta *Clean Water Act*, s.19 is only $25,000.

152. *Penalties and Proceeds Forfeitures Regulations*, C.R.C. 1978, c.827 [hereinafter *Forfeitures Regulations*].

153. Information for this case description was obtained from the Canadian Environmental Law Association and Department of Environment files, newspaper accounts (as noted *infra*), a telephone conversation with Dr. Brockman, and the case decision, *supra*, note 4. An earlier version of this case description appeared in K. Webb, *Industrial Water Pollution Control and the Environmental Protection Service*, Law Reform Commission of Canada Background Study (1983) [unpublished][hereinafter *Industrial Water Pollution*].

154. R.S.O. 1980, c.141 [hereinafter *E.P.A.*].

155. R.S.O. 1980, c.361.

156. Letter from Mr. Neil Mulvaney. Director of Legal Services Branch, Ontario Ministry of Environment, to Professor M. Dickman, dated April 10, 1979.

157. Letter from the Honourable James Auld, Ontario Minister of Natural Resources, dated December 19, 1980; Letter from the Honourable Harry Parrot, Ontario Minister of Environment, to Mr. Robert Timberg, Counsel for C.E.L.A., dated January 5, 1981.

158. Letter from the Honourable John Roberts, federal Minister of Environment, to Mr. Robert Timberg, C.E.L.A., dated January 5, 1981.

159. *E.g.* see "Chemical Producer Charged by Biologist" *The [Toronto] Globe and Mail* (3 March 1981) A5; "Trout Die in Discharge From Plant, Court told" *The [Toronto] Globe and Mail* (24 June 1981) A2; "Firm is fined $1 for pollution, given a month to pay by the judge" *The [Toronto] Globe and Mail* (29 August 1981) A12.

160. *Supra*, note 4 at 152.

161. *Ibid.*

162. *Ibid.*

163. *Ibid.*

164. *Ibid.* at 153–54.

165. *Ibid.* at 154.

166. Most notably a lack of chemical analysis, so that there was no conclusive evidence of ammonia in the effluent other than a notable odour detected at the time. *Ibid.*

167. *Ibid.*

168. *Ibid.* at 158.

169. *Ibid.* at 159.

170. *Ibid.*

171. *Ibid.* at 160.

172. *Ibid.* at 160–61.

173. *Ibid.* at 161.

174. Telephone conversation with Prof. Dickman, October 9, 1990.

175. *Supra*, note 4. Information concerning *Crown Zellerbach* derived from federal Department of Environment files, L. Kolankiewicz, *Implementation of B.C.'s Pollution Control Act in the Lower Fraser River* (M.Sc. Thesis, Faculty of Graduate Studies, School of Community and Regional Planning, University of British Columbia, 1981) [unpublished], and telephone conversations with federal officials. An earlier version of this case description was included in *Industrial Water Pollution*, *supra*, note 153.

176. S. Fournier, "River Crusader wins $14,000" *The Province* (30 April 1981) 1.

177. *Crown Zellerbach*, *supra*, note 4 at 105.

178. *Ibid.*

179. Fournier, *supra*, note 176.

180. *R. v. Crown Zellerbach Properties Ltd.* (1984), 4 F.P.R. 117.

181. *Ibid.* at 127.

182. *Ibid.* at 125.

183. Information for *Suncor* case study was derived from federal Department of Environment files, three reported decisions (*R. v. Suncor Inc.* (1982), 3 F.P.R. 264 (Alta. Prov. Ct) [hereinafter *Suncor 1982*], *R. v. Suncor Inc.* (1983), 4 F.P.R. 409 (Alta. Prov. Ct) [hereinafter *Suncor 1985*]) and Environmental Law Centre, *Enforcement of Environmental Law in Alberta: A Critical Examination of Alberta Government Law, Policy and Practice with Illustration from the Case R. v. Suncor Inc.* (Edmonton: Environmental Law Centre, Alberta Law Foundation, 1983) [hereinafter E.L.C.].

184. *Suncor 1985*, *ibid.* at 411.

185. *Suncor 1983*, *supra*, note 183 at 274.

186. *Suncor 1985*, *supra*, note 183 at 413.

187. *Ibid.* at 415.

188. *Suncor 1983*, *supra*, note 183 at 295. Horricks, Prov. Ct. J., stated:

> It [Suncor] was the first one of its type, and clearly it suffers from defects of design with respect to the treatment of wastewater that would not be permitted now in the light of experience and indeed as we aware, because it appeared in the evidence, the only other oil sands recovery plant, being Syncrude works on a closed water system, but then everybody by then perhaps had smartened up about what was necessary.

189. *Petroleum Refinery Liquid Effluent Regulations*, C.R.C. 1978, c.828.

190. Horricks, Prov. Ct. J. in *Suncor 1983*, *supra*, note 183 at 295: "[I]n fifteen years the people responsible for producing regulations for Plants have not seen fit to produce regulations for Plants of this nature and it's a factor I take into account."

191. See M. Dent, "Will Prosecutor Be Ready at Suncor Trial?" *Fort McMurray Today* (21 January 1983) 5.

192. *Suncor 1985*, *supra*, note 183 at 420.

193. Dent, *supra*, note 191.

194. *Ibid.*

195. *E.g.*, apparently, a similar wastewater problem to the 1982 discharges under consideration in this case study occurred as early as the winter of 1967–1968 (see

Suncor 1985, supra, note 183 at 472), and there were proceedings under the *Fisheries Act* in 1977 and 1978 concerning a deposit unlike the 1982 situation (*supra* at 431).

196. In place at the time was the Canada-Alberta Accord for the Protection and Enhancement of Environmental Quality, Alta. Reg. 87/75.
197. *Supra*, note 151.
198. E.L.C., *supra*, note 183 at 57.
199. *Suncor 1985, supra*, note 183 at 414.
200. *Suncor 1983, supra*, note 183 at 278.
201. *Ibid.*
202. E.L.C., *supra*, note 183 at 45; see also *Suncor 1985, supra*, note 183 at 419.
203. E.L.C., *ibid.* at 19–20.
204. *Suncor 1985, supra*, note 184 at 415.
205. *Ibid.*
206. *Ibid.*
207. E.L.C., *supra*, note 183 at 53.
208. Dent, *supra*, note 191.
209. *Suncor 1985, supra*, note 183 at 416.
210. *Ibid.* at 418.
211. *Ibid.*
212. *Ibid.*
213. *Suncor 1983, supra*, note 183 at 294.
214. E.L.C., *supra*, note 183 at 53.
215. *Suncor 1985, supra*, note 183 at 420.
216. *Suncor 1983, supra*, note 183 at 271.
217. Dent, *supra*, note 191. But, the same article goes on to note that under cross-examination, McDonald admitted she had no proof that it was Suncor effluent which made members of the band sick.
218. "Suncor trial moved" *Fort McMurray Today* (14 July 1983) 9.
219. *Suncor 1982, supra*, note 183 at 267.
220. *Suncor 1983, supra*, note 183 at 271.
221. *Suncor 1982, supra*, note 183 at 268.
222. *Suncor 1983, supra*, note 183 at 271.
223. *Ibid.* at 273. This finding is questionable, because the nature of the offence in the case of the *Fisheries Act* — depositing deleterious substances — is potentially broader than that of exceeding specific licence terms under the Alberta licence.
224. *Ibid.* at 287.
225. *Ibid.* at 292.
226. *Ibid.* at 294.
227. *Ibid.* at 295. This presumably alludes to the fact that there are federal regulations for conventional petroleum refineries, but not oil sands extraction and recovery facilities.
228. *Ibid.*
229. *Ibid.* at 296.
230. *Ibid.* at 270.
231. The Court relied on the Supreme Court of Canada decision *Northwest Falling Contractors Ltd.* v. *R.*, [1980] 2 S.C.R. 292, 53 C.C.C. (2d) 353 upholding the validity of s.33(2) (*Suncor 1985, supra*, note 183 at 432). The Court also upheld the reliability of the measurement made by Suncor, and rejected the due diligence defence (*supra* at 474).
232. See comments of E. Kupchanko, Assistant Deputy Minister of the Alberta Environment Department, as reported in "Prosecuting Polluters is Effective Strategy, Ministry Lawyer Says" *The [Toronto] Globe and Mail* (24 May 1984) A13.
233. *Suncor 1985, supra*, note 183 at 471.
234. Review Panel on Environment Law Enforcement, *An Action Plan for Environmental Law Enforcement in Alberta* (1988).
235. J. Flett (Ministry of Environment), "New Directions in Environmental Law Enforcement in Alberta" (Insight paper, September 19, 1990) at 4–5.
236. *Ibid.*
237. Proposed Alberta Environmental Protection and Enhancement Legislation.
238. Flett, *supra*, note 235 at 3–4.
239. September 26, 1990 phone call with Mr. Tom Dixon, Pollution Control Division.
240. According to Ms. Jillian Flett, Branch Head, Compliance Branch, Pollution Control Division, in a phone call of Oct. 26, 1990, private prosecutions were attempted in 1988, in relation to the Daishowa pulp and paper mill permit to construct (stayed), and subsequently three prosecutions concerning the Old Man Dam have been attempted, of which two have been stayed and the third is still alive.
241. Such separate enforcement staff exist in several jurisdictions, including Ontario, Quebec, B.C. and Alberta.
242. Most notably, the creation of enforcement and compliance policies.
243. On move toward technical environmentalism, see R. Paehlke, "Democracy and Environmentalism: Opening a Door to the Administrative State" in Paehlke & Torgerson, eds., *supra*, note 92, 35 at 45.
244. As was discussed in part III. C. above.
245. In Ontario, Quebec, Newfoundland, Nova Scotia, Manitoba, British Columbia and Alberta.

Three
Assessing Environmental Change

A. Environmental Assessment

(a) "Assessing Environmental Impacts in Canada"
Thomas Meredith

Baumol, W.J. 1986. *Superfairness*. Cambridge, Mass.: MIT Press.

Beanlands, G.E., and P.N. Duinker. 1983. *An Ecological Framework for Environmental Impact Assessment in Canada*. Ottawa: FEARO.

Berger, T.R. 1978. *Northern Frontier, Northern Homeland*. Ottawa: Ministry of Supply and Services Canada.

CEARC (Canadian Environmental Assessment Review Council). 1988. *Evaluating Environmental Impact Assessment: An Action Prospectus*. Ottawa: Ministry of Supply and Services Canada.

CEQ (Council on Environmental Quality). 1973. *Preparation of Environmental Impact Statements, Proposed Guidelines*. Washington, DC: US Government Printing Office.

Couch, W.J. 1985. *Environmental Assessment in Canada: 1985 Summary of Current Practice*. Ottawa: FEARO.

———. 1994 *The Creation and Evolution of EARP: Chronology of Events*. Unpublished report. Ottawa: FEARO.

Dirschl, H.J. 1982. *The Lancaster Sound Region: 1980–2000*. Ottawa: Ministry of Indian and Northern Affairs.

Dunlap, R.E. 1987. 'Public Opinion on the Environment in the Reagan Era'. *Environment* 29: 7–37.

Emond, D.P. 1978. *Environmental Assessment Law in Canada*. Toronto: Emond-Montgomery Ltd.

Environmental Quality Act. 1978. Government of Quebec.

FEARO. 1978 *Federal Environmental Assessment and Review Process — Guide for Environmental Screening*. Ottawa: Environment Canada.

———. 1979. *Detailed Outline of the Cabinet Memorandum Establishing the Federal Environmental Assessment and Review Process*. Ottawa: Ministry of Supply and Services Canada.

———. 1987. *Reforming Federal Environmental Policy*. Ottawa: Ministry of Supply and Services Canada.

———. 1988. *The National Consultation Workshop on Federal Environmental Assessment Reform*. Ottawa: Ministry of Supply and Services Canada.

FEARO (Federal Environmental Assessment Office). 1993. *A Guide to the Environmental Assessment Act (Draft)*. Hull: Policy and Process Development, FEARO.

Franson, R., and A. Lucas. 1978. *Environmental Law Commentary and Case Digest*. Scarborough, ON: Butterworths.

Government of Canada. 1992. *Canada Gazette*. Ottawa: House of Commons.

Government of Quebec. 1992. 'Projet de loi 61: Loi modifiant la loi sur la qualité de l'environnement', *Gazette Officielle du Quebec*, 447–60.

———. 1993. 'Draft regulations to the Environmental Quality Act', *Gazette Officielle du Quebec*, 3302–13.

Harper, J.L. 1977. *Population Biology of Plants*. London: Academic Press.

Illich, I. 1982. 'Vernacular Gender'. *Alternatives* 13:381–448.

Joyce, J. 1922. *Ulysses*. London: Bodley Head Ltd.

Lang, R., and A. Armour. 1981. *The Assessment and Review of Social Impacts*. Ottawa: FEARO.

Liberal Party of Canada. 1993. *Creating Opportunity: The Liberal Plan for Canada*. Ottawa: The Liberal Party.

Livingston, J. 1981. 'Environmental Impact Assessment — It's Whatever You Make of It'. *Probe Post* (November):12–14.

Lucas, A.R. 1981. 'The Assessment Process: The Canadian Experience'. In *Environmental Assessment in Australia and Canada*, edited by S.D. Clark. Vancouver: Westwater Research Centre, University of British Columbia.

———, and J.B.R. Whitney, eds. 1985. *New Direction in Environmental Impact Assessment in Canada*. Toronto: Methuen.

Malvern, R.J., et al. 1992. *A Reference Guide to Environmental Legislation in Canada*. Toronto: Environmental Studies and Assessment Department, Ontario Hydro.

McHarg, I.L. 1969. *Design with Nature*. New York: Natural History Press.

Meredith, T.C, 1988. 'Impact Assessment in Cross-Cultural Situations: The Case of Northern Quebec'. In *Human Ecology: Research and Application*, edited by R.J. Borden and J. Jacobs, 198–205. College Park, MD: Society for Human Ecology.

———. 1992. 'Environmental Impact Assessment, Cultural Diversity and Sustainable Rural Development'. *Environmental Impact Assessment Review* 12:125–38.

Miles, I. 1985. *Social Indicators for Human Development*. London: Frances Printer.

Munro, D.A., et al. 1986. *Learning from Experience: A State of the Art Review and Evaluation of Environmental Impact Assessment Audits*. Ottawa: Canadian Environmental Assessment Research Council.

NEPA (National Environmental Policy Act). 1969. *National Environmental Policy Act*, (US)>

Pushchak, R., and I. Burton. 1983. 'Risk and Compensation in Siting Low-Level Nuclear Waste Facilities: Dealing with the NIMBY Syndrome'. *Plan Canada* 23:68–79.

Regulatory Advisory Committee. 1993. *Report of the CEAA Regulatory Advisory Committee: Report No. 1*. Hull: FEARO.

———. 1994. *Report of RAC Meeting 10.0*. Hull: FEARO.

Rosenberg, D.M., et al. 1981. 'Recent Trends in Environmental Impact Assessment'. *Canadian Journal of Fisheries and Aquatic Science* 38:591–624.

Sadler, B. 1994. *International Study on the Effectiveness of Environmental Assessment*. Hull: FEARO.

Smith, G. 1993. *Impact Assessment and Sustainable Resource Management*. Harlow, UK: Longman Scientific and Technical.

Standing Committee on Environment and Sustainable Development. 1994. *The Commissioner of the Environment and Sustainable Development*. Report to the First Session of the Thirty-fifth Parliament, Ottawa.

Thompson, A.R. 1980. *Environmental Regulation in Canada*. Vancouver: West-water Research Centre, University of British Columbia.

UNCED (United Nations Conference on Environment and Development). 1993. *Agenda 21*. Geneva: UNCED Secretariat.

Wells, H.G. 1922. *An Outline of History*. London: Cassell Publishing.

Westman, W. 1985. *Ecology, Impact Assessment and Environmental Planning*. New York: John Wiley.

Whitney, J.B.R., and V.W. Maclaren. 'A Framework for the Assessment of EIA Methods'. In *Environmental Impact Assessment: The Canadian Experience*, edited by J.B.R. Whitney and V.W. Maclaren, 1–32. Toronto: Institute for Environmental Studies, University of Toronto.

———. 1985b. *Environmental Impact Assessment: The Canadian Experience*. Toronto: Institute for Environmental Studies, University of Toronto.

(b) "The New *Canadian Environmental Assessment Act* — Bill C-78"
Michael I. Jeffrey

1. The environmental assessment process at the federal level in Canada began not as legislation, but rather as a series of Cabinet directives dated June 3, 1972 and December 20, 1973. A further Cabinet directive in 1977 initiated some additional improvements, and the *Government Organization Act, 1979*, S.C. 1978–79, c.13 effectively reaffirmed the responsibility of the federal Minister of the Environment for E.I.A. of the activities of the federal government and related bodies. These early efforts were consolidated in the Environmental Assessment and Review Process Guidelines Order, SOR/84-467 (June 22, 1984) [hereinafter Guidelines Order or E.A.R.P.]. Following a series of decisions by the Federal Court (discussed *infra*, notes 9-29 and accompanying text), the federal government recently moved to legislate the environmental assessment process in Bill C-78, *An Act to Establish a Federal Environmental Assessment Process*, 2d Sess., 34th Parl., 1990 [hereinafter *Canadian Environmental Assessment Act* or *C.E.A.A.*]. The Bill was tabled June 18, 1990 and received second reading on October 30, 1990. It was then considered by the Special Committee on the Federal Environmental Assessment Process. Public hearings have been held, and while the bill died on the order paper, it has been reintroduced in identical form as Bill C-13, *An Act to Establish a Federal Environmental Assessment Process*, 3d Sess., 34th Parl., 1991 and has been referred to a legislative committee.

2. 83 Stat. 852 (1970), as amended, 42 U.S.C. § 4321 (1975) [hereinafter *N.E.P.A.*]. The Act was proclaimed in force January 1, 1970.

3. *Ibid.*, s.102.

4. 464 F.2d 254 (1972).

5. *Ibid.* at 257, quoting 36 Fed. Reg. 7724 (1971); see also *Chelsea Neighbourhood Association* v. *U.S. Postal Service*, 389 F. Supp. 1171 (1975) at 1182; *Conservation Society of Southern Vermount* v. *Secretary of Transportation*, 362 F. Supp. 627 (1973); and *Indian Lookout Alliance* v. *Volpe* 484 F. 2d 11 (1973).

6. See F.R. Anderson, *N.E.P.A. in the Courts* (Washington: Resources for the Future, 1973).

7. Part I of the *Constitution Act, 1982*, being Schedule B of the *Canada Act 1982* (U.K.), 1982, c.11.

8. See S.D. Clark, ed., *Environmental Assessment in Australia and Canada* (Vancouver: Westwater Research Centre, University of British Columbia, 1981) at 43.

9. *Canadian Wildlife Federation Inc.* v. *Canada (Minister of Environment)*, [1989] 3 F.C. 309, [1989] 4 W.W.R. 526 (T.D.), Cullen J. [hereinafter *Rafferty Alameda No. 1* cited to F.C.], aff'd *Saskatchewan Water Corp.* v. *Canadian Wildlife Federation Inc.* (sub nom. *Canadian Wildlife Federation Inc.* v. *Canada (Min. of Environment)*) (1989), [1990] 2 W.W.R. 69, 38 Admin. L.R. 138 (F.C.A.) [hereinafter *Rafferty Alameda No. 2.*]. Since the first *Rafferty Alameda* decision on April 10, 1989, four decisions have been rendered by the Federal Court regarding the environmental assessment of the Rafferty and Alameda dam projects in Saskatchewan. See *infra*, notes 15–29 and accompanying text.

10. Originally s.6(2) of the *Government Organization Act, 1979*, *supra*, note 1, s.14; now s.6 of the *Department of the Environment Act*, R.S.C. 1985, c. E-10 [hereinafter *Department of the Environment Act*].

11. *Rafferty Alameda No. 1*, *supra*, note 9 at 322.

12. See *infra*, discussion accompanying notes 15–28.

13. See *infra*, discussion accompanying notes 29–38.

14. Guidelines Order, *supra*, note 1, ss.2–6.

15. *Rafferty Alameda No. 1*, *supra*, note 9.

16. R.S.C. 1985, c.I-20, s.4.

17. R.S.C. 1985, c.I-21.

18. *Rafferty Alameda No. 1*, *supra*, note 9 at 322.

19. R.S.C. 1985, c.I-17.

20. R.S.C. 1985, c.M-7.

21. *Rafferty Alameda No. 1*, *supra*, note 9 at 323.

22. *Ibid.* at 325.

23. *Rafferty Alameda No. 2*, *supra*, note 9.

24. See *Canadian Wildlife Federation Inc.* v. *Canadian (Minister of Environment)* (1989), [1990] 31 F.T.R. 1, Muldoon J. (T.D.) [hereinafter *Rafferty Alameda No. 3*]. The decision was rendered December 28, 1989.

25. *Tetzlaff* v. *Canada (Min. of Environment)* (21 December 1990), T-2729-90 (F.C.A.) [unreported] [hereinafter *Rafferty No. 4*].

26. *Ibid.* at 18.

27. *A.G. Canada* v. *Saskatchewan Water Corp.* (15 November 1990), QB-4277/90 (Sask. Q.B.), MacPherson C.J. [unreported].

28. See *Tetzlaff* v. *Canada (Minister of Environment)* (8 February 1991), T-2230-89 (F.C.T.D.) at 9 [unreported].

29. *Ibid.*

30. *Friends of the Oldman River Society* v. *Canada (Min. of Transport and Min. of Fisheries and Oceans)* (1989), [1990] 1. F.C. 251, 30 F.T.R. 108 (T.D.) [hereinafter *Oldman River No. 1*, cited to F.C.], rev'd [1990] 2 F.C. 18, 68 D.L.R. (4th) 375 [hereinafter *Oldman River No. 2*, cited to D.L.R.].

31. R.S.C. 1985, c.N-22 [hereinafter *Navigable Waters Protection Act*].

32. *Oldman River No. 1*, *supra*, note 30 at 274.

33. *Oldman River No. 2*, *supra*, note 30.

34. *Supra*, note 9.

35. *Oldman River No. 2*, *supra*, note 30 at 392–93.

36. "Proposal" is defined in s.2 of the Guidelines Order, as "any initiative, undertaking or activity for which the Government of Canada has a decision making responsibility."

37. *Oldman River No. 2*, *supra*, note 30 at 396.

38. R.S.C. 1985, c.F-14.

39. *Oldman River No. 2*, *supra*, note 30 at 396.

40. R.S.C. 1985, c.A-1.

41. The process of the Ontario Environmental Assessment Board, for example, is quasi-judicial in nature. As a statutory administrative tribunal with decision making powers, the Board is governed by the provisions of the *Statutory Powers Procedure Act*, R.S.O. 1980, c.484, which provides for the cross-examination of witnesses (s.10(c)), as well as other adversarial procedures. Some commentators have expressed the view that an adversarial hearing format allows for a more rigorous testing of scientific evidence and, based upon my own experience, their view is well-founded. See, for example, S.L. Smith, "Science in the Courtroom: The Value of an Adversarial System" (April/May 1988) 15 Alternatives 18, and M.I. Jeffrey, Q.C., "Science and the Tribunal: Dealing with Scientific Evidence in the Adversarial Arena" (April/May 1988) 15 Alternatives 24.

42. See, *e.g.*, the Ontario *Environment Assessment Act*, R.S.O. 1980, c.140, s.23; and the *Consolidated Hearings Act, 1981*, S.O. 1981, c.20, s.13.

43. Study Group on Environmental Assessment Hearing Procedures, *Public Review: Neither Judicial nor Political, but an Essential Forum for the Future of the Environment — A Report Concerning the Reform of Public Hearing Procedures for Federal Environmental Assessment Reviews* (Ottawa: Supply & Services, January 1988) (Chair: A.M. Walsh).

44. Environment Canada, F.E.A.R.O., *Reforming Federal Environmental Assessment — A Discussion Paper* (Ottawa: Supply & Services, 1987) [hereinafter Green Paper].

45. See "Statement of the Honourable Robert de Cotret, Minister of the Environment, Introducing the *Canadian Environmental Assessment Act*" (June 18, 1990) at 6 [hereinafter Minister's Statement].

46. *C.E.A.A.*, s.2.

47. *Ibid.*, s.5. It is to be noted here that s.5 narrows considerably the application of the review process from the broad requirement of an environmental effect on an area "federal responsibility" under s.6(b) of the Guidelines Order.

48. *Ibid.*, s.55(1)(b)–(e).

49. *Ibid.*, ss.57–59.

50. *Ibid.*, s.16.

51. *Ibid.*

52. *Ibid.*

53. *Ibid.*, ss.21, 24 & 25.

54. *Ibid.*, s.36.

55. *Ibid.*, s.11.

56. *Ibid.*, s.51.

57. *Ibid.*, s.37.

58. The government considered it to be a significant improvement upon the existing E.A.R.P. to empower the Minister of the Environment with the discretion to establish a panel, appoint its membership and provide its terms of reference. The government failed, however, to seize the opportunity to depoliticize the process by establishing an independent tribunal with decision making authority.

59. See, *e.g.*, the report of submissions to the House of Commons Special Committee examining the draft legislation by the Canadian Bar Association and the Environmental Assessment Caucus: "Lawyers' Groups Urge Changes to Proposed Assessment Process" (1990) 1 Envt. Pol. & L. 121.

60. See R. Ray, "Provinces, Lawyers See Disputes over Jurisdiction" (October 1990) 1 Envt. Pol. & L. 85.

61. The James Bay II project slated for commencement of construction in 1992 will likely provide the litmus test with respect to federal/provincial cooperation in the environmental arena: see "Federal-Provincial Tangles over a Shared Environment" *The Toronto Globe and Mail* (22 November 1990) A18.

62. These shortcomings were acknowledged by Raymond Robinson, Executive Chairman of F.E.A.R.O., who stated at a pre-introduction media briefing on the proposed *C.E.A.A.*: "The scope of this Act cannot be determined by what you have before you." Cited in K. Pole, "Proposal Labelled World's 'Most Comprehensive'" (1990) 1 Envt. Pol. & L. 41.

63. A participant funding program had been announced by the Minister as part of his earlier reform package and was referred to in the Minister's Statement, *supra*, note 45 at 5.

64. See *supra*, notes 41–42 and accompanying discussion.

65. *C.E.A.A.*, *supra*, note 1, s.32.

66. *Ibid.*, s.2.

67. Guidelines Order, s.2.

(c) "'The Nasty Game': The Failure of Environmental Assessment in Canada" Andrew Nikiforuk

6. The panel reports on the Oldman Dam, Rafferty-Alameda Project and Northumberland bridge all clearly document a process betrayed by federal and provincial politicians.

7. See Fred Roots, "Environmental Impact Assessment: What Does it Mean in the 1990s and What is the Role of the University?," p. 17.

8. See Thomas Berger, *Northern Frontier: Northern Homeland, Report of the Mackenzie Valley Pipeline Inquiry*, Volume 1, p. 16.

...

10. See William Rees and Peter Boothroyd, "A Background Paper on EARP Reform — Activities," pp. 6–11.

11. See Rees and Boothroyd, *Process and Structure*, p. 15.

12. See *Alberta Environmental Protection*, 1996, Northern River Basins Study: Report to the Ministers, pp. 89–102.

13. Source: William Ross.

14. See Northey, pp. 255–274.

15. See Northey, p. vii.

16. See Alison Delicaet, "The New Canadian Environmental Assessment Act: A Comparison with the Environmental Assessment Review Process," p. 500.

17. For the best review of the new act's deficiencies see Robert Gibson, "The New Canadian Environmental Assessment Act: Possible Responses to its Main Deficiencies." See also Northey's comprehensive overview, pp. 585–754.

...

20. A news release from the Canadian government (1-9632 Backgrounder #5) simply states, "there is little data about this huge region, especially in relation to the possible cumulative effects of the various potential mining and related infrastructure developments." Ottawa's million-dollar panel review on BHP didn't change this reality.

21. *Northern Perspectives*, Fall/Winter 1996, pp. 1–4. See also Susan Wismer, "The Nasty Game: How Environ-

mental Assessment Is Failing Aboriginal Communities in Canada's North."

22. See *Draft Final Memorandum of Understanding on Environmental Assessment of the Proposed Voisey's Bay Mining Development*, p. 10.

23. *U.S. Code of Federal Regulations*, 40, p. 283.

24. See Derek Doyle, *Canadian Case Studies on the Effectiveness of Environmental Assessment*, pp. 51–54.

25. See Appendix 2, Panel Review 45.

26. See Article 14, Submission made by the Friends of the Oldman River to the Commission for Environmental Cooperation, October 1, 1996.

27. In a document on problems encountered with CEAA, the Mining Association of Canada makes the following points on law evasion: "The many law list triggers are all laws and regulations created for other purposes. Many are not designed to be clear-out triggers for an assessment process. To make matters worse, officials are reluctant to launch an assessment. An assessment absorbs scarce departmental resources, and there are no incentives in the process to make launching an assessment desirable for an official. Requests for a decision can languish for months or years.... Moreover, ministerial discretion for setting conditions on an approval following a CEAA process is seen as limitless, and beyond strictly environmental issues. Thus the careful work of Parliament in defining the scope of an act or regulation, based on clear federal jurisdiction, may in practice be turned into discretionary decisions, without accountability to Parliament."

28. This has always been the case. "Bulletins of Initial Assessment Decisions" published annually by the government in the 1990s show that 99 per cent of all screenings resulted in a go with no adverse effects or a go "because the potentially adverse impacts may be mitigated with known technology."

29. Even today, David Schindler's short 1976 essay on "The Impact Statement Boondoggle" accurately reflects the poor use of science in most environmental assessments. See Appendix 3.

...

31. See Rees and Boothroyd, *Process and Structure*, p. 15.

32. Larry Pokok Aknavigak, chair of the Nunavut Impact Review Board, spells out his position clearly: "We will manage our own resources.... Environmental assessment in the Nunavut Settlement Area will be done by our Impact Review Board and not CEAA."

33. See *CEAA, International Study of the Effectiveness of Environmental Assessment*, p. 25.

34. Interviews with K.D. Ferguson of Placer Dome Canada Limited, Vancouver and Peter Campbell of Princeton Mining, Vancouver.

...

39. See Husain Sadar and William J. Stolte, "Canadian Experience in Environmental Impact Assessment," pp. 13–25.

...

41. Source: David Schindler and Charlie Ferguson.

Selected Bibliography

Bankes, Nigel. 1996. "Environmental Security and Gas Exports," *Resources*. 53:1–5.

Beattie, Robert, 1995. "Everything You Already Know About EIA (But Don't Often Admit)." *Environmental Impact Assessment Review* 15:109–114.

Berger, Thomas. 1977. *Northern Frontier, Northern Homeland; Report of the Mackenzie Valley Pipeline Inquiry*, Volume 1 and 2. Ottawa.

Berry, Wendell. 1993. *Sex, Economy, Freedom & Community: Eight Essays*. New York: Pantheon Books.

CEAA. 1996. *The Canadian Environmental Assessment Act: Training Compendium*. Ottawa.

CEAA. 1996. *Discussion Paper On Cost Recovery, Environmental Assessment*. Ottawa.

CEAA. 1996. *Position Paper On Process Efficiency, Environmental Assessment*. Ottawa.

CEAA. 1996. *Environmental Assessment in Canada: Achievements, Challenges and Directions*. Ottawa.

CEAA. 1995. *First Annual Report*. Ottawa.

CEAA. 1995. *Military Flying Activities in Labrador and Quebec, Report of the Environmental Assessment Panel*. Ottawa.

CEAA. 1996. *NWT Diamonds Project, Report of the Environmental Assessment Panel*. Ottawa.

Cobb, Clifford et al. 1995. "If the GDP Is Up, Why is America Down?" *Atlantic Monthly*. October:59–78.

DeLury, R.T. 1993. *Annotated Inuvialuit Final Agreement*.

Delicaet, Alison. 1995. "The New Canadian Environmental Assessment Act: A Comparison with the Environmental Assessment Review Process." *Environmental Impact Assessment Review*. 15:497–505.

Doyle, Derek. 1996. *Canadian Case Studies On the Effectiveness of Environmental Assessment*. UMA Engineering Ltd. Toronto.

Doyle, Derek and Barry Sadler. 1996. *Environmental Assessment in Canada: Frameworks, Procedures and Attributes of Effectiveness*. Ottawa.

Elder, Philip. 1991. "Environmental and Sustainability Assessment." *Journal of Environmental Law and Practice*. 2:125–149.

Federal Environmental Assessment Review Office. 1991. *Rafferty-Alameda Project, Report of the Environmental Assessment Panel*. Ottawa.

Federal Environmental Assessment Review Office. 1992. *Oldman River Dam, Report of the Environmental Assessment Panel*. Ottawa.

Gardner, Alex. 1994. "Federal Intergovernmental Co-operation on Environmental Management: A Comparison of Developments in Australia and Canada in Reviewing CEPA." *The Issues. #17*, Environment Canada. Ottawa.

Gibson, Robert. 1992. "The New Canadian Environmental Assessment Act: Possible Responses to its Main Deficiencies." *Journal of Environmental Law and Practice*. 2:223–255.

Hardin, Garrett. 1985. *Filters Against Folly: How to Survive Despite Economists, Ecologists and the Merely Eloquent*. New York: Penguin Books.

Hegmann, George and G.A. Yarranton. 1995. *Cumulative Effects and the Energy Resources Conservation Board's Review Process*. Macleod Institute for Environmental Analysis. University of Calgary. Working Paper #1.

Keith, Robbie. 1996. "Mining in Aboriginal Homelands." *Northern Perspectives*. 23:1–12.

Kostuch, Martha. 1996. *Revised Submission on Enforcement Matters Under Article 14 of the North American Agreement on Environmental Cooperation*. Montreal.

Leopold, Aldo. 1996. *A Sand County Almanac*. New York: Ballantine Books.

National Energy Board/CEAA. 1996. *Express Pipeline Project, Report of the Joint Review Panel*. Calgary.

Northey, Rodney. 1994. *The 1995 Annotated Canadian Environmental Assessment Act and EARP Guidelines Order.* Toronto: Carswell.

Nunavut Impact Review Board. 1996. "Mission Statement." Cambridge Bay.

O'Reilly, Kevin. 1996. "Diamond Mining and the Demise of Environmental Assessment in the North." *Northern Perspectives.* 24:1–4.

Page, Robert et al. 1996. *Banff-Bow Valley: At the Crossroads: Summary Report of the Bow Valley Task Force.* Heritage Canada: Ottawa.

Pratt, Larry and Ian Urquhart. 1994. *The Last Great Forest: Japanese Multinationals and Alberta's Northern Forests.* Edmonton: NeWest Press.

Rees, William. 1995. "More Jobs, Less Damage." *Alternatives.* 21:24–30.

Rees, W.E., and P. Boothroyd. 1987. "Background Papers on EARP Reform-Activities/Process and Structure." Ottawa: Canadian Environmental Assessment Research Council.

Roots, Fred. 1993. "Environmental Impact Assessment: What Does it Mean in the 1990s and What is the Role of a University?" Ottawa: Impact Assessment Centre.

Sadar, H. and W.J. Stolte. 1996. "Canadian Experience in Environmental Impact Assessment." *Impact Assessment.* 14:215–228.

Sadar, H. 1995. "Environmental Impact Assessment in Canada: An Overview of the Past Performance of the Federal Process." Ottawa: Impact Assessment Centre.

Sadar, H. 1996. "The Need to Review the Federal Contribution to Environmental Impact Assessment (EIA) Effectiveness in Canada." Unpublished.

Sadler, Barry. 1996. *International Study of the Effectiveness of Environmental Assessment.* Ottawa.

Schindler, David. 1976. "The Impact Statement Boondoggle." Science 192:509.

Struzik, Edward. 1996. "The Last Tundra." Unpublished.

Tilleman, William. 1995. "Public Participation in the Environmental Impact Assessment Process: A Comparative Study of Impact Assessment in Canada, and the United States and the European Community." *Columbia Journal of Transitional Law.* 33:337–439.

UNEP Secretariat. 1993. Concepts and Principles in "A Statement by Banks on the Environment and Sustainable Development." Geneva.

U.S. Code of Federal Regulations. 1995. "Protection of the Environment." 40:276–315.

Wismer, Susan. 1996. "The Nasty Game." *Alternatives.* 22:10–17.

World Wildlife Fund. 1996. "WWF Seeking Clarification of Cabinet Decision on BHP Diamond Mine." Toronto: WWF News release.

(e) "Environmental Impact Assessment and the Fallacy of Unfinished Business" Kristin Shrader-Frechette

1. See J.M. Deutsch and the Interagency Review Group on Nuclear Waste Management, *Report to the President*, TID-2817 (Springfield, Va.: National Technical Information Service, October, 1978); hereafter cited as IRG, *Report.*

2. See J.J. Stukel and B.R. Keenan, *Ohio River Basin Energy Study Report*, vol. 1, p. 16; hereafter cited as OTA, *Auto.*

3. Robert Stobaugh and Daniel Yergin, "Conclusion: Toward a Balanced Energy Program," in Stobaugh and Yergin, eds., *Energy Future* (New York: Random House, 1979), p. 227. See also Yergin, "Conservation: The Key Energy Source," in Stobaugh and Yergin, *Energy Future*, pp. 136–182.

4. U.S. Congress, OTA, *Technology Assessment of Changes in the Future Use and Characteristics of the Automobile Transportation System*, 2 vols. (Washington, D.C.: U.S. Government Printing Office, 1979). See vol. 1, p. 16; hereafter cited as OTA, *Auto.*

5. See note 17.

6. K.E. Boulding, "Fun and Games with the Gross National Product: the Role of Misleading Indicators in Social Policy," in R.T. Roelofs, J.N. Crowley, and D.L. Hardesty, eds., *Environment and Society* (Englewood Cliffs, N.J.: Prentice Hall, 1974), p. 136.

7. Stobaugh and Yergin, "The End of Easy Oil," in Stobaugh and Yergin, *Energy Future*, pp. 4–11. See also Stobaugh and Yergin, "Conclusion," p. 227.

8. In addition to the automobile and energy studies already cited, see, for example, U.S. Congress, OTA, *A Technology Assessment of Coal Slurry Pipelines* (Washington, D.C.: U.S. Government Printing Office, 1979), where ethical, legal, and social parameters involved in use of slurries are disregarded; hereafter cited as OTA, *Coal.* See also, U.S. Congress, OTA, *Policy Implications of the Computed Tomography (CT) Scanner* (U.S. Government Printing Office: Washington, 1978), which neglected to consider alternative social, regulatory, legal, political, and ethical frameworks within which the scanners might best be used and misuse avoided. The same failure to evaluate alternative social, political, and ethical frameworks within which a technology is used, or within which environmental impacts occur, appears in nearly all assessments. See, for example, (1) U.S. Atomic Energy Commission, *Comparative Risk-Cost-Benefit Study of the Alternative Sources of Electrical Energy*, WASH-1224 (Washington, D.C.: U.S. Government Printing Office, 1974); hereafter cited as AEC, *Risk*; (2) Congress, OTA, *An Evaluation of Railroad Safety* (Washington, D.C.: U.S. Government Printing Office, 1978); hereafter cited as OTA, *Railroad*; (3) Congress, OTA, *Pest Management Strategies*, vol. 3 (Washington, D.C.: U.S. Government Printing Office, 1979); hereafter cited as OTA, *Pest.* The one significant exception to this rule is U.S. Congress, OTA, *Application of Solar Technology to Today's Energy Needs*, vol. 1 (Washington, D.C.: U.S. Government Printing Office, 1975), hereafter cited as OTA, *Solar*, in which alternative social, political, and ethical frameworks are considered.

9. In this regard, see K.S. Shrader-Frechette, *Environmental Ethics* (Pacific Grove, Calif.: Boxwood Press, 1981), pp. 154–94.

10. Ibid., p. 162.

11. K. Keniston, "Toward a More Human Society," in H.K. Girvetz, ed., *Contemporary Moral Issues* (Belmont, Calif.: Wadsworth, 1974), pp. 401–02.

12. G.E. Moore, *Principia Ethica* (Cambridge: Cambridge University Press, 1951), p. 40.

13. A discussion of this error, as applied to assessment of nuclear fission, may be found in Shrader-Frechette, *Nuclear Power and Public Policy* (Boston: D. Reidel, 1980), pp. 136–37.

14. Moore, *Principia Ethica*, pp. 23–24; see also p. 36. Although Moore argues that ethical judgments ought not

be reduced to purely scientific ones, he does not deny that causal or empirical propositions are a part of ethics. In this regard, see F. Snare, "Three Skeptical Theses in Ethics," *American Philosophical Quarterly* 14 (1977): 129–30.

15. For discussion of this point, see Stukel and Keenan, *ORBES*, IV (1978), pp. 50 ff.

16. For example, one of the forms the naturalistic fallacy has taken is the attempt to derive "ought" statements from "is" statements. This definition of the *fallacy* is controversial, in large part, because it appears to presuppose a fact-value distinction. In this regard, see J.R. Searle, "How To Derive 'Ought' from 'Is'," *Philosophical Review* 73 (1964): 43–58. See also Moore, *Principia Ethica*, pp. 73, 108. A number of philosophers (e.g., Bruening, Frankena, White, as well as Snare), however, do not believe that the naturalistic fallacy is committed whenever one attempts to derive an "ought" from an "is." See, for example, L. Kohlberg, "From Is to Ought: How to Commit the Naturalistic Fallacy and Get Away with It...," in T. Mischel, ed., *Cognitive Development and Epistemology* (New York: Academic Press, 1971), p. 154. Failing to consider the open question has also been considered by authors such as Kohlberg and Giarelli to be another variant of the naturalistic fallacy. See J.M. Giarelli, "Lawrence Kohlberg and G.E. Moore," *Educational Theory* 26 (1976): 350. This variant is also controversial, however, because not all philosophers are willing to challenge the analyticity of definitions of good.

17. U.S. Congress, OTA, *Annual Report to the Congress for 1978* (Washington, D.C.: U.S. Government Printing Office, 1978), p. 73.

18. Shaul Ben-David (Department of Economics, University of New Mexico), Allen V. Kneese (Resources for the Future, Washington, D.C.), and William D. Schulze (Department of Economics, University of Wyoming), "A Study of the Ethical Foundations of Benefit-Cost Analysis Techniques," unpublished research done under EVIST funding, working paper, August 1979, p. 130.

19. Sukel and Keenan, *ORBES*, I (1977).

20. See U.S. Congress, OTA, *Railroad Safety — US-Canadian Comparison* (Washington, D.C.: U.S. Government Printing Office, 1979), pp. vii–viii. See also OTA, *Railroad*, esp. pp. 14, 37, 141, 156.

21. Robert Van Den Bosch, *The Pesticide Conspiracy* (Garden City, N.Y.: Doubleday, 1978), pp. 147–51; see also pp. 152–78. The late Van Den Bosch, a Berkeley entomologist, spent his life doing research on nonchemical forms of pest control.

22. See Goran Backstrand and Lars Ingelstam, "Should We Put Limits on Consumption?" *The Futurist* 11 (1977): pp. 157–62.

23. See OTA, *Auto*.

24. See M.R. McDowell and D.F. Cooper, "Control Methodology of the U.K. Road Traffic System," in D.F. Burkhardt and W.H. Ittelson, eds., *Environmental Assessment of Socioeconomic Systems* (New York: Plenum, 1978), pp. 279–280. Cf. OTA, *Auto*, vol. 1, pp. 16, 21–25, 31.

25. Core-melt probabilities were computed in the only allegedly complete study of nuclear reactor safety, WASH-1400, known as the Rasmussen Report. Released in 1975, this study concluded that fission reactors presented only a minimal health threat to the public. Early in 1979, however, under growing knowledge of core-melt hazards, the Nuclear Regulatory Commission withdrew its support from WASH-1400. See U.S. NRC, *Reactor Safety Study*. WASH-1400, NUREG-75/014 (Washington, D.C.: U.S. Government Printing Office, 1975). See also Shrader-Frechette, *Nuclear Power*, pp. 3–4.

26. In fact, the U.S. government says it will not know the answer to this question until well beyond the year 2000, since the first test-model storage facility will not be built until then. See IRG, *Report*, p. xxiii.

27. OTA, *Solar*, vol. 1, p. 11.

B. Science and the Law: Facts and Values and Interpretation

(a) "The Conflict between Law and Science"
Hajo Versteeg

1. *Palmer* v. *Stora Kopparbergs Bergslags Aktiebolag* (1983), 12 C.E.L.R. 157 (N.S.S.C., T.D [hereinafter *Palmer* v. *Stora Kopparbergs* or *Palmer*].

2. *Ibid.* at 230.

3. See generally H. Hart & Honoré *Causation in the Law* (Clarendon Press, 1959); J.G. Fleming, *The Law of Torts*, 5th ed. (Sydney: The Law Book Company, 1977); E.J. Weinrib, "A Step Forward in Factual Causation" (1975) 38 Modern Law Rev. 518; J. Krier, "Environmental Litigation and The Burden of Proof" in Baldwin & Page (eds.), *Law and the Environment* (Walker, 1970) at 105; G. Calabresi, "Concerning Cause and the Law of Torts: An Essay for H. Kalven, Jr." (1975) 43 U. Chicago L. Rev. 69; T. Page, "A Generic View of Toxic Chemicals and similar Risks" (1978–79) 7 Ecology L. Q. 207; W.H. Pedrick, "Causation, The 'Who Done It' Issue, and A. Becht" (1978) Washington U. L. Q. 645.

4. Page, *supra* note 3, esp. at 233–234.

5. See generally sources cited in note 3, *supra*.

6. See generally sources cited in note 3, *supra* esp. J. Fleming at 7–12.

7. *Ibid.* See also R. Solomon, B. Feldthusen & S. Mills, *Cases and Materials in the Law of Torts* (Carswell, 1982) at 14–21.

8. G. Robinson, "Multiple Causation in Tort Law: Reflections on the DES Cases" 68 Virginia L. Rev. 713 (1982).

9. Thode, "Tort Analysis: Duty-Risk v. Proximate Cause and the Rational Allocation of Functions Between Judge and Jury" [1977] Utah L. Rev. 1, 2 quoted in R. Delgado, *"Beyond Sindell:* Relaxation of Cause-in-Fact Rules for Indeterminate Plaintiffs" (1982) 70 California L. Rev. 881, at 883 note 12.

10. See, for example, D. Stuart, *Canadian Criminal Law* (Carswell, 1982) at 32–41.

11. Krier, *supra* note 3 at 107–111; J. Sax, *Defending the Environment* (A. Knopf, 1971) at 137–157. See also an excellent book by J. Dales, *Pollution Property and Prices* (U. of T. Press, 1968), esp. at 58–76.

12. Krier, *supra* note 3 at 107–108.

13. See, for example, Note, "Tort Actions for Cancer: Deterrence, Compensation, and Environmental Carcinogenesis" (1981) 90 Yale L.J. 840; D. Large & P. Michie, "Proving that the Strength of the British Navy Depends on the Number of Old Maids in Eng-

land: A Comparison of Scientific Proof with Legal Proof" (1981) 11 Environmental L. 555: R. Rabin, "Environmental Liability and the Tort System (1987) 24 Houston L. Rev. 27.

14. R. Carson, *Silent Spring* (Houghton Mifflin, 1962); B. Commoner, *The Closing Circle* (A. Knopf, 1971); B. Ward & R. Dubos, *Only One Earth* (W. Norton, 1972).

15. W. Ruckelshaus, "Risk Science and Democracy" (Nov. 87) Chemtech: "Risk Assessment and Management: Framework for Decision Making," (Dec. 1984) U.S.E.P.A.

16. See Page, *supra* note 3 at 207–223; M. Gelpe & A. Tarlock, "The Uses of Scientific Information in Environmental Decision Making" (1974) 48 Southern California L. Rev. 371; L. D. Silver, "The Common Law of Environmental Risk and Some Recent Applications" (1986) 10 Harvard Environmental L. Rev. 61.

17. A number of articles are extremely helpful in understanding the environmental science/law interface. They include:

Page, *supra* note 3; Delgado, *supra* note 9; Large & Michie, *supra* note 13; Council on Environmental Quality (Washington, D.C.: Government Printing Office), 6th Annual Report (Dec., 1975); K. Feinberg, "The Toxic Tort Litigation Crisis: Conceptual Problems and Proposed Solutions" (1987) 24 Houston L. Rev. 155; J. Forstrom, "Victim Without a Cause: The Missing Link Between Compensation and Deterrence in Toxic Tort Litigation" (1987) 18 Environmental L. 151; Gelpe & Tarlock, *supra* note 16; Interagency Regulatory Liaison Group — Work Group on Risk Assessment, "Scientific Bases for Identification of Potential Carcinogens and Estimation of Risks" (July 1979) 63 Journal of the National Cancer Institute 241; H. Latin, "The Significance of Toxic Health Risks: An Essay on Legal Decisionmaking Under Uncertainty" (1982) 10 Ecology L. Q. 339; J. Leape, "Quantitative Risk Assessment in Regulation of Environmental Carcinogens" (1980) 4 Harvard Environmental L. Rev. 86; J. McElveen & P. Eddy, "Cancer and Toxic Substances: The Problem of Causation and the Use of Epidemiology" (1984–85) 33 Cleveland State L. Rev. 29; "Rethinking Tort and Environmental Liability Laws: Needs and Objectives of the Late 20th Century and Beyond" (1987) 24 Houston L. Rev. 1; "Tort Actions for Cancer: Deterrence, Compensation, and Environmental Carcinogenesis" (1981) 90 Yale L. J. 840; H. Versteeg, "Environmental Risk Assessment: A Rational Approach to the Management of New Brunswick's Spruce Budworm Enigma" (1982) 11 Canadian Environmental L. Rep. 109; H. Versteeg, "The Spruce Budworm Spray Programme and the Perception of Risk in New Brunswick" (May 1984) Friends of the Earth; D. Harvey, "Epidemiologic Proof of Probability: Implementing the Proportional Recovery Approach in Toxic Exposure Torts" (1984) 89 Dick. L. Rev. 233; R. Rabin, "Environmental Liability and the Tort System" (1987) 24 Houston L. Rev. 27.

18. *Cook* v. *Lewis*, [1952] 1 D.L.R. 1 (S.C.C.).

19. Fleming, *supra* note 3 at 301. See also Weinrib, *supra* note 3.

20. *Sindell* v. *Abbott Laboratories*, 26 Cal. 3d 588; 607 P. 2d 924.

21. The California Court extended principles developed in *Summers* v. *Tice*, 33 Cal. 2d 80 (1948). The facts in the *Tice* case were virtually identical to those in *Cook* v. *Lewis*. See Delgado, *supra* note 9 at 881–883.

22. *Supra* note 20 at 936.

23. Delgado, *supra* note 9; Weinrib, *supra* note 3.

24. See generally Council on Environmental Quality (CEQ) *Annual Reports, supra* note 17; Versteeg, *supra* note 17 (Perception of Risk, esp. ch. 4 and 5). Note: This paper will focus on the potential adverse human health impact of toxic substances. However, it must be clearly understood that the potential impact on the natural environment is also profound. See, for example. Versteeg, *supra* note 17 (Perception of Risk, ch. 6) and CEQ *Annual Reports*.

25. See CEQ *Annual Reports*, esp. the 6th Annual Report, ch. 2. See also S. Epstein, *The Politics of Cancer* (Garden City: Doubleday, 1979) esp. Part I.

26. *Ibid.* See also Harvey, *supra* note 17 at 234–235; Leape, *supra* note 17; Interagency Regulatory Liaison Group, *supra* note 17.

27. See, for example, interagency Regulatory Liaison Group, *supra* note 17; Epstein, *supra* note 25.

28. See, for example, A. Feinstein & R. Horwitz, "Double Standards, Scientific Methods, and Epidemiological Research" (Dec. 1982) 307 The New England J. of Medicine 1611; G. Hutchison, "The Epidemiological Method" in Schottenfeld & Fraumeni, *Cancer Epidemiology and Prevention* (1982); McElveen & Eddy, *supra* note 17, esp. at 37–47; Harvey, *supra* note 17, esp. at 236–240.

29. *Ibid.* But see esp. Harvey, *supra* note 17 at 241–242; McElveen & Eddy, *supra* note 17 at 47–56; Large & Michie, *supra* note 17; Feinberg *supra* note 17 at 159–164; C. Cranor, "Epidemiological and Procedural Protections for Workplace Health in the Aftermath of the *Benzene* Case" 5 Industrial Relations L.J. 372 at 379–393.

30. *Ibid.* esp. Cranor at 385–394.

31. McElveen & Eddy, *supra* note 17 at 46–47.

32. This example, somewhat modified, is taken from Harvey, *supra* note 17 at 237–240. See also Feinstein & Horwitz, *supra* note 28 at 1612.

33. See, for example, Fleming, *supra* note 3 at 179 191; Large & Michie, *supra* note 13 at 594–614.

34. *Ibid.* See also Delgado, *supra* note 9 at 887, esp. authorities cited in note 30.

35. *Supra* note 18.

36. [1972] 3 All E.R. 1008 (H.L.).

37. *Ibid.* at 1012.

38. See generally authorities cited in note 17, *supra*. See also H. Schiefer, D. Irvine & S. Buzik, *You and Toxicology* (Saskatoon, 1986).

39. Schiefer, *supra* note 35 esp. at 4–11 gives an excellent overview of the various tests used in toxicological studies. See also Interagency Regulatory Liaison Group, *supra* note 17 at 248–256.

40. Interagency Regulatory Liaison Group, *supra* note 17 at 248.

41. See generally authorities cited in note 17, *supra*.

42. The rationale for high dosage feeding has been gravely misunderstood by many lay people. There is little evidence that any chemical fed to animals in large quantities will cause cancer. However, there is clear scientific evidence that the higher the exposure of a

subject to a chemical, the greater the likelihood the disease of concern will be contracted. Detecting an incidence of cancer as low as .01% in experimental animals (1 case in 10,000; 10 cases in 100,000; 100 cases in 1,000,000). Since such experiments would be prohibitively expensive and impossible to manage, researchers *reduce* the number of test animals but *increase* the dosage in order to increase in probability of including the disease in question in a particular animal (*or to* establish evidence of no observable effect). An illustration is helpful. Suppose that feeding the equivalent of 1,000 cans of saccharin-containing pop produces one significant cancer in 50 rats. The toxicologist may then assume, all other things being equal, that 100 cans will produce 1 tumor in 500 rats, 10 cans will produce 1 tumor in 5,000 rats, and 1 can will produce 1 tumor in 50,000 rats. Note that Justice Nunn in the Nova Scotia Herbicide Trial expressed grave concerns about the high dosage levels fed to animals in the dioxin studies — see text accompanying note 50, *infra*. See generally, Cranor, *supra* note 29 at 381; Epstein, *supra* note 25 at 61–64; CEQ, *6th Annual Report, supra* note 17.

43. Cranor, *supra* note 29 at 381.

44. *Ibid.* See also V. Covello, "Informing People About Risks From Chemicals, Radiation, and Other Toxic Substances", unpublished manuscript, submitted for publication. Available, subject to permission from author, from H. Versteeg.

45. *Ibid.*

46. *Reserve Mining Co.* v. *EPA*, 514 F. 2d 292 (8th Cir. 1975) [hereinafter *Reserve Mining*].

47. *Federal Water Pollution Control Act* § 504(a), 33 U.S.C. § 1364(a) (1982), quoted in Silver, *supra* note 16 at 88–89.

48. See Large & Michie, *supra* note 13 at 560–561.

49. See J.F. Castrilli, "Problems of Proof and Credibility Issues in Relation to Expert Evidence in Toxic Tort Litigation" (1984–85) 10 Queen's L.J. 71 at 73–74.

50. *Supra* note 46 at 506 *et seq.*

51. *Ibid.* at 535–537.

52. *Supra* note 1 at 229–230.

53. See text accompanying note 2.

54. *Supra* note 1 at 234–235.

55. *Ibid.* at 237. See also Castrilli, *supra* note 45; B. Wildsmith, "Of Herbicides and Humankind: Palmer's Common Law Lessons" (1986) 24 Osgoode Hall L.J. 161.

56. *McGhee, supra* note 36 at 1011.

57. See authorities cited in Delgado, *supra* note 9 at 891.

58. Weinrib, *supra* note 3 at 533.

59. *Ibid.* at 530.

60. See Harvey, *supra* note 17 at 245; D. Rosenberg, "Toxic Tort Litigation: Crisis or Chrysalis?" (1987) 24 Houston L. Rev. 183 at 190–193; Delgado, *supra* note 9 at 891–895.

61. See text accompanying note 4, *supra*.

62. See authorities cited in note 11, *supra*.

63. Page, *supra* note 3 at 230–236; Versteeg, *supra* note 17 (Perception of Risk) at 86–91.

64. Feinberg, *supra* note 17 at 167–174; Rabin, *supra* note 17.

65. Forstrom, *supra* note 17 at 163–168.

66. Harvey, *supra* note 17 at 248; Forstrom, *supra* note 17 at 171–176.

67. Note "Toxic Substance Contamination: The Risk-Benefit Approach to Causation Analysis" 14 U. of Mich. J.L. Ref 53; Harvey, *supra* note 17 at 244.

68. Harvey, *supra* note 17 at 244–246; Delgado, *supra* note 9 at 897; Gelpe & Tarlock, *supra* note 17.

69. See Delgado, *supra* note 9 at 899–908; Forstrom, *supra* note 17 at 168–169; Harvey, *supra* note 17 at 245–248; Rosenberg, *supra* note 56 at 190–194.

70. Rosenberg, *supra* note 56 at 192–193; Harvey, *supra* note 17 at 245.

71. See text accompanying note 19, *supra*.

72. Delgado, *supra* note 9 at 903; Harvey, *supra* note 17 at 258; Rosenberg, *supra* note 56 at 192.

73. See generally: Note, "Toxic Tort Contamination: The Risk-Benefit Approach to Causation Analysis", *supra* note 64 esp. at 60–67; Note: "Reserve Mining — The Standard of Proof Required to Enjoin an Environmental Hazard to the Public Health" (1975) 59 Minnesota L. Rev. 893 esp. at 901–913.

74. See for example Wildsmith, *supra* note 51 at 176–179; Castrilli, *supra* note 45 at 76–80; Krier, *supra* note 3.

75. See Harvey, *supra* note 17 at 243–244.

76. *Supra* note 1 at 232–233.

77. See for example, A. Kantrowitz, "The Science Court Experiment: Criticisms and Responses: (April 1977) Bull. Atomic Scientists; Martin," The Proposed Science Court" (1977) 75 Mich. L. Rev. 1058; R. Carpenter, "Ecology in Court, and Other Disappointments of Environmental Science and Environmental Law" 15 National Resources Lawyer 573 at 593.

78. See Carpenter, *supra* note 74 at 593.

79. H. Markey, "Science and Law: A Dialogue on Understanding" (1982) 68 American Bar Association J. 154.

80. *Ibid.* See also Carpenter, *supra* note 74; D. Bazelon, "Science and Uncertainty: A Jurist's View" (1981) 5 Harvard Environmental L. Rev. 209; W. Thomas (ed.) *Scientists in the Legal System* (Ann Arbor Publishers, 1974).

81. G. Bingham & L. Haygood, "Environmental Dispute Resolution: The First Ten Years" (1986) 41 Arbitration J. 3; Canadian Environmental Mediation Newsletter, published by Conflict Management Resources of York University, Toronto, Canada.

(b) "Science and the Tribunal"
Michael I. Jeffery

1. *McGraw-Hill Dictionary of Scientific Technical Terms*, 2nd edition, p. 1414.

2. John Burke, ed., *Osborn's Concise Law Dictionary*, (Sweet & Maxwell: sixth edition), p. 196.

3. See, for example, S. 1(c) of the *Environmental Assessment Act*, Revised Statutes of Ontario 1980, c.140, which incorporates socio-economic and cultural conditions into the definition of the term "environment." See also (Saskatchewan) *Environmental Assessment Act*, ss.1980, c.e.10.1 and (Newfoundland) *Environmental Assessment Act*, S. Nfld. 1980, c.3.

4. For example, courts will rarely admit hearsay evidence and often rely upon the "best evidence" rule; S.15 of the *Statutory Powers Procedure Act*, Revised Statutes of Ontario 1980 c.484, on the other hand, allows tribunals having a decision-making power to admit almost any type of evidence, whether oral or documentary, and this includes hearsay evidence, opinions and conclusions of a witness. The tribunal is then at liberty to weigh this evidence as it sees fit and is not circumscribed in any way by the fact that such evidence may be inadmissible in a court of law.

5. (1947) 2 All England Reports 372.

6. *Ibid.*, p. 374; see also *Smith v. Smith and Smedman* (1952) 2. Supreme Court Reports 312 p. 331–332; *Clark* v. *The King* (1921), G.1 Can. Supreme Court Reports 608 p. 616.

7. See Sopinka and Lederman, *The Law of Evidence in Civil Cases* (Toronto: Butterworth, 1974), p. 384, for a comprehensive discussion of the extent and allocation of burden of proof.

8. See Nicholas A. Ashford, "Examining the Role of Science in the Regulatory Process," *Environment*, 25:5 (June 1983), p. 7.

9. See Jerome Ravetz, "Scientific Uncertainty Looms Large Over Environmental Policymakers," *Transatlantic Perspectives*, 11 (April 1984), p. 11.

10. M. Frankel, "The Search for Truth: An Umpireal View," 123 *University of Pennsylvania Law Review* 1031 (1975), pp. 1036–1037.

11. Dr. Stuart L. Smith, "Science in the Courtroom: the Value of an Adversarial System," *Alternatives*, Volume 15:2 (1988), p. 18.

12. See, for example, S.38(2) (e) of the *Environmental Protection Act*, Revised Statutes of Ontario 1980, c.141.

13. See S.18(9) of the *Environmental Assessment Act*, Revised Statutes of Ontario 1980, c.140 and also S.10 of the *Consolidated Hearings Act, 1981*, c.141.

14. At the date of this writing, the Ontario Government is implementing a trial intervenor funding programme which will initially cover hearings held pursuant to environmental legislation. The Ontario Minister of the Environment, Jim Bradley, has publicly stated his support for the concept of intervenor funding and his Ministry has taken a number of interim measures in connection therewith pending the approval by Cabinet of a formal programme.

    In October and November of 1984, a Joint Board chaired by this writer awarded costs in advance to two groups of intervenors pursuant to a cost power contained in the *Consolidated Hearings Act, 1981* (S.7); see Orders and Reasons for Order dated October 16 and November 5, 1984 (*Hamilton-Wentworth East-West/ North South Transportation Corridor — Redhill Creek Expressway Application*), Registrar's File CH-82-08. These Orders awarding costs in advance were challenged by way of judicial review and quashed by the Divisional Court of the Supreme Court of Ontario; see *Re Regional Municipality of Hamilton-Wentworth and Hamilton-Wentworth Save the Valley Committee, Inc. et al.* (1985), 51 Ontario Reports (2d) 23. The Respondent sought leave to appeal which was refused.

    Concurrently, the Ontario Energy Board stated a case to the Divisional Court concerning its statutory power to award costs in advance and this stated case was heard by the same panel. The Court reached the same conclusion and held that neither the Joint Board nor the Energy Board had jurisdiction to award costs except at the conclusion of a hearing. (1985), 51 Ontario Reports (2d) 333.

    Although of the opinion that the statutory cost power as worded could not support a funding order, both the Divisional Court and Court of Appeal indicated in their judgements that "this issue (intervenor funding) is fast becoming one which should receive early legislative consideration."

    The Court of Appeal went even further with an endorsement on the record in the following words:
    We wish to add that like the Divisional Court we feel it appropriate to say that the Legisla-
ture might at an early date, consider the problem raised in this application and determine whether an amendment to the legislation under review, somewhat in terms of S.6 of the *Energy Resources Conservation Amendment Act, 1981* of the Statutes of Alberta, might be appropriate.
    To this writer's knowledge, only Alberta's *Energy Resources Conservation Act* contains specific statutory authority for the awarding costs *in advance* to intervenors.

    Following the court decision referred to above, the Ontario Ministry of the Environment has provided funds for specified intervenors in relation to several applications. Special funding panels comprised of members of the Environmental Assessment Board (EAB) other than sitting panel members entertain motions for funding from intervenors and award funds in accordance with criteria set out in the Orders-in-Council allocating the said funds. The Minister stated that this *ad hoc* funding would apply to certain applications until a specific intervenor funding programme is endorsed by Cabinet; see Order-in-Council No. 12395/85 and Orders of the Funding Panels dated October 19, 1985 and October 30 1985 — Registrar's Files EP-85-01 (F) (3Mm Canada Inc. Application) and CH-85-02 (F) (Tricil-Sarnia Application).

    See Scott and Anand, "Financing Public Participation in Environmental Decision Making," *Canadian Bar Review 60* (1982) p. 81; Dewees, Prichard and Trebilcock, "An Economic Analysis of Cost and Fee Rules for Class Action," Working Paper Series Number 79/8. (Institute for Policy Analysis, University of Toronto, 1979); "Intervenor Funding — Public Participation in Rulemaking," *At Home With Consumers*, 1:3 (January, 1980).

15. See William A. Thomas ed, *Proceedings of Symposium of Law-Science Cooperation under the National Environmental Policy Act* (October 8, 1982), p. 593.

16. For a detailed analysis see Kenneth R. Hammond, Jeryl Mumpower, Robin Q. Dennis, Samuel Fitch and Wilson Crumpacker, "Fundamental Obstacles to the Use of Scientific Information in Public Policy Making," *Technological Forecasting and Social Change* (1983), p. 287.

17. Revised Statutes of Ontario 1980, c.411.

(c) "Science in the Courtroom"
Stuart L. Smith

1. In this, I speak for myself and not necessarily for the other members of the Science Council, whose views I have not canvassed.

2. J.M. Doyle, *William and Mary Law Review*, 25 (1984), p. 647.

3. Lloyd Tataryn, *Formaldehyde on Trial* (Toronto: James Lorimer and Company, 1983).

4. Gulf South Insulation et al. versus United States Consumer Product Safety Commission, US *Federal Reporter*, 2nd series, 701 (1983), p. 1137.

5. Palmer et al. vs. Nova Scotia Forest Industries, *Nova Scotia Reports*, 2nd series, 60 (1983), p. 271.

6. Science Council of Canada, *Regulating the Regulators — Science, Values and Decisions*, (Ottawa: ScCC, October 1982).

7. H.T. Markey, *William and Mary Law Review*, 25 (1984), p. 527.

8. R. Albury, "The Politics of Truth," in M. Ruse (ed.), *Nature Animated*, cited by D. Bartels in *Science, Technology and Human Values*, 10 (1985), pp. 69–74.

9. Kriss Boggild, "The Amax Controversy," *Alternatives*, 10:2/3, (1982), pp. 40–46 and Bill Skidmore, "Documents point to government culpability in Amax Affair," *Alternatives*, 11:3/4, (1983), pp. 6–7.

10. A. Kantrowitz, *Congressional Record* 113 (1967), pp. 15, 256.

11. The Science Court Experiment: An Interim Report, *Science* 193 (1976), p. 653.

(d) "Ethics, Science and Environmental Regulation"
Donald Brown

1. *McGraw-Hill Dictionary of Scientific Technical Terms*, 2nd edition, p. 1414.

2. John Burke, ed., *Osborn's Concise Law Dictionary*, (Sweet & Maxwell: sixth edition), p. 196.

3. See, for example, S.1(c) of the *Environmental Assessment Act*, Revised Statutes of Ontario 1980, c. 140, which incorporates socio-economic and cultural conditions into the definition of the term "environment." See also (Saskatchewan) *Environmental Assessment Act*, ss.1980, c.e.10.1 and (Newfoundland) *Environmental Assessment Act*, S. Nfld. 1980, c.3.

4. For example, courts will rarely admit hearsay evidence and often rely upon the "best evidence" rule; S.15 of the *Statutory Powers Procedure Act*, Revised Statutes of Ontario 1980 c.484, on the other hand, allows tribunals having a decision-making power to admit almost any type of evidence, whether oral or documentary, and this includes hearsay evidence, opinions and conclusions of a witness. The tribunal is then at liberty to weigh this evidence as it sees fit and is not circumscribed in any way by the fact that such evidence may be inadmissible in a court of law.

5. (1947) 2 All England Reports 372.

6. *Ibid.*, p. 374; see also *Smith* v. *Smith and Smedman* (1952) 2. Supreme Court Reports 312 p. 331–332; *Clark* v. *The King* (1921), G.1 Can. Supreme Court Reports 608 p. 616.

7. See Sopinka and Lederman, *The Law of Evidence in Civil Cases* (Toronto: Butterworth, 1974), p. 384, for a comprehensive discussion of the extent and allocation of burden of proof.

8. See Nicholas A. Ashford, "Examining the Role of Science in the Regulatory Process," *Environment*, 25:5 (June 1983), p. 7.

9. See Jerome Ravetz, "Scientific Uncertainty Looms Large Over Environmental Policymakers," *Transatlantic Perspectives*, 11 (April 1984), p. 11.

10. M. Frankel, "The Search for Truth: An Umpireal View," 123 *University of Pennsylvania Law Review* 1031 (1975), pp. 1036–1037.

11. Dr. Stuart L. Smith, "Science in the Courtroom: the Value of an Adversarial System," *Alternatives*, Volume 15:2 (1988), p. 18.

12. See, for example, S.38(2) (e) of the *Environmental Protection Act*, Revised Statutes of Ontario 1980, c.141.

13. See S.18(9) of the *Environmental Assessment Act*, Revised Statutes of Ontario 1980, c.140 and also S.10 of the *Consolidated Hearings Act, 1981*, c.141.

14. At the date of this writing, the Ontario Government is implementing a trial intervenor funding programme which will initially cover hearings held pursuant to environmental legislation. The Ontario Minister of the Environment, Jim Bradley, has publicly stated his support for the concept of intervenor funding and his Ministry has taken a number of interim measures in connection therewith pending the approval by Cabinet of a formal programme.

In October and November of 1984, a Joint Board chaired by this writer awarded costs in advance to two groups of intervenors pursuant to a cost power contained in the *Consolidated Hearings Act, 1981* (S.7); see Orders and Reasons for Order dated October 16 and November 5, 1984 (*Hamilton-Wentworth East-West/ North South Transportation Corridor* — Redhill Creek Expressway Application), Registrar's File CH-82-08. These Orders awarding costs in advance were challenged by way of judicial review and quashed by the Divisional Court of the Supreme Court of Ontario; see *Re Regional Municipality of Hamilton-Wentworth and Hamilton-Wentworth Save the Valley Committee, Inc. et al.* (1985), 51 Ontario Reports (2d) 23. The Respondent sought leave to appeal which was refused.

Concurrently, the Ontario Energy Board stated a case to the Divisional Court concerning its statutory power to award costs in advance and this stated case was heard by the same panel. The Court reached the same conclusion and held that neither the Joint Board nor the Energy Board had jurisdiction to award costs except at the conclusion of a hearing. (1985), 51 Ontario Reports (2d) 333.

Although of the opinion that the statutory cost power as worded could not support a funding order, both the Divisional Court and Court of Appeal indicated in their judgements that "this issue (intervenor funding) is fast becoming one which should receive early legislative consideration."

The Court of Appeal went even further with an endorsement on the record in the following words:

> We wish to add that like the Divisional Court we feel it appropriate to say that the Legislature might at an early date, consider the problem raised in this application and determine whether an amendment to the legislation under review, somewhat in terms of S.6 of the *Energy Resources Conservation Amendment Act, 1981* of the Statutes of Alberta, might be appropriate.

To this writer's knowledge, only Alberta's *Energy Resources Conservation Act* contains specific statutory authority for the awarding costs *in advance* to intervenors.

Following the court decision referred to above, the Ontario Ministry of the Environment has provided funds for specified intervenors in relation to several applications. Special funding panels comprised of members of the Environmental Assessment Board (EAB) other than sitting panel members entertain motions for funding from intervenors and award funds in accordance with criteria set out in the Orders-in-Council allocating the said funds. The Minister stated that this *ad hoc* funding would apply to certain applications until a specific intervenor funding programme is endorsed by Cabinet; see Order-in-Council No. 12395/85 and Orders of the Funding Panels dated October 19, 1985 and October 30 1985 – Registrar's Files EP-85-01 (F) (3Mm Canada Inc. Application) and CH-85-02 (F) (Tricil-Sarnia Application).

See Scott and Anand, "Financing Public Participation in Environmental Decision Making," *Canadian Bar Review 60* (1982) p. 81; Dewees, Prichard and Trebilcock, "An Economic Analysis of Cost and Fee Rules for Class Action," Working Paper Series Number 79/8. (Institute for Policy Analysis, University of Toronto, 1979); "Intervenor Funding — Public Participation in Rulemaking," *At Home With Consumers*, 1:3 (January, 1980).

15. See William A. Thomas ed, *Proceedings of Symposium of Law-Science Cooperation under the National Environmental Policy Act* (October 8, 1982), p. 593.

16. For a detailed analysis see Kenneth R. Hammond, Jeryl Mumpower, Robin Q. Dennis, Samuel Fitch and Wilson Crumpacker, "Fundamental Obstacles to the Use of Scientific Information in Public Policy Making," *Technological Forecasting and Social Change* (1983), p. 287.

17. Revised Statutes of Ontario 1980, c. 411.

18. See James P. Leape "Quantitative Risk Assessment in Regulation of Carcinogens." Harvard Environmental Law Review 4 (1980): 86–116..

19. Mark Sagoff, "On Markets for Risk," Maryland Law Review 41 (1982): 755–773.

20. K.S. Shrader-Frechette, Nuclear Power and Public Policy (Dordreut and Boston: D. Riechel Publishing Company, 1980). See also, Ernest Partridge's review of the book in Environmental Ethics 4 (1982): 261–71.

21. See James H. Ware, "Health Risk Assessment: The Role of Statistical Analysis," in Magat, *Reform of Environmental Regulation*.

(e) "Using Science in Environmental Policy"
Ted Schrecker

1. J.A. Hutchings, C. Walters and R.L. Haedrich, 'Is Scientific Inquiry Incompatible with Government Information Control?' *Canadian Journal of Fisheries and Aquatic Science* 54 (1997): 1198–1210.

2. J.A. Hutchings and R.A. Myers, 'What Can Be Learned from the Collapse of a Renewable Resource? Atlantic Cod, *Gadus morhua*, of Newfoundland and Labrador,' *Canadian Journal of Fisheries and Aquatic Sciences* 51 (1994): 2126–46; J.A. Hutchings, The Biological Collapse of Newfoundland's Northern Cod,' in D. Newell and R.E. Ommer, eds, *Fishing Places, Fishing People: Traditions and Issues in Canadian Small-Scale Fisheries* (Toronto: University of Toronto Press, 1999), 260–75.

3. Hutchings, Walters, and Haedrich, 'Scientific Inquiry,' 1199.

4. Ibid., 1204–5; B. Christensen, *Too Good to Be True: Alcan's Kemano Completion Project* (Vancouver: Talonbooks, 1995), 147–57; A. Thompson et al., 'Rivers Defence Coalition Final Argument, Phase V, Kemano Completion Project Review,' BC Utilities Commission (Vancouver, mimeo, 1993; on file with West Coast Environmental Law Association and author), 11–20.

5. Thompson et al., 'Final Argument,' 18.

6. J.F. Castrilli and C.C. Lax, 'Environmental Regulation-Making in Canada: Towards a More Open Process,' in J. Swaigen, ed., *Environmental Rights in Canada* (Toronto: Butterworth, 1981), 334–95; M. Rankin, 'Information and the Environment: The Struggle for

Access,' in ibid., 285–333; T. Schrecker, *Political Economy of Environmental Hazards*, Study paper, Protection of Life, Health and the Environment Project (Ottawa: Law Reform Commission of Canada, 1984), 17–20, 34–7; K. Harrison and G. Hoberg, *Risk, Science and Politics: Regulating Toxic Substances in Canada and the United States* (Montreal: McGill-Queen's University Press, 1994), 52–4, 62–3, 176–9; G. Hoberg, 'Governing the Environment: Comparing Canada and the United States,' in K. Banting, G. Hoberg, and R. Simeon, eds, *Degrees of Freedom: Canada and the United States in a Changing World* (Montreal: McGill-Queen's University Press, 1997), 350–6; W. Leiss, 'Between Expertise and Bureaucracy: Risk Management Trapped at the Science/Policy Interface,' in G.B. Doern and T. Reed. eds, *Risky Business: Canada's Changing Science-Based Policy and Regulatory Regime* (Toronto: University of Toronto Press, forthcoming).

...

14. C. Lindblom, *Politics and Markets* (New York: Basic Books, 1977), 170–221; Schrecker, *Political Economy of Environmental Hazards*, 16–23; T. Schrecker, 'Resisting Environmental Regulation: The Cryptic Pattern of Business-Government Relations,' in R. Paehlke and D. Torgerson, eds, *Managing Leviathan: Environmental Politics and the Administrative State* (Peterborough, ON: Broadview, 1989), 165–99.

15. C. Offe, *Contradictions of the Welfare State*, ed. John Keane (Cambridge, MA: MIT Press, 1984), 151.

16. T. Schrecker, 'Of Invisible Beasts and the Public Interest: Environmental Cases and the Judicial System,' in R. Boardman, ed., *Canadian Environmental Policy* (Toronto: Oxford University Press Canada, 1992), 83–8.

17. R. Kazis and R. Grossman, *Fear at Work: Job Blackmail, Labor, and the Environment* (New York: Pilgrim Press, 1982). In a relatively simple illustration, an Ontario Ministry of the Environment spokesperson explained the province's choice of permissible effluent levels for the chemical industry in 1994 by saying: 'We could say zero discharge but they would all close their plants and move to Mexico'; quoted in D. Westell, 'New rules to cut toxic wastes 47%,' *Globe and Mail*, 14 Sept. 1994: B2. As this example illustrates, the threat of disinvestment need not be explicit to be effective; it can operate instead by way of the mechanism of anticipated reaction.

18. S. Jasanoff, 'Acceptable Evidence in a Pluralistic Society,' in D.G. Mayo and R.D. Hollander, eds, *Acceptable Evidence: Science and Values in Risk Management* (New York: Oxford University Press, 1991), 29–47; T. Schrecker, 'Environmental Law and the Greening of Government: A Cynical Guide,' in G. Thompson, M. McConnell and L. Huestis, eds, *Environmental Law and Business in Canada* (Aurora, ON: Canada Law Book, 1993), 164–8; Hoberg, 'Governing the Environment,' 355–6.

19. R. Inglehart, *Culture Shift in Advanced Industrial Society* (Princeton, NJ: Princeton University Press, 1990).

20. A category that is by no means coextensive with the entire electorate: cf. the observations of E.E. Schattschneider that '[p]robably about 90 percent of the people cannot get into the pressure system' so crucial not only to setting the electoral agenda but also to the political exchanges that occur during the period between elections, and of Lynton Caldwell to the effect that even in formally democratic states, '[p]oliticians generally know whom they must regard

as important and whom they can afford to neglect. 'Schattschneider, *The Semisovereign People: A Realist's View of Democracy in America* (Hinsdale, IL: Dryden Press, [1960] 1975), 34–5, see generally 30–45; Caldwell, *Between Two Worlds: Science, the Environmental Movement, and Policy Choice* (Cambridge: Cambridge University Press, 1990), 88.

21. Canadian Endangered Species Coalition, 'Federal Endangered Species Legislation — Background' [handout] (Ottawa, 8 Aug. 1997).

22. Because of that high level of urbanization, an intriguing area for future research, which unfortunately is outside the scope of this chapter, involves the effects on environmental policy of the consistent overrepresentation of the rural electorate in parliament and in provincial legislatures.

23. A. Eadie, 'On the grid: Net balances for Canada's exports and imports,' *Globe and Mail*, 17 Sept. 1998: B15.

24. N. Klein, 'The Real APEC Scandal,' *Saturday Night*, February 1999: 48.

25. For example, in August 1999 the governments of Canada and the Northwest Territories jointly agreed to assume liability for disposal of toxic tailings generate by the operation of the Giant gold mine, in order to facilitate that mine's sale to a new operator following the bankruptcy of its current owner, Royal Oak Mines Inc. Cost was estimated at $250 million. A. Robinson, 'Ottawa, NWT to pay for Giant cleanup,' *Globe and Mail*, 28 Aug. 1999.

26. K. Harrison, *Passing the Buck: Federalism and Canadian Environmental Policy* (Vancouver: UBC Press, 1996).

27. Patricia Marchak has suggested that a similar outcome may be in store for the forest-products industry in British Columbia: see her *Logging in Globe* (Montreal: McGill-Queen's University Press, 1995). Such an outcome would be in keeping with the historical pattern of exhaustion of renewable resources documented in H. Regier and G.L. Baskerville, 'Sustainable Redevelopment of Regional Ecosystems Degraded by Exploitive Development,' in W. Clark and R.E. Munn, eds, *Sustainable Development of the Biosphere* (Cambridge: Cambridge University Press, 1986), 75–100.

28. In the words of a fishery industry executive quoted by S. Feschuk, 'Only one big processor ready for cod clobbering,' *Globe and Mail*, 3 July 1992.

29. Some time before the last merchantable tree is cut down in British Columbia, the provincial government will probably end up paying forest-product firms to harvest trees for export. The strategy will in turn probably be frustrated, at least as it applies to the U.S. market, by understandable protests from competitors in the Pacific northwest, Meanwhile, the Japanese will be quite happy to have Canadian taxpayers continue to help finance their imports of forest products from both BC and Alberta.

30. M. Trebilcock, *The Political Economy of Economic Adjustment: The Case of Declining Sectors*, Royal Commission on the Economic Union and Development Prospects for Canada, Collected Research Studies Series vol. 8 (Toronto: University of Toronto Press, 1986), 24–5, 34.

31. D.A. Bella, 'The Pressures of Organizations and the Responsibilities of University Professors,' *Bio Science* 46 (1996): 772.

32. J. Elster, *Ulysses and the Sirens: Studies in Rationality and Irrationality* (Cambridge: Cambridge University Press, rev. ed., 1984), 30.

...

34. D.J. Mattson, 'Ethics and Science in Natural Resource Agencies,' *Bio Science* 46 (1996): 767–71.

35. See generally D.J. Savoie, *Governing from the Centre: The Concentration of Power in Canadian Politics* (Toronto: University of Toronto Press, 1999). The 1996 report of a task force on the federal government's policy capacity similarly noted that line departments 'rarely control the interdepartmental allocation of resources, so they are lacking a key lever — and when a line department does lead in the allocation of resources, as happened under the Green Plan, other departments can challenge its objectivity. Typically lead departments also have only weak levers in relation to the process of decision making and they have none of the broader influence that comes from the Prime Minister's and the Clerk's [i.e., the Clerk of the Privy Council's] role in Ministerial and deputy ministerial appointments.' I. Fellegi (chair), *Strengthening Our Policy Capacity: Task Force Report* (Ottawa: Privy Council Office, December 1996), 18.

36. Savoie, *Governing from the Centre*, 108; see generally 71–108.

37. On the role of deputy ministers see ibid., 248–59, 275–81, 314–17.

38. Ibid., 277.

39. Ibid., 255; see also 275–6, 315 and G.B. Doern, *The Peripheral Nature of Scientific and Technological Controversy in Federal Policy Formulation*, Background study no. 46 (Ottawa: Science Council of Canada, 1981).

...

42. Schrecker, 'Invisible Beasts' and 'The Greening of Government.'

43. E. Silbergeld, 'Risk Assessment and Risk Management: An Uneasy Divorce,' in Mayo and Hollander, eds, *Acceptable Evidence*, 99–114.

44. The classic discussion of the internal structure of interest representation within the Canadian state remains R. Mahon, 'Canadian Public Policy: The Unequal Structure of Representation,' in L. Panitch, ed., *The Canadian State: Political Economy and Political Power* (Toronto: University of Toronto Press, 1977), 165–98. The continuing importance of Mahon's analysis for environmental policy was illustrated by the first report of the Commissioner of the Environment and Sustainable Development to Parliament. The report noted that the approach taken by Industry Canada and Natural Resources Canada to regulation of industrial chemicals tends to be quite different from that taken by Health Canada, Environment Canada, and DFO. In specific cases, such as those involving regulation of aquatic herbicides and activities that may result in increased discharges of mercury into the aquatic environment, the effect of such disagreements has been a policy impasse. This amounts, of course, to a tacit endorsement of the status quo, which may be precisely what the development-oriented departments and their clients had in mind. See Commissioner of the Environment and Sustainable Development, *Report to the House of Commons* (Ottawa: Public Works and Government Services Canada, 1999), chap. 3.

45. T. Page, 'A Generic View of Toxic Chemicals and Similar Risks,' *Ecology Law Quarterly* 7 (1978): 207–44;

Schrecker, *Political Economy of Environmental Hazards*, 25–37; Harrison and Hoberg, *Risk, Science and Politics*, 20–7.

46. J. Maienschein, J.P. Collins, and D.S. Strouse, 'Biology and Law: Challenges of Adjudicating Competing Claims in a Democracy,' *Jurimetrics Journal* 38 (1998): 153–4, 159–65; K.S. Shrader-Frechette and E.D. McCoy, *Method in Ecology: Strategies for Conservation* (Cambridge: Cambridge University Press, 1993), 86–92, 198–239; B.L. Taylor and T. Gerrodette, 'The Uses of Statistical Power in Conservation Biology: The Vaquita and Northern Spotted Owl,' *Conservation Biology* 7 (1993): 489–500.

47. Page, 'Generic View.'

48. T.D. Crocker, 'Scientific Truths and Policy Truths in Acid Deposition Research,' in T. Crocker, ed., *Economic Perspectives on Acid Deposition Control*, Ann Arbor Science Acid Precipitation Series (Boston: Butterworth, 1984), 8: 66–7.

49. J.S. Weis, 'Scientific Uncertainty and Environmental Policy: Four Pollution Cases Studies,' in J. Lemons, ed., *Scientific Uncertainty and Environmental Problem Solving* (Cambridge, MA: Blackwell Science, 1996), 169.

50. W. Darby, 'An Example of Decision-Making on Environmental Carcinogens: The Delaney Clause,' *Journal of Environmental Systems* 9 (1979): 116.

51. S.D. Jellinek, 'On the Inevitability of Being Wrong,' *Annals of the New York Academy of Science* 363 (1981): 43–4.

52. Maienschein et al., 'Biology and Law,' 156–8; T.O. McGarity, 'Substantive and Procedural Discretion in Administrative Resolution of Science Policy Questions,' *Georgetown Law Journal* 67 (1979): 732–40.

53. McGarity, 'Substantive and Procedural Discretion,' 748–9; Stewart Cohen et al., 'Climate Change and Sustainable Development: Towards Dialogue,' *Global Environmental Change* 8 (1998): 360–2.

54. Page, 'Generic View,' 233–4.

55. Shrader-Frechette and McCoy, *Method in Ecology*, 84–101. Their discussion relies on a more extensive, if somewhat impenetrable, treatment of the issues by Helen Longino, *Science as Social Knowledge: Values and Objectivity in Scientific Inquiry* (Princeton: Princeton University Press, 1990).

56. Shrader-Frechette and McCoy, *Method in Ecology*, 84.

57. Such methodological value judgments, and the inability of science to provide resolution of the disagreements that result, are discussed at length in a detailed case study of Canadian decision-making concerning two particular herbicides: C. Brunk, L. Haworth, and B. Lee, *Value Assumption in Risk Assessment: A Case Study of the Alachlor Controversy* (Waterloo, ON: Wilfrid Lurier University Press, 1991).

58. The importance of such judgments is evident in the report of a panel that considered the impact of a proposed pulp mill in northern Alberta, under the terms of an agreement between the federal and Alberta governments. The members of the panel insisted on considering the impact of discharges from the proposed mill in combination with those from other existing or anticipated industrial developments, and on that basis recommended that the mill not be approved pending the completion of additional environmental-impact studies. However, they were instructed in their terms of reference, which were drafted jointly by the federal and Alberta governments, not to address the environ-

mental impacts of the forest harvesting without which the proposed mill would lack a supply of fibre. The panel identified this limitation as 'a serious shortcoming in the process': Alberta-Pacific Environmental Impact Assessment Review Board, 'The Proposed Alberta-Pacific Pulp Mill: Report of the EIA Review Board' (Edmonton: Alberta Environment, March 1990). On the history of the panel report, and subsequent developments, see L. Pratt and I. Urquhart, *The Last Great Forest: Japanese Multinationals and Alberta's Northern Forests* (Edmonton: NeWest Press, 1994), 135–200.

59. B. Paigen, 'Controversy at Lover Canal,' *Hastings Center Report* 12 (June 1982): 32.

60. See, e.g., R.A. Carpenter, 'Uncertainty in Managing Ecosystems Sustainably,' in J. Lemons, ed., *Scientific Uncertainty and Environmental Problem Solving*, 118–59; J. Lemons, 'The Conservation of Biodiversity: Scientific Uncertainty and the Burden of Proof,' in ibid., 206–32.

61. R.M. M'Conigle et al., 'Taking Uncertainty Seriously: From Permissive Regulation to Preventive Design in Environmental Decision Making,' *Osgoode Hall Law Journal* 32 (1994): 158.

62. R.C. Earll, 'Commonsense and the Precautionary Principle — An Environmentalist's Viewpoint,' *Marine Pollution Bulletin* 24 (1992): 184; see also R.M. Peterman and M. M'Gonigle, 'Statistical Power Analysis and the Precautionary Principle,' *Marine Pollution Bulletin* 24 (1982): 231–4.

63. 'In the face of threats of irreversible environmental damage, lack of full scientific understanding should not be an excuse for postponing actions which are justified in their own right. The precautionary approach could provide a basis for policies relating to complex systems that are not yet fully understood and whose consequences of disturbances [sic] cannot yet be predicted.' UN Conference on Environment and Development [UNCED], 'Agenda 21,' in J. Quarrie, ed., *Earth Summit '92* (London: Regency Press, 1992), chap. 35.

64. M'Gonigle et al., 'Taking Uncertainty Seriously,' 161.

65. Weis, 'Scientific Uncertainty,' 161.

66. W. Leiss, *Governance and the Environment*, Working Paper Series 96-1 (Kingston, ON: Environmental Policy Unit, School of Policy Studies, Queen's University, 1996), 19–20.

67. M.E. Paté, 'Acceptable Decision Processes and Acceptable Risks in Public Sector Regulation,' *IEEE Transactions on Systems, Man, and Cybernetics* 13 (March/April 1983): 114; see also D. MacLean, 'Risk and Consent: Philosophical Issues for Centralized Decisions,' *Risk Analysis* 2, no. 2 (1982): 59–67; K.S. Shrader-Frechette, *Risk and Rationality: Philosophical Foundations for Populist Reforms* (Berkeley: University of California Press, 1991).

...

72. Paté, 'Acceptable Decision Processes,' 120.

73. The idea of a firewall is borrowed from the financial-services sector, where there are clear synergies among (for example) investment banking, brokerage, and other business lines. At the same time, it is imperative that firms operating in several such areas have some level of credibility with respect to the effective segregation of each operation; otherwise, there would be grounds for suspicion that they were favouring their own interests at the expense of their clients'. Since governments often have a stake, both financial and po-

litical, in the extractive or industrial activities whose environmental impacts they are simultaneously charged with managing, the term is uniquely apposite here.

74. Hutchings, Walters, and Haedrich, 'Scientific Inquiry,' 1206–8.

75. W. Leiss, 'The Trouble with Science: Public Controversy over Genetically-Modified Foods,' paper presented at eastern regional meetings of Canadian Society of Plant Physiologists, Queen's University, 12 Dec. 1999; <http://www.ucalgary/ca/-wleiss/news/trouble_with_science.htm>.

76. Quoted in W.G. Doubleday, D.B. Atkinson, and J. Baird, 'Comment: Scientific Inquiry and Fish Stock Assessment in the Canadian Department of Fisheries and Oceans,' *Canadian Journal of Fisheries and Aquatic Sciences* 54 (1997): 1424; emphases added.

77. See also J.E. Halliwell and W. Smith, *Scientific Advice in Government Decision-Making: The Canadian Experience*, report to Council of Science and Technology Advisors (Gloucester, ON: JEH Associates Inc., March 1999), app. I, 14 on the perceived need at the Canadian Food Inspection Agency 'to develop a clear code on what scientists can and should say in public to ensure balance of openness and respect for Cabinet solidarity.'

78. V.R. Walker, 'Keeping the WTO from Becoming the "World Trans-science Organization"' Scientific Uncertainty, Science Policy, and Factfinding in the Growth Hormones Dispute,' *Cornell International Law Journal* 31 (1998): 291.

79. 'There is literally no information content in a negative finding unless there is an analysis of ... the probability of a false negative.' T. Page, 'A Framework for Unreasonable Risk in the Toxic Substances Control Act (TSCA),' *Annals of the New York Academy of Science* 363 (1981): 162; see also Page, 'Generic View,' 231.

80. Walker, 'Keeping the WTO,' 291.

81. In a number of situations, the secrecy of Canadian regulatory procedures has been defended with reference to the proprietary nature of the data submitted in support of applications for product approval, such as those involving pesticides or veterinary biologicals; see Schrecker et al., 'Biotechnology, Ethics and Government,' 226–7. However, such information as a list of study titles and topics cannot reasonably be considered proprietary, and both the extent of regulatory reliance such studies and the fact that they cannot have undergone the usual process of scientific peer review are important items of information in themselves.

82. W. Smith and J. Halliwell, *Principles and Practices for Using Scientific Advice in Government Decision Making: International Best Practices*, report to the Science and Technology Strategy Directorate (Ottawa: Industry Canada, January 1999), 14.

83. Task Force on Incomes and Adjustment in the Atlantic Fishery, *Charting a New Course: Towards the Fishery of the Future* (Ottawa: Communications Directorate, Dept. of Fisheries and Oceans, 1993); see also R. Ommer, 'Deep Water Fisheries, Policy and Management Issues, and the Sustainability of Fishing Communities,' in A.G. Hopper, ed., *Deep Water Fisheries of the North Atlantic Slope*, Proceedings of the NATO Advanced Research Workshop (Dordrecht: Kluwer, 1995), 307–322.

84. M. Trebilcock et al., *The Political Economy of Business Bailouts* (Toronto: Ontario Economic Council, 1985), 276–93.

85. On the strategic significance of the ability to define the scope and terms of political conflict, see Schattschneider, *The Semisovereign People*, 60–75.

86. W. Leiss and C. Chociolko, *Risk and Responsibility* (Montreal: McGill-Queen's University Press, 1994) 54.

87. Two examples will suffice. First, at least as of the late 1990s one of the objectives of Health Canada's Health Protection Branch, as part of its overall policy framework, was 'to maintain an effective and efficient regulatory system that is in balance with those of competitor nations so Canada is not economically disadvantaged.' Halliwell and smith, *Scientific Advice in Government Decision-Making*, app. I, 46.

Second, an exhaustive study of Canada's re-evaluation of the herbicide Alachlor, after its original registration turned out to have relied on fraudulent safety data (Brunk, Haworth, and Lee, *Value Assumptions in Risk Assessment*), pointed out that no regulatory decision-makers took seriously the option of cancelling the registrations both of Alachlor and a substitute herbicide produced by a competing agrochemical firm. The clear inference is of an a priori conclusion that the economic disruption of corn and soybean farming associated with cancelling both registrations would be politically unacceptable — a conclusion that turned the review process into a purely scholastic exercise in risk comparison.

...

112. See e.g. Council of Science and Technology Advisors, *Building Excellence in Science and Technology (BEST): The Federal Roles in Performing Science and Technology* (Ottawa: Industry Canada, 1999), 31-3; Commissioner of the Environment and Sustainable Development, *Report to the House of Commons* (1999), chaps 3 and 4; G.B. Doern, '"Patient Science" versus "Science on Demand": The Stretching of Green Science at Environment Canada,' paper prepared for Conference on Science, Government and Global Markets (Ottawa: Carleton Research Unit on Innovation, Science and Environment [CRUISE], 20 Sept. 1998: 2; and M. Wiktorowicz, 'Shifting Priorities at the Health Protection Branch: Challenges to the Regulatory Process,' *Canadian Public Administration* 43 (2000): 1–22.

113. Impact Group, 'The Roles of the Federal Government in Performing Science and Technology: The Canadian Context and Major Forces,' report prepared for Council of Science and Technology Advisors (Ottawa: Industry Canada, 1999), 1.

114. G.B. Doern, 'Science and Scientists in Federal Policy and Decision Making,' paper prepared for Policy Research Secretariat, Government of Canada (Ottawa: Carleton Research Unit on Innovation, *Science and Environment* [CRUISE]), 1999, part I; Halliwell and Smith, *Scientific Advice*, 8, 32.

C. Risk Assessment

(a) "A Critical Review of Current Issues in Risk Assessment and Risk Management"
Steve E. Hrudey

References

Anderson, C. 1991. Cholera epidemic traced to risk miscalculation. *Nature*. 354, 28 November, 255.

Canadian Standards Association. 1996. Draft 7: Q850 Risk Management: Guideline for Decision-Makers. Toronto, Ontario: Canadian Standards Association. 49pp.

Finkel A.M. 1990. *Confronting Uncertainty in Risk Management — A Guide for Decision-Makers*. Washington, D.C.: Centre for Risk Management, Resources for the Future. 68pp.

Graham, J.D. and J.B. Wiener. 1995. Risk vs. Risk: Tradeoffs in Protecting Health and the Environment. Cambridge, Massachusetts: Harvard University Press. 337pp.

Hattis, D. and D. Kennedy. 1986. Assessing risks from health hazards: An imperfect science. *Technology Review*. 89, 4, 60–71.

Hoffman, F.O. 1996. Senes Oak Ridge; Oak Ridge, Tenn., Personal communication.

Hrudey, S.E. and D. Krewski. 1995. Is there a safe level of exposure to a carcinogen? *Environmental Science and Technology*. 29, 370A–375A.

Hurd, D. 1996. The beef scare and the balancing of risks. *The Globe and Mail*, Friday, May 31, A19.

Jardine, C.G. and S.E. Hrudey. 1996. Mixed messages in risk communication. *Environmental Risk Management Working Paper*, ERC 96-4, Edmonton, Alberta: Eco-Research Chair in Environmental Risk Management, University of Alberta.

Kaplan, S. and B. Garrick. 1981. On the quantitative definition of risk. *Risk Analysis*. 1, 1–27.

Kraus, N., T. Malmfors and P. Slovic. 1992. Intuitive toxicology: expert and lay judgments of chemical risk. *Risk Analysis*. 12, 215–232.

Leiss, W. and C. Chociolko. 1994. *Risk and Responsibility*. Montreal and Kingston: McGill-Queen's University Press. 405pp.

Morgan, M.G. 1981. Choosing and managing technology-induced risk. *IEEE Spectrum*. 18, 12, 53–60.

National Academy of Sciences. 1983. *Risk assessment in the Federal Government: Managing the Process*. Washington, D.C.: National Academy Press.

National Research Council. 1994. *Science and Judgment in Risk Assessment*. Washington, D.C.: National Academy Press, 651pp.

Paulos, J.A. 1995. A Mathematician Reads the Newspaper. New York, NY: Anchor Books, 212pp.

Rothman, K.J. 1988. Inferring causal connections — habit, faith or logic? In: K.J. Rothman (Ed.) *Causal Inference*. Chestnut Hill, Mass.: Epidemiology Resources. 3–12.

Slovic, P., T. Malmfors, D. Krewski, C.K. Mertz, N. Neil and S. Bartlett. 1995. Intuitive toxicology II. Expert and lay judgments of chemical risks in Canada. *Risk Analysis*. 15, 661–675.

Susser, M. 1988. Rational science versus a system of logic. In: K.J. Rothman (Ed.) *Causal Inference*, Chestnut Hill, Mass.: Epidemiology Resources Inc. 187–199.

(b) "Is a Scientific Assessment of Risk Possible? Value Assumptions in the Canadian Alachlor Controversy"
Conrad Brunk, Lawrence Haworth and Brenda Lee

1. This article is a condensation of the first four chapters of the authors' book, *Value Assumptions in Risk Assessment: A Case Study of the Alachlor Controversy* (Waterloo, ON: Wilfrid Laurier University Press, 1991). The authors would like to thank the Institute for Risk Research at the University of Waterloo and Social Science and Humanities Research Council of Canada for substantial assistance in the carrying out of the research upon which this paper is based and the preparation of the paper.

2. The term "mandated science" is taken from a recent, excellent book by Liora Salter, *Mandated Science* (Dordrecht: Kluwer Academic Publishers, 1988).

3. The term "risk assessment" is generally used to refer to this first stage of risk analysis, so that the most fundamental distinction is that between risk assessment and risk management. Sometimes, risk assessment and risk estimation are distinguished: risk estimation is construed as one phase of risk assessment, the phase at which the level of risk or magnitude of risk is determined. Among those who make this distinction, there is little consensus concerning how the other phases of risk assessment should be identified. One example, though, would be hazard identification. We are focussing on risk *estimation*, determination of the level of risk. In this paper, the reader should regard the terms "risk estimation" and "risk assessment" as synonymous.

4. Of course the concept of "harm" is itself a normative one, but if it can be given a naturalistic definition (e.g., "incidence of cancer deaths in a population"), then the measuring of this harm is thought to be a purely empirical matter.

5. We mean by "normative" any judgment that reflects a political, moral, personal, or other value preference. These are generally recognizable by the presence of terms such as "good," "better," "ought," "should," and the like. Debates over these judgments generally are not settled solely by appeal to empirical evidence, since they are not debates about the facts alone, but also about the relative worth of various facts. For example, in the Alachlor debate the question, "How many farmers wore adequate protective gloves?" was primarily an empirical (non-normative) one. The question, "Should the exposure incurred by farmers who do not wear such gloves be included in estimates of applicators' exposure to Alachlor?" since it raised the issue of whether doing so would be fair to Monsanto, was a normative question.

6. Numerous authors have argued, as we do here, that risk assessment is not a value-free enterprise. Generally speaking, they fall into two groups. Some, looking to specific examples, represent the presence of values in the assessments as a sign that they are flawed. These critics, then, implicitly accept the ideal held forth by the classical view. They assume that value-free risk assessments are both possible and desirable; their contribution is to show that the ideal is seldom achieved. Others hold that the ideal is impossible to achieve, but base their argument on some general philosophical position, for example, the sociology of knowledge or a critique of the "fact-value" distinction. Our approach is similar to that taken by the first group (and unlike that taken by the second group) in that we do not argue from general principles but base our conclusion on an examination of particular cases. It is similar to that taken by the second group (and unlike that taken by the first group) in that we do not regard value-free risk assessments as possible. Nor do we regard assessments which fail to be value-free as necessarily flawed. For a view concerning risk assessment which is in many respects similar to our own,

see Brian Wynne, *Risk Management and Hazardous Waste* (Berlin: Springer-Verlag, 1987), and, with L. Aitken, "The System's Ability to Learn: Some Basic Problems in Post-hoc Accident Assessment," in *Policy Responses to Large Accidents*, edited by B. Segerstahl and G. Krömer (Vienna: IFASA, 1989), pp. 185–205. But see also P. Thompson, "Risk Subjectivism and Risk Objectivism: When are Risks Real?" *Risk*, 1 (1990); K. Shrader-Frechette, "Scientific Method, Anti-Foundationalism and Public Decisionmaking," *Risk*, 1 (1990); Thomas McGarity, "Substantive and Procedural Discretion in Administrative Resolution of Science Policy Questions: Regulating Carcinogens in EPA and OSHA," *Georgetown Law Review*, 67 (1979); Nicholas Ashford et al., "A Hard Look at Federal Regulation of Formaldehyde," *Harvard Environmental Law Review*, 7 (1983); Sheila Jasanoff, "Contested Boundaries in Policy-Relevant Science," *Social Studies of Science*, 17 (1987); Alvin Weinberg, "Science and its Limits: The Regulator's Dilemma," *Issues in Science and Technology* (Fall 1985); Alvin Weinberg, "Science and Trans-Science," *Minerva*, 10 (1972); Sheila Jasanoff, *Risk Management and Political Culture* (New York: Russel Sage, 1986); Ronald Brickman et al., *Controlling Chemicals* (Ithaca, NY: Cornell University Press, 1985); and Nicholas Rescher, *Risk: A Philosophical Introduction to the Theory of Risk Evaluation and Management* (Washington, DC: University Press of America, 1985). The Weinberg and McGarity papers place particular stress on the ways uncertainty in risk assessments leads to importation of assessors' value perspectives; in this way they anticipate what we shall refer to as "conditionally normative issues" in risk assessment.

7. The findings of the Review Board are printed in the *Report of the Alachlor Review Board* (Ottawa, ON: Alachlor Review Board, 1987). The transcripts of the hearings are published as the *Alachlor Review Board Hearings* (Toronto, ON: Atchison & Denman Court Reporting Services, 1986, 1987).

8. "Amortization" means simply the dividing of an exposure level by a fraction equal to that of the period of time out of a lifetime during which a person is exposed. For example, if a person is exposed to 2.5 mg/kg/day for a total of 180 days out of an expected life-span of 72 years, the exposure of 2.5 would be reduced by a fraction of approximately 1/144. The assumption is that the carcinogenic effects of the chemical are not due to "one-shot" exposure, but are incremental with the length of exposure.

(c) "Comparative Risk Assessment and the Naturalistic Fallacy"
Kristin S. Shrader-Frechette

1. Weinberg, A. (1988) in *Phenotypic Variations in Population* (Woodhead, A., Bender, M. and Leonard, R., eds), pp. 121–128, Elsevier.
2. Whipple, C. (1989) in *The Risk Assessment of Environmental and Human Health Hazards* (Paustenbach, D., ed.), pp. 1116–1123, Wiley.
3. Cooke, R. (1992) *Experts in Uncertainty: Subjective Probability and Expert Opinion.* Oxford University Press.
4. Shrader-Frechette, K. (1991) *Risks and Rationality*, University of California Press.
5. Moore, G. (1959) *Principia Ethica*, Cambridge University Press.

Four
Responses to Environmental Conflict

A. Avenues for Citizen Participation

(c) Conclusion: Continuing the Process..."
Gerald Cormick et al.

14. For example, the Department of Fisheries and Ocean's Policy for the Management of Fish Habitat affords many opportunities for cooperative, adaptable solutions to potential ·habitat problems. These can be best explored through multiparty discussions involving the Department and proponents and opponents of development projects with potential environmental impacts.

B. Environmental Mediation

(a) "Alternative Dispute Resolution and Environmental Conflict"
Elizabeth J. Swanson

1. For an overview of the legal issues relevant to the use of ADR, see E. Swanson, "Alternative Dispute Resolution Processes: The Legal Issues" (1995) 10:2 News Brief 1.
2. G. Bingham, *Resolving Environmental Disputes: A Decade of Experience* (Washington, D.C.: The Conservation Foundation 1986) at 4–5.
3. This definition is based on G.W. Cormick's definition of "consensus building" and "policy dialogues" as given in "The Myth, The Reality, and The Future of Environmental Mediation" (1982) 24:7 Environment 14 at 16.
4. As defined by J.R. Nolan *et at.*, *Black's Law Dictionary*, 6th ed. (St. Paul: West Publishing Co., 1990) at 472, "dispute" means "[a] conflict or controversy; a conflict of claims or rights; an assertion of a right, claim or demand on one side, met by contrary claims or allegations on the other. The subject of litigation...."
5. For a comprehensive discussion of the nature of environmental disputes and the use of alternative dispute resolution techniques to resolve them, see E. Swanson, "Towards Resolution: Alternative Dispute Resolution Processes, Environmental Conflict and the Law" (Edmonton: Environmental Law Centre, 1995) [unpublished].
6. In distinguishing between conflicts arising out of differences in values and those arising out of differences in interests, I adopt the definitions provided by A.H.J. Dorcey & C.L. Rick, "Negotiation-Based Approaches To The Settlement of Environmental Disputes in Canada" in *The Place of Negotiation in Environmental Assessment* (Hull: Canadian Environmental Assessment Research Council, 1989) 7 at 8 [emphasis in original]:
   Value conflicts stem from different preferences about the outcome....
   Interest conflicts occur when there are disagreements about the distribution of costs and benefits.

7. See *e.g.* D.P. Emond, "Accommodating Negotiation/ Mediation Within Existing Assessment and Approval Processes" in *The Place of Negotiation in Environmental Assessment, ibid.*, at 45.
8. T.J. Sullivan, *Resolving Development Disputes Through Negotiations* (New York: Plenum Press, 1984) at 182.
9. *Supra* note at 37.
10. The results of the study are presented in an unpublished paper by E. Swanson, *supra* note 5.
11. E. Vanderburgh & A. Hope, "Alternative Dispute Resolution" in C. Sandborn, ed., *Law Reform for Sustainable Development in British Columbia* (Vancouver: Canadian Bar Association, British Columbia Branch, 1990) 16 at 18. See also L.R. Freedman & M.L. Prigoff, "Confidentiality in Mediation: The Need For Protection" (1986) 2 Ohio St. J. Dispute Res. 37; J.B. Stulberg, "Mediator Immunity" (1986) 2 Ohio St. J. Dispute Res. 85; E. Swanson, "Legislative Reform and the Institutionalization of ADR" (Edmonton: Environmental Law Centre, 1995) [unpublished].
12. M.C. Berstein, "The Desirability of a Statute for the Enforcement of Mediated Agreements" (1986) 2 Ohio St. J. Dispute Res. 117 at 117–118.
13. See generally R.P. Burns, "The Enforceability of Mediated Agreements: An Essay on Legitimation and Process Integrity" (1986) 2 Ohio St. J. Dispute Res. 93; A.A. Chaykin, "The Liabilities and Immunities of Mediators: A Hostile Environment for Model Legislation" (1986) 2 Ohio St. J. Dispute Res. 47; E. Green, "A Heretical View of the Mediation Privilege" (1986) 2 Ohio St. J. Dispute Res. 1.
14. (Toronto: Canadian Environmental Law Association, 1987) [unpublished].
15. *Ibid.*, at 103.
16. This might be achieved, for example, by establishing rights of participation including: (a) the right to notice of ADR processes; (b) the right of funding to facilitate participation; and (c) the right to access information.
17. Keeping in mind that arbitration is considered here as a *traditional* dispute resolution process, the author is not aware of any similar legislation in Canada.
18. Pub. L. No. 101–152, 104 Stat. 2736 (1990).
19. Title 13, Article 22, Part 3.
20. *Ibid.*, §581(2) at 2738.
21. *Ibid.*, §582(b)(1)–(6) at 2739.
22. *Supra* note 19, 13-22-305.
23. S.C. 1992 c. 37.
24. *Ibid.*, s. 20.
25. As defined in s. 2 of the CEAA, an "interested party" any person or body having an interest in the outcome of the environmental assessment for a purpose that is neither frivolous nor vexatious...." While not expressly stated, it is likely that the Minister of the Environment would settle the issue of who is (or is not) an "interested party," though it should be noted that the mediator has the authority to add parties during the course of a mediation (*ibid.*, ss. 29(2) 31).
26. S.N.S. 1994–95, c. 1.

27. S.M. 1987–88, c. 26.
28. *Ibid.*, s. 6(5)(d).
29. See the *Environmental Protection Act*, R.S.N.W.T. 1988, c. E-7, s. 2.2(f); *Environment Act*, S.Y. 1991, c. 5, s. 23(3)(b).
30. S.O. 1993, c. 28, ss. 24(1), 34.
31. J. Titerle, "Politics and BC's New Environmental Legislation" (April 1995) Compliance Report 5.
32. 5 U.S.C. §581, Pub. L. No. 101–648, 104 Stat. 4969 (1990).

(b) "Environmental Mediation"
Steven Shrybman

1. See Gerald Cormick "The Myth, The Reality and the Future of Environmental Mediation" *Environment* 24, 7: 14–39, 1982.

...

4. See Emrich "New Approaches to Managing Environmental Conflict: How Can the Federal Government Use Them." Prepared for the Council on Environmental Quality. Reston, Virginia 1980, at p. 6.
5. See "Environmental Conflict Management Practitioners Workshop." A report of the proceedings of conference convened at Florissant, Colorado, October, 1982, at pp. 3–11....

...

9. The facts of this particular dispute are discussed in some detail in "Conflict Assessment: A Consumers Guide".

...

11. See First Interim Report, Northern Flood Agreement case study. In this regard, among the various provisions of the Agreement are several that directly address issues pertaining to resource management. With respect to natural wildlife, the Agreement provides for the establishment of a Wildlife Planning and Development Board that includes Indian people. The economic development program provided for by the Agreement is designed to facilitate the commercial development of indigenous resources by the Indian residents of the area.
12. See First Interim Report, case study bibliography.
13. In this regard, it would be very problematic to dispense with the public hearing process established to oversee the siting by Ontario Waste Management Corporation of a hazardous and toxic waste disposal facility on the basis of a mediated agreement that would involve the payment of compensation to the host municipality.
14. See the keynote remarks of Charles Warren, then Chairman of the Council of Environmental Quality in "Environmental Mediation: An Effective Alternative?" A report of a conference held in Reston, Virginia; Resolve 1978 at pp. 11 and 12.
15. Supra Part I — Mediation Models.
16. See First Interim Report: Part III Questionnaire.
17. Supra Part III Fn. 5.
18. Supra Fn. 1: Questionnaire respondents frequently identified these attitudinal barriers as needing to be overcome.
19. See two excellent articles by Leah Patton who canvasses the impediments thoroughly: "Problems in Environmental Mediation: Human, Procedural and Substantive", *Environmental Comment*, November 1981, 7–10; "Settling Environmental Disputes", Speech presented to the National Conference on Dispute Resolu-

tion sponsored by the Conservation Foundation, Washington D.C., January 24, 1983. Seattle, Wash.: Institute for Environmental Mediation.
20. Idem.

...

22. See Supra Part II: "Do Sufficient Incentives Exist" and Part III: "Conflict Assessment: A Consumers Guide".
23. Kim Roberts, who is a staff lawyer with the West Coast Environmental Law Association, also makes many of these points in his "Address to Malaspina College Conference on Mediation" ... Malaspina College, Nanaimo, B.C. April, 1983.
24. An excellent survey of the criteria that have been advanced in this regard is provided by Douglas Amy in "The Politics of Environmental Mediation", *Ecology Law Quarterly*, vol. II no. 1.
25. Idem at p. 14.
26. Idem at p. 3.

(c) "How Efficient Are Environmental Dispute Resolution Processes?"
Gail Bingham

1. Roscoe Pound, "The Causes of Popular Dissatisfaction with the Administration of Justice," American Bar Association *Reports* 29 (1906): 395; reprinted in *Judicature* 46 (1962): 55.
2. Jerald S. Auerback, *Justice Without Law* (New York: Oxford University Press, 1983).

...

4. Allan R. Talbot, *Settling Things: Six Case Studies in Environmental Mediation* (Washington, D.C.: The Conservation Foundation, 1983), pp. 7–24.
5. Ibid., p. 1.
6. The number of civil suits, filed in U.S. District courts, that reached trial has declined steadily from 10 percent in 1970 to 5.4 percent in 1983. See Judicial Conference of the United States, *Annual Report of the Director of the Administrative Office of the United States Courts 1983* (Washington, D.C.: U.S. Government Printing Office, 1983), p. 142.

...

8. Judicial Conference of the United States, "Analysis of the Workload of the Federal Courts during the Twelve Month Period Ended June 30, 1983," *Annual Report of the Director of the Administrative Office of the United States Courts 1983*, p. 114.
9. Ibid., p. 97.
10. Ibid., p. 114.
11. Ibid., p. 97.

...

13. Council on Environmental Quality, *Annual Report 1978* (Washington, D.C.: U.S. Government Printing Office); Council of Environmental Quality, *Annual Report, 1983* (Washington, D.C.: U.S. Government Printing Office).
14. *Annual Report of the Director of the Administrative Office of the United States Courts 1983*, p. 122.

...

17. The author particularly would like to thank Joe Cecil and Eric Armen from the Federal Judicial Center for their assistance.
18. For example, lawsuits over many kinds of land-use issues more likely would be brought at the local or state level. The environmental lawsuits included in figure 16 involved a federal agency as either the plaintiff

or a defendant; or if they did not involve a federal agency, the complaint cited a federal statute.

19. For example, the negotiated agreement in a dispute between the U.S. Environmental Protection Agency and the Brown Company over control of sulfur emissions at the company's pulp and paper mill in Berlin, New Hampshire resulted in significant economic gains for the company and in environmental gains for the agency. See David Gilmore, "Successful Regulatory Negotiation (The Brown Company Case)," in Lawrence Susskind, Lawrence Bacow, and Michael Wheeler, eds., *Resolving Environmental Regulatory Disputes* (Cambridge, Mass.: Schenkman Publishing Company, 1983), pp. 5–29.

20. For example, a Minnesota Mining and Manufacturing, Inc. (3M), tape coating plant in Bristol, Pennsylvania, reportedly can reduce its emissions of volatile organic compounds far below the levels required by conventional regulation, at far less cost, through use of a bubble. 3M is substituting water-based solvents as part its bubble proposal. See Richard A. Liroff, *Reforming Air Pollution Regulation: The Toil and Trouble of EPA's Bubble*, (Washington, D.C.: The Conservation Foundation, forthcoming).

21. Lawrence S. Bacow and Michael Wheeler, *Environmental Dispute Resolution* (New York: Plenum Press, 1984), pp. 46–50.

22. For example, in the CREST case, the parties actually first contacted The Mediation Institute several years before the mediation process began. At that stage, the parties were able to proceed on their own in resolving many of the issues through the planning process. Ultimately, the parties reached an impasse, however, and returned for assistance from the mediators. In such cases, the mediation process will be measured from the later contact.

* Although the information available about how much time it took to resolve the environmental disputes examined for this study is incomplete, it is sufficient to provide general answers to some important questions about the duration of mediation-type processes. For about two thirds of the cases studied, information is available on when the mediators were contracted, how long the dispute assessments took, when the first meetings took place, how many meetings there were, the dates of the last meetings, when the agreements (if they were put in writing) were signed, and when any formal ratifications that might have occurred took place.

23. Testimony by Sam Gusman before the Senate Select Committee on Small Business, July 29–30, 1980, p. 79.

(d) "The Politics of Environmental Mediation"
Douglas J. Amy

1. In this essay, the term "environmental mediation" refers to a number of different dispute resolution approaches that use a neutral intervener. For a discussion of the distinctions between the various forms of environmental mediation, see Bellman, Bingham, Brooks, Carpenter, Clark & Craig, *Environmental Conflict Resolution*, Envtl. Consensus, Winter 1981, at 1.

2. *See, e.g.,* S. Mernitz, Mediation of Environmental Disputes (1980); Northern Rockies Action Group, *Selected Transcripts From the NRAG Conference on Negotiations,*

NRAG Papers, Fall 1980 ([hereinafter cited as *NRAG Transcripts*]; O'Gara, *Should This Marriage Be Saved?*, Envtl. Action, Mar. 11, 1978, at 10.

3. Mernitz, *supra* note 2, at 48–49.

4. *Id.* at 50.

5. Bellman, Bingham, Brooks, Carpenter, Clark & Craig, *supra* note 1, at 5.

6. For a description of some of the successes and failure of environmental mediation, see Mernitz, *supra* note 2, at 79–121.

7. Telephone interview with James Benson, Director of the Institute for Ecological Studies (November 17, 1981).

8. *Quoted in* J. Crowfoot, *Negotiations: An Effective Tool for Citizen Organizations?*, NRAG Papers, Fall 1980, at 25.

9. O'Gara, *supra* note 2, at 11–13.

10. *See, e.g.,* Abel, *The Contradictions of Informal Justice,* in The Politics of Informal Justice 267–320 (Abel ed. 1982).

11. *E.g.,* Mernitz, *supra* note 2; A Talbot, Environmental Mediation: 3 Case Studies (1981).

12. There are some exceptions to this. Two notable attempts to begin to deal with the possibility of political bias in environmental mediation are Crowfoot, *supra* note 8 and Cormick, *Intervention and Self-determination in Environmental Disputes: A Mediator's Perspective,* Envtl. Consensus 1 (Winter 1982), at 1.

13. See Arnstein, *A Ladder of Citizen Participation,* 1969 J. Am. Inst. Planner, 216, 216–24.

14. Benson, *supra* note 7.

15. *Id.*

16. *Id.*

17. Mernitz, *supra* note 2, at 157.

18. Telephone interview with Gail Bingham of the Conservation Foundation (September 22, 1981).

19. Carpenter & Kennedy, *Environmental Conflict Management*, 2 The Envtl. Prof. 71 (1980).

20. ROMCOE, or the Rocky Mountain Center on the Environment, is located in Denver, Colarado, and has been at the forefront of the attempt to bring together business, government, and public interest groups to address environmental problems in that region.

21. Carpenter & Kennedy, *supra* note 19.

22. Bingham, *supra* note 18.

23. G. Cormick, Environmental Mediation in the U.S.: Experience and Future Directions 11 (1981)(unpublished paper presented to the American Association for the Advancement of Science Annual Meeting).

24. Interview with Howard Bellman, regional director for the Institute for Environmental Mediation, in Oberlin, Ohio (September 25, 1981).

25. In fact, environmentalists sometimes offer this very interpretation of the problem. For example, James Benson attributed much of it to the fact that many environmental negotiators are simply too polite and not feisty enough. See *supra* text accompanying note 16.

26. *See* Crowfoot, *supra* note 8, at 39.

27. Benson, *supra* note 7.

28. Bellman, *supra* note 24.

29. For example, one controversy involving the expansion of Boston's subway system eventually involved more than 50 different governmental organizations, environmental groups, business groups, and neighborhood organizations. L. Susskind, The Importance of Citizen Participation and Consensus Building in the Land Use Planning Process 7 (1977)(unpublished paper from En-

vironmental Impact Assessment Project at the Massachusetts Institute of Technology).

30. Many of the criticisms of pluralist democratic theory bear a resemblance to the criticisms this essay makes about environmental mediation. For a classic critique of pluralist theory in general and the problem of access in particular, see R. Wolff, *Beyond Tolerance*, in A Critique of Pure Tolerance (1965).

31. It should be pointed out that groups can be left out of mediation attempts for other reasons besides lack of power. For example, some groups may not be aware of the mediation and others may be unorganized. One might also include future generations as a group that is often left out of mediation efforts.

32. Resolve Center for Environmental Conflict Resolution, Environmental Mediation: An Effective Alternative? 41 (1978) [hereinafter cited as Resolve Conference Report].

33. For example, the developers agreed that there would be no access to the shopping center through the neighborhood. *Id.* at 42.

34. *Id.*

35. Cormick & Patton, *Environmental Mediation: Defining the Process Through Experience* (1978) in Environmental Mediation: The Search for Consensus 84 (Lake ed. 1980).

36. *Id.*

37. Cormick, *supra* note 23, at 15.

38. As Cormick has observed, "[w]here there has not been this opportunity for the challenging party to establish a power base, the more established party may seek to select or initiate an intervention process and may even underwrite the expense of the intervention or the intervener." Cormick, *supra* note 12, at 4.

39. Mernitz, *supra* note 2.

40. *See, e.g.*, Lake, *Environmental Conflict and Decision-making* in Environmental Mediation: The Search for Consensus 8 (Lake ed. 1980).

41. Benson, *supra* note 7.

42. Mernitz, *supra* note 2, at 49–50.

43. Harrington, *Voluntariness, Consent, and Coercion in Adjusting Minor Disputes: The Neighborhood Justice Center*, in Policy Implementation 131 (1980).

44. *Id.* at 149.

45. Benson, *supra* note 7.

46. Crowfoot, *supra* note 8, at 36.

47. See *supra* note 32 and accompanying text.

48. Resolve Conference Report, *supra* note 32, at 42.

49. P. Clark & W. Emrich, New Tools for Resolving Environmental Disputes (1980) (Report for the Council on Environmental Quality and the Geological Survey, U.S. Department of the Interior).

50. *Id.* at 2.

51. *Id.* at 12 (emphasis in original).

52. *NRAG Transcripts*, *supra* note 2, at 13.

53. Arnstein, *supra* note 13.

54. In Cormick's words, "there will be legitimate differences in priorities among persons with varying perspectives and divergent aspirations. These differences cannot be dealt with in terms of 'right' and 'wrong' —

all are 'right' or legitimate concerns." Cormick, *Mediating Environmental Controversies: Perspectives and First Experience*, 2 Earth L.J. 215 (1976).

55. One can draw parallels here between the perspective on political issues fostered by environmental mediation and the perspective fostered by the theory of interest-group pluralism. Pluralism also defines a just policy outcome as one in which the interest groups involved achieve some of their goals. *See* Wolff, *supra* note 30.

56. As Scott Mernitz pointed out in his book on environmental mediation, one of the main "goal[s] of mediation is to encourage responsible, planned and progressive development." Mernitz, *supra* note 2, at 163.

57. Mernitz has stated that "future, mediated environmental settlements will tend to favor developmental interests in the sense that some development will occur." *Id.*

58. *Id.* at 158.

59. *E.g.*, H. Daly, Steady-State Economics (1977); W. Ophuls, Ecology and The Politics of Scarcity (1977); L. Schumacher, Small Is Beautiful (1973).

60. Ophuls, *supra* note 59, at 1–137.

61. Daly, *supra* note 59, at 2–49.

62. *NRAG Transcripts*, *supra* note 2, at 21.

63. Abel, *supra* note 10.

64. *Id.* at 287–89.

65. *Id.* at 289.

66. *Id.* at 285.

67. Cormick, *supra* note 54, at 218.

68. *Id.*

69. For one description of Goldaber's work, see Dowie, *Atomic Psyche-Out*, Mother Jones, May 1981, at 21.

70. Dowie, *supra* note 69, at 50.

71. *Id.*

72. *Id.*

73. Mernitz, *supra* note 2, at 60.

74. *See, e.g.*, Golten, *Mediation: A "Sellout" for Conservation Advocates, or a Bargain?* 2 The Envtl. Prof. 62, 65 (1980); Carpenter & Kennedy, *supra* note 19.

75. Golten, *supra* note 74.

76. This line of reasoning was apparent in a recent attempt by the ROMCOE Center for Environmental Problem Solving to mediate another uranium mine dispute in Utah. Carpenter & Kennedy, *supra* note 19. From the very beginning, the ROMCOE mediators made it clear that because of time limitations it would be most efficient to address only a limited agenda of issues: "In our opening remarks, we addressed the issue of nuclear warfare explicitly by pointing out that it was unlikely that we would solve that problem in one day, but it could easily absorb the entire time available. We suggested that the groups agree not to address the nuclear warfare issues because we wanted to know about the plans for the uranium mine." *Id.* at 73.

77. For examples of mediation efforts that have benefitted environmentalists, see Resolve Conference Report, *supra* note 32, at 37–46.

78. For an excellent discussion of how citizens' groups should go about deciding if mediation is appropriate in a particular situation, see Crowfoot, *supra* note 8.

Glossary of Terms and Concepts

A PRIORI: Latin term meaning "what comes before"; an *a priori* proposition is one that can be known to be true or false without reference to experience [*A Dictionary of Philosophy*].

ABATEMENT: putting an end to an activity (such as pollution), or at least reducing its impact in degree or intensity.

ABSOLUTE LIABILITY: see **Liability**

ACTUS REUS: The "guilty deed", an action attracting guilt; the elements of an offence, not including the intent.

ADJUDICATION: The formal judgment or decision of court or tribunal; the legal process of resolving a dispute — it implies a **hearing** by a court, after notice, of legal evidence, conducted in accordance with rules of **civil procedure**.

ADMINISTRATIVE PENALTIES: Penalties (usually fines) that an administrative agency or **tribunal** may itself impose for a breach of a regulation, without having to prosecute the violator (i.e., to take the violator to court). Administrative penalties are contrasted with criminal and quasi-criminal sanctions, which are imposed by a court upon conviction of the accused. For example, the penalty for late filing of an income tax return is an administrative penalty; tax evasion is a criminal offence.

ALTERNATIVE DISPUTE RESOLUTION (ADR): Use of a neutral third party to resolve disputes through a process the procedure of which is less formalized, less structured, and less legalistic than that of a court; ADR includes **arbitration**, **mediation**, and **negotiation**. See Editors' Notes to Section Four, Part B.

ANTHROPOCENTRIC/ANTHROPOCENTRISM: (derived from Greek *anthropos* = man/human and Greek *kentrikos* = centre) human-centred; conceiving of everything in the universe in terms of human values and interests; only humans have moral standing; assumption that moral obligation is a function of human interests; human interests determine what obligations human beings have regarding the environment.

ARBITRATION: A process of dispute resolution in which a neutral third party (arbitrator) renders a decision after a **hearing** at which both parties have an opportunity to be heard". [*Black's Law Dictionary*] Usually a voluntary, binding quasi-judicial process. See Editors' Notes to Section Four, Part B.

AUDIT/AUDITING: An audit is a formal examination of an organization's or an individual's accounts. As currently used in environmental management, an audit is a formal comparison of an organization's current practices with approved environmental standards or procedures; an examination of an organization's accounts to demonstrate its ability to comply with environmental laws. In Canada's environmental assessment practice, the document that formally compares environmental losses with potential benefits is sometimes referred to as an audit.

BIOCENTRIC/BIOCENTRISM: Life-centred; all living beings have moral standing; moral consideration is extended to all life; human beings have duties to all living beings.

BREACH: "The invasion of a right, or the violation ... of a legal duty", or a failure to perform a legal duty. I. In the context of the tort of **negligence**, the term "breach of duty" signifies the "omission to do something" which a reasonable person would do, or "doing something which a reasonable person would not do". II. In the context of **contract**, a breach of contract is a "failure to fulfil a contractual obligation, entitling the innocent party to a **remedy**". [*Osborn's Concise Law Dictionary*].

BYLAW: A form of subordinate legislation made by some authority subordinate to a legislature, for example, a law that a municipality makes [*Osborn's Concise Law Dictionary*]; a rule or resolution adopted by a corporation to regulate its operations.

CABINET: In a parliamentary system of government such as Canada's, the Cabinet consists of the Prime Minister or Premier and the Ministers responsible for the various departments and ministries of the government. Members of Cabinet are usually members of the legislature who belong to the governing party, and are appointed to Cabinet by the PM or Premier. The Cabinet is responsible for overseeing the executive branch of government (i.e., the bureaucracy) and also controls the agenda of the **legislature**.

CAPITALISM: A type of economic system characterized by the following: "(1) private ownership and control of the economic instruments of production, i.e., capital; (2) the gearing of economic activity to making profits; (3) a market framework that regulates this activity; (4) the appropriation of profits by the owners of capital (subject to taxation by the state); (5) the provision of labour by workers who are free agents" [*Dictionary of Sociology*].

CAPTURE: The process by which the members of a regulatory agency, or the agency itself, come to identify with the interests of the regulated; a situation in which the ties between regulators and the regulated (includes risk creators) are stronger than the ties between regulators and the public (includes risk bearers).

CERTIFICATE OF APPROVAL: The term used in Ontario law for a licence or permit to pollute, issued in accordance with the *Ontario Environmental Protection Act* or the *Ontario Water Resources Act*. The Certificate of Approval establishes site or firm specific standards. Polluters in violation of the terms of the Certificate of Approval may be ordered to stop (Stop Order), to come into compliance or to abate the pollution according to a specified timetable; they may also be prosecuted.

CIVIL LAW: 1. Roman Law embodied in the Justinian Code (*Codex Justinianeus*); legal systems that are descendants of Roman law (and are prevalent in Western European countries), as distinct from the English system of **common law**; 2. The private law of the province of Quebec is governed by the *Civil Code* of Quebec (governing substantive law) and the *Code of Civil Procedure* [*Canadian Law Dictionary*]; 3. Private law, or the part of the law concerned with non-criminal matters, distinct from administrative, military, and ecclesiastical law [*A Dictionary of Law*]; Civil Actions are legal actions pursued to protect civil rights and to compel a civil **remedy**, and they are distinguished from criminal **prosecutions**.

CIVIL LIABILITY: see **liability**

CIVIL LIBERTIES: Democratic rights and freedoms that govern the relationship between the individual and the institutions of society [*A Dictionary of Law*]; constitutionally, they are restraints on government (*Black's Law Dictionary*). For instance, in Canadian law, civil liberties are enshrined in the *Canadian Charter of Rights and Freedoms*.

CIVIL PROCEDURE: The body of law concerned with methods and practices used in civil litigation [*Black's Law Dictionary*].

CIVIL RIGHTS: Proprietary, contractual and tortious rights between individuals in society [*A Dictionary of Law*]; Section 92(13) of the *Constitution Act* confers upon the provincial legislatures the power to make laws in relation to "property and civil rights in the province".

CIVIL WRONG: An infringement of a person's rights for which the wronged person may sue for damages or some other civil **remedy**. Includes Breach of **Contract** and **Torts** [*A Dictionary of Law*].

CLASS ACTION: Also referred to as "representative action". "A class action provides a means by which, where a large group of persons are interested in a matter, one or more may sue or be sued as representatives of the class without needing to join every member of the class" [*Black's Law Dictionary*]. There must be a well-defined common interest in the questions of law and fact that justifies allowing the parties to be represented this way. To maintain a class action, it is necessary to show that the persons constituting the class are so numerous it would be impracticable to bring them all before the court at once, and the named representatives must insure adequate representation for all concerned. A trial court must certify a lawsuit as a class action [*Black's Law Dictionary*]. Class actions were first developed in the United States, and they have since been legislatively authorized in several Canadian provinces. (Bowal, 2002: 11).

CLOUT: The ability to pursue one's objectives effectively in negotiations due to the resources at one's disposal (what one brings to the bargaining table); bargaining power.

COMMON LAW: "The system of jurisprudence, which originated in England and was later applied in Canada, that is based on judicial **precedent** rather than legislative enactments [**legislation**].... Common law depends for its authority upon the recognition given by the courts to principles, customs, and rules of conduct previously existing among the people. It is now recorded in law reports that embody the decisions of judges, together with the reasons they assign for their decisions" [*Canadian Law Dictionary*]. Common law is contrasted with **civil law** and with **equity**.

COMMON PROPERTY RESOURCE: A resource to which there do not exist private property rights; economics predicts that profit-seeking behaviour (which may be otherwise beneficial) may have undesirable outcomes in the case of common property resources, because there is no incentive to either conserve or invest in a resource that others have free access to ("tragedy of the commons"), for which the object in question can be exchanged [*The Penguin Dictionary of Economics*]. see also **property**

COMPLIANCE: Obedience; conformity in fulfilling official requirements.

CONSENSUS STANDARDS: see **standard**

CONSENTS: Schedules for achieving compliance with performance standards. This is a British term; the term "permit" is used in some other jurisdictions, and **Certificate of Approval** is the term used in Ontario.

CONSEQUENTIALISM: A moral theory in which the moral worth of an action or policy is determined solely by the consequences of that action or policy; compare **deontology**

CONSTITUTION: "The system or body of fundamental principles according to which a nation, state, [or other organization] ... is constituted and governed" [*Oxford English Dictionary*]. The Canadian Constitution — like that of the United States and unlike that of Britain — is set out in a single comprehensive statute. The *Constitution Act of 1982* built upon Canada's original constitution, the *1867 British North America Act*. The *Constitution Act* establishes the structure and jurisdictions of the federal and provincial governments, and the procedures by which valid laws may be enacted. The 1982 Act (unlike the previous *B.N.A. Act*) also includes a Charter of Rights and Freedoms, which guarantees freedom of expression, religion, association, etc., and equality before the law, among other things. As the most fundamental law, the *Constitution Act* is "entrenched", which means that it is much more difficult to amend than is an ordinary piece of legislation. See "The Constitutional Structure of Government", in Section One, Part C of this book.

CONTRACT: An agreement that binds the parties and is enforceable at law. An essential feature of contract is a promise by one party to another to do or forbear from doing certain specified acts. The offer of a promise becomes a promise by acceptance. The content of the legal obligation is constituted and defined by the parties to the contract. For a contract to be valid and legally enforceable, there must be: (i) capacity to contract, (ii) intention to contract, (iii) *consensus ad idem* (Latin = agreement to the same point; in effect, a meeting of minds), (iv) valuable consideration, (v) legality of purpose, (vi) sufficient certainty of terms. [*Osborn's Concise Law Dictionary*]. Some legal obligations arise without agreement — for example, in the law of **torts**.

COST: What has to be given up in order to achieve or attain something; see also **opportunity cost**

COST-BENEFIT ANALYSIS: Technique that attempts to set out and evaluate the social costs and social bene-fits (in addition to economic costs and benefits) of projects to help decide whether the project should be undertaken; cost-benefit analysis is also used to evaluate regulation.

COURT ORDER: A legally binding set of instructions specifying behaviours one is obliged to perform.

CRIMINAL LIABILITY: see **liability**

DAMAGES: A pecuniary (monetary) compensation, "which may be recovered in the courts by any person who has suffered loss, detriment, or injury, whether to his person, property, or rights, through the unlawful act or omission or negligence of another". A sum of money awarded to a person injured by the **tort** of another [*Black's Law Dictionary*]. Damages can be divided into several categories: (1) "actual", or "compensatory" or "**general**" damages; (2) "nominal" damages; (3) "punitive" or "exemplary" damages. The first refers to real and substantial damages awarded as compensation for actual loss or injury. Nominal damages are "a trifling sum" awarded "where there is no substantial loss or injury to be compensated, but still the law recognizes a technical invasion" of the plaintiff's rights or breach of the defendant's duty. Punitive, or exemplary, damages are awarded in cases where the wrong done to the plaintiff was "aggravated by circumstances of violence, oppression, malice, fraud, or wanton and wicked conduct on the part of the defendant". Such damages are "intended to solace the plaintiff" for emotional suffering and mental anguish, or else to "punish the defendant" for evil behaviour, or to make an example of the defendant [*Black's Law Dictionary*]. Punitive, or exemplary, damages are based on different public policy considerations than compensation — punishment or deterrence.

DEFENDANT: A person against whom an action, information or other civil proceeding is brought; a person charged with a criminal offence is usually referred to as the "accused" [*Osborn's Concise Law Dictionary*].

DEONTOLOGY: (derived from Greek *deon* = necessity, obligation) the theory of duty or obligation. According to deontological ethical theories, an action or policy is morally worthy only if it derives from a moral principle, such as the categorical imperative (see **Kantianism**), respect for persons or fairness (see **Rawls**). The results of actions are not morally relevant.; compare **consequentialism, utilitarianism**

DEREGULATION: A term "used both to describe and to effect [bring about] the privatization of major public sector" institutions and industries. The "systematic restructuring of forms of public provision and control and their replacement with those derived more directly from commercial, market operations". The reorganization of public monopolies, and state-funded and state-controlled agencies in order that they may "compete more directly according to market forces of profitability, investment and consumer demand. The *de* in de**regulation** therefore implies the positive removal or 'rolling back' of the power of the state and public authority as sectors are 'opened up' to commercial competition" [*Key Concepts in Communication and Cultural Studies*].

DESIGN STANDARD: see **standard**

DETERRENCE: Deter: generally, to discourage or prevent from acting by fear; specifically, **punishment** is a deterrent to crime; using the prospect of legal sanctions (for example, fines or imprisonment) to discourage undesirable behaviour (such as crime or pollution). "Specific Deterrence" refers to the effect of punishment on the offender, discouraging the one punished from repeating the offence, or re-offending. "General Deterrence" refers to the effect of punishment of an individual on the general population; it is directed at others who will be discouraged from offending in the first place. "General Deterrence" works by "making an example" of the offender.

DIALECTICAL: "The notion of dialectic expresses the view that development depends on the clash of contradictions and the creation of a new, more advanced synthesis out of these clashes. The dialectical process involves the three moments: thesis, antithesis and synthesis. Karl Marx used the notion to account for social and historical events" [*Dictionary of Sociology*].

DIMINISHING MARGINAL UTILITY: see **Marginal Utility**

DISTRICT COURT (U.S.): Trial courts in the federal court system in the United States. The appeal level above the district courts consists of twelve regional "Circuit Courts of Appeal". Above those circuit courts is the United States **Supreme Court** (Bowal, 2002: 10).

DOSE RESPONSE: The dose-response relationship in **toxicology** is used to determine the safe and harmful concentrations of an environmental contaminant for humans and other organisms. It relates the level of contaminant exposure to an organism's responses in terms of illness or death. Because the sensitivity to a toxin can vary significantly between species, extrapolation of the dose-response relationship from one animal species to another (from laboratory animals to humans), as in **risk assessment**, is controversial.

DUE DILIGENCE: A defence available to those charged with some regulatory offences; the person/entity wishing to rely upon the defense of due diligence must have undertaken reasonable measures to comply with the requirements of the act, and taken reasonable care to prevent the prohibited act, and be able to provide evidence to that effect; see **quasi-crime/quasi/criminal**

ECOCENTRIC/ECOCENTRISM: Oral standing is attached to ecosystems; moral consideration is extended to all of nature, including living and non-living nature (animals, birds, insects, plants, trees, rivers, rocks, soil ...).

ECONOMY: Derived from the Greek word *oikonomia*, management of a household or state; management of the income, expenditures, etc., of a household, private business, community, or government; system of producing, distributing, and consuming wealth [*The Penguin Dictionary of Economics*].

ECONOMIC EFFICIENCY: Economic efficiency is the state in which it is not possible to rearrange production and consumption so as to make at least one person better off except by making one or more other individuals worse off; Pareto Optimality [*The Penguin Dictionary of Economics*]. Less formally, the state in which resources are so allocated (among alternative uses) as to maximize aggregate wealth or **utility**.

ECOSYSTEM: "A complex system of living organisms (plants, animals, fungi and microorganisms) together with their abiotic environment (soil, water, air and nutrients) that function together to circulate nutrients and create a flow of energy; A unit of land or water comprising populations of organisms considered together with their physical environment and the interacting processes between them" [*Dictionary of Natural Resource Management*]. "Natural ecosystems are theoretically self-sustaining, but increasing human interference is threatening their sustainability in many parts of the world, and various methods of ecosystem management have been introduced in an attempt to preserve and protect characteristic natural ecosystems" [*The Environment Dictionary*].

ENFORCEMENT: Carrying something out effectively. The act of putting something such as a law into effect; the execution of a law [*Black's Law Dictionary*].

ENVIRONMENTAL ASSESSMENT (EA): EA is an evaluation of the effects of a proposed project on natural and human environments. Its purpose is to predict how a project may damage or harm the environment, and whether unacceptable environmental impacts can be avoided or reduced before significant environmental changes occur. As a document, an environmental assessment has three main elements: (i) description of the project and the environment to be affected; (ii) prediction of the project's impacts; and (iii) an evaluation of the significance of the impacts. As a process, it includes public input in setting the scope of the investigation, reviewing the assessment, and participating in a **hearing** on the validity of the results where they are in question.

ENVIRONMENTAL ASSESSMENT AND REVIEW PROCESS (EARP): The first attempt by the Canadian government in 1973 to establish an environmental assessment process of its own, following the passage of the *National Environmental Policy Act* (**NEPA**) in the United States. It was originally established as a Cabinet Directive, rather than a law passed by **Parliament**. It directed the Minister of the Environment to establish a process to ensure that environmental effects were taken into account early in the planning of new federal projects. It also directed the Minister to ensure that an environmental assessment (EA) would be carried out for projects that may have an adverse effect on the environment, *before* the project was executed. See Editors' Notes for Section Three, Part A for further elaboration.

EPIDEMIOLOGY: The statistical study of the occurrence, rates, distribution and determinants of diseases in human populations, and the use of this knowledge to control health problems. Epidemiologists, for example, will attempt to estimate the risk to human health of a particular hazard by comparing rates of illnesses among human populations exposed (to a greater or lesser degree) to the hazard in question — while using statistical techniques to try to take into account the confounding effects of other factors that affect the health of these populations; compare **toxicology**

EQUITY: 1. Fairness, freedom from bias or favouritism. 2. "Justice administered according to fairness as contrasted with the strictly formulated rules of common law" [*Black's Law Dictionary*]. Body of rules formulated and administered by the Court of Chancery to supplement the rules and procedures of the common law [*Osborn's Concise Law Dictionary*]; legal principles serving as the source of equitable rights, claims or **remedies**. See Editors' Notes to "The Elements of the Legal System", Section One, this book, for a discussion of the latter meaning of equity.

ETHICS: Derived from the Greek word *ethos*, meaning "character" and connected to the Latin word *moralis*, meaning customs or manners; study of human duties, conduct and values.

EXCHANGE VALUE/USE VALUE: Terms in classical and Marxian economics. "Exchange value" refers to the market value of some commodity, i.e., the amount of some other commodity that a unit of the commodity will fetch in the market; in monetary terms, its price. "Use value" refers to the actual use of a resource or product for which it is desired, for example, food for eating, housing for shelter, etc. Exchange value is an abstract, quantitative attribute, while use value is a concrete, qualitative attribute. Most commodities only have exchange value because they have some use value, but the exchange value (i.e., the price) does not depend upon the nature of the use value. To compare the neoclassical economic theory's approach to this issue of economic value, see **utility**, and **marginal utility**.

EXTERNALITIES: Costs or benefits, in production or consumption, that are not reflected in market prices; externalities are addressed by the imposition of taxes on activities that decrease welfare or increase costs or the payment of subsidies on activities that increase welfare or lower costs [*The Penguin Dictionary of Economics*]. Externalities, more simply, are unpriced effects in the relations between producers and consumers that affect a third party. A common example of a negative externality is pollution. A front-yard garden or shade tree planted at private expense but also enjoyed by passersby would be an example of a positive (benefit) externality. Externalities distort the operation of the market, making it less efficient; see **economic efficiency**, and **invisible hand**

FACT/VALUE DISTINCTION: Generally, facts are descriptions of the way things actually are in the world, accounts of the states of affairs that obtain. Factual claims are supported by appeal to empirical evidence and proof. Values are judgments of importance, and are prescriptive; values are supported by appeals to human needs and interests. More specifically, in the philosophical literature, "[d]istinction is made between two classes of assertions: the factual and the moral (evaluative). Premises and conclusions of one [kind of claim] can neither entail nor be derived from those of the other" (as a matter of logic) [*A Dictionary of Philosophy*]; see also **naturalistic fallacy**

FALSE NEGATIVE: Type II Error; false finding that harm does not exist when in fact harm does exist.

FALSE POSITIVE: Type I Error; false finding that harm does exist when in fact harm does not exist.

FEDERALISM: A system of government in which regional units (provinces, states) within a country or federation have governments with their own powers and responsibilities distinct from those of the central (federal) government of the country or federation. Canada and the United States are both federal countries; England is a unitary (non-federal) country, but is now part of the federation that comprises the European Community. In Canada, the **Constitution** spells out which matters fall under provincial jurisdiction, and which matters fall under federal jurisdiction. The federal government cannot make laws concerning matters of provincial jurisdiction and vice versa. See the readings in "The Constitutional Structure of Canadian Government", in Section One, Part C.

FIDUCIARY: Designating a person who holds something in trust for another; held in trust.

FALSE FIDUCIARY: Someone who does not act properly as a fiduciary; a regulator who subordinates the realization of public values to self interest.

PURE FIDUCIARY: A regulator who exercises responsibility delegated for reducing harm by employing the most effective techniques available for reducing harm to risk bearers.

FISH TOXICITY TEST: An impact standard (see **standard**). Rainbow trout are placed in a tank containing a solution of a pollutant (e.g., pulp mill effluent) that has been diluted by 35%. If, after four days, more than 20% of the trout die, the solution is lethal, and an offence has been committed.

FORBEARANCE: A decision to overlook regulatory non-compliance because (1) violation poses no serious risk, (2) the cost of compliance is too great, (3) reasonable time is needed to achieve compliance, or (4) good faith efforts have been made.

FREE RIDERS: Those who take a "free ride" are those who benefit, without paying, from a collective good (for example, a resource which is supplied communally), for which others pay the costs.

GENERAL DAMAGES: see **damages**

GUIDELINES ORDER: Pertains to the Environmental Assessment Review Process (EARP) Guidelines Order, which was replaced by the *Canadian Environmental Assessment Act* (1995). Under the EARP Guidelines Order, federal projects had to be screened to determine if they might have significant environmental impacts. If the screening indicated that significant impacts were likely to occur, the guidelines order required the project to be referred to an Environmental Assessment **Panel** for a **hearing**. See Editors' Notes to Section Three, Part A, for further elaboration.

HEARING: "A proceeding of relative formality (though generally less defined than a **trial**), generally public, with definite issues of fact or law to be tried, in which witnesses are heard and evidence presented." The term is also used in a broader sense to include hearings before administrative agencies and, thus, consists of "any confrontation, oral or otherwise, between an affected individual and an agency decision-maker sufficient to allow the individual to make his/her case in a meaningful manner" [*Black's Law Dictionary*]. See Editors' Notes to Section Two for discussion of hearings and tribunals in the regulatory context. See Editors' Notes to Section Three, Part A for discussion of hearings and tribunals in the context of environmental assessment.

HOLISM: The contention that wholes, or some wholes, are more than the sum of their parts; the claim that the value of a whole (e.g., an ecosystem) is not reducible to the value of the sum of its parts.

IMPACT STANDARD: see **standard**

IMPLEMENTATION: To give practical effect to, and ensure fulfilment of, policy goals, objectives and plans, by concrete measures; see Editors' Notes to Section Two and Section Three, Part A for discussion of implementation in the context of the regulatory system, and environmental assessment, respectively.

INCENTIVE: An inducement to take, or refrain from taking, a given action.

INHERENT WORTH/INTRINSIC VALUE: Something with inherent worth or intrinsic value is valuable in and of itself [*Dictionary of Philosophy*]; compare **instrumental/ extrinsic value**

INJUNCTION: An order or decree by which a party to an action is required to do, or refrain from doing, a particular thing; injunctions are either restrictive (preventive) or mandatory (compulsive); as regards time, injunctions are either interlocutory (i.e., interim or temporary) or perpetual [*Osborn's Concise Law Dictionary*].

INSTRUMENTAL/EXTRINSIC VALUE: Something with instrumental or extrinsic value is valuable as a means to some other end [*Dictionary of Philosophy*]; compare **inherent worth/intrinsic value**

INSTRUMENTS: The legal means by which policies are implemented. Instruments aim to affect behaviour of individuals and organizations (for example, corporations) by creating incentives and disincentives. For example, legal instruments for controlling pollution include criminal prohibitions; subsidies for control technology; regulatory standards applying to all polluters of a certain type; site-specific regulations in the form of permit conditions (see **consent, certificate of approval**) and voluntary initiatives. Other instruments (often called economic instruments) include pollution taxes, and tradeable pollution rights (tradeable emission permits).

INVISIBLE HAND: Adam Smith, an economist, claimed that individualistic self-seeking behaviour by consumers and firms will be guided by the invisible hand (of market forces) to achieve the highest level of welfare for society as a whole [*The Penguin Dictionary of Economics*]. The "invisible hand" can operate only if the market is not significantly distorted by **market failures**, such as monopolies and **externalities**.

JUDICIAL REVIEW: The "[p]ower of courts to review decisions" of government. In Canada, courts can review legislative enactments passed by the federal or provincial governments to ensure that a law is *intra vires* (Latin = within the powers), or inside the valid jurisdiction of that government. The **Constitution** (*Constitution Act of 1982*) sets out the limits of powers for each level of government. In the context of administrative law, judicial review is a "form of appeal from an administrative body to the courts for review" in cases of "error of law", or where the administrative body is acting *ultra vires* (Latin = beyond the powers), or outside of its valid jurisdiction [*Black's Law Dictionary*].

KANTIANISM: Immanuel Kant is one of the most influential proponents of deontology (theory of obligation). Kant said that the only absolutely valuable thing is the good will, the determination to do what is right. For Kant, the moral worth of an action or a choice is determined, not by the consequences of the action or the choice (as in utilitarianism), but by whether the action or choice satisfies a duty or obligation. Kant called his theory the Categorical Imperative (categorical meaning absolute or unqualified, and imperative referring to command). There are two formulations of the Categorical Imperative: (1) Act in such a way that the general rule behind your action could consistently be willed to be a universal law, and (2) Always treat persons (including yourself) as ends, never as means only: always treat persons with respect [*Dictionary of Philosophy*].

LAISSEZ FAIRE: A doctrine opposing governmental interference in economic affairs beyond the minimum necessary for the maintenance of peace and property rights; philosophy or practice characterized by a usually deliberate abstention from direction or interference especially with individual freedom of choice and action [*The Penguin Dictionary of Economics*]. This became a principle of classical economics, and amounted to a condemnation of government interference with industry on the grounds that such interference is considered inappropriate and harmful except insofar as it is necessary to break up private monopoly; reliance upon the "invisible hand", which would guide business activities in a socially beneficial direction more effectively than any public official or body of officials could.

LEGAL STANDING: A person or legal entity determined to have suffered a legal wrong has standing to sue; compare **moral standing**

LEGISLATION: "Acts or **statute**s passed by a governing authority. Statutes and instruments of **Parliament** are referred to as federal legislation. Likewise, enactments of the provincial legislatures are referred to as provincial legislation" [*Canadian Law Dictionary*].

LEGISLATURE: The body having primary power to make written law. In Canada, laws are made by **Parliament** or a provincial legislature.

LIABILITY: Obligation in law; responsibility for one's conduct, such as contractual liability, tort liability or criminal liability. **'TRUE' CRIME/CRIMINAL LIABILITY**: Both *actus reus* ("guilty act") and *mens rea* ("guilty mind") must be established for liability. Criminal offences are very rare outside the criminal code. Regulatory offences (arising from non-Criminal Code legislation) can involve strict or absolute liability. **ABSOLUTE LIABILITY**: Liability regardless of intention. The **prosecution** need only prove the *actus reus* of the offence, and conviction will follow automatically. **STRICT LIABILITY**: As with absolute liability, it is also liability without intention, but after the *actus reus* has been established by the prosecution (beyond a reasonable doubt), then the accused has the option of invoking a "**due diligence**" defence (to be established on a balance of probabilities). The due diligence defence requires showing that the defendant took reasonable precautions to avoid the offence. Strict Liability Crimes are "usually limited to minor offences or regulatory offences". They are also referred to as public welfare or statutory offences, or strict responsibility [*Canadian Law Dictionary*].

NOTE—There is also a **tort** of strict liability, which consists of liability for harm arising from lawful activity that exposes others to extraordinary risks or injury (ultra-hazardous activity), even though no fault is involved on the part of the "wrongdoer"; liability without a showing of negligence; see also **quasi-crime/quasi-criminal**

LIBERALISM: A political philosophy that developed in the eighteenth century, and was "historically associated with the idea of freedom; the civil freedom of the individual; free political institutions; freedom of religion"; freedom of expression; freedom of association; "free enterprise and free trade in economics" [*Fontana Dictionary of Modern Thought*].

MARGINAL UTILITY: Increase in total utility of consumption of a good that results from increasing the quantity of the good consumed by one unit; marginal utility determines price. Something may have high total utility, but low marginal utility; for example, water. **DIMINISHING MARGINAL UTILITY**: after some point, successive equal increments (increases) in the quantity of a good will yield smaller and smaller increases in utility [*The Penguin Dictionary of Economics*].

MARKET: A system of exchange where the demands of buyers interact with the supply made available by the sellers, determining the resulting prices (in free markets); in a free market economy, the market is the mechanism by which resources are allocated.

MARKET FAILURE: Occurs when the market system produces an allocation of resources that is not Pareto efficient — when it is possible to change resource allocation to make some consumer(s) better off and no one worse off; the prevalence of market failure calls into question the "invisible hand" theory. Examples of market failures include: monopoly (market situation in which a single seller controls the entire output of a good or service), oligopoly (type of market with relatively high degree of concentration, in which a small number of firms account for large proportion of output, employment, etc.), **common property resources**, **public goods**, and **externalities** [*The Penguin Dictionary of Economics*]. The classic examples of market failures, in the environmental context, include: pollution (negative externality), resource depletion (fisheries as a common property resource), and the consistent underproduction of clean air or water (environmental protection being a public good, or positive externality); see **economic efficiency**, **invisible hand**

MARXISM: "For Marx, the relations of production necessarily involve conflict because the owners of the means of production, for example capitalists within a capitalist society, effectively exploit workers by appropriating the product of their labour ... [t]his conflict or contradiction ... at the heart of class societies also suggests a theory of social change. Marx argues that class struggle is the 'motor of history'; the rising capitalist class overthrew the feudal aristocracy and will be similarly displaced by the working class" [*Dictionary of Sociology*].

Interpretive Note—"Marx is best known for his views on the relationship between economic life and other social institutions. It is often suggested that he was an economic determinist, believing that the nature of a society was determined by the manner in which its economy was owned and organized. This is certainly not the case. Although he thought that human labour was the basis of social activity, he also held that social institutions, like the state or the family [or law], were relatively independent of the economy in their development and even had an influence on the operation of the economy" [*Dictionary of Sociology*].

MEANS OF PRODUCTION/RELATIONS OF PRODUCTION: Means of Production refers to the material factors of production, i.e., the resources necessary for production. Examples include tools, machinery, land, etc. Relations of production refers to the relations between those who have control of the means of production and, thus, capacity to possess the products and those who do not [*Dictionary of Sociology*].

MEDIATION: A voluntary, non-binding, relatively informal approach to finding a mutually acceptable agreement that can form the basis for a settlement between the parties; it involves the assistance of a third party. See Editors' Notes to Section Four.

MENS REA: Guilty mind; an evil intention or a knowledge of the wrongfulness of an act. "There is a presumption that it is an essential ingredient in every criminal offence.... Many minor statutory offences, however, are punishable irrespective of the existence of *mens rea*" — see **liability; strict liability** [*Osborn's Concise Law Dictionary*].

MITIGATION: Reduction in the amount of harm that is achieved by remedying or removing existing sources of harm; often involves redesign or restructuring of relationships so that the reduction becomes long-term rather than temporary.

MONITORING: To watch, observe, or check for a special purpose; in the environmental context, monitoring is the observation or measurement of changes in the environment, in order to determine whether to take action, or after an action has been taken. See the Editors' Notes to Section Two for discussion of the role of monitoring in the context of the regulatory system. See the Editors' Notes to Section Three, Part A for a discussion of the role of monitoring in the Environmental Assessment Process.

MORAL STANDING: The interest or well-being of certain beings or organisms must be counted or considered in deciding what it is permissible to do; the harm that would be suffered by any entity with moral standing counts against the moral worth of any action or policy that would cause the harm (that harm must then be justified, or else avoided).

NATIONAL ENVIRONMENTAL POLICY ACT (NEPA): The first general environmental policy passed by the United States Congress in 1969. NEPA not only established a comprehensive environmental policy statement, it also created the Environmental Protection Agency (EPA) as the independent federal agency responsible for environmental protection.

NATURAL JUSTICE: "A duty of procedural fairness to persons", in the context of legal proceedings. The term is "generally understood to apply to statutory **tribunal**s charged with adjudicating disputes ... where legal rights and interests may be affected". Such decision-making bodies must "adhere to and apply the principles of natural justice — that is, (i) give persons specially affected by the decision a reasonable opportunity of presenting their case, (ii) listen fairly to both sides (*audi alteram partem*) and (iii) reach a decision untainted by bias". In Canada, there is often a distinction drawn between the principles of natural justice — which "apply to statutory boards exercising only judicial or quasi-judicial functions", and the duty of fairness — somewhat less stringent than natural justice. The latter is thought to apply to "those bodies exercising administrative functions". There is, nevertheless, some debate about this difference, and "the matter remains unsettled" [*Canada Law Dictionary*].

NATURAL LAW: Term of the Roman jurists — *jus naturale*; the law of nature. The term denotes "a system of rules and principles for the guidance of human conduct which, independently of enacted law" of the legal systems of any particular societies, "might be discovered by the rational intelligence" of human beings [*Black's Law Dictionary*]. It also refers to law as divine command; law derived from human nature; "a principle of proper human action or conduct taken to be God-given or to be a consequence of human nature" [*The Philosopher's Dictionary*]. As a theory of law, natural law theory holds that the validity of a legal system depends on the coherence of law with objective morality.

NATURALISTIC FALLACY: The mistake in reasoning (which is not universally agreed always is a mistake) of deducing conclusions about what ought to be from premises that state only what is the case; or the other way around [*Dictionary of Philosophy*].

NEGLIGENCE: "As a **tort** negligence is the **breach** by the defendant of a legal duty to take care, which results in damage to the plaintiff". Duty of care is a term of art, which characterizes the interests of persons to be protected by the tort of negligence. "It determines whether the type of loss suffered by the **plaintiff** in a particular way in which it occurred can, as a matter of law, be actionable" [*Osborn's Concise Law Dictionary*].

NEGOTIATION: Any process directed towards an agreed resolution, in situations of conflict, in which no third party plays a significant part; discussion and bargaining towards an agreement among individuals and/or their agents; see Editors' Notes to Section Four.

NEOLIBERALISM: Many changes in the global political economy are thought to be associated with the ascendency of neoliberal, or radical free-market, ideas. Neoliberalism is said to be characterized by a redefinition of the "relationship between 'public' and 'private' in contemporary capitalism", and adoption and implementation of deregulatory policies favouring market forces (Gill, 1994: 75–76). Associated developments include the restructuring of capital, the rolling back of the public sector, and the liberalization and expansion of international trade, often under pressure from multilateral organizations such as the International Monetary Fund and the World Bank (ibid: 82). Also sometimes identified as economic liberalism.

NON-COMPLIANCE: Failure to perform as prescribed.

NUISANCE: 1. "A private nuisance is a **tort** consisting of (i) any wrongful disturbance or interference with a person's use or enjoyment of land; (ii) the act of wrongfully causing or allowing the escape of deleterious things into/onto another person's land" (for example, fumes, gas, smoke, water, vibrations). Nuisance is actionable only by the "person in possession of land injuriously affected; there must be actual damage to the plaintiff". The remedies for private nuisance include damages (monetary compensation), injunction or abatement (cessation, stopping the nuisance). 2. A public nuisance "is an act which interferes with the enjoyment of a right which all members of the community are entitled to, such as the right to fresh air" or common sources of clean water. An action for public nuisance is normally undertaken by the Attorney-General; remedies include injunction or abatement [*Osborn's Concise Law Dictionary*].

NULL HYPOTHESIS: The hypothesis — a testable, tentative explanation — that "an observed difference ... is due to chance alone and not due to a systemic cause" [*Webster's Collegiate Dictionary*].

OPPORTUNITY COST: The value of alternatives or other options that have to be foregone in order to achieve something; what is foregone by choosing a particular alternative.

ORDERS: In the context of provincial environmental law in Ontario, orders are administrative remedies that may be imposed by the Ministry of the Environment in the event that a polluter is found to be not in compliance with the terms of their **Certificate of Approval**. These remedies may be imposed in lieu of, or in addition to, **quasi-criminal** prosecution. There are several kinds of orders (control orders, stop orders, remedial orders and preventive orders). **CONTROL ORDERS:** "Control orders are intended to stop or reduce existing pollution.... If the Ministry is not satisfied that efforts to obtain pollution abatement voluntarily are succeeding, it may issue a control order". The order can be issued only after a "finding that a contaminant has been discharged into the natural environment in contravention" of legislation. The order will set out a pollution abatement program. The orders "may direct the persons to whom they are directed: to limit or control the rate of discharge of a contaminant; to stop the discharge permanently or for a specified period of time; ... or to install or replace or alter any pollution control equipment". They may also "require the person to monitor and record the discharge" [Estrin and Swaigen, 1993: 445]. **STOP ORDERS:** "Stop orders

may be issued by the Ministry [of the Environment] when [there are] reasonable and probable grounds to believe that contaminant emissions may cause an immediate danger to life, health or property". Stop orders take effect immediately, but they are rarely used [Estrin and Swaigen, 1993: 447]. **REMEDIAL ORDERS**: Remedial orders can be used both to prevent harm and to rectify it. These orders may be appealed to the Environmental Appeal Board [Estrin and Swaigen, 1993: 448]. **PREVENTIVE ORDERS**: Preventive orders are "intended to anticipate and prevent pollution whenever the nature of an undertaking, or of anything on the property where an undertaking is being carried on, is such that if a contaminant were discharged from the undertaking or from the property, it would be likely to result in an adverse effect" [Estrin and Swaigen, 1993: 448].

ORDINANCE: Enactment of a municipal government.

PANEL: "A list of jurors summoned to serve in a particular court ... or a [g]roup of judges (smaller than the entire court) which decides a case; may also refer to members of a commission". Commission: "a body composed of several persons acting under lawful authority to perform some public service" [*Black's Law Dictionary*]. See Editors' Notes to Section Three, Part A for discussion of the distinct aspects of Environmental Assessment Panels.

PARETO CRITERION: A principle of policy evaluation that says to accept only those policies that benefit some people while harming no one; it is not widely accepted by economists, since few policy proposals do not impose some costs on some people; this criterion would rule out any policies that have the effect of redistributing resources (because those redistributive policies would make the previously well off less well off and thus harm them) [*The Penguin Dictionary of Economics*]. In the environmental context, measures that would improve environmental quality at no cost to anyone would satisfy the criterion.

POTENTIAL PARETO CRITERION (Kaldor-Hicks Criterion): The most widely accepted economic principle asks whether the aggregate of the gains to those made better off measured in money terms is greater than the money value of the losses of those made worse off; if gains exceed losses, the policy is accepted by this criterion [*The Penguin Dictionary of Economics*]; see **economic efficiency**

PARETO OPTIMUM/OPTIMALITY: State of equilibrium; an economy has reached a state of Pareto Optimality if it is not possible to rearrange production and consumption activity so as to make at least one person better off except by making one or more individuals worse off; economic theory assumes that in a perfect market a state of Pareto Optimality will be reached through free exchange; what the Optimum will be depends upon the initial distribution of entitlements.

NOTE—there can be many different Pareto Optimal states, each of which represents the best that can be attained given the pre-existing distribution of entitlements (assets people own or have the right to benefit from) [*The Penguin Dictionary of Economics*]; see **economic efficiency**

PARLIAMENT: In Canada, the federal **legislature**, consisting of the House of Commons and the Senate. The members of the House of Commons are elected representatives of their constituencies, and the members of the Senate are appointed by the Prime Minister. The provincial legislatures are referred to as Legislative Assemblies (National Assembly in Quebec), and are similar to Parliament, except that there is no appointed upper house (i.e., the Senate) at the provincial level.

PERFORMANCE STANDARD: see **standard**

PLAINTIFF/DEFENDANT: In civil law, the one who brings an action is the "plaintiff"; the action is a "law suit" and the one against whom the action is brought is a "defendant". Hence, we say that the plaintiff sued the defendant. A civil defendant is found either "liable" or "not liable"; see **liability**

POSITIVE LAW: Law that has been "posited", i.e., put in place; law that is created by political authority; positivism is a legal theory premised upon the conceptual separation of law and morality; positivism insists that there is no necessary connection between morality and the existence or validity conditions of law.

POTENTIAL PARETO CRITERION: see **Pareto Criterion**

PRECAUTIONARY PRINCIPLE: The principle that action should be taken to reduce or eliminate likely environmental hazards even if the causal link between the suspected hazard and harm is not yet proven or fully understood scientifically. See Section Three, Part C for elaboration.

PRECEDENT: "The doctrine [of judicial precedent] whereby a previously described case is recognized as authority for the disposition of future cases. In the common law, precedents are regarded as a major source of law. A precedent may involve a novel question of common law [principles] or it may involve the interpretation of a **statute**." Under the doctrine of *stare decisis* (Latin = to stand by that which was decided, to abide by precedent), future cases rely upon previous cases as precedent, or are distinguished from them. See Editors' Notes to Section One — "Elements of the Legal System", for elaboration.

PRESCRIPTIVE STANDARD: see **standard**

PRICE: Quantity of money that must be exchanged for one unit of a good or service.

PRIMA FACIE: On first appearance; a *prima facie* moral claim may be overridden by another and stronger moral obligation; a *prima facie* legal case is one for which there is some evidence of the allegation made that will stand unless it is rebutted.

PRIVATIZATION: Reduction in the amount of public sector ownership and managements rights undertaken to increase the private sector ownership and management rights.

PROPERTY: That which is capable of ownership; in effect, anything that can be owned exclusively by a person. The term "property" may denote "the thing or object to which the rights or interests apply *or* the legal relation[s] that exist with respect to those rights" [*Canadian Law Dictionary*]. Distinctions are drawn between real property — land, for instance; and personal property — all other kinds of property. Property may relate to a tangible, corporeal object with a physical existence, or it may pertain to intangible, incorporeal or abstract objects that are the subject matter of intellectual property rights (patents, copyright, trademarks, trade secrets).

PROSECUTION: The act of bringing a legal action against someone, when the action involves public (criminal or quasi-criminal), as opposed to civil, law. In criminal law, the one who prosecutes is a "prosecutor" (usually, in Canada, a Crown attorney) and the one who is prosecuted is the "accused". Hence, we say that the Crown prosecuted the accused (in the name of the Queen, *Regina*). An accused is "convicted" if found guilty and "acquitted" if found not guilty. A civil defendant, on the other hand, is found either "liable" or "not liable"; compare **plaintiff/defendant**

PUBLIC GOODS: Goods that must be supplied communally because they cannot be withheld from one individual without withholding them from everyone (e.g., national defence, police protection); since the state can raise revenues by taxation, it alone can finance provision of public goods; a private entrepreneur would not undertake to supply public goods because he would not have the power to force the community as a whole to pay, and he/she could not exclude anyone who did not pay for the goods [*The Penguin Dictionary of Economics*].

PUNISHMENT: A penalty imposed on a criminal defendant by an authorized court. Punishment is declared in the sentence of the court. [see **sentence**] There are a number of different theories of punishment, which set out to articulate, and potentially justify, the aims and purposes of the criminal justice system. These theories include, for instance, Retributivism and Deterrence.

PUNITIVE DAMAGES: see **damages**

QUANTITATIVE STANDARD: see **standard**

QUASI-CRIMINAL: Category of law dealing with regulatory or "public welfare" offences, such as most pollution offences. Quasi-criminal laws, like "true" criminal laws, are enforced through **prosecution**. The main difference between quasi-crimes and "true" crimes is that the latter involve an element of criminal intent (*mens rea*). To obtain a conviction under quasi-criminal law, by contrast, the Crown need not prove that the accused intended to commit the offence, provided that the accused cannot show that they exercised "**due diligence**" (i.e., took reasonable precautions to avoid the offence). See **liability**, **strict liability** and the Editors' Notes to Section One — "Elements of the Legal System".

RAWLS: John Rawls developed a theory of justice as fairness; Rawls claimed that certain principles of justice would be chosen by people who reasoned behind a "veil of ignorance" in an "original position"; the principles are: First: each person is to have an equal right to the most extensive basic liberty compatible with a similar liberty for others. Second: social and economic inequalities are to be arranged so that they are both (a) to the greatest benefit of the least advantaged (*Difference Principle*), and (b) attached to offices and positions open to all under conditions of fair equality of opportunity.

(RAWLSIAN) ORIGINAL POSITION: Purely hypothetical situation in which persons reach agreement on the conception of justice to regulate and structure social institutions and their reform; part of a social contract model in which parties contract to adopt certain moral principles; a contract view holds that certain principles would be adopted in a well-defined initial situation.

(RAWLSIAN) VEIL OF IGNORANCE: The situation in which no one knows his/her place in society, his/her class position or social status, his/her fortunes in the distribution of natural assets and abilities, his/her intelligence, strength, and so on (includes gender, age, race, ethnicity) [*Dictionary of Philosophy*].

REGULATION: Regulations are detailed rules made according to some statute but not included in the statute. For example, a piece of environmental legislation might make it an offence to pollute in excess of some levels to be specified in the regulations, and to indicate that the regulations are to be set by the Minister of the Environment. The statute in this case is said to be a piece of "enabling legislation" because it empowers an official to make legally enforceable rules. The enabling legislation specifies the legal means by which its regulations are to be enforced. Most regulatory violations are subject to **quasi-criminal** sanctions, but some are subject to **administrative penalties**.

REGULATORY STANDARD: see **standard**

REMEDY/REMEDIES: "The means by which a right is enforced or the violation of a right is prevented, redressed, or compensated" [*Black's Law Dictionary*]. "The most common remedy at law consists of **damages**" — monetary compensation to one who has suffered loss or injury by the wrongdoing of another, such as **breach** of **contract**, or a **tort**ious act. "The courts of chancery developed a number of equitable remedies where none could be had at common law";

for example, injunction [*Canada Law Dictionary*]. A civil remedy is one "afforded to a private person in the civil courts" whose **civil rights** have been infringed or violated, "as distinguished from the remedy by criminal **prosecution** for the injury to the rights of the public" [*Black's Law Dictionary*].

RESOURCES: Factors of production classified into land (including natural resources), labour (manual and non-manual), capital (services provided by machinery, buildings, tools and other productive instruments); the most important characteristic of resources is that they are relatively scarce [*The Penguin Dictionary of Economics*].

RESOURCE ALLOCATION: The process by which scarce resources in the economy are distributed among alternative uses [*The Penguin Dictionary of Economics*].

RIGHTS LEGAL RIGHTS: Interests of persons that are "recognized and protected by law, respect for which is a duty and disregard of which is wrong" [*Osborn's Concise Law Dictionary*]. Legal rights provide the basis for **legal standing**. **MORAL RIGHTS:** a being is said to have a right to something or some action when it is thought that nobody should be allowed to prevent that being from having that thing or from doing that action.

RIPARIAN RIGHTS: Rights connected to land that is adjoining or abutting a river or stream. Specifically, "the rights of the owners of lands on the banks of watercourses, relating to the water, its use, ownership of soil under the stream, etc.". Being able to benefit from the water as it passes through/over land, "for all useful purposes", such as irrigating, fishing, boating [*Black's Law Dictionary*].

RISK: The likelihood that an event, activity, decision, etc. will give rise to an unwanted, negative consequence; i.e., the likelihood that a given hazard will result in a given harm. **RISK ANALYSIS/RISK ASSESSMENT:** see Editors' Notes to Section Three, Part C. **RISK BEARERS:** all those exposed to potential harm as a result of decisions or activities of others. **RISK CREATORS:** those individuals, firms, and organizations who engage in activities that are potentially harmful to others. **RISK PERCEPTION:** "[P]eople's beliefs, attitudes, judgments and feelings, as well as the wider social or cultural values and dispositions that people adopt, towards hazards and their benefits" [Royal Society of Canada: *Risk: Analysis, Perception and Management*, 1992, 5.1.1.].

RULE OF LAW: "Form of government in which no power can be exercised except according to procedures, principles, and constraints contained in the law, and in which any citizen can find redress against any other, however powerfully placed, and against the officers of the state itself, for any act which involves a breach of the law" [Roger Scruton, *A Dictionary of Political Thought*].

RULING CLASS: "The ruling class has come to mean a social class, usually the economically dominant class, that controls a society through whatever political institutions are available" [*Dictionary of Sociology*].

SENTENCE: Punishment ordered by the court; "also any order of the trial court made on conviction in addition to, or substitute for fine and imprisonment" [*Canada Law Book*].

SENTIENT/SENTIENTISM: Having the capacity for feeling or perception, having the capacity to experience pleasure and pain. Sentientism: the theory that the interests of sentient beings determine our (human beings') obligations regarding the environment; only sentient beings have moral standing. (Which beings count as sentient is an open question.)

STANDARD: A standard defines a threshold, the point at which behaviour becomes minimally acceptable. Standards may be classified in various ways. One contrast is between **prescriptive standards** — which specify what must be done (how to meet the standard) — and **performance standards** — which specify, instead, an outcome. An example of prescriptive standards are **design standards**, ones specifying procedures, methods, and/or technologies one is required to adopt in order to reduce harm. **Performance standards**, by contrast, specify the amount of harm reduction to be achieved without specifying the means by which the harm is to be reduced. **Impact standards** (see, for example, **fish toxicity test**) and **quantitative standards** — such as Ontario's ozone standard of 80 parts per billion (measured using hourly averages) — are both performance standards. We can also distinguish between **regulatory standards**, which are imposed by the government pursuant to **legislation**, and may be enforced through **quasi-criminal** law, and **voluntary standards**. Voluntary standards are ones that are developed by trade associations, or non-governmental certifying bodies such as the International Standards Organization (ISO). Such standards are not imposed by government, and are adopted by firms out of self-interest (for example, in order to gain access to markets and to gain consumer confidence and approval), but they may have legal consequences, nevertheless. See Kernaghan Webb, "Voluntary Initiatives and the Law", in Section Two, Part C. **Consensus standards** are regulatory or voluntary standards developed through a consultative process which seeks to involve all affected interests so that the output will be viewed as legitimate by all.

STANDING: see **Legal Standing** and **Moral Standing**

STATUTE: "An act of the **legislature**; in Canada an act of a provincial legislature or the Federal **Parliament**. Statutes are a primary source of law and are enacted, for example, to prescribe conduct, define crimes, create inferior government bodies, appropriate public monies, and in general promote the public good and welfare". In Canada, the **Constitution** (*Constitution Act, 1982*) divides up legislative power between the federal and the provincial governments [*Canada Law Dictionary*].

STATUTE OF LIMITATIONS: "Any law that fixes the time within which parties must take judicial action to enforce rights or else be thereafter barred from enforcing them" [*Canada Law Dictionary*].

STRICT LIABILITY: see **liability**

SUASION: Exhortation to change behaviour.

SUPREME COURT: The highest court of appeal in Canada. The Supreme Court of Canada has "final authority over all public and private law throughout Canada", including all municipal, provincial, federal law, common law and constitutional interpretation (Bowal, 2002: 10). In the United States, the "Supreme Court has a more limited mandate: it deals only in federal legislation and the US Constitution" (Ibid.).

SUSTAINABLE DEVELOPMENT: The term is derived from the 1987 Bruntland Commission Report, *Our Common Future*. That report defined sustainable development as a process that meets the needs of the people of today without jeopardizing the needs of future generations. As per current usage, the term suggests an environmental goal for human activity, and it implies a long-term view of development that protects the integrity of environmental systems. The concept suggests that all actors in society are expected to actively participate in ensuring that sustainable development occurs — including governments in passing environmental laws that lead to sustainable development, and legal officials in rendering decisions that support it.

TORT: A **civil wrong** arising from **breach** of a duty imposed by law, *other* than a **breach of contract**. The victim (plaintiff) acquires a right of action for **damages**, as a **remedy** for the wrong. A tort consists of harm done to a person or their property, for which the victim can sue the person or company responsible (defendant). In Canada (outside of Quebec), as in other English-speaking countries, torts are mostly a matter of **common law**, but torts may also be created by statute. See the common law torts of **negligence**, **nuisance**, **riparian rights** and **trespass**.

TOXIC TORT: A **tort** in which the harm to the victims' health or property is due to exposure to toxic substances. "Toxic tort" is not a legal category: the specific legal cause of action could be **negligence**, **nuisance**, **trespass**, **riparian rights**, **strict liability** (tort), etc., depending on the particular facts of the case. Toxic tort cases are "civil lawsuits brought by plaintiffs to address exposure to toxic agents (chemical, biological, or radiological)" (William Charles and David VanderZwaag, this volume — Section One, Part B). Some commentators call toxic tort cases a "subspecies of product liability cases", but the category can be broader than that. Toxic tort lawsuits raise distinctive problems, however, to do with the difficulty of proving scientifically that the plaintiffs' specific illnesses or injuries are cause by the specific substances released by the defendant. Toxic tort cases are often **class action** lawsuits (ones involving large numbers of plaintiffs not all of whom are affected in exactly the same way), which adds further complications. See the Editors' Notes to Section Three, Part B ("Science and the Law" for elaboration on toxic torts, scientific uncertainty, and problems of admissibility of evidence.

TOXICOLOGY: The experimental study of whether, to what extent, and by what means, substances have harmful effects on organisms. Toxicologists, for example, attempt to estimate the risk to human health of a particular substance on the basis of its chemical properties, and its effects on laboratory animals in controlled experiments; compare **epidemiology**

TRESPASS: "An unlawful interference with one's person, property, or rights. At **common law**, trespass was a form of action brought to recover **damages** for any injury to one's person or property or relationship with another". As a **tort**, trespass to land covers "unauthorized and direct **breach** of the boundaries of another's land" [*Black's Law Dictionary*].

TRIAL: Examination of a case and decision in that case by a court of law. "A judicial examination and determination of issues between parties to an action, whether they be issues of law or of fact, before a court that has jurisdiction" [*Black's Law Dictionary*].

TRIBUNAL: "An officer of body [of persons] having authority to adjudicate judicial or quasi-judicial matters" [*Canada Law Dictionary*]. An administrative tribunal is a body established by a legislature "to decide claims and disputes arising in connection with the administration of legislative schemes, normally of a welfare or regulatory nature.... They exist outside the ordinary courts of law", but their decisions may be subject to **judicial review** [*A Dictionary of Law*]. See Editors' Notes to Section Three, Part A for discussion of hearings and tribunals in the context of environmental assessment.

TYPE 1 ERROR: False positive; finding a causal link or statistical association where none actually exists.
TYPE 2 ERROR: false negative; finding no causal link or statistical association where one actually exists. Academic scientific practices, such as conventional standards of statistical significance, seek to avoid Type 1 errors at the cost of incurring some Type 2 errors. Proponents of the **precautionary principle** argue that this priority is inappropriate when assessing environmental **risks**.

UNDERCONTROL: Rules that are inconsistently employed, and that are not enforced when broken, as a result of too much regulatory flexibility and too much discretion on the part of individual regulators.

UNDERTAKINGS: In the *Ontario Environmental Assessment Act*, undertakings are proposed actions that might create environmental effects for which an envi-

ronmental assessment is done. See Editors' Notes to Section Three, Part A for further elaboration.

USE VALUE: see **exchange value/use value**

UTILITY: Happiness, pleasure, usefulness, desirability; satisfaction, pleasure or fulfilment of needs derived from consuming some quantity of a good; utility is essentially a psychological concept that is incapable of direct measurement in absolute units; the theory of utility is recast in terms of ordinal utility for economic analysis (ordinal = expressing order), in which it is assumed that consumers are able to rank quantities of goods on the basis of preferences; do say that one combination of goods (or goods and services) has "greater utility" than some other combination simply means that the consumer prefers the first one to the second.

Utility in economic analysis is measured by Willingness to Pay.

UTILITARIANISM: The principle of utilitarianism is, "maximize the greatest good or happiness for the greatest number"; the right action or policy is the one that will make as many people happy as possible; the requirement of utilitarianism is to choose the action or policy (from all the feasible alternatives) that will maximize the total net benefit (benefits minus costs: happiness minus unhappiness) for all those affected by the action; the utility of every individual is to count equally; utility is to be summed across persons, and the distribution of utility among persons is not morally relevant; Bentham thought that only the quantity of utility mattered, but Mill thought quality of utility was also important (Mill distinguished between higher and lower pleasures).

VALUE: (derived from Latin, *valere* = to be strong, to be of worth) something that is of value is the object of a preference or the object of a judgement of importance; values are classified into categories — moral, aesthetic, economic, religious, political, legal, etc. "A theory of value is a theory about what things in the world are good, desirable, and important" [*A Dictionary of Philosophy*]; see also **Fact/Value Distinction**

VOLUNTARY INITIATIVES: Policies and programs for environmental protection adopted voluntarily by industry. Voluntary initiatives "have ranged from commitments by individual companies to achieve environmental targets that go beyond existing regulations, to codes of conduct adopted unilaterally at the national or international level by sectoral industry associations, to agreements on environmental performance targets between a government and a company, a group of companies or industry sector" [United Nations Environment Program, Division of Technology, Industry and Economics (http://www.uneptie.org/outreach.vi/background.htm)].

WELFARE STATE: "Colloquial term ... for a state which makes substantial provision through law and administration for those in need, e.g., the sick, poor, elderly, disabled and indigent". The welfare state typically provides for health services, education, and unemployment benefits out of government funds. These policies, however, "have met with opposition on the ground that [they] involve illegitimate government expenditure, and therefore illegitimate taxation", and are thought by some critics to "encourage indigence and discourage self-help". On the other hand, the favoured alternative approach, of private insurance, is "often attacked for the abuses and injustices to which it" gives rise. The welfare state, then, is "defended as involving not only social justice", but also as pertaining to activities and tasks which could not be effectively performed by any other agent or institution [*A Dictionary of Political Thought*].

REFERENCES

Abercrombie, Nicholas, Stephen Hill, and Bryan S. Turner. 1994. *Dictionary of Sociology*, Third Edition. London, UK: Penguin Books.

Bannock, Baxter and Rees. 1984. *The Penguin Dictionary of Economics*, Third Edition. New York, NY: Penguin.

Black's Law Dictionary. 1991. Abridged Sixth Edition. St. Paul, MN: West Publishing.

Bottomore, Tom (ed.). 1991. *A Dictionary of Marxist Thought*. Second Edition. Oxford, UK: Blackwell.

Bowal, Peter. 2002. "Ten Differences." *Law Now* (June/July): 9–11.

Bullock, Alan and Oliver Stallybrass (eds.). 1977. *The Fontana Dictionary of Modern Thought*. London UK: Fontana/Collins.

Dunster, Julian and Katherine. 1996. *Dictionary of Natural Resource Management*. Vancouver, BC: University of British Columbia Press.

Estrin, David and John Swaigen. 1993. *Environment on Trial: A Guide to Environmental Law and Policy*, Third Edition. Toronto: Emond-Montgomery.

Gill, Stephen. 1994. "Knowledge, Politics, and Neo-Liberal Political Economy". In *Political Economy and the Changing Global Order*, ed. Richard Stubbs and Geoffrey R.D. Underhill. Toronto: McClelland and Stewart Inc.

Kemp, David D. 1998. *The Environment Dictionary*. London and New York: Routledge.

Martin, Robert. 1997. *The Philosopher's Dictionary*. Peterborough, ON: Broadview Press.

Merriam Webster. 1993. *Webster's Collegiate Dictionary*, Tenth Edition. Springfield, MA: Merriam-Webster.

O'Sullivan, Tim, John Hartley, Danny Saunders, Martin Montgomery, and John Fiske. 1994. *Key Concepts in Communication and Cultural Studies*, Second Edition. London and New York: Routledge.

Oxford Reference. 1994. *A Dictionary of Law*, Third Edition. Oxford, UK: Oxford University Press.

Pan Reference. 1984. *A Dictionary of Philosophy*. London, UK: Pan/Macmillan.

Rutherford, Leslie, and Sheila Bone (eds.). 1993. *Osborn's Concise Law Dictionary*, Eighth Edition. London, UK: Sweet and Maxwell.

Scruton, Roger. 1996. *A Dictionary of Political Thought*. London, UK: Macmillan.

The Shorter Oxford English Dictionary. 1973. Oxford, UK: Oxford University Press.

Webster's Ninth New Collegiate Dictionary. 1983. Markham, ON: Merriam-Webster.

Yogis, John. 1995. *Canadian Law Dictionary*, Third Edition. New York, NY: Barron's Educational Series Inc.